THE AMERICANA ANNUAL

2001

AN ENCYCLOPEDIA
OF THE EVENTS OF 2000

YEARBOOK OF THE
ENCYCLOPEDIA AMERICANA

GROLIER

This annual has been prepared as a yearbook for general encyclopedias.
It is also published as *Encyclopedia Year Book.*

© GROLIER INCORPORATED 2001
Copyright in Canada © by Grolier Limited
Library of Congress Catalog Card Number: 23-10041
ISBN: 0-7172-0233-x
ISSN: 0196-0180

Printed and manufactured in the United States of America

Contents

Feature Articles of the Year

Many predicted a tight race. Nobody anticipated the unprecedented events that would unfold in the 2000 presidential election. Veteran political correspondent Robert Shogan tells the complete story. The electoral process and machinery are analyzed in a separate sidebar. There also is a report on First Lady Hillary Rodham Clinton's successful run for the U.S. Senate.

When the U.S. economy emerged from recession in March 1991, few dared believe that the period of economic growth would evolve into the great expansion of the 1990s, and continue on into the new millennium. John Cunniff, the Associated Press' Business News Analyst, takes a look at the economic boom and its impact on U.S. society.

Africa, seen as so vital to U.S. national security during the Cold War era, has essentially been abandoned. The new world order and globalization have bypassed it. Peter Schwab, a professor of political science at Purchase College, examines the many problems facing this troubled continent.

A dramatic breakthrough in relations between South Korea and North Korea occurred in Pyongyang, North Korea, in June 2000. The first-ever summit meeting between the leaders of the two countries opened a floodgate for high-level official exchanges, economic assistance, and family reunions. Han-Kyo Kim, a specialist on Korean affairs, comments on this stirring development. The Korean War—which began 50 years ago, in 1950—is recalled in a sidebar.

David A. Klinger, an associate professor in the Department of Criminology and Criminal Justice at the University of Missouri, points out that certain events of 2000 serve to remind us that the process of policing a democratic society is a problematic enterprise.

The overwhelming interest in and reaction to the passing of Charles M. Schulz of *Peanuts* fame suggest that the popularity of newspaper comic strips is still strong. Stephen Charla, curator of the International Museum of Cartoon Art, in Boca Raton, FL, outlines the history of this unique art form. Mr. Schulz' life and legacy are recalled by Rheta Grimsley Johnson, the author of the authorized biography *Good Grief: The Story of Charles M. Schulz.*

Close to 20% of the world's primates stand a reasonable chance of disappearing within the next ten to 20 years, according to a major new report. Jenny Tesar, the author of numerous books on the world's wildlife, describes the 25 primates most endangered with extinction.

One new phrase television viewers happily became familiar with in 2000 was: "Is that your final answer?" Freelance writer Brad Herzog, an actual contestant on the very popular *Who Wants to Be a Millionaire,* articulates the quiz-show revival as he recalls the genre phenomenon in the 1950s.

© AP/Wide World Photos

© Mike Theiler/Reuters/Archive Photo

© Scott Daniel Peterson/Liaison Agency

© United Features Syndicate, Inc.

© Frans Lanting/Minden Pictures

The Alphabetical Section

Entries on the continents and major nations of the world will be found under their own alphabetical headings.

A Review of the Year 2000

On the stroke of midnight, the year 2000 began and the world breathed a sigh of relief. The much feared Y2K computer bug proved to be a nonevent.

With the 2000s under way, it was time to search for new beginnings. Accordingly, the largest gathering of world leaders in history occurred at the United Nations in September. More than 150 heads of state and high-ranking officials from more than 40 countries assembled for the Millennium Summit (*photo above*). The purpose of the summit was to consider the role of the United Nations in the 21st century, and the subject of globalization received much attention.

In other ways, too, the year was one of new beginnings. For the first time in modern history, Russians saw the transfer of power from one popularly elected president to another. A more democratic administration took over in Yugoslavia as Slobodan Milosevic was ousted from power. In Mexico, Vicente Fox Quesada of the National Action Party (PAN) defeated the candidate of the Institutional Revolutionary Party (PRI), which had governed the nation for 71 years. The first meeting between the leaders of North and South Korea was a hopeful sign. China looked toward membership in the World Trade Organization (WHO).

In certain areas, the year saw little change, just more of the same. Israel's Prime Minister Ehud Barak and Palestinian leader Yasir Arafat continued their shuttle diplomacy on behalf of the peace process. However, outbreaks of violence between Israel and the Palestinians intensified and stalled the peace process. Saddam Hussein remained in power in Iraq, perhaps with more clout. Conflict, poverty, and AIDS grew worse in Africa. India and Pakistan continued their dispute over Kashmir.

The presidential race between Democratic Vice-President Al Gore and Republican Texas Gov. George W. Bush was tight enough to require weeks of recounts in the decisive state of Florida. In the end, the Texas governor would be president-elect. President Bill Clinton traveled the globe, while his wife became Senator-elect Hillary Rodham Clinton from New York. Early in the year, the nation's attention was focused on Elián González, a six-year-old Cuban boy who was found in U.S. waters, only to spark a seven-month debate about where he should call home. Americans also were counted in the 22d census, and became concerned following a terrorist attack on the USS *Cole* while it was docked in a port in Yemen.

U.S. unemployment fell to a 30-year low of 3.9%, consumers again faced high gas prices, and fears arose about the fate of the record period of economic growth. America Online and Time Warner took steps toward a union.

Science saw the announcement that a "working draft" of a human genome had been achieved. Space exploration was marked by the first live-in crew aboard the International Space Station. *The Music Man* returned to Broadway, and moviegoers awaited Tom Hanks in the December release, *Cast Away (photo above)*. Television belonged to *Who Wants to Be a Millionaire* and the wildly popular *Survivor*. In baseball, there was New York City's "Subway Series," with the Yankees defeating the Mets in five thrilling games; the Sydney Olympics had its heroes; but Tiger Woods *(photo above, right)* was just about everyone's choice as "athlete of the year."

The Editors

Photo (left): © Harry How/Allsport   © Zade Rosenthal/Photofest

© Corbis-Sygma

IN GOD WE TRUST

U.S. President Bill Clinton traveled to Capitol Hill, Jan. 27, 2000, to deliver the annual State of the Union message. The president declared: "Never before has our nation enjoyed, at once, so much prosperity and social progress with so little internal crisis and so few external threats."

1 The year 2000 arrives with worldwide festivities. Feared worldwide computer glitches—the "Y2K bug"—are relatively minor.

5 Under the terms of a September 1999 peace accord, Israel transfers an additional 5% of the West Bank to Palestinian control.

10 Israel and Syria complete weeklong peace negotiations in Shepherdstown, WV, without an agreement.

America Online, Inc. (AOL), the world's largest Internet service provider, announces plans to purchase Time Warner, Inc.

11 The Bill Clinton administration proposes a two-year, $1.3 billion emergency-aid program for Colombia. The assistance is intended primarily to stop the flow of illegal narcotics to the United States from Colombia.

14 Guatemala's President-elect Alfonso Portillo Cabrera takes the oath of office.

16 Ricardo Lagos Escobar, a Socialist, is chosen president of Chile in a runoff election.

20 The foreign ministers of Greece and Turkey sign five accords to build confidence between the two nations.

22 Ecuador's Vice-President Gustavo Noboa Bejarano is named president following the overthrow of President Jamil Mahuad Witt amid widespread protests.

24 The U.S. Supreme Court upholds a Missouri law that limits the contributions that individuals can donate to a candidate during a single election.

27 U.S. President Clinton delivers the annual State of the Union address. Proposals regarding education, health care, and gun control are among the items receiving prime attention.

30 The St. Louis Rams defeat the Tennessee Titans, 23–16, to capture pro football's Super Bowl XXXIV.

February

1 The U.S. economic expansion that began in March 1991 enters its 108th month, becoming the longest in history.

3 The U.S. Senate confirms the nomination of Federal Reserve Board Chairman Alan Greenspan to a fourth four-year term.

4 Austria's President Thomas Klestil administers the oath of office to a new coalition government that included Wolfgang Schüssel's Christian Democratic Austrian People's Party and Jörg Haider's right-wing Freedom Party. The inclusion of Haider's anti-immigration party stirs national and international concern because of its racist views.

6 Russia's acting President Vladimir Putin announces that the Russian military has captured Grozny, the capital of the breakaway Russian republic of Chechnya, from Chechen rebels. The capital had been under Russian attack since December 1999.

In Finland, Foreign Minister Tarja Halonen of the Social Democratic Party is the first woman to be elected president.

U.S. First Lady Hillary Rodham Clinton formally declares that she is a candidate for a U.S. Senate seat from the state of New York.

7 In Croatia, Stipe Mesic, 65-year-old former communist, is elected president in a runoff election. The ruling Croatian Democratic Union (HDZ), the party of President Franjo Tudjman, who died in December 1999, had been defeated by a coalition of center-left parties in parliamentary elections in early January 2000.

President Clinton presents to Congress a $1.84 trillion budget for fiscal year 2001.

11 Great Britain suspends self-rule in Northern Ireland. According to legislation passed by the British Parliament, direct rule over Northern Ireland's legislative and executive affairs is returned to Britain. The suspension comes after the Irish Republican Army (IRA), the largest paramilitary organization in Northern Ireland, had failed to begin decommissioning (disarming) by a February deadline.

Peter Caruana of the Gibraltar Social Democrats is reelected chief minister of the British-controlled province of Gibraltar, located on Spain's southern coast.

12 U.S. cartoonist Charles Schulz, creator of the comic strip "Peanuts," dies at the age of 77.

18 In Iran's elections for the Majlis (parliament), candidates considered to be moderates win a majority of the seats.

The U.S. Commerce Department reports a deficit in trade in goods and services of $271.3 billion in 1999. It is the largest calender-year trade gap in U.S. history.

25 In Albany, NY, a jury acquits four New York City police officers of second-degree murder and lesser charges in the February 1999 shooting death of Amadou Diallo, an unarmed black immigrant from Guinea. The acquittals lead to protests in the streets of New York City.

28 As national and international protest against Austria's new coalition government continues, Jörg Haider resigns as leader of Austria's Freedom Party.

© Kare Prinsloo/AP/Wide World Photos

Beginning in February, Mozambique suffered from the worst flooding in some 50 years as Cyclone Eline struck the southern African nation following two weeks of heavy rain. More than 1 million people were left homeless.

March

1 The Los Angeles Police Department (LAPD) releases the findings of its investigation into a departmental corruption scandal.

2 In Great Britain, Chile's former President Augusto Pinochet Ugarte is freed from house arrest and allowed to return to his homeland after Britain's Home Secretary Jack Straw concludes that Pinochet was mentally and physically unable to stand trial. Belgium, France, Spain, and Switzerland had sought to try the former Chilean leader on human-rights violations.

Team New Zealand, known as the Kiwis, retains yachting's America's Cup, marking the first time that a non-American syndicate successfully defended the Cup.

9 After U.S. Vice-President Al Gore (D) and Texas Gov. George W. Bush (R) score major victories in their parties' presidential primaries on Super Tuesday, March 7, former U.S. Sen. Bill Bradley withdraws "from the Democratic race for the presidency," and Sen. John McCain announces that he no longer is "an active candidate" for the Republican nomination.

16 Independent Counsel Robert Ray issues a report clearing the Clinton administration of criminal wrongdoing in connection with the improper acquisition of confidential files of the Federal Bureau of Investigation in 1993 and 1994.

17 In Norway, Jens Stoltenberg of the Labour Party takes office as prime minister. The coalition government of Kjell Magne Bondevik had resigned on March 9 as a result of an environmental dispute.

U.S. Secretary of Defense William Cohen ends a weeklong tour of Southeast Asia, during which he became the first U.S. defense secretary to visit Vietnam since the Vietnam war ended in 1975.

18 In Taiwan, voters elect Taipei Mayor Chen Shui-bian of the opposition Democratic Progressive Party (DPP) president. It is the first defeat for the ruling Nationalist Party (the Kuomintang) since 1949, when the Nationalists fled mainland China for Taiwan.

19 In Senegal, Abdoulaye Wade of the opposition Senagalese Democratic Party (PDS) is elected president.

21 The U.S. Supreme Court rules, 5–4, that the U.S. Food and Drug Administration overstepped its regulatory authority when it sought to curb the marketing of cigarettes to youngsters.

23 The executive board of the International Monetary Fund (IMF) elects Horst Koehler of Germany to succeed Michel Camdessus as its managing director.

26 Russia's acting President Vladimir Putin is elected president outright, winning sufficient votes to avoid a runoff.

En route home from a visit to Bangladesh, India, and Pakistan, President Clinton confers with Syria's President Hafiz al-Assad in Geneva. Efforts to renew the Israeli-Syrian peace talks, which broke off in January, are unsuccessful.

Pope John Paul II returns to Rome after a seven-day pilgrimage to the Middle East, during which the pontiff met with political and religious leaders and visited Holy Land sites.

31 In Uganda, officials set the number of deaths linked to a doomsday religious cult, the Movement for the Restoration of the Ten Commandments, at more than 900. A March 17 fire at the cult's church in the town of Kanungu had taken the lives of 530 members, and authorities subsequently found mass graves at various sites linked to the cult.

Порядочный
Умный
Твердый
Инициативный
Настойчивый
    Президент России

At a Russian campaign rally, a woman held a poster depicting Vladimir Putin, with the words "honest, intelligent, firm, active, persistent." The acting president was elected to the presidency outright on March 26.

April

3 U.S. District Court Judge Thomas Penfield Jackson concludes in a 43-page "findings of law" that Microsoft Corporation, the world's largest computer-software company, had violated the 1890 Sherman Antitrust Act by employing unfair tactics to gain and maintain dominance in its market.

Michigan State University wins the National Collegiate Athletic Association (NCAA) men's basketball title by defeating Florida, 89–76. The University of Connecticut had taken the women's crown on April 2, with a 71–52 victory over Tennessee.

5 Japan's Diet (parliament) names Yoshiro Mori, who earlier had been selected by the ruling Liberal Democratic Party (LDP) to replace Keizo Obuchi as its secretary-general, as prime minister. Obuchi was in a coma after suffering a stroke on April 2.

Independent Counsel Ralph I. Lancaster, Jr., clears U.S. Secretary of Labor Alexis Herman of wrongdoing in relationship to an alleged influence-peddling scheme.

6 In Pakistan, Mohammad Nawaz Sharif, who was deposed as prime minister in an October 1999 coup, is found guilty of hijacking and terrorism. He is sentenced to life imprisonment.

7 President Clinton signs legislation removing the limits on how much retired people age 65 to 69 may earn without losing Social Security benefits.

9 Greece's Panhellenic Socialist Movement (Pasok) is reelected by a narrow margin.

Fiji's Vijay Singh wins the 64th Masters golf tournament in Augusta, GA.

10 Monitors from the Organization for Security and Co-operation in Europe (OSCE) report irregularities in the voting in Georgia's presidential election on April 9 as President Eduard Shevardnadze is reelected to a new five-year term.

14 In parliamentary elections in South Korea, both the Millennium Democratic Party of President Kim Dae Jung and the opposition Grand National Party win an increased number of seats.

The U.S. stock market concludes a particularly volatile week. Both the Dow Jones industrial average and the composite index of the Nasdaq underwent record single-day plunges.

17 In Rwanda, Maj. Gen. Paul Kagame, who took over as the nation's interim president after President Pasteur Bizimungu resigned in March, is chosen president by government ministers and legislators.

22 Earth Day 2000, the 30th anniversary of the first Earth Day, is marked worldwide.

26 A new government, with Giuliano Amato as prime minister, takes office in Italy. The center-left coalition of Prime Minister Massimo D'Alema had been defeated in regional elections.

27 Spain's Prime Minister José María Aznar is sworn in for a second term and appoints a new cabinet. Aznar's Popular Party had won an absolute majority of seats in the lower house of parliament (the Congress of Deputies) in elections on March 12.

30 A major march to rally support for the gay- and lesbian-rights movement is held in Washington, DC.

© Michael Laughlin/"The Sun-Sentinel"/Corbis-Sygma

In the early morning hours of April 22, U.S. immigration agents removed Elián González from the Miami, FL, home of his U.S. relatives and transported him to Maryland for a reunion with his father. The six-year-old Cuban boy, who had been rescued off the Florida coast in November 1999 after his mother drowned while escaping from Cuba, had been the center of an international custody battle.

5 Turkey's parliament elects Ahmet Necdet Sezer, the current chief justice of Constitutional Court, as the nation's president.

7 After being inaugurated as president of Russia, Vladimir V. Putin names First Deputy Premier Mikhail Kasyanov as premier.

11 In New Mexico, a fire that the National Park Service had set intentionally to prevent accidental fires becomes a raging wildfire, sweeping the towns of Los Alamos and White Rock.

© Heinz-Peter
Bader/Reuters/Archive Photos

© Estelito Cortero/
Asia Pix/Liaison
Agency

```
Date:       04/05/2000 3:29:02 PM
From:       xxxxxxxxx, xxxxx
Subject:    ILOVEYOU
To:         BADER, Heinz-Peter

kindly check the attached LOVELETTER coming from me

rem  barok -loveletter(vbe) <i hate go to school>
rem       by      yder / ispyder@mail.com / @GRAMMERSof
On Error Resu    ext
dim fso            dirwin,dirtemp,eq,ctr,file,vbscopy,dow
eq                 
                   ect("Scripting.FileSystemObject")
                   extFile(WScript.ScriptFullname,1)
                   ll
```

In early May, a computer virus, above—dubbed the "Love Bug" and described technically as a "worm" rather than a virus because of its ability to spread to other computers—crippled business and government agencies worldwide. After the virus was traced to the Philippines, Onel de Guzman, a computer-school dropout, and his sister Irene, right, became the center of the government's investigation into the case.

15 Israeli troops and Palestinian security forces engage in a four-hour gun battle in the Israeli-occupied West Bank.

16 In an effort to slow the U.S. economy and control inflation, the Federal Reserve Board (the Fed) increases both the federal funds rate—the interest rate that banks charge other banks on overnight loans—and the discount rate—the interest rate the Fed charges banks for direct loans—by a half of one percentage point.

18 In the Dominican Republic, Hipólito Mejía Dominguez of the center-left Dominican Revolutionary Party (PRD) is declared president-elect. Although Mejía had failed to win a majority in first-round voting on May 16, he had captured such a large percentage of the vote that his two major opponents withdrew, averting a runoff.

21 In Haiti, parliamentary and local elections, which had been delayed since late 1999, are held.

24 Israel completes the withdrawal of its forces from southern Lebanon, ending its 22-year occupation of the region.

27 In Northern Ireland, the Ulster Unionist Party (UUP) endorses a proposal by which the Irish Republican Army (IRA) agrees to put its arms "beyond use" and to allow weapons inspections by third parties. Following the vote, Britain restores home rule to the province, and the local government, which had been suspended by Britain in February, resumes power.

28 Peru's President Alberto Fujimori is reelected in a runoff vote that the opposition and international observers declare to be unfair.

29 Fiji's military takes control of the Pacific island nation and declares martial law following a coup attempt by indigenous Fijians in mid-May. President Kamisese Mara had resigned after earlier dismissing Prime Minister Mahendra Chaudhry.

June

4 Bill Clinton concludes two days of talks with Russia's President Putin in Moscow. Arms control is reported to have dominated the discussions. The U.S. president also had made stops in Portugal, Germany, and Ukraine during the six-day trip.

7 U.S. Federal Judge Thomas Penfield Jackson orders the breakup of Microsoft Corporation. The judge declares that "there is credible evidence in the record to suggest that Microsoft, convinced of its innocence, continues to do business as it has in the past and may yet do to other markets what it has already done" to dominate operating systems and Internet software.

9 Canada and the United States sign a border-security agreement, calling for the establishment of a border-enforcement team.

10 The New Jersey Devils win the National Hockey League's Stanley Cup, defeating the Dallas Stars by four games to two.

13 North Korea's leader Kim Jong Il welcomes South Korea's President Kim Dae Jung to Pyongyang for a three-day summit. It is the first such meeting between the leaders of North and South Korea.

16 U.S. Secretary of Energy Bill Richardson reports that an employee at the Los Alamos National Laboratory in New Mexico had discovered two missing computer hard drives containing classified information about nuclear weapons. The drives had been discovered to be missing in early May.

18 In Algiers, Algeria, the foreign ministers of Ethiopia and Eritrea sign a preliminary cease-fire accord and agree to work toward a permanent settlement of their nations' two-year border war.

19 The U.S. Supreme Court rules that group prayer led by students at public-school football games violates the 1st Amendment's principle calling for the separation of church and state.

The Los Angeles Lakers defeat the Indiana Pacers, 116–111, to win the National Basketball Association championship, four games to two.

25 In elections for the lower house of Japan's Diet (parliament), the ruling coalition led by the Liberal Democratic Party (LDP) retains its majority but suffers a loss in its number of seats.

Zimbabwe's opposition party, the Movement for Democratic Change, scores major gains in two-day parliamentary elections.

26 The Human Genome Project, an international, publicly financed consortium working to map the human genome, and Celera Genomics Corp., a private U.S. company involved in similar work, announce jointly that they each had created a working draft of the human genome.

28 Six-year-old Elián González, who had been the center of an international custody dispute, returns with his father to Cuba from the United States.

29 Some 500 people drown when an overloaded wooden ferry capsizes during a severe storm off Sulawesi Island, Indonesia. The ferry was carrying refugees who were escaping religious strife in the Moluccas island chain. On June 26, Indonesia's President Abdurrahman Wahid had declared a state of emergency in the Moluccas in light of escalating fighting between Christians and Muslims.

© Bassem Tellawi/AP/Wide World Photos

Following the death of Syria's longtime president, Hafiz al-Assad, on June 10, supporters gathered outside parliament to mourn their late president and support his son Bashar (poster right) as the new national leader.

July

A motorist dramatically photographed an Air France Concorde as it burst into flames shortly after takeoff near Paris on July 25, taking 113 lives. The tragedy marked the first crash by a supersonic plane since the Concorde began operation in 1976.

2 In Mexico's presidential election, Vicente Fox Quesada of the National Action Party (PAN) outpolls Francisco Labastida Ochoa of the governing Institutional Revolutionary Party (PRI). The PRI had controlled Mexico's presidency since the party's founding in 1929.

The Mongolian People's Revolutionary Party (MPRP), Mongolia's former Communist Party, wins 72 of 76 seats in parliamentary elections.

8 The 13th International AIDS Conference opens in Durban, South Africa.

9 Pete Sampras of the United States defeats Australia's Patrick Rafter to capture the men's singles tennis championship at Wimbledon. It was Sampras' 13th Grand Slam title, a record. On July 8, Venus Williams of the United States had defeated Lindsay Davenport for the women's singles crown.

13 Fiji's Great Council of Chiefs elects Ratu Josefa Iloilo, a former vice-president, as president hours after indigenous Fijians had released some 40 hostages, including Prime Minister Mahendra Chaudhry, who were taken captive in May.

The United States and Vietnam sign a major trade agreement. The pact now must be approved by the U.S. Congress.

Sprint Corp. and WorldCom cancel their planned merger in light of opposition by regulators in the United States and Europe.

21 Former U.S. Rep. Norman Mineta (D-CA) is sworn in as U.S. secretary of commerce. He succeeds William Daley, who resigned the post to become chairman of the presidential campaign of Vice-President Al Gore.

23 Leaders of the Group of 8 (G-8) industrialized nations conclude their annual summit in Okinawa, Japan.

25 President Clinton announces that the leaders of Israel and the Palestinians have been unable to reach an agreement "at this time." The two sides had been holding peace negotiations at Camp David, MD, for two weeks.

30 In accord with a new constitution in Venezuela, voters elect President Hugo Chávez Frías to a new six-year term.

31 In a vote in Israel's parliament, Moshe Katsav of the opposition Likud Party defeats former Prime Minister Shimon Peres for the nation's presidency. Ezer Weizman had been forced to resign as president due to allegation of fraud.

August

3 At the Republican National Convention in Philadelphia, Texas Gov. George W. Bush accepts the Republican Party's nomination for the presidency. Earlier, Richard B. Cheney, a former U.S. congressman from Wyoming and a former secretary of defense, had been nominated as the party's vice-presidential candidate.

© Eric Draper/AP/Wide World Photos

4 Great Britain's Queen Elizabeth the Queen Mother celebrates her 100th birthday.

8 Eight people are killed and dozens are injured as the result of a bomb explosion in a pedestrian underpass in Moscow, the Russian capital.

9 Tire manufacturer Bridgestone/Firestone announces that it is recalling 6.5 million Firestone tires because of safety concerns.

10 In Baghdad, Iraq, Venezuela's President Hugo Chávez is the first head of state to meet with Iraq's President Saddam Hussein since the 1991 Persian Gulf war.

17 At the Democratic National Convention in Los Angeles, Vice-President Al Gore formally accepts the Democratic Party's nomination for the presidency. Earlier the vice-president had selected Sen. Joseph I. Lieberman (CT) as his running mate.

As major wildfires rage in a dozen Western states, the National Interagency Fire Center (NIFC) reports that some 5 million acres (2.02 million ha) of U.S. land has burned during the year.

© Bob Childs/AP/Wide World Photos

20 Verizon Communications, the largest U.S. telecommunications employer, and the two unions representing some 86,000 telephone workers reach a contract agreement, ending a 15-day strike.

21 British and Norwegian divers confirm that all 118 crew members aboard the Russian submarine the *Kursk*, which sank during a military exercise in the Barents Sea on August 12, had perished.

23 The National Institutes of Health (NIH) issues regulations permitting federally financed researchers to perform human embryonic stem-cell research.

A Gulf Air Airbus crashes off Bahrain, killing all 143 people on board.

24 President Clinton confers with Mexico's President-elect Vicente Fox Quesada at the White House.

26 President Clinton begins a four-day visit to Africa, meeting with Nigeria's President Olusegun Obasanjo in Abuja, Nigeria's capital.

30 Abdikassim Salad Hassan, who was chosen as president of Somalia at a peace conference in Djibouti, arrives in the Somalian capital of Mogadishu and prepares to try to restore the nation's central government. Somalia had undergone a prolonged civil war and had been without a government since 1991.

During a one-day stopover in Cartagena, Colombia, President Clinton defends the U.S. plan to grant Colombia $1.3 billion in military aid to fight drugs.

The Republicans and the Democrats officially nominated their presidential tickets in August. The GOP chose Texas Gov. George W. Bush (top right) for its top spot and former Defense Secretary Richard B. Cheney as his running mate. The Democrats selected Vice-President Al Gore (bottom left) and Sen. Joseph I. Lieberman for their Number 1 and 2 positions, respectively.

September

1 President Clinton announces that he has "decided not to authorize deployment of a national missile defense at this time."

8 The three-day United Nations Millennium Summit—the largest gathering of world leaders ever held—concludes with a declaration of common values.

10 The Palestinian Central Council defers the declaration of a Palestinian state, scheduled for no later than September 13, and recommits itself to the Middle East peace process.

11 Following a yearlong study, the Federal Trade Commission (FTC) issues a report on the marketing of violent entertainment to children. The report concludes that the vast majority of best-selling restricted movies, music, and video games were marketed deliberately to children under the age of 12.

13 Former Los Alamos scientist Wen Ho Lee pleads guilty to a single charge of mishandling nuclear secrets and is released after spending nine months in prison.

The U.S. House of Representatives fails to override President Clinton's veto of a bill cutting taxes for some married couples by $292 billion over ten years—the so-called marriage-penalty bill. On September 7 the House had upheld the president's veto of a bill repealing estate taxes.

19 The U.S. Senate passes a bill removing curbs on U.S. trade with China. The House of Representatives had passed similar legislation in May.

20 U.S. Independent Counsel Robert Ray issues a statement concluding that there is "insufficient" evidence to prove that President Clinton or First Lady Hillary Rodham Clinton committed a crime in connection with the Whitewater land-development deal.

22 In view of rising oil prices, President Clinton orders the release of 30 million barrels of oil from the Strategic Petroleum Reserve.

28 The U.S. Food and Drug Adminstration (FDA) announces that it has approved the marketing of an abortion-inducing drug, mifepristone (Mifeprex, RU-486).

29 Four Palestinians are killed at Temple Mount, called al-Haram al-Sharif in Arabic, in Jerusalem's Old City following a visit by Israeli opposition leader Ariel Sharon to the Muslim compound.

In Yugoslavia on September 26, the Federal Election Commission announced that opposition candidate Vojislav Kostunica had defeated President Slobodan Milosevic in the presidential election two days earlier, but that a runoff election would be required since Kostunica had not obtained a majority of the votes. Opposition leaders challenged the results and refused to participate in a runoff, and massive demonstrations in support of Kostunica's victory occurred in Belgrade, right, and other cities.

October

1   The XXVII Olympic Games conclude in Sydney, Australia.

3   U.S. presidential candidates Texas Gov. George W. Bush (R) and Vice-President Al Gore (D) engage in the first of three scheduled debates.

7   In Yugoslavia, Vojislav Kostunica is sworn in as president, one day after Slobodan Milosevic formally steps down.

  In Luxembourg, Crown Prince Henri becomes grand duke following the abdication of his father, Grand Duke Jean.

8   Poland's President Aleksandr Kwasniewski is elected to a second five-year term.

8   President Clinton signs legislation granting China normal trade-relations status on a permanent basis.

  In parliamentary elections in Sri Lanka, the ruling People's Alliance coalition of President C.B. Kumaratunga is returned to power but fails to win a majority.

13   The Norwegian Nobel Committee awards the Nobel Peace Prize to South Korea's President Kim Dae Jung.

© Reuters/ Archive Photos

© Sgt. Don L. Maes/U.S. Marine Corps. via Newsmakers/Liaison Agency

17   At a summit meeting in Sharm el-Sheikh, Egypt, Israeli Prime Minister Ehud Barak and Palestinian leader Yasir Arafat agree to a cease-fire to end nearly three weeks of clashes between Israelis and Palestinians.

  Missouri Gov. Mel Carnahan, a Democratic candidate for the U.S. Senate, is killed in a plane crash during a campaign trip.

22   As clashes between Israelis and Palestinians in the West Bank and Gaza Strip continue despite the cease-fire, Israel's Prime Minister Barak declares that Israel will take a "time-out" from the peace process. On October 20 the UN General Assembly had voted to condemn Israel for the use of excessive force against Palestinian civilians.

23   Lebanon's President Emile Lahoud names Rafiq Hariri, the owner of a construction and engineering company, prime minister.

24   U.S. Secretary of State Madeleine Albright concludes a two-day visit to North Korea during which she met with North Korea's leader Kim Jong II.

25   AT&T Corporation releases a plan that would split the telecommunications giant into four different units.

26   The New York Yankees win Major League Baseball's World Series, defeating the New York Mets, four games to one.

27   The newly elected president of the Ivory Coast, Laurent Gbagbo, forms a government of national unity.

31   A Russian *Soyuz* rocket carrying the first crew of the International Space Station—one U.S. astronaut and two Russians—is launched from Baikonur Cosmodrome in Kazakhstan.

On October 12, a small boat exploded alongside the USS Cole, a U.S. Navy destroyer that was refueling in Yemen, killing 17 U.S. sailors and wounding 39 others. The explosion, which U.S. officials termed a terrorist attack, tore a hole, top, 40 ft by 40 ft (12 m by 12 m) in the port side of the ship. By month's end, the guided missile destroyer was returning to the United States for repair that would cost $150 million.

November

1 Yugoslavia is readmitted to the United Nations.

7 On U.S. Election Day 2000, the presidential race ends undecidedly as a recount vote is scheduled in Florida. The Republican Party retains control of the U.S. House of Representatives. The margin in the U.S. Senate is 50 Republicans and 49 Democrats, with the race in Washington in doubt. Eleven governorships are decided.

10 A cease-fire between the Sierra Leone government and the Revolutionary United Front (RUF) is signed in Abuja, Nigeria.

12 The Organization of Petroleum Exporting Countries (OPEC) decides to delay an increase in oil output until at least January 2001.

13 China's President Jiang Zemin becomes the first Chinese head of state to visit Cambodia since 1963.

15 Egypt's National Democratic Party (NDP) retains a two-thirds majority in three-stage parliamentary elections.

16 In Brunei, representatives of the 21 members of the Asia-Pacific Economic Cooperation (APEC) forum end their annual summit.

19 President Clinton concludes a three-day visit to Vietnam during which U.S.-Vietnam trade development was a major focus.

India's Prime Minister Atal Bihari Vajpayee announces that India would maintain a unilateral cease-fire for one month in Nammu and Kashmir states. The Indian army has been fighting Muslim separatist rebels in the region since 1989.

21 Egypt recalls its ambassador to Israel in response to Israeli air strikes against Palestinians.

Members of Peru's legislature reject the resignation of Alberto Fujimori as the nation's president and approve a measure removing the president from office on the grounds that he is "morally unfit."

25 In The Hague, the Netherlands, discussions among representatives of more than 170 nations regarding a treaty to curb global warming collapse.

29 Official results of Haiti's presidential election of November 26 reveal that Jean-Bertrand Aristide has been returned to the presidency. Aristide had held the office in the early and mid-1990s.

© Fred Chartrand/AP/Wide World Photos

Canadians went to the polls on November 27, and Prime Minister Jean Chrétien and his wife Jean (right) were delighted with the results. Chrétien's ruling Liberal Party was returned to power with 172 parliamentary seats—a gain of 13. Stockwell Day's Canadian Alliance, which had been formed in March following the dissolution of the Reform Party, finished second with 66 seats.

December

1 Vicente Fox Quesada is sworn in as president of Mexico.

Democrat Maria Cantwell is declared the winner of the undecided U.S. Senate race in Washington.

5 Japan's Prime Minister Yoshiro Miro reshuffles his cabinet.

9 Israel's Prime Minister Ehud Barak resigns. New elections for the office of prime minister would be held within 60 days.

10 In a runoff election in Romania, former President Ion Iliescu is elected president.

11 At a summit in Nice, France, leaders of the European Union (EU) sign a treaty in which they agree to revisions of the EU's structure and to a reallotment and reform of each nation's voting power on the Council of Minister. The agreement prepares the EU for the admission of new members.

The space shuttle *Endeavour* completes a ten-day space flight during which it attached a large array of electric-generating solar panels to the International Space Station.

12 In Algiers, Algeria, Ethiopia's President Meles Zenawi and Eritrea's President Isaias Afeworki sign a peace agreement formally ending their border war.

13 After the U.S. Supreme Court on December 12 blocked further recounting of the ballots in Florida, Vice-President Al Gore, the Democratic presidential candidate, concedes defeat to Texas Gov. George W. Bush (R).

15 The 106th U.S. Congress adjourns.

18 Popocatepetl, the Mexican volcano, begins to erupt.

22 The World Bank and the International Monetary Fund (IMF) announce that the industrial nations, including the United States and Japan, will forgive loans to 22 of the world's poorest nations.

23 The United Nations General Assembly approves a major overhaul of UN financing. Under the plan, U.S. dues to the world body are reduced.

26 Michael McDermott, a 42-year-old software tester at an Internet consulting company in Wakefield, MA, kills seven of his coworkers with a rifle and a shotgun.

28 The U.S. Census Bureau begins releasing data from the 22d decennial census. The nation population is 281,421,906—a 13.2% gain since 1990.

29 The U.S. stock market closes for 2000, with the Dow Jones Industrial Average and the Nasdaq Composite Index down 6.2% and 39.3%, respectively, for the year.

In Ghana, opposition leader John Agyekum Kufuor is declared the winner of the recent runoff presidential election.

© Jeff Mitchell/Reuters/Corbis

After being declared president-elect on December 13, George W. Bush named retired Gen. Colin Powell (left), former chairman of the Joint Chiefs of Staff, as his secretary of state.

E lection Day 2000 *(photo, above)* ended in the United States with neither the Republican candidate Texas Gov. George W. Bush nor the Democratic nominee Vice-President Al Gore being the president-elect. Both candidates were short of electoral votes. National eyes then focused on the Sunshine State of Florida as it began a recount. Five weeks of laborious vote tallies and re-tallies and a flurry of lawsuits by both sides followed. During that time, antiquated voting machines, the design of ballots, the media's role in the election process, voter apathy, and the Electoral College all came under fire. Finally, a U.S. Supreme Court decision led to Gore's concession, and Bush was declared president-elect on December 13. In what became somewhat of an aside, for the first time in history, a first lady had sought—and won—electoral office. Accordingly, the annual opens with an in-depth section: The 2000 U.S. Presidential Election—One Unlike Any Other.

Meanwhile, in Africa, tribal conflict, disease, and starvation *(photo, left)* were among the devastating troubles facing the continent. On a more positive note, efforts for peace brought the leaders of bitter rivals North Korea and South Korea to a summit, and an era of détente—symbolized gallantly when athletes from both the North and South carried the Korean flag at the Opening Ceremonies at the 2000 Olympic Games in Sydney, Australia *(photo at top left of page 21)*—began.

In the United States, economic expansion would be of record duration; and the nation was gripped by

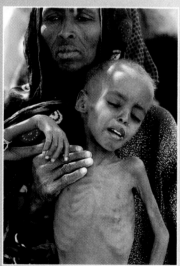

© Andy Clark/Reuters/Archive Photos

© Reed Saxon/AP/Wide World Photos

HOW MANY
OF OUR
LOVED ONES
ARE IN JAIL
BECAUSE
OF POLICE
LIES!

© D.Kirkland/Corbis-Sygma

high-profile headline stories, trials, and protests *(photo, above, right)* involving the police. Television viewers were enthralled by ABC's quiz show, *Who Wants to Be a Millionaire (photo, below)*. The sadness evident with the death of Charles M. Schulz *(photo, right)*, the creator of the beloved *Peanuts* series, testified to the lasting lure of newspaper comic strips. An authoritative new listing of the 25 most endangered primates was serving as a wake-up call. Accordingly, the yearbook features the following special articles: the U.S. Economy—The Great Expansion; Africa: A Continent of Problems; The Koreas—A Rapprochement; Policing—A Problematic Enterprise; Cartooning: The Comics Are Here to Stay; Primates in Peril; and The Quiz-Show Craze.

© Maria Melin/2000 ABC, Inc.

The 2000 U.S. Presidential Election— One Unlike Any Other

By Robert Shogan

The 2000 presidential election featured two familiar political names as Republican nominee George W. Bush, the son of the former president, and Democratic nominee Al Gore, the son of a former longtime U.S. senator, engaged in a historic race for the White House. Vice-President Gore won the popular vote; Governor Bush took the decisive electoral vote. The outcome was not known until five weeks after Election Day.

The first meaningful votes of the 2000 presidential campaign were cast a year before the contest officially got under way, far from the traditional early battlegrounds of Iowa and New Hampshire. The unlikely venue was the floor of the U.S. Senate. It was in that hallowed chamber on Feb. 12, 1999, that senators of both parties rendered judgment on the impeachment charges against President Bill Clinton.

The immediate result was that the president was acquitted. But the Senate's actions had broader significance, reflecting and reinforcing growing public concern about presidential character that cast a long shadow over the forthcoming campaign to choose Clinton's successor. Clinton's foes in the Senate could not muster the two-thirds vote required to remove him from office. But in addition to the 50 who voted to convict him of obstruction of justice, another 32 signed a statement censuring his conduct as "shameful, reckless, and indefensible." That made a total of 82 senators, more than four-fifths of the membership, who went on record as denouncing the president's behavior. That response to the revelations of Clinton's affair with a White House intern was an early warning of the dramatic emergence of the character issue as a potent influence on voter choices in the 2000 campaign. More than ever before, the public and the media seemed to be paying attention to the personal experiences and behavior of presidential candidates, seeking to measure their sincerity and integrity.

The Character Issue. The search for a trustworthy president did not supplant or necessarily trump other issues on the political agenda. In the fall campaign, Texas Gov. George W. Bush, the Republican standard-bearer, pushed a bold idea for partly privatizing Social Security, along with proposals for across-the-board tax cuts and a limited scheme for linking prescription drugs to Medicare. For his part, Vice-President Al Gore, the Democratic nominee, favored stabilizing the existing Social Security system, targeted tax cuts, and a more ambitious prescription-drug plan. Voters pondered these and other substantive matters, such as education, gun control, and the future makeup of the Supreme Court. But the increased importance attached to character colored the debate over public policy, and thus probably played a part in making the outcome of the first election of the new century unlike any other in more than 200 years of American history.

To begin with, the character issue complicated the efforts of Bush, the early frontrunner in the Republican contest, and Gore, the heavy favorite among the Democrats, to gain their party's nominations. Each man faced a special character problem. To offset his reputation as a free-living, hard-drinking young man, Bush claimed to have sobered up and calmed down, a change underlined by his strict teetotalism. If elected, former President Bush's eldest son vowed to usher in the "responsibility era," departing from the current attitude that "if it feels good, do it." Nagged by the press, he claimed that he had used no illegal drugs for the past 25 years, but refused to answer further questions on that subject.

About the Author. Robert Shogan served as national political correspondent in the Washington Bureau of the *Los Angeles Times* for more than 25 years. A longtime observer of the U.S. political scene, Mr. Shogan has written several books on the presidency and presidential politics, including the forthcoming *Bad News; Where the Press Goes Wrong in the Making of the President* and *The Double-Edged Sword: How Character Makes and Ruins Presidents, from Washington to Clinton* (1998). He also is an adjunct professor at Johns Hopkins University, where he teaches a course in presidential politics and the media.

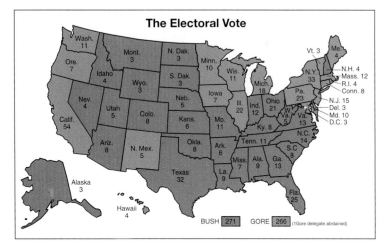

The Electoral Vote

Wash. 11
Ore. 7
Mont. 3
N. Dak. 3
Minn. 10
Vt. 3
Me. 4
N.H. 4
Mass. 12
Idaho 4
Wyo. 3
S. Dak. 3
Wis. 11
Mich. 18
N.Y. 33
R.I. 4
Conn. 8
Nev. 4
Utah 5
Colo. 8
Neb. 5
Iowa 7
Ill. 22
Ind. 12
Ohio 21
Pa. 23
N.J. 15
Del. 3
Calif. 54
Kans. 6
Mo. 11
Ky. 8
W. Va. 5
Va. 13
Md. 10
D.C. 3
Ariz. 8
N. Mex. 5
Okla. 8
Ark. 6
Tenn. 11
N.C. 14
S.C 8
Texas 32
La. 9
Miss. 7
Ala. 9
Ga. 13
Alaska 3
Hawaii 4
Fla. 25

BUSH 271   GORE 266   (1Gore delegate abstained)

Republican Sen. John McCain of Arizona (top) had unsuccessfully challenged Governor Bush for the GOP nomination, while former U.S. Sen. Bill Bradley (above), had been overwhelmed by Vice-President Gore in the Democratic primaries.

As for Vice-President Gore, he had to live down his involvement in the fund-raising abuses of the 1996 presidential campaign. He pointed out that the Justice Department had cleared him of criminal wrongdoing, and counted on his advocacy of campaign-finance reform to help erase the stain on his integrity. Gore also sought to separate himself from the sleazy side of the Clinton presidency, lamenting the time the nation had wasted because of the Lewinsky affair and labeling Clinton's behavior "inexcusable."

Skepticism about Gore's transformation helped boost the candidacy of his only rival for the Democratic nomination, former Sen. Bill Bradley of New Jersey, a Rhodes Scholar and athletic hero whose integrity had never been questioned. But Bradley, jealous of his privacy, on one occasion kept to himself the fact that he had suffered an attack of his chronic heart arrhythmia, even though it forced him to curtail his campaign schedule. And the controversy about his failure to be more forthcoming hindered his efforts to catch up with Gore.

On the Republican side, Sen. John McCain of Arizona used the appeal of his character to vault into prominence in the race. A bona-fide war hero as a result of his brutal imprisonment by the North Vietnamese, McCain's advocacy of campaign-finance reform, despite the opposition of most other Republicans to the idea, had stamped him as a man of principle. It also helped that McCain exuded humor and candor, qualities that he exploited by making himself totally accessible to reporters while driving through the hustings in a van labeled the "Straight Talk Express."

Caucuses and Primaries. To conserve his limited resources, McCain did not compete in the Iowa precinct caucuses, which launched the delegate-selection process on January 24. Bush won that contest easily with 41% of the vote, and publisher Steve Forbes, who many had considered Bush's strongest challenger, came in second with 30%. Trailing were talk-show host Alan Keyes, conservative activist Gary Bauer, McCain, and Utah Sen. Orrin Hatch, who then dropped out of the race.

The results were far different on February 1 in the first primary—New Hampshire, where McCain had been campaigning furiously. He had counted on his maverick style of appealing to the state's Independent voters, who were allowed to participate in the Republican contest, and primary day proved him right. McCain won with 49% of the vote to 30% for Bush. That soon put an end to the candidacies of Forbes, who got 13%, and Bauer, who received 1%; Keyes—who received 6% of the vote in New Hampshire—stayed in the race, mainly to promote his conservative beliefs. More than one-third of voters in the Republican contest told the Voter News Service (VNS) exit poll that the most important factor in making their choice was whether a candidate "stands up for what he believes." Three out of five of those voters cast their ballots for McCain. Independent voters, who made up about 40% of the Republican vote, supported McCain by a margin of better than three to one. Yet among registered Republicans, Bush had an edge over McCain.

That was an ominous sign for McCain, as was demonstrated in the next major test, the South Carolina primary on February 19. Bush won with 53% of the vote to 42% for McCain and 5% for Keyes. Exit polls showed that while character mattered in South Carolina, particularly to Independents, it mattered less to registered Republicans. Attracted by Bush's conservative views and his support from party leaders, registered Republicans backed Bush by two to one.

McCain fought back on February 22, winning the primary in his own state of Arizona by 60% to 36% over Bush, and upsetting Bush in Michigan with 53% to 42%. In the Wolverine State, the senator once again won strong support from Democrats and Independents; on the other hand, regular Republicans backed the Texas governor by more than two to one. But in the Super Tuesday balloting on March 7, Bush captured nine states to four for McCain and effectively clinched the nomination. Exit polls in California and New York, the two largest states that balloted, showed Bush getting about 60% of the Republican vote—the same share he had gotten elsewhere. McCain still captured most of the Independents and the majority of voters who most wanted a candidate "who stands up for what he believes." McCain's rise from little-known underdog to Bush's principal challenger illustrated the political potency of the character issue. Bush's ultimate victory demonstrated character's limitations in the intraparty contest for the presidential nomination, where partisan loyalty and ideology counted most.

Among the Democrats, Gore had relatively little trouble defeating Bradley. In their debates, Gore was generally more aggressive, charging that the health-care reform—the centerpiece of Bradley's policy agenda—

Like other presidential races, Campaign 2000 featured third-party candidates: Commentator Patrick Buchanan (bottom) represented the Reform Party, founded by Ross Perot, and Ralph Nader, the consumer advocate, ran on the Green Party.

© Carlos Osorio/AP/Wide World Photos

© Ben Margot/AP/Wide World Photos

would undermine Medicare. Bradley struck back, accusing Gore of distorting his proposals and record. Demanded Bradley: "Why should we believe that you will tell the truth as president if you don't tell the truth as a candidate?"

After defeating Bradley by 63% to 35% in Iowa and 52% to 48% in New Hampshire, Gore, like Bush, clinched the nomination on Super Tuesday when he swept all 15 Democratic contests. But as would become clear, Bradley's counterattack on Gore's truthfulness heightened the vice-president's vulnerability on the character issue in the general-election campaign against Bush.

Third-Party Candidates and the Conventions. Experience suggested that in view of the salubrious national condition, Gore would have an easy time against Bush. Instead, the Republican jumped out in front. This was all the more surprising because the same surveys that put Gore in second place also showed that most voters favored the policies he advocated over Bush's positions. The only explanation for this contradiction offered by the polls was Gore's old nemesis, the character issue. "While many Americans find Vice-President Al Gore's stands on issues more appealing, he is not as well liked or considered as commanding a leader as Gov. George Bush," *The New York Times* reported in May. Gore's "lackluster personal favorability ratings," the story noted, accounted for his trailing Bush by 39% to 47%.

Gore faced another problem in the person of longtime consumer activist Ralph Nader, who in late June was nominated for president on the Green Party ticket. While Nader was scornful of both parties, his attacks on what he called corporate corruption of American life seemed certain to appeal more to potential Gore voters than to backers of Bush. To be sure, there was also an independent presidential candidate on the ideological right, Pat Buchanan, who in August was nominated by the Reform Party, which had been founded by Ross Perot. But most analysts felt—correctly, as it turned out—that divisions within his new party would limit Buchanan's potential for drawing away conservatives from George Bush.

Meanwhile, the governor appeared to bolster his own

© Joel Page/AP/Wide World Photos

Governor Bush looked to Washington experience as he selected Dick Cheney (top), a former U.S. congressman and veteran of the Ford and Bush administrations as his running mate. Democratic vice-presidential nominee Joseph Lieberman (below), a U.S. senator from Connecticut, entered the history books by being the first Jew to run on a national ticket.

www.GoreLieberman.com

© James A. Finley/AP/Wide World Photos

position by announcing the selection of his father's former defense secretary, Richard Cheney, as his running mate. A former House Republican leader in the Reagan era, and before that chief of staff to President Gerald Ford, Cheney brought to the GOP ticket the Washington experience and the understanding of foreign policy that critics contended Bush lacked.

Addressing the GOP convention in Philadelphia in July, Bush argued that the Democratic administration had squandered the opportunities provided by the booming economy and the end of the Cold War. "This administration had its chance," he declared. "They have not led. We will." In an unmistakable allusion to Gore, he questioned his opponent's sincerity when he said: "I do not need to take your pulse before I know my own mind. I do not reinvent myself at every turn. I am not running in borrowed clothes." The convention was judged a success, and Bush's stock soared even higher in the polls.

But then Gore acted dramatically to remedy his character problems by announcing his selection of a vice-presidential candidate, U.S. Sen. Joseph Lieberman of Connecticut, who became the first Jew to run on the national ticket of a major political party. Of more immediate significance, many analysts said, was that Lieberman had been the first prominent Democrat to denounce President Clinton's conduct in the Lewinsky affair. The senator had called Clinton's behavior "not just inappropriate" but "immoral." Lieberman's criticism of Clinton was consistent with the high moral tone he had sought to establish throughout his political career. For example, he had joined leading conservatives in criticizing the entertainment industry for excessive depictions of violence and sexuality. Beyond Lieberman's record, Gore won extra character points from the media by acting to sever his symbolic link to the Clinton scandals even at the risk of stirring latent feelings of anti-Semitism against the Democratic ticket.

Gore reinforced the impression of boldness in his acceptance speech. Instead of resting on the laurels of the booming economy, the vice-president promised to improve the lot of those who had not thrived in the so-called "new economy." "Let's make sure our prosperity enriches not just the few but all working families," he declared. And he used his speech to portray himself as the defender of "working families" against "powerful interests" such as "the big polluters," "the big drug companies," and "bean-counters at HMOs [health-maintenance organizations]."

The Debates and the Fall Campaign. Right after the convention, Gore's poll standings soared. Suddenly it was Bush

The presidential campaign was a family affair for both candidates. George P. Bush (top), the son of Florida Gov. Jeb Bush, gave a passionate speech in behalf of his uncle at the Republican National Convention. In turn, Karenna Gore Schiff (above) seconded her father's nomination at the Democratic National Convention.

Nominees Bush and Gore engaged in a series of three televised debates, sponsored by the Commission on Presidential Debates. Jim Lehrer of PBS served as moderator. The overall effect of the exchanges on the electorate was debatable.

who was on the defensive, forced to defend his policies and explain away tactical blunders, one of which appeared to be his reluctance to agree to the three debates with Gore proposed by the Commission on Presidential Debates. In the face of charges that he was fearful of confronting Gore one-on-one, Bush backed down and accepted the debate commission's proposals. In the debates, Bush benefited from the lower expectations for his performance, because he lacked Gore's experience in debating and the vice-president's grounding in national and foreign policy. Bush was also aided by the media's focus on style and performance as aspects of the character issue. In the first debate, on October 3, moderated by Jim Lehrer of Public Broadcasting Service (PBS), analysts agreed that Gore dominated the exchanges between the two men, seeming more confident and forceful and better informed. A poll for *Time* magazine gave Gore the edge by an average margin of more than 20 points on having "more to say on the issues" and having better "command of the facts." Yet the notion soon took hold that Bush actually had won because he had not committed any great blunder.

"I think they held their own. They both did. And in the end, that has to favor Bush," reported CNN correspondent Candy Crowley in a typical judgment. Also, influential journalists faulted Gore for what they regarded as his condescending mannerisms—sighing and grimacing while Bush answered question. "The vice-president's boorishness gets in the way of his message," wrote *The New York Times* columnist Bob Herbert, while Bush "benefits from a more conversational tone and the demeanor of an ordinary guy."

Even more injurious to Gore were misstatements he made during the debate. He denied that he had questioned whether Bush possessed the experience required for the presidency, though he had been quoted saying just that in *The New York Times*. And Gore claimed that he had traveled to Texas with the head of the Federal Emergency Management Agency (FEMA) on a postdisaster inspection trip, when he actually had only done an aerial inspection on his

(Continued on page 33.)

Spotlight Falls on the Electoral Machinery

In modern U.S. politics, presidential campaigns are supposed to be interminable and tumultuous, while elections are supposed to be swift and bloodless.

The 2000 presidential race turned that rule book inside out. The campaign never ignited the imagination of the public, but the freakishly close vote on Election Day opened the floodgates to a torrent of legal, political, and constitutional wrangling that kept the nation transfixed, in a mixture of fascination and horror, for more than a month. This was "the election from hell," to be remembered not for what happened before the polls opened, but after they closed.

Yet there was a thread that connected the humdrum campaign to its topsy-turvy overtime: The entire spectacle, start to finish, exposed the barnacles on some of the nation's most basic electoral machinery. Among the systems that misfired were an antiquated Electoral College, which produced a president who did not get the most popular votes; outmoded voting machines, which were revealed to have margins of error that in 2000 were greater than the presidential margin of victory; loophole-ridden campaign-finance laws, which could not prevent a record $4 billion from pouring into the campaign—much of it in six- and seven-figure checks from special interests; and the national broadcast networks, which sharply cut back on coverage throughout the campaign and then, on Election Night, blew the call of the pivotal state of Florida—not once but twice.

Then there was this: As has become the norm for the past generation, barely half of eligible adults bothered voting for president—this despite the record sum of money that candidates, parties, and issue groups lavished on trying to capture the electorate's attention and win their votes.

It was not democracy's finest hour. A roundup of the big things that went wrong in Campaign 2000, and a review of the prospects for a fix follow.

The Mechanics: Electoral College and Voting Machines. For the first time since 1888, and the fourth time in U.S. history, the winner of the national popular vote for president was not the winner of the Electoral College vote. Al Gore defeated George Bush by more than 500,000 votes, or 0.5% of some 105 million votes cast, but Bush prevailed in the Electoral College vote, 271–267. Predictably, this "inversion" triggered a fresh wave of calls for the abolition of an institution that Americans have long regarded as a relic. Just as predictably, however, the Electoral College seems likely to outlast its critics. It was written into the Constitution by Founding Fathers who were openly skeptical of the idea that ordinary citizens had the wisdom to decide who should be president; this would be like blind men picking out colors, George Mason of Virginia opined in 1787. Instead, the framers created a system in which the voters or legislatures of each state would choose a national college of electors— and these wise men, in turn, would choose a president of the nation.

In the ensuing two centuries, the proposition that the people should be their own rulers has become a cornerstone of the notion of democracy. As a result, the Electoral College has long since been reduced to a mere rubber stamp of the will of the voters of the states. But there remains one key feature of the College that, as a matter of practical politics, makes its elimination

© B. Daemmrich/Corbis-Sygma

The low percentage of Americans that go to the polls has dismayed observers for years. In the presidential race of 2000, voter turnout was slightly above 50%.

unlikely. It gives extra weight to the votes of citizens from smaller states, by apportioning electors to each state on the basis of its combined total of U.S. congressmen and senators. The idea was to guard against a strict majoritarian regime that might cause candidates for president to concentrate their campaigns exclusively on major population centers. It was this small-state "bonus" that tipped the Electoral College vote to Bush in 2000. And it is this same small-state bonus that makes the institution so resilient. All constitutional amendments must be approved by three-quarters of all states—a remote prospect, given the heavy small-state stake in the status quo.

What is far more likely is that the excruciatingly close popular vote in 2000 will serve as a wake-up call to elected officials to modernize U.S. voting equipment. The tangled recount drama in Florida turned in part on how to deal with the fact that old-fashioned punch-card voting machines—which are used in about one-third of all voting precincts nationwide—have difficulty reading the votes of citizens who do not punch their ballots all the way through. Even before the courts finally put an end to these "chad wars," the halls of the U.S. Congress had filled with proposals to create bipartisan national commissions and provide federal funding for local governments to update their machines.

While a new infusion of money could help modernize the equipment, it was less clear as the year ended whether other problems exposed by Campaign 2000 could be so easily repaired. The revelation that roughly 2% of ballots routinely go uncounted in a national election—either because the voter has not followed the proper procedure or because a machine cannot discern the voter's intention—doubtless came as a blow to the already tenuous grip that the phrase "every vote counts" has on the civic imagination. Will it further dampen

© AP/Wide World Photos

The media added to the confusion of Election Night 2000 as the television networks and cable news programs miscalled the results in Florida and major newspapers published editions with headlines that proclaimed the winner prematurely.

turnout? Or will the razor-thin margin of 2000 spark a new interest in voting? That is a tug-of-war sure to play out in the hearts and minds of the electorate for years to come.

The Media—Networks Missed the Campaign; Bombed on Election Night. Two different times on Election Night, all the major U.S. networks and cable news programs miscalled the results in Florida, a reporting debacle that conceivably influenced the voting and surely shaped the politics of the postelection recount. It was the biggest reporting blunder in television history. "We don't just have egg on our face," lamented NBC anchorman Tom Brokaw, "we have an omelet."

Shortly before 8:00 P.M. East Coast time—50 minutes after the polls had closed in most of Florida, but about 10 minutes before they closed in a handful of counties in the state's Panhandle—all three broadcast networks and all the major cable news networks declared that Gore had carried the state. The projections were based on interviews with voters leaving the polling places in sample precincts selected by the Voter News Service (VNS), an exit-polling consortium that, in a cost-cutting move, all the networks jointly financed. But it turned out the VNS samples were off, a discovery that ashen-faced TV anchors disclosed to their viewers a few hours later, when they switched Florida to the "too close to call" column. Then, shortly after 2:00 A.M., with more than 95% of the actual Florida vote in, the networks made their second blunder—they all reported that Bush had carried the state, and declared that he was the next president of the United States. This led Gore to phone Bush, congratulate him, and prepare to give his concession statement. But on the way to deliver it, Gore learned—and the networks learned—that those last late-reporting precincts in Florida had shrunk Bush's lead to just a few thousand votes. The vice-president promptly made a second call to Bush, awkwardly rescinded the concession, and spent the next five weeks pressing, in vain, for a conclusive manual

Politics and money long have been intertwined, and campaign-finance reform has become a major issue. During the year, New Mexico Attorney General Patricia Madrid (above) spoke in favor of campaign-reform amendments in her home state.

campaign, the broadcast industry reenforced a "pay-to-talk" campaign culture in which candidates who want to be seen and heard on television must pay their way on—30 seconds at a time. Throughout 2000, more than 1 million political advertisements aired on broadcast television, at an estimated cost of nearly $1 billion. It was a record-breaking bonanza for the broadcast industry, which sold more political ads than fast-food ads. But it helped fuel the nonstop political-money chase that has become the defining characteristic of modern politics.

recount in Florida. In that effort, Gore was handicapped from the start by the public perception, first fixed by the network declaration on Election Night, that Bush had in fact won the state and the election.

The blunders triggered a round of calls for the networks to resist making any projection until all polls in a state had closed, along with proposals for a uniform nationwide poll closing time, to prevent the possibility that early projections in some states might dampen turnout in other states. The networks pledged to reexamine their projection standards, and said they would no longer rely on a single exit-polling consortium, such as VNS.

But while Election Night was the most visible network foul-up in Campaign 2000, it was not the only one. This was a year in which the presidential campaign largely migrated on television from the traditional networks to the cable news shows, which draw just a fraction of the networks' audience. Overall coverage on ABC, NBC, and CBS was down substantially from previous campaigns. Coverage of the national-party conventions continued to drop, and, for the first time ever, two of the three networks did not carry some or all of the presidential debates in the fall. "We basically forfeited the field" to cable, veteran ABC reporter Sam Donaldson said of his network's nightly news coverage. The paucity of campaign coverage was even more pronounced on local stations, which provided minimal coverage of local and state races. By scaling back on coverage of the

The Money—Loopholes Swallow the Law. When it comes to money and politics, virtually everything that happened in Campaign 2000 set a record. The Center for Responsive Politics, a leading campaign-finance-watchdog group, estimated that $3 billion was spent on all federal campaigns, and another $1 billion on state and local races. It was not just this record amount of money, but the way it found its way into the campaign, that made a mockery of the campaign-finance laws of the mid-1970s. Those laws, enacted after the Watergate scandal, created a system of contribution limits designed to keep large donations out of federal elections, in order to avoid the appearance or reality of corruption

However, nearly $500 million was donated in 2000 to the national political parties in the form of "soft-money"—unlimited five-, six-, or seven-figure checks from businesses, unions, and wealthy individuals. The soft-money loophole was created in the late 1970s to allow wealthy donors to provide parties with resources for party-building activities. It was never intended to be used interchangeably with "hard money"—donations subject to contribution limits—to fund campaign ads. Since the mid-1990s, however, a series of court and administrative rulings have allowed soft-money to be used in this manner, effectively undermining the entire post-Watergate regime of contribution limits. And as the loophole has opened, the money has flooded in—party soft money

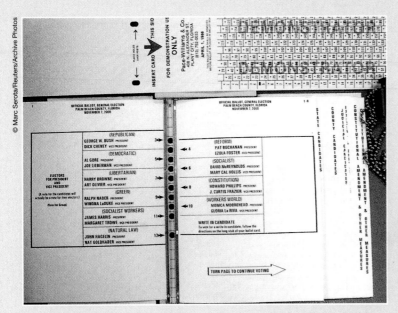

Outmoded voting machines and various ballots came under fire following the tight presidential race of 2000. The "butterfly ballot," above, that was used in Florida's Palm Beach County was considered particularly confusing since the candidate's name and the spot to indicate one's choice were not side by side.

funding. Meantime, a Wall Street mogul named Jon Corzine shattered a different kind of record: He dipped into his personal fortune for $62 million to finance his first race for public office—a successful bid for a U.S. Senate seat from New Jersey. While the size of Corzine's personal investment in his campaign was eye-popping, it was also part of a trend. Increasingly, both major parties took to recruiting millionaire candidates, figuring that every time they snared a candidate who could bankroll his or her own race, it meant the parties could stretch their dollars further among candidates who needed their financial help.

receipts tripled from 1992 to 1996, then doubled again from 1996 to 2000.

But that was not the only gaping loophole that widened in 2000. The campaign also saw hundreds of millions of dollars go into campaign advertising by special-interest groups. Some of the groups were well known, such as the Sierra Club, the National Rifle Association (NRA), the U.S. Chamber of Commerce, the AFL-CIO. Others sought to hide their identity, such as a group that called itself Citizens for Better Medicare, even though it was really a consortium of major pharmaceutical companies. None of these expenditures was subject to contribution limits. In a number of U.S. congressional races, the issue groups spent more money than either the candidates or the parties—creating a complex, hydra-headed world of political spending that becomes more difficult to rein in with each new election.

Even without these loopholes, the booming economy created so much disposable income among America's wealthiest citizens that all forms of traditional fund-raising increased. Bush became the first presidential candidate ever to raise more than $100 million in "hard money"—money subject to the $1,000 per-person contribution limit. He also became the first nominee of a major party to forgo federal matching funds in the primaries because he did not want to operate within the spending limit required of candidates who accept such public

As Washington, DC, continued to fill up with elected officials who got to town on the strength of their own fortunes or the largesse of special interests, the public continued to grow disenchanted with the whole political-money game. For a brief moment during the 2000 primary season, Sen. John McCain (R-AZ) tapped into a yearning for something better; he became the first presidential candidate in modern history to build his candidacy around a call for campaign-finance reform. McCain did not prevail, but his unexpectedly strong showing in the primaries added to his clout in the Senate as the coauthor of the leading bipartisan campaign-finance-reform measure. It has been a generation since the nation undertook a major overhaul of the rules governing money and politics. The last time a major bill passed, the spark was the illegal fund-raising practices uncovered during the Watergate scandal. This time, if and when reform comes, the spark will be not what is illegal, but that what is considered legal is also considered scandalous.

PAUL TAYLOR

Editor's Note. Paul Taylor is the founder and executive director of the Alliance for Better Campaigns, a public-interest group that "seeks to improve elections by promoting campaigns in which the most useful information reaches the greatest number of citizens in the most engaging way." Previously, Mr. Taylor had been a journalist for some 25 years, covering national politics and social issues.

own. Bush's running mate Cheney seized upon these instances as evidence that Gore had an "uncontrollable desire" to exaggerate, and other Republicans joined in making the argument that the vice-president lacked the integrity to lead the country. Gore claimed his controversial statements were merely innocent mistakes. But he was clearly shaken by the criticisms.

In his second encounter with Bush—in Winston-Salem, NC, on October 11—Gore felt obliged to offer an apology for his "getting some of the details wrong" the previous week. Also, Gore abandoned the aggressive style that had drawn criticism in the first encounter with Bush, and appeared unnaturally subdued. Bush, on the other hand, won praise for handling foreign-policy questions without error. Most journalists and opinion surveys judged Bush the winner. In the third debate, on October 17 in St. Louis, Gore abandoned attempts to alter his personality and went after Bush hammer and tongs. The Republican standard-bearer responded in kind. The result, in the judgment of pundits and pollsters, was a draw. "No body slams; both candidates are still in the ring and still standing," said NBC's Tom Brokaw. But most analysts agreed that the debates had on balance helped Bush by blurring the policy differences between the two men, which polls showed worked in Gore's favor, and by focusing attention instead on character, Gore's weakness.

As the campaign headed into its closing days, the polls showed the race to be almost even, with Bush enjoying a slight edge. Then, five days before the voting, the Republican's campaign was jarred by the disclosure that the governor had been convicted of driving under the influence of alcohol in 1976. Pressed about why he had not previously disclosed this episode, even though he had been asked by reporters whether he had ever been guilty of such an offense, Bush explained that he did not want to reveal it to his twin daughters. On the campaign trail, he went back to stressing one of his favorite themes—the importance of character and integrity to presidential leadership.

Election Day, the Results, and the Challenges. As Election Day—November 7—arrived, everyone expected the result would be very close. But no one anticipated the photo finish that left the identity of the winner a question mark for weeks and set off an unprecedented political and legal battle.

The first returns for the most part sustained the forecasts of the polls. Bush's strength was spread evenly through the Southwest, the Plains States, and the South. His biggest conquests were his own state of Texas, with 32 electoral votes, and the traditional Republican stronghold of Ohio, with 21 electoral votes. Gore's strength was concentrated on the West Coast, where he was winning the election's richest prize, California, with its 54 votes, and the East, where he claimed New York, with 33 electoral votes. It became clear that the election would probably be decided by the results in three closely fought states: Michigan, with 18 electoral votes; Pennsylvania, with 23; and Florida, with 25. Gore took an early lead in the first two and won them both. That meant Florida held the key to the election. At first, the television networks, relying on exit polls and tabulated voting data, thought that the vice-president had prevailed in that state, too. But later in the evening, the networks withdrew their initial projection for the state and anointed Bush as the winner—not just of Florida, but of the presidency. Resignedly, Gore called Bush to concede defeat, and began to draft his concession speech. Then the networks, realizing they had miscalculated, retracted their award of Florida to Bush, declaring the state too close to call. Gore promptly phoned Bush back to cancel his concession. On the day after the election, Bush led in Florida by only 1,784 votes out of 6 million cast, or about three-hundredths of 1% of the total vote in the state. Nader received a total of 100,000 votes—which, as Gore supporters pointed out, would have been more than enough to give their candidate victory.

© Charles Rex Arbogast/AP/Wide World Photos

Judge Charles Burton, chairman of the Palm Beach County canvassing board, was surrounded by lawyers representing both the Republicans and the Democrats as he considered ballots during Florida's vote-recount process.

With some votes still to be counted and recounted, Gore led in the popular vote, with about 48.5% to 48.4% for Bush, 3% for Nader, and 1% to Buchanan. Gore enjoyed an Electoral College lead of 255 votes to 246 for Bush. Oregon, with 7 electoral votes, and New Mexico, with 5, were still judged too close to call, though both ultimately went to Gore. But neither candidate could gain an Electoral College majority of 270 without Florida, and the Sunshine State's 25 votes were knotted in a legal tangle that would continue for five turbulent weeks.

A machine recount, mandatory under Florida law, went forward, cutting Bush's initial lead to 327 by November 10. But Democrats were not satisfied. They complained about ballot irregularities, particularly in Palm Beach County, where they charged an oddly designed "butterfly ballot" had fooled thousands of would-be Gore voters into casting ballots for Pat Buchanan. They also contended that punch-card ballots had cost Gore votes because the voting machines had failed to register the indentations Gore supporters had made on the ballots. A huge controversy erupted, and "chad"—the disk on the ballot that was supposed to be perforated to mark a vote—and "dimple"—the mark left on a chad, became part of the political lexicon.

Four heavily Democratic counties—Volusia, Palm Beach, Broward, and Dade—began hand-counting ballots to find votes that the machines overlooked. The process was prolonged by bitter arguments about standards for counting—whether "dimpled chads" should be considered a vote or whether a clean perforation should be required. On Tuesday, November 14, when Florida Secretary of State Katherine Harris, who had been cochair of Bush's campaign in the state, was scheduled to certify the statewide vote, Bush's lead was 300 votes, and only the hand-counted ballots from Volusia County were part of the tally. The day before, Harris had said that she would enforce a deadline of 5:00 P.M., November 14, for counties to complete manual recounts. Leon County Court Judge Terry Lewis agreed with Harris' deadline, but ruled that she must consider requests for amended results after the deadline, and could not reject hand counts arbitrarily. On Saturday, November 18, absentee ballots boosted the Bush margin to 930 votes, setting off another series of protests, this time from Republicans. They claimed that Bush's gains would have been greater if Democrats had not insisted on disqualifying more than 1,000 absentee ballots from members of the armed forces abroad because they had not been properly postmarked.

Then, on Tuesday, November 21, the Florida Supreme Court stepped into the dispute, overruling Harris and extending the certification deadline until Sunday, November 26, to give Broward, Palm Beach, and Miami-Dade counties time to finish their hand counting. Charging that the court had rewritten the Florida statute book, the Bush campaign appealed the decision to the U.S. Supreme Court, while the Gore campaign celebrated. But that turned out to be premature. Deciding that there was not enough time to meet the new deadline, election officials of Democratic Miami-Dade, the largest county in the state, abandoned the manual recount. Palm Beach County also struggled against the clock, submitting an incomplete count to Harris, who refused to consider it. On November 26, Harris certified Bush as the winner of Florida by a 537-vote margin, including only the recounted ballots from Broward County in her tally.

Bush claimed victory and began planning his administration. He appeared to get a partial boost on December 4, when the U.S. Supreme Court granted the Texas governor's request to vacate the Florida Supreme Court's decision extending the certification deadline, and sent the ruling back to the Florida court for clarification. Gore refused to give up. He launched a new legal effort, contesting the certified results that would have given the state's electors to Bush, and asking the Florida courts to restart the recount in Palm Beach and Miami-Dade. Rebuffed by a Florida circuit court, Gore appealed to the state's Supreme Court, which on December 8, gave the vice-president most of what he wanted. By a four-to-three decision, the justices not only ordered manual recounts to proceed in Palm Beach and Miami-Dade counties, as Gore had asked, but also ordered a recount of about 45,000 "undervotes"—ballots that registered no vote for president—in every other county in Florida, too. The Florida court also directed that the recounted votes that Secretary Harris had refused to certify be added to Gore's tally, reducing Bush's total to 154. The court set a December 10 deadline for counting to assure making the December 12 federal statutory deadline for certifying Florida's electors.

But Gore faced two obstacles. Fearful that the courts would take away Bush's victory, leaders of Florida's Republi-

Although Florida's Secretary of State Katherine Harris signed the certificate declaring Governor Bush the winner of Florida's electoral votes and essentially the president-elect on November 26, legal challenges continued for more than two weeks.

© Rick Wilking/Reuters/Archive Photos

While awaiting the final outcome, the GOP ticket conferred at the governor's Texas ranch. After the U.S. Supreme Court ruled on December 12 that the Florida recount should be stopped, Vice-President Gore conceded defeat and George W. Bush was president-elect.

can-controlled legislature convened a special session. Their goal was to select a slate of electors pledged to support Bush's candidacy when the Electoral College met on December 18, regardless of what the court-ordered recount might show. Another, even more formidable, roadblock was the U.S. Supreme Court. On December 9, in response to an appeal from Bush, the high court called a halt to the recount ordered by the Florida court and agreed to consider the case. Interest in the case ran high, and audiotapes of the arguments on December 11 were released for broadcast to the public. The give-and-take between the justices and the lawyers for each side made obvious that the Supreme Court was sharply divided, and this split was underlined by the rulings handed down on December 12. Seven justices agreed that the Florida Supreme Court ruling to allow recounts had raised constitutional problems. But the key decision—that there was no constitutional way to solve these problems within the time available—produced a five-to-four split along ideological lines. Ruling in Bush's favor were the court's most conservative justices—Chief Justice William Rehnquist and Justices Sandra Day O'Connor, Antonin Scalia, Anthony Kennedy, and Clarence Thomas. Opposed were the more liberal justices—David Souter, Stephen Breyer, Ruth Bader Ginsburg, and John Paul Stevens. In a stinging dissent, Stevens contended that while doubt might still remain over who really won the presidential election, "the identity of the loser is perfectly clear. It is the nation's confidence in the judge as an impartial guardian of the rule of law."

The Outcome. By ending the contest in Florida, the high-court ruling in effect gave Bush 271 electoral votes to 267 for Gore. It was the narrowest electoral-vote margin in a presidential contest since Thomas Jefferson and Aaron Burr deadlocked in 1800, throwing the election into the House of Representatives. Bush trailed in the popular vote, getting 50,456,169, more than 500,000 fewer that Gore's 50,996,116. Only three other candidates had won the White House after losing the popular vote—John Quincy Adams (1824), Rutherford B. Hayes (1876) and Benjamin Harrison (1888).

On December 13, the day after the Supreme Court ruled against the vice-president and 36 days after Americans went to the polls, Gore in a brief televised speech officially conceded to Bush. Displaying no bitterness or rancor, Gore said that while he disagreed with the adverse ruling of the high court, he would accept it. He added a pledge to help Bush "bring Americans together." President-elect Bush, in his own remarks later that night, matched Gore's conciliatory tone. "I was not elected to serve one party, but to serve one nation," Bush said. "Whether you voted for me or not, I will do my best to serve your interests."

The First Lady Becomes Senator-elect

In 1998, Daniel Patrick Moynihan, nearing the end of his fourth term as a Democratic U.S. senator from New York, said he would not seek reelection. Almost immediately, prominent Democrats began suggesting that First Lady Hillary Rodham Clinton should be the party's candidate for the post. After months of deliberation, exploratory work, and fact-finding tours of New York State, Mrs. Clinton decided to run, becoming the first wife of a sitting president to seek elective office.

The Campaign. New York Mayor Rudolph W. Giuliani, the apparent Republican candidate for the Senate seat, began portraying the first lady, who was raised in Illinois and had been a resident of Arkansas since her marriage to Bill Clinton in 1975, as a carpetbagger, and accused her of relying on "soft money"—the unregulated donations that political parties route to individual campaigns. She made limp efforts to counter the carpetbagger criticism, but was more effective in handling questions regarding education and racial problems. Mrs. Clinton (shown at right, campaigning with her daughter Chelsea) plunged into a dogged traverse of the state that began in July 1999, seven months before she formally declared her candidacy, and continued until Election Day. The traveling raised her visibility in upstate Republican strongholds and immersed her in firsthand stories of economic deprivation, energy costs, taxes, health crises, and troubled schools.

In May 2000, Giuliani withdrew from the Senate race. He earlier had announced that he had prostate cancer, and had surprised his wife of 16 years by announcing his intention to separate. With less than six months to Election Day, the Republicans then turned to a young U.S. congressman from Long Island, Rick A. Lazio, as their nominee. By plane and bus, Lazio headed out across the state, emphasizing his New York roots, fiscal restraint, history as a public servant, and his character and integrity. He made the traditional Republican proposal for a tax cut. Ads showed him as a devoted family man, subtly raising the issue of President Clinton's sexual indiscretions, and

Mrs. Clinton's decision to remain in their marriage. Lazio's war chest swelled with donations not only from New Yorkers but from people nationwide who disliked the first lady.

In pressing the attack over soft money, Lazio walked up to Mrs. Clinton's podium during a debate to demand that she sign a pledge to

© Chris Hondros/Newsmakers/Liaison Agency

forgo such funding, a move seen as menacing. He tried to cast doubt on her commitment to Israel, and criticized her for collecting $50,000 in campaign contributions at a fund-raiser held by a Muslim-American organization that had been criticized for expressing support for terrorist groups. She returned the money, but any Republican advantage was lost in popular outrage against a statewide party telephone campaign that tried to link some of the first lady's supporters to terrorism just after the bombing of the USS *Cole* in a Yemeni port in October.

The Outcome. Despite spending nearly $40 million to Mrs. Clinton's $29 million—helping to make it the most expensive U.S. Senate race in history—Lazio could not match her fame, her upstate focus, or a Democratic get-out-the-vote campaign. Mrs. Clinton piled up big vote margins in New York City, held on in the suburbs, and ran strong upstate. She won 3,747,310 votes to Lazio's 2,915,730. She then headed back to Washington to finish her duties as first lady and prepare for her role as one of 13 female senators in the 107th Congress.

ANDREA KANNAPELL, *"The New York Times"*

THE U.S. ECONOMY— THE GREAT EXPANSION

By John Cunniff

Soaring stock prices for much of the 1990s and into 2000 kept traders on the New York Stock Exchange, above, busy, increased the personal wealth of many Americans, and fueled consumer confidence.

About the Author. John Cunniff, Associated Press' (AP's) Business News Analyst and author of the daily column "Business Mirror," has been a reporter, commentator, and critic of consumer, business, and economic events for more than three decades. Accordingly, his reporting and comments have appeared in hundreds of newspapers and other publications. Mr. Cunniff has been the recipient of numerous journalism honors, including the George Polk Award for national reporting and the Distinguished Achievement Award of the Society of American Business Editors and Writers. His books include *Live Within Your Income.*

As the U.S. economy emerged from recession in March 1991, few would have dared believe that the period of economic growth would evolve into the great expansion of the 1990s, and continue on into the new millennium as the longest in American history, 118 months as the year 2000 ended. The experience of post–World War II had conditioned Americans to expect a cycle of economic expansions and contractions every few years. It was the way things were.

That the economy continued to charge ahead without interruption in the 1990s was, therefore, a constant surprise. Warnings of a downturn were repeatedly contradicted by a soaring stock market, and by monthly statistics that showed wages, profits, and gross domestic product (GDP) rising, while unemployment, inflation, and other negative readings remained low or falling. Much else evolved that preexpansion Americans would have had difficulty imagining, including huge annual U.S. budget surpluses, an explosion of consumer electronic devices, "instant" entrepreneurial billionaires, and a huge gain in output per work-hour that made economists question theories. The expansion was energized by a massive rethinking and reexpression of the economic world in terms of electronics, exemplified largely by the electronic chip that drove computers and other communication and information devices. In a sense, the chip condensed the elaborate pipe and wire designs of the mechanical age to nearly invisible electronic circuitry printed on a tiny silicon wafer.

The good times led not only to changes in the way people lived and worked, but to extravagances without limit. Many new suburban homes, triple the standard-sized three- or four-bedroom homes, sold quickly. The ocean-cruise industry became a hot ticket. Prices of electronic stocks soared to unheard-of multiples. Tickets to sporting events were scalped for thousands of dollars. Fancy restaurants attracted customers not just for their food but for elegant, architect-designed rest rooms.

To some extent, the greatest doubts and fears were contained mainly among professional reviewers of the economy and to the older members of the population, who earlier had experienced recession disappointments. The fearlessness and enthusiasm of the so-called baby boomers of the post–World War II era, and, increasingly, their children, provided much of the thrust, characterized by innovation, exuberance, and an impatient desire for a better material life.

As the expansion continued, exceeding the old record of 106 months early in the new millennium, half of all U.S. households were connected to the Internet and using it to buy merchandise, deliver messages, sell stocks, make travel arrangements, and even attend college courses. It literally opened a new world of information and communications, with access to most of it free for the clicking. While estimates varied, industry figures placed the number of cellular telephones in use at more than 86 million, and the sight of lone pedestrians conversing as they strolled became commonplace. Expensive new houses were electronically equipped to allow for remote operation of appliances, and drivers of vehicles were beginning to be guided by global positioning systems that pinpointed locations and routes within yards. Speed and efficiency became more necessary than ever in business and personal life, and some complained that the new demands were accompanied by a decline in privacy and interpersonal services. Perhaps most telling of the changes, family life became the working life: For the first time in U.S. Census history, by 1998 the majority of parents were employed at least some of the time, compared with 33% in 1976. Feminists tended to view changes in terms of success. Indeed, and in spite of complaints about a glass ceiling that was said to limit advancement, women became increasingly successful in creating and occupying the top ranks in companies.

Technological and communications gains—such as the mobile phone, above—changed life and work styles in the 1990s. Meanwhile, people with growing incomes sought ever-larger houses equipped for the new technologies.

New Worries, Too. Nevertheless, big changes created new worries. Academics worried about a population with eyes fixed on the future and with disdain for the lessons of the past. Religious leaders expressed fears about new

© Spencer Grant/PhotoEdit

Gross Domestic Product

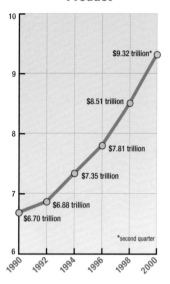

- $9.32 trillion* (2000)
- $8.51 trillion
- $7.81 trillion
- $7.35 trillion
- $6.88 trillion
- $6.70 trillion

*second quarter

The growth of technology companies—many of which were listed on the Nasdaq stock exchange—created talk of a "new economy." Whether the economy was "old" or "new," the U.S. gross domestic product (GDP) increased from $6.7 trillion in 1990 to $9.32 trillion in the second quarter of 2000.

freedoms in sexual behavior and what they viewed as a decay of moral values. The Federal Reserve worried about the propensity of the young to live for the moment, while borrowing against future income to buy cars, houses, and nonessential luxuries—such as cruises and ski trips. Even the worrywart Fed worried others; some criticized it for what they viewed as overly restrictive, tied-to-the-past monetary policies, and others complained that it made borrowing too easy for individuals and businesses. In general, headlines that began with "Economists" often were followed by "warn," suggesting economic professionals feared heights more so than did most Americans. Curiously and significantly, after a nationwide survey, The Conference Board reported that more Americans were dissatisfied with their jobs than five years earlier, and that the most dissatisfied of all were the baby boomers, ages 45 to 54.

The times also were lamented by some as coldly materialistic, the point illustrated prolifically in popular "how-to" money magazines and cover stories featuring successful young couples. Television's highest-rated show in the year 2000 was *Who Wants to Be a Millionaire*, in which contestants sought to win $1 million by successfully answering questions on camera; and *The Millionaire Next Door*, a 1996 book by Thomas J. Stanley and William D. Danko on the emerging wealth of families, remained a best-seller. While wages rose after having remained stagnant throughout the 1980s, and unemployment fell to under 4% of the labor force, the gap between rich and poor widened. Repeated increases of the mandated federal minimum wage to $5.15 per hour were minimized by explosive increases in the incomes of personnel in entertainment, sports, business start-ups, the executive suite, and legal and financial services. Spectrum Financial Group, a research firm, provided specifics on the "wealthiest one percent," a much-used term. The richest 1%, it said, was made up of 1.1 million households with an average annual income of $671,000 and a net worth of $4.2 million. Most shocking of all—to old-timers, at least—were the incomes and assets of the creators of high-tech companies and their early investors. Bill Gates, cofounder of Microsoft Corporation, the world's largest computer-software firm, was entrenched as the world's richest person, with assets of more than $60 billion, but he was followed closely by Larry Ellison, founder of Oracle Corporation, also a software company. Not far behind was Michael Dell, whose Dell Computer Corporation began as a college enterprise and gained him assets of more than $17 billion by age 35. Following were scores of high-tech enterprisers whose assets sometimes soared to nine digits when they sold shares to the public.

With General Electric a notable exception, many old blue-chip companies ran into trouble, misreading the market or unable to smoothly make the transition to what had become known as the new economy. The new economy included not just computing and telecommunications, but biotechnology firms that produced a cornucopia of pharmaceuticals, some genetically engineered. The expansion's impact spread through every aspect of American life, and some of the older industrial concerns benefited as well as the new. But the number of mature companies that tripped on the new or became involved in product litigation read like a *Who's Who* of the old economy—American Telephone & Telegraph, Xerox, Campbell Soup, Procter & Gamble, Gillette, Coca-Cola, Eastman Kodak, Owens Corning, and scores of retailing, media, and manufacturing companies. The tobacco companies, in constant litigation that already had cost them well more than $1 billion in expenses and penalties, were a separate case in an increasingly health-conscious, antitobacco world. But even Microsoft ran into trouble, being declared a monopoly and threatened with a federal court-ordered split up. Even newer companies—such as Lucent, a high-tech spin-off from AT&T; on-line marketer Amazon.com; and priceline.com, whose software offered low-cost tickets and other products and services—ran into problems. In a wry twist, directors increasingly sought the experience of old-economy executives, a sign—some said, that old and new concepts were merging.

The Beginning. The great upheaval in business and lifestyles began as crankily as an old diesel locomotive, quickened after a few years, and, from 1995 on, jetted onward. Statistics documented its power:

• In 1990 the gross domestic product (GDP), the broadest measure of the output of goods (from bread to automobiles) and services (health care, education, and the like), was $6.71 trillion. Measured for consistency by the same 1996 dollar, the GDP in the April–June quarter of 2000 totaled $9.32 trillion at an annual rate. An economy which was centuries old had leaped nearly 40% in one decade.

• Technology-induced productivity gains (hourly output of all workers) in the nonfarm business sector rose from 1.1% in 1990—and under 1% in 1993 and 1995—to 2.9% in 1999, with quarterly rates as high as 8% in the final quarter of 1999. Productivity gains are the most direct way in which wages and profits can improve simultaneously without serious inflation.

• Measured in 1982 dollars, the average hourly wage, at $7.39 in 1995, rose to $7.90 in August 2000, when the biggest monthly gain occurred. Increasingly, however, incomes were raised by investment returns and transfer payments, the latter including Social Security benefits to an aging population.

• After-tax corporate profits more than doubled from $261 billion in 1990 to $567 billion in 1999. And, measured by consumer prices, the inflation rate fell to 2.7% in 1999 from 6.1% in 1990.

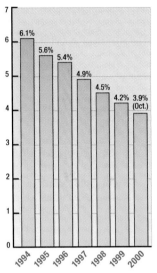

Unemployment

6.1% (1994)
5.6% (1995)
5.4% (1996)
4.9% (1997)
4.5% (1998)
4.2% (1999)
3.9% (Oct.) (2000)

© Mark Richards/PhotoEdit

Most Americans were working in the 1990s, with unemployment reaching 30-year-lows of 3.9% in 2000. Productivity was up with workers, as the computer became the office mainstay.

• Unemployment, 5.6% in 1990, dropped to 30-year lows of 3.9% in three months of 2000—April, September, and October. Civilian jobs rose from 118.7 million in 1990 to 135 million in 2000. Much of the gain was among women, minorities, and the least skilled.

• The poverty rate as 2000 began fell to a 21-year low of 11.8%. During 1999 more than 2 million people rose above the poverty level of $17,029 for a family of four, as median income rose for the fifth consecutive year. The bottom 20% of incomes rose 5.4% in 1999, the fastest rate of all. The top 20% rose only 3.9%, but the gap between rich and poor widened, the wealthiest increases being from a larger dollar base. The poverty rates for minorities were sharply reduced. The rate for African-Americans fell to 23.6%, the lowest ever. The rate for Hispanics declined to 22.8%, and for Asians to 10.7%.

• Matching a record high, more than 67% of American families owned their own homes in 2000. As the decade neared its end, new-home sales rose to more than 900,000 units, and existing home sales to more than 5 million units, both records.

• Retail sales of passenger vehicles exceeded 17 million units by 2000, compared with 9.3 million units in 1990. The latest figures included so-called sport-utility vehicles (SUVs), which were popular with families.

Inflation Rate

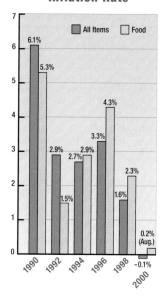

Taking Credit. Predictably, the accomplishments provided opportunities for elected officials of all political parties to take credit and, in rarer instances, to assess blame. The Clinton administration presided over much of the expansion period, and the president made efforts to remind people of it, but credit was not easily granted. Federal Reserve chairman Alan Greenspan, responsible for six interest-rate increases between June 1999 and May 2000, was extolled by Democrats and Republicans alike for having prolonged the expansion by slowing it to sustainable levels. Republican critics conceded Clinton may have nurtured the good times, but they frequently attributed it to renewed confidence generated by tax cuts of the Reagan administration. Technologists were more inclined to attribute the expansion to university research and entrepreneurship. Others, including Greenspan, simply mentioned the productivity explosion. In time, historians may find more contributors and conclude that all played a role in the grand design. Whatever, the great expansion left the United States vastly changed, but in the view of some, not always for the better.

© Mike Theiler/Reuters/Archive Photos

Alan Greenspan, above, began his fourth term as chairman of the Federal Reserve Board in 2000. He was credited with helping to prolong the economy's expansion by instituting interest-rate increases at appropriate times to keep the growth at sustainable levels.

The Good and the Bad. As companies grew or merged, retail casualties abounded. Wal-Mart, a general-merchandise store founded by Sam Walton of Arkansas in the early 1960s, grew into such a vast international chain that its sales exceeded any other retail enterprise ever created. At the same time, some accused it and other large stores, such as Home Depot, of devastating downtown areas by attracting buyers to their warehouse-style structures at outlying fringes.

The economy, it was often said, was driven by the courage of consumers in spending lavishly, but concerns were increasingly expressed by the level of consumer credit outstanding—$789 billion in 1990 and $1.4 trillion in August 2000. The savings rate flirted with zero. However, it was argued, the statistic was a bit dated in failing to recognize that people now invested in stocks and saved through rising home equity.

The U.S. budget surpluses, which began in 1998 and totaled $237 billion in fiscal year 2000, with further surpluses for years more, were welcomed after deficits that often ran more than $200 billion in the 1980s and early 1990s. But the country seemed divided on how to use the surpluses—cut taxes; reduce the federal debt, which had swelled from $3.2 trillion in 1990 to $5.7 trillion in 2000; use the money to bolster Social Security; or create new government benefits. It became a big issue in the fight for the presidency between Vice-President Al Gore and Texas Gov. George W. Bush.

With many households involved in the stock market either as owners of corporate shares or mutual funds, or vested in pension funds, most people cheered as the Dow Jones Industrial Average (DJIA) rose from just above 3,000 points in 1991 to an all-time 11,722.98 points in January 2000, creating enormous paper wealth for individuals and institutions. Harvard University's endowment surged to $19.2 billion in 2000, a gain of $4.8 billion in one year. But such heights caused concern over triple-digit price-earnings ratios, especially among Internet merchandisers. The DJIA closed the year at 10,786.85.

Consumer Credit

$1,482 billion (Aug.)

- 1990: $789.1 billion
- 1993: $838.3 billion
- 1996: $1,182.6 billion
- 1999: $1,393.7 billion
- 2000: (to 1,500)

U.S. exports soared, especially as the dollar strengthened against foreign currencies, but so did imports, leaving a huge and growing net trade imbalance. Economists were concerned that the country, including the securities markets, had become too dependent on foreign money.

Families enjoyed stable food prices, a consequence of rising corporate-farm productivity, but small farmers were often distressed, From mid-1996 on, the gap widened between farmer costs and prices received. Meanwhile, increasing gasoline and fuel prices became a worry for almost everyone.

© David Young-Wolff/PhotoEdit

Although shoppers welcomed stable food prices, small farmers did not fare well. Some experts warned that the tendency of Americans to overuse the credit card and save little was a dark side of the expansion era.

Still, the ordinary folks who helped create the great expansion, and who now faced the challenge of maintaining the momentum, were encouraged. While concerned with great heights, they seemed enthusiastic about new possibilities. And, so typical of their parents, the youngest of them declared that the best was yet to come.

AFRICA:
A Continent of Problems

By Peter Schwab

The first year of the new millennium provided a continuation of the virtual collapse of the nation-state in Africa south of the Sahara, a breakdown that can be traced to the demise of the Soviet Union and the end of the Cold War in 1991. At the time, U.S. President George Bush, in a spasm of optimism, heralded the onset of a "new world order" of vast political, social, and economic opportunity that soon would be available to both the impoverished and the developed world. Bill Clinton, who succeeded Bush as president in 1993, waxed eloquently as he successfully nudged much of the world toward the benefits of globalization and free trade.

But globalization has bypassed Africa, particularly those countries south of the Sahara. Africa, a continent rich in resources which during the Cold War was seen as vital to U.S. national security, has essentially been aban-

Famine and drought are but two of the problems that continue to plague the African continent. An estimated 16 million people were affected by one or the other calamity during 2000. In Ethiopia, malnourishment affected children as well as families living in hillside huts, right and below.

doned by the sole remaining superpower. Since 1991 the United States has seen no strategic interest in Africa, has drastically reduced its aid to the region, and has concentrated its foreign-policy initiatives toward other, more-vital geopolitical regions. For Africa, the new world order and globalization have proved to be merely a grotesque chimera. That is due in some part to the continent's colonial heritage and its confined geographic location; in larger part, it is due to its intractable social, political, and ethnic problems.

The Heritage of Colonialism and the Cold War. Most African borders were created out of the needs of European rather than African states. Ethnic groups were divided between nations because a river or ridge served as a demarcation point for a boundary. European colonizers, not to mention the European slave traders

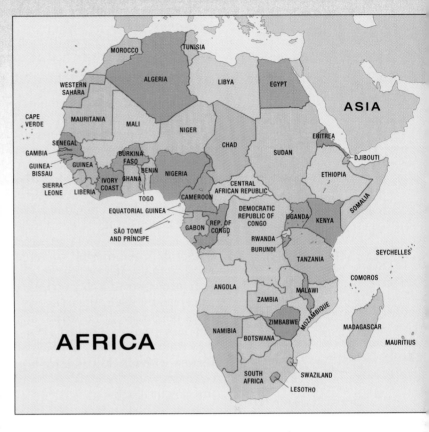

of a previous era, had little interest in the people or territories they controlled. The Europeans were absorbed with their own advantages. In many cases, unrealistic borders encompassed groups with little in common culturally or sociologically. In Nigeria, Sudan, and Kenya, for example, different ethnic groups or nationalities were forced to coexist.

Often European states selected one tribe to serve the colonial bureaucracy, creating a dependence upon the colonizing nation, while other cultures then were politically marginalized. As independence came in the 1960s, these preferred ethnic groups commonly, though not always, gained control over the new state. Resentment by other groups or nationalities intensified.

After colonial rule collapsed, the Soviet Union, the United States, and European states moved into the vacuum and extended the divisions so that their own interests could be served. The superpowers either buttressed the elites empowered by the colonial powers, or backed the opposition, as each superpower supported a different client and a different agenda. In Angola and Somalia, for example, different political entities were served by one or the other of the major powers. By continuing the colonial intrusion, and by pouring hundreds of millions of dollars of weaponry into client states, political elites were trained to use the arms to support the interests of the respective superpower and to resist competing indigenous forces.

Since clans, ethnic groups, or nationalities in a given state, frequently did not consider other cultures part of their tribal nation, there were few constraints limiting political behavior. Thus, the violence that often accompanied the ensuing struggle for power was repeatedly awesome and destructive. In Africa, those not seen as part of the national sphere frequently were viewed as being outside the boundaries of normal political discourse, and were deemed to be threatening.

The tribal-divisive "nations" being described are, in many cases, merely 40 years old. They achieved independence only in the 1960s. As a consequence, they have usually not been able, or in many cases willing, to create the political, cultural, social, or economic infrastructures that could bind their various communities together, support social or economic advancement, or deal with the new crisis ravaging the continent—AIDS. They often are either agricultural states with a one-crop economy, and sometimes no-crop economies, or mineral-rich states where the resources frequently are used to fund civil strife. Many of these states find themselves characterized by the United Nations as among the least developed countries of the world, as opposed to the potentially rich and resource-abundant Republic of South Africa. Thus, the struggle for power in much of Africa is seen as a contest for survival, and little quarter is given to opponents. In 2000, as throughout the 1990s, war and ethnic horrors rampaged through the continent.

Civil Strife, Wars, and Political Collapse. In 2000, Sierra Leone ceased its existence as a coherent state; the Democratic Republic of the Congo spiraled further into complete disintegration; Zimbabwe's President Robert Mugabe, in an effort to hold on to power, pushed his country into raucous tyranny; and Ethiopia and Eritrea battled furiously in a convulsive finale to their two-year war over a tiny piece of barren land separating the two countries.

In Sierra Leone, rebel soldiers of the Revolutionary United Front (RUF), led by Foday Sankoh, and supported by Liberia, went on a reign of terror in 1999 and 2000 so as to wrest power from President Ahmad Tejan Kabbah. Terrorizing the population into submission by mutilating thousands of civilians, the RUF controlled more than 60% of the country in 2000. When those killers were on the verge of capturing Freetown, the capital, Great Britain, the former colonial ruler, sent in troops to halt the advance. The British forces had moved in to support Kabbah as the remaining Nigerian troops who made up the core group of fighters of the Economic Community of West African States Monitoring Group (ECOMOG), which supported the government, and the UN's 13,000 peacekeepers, who were permitted to carry only light arms, were unable to prevent the rebel advance.

About the Author. Peter Schwab is professor of political science at Purchase College, the State University of New York. He has written several books including *Decision-Making in Ethiopia, Ethiopia: Politics, Economics and Society,* and *Cuba: Confronting the U.S. Embargo.* Dr. Schwab has lived in Liberia and Ethiopia, and has traveled extensively in Africa. He also has authored and coedited (with Adamantia Pollis) three books on human rights—*Human Rights: Cultural and Ideological Perspectives,* which was selected by the United Nations Commission on Human Rights as a "primary reference work" on the subject; *Toward a Human Rights Framework;* and most recently, *Human Rights: New Perspectives, New Realities.*

Between 150,000 and 200,000 civilians were displaced in Freetown, while scores of thousands of refugees roamed the countryside fleeing RUF forces. During 2000, some 500 UN peacekeepers were captured and 233 trapped until their release was negotiated or they were rescued.

Sankoh, in an attempt to halt his campaign by a flawed and questionable U.S.–sponsored peace plan, had in 1999 been let *in* to a reorganized government and put in charge of minerals, largely diamonds, which he had been using to subsidize his war and enrich himself and his supporters, Presidents Charles Taylor, of Liberia, and Blaise Compaore, of Burkina Faso. Sankoh was also given an amnesty for the war crimes his fighters had committed. His struggle for power, however, continued. By mid-2000, he was captured—which, along with the presence of the British armed forces, only temporarily calmed the fractured country.

Congo's civil war erupted in 1998 against President Laurent Kabila, who had taken power in 1997 after leading a revolt that overthrew the massively corrupt tyrant President Mobutu Sese Seko. By 2000 the hostilities had involved Uganda, Rwanda, Zimbabwe, Angola, Namibia, Zambia, the Central African Republic, Chad, Burundi, and scores of contending rebel groups within Congo itself. The motives for the multiple involvement were: a struggle for power by indigenous groups; the grabbing of diamonds for personal and political benefit, as in Sierra Leone; Rwanda's attempt to eliminate its Hutu killers who had fled into eastern Congo (then called Zaire) in 1994 after the attempted genocide of Rwandan Tutsi; hubris and dubious glory as Zimbabwe's president sent one-third of his 30,000-man army to the Congo, helping to practically bankrupt his country; and Angola's aspiration to secure its border from rebel National Union for the Total Independence of Angola (UNITA) forces, led by Jonas Savimbi. Savimbi's movement, which once had been supported by the United States and fueled by diamond smuggling, has been fighting the government for more than 25 years—to the cost of 2 million lives and the destruction of a large part of the country.

Congo's civil/African war threatened to spiral out of control. The potential for this was evident as Uganda and Rwanda briefly entered into hostilities against each other in Kisangani, in eastern Congo, while civilian refugees poured into neighboring countries. In 2000 the UN agreed to send in 5,537 "observers" and troops to "verify" that the multiple countries and rebel groups pulled back and eventually with-

Civil strife was rampant in Africa in 2000 as numerous governments collapsed. In Sierra Leone, rebel soldiers, top, led by Foday Sankoh, wrested power from President Ahmad Tejan Kabbah. UN peacekeepers, bottom, were unable to stop the rebel advance. Other attempts at peace also failed, but by midyear there was some calm as Sankoh was captured.

drew their forces. But the observers would not enter the Congo until *after* the respective forces pulled back—something they had been unwilling to do even in the face of a cease-fire signed in 1999.

And while the UN imposed a global ban on diamond exports from Angola in 1998, and did the same in July 2000 to Sierra Leone, no sanctions were imposed on gems from the Congo. Ban enforcement on diamonds from countries ravaged by civil strife was left to private marketing groups, largely based in Belgium. Extremely lax controls have made all embargoes ineffective. In 1999, Liberia alone exported $300 million worth of smuggled Sierra Leonean stones. The UN and the West chose to skirt real commitment, enabling the Congolese war to continue.

United Nations Secretary-General Kofi Annan, a native of Ghana, actively sought to maintain order in Africa. In January 2000, he met with Zimbabwe President Robert Mugabe at the UN headquarters. Violence erupted in Zimbabwe during 2000 as Mugabe sought to redistribute the country's white-owned farms to blacks.

In a deleterious effort to secure black support in the 2000 parliamentary elections, President Robert Mugabe enlisted thousands of his supporters to storm and either seize or destroy the farms of white Zimbabweans. By midyear, squatters had occupied more than 1,000 farms, many of them having been burned to the ground. Five white farmers and scores of African employees were murdered, while thousands of black agricultural workers lost their jobs. Of 4,500 white settlements, the government listed more than 3,270 farms for confiscation and redistribution under its black resettlement program. Despite the raging chaos, Mugabe proclaimed he would brook no domestic opposition nor accept any foreign criticism of the policy. Court orders declared the occupations illegal, yet Mugabe received support from southern African leaders. With tobacco being Zimbabwe's largest currency earner, the occupation of the tobacco farms only added to the nation's economic misery. Many white farmers fled the country; others were forced to halt planting or harvesting. Meanwhile, the economy spiraled further downward. In the election, the opposition group Movement for Democratic Change (MDC) increased its representation dramatically, but to little avail.

Africa's bloodiest war was fought over a barren piece of wasteland—the Yiagra Triangle—separating Ethiopia and Eritrea. In a titanic struggle, by means of trench warfare, air bombardment, and tank combat that lasted from 1998 to 2000, 70,000 soldiers were killed, 500,000 Eritrean civilians were turned into refugees, and the economies of both countries fell into disrepair. Even without the war, both nations had been labeled by the UN as among the ten least developed countries in human terms. The raging battles took place in the midst of an extraordinary drought and famine that affected 8 million Ethiopians and 800,000 Eritreans. With Eritrea's military forces and civilian population reeling, it agreed to a humiliating cease-fire that was hammered out in Algeria under the auspices of the UN, the Organization of African Unity (OAU), the United States, and Algeria. But in fact, the war was concluded on the battlefield. The UN, pressured by the West, refused to use its clout to intercede effectively. Ethiopia, Eritrea, and indeed, Africa as a whole were footnotes to the larger and more prominent foreign-policy interests of the West. What the West did arrange was the shipment of 1 million tons of food to Ethiopia and Eritrea; this aid helped to stem the onset of a portentous famine.

Whither Human Rights? The continued violation of human rights by African leaders and the ignoring or playing down of such violations by Western powers and the UN Security Council calls into question the importance of human rights in Africa. In 1994, Africa's most profound contemporary calamity occurred in Rwanda when the *interahamwe*, the strike force of the Hutu government, murdered some 800,000 Tutsi in a three-month holocaust in which genocide became state policy. While the United States did everything conceivable to keep the UN from taking action, France, under then-President François Mitterrand, militarily supported the Hutu initially before leading a "neutral" mission to the country. The massive violation of human rights in Rwanda by Hutu warriors was truly of insignificance to the Great Powers, whose national-security interests were directed to other regions. The slaughter ended only when a Tutsi-dominated strike force, led by Gen. Paul Kagame, overthrew the *génocidaires* and took over in July 1994. In 1998, President Clinton briefly visited Rwanda to apologize for U.S. policy; he vowed the United States would no longer remain aloof. But Hutu attacks on Tutsi continued.

Hutu/Tutsi violence is also a hallmark of Burundi politics, where, since 1993, well over 200,000 people have been killed

Violence between the Hutu and Tutsi, including in Burundi, below, continued to dominate concerns about human rights in Africa as hundreds of thousands of people have been killed and hundreds of thousands of others were in displacement camps.

and 500,000 remained in displacement camps. Attempts at a peace accord—brokered by former South African President Nelson Mandela, and supported by Clinton, who visited Tanzania in August 2000 to encourage the peace process—proved elusive. In 1999 the president of Niger was assassinated, while military coups took place in the Ivory Coast, a hallmark of stability for four decades, and Guinea-Bissau.

Violence continued in Somalia, a country divided among clans. Some 500,000 people have fled, and two autonomous regions—Somaliland and Puntland—have been established. No government has existed in Somalia since 1991, despite the August 2000 selection of a three-year transitional administration chosen by a 245-member self-appointed assembly meeting in Djibouti. The administration was rejected by Somali warlords. The United States and the UN had dispatched peacemakers to Somalia in the early 1990s in an abortive attempt to create a stable and legitimate government; their respective failures, with the attendant military casualties and deaths, are what is generally, though erroneously, seen as the reason for U.S. hesitancy to get involved in African crises.

In Sudan, which has been engaged in a civil war for more than two decades, the conflict between north and south, Islamic and Christian, has left more than 1 million dead. The Congo Republic (not to be confused with the Democratic Republic of the Congo) has been convulsed by civil war since 1997, although a peace accord was reached in late 1999. During the fighting, the capital, Brazzaville, was demolished and much of its citizenry dislocated. In Togo, President Gnassingbé Eyadéma has, with French support, dominated a totalitarian regime for some three decades. In Kenya, where corruption and political assassination are rampant, dissidents in the streets of the capital Nairobi often are whipped by soldiers and police. Chad, Cameroon, and Nigeria have been ranked the world's most corrupt countries by Transparency International—a nonprofit anticorruption organization. In the Ivory Coast, ethnic heritage is used to define citizenship and deny qualification for seeking political office.

"Since the early 1990s, 42 of 48 sub-Saharan states have held multiparty presidential or parliamentary elections. But one in five Africans still lives in a country severely disrupted by conflict. Excluding the region's former wars of independence, nearly 20 African countries have experienced at least one period of serious civil strife since 1960. This has imposed massive costs and increased poverty which in turn has led to increased violence."

**"Can Africa Claim the 21st Century?,"
World Bank, May 2000**

Poverty. According to the World Bank, Africa accounts for merely 1% of global gross domestic product (GDP) and only 2% of world trade. Since the era of independence, Africa has lost market share in global trade. The continent's per-capita income is lower than in the 1960s, while sub-Saharan Africa's total income is equivalent to that of Belgium. Only 16% of Africa's roads are paved, and just 30% of its people live near an all-weather road. The entire continent, excluding South Africa, has fewer roads than Poland. Eighty percent of Africans have no access to electricity. Safe drinking water is atypical, while two-thirds of rural Africa lacks adequate water supplies. Seventy-five percent of its people live without appropriate sanitation. The deficient infrastructure is "a major barrier to growth and reducing poverty." Some 20,000 professionals abandon the continent annually.

UN reports document that 2 million of the continent's children die before their first birthday each year, while

Efforts to battle the newest, and perhaps most devastating African crisis, the AIDS epidemic, included the posting of newspaper headlines, above, *in prominent places.*

Africa's malaria-infection rate has soared by 60% over the past 30 years. Parasitic invasions, leading to sleeping sickness and schistosomiasis, are rampant; cholera remains pervasive. Famine and drought are periodic occurrences; in 2000, 16 million people in Ethiopia, Eritrea, Somalia, Sudan, Djibouti, Kenya, and Uganda were struck by the dual calamities. Life expectancy throughout the region is unusually low—38 to 50 years, depending on the country. Africa's rate of maternal mortality is 100 to 500 times Western European rates. Between 1960 and 1990, average schooling for African women increased by only 1.2 years, the lowest gain of any region. Overall literacy rates are abysmal, normally between 10% and 35%. In part, this is due to multiple languages within each country. In larger part the cause is a bifurcated education system where emphasis is placed on developing schools in urban areas, while the interior is habitually disregarded. Health-care facilities and housing are also unequally split along the urban and rural divide.

Africa's apparent hopelessness—political, economic, and social—clearly deters foreign and domestic investors despite the U.S. trade initiative instituted in 2000, to expand duty-free access to African nations. The violence evident throughout the continent has imposed massive costs—not the least of which are extreme poverty and underdevelopment. The surge in poverty has a cyclical effect as it, in turn, leads to ever more violence. The spiral of decline has accelerated.

AIDS. Perhaps no other crisis highlights the turmoil in Africa south of the Sahara more so than does the explosion of AIDS and its cause, the HIV virus. Of those infected with the HIV virus worldwide, 70%—some 24 million people—live in Africa, where AIDS is largely a heterosexual disease. The continent is the epicenter of an AIDS pandemic. Botswana and Zimbabwe, for example, have an HIV infec-

U.S. President Clinton was in Nigeria in August 2000 to support the efforts of President Olusegun Obasanjo (right) to restore civil rule to the continent's most populous country.

tion rate of 25.1% and 25.84%, respectively. In the Ivory Coast, where the infection rate is 11%—the highest in West Africa—72,000 people died of AIDS in 1999. In addition, 64% of all teachers' deaths were AIDS-related. In 1993 the HIV virus affected 4% of South Africa's adult population; by 2000 the figure was 20%. The Democratic Republic of the Congo, Zambia, Malawi, the Central African Republic, Kenya, Burundi, Tanzania, and Rwanda also have exceedingly high infection rates.

In July 2000 at the 13th International AIDS Conference, held in Durban, South Africa, Dr. Peter Piot, head of UNAIDS, a UN program that monitors the spread of the disease, maintained it would take $3 billion per year to take basic measures to deal with AIDS in Africa. In addition, it would take tens of billions of dollars yearly to provide the continent with the standard drugs used to combat the disease in developed nations. Merely $300 million was spent on AIDS in Africa in 2000. As the conference concluded, the U.S. Export-Import Bank offered 24 sub-Saharan African states $1 billion in annual loans to finance the purchase of AIDS drugs and medical services from the United States. Some nations, including Namibia and South Africa, declined the Export-Import Bank offer, averring they already were overwhelmed by foreign debt. The Bill & Melinda Gates Foundation and Merck & Co. donated $50 million each toward battling AIDS in Botswana.

Education, free clinics to treat sexually transmitted infections, counseling, testing, the willingness of political and religious leaders to enlighten populations so as to promote safe sex and reduce the stigma of the disease, and an aggressive prevention campaign are also vital components of any battle against this scourge. In fact, Senegal, using precisely this framework, has an HIV infection rate of only 1.8%. Under the progressive leadership of President Yoweri Museveni, Uganda, which in 1988 was the most AIDS-affected country in the world, reduced its infection rate from 14% to 8%. Through the use of midwives, public-health centers, and tech-

"Let us not equivocate. A tragedy of unprecedented proportions is unfolding in Africa.... AIDS is clearly a disaster, effectively wiping out the development gains of the past decade and sabotaging the future."

Nelson Mandela
13th International
AIDS Conference
July 14, 2000

nology, Uganda's rate of maternal mortality was halved. U.S. pharmaceutical companies should be prepared to lower the cost of drugs that combat AIDS.

Will Africa Survive? Certainly some African states have made real progress. South Africa, despite a murder rate that is among the highest in the world, has thrust aside apartheid and is a vibrant democracy. Mozambique and Ghana, through liberalizing markets and trade, and improving economic management, have seen poverty reduced and incomes rise. Mozambique has in recent years avoided military strife through the creation of a party-neutral army. Though still poor, and hit with violent floods early in 2000, it is one of the fastest-growing economies in Africa. Botswana's democracy is real and its economy is soaring, although the country's escalating HIV/AIDS rate may, unless confronted, reverse recent gains. Equatorial Guinea soon will begin to benefit from the vast deposits of oil discovered off its coastal shores.

In Nigeria, despite ethnic unrest, and tension between the Muslim north and the Christian south over the extension of Islamic Shariah law, the first free elections in 20 years took place in 1998–99. Since Nigeria is a major oil-producing state with one-quarter of the population of sub-Saharan Africa, the return of democracy after decades of intermittent military dictatorship has consequences far beyond the nation's borders. Elections also were held in Namibia, Benin, the Central African Republic, and Malawi in 1999. But elections are merely one indicant of the democratic process, and they are not worth very much if one leader, party, or group totally dominates the system. After all, Togo had elections in June 1998, but it remained a totalitarian state. In Liberia in July 1997, Charles Taylor was elected president through a process of controlled mayhem.

Although exceptions do exist, pandemonium, war, predatory governments, disease, and poverty have replaced the expectations of the 1960s. Until African leaders turn away from the violence and the destructive struggle for power that has consumed the continent virtually since independence, and until they move to a political framework that incorporates human rights and more-orderly democratic processes, their national budgets will continue to be monopolized by their militaries. So, too, the West must be far more willing to incorporate Africa into the advancing globalized network. Unless the United States, the former European colonizers, the World Bank, and the International Monetary Fund (IMF) are more forthcoming with aid and debt forgiveness, and until more truly democratic African leaders emerge to commit themselves to economic development and democratic processes, the continent will survive, but barely. Without fundamental change, the 1990s will have been simply a prologue to the future. And the future may well be a continuing series of coups, countercoups, wars, and ethnic explosions that will be publicized for a while, and then replaced by the next and future tribal event. States likely will continue to crumble and be replaced by internecine ethnic warfare.

"Can Africa change? Yes, it can. There are instances from all over the continent that, in the right circumstances, Africans can greatly improve their lives.... More than anything, Africa's people need to regain their self-confidence. Only then can Africa engage as an equal with the rest of the world, devising its own economic programmes [programs] and development policies. Its people also need the confidence to trust each other. Only then can they make deals to end wars and build political institutions: institutions that they actually believe in."

**"The Economist"
May 13, 2000**

THE KOREAS — A RAPPROCHEMENT

By Han-Kyo Kim

A first-ever summit between South Korean President Kim Dae Jung, right in both photos, and Chairman Kim Jong Il of North Korea, left in both photos, ended on June 15, 2000, with a symbolic hug. The South Korean president had been greeted with full honors on his arrival in Pyongyang, North Korea, two days earlier, bottom.

A dramatic breakthrough in inter-Korean relations took place in Pyongyang, North Korea, June 13–15, 2000. The first-ever summit meeting between the leaders of South Korea and North Korea opened a floodgate for high-level official exchanges, economic assistance, and family reunions. It raised hopes within and beyond the Korean peninsula for peace and reconciliation—after half a century of hostile confrontation. President Kim Dae Jung of South Korea took the initiative, and Chairman Kim Jong Il of North Korea responded with surprising enthusiasm. The joint declaration, announced at the conclusion of the historic summit, appeared to herald a possible change in North Korea's isolationist policy, and raised the hope for an eventual reunification of the two Koreas.

Kim Jong Il, chairman of the National Defense Commission (NDC), and son of late President Kim Il Sung, surprised his southern visitors by greeting them personally at the Sunan Airport outside Pyongyang. The two Kims rode together from the airport amid cheers from a welcoming crowd. They were the center of media attention as they held meetings, toasted each other at banquets, and signed the joint agreement. Kim Jong Il, a reputed recluse, was spontaneous and decisive in demeanor, and warmly embraced Kim Dae Jung as he departed. It was a carefully choreographed public-relations coup that projected new images of North Korea and its leader.

About the Author. Han-Kyo Kim is a professor emeritus of political science at the University of Cincinnati. He studied at the Seoul National University, Swarthmore College, and the University of Chicago. His publications include *Korea and the Politics of Imperialism*, *Studies on Korea: A Scholar's Guide*, and *The Spirit of Independence* by Syngman Rhee.

The June 15 Declaration. Five major points highlighted the June 15 declaration: (1) both sides "agreed to solve the question of the country's reunification independently by the concerted efforts of the Korean nation;" (2) they recognized that the North's proposal for "federation of lower stage" and the South's proposal for "confederation" had common "elements," and they agreed "to work for reunification in this direction;" (3) they agreed to settle humanitarian issues, including the exchange of visiting family members and the return of unconverted political prisoners held in the South, "as soon as possible . . . this year;" (4) they agreed "to promote the balanced development of the national economy through economic cooperation," and to "build mutual confidence by activating cooperation and exchanges in all fields, social, cultural, sports, public health, environmental, and so on;" and (5) they agreed to "hold dialogues between the authorities as soon as possible to implement the above-mentioned agreed points in the near future." In its last sentence, the declaration announced Chairman Kim Jong Il's accep-

© Newsmakers/The Liaison Agency

Residents of North and South Korea enthusiastically supported the diplomatic breakthrough between their countries. North Korean residents, left, waved artificial flowers to welcome the two leaders to the summit.

tance of President Kim Dae Jung's invitation to visit Seoul "at an appropriate time in the future."

Far-reaching as the ramifications of these agreements were, some important omissions were equally, if not more, significant. There was no mention of the pressing need to defuse military tension along the heavily fortified border, the Demilitarized Zone (DMZ). Nothing was said about the nuclear and missile programs in the North, and there was no reaffirmation of the mutual nonaggression pledge both sides signed in 1991. Issues raised by opposition-party politicians in the South—such as abducted South Koreans or unreturned southern POWs in the North—also were ignored.

These reservations—voiced by some in South Korea and abroad—failed to minimize the psychological impact of the summit. Televised images of the smiling leaders were dramatic. President Kim's "sunshine policy" (recently renamed "engagement policy") was credited for inducing the North to alter its policy toward the South and the rest of the world.

Preludes to the Summit. The first summit proposal came in 1972, when an initial attempt at peaceful dialogue was made through clandestine contacts, leading to the so-called "July 4 Joint Communiqué." As if to emulate the meeting between U.S. President Richard Nixon and China's Mao Tsetung in Beijing, Kim Il Sung proposed meeting his counterpart, President Park Chung Hee, but no meeting resulted. In 1982, President Chun Doo Hwan publicly stated his willingness to meet the northern leader. Even after he narrowly escaped an assassination attempt—allegedly by North Korean agents, while visiting Burma (Myanmar) in 1983—Chun repeated his call for a summit. There was an exchange of secret visits by high-level emissaries from each side in 1985, to prepare for Chun's meeting with Kim Il Sung, but the project swiftly crumbled.

In 1988 a proposal for a summit was included in public addresses by the next South Korean president, Roh Tae Woo, but Pyongyang ignored it. In 1994, however, Kim Il Sung accepted former U.S. President Jimmy Carter's suggestion, and preparations were set in motion for his meeting with President Kim Young Sam, Roh's successor. This time the sudden death of the northern leader, weeks later, halted the project in midstream.

Following his inauguration in 1998, President Kim Dae Jung took every opportunity to publicize a more conciliatory policy toward Pyongyang, and to encourage more peaceful exchanges, including aid to alleviate the economic hardship in the North. Private business

(Continued on page 60.)

Interest in the historic summit was widespread as news media around the world gave it full coverage. A monk in Seoul, South Korea, left, kept up on the latest details.

The Korean War—50 Years Later

Wreaths dotted the Korean War Veterans Memorial in Washington, DC, in June 2000 as the United States recalled the start of the Korean conflict, 50 years earlier. More than 36,000 American lives were lost in "the forgotten war."

June 25, 2000, was the 50th anniversary of the beginning of the Korean war. Most commemorations of the event in the United States portrayed the conflict as "the forgotten war," a war that faded into history as a bloody interlude between the end of World War II and the beginning of the Vietnam war. If forgotten in the United States, the war continued to hover over the scarred Korean peninsula as South Korea and North Korea continued to confront each other across a tense border. But with the anniversary, the North made a series of diplomatic moves, including a historic summit between the leaders of the two nations, aimed at bringing the North out of isolation. In view of the rapprochement, both North Korea and South Korea canceled or reduced their planned ceremonies marking the war's anniversary.

Anniversary-Year Developments. New information—and new controversy—about the conflict arrived during the 50th-anniversary year. In June, the U.S. Department of Defense officially announced a new total in the number of U.S. deaths in the war: 33,686 "battle deaths" and 2,830 "nonbattle deaths," for a war toll of 36,516. The new total replaces the 54,246 figure printed in history books and engraved in stone on the Korean War Veterans Memorial in Washington, DC. The Pentagon explained that 17,730 service deaths outside Korea during the

three-year war had been erroneously added to the total.

The National Security Agency (NSA) made news by releasing a report revealing that in 1948, a spy—in what was then the Armed Forces Security Agency—had told his Soviet Union spymasters that the United States had cracked Soviet codes. "In rapid succession," the report said, every Soviet cipher system "went dark." As a result, U.S. electronic eavesdroppers also were in the dark when the war started in 1950. The report helped to explain why the vaunted U.S. message-intercept network had not been able to decrypt Soviet–North Korean communications. Historians, assuming that the network was reading Soviet messages, over the years had criticized the U.S. intelligence community for failing to predict either North Korea's invasion or China's entrance into the war.

A sensational 1999 report, which won the Associated Press the Pulitzer Prize in 2000, claimed U.S. troops killed hundreds of South Korean civilians in the village of No Gun Ri, in the early days of the war. The story's credibility suffered in 2000, as two key witnesses acknowledged they had not been at No Gun Ri. U.S. Army records showed no massacre, but the story rekindled allegations of the killings of civilians, suspected of being North Korean guerrillas. Meanwhile, the Defense Department's investigation of the incident was continuing during the year.

Background to the Conflict. The Korean peninsula had been sundered since the dawn of the Cold War. The Allied victory in World War II had liberated Korea, which had been part of the Japanese Empire since 1910. Under joint U.S.-Soviet occupation, the country was divided into two zones at the 38th parallel, which roughly ran across the middle of the peninsula. The occupation created two nations: North Korea—the Democratic People's Republic of Korea, with a Soviet-installed communist regime; and South Korea—the Republic of Korea, with U.S. backing. The occupation officially ended in 1949, when U.S. and Soviet troops withdrew. But North Korea remained a communist dictatorship, and a well-armed threat to South Korea.

By then, the U.S.-Soviet Cold War had begun. U.S. interests focused on Germany and China, where a civil war had ended with the Communists victorious and allied with the Soviet Union. U.S. policy in Asia, as defined by Secretary of State Dean Acheson in January 1950, put South Korea outside the U.S. defensive perimeter in the Far East. So, when North Korea invaded South Korea on June 25, 1950, the possibility of U.S. intervention was unclear.

The Conflict Itself. On June 27, however, as the North Korean invaders poured down the peninsula, President Harry S. Truman ordered U.S. air and sea support of South Korean defenders, and the United Nations Security Council, which the Soviet Union was boycotting, called on member nations to give aid. On June 29, North Korean troops took Seoul, the capital of South Korea, and the next day Truman committed U.S. ground troops to Korea. When a reporter asked if this could be called a United Nations "police action," the president agreed. The term would haunt Truman through what would be a long and bloody war.

Joining the United States, in an unprecedented UN military commitment, were some 20 other nations, 15 of which contributed combat forces; the others provided noncombatant medical units. U.S. officials viewed the invasion as inspired by the Soviet Union, possibly to deflect Western attention from Europe. The invasion, in fact, surprised the Soviets as much as the Americans. Soviet leader Joseph Stalin gave his support to the invasion, sending supplies, advisers, and MiG pilots.

The North Koreans overwhelmed the South Korean army, quickly taking Seoul's port of Inchon. Ill-equipped

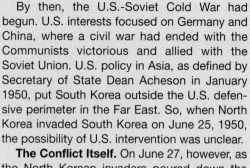

© AP/World Wide Photos

© CNP/Archive Photos

© Bert Hardy/Liaison Agency, Inc.

After North Korea invaded South Korea in June 1950, the United States sent ground troops (inset) to Korea. Before the conflict ended, the United States and its UN allies were fighting not only North Korean but Chinese troops (above) as well. Heavy casualties resulted.

U.S. troops, rushed to Korea from Japan, established a beachhead at Pusan on the southeastern tip of the peninsula. While the Pusan defenders fought to hold the beachhead, U.S. Army Gen. Douglas MacArthur, supreme commander of UN forces in Korea, planned a bold outflanking move: an amphibious landing at Inchon, on the west coast. The landing liberated Seoul and severed North Korean supply lines. At the same time, UN troops broke out of Pusan, and a drive began to force the North Koreans back to the 38th parallel.

MacArthur captured the North Korean capital of Pyongyang in October, and then, challenging Washington's limits on the war, authorized a drive to the Yalu River, the North Korean–Chinese border. In a meeting with President Truman on Wake Island, MacArthur dismissed the possibility of Chinese intervention and said that UN troops could be withdrawn from Korea as early as Christmas. But, as frontline UN troops neared the border, they found themselves fighting 300,000 Chinese soldiers. The Chinese, in "human wave" attacks, inflicted so many casualties that U.S. officials contemplated using nuclear weapons, but declined fearing Soviet nuclear retaliation.

On November 27, in freezing cold, nearly 100,000 Chinese attacked the 1st Marine Division at the Chosin Reservoir. More than 40,000 U.S. Marines and soldiers, in an epic fighting withdrawal, reached the port of Hungnam, where they were evacuated. The Communist troops retook Pyongyang and surged southward, occupying Seoul in January 1951. The UN forces reorganized and launched an offensive in February; they took Seoul in March, drove the Chinese from South Korea, and advanced to just north of the 38th parallel.

The unforeseen Chinese intervention had put President Truman on a collision course with General MacArthur. In what Truman saw as a reckless crusade for a war with China, the general continually ignored orders from Washington. On April 11, the president relieved

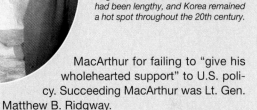

In July 1953, generals from both sides signed an armistice in Panmunjom. Negotiations to end the brutal conflict had been lengthy, and Korea remained a hot spot throughout the 20th century.

MacArthur for failing to "give his wholehearted support" to U.S. policy. Succeeding MacArthur was Lt. Gen. Matthew B. Ridgway.

Fighting went on for two more years, with U.S. airmen unaware they sometimes were fighting Soviet pilots in North Korean MiGs. The fighting did little to change the war, but the battles—Heartbreak Ridge, Pork Chop Hill, T-Bone, Old Baldy—would reverberate in the memories of veterans. For them, this would not be a forgotten war.

Negotiations to end the war deadlocked on two issues: prisoners and an armistice border. The death of Soviet leader Joseph Stalin on March 5, 1953, helped to end the stalemate. Stalin had goaded the Chinese into intervening, according to documents released after the end of the Cold War. Stalin's successor, Georgy M. Malenkov, swiftly made conciliatory gestures toward the new administration of Dwight D. Eisenhower. The incoming president had used "I will go to Korea" as a campaign slogan that implied he would end the unpopular war.

In June 1953, negotiators reached agreement on the prisoner issue and on a border that gave South Korea some territory north of the 38 parallel. On July 27, at Panmunjom, just south of the 38th parallel, generals from both sides signed an armistice. The war ended, but through the rest of the 20th century, Korea would be a crisis point where North Korea and South Korea confronted each other. With the dawn of the 21st century, the confrontation was easing. But there still were troops along both sides of the border, including some 37,000 U.S. soldiers whose presence gave South Korea a shield against another invasion.

THOMAS B. ALLEN

About the Author. Thomas B. Allen, a freelance writer and editor based in Bethesda, MD, includes military history among his specialties and interests. He is coauthor of World War II: America at War, 1941–1945 (Random House, 1991) AND CNN: WAR IN THE GULF (TURNER PUBLISHING, 1991).

(Continued from page 56.)

groups in the South steadily developed joint ventures in the North. In 1998, for example, thousands of southern tourists were allowed to travel to the scenic Kumgang Mountains, immediately north of the DMZ. In March 2000, President Kim spoke in Berlin, the capital of the reunified Germany, announcing Seoul's willingness to offer government-to-government cooperation, while renewing the call for resuming formal dialogue.

Following the Berlin speech, special envoys from both sides met secretly in Shanghai and Beijing, and reached an agreement to hold a summit meeting June 12–14. The bombshell announcement of the forthcoming meeting was made simultaneously in the two capitals—Seoul and Pyongyang—on April 10, only three days before hotly contested general elections for the National Assembly in the South. Pyongyang carefully noted that President Kim had requested the summit, using his official title as president of the Republic of Korea for the first time.

In recognition of the momentous impact the summit would bring to the Korean peninsula and beyond, the two Koreas consulted and sought support from their respective allies. Particularly noteworthy was Chairman Kim's May trip to Beijing, just weeks prior to the summit, likely intended to underscore or demonstrate the strength of the Beijing-Pyongyang alliance.

After the Summit. The June summit produced far-reaching consequences within Korea and around the world. South Koreans expressed overwhelming (90%) approval for the diplomatic breakthrough. The public perception of Kim Jong Il changed overnight from that of a sinister and enigmatic adversary to that of an able leader and potential partner. Although partisan sniping against President Kim's "appeasement" policy continued, South Korea embraced the declaration he made upon his return from Pyongyang—that the war on the peninsula was finally over.

Kim Dae Jung

The Nobel Peace Prize for 2000 was awarded to Kim Dae Jung, president of the Republic of Korea (South Korea). In awarding the prize, the Norwegian Nobel Committee commended Kim, who is known as DJ, for his contribution "to democracy and human rights in South Korea and East Asia in general, and for peace and reconciliation with North Korea in particular." Responding, the new Nobelist noted: This "honor is due to public support for democracy, human rights, peace, reconciliation, and cooperation between South Korea and North Korea during the past 40 years."

Kim Dae Jung, who was born on Dec. 3, 1925, took office as the 15th president of South Korea on Feb. 25, 1998. For Kim, it was a moment of personal triumph after a political journey of more than four decades that included imprisonment, exile, kidnapping, and a death sentence. For South Korea, the occasion marked the first peaceful transfer of power to an opposition leader in the nation's history.

Symbols of the new diplomatic relationship between North and South Korea could be seen in many forms, including a joint performance of the two state orchestras in Seoul, left, *and the combined entrance of athletes from both countries at the opening ceremony of the Olympic Games in Sydney, Australia,* below.

In the months following the Pyongyang summit, measures to implement the June agreement were taken by both sides. Seoul scaled back long-planned activities to commemorate the 50th anniversary of the Korean War (*see* THE KOREAN WAR—50 YEARS LATER, PAGE 57), while Pyongyang canceled all similar activities. An annual joint U.S.–South Korean military exercise in August also was downsized. The defense chiefs of the two sides held their first meeting on September 25 and 26, and pledged joint efforts for easing the threat of war. They also agreed to cooperate in removing land mines in a narrow corridor of the DMZ, in order to build rail connections.

Cabinet ministers, responsible for inter-Korean affairs for both sides, met three times between July and September, and agreed to reopen liaison offices at Panmunjom, to reconnect the Seoul-Pyongyang railroad line across the DMZ, and to create a working-level structure for economic cooperation. A separate set of meetings to facilitate capital investments in North Korea—through governmental guarantees and avoidance of double taxation—also began in September. An even-higher-level contact took place in mid-September when Kim Yong-sun, the North's veteran party official in charge of South Korean affairs, went to Seoul, as Kim Jong Il's special emissary, presumably in preparation for the latter's visit sometime in early 2001.

In response to the urgent food crisis in North Korea, Seoul shipped 200,000 tons of fertilizer in May and June, and pledged a loan of 500,000 tons of grain, including 200,000 tons of rice from Thailand and 300,000 tons of corn from China, at a cost of about $100 million. The products began to arrive in the North in early October.

© Lee Jae-won/AP/
Wide World Photos

© Yun Suk-bong/Reuters/Archive Photos

In August 2000, for the first time since 1985, relatives who lived on opposite sides of the border had a chance to reunite. The reunions were emotionally charged and tearful as a brother and sister, top, *and a mother and daughter,* above, *greeted each other and then said goodbye.*

Of all the cross-border exchanges, the most emotionally charged were between families separated for half a century. For the first time since 1985, and only the second time ever, 100 mostly elderly visitors from each side crossed the border in August for tearful, three-day reunions with family members. Two more family reunions were promised before the end of the year. Under further humanitarian premises, Seoul returned, on September 2, all 63 "unconverted" political prisoners and former North Korean agents imprisoned in the South.

Other notable exchanges included a trip by 46 executives representing the South Korean media, who were given a red-carpet tour of the North and a lengthy interview with Kim Jong Il; the attendance of 42 South Koreans—many of whom represented religious, labor, and farmers' organizations—at the celebration of the 55th anniversary of the founding of the Korean Workers' Party in Pyongyang; and performances by a North Korean symphony orchestra and a circus troupe in the South. A moving demonstration of the new inter-Korean relationship was the entrance of North and South Korean athletes, as a single group, at the opening ceremony of the Olympic Games in Sydney. They marched together, wearing similar uniforms, behind a flag depicting a map of the Korean peninsula.

Apparently, the quick pace and the wide-ranging scope of these contacts were somewhat overwhelming for the North Korean bureaucracy, especially because of Pyongyang's recent interest in establishing formal relations with more than a dozen other countries, including the United States, Japan, and the European Union (EU) members. Pyongyang requested a delay in convening the second session of economic talks, and the dates for the second and the third family-reunion visits also have been pushed back.

North Korea's International Relations. North Korean diplomats have been busy negotiating for formal relations with foreign powers and international organizations. Only days after the beginning of the new millennium, Italy became the first Group of 7 (G-7) nation to grant diplomatic recognition to North Korea. In May, Australia followed suit. Within a month after the June summit, the Philippines established formal relations with North Korea, and similar steps were taken by Canada and New Zealand. Britain, Germany, the Netherlands, and Spain also were expected to set up ties with Pyongyang.

North Korea has long recognized the importance of its relations with the United States. Despite its tirade against

U.S. imperialism, North Korea has sought, in recent years, an improved bilateral relationship. The United States holds the key both to economic assistance and the formal termination of the state of war on the peninsula. Washington, on its part, desires peace and stability in Korea, and, since the early 1990s, it had been particularly concerned about Pyongyang's development of nuclear weapons and long-range missiles. It also had placed North Korea on the U.S. list of states sponsoring international terrorism.

Both before and after the 1994 Agreed Framework— which froze the nuclear project in North Korea, in exchange for "safer" light-water reactors to be built by an international consortium, including the United States, Japan, and South Korea—Pyongyang and Washington had been engaged in tough bilateral negotiations. Seoul, under previous administrations, was suspicious, if not resentful, for being sidelined while Pyongyang chose to ignore its southern rival. President Kim Dae Jung, however, has welcomed, and even encouraged, any effort by Washington or Tokyo to engage Pyongyang in peaceful dialogue. When the [Special Envoy and former U.S. Secretary of Defense William] Perry Report was made public in 1999—recommending a carrot-and-stick strategy in dealing with Pyongyang, and intimating an eventual normalization of U.S.–North Korean relations—Seoul openly welcomed the report, and the U.S. decision to lift some economic sanctions against North Korea.

The June 2000 summit provided the impetus for a new phase in Pyongyang's relations with Washington. Only days after the summit, the United States announced the lifting of some of the remaining economic sanctions on North Korea, while U.S. Secretary of State Madeleine Albright hurried to Seoul, to be briefed directly by President Kim on the meet-

In September workers began rebuilding a railway line connecting Seoul and Pyongyang for the first time in 50 years. At the groundbreaking ceremony in Seoul, above, South Koreans wrote their wishes for reunification on railroad ties.

Though just a few hundred miles apart, Pyongyang, top, and Seoul, above, are vastly different. Pyongyang's two million people have relied since 1995 on outside food aid. The 10 million residents of Seoul were riding the economic wave of a high-tech boom in 2000.

ing in Pyongyang. Washington wanted, and received, Seoul's assurance that the Korean conferees had not made any secret deal affecting the continued presence of U.S. troops in Korea. The South Korean press even reported that Chairman Kim had privately agreed with President Kim that the U.S. soldiers should remain even after Korea's reunification to serve as a regional peacekeeping force. In July, Secretary Albright had a "symbolically historic" meeting with her North Korean counterpart, at a Bangkok meeting of the Association of Southeast Asian Nations Asian Regional Forum (ASEAN ARF), to which North Korea was admitted as the 23d member.

Although a minor note of discord was struck when the titular head of the North Korean state, Kim Yong-nam, abruptly gave up his plan to board a New York–bound flight from Frankfurt—over the issue of diplomatic protocol, thereby scrapping his plans to meet U.S. and other world leaders at the United Nations (UN) Millennium Summit—the momentum for improving relations continued. Vice-Marshal Jo Myong-rok, the first vice-chairman of the NDC, and the person widely recognized as the penultimate official in the North Korean hierarchy, visited Washington, and called on U.S. President Bill Clinton in full military uniform on Oct. 10, 2000, to deliver Chairman Kim's message. Jo also had meetings with Secretary Albright and Defense Secretary William Cohen.

Washington gave a cordial reception to the vice-marshal, the highest North Korean official ever to visit the United States. A joint U.S.–North Korean communiqué, dated Oct. 12, 2000, declared that both sides were determined to improve relations and to replace the Korean armistice with a peace agreement. Subsequently, Pyongyang reaffirmed its willingness to continue the suspension of long-range missile tests, an issue that concerned both Washington and Tokyo. The communiqué closed with an announcement of Secretary Albright's visit to Pyongyang. Secretary Albright's two-day visit October 23–24 included six hours of "serious and constructive talk" with Chairman Kim on a wide range of topics, and made "important progress." There were speculations that the United States would remove North Korea from its list of terrorism-sponsoring states.

In contrast to progress with Western nations, Pyongyang's negotiations with Japan have been stymied for years over issues involving a Japanese apology and compensation for the colonial occupation of Korea. Three ambassadorial-level talks were held in 2000, but failed to reach any accord. Tokyo's new promise of 500,000 tons of rice, to relieve Pyongyang's grain shortfall, was meant to be more than a pure humanitarian gesture, however. A dramatic event such as the June summit may be required to break the deadlock.

With respect to multilateral international organizations, President Kim of the South has been a staunch advocate of Pyongyang's participation in such forums that would provide additional dimensions of international experience to the "hermit" republic, thereby inducing changes in its policies, both diplomatic and domestic. It was President Kim who urged Pyongyang's participation in ASEAN ARF. At the ASEM (Asia-Europe Meeting) in Seoul in October, South Korea also publicly supported Pyongyang's membership in the Asian Development Bank (ADB).

It is an understatement to call 2000 a turning point in North Korea's relations with South Korea, the United States, and the rest of the world. In less than six months, there was a drastic shift away from tense confrontation, and toward reconciliation and stability on the Korean peninsula and in Northeast Asia. Undoubtedly, North Korea's economic and political situation drove Chairman Kim Jong Il's momentous decision to invite President Kim Dae Jung and usher in a new era. It was equally obvious that President Kim's vision and efforts have borne fruit. For that reason, he was awarded the prestigious Nobel Peace Prize for 2000, the first Korean ever to receive a Nobel award.

"Please give me your E-mail address."

North Korea's Chairman
Kim Jong Il to
U.S. Secretary of State
Madeleine Albright
Pyongyang, North Korea
Oct. 24, 2000.

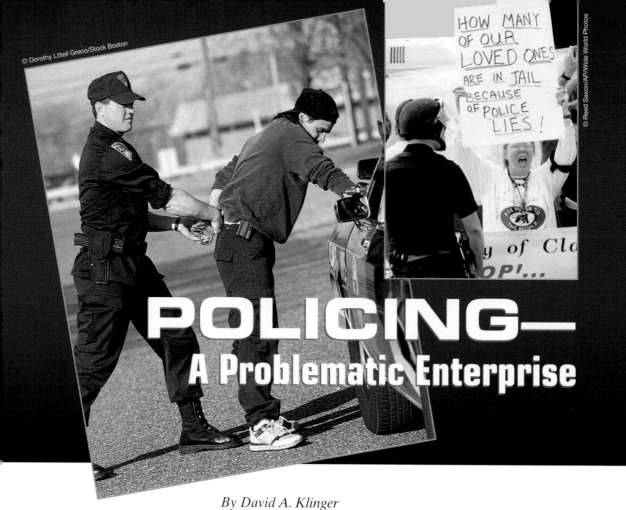

HOW MANY
OF OUR
LOVED ONES
ARE IN JAIL
BECAUSE
OF POLICE
LIES!

y of Cla

OP!...

POLICING—
A Problematic Enterprise

By David A. Klinger

A major corruption scandal in Los Angeles, photo, above right, *the second-degree murder trial of four New York City police officers, as well as the continuing issue of racial profiling focused national attention on the police and the process of policing during 2000.*

In 1899, during the initial stages of the Progressive movement that animated great interest in reforming inefficient and corrupt government institutions across the United States, an editorial in the widely read *Harper's Weekly* opined that "there is no doubt that the police problem is one of the most important with which we have to deal." Major news stories of the year 2000 demonstrate that a century later, these words clearly still ring true. From a multitentacled corruption scandal that continued to unfold in Los Angeles; to the trial and acquittal of four New York City officers who mistakenly killed an unarmed man in a hail of 41 bullets; to cries of "racial profiling" across the land; to the conviction of two New York City police officers and one former officer of conspiracy to obstruct justice in the August 1997 torture of Abner Louima, a Haitian immigrant, in a police station; and to legions of other controversies that made lesser headlines, 2000 was a year that reminded us time and again that the process of policing a democratic society is a problematic enterprise.

The ongoing "police problem" is a result primarily of two features of policing in the United States. The first is that the police stand at the intersection of society's oftentimes-competing demands for freedom and order. At the same time that Americans clamor for protection from criminals who are inclined to take their property, physically accost them, or both, they also demand freedom from the government intrusion that is sometimes part and parcel of providing security. As a consequence, officers are pushed and pulled in contrary directions as they seek to promote order among a citizenry whose birthrights include a remarkable dose of liberty.

The second major source of the "police problem" is that officers have a great deal of discretion about how to handle the matters that come their way. This latitude stems from two features of police work that are unique among public-service occupations. One is that it is difficult to craft precise rules about how officers should behave because no two police tasks of any type (traffic stops, for example) are exactly alike. The other is that officers labor with very little supervision because most police work is conducted on local streets, in businesses, and in homes. Since it is difficult for police managers to craft rules to guide officers' conduct, and because police work with only limited supervision, officers have a great deal of freedom to act as they see fit while working the streets. Unfortunately, the major policing stories of 2000 revolve around the sorts of problems that sometimes arise when officers have considerable freedom from oversight in a society that clamors for order.

A Scandal in Los Angeles. The roots of the corruption scandal in the Los Angeles Police Department (LAPD) extend back to March 1998, when 6.6 lbs (3 kg) of cocaine came up missing from the department's main property room. An investigation into the missing cocaine identified an officer named Rafael Perez, who was assigned to an antigang unit in the city's crime-ridden Rampart Division, as the likely culprit. Officer Perez was arrested and charged with theft

About the Author. David A. Klinger is an associate professor in the Department of Criminology and Criminal Justice at the University of Missouri in St. Louis. His many writings on the police profession have appeared in such journals as *Criminology*, the *Journal of Quantitative Criminology*, and the *Journal of Research in Crime and Delinquency*. His recent research endeavors include federally funded studies of police Special Weapons and Tactics (SWAT) teams and the use of deadly force by officers. Prior to pursuing an academic career, Dr. Klinger was a street policeman in Los Angeles and in Redmond, WA.

Los Angeles Police Chief Bernard Parks was in the forefront throughout the investigation of a corruption scandal within the antigang unit of the department's Rampart Division.

© Nick Ut/AP/Wide World Photos

and other crimes related to the missing cocaine in August 1998. His trial, which began in early December 1998, ended in a mistrial when the 12-person jury hearing his case could not reach the unanimous verdict required to convict in California courts. A retrial then was set for the second half of 1999.

As detectives continued their investigation of Officer Perez in anticipation of the second trial, they developed information that linked him to other crimes, including allegations that he and another officer had planted evidence on citizens they had arrested. Faced with mounting evidence against him, Perez, in exchange for a lesser prison sentence, offered to plead guilty to the crimes with which he was charged, and to cooperate with the detectives who were investigating the other illegal activities in which they believed he was involved. After finalizing a plea-bargain deal with the district attorney's office, Perez told detectives about numerous cases where he and other Rampart antigang officers allegedly had committed illegal acts, such as planting evidence on arrestees, giving false testimony in judicial proceedings, administering unnecessary beatings, and even shooting citizens without justification.

The investigation into Perez' claims led to one of the largest police-corruption scandals in recent U.S. history when it uncovered evidence corroborating many of his allegations. After immediately suspending 11 officers who had ties to Perez, the LAPD convened a special Board of Inquiry that consisted of some 300 officers of various ranks to assess the scope and nature of the corruption in Rampart and make recommendations designed to address any organizational problems that may have contributed to the scandal. The board's report, which was released in March 2000, identified several problems and called for sweeping changes in areas such as the hiring of new personnel, supervisory practices, organization structure, and investigations into officers' actions. As the department moved forward to implement the changes the board called for, the corruption investigation proceeded apace and proceedings emanating from it moved

Protesters face-off against Los Angeles police officers during a demonstration against police actions uncovered during the investigation of the Rampart Division scandal. A Board of Inquiry called for sweeping changes as a result of the case.

Saikou and Kadiatou Diallo, left, parents of Amadou Diallo, an unarmed West African immigrant killed by New York City police officers in a barrage of 41 bullets, attended the trial of the four police officers accused of the killing. After the verdict was announced, acquitting the four officers, defendants Kenneth Boss and Sean Carroll, below, embraced. The Diallos criticized the verdict, but pleaded for calm.

on. By late summer 2000, more than 100 criminal convictions had been overturned by judges who were presented with evidence that the convictions were based on false evidence or false testimony from LAPD officers; some 70 officers remained under investigation for administrative infractions; at least six officers were charged with violating departmental rules; and one officer had been charged with attempted murder stemming from an incident where he allegedly shot an unarmed man and then planted a gun on him.

A Shooting in the Bronx. As was the case with the LAPD scandal, the roots of the second major police story of 2000 lie in a previous year. It all began at about half-past midnight one February morning in 1999, when four New York City plainclothes officers assigned to the department's Street Crimes Unit, riding together in an unmarked car, spotted a young male—later identified as Amadou Diallo, an immigrant from West Africa—ducking in and out of the entrance to an apartment house in the South Bronx. According to police accounts of what happened next, Diallo stuck his right hand into a pocket and retreated out of sight into the apartment's vestibule when the officers stopped to investigate. Fearing that the man they wished to question might be armed, two of the officers drew their weapons and ran up the stairs in front of the apartment house after Diallo. When they got to the top of the steps, they saw that the man they were chasing still had his right hand in his pocket while he tried to open the vestibule's inner door with his left hand. As the officers pointed their guns at Diallo and ordered him to halt, he suddenly pulled a black object from his pocket. Both of the officers at the top of the steps thought that the black object was a gun and began to fire. In his haste to get away from the danger he perceived, one of the officers tripped and fell backward down the steps. Believing that one of their partners had just been shot, the other two officers ran to the foot of the stairs. When the second pair of officers arrived at the scene, they looked up, saw Diallo standing with the black object in his hand, and began to fire at him. When the smoke cleared, it turned out that the four officers had fired a total of 41 rounds, that 19 of the bullets had struck Diallo, and that Diallo was dead. It also turned out that Diallo did not have a gun; that what the officers thought was a pistol was actually his wallet.

The news that four white officers had killed an unarmed black man in a hail of 41 bullets led to outrage in many quarters of U.S. society, and massive press coverage throughout the land, as the nation tried to understand how such an event could have occurred. Critics of the New York Police Department (NYPD) and of the city's mayor, Rudolph Giuliani, claimed that it was a simple case of racially motivated murder perpetrated by four white cops whose disdain for blacks was consistent with the mayor's own animus for minorities. They asserted that the NYPD routinely stopped and "hassled" young blacks for no legitimate reason, that Diallo was stopped because he was black, and that the notion that officers could mistake a wallet for a gun was absurd and that the officers had simply killed Diallo in cold blood. On the other hand, others, including the mayor and many in the law-enforcement community argued that what had happened that cold February morning was indeed a tragic mistake, not murder. When the district attorney for the Bronx reviewed the case, he sided with the critics' version of events and filed second-degree-murder charges against all four of the officers.

Public outcry about the Diallo shooting continued throughout 1999 as the criminal case against the officers moved through the New York State legal system. It reached an apex when the courts granted the officers' request to hold the trial somewhere other than the city because it was felt that the officers could not get a fair trial there. The change-of-venue ruling angered many in the South Bronx and other minority communities around the nation who felt that officers should be held accountable by a jury from the community where the incident happened. Among the voices espousing this position were some who rallied around the cry "no justice, no peace!"—and threatened to engage in retaliatory violence if the officers were not punished for their actions.

When the trial was held in the state capital of Albany in February 2000, the prosecution argued that the officers had murdered Diallo, but the prosecutors chose not to present evidence relating to racial bias against young black males as a motive. The defense—consistent with the initial police version of events—argued that the officers had made a terrible, but simple, mistake when they shot Diallo as he grabbed his wallet. In the end, the jury sided with the defense and acquitted all four officers. The verdict led to additional spasms of protest in some minority communities—but fortunately, resulted in virtually none of the violence that had been threatened before the verdict came in.

Racial Profiling. The assertion that Diallo was stopped, and ultimately killed, merely because he was black dove-

tailed with the third major policing story of the year: racial profiling. Many critics of law enforcement saw the Diallo case as the most egregious example of an allegedly widespread practice where police officers throughout the United States routinely stop and question minority (and especially black) citizens without just cause.
According to those who voice this claim, the police single out minorities because officers believe that minorities are more likely to be criminals. Concerns that the police might be stopping people based on the color of their skin rather than the nature of their conduct led to a great deal of public discussion, investigations by law-enforcement agencies at all levels of government, and legislative hearings.

Many people in and out of law enforcement challenged the assertion that officers were discriminating against blacks and members of other minority groups, pointing out that the available evidence generally showed that minorities were stopped in proportion with minority involvement in criminal activity. That is, data indicated that while minorities were indeed more likely to be stopped by the police, minorities also were more likely to be involved in criminal activity. Whatever the evidence showed, critics of the police seemed to carry the day as many police agencies mandated that their officers collect information on the race of each and every citizen they stop. Several states passed legislation that outlaws racial profiling and mandates the collection of racial characteristics of the people the police stop.

The police department in Miami, FL, also made news in 2000. Following the resignation of Chief of Police William O'Brien in the wake of the federal government's removal of Elián González, a 6-year-old Cuban refugee, from the home of his Miami relatives, Raul Martinez, a 24-year veteran of the police force, was appointed to the post. A Cuban immigrant, Martinez became the first Hispanic police chief in the largely Hispanic city.

Why the Problems? Consideration of the social context in which the police in the United States operate at the dawn of the 21st century offers some ideas about why the problems behind the policing stories that dominated the headlines in 2000 occurred. The first point to be made flows from the previous discussion about the large dose of freedom that officers enjoy from supervisory oversight as they seek to control crime in a society that cherishes liberty. This freedom creates a climate where officers can make two sorts of errors in the course of their duties. The first sort of error is engaging in *corrupt* activity. When officers purposely violate laws regarding their arrest powers, bribery, and even ordinary laws such as those forbidding common crimes such as robbery and theft, they engage in corruption. The other sort of wrongs that officers may commit are those that result from errors of judgment or action. When officers believe an innocent citizen is a wanted criminal, for example, and treat him as they would a criminal, their actions constitute a mistake. By viewing the stories from Los Angeles and New York through this lens, it seems apparent that the LAPD corruption scandal stemmed from the purposeful abuse of freedom and power

Community relations remained an important part of policing in 2000. Officers in many towns and cities visited schools to talk with students about police work.

by the involved officers, while the Diallo shooting was the result of mistaken judgment.

While the distinction between mistakes and corrupt activities can help identify the nature of some police problems, it does not explain *why* the officers in Los Angeles chose to break the law, why the officers in New York made their fatal error, or why some officers might engage in racial profiling. To do so requires a look at other aspects of the social climate in which the police operate.

One of the challenges that police organizations always face is hiring competent people with the proper ethical character. Meeting this challenge has become more difficult in recent years as the red-hot economy has taken people who might otherwise have been interested in careers in law enforcement and has drawn these prospective police officers into more-lucrative occupations. With fewer highly qualified individuals to choose from, some police agencies have had to turn to less-qualified applicants. A second factor that has let less-qualified people into the police ranks is court rulings that make it more difficult to decline the applications of those deemed unfit by the police agencies they seek to work for. This second factor clearly played a role in the Rampart scandal as the LAPD initially rejected Rafael Perez when he applied, but was forced to hire him when he appealed to the city's civil-service board, who ruled in his favor. With more and more young people who lack the requisite qualifications and character coming into the police service across the country, it is likely that in the near future, we will see more scandals like the one that rocked Los Angeles.

Another matter that seems to be relevant to the troubles of 2000 is training. Both common sense and evidence from decades of research indicate that well-trained officers perform better than do officers who lack sound training. This is particularly true where the use of force is concerned. Evidence shows that good training can reduce the incidence of force by officers. While the precise reason why the officers who shot Diallo mistook his wallet for a gun, fired so many rounds, and missed what they were aiming at with more than half of their shots is not known, it is possible that had the officers received more-intensive training, that they might have recognized the wallet for what it was and avoided the shooting entirely—or, if they had fired, might not have done so in such a haphazard fashion.

On the other hand, it is entirely possible that poor training may have had nothing to do with the error that led to the terrible tragedy in the Bronx; that the best-trained officer could have mistaken Diallo's wallet for a gun. Humans—no matter how well trained they might be—after all, make mistakes. If even the best-trained officer could indeed have made such a fatal error, the Diallo shooting raises an issue that goes far deeper than training, to the core issue of how the police should work to promote social order. The officers who shot Diallo sought to stop him because they were doing what officers are trained to do in the crime-fighting mind-set that currently dominates police thinking: Stop crime by actively seeking out and stopping suspicious people. If officers are bound (by their status as humans) to make mistakes, and, if officers are bound (by their crime-fighting mandate) to stop and question suspicious people, then tragedies such as the Diallo shooting are an inevitable by-product of the tactics the police currently use to fight crime and promote order. If this is the case, then tragedies such as the Diallo shooting can be avoided only by changing current police practices and having officers avoid suspicious citizens. Doing so, however, would almost certainly lead to a substantial increase in crime and disorder, something that a citizenry that demands order and protection from predatory criminals would certainly not countenance.

The policeman on the street is an important presence—not only in terms of law enforcement but also for rapport with local citizens.

The same limitation prevails where corruption goes. The only way that scandals such as the one swirling around the LAPD can be completely eliminated is if police managers were to somehow restrict officers' freedom so greatly that officers could not independently respond to citizens' requests for service. Such a practice would, like moving away from stopping and questioning suspicious people, lead to an increase in crime and disorder that the public would not accept. Because complete elimination of the scandals and mistakes that made headlines in 2000 would almost certainly lead to an increase in crime and disorder that the people will not accept, it would appear that the changes needed to accomplish this goal will not be forthcoming, and, therefore, that the "police problem" discussed in *Harper's Weekly* at the dawn of the 19th century will remain in the 21st century.

Cartooning:
The Comics
Are Here To Stay

© Mary Kate Denny/
PhotoEdit

© Walter Sanders/TimePix

By Stephen Charla

Newspaper comic strips are as popular today (above left) *as they were some 50 years ago* (above right). *In fact, the comic strips have been a fixture of the American scene for more than a century.*

On Feb. 12, 2000, Charles M. Schulz—the creator of the comic strip *Peanuts*, which was appearing in more than 2,600 newspapers worldwide at the time—died following a battle with colon cancer. The overwhelming interest in and reaction to Schulz' passing are evidence of the continued popularity and influence of newspaper comic strips.

The comics are a unique narrative art form in which text and pictures are interdependent. Neither component makes complete sense without the other, and each is changed by the presence of the other. Even more crucial to the way comic strips work is the fact that they are composed of separate images arranged in a sequence. The "language" of the comics—which utilizes panels, speech balloons, thought balloons, motion lines, onomatopoeic sound effects, and other symbols—was developed by the early comic-strip artists during the late 19th and early 20th centuries. Later the language of comic strips was applied to comic books, underground or alternative "comix," and modern graphic novels.

The History. The 18th- and 19th-century European picture stories of William Hogarth, Thomas Rowlandson, Rodolphe Töpffer, and Wilhelm Busch can be seen as antecedents to the comic strip. Unlike comics, however, the text and illustrations in these stories were usually kept separate from one another. The first true comic strips appeared in U.S. newspapers late in the 19th century.

Daisy Mae and Li'l Abner

About the Author. Stephen Charla is curator of the International Museum of Cartoon Art, located in Boca Raton, FL. Begun in 1974 and open to the public in its current location since March 1996, the museum is a collection of more than 160,000 original drawings that include every genre of the art—animation, comic books, comic strips, gag cartoons, illustration, editorial cartoons, greeting cards, caricature, graphic novels, sports cartoons, and computer-generated art. Cartoonists from more than 50 countries are represented in the museum's collection.

In 1894, newspaper publisher Joseph Pulitzer added a color humor supplement to the Sunday edition of his *New York World* to boost its circulation. This newspaper supplement was not a collection of comic strips. It contained cartoons, jokes, and humorous text pieces. Its content was similar to that of the popular humor magazines of the time, such as *Judge*, *Puck*, and *Life*. Two years later, rival publisher William Randolph Hearst added an eight-page color comic supplement to the Sunday edition of his *New York Morning Journal*. These humor supplements evolved into the Sunday comics section, which eventually became a familiar component of U.S. newspapers.

Cartoonist Richard F. Outcault began producing a comic feature for the Sunday *World* in 1895. Eventually called *Hogan's Alley*, the cartoon depicted humorous scenes in an Irish slum in New York City. By 1896 a little boy in a bright yellow nightshirt began to appear in *Hogan's Alley* on a regular basis. "The Yellow Kid" was enormously popular with the *World*'s readers, and he ultimately became the star of the cartoon. Like many latter-day comic-strip characters, he was merchandised heavily. People bought Yellow Kid dolls, toys, books, buttons, fans, and cracker tins. Often referred to as the first comic strip, *Hogan's Alley* rarely appeared in strip form. It was nearly always a single illustration, as opposed to a sequence of panels. Nevertheless, the popularity of *Hogan's Alley* and the Yellow Kid led to the proliferation of comic strips.

The Katzenjammer Kids

Dagwood and Blondie

Dick Tracy

Recognizing the potential of cartoons to increase newspaper circulation, Hearst hired Outcault away from Pulitzer and put him to work on the *Journal*'s Sunday comic supplement, "The American Humorist." Another of Hearst's artists, the German-born Rudolph Dirks, produced the earliest successful comic feature to appear regularly in the strip format. *The Katzenjammer Kids*, which began publication in late 1897, was based loosely on Wilhelm Busch's *Max und Moritz* picture books. Dirks' feature was about two boys, Hans and Fritz, who liked to play cruel pranks on the strip's adult characters. As with many early comic strips, the gags consisted mainly of slapstick and ethnic humor. Although the strip originally had typeset captions beneath the panels, Dirks later began to use speech balloons to incorporate the dialogue into the pictures.

Soon other newspapers began adding comic supplements to their Sunday editions. By the end of the first decade of the 20th century, most of these were devoted exclusively to cartoons and comic strips. The verses, jokes, and other text features were dropped. After the success of Bud Fisher's *Mutt and Jeff*, comic strips started to appear in the daily newspapers as well. The major newspapers began to syndicate their more popular comic strips to smaller papers in other parts of the country. Eventually newspaper syndicates hired cartoonists to create comic strips directly for syndication. Many local newspapers also produced their own strips.

Krazy Kat

Winsor McCay's *Little Nemo in Slumberland* and George Herriman's *Krazy Kat*, both of which made their first appearance in the early decades of the 20th century, have been recognized as classics of the art form. These two strips demonstrated the unlimited potential of the comics. *Little Nemo in Slumberland* followed its protagonist, based on McCay's own son, on a series of adventures in the land of dreams. The strip was illustrated beautifully in painstaking detail. McCay experimented with the layout of the page, changing the size and shape of the panels to suit the situation. Comics critic Robert C. Harvey has noted that McCay was so far ahead of his contemporaries that most of his discoveries had to be rediscovered decades later.

Herriman's *Krazy Kat* was a surreal comic strip about a love triangle involving the title character, a mouse named Ignatz, and a dog named Offissa Pupp. In many of the strips, Ignatz would attempt to hit Krazy Kat in the head with a

Hi & Lois

brick. *Krazy Kat* then would interpret this as an expression of love. Like McCay, Herriman would vary the layout of the page. He also was fond of changing the appearance of the backgrounds from panel to panel, even if his characters were standing still. *Krazy Kat* was not especially popular when it originally was published, but it was embraced by intellectuals, such as the literary critic Gilbert Seldes and poet e.e. cummings. It also was William Randolph Hearst's favorite comic strip. Hearst made it clear that he would continue to publish *Krazy Kat* for as long as Herriman wanted to draw it.

Newspaper comic strips encountered some opposition during the early part of the 20th century. Some denounced the comics as vulgar and a bad influence on children. Comics historian Ron Goulart has pointed out that these kinds of complaints were slowly overcome when comic strips began to target a middle-class audience. Comic strips about families were especially successful. These included Sidney Smith's *The Gumps*, George McManus' *Bringing Up Father*, and, later, Chic Young's *Blondie*. Comic strips with a domestic setting remain a popular genre.

Mutt and Jeff

Little Orphan Annie

In addition to comic strips that provided a joke a day, there were strips with continuing story lines that readers could follow from episode to episode. Among these were Frank King's *Gasoline Alley*, Billy DeBeck's *Barney Google*, E.C. Segar's *Thimble Theatre*, and Harold Gray's *Little Orphan Annie*—all of which began publication in the 1910s and 1920s.

In 1924, Roy Crane began to change his humorous strip, *Wash Tubbs*, into the first successful adventure strip. During the 1930s, Hal Foster, who drew *Tarzan* and *Prince Valiant*, and

(Continued on page 80.)

The Life and Legacy of Charles M. Schulz

Charles Monroe Schulz, who was called "Sparky" by his friends and family, died at his Santa Rosa, CA, home on Saturday, Feb. 12, 2000—just hours before Sunday newspapers across the United States carried his last original *Peanuts* strip. Schulz, 77, had drawn Charlie Brown and his friends for nearly 50 years, and in the process created a $1 billion-a-year industry.

Early Life. Charles Schulz was born on Nov. 26, 1922, the son of a St. Paul, MN, small businessman, self-made Carl Schulz, who dropped out of school after the third grade and later paid his own way through barber school. Nothing in Charles Schulz' early working-class existence prepared him for the fame and phenomenal

© D. Kirkland/Corbis-Sygma

financial success that *Peanuts* would bring. "None of us know the meaning of a dollar anymore," Schulz once complained. "My father knew. He knew exactly how many haircuts he had to finish to have a dollar. Now, it's all so confusing."

Carl Schulz, who owned and ran The Family Barbershop for 45 years, loved the funny papers, and he nicknamed his only child—at the age of two days—after Barney Google's racehorse, Spark Plug. Sparky made his own first dollar at the age of 8, modeling knickers at the Emporium department store in St. Paul at the behest of a neighbor. He immediately went out and spent 20 cents of the largess on a ceramic frog for his mother, Dena.

It was never the pursuit of money, but a passion for his comic-strip art that motivated

Charles Schulz. His kindergarten teacher was the first outside of the family to notice his ability when she passed around fat crayons and butcher paper for drawing. Young Sparky's picture of a man shoveling Minnesota snow included a palm tree, exotic and misplaced flora suggested by letters from relatives in Needles, CA. The teacher took one look at the palm tree and, to her everlasting credit, told him: "Someday, Charles, you're going to be an artist." Young lives pivot on fine points, and Schulz' was no exception.

At Richard Gordon Elementary School, Sparky shone academically, skipping two half-grades. But his school career soured at puberty. He became a shy, skinny kid with pimples and big ears, nearly 6′ (1.8 m) tall and weighing only 136 lbs (62 kg). Girls ignored him. His scholarship faltered. In the annual, where they list the extracurricular activities of each student, Sparky had only the annual staff to his credit. He was on the golf team, too, but they forgot to mention that. The socially inept Sparky submitted a series of cartoons for the Central High School senior annual his senior year. "I waited and waited for the annual to come out. When it did, my drawings were not in it," Schulz said decades later. He had an uncanny ability to remember the slights and humiliations of childhood and adolescence, never letting go of life's sad moments, defeats, and losses. Instead, he used them as grist for his genius.

It was his doting mother, Dena, who noticed an advertisement in the local newspaper for Federal Schools, a correspondence plan for aspiring artists. (It later would become known as Art Instruction Schools, the famous "Draw Me" folks.) Carl Schulz paid the $170 tuition, in installments, for his son to learn lettering, perspective, and the other basics of cartooning. There were 12 divisions. Instructor Frank Wing gave Schulz a C+ in Division Five: Drawing of Children. When he completed the art course, Schulz began trying unsuccessfully to sell gag cartoons to magazines. But in 1943, fate and World War II interrupted the young cartoonist's efforts. Schulz was drafted and sent to the European theater. His mother died of cancer the same year. Schulz became an infantry staff sergeant and the leader of a machine-gun squad. He saw little combat during the war, but gained the confidence he had lacked, and came home determined to draw and sell.

Career. Charles Schulz came close to accepting a job lettering tombstones. Instead, he made his breakthrough into professional cartooning when an editor at *Timeless Topix,* a comic magazine owned by the Roman Catholic Church, hired him to letter adventure cartoons already drawn. The work was menial, but the journey of a thousand miles had begun. Soon he was hired by his alma mater, Art Instruction Schools, to correct student lessons that were returned by mail. It was there that he met and fell in love with Donna Johnson, a pretty, red-headed secretary. Schulz later would immortalize her in his comic strip as "The Little Red-haired Girl." Donna turned down Schulz' earnest proposal and married a fireman. Her mother encouraged the decision, warning her daughter that a cartoonist never would amount to anything. (Schulz later married Joyce Halverson, and together the couple reared five children. They were divorced in 1972, and Schulz married Jeannie Forsyth the following year.)

Between 1948 and 1950, Schulz sold 15 cartoons to *The Saturday Evening Post.* The magazine paid $40 for his first, one-column cartoon. He also made his first newspaper sale, a weekly comic feature called *Li'l Folks*, to the *St. Paul Pioneer Press.* One June day in 1950, Schulz took the train from St. Paul to New York City, armed with his art, ready to meet with an encouraging editor at United Feature Syndicate. The syndicate liked what it saw and outlined a deal. Schulz took it and treated himself to a steak on the jubilant train ride home.

It was Oct. 2, 1950, when the first *Peanuts* strip appeared in seven newspapers. Growth was slow that first year. Fellow cartoonist Mort Walker remembered feeling sorry for Schulz, whose strip came in dead last when the *New York World-Telegram* took a readers' poll. Nobody would have to worry long. Schulz parlayed human angst, melancholy, and frustrated expectation into funny pictures and memorable lines. The strip eventually became the world's most widely read comic strip—in 2,600 news-

papers in 75 countries and 21 languages. Guinness recognized his readership at 90 million. As the syndicate and Schulz prepared to celebrate the 50th anniversary year of *Peanuts,* in 2000, the cartoonist, already suffering from Parkinson's disease, had several small strokes. During emergency surgery, doctors diagnosed Schulz with colon cancer. He regretfully announced his retirement in late 1999, saying there would be no new daily strips after Jan. 3, 2000, and new Sunday cartoons would cease after February 13.

Legacy. Schulz and his creation became legendary. He dined with presidents, was grand marshal of a Rose Parade, fielded the questions of television newsman David Brinkley, and was photographed by Yousuf Karsh. The tributes to Schulz and *Peanuts* were endless. Violinist Robert McDuffie composed a serenade to Schulz. At the height of Snoopy-mania, in 1966, a Florida rock group called the Royal Guardsmen sold 3 million copies of the song "Snoopy vs. the Red Baron." In 1969 the lunar module on the *Apollo 10* flight was given the name Snoopy. The musical *You're a Good Man, Charlie Brown* was a hit first off—and then on—Broadway. And the TV specials inspired by the strips—including the Emmy-winning *A Charlie Brown Christmas*—began appearing in 1965 and have been popular reruns ever since. The strip spawned three amusement parks, four movies, and reprint books that have sold 300 million copies. Numerous items—including cards, toys, and clothes—with a "Peanuts" theme became best-sellers with children of all ages.

"A cartoonist is someone who has to draw the same thing every day without repeating himself," Schulz said. Schulz did that for nearly five decades.

RHETA GRIMSLEY JOHNSON

Editor's Note. Rheta Grimsley Johnson, a columnist with *The Atlanta Journal/Constitution,* is the author of *Good Grief: The Story of Charles M. Schulz.* Her authorized biography of Mr. Schulz was published in 1989.

Photo Credit: © United Features Syndicate, Inc.

Alex Raymond, who is best known for *Flash Gordon*, raised the standard for adventure comics with their illustrative drawing styles. Milton Caniff was another acknowledged master of the adventure comic strip. His *Terry and the Pirates* is considered one of the classics of the genre. The strip followed a teenager named Terry Lee and his guardian Pat Ryan on a series of adventures in the Orient. Caniff has been praised for his use of "cinematic" techniques, his outstanding use of light and shadow, his sense of drama, and his ability to create memorable characters. Adventure comics of all kinds flourished in the 1930s and 1940s. Although not an adventure comic, Al Capp's *Li'l Abner*, which debuted in the mid-1930s, enjoyed particular popularity.

One of the most significant strips to begin publication during the 1940s was Walt Kelly's *Pogo. Pogo,* a humor strip about the anthropomorphized talking animals who inhabited the Okefenokee swamp, is considered a masterpiece of the medium. Within a few years of its initial publication, Kelly was using the strip as a vehicle for social and political satire. Although comic-strip artists occasionally expressed political opinions, most avoided it for fear of alienating readers. Kelly caused a controversy by publishing a story line that criticized Sen. Joseph McCarthy. Although *Pogo* was not exclusively a political comic strip, characters based on political figures (such as J. Edgar Hoover, Nikita Khrushchev, Fidel Castro, Lyndon Johnson, and Richard Nixon) continued to make appearances. Kelly's success helped make it possible for later cartoonists—such as Jules Feiffer (*Feiffer*), Garry Trudeau (*Doonesbury*), and Berke Breathed (*Bloom County*)—to use comic strips to convey political messages.

By the middle of the 20th century, many different genres of comic strips were appearing in newspapers. Today, humor strips dominate the comics sections. During the 1950s, newspapers began reducing the size of the comics in order to save space. Because they were more simply drawn, humor strips were more able to survive a reduction in size than were the detailed, realistically drawn adventure and soap-opera strips. After the arrival of television, newspaper editors came to believe that readers would not want to follow a single story in the comics for months when they could see several complete stories on TV every night. This made them reluctant to buy new continuity strips.

Comics critic Robert C. Harvey has written that Mort Walker's *Beetle Bailey* and Charles Schulz' *Peanuts*, both of which first appeared in the fall of 1950, became the models for most subsequent humor strips. Both comic strips told a joke a day and were drawn in a clean, simple, almost abstract style. Many of today's popular humor strips premiered in the 1970s, including Cathy Guisewite's *Cathy*, Dik Browne's *Hagar the Horrible*, Jeff MacNelly's *Shoe*, Jim Davis' *Garfield*, and Lynn Johnston's *For Better or For Worse.*

Reprinted with
special permission of
King Features Syndicate

Flash Gordon

To mark the 50th anniversary of the comic strip "Beetle Bailey" in 2000, Secretary of the Army Louis Caldera (second from left) *honored its creator, Mort Walker, at a Pentagon ceremony. Bailey (right) and Sarge were proud to attend the festivities.*

Today and the Future. Successful comic strips can run for decades. With fewer newspapers being published, and with less space allotted to comic strips in those papers, it has been difficult for new material to be noticed. Even under these circumstances, however, some comic strips have been able to attract attention. Bill Watterson's *Calvin and Hobbes*, which premiered in 1985 and ran for ten years, is already considered a classic. Scott Adams' *Dilbert*, an irreverent strip about the workplace, became extremely popular during the 1990s.

The future of comic strips seems to be tied to that of newspapers. The comics became a part of American life at a time when newspapers were the most important source of information and entertainment. Comic strips have remained popular even as various audiovisual media have challenged the importance of newspapers. Although some have predicted that computers and the Internet will lead to a "paperless" society, it seems unlikely that newspapers will disappear. After all, some predicted that television would make movie theaters obsolete. As newspapers, syndicates, and individual cartoonists make comic strips available on-line, space considerations may be less of an issue, and artists may have more freedom in drawing and designing the layouts of their strips. The new media may change the comics in other ways. For example, cartoonist Scott McCloud creates each panel of his on-line comic strip, *Choose Your Own Carl*, after consulting suggestions from his readers. There is no scarcity of talented new comic-strip artists with original ideas. The late 1990s saw the arrival of Patrick McDonnell's warm and slightly offbeat *Mutts*, Aaron McGruder's daring *The Boondocks*, and Frank Cho's superbly drawn *Liberty Meadows*, among others. The comics, it seems, are here to stay.

PRIMATES
IN PERIL

© Lynn M. Stone/Bruce Coleman, Inc.

By Jenny Tesar

The golden lion tamarin, above, is among the 25 most endangered primates, according to a new study released in early 2000. Noted for its golden-yellow fur, the golden lion tamarin is native to the Atlantic rain forests of eastern Brazil. The species was the focus of an international captive breeding program in the 1970s. Today, the golden lion tamarin numbers about 800, with another 500 in captivity.

A pes, monkeys, and lemurs—mankind's closest living relatives—are being driven to extinction. Man fragments and destroys the forest homes of nonhuman primates to create farms, pasture land, and urban settlements; to extract timber and mineral resources; and to fight their wars. Man captures species of primates for pets and kills them for food and traditional medicines. "Close to 20% of the world's primates stand a reasonable chance of disappearing within the next ten to 20 years unless we take decisive action," warned William Konstant, coauthor of the report "Primates in Peril," which was released in early 2000 by Conservation International and the World Conservation Union's Species Survival Commission.

In an effort to stress the seriousness of the situation, the report listed the world's 25 most endangered primates. The animals range from tiny lion tamarins to lumbering mountain gorillas. They include not only species with the fewest numbers but also recently discovered or rediscovered primates whose populations are unknown but presumed to be dangerously small. "Species whose populations were stable only a few years ago but are now under serious threat of extinction" as well as those "that have only recently been recognized as distinct, and therefore have not been the specific focus of conservation measures" also are featured on the list. All but one of the species are found in seven of the world's 25 biodiversity hotspots—regions with a wide variety of species as well as some of the most severe habitat destruction. For example, the rain forest that once covered almost the entire Atlantic coast of Brazil now is less than 8% its original size; it is home to five monkeys on the list.

Conservation groups stress the importance of worldwide education campaigns that describe the causes, consequences, and appropriate solutions to the crisis. They are working to expand national parks and other protected areas, and to strengthen enforcement of laws against exploitation of wildlife and habitats. Also critical are efforts to aid the millions of impoverished people who depend on the same habitats as the primates for food, fuel, and shelter.

Zoos and research centers worldwide have captive breeding programs for some of the primates, planning to try to reintroduce those born in captivity to the wild. This already has been done successfully with golden lion tamarins, but the lack of appropriate forest habitat limits the feasibility of such reintroduction.

About the Author. Jenny Tesar, a free-lance writer and editor, living in Bethel, CT, is a member of the National Association of Science Writers. She is the author of nearly 40 books, many of which are concerned with the world's wildlife and the environment generally. The American Association for the Advancement of Science judged two of her books—*Mammals* (1993) and *What on Earth is a Tuatara?* (1994)—as the year's best books for children. Ms. Tesar is coauthor of *The Penguin Desk Encyclopedia of Science and Mathematics*, which was published by Viking/Penguin in late 2000.

The 25 Most Endangered Primates

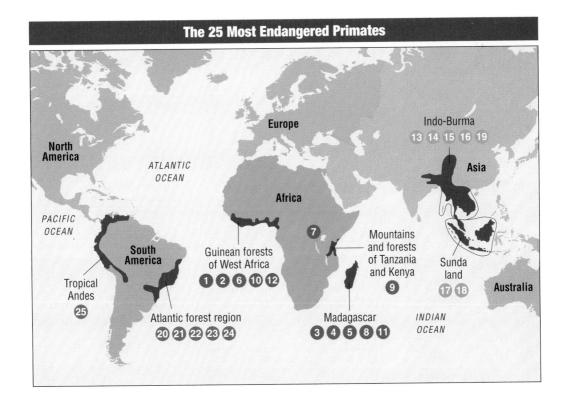

AFRICA

1 Cross River gorilla

Gorilla gorilla diehli

This subspecies of gorilla is distinguished by its comparatively short skull and small braincase. It also has a narrower palate and other unique mouth features, possibly related to its diet, which consists of drier, harder foods than the diets of other gorillas.

Habitat: dense forests on hills along the Nigeria-Cameroon border
Estimated Population: 150 to 200
Primary Threat: hunting for its meat

2 Drill

Mandrillus leucophaeus

The drill is a large-bodied primate, weighing about 50 lbs (23 kg). Its fur is grayish brown; the face is purplish black with a white beard. Hard buttock pads are reddish purple, brightening when the animal is excited. Drills typically live in large, male-dominated troops that may number 100 or more. Primarily terrestrial, they feed on small animals, nuts, fruits, and plants.

Habitat: forests of Cameroon, Equatorial Guinea, and Nigeria.
Estimated Population: unknown
Primary Threat: hunting for its meat

© Zig Leszczynski/Animals Animals/Earth Scenes

3 Golden bamboo lemur

Hapalemur aureus

One of three species of bamboo lemurs, this animal was discovered in 1985. It is named for its golden facial color and its primary food—shoots of giant bamboo. The bamboo contains high levels of cyanide, but this does not appear to harm the lemur. The animal weighs about 3.5 lb (1.6 kg) and has a tail as long as its body. It lives in small groups and is most active at dawn and dusk.

Habitat: eastern rain forests of Madagascar
Estimated Population: about 1,000
Primary Threat: habitat loss from agriculture

©: Frans Lanting/Minden Pictures

4 Golden-crowned sifaka

Propithecus tattersalli

Characterized by mostly white fur and a golden-orange crown, these lemurs were photographed for the first time in 1974. They live in small groups that usually include two adults of each sex. They are active during the day, feeding mainly on seeds, fruits, leaves, and flowers. At night they sleep in tall trees. People who are native to the area where golden-crowned sifaka live consider hunting these animals taboo, but newcomers to the area do not.

Habitat: dry forests of northeastern Madagascar
Estimated Population: fewer than 8,000
Primary Threat: habitat loss from human settlements and mining; hunting for its meat

© David Haring/Animals Animals/Earth Scenes

5 Lac Alaotra bamboo lemur

Hapalemur griseus alaotrensis

About the size of a guinea pig and garbed in gray fur, the Lac Alaotra bamboo lemur occupies wetlands of reeds and papyrus, a unique niche for primates. It feeds mainly on the plants in its watery habitat. It lives in small social groups and is active throughout the day.

> **Habitat:** reed and papyrus beds around Lac Alaotra, Madagascar's largest lake
> **Estimated Population:** fewer than 5,000
> **Primary Threats:** habitat loss from agriculture and irrigation; cutting of reeds and papyrus; hunting for its meat; capture for pets

© Russell A. Mittermeier

6 Miss Waldron's red colobus

Procolobus badius waldroni

First identified in 1933 and last sighted in the 1970s, this subspecies of red colobus was declared extinct in late 2000—the first primate known to become extinct since the early 1700s. Unlike other primates, which have a one-chambered stomach, colobine monkeys have a complex four-chambered stomach that enables them to digest leaves that cannot be digested by other primates. Red colobus monkeys also eat large amounts of unripe fruits. Named for their reddish-orange coat, they live high in trees and are active mainly during the day.

> **Habitat:** rain forests of Ghana and Ivory Coast
> **Estimated Population:** unknown
> **Primary Threat:** hunting for its meat

7 Mountain gorilla

Gorilla gorilla beringei

Gorillas are the largest of the primates, with males averaging 350 lbs (159 kg); females are significantly smaller. Gorillas are gentle and intelligent creatures that live in small groups composed of an adult male and two or three females and their young. They are active during the day, feeding on plant matter. As darkness falls, they build nests of leaves on which they sleep through the night.

> **Habitat:** montane forests on the Virunga volcanoes of Uganda, Rwanda, and the Democratic Republic of Congo
> **Estimated Population:** 320
> **Primary Threats:** habitat loss from farming, human settlements, and war; hunting for its meat

© Art Wolfe

8 Perrier's sifaka

Propithecus diadema perrieri

This all-black lemur—a subspecies of diademed sifaka—lives in small groups of two to six individuals. Excellent jumpers, they travel through the treetops, stopping to feed on leaves, flowers, stems, and unripe fruits. In the group, they hop along on their hind legs. Like other sifakas, they confront enemies with the alarm call, siFAHK!

> **Habitat:** dry deciduous forests of northern Madagascar
> **Estimated Population:** 1,000 to 2,000
> **Primary Threats:** habitat loss from agriculture, logging, and charcoal production; mining

9 Sanje mangabey

Cercocebus galeritus sanjei

A subspecies discovered in 1981, the Sanje mangabey ranges in color from fawn to smoky brown, with a pale belly. It has white eyelids and short, erect hairs above the brow. It is a fairly large, though slender monkey, with cheek pouches and powerful jaws that help it crack shells. Strictly arboreal, it moves through the forests on all fours. It communicates with others in its group through a variety of calls and visual displays.

Habitat: forests on the Udzungwa Mountains of Tanzania
Estimated Population: fewer than 1,500
Primary Threats: habitat loss; hunting for its meat

10 Sclater's guenon

Cercopithecus sclateri

Sclater's guenon is a small arboreal monkey with long legs and an extremely long tail that aids in balance. Active mainly in early morning and late afternoon, it eats a variety of plant matter as well as insects. When alarmed, it becomes very vocal, grimaces, and exposes its teeth (guenon derives from the French word meaning "fright").

Habitat: forests of eastern Nigeria
Estimated Population: 2,000 to 3,000
Primary Threats: hunting for its meat; habitat loss from agriculture, timber cutting, and oil-industry activities

11 Silky sifaka

Propithecus diadema candidus

A subspecies of diademed sifaka, the silky sifaka is easily recognized by its completely white coat. It is one of the largest lemurs, weighing up to 15 lbs (7 kg). It lives in small groups that usually are found high in tall trees. It is active during the day, feeding mainly on leaves, fruits, and flowers. These sifakas are monogamous, with a pair and its offspring forming the basic social group.

Habitat: rain forests of northeastern Madagascar
Estimated Population: 100 to 1,000
Primary Threats: habitat loss from agriculture, logging, and charcoal production; hunting for its meat

12 White-naped mangabey

Cercocebus atys lunulatus

A slender, medium-sized monkey with a long tail, the white-naped mangabey is distinguished by the white fur on the back of its neck. The rest of the coat is mostly sooty black. Mangabeys have a long tail, which often is carried parallel over the back. They live in groups, are strictly arboreal and diurnal, and feed on both plant and animal matter. Like other mangabeys, they use their faces to express aggression, respect, and a desire to be groomed.

Habitat: forests of Ghana and Ivory Coast
Estimated Population: fewer than 3,000
Primary Threats: hunting for its meat; habitat destruction

© Russell A. Mittermeier

ASIA

13 Cat Ba Island golden-headed langur

Trachypithecus poliocephalus

This extremely rare langur, or leaf-eating monkey, is known only from a small island off the coast of mainland Vietnam. It appears to be most active in early morning and late afternoon, when small groups can be seen foraging on the ground for the plant matter that composes its diet.

Habitat: rocky areas on the island of Cat Ba, Vietnam
Estimated Population: 100 to 200
Primary Threat: hunting for use in traditional medicines

© Russell A. Mittermeier

14 Delacour's langur

Trachypithecus delacouri

This slender, long-tailed langur, or leaf-eating monkey, was first described in 1932. It is about 2 ft (.6 m) long. It has white fur on its cheeks, lower back, and outer thighs; the rest of the fur is black. It lives in forest trees. A portion of its population resides in Cuc Phuong National Park, Vietnam's first national park, established in 1962.

Habitat: forests of Vietnam
Estimated Population: 200
Primary Threats: habitat loss; hunting for use in traditional medicines

15 Gray-shanked douc langur

Pygathrix nemaeus cinerea

Once considered a variant of its black- and red-shanked cousins—also native to wooded habitats of Vietnam—this monkey now is recognized as a distinct subspecies. Like other douc langurs (often called leaf-eaters), it lives in small groups generally composed of one or more adult males, twice the number of females, and their young. They are arboreal and diurnal, traveling from tree to tree in search of leaves, buds, and other plant food.

© Tilo Nadler

Habitat: forests in the central highlands of Vietnam
Estimated Population: fewer than 100
Primary Threats: habitat loss; hunting

16 Hainan gibbon

Hylobates concolor hainanus

Like all gibbons, Hainan gibbons are small, lightweight apes with a slender body and arms longer than the legs. They lack a tail. They are strictly arboreal and very dexterous, moving rapidly and gracefully through the treetops in search of pulpy fruit, young leaves, insects, and other food. They live in groups and are active during the day. Male Hainan gibbons are all-black, while females are brownish yellow with black patches on the head.

Habitat: the island of Hainan, China
Estimated Population: fewer than 50
Primary Threats: habitat loss from human settlement; capture for pet trade

17 Javan gibbon

Hylobates moloch

Also known as the silvery gibbon, this animal is extremely agile, leaping through the treetops and using the fingers of its hands as a hook to grab onto branches. It eats mainly fruits and leaves. Because each group of Javan gibbons lives all year round in a home range, the forest must have a great diversity of tree species to fulfill dietary needs.

Habitat: rain forest of western and central Java, Indonesia
Estimated Population: 300 to 400
Primary Threats: habitat loss; capture for pet trade

© Russell A. Mittermeier

18 Sumatran orangutan

Pongo abelii

A heavy-bodied animal with a shaggy coat of long reddish-brown hair, the orangutan seldom leaves the trees of its forest home. It moves slowly, using its powerful arms to swing from one branch to another, and grasping branches with both hands and feet. Active during the day, it builds a sleeping nest, or platform, on which it spends the night. Its diet consists primarily of fruit. Males may weigh 220 lbs (100 kg); females are smaller.

Habitat: forests on the island of Sumatra, Indonesia
Estimated Population: fewer than 5,000
Primary Threats: habitat loss from agriculture, logging, and human settlement; hunting for food and sport; capture for pet trade

© Tom Brakefiield/Bruce Coleman, Inc.

19 Tonkin snub-nosed monkey

Rhinopithecus avunculus

This large-bodied monkey is named after its upturned nose, with nostrils opening toward the front. It is a social animal; there are all-male bachelor groups as well as groups consisting of an adult male and several adult females and their young. Groups often meet at feeding trees and sleeping sites. Strictly arboreal, it feeds primarily on leaves and fruits.

Habitat: forests on limestone hills in northern Vietnam
Estimated Population: 100 to 200
Primary Threats: habitat loss; hunting for its meat; and use in traditional medicines

© Tilo Nadler

SOUTH AMERICA

20 Black-faced lion tamarin

Leontopithecus caissara

Unknown to science until 1990, the black-faced lion tamarin has black fur on the head, limbs, and tail; the rest of the body is covered with golden fur. Long fingers are used to capture small insects and vertebrates, but soft fruits make up most of the diet. An adult averages 21 oz (600 kg). This tamarin lives in small groups high in the trees and is most active in early morning and late afternoon.

Habitat: Atlantic rain forest of eastern Brazil
Estimated Population: 400
Primary Threat: habitat loss

21 Black lion tamarin

Leontopithecus chrysopygus

Black with a golden rump, this species has long fingers, which it uses to forage for small insects and vertebrates; it also eats fruits and other plant matter. It is arboreal and active during the day, sleeping in tree holes at night. Groups usually contain two or three adults plus their young.

Habitat: Atlantic rain forest of eastern Brazil
Estimated Population: 900 or more (plus about 100 in captivity)
Primary Threat: habitat loss

22 Buff-headed capuchin

Cebus xanthosternos

This species is one of the tufted capuchin monkeys, with a ridge of short, erect black hairs on either side of the crown. Adults weigh about 6 lbs (2.7 kg). Buff-headed capuchins form small groups in which one male is dominant. They live in the highest trees. Fruits are their main food.

Habitat: Atlantic rain forest of eastern Brazil
Estimated Population: fewer than 5,000
Primary Threats: habitat loss; hunting for its meat; capture for pets

© Russell A. Mittermeier

23 Golden lion tamarin

Leontopithecus rosalia

This monkey, weighing just more than 1 lb (about 500 g), is among the most brilliantly colored of mammals, with iridescent golden-yellow fur. It lives in trees, feeding during the day and sleeping at night in tree holes.

Habitat: Atlantic rain forest of eastern Brazil
Estimated Population: 800 (plus about 500 in captivity)
Primary Threats: habitat loss from agriculture and human settlement; capture for pet trade

24 Northern muriqui

Brachyteles hypoxanthus

Also known as woolly spider monkeys, muriquis have short thick fur, a long prehensile tail, and strong arms used to swing from tree to tree. They live in groups that include several adults of both sexes. The diet consists of fruits and leaves. Adults weigh 20 lb (9 kg) or more.

Habitat: Atlantic rain forest of eastern Brazil
Estimated Population: 300
Primary Threat: habitat loss

© Andrew Young

25 Yellow-tailed woolly monkey

Lagothrix flavicauda

Weighing up to 24 lbs (11 kg), this monkey has thick, woolly fur and a yellow, prehensile tail that serves as a fifth arm as the animal travels through its forest home. It spends most of its life high above the ground and active during the day, feeding mainly on fruits and flowers. Yellow-tailed woolly monkeys live in groups numbering four to 14.

Habitat humid cloud forests in the Andes of northern Peru
Estimated Population: fewer than 5,000
Primary Threats: hunting for its meat; habitat loss from agriculture and cattle ranching; capture for pets

THE QUIZ-SHOW CRAZE

By Brad Herzog

Appearing on television's latest sensation—"Who Wants to Be a Millionaire"—Brad Herzog (left) *told host Regis Philbin about his career as a freelance writer.*

Who would have guessed that five simple words uttered by the host of a quiz show would emerge as the catch-phrase of the new millennium? But from the first time Regis Philbin pointed to a contestant and asked: "Is that your final answer?", a sensation was created and a television network was transformed.

Who Wants to Be a Millionaire debuted on ABC on Aug. 16, 1999, as an inexpensive summer substitute program. But by its second run during November sweeps, the show was an American obsession, drawing some 24 million television viewers nightly and becoming the subject of countless water-cooler conversations.

The Format and Success of "Millionaire." When producer Michael Davies brought *Millionaire* to the United States from Britain, he imported the exact format that had been so successful overseas—including a futuristic set; flashing lights; a relentless, tension-inducing sound track; and a simple concept. The show begins with ten contestants seated in a semi-circle. They are asked a "fastest finger" question, requiring them to put four subjects in chronological or geographic order. Whoever answers correctly in the fastest time earns a trip to the center of the stage and the "hot seat," which has become as iconic as Archie Bunker's easy chair.

Starting with a simple $100 question, contestants must then answer 15 increasingly difficult multiple-choice trivia testers in a row to win the $1 million grand prize. They may decline to continue, and thus keep the money earned at any time, even after seeing the next question. But an incorrect answer drops them to either the $0, $1,000, or $32,000 plateau, depending on how far they have progressed. Perhaps the most appealing element of the show is the availability of three "lifelines" to help the contestants answer the questions. Contestants may poll the members of the studio audience, phone a friend, or opt for the "50-50" lifeline, which removes the two least likely of the four possible answers.

While strategy and courage emerged as integral parts of the game, critics began to wonder how much sheer smarts was required, contending that the subject matter and format were evidence of the "dumbing down" of America. When several contestants won the million-dollar prize, Millionaire's London-based insurance company filed suit to end its contract with the show, claiming the questions were too easy.

Regardless, *Who Wants to Be a Millionaire*, airing several times a week during the regular television schedule, usually earned the top three spots in the Nielsen ratings. ABC became the Number 1 U.S. network, and longtime daytime talk-show host Philbin became television's man of the moment, renegotiating his contract to earn millions himself. Several contestants added unexpected fame to their newfound fortune as well. IRS employee John Carpenter, the first person to win $1 million, even found himself on the cover of *People* magazine. Not surprisingly, approximately 250,000 people a day called ABC's special hot line to try out for the show.

Imitation. Contestants were not the only people to reap the benefits of the quiz-show craze in 2000. Producers realized that such shows are much cheaper to produce than dramas or sitcoms, while advertisers discovered that they constitute one of the few genres that gets the whole family watching television together. As a result, not only did *Who Wants to Be a Millionaire*

About the Author. In April 2000, freelance writer Brad Herzog won $64,000 on *Who Wants to Be a Millionaire*. He then watched as his book *States of Mind* was catapulted toward the top of a national best-seller list after he discussed it on the show. *States of Mind* also was named one of the Ten Outstanding Books of 1999 by Independent Publisher. Mr. Herzog has been awarded three gold medals for feature writing from the Council for Advancement and Support of Education (CASE).

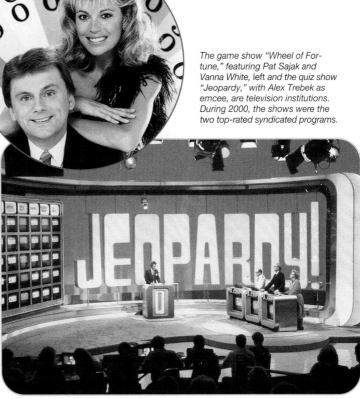

© NBC Photo/The Kobal Collection

The game show "Wheel of Fortune," featuring Pat Sajak and Vanna White, left and the quiz show "Jeopardy," with Alex Trebek as emcee, are television institutions. During 2000, the shows were the two top-rated syndicated programs.

© Everett Collection

spawn a flood of ancillary merchandise, from calendars to clothing lines, it also led to a series of prime-time imitators.

As TV personality Fred Allen stated nearly 50 years ago, "Imitation is the sincerest form of television." The other major networks quickly lined up a series of shows in an attempt to capitalize on the phenomenon. CBS offered *Winning Lines*, with ever-youthful Dick Clark hosting. Fox created *Greed*, a team-based show in which teammates have the chance of eliminating one another. And NBC aired *Twenty One*, which offered a theoretically unlimited top prize.

If as much as 6 $\frac{1}{2}$ hours of prime-time network quizzing a week were not enough, another type of program arrived that seemed a cross between game shows and reality television. Fox trotted out an embarrassing one-time effort called *Who Wants to Marry a Multi-Millionaire?*, a program that met its demise when the so-called winner selected from 50 would-be brides decided to annul the marriage. In the summer of 2000, CBS debuted a much more successful show, *Survivor*, in which 16

© Photofest

Quiz shows were mainstays of television in the 1950s. Charles Van Doren (left, photo right), *an English instructor at Columbia University, became a national celebrity after defeating Herbert Stempel* (right) *on "Twenty-One" in 1957. In November 1959, Van Doren admitted before a U.S. House of Representatives subcommittee that he had been briefed on questions and answers prior to the programs. The subcommittee also learned that "The $64,000 Question,"* below, *which also was immensely popular, was manipulated, and the quiz-show craze of the 1950s quickly ended.*

© Archive Photos

Comedy Central had its own quiz show in 2000, as "Win Ben Stein's Money" offered contestants a chance to match knowledge of historic and current tidbits with Mr. Stein.

people were stranded on an island in the South Pacific, then voted to eliminate each other one by one. The winner received $1 million; CBS received the summer's top-rated show.

The Genre's History. Some industry observers attributed the surge in game-show popularity to a get-rich-quick environment fostered by a booming economy. Others, however, suggested the phenomenon was merely an example of television's cyclical nature. Indeed, this was not the first time that a summer prime-time quiz show promised astonishing prizes, earned a spot on the fall schedule, became a Number 1 hit, and then spawned imitators. *The $64,000 Question*, sponsored by Revlon, was the *Who Wants to Be a Millionaire* of its day. It was not the first TV game-show series (the DuMont Network debuted *Cash and Carry* in 1946), but *The $64,000 Question* was the first quiz-show phenomenon. First airing on June 7, 1955, it featured ordinary people with big pockets of expertise.

The $64,000 Question was so successful that, by 1958, 23 game shows were airing in prime time, including the original *Twenty-One*, which featured two contestants answering a series of questions while standing in isolation booths. Soon, however, allegations that some shows were fixed led to congressional hearings, where it became clear that there was widespread quiz-show tampering. Eventually, most shows were canceled due to the backlash.

While nearly four decades passed between prime-time game-show eras, they long have been a staple of daytime TV. CBS's *The Price is Right* has prospered since 1956, and *Jeopardy!* and *Wheel of Fortune*—which began in 1964 and 1975, respectively—now are the two top-rated syndicated programs. Of course, five-time *Jeopardy!* champions may take home only about $50,000 despite facing tough questions. But, as the show's host, Alex Trebek, quipped: "Our contestants make money the old-fashioned way. They earn it."

© Steven Senne/AP/Wide World Photos

© Bebeto Matthews/AP/Wide World Photos

O peration Sail was envisioned by President John F. Kennedy in 1961 to foster "the importance of the ship, the ocean, and the waterways" in U.S. history. To mark the year 2000, Operation Sail staged OpSail 2000, during which the tall ships visited San Juan, Puerto Rico, and ports along the U.S. East Coast.

© Joel Page/AP/Wide World Photos

A majestic highlight of OpSail 2000 occurred on Independence Day, July 4, when 180 tall ships—including the U.S. frigate the *Rose* and New Zealand's *Soren Larsen* (*r–l, bottom, photo, page 95*)—military craft; and pleasure boats were on parade in New York's Harbor and along the Hudson River. A replica of the 129-ft (39-m) Spanish schooner *Amistad, (photo, directly above)* captured the emotions of many spectators. Slaves being carried aboard the *Amistad* had revolted against their Spanish slave traders in 1839. Three years later the slaves won their freedom following historic arguments before the U.S. Supreme Court.

As part of the millennium voyage, tall ships sailed into Boston Harbor *(photo, above top)*, and Argentina's *Libertad* was viewed in Portland, ME *(photos, left, and top, page 95)*. Previously, tall-ship events had honored the 1964 World's Fair, the nation's bicentennial, the 1986 salute to the Statue of Liberty, and the Christopher Columbus quincentennial.

© Joel Page/AP/Wide World Photos

© Keith Meyers/"The New York Times" Pictures

Accidents and Disasters

AVIATION

Jan. 30—A Kenya Airways Airbus A310 jet crashes off the African coast shortly after takeoff from Abidjan, Ivory Coast; 169 people perish.

Jan. 31—An Alaskan Airlines MD-80 passenger jet en route from Puerto Vallarta, Mexico, to San Francisco plunges into the ocean off the coast of southern California, killing all 88 aboard.

Feb. 3—Eight Iranian soldiers are killed when their Hercules C-130 plane collides on the ground with an Iran Air Airbus A300 at an airport in Tehran, according to Iran's Civil Aviation Authority.

March 30—Forty people are killed when a Sri Lankan Air Force plane crashes while trying to land at Thalawa, Sri Lanka.

April 8—A Marine Corps V-22 Osprey aircraft crashes in the process of landing at an airfield in Marana, AZ, killing 19 U.S. marines.

April 19—An Air Philippines jet crashes in the southern Philippines, killing 131 people aboard.

May 21—Nineteen people are left dead when a charter airplane crashes near Wilkes-Barre, PA.

June 22—A helicopter carrying film crew members from a Los Angeles, CA, production company crashes into a glacier in British Columbia, Canada, while the unknowing film crew is shooting the site. All four people aboard are killed.

June 22—Forty-two people are killed when a Chinese domestic airliner flying in a thunderstorm plummets to the ground in a suburb of Wuhan city in Hubei province while trying to land at Wuhan.

July 17—An Alliance Air Boeing 737 crashes into a housing complex after trying to land near Patna, eastern India; 55 passengers aboard the aircraft and five people on the ground are killed. At least nine others are injured.

July 25—An Air France Concorde jetliner en route to New York City crashes 9 mi (14 km) outside Paris in Gonesse; 113 people are killed.

Aug. 23—At least 143 people are killed when a Gulf Air Airbus A320 on a flight from Cairo, Egypt, crashes in the Persian Gulf while attempting to land in Bahrain.

Oct. 31—A Singapore Airlines Boeing 747 bound for Los Angeles crashes on takeoff from Taipei, Taiwan; 83 passengers are killed.

Nov. 1—Forty-eight people are killed when a charter Antonov 26 plane crashes into a remote jungle in Angola.

FIRES AND EXPLOSIONS

March 9—Fire sweeps through a high-school dormitory in the South Pacific island nation of Tuvalu, killing 18 students and a matron.

March 11—Eighty-one coal miners are killed when a powerful underground explosion occurs in a mine in Krasnodon, Ukraine.

March 27—An explosion at a Phillips Petroleum Co. petrochemical plant in Pasadena, TX, kills one plant worker and injures 71 others.

June 23—Fifteen people are killed and ten injured when a fire breaks out at a hostel in the town of Childers, Queensland, Australia.

July 10—An oil pipeline explosion in Adeje, southern Nigeria, kills at least 200 people.

Aug. 8—Eight people are killed and dozens wounded by a bomb explosion in a pedestrian underpass in Moscow, Russia.

Aug. 19—Twelve people from two families are killed while camping along the Pecos River near Carlsbad, NM, when an underground pipeline explodes, engulfing the campsite with flames.

Sept. 8—Sixty people are killed when a truck taking explosives for disposal explodes in Northwest China.

Oct. 20—At least 20 people die and at least 39 are injured when a fire destroys the Lobohombo nightclub in Mexico City, Mexico.

Nov. 11—At least 159 skiers are killed in an Alpine tunnel fire above the Alpine village of Kaprun, Austria, near Salzburg.

Dec. 1—When a leaking oil pipeline explodes near the Lagos, Nigeria, lagoon, at least 30 people are killed.

Dec. 25—When fire sweeps through a shopping center in the Dongdu Commercial building in the city of Luoyang in central China, at least 309 people are killed.

LAND AND SEA TRANSPORTATION

Feb. 10—A van carrying athletes from Texas A&M University's men's track and field team crashes near Karnack, TX, killing four members and injuring six others.

March 29—When two passenger buses collide head-on near Kericho, western Kenya, at least 60 people are left dead.

April 13—At least 56 people are killed when an overloaded Philippine ferryboat headed for Malaysia capsizes. As many as 65 others are feared dead.

June 22—When a ferryboat tips over on a stretch of the Yangtze River in the southwestern province of Sichuan, China, up to 131 people are killed.

June 29—Around 500 people drown when an overloaded wooden ferry capsizes in a storm off the northern tip of Sulawesi Island, about 1,440 mi (2 317 km) northeast of Indonesia's capital, Jakarta. Only ten survivors are found.

July 6—Twenty-eight people are killed after a truck collides head-on with a bus outside the town of Soria, Spain, northeast of Madrid.

Sept. 30—At least 76 of more than 500 people aboard a Greek ferry are killed after it strikes a patch of rocks in the Aegean Sea.

Oct. 10—Five Haitian migrants are killed and 23 feared drowned when their sailboat collides with a Bahamian mail boat.

STORMS, FLOODS, AND EARTHQUAKES

Jan. 14—Five people are killed, 1,500 injured, and 31,064 houses damaged or destroyed in an earthquake in Yaoan County of Yunnan, China.

Feb. 14—A series of deadly tornadoes touches down near Camilla, GA, killing 18 people and seriously injuring more than 100 others.

March 28—Tornadoes wreck havoc in Fort Worth and Arlington, TX. At least five people are killed and more than 100 are injured.

May 4—An earthquake kills at least 46 people and injures 264 others in the Luwuk area, Sulawesi, and on nearby islands of Sulawesi, Indonesia.

May 18—Floods kill at least 93 people when heavy rains sweep away villages in West Timor, Indonesia.

June 4—At least 103 people are killed, 2,174 are injured, and 25,000 are left homeless in Southern Sumatera, Indonesia, after an earthquake occurs.

June 6—At least two people are killed, more than 80 are injured, and at least 4,600 homes are destroyed or damaged in an earthquake that rattles the Cerkes-Cubuk-Orta area of Turkey.

July 6—A strong earthquake in Masaya, Nicaragua, leaves seven people dead, 42 injured, and 357 houses destroyed.

July 14—Eleven people are killed and more than 130 injured when a tornado descends on an Alberta, Canada, campsite.

Aug. 23—Typhoon Bilis strikes Taiwan, killing at least 11 people. The storm also causes massive damage to crops and destroys temporary housing built for earthquake victims in 1999.

Sept. 16—At least 19 people are killed in Guatemala by flooding and mudslides resulting from Hurricane Gordon.

Oct. 3—Tropical Storm Leslie causes serious flooding across southeast Florida, including Miami-Dade and southeast Broward counties. At least 214,000 people are left stranded or homeless due to flood waters, and three people are killed.

Oct. 4—More than 700,000 Bangladeshis are left without homes and more than 110 are dead due to flooding by rivers swollen by monsoon rains in Dhaka, Bangladesh.

Oct. 6—In western Honshu, Japan, more than 2,000 homes are destroyed or damaged and 130 people are killed in a serious earthquake.

Oct. 7—More than 1,000 people are reported dead due to floods occurring over the past month in the Indian state of West Bengal.

MISCELLANEOUS

March 29—An avalanche strikes an area south of Salzburg, Austria, killing at least 11 skiers.

July 10—At least 218 people are killed when a mountain of garbage collapses onto a shanty town in the capital city of Manila, Philippines.

Advertising

A huge account shift, a five-month actors' strike, a boom in Internet ad spending, and continued consolidation among leading ad agencies contributed to make 2000 a tumultuous and exciting year for the U.S. advertising industry.

Ad Spending. The healthy economy continued to positively affect U.S. advertising. The McCann-Erickson ad agency predicted that U.S. ad spending in 2000 would reach $236.3 billion, a gain of 9.8%. Significant ad dollars were spent on the U.S. Census, national elections, and the Summer Olympics. Among measured media, ad spending on cable television once again was expected to show the largest increase at 20%, compared with 15% for radio. Network television and newspapers were expected to each show a 12% increase; and magazines, a 7.5% increase. For 2001, McCann said U.S. ad spending would be $250 billion, up 5.8%.

Internet. According to New York–based investment-banking firm Veronis Suhler, ad spending on the Internet skyrocketed to $7.7 billion in 2000, compared with $4.6 billion in 1999—a 67% increase. The company predicted Internet ad spending would grow at a 39.5% compound annual rate in four years, reaching $24.4 billion by 2004. But critics doubted that figure, claiming much of it represented barter deals rather than hard money. Top Internet ad spenders included Microsoft ($36.2 million), IBM ($27.1 million), and General Motors ($27.1 million).

Agencies. Times were prosperous for U.S. ad agencies. In the first six months of 2000, revenues for the major, publicly traded holding companies—Omnicom, True North, Interpublic, Young & Rubicam, WPP, Grey, Cordiant, and Saatchi—were $10.3 billion, a 17% increase over 1999 revenues. Pretax profits rose almost 25%, to nearly $1.3 billion. Meanwhile, mergers and consolidations continued unabated. The market belonged to the sellers, with general-market agencies going for six to seven times operating profits. The activity was driven by agencies' need to expand the sectors they operate in to satisfy client demand for a full range of services. Holding companies also had become dependent on acquisitions to achieve high growth rates for stockholders.

The most-significant mergers and acquisitions in 2000 included the creation of a new holding company—Bcom3—which was formed when BDM, consisting of the previously merged Leo Group and MacManus Group, teamed with Japan's Dentsu. In addition, Young & Rubicam was acquired by WPP Group, and Saatchi & Saatchi was acquired by Publicis, which also purchased Fallon McElligott in Minneapolis and Frankel & Co. in Chicago. Snyder Communications, owner of Arnold Communications, was acquired by Havas Advertising. Deutsch, one of the last of the large, independent agencies, was acquired by the Interpublic Group of Companies.

In the largest account shift in automotive-advertising history, the Chrysler Group moved its estimated $1.8 billion account to Omnicom Group in November. The loser was True North Communications, which was expected to lose an estimated $140 million in annual revenue. Omnicom said it would form a new agency called PentaMark to handle the consolidated account.

Actors' Strike. A disruptive and well-publicized event was the six-month strike begun on May 1 by 135,000 commercial actors who are members of the Screen Actors Guild (SAG) and the American Federation of Television and Radio Artists (AFTRA) against the U.S. advertising industry. At issue was the pay structure for union actors who appear in such media as cable TV and the Internet. A settlement was reached in late October.

Creative. Nike, known for its award-winning creative work from ad agency Wieden & Kennedy in Portland, OR, became embroiled in two controversies. First, an ad featuring U.S. Olympic runner Suzy Hamilton being chased by a chain-saw-wielding man was pulled from Olympic TV advertising. Nearly two months later, Nike publicly apologized for offending the disabled with an ad for a trail-running shoe.

Meanwhile, beer ads captured top broadcast and print awards at the International Advertising Festival in Cannes, France. The broadcast winner was a Budweiser television campaign that supplied America with a new catchphrase—"Whassup?"—from ad agency DDB in Chicago. In it, a group of young men are shown talking on the telephone, continually asking each other "Whassup?" in exaggerated tones. In print, ad agency Lowe Lintas in London captured the Grand Prix for a magazine campaign for the Whitbread Beer Company. The ads showed Whitbread bottle caps placed in strategic locations on such objects as a scooter, electric guitar, and wooden chair.

John WOLFE, *Senior Vice-President*
American Association of Advertising Agencies

Afghanistan

War, disease, poverty, and approaching famine held sway in Afghanistan in 2000, while a Taliban-dominated government remained an international pariah.

Civil War. In early 2000 the Northern Alliance, made up mainly of Tajiks, Uzbeks, and Hazaras, controlled the northeastern 15% of Afghan territory, but by year's end held only 5%. It was inferior to its Taliban (mainly Pashtun) enemy in arms, manpower, and transportation. In early September the Taliban took Taloqan, a key supply staging area.

Foreign patrons supported both sides. Russia and possibly Iran gave arms to the Northern Alliance, whereas the Taliban procured arms, manpower, and funding from Pakistan (especially the Pakistani intelligence service), the United Arab Emirates (UAE), and Arab-world sources.

In November the United Nations (UN) won written agreement from both Taliban and the Northern Alliance to broker indirect peace talks. Representatives of the exiled former Afghan king, Zahir Shah, also held separate exploratory talks with leaders of the Taliban, Pakistan, the Northern Alliance, and several Central Asian Republics about a peaceful settlement, but without immediate concrete results.

Economy. In October the UN called Afghanistan the world's "second-hungriest country" (after Haiti), with an average daily intake per person of 480 calories. An ongoing drought, the worst in 30 years, devastated all agriculture, threatening starvation for up to 1 million Afghans in 2001, and by November forcing more than 30,000 new refugees into Pakistan. The only strong branches of the economy were illegal opium exports—3,275 metric tons or 75% of the world's total—and smuggling. By mid-2000, opium-poppy acreage had grown to 64,000 from 51,000. However in September, the Taliban banned opium-poppy growing and burned 25 heroin-producing laboratories. Over the year, the unit of currency (afghani) fell from an unofficial rate of 51,000 to the dollar to an all-time low of 68,000.

Society. Twenty-one years of warfare had decimated the male population. Despite labor shortages and women's need for jobs, the Taliban abolished bakeries and handicraft enterprises where foreign supporters had employed war widows. By year's end, women could be legally employed only in health services.

The Taliban's rigid interpretation of Islam was reflected in public executions and amputations, arbitrary beatings of women and men for improper dress or grooming, mandatory five-times-daily prayers, and prohibitions against most games and all public music. Enforcement of these measures was in the hands of the all-powerful Department to Propagate Virtue and Eliminate Vice.

Foreign nongovernmental organizations (NGOs), mostly UN-sponsored, provided virtually the only medical and other social services. Malaria cases, which had dropped to 30,000 in the mid-1970s, stood at 3 million, and the tuberculosis rate was climbing steeply. Vaccination campaigns were helping, but various diseases—rabies, cholera, polio, and measles—ran rampant.

Foreign Affairs. Afghanistan remained a pariah nation thanks to its human-rights record, its opium exports, its harboring of suspected Saudi terrorist Osama bin Laden (*see* TERRORISM), and its reported camps for training Islamic militants for "holy wars" against non-Muslim nations. Pakistan, the UAE, and Saudi Arabia were the only countries that recognized the Kabul government, and the Saudis had broken diplomatic relations. The UN seat for Afghanistan still belonged to Burhanuddin Rabbani's government (Islamic State of Afghanistan), which headed the Northern Alliance, and the UN sanctions that were imposed in 1999 against the Taliban remained in force.

In October, Russian Defense Minister Igor Sergeyev met openly with the Northern Alliance defense chief, Ahmad Shah Massoud, in Dushanbe, Tajikistan, to discuss Russian arms aid. In November, ranking U.S. diplomats initiated ongoing talks with Taliban representatives in Pakistan to discuss differences.

ANTHONY ARNOLD
Freelance Writer on Afghanistan

AFGHANISTAN • Information Highlights

Official Name: Islamic State of Afghanistan.
Location: Central Asia.
Area: 251,672 sq mi (652 000 km²).
Population (2000 est.): 25,838,797.
Chief Cities (1988 est.): Kabul, the capital, 1,424,400; Kandahar, 225,500; Herat, 177,300.
Government: Declared an "Islamic state" by the Taliban militia group in 1996. De facto government is under Taliban, administered by an interim Council of Ministers.
Monetary Unit: Afghani (4,726.2500 afghanis equal U.S.$1, official rate, Nov. 14, 2000).
Gross Domestic Product (1999 est. U.S.$): $21,000,000,000 (purchasing power parity).

Africa

In 2000, Africa stumbled seriously in its efforts to move toward democracy. Civil war continued in Angola and Sierra Leone; the Ivory Coast, once an island of stability, entered a period of chaos; Zimbabwe advanced toward absolutism; and civil strife persisted in Burundi. Elsewhere, on December 12, Ethiopia and Eritrea formally ended their two-year border war by signing a comprehensive peace agreement; the Democratic Republic of the Congo remained consumed by conflict; and Liberian armed forces made forays into border areas of Guinea, where 460,000 Liberian and Sierra Leonean refugees were living.

On the positive side of the ledger, elections were held in Mauritius in September, with the opposition alliance headed by former Prime Minister Anerood Jugnauth winning 54 of the 62 seats in the National Assembly. In October, elections were also held in Tanzania. And in Somalia a government administration—though of questionable legitimacy— was selected by 2,000 representatives of Somalia's clans.

In September the International Monetary Fund (IMF) and the World Bank, supported by the United States and the European Union (EU), pledged debt relief to eight sub-Saharan African states. The debt of Cameroon is to be reduced by 30%, Chad 27%, Ethiopia 23%, Guinea 34%, Guinea-Bissau 73%, Malawi 43%, Rwanda 71%, and Zambia 62%. This almost tripled the number of African countries offered debt relief by the financial institutions since 1999 in an effort to reduce the burden borne by some of the world's poorest nations.

Somalia. Some 2,000 representatives of Somalia's many clans met for five months in Arta, Djibouti, in an effort to form a central government, something Somalia has been without since 1991. Although bearing no electoral legitimacy, the group of 2,000 appointed 245 of its members to a Transitional National Assembly that in August selected Abdikassim Salad Hassan as president. Both the assembly and the president are to serve for three years as a transitional government. The conference had been organized by Djibouti's President Ismail Omar Guelleh, who feared that with Ethiopia and Eritrea at war and Somalia in a state of anarchy, his tiny country could be engulfed by chaos.

The selection of Salad Hassan as president was rejected by the heads of four major clans, most importantly Hussein Muhammad Aidid. The four indicated that the peace conference included officials of the country's former dictator, Mohamed Siad Barre, who fell from power in January 1991, and they called upon other nations to disavow its outcome.

The new "president"—who was deputy prime minister under Siad Barre—heads a state that is fragmented into three separate entities and whose capital, Mogadishu, is without water, electricity, police, or schools. Half a million Somali refugees remained in Yemen, where they fled to escape the fighting. Whatever the basis of Salad Hassan's legitimacy, it was clear that he had a formidable job in administering a divided state convulsed by bedlam.

Burundi. Despite intensive efforts, little progress was made in 2000 to resolve Burundi's eight-year civil war. Former South African President Nelson Mandela, who in December 1999 had taken on the task of mediating the conflict in Burundi between the Tutsi-controlled government and army and Hutu rebel groups, convened an August

© Brennan Linsley/AP/Wide World Photos

The Democratic Republic of the Congo remained consumed in conflict in 2000. Congolese President Laurent Kabila, right, and U.S. Ambassador to the United Nations Richard Holbrooke met in Kinshasa on May 4 to discuss an unstable cease-fire.

conference in Arusha, Tanzania, in which 19 separate Burundian groups were to attend to sign a peace accord. On the eve of the conference, however, Hutu rebels and Tutsi hard-liners launched attacks on Burundi's capital, Bujumbura, while President Pierre Buyoya, in an indication of his weak political position, warned Tutsi militants, who opposed the conference, not to stage a coup.

The peace accord called for the eventual return to power of the Hutu majority, who make up 85% of the population, but with rights and protection for the Tutsi. A three-year transitional government would be established before new general elections are held. A legislative body to be evenly split by ethnicity would be created, while the army would also be divided equally for ten years. A genocide tribunal and a peace-and-reconciliation commission would be set up to consider the torture and murder of more than 200,000 people since 1993.

U.S. President Bill Clinton made a one-day visit to Tanzania, hoping to pressure the warring factions to sign the accord, but it did not work. Two of the main Hutu rebel groups refused to attend, some parties refused to sign the accord, and Mandela concluded the meeting by lecturing the attendees on their embarrassing failure. A follow-up summit meeting held in Nairobi, Kenya, in September to firm up the Arusha accord also ended in failure as the parties refused to agree to a cease-fire. Burundian authorities did agree prior to the meeting to release 350,000 of the 850,000 civilians in displacement camps.

Ivory Coast. Long one of the few stable and prosperous countries in Africa, the Ivory Coast has become an ethnically divided state. In December 1999, troops overthrew the unpopular President Henri Konan Bédié because of unpaid wages, corruption, unemployment, and government-supported ethnocentrism aimed at separating Christian southern Ivorians from northern Muslim "outsiders." About 40% of Ivorians are Muslims, and 30% Christians.

Gen. Robert Gueï took power as head of a military junta, promising quick elections and a return to democracy and civilian rule. But within months, he worsened the ethnic divisions and decided to run for president. Soon after, the Supreme Court, intimidated by Gueï, ruled that the popular Alassane Ouattara, an economist with the IMF and head of the opposition party Rally of the Republicans, and eight other Muslim candidates were ineligible to run for the presidency. Five Christian candidates, including Laurent Gbagbo, leader of the third-largest party, the Ivoirian Popular Front, were allowed on the ballot. Gbagbo, a socialist, organized his campaign around Christian ascendancy. The Rally of the Republicans, along with the Democratic Party, announced a boycott of the election.

The election took place on October 22, and it became clear within two days that Gbagbo was far ahead in the vote count. Gueï dissolved the electoral commission and declared himself the winner. Tens of thousands took to the streets of the capital, Abidjan, to condemn the electoral putsch, and were joined by elements of the armed forces, police, and security services. On October 25, Gueï relinquished power; Gbagbo declared himself president and was inaugurated swiftly. Ouattara, however, rejected Gbagbo's authority to govern, and called for new and fair elections. Gbagbo, supported by the military, defied Ouattara's demand, setting off street battles between Christians and Muslims, during which scores were killed and a number of Abidjan's mosques and churches burned. The strife continued as Ouattara was barred from running for parliament in December.

Sierra Leone. In May, despite having signed on to the 1999 Lomé Peace Agreement in which all parties acceded to an end to hostilities in Sierra Leone, Foday Sankoh, leader of the rebel Revolutionary United Front (RUF), renewed his war against the government. At the same time, 500 United Nations peacekeepers were taken hostage by the RUF. Over the next two months, they were released or plucked from captivity. Because UN peacekeepers and the Nigerian troops of the Economic Community of West African States Cease-Fire Monitoring Group (ECOMOG) could not stop RUF forces from besieging Freetown, Great Britain sent 1,000 troops to secure the capital. Sankoh was finally arrested in May by combatants supporting President Ahmad Tejan Kabbah.

As conflicts arose among the various peacekeeping forces because of their inability to bring the civil war to a halt, India announced in September that it would withdraw its contingent of 3,150 soldiers under UN command, the largest force of the 13,000-strong UN peacekeeping team. Soon thereafter, Jordan said that it would withdraw its 1,800 troops.

As a result of the ensuing chaos, the United States began to dispatch soldiers to

Mozambique

In February 2000 the East African nation of Mozambique suffered one of the worst disasters in its history when weeks of torrential rain followed by Cyclone Eline caused massive flooding. Mozambique's major river, the Limpopo, and many other rivers burst their banks, causing devastation in the south and central portions of the country.

In the Limpopo Valley, one of the worst-hit areas, hundreds of people clung to treetops, and thousands were stranded on rooftops, where they remained for days without food or water. Chokue, about 125 mi (201 km) north of the capital city of Maputo, and the coastal town of Xai-Xai were all but submerged. The floods destroyed crops, homes, bridges, and roads, and thousands of cattle and other animals were drowned. In some areas, there was a shortage of clean drinking water.

By the end of March, with an estimated 1 million people homeless, refugee camps were set up in different parts of the country. President Joaquim Chissano expressed concern about starvation and the danger of malaria and cholera epidemics.

About one-third of Mozambique's population was affected by the floods, and 10% of cultivated lands were destroyed. Several hundred people died, but many of the stranded were saved with the assistance of helicopters from South Africa, Malawi, Britain, Germany, and the United States. The United States also sent food, clothing, and blankets, and pledged $12.8 million in disaster relief. Foreign lenders agreed to additional substantial debt reductions. Still, Mozambican leaders were critical of the slow international response to the disaster.

It was estimated that the country would have to raise $427 million for the rebuilding of roads, housing, and utilities and for health care and agricultural needs. The devastation came at a time when Mozambique was reestablishing its infrastructure and making market reforms after the 16 years of civil warfare that ended in 1992. There was strong economic growth, and peasants who had fled the war had returned to their lands and were growing crops again. In April the Mozambican government maintained that despite the floods, if the country could raise the necessary funds for reconstruction, it would experience economic growth of between 6% and 8% in 2000.

PATRICK O'MEARA
Indiana University

Nigeria in August to train 7,500 troops from Ghana and Nigeria to bolster the UN force. This would bring the total number of peacekeepers to 20,500 by December 31. Concurrently, the UN Security Council voted to increase the force's number and security functions and to establish a war-crimes tribunal to try Sierra Leonean "crimes against humanity." It also imposed a global ban on diamond exports from Sierra Leone, because the gems have largely fueled the civil war. Liberia, supportive of the Sierra Leonean rebels and claiming that Guinea was giving refuge to Liberian rebels, in September sent its armed forces on intermittent forays into Guinea.

Angola. The civil war in Angola continued to simmer in 2000. In July, Great Britain accused Jonas Savimbi, head of the rebel National Union for the Total Independence of Angola (UNITA), of continuing to break the 1998 UN embargo on the sale of diamonds used to finance his war against the Angolan government. Angola, which has huge offshore oil reserves, continued to use the bulk of its oil revenues to procure arms.

In February, in the capital of Luanda, civilians organized protests against corruption and the waste of oil revenues on the military. The protests culminated in a June rally in which more than 6,000 people demanded peace. Angola is the eighth-largest supplier of oil to the United States. Yet, it is one of the world's poorest nations, with 82% of the country's 11 million people living in poverty, 80% unemployment, and life expectancy a mere 42. Three out of ten children die before the age of 5. In September the government of President José Eduardo dos Santos and the IMF agreed on a threefold increase in spending on health and education, and to permit IMF auditors to analyze Angolan figures on oil revenues, which make up 90% of the country's export income. Angola's leaders wished to gain access to IMF low-interest loans and to shed their image of corruption.

See also AFRICA: A CONTINENT OF PROBLEMS, page 44; *see* INDEX for African nations on which there are separate articles.

PETER SCHWAB
Purchase College, State University of New York

Agriculture

Drought restricted food production in several important production areas—including northeastern China, Eastern Europe, North Africa, Russia, the Ukraine, the western edge of the U.S. Corn Belt, and parts of the southern United States—in 2000. The North China Plain experienced one of the worst droughts of the past century.

Wheat Stocks and Production Trends. With adverse weather, global wheat production rose by a meager 0.16% from the previous year. That was well below the long-term average annual increase in demand of 0.6%, and was expected to reduce wheat carryover stocks in 2001. Since wheat is the world's most important food grain and is a staple in the diets of billions of people, world wheat carryover stocks are considered a key indicator of global food security. Global wheat stocks were projected at a record low 19% of annual use by the end of the marketing year in mid-2001, about the minimum level considered necessary for global food security. The previous record low in global wheat stocks was in 1995–96, when wheat prices reached record highs. The stocks-to-use ratio measures the reserve supply remaining at the end of the marketing year to offset possible adverse weather and low yields the next year. Excessive rain during harvest also reduced the amount of milling-quality wheat in Canada and Europe, and increased the amount of wheat potentially available for livestock feed.

World rice production was estimated to be up only 0.4% from the previous year because of adverse weather. Fall flooding in southeastern Asia threatened to further reduce the quality and quantity of production. The global cotton crop was estimated to be down 0.1% from 1999, with declines in the United States, China, Pakistan, Europe, Africa, and Turkey. Small increases were estimated for Australia and Brazil.

Because of large U.S. crops, world feed-grain supplies were slightly more adequate than for wheat. World feed-grain production increased by an estimated 0.5% from the previous year, also moderately below the long-term annual rate of demand growth. Good U.S. yields helped offset sharply lower production in China as well as drought-reduced production in Eastern Europe and the Ukraine.

Despite regional droughts, U.S. corn production reached a new record high. The United States normally supplies about 67% of world corn exports, and its production is a major source of feed for dairy and beef cattle, pigs, chickens, turkeys, and other poultry. Corn also is processed into sweeteners for manufactured foods and soft drinks. Other products derived from the corn crop include starch, corn oil, and ethanol for beverage alcohol and motor fuel. The large crop kept prices to corn growers at levels near those of the mid-1980s, when a farm financial crisis forced thousands of families to leave their farms. However, record large 2000 government payments avoided another agricultural financial crisis, with farm foreclosures and rural bankruptcies. Government payments accounted for nearly half of all net farm income, but went mainly to crop farmers. For some major crops, government payments were significantly greater than total net farm income.

In response to large sugar supplies and low prices, the U.S. government paid sugar producers to destroy part of their 2000 harvest. This move was highly unusual, and was made to avoid extreme financial pressures on sugar-producing farmers.

Trade Developments. China, in preparing to join the World Trade Organization (WTO), lowered its support prices for corn and wheat, and reduced corn-export subsidies in the last third of the year. Lower price supports shifted land area from these crops into soybeans, where Chinese prices had been at world levels. China's estimated land area in corn declined by 8% from the previous year, while its estimated area planted in soybeans increased by 14%. International grain buyers prepared for a decline in availability of Chinese corn in global markets, along with some reduction in its soybean-import needs. China for many years has been the world's second-largest corn exporter. Since 1996, it has been a large soybean importer. Chinese agricultural specialists anticipated that entry into the WTO would create new export opportunities for its silk, tea, textiles, and spice. China also hoped that WTO entry would create export opportunities for its meat and for producers of high-value "organic" or "green" foods that are raised without use of synthetic chemicals or genetically modified seeds.

Late in the year, the United States lifted four decades of sanctions against food and medicine trade with Cuba. The action was not accompanied by removal of restraints on U.S. financing of such trade, but allows U.S. institutions to be intermediaries in arranging foreign financing. Cuba may eventually import U.S. corn, while exporting sugar to the United States.

Gradual phase-in of provisions from previous WTO negotiations required the European Union (EU) to reduce substantially its volume of subsidized wheat exports. The EU expected to comply with this provision through exports to several Central and Eastern European nations that plan to join the EU. These nations have agreements allowing imports of EU wheat without tariffs, and without EU export subsidies. Drought created a need for wheat imports in this region.

Farmers in the Dakotas and Montana complained about wheat imports from Canada, resulting from a strong U.S. dollar and the North American Free Trade Agreement (NAFTA). Wheat growers in those areas believed that the Canadian Wheat Board (CWB) acts as a monopolist in export sales, unfairly undercutting prices in the United States. In Mexico, the sugar industry alleged that the United States unfairly restricts imports of its sugar.

Genetically Modified Organisms. Genetically modified organisms (GMOs) were a controversial issue, because of lack of consumer acceptance in some foreign markets, especially in Europe and parts of the Pacific Rim. With uncertain markets, U.S. farmers reduced their plantings of GMO corn and soybeans to 25% and 54% of the crops, respectively. These were declines from 33% and 57% the previous year.

Genetically modified soybeans contain a gene from an unrelated plant protecting them from a normally toxic broad-spectrum herbicide, Roundup. Roundup herbicide greatly simplifies weed control for soybean farmers. For corn, genetic modifications involve insertion of genes from an unrelated fungus or bacterium that causes plants to manufacture an internal pesticide for killing the European corn borer (ECB). The ECB can cause a very serious reduction in yields in some area. Other types of GMO corn resist the Roundup herbicide, and still others—called "stacked events"—have both of these GMO features. Biotechnology firms, government, and university researchers worked to develop herbicide-resistant wheat, rice with increased vitamin content, and other products intended to add value for consumers.

Plant breeders experimented with native corn from South America that has resistance to several insects common in U.S. corn-growing areas. Some scientists believe this corn may replace controversial GMO varieties.

A harvesttime survey indicated that more than half of the grain elevators in the Midwest were either requiring or encouraging farmers to segregate GMO corn and soybeans from non-GMO varieties to channel supplies more effectively to appropriate customers. One type of GMO corn, Starlink—which has been approved only for use as livestock feed and for nonfood industrial uses—was recalled from the

© Todd Stone/AP/Wide World Photos

U. S. farmers, such as Tommy Daughtry, left, in Lenox, GA, were concerned about the impact increased fuel prices would have on their profits in 2000.

market. It was found in food products. The U.S. Department of Agriculture (USDA) and the corn's developer, Aventis Crop-Science, jointly bought 2000 production and isolated it from nonfeed marketing channels. Seed suppliers halted sales of the product late in the year.

Increased U.S. and global concentration of ownership in the seed industry and in farm-supply, agricultural-processing, and marketing firms caused concern among farmers and farm-state legislators. Iowa Beef Packers (IBP), the largest U.S. beef processor, was purchased by an investment company owning other agricultural interests. A major corporate hog-producing firm was absorbed by a competing company, continuing the dramatic shift of the past decade to fewer and larger hog-producing businesses. This change brought a further decline in the market share of smaller and medium-size independent family hog farms. (*See also* FOOD—Genetically Modified Foods.)

South America. South America is the last area with the potential for large-scale agricultural expansion. Estimates of the amount of undeveloped land potentially suitable for production of soybeans, wheat, rice, corn, beef, and other agricultural products range up to 180 million acres (73 million ha) or even higher. For comparison, the United States is by far the largest producer of corn and soybeans in the world, and the largest exporter of these products. Its combined corn and soybean area is about 155 million acres (63 million ha). Although agricultural development in the region is a sensitive issue with environmentalists and indigenous tribes, South American governments see it as a way of creating rural jobs and income.

Farmers in parts of South America accelerated their development of vast grasslands just below the Amazon rain forest. The most extensive land development is in Brazil's Center-West, and is in response to the opening of barge transportation on the Madeira River, a tributary of the Amazon, and the construction of a floating grain elevator on the Amazon River. The floating elevator is approximately 700 mi (1 126 km) upstream from the Atlantic Ocean, but it can load directly into ocean vessels. Construction of a second floating elevator was under way.

In addition, firms in central and southern Brazil were working to upgrade railroad lines to reduce the cost of transporting soybeans and other crops from landlocked areas to ports for shipping. Other countries where parts of the savanna were being converted to farmland include Bolivia and Paraguay. While development of navigation on other rivers to encourage agricultural development has been discussed, major challenges from environmental interests limited such activity.

The Environmental Influence. While U.S. agriculture has reduced its negative impacts on groundwater quality in recent years through improved management of fertilizer, livestock wastes, and soil tillage, serious concerns still remain. A major one in 2000 was the impact of agriculture on water quality in the lower Mississippi River and in the Gulf of Mexico. Nitrogen concentration of waters in the area has increased substantially in recent decades, causing periods in which oxygen content drops to levels threatening fish, lobster, shrimp, crabs, clams, snails, and other important aquatic life. Similar concerns also were focused on parts of the Chesapeake Bay. Even-more-serious problems in the Baltic and Black seas and in some coastal areas of China received adverse publicity.

Nitrogen fertilizer is believed to be a primary contributor to these water-quality problems. In the United States, to reduce the problem, the U.S. Conservation Reserve Program (CRP) of the USDA placed increased emphasis on partnering with farmers to create filter strips to absorb runoff of nitrogen-contaminated waters. Filter strips are stream-bordering areas that have been converted to grass cover to slow the runoff and allow water to soak into the soil instead of running directly into streams and rivers. Also, incentives were created for farmers to restore wetlands that were drained and converted to cropland decades ago.

Another area of environmental concern was the Loess Hills region of western Iowa and northwestern Missouri. This area of hills on the eastern side of the Missouri River valley was formed as winds deposited finely textured soil particles centuries ago. The region still is mainly rural, being used for pasture, timber, hunting, and recreation. However, in areas near urban centers such as Omaha, NE, and Council Bluffs, IA, development prospects concerned some residents and officials. These soils are extremely fragile and erode easily. Residential development could threaten to significantly change the character of the region, increase soil erosion, and create problems in adjacent streams and rivers.

ROBERT WISNER
Department of Economics, Iowa State University

Albania

During 2000, Albania held local elections that confirmed public support for the Socialist administration. The government continued to consolidate the law and order system, intensified its campaign against criminality and corruption, and made progress stabilizing the economy.

Political Polarization. Local elections in October were won by the ruling Albanian Socialist Party (PS), which gained a majority of district and municipal seats, many previously held by the oppositionist Democratic Party (PD). The Socialists won control of 252 out of 398 towns and districts, and gained more than 50% of the vote. The Democrats obtained only 33% of the popular vote. The ballot was widely viewed as a test of political strength in the run up to the scheduled 2001 legislative election. The Democrats boycotted the second round of the local ballot to protest what they claimed was fraud and irregularities in the first round. Most international observers described both rounds of elections as free and fair.

Albanian politics remained polarized between the two major parties. Former Albanian President Sali Berisha, the Democratic Party leader, continued to insist that the government was illegitimate, and called for early general elections. His supporters organized several demonstrations demanding the resignation of the Socialist administration. However, after the opposition loss in the local balloting, some Democratic leaders called for Berisha's resignation from the party leadership.

Anticrime Campaigns. With the help of international agencies, the government intensified its campaign against criminal gangs and corrupt officials. In March the Justice Ministry announced that the country's Supreme Justice Council had fired 70 judges for corruption and incompetence. Albania increased cooperation with Italian experts and several neighboring Balkan states to fight organized crime and combat trafficking of illegal immigrants, prostitutes, drugs, weapons, and stolen cars between the Balkans and Western Europe.

In January, Prime Minister Ilir Meta sacked the privatization minister and the state minister, charging them with irregularities in awarding business contracts. In February the Albanian parliament elected law professor Emir Dobjani as Albania's first-ever ombudsman. The position was provided for in the 1998 Albanian constitution at the recommendation of the Organization for Security and Co-operation in Europe (OSCE). Dobjani was empowered with investigating citizens' complaints against officials believed to be inefficient, incompetent, or corrupt.

Ethnic Tensions. Although the position of the Greek minority in Albania was not a subject of international concern, ethnic tensions were raised during local elections in October. In the southern town of Himara, Socialists and Democrats joined forces against the mayoral candidacy of a member of the Greek minority. Many ethnic Albanians resented what they viewed as too close a relationship between local Greek leaders and the government in Athens. Greece protested that Albanian border officials refused to let ethnic Greek guest workers in Greece return to Albania to vote.

Although the Socialist candidate eventually won in Himara, local Greek leaders from the ethnic-Greek Unity for Human Rights Party (PBDNJ) charged the government with fraud. Meanwhile, Albanian politicians accused Greek leaders of attempting to buy votes by promising that development aid and business investment would come from nearby Greece if the PBDNJ won. PBDNJ spokesmen denied they were trying to increase Greek influence in the border region, or promote separation and annexation by Athens.

Economic Developments. Economic conditions continued to improve in Albania after years of stagnation. According to official statistics, the unemployment rate dropped to about 17% during the year, with the Socialist government claiming it had created 60,000 new jobs since 1997. The opposition charged that some 30% of the popula-

---

ALBANIA • Information Highlights

Official Name: Republic of Albania.
Location: Southern Europe, Balkan peninsula.
Area: 11,097 sq mi (28 748 km²).
Population (2000 est.): 3,490,435.
Chief City (1990 est.): Tiranë, the capital, 244,200.
Government: *Head of state,* Rexhep Meidani, president (took office July 1997). *Head of government,* Ilir Meta, prime minister (appointed October 1999). *Legislature* (unicameral)—People's Assembly.
Monetary Unit: Lek (142.7500 leks equal U.S.$1, Dec. 31, 2000).
Gross Domestic Product (1999 est. U.S.$): $5,600,000,000 (purchasing-power parity).
Economic Index (1999, 1992 = 100): *Consumer Prices,* all items, 454.5; food, 445.8.
Foreign Trade (1999 est. U.S.$): *Imports,* $1,151,000,000; *exports,* $275,000,000.

tion had no regular work. Observers indicated the real figure was impossible to determine, especially because many Albanians worked in the gray economy and did not report incomes to authorities.

The Ministry of Economic Cooperation and Trade announced that more than 15% of Albania's 3.4 million people had emigrated from the country during the previous ten years. About 400,000 Albanian emigrants lived in Greece, and more than 150,000 in Italy. A further 50,000 reportedly emigrated to Germany, the United States, Great Britain, and other Western countries. Although much of the emigration was legal, large numbers of illegal migrants were believed to have settled in Italy and Greece. Émigré earnings constituted an important source of revenue both for Albanian families and the national economy.

Officials of the International Monetary Fund (IMF) agreed to approve a further $13 million credit package for Albania. The IMF praised the country's stabilization and economic growth, despite disruptions caused by the Kosovo crisis and the wave of refugees that Albania accommodated the previous year. The country's gross domestic product (GDP) was projected to grow by nearly 8% in 2000, while the inflation rate remained near zero. IMF officials commended the achievements of the Albanian authorities in pursuing sound macroeconomic policies, and for keeping currency reserves at a comfortable level. However, international financial institutions also asserted that Albania must pursue extensive structural reforms.

Foreign Relations. Officials of the European Union (EU) praised Albania's economic progress, but set no timetable for possible Albanian membership in the EU. In June the EU reported that Albania had made significant progress in stabilizing the macroeconomic situation, adopting laws on the police and civil service, and also privatizing the mobile-telephone monopoly. However, there was much that still remained to be accomplished to strengthen the nation's judicial system; speed up reforms in the financial sector; and privatize banks, utilities, and the fixed-telephone monopoly.

The EU also announced that it would establish a large free-trade zone for industrial and agricultural products from Albania, Bosnia and Herzegovina, Croatia, and Macedonia, and that it would pursue infrastructural projects such as road construction to better integrate the Balkan states. Albania continued to develop bilateral relations with its neighbors, including Macedonia, Montenegro, and Croatia. The focus for improvement included trade, transportation, and telecommunications.

JANUSZ BUGAJSKI
Center for Strategic and International Studies

Algeria

Some 6,000 guerrillas laid down their arms in Algeria in response to President Abdelaziz Bouteflika's offer of amnesty by the deadline of Jan. 13, 2000. The president extended the deadline in hopes of rallying remaining holdouts to his policy of "civil concord," but by midyear, acts of terrorism were again on the rise. In August, President Bouteflika named a new prime minister in order to get a firmer grasp on economic policy. Bouteflika also devoted much of his energy to foreign policy, notably during a high-profile trip to France.

Amnesty and Terrorism. The minister of the interior announced on January 19 that 80% of the armed Islamic guerrillas had surrendered to the government. Most of these were members of the Islamic Salvation Army (AIS), to which Bouteflika offered a blanket pardon on January 11. The AIS threatened to back out of the amnesty deal when some of its members were punished for their activities during the rebellion. Many AIS guerrillas were integrated directly into the national army in order to root out remaining dissident elements of the Armed Islamic Group and the Salafist Group for Preaching and Combat. Despite the conversion of the AIS to the government side, the violence that marked the past years did not come to a complete end; gruesome acts of terrorism—such as the May torching of a bus near Medea, in which 23 innocent civilians were burned to death—continued. Hostilities claimed some 1,200 victims in the first six months of the year, four times the number for the second half of 1999. Nonetheless, major cities were considerably more secure than during much of the 1990s.

Government and Politics. At the end of August, following enduring criticism over lack of direction and the immobility of Prime Minister Ahmed Benbitour's government, the president named one of his closest aides, Ali Benflis, to the post. A lawyer, human-rights activist, and former minister of justice, Benflis had managed Bouteflika's election campaign in 1999 and served as his head of staff at the presidency. The appointment of Benflis created a tight alliance at the top of the government, which had been lacking under Benbitour. Most of the cabinet remained in place, including the minister of privatization, Hamid Temmar, who had publicly criticized Benbitour's economic policies in June. Temmar favored a more rapid pace of privatization than did Benbitour. In his letter of resignation, Benbitour accused the president of impinging upon his constitutional prerogatives in several domains, notably with regard to certain financial holdings of the state. He complained of having had certain key ministers—such as Temmar—imposed upon him, creating a "presidential administration" that Benbitour argued was contrary to the intent of the constitution. The departure of Benbitour thus accentuated Bouteflika's growing authority over government policy.

In September, Benflis officially presented the new government's program to the parliament. On key economic issues, he emphasized a strong market orientation, including privatization of such sectors as the oil and natural-gas industries, the production of electricity, and the construction of public housing—all areas in which the state had long exercised a monopoly. While only two small leftist parties voted against this program in the legislature, there was opposition to it in the national trade union and within those classes of society that had benefited from state control over the economy.

In a significant change of policy, Bouteflika invited several prominent international human-rights organizations to visit the country. Amnesty International sent a delegation in May that found a "very marked improvement in the human-rights climate: less violence, fewer assassinations, fewer instances of torture and disappearances." Human Rights Watch, the International Human Rights Federation, and Reporters Without Borders also visited the country.

The government refused to accredit the new Islamic party of Ahmed Taleb Ibrahimi, the Wafa, on the grounds that it was a reconstitution of the banned Islamic Salvation Front (AIS).

Economy. Rising oil prices swelled the public coffers—almost $10 billion in revenues beyond the year's budgetary forecast. Social tensions rising out of the poor performance of the nonenergy economy, however, were abundantly evident. The General Union of Algerian Workers organized protests against the government's plans to privatize several key industries. Unemployment remained more than 30%. The social climate appeared potentially explosive as people became tired of waiting for the government to get the economy turning again.

Foreign Policy. President Bouteflika devoted considerable attention to representing Algeria abroad. He undertook major state visits to Canada and France, attended the Millennium Summit of the United Nations (UN), and carried out several missions in Africa. In France, he delivered a major address to the National Assembly, in which he evoked emotionally charged issues growing out of the long history of French colonialism in Algeria, while calling for a "veritable reconciliation between the two peoples." Bouteflika visited the memorial at Verdun, dedicated to Algerians who died for France during World War I. He summed up his message with an appeal for "extraordinary . . . exemplary, exceptional relations with France," not an uncontroversial position in Algerian politics.

African policy revolved around Algeria's role as head of the Organization of African Unity (OAU) during the year following the July 1999 OAU summit in Algiers. President Bouteflika mediated the proximity talks concerning the war between Ethiopia and Eritrea, and participated with other African heads of state in an effort to reduce tensions surrounding a contentious presidential election in the Ivory Coast. Relations with Morocco and Israel—which had shown signs of improvement in 1999—deteriorated again as a result of events in Western Sahara and the Palestinian territories. Algeria reestablished diplomatic relations with Iran.

ROBERT A. MORTIMER, *Haverford College*

ALGERIA • Information Highlights

Official Name: Democratic and Popular Republic of Algeria.
Location: North Africa.
Area: 919,591 sq mi (2 381 740 km²).
Population (2000 est.): 31,193,917.
Chief Cities (1987 census): Algiers, the capital, 2,561,992 (provisional census June 1998); Oran, 609,823; Constantine, 443,727.
Government: *Head of state,* Abdelaziz Bouteflika, president (elected April 15, 1999). *Head of government,* Ali Benflis, prime minister (named August 2000). *Legislature*—Parliament: National People's Assembly and Council of Nations.
Monetary Unit: Dinar (73.4200 dinars equal U.S.$1, Dec. 31, 2000).
Gross Domestic Product (1999 est. U.S.$): $147,600,000,000 (purchasing power parity).
Economic Index: *Consumer Prices* (Algiers, 1999; 1990 = 100): all items, 452.4; food, 470.5.
Foreign Trade (1999 est. U.S.$): *Imports,* $9,300,000,000; *exports,* $13,700,000,000.

Anthropology

In anthropology, the year began and ended with the publication of highly controversial books, both of which stimulated considerable substantive debate, although both are possibly wrong in their basic arguments.

Signs of Life. After several decades of eclipse from the fame of the Leakeys and "Lucy" in East Africa, South Africa is beginning to turn up extraordinary new fossil hominids. The year 2000 saw the announcement regarding "Orpheus" and "Eurydice," representatives of *Paranthropus robustus* (or robust australopithecines), nearly 2 million years old. "Orpheus" is a male jawbone, and "Eurydice" is a complete female skull, permitting anthropologists to study the physical differences between males and females in this bipedal, and possibly tool-using, cousin of our species.

Highlighting the ecological precariousness of most of the world's primate species, threatened by deforestation, predation, and human encroachment, anthropologists announced the first formal extinction of a known kind of primate since the 18th century. This was a subspecies of red colobus monkey, known formally as *Procolobus badius waldroni*, or "Miss Waldron's red colobus." Once plentiful in West Africa, none has been seen in years, due to hunting and deforestation. (*See also* PRIMATES IN PERIL, page 82.)

A man known only as Ishi survived the massacres of his family and friends at the hands of the white settlers of California, and was found near Oroville, CA, in 1911. In the next few years, he became known as "the last wild Indian of California," allowing anthropologists to record his language and folktales. Ishi died of tuberculosis in 1916 and was cremated according to his wishes, but it was discovered in 1997 that his brain had been removed and sent to the Smithsonian Institution, where it sat for more than 80 years. Under the 1990 Native American Graves Protection and Repatriation Act (NAGPRA), California Indians petitioned the return of Ishi's brain. Following a political struggle, the Smithsonian returned Ishi's brain to his closest living relatives—members of the Pit River and Redding Rancheria tribes—who reunited Ishi's remains in a private ceremony in August.

Perhaps the most important hominid fossil finds of the 1990s were well-dated remains from Dmanisi, Georgia (in eastern Europe), that provide the best evidence for the early emigration of hominids out of Africa. Dated to 1.7 million years ago, the fossils are attributed to *Homo ergaster*, an early ancestor of the better-known Java man and Peking man (*Homo erectus*), known outside of Africa a million years later. This tells us that by this early date, hominids were exploring diverse geographic and climatic regions.

Controversial Books. The newly published book *A Natural History of Rape* by Randy Thornhill and Craig Palmer is a work of evolutionary psychology, purporting to explain specific human behaviors by recourse to their Darwinian origins. An analysis of rape suggests that coercive sexuality is a last-ditch reproductive strategy in certain species, such as ducks and scorpion flies. By analogy, then, rape can be understood as a reproductive strategy in humans as well. Sexuality in humans, however, is far more diverse in purpose and context than in ducks and scorpion flies. To interpret the act of rape solely as a reproductive crime is to misrepresent quite egregiously the evolved functions of human sexuality.

The year 2000 ended with the publication of *Darkness in El Dorado* by journalist Patrick Tierney, leveling a series of extraordinary accusations against the geneticists and anthropologists who studied the Yanomamo of Brazil and Venezuela for the past 40 years. Tierney accuses U.S. anthropologist Napoleon Chagnon of causing the very violence he documented in his bestselling *Yanomamo: The Fierce People*, and of exploiting the people ruthlessly; Tierney accuses French anthropologist Jacques Lizot of promiscuous sexual exploitation; and U.S. geneticist James Neel of near-genocidal malice in causing the measles epidemic that decimated the tribe in the 1960s. It was clear that all charges were not equally credible, and the American Anthropological Association was investigating.

JONATHAN MARKS
University of North Carolina at Charlotte

Archaeology

The world of archaeology in 2000 generated discoveries of a fresco-laden inn in Pompeii; a 350-year-old bottle of wine in the North Sea; a new Maya palace in Guatemala; and the raising of the Confederate submarine *H.L. Hunley* from the waters off Charleston, SC (*see* PEOPLE, PLACES, AND THINGS, page 400).

Eastern Hemisphere

Saving Zeugma. When waters reached their full height behind a new dam on the Euphrates River in southeastern Turkey in October 2000, nearly one-tenth of the classical site of Zeugma was flooded. Founded in about 300 B.C. by Seleucus I, a successor of Alexander the Great, Zeugma (the name means "bridge") was a key link in east-west trade until it was sacked by the Parthians in A.D. 256. As Turkish archaeologists, with a few French and Australian colleagues, conducted salvage excavations at the site early in the year, they uncovered exquisite mosaics. Concern over the loss of such artworks led the Packard Humanities Institute of California to commit $5 million to assess and excavate larger areas threatened by the rising waters. A large-scale rescue operation was mounted, much of the area was ultimately excavated, and additional mosaics were recovered.

Neanderthal Meat Eaters. New evidence from the analysis of carbon and nitrogen isotopes suggested that meat was a major part of the Neanderthal diet. Collagen was extracted from Neanderthal bones from Vindija Cave, Croatia, radiocarbon-dated to between 28,000 and 29,000 years ago. Nitrogen isotopes helped to determine whether animal or plant proteins were of greater importance, while carbon isotopes could distinguish between terrestrial and marine dietary protein. The results, announced by Michael Richards of the University of Oxford and his colleagues in the June 20 *Proceedings of the National Academy of Sciences*, placed the Vindija specimens closer to carnivores (wolf and fox) than to omnivores (cave bear) or herbivores (mammoth and bovid).

Stonehenge: Skeleton and Bones. Stonehenge, the circle of megalithic standing stones built in southwestern England around 2100 B.C., continued to yield surprises. When the Royal College of Surgeons in London was bombed during World War II, it was thought that skeletons excavated at Stonehenge were among the casualties. Archaeologist Mike Pitts, however, has discovered at least one, the remains of a man aged 35. The skeleton has now been radiocarbon-dated, a technique not known when it was found, and shown to date to only A.D. 650 to 700, much later than the construction of Stonehenge.

Early Vintages. Two centuries-old wine bottles, found still corked, contained vastly different vintages. A 350-year-old bottle, recovered from the remains of a Dutch warship in shallow waters between the Netherlands coast and the North Sea, proved to hold wine flavored with elderberry, a vintage known to have been produced in northeastern Portugal at the time. British archaeologists were less fortunate than their Dutch colleagues: The 300-year-old bottle they found at Reigate, south of London, proved to hold not wine but urine and bent brass

© Liaison Agency

© Staton R. Winter/Liaison Agency

In October 2000, flood waters threatened the site of Zeugma, Turkey, but a large-scale rescue operation managed to preserve much of the area and many precious stone-masonry pieces, left. Exquisite mosaics, above, also were recovered.

pins. The combination suggests that this was a "witch bottle." Such bottles were intended to protect houses and people from evil.

Pompeii. Excavation in advance of highway construction just south of Pompeii has revealed an inn decorated with magnificent frescoes preserved by the ash from the eruption of Mount Vesuvius in A.D. 79. The two-story building had five dining rooms and a kitchen, along with an adjacent bath complex. Walls of the dining rooms were decorated with well-preserved frescoes. Skeletons of five people, victims of the volcano, were found in the bath complex.

Black Sea Flood? Claims of the discovery of a Neolithic structure, submerged in a catastrophic flooding of the Black Sea around 5600 B.C., remained to be evaluated. Following up on a theory proposed by two geologists—that the Black Sea had been a freshwater source until a catastrophic flood occurred during the Neolithic period—Robert Ballard of the Institute for Exploration in Mystic, CT, set out to locate evidence of the flood in the form of submerged Neolithic villages, using sophisticated sonar gear and remote-controlled vehicles equipped with sonar and cameras. According to William Ryan and Walter Pitman of the Lamont-Doherty Geological Observatory of Columbia University in their 1998 book *Noah's Flood*, water from the melting glaciers initially drained southward but, after a brief return to a colder climate, flowed to the west, across Europe rather than south to the Black Sea.

On Sept. 9, 2000, Ballard's group claimed to have found the remains of a wattle-and-daub structure with stone tools and pottery on the floor of the Black Sea. The evidence offered, however, consisted of a few photographs and a sketch of what such a hut might have looked like. The photographs were not distinct, however, and no archaeologists working independently of the project examined the material firsthand.

China Cracks Down. China has long been passive about the plundering of its archaeological sites—a problem that has worsened in recent years because of the growing popularity of Chinese antiquities among collectors. The year 2000, however, may have marked a turning point in China's policy. In January, three looters were executed for stealing 15 Tang dynasty (A.D. 618–907) murals from a museum in Shaanxi Province, and in March, U.S. Customs, in cooperation with Chinese authorities, seized a 10th-century sculptured wall panel, stolen from a tomb in Hebei Province, that was up for sale at a New York City auction house.

Western Hemisphere

A Maya Palace. A third look at Cancuén, a Maya site in the Guatemalan jungle, paid off for archaeologist Arthur Demarest of Vanderbilt University, who found one of the largest Maya palaces ever discovered, buried beneath thick vegetation. Earlier investigations failed to identify the massive palace's more than 170 rooms built around 11 courtyards and covering some 270,000 sq ft (25 110 m^2). Inscriptions attribute construction of the three-story palace to Tah ak Chaan, a mid-8th-century A.D. king.

Amazonian Burial Urns. Archaeologists have pinpointed the source of unusual burial urns in the Amazon rain forest. Until 2000 the type was known from only a few examples, such as one given to the Goeldi Museum in Belém, Brazil, in 1896, whose findspot was unknown. Early in 2000 a hunter led scientists from the museum to three caves near the Maraca River, which flows into the Amazon River near its delta. The largest cave held 20 of the urns, which are shaped like seated men or women. They average about 2.5 ft (0.8 m) in height and have hollow, cylindrical bodies in which the bones of the deceased were placed.

Repatriation Debate: Spirit Cave and Kennewick. Two important decisions were made in the ongoing debate about the repatriation of ancient Native American skeletal remains to modern-day tribes. The rulings concerned human remains that are among the earliest to have been found in North America: those of a 45- to 50-year-old man found near Kennewick, WA, in 1996, and dated about 9,000 years ago; and those of a 45- to 55-year-old-man found at Spirit Cave, NV, in 1940, but only recently radiocarbon-dated to 9,400 years ago. Under the 1990 Native American Graves Protection and Repatriation Act, remains found on federal land, and that can be shown to be related to modern tribes, can be claimed by them and reburied. Secretary of the Interior Bruce Babbitt ruled on September 21 that the evidence supports the claim of five tribes (Colville, Umatilla, Yakama, Nez Percé, and Wanapum) that Kennewick Man is affiliated with them, but a July 26 Bureau of Land Management decision found evidence lacking for affiliation between Spirit Cave Man and the Fallon Paiute-Shoshone tribe.

MARK ROSE, *Managing Editor, "Archaeology"*

Architecture

Large-scale planning for cities and new communities, concern for the natural environment, buildings designed to fit their surroundings, as well as restorations and renovations occupied architects during 2000. The top award in architecture, the Pritzker Prize, went to Dutch architect Rem Koolhaas. His completed projects include the Netherlands Dance Theater; the Nexus Housing in Fukuoka, Japan; and his largest urban-planning design, the Grand Palais in Lille, France. In 1978, Koolhaas published *Delirious New York*, which changed the way many viewed modern architecture.

The historic merit of modern architecture was discussed as many of the concrete, glass, and steel buildings of New York City, built in the 1960s, reached an age where the city's landmark law makes them eligible for protection. Led by Robert A.M. Stern and other architects, advocates of preserving masterpieces of the era acknowledged the irony in their effort, since it was construction of the glass and concrete buildings that spurred the movement to preserve earlier Beaux Arts and Art Deco buildings.

AIA Honor Awards The American Institute of Architects (AIA) issued 38 Honor Awards in 2000, its largest number to date. The high number reflected how busy most architects were as a strong U.S. economy fueled demand for new projects.

Although projects making independent "statements" have won many past awards, the 2000 focus was on renovation and rehabilitation, as well as on new structures that fit in with their neighbors or expressed their locations. Such thinking was seen in the AIA's choice of Gensler as Firm of the Year. In the words of founder M. Arthur Gensler, Jr., the firm emphasized service—"listening to clients and solving their problems."

Regional and urban design projects received 11 awards. Bahcesehir, a new satellite city west of Istanbul, Turkey, was designed by architects Torti Gallas and Partners-CHK, Inc. with associate Oner Ozyar Inas A.S., as a self-sufficient urban entity. Architect Daniel Williams created a plan that extended his 1999 award-winning ecology project northward to protect not just watersheds but farmland in southeast Florida. Ecological preservation also was the base of a project by Skidmore, Owings & Merrill LLP (SOM), which won the most AIA awards in 2000. SOM was commissioned by a group opposing the government's plans to fill in more of Hong Kong's harbor for commercial use. The firm proposed a waterfront park for recreational and cultural purposes. For Windsor Town Centre in Vero Beach, FL, Merrill and Pastor Architects designed traditional Spanish-style buildings with steep roofs and balconies.

Urban Planning. AIA winners in urban planning included SOM's remodeling of a

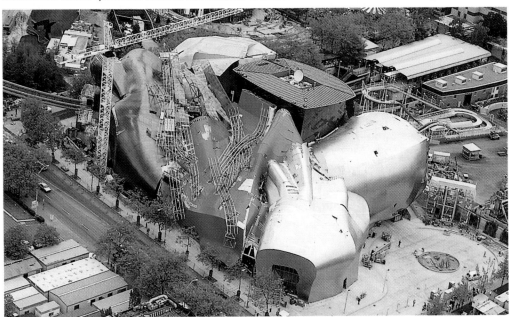

Architect Frank Gehry's Experience Music Project (EMP), below, designed in the shape of smashed guitars, opened in Seattle, WA, in June 2000. Financed by Microsoft cofounder Paul Allen, EMP is an interactive museum devoted to the history of rock music.

New York City post office, designed by McKim, Mead & White at the turn of the 20th century, into a new Pennsylvania Railroad Station that reproduced some of the original station's grandeur. The 1963 demolition of the old station, also designed by McKim, Mead & White, had sparked the nationwide preservation movement.

SOM's plan for the Shanghai, China, fast-growing waterfront across the river from the colonial-era downtown was to coordinate the development of offices, tourist attractions, housing, and recreational facilities around large parks stretching into the countryside. In Detroit, the $40 million first phase of the Harmonie Park/Madison Avenue Development Project, by Schervish Vogel Consulting Architects, relied on adaptive reuse of existing structures, augmented by new residential and office construction.

To revive pedestrian traffic and enliven street life around Philadelphia's City Hall, Thompson, Ventulett, Stainback & Associates added onto and converted the nearby 1893 Reading Terminal Train Shed into a convention center. Consulting architects were Kelly/Maiello. The associate architect was Vitetta. In San Francisco, greater waterfront use was promoted by ROMA Design Group's Mid-Embarcadero Open Space/Ferry Terminal project.

Suitable Buildings. Among AIA's 2000 award winners that paid tribute to new structures that fit in with their neighbors or were built in unique locations was the Seiji Ozawa Hall at Tanglewood in Lenox, MA, designed by William Rawn Associates, Architects. The jury noted that this detailed wood structure "recalled New England meetinghouses." Another winner—Turnbull Griffin Haesloop's Long Meadow Ranch Winery in St. Helena, CA, a post-and-beam structure with a roof supported by heavy wood trusses—is a refined version of utilitarian structures in the local countryside.

Similarly, two houses expressed their individual locations. James Cutler Architects designed the Methow Valley Cabin in Winthrop, WA, to expose as much of its structure as possible and make the vertical elements blend in with the surrounding trees. The Hill County Jacal in Pipe Creek, TX, was designed by Lake/Flato Architects to appear indigenous and as if it had always been there. Jacal is a Mexican term for "lean-to structure." As such, wide-sloping roofs were anchored into a rock ledge, and simply framed glass walls make the structure appear open to the elements.

The brightly colored buildings of Mexico's Ricardo Legorreta, winner of the 2000 AIA Gold Medal, reflected climate-control concerns and were evocative of modest adobe structures blown up to a large scale.

Renovation and Restoration. Compared with previous years' awards, a proportionally large number of honors in 2000 went to renovation projects. Le Fresnoy National Studio for Contemporary Arts in Tourcoing, France, was converted from a large, historic utilitarian building by Bernard Tschumi Architects. The firm designed a large roof over the original structure, thus creating new studio space. Weiss/Manfredi Architects' park and community center in Olympia Fields, IL, made use of early- 20th-century farm buildings for offices, meeting spaces, and libraries. Bruner/Cott & Associates' remodeling of a 19th-century manufacturing complex in North Adams, MA, preserved the 19th-century patina, while creating large, airy galleries for the Massachusetts Museum of Contemporary Art (MASS MoCA).

Other restorations included Marmol and Radziner Architects' work on Richard Neutra's 1946 Kaufmann House in Palm Springs, CA. Mies van der Rohe's Farnsworth House in Plano, IL, was restored by Lohan Associates after river waters flooded it, destroying all finishes, utilities, and furniture. In restoring New York City's monumental Beaux Arts Grand Central Terminal, Beyer Blinder Belle Architects & Planners LLP stripped away latter-day intrusions and grime, built a staircase intended in Warren and Wetmore's original design, and restored the ceiling constellations. Another restoration receiving a 2000 award was the San Francisco City Hall Improvement Project. The work included structural reinforcements to protect against potential earthquake damage. The supervising architects were Heller Manus Architects, who worked with Komorous-Towey Architects/Finger & Moy Architects.

Several completed monuments deserved notice in 2000, but only one, the Women's Memorial and Education Center in Arlington, VA, received an AIA award.

Richard Meier & Partners received two awards for new structures—the Getty Center in Los Angeles, CA, and a Neugebauer House in Naples, FL. Richard Meier also received the 25-year award for his 1968 Smith House in Darien, CT.

CHARLES K. HOYT, *Fellow*
American Institute of Architects

Argentina

Upon taking office as president of Argentina in December 1999, Fernando de la Rúa planned to restore confidence in Argentina by lifting it out of recession, creating jobs, punishing criminals, combating corruption, and restructuring the public debt. The governing center-left Alliance coalition, made up of de la Rúa's Radical Civic Union (UCR) and the Front for a Country in Solidarity (FREPASO), had no intention of deepening, or even maintaining, the close relationship with the United States established by the previous administration.

Government and Politics. The strategy for lowering the 15% unemployment rate was to create jobs by cutting costs of hiring more people. A prolabor code passed in the 1950s contained a 30-day probationary period for new workers. Under the code, modified on April 26, probation for new employees was extended to six months in larger firms and to a year in smaller businesses. Payroll taxes on new hires were reduced from 17.5% to 12%, and no severance pay was available to workers dismissed after being on the job for up to 12 months.

In July it was alleged that the government, which was elected on an anticorruption platform, had utilized some $10 million as bribes to assure Senate passage of the crucial labor reforms. While the president denied involvement, his labor minister and intelligence chief were suspected. Carlos "Chacho" Alvarez, the vice-president and head of the Senate, quit over the president's failure to resolve the scandal involving seven opposition senators and a progovernment one. Resignations followed from the chief of staff and head of intelligence, and the Senate's stature was badly shaken. In November, de la Rúa's popularity plunged to 23% of those polled.

Having inherited a deficit of $7 billion from the outgoing administration, de la Rúa responded with new tax levies. Obligated by the International Monetary Fund (IMF) to cut expenditures in order to receive fresh funding, Buenos Aires took aim at the wasteful provinces that were in debt by $18 billion, with the federal government as guarantor. Tax evaders, who cost the government $20 billion yearly, were targeted. An anticorruption bureau was established, and more than 50 people identified with the previous regime were to be questioned. High on that list were Victor Alderete, who was suspected of abusing his position as head of the state health service, and María Julia Alsogaray, who was responsible for important privatizations in the telecommunications and steel industries, and who tried to explain the spectacular rise in her personal wealth while a part of the government.

Late in 1999, Spanish Judge Baltazar Garzon ordered a search for and detention of 98 Argentine military men on charges of genocide, terrorism, and torture during the so-called "dirty war" in Argentina (1976–83). The list included former Presidents Jorge Videla and Leopoldo F. Galtieri, along with ranking junta members who served during their dictatorships. Unlike his predecessor, Carlos Menem, de la Rúa indicated that his administration would hear the charges, and that some of those charged would be turned over to Argentine courts. Many of those sought by Garzon had previously been convicted of grave human-rights violations in Argentine trials and sentenced, only to be set free through later amnesties. Not covered in amnesties were cases where military men had seized babies, perhaps as many as 500, born to dissident mothers while detained. The newborns were handed over to military couples to raise as their own. After

© Enrique Marcarian/Reuters NewMedia Inc./Corbis

In late May 2000, Argentines, weary of more austerity, protested a visit by delegates from the International Monetary Fund (IMF). The delegation was in Argentina to monitor the government's economic policies.

giving birth, the mothers were killed. More than 60 of the kidnap victims have been reunited with their biological families.

Economics. The financial world doubted Argentina's viability because of disappointing tax returns, a large deficit, and less than 1% growth projected for 2000. A $123 billion foreign debt had to be serviced in the 2001 budget submitted to the National Congress in October. To do so required borrowing at least $19.5 billion, most of it from abroad. Borrowing costs had already doubled to 15% between July and November, when the government sold treasury bills worth $1.1 billion. Pledges of nearly $40 billion were received from the World Bank and the Inter-American Development Bank, as well as from foreign governments and local banks. Terms for the assistance included reducing the 2001 budget by $700 million, lowering taxes on corporations, trimming public-sector salaries by 12%-15%, slicing pensions, and privatizing all pension funds. Governments at both the provincial and federal levels had to agree to retain current spending levels until 2005, something that 14 opposition Peronist governors resisted, causing the federal executive to threaten implementation of a freeze by decree. The dissidents finally accepted the fiscal arrangement on November 20.

A weary public reacted to the prospect of more austerity. A general strike was called for November 23–24, to coincide with a visit from an IMF delegation. In the largest union-led protest of recent years, millions of strikers virtually paralyzed the country, blocking highways, disrupting transportation. and closing schools. Instead of cuts, the strikers sought additional funding for social services as unemployment approached 16%. Growing underemployment affected nearly 50% of the workforce.

The slow progress of trade-pact negotiations with Europe and North America shifted attention to advancing the Southern Cone Common Market (Mercosur). At a June summit in Buenos Aires, Mercosur leaders moved ahead on establishing macroeconomic convergence, lowering the common external tariff, incorporating new members such as Chile, and widening the market's scope to include social issues. Separately, Argentina and Brazil agreed to new rules for the auto sector.

Foreign Affairs. In spite of Argentina's intention to reorient its foreign policies more toward Europe, contacts with the U.S. government were frequent. In February, U.S.

ARGENTINA • Information Highlights

Official Name: Argentine Republic.
Location: Southern South America.
Area: 1,068,297 sq mi (2 766 890 km²).
Population (2000 est.): 36,955,182.
Chief Cities (1991 census): Buenos Aires, the capital, 2,960,976; Cordoba, 1,148,305; San Justo, 1,111,811; Rosario, 894,645.
Government: *Head of state and government,* Fernando de la Rúa, president (inaugurated Dec. 10, 1999). *Legislature*—National Congress: Senate and Chamber of Deputies.
Monetary Unit: Peso (0.9994 peso equals U.S.$1, Nov. 16, 2000).
Gross Domestic Product (1999 est. U.S.$): $367,000,000,000 (purchasing power parity).
Economic Index (Buenos Aires, 1999; 1990 = 100): *Consumer Prices,* all items, 405.9; food, 378.6.
Foreign Trade (1999 U.S.$): *Imports,* $25,538,000,000; *exports,* $23,309,000,000.

Secretary of Commerce William Daley went to Buenos Aires with a delegation of business leaders. The delegates heard complaints from Vice-President Alvarez that Argentina was opening its markets to the world, but was finding world markets closed to Argentine goods. Visitors indicated that they were "favorably disposed" to boosting trade with their southern neighbor. Argentina defended itself against U.S. charges of inadequate patent protection with a new law obligating its pharmaceutical manufacturers to pay patent holders for products made locally. Because of heavy losses by Argentine airlines, Buenos Aires announced in February that it was suspending an open-skies accord signed with the United States in 1999 that had provided for a total deregulation of commercial aviation between the two countries by 2003.

President de la Rúa paid a state visit to the United States in June. He sought new private investments, especially in telecommunications, while in New York City. In Washington D.C., de la Rúa signed agreements on extradition, corruption, environment, and satellite cooperation. He also pushed for lower trade barriers, mainly on steel pipe, orange juice, and beef. During a stopover in Buenos Aires in August, U.S. Secretary of State Madeleine Albright asked for help in the drug war. She was deluged with requests from human-rights groups to declassify U.S. documents that could shed light on the whereabouts of dissidents' children who became victims of "dirty war" officers trained at the U.S.-operated School of the Americas.

Two prisoners suspected in a 1999 assassination of Paraguayan Vice-President Luis María Argaña escaped on September 17 from a maximum-security jail in Buenos Aires, where they had been awaiting extradition. The incident led to the firings of 25 police and prison guards. The head of the prison resigned. It was rumored that a former Paraguayan general, Lino Oviedo, believed to have masterminded Argaña's demise, paid $300,000 for the breakout in Buenos Aires. One escapee was recaptured in November and sent to Asunción.

LARRY L PIPPIN, *University of the Pacific*

Armenia

In 2000, Armenia experienced reverberations from the October 1999 assassination of its top leaders. President Robert Kocharian, however, overcame political isolation and weakness through the co-optation of former opponents into the administration.

Domestic Politics. The New Year brought opposition calls for the resignation of President Kocharian and new parliamentary elections. The 1999 assassination implicated leading figures in Armenian society—including Aleksan Harutiunian, Kocharian's aide. The military prosecutor responsible for the pretrial investigation claimed there was a massive conspiracy aimed at overthrowing the government, but within months conceded that he had no evidence against anyone except the five gunmen directly involved in the killing. Parliamentary parties blamed Kocharian for political chaos, and the majority Unity Bloc demanded Kocharian dismiss his presidential chief of staff for interfering in the investigation of the 1999 murders.

Attacked by his own prime minister, Kocharian reasserted control over the military by appointing members of the Yekrapah Union, a source of potential opposition in parliament, to top military posts. In May,

---

ARMENIA • Information Highlights

Official Name: Republic of Armenia.
Location: Southwest Asia.
Area: 11,506 sq mi (29 800 km²).
Population (2000 est.): 3,344,336.
Chief Cities (July 1990 est.): Yerevan, the capital, 1,254,400; Gyumri, 206,600; Vanadzor, 170,200.
Government: *Head of state,* Robert Kocharian, president (sworn in April 9, 1998). *Head of government,* Andranik Markaryan, prime minister (appointed May 12, 2000). *Legislature* (unicameral)—National Assembly.
Monetary Unit: Dram (553.8700 dram equal U.S.$1, Nov. 28, 2000).
Gross Domestic Product (1999 est. U.S.$): $9,900,000,000 (purchasing power parity).
Foreign Trade (1999 est.U.S.$): *Imports,* $800,000,000; *exports,* $232,000,000.

Kocharian replaced his prime minister and defense minister. The new prime minister—Andranik Markaryan—was chairman of the Republican Party, one of the two partners in the Unity Bloc, and the new defense minister was a powerful Kocharian ally. Ultimately, talk of impeachment ended, and Kocharian benefited for the rest of the year from parliamentary jealousies and conflicts. In October, however, a large demonstration in Yerevan called for Kocharian's resignation on economic grounds.

The Economy. Armenia's economic stability depends in large part on the Medzamor nuclear-power station, which produces 40% of the country's electricity supply. In 2000 the power station's life was extended another ten years despite a promise to the European Union (EU) to close it in 2004. The Ministry of Industry and Trade reported a 22% increase in industrial production over the first six months of 2000 as a result of the reactivation of mining, smelting, and chemical plants, but the first half registered only 2.9% growth in gross domestic product (GDP). In August, there was still a 45% shortfall in the collection of taxes, and the budget passed in March 2000 anticipated a deficit equal to 5% of GDP. Foreign debt continued to rise in 2000 with approximately 20% of state revenues used to service it. The population's economic woes were exacerbated by a summer drought that caused $100 million worth of damage and severe shortages.

Foreign Policy. President Kocharian engaged President Heydar Aliyev of Azerbaijan in a number of direct meetings to try and resolve the Nagorno-Karabakh territorial dispute, but without success. Armenia continued to be dependent on Russia in its conflict with Azerbaijan, and in September, Kocharian traveled to Moscow to sign more agreements on energy cooperation and a rescheduling of Armenia's debt.

Relations with Iran continued to prosper, and in August, both governments agreed to build a gas pipeline linking the two countries. At the same time, Armenia was awaiting final acceptance into the Council of Europe. Agreements on military assistance were signed with the United States and Greece. Even though Turkey continued to back Azerbaijan in the Nagorno-Karabakh dispute, Armenia insisted that Turkey's recognition of the 1915 genocide of Armenians in Ottoman Turkey would lead to normal relations.

STEPHEN F. JONES, *Mount Holyoke College*

Art

On Dec. 31, 1999, art thieves used millennium festivities as a cover to break into Oxford University's Ashmolean Museum and steal Paul Cézanne's Postimpressionist painting "Auvers-sur-Oise" (1879–82). The painting, valued at more than $3.2 million, had not been recovered by late in 2000.

Death took three key figures in American 20th-century representational art in 2000—painter Jacob Lawrence (b. 1917), printmaker Leonard Baskin (b. 1922), and sculptor George Segal (b. 1924). (*See also* OBITUARIES.)

Trends. Globalism was a hot buzzword in art in 2000. Chinese artists such as Xu Bing, Cai Guo-qiang, and Wenda Gu, who linked Chinese traditions to international concerns, achieved worldwide acclaim. At the Biennale in Lyon, France, for example, Gu installed his "United Nations—Temple of Exoticism," which used his trademark, human hair, woven into a tent decorated with Ming and Louis XV furniture.

Artworks created on, and for, the Internet sped around the globe, seeming to exist everywhere and nowhere simultaneously. Artists did, too, as international contemporary-art exhibitions proliferated from Sydney, Australia, to Santa Fe, NM. The term "cultural nomadism" designated creators, critics, and curators wandering the globe from exhibition to exhibition. While artists roamed, many new artworks were "site specific"—that is, created for, and rooted to, a single exhibition space. This led to some criticism that curators often have given up their obligation to judge specific works of art in favor of simply inviting known artists to come and create something new but of unknown quality.

Controversy. The 1999 controversy over the Brooklyn Museum of Art's showing of "Sensation: Young British Artists from the Saatchi Collection" was settled quietly as both sides agreed in March 2000 to drop litigation. New York City had threatened to terminate the museum's lease and replace its board of trustees. The museum answered by filing a 1st Amendment suit against the city. The controversy had been sparked by Mayor Rudolph W. Giuliani's objection to the use of cow dung and pornographic magazine cutouts in Chris Ofili's 1996 painting "The Holy Virgin Mary." Questions later arose concerning financial interests in "Sensation." Evidence of a possible conflict of interest led the American Association of Museums (AAM) to issue new guidelines on exhibition sponsorship in July. The guidelines urged museums to "maintain intellectual integrity and institutional control" in mounting exhibitions.

Controversy also arose at New York City's Whitney Museum of

The Tate Modern, Britain's new home for modern and contemporary art, opened in a former London power station in 2000. An exhibit by Louise Bourgeois, left, was featured in the Turbine Room.

American Art's Biennial show 2000, where Hans Haacke's contribution, "Sanitation," featured art-critical quotes from contemporary American politicians written on the wall in the Gothic script favored in Nazi Germany. Those who objected included Jewish groups who found the parallel drawn between contemporary America and Nazi Germany invalid and disrespectful. Haacke, a German-born artist residing in New York since the early 1960s, returned to Germany to attempt to execute a work at the Reichstag building in Berlin, newly renovated by British architect Sir Norman Foster. Haacke's piece for the restored capital of the reunited Germany also proved controversial. He proposed changing the inscription over the building's entrance from "To the German People"—which had been there since 1917—to "To the Population," and to surround the entrance with soil gathered from throughout Germany. Haacke's changes called attention to the great number of non-Germans living on German soil.

© 2000 The Detroit Institute of Arts

Martin Johnson Heade's "Cattleya Orchid and Three Brazilian Hummingbirds," above, was exhibited at the National Gallery of Art. The "Van Gogh: Face to Face" exhibit, which was seen at the Detroit Institute of Arts and elsewhere, viewed the artist's evolving approach to portraits, including Camille Roulin, left.

One peripatetic piece found a comfortable summer resting place, as American artist Jeff Koon's "Puppy," created first for an exhibition in Germany in 1992, sat on its haunches outside New York's Rockefeller Center. The 43-ft (13-m)-high terrier previously had been shown in Sydney, Australia. Another version is on view at the Guggenheim Museum in Bilbao, Spain, where it was attacked by Basque separatists disguised as gardeners. (*See also* PEOPLE, PLACES, AND THINGS, page 402.)

Exhibitions and Installations. A series of exhibitions at U.S. museums highlighted the works of women artists since the 1940s. Each reflected the period in which the artist came of age. Fifty years of realist portraits by Alice Neel (1900–1984) were shown at the Philadelphia Museum of Art; the Whit-ney Museum of American Art; the Addison Gallery of American Art in Andover, MA; and the Walker Art Center in Minneapolis.

Paintings and collages by abstract expressionist Lee Krasner (1911–84), wife of Jackson Pollock, were shown in a retrospective curated by Robert Hobbs and seen at the Los Angeles County Museum of Art, the Des Moines Art Center, the Akron Art Museum, and the Brooklyn Museum of Art. Another kind of abstraction—the vision-blurring op art of the 1960s—was resurrected in a retrospective of the British artist Bridget Riley (b. 1931) at New York's Dia Center for the Arts. An icon of the 1960s, Yoko Ono had her first major U. S. retrospective, "YES Yoko Ono," consisting of more than 150 pieces. The show was organized by, and first seen at, the Japan Society Gallery in New York. It was to travel in 2001 to the Walker Art Center in Minneapolis; the Contemporary Arts Museum in Houston; the List Visual Arts Center at the Massachusetts Institute of Technology (MIT) in Cambridge, MA; the Art Gallery of Ontario in Toronto; and the San Francisco Museum of Modern Art.

The political videos and installations of Martha Rosler, who came to prominence in the 1970s, were seen at the New Museum of Contemporary Art in New York. Another 1970s artist, Eleanor Antin, had a retrospective organized by the Los Angeles County Museum of Art. This show also was seen at the Washington University Gallery of Art in St. Louis. The retrospective of Barbara Kruger, who in the 1980s had made a strong graphic impression with posterlike photomontages pointing out common gender stereotypes, was organized by the Museum of Contemporary Art in Los Angeles and was seen at the Whitney.

Women artists of the 1990s and 2000s were represented by the first museum shows for two rising painting stars. The works of Ellen Gallagher, which deal with stereotypes of African-Americans, were seen at the Institute of Contemporary Art in Boston. Lisa Yuskavage's show of more than 80 paintings—many of women in pinup poses with less-than-"perfect" bodies—was seen at the Institute of Contemporary Art, Philadelphia. Much further back in time were exhibits such as "Ancient Faces: Mummy Portraits from Roman Egypt." This exhibit presented some 70 painted panel portraits, also known as Fayum portraits, created from the 1st to 3rd centuries A.D.. The show originated at the British Museum and was seen in 2000 at the Metropolitan Museum of Art in New York.

The most comprehensive showing of late Baroque and Neoclassical art from Rome was on view in "The Splendor of 18th-Century Rome," an exhibit organized by the Philadelphia Museum of Art and seen also at the Museum of Fine Arts in Houston. The National Archaeological Museum of Naples, Italy, opened its galleries of ancient erotic art for the first time in 40 years, and the Guggenheim Museum in New York looked back 100 years in the comprehensive "1900: Art at the Crossroads," which featured 240 works by more than 170 artists.

"Painting on Light: Drawing and Stained Glass in the Age of Dürer and Holbein," organized by the J. Paul Getty Museum in Los Angeles and also seen at the St. Louis Art Museum, illuminated the Renaissance use of an art form more commonly associated with Gothic cathedrals. Calligraphy, illustrated books, lacquer work, and ceramics created by Japanese artist Hon'ami Koetsu (1558–1637) were shown abroad extensively for the first time in an exhibition at the Philadelphia Museum of Art.

Facilities, Gifts, and a Return. Great Britain's new home for its national collection of modern and contemporary art is the Tate Modern, which resulted from the $241 million renovation of a power station by the Swiss architectural firm of Herzog & de Meuron. The Museum of Fine Arts in Houston's $50 million addition, designed by José Rafael Moneo, makes it the sixth-largest art museum in the United States. A new wing to the Portland Art Museum in Oregon added 60,000 sq ft (5 574 m²). The Denver Art Museum chose Daniel Libeskind to design its $62.5 million addition.

Collectors Peter and Eileen Norton announced a gift of about 1,000 works of contemporary art to 28 American museums and the Tate Gallery. The Weitzenhoffer family gave its Impressionist and Postimpressionist paintings to the University of Oklahoma. The General Motors Corporation gave $5 million to the Detroit Institute of the Arts to support creation of the Center for African American Art.

In November, the National Gallery of Art announced that it would return "Still Life with Fruit and Game," a 17th-century Flemish painting by Frans Snyders, to the heirs of Marguerite Stern, the widow of a Jewish banker from France whose art collection had been seized by the Nazis during their occupation of Paris.

Staff and Honors. Lowery Stokes Sims became director of the Studio Museum in Harlem. Katharine Lee Reid went from the Virginia Museum of Fine Arts to the Cleveland Museum of Art. Australian Michael Brand took over at the Virginia Museum. Michael E. Shapiro replaced Ned Rifkin as director of the High Museum of Art in Atlanta, and Rifkin became director of The Menil Collection in Houston. Deborah Gribbon took over as director of the J. Paul Getty Museum in Los Angeles, while Alfred Pacquement, a contemporary-art specialist, succeeded German modern-art scholar Werner Spies as director of the Musée national d'art moderne at the Centre Pompidou in Paris.

Robert Rauschenberg won the $50,000 Wexner Prize. MacArthur Foundation fellows in the arts included sculptor Alfredo Jaar and critic and curator Deborah Willis. Sculptor Robert Gober will represent the United States at the 2001 Venice Biennale. Critic Dave Hickey will curate the 4th SITE Santa Fe Biennial in summer 2001.

PETER CHAMETZKY, *School of Art and Design Southern Illinois University, Carbondale*

Art Market

Despite the ongoing U.S. Department of Justice's criminal investigation of the auction industry over price-fixing and signs of possible softening within the international art market, stunning prices for world-class works of art were still achieved at auction in the year 2000.

In January the art world was rocked by revelations that auction-giant Christie's had cooperated with the Justice Department's investigation and received conditional amnesty for its role in colluding with Sotheby's over setting commissions on the sale of art and objects at auction. The subsequent resignations of Sotheby's chairman and chief executive officer in February further strained the credibility of the world's two largest auction houses, who together account for close to 95% of the auction industry.

Spring and Summer Auctions. Against that headline-grabbing atmosphere, price seemed to be no object during the spring-summer auction season in New York and London. Claude Monet's dazzling interpretation of the Rouen Cathedral, "The Portal (Sun)," fetched $24.2 million, while Paul Cézanne's gravity-defying composition, "Still Life with Fruit and a Pot of Ginger" hit $18.1 million.

On the modern front, Pablo Picasso's arresting "Still Life With Tulips," featuring the visage of his young lover, Marie-Thérèse Walter, climbed to $28.6 million. Even lesser-known names of the Impressionist epoch broke into the record books as Gustave Caillebotte's "Man on the Balcony, Boulevard Haussmann" from 1880 soared to $14.3 million.

Sculpture continued its red-hot pace as a sultry bronze by Henri Matisse, "La Serpentine," made a record-setting $14 million. Edgar Degas' "The Little 14-Year-Old Dancer" shot to a record $11.5 million.

November Sales. In sharp contrast, sales at the major houses in November registered the highest failure rates since May 1994, a sure sign the market was cooling for anything less than stellar material. That was certainly the case for Picasso's Blue Period painting "Woman with Crossed Arms," which sold to an anonymous telephone bidder for a staggering $55 million, the highest price ever for a 20th-century work of art.

Though the bloom was clearly off in the Impressionist-Modern field, prices for post–World War II and contemporary art remained buoyant. Mark Rothko's luminous and haunting abstraction, "no. 2 (Blue, Red and Green)," sold for $11 million, and Yves Klein's sponge relief, "RE 1," made $6.7 mil-

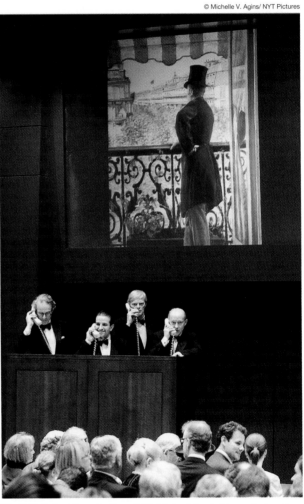

© Michelle V. Agins/ NYT Pictures

The U.S. federal investigation of Christie's did not deter collectors from spending record sums. Gustave Caillebotte's "Man on the Balcony, Boulevard Haussmann," above, sold for $14.3 million.

lion. Sculpture continued its rise as Alexander Calder's gigantic and painted steel stabile "Stegosaurus" from about 1972 brought $4.1 million, and Alberto Giacometti's towering bronze "Grande Femme Debout I" from 1960 climbed to $14.3 million. Million-dollar results also greeted some contemporary stars, including Charles Ray.

JUDD TULLY, *"Art & Auction"*

Asia

The three most prominent Asian international organizations—the Association of Southeast Asian Nations (ASEAN), the ASEAN Regional Forum (ARF), and the Asia-Pacific Economic Cooperation (APEC) forum—experienced serious disagreements during their meetings in 2000. These difficulties mirrored the continued unsettled political and economic situations in Asia.

ASEAN. Consisting of all ten Southeast Asian states, ASEAN met twice: a July foreign ministers conference and a November-December informal summit that also included Japan, South Korea, and China. Both meetings displayed the ongoing division within ASEAN between its two democratic members (Thailand and the Philippines) and their more authoritarian counterparts (Malaysia, Vietnam, and Myanmar) over questions of whether and when it is appropriate for ASEAN to become involved in the internal affairs of its members. The issue came to the fore in the aftermath of Indonesia's 1999 East Timor crisis. It expanded in 2000 to encompass Muslim extremist activities in the region, highlighted by the kidnappings committed in the Philippines and Malaysia by the Philippine radical Muslim group Abu Sayyaf.

To cope with these potential threats to regional peace and stability, ASEAN foreign ministers at their July meeting crafted a typical compromise between the interventionists and those who wished to maintain exclusive control over their domestic affairs. ASEAN established a tripartite ministerial subgroup, consisting of three members, that would convene if a situation arose in the region that affected ASEAN security. While this troika mandate would be set by ASEAN foreign ministers, it presumably would honor the noninterference principle in members' internal affairs. How these contradictory mandates would be reconciled was not determined. Despite ASEAN's reticence about becoming involved in members' internal affairs, the foreign ministers unanimously issued a statement supporting Indonesia's territorial integrity against secessionist movements within that vast archipelagic state.

On economic matters, ASEAN further weakened the Common Effective Preferential Tariff (CEPT) under the ASEAN Free Trade Area (AFTA) to allow member countries more flexibility in meeting their obligations. This retreat from ASEAN free trade followed Malaysia's decision to continue to protect its automobile industry. Nevertheless, ASEAN as a whole remained committed to a common external tariff of 5% on many products by 2003.

At November's ASEAN informal summit, other contentious issues arose. ASEAN and China had been working on a code of conduct for the South China Sea, in order to control disputes among the claimants to the Spratly Islands. Conflicts between the Philippines, Vietnam, and China had led to low-level naval skirmishes in recent years. However, no agreement on the code was reached as Vietnam insisted that the Paracel Islands be added to the Spratlys. China, which had seized the Paracel Islands from the former Republic of Vietnam in 1974, refused. So, although the Philippines and China had reached an agreement on no new occupation or structures on the Spratly Islands, the code of conduct—which in any case would be voluntary—was not formalized.

The third Asia-Europe Meeting (ASEM), hosted by South Korea's President Kim Dae Jung (right) in Seoul in October 2000, issued a declaration for peace on the Korean Peninsula.

Representatives of the 21 member nations of the Asia-Pacific Economic Cooperation (APEC) forum assembled in Brunei in November 2000. The summit called for new global trade discussions.

© Brunei Information Department/AP/Wide World Photos

Also during 2000, ASEAN could not reach consensus on endorsing the case of Myanmar to the International Labor Organization (ILO) that Yangon (Rangoon) had stopped the practice of employing forced labor. Thailand, which for some time had experienced serious border and refugee problems with Myanmar, refused to support the latter's claim, arguing that forced labor in that country has been a significant source of refugees fleeing into Thailand, where as many as 1 million illegals were located during 2000.

The ASEAN summit succeeded in crafting an E-commerce treaty. But different levels of economic development within the members of the association hampered its effectiveness. Indeed, Singapore—a highly developed city-state—had chosen to go well beyond ASEAN, halting free-trade area plans to negotiate more advanced trade relations bilaterally with several states, including the United States. Singapore's moves in the trade field upset several ASEAN members.

ARF. Founded in 1994, ARF added most remaining nations of East Asia, Russia, the United States, Canada, the countries of the European Union (EU), India, Australia, and New Zealand to ASEAN. North Korea was admitted to the ARF in July. The 2000 ARF provided a venue for talk of pressing security issues by national leaders. China, Russia, and the United States discussed the latter's controversial National Missile Defense (NMD) system. Thailand tried to raise the issue of the Spratly Islands, but China insisted it would not discuss its claims in a forum dominated by nonclaimants.

The ARF's security agenda included threats posed by organized crime, narcotics, arms, and human trafficking. Thailand drove this initiative, concerned particularly with narcotics smuggled from Myanmar. The chairman's statement at the end of the meeting welcomed ARF progress in developing proposals that began to move from confidence building to preventive diplomacy, though the forum was still engaged in defining the latter concept and how it could be applied to ARF concerns. The statement also took note of contributions made to ARF deliberations by the Councils for Security Cooperation in the Asia-Pacific (CSCAP), its counterpart organization that included nongovernment experts. Finally, the ARF published the initial volume of its *Annual Security Outlook*, produced by individual states on a voluntary basis.

APEC. In November the APEC forum met in Brunei. Reflecting the split between developed and developing states, the United States called for accelerated global-trade liberalization, while Malaysia insisted talks should reconvene only after a specific agenda had been determined. Moreover, the developing countries complained about U.S. demands for labor and environmental standards. Discussions generally revealed ambivalence toward globalization. Developed states viewed globalization as expanding economic growth for all; developing countries saw the downside in losing control over their economies.

Trade liberalization commitments scheduled over ten to 20 years remained strictly voluntary, as the United States and other industrial countries lost their bid to establish a binding schedule for tariff reduction. The APEC members did agree that a "broad-based agenda" for eliminating trade barriers "should be formulated and finalized as soon as possible in 2001."

See INDEX for Asian nations on which there are separate articles.

SHELDON W. SIMON, *Arizona State University*

Astronomy

At a time of maximum solar activity, scientists used a solar-observation satellite called TRACE (Transition Region and Coronal Explorer) to photograph coronal loops so immense that they would engulf 30 Earths. In addition, astronomers studying the Sun have developed a technique for "seeing" the far side of the Sun. They hope this will enable them to detect dangerous electromagnetic storms that could affect Earth-based satellites and power systems.

Planetary scientists using the Galileo spacecraft in orbit around Jupiter and its moons have found that the giant planet has clear, dry "holes" in the clouds near the planet's equator—some as high as 62 mi (100 km). They have also found that Jupiter's closest Galilean moon, Io, contains many more volcanoes than scientists had thought, and that many have changed dramatically from previous observations. And magnetic readings from the Jovian moon Europa suggest that this body has a salty liquid ocean far beneath its thick, icy crust.

The Hubble Telescope has helped astronomers see what they think might be an icy mountain range on the surface of Titan, Saturn's largest moon. They hope to clear up this mystery with a probe that will visit this moon in 2004.

Rocks from space made headlines during 2000 as well. A rare meteorite that was seen as it fell into a frozen lake in the Canadian Yukon in January 2000 was recovered and analyzed. It was shown to contain material that is unchanged since the birth of the solar system. This find has been hailed as one of the most important discoveries in the history of the field of meteorite studies. In addition to this meteorite, scientists recorded the 14th meteorite set believed to be chunks blasted by an ancient asteroid impact on the planet Mars.

Astronomers released the results of the NEAR (Near Earth Asteroid Rendezvous) survey of the asteroid Eros. The spacecraft took more than 100,000 images of the asteroid at distances ranging from 22 mi to 218 mi (35 km to 350 km). And 8 million measurements by the laser rangefinder on board the spacecraft indicate that it is a single solid object from the solar system's birth, rather than a loosely collected "rubble pile."

From data gathered through the asteroid-tracking effort called Spacewatch, scientists estimated that there are some 900 asteroids at least 0.6 mi (1 km) in size whirling around near the Earth. The scientists said that they had found about 40% of them.

Astronomers studying Comet LINEAR, one of the brightest comets in several years, watched as a chunk the size of a house came off of the comet. Later, as the comet rounded the Sun, all of the ice in the comet's nucleus—the glue that held it together—completely evaporated, and the comet dissolved before their eyes.

In late 1999, astronomers discovered what they believed to be the most distant object ever seen in our solar system. Located in the Kuiper Belt, more than 60 AUs away from the Earth, the object is thought to be a ball of ice 62 mi (100 km) across.

In the Milky Way. The number of planets that astronomers have discovered in orbit around other stars reached 50 in 2000. They found the second new multiple-planet system that contains two Saturn-sized planets, one orbiting every 2.98 days, and the other every 29.8 days. Another planet orbits a nearby star named Epsilon Eridani—only 10.5 light-years from Earth. This is exciting because the system's relative proximity to Earth may mean that the Hubble Telescope might be able to photograph it.

In October, astronomers announced their discovery of 18 planetlike objects drifting through the constellation of Orion. Since they seem to exist without a "parent" star, these "free-floaters" may challenge the traditional theories about how planets form.

New gamma-ray observations showed that about half the previously unidentified sources of high-energy gamma rays are emanating from a new class of objects. These emit gamma rays continuously, rather than in the flashes or bursts of the most famous gamma-ray-emitting objects. The discovery has implications for gamma-ray astronomy.

Astronomers using the European Southern Observatory's (ESO's) Very Large Telescope (VLT) have discovered a neutron star 12.4 mi (20 km) across, moving through space at 62 mi (100 km) per second. Its motion has caused a bow shock–shaped nebula to form around the neutron star as it slams into the interstellar environment.

After analyzing 13 years of data gathered by the Jodrell Bank Observatory in England, astronomers believed they had found the first wobbling pulsar. Like many pulsars, this supernova remnant is only the size of a city, weighs a million times more than Earth, and spins 2.5 times per second. However, it wobbles like a slowing top, with a period of 1,000 days.

Astronomers continue to discover new planets orbiting around other stars. The artist's rendering, above, illustrates the Saturn-sized planet around the star 79 Ceti, which is 117 light years away in the constellation of Cetus, the sea monster.

In January 2000 a blast of X rays from a nearby binary-star system led astronomers to suspect that the X rays were caused by the closest black hole ever discovered—only 1,600 light-years away. And astronomers using the giant Keck Observatory on Mauna Kea pinpointed an immense black hole at the core of the Milky Way. With the mass of more than 2 million Suns, this black hole causes nearby stars to speed up as they revolve around the galactic core.

In a cloud of gas and dust near the center of the Milky Way, astronomers found evidence of simple sugar molecules. This suggests that the precursors to life are formed in early solar systems—even before planets themselves exist.

The Universe Beyond. A 3,000–light-year-diameter magnetic bubble—unlike anything ever before seen—was found in the nearby galaxy known as M82.

Deep within the core of the distant galaxy NGC 4395, astronomers discovered a relatively tiny "supermassive" black hole pulling in as much matter and radiating as many X rays as much larger holes. It appeared to be part of a new classification of mid-mass black holes with, perhaps, the mass of 10,000 to 100,000 Suns.

Astronomers using the 33-ft (10-m)-diameter Keck Telescope in Hawaii located the most distant object ever. The quasar is believed to lie so distant that its light was visible when the universe was less than a bil-lion years old. Italian scientists plotting a "temperature map" of the extremely young universe believe they have found evidence that the universe is "flat," and could continue to expand forever.

Astrotechnology The newly converted telescope at the Multiple Mirror Telescope Observatory (MMTO)—a joint project of the University of Arizona and the Smithsonian Institution—on Mount Hopkins, AZ, took its first wide-field picture on September 6. The new MMTO telescope is actually a conversion in which the six existing mirrors were replaced by a new 21–ft (6.4–m) mirror. The telescope's first target is an immense spiral galaxy known as 'NGC 7479—similar in size and shape to our own Milky Way Galaxy. In May 2000, the new $4 million Australian-Japanese telescope CANGAROO II—designed to seek out and understand black holes—began operation under the clear, dark skies of the Australian Outback. And in September, astronomers and dignitaries attended a groundbreaking ceremony near Sutherland, South Africa, for the construction of the ESO's Southern African Large Telescope (SALT). This telescope's main mirror is composed of an array of hexagonal 3-ft- (1-m-) diameter mirrors, making it the equivalent of a 33-ft (10-m) telescope. The observatory will cost about $15 million to build.

DENNIS L. MAMMANA
SkyScapes (www.skyscapes.com)

Australia

Sydney's highly successful staging of the Olympic Games (*see* SPECIAL REPORT, page 126)—along with nationwide preparations to celebrate the first century of Australia's nationhood at year's end—made 2000 an evocative and prideful year that strengthened the dedication of Australians to their traditional democratic values of tolerance during a time of increased tension and instability in many countries.

The Economy. In the fifth year under the prime ministership of John Howard, leader of the Liberal-National Party coalition, the nation enjoyed continued prosperity with sustained gross domestic product (GDP) growth. Only rural and regional communities were under any severe economic pressure. Positive moves were made to redress earlier mistreatment and deprivation of the indigenous people.

The general level of income tax was lowered from midyear to coincide with the introduction of a 10% goods-and-services tax (GST), which replaced other indirect taxes, including wholesale-sales tax. However, this new tax system—along with higher gasoline prices—brought uncertainty to the small-business sector and resulted in mixed economic signals. Inflation rose as a result of the GST's initial impact, and ran at about 6% in the third quarter; unemployment was at an 11-year low of 6.3%.

A 15% fall in the exchange rate of the Australian dollar helped lift the number of international visitors to record levels and provided a stimulus to Australian exports, resulting in marked improvement in the balance-of-payment figures. In industrial relations, the zeal for reform faltered after a decade-long phase during which enterprise bargaining and productivity-based wage rises largely supplanted the traditional "needs-based" arbitration system of wage setting. However, the coalition remained committed to strengthening the primacy of enterprise bargaining, and reducing the role of the Industrial Relations Commission. By contrast, the new Australian Labor Party (ALP) policy, developed under union pressure, sought to strengthen "the right of employees to act, organize, and protect themselves collectively."

The Budget. The federal budget for fiscal 2000–2001 benefited from sustained economic growth and projected an underlying cash surplus of A$2.8 billion (U.S.$5.2 billion). Reaction to the budget was mixed. Most analysts considered it bland, and many financial experts expected its expansionary fiscal policy to pressure interest rates. In a November review of economic progress, Treasurer Peter Costello revised the budget revenue to an enhanced annual surplus of A$4.8 billion (U.S.$8.8 billion). He announced a further spending initiative: an additional A$1.5 billion (U.S.$2.8 billion) for the improvement of rural roads—a measure clearly designed to lessen dissatisfaction over the sharp rise in gasoline costs.

Meanwhile, after heavy rains in the states of New South Wales and Queensland, floodwaters inundated widespread farming areas, destroying crops of wheat, sorghum, and cotton. The government arranged emergency support because of the flood damage and promised further assistance.

Aboriginal Policy and Reconciliation. With aspects of Aboriginal deprivation receiving international attention, indigenous-affairs policy was to the fore in the nation's unfinished business leading up to the centenary of federation. An anthology titled *Reconciliation* was published in April. In analyzing Australia's reconciliation process, it presented the views of 40 leading authorities, indigenous and nonindigenous leaders, social commentators, politicians, and writers. This was followed by the release of the final report by the Council for Aboriginal Reconciliation—a representative body set up in 1991—which called for a range of measures on symbolic and action-oriented aspects of Aboriginal-affairs policy.

A May ceremony at the Sydney Opera House during Corroboree 2000 brought together all interested groups for the formal

---

AUSTRALIA • Information Highlights

Official Name: Commonwealth of Australia.
Location: Southwestern Pacific Ocean.
Area: 2,967,896 sq mi (7 686 850 km²).
Population (2000 est.): 19,169,083.
Chief Cities (June 30, 1997 est., metro. areas): Canberra, the capital, 309,500; Sydney, 3,934,700; Melbourne, 3,321,700; Brisbane, 1,548,300.
Government: *Head of state,* Elizabeth II, queen; represented by Sir William Deane, governor-general (took office February 1996). *Head of government,* John Howard, prime minister (took office March 1996). *Legislature*—Federal Parliament: Senate and House of Representatives.
Monetary Unit: Australian dollar (0.5226 A$ equals U.S.$1, Nov. 28, 2000).
Gross Domestic Product (1999 est. U.S.$): $416,200,000,000 (purchasing power parity).
Economic Indexes (1999, 1990 = 100): *Consumer Prices,* all items, 119.1; food, 126.4. *Industrial Production,* 117.2.
Foreign Trade (1999 U.S.$): *Imports,* $69,160,000,000; *exports,* $56,087,000,000.

© Russell Boyce/Reuters NewMedia Inc./Corbis

In mid-March 2000, Britain's Queen Elizabeth began a 16-day tour of Australia. The visit—the queen's 13th to that nation—followed a November 1999 referendum in which Australians had endorsed retaining the British monarchy as the nation's head of state.

meant that Labor failed to make any notable gains in public-opinion polls. The balance of party support continued to fluctuate, suggesting a tight race in the late-2001 general election.

In the search for policy proposals that would be suited to election campaigning, the main parties prepared to offer greater federal funding for schools and hospitals, and improved accommodation for the elderly. A government review of Australia's science capacity suggested comprehensive methods to strengthen the nation's position as a globalized and ideas-based economy, and canvassed a shift toward greater funding for applied science.

presentation of the Reconciliation Council's recommendations. While expressing broad general support, Prime Minister Howard rejected the call for customary law, self-determination, and a treaty, and also was unwilling to offer a national apology for any past wrongs.

Headlines followed the political storm raised when a skeptical report on the so-called "stolen generation," prepared in the office of Minister for Aboriginal Affairs John Herron, was leaked to the media. Referring to the thousands of Aboriginal children removed from their mothers and placed with white families or orphanages, as part of the assimilation policy of earlier decades, the report claimed that because no more than 10% of Aboriginal children were affected, the widely used term "stolen generation" was inaccurate. After some Liberal Party members threatened to rebel, Howard expressed regret for any offense the report had caused.

Politics. At the national congress of the ALP in August, the party endorsed the policy line of federal opposition leader Kim Beazley in his persistent attacks on the GST and other government measures. However, factionalism within the ALP was evident, and this, combined with patchy performances in some ALP-governed states,

Meanwhile, financial experts and business economists were urging all parties to refrain from promising overgenerous spending initiatives, which were seen as likely to erode future budgetary surpluses.

A last-ditch stand by a minority of union leaders—in favor of protectionism as a bulwark against globalization and the closing of many manufacturing enterprises—was lost at the ALP's policy-making conference, when the party's parliamentarians were able to have the proposal defeated, 105 to 82.

Defense and Foreign Affairs. A November report on the public's perceptions of the most appropriate defense role for Australia indicated widespread support for a substantial increase in defense outlays. The report's findings became an element in the comprehensive reevaluation contained in the government's draft paper on longer-term defense strategies. At meetings of the South Pacific Forum and the Asia-Pacific Economic Cooperation(APEC), Howard gave assurances that Australia was ready to continue its role in maintaining regional security.

Foreign Minister Alexander Downer visited Pyongyang to seal diplomatic relations between Australia and North Korea after a 25-year break.

R.M. YOUNGER
Author, "Australia and the Australians"

Sydney—An Olympic City

© Nick Wilson/Allsport

Sydney's hosting of the XXVIIth Olympiad was a sign that this Australian city is a modern, international metropolis. The Olympic Park, above, was built west of Sydney's center, and included arenas for track and field as well as the opening ceremonies.

With its magnificent harbor resplendent in spring sunshine, Sydney, Australia's showcase city, was in a festive mood in September 2000 for the staging of the Games of the XXVIIth Olympiad of the modern era. For Sydneysiders in particular, and Australians in general, the Sydney Games gave a sense of occasion to the nation's long-established love of sport and accompanying hero worship.

The 16-day international sports extravaganza, from September 16 to October 1, attracted 15,000 athletes and officials from 200 countries and 21,000 media representatives as well as an estimated 500,000 visitors. Opulent cruise ships and some of the world's most luxurious yachts were moored in the harbor, adding to the splendor of the occasion. Much of Sydney's everyday life was suspended for two weeks, with many factories and businesses operating with reduced staff and all universities and

schools closed. The latter freed school buses for Olympic transport use. By providing a focus for emotion and patriotism, the Games marked a milestone in Australia's quest for national identity. Thanks to the participation of high-profile Aboriginal sprinter Cathy Freeman, they also proved important in advancing the cause of reconciliation with Australia's indigenous people.

For the 4 million Sydneysiders, it was a long-awaited opportunity to show the world Australia's technological advancement and cultural achievement, and to display the readiness of Australians to remain true to their openhearted traditions. A continent-wide sense of involvement was fostered with the preceding 100-day torch relay—in which the flame kindled on Greece's Mount Olympus began its Australian odyssey at the sacred Aboriginal site Uluru, or Ayers Rock, in central Australia. Thousands of communities in regional and remote parts, as well as the main centers of population, took part in the relay.

In the lead-up to the Games, there were concerns about the ability of Sydney's transport system to handle the crowds, and arrangements for ticket sales brought criticism of the Sydney Organizing Committee for the Olympic Games (SOCOG) at a time when revelations about some members of the International Olympic Committee (IOC) generated publicity adverse to the Olympic movement. However, the Games were handled competently. Every aspect of the staging of the Games, and Sydney's attention to forestalling potential problems, brought praise.

Almost 50,000 volunteers were enlisted for the countless courtesy tasks that smoothed the way for athletes, officials, media representatives, and visitors, and helped provide a pervading air of friendship and goodwill. In all, nearly 6 million tickets were sold to Olympic events in Sydney—a record total.

Preparation and the Venues. For seven years, SOCOG had been preparing for the event. Ample funds were allocated. The main venues and facilities were built for the 28 sports at a cost of Australian (A)\$3 billion. Most sites were within the 1,870-acre (757-ha) Olympic Park in the suburb of Homebush Bay, about 9 mi (14 km) west of the city's heart. The park's centerpiece was the 110,000-seat Olympic Stadium, the arena in which track-and-field events and the opening and closing ceremonies were conducted. The 14-story structure, costing A\$690 million, took 12,000 tons of structural steel and 10,000 tons of reinforcing steel as well as 3 million cu ft (84 951 m³) of concrete. Its two enormous arching roof structures of translucent polycarbonate were designed to shelter the stadium, while minimizing shadows and harsh light for competitors, spectators, and television cameras.

Other venues within Olympic Park included the SuperDome, which was used for basketball and gymnastics, and the Dome and Pavilions, with venues

The challenge of transporting more than 500,000 Olympic athletes, reporters, and visitors was eased by a monorail, right, *connecting Darling Harbour to downtown Sydney.*

for volleyball, handball, modern pentathlon, and rhythmic gymnastics. Both were located north of the main stadium. To the south were the Aquatic Centre, for swimming, diving, synchronized swimming, and water polo; the Tennis Centre; the State Sports Centre, for table tennis and Tae Kwon Do; and the field-hockey center. Beyond Olympic Park were facilities for marksmanship, cycling, boxing, fencing, judo, weight lifting, and wrestling, as well as Horsley Park for equestrian events. A train station built to serve the new rail link to Olympic Park was able to handle the arrival of up to 50,000 passengers per hour. At the Olympic Village for athletes and officials—designed for later residential use—meals were prepared according to multiethnic cuisines and served on an unrestricted—"all you can eat"—basis.

Background. Sydney's bid for the 2000 Olympics, made in 1993, was based on the city's buoyant quality and technological expertise. While the Olympic facilities were being built, prosperity was rising, and Sydney led other Australian cities in employment. The city had long since outgrown its onetime role as a shipping port for wool and other rural products. Manufacturing and general commerce had grown steadily, and by the 1960s, Sydney was establishing its place among the world's leading cities. High-rise office blocks reshaped the city skyline, and on the harbor front, one of the world's most notable buildings—the Sydney Opera House, with its soaring white-tiled "sails"—took shape. By the 1990s, Sydney was welcoming more than 2 million visitors annually. New strength as an international tourism and trade center hastened its progress in world

© Adam Pretty/Allsport

financial markets. A greater maturity in outlook, and in the arts and education, was evident. The city's six universities had a total enrollment of 90,000 full-time and 45,000 part-time students.

Sydney owed its founding in 1788 to two factors. These were Captain James Cook's defining voyage along Australia's east coast in 1770 and the loss of Britain's American colonies in 1783, which led to London's decision to establish a penal colony in the southern continent. The settlement was established at Sydney Cove on the harbor's southern shore, about 3 mi (5 km) from the harbor's entrance. In the 19th century, Sydney prospered as a port and trade center. Throughout, Sydney drew strength from its role as a commercial channel as well as being the political and administrative capital of New South Wales, a state almost twice the size of California. Gold discoveries in 1851 quickened the pace of growth at a time when Pacific commerce was developing, and in the 1870s a regular shipping link with San Francisco was added to the British lines that continued to handle the bulk of the port's freight.

In May 1908 more than 500,000 people flocked to harborside vantage points to welcome the U.S. Navy's 16-ship squadron with a 15,000-man complement during its extensive Pacific cruise. Five years later, Sydney became the base for Australia's own fleet. By the 1930s, Pan American Airways had developed the first San Francisco/Sydney airmail and passenger service, strengthening American links.

Domestically, the opening of the Sydney Harbour Bridge in 1932 gave road and rail access to North Sydney and encouraged further suburban expansion. World War II strengthened contact with the United States when American troops and supplies poured in to assist in the defense of Australia. And postwar, a transforming impact came with the big influx of refugees and migrants from Europe after the 1950s and from Asia after the 1980s. The result was the emergence of a multiethnic society in which at least 15 languages—other than English—are spoken. In addition, the steady influx of young people from the state's rural areas brought fast-paced population growth to the city. Sydney now has 62% of the 6.4 million people of New South Wales, and more than one-fifth of Australia's 18.7 million people. Included are some 35,000 Australians of indigenous origin.

Olympic Events. Images drawn from Aboriginal lore as well as icons of modern Australia blended as the spectacular opening ceremony of the 2000 Games offered a flight of fancy and humor expressing Australia's uniqueness. The spirited, hour-long show involved 12,697 performers, a backstage crew of 4,600, and a price tag estimated at A$5 million. The spectacle of 120 horseback riders holding aloft an Australian flag and cantering across the stadium was the prelude to a series of tableaux interpreting many of the strands woven into Australian society. The climax was the arrival of the Olympic flame at the end of its three-month relay run. On entering the stadium, the torch was passed through the hands of six Australian female athletes for a final stadium lap. The last of the six, Aboriginal runner Cathy Freeman, emerged from the shadows to accept the honor of lighting the cauldron.

On the final day, after the passing of the Olympic flag to the next host city, Athens, the grand closing ceremony brought together some of Australia's international celebrities, including Elle MacPherson and Greg Norman, to participate with 7,000 performers at center stage. Performers included 1,000 ballroom dancers, two 100-voice choirs, and 48 trumpet players leading a fanfare. The Games closed on a dramatic note when, as the Olympic flame was extinguished, an F-111 jet swept past, its afterburner glowing orange as it symbolically carried the flame away into the night sky. Along the Parramatta River, this was the moment to send a river of lightning racing on its way, with grand fireworks exploding successively from a series of six barges in a torrent of fire that burst over the Sydney Harbour Bridge in a sky-filling crescendo.

Ancillary aspects of the official Olympic effort included the Arts Festival, which, like the Games, was on a lavish scale. The first of its 53 productions and 50 exhibitions began on September 2 with a wide range of performing-arts events, most of which ran throughout the month. At the Sydney Opera House, there were operas and concerts. At the same time, 16 visual-arts exhibitions began seasons of six weeks or more. They included "Australian Icons," at the Art Gallery of New South Wales, and "Sydneysiders," at the Museum of Sydney.

Australians were strengthened in their belief that Sydney's efforts as Olympic host had demonstrated a mature and deeply held pride in the nation's achievements. A commentator was moved to write that the Games had turned out to be "a celebration of life, love, hope, optimism, courage, pride, patriotism, and can-do."

See SPORTS—The XXVII Summer Games.

R. M. YOUNGER

Austria

Austria began the year 2000 in a state of political deadlock, as the nation's major parties were unable to agree on the establishment of a new coalition government after the national elections held in October 1999.

Political Deadlock. In the 1999 elections, Austria's Social Democratic Party (SPÖ) received 33.15% of the vote and 65 seats in the Austrian Parliament; the Christian Democratic Austrian People's Party (ÖVP) received 26.91% and held its 52 seats; the Freedom Party of Austria (FPÖ) extended its winning record under the leadership of Jörg Haider, also receiving 26.91% of the vote and 52 seats; and the Green Party took 7.4% of the vote. The Liberal Forum, a party established by a splitter faction of liberal FPÖ parliamentarians in 1995 who were dissatisfied with the ideological drift of the party to the right under Haider, received 3.65% and fell below the threshold necessary to be represented in the legislature.

Many observers found the success of the FPÖ disturbing because Haider, a right-wing populist, had made isolated apologetic or ambiguous remarks about National Socialism in the past and openly appealed to Austrian anxieties regarding immigration and the challenges of modernization related to European Union (EU) membership.

Austria's political deadlock was related to preelection promises made by the parties in the SPÖ-ÖVP government, a coalition that had ruled the country since 1986. The SPÖ said it would not consider a coalition government with the FPÖ under any circumstances, and the ÖVP promised to go into opposition should it lose its position as the second-largest party in Austria. Although the ÖVP and the FPÖ each finished with 52 seats in parliament, the ÖVP technically finished third—a mere 415 votes behind the FPÖ—and decided to honor its preelectoral promise. This left Austria with no viable parliamentary majority. The SPÖ and the ÖVP did attempt to negotiate a new coalition agreement, but during the course of their failure to do so in January, the ÖVP and the FPÖ began to discuss the conditions under which they might form a coalition government. With their 104 of 183 seats in parliament, they had a sound majority.

In January the 14 other member states of the EU expressed their disapproval of the ÖVP-FPÖ negotiations. They warned that they would not "promote or accept any bilateral contacts at a political level with an Austrian government integrating the FPÖ" and threatened to impose predominantly symbolic sanctions on the traditional bilateral diplomatic level, including no bilateral visits on the ministerial level, and "no business as usual."

This was an unprecedented measure in the EU. The EU member states not only expressed their disapproval of Haider and the FPÖ, they threatened to sanction a member state and intervene in its domestic

On Feb. 4, 2000, a new coalition government was installed in Austria. It included Wolfgang Schüssel (foreground) as federal chancellor and members of the controversial Freedom Party, led by Jörg Haider (driver), in key posts. The coalition came under international fire, including sanctions by the European Union. Haider later resigned as party leader.

affairs, which raised the issue of the sovereignty of member states in the EU.

New Government and Sanctions. The establishment of an ÖVP-FPÖ coalition government on February 4, with ÖVP Chair Wolfgang Schüssel as federal chancellor and FPÖ Vice-Chair Susanne Riess-Passer as vice-chancellor, was accompanied by waves of antigovernment protest in Austria. There also was a considerable international discussion about the implications of the FPÖ participation in the government as well as the EU sanctions, which went into effect.

Advocates of the sanctions justified them as necessary, and emphasized that the EU as a "community of values" could not tolerate the participation of a party such as the FPÖ in an EU government. Critics of the sanctions considered them a rash, sanctimonious, and illegitimate intervention in Austria's domestic affairs. Although the sanctions of the 14 member states of the EU ostracized Austria on a bilateral level, they did not infringe on Austria's rights and obligations as a full member of the EU or the role of Austria in EU bodies. Furthermore, when the 14 member states imposed the sanctions, they did not state the conditions under which they would be lifted. There effectively was no exit strategy.

In late February, Jörg Haider, the most controversial figure in the entire affair, announced his resignation as FPÖ party chairman; Riess-Passer filled his position.

The establishment of the ÖVP-FPÖ government had marked a watershed in Austrian politics. The shift from a center-left to a center-right government ended 14 years of SPÖ-ÖVP coalition governments. It also marked the end of 30 years in government for the SPÖ, the longest-reigning social democratic party in Europe. Furthermore, the shift in government represented the "normalization" of the FPÖ, insofar as it had to abandon its traditional role in the opposition and assume responsibility in the government.

Agreement and Subsequent Developments. In June, a Portuguese initiative eased the quandary of EU sanctions against Austria. Three "wise men"—Martti Ahtisaari, the former president of Finland; Jochen Frowein, a German expert on human rights; and Marcelino Oreja, former foreign minister of Spain and former secretary-general of the Council of Europe—were mandated to report on "the Austrian government's commitment to common European values," and "the evolution of the political nature of the FPÖ." Their report, presented at the beginning of September, exonerated the Austrian government; ascertained that the FPÖ was "a right-wing populist party with radical elements"; and recommended that the sanctions imposed against Austria be lifted. This report and recommendation led to a normalization of Austrian-EU relations.

The domestic situation in Austria slowly began to normalize, and the new ÖVP-FPÖ government began drawing up legislation to address a backlog of structural reform in Austria. Austerity budgets for 2001 and 2002, with the target of a zero deficit for 2002, were passed in October.

In late October, bilateral agreements with Belarus, the Czech Republic, Hungary, Poland, and the United States were concluded under the auspices of the Reconciliation Fund set up by the Republic of Austria to compensate 150,000 former slave laborers. Most of the former slave laborers had been from Central and Eastern Europe and had been forced by Nazi Germany to work in Austria during World War II. The conclusion of these agreements coincided with the beginning of negotiations on compensation for "Aryanization victims" of the Nazi era designed to identify gaps in previous and existing compensation laws.

A Disastrous Fire. On November 11, a fire in a funicular lift that ran in an underground tunnel between the village of Kaprun and Kitzsteinhorn glacier in the Austrian province of Salzburg claimed the lives of 155 people. Many of those killed were young skiers and snowboarders.

LONNIE JOHNSON, *Author*
"Central Europe: Enemies, Neighbors, Friends"

AUSTRIA • Information Highlights

Official Name: Republic of Austria.
Location: Central Europe.
Area: 32,378 sq mi (83 858 km²).
Population (2000 est.): 8,131,111.
Chief Cities (Dec. 31, 1998 est.): Vienna, the capital, 1,606,843; Graz, 240,513; Linz, 189,073; Salzburg, 143,991; Innsbruck, 110,997.
Government: *Head of state,* Thomas Klestil, president (took office July 8, 1992). *Head of government,* Wolfgang Schüssel, chancellor (took office February 2000). *Legislature*—Federal Assembly: Federal Council and National Council.
Monetary Unit: Schilling (15.0821 schillings equal U.S. $1, Dec. 11, 2000).
Gross Domestic Product (1999 est. U.S.$): $190,600,000,000 (purchasing power parity).
Economic Indexes (1999, 1990 = 100): *Consumer Prices,* all items, 126.4; food, 122.7. *Industrial Production,* 137.6.
Foreign Trade (1999 U.S.$): *Imports,* $68,757,000,000; *exports,* $63,408,000,000.

Automobiles

The market for new cars and trucks held firm through the 2000-model year above the all-time-record level of 1999, shrugging off forecasts of an "inevitable" downturn after nearly a decade of strong sales and profits for manufacturers and dealers.

After ten months of 2000, the annualized rate of retail deliveries for the full year stood at a new peak of 17.3 million units. If realized, this would exceed the previous high of 16,958,347 attained in 1999.

New-vehicle-demand levels remained buoyant thanks in part to a strong U.S. economy and related growth in incomes. Prices of 2000 models were held to single-digit increases, and the 1990s phenomenon of vehicle leasing rose in every segment of the market, prompting new-vehicle replacements every two to three years. Interest-rate increases ordered by the Federal Reserve Board failed to stem the brisk auto-sales pace. Historically, as well, presidential-election years have not been recorded as auto-sales deterrents. Promises of tax reductions and health-care-income enhancements again filled the air during the 2000 campaign, creating a buying atmosphere that automakers sweetened with hefty incentives to clear out 2000 models.

Despite the upbeat mood across U.S. auto rows, several challenges awaited the 2001-model year, which began October 1. Market shares of each of the U.S. Big Three auto producers declined in the January–August period, giving up ground to Asian and European brands. Number 2 automaker Ford Motor Company was confronted by an Explorer sport-utility-vehicle (SUV) recall of 6.5 million Firestone tires, which could impact demand of one of its top-selling products, and create a ripple effect on other popular SUVs (*see* SIDEBAR). And, as gasoline prices hovered close to modern-day highs, the potential backlash could see potential new-vehicle buyers choose pre-owned units that are more fuel-efficient (*see* ENERGY—Gas Prices).

General Motors. The decline in market penetration was especially troubling for Number 1 automaker General Motors (GM) Corporation. Headed, as of June 1, by a new president and chief executive officer (CEO), 47-year-old G. Richard Wagoner, Jr., GM was determined to reverse a slide to 28.6% of the total market in the January–October period. This was 0.9 percentage points below the comparable 1999 share,

2001 Pontiac Aztek GT

and extended a downturn of nearly 20 points in the past two decades. Ford's market share fell 0.5 points to 24.3%, and DaimlerChrysler's share fell 1.1 points to 15.7%.

Like Ford and DaimlerChrysler, GM looked to foreign-expansion opportunities in 2000 to bolster global positions against any future decline in the North American market. This quest took on a highly competitive tone, as both Ford and GM bid for the Korean automaker Daewoo Corporation, and Ford purchased the British SUV producer Land Rover Group Limited from BMW AG without the German automaker's notifying GM or DaimlerChrysler that Land Rover was for sale.

But at home the three automakers, for the first time in the century-long history of the U.S. auto industry, organized an industry-owned venture. Covisint, as it was named, went into business on the Internet late in 2000, as an exchange for ordering and purchasing auto parts by automakers from their suppliers. Cleared under the antitrust laws in mid-September by the Federal Trade Commission (FTC), Covisint planned to go on-line with supplier transactions both from its founders—GM, Ford, and Daimler-Chrysler—and with overseas-based competitors Toyota, Nissan, and Renault as participants in an electronic bazaar.

On-line Sales. The Internet played an increasingly prominent role in auto sales, as well as in supplies and parts. Sales-oriented Web sites were springing up almost monthly. Ford launched a pilot operation allowing customers to order vehicles on-line from the automaker and some of its Canadian dealers. GM began a similar pilot site among seven Oldsmobile dealers in the Twin Cities of Minneapolis/St. Paul.

Ford—in a departure designed to heal wounds created by a rescinded initiative to create urban "collections" of factory-owned dealerships—created FordDirect.com. It is 80% owned by dealers and 20% by the

131

manufacturer, and went into operation in October in San Diego.

Already in operation were such on-line sales sites as CarsDirect.com and Greenlight.com, as well as sales sites established by dealer consolidators, paced by the Number 1 megadealer network, AutoNation, Inc. The original "dot coms" in auto sales were generators of leads to dealers, such as Auto-By-Tel. Now individual dealers also were joining the parade with their own Web sites and "dedicated" sales personnel handling on-line vehicle orders, sales, and deliveries in the dealership or at homes, if customers desire it. Though executives were enthusiastic about the future of the Internet as a sales tool, actual sales transactions, completed entirely via computer, averaged 5% or less for most dealers in 2000.

Global Trends. For its part, DaimlerChrysler became the second European-based automaker to buy a portion of a Japanese automaker. Formed in 1998 when Daimler-Benz AG acquired Chrysler Corporation, DaimlerChrysler obtained 34% of the ailing Mitsubishi Motors Corporation and proceeded to assign German executives to the company late in 2000. It also bought 10% of Korea's Hyundai Motor Company. In a move signifying that the former Daimler-Benz was fully in control of the Chrysler Corporation it acquired in 1998, former Chrysler Chairman and CEO Robert J. Eaton retired March 31, 2000, as co-CEO of DaimlerChrysler. Juergen E. Schrempp, his co-CEO, became the sole CEO.

Also underscoring the stepped-up globalization of the auto industry, DaimlerChrysler announced plans to build a second assembly plant in Vance, AL, next to its four-year-old M-class (SUV) plant. Honda said it would open an Odyssey minivan plant in Lincoln, AL, in late 2001. Ford followed GM in spinning off its parts plants into a separate corporate entity, called Visteon Corporation. GM had divested its parts plants in 1999 into Delphi Automotive Systems. Nissan said it would build its second U.S. assembly plant near Jackson, MS.

Reflecting the buoyant demand for high-profit truck models—such as SUVs, minivans, and pickups—worldwide revenues increased in the second quarter from 1999 levels to $48.7 billion at GM and $44.5 billion at Ford. DaimlerChrysler reported $80.8 billion in first-half revenues, up 17% from the prior year.

The 2001/2002 Models. All-new and revamped SUVs and minivans were dominating the 2001–2002 field for both U.S. and overseas-based producers. Many of the new SUVs combined features adapted from passenger cars and minivans, such as softer suspensions, removable rear seats for extra room, and all-wheel drive. In the compact segment, all-new SUVs included the Ford Escape and its sibling Mazda Tribute, the Hyundai Santa Fe, and the "hybrid" Pontiac Aztek. The Escape was Ford's first small SUV in a fast-growing segment.

DaimlerChrysler, seeking to retain the flagship position in the minivan arena it created in the early 1980s, unveiled restyled models for the Chrysler Voyager, Town & Country, and Dodge Caravan lines. The Voyager name was transferred to Chrysler from Plymouth. The latter would be dropped as a nameplate at the end of 2001, after 73 years in existence.

Chrysler minivans introduced a power-oriented rear tailgate and an easily removable row of third seats. Unlike the Honda Odyssey, they do not fold onto the floor. Technical "breakthroughs" were expected when Chevrolet rolls out its Avalanche hatchback crew cab for 2002, and Buick checks in with the Rendezvous minivan SUV. Cadillac was planning a 2002 roadster, tentatively called the Evoq, and Oldsmobile will debut a restyled Bravada SUV in the full-size segment. Adding new models to strengthen increasing market shares in the North American market, Toyota introduced the Sequoia full-size SUV, while Honda redesigned the top-selling Civic subcompact.

Motoring Briefs. Ford linked half of its executives' future bonuses to customer-satisfaction ratings. . . . Lincoln became the first domestic brand to offer free maintenance during the warranty period. Ford dropped the Mercury brand in Canada.

MAYNARD GORDON, *Senior Editor*
Ward's Dealer Business Magazine

Courtesy, DaimlerChrysler

2001 Chrysler Town & Country Limited

The Ford-Firestone Tire Story

Two of the most venerable names in the century-old history of the automobile industry—Ford and Firestone—became embroiled in a far-ranging consumer-safety crisis during the summer of 2000.

The Crisis and Responses. Sudden failures of Firestone tires on Ford's highly popular Explorer sport-utility-vehicles (SUVs) were blamed for rollovers that caused 119 deaths in the United States and 47 in Venezuela, and more than 500 serious injuries. Disclosure of the rollover problem, which began as early as 1996, caused Bridgestone/Firestone, Inc., to recall an estimated 6.5 million Firestone light-truck tires on Aug. 9, 2000. Most were original equipment on Explorers.

Responding quickly to what Ford Motor Company perceived might be a threat to the integrity of the Explorer—and other Ford vehicles—in the eyes of the public, the company offered to take Firestone tires used on Explorers and to replace the tires—free of charge—at its dealerships or tire stores. As Ford and Firestone embarked on a touchy and highly publicized exercise in apologies to a worried audience of Explorer owners, friction between the two companies reached the boiling point as to whether to blame the tire or the vehicle—or both—for the rollover epidemic.

Exchanges between executives of the two companies moved from the private to the governmental level when House and Senate Commerce Committee subcommittees conducted hearings in September on what action should be taken to give the National Highway Traffic Safety Administration (NHTSA) greater authority to increase the safety of tires, and to monitor accident data known to the manufacturers, but not reported to public agencies.

The role of the Ford Motor Company in the developing "tiregate" scandal was complicated at the top-executive level by the fact that its chairman, William Clay Ford, Jr., is the great-grandson of company founder Henry Ford, and also is the great-grandson of Harvey Firestone, whose tire company has supplied Ford Motor Company with tires since 1906.

Jacques A. Nasser, Ford president and chief executive officer (CEO), undertook the task of explaining the company's position on the tire-replacement offer, and the issue of who was to blame for the rollovers. He appeared on numerous television commercials and ordered three Explorer and light-truck plants closed for three weeks to assure that dealers and tire stores had enough tires on hand to accommodate Explorer owners. Testifying before a House Commerce subcommittee, whose members joined U.S. senators in lambasting both companies for withholding data about earlier rollovers, Nasser called the cause "a tire issue and not a vehicle issue."

For his part, Bridgestone/Firestone chief Masatoshi Ono apologized "to the American people," but denied that tire failures alone were at fault. He and his successor-to-be at the tire-maker, John Lampe, admitted internal cracks could develop in tires, thus causing tread separations, but they pointed fingers at an Explorer suspension or wheel problem as a root cause of the tire breakdown. Lampe—named to replace Ono in October, after a 27-year career with the Firestone and its Japanese parent, Bridgestone—promised to rebuild the company's reputation while at the same time keeping pressure on Ford, Firestone's top customer, to "share the blame" for tire failures.

Federal Legislation and the Effect. As a result of legislation passed by Congress and signed by President Bill Clinton with minimal delay after the committee hearings, the NHTSA was given three months to write a rule on reporting sales of recalled tires; a year to require low-tire-pressure warning devices; 18 months to write tire-safety and -labeling standards; and two years to develop a handling test for rollovers. More severely, the new measure imposes criminal penalties on executives—of any industry—who knowingly make defective products that result in deaths or injuries. Rarely in NHTSA's sometimes controversial 30-year history had the agency's powers been so broadened without formidable auto-industry opposition. In the public hearings, the Republican chairmen of the inquiring committees, however, chastised Ford and Firestone officers and the new administrator of NHTSA, Dr. Sue Bailey, for their conduct after the first disclosures of the rollover deaths.

As for Ford, fears that the Explorer would "take a hit" that might rub off on sister vehicles proved premature. Sales of the leftover 2000 model did slow down in October, ebbing about 16% from the previous year to 29,611 vehicles. However an "all-new" and "safer" restyled 2002 Explorer was on the road for a marketing rollout in April 2001, with a significant industry first: Purchasers can choose any brand of tires on an optional no-cost basis.

MAYNARD GORDON

Azerbaijan

Azerbaijan continued to pursue its pro-Western policy in 2000, but civil rights remained weak under President Heydar Aliyev's authoritarian government. Major issues in 2000 were the president's health and questions of succession, tense relations with Russia and Iran, electoral fraud in the November parliamentary elections, continuing pipeline negotiations for the transport of Azerbaijan's oil, economic stagnation, and fruitless talks over Nagorno-Karabakh and other Azerbaijani territories occupied by Armenian forces.

Domestic Politics. Despite Azerbaijan's application to join the Council of Europe, which has high democratic requirements for membership, the government continued to intimidate both the opposition and the press. Parties and demonstrations were banned, newspaper editors were imprisoned, papers were shut down, and opposition candidates were excluded from participation in the November elections. Under pressure from street demonstrations and Western governments, the electoral law was ultimately liberalized, and most parties were eventually permitted to participate in the elections. In July, Aliyev granted political amnesty to 87 former oppositionists. Yet, the political opposition, despite its ability to upset the government, has been hampered by its own disunity. Agreements between opposition parties were overshadowed by a split in the major opposition movement—the Popular Front. To make matters worse, its leader and most prominent opposition leader, Abulfaz Elchibey, died in August while undergoing treatment for prostate cancer in Turkey.

President Heydar Aliyev casts his ballot during parliamentary elections on Nov. 5, 2000. The official election results would assure President Aliyev a compliant parliament.

On November 5, new parliamentary elections were held. Unofficially, the two strongest contenders were the opposition Musavat Party and the Popular Front, but official results gave the ruling Yeni (New) Azerbaijan Party (YAP) more than 70% of the vote. The Musavat did not overcome the 6% barrier needed to ensure representation. As of November 15, the YAP won 62 seats, and the independents received 26 from the 100 allocated to single-mandate constituencies. (Twenty-five additional seats are allocated to party lists). The results, unanimously condemned by opposition parties, assured President Aliyev a compliant National Assembly. It was likely that President Aliyev's son would be elected speaker of parliament and would succeed his ailing 77–year-old father.

Economic Situation. Azerbaijan moved toward a positive trade balance and had $200 million in its oil fund. In 2000, inflation was officially 4% to 5%, and gross domestic product (GDP) growth was between 6% and 8%. But oil investments did not improve an economy still dogged by a budget deficit of $93 million—or 1.7% of GDP—much of it due to military expendi-

---

AZERBAIJAN • Information Highlights

Official Name: Azerbaijani Republic.
Location: Southwest Asia.
Area: 33,436 sq mi (86 600 km²).
Population (2000 est.): 7,748,163.
Chief Cities (January 1990 est.): Baku, the capital, 1,149,000; Gyanja, 281,000; Sumgait, 235,000.
Government: *Head of state,* Heydar Aliyev, president (took office June 1993). *Head of government,* Artur Rasizade, prime minister (took office November 1996). *Legislature* (unicameral)—National Assembly.
Monetary Unit: Manat (4,552.0000 manats equal U.S.$1, Nov. 17, 2000).
Gross Domestic Product (1999 est. U.S.$): $14,000,000,000 (purchasing power parity).
Economic Index (1999, 1993 = 100): *Consumer Prices,* all items, 10,182.1; food, 9,630.3.
Foreign Trade (1999 U.S.$): *Imports,* $1,620,000,000; *exports,* $885,000,000.

---

tures and support of 800,000 Azerbaijani internally displaced persons (IDPs). Despite President Aliyev's decree in February designed to stem corruption, and a new privatization program launched in March, there was little progress. Sixty percent to 70% of the population remained on the poverty line, and pensions, when paid, averaged only $10-$12 dollars per month. A serious summer drought exacerbated the nation's economic ills.

Foreign Policy. The manipulation of the November elections raised questions about Azerbaijan's admission into the Council of Europe. Relations with Turkey were strengthened with the visit of new Turkish President Ahmed Necdet Sezer in July. Turkey signed agreements to train the Azerbaijani army and supply it with direct military assistance.

Azerbaijan's relations with Russia remained tense, with disputes over the status of the Caspian Sea and Russian claims that Azerbaijan was sheltering Chechen "terrorists." Russia continued to support Armenia in the dispute over Nagorno-Karabakh, and opposed Azerbaijani- and U.S.-supported oil- and gas-pipeline routes from Central Asia and Baku, across South Caucasia. A series of agreements between Azerbaijan, Georgia, and Turkey were signed in 2000, setting the legal and financial conditions for constructing the Baku-Ceyhan oil pipeline.

President Aliyev visited the United States twice in 2000 while U.S. oil companies continued to press for the removal of legal restrictions on U.S. trade with Azerbaijan. Meanwhile, relations with Iran remained tense. The Azerbaijani foreign minister complained in May of Iranian mistreatment of the large Azerbaijani population living in northern Iran.

STEPHEN F. JONES, *Mount Holyoke College*

Baltic Republics

The year 2000 in the Baltic region was dominated by domestic politics in two of its three countries. Latvia was racked by governmental crisis, while elections in Lithuania established a major power shift. Economically, the region was in recovery from the effects of Russia's 1998 financial crash, but Lithuania's economy lagged well behind the others, impacting the election process in that country. Finally, it was a banner year for foreign relations in the Baltic region, as all three countries made efforts to join the European Union (EU) and gain North Atlantic Treaty Organization (NATO) membership.

Politics. By the end of 1999, the furor over the language issue—which had roiled Latvian politics during the year—had barely subsided when Prime Minister Andris Skele's government found itself in crisis. In December 1999, after much controversy, President Vaira Vike-Freiberga signed a new language law—somewhat more accommodating to the large Russian-speaking minority. The new legislation would become effective in September 2000. Then, early in 2000, the government was rocked by allegations that several cabinet ministers were involved in a pedophilia scandal. A parliamentary investigation was launched.

Complicating the governmental crisis, Economics Minister Vladimirs Makarovs fired the chief of the state privatization agency over a major policy difference. In April, Prime Minister Skele dismissed Makarovs from the cabinet, causing two of the three political parties to withdraw support from the ruling coalition over the underlying privatization issue. Facing his government's collapse, as well as the impending report on the sex scandal to be released the next day, Skele resigned on April 12. The subsequent report was anticlimatic, based largely on circumstantial evidence, but the unfounded allegations had done their damage. The president then invited Andris Berzins, the mayor of Riga, Latvia's capital, to form a new government. Prime Minister Berzins, his cabinet, and his pro-Europe and proprivatization governmental program quickly gained approval of a parliamentary majority. By fall, however, the government had to again cope with controversy—as well as criticism from Russia—over implementation of Latvian as the official language.

In Lithuania, two sets of elections generated a significant political and generational shift in power. The outcome of the local elections in March signaled the decline of the ruling Homeland Union/Lithuanian Conservatives, as the party went from nearly 500 local council seats to less than half nationwide. Conversely, radical and populist parties made substantial gains, a harbinger of the fall elections. One such party was the Lithuanian Farmer's Party, resembling a social-protest movement espousing protectionist trade policies for agriculture, and a skeptical attitude toward EU integration. In the run-up to the October parliamentary elections, polls reflected a popular backlash

BALTIC REPUBLICS • Information Highlights

Nation	Population (in millions)	Area (sq mi)	Area (km²)	Capital	Head of State and Government
Estonia	1.4	17,462	45 226	Tallinn	Lennart Meri, president / Mart Laar, prime minister
Latvia	2.4	24,938	64 589	Riga	Vaira Vike-Freiberga, president / Andris Berzins, prime minister
Lithuania	3.6	25,174	65 200	Vilnius	Valdas Adamkus, president / Rolandas Paksas, prime minister

against the ruling coalition over economic conditions and delayed social reforms. This was confirmed by the election. The winners of the party vote, under proportional-repre-sentation rules, were the left Social Demo-cratic Party (31%), the New Alliance/Social Liberals (19.5%), and the Liberal Union (17%). The conservatives won 8.6% of the vote and fell from power.

Lithuania's President Valdas Adamkus invited former Prime Minister Rolandas Paksas, now of the Liberal Union, to head a minority government. The Social Demo-crats, excluded from the coalition, went into opposition as the largest faction in parlia-ment. On November 9, the new govern-ment's program won parliamentary approv-al by a narrow margin. Nonetheless, a change in Lithuania's political landscape had taken place, along with a generational shift from older to younger officeholders and from political veterans to the inexperi-enced—with 103 of the 141 deputies never having had legislative experience.

Estonia, in contrast, had a relatively quiet year politically. With a number of economic reforms completed in 1999, Prime Minister Mart Laar's coalition government turned its attention to political reforms, most of which will require constitutional amendments.

Economy. Estonia continued to be the Baltic region's economic success story. Due to the 1998 Russian crisis, 1999 had been Estonia's worst year since regaining inde-pendence. Privatization of state-owned property had nearly been completed during the year, but the economic growth rate was negative, albeit marginally. By June 2000, the recession ended. Aided by rising exports to the West and greater consumer demand, the economy was growing at a rapid pace. Still, unemployment rose among the less educat-ed, and inflation reached 5.4%, due in part to higher energy and food prices.

Latvia's economic progress was more lin-ear. By the end of 1999, economic growth was minuscule; foreign trade was down slightly; and 10% of the population lived below the poverty line, while 67% were clas-sified as "poor." In the first quarter of 2000,

however, growth surged 5.1% on a year-to-year basis. For the first six months, foreign-trade volume was up, as the percentage of trade with EU countries rose. By the end of the third quarter, while inflation driven by world oil prices was 2% higher year to year, unemployment in Latvia decreased to 7.8%.

Lithuania continued to struggle to over-come the effects of the earlier economic cri-sis in Russia, its largest trading partner. In January, unemployment reached 10.8%, a 40% increase over the same period in 1999, and a record high since regaining indepen-dence. Growth was relatively anemic at 1.9% for the first half of the year, during which inflation rose by 2% due to higher energy costs. Foreign trade grew dramatical-ly by midyear, but by summer the number of bankruptcies increased, while the slow eco-nomic recovery was not felt by individuals, whose cash income was down by 7% on a year-to-year basis. The decline in business income was even greater.

Foreign Affairs. The Baltic states com-pleted steps in connection with hopes of joining NATO, while all three found them-selves on track to eventual EU accession. BALTNET, a regional air-surveillance sys-tem based in Lithuania, went on-line in June. In Estonia the Baltic Defense College prepared to graduate its first class of staff officers trained to NATO standards. George Robertson, the secretary-general of NATO, visited Latvia to assess preparations. Lithua-nian troops worked with U.S. military instructors on NATO procedures, and Esto-nia increased its commitment to United Nations (UN) peacekeeping operations.

In the last days of 1999, the EU had invit-ed Latvia and Lithuania to begin accession negotiations, which got under way in the new year. Meanwhile, Estonia forged ahead with the complex process of adjusting its legislation—including its language law—to conform to the requirements of the EU. Symbolic of the Baltic states' reorientation toward the West, late in 2000, Latvia took over the rotating presidency of the Council of Europe.

ROBERT SHARLET, *Union College*

Bangladesh

The year 2000 saw a deterioration in law and order in Bangladesh, which weakened the economy, hindered development, and jeopardized democracy.

Politics. The major political event of 2000 was the formation of a four-party opposition alliance to participate jointly in the national election scheduled for 2001. The major opposition party, the Bangladesh Nationalist Party (BNP), allied itself with the Jatiya Party (JP) of former President Gen. Hussain Mohammad Ershad, as well as with the Jamaat-E-Islami (JI), and the Islami Oikkya Jote (IOJ). This four-way alliance demanded an early election and called *hartals* (strikes) to support this demand.

Early in 2000, the Awami League (AL) government appointed a new chief election commissioner after the former commissioner resigned for health reasons. Although opposition parties had demanded the removal of the former commissioner, they also opposed the new one. Other important political events included a court verdict against former President Ershad in connection with the Janata Tower corruption case. This case was filed initially during the BNP regime and now threatened Ershad's election bid. Meanwhile, the AL government initiated several corruption cases against BNP chief Begum Khaleda Zia and other leaders of the party.

A lawsuit for contempt was brought against Prime Minister Sheikh Hasina Wajed by the opposition, based on her remarks concerning the nation's court system in an interview with the British Broadcasting Corporation (BBC) in August. The prime minister said the court had become a safe haven for criminals and terrorists since it indiscriminately granted bail to the accused. The suit was dismissed in October, with a warning to the prime minister.

Economy. Bangladesh's economy suffered from frequent *hartals*, increased political polarization, and a very slow pace of institutional reforms. Corruption, insecurity, and extortion increased, discouraging capital investment and disrupting economic activities—particularly by the poor.

A controversy over the exploitation of vast natural-gas reserves found in the country has surfaced in recent years. Several foreign energy companies have been interested in this resource and favored exporting it to India. However, the four-party opposition alliance claimed that exporting natural gas would not bring any economic benefit to the country and could lead to a serious crisis.

Social Issues. The Bangladesh government introduced the Public Safety Act in January, but the act did little to improve law and order within the country. Violence was so widespread that many people did not feel safe at work, on the street, or even at home. Nearly 3,000 people were murdered, and several thousands fell victim to criminal activities in the first nine months of 2000.

Corruption at all levels reached new peaks. A foreign panel report claimed that more than $2.3 billion had been drained from government accounts in the first six months of 2000 through corruption in different public sectors. The report identified the nation's law-enforcing agencies as the most corrupt area, followed by local governments and the education sector.

An outbreak of dengue fever in July 2000 claimed more than 100 lives, with some 4,000 cases reported. The government initiated a five-year action plan to combat the disease. In late September and early October, eight districts in the southwest suffered from severe flooding. Four million people were marooned or left homeless by the flood; crop loss was some $111 million.

Foreign Relations. Relations between Bangladesh and Pakistan deteriorated after Bangladeshi Prime Minister Hasina made oblique remarks about Pakistan's role in the Independence War of 1971 at the United Nations Millennium Summit. Despite numerous border clashes, relations between India and Bangladesh remained unchanged. Prime Minister Hasina met with President Bill Clinton in Washington on Oct. 19, 2000.

BIMAL KANTI PAUL, *Kansas State University*

BANGLADESH • Information Highlights

Official Name: People's Republic of Bangladesh.
Location: South Asia.
Area: 55,598 sq mi (144 000 km²).
Population (2000 est.): 129,194,224.
Chief Cities (1991 census): Dhaka, the capital, 3,637,892; Chittagong, 1,566,070; Khulna, 601,051.
Government: *Head of state,* Shahabuddin Ahmed, president (took office October 1996). *Head of government,* Sheikh Hasina Wajed, prime minister (sworn in June 1996). *Legislature*—unicameral National Parliament.
Monetary Unit: Taka (54.1 takas equal U.S.$1, Nov. 19, 2000).
Gross Domestic Product (1999 est. U.S.$): $187,000,000,000 (purchasing power parity).
Economic Indexes: *Consumer Prices* (1998, 1990 = 100): all items, 128.7; food, 130.1. *Industrial Production* (1999, 1990 = 100): 182.1.
Foreign Trade (1999 U.S.$): *Imports,* $7,687,000,000; *exports,* $3,919,000,000.

Banking and Finance

The impact of the 1999 Gramm-Leach-Bliley Act (GLBA) was felt in 2000 as banks merged with securities firms to form financial-services holding companies. The U.S. Congress, meanwhile, debated bankruptcy reform, privacy, and retirement savings, and passed an electronic -signature law. The Federal Reserve raised interest rates, and banking-industry profitability decreased for the first time since 1992.

Legislation. The Electronic Signatures in Global and National Commerce Act, signed into law by President Bill Clinton on June 30, gives digital signatures the same legal standing as those on paper. Consumers now can sign contracts on-line and receive financial disclosure statements and records over the Internet. The act was expected to expand electronic commerce as consumers and businesses made the transition to more Internet and E-mail transactions.

Bankruptcy-reform legislation again proved controversial. The proposed legislation, which would require more bankruptcy filers to use Chapter 13 rules, where debts are repaid rather than eliminated as in Chapter 7, was debated in Congress. President Clinton vetoed the act as passed by the House in October and the Senate in December. Congress adjourned without voting to override the president's veto.

Predatory lending or abusive lending practices where mortgagees are faced with unaffordable payments and are eventually forced into foreclosure were the subjects of Federal Reserve hearings and a joint task force made up of 11 regulatory agencies. The Federal Reserve and other agencies considered how to use the Home Ownership and Equity Protection Act (HOEPA) of 1994 to prevent predatory lending, while bills were introduced to amend the act.

Congress also debated, but did not pass, the Retirement Security and Savings Act of 2000, which would have increased the amount individuals were allowed to contribute annually to their individual retirement accounts (IRAs) and their 401(k) and 403(b) plans. The personal-savings rate for the United States had fallen drastically, and the act was designed to reverse the trend. Another bill that came close to passing allowed banks to pay interest on business checking accounts.

Regulatory Agencies. Alan Greenspan, originally appointed chairman of the Federal Reserve Board in 1987 by President Ronald Reagan, was sworn in for his fourth four-year term on June 20, 2000. President Clinton credited Greenspan with wise leadership in directing the current strong economy. Meanwhile, several appointments to the boards of the Federal Reserve and the Federal Deposit Insurance Corporation (FDIC) were held up by election-year politics. The confirmations of Carol J. Parry and Roger W. Ferguson, Jr., as members of the Federal Reserve Board were delayed, as was Donna Tanoue's renomination as chairman of the board of the FDIC. Two other nominees for the FDIC Board, John M. Reich and Richard C. Houseworth, also remained unconfirmed by the U.S. Senate.

Deposit-insurance reform was the topic of an "options paper" issued by the FDIC in August. The paper presented potential reforms to the system, including doubling the amount of deposits covered by federal deposit insurance. Deposit accounts had been insured up to $100,000. Additional issues included the amount banks should pay for federal deposit insurance, and restructuring of the insurance fund.

The Federal Reserve's Open Market Committee raised interest rates twice. In March the Fed raised the federal-funds rate—the rate commercial banks charge each other for overnight loans—to 6%, the fifth one-quarter-point increase since the previous June. In May, with the economy not slowing down enough and inflation still feared, the Fed boosted the federal-funds rate by half a point to 6.5%, the largest increase in five years. The Fed also raised the discount rate—the rate at which banks borrow from the Federal Reserve—a half point to 6%.

Court Cases. At the end of June, the U.S. District Court for the Northern District of California ruled that banks could require noncustomers to pay surcharges at automated-teller machines (ATMs). The court said that any local laws or referendums restricting surcharges were a violation of the National Banking Act and the Home Owners Loan Act.

In Washington the federal government's antitrust case against MasterCard and VISA opened in June. The Justice Department's case revolved around its belief that MasterCard and VISA had restricted credit-card competition by forbidding member banks from issuing competing brands, and had delayed adoption of smart-card technology. Meanwhile, MasterCard and VISA also faced a class-action suit brought by mer-

Douglas A. Warner III (left), chairman and chief executive officer (CEO) of J. P. Morgan, and his counterpart at Chase Manhattan Corporation, William B. Harrison, Jr, announced the pending merger of their two major banks in September 2000.

chants who objected to being required to accept Visa Check and MasterMoney debit cards if they accept those particular brands of credit cards.

Mergers. The number of major bank mergers increased, as did mergers with securities firms, following passage of GLBA. In January, Charles Schwab Co., a leading discount-brokerage firm, announced creation of the first financial conglomerate under the new law. With its acquisition of U.S. Trust Corporation, one of the nation's leading wealth-management firms, Schwab reached its goal of being able to offer all investors, both new and high net worth, investment and wealth-management services. Two foreign financial institutions also expanded their base in the United States. UBS's acquisition of PaineWebber Incorporated in July was followed by Credit Suisse Group's purchase of Donaldson, Lufkin & Jenrette, Inc. in August. With the Swiss banks UBS and Credit Suisse being among the largest banks in the world, the globalization of the financial-services industry continued.

In September, Citigroup, one of the nation's largest financial-services companies, acquired Associates First Capital Corporation, the nation's largest consumer-finance company. Meanwhile, Chase Manhattan Corporation and J.P. Morgan, two of the top U.S. banks, announced a merger. Together, Chase, a leader in consumer and business banking, and Morgan, a powerful name in investment banking, form an institution with almost $700 billion in assets. In October, FleetBoston Financial Corporation bought Summit Bancorp, the

largest independent New Jersey bank, to expand its share of the market in that state. Within days, Firstar Corporation of Milwaukee announced its acquisition of U.S. Bancorp of Minneapolis, thus creating a Midwest bank with branches in 24 states. Then, in November, two other Midwest banks—Fifth Third Bancorp of Cincinnati, and Old Kent Financial of Grand Rapids, Michigan—agreed to merge

Other mergers having an impact on bank customers involved the automated-teller networks, an industry now dominated by several regional organizations. In October, Concord EFS, Inc., owner of the MAC network, acquired Star Systems, Inc., and Pulse EFT Association bought Money Station. The MAC-Star merger created the largest regional ATM network, with 195,000 ATMs.

Bank and Thrift Profitability. The commercial-banking industry's earnings totaled $53.4 billion for the first nine months of 2000, off 1.4% from the same period in 1999. The second quarter, however, produced the lowest quarterly earnings since the second quarter of 1997, as a few large banks reported higher overhead expenses and loan-loss provisions as well as slower growth in noninterest income. In addition, the industry's return on assets fell below 1% for the first time since 1992.

The number of banks continued to decline, with a total of 8,375 in September. There were 344 banks absorbed by mergers, and 140 new banks chartered in the first nine months. By October, five commercial banks had failed. The thrift industry reported reduced earnings of $2.6 billion in the third quarter, although noninterest income, including fee income, was up $564 million from a year earlier. The number of savings institutions stood at 1,613 in the third quarter, with 35 savings institutions being acquired by commercial banks in the first nine months, and eight converting to commercial-bank charters.

ANN KESSLER, *American Bankers Association*

Belarus

The year 2000 saw a general tightening of repression in Belarus. The major event was the parliamentary election of October 15, which many observers regarded as a prelude to the anticipated presidential election of 2001. The opposition parties, for the most part, boycotted the election, but some politicians chose to stand on an individual basis.

© Itar-Tass/AP/Wide World Photos

Although Russia's new president, Vladimir Putin, conferred with Belarus' President Aleksandr Lukashenko (right) in Minsk in May, implementation of the planned union of the two nations appeared to be protracted in 2000.

However, the Electoral Commission disqualified more than 60 democratic candidates for alleged registration irregularities. On October 15 the official figures indicated a turnout of 60.6%, with more than 40 deputies elected outright.

Politics. On October 29 a runoff election took place, with a 52% turnout that was valid in all 56 constituencies. Ninety-seven deputies were elected to the 110-seat parliament. The Organization for Security and Co-operation in Europe (OSCE) called upon its Advisory and Monitoring Group (AMG), in Minsk, which declared the elections undemocratic. The AMG has tried to develop a dialogue between the government of President Aleksandr Lukashenko and the opposition. Prerequisites for such a discussion remained the end of political repressions, a more powerful legislature, elections that conform to democratic standards, and access of opposition forces to the state media. None were forthcoming.

The opposition held several protest marches during the year. On March 25, on the annual march to remember the 1918 independent state, scores of demonstrators and several journalists, including Russian television crews, were arrested. The largest such march—a commemoration of the 1986 Chernobyl nuclear-power disaster—attracted more than 10,000 people on April 26. On June 29 more than 1,500 delegates met in Minsk for an All-Belarusian Congress, which adopted an Independence Act. The latter legislation emphasized the importance of independence and state sovereignty. Lukashenko responded with a Congress of Soviets, with 2,500 delegates on September 29.

In February, Prime Minister Sergey Ling was replaced with Vladimir Yermoshin, a native Russian. In May, former Prime Minister Mikhail Chigir was tried for alleged embezzlement of funds, and fined $220,000, with a three-year suspended sentence.

Economy and Union With Russia. Under President Lukashenko, Belarus continued to suffer a decline in living standards. In real terms, the average salary was only $35 a month in 2000, and pensions were under $20. Though the gross domestic product (GDP) rose by 4% in the first half of the year, consumer prices rose 45% over the same period, with very high rates of inflation—more than 200% per annum. The government continued to focus on the collective-farm system in agriculture. A new ambitious five-year plan for economic development called for a 5.5% rise in agricultural output in 2001.

Belarus has agreed to coordinate its foreign and economic policies with those of Russia via a single currency (the Russian ruble) for the Russia-Belarus Union. However, the practical implementation of this decision was likely to be protracted. Russia officially approved the October parliamentary elections in Belarus, but appeared less committed to deepening the union.

DAVID R. MARPLES, *University of Alberta*

BELARUS • Information Highlights

Official Name: Republic of Belarus.
Location: Eastern Europe.
Area: 80,155 sq mi (207 600 km²).
Population (2000 est.): 10,366,719.
Chief Cities (January 1999 est.): Minsk, the capital, 1,725,100; Gomel, 503,700; Mogilev, 371,300.
Government: *Head of state,* Aleksandr Lukashenko, president (took office July 1994). *Head of government,* Vladimir Yermoshin, prime minister (took office February 2000). *Legislature*—Parliament: Council of the Republic and Chamber of Representatives.
Monetary Unit: Belarusian ruble (1,180.00 rubles equal U.S.$1, Dec. 31, 2000).
Gross Domestic Product (1999 est. U.S.$): $55,200,000,000.
Economic Index (1999, 1992 = 100): *Consumer Prices,* all items, 4,130,517.6; food, 5,264,124.2.
Foreign Trade (1999 est. U.S.$): *Imports,* $6,664,000,000; *exports,* $5,922,000,000.

Belgium

The year 2000 provided relief from the previous mistrust of government and judicial officials that was brewed by proof of kickbacks, bumbling prosecution of pedophile and murder cases, and dioxin scares.

Royal Wedding. The year opened amid good feelings following the Dec. 4, 1999, marriage of Mathilde d'Udekem c'Acoz, 26, to Crown Prince Philippe, 39. Mathilde's ancestors dwelled in Flanders; she grew up in Wallonia, and later moved to Brussels, where she opened a speech-therapy practice. Her background enhanced the unifying role played by the royal family in the linguistically divided country.

Foreign Affairs. The Belgian government articulated principled positions in two European controversies. When success in Austrian elections allowed the right-wing Freedom Party led by Jörg Haider to become a coalition partner in that nation's government, Brussels officials were outspoken in their criticism. They, along with other members of the European Union (EU), found Haider's views—including statements that suggested sympathy with some of those of the late German Chancellor Adolf Hitler—incompatible with the values held by the EU. Belgium urged and participated in EU measures tending to isolate Austria, measures that were relaxed by the end of the year.

Belgium—like Spain, France, and Switzerland—issued a warrant for the arrest of former Chilean dictator Gen. Augusto Pinochet on the basis of crimes formerly committed against individuals currently resident in Belgium. The aged Pinochet, in exile in Britain, was judged by British Home Secretary Jack Straw to be mentally and physically unfit to stand trial and was returned to Chile. Belgium joined human-rights groups to request the British high court to review Straw's decision. When the high court upheld Straw's decision, the Belgians decided to pursue the case in Chile's courts.

In January a special amnesty was offered to resident illegal immigrants. Borders with neighboring states were closed to prevent influx of illegals from those regions. A Commission for Regularization reviewed the cases of nearly 20,000 illegals who registered. For the most part, legal-resident status was granted to immigrants coming from what were deemed "risk" countries if the immigrants had been resident for six years (five if they had school-age children). The remainder were required to leave Belgium.

BELGIUM • Information Highlights

Official Name: Kingdom of Belgium.
Location: Northwestern Europe.
Area: 11,780 sq mi (30 510 km²).
Population (2000 est.): 10,241,506.
Chief Cities (Dec. 31, 1998): Brussels, the capital (incl. suburbs), 954,460; Antwerp (including suburbs), 447,632; Ghent, 224,074; Charleroi, 202,020; Liège, 187,538; Bruges, 115,991.
Government: *Head of state,* Albert II, king (acceded Aug. 9, 1993). *Head of government,* Guy Verhofstadt, prime minister (took office July 1999). *Legislature*— Parliament: Senate and Chamber of Deputies.
Monetary Unit: Franc (42.8169 francs equal U.S.$1, Dec. 31, 2000).
Gross Domestic Product (1999 est. U.S.$): $243,400,000,000 (purchasing power parity).
Economic Indexes (1999, 1990 = 100): *Consumer Prices,* all items, 119.5; food, 109.3. *Industrial Production,* 110.8.
Foreign Trade (1999 with Luxembourg, U.S.$): *Imports,* $160,770,000,000; *exports,* $176,140,000,000.

A United Nations (UN) report in March criticized Belgium for allegedly violating UN sanctions against the rebel National Union for the Total Independence of Angola (UNITA). To gain money for arms purchases, UNITA sold diamonds through other African countries. Belgium was accused of "extremely lax controls and regulations" regarding the sale of gems that allowed UNITA to gain substantial funds. An old African problem arose when Belgian historian Ludo de Witte asserted that Belgian authorities had arranged the entire assassination of former Congolese Prime Minister Patrice Lumumba in 1961. A government investigation of the matter began.

Fuel Costs. Rising fuel prices led Belgian truckers to block the major boulevard in Brussels in September. Although there was little violence, the city was nearly paralyzed. On September 12 the blockade spread to the port of Antwerp. Government officials have permanently refused to reduce gasoline taxes as a way of reducing fuel costs, claiming that EU rules prevented it. (On September 4, gasoline cost $3.63 per gallon, with 64.5% of that going to taxes). On September 14 the truckers accepted the government's $85 million compensation package that included reduction in social-security taxes.

Other. During the first third of the year, production and investment grew, unemployment fell, and prices rose. In August, Belgium banned import of British pigs and pork products for health concerns. . . . The World Health Organization (WHO) ranked Belgium third among its 191 members in successfully distributing health-care costs.

JONATHAN E. HELMREICH, *Allegheny College*

Biochemistry

During the year 2000, biochemists got a glimpse of the innermost structure of key molecules and made progress toward a dream of using carbohydrates as drugs.

Key Protein. After more than ten years of work, scientists at Stanford University in California determined the three-dimensional molecular structure of RNA polymerase. This molecule of heredity has been called "the most important protein in biology."

RNA polymerase is critical in the transfer of genetic information from genes to proteins. Genes store information for hereditary traits in the form of DNA. But that information remains silent, and has no influence on heredity or body processes, until RNA polymerase acts. It transcribes, or "copies," DNA into strands of messenger RNA. Protein-making machinery in cells then uses the messenger RNA as a pattern or template to make enzymes and other proteins that control biochemical processes in the body. The structure is an image showing the exact location of each atom in RNA polymerase's molecular skeleton. Scientists get molecular structures by beaming X rays through crystals of proteins such as RNA polymerase. Analysis of the resulting X ray shows how the molecule is put together. Roger Kornberg, who headed the research team, predicted that it will help scientists unlock the secrets of biological processes, including how a single fertilized egg cell develops into an animal with hundreds of different types of cells.

Making Carbos. Huge carbohydrate molecules called oligosaccharides could become the next generation of drugs for infections, autoimmune diseases, cancer, and other conditions. The major barrier is the lack of an easy way to synthesize, or make, oligosaccharides. Existing methods take a long time and are expensive.

A team of scientists led by Peter Seeberger at the Massachusetts Institute of Technology (MIT) reported progress toward an automated oligosaccharide synthesizer. The machine may cut the time and cost of making oligosaccharides in the lab. It automatically links together monosaccharides, the building blocks of oligosaccharides, in the order needed to make a specific carbohydrate molecule. Seeberger's team used the device to make one oligosaccharide in 19 hours. It takes about 14 days to make the same compound by hand. The machine produced quadruple the amount per batch,

compared with a synthesis done by hand. The scientists were working to improve the machine so it can be put into wide use.

Sending Signals. Cells that respond to light, hormones, and other external stimuli face a challenge. They must transmit word of the encounter to the cell's interior, so that it can respond. A cell in the light-sensitive retina of the eye would respond with biochemical reactions that the brain interprets as vision. The process of converting such a signal from one form into another is called signal transduction. G-protein-coupled receptors (GPCRs) are the most common signal-transducing molecules in humans. They work in processes ranging from vision to the immune system's battle against disease-causing microbes. For years, scientists dreamed of glimpsing the three-dimensional structure of a GPCR molecule.

Krzysztof Palczewski and associates at the University of Washington, Seattle, determined the three-dimensional structure of the first GPCR. It was rhodopsin, the protein in the retina in the eye that changes light into the biochemical signals that produce sight. The find will help scientists understand GPCRs. It could speed development of new drugs for diseases that occur when GPCRs do not signal normally.

Appetite Switch. Biochemists at Johns Hopkins University announced synthesizing, or making, a chemical compound that turns off appetite in mice, causing weight loss. When injected into mice, the compound—called C75—eliminates their interest in food within 20 minutes. One injection lasts for several days. Researcher Frank Kuhajda said C75 probably does the same in people, but more research will be needed, however, before scientists decide whether to test C75 or a related compound in people.

Insect Antifreeze. Insects that damage food crops survive freezing winter temperatures by making natural antifreeze proteins (AFPs). Canadian scientists identified the chemical structure of an insect AFP. It is about 100 times more powerful than similar proteins found in cold-water fish. Peter Davies, who headed the team of scientists from Queen's University and the University of Alberta, said the discovery may boost food production. Plants, he indicated, could be genetically engineered to produce the protein. It would lengthen growing seasons by enabling plants to survive frosts.

MICHAEL WOODS, *Science Editor*
Washington Bureau, "The Toledo Blade"
and "The Pittsburgh Post-Gazette"

Biography

A selection of profiles of 2000 newsmakers appears on pages 143–154. The affiliation of the contributor is listed on pages 591–94; A few biographies were written by the editors. Included are profiles of:

ASSAD, Bashar al-

Following the death of Syria's President Hafiz al-Assad on June 10, 2000, the nation's establishment rapidly and deftly transferred power to his son, Bashar al-Assad. The constitution was changed to permit his becoming president at 34; the party organs rubber-stamped his claim to power; the Syrian parliament appointed him president; and the appointment was confirmed overwhelmingly by a referendum on June 25. Bashar presided with dignity and competence at his father's funeral, and did not stumble in any way during the first months of his presidency.

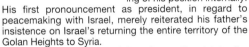

Bashar al-Assad

Immediately, Bashar's top priority was the strengthening of his position internally. His first pronouncement as president, in regard to peacemaking with Israel, merely reiterated his father's insistence on Israel's returning the entire territory of the Golan Heights to Syria.

Background. Bashar al-Assad was thrust into the spotlight in January 1994, when his elder brother Basil, already well along in his apprenticeship for eventual succession to the presidency, died in a car accident. Bashar, then 28, the third of five children and two years younger than Basil, had been of slight importance up to that moment. He was quiet, thoughtful, and scholarly, interested in science, modest in demeanor. He had a strong facial resemblance to his father.

Following high school, Bashar became a medical student at Damascus University, going on to specialized training in ophthalmology at Teshreen Military Hospital. He then moved to London to continue his training as an eye doctor. In these years in London, he was not one of the young, rich, Arab playboys of whom the city had an ample supply. He lived in a modest flat near Oxford Street, and worked at St. Mary's Hospital.

Following Basil's death, Bashar pursued a well-planned, sensible training that had several facets. His shyness melted away, and his competence grew. His military credentials had been nil, but he speedily acquired what was requisite. He attended the military school in Homs, Syria. Passing a crash course as tank battalion commander, he was graduated as lieutenant. Soon he was promoted to major in the Republican Guard, later becoming colonel and brigade commander.

Bashar has been dedicated to moving Syria into the new world of communications. He has struggled passionately to enhance the use of computers and innovative techniques within government departments. In the late 1990s, the Internet became accessible to some Syrians, and satellite dishes were permitted.

On Jan. 1, 2001, the Syrian president married the British-born Asma al-Akhrass, 25, a member of a prominent Muslim Sunni family from Homs.

ARTHUR CAMPBELL TURNER

BENING, Annette

The year 2000 was a good one for actress Annette Bening. Not only was she nominated for an Oscar for best actress in the black comedy *American Beauty*, she also gave birth to her fourth child with actor and director Warren Beatty. Although Hilary Swank took the Academy Award as best actress for her outstanding performance in *Boys Don't Cry*, Bening saw her husband honored with the Irving Thalberg Memorial Award for lifetime achievement at the Oscar presentations.

Bening's baby daughter Ella arrived on April 8, bringing further attention to her personal life with Beatty. The durability of their 1992 marriage has been noted by Hollywood scribes, with Bening, whose previous marriage to theater director J. Steven White ended in divorce, cited as that special bright and attractive woman who finally got bachelor Beatty to settle down. They also have worked together professionally, in *Bugsy* (1991) and *Love Affair* (1994), which Beatty directed.

The tall, imposing actress has earned a reputation as one of Hollywood's best, with a unique aura that enables her to stand out from the crowd. On-screen, she can project a combination of intelligence and sexiness, brains and beauty, as she did in *The American President* (1995), in which she was wooed in the White House by Michael Douglas, portraying the chief executive. In *American Beauty*, demonstrating ability at gallows humor, she played a disgruntled husband's overwrought wife, over-the-edge yet sympathetic, comic yet pathetic. In a sense, she is an updated version of Hollywood actresses who showed such dynamism in films of the 1930s and 1940s.

Annette Bening

Background. Annette Bening was born on May 29, 1958, in Topeka, KS, to insurance salesman A. Grant Bening and homemaker Shirley Bening. The actress grew up in San Diego, CA, where she fell in love with the stage when she saw her first play, Shakespeare's *The Merchant of Venice*. She pursued an acting career by studying at San Diego Mesa College, San Francisco State University, and the American Conservatory Theater.

Her breakthrough came on stage in New York City in 1986 when she won a Tony nomination for her perfor-

143

mance in the play *Coastal Disturbances*. Major film recognition followed with a best-supporting-actress Oscar nomination for playing an unscrupulous con woman in *The Grifters* (1990). Among her other films are *Valmont* (1989), *Postcards from the Edge (1990), Guilty by Suspicion* (1991), *Regarding Henry* (1991), *Richard III* (1995), *Mars Attacks!* (1996), *The Siege* (1998), *In Dreams* (1999), and *What Planet Are You From?* (2000). She has also been active in television.

Bening, Beatty, and their children—Kathlyn, Benjamin, Isabel, and Ella—live in Beverly Hills, CA. In interviews, Bening has made much of her desire to balance her personal and professional lives. She has been able to pursue her life as a mother and wife and still build her reputation as a busy actress, who at 41 was able to both expand her family and further enhance her career. She is also supportive of her husband's projects, including his liberal political activities.

WILLIAM WOLF

BLAIR, Cherie Booth

Until May 20, 2000, the career of Cherie Blair was running in close parallel to U.S. First Lady Hillary Rodham Clinton's in two striking respects. As the loyal wife of Britain's Prime Minister Tony Blair, she was at the epicenter of political power; she also was a strong-willed, successful attorney. But at age 45, Mrs. Blair gave birth to son Leo—the Blairs' fourth child—making history by bringing diapers and baby bottles to 10 Downing Street for the first time since 1848.

Working under her maiden name of Booth, Mrs. Blair is a Queen's Counsel— one of an elite group of High Court advocates. She specializes in employment law and human rights, and although for the most part she tries to adopt a low public profile politically, commentators say she shares her husband's Labour Party beliefs and offers him advice.

Mrs. Blair is determined to combine the roles of mother and lawyer. Only days before the birth of Leo, she was in the High Court, arguing a complex parental-leave case. Less than a month later, she was helping to build up a newly established law firm she cofounded that specializes in human-rights cases.

©Ian Waldie/Reuters NewMedia, Inc./Corbis

Cherie Blair

Her attempts to stay out of the political limelight have not always been successful. In August, writing as Cherie Booth, she published an article in London's *Daily Telegraph* supporting the Blair government's plans to adopt European human-rights legislation. An opposition Conservative Party spokesman alleged that Mrs. Blair had broken a "long-standing convention" that prime ministers' spouses do not use their position to promote their own political agendas. Later it was announced that she intended to chair a fringe meeting on government policy toward woman at the Labour Party's annual conference.

Mrs. Blair and her husband, who also is a lawyer, are fiercely protective of their family's privacy. The couple attempted to prevent news photographers at the christening of baby Leo, and they were reported to be devastated when newspapers reported that police in London's Leicester Square had arrested their teenage son Euan for drunkenness.

Mrs. Blair's voice is scarcely ever heard by the British public, but in court, wearing close wig and gown, she speaks with great fluency, seldom using notes. A colleague has callled her "intellectual and unflappable."

Background. Cherie Booth Blair was born in the borough of Bury on Sept. 23, 1954, the eldest child of Tony Booth, an actor who fathered seven daughters. She was raised in Liverpool.

A Labour Party activist at 16, Mrs. Blair ran for Parliament in June 1983, but lost in the same general election in which her husband won the seat he continues to hold. She has told friends she is proud to be the first British prime minister's wife with her own career, and has been quoted as saying she hopes to become a judge.

The Blairs were married in 1980.

ALEXANDER MACLEOD

BUSH, George Walker

By winning the U.S. presidency in 2000, Texas Gov. George W. Bush became the first son of a president to be elected to the White House since John Quincy Adams, son of John Adams, in 1824. And as even Bush's admirers acknowledged, his father's example set him on the path to the presidency. Yet the Texas governor himself realized that if he were to achieve that goal, he would first have to change the image of the party his father once led.

"I have no stake in the bitter arguments of the last few years," George W. Bush said in accepting his party's nomination. He thus sought to distinguish himself from the confrontational stance of the Republican congressional leadership during Democrat Bill Clinton's presidency. Bush went on to tell the GOP convention that he decried the wall between wealth and ambition on one side and poverty and despair on the other, and vowed: "My fellow Americans, we must tear down that wall."

Following an election that ended without a clear winner and five turbulent weeks of vote recounts in Florida and court decisions, the Texas governor was declared the nation's 43rd president. In his first national address as president-elect, Bush picked up his earlier theme. "I was not elected to serve one party, but to serve one nation," he told the American people on December 13. He then began assembling his cabinet and administration. Many of his nominees had service in the first Bush administration on their resumes.

Background. In charting a new course for the GOP during the presidential campaign, the Texas chief executive had drawn on his own personal and political heritage. George Walker Bush was born on July 6, 1946, in New Haven, CT, where his father, who had just returned from World War II combat as a much-decorated navy flier, was attending Yale University. After graduating from Yale and hoping to make a fortune in the oil business, the elder Bush—together with his wife, Barbara, and their young son—settled in the Texas town of Odessa in 1948 and moved to Midland two years later. Young George had a relatively carefree childhood, marred only by the death of his sister Robin, from leukemia. Bush has another sister, Dorothy, along with three brothers—John, known as Jeb, and now governor of Florida; Neil; and Marvin.

After early schooling in Texas, George W. Bush went East to attend the same elite schools as his father— Phillips Academy in Andover, MA, and Yale. He was not an outstanding student or athlete; his greatest strength was getting along with his fellow students. Unable to make any of the varsity teams at Andover, he settled for winning election as head cheerleader. At Yale, where the future politician majored in history, he again made friends easily and was elected president of his fraternity. In 1968, a few months before leaving Yale, the young man qualified for the Texas Air National Guard. Although critics later contended that he signed up to avoid combat in Vietnam, the future presidential candidate claimed that he joined to become a fighter pilot like his father.

After a period of drifting following college, he entered the prestigious Harvard Business School, earning a master's degree in business administration in 1975. Bush decided to make his start in the business world where his father began, in Texas, at a time when the oil industry was still booming because of the 1973 Arab oil embargo. Politics was still part of his heritage, though, and in 1978 he staged an unsuccessful campaign for a seat in the U.S. House of Representatives.

Meanwhile, he had met and married Laura Welch, a librarian, whom friends credit with being a stabilizing influence on her husband. Their twin daughters, Barbara and Jenna, were born in 1981. Still, when the oil business slumped, Bush drank heavily, until his 40th birthday, when he swore off alcohol entirely. He sold his business and became managing partner of the Texas Rangers baseball team, a position that helped open the way for his political career. As George W. Bush told *Time* magazine, the biggest liability to his running for office in Texas was that people would think he was simply taking advantage of his father's name. "Now I can say, I've done something—here it is," Bush explained.

In 1994 he gained the Republican nomination for governor of Texas and defeated incumbent Democrat Ann Richards in November. During the campaign, he concentrated on four issues—welfare, education, juvenile crime, and legal reform to limit damages from lawsuits. As governor, he soon signed most of his programs into law. Governor Bush also made a vigorous effort to reach out to Hispanic-Americans. He gave his qualified support to bilingual education, and his 1998 reelection-campaign commercials included a Spanish-language song called "Juntos con Bush" ("Together with Bush"). He was rewarded with about half of the Hispanic vote, part of his landslide reelection majority.

Governor Bush's impressive victory in the nation's second-largest state gave his White House prospects a big boost and helped get his candidacy off to a fast start. He collected more endorsements from Republican leaders than any other candidate, and he also raised far more money, enough so that he decided not to accept federal matching funds. Even so, the governor's path to the nomination was not altogether smooth. Rivals charged that he lacked experience, particularly in foreign policy. And he had to overcome a defeat in the New Hampshire primary by Arizona Sen. John McCain by winning a series of Southern primaries that assured him of the nomination.

ROBERT SHOGAN

BUSH, Laura Welch

There was little of the shy, elementary-school librarian evident in Laura Welch Bush's demeanor in 2000 as she hit the campaign trail for her husband, George W. Bush. But give this native Texan—who was to become the nation's new first lady when her husband assumes the presidency in January 2001—a choice between politics or a good book, and she is likely to choose the latter.

Unlike her predecessor, Hillary Rodham Clinton, Laura Bush does not have a political agenda of her own. Her role, she is the first to point out, is to support her husband. And, in a strong but unobtrusive way, that is just what she has done since the two met and married after a whirlwind three-month courtship in 1977. Their relationship, which is often likened to that of a schoolmarm and

Laura Bush

a troublesome child, is one of opposites. He is garrulous; she is quiet. He can be mischievous and arrogant; she reins him in. And in 1986, when his drinking threatened their marriage and family life, she got him to stop.

One of Laura Bush's primary interests, and one that she was expected to pursue as first lady, is education, especially reading. As first lady of Texas since 1995, she launched an early-childhood-development initiative that helps parents and guardians prepare infants and young children for learning before they enter school. She also actively influenced legislation reforming education and launched a book festival that has become an annual fund-raiser for Texas public libraries. Mrs. Bush's other interests include breast-cancer awareness and women's-health issues.

Background. Laura Welch Bush was born Nov. 4, 1946, in Midland, TX. Her father, Harold G. Welch, was a builder, while her mother, Jenna, worked as a corporate secretary in his company. Laura attended schools in Midland, as did her husband, although the two did not know each other well. She received a bachelor's degree in education from Southern Methodist University in 1968, and began teaching in racially mixed elementary schools in Dallas and Houston. She received a master's degree in library science from the University of Texas at Austin in 1973. Laura continued working in the public-school system until her marriage in 1977.

George W. Bush lived in the same apartment complex as Laura in the early 1970s, but their paths did not cross until a summer barbecue in 1977. They were quickly married and, although she had vowed never to make a political speech, she made her first of many in 1978 when her husband unsuccessfully ran for Congress.

Following the birth of twin daughters, Barbara and Jenna, in 1981, Laura devoted herself to being a mother. By 1994, she was back on the political scene when George W. successfully sought the Texas governorship. By 2000, she was a very capable public speaker.

KRISTI VAUGHAN

CHEN Shui-bian

Winning 39% of the ballots cast in Taiwan's second presidential election in March 2000, Chen Shui-bian bested his two rival candidates to become the first opposition-party candidate to take power in a Chinese democracy. His victory brought an end to the 55-year-long rule of the Nationalist Party (Kuomintang, or KMT) on Taiwan. Chen's candidacy was helped by a split within the KMT ranks. This occurred when former President Lee Teng-hui chose his vice-president, Lien Chan, as his favored successor, thereby thwarting the aspirations of former Taiwan Gov. James Soong. Despite Beijing's strenuous attempts to sway the Taiwan electorate away from Chen by threatening to counter any move toward independence with military force, he pulled ahead of Lien, who ran a lackluster campaign, and Soong, who ran as an independent candidate.

Background. Chen Shui-bian was born in poverty on Feb. 18, 1951. His father was an agricultural day laborer, and his mother worked at odd jobs. Chen excelled at school, gaining admission to the prestigious National Taiwan University. He first studied business, but graduated with a law degree in 1975. He joined a local law firm after graduation and became a corporate lawyer. He married Wu Shu-chen, the daughter of a physician.

Chen entered into politics by a side door when he defended a group of dissident protesters on trial for sedition in 1980. Among the defendants was Annette Lu, a U.S.-trained lawyer who, 20 years later, was elected as Chen's vice-president. While Chen lost his case, he became convinced of the validity of the protesters' cause—an independent Taiwan.

The following year, he won a seat on the Taipei City Council, running as an independent because opposition parties were forbidden under the martial law then in effect. In 1985 he lost an election in his native Tainan County, where, in a postelection rally, his wife was struck by a truck. She suffered injuries that permanently para-

©Wally Santana/AP/Wide World Photos

Chen Shui-bian

lyzed her from the chest down. Despite sketchy evidence, Chen remains convinced that the incident was politically motivated.

Sued in a libel case by a Nationalist politician, Chen spent eight months in jail in 1986. Coincident with his release, martial law was lifted, and he immediately joined the now-legal Democratic Progressive Party (DPP). He was elected to the national legislature in 1989 and, in 1994, he became mayor of Taipei—a victory that marked a major milestone in the rise of the DPP. He earned a reputation during his mayoral term as a rather-too-rigid moralizer. This resulted, in large measure, from his campaign to eliminate prostitution in Taiwan.

After a single term in office, Chen lost his reelection bid to the Nationalist candidate, Ma Ying-jeou, who formerly had served as minister of justice and who ran on a popular anticrime and anticorruption platform. The defeat was a sobering experience for Chen that taught him the need for nuance rather than dogmatism. He put this lesson into practice immediately—in a fashion reminiscent of Bill Clinton with the U.S. Democratic Party in the early 1990s and Tony Blair with Great Britain's Labour Party in the late 1990s. In the months before the 2000 presidential election, Chen gradually moved the DPP away from its shrill insistence on an independent Taiwan. While the party platform continued to support an independent Taiwan, Chen abandoned that position in favor of promoting a modus vivendi with the mainland government—a policy he continued to follow after his inauguration in May.

JOHN BRYAN STARR

CHENEY, Richard Bruce

In 1989, when newly inaugurated President George Bush needed someone he could count on to run the Pentagon and get confirmed by the Senate, after his first choice—U.S. Sen. John Tower (R-TX)—was turned down, he selected Dick Cheney to be his secretary of defense. So it was not surprising that when President Bush's son and 2000 GOP presidential nominee George W. needed someone to provide gravitas to the party's national ticket, he chose Dick Cheney to be his vice-presidential running mate.

Cheney's record of helping out Republican presidents goes back to the Gerald Ford presidency, when he helped steer that administration through Washington's post-Watergate shoals. Through the years, on Capitol Hill and in the executive branch, he was the consummate Washington insider. Except for a relatively brief interval during the 1991 Persian Gulf War, he operated without much public exposure.

His nomination as vice-president changed that, of course, and the different treatment was not always easy for Cheney to take. When he was chosen as defense secretary, Democrats joined Republicans in praising him, a mark of their respect for his savvy and their admiration for his civility. But in 2000, with the presidency at stake, the opposition abandoned restraint and pounded away at Cheney's conservative votes while a member of the House of Representatives (1979–89) on issues from abortion to environmental safety to gun control. In view of the tightness of the election, however, it was hard to tell whether the tactic was successful or unsuccessful.

Cheney served as a prime adviser to Bush during the days in November and December when the election outcome was undecided. He maintained that position after the GOP nominee was declared president-elect and began assembling his new administration. The former

defense secretary was expected to be a very active vice-president and a key presidential confidant.

Background. Cheney's conservatism, his friends point out, is deeply ingrained, reflecting his personal beliefs and the fierce individualism of the Big Sky country where he was raised. Richard Bruce Cheney was born in Lincoln, NE, on Jan. 30, 1941. But his family soon moved to Casper, WY, a rough-and-ready oil town, where young Dick became a captain of his high-school football team and president of his senior class. Cheney learned the value of hard work and self-reliance living among ranchers. And he found out about the treacherous vagaries of economic life as he watched his neighbors strike it rich in Casper's oil fields, and then go broke because of the oil industry's relentless economic boom-and-bust cycle.

A scholarship lured the young man East to Yale University, but he dropped out in his second year because of poor grades. He switched to the University of Wyoming, earning bachelor's and master's degrees in political science. He married his high-school sweetheart, Lynne, who would become head of the National Endowment for the Humanities. The Cheneys have two grown daughters, Mary and Elizabeth.

Cheney came to Washington at the start of the Nixon administration as a congressional fellow and soon caught the eye of Donald Rumsfeld, who was running the Office of Economic Opportunity (OEO). He followed Rumsfeld to the Ford White House. After President Ford's defeat in 1976, Cheney returned to Wyoming to run for Congress. Entering the House in 1979, he rose rapidly in the leadership to become chairman of the House Republican Policy Committee and then Republican House whip.

Following President Bush's defeat in 1992, Cheney considered running for president, but dropped the idea in favor of becoming chief executive officer of the Dallas-based Halliburton Company, a leading oil-services and construction firm. He served in that post from 1995 until Bush tapped him for the vice-presidential nomination.

After suffering three heart attacks, Cheney underwent quadruple-coronary-bypass surgery in 1988. He was hospitalized briefly after suffering another heart attack a few weeks after the election. Although doctors pronounced him fit to be vice-president, others expressed concern about his health.

ROBERT SHOGAN

EGAN, Edward Michael

When Archbishop Edward Michael Egan was installed as the ninth archbishop of New York on June 18, 2000, his credentials included 12 years heading the neighboring diocese of Bridgeport, CT, and 23 years in Rome as a student, teacher, and judge on the top Vatican court.

From the start of his tenure in the large and influential New York archdiocese, with its 2.4 million Catholics in three New York City boroughs and seven counties to the north, he made promoting new vocations to the priesthood a priority, something he had had much success with in Bridgeport. Archbishop Egan also made clear right away his support for tax-funded school-tuition vouchers, joining a number of local officeholders who have backed voucher proposals. As his first major appointment in New York on October 11, the archbishop named Bridgeport financial expert Bernard Reidy his delegate for administration and finance, signaling that fiscal affairs of the archdiocese also will be a priority.

Archbishop Egan had served in the New York archdiocese for more than three years in the 1980s as an auxiliary bishop in charge of the Catholic school system before his 1988 appointment to Bridgeport. In the Connecticut diocese, he was known for attracting vocations, overhauling the school system, expanding Catholic Charities, and success as a fund-raiser.

Background. Born on April 2, 1932, in Oak Park, IL, a comfortable Chicago suburb, Edward Michael Egan was one of four children of Thomas and Genevieve Egan. He studied for the priesthood at St. Mary of the Lake Semi-

Archbishop Edward Egan

nary of the Chicago archdiocese in Mundelein, IL, and at the Pontifical North American College in Rome. He was ordained as a priest of the Chicago archdiocese in Rome on Dec. 15, 1957.

He continued studies at Rome's Pontifical Gregorian University, receiving a licentiate in sacred theology in 1958 before going home to Chicago, where he served two years as secretary to Cardinal Albert Meyer. He returned to Rome for doctoral studies in canon law, while serving on the faculty of the Pontifical North American College.

Back in Chicago from 1966 to 1971, he was named secretary to Cardinal John Cody, who appointed him in 1968 to head the newly created Archdiocesan Commissions on Ecumenism and Human Relations. His final Rome assignment lasted from 1971 to 1985 as a judge of the Sacred Roman Rota, which functions as the supreme court of the Roman Catholic Church. In 1982 he was one of six canonists chosen to brief Pope John Paul II on the new Code of Canon Law before it was promulgated the following year. He was ordained a bishop in Rome in May 1985, and assigned as auxiliary bishop of New York under Cardinal John J. O'Connor, whom he was to succeed after the cardinal's death in May 2000. Archbishop Egan was named a cardinal in January 2001.

A cultured and learned man, Archbishop Egan is fluent in Latin and several European languages, plays classical piano, and enjoys attending the opera. He is a polished preacher who often weaves personal anecdotes into his sermons to illustrate a spiritual message.

MARY ANN POUST

FOX QUESADA, Vicente

Vicente Fox Quesada attracted numerous dignitaries to his Dec. 1, 2000, inauguration as Mexico's president. This event was historic, because Fox—as candidate of the center-right National Action Party (PAN)—had ousted from power the Institutional Revolutionary Party (PRI), which had governed Mexico since 1929.

Background. The 6′ 5″ (2-m) tall Fox—whom admirers call the "Marlboro Man" because of his craggy good looks and his love of horseback riding—was born in Mexico City on July 2, 1942, the second of nine children. Fox attended Jesuit schools before entering the Iberoamerican University in Mexico City. There, he concentrated more on his courses in business administration than on politics, although he managed to attend bullfights and play soccer and chess.

His diligence won him a job with Coca-Cola in 1964. The soft-drink company enabled Fox to learn about Mexico while he earned a living "without having to wear a coat and tie". He promoted Coke in the Mexico City area, in the North, and in several Pacific-coast states before rising to the presidency of Coca-Cola for Mexico and Latin America in 1975. Four years later, he left the corporation to concentrate on his family's shoe-production and ranching businesses in Guanajuato State.

Fox excoriated the PRI for corruption and hostility to free enterprise. Yet he entered the political arena in 1988 only at the request of the PAN's presidential nominee, a respected businessman. His party lost the general election that year, but Fox captured a congressional seat—a post he used to attack the PRI regime. In 1995 he won the governorship of Guanajuato. Soon after taking office, Fox launched his bid for the PAN's 2000 presidential nomination.

Fox grew accustomed to denouncing Mexico's authoritarian system even as his party forged mutually beneficial accords with PRI officials. PAN traditionalists, however, berated Fox as an outsider, upstart, and "Northern Barbarian." This term applies to aggressively impatient members of the business community who have joined the party in the past dozen years and disdain dealmaking with the PRI.

To overcome such resistance within the PAN and to gain name recognition, Fox began barnstorming the country, often wearing blue jeans, open-necked shirts, and his signature cowboy boots. He complemented this crowd-pleasing attire with bombastic speeches, garnished with earthy, even crude, words. He continuously castigated the PRI for venality, incompetence, drug trafficking, and a dearth of new ideas.

The "Marlboro Man" also created "Amigos de Fox" (Friends of Fox), a personal organization designed to raise funds, demonstrate his broad appeal, and pressure the skeptical PAN hierarchy to fall in behind him. Old-line chiefs scoured the party's ranks for an alternative; however, the indefatigable Fox swept the nomination unopposed in September 1999.

Fox benefited from a remarkably efficient campaign, success in television debates, the public's acute hunger for change after 71 years of single-party dominance, and a lackluster PRI candidate. As a result, he garnered 42.5% of the vote in a five-way election race.

The new chief executive shares custody of four adopted children with his former wife, Lillian de la Concha Estrada.

GEORGE W. GRAYSON

GORE, Albert, Jr.

Albert Gore's rise in politics was greatly aided by Bill Clinton, who, by selecting Gore as his vice-presidential running mate in 1992, positioned him to seek the presidency. But when Gore ran for the highest office in the land in 2000, the vice-president had to distinguish himself from the president in order to establish his own claim to leadership.

As vice-president, Gore had loyally supported Clinton in the midst of the scandals that plagued him. But as a presidential candidate, Gore pointedly promised to "take my own values of faith and family to the presidency." And just before his nomination, he selected as his running mate U.S. Sen. Joseph Lieberman of Connecticut, who had been the first prominent Democrat to publicly criticize Clinton for his behavior in the Monica Lewinsky affair, which had led to the president's impeachment.

Background. Long before he separated himself from Clinton, Gore had moved out of the shadows of a famous father to launch his own political career. Albert Gore, Jr., was born in Washington, DC, on March 31, 1948, to Pauline La Fon and Albert Gore, Sr., then in his fifth term as a Democratic congressman from Tennessee. As the future presidential candidate grew older, his father, who served two more terms in the House and three in the Senate, drew on his experiences to lecture his son regularly about the inner workings of politics.

From the beginning the boy strove to live up to the example set by his prominent father and to the high expectations of his parents. At the exclusive St. Albans School, where he ranked in the middle of his class and was captain of the football team, he had to work hard both for his grades and his athletic success.

Gore went on to study government at Harvard University, while the Vietnam War was raging half the world away. Gore opposed the war and joined in protest demonstrations against the fighting. And after graduating in 1969, he thought of going to Canada to avoid military service. Instead, he enlisted in the army to prevent embarrassment to his father, who would be seeking reelection to the Senate in 1970. The senior Gore was defeated anyway, and his son went to Vietnam to serve as an army journalist. By that time, he had married Mary Elizabeth Aitcheson, known as Tipper, whom he had met at a school dance at St. Albans. The couple now have three daughters—Karenna, Kristin, and Sarah—and a son—Albert.

Gore's father's defeat left the future vice-president disillusioned with politics. When he left the army, instead of seeking office, as his friends expected, he went to work for *The Tennessean*, covering local government for the Nashville newspaper. He also attended divinity school and law school at Vanderbilt University.

But in 1976, when the congressman who had held Gore's father's old House seat retired, Gore decided to seek the office himself. In telling his father of his plans, he made it clear that he wanted to run on his own, rather than as the heir to a celebrated Tennessee political name. His father obediently stayed on the sidelines. Gore defeated eight other candidates to win the Democratic nomination that assured his election. Gore easily won reelection three times, and then moved up to the Senate in 1984. On Capitol Hill, he became an expert on issues involving science and technology, particularly arms control. He also gained recognition as a defender of the environment and published a book—*Earth in the Balance: Ecology and the Human Spirit*—that strengthened that reputation. Gore's familiarity with national issues and foreign affairs led to his selection as the vice-presidential candidate by Clinton, whose own background was limited to state government. After the Democrats won the 1992 election, Clinton put Gore in charge of his so-called Reinventing Government program, intended to make the federal bureaucracy more efficient and less expensive.

During his political career, Gore's public behavior has usually been formal and reserved. But at the 1996 Democratic convention that renominated him and Clinton, he gave an emotional speech about the death of his older sister, Nancy, in 1984 from lung cancer, which he blamed on cigarette smoking. Some critics pointed out that Gore had received substantial financial support from the tobacco industry for years after his sister's death.

Gore's efforts to raise money for the Democratic Party during the campaign, notably his attending a fund-raising event at a Buddhist temple in Los Angeles, brought criticism. But the vice-president denied any wrongdoing, and the Justice Department rejected calls for a special prosecutor to investigate the charges.

Gore emerged from the 1996 election as the clear favorite for the Democratic nomination in 2000, but many criticized him as being dull and stiff. He faced a serious challenge for the Democratic nomination from former U.S. Sen. Bill Bradley of New Jersey. Gore tried to make himself more interesting by changing his speaking style. With the strong help of party leaders, he easily defeated Bradley for the nomination.

Following a campaign that featured three presidential debates, Election Day 2000 ended without a clear winner. The vice-president was ahead of Governor Bush in terms of popular votes but was short of the necessary 270 electoral votes. Five weeks of vote recounts in the key state of Florida then occurred. After the U.S. Supreme Court blocked further manual recounts of the votes in Florida on December 12, Gore gracefully conceded defeat to Governor Bush. The vice-president was the fourth person in U.S. history to win the popular vote but not the all important electoral votes in a presidential race. He received more popular votes than any presidential candidate in history, except for Ronald Reagan in 1984.

ROBERT SHOGAN

JACKSON, Philip D.

In his first season as head coach of the Los Angeles Lakers, Phil Jackson proved decisively that, once again, he is professional basketball's best—and most unusual—coach. Jackson and his talented Lakers won the 1999–2000 National Basketball Association (NBA) title as he turned what had been an underachieving team into a powerhouse. And he did so in his own unorthodox way.

Neither a screamer nor a pacifist, Jackson uses what has been called a "benevolent dictator approach" to mold his players into a winning combination. He can be

©Mike Blake/ReutersNewMedia Inc./Corbis

Phil Jackson

intimidating—after all, he stands 6'8" (2 m)—but he would rather appeal to his players' minds than rely on fear and screaming. Applying consistent mental pressure, Jackson convinced the Lakers they could win doing it his way, which means playing basketball with discipline, yet with a large touch of freedom that allows individual talent to blossom.

This was Jackson's seventh NBA crown as a coach. He had won six with the Bulls, relying heavily on the abilities of Michael Jordan to help those teams excel. No one knew if Jackson would be a good fit with the Lakers or with Los Angeles, since he spends the off-season isolated in a cabin in Montana. But Jackson has a rare gift that allows him to sense the pulse of a team and adjust accordingly. It helps, of course, that he comes into any new situation as a winner. But beyond that, he purposely maintains a sense of mystery. He is eccentric, liberal, spiritual, and unconventional. He has interests in philosophy, Eastern thought, and Native American mysticism, and calls himself a Zen Christian. Jackson believes in developing players' minds beyond the court; during the season, he handed his players books such as Toni Morrison's *Jazz* and Friedrich Nietzsche's *Ecce Homo* ("How One Becomes What One Is"). The latter went to superstar center Shaquille O'Neal. Jackson practices the team in silence and another time without a ball, and uses Indian rituals to cleanse rooms of demons. Sometimes during time-outs, he hardly gives any instructions. Instead, he relies on his players to analyze the situation and produce results.

His methods certainly work. O'Neal and Kobe Bryant, the team's other star player, meshed well enough to combine into dominating forces. The squad adapted to Jackson's beloved triangle offense, which had been used so well by the Bulls and is based on what Jackson calls "awareness in action". The Lakers won the NBA Pacific Division title and had the best regular-season record, then survived close play-off series against Sacramento and Portland before breezing past the outmanned Indiana Pacers in the finals.

Background. Philip D. Jackson was born on Sept. 17, 1945, in Deer Lodge, MT, the son of Pentecostal, fundamentalist preachers. His parents took a vow of poverty, and he grew up without movies, comic books, dances, or other distractions. He attended church and played music (piano and trombone). While excelling at high-school sports, he pitched, played defense in football, and was the center in basketball. Now living in South Dakota, he attended the University of North Dakota, where he excelled in basketball. After college, he was drafted by the New York Knicks and played 13 years in the NBA with the Knicks and, later, the New Jersey Nets.

Before winding up as coach of the Bulls, he coached in the Continental Basketball Association (CBA) and in Puerto Rico; he also ran a health club, and was a television commentator and an assistant coach in the NBA. He became the Bulls coach in 1989 and won his first title in 1990–91. Jordan quit after the third championship, only to return to basketball two years later. The Bulls then won three more titles before both Jackson and Jordan retired after the 1998 season. Jackson sat out a season before joining the Lakers.

He and his wife, June, have four grown children—Ben, Charley, Brooke, and Chelsea. The successful coach also has a daughter, Elizabeth, by a previous marriage.

PAUL ATTNER

JONES, Marion

No female had ever won five track and field medals in a single Olympics, yet when Marion Jones captured three golds and two bronzes at the 2000 Sydney Olympic Games, some sensed a letdown. That is because she had long predicted all her medals would be gold, touting her efforts as the "Drive for Five". She also encountered scandal, when her husband, C.J. Hunter, one of the world's top shot-putters, reportedly tested positive for a steroid. The news broke in the midst of her Olympic quest, but Jones rose above the clamor to compete with cool grace on the track.

In Sydney, Jones coasted to gold in the 100-m (10.75), 200-m (21.84), and 1600-m relay. Only the poor performance of the rest of the U.S. 400-m relay team—and her inconsistent long jumping—prevented her from reaching her goal, resulting in a pair of bronze medals.

Marion Jones

Background. Jones was born October 12, 1975, in Los Angeles, and grew up in Palmdale, just north of the city. She was deeply inspired, at age 9, when the 1984 Olympic Games overtook the metropolis—it was her first exposure to the Olympic competition, and she was immediately hooked. Her career has been a steady progression of excellence. At 15, she ran the 100–m in 11.17 seconds, and the 200–m in 22.76 seconds, both Olympic-quality performances. A year later, offered a spot on the U.S. 400-m relay squad for the 1992 Olympics, she declined. A California high-school star, she attended college at North Carolina, splitting her time between track and basketball. She helped the Tar Heels to their 1994 NCAA women's basketball title.

In 1997, after three years out of the limelight, she returned to sprinting with a vengeance, winning the world title in the 100-m, with a time of 10.76 seconds. In 1998, she was faster still, in both the 100–m (10.65) and 200–m (21.62), winning World Cup titles in both sprints. By 1999, Jones reigned as the world's fastest woman. At the World Championships, she ran to another 100-m gold, but was injured in the 200–m semifinal race. Many placed the blame on her poor long-jump style, suggesting it could hamper her Olympic goals.

But in 2000, Jones was more dominant than ever before. She produced one of the world's fastest 400–m times, to guarantee her place on the Olympic 1600–m squad. That, along with a supremely confident, no-bull approach to her work—when David Letterman asked how she won all those races, she replied dryly, "Run fast"—has made Marion Jones an Olympic legend.

JEFF HOLLOBAUGH

KOSTUNICA, Vojislav

Vojislav Kostunica, the newly elected president of the Federal Republic of Yugoslavia, became the flag bearer for those hoping to sweep former President Slobodan Milosevic and his Socialists—blamed by the West for four Balkan wars—from power completely.

Upon his election in the fall 2000, Western governments hailed Kostunica as a democrat and rushed to offer him support. Throughout the revolutionary upheaval following the September elections, Kostunica urged caution, and restrained the public from attacking government targets. Subsequently, his negotiations for power sharing with elements of the Socialist apparatus, and his opposition to extraditing Milosevic and other indicted war criminals to the Hague, became subject to increasing criticism, both inside and outside the country. Still, he was viewed by many as a breath of fresh air—and a symbol of hope for Yugoslavia.

Background. Vojislav Kostunica was born in Belgrade in 1944. He received a doctorate in law from the University of Belgrade in 1974. He was elected assistant lecturer to the university's Faculty of Law in 1970, but was purged from the university in 1974 as a result of his staunch opposition to changes in the Yugoslav constitution that gave increasing powers to the country's six federal republics and two autonomous regions. As a Serbian nationalist, Kostunica wanted to preserve a centralized Yugoslav state, but as an anticommunist, he favored the creation of a pluralistic party system.

Throughout the 1980s, Kostunica worked with the Belgrade-based Institute of Philosophy and Social Theory. He edited several highly acclaimed periodicals in the fields of law and philosophy, and was active in the dissident Committee for the Protection of Freedom of Thought and Expression.

Kostunica was one of the founding members of the Democratic Party in 1989. Following disputes with his former colleagues, he founded his own Democratic Party of Serbia (DPS) in 1992, and was elected a member of the Serbian parliament twice between 1990 and 1997.

Unlike several other opposition leaders during the 13 years of Milosevic's rule, Kostunica was never corrupted or co-opted by the ruling party, or smeared by financial scandals. This clearly raised his stature among ordinary voters during the election campaign for the federal presi-

Vojislav Kostunica

dency. However, his small political organization remained marginal throughout the 1990s even though it participated in several projects against the Socialists.

With the disintegration of Tito's Yugoslavia in 1991, Kostunica supported the creation of a new Yugoslav state in which Serbia would become the dominant republic. He therefore sympathized with Serbian separatists in Croatia and Bosnia and Herzegovina even though he did not explicitly support their policies of "ethnic cleansing."

Kostunica opposed the internationally arranged Dayton Accords in November 1995, claiming they sanctioned the loss of historic Serbian territories in Bosnia and Herzegovina. He staunchly opposed the independence of the Albanian-dominated region of Kosovo, and openly condemned Western policy throughout the former Yugoslavia, claiming it favored the non-Serb nationalities. At the same time, he strongly criticized Milosevic for his mishandling of the crisis throughout Yugoslavia and for his repressive policies inside Serbia.

The new president speaks several languages, including English, French, and German. His wife, Zorica Radovic, also is a lawyer.

JANUSZ BUGAJSKI

LEE, Wen Ho

Until the spring of 1999, Wen Ho Lee lived the American dream. He and his wife, Sylvia, had two children—a son, Chung, and a daughter, Alberta. He did important work as a research scientist at the U.S. government's Los Alamos National Laboratory in New Mexico; owned his own home in the Los Alamos suburb of White Rock; and filled his spare time with fishing, gourmet cooking, and listening to classical music.

That dream crumbled in April of that year, when, in the wake of a sensational article in *The New York Times*, examining security lapses at Los Alamos, Lee was fired and accused of being a spy for the People's Republic of China. Government agents suspected that Lee had given the Chinese government highly sensitive information about the most advanced weapon in the U.S. nuclear arsenal, the W-88 warhead, mounted on ballistic missiles fired from Trident submarines.

©Mike Fiala/AFP/Corbis

Wen Ho Lee

After a grand jury indicted him in December 1999 on 59 felony counts of breaching national security—36 of which carried a life sentence—the 60-year-old Lee spent nine months in prison under extremely harsh conditions. He was held in solitary confinement in a 7 ft (2 m) by 13 ft (4 m) cell for most of the day, and, during his one hour of exercise, was forced to wear leg irons.

Then, in September 2000, Lee's troubles seemed to vanish as suddenly as they appeared, when the government's case against him collapsed for lack of solid evidence. After a Federal Bureau of Investigation (FBI) investigator admitted deceiving U.S. District Judge James Parker on several points of testimony, attorneys for the U.S. Justice Department allowed Lee to plead guilty to a single felony count of improper holding of files, with the only punishment being prison time already served. As he set Lee free, Judge Parker apologized to him for the government's conduct.

Background. Wen Ho Lee was born in Nantou, Taiwan, in 1939. His intelligence was such that, after receiving a bachelor's degree from Taiwan's Cheng Kung University, he was admitted to Texas A&M for postgraduate work. Lee earned a doctorate in mechanical engineering in 1970, and four years later became a citizen of the United States. He began working at the Los Alamos laboratory in 1978, concentrating on applied mathematics and fluid dynamics.

The FBI opened an investigation on Lee in late 1982, after he telephoned a former scientist at another national laboratory who was suspected of passing classified information to China. Lee was interviewed by government agents several times and given a lie detector test. The FBI closed that investigation in 1984.

The Bureau opened a new investigation in 1996, after special software monitoring the Los Alamos computer network showed that Lee was downloading large amounts of information to a personal computer system. Lee's defenders acknowledged that he downloaded information to an unsecured computer, but point out this is a common practice among working scientists. As the government's case unraveled, FBI agents admitted the information was not nearly as sensitive as they had initially claimed, and that it all had to do with specific projects assigned to Lee.

JIM ANDERSON

LIEBERMAN, Joseph Isador

In 1998, when U.S. Sen. Joseph Lieberman of Connecticut denounced President Clinton's behavior in the Monica Lewinsky affair, the senator's action seemed likely to win him admiration from the public but also to invite retribution from his peers. As expected, Lieberman's criticism of Clinton, the first by a Democratic lawmaker, did enhance the senator's reputation as a man of conscience. Surprisingly, his apostasy was one of the main reasons that Democratic presidential nominee Albert Gore, Jr., chose him as his running mate. Lieberman thus became the first Jew to be on the national ticket of a major political party.

In picking Lieberman, a move that seemed designed to help separate Gore from the taint of the Clinton scandals, the vice-president was running considerable risks. Some Democrats worried that his candidacy might stir anti-Semitism and cost their party votes. In addition, Lieberman's past views on some issues—his support for some forms of private-school vouchers, his interest in proposals to make some part of Social Security voluntary, and his opposition to affirmative action—led Republicans to claim that Lieberman had more in common with their presidential candidate, George W. Bush, than with Vice-President Gore, an argument that Lieberman himself quickly dismissed.

The other questions about his candidacy, having to do with his religious faith, were not so readily answered. But Lieberman had been dealing with such issues all his political life, and there were some indications that the senator's devotion to his religion worked in his favor.

During the five weeks in November and early December that the presidential election remained undecided,

Lieberman served as a major supporter and spokesperson for Gore. Then after the Democratic ticket conceded the election to Bush-Cheney, Lieberman prepared to return to the Senate where he was expected to be an active force in Democratic circles. To some people's consternation, he easily had won a third Senate term in November, while running for the vice-presidency as well.

Background. Joseph Isador Lieberman was born in Stamford, CT, on Feb. 24, 1942, to Henry Lieberman, a liquor-store owner and real-estate agent, and his wife, Marcia. Educated in Stamford's public schools, the future politician went on to Yale University, where he earned a bachelor's degree in 1964 and his law degree in 1967. He got his first taste of politics as a Washington intern on Capitol Hill, and then, after a brief stint at practicing law, won a state Senate seat in 1970. After ten years in the Connecticut Senate, Lieberman ran for the U.S. Congress and lost. But two years later, he won election as state attorney general, a post he used to push efforts to protect consumers and safeguard the environment. After his reelection in 1986, Lieberman moved on to the U.S. Senate in 1988, upsetting the popular three-term Republican incumbent, Lowell Weicker. Lieberman coasted to reelection in 1994. Lieberman generally has taken much the same centrist positions as Clinton and Gore during his Senate service.

In keeping with Orthodox practices, Lieberman observes the Sabbath, and refused to attend the Democratic convention that nominated him for the Senate because it was held on a Saturday. He sent a videotape instead. But when U.S. Senate roll-call votes were taken on a Saturday, Lieberman reconciled his religious beliefs with his governmental obligations by walking the 5 mi (8 km) to Capitol Hill from his home in Georgetown to cast his ballot.

Lieberman is married to the former Hadassah Freilich, the daughter of Holocaust survivors, with whom he has had one child. He also has two children from a previous marriage.

ROBERT SHOGAN

MANNING, Peyton Williams

Peyton Manning, in only his third season in the National Football League (NFL) in 2000, drew comparison with quarterback legends such as Joe Montana, Johnny Unitas, and, naturally, Archie Manning, his quarterback father who toiled for seasons with the lowly New Orleans Saints.

The 24-year-old Peyton continued his assault on the record books in 2000, throwing for 4,413 yards and 33 touchdowns. His 10–6 Indianapolis Colts surged into the postseason as a wild-card, before losing an overtime barn burner to the Miami Dolphins, 23–17. Peyton has won with his team—something Archie's Saints did infrequently—but it was to Archie's credit that Peyton remained as poised, mature, and dedicated a football player as he was.

Background. Growing up the son of a legendary NFL signal caller, playing quarterback was Peyton's goal from the start. Often the Manning boys—Peyton and his brothers, Eli and Cooper—and a legion of neighborhood friends would spend afternoons in the yard of the Mannings' New Orleans home, waging gridiron battles. Archie guided his sons with a philosophical, hands-off approach. He kept the game of football fun, generating Peyton's love for the sport; a passion that blended nicely with undeniable physical gifts.

As a senior at Isidore Newman High, he was named Gatorade Circle of Champions National Player of the Year and was given a scholarship to Tennessee. Again under the microscope, Peyton achieved the remarkable. He quickly became a star at Tennessee, and following his junior season, the experts felt Peyton was ready for the NFL. Academics could not hold him back—he completed his speech-communications degree in three years, graduating cum laude. But he chose to stay for his senior year—despite the lure of millions of dollars—honoring a commitment to his teammates and coaches.

Peyton Manning

©RickStewart/Allsport

Many felt he was crazy; others simply admired his loyalty. It was a decision Peyton claimed he will never regret, and it was worth it.

After a remarkable senior season in 1997 (3,817 yards and 36 touchdowns), Peyton left Tennessee as the school's all-time leading passer with 11,201 yards and 89 touchdowns, compiling a 39–6 record as a starter. He set two NCAA, eight SEC, and 33 Tennessee records.

As the 1998 NFL draft drew near, experts debated whether Manning or Washington State quarterback Ryan Leaf deserved to go first—undoubtedly, Indianapolis made the right pick. As a rookie in 1998, Manning's 26 touchdowns and 3,739 yards capped the finest rookie-quarterback campaign in league history. He set rookie records with four 300-yard passing performances and four three-touchdown games. Along the way, he set a Colts record for being the only team quarterback in history to take every snap of the entire season.

Despite the heroics, Indianapolis was 3–13 in 1998, and some wondered if Peyton would endure a string of losing seasons as Archie had with the Saints. But in 1999, Peyton led the team to a 13–3 regular season and the play-offs. Few quarterbacks dominated the professional ranks so early in their careers as Manning. He helped transform Indianapolis from a cellar dweller to a Super Bowl contender: a stunning turnaround for a team used to losing, directed by a young man accustomed to winning.

MARC SESSLER

MCCAIN, John Sidney, III

After delivering an endorsement of Republican presidential nominee George W. Bush at the party's nominating convention in Philadelphia, U.S. Sen. John McCain of Arizona packed up and went back to Washington. But then McCain received an urgent call from Governor Bush, his former rival for the GOP nomination, urging him to return to Philadelphia for Bush's acceptance speech on the final night of the convention. McCain's conspicuous presence at the convention that night signaled that despite his failed bid for the presidency, the three-term senator had become one of the country's most esteemed politicians.

McCain, a former Vietnam prisoner of war (POW), achieved this status by making campaign-finance reform

©Stephan Savoia/AP/Wide World Photos

John McCain

the centerpiece of his presidential candidacy and by casting himself as the messenger of truth and candor. He even dubbed his campaign van the "Straight Talk Express." Although McCain was overwhelmed by Bush after capturing the New Hampshire primary, the Arizona senator emerged with his reputation for integrity enhanced.

As the son and grandson of admirals, and himself a decorated navy flier who endured five years in the "Hanoi Hilton" prison after being shot down over Vietnam, McCain's career had a legendary quality. The legend had blemishes, however. McCain divorced his first wife, who had waited for him through his captivity after admitted affairs on his part. His links to Arizona developer Charles H. Keating ensnared him in a Senate scandal. Yet McCain managed to rebound from these experiences as he had from the rigors of his early life.

Background. John Sidney McCain III was born Aug. 29, 1936, in the Panama Canal Zone, where his father then was stationed. Like most other so-called military brats, his childhood was spent bouncing from school to school as his father's assignments changed. Entering Annapolis like his father and grandfather before him, the young man rebelled against the rigidity of the Naval Academy and was graduated fifth from the bottom of his class in 1958.

In Vietnam, where he was posted in 1967, he flew 22 bombing missions against the North before he was shot down. Early in his imprisonment, McCain turned down a Vietnamese offer to go home, realizing it was a ploy to embarrass his father, then a high-ranking officer in the Pacific. After being freed in 1973, and commanding a naval squadron in Jacksonville, FL, he was named navy liaison to the Senate, which helped to focus his growing interest in a political career.

McCain won election to the House of Representatives in 1982 and gained another term in 1984. He moved to the Senate in 1986, easily winning reelection in 1992 and 1998. His first Senate term was marred by the Keating scandal, which also involved four other senators. McCain, who had received campaign contributions from Keating but never intervened on his behalf, ultimately was declared guilty only of "poor judgment." His most notable legislative efforts in the Senate have been on proposals to tighten regulation of campaign financing and of tobacco-company advertising.

In 1980, after divorcing his first wife, McCain married Cindy Hensley and moved to her hometown of Phoenix, AZ. The couple have four children, in addition to McCain's three from his first marriage. Shortly after appearing at the Republican convention, McCain was operated on for two malignant skin tumors; afterward, his doctor declared him cancer-free. His biographical book *Faith of My Fathers* was a best-seller early in 2000.

ROBERT SHOGAN

MORI, Yoshiro

On April 5, 2000, Yoshiro Mori was selected by both houses of Japan's Diet (parliament) to be Japan's 85th prime minister. His choreographed succession within the Liberal Democratic Party (LDP) had been marked by secrecy after his mentor, Prime Minister Keizo Obuchi, suffered a stroke on April 2. (Obuchi died on May 14.)

During 30 years in the Diet, Mori had concentrated on educational issues. He had little experience in foreign affairs or in finance, where most of his predecessors had concentrated. He had favored the controversial inclusion of the New *Komeito* (a party linked to a Buddhist group) in the governing coalition, and promptly reappointed the entire Obuchi cabinet. In his first policy speech to the Diet, April 7, the new prime minister promised a "rebirth of Japan" with revival of the economy. On June 2, however, facing weak support in polls, the prime minister dissolved the Diet, calling for a national election.

In the June 25 poll for the (lower) House of Representatives, the LDP-led coalition won "by default," as one expert observed. In urban areas, opposition to the government was strong. With a sparse majority held by the coalition of the LDP, the New *Komeito*, and the New Conservative Party, Mori formed his second cabinet on July 4. It included holdovers in the foreign affairs and finance ministries.

Meanwhile, Mori's reputation was enhanced by a number of well-publicized summit meetings. On April 29 in St. Petersburg, two new leaders—Russia's President Vladimir Putin and Prime Minister Mori—promised to negotiate further on a long-delayed peace treaty between Japan and Russia. On May 6, Mori made the required trip to Washington, consulting with U.S. President Bill Clinton on matters of trade. Mori also met with both Putin and Clinton in Okinawa during the meeting of advanced industrial nations (G-8) in July, the first such summit hosted by Japan outside of Tokyo. Obuchi and Mori had planned the summit's site to encourage development of the relatively neglected island-prefecture.

©Koji Sasahar/AP/Wide World Photos

Yoshiro Mori

Background. Yoshiro Mori was born July 14, 1937, in Neagari, Ishikawa Prefecture. He was reared in a middle-class, rice-farming family; his grandfather and father had served as mayor of their town. After middle school, Mori enrolled in the School of Commerce, Waseda University. There he joined the debating club, where he first met Keizo Obuchi. Having been graduated from Waseda, Mori joined the staff of the *Sankei Shimbun*, a major financial newspaper.

In 1962 the future leader took the first step in a long political career by becoming a secretary to a member of the lower house. In December 1969, Mori stood as a candidate for the House of Representatives, finishing first in Ishikawa Prefecture and winning a Diet seat at age 32. He has been reelected ten consecutive times. Prior to becoming prime minister, Mori had varied political experience, mainly in his party. Twice he was appointed LDP secretary-general (1993 and 1998). He also has served in cabinet positions—including minister of education (1983), minister of international trade and industry (1992), and minister of construction (1995).

Mori married Chieko Maki, a fellow student at Waseda, in 1961. They have a son, Yuki; a daughter, Yoko; and a granddaughter, Reiko. The prime minister enjoys a game of golf.

ARDATH W. BURKS

PUTIN, Vladimir Vladimirovich

A relatively obscure public official who had served as a KGB counterintelligence officer, Vladimir Putin emerged during the year 2000 as the second president of the Russian Federation. His surprise appointment as the nation's prime minister by President Boris Yeltsin in August 1999 had set him on course to the presidency less than a year later.

Putin's tenure as prime minister coincided with a resumption of the Chechen war, the fighting between the central government and its rebellious Caucasian province that had ended in political settlement in 1996. This time, public opinion supported Moscow's Chechen operations, and the prime minister's popularity rose commensurably. After the fall 1999 parliamentary elections reflected strong support for Prime Minister Putin, Yeltsin surprised the world on New Year's Eve by suddenly resigning office, which automatically made the prime minister Russia's acting president, pending a special election.

On March 26, 2000, after a brief campaign involving several candidates, Putin was elected president with 52.94% of the vote, thus avoiding a runoff. The race later was criticized for electoral fraud. President Putin devoted his first 100 days in office to strengthening the Russian state by recentralizing control over the provinces, reducing the political leverage of "big business," and reasserting Russian influence abroad.

Background. Vladimir Vladimirovich Putin was born in Leningrad on Oct. 7, 1952. As a teenager, he became entranced with the romance of being a foreign agent. Advised to first study law, Putin received his law degree in 1975 from Leningrad University's law school, where he encountered his later mentor, Professor Anatoly Sobchak. Upon graduation, Putin became a career officer in the KGB, the Soviet Union's main intelligence organization. His initial duties in Leningrad involved trying to recruit foreign visitors as agents for the KGB. After advanced training, Putin was posted to East Berlin in the German Democratic Republic, where he worked from 1986 to 1989.

Then, with the Cold War waning, he returned to the USSR. Finding himself shunted off to a minor post back in Leningrad, Putin retired from the KGB and turned to politics. In his new career in Leningrad's democratic politics, the future president was inspired by the political reforms of Mikhail Gorbachev, the last leader of the Soviet Union.

As a protégé of Mayor Anatoly Sobchak, a well-known reformer, Putin became deputy mayor of St. Petersburg (formerly Leningrad) in 1994. Two years later, he moved to the Kremlin in Moscow to work in the administration of President Yeltsin. Soon recognized as an efficient and highly competent administrator, Putin began his rapid ascent in national politics, beginning with appointment as deputy director of the presidential staff in 1997, and as the Kremlin's coordinator of relations with Russia's 89 provincial governments in 1998. Just a few months later, Yeltsin made Putin head of Russia's internal-security agency, the Federal Security Service (FSB), and asked him to run the powerful Security Council as well. Then, on Aug. 9, 1999, the president chose Putin as his new prime minister.

The new Russian president, and his wife, Lyudmila, are the parents of two teenage daughters. He has admitted to being a practicing Orthodox Christian, and is known to have a fondness for the martial arts.

ROBERT SHARLET

ROWLING, J[oanne] K[athleen]

Following its publication in July 2000, *Harry Potter and the Goblet of Fire*, the fourth in the Harry Potter series of books written by J.K. Rowling, became the fastest-selling book in history. The four Potter books—part of a projected series of seven—are all award winners and fixtures on best-seller lists. And no one is more surprised at the books' overwhelming success than their creator, J.K. Rowling.

Prior to 1997, few people had heard of Rowling. Now there is hardly a child in the United States, Canada, or overseas who does not know her and her literary creation, Harry Potter. The four Harry Potter books—*The Sorcerer's Stone*, *Chamber of Secrets*, *Prisoner of Azkaban*, and *Goblet of Fire*—have transformed the life of the author from a single mother on welfare when she sat down to write the first book to one of *Forbes'* 100 most-powerful celebrities. She was not expecting fame and fortune. In fact, her greatest hope for the first book was that she could go to a bookstore and see it on the shelf.

J K Rowling

©Ian Waldie/Reuters NewMedia, Inc./Corbis

Background. Joanne Kathleen Rowling was born on July 31, 1965, in the small English village of Chipping Sodbury, near Bristol. She began writing at an early age, reading her stories aloud to her younger sister.

Her family moved to the town of Tutshill near the Forest of Dean when Joanne was 9. As a teenager, she attended the Wyedean School. Taking her parents' advice, she went to the University of Exeter, where she studied French and literature and was graduated with honors. Unwilling to risk being a full-time writer, Rowling took a series of undistinguished jobs, all the while writing. It was during a train breakdown as Rowling was commuting between her home in London and her job in Manchester that Harry Potter was born. Staring out the window at a field of cows, Rowling saw a boy who attends a school for wizards, and she began jotting notes for stories about the boy she named Harry Potter.

In September of 1990, Rowling took a teaching position in Portugal, where she met and married a journalist. Their daughter, Jessica, was born in 1993. When the marriage ended in divorce, Rowling moved to Scotland to live near her sister. Once in Scotland, Rowling made the commitment to finish her book about Harry Potter. She decided not to take a teaching job, but rather, went on public assistance so that she could write full-time.

When the manuscript was finished, she found the name of an agent in a library book. *Harry Potter and the Philosopher's Stone*, as it was called in England, was rejected by numerous publishers, but in 1996 the British publisher Bloomsbury agreed to buy it for an advance of about $3,500. Word of mouth about Harry became so strong that in 1997 an auction at the Bologna (Italy) Children's Book Fair took place, with the rights going for $100,000 to Scholastic Press.

Although there has been some controversy, especially in the United States, about the element of witchcraft in the books, the series has been elevated to classic status and is published in dozens of countries.

ILENE COOPER

SANTANA, Carlos

Carlos Santana, the singer-guitarist who burst to fame after he played at the 1969 Woodstock Festival, made a dramatic comeback in the music world with his 1999 album *Supernatural*. It dominated the Grammy Awards in 2000, garnering ten nominations and winning eight awards—including two for the single "Smooth," which featured singer Rob Thomas of Matchbox 20. With the album, Santana tied Michael Jackson's 1983 record for the most Grammys won by a single performer.

Carlos Santana

Santana had not released a hit record in nearly two decades, but *Supernatural*'s savvy pairing of the guitarist with such contemporary stars as Dave Matthews, Everlast, and Lauryn Hill proved appealing to both baby-boom fans and their children. The album quickly sold more than 20 million copies worldwide.

Santana's Grammy-sanctified career revival was reminiscent of Bonnie Raitt's success following four Grammy wins in 1990 for *Nick of Time*. One minute, Santana and Raitt were highly regarded musicians and consistent concert draws whose albums had fallen out of commercial favor; the next moment, they were middle-aged pop stars with hit records. The sales of *Supernatural* also confirmed that there is a growing market of older music buyers—roughly one-quarter of all recorded music is bought by people over the age of 45. But it mostly reflected the fact that Santana is one of those rare musicians who truly speaks through their instrument. Nobody plays the guitar quite like Santana.

Background. Carlos Santana was born in the Mexican village of Autlán de Navarro on July 20, 1947, and was introduced to music by his father, José, an accomplished mariachi violinist. When Carlos was 7, the family moved to Tijuana, where he started playing guitar and was drawn to the sounds of such blues musicians as B.B. King, T-Bone Walker, and John Lee Hooker. Santana was a regular club musician in the busy border town before relocating with his family to San Francisco, where he formed the Santana Blues Band in 1966, and found a receptive audience at the legendary Fillmore Auditorium. Fillmore promoter Bill Graham encouraged the band to learn what became one of its breakthrough songs, a Willie Bobo salsa called "Evil Ways." Graham also became the band's manager and got the local favorites a slot at Woodstock. Santana signed his first record deal with Clive Davis, the same music executive behind *Supernatural*.

But the people who have had the most influence on Santana are such musicians as John Coltrane, Miles Davis, and Jimi Hendrix—genius players who were masters of their musical instruments. Santana's guitar solos are characterized by richly sustained notes and the explosive release of rhythmic tension. He plays with the knowledge that every note counts, and it is the signature wail of his guitar, defined on such seminal albums as *Abraxas* and *Caravanserai,* that has helped him thrive despite a somewhat inconsistent recording career. Always an inspired live performer, the guitarist was one of the few acts from the original festival to play Woodstock '94. Five years later, Santana surprised the world by producing one of the most successful albums in the history of pop music.

JOHN MILWARD

SCHLESSINGER, Laura

Dr. Laura Schlessinger, the controversial host of the popular radio talk show *The Dr. Laura Schlessinger Program*, publicly apologized in March 2000, and again in October, for what she called "poorly chosen" words in discussing homosexuality. These apologies did little to mitigate criticism from gay activists, who characterized her comments—in which she referred to homosexuality as a biological error and deviant—as hate speech.

In September, when she launched a syndicated television show, *Dr. Laura*, on a number of CBS stations, the success of her radio show did not immediately follow. Just two weeks after its debut, the television show was briefly halted. The official reason was a preplanned production hiatus, but gay-rights activists—many citing her public apology to the gay community as insincere—had tried to stop television stations from broadcasting it, and several top advertisers dropped sponsorship. By October, the show was back on the air in more than 90% of the country. However in early November, CBS moved Dr. Laura's show from afternoons to the red-eye time slot of 2 A.M. on stations in the cities throughout the nation.

Schlessinger, who holds a doctorate in physiology, has worked in radio since the mid-1970s. *The Dr. Laura Schlessinger Program*, with more than 18 million listeners, has been syndicated since 1994. As a sharp-tongued host, Schlessinger lectures and offers advice on morality, mostly from a conservative viewpoint. In an interview with *Time* magazine, Schlessinger said she believed she was tapping into "a basic moral intuition about what was right and wrong."

Background. Laura Schlessinger was born on Jan. 16, 1947, in Brooklyn, NY. She was the eldest child of Monroe Schlessinger, a civil engineer, and Yolanda Ceccovini. Her childhood was troubled as her father reportedly was physically and verbally abusive, and his Jewish family never accepted her Roman Catholic mother. Although raised without religion, Schlessinger became an Orthodox Jew as an adult.

Laura Schlessinger

She grew up in Jericho, NY, and attended the State University of New York at Stony Brook, graduating in 1969 with a bachelor's degree in biology. She received a Ph.D. in physiology from Columbia University Medical School in 1974. While she was teaching biology, physiology, and human sexuality at the University of Southern California in 1975, she got involved with radio talk shows—first as a guest and later as a host.

The Dr. Laura Schlessinger Program was launched in 1990 on a Los Angeles radio station. By 2000 it was playing on more than 450 stations nationwide. On her broadcasts, in her books, and in her syndicated newspaper column, Schlessinger promotes what she calls "traditional family values." According to these values, premarital and extramarital affairs are inexcusable; abortion is justifiable only to save the life of the mother; and the needs of the children must always come before those of their parents.

Schlessinger is married to Dr. Lewis G. Bishop, her manager and business partner. The couple have a 14-year-old son, Deryk.

KRISTI VAUGHAN

Biotechnology

Biotechnology experienced exciting advances in 2000, including the first successful human gene-therapy procedure, a program for crop improvement through gene activation, the use of a DNA vaccine against the AIDS virus, and a novel method for control of insect populations.

Successful Gene Therapy. Since the first gene-therapy procedure in 1990, more than a dozen diseases have been treated, but in no case has there been a complete cure. Early in 2000, M. Cavazzana-Calvo and her colleagues at the Gene Therapy Laboratory in Paris, France, announced they had cured two male children of an X-chromosome-linked form of the disease, *severe combined immunodeficiency (SCID-X1).* Affected individuals suffer a mutation that blocks the action of a gene needed to make the type of white blood cell called the T cell. Without such cells, the individual cannot successfully combat infections, and dies at a young age.

The scientists extracted blood-forming stem cells from the bone marrow of both patients. Each child's cells were incubated separately with viruses that contained the normal form of the SCID-X1 gene. During incubation, the viruses entered the stem cells, and their DNA became incorporated in one of the individual's chromosomes. The stem cells were then transfused back into the respective SCID-X1 patient, where they produced normal amounts of T cells. Whether the cure is permanent was to be determined.

Crop Improvement Through Gene Activation. Richard A. Jefferson of the Center for the Application of Molecular Biology to International Agriculture (CAMBIA) in Canberra, Australia, reported on a new project designed to produce crop plants (rice, corn, wheat) with enhanced desirable traits, including increased food production, pest resistance, and temperature tolerance. The project involves the insertion of a gene-regulating DNA sequence from a bacterium, yeast, or other plant into a recipient plant's DNA. The inserted genetic segment is capable of activating one or more of the plant's normally dormant genes. One can then choose plants with desirable traits for further propagation.

This approach assumes that in its evolutionary history, each crop species has developed and then, for reasons unknown, suppressed the expression of many genes that, if activated, could benefit humans. Whether this is the case, remained to be seen. If the project is successful, it will make unnecessary the transfer of foreign genes into crop species for crop improvement.

DNA Vaccine and the AIDS Virus. Injections of killed or weakened disease-causing microbes stimulate a person's immune system to produce various types of white blood cells that will neutralize any future infection by the particular pathogen. Attempts to vaccinate people against the AIDS virus using this approach have proved unsuccessful.

Norman L. Letvin and colleagues at Harvard Medical School in Massachusetts injected eight rhesus monkeys with molecules of DNA containing two AIDS-virus protein-producing genes. Eight other rhesus monkeys were injected with molecules of DNA that did not contain any AIDS-virus genes. After a period of time, all 16 animals were infected with an AIDS virus that would ordinarily kill them in a few months. Those monkeys who received DNA with the viral genes survived with no signs of ill health, while half of the others died within the 140-day experimental period. This clearly showed that, at least in the case of rhesus monkeys, DNA containing AIDS-virus genes can serve as a vaccine against the disease. It is hoped that similar results will occur in human beings.

Insect Population Control. A number of diseases are transmitted from person to person by insects, including sleeping sickness by the tsetse fly, and malaria by the anopheles mosquito. Dean D. Thomas and colleagues at the University of Oxford in England reported on a method to limit, and possibly even eradicate, an insect population in a given area. Their experimental insect was the fruit fly, *Drosophila melanogaster,* which is not known to transmit any human disease.

Through the use of a complicated breeding program, a strain of *D. melanogaster* was produced containing a dominant lethal gene that killed female—but not male—flies. Huge numbers of male flies were produced and released into a controlled natural environment. They were able to mate with some of the females in the area, but only male offspring were produced from these matings. Continuation of this procedure for a number of generations should result in the eradication of the fruit-fly population in the particular area. Similar projects involving disease-transmitting insects would lead to a reduction in illnesses and loss of life.

Louis Levine, *Department of Biology*
City College of New York

Bolivia

With less than two years before the next general election, 2000 was a year of political, economic, and social upheaval for the government of Hugo Banzer, and for Bolivia.

Politics. Municipal-election results in December 1999 highlighted the diminishing popularity of Banzer's administration, which was further tested by social unrest in April and September. Both occasions reflected social discontent over a range of issues. April demonstrations were sparked by protests against water-rate hikes in Cochabamba and low police wages. The government was forced to make concessions, including renationalization of the recently privatized water company in Cochabamba and a 50% wage increase for the police force. In September, social unrest was widespread, mobilized around the teachers, union demanding higher wages, and the Cocalero movement in Chapare against coca eradication. After several weeks of violent confrontation, a precarious agreement was reached between the government and coca producers, centering on the provision for— and management of—alternative agricultural-development resources. At the heart of this social unrest was deep discontentment over persistent poverty and hardship.

Economy. Following 1999's dismal economic performance, a reactivation of the economy was expected for 2000, given the more favorable international context of higher commodity prices; the gradual recovery of the Southern Cone economies; and natural-gas sales to Brazil, following the 1999 completion of the Bolivia-Brazil gas line. The economy took longer than expected to emerge from recession, however, growing by only 2.1% year on year, in the first half of 2000.

The government tried to stimulate domestic demand with an April legislative package, which included measures to offset bank-lending restrictions, tax incentives for business, improvements in road infrastructure, and new public-spending initiatives. But by the final quarter of the year, these measures generally had failed to yield results. After the austerity of 1999, the government relaxed fiscal policy somewhat, but without jeopardizing 2000 fiscal targets. Poverty alleviation and institutional reform measures were to be financed from aid of U.S. $1 billion pledged by foreign donors for 2000–2002.

In October 2000, the Bolivian government agreed to various demands by Indian peasants. For three weeks the peasants had blocked roads, below, *paralyzing the economy, causing food shortages, and threatening the presidency of Hugo Banzer.*

BOLIVIA • Information Highlights

Official Name: Republic of Bolivia.
Location: West-central South America.
Area: 424,162 sq mi (1 098 580 km²).
Population (2000 est.): 8,152,620.
Chief Cities: Sucre, the legal capital (1997 est.),
163,563; La Paz, the administrative capital (1998 est.),
894,000; Santa Cruz de la Sierra (1998 est.), 953,000;
Cochabamba (1997 est.), 560,284.
Government: *Head of state and government,* Hugo
Banzer Suarez, president (took office August 1997).
Legislature—National Congress: Chamber of Senators
and Chamber of Deputies.
Monetary Unit: Boliviano (6.36 bolivianos equal U.S.$1,
Dec. 21, 2000).
Gross Domestic Product (1999 est. U.S.$):
$24,200,000,000 (purchasing power parity).
Economic Indexes (1999): *Consumer Prices* (1990 =
100): all items, 227.3; food, 220.5. *Industrial Produc-
tion* (1990 = 100): 132.0.
Foreign Trade (1999 U.S.$): *Imports,* $1,227,000,000;
exports, $1,033,000,000.

The mining sector showed important signs of recovery following the final stages of privatization of zinc and tin mines, and a rise in the price of Bolivia's mineral exports. After a poor harvest in 1999, agriculture recovered somewhat, led by an estimated 19% increase in soybean yields.

Coca Eradication. The coca-eradication program assumed a particular importance amid a sluggish economy and the enduring problem of underemployment. During an August visit to Bolivia, U.S. Secretary of State Madeline Albright congratulated the government on the success of the program, and claimed an additional $110 million has been approved for alternative development projects. The secretary was less forthcoming when probed about the issue of lifting U.S. duties on textile imports from Bolivia.

PILAR DOMINGO, *University of London*

Bosnia and Herzegovina

During 2000, Bosnia and Herzegovina remained divided into two national-based entities, and the central government in Sarajevo remained weak. Nevertheless, there were signs that with democratic changes in Croatia and Serbia, separatist pressures would be eased within Bosnia itself.

Political Challenges. Sarajevo's central government remained fragile and divided, despite efforts of the international community to construct an effective multiethnic administration. In early June the Bosnian parliament approved a new central government led by Spasoje Tusevljak. He served until mid-October when he was replaced as prime minister by Martin Raguz.

In February, Muslim leader Alija Izetbegovic assumed the rotating chair of Bosnia's joint presidency, and was due to remain in office until October, when he was set to retire from political life. Halid Genjac succeeded Izetbegovic, who had led the Muslim population in Bosnia's tripartite presidency throughout the difficult years of Bosnia's independence. International officials expected that Izetbegovic's retirement would compel the other presidency members, Serb Zivko Radisic and Croat Ante Jelavic, to resign. New elections would provide an opportunity to remove Radisic and Jelavic, who were viewed as obstructions to implementing the 1995 Dayton Agreement for a unified state.

Political conflicts were also evident in the Serb entity between separatists and pragmatists. The presidential post had remained vacant since the nationalist Nikola Poplasen was removed by the Office of the High Representative in March 1999. Vice-President Mirko Sarovic announced he would assume the presidency, but was blocked by Wolfgang Petritsch, the new international-community representative, who considered this move unconstitutional.

In February the Socialist Party (the Bosnian branch of Slobodan Milosevic's ruling party in Serbia) left the governing coalition in the Serb entity. The decision was viewed as an attempt by Milosevic to undermine the governing coalition and the Dayton Agreement. In September the Serb-entity parliament passed a no-confidence motion in the government of Western-backed Premier Milorad Dodik.

With the victory of democratic parties in the Croatian and Serbian elections, observers hoped that radical forces would be undermined in Bosnia. April's municipal elections showed mixed success. Serb nationalists won in 49 municipalities, while Croatian nationalists captured 25. The Muslim Party of Democratic Action won 23 individually, and 11 in coalition with the more moderate Party for Bosnia and Herzegovina. There were encouraging signs in that the multiethnic Social Democrats were victorious in 15 municipalities and made important electoral advances.

Parliamentary elections took place in November, after the international community approved an election law designed to break the nationalist grip on power, and enable moderates to win more offices. Although centrist and civic forces proved more successful than in previous ballots, the

Early in 2000, the Bosnian town of Brcko was officially proclaimed a multi-ethnic district. In October, Bosnian-Serb students marched through the streets to protest the multiethnic school program.

© Amel Emric/AP/Wide World Photos

cratic Union obtained five of the 42 seats in the House of Representatives and 25 out of 140 seats in the Federation. The Social Democrats also performed well in the Federation and sought to bridge the ethnic divide, but was not prepared to enter a coalition with a nationalist party.

Ethnic Divisions. Bosnia remained divided among the three ethnic communities, but progress was registered in areas such as interentity law enforcement and cooperation between the two interior ministries. International agencies pressed for greater refugee returns as some 1.2 million people were still displaced as a result of the 1992–95 war.

In March the Bosnian town of Brcko was officially proclaimed a multiethnic district to be run jointly by Muslims, Serbs, and Croats, while remaining under the sovereignty of the Bosnian state. The final status of Brcko, which was populated predominantly by Muslims and Croats before the war, but was "ethnically cleansed" by Serb nationalists, had been the only territorial issue left unresolved by the Dayton Agreement.

Crime and Corruption. International organizations arrested several war-crimes suspects, although former Bosnian Serb leader Radovan Karadzic continued to evade capture. In April, NATO-led Stabilization Forces (SFOR) troops apprehended Serb leader Momcilo Krajisnik and delivered him to the International Criminal Tribunal in The Hague. Krajisnik, a former speaker of the Bosnian parliament and member of the postwar collective presidency, was charged with genocide and crimes against humanity.

Crime and corruption remained widespread in the country and were increasingly identified as the main obstacles to effective economic reform. Bank fraud, customs evasion, tax fraud, bribery, embezzlement, extortion, and an organized-crime network undermined efforts to rehabilitate the economy, and were the most serious obstacles to foreign investment. According to analysts, $500 million of domestic revenue was lost due to smuggling each year.

Economic Performance. The Bosnian economy remained heavily reliant on foreign aid, both to shore up the budget and to finance a massive trade deficit. The international community had provided the republic

three nationalist parties gained sufficient representation to obstruct multiethnic integration. The Serbian Democratic Party (SDP) took 36% of the vote to the Serb Assembly and garnered a total of 31 seats. Mirko Sarovic of the SDP won the presidency. The Party of Democratic Action gained eight out of 42 seats in the House of Representatives and 38 out of 140 seats in the Federation parliament. The Croatian Demo-

---

BOSNIA AND HERZEGOVINA
Information Highlights

Official Name: Bosnia and Herzegovina.
Location: Southeastern Europe.
Area: 19,735 sq mi (51 129 km²).
Population (2000 est.): 3,835,777.
Chief Cities (1991 census): Sarajevo, the capital, 415,631; Banja Luka, 142,644.
Government: *Head of state,* Halid Genjac (Muslim), Zivko Radisic (Serb), Ante Jelavic (Croat), presidents. *Head of government,* Martin Raguz, prime minister. *Legislature* — Parliamentary Assembly: National House of Representatives and House of Peoples.
Gross Domestic Product (1999 est. U.S.$): $6,200,000,000 (purchasing power parity).

with more than $5 billion in assistance over the previous five years. Much of the economic infrastructure had been reconstructed, giving a possibility for economic recovery. Although growth in the gross domestic product (GDP) was projected at 15% for the year, other economic indicators remained disappointing. The unemployment rate, for example, stood at some 35% of the working population.

Foreign Relations. NATO forces continued to assist the civilian authorities in their efforts to create a stable political environment. SFOR provided logistical support for internationally monitored elections, and offered assistance in refugee resettlement. However, the military presence continued to be reduced in size, and numbered some 23,000 troops by the end of the year.

Bosnia and Herzegovina remained heavily reliant on foreign aid. The international community contributed to the country's development, launching projects in various fields, including infrastructure, housing, job creation, protection of minority rights, and support of an independent media.

Relations between Bosnia and Croatia improved during the year. In March, Croatian President Stipe Mesic visited Sarajevo and announced that Zagreb would no longer interfere in Bosnia's internal affairs, or finance the Croatian separatists. Bosnia and Croatia signed a trade and economic-cooperation agreement on December 19. Bosnia's relations with the democratic government in Montenegro also improved, and the ouster of Yugoslavia's President Milosevic in October generated hope that Sarajevo's contacts with Belgrade would be placed on a more constructive footing.

JANUSZ BUGAJSKI
Center for Strategic and International Studies

Brazil

Although Brazil's economy registered marked improvement during the year 2000, the public awarded low grades to President Fernando Henrique Cardoso. Lofting the anticorruption banner, the leftist Workers' Party (PT) scored victories in the October municipal elections. These contests brought to the fore several new presidential contenders for 2002, including a glamorous female sexologist.

Politics. No sooner was one set of elections completed than Brazilian politicians prepared for the next. The leftist PT

BRAZIL • Information Highlights

Official Name: Federative Republic of Brazil.
Location: Eastern South America.
Area: 3,286,473 sq mi (8 511 965 km²).
Population (2000 est.): 172,860,370.
Chief Cities (Aug. 1, 1996): Brasília, the capital, 1,821,946; São Paulo, 9,839,066; Rio de Janeiro, 5,551,538; Salvador, 2,211,539; Belo Horizonte, 2,091,371.
Government: *Head of state and government,* Fernando Henrique Cardoso, president (sworn in Jan. 1, 1995). *Legislature*—National Congress: Federal Senate and Chamber of Deputies.
Monetary Unit: Real (1.9535 reales equal U.S.$1, Dec. 21, 2000).
Gross Domestic Product (1999 est. U.S.$): $1,057,000,000,000 (purchasing power parity).
Economic Indexes: *Consumer Prices* (1999, 1994 = 100): all items, 222.3; food, 179.8. *Industrial Production* (1999, 1990 = 100): 119.9.
Foreign Trade (1999 U.S.$): *Imports,* $49,214,000,000; *exports,* $48,011,000,000.

---

emerged as the big winner in the fall local-government races, capturing 13 of 16 of the nation's major cities. Still, the PT garnered only 14% of the total vote, and two parties in Cardoso's four-party, center-right coalition came out of the balloting relatively unscathed. The catchall Brazilian Democratic Movement (PMDB) saw its contingent of mayors slip from 1,323 to 1,253–not a bad showing in light of Cardoso's unpopularity. The Liberal Front Party (PFL) picked up 65 city halls, elevating its total to 1,027.

The PT standard-bearer who attracted the most attention was Marta Suplicy. She garnered 58.5% of the ballots cast to win the São Paulo mayorship, defeating veteran politician Salim Maluf of the conservative Brazilian Progressive Party (PPB). Suplicy, 55, entered the race with widespread name recognition, derived from her fame as a television psychologist in the 1980s who talked openly about sexual intimacy. As a federal deputy, Suplicy attracted the spotlight by championing gay rights and access to abortion—subjects that resonated with cosmopolitan voters, but are not associated with the PT's traditional focus on poverty. During her mayoral campaign, though, she stressed the need to diminish the school dropout rate, promote adult education, and double the number of police officers to combat the violence besetting her city. Although personalities and local issues often determine the results of local elections, Suplicy's triumph in the nation's biggest metropolis vaulted her onto the shortlist of possible candidates to succeed Cardoso. Before aspiring seriously to the presidential palace, she must figure out how to avoid drastic budget cuts in a city beset by a $9.3 billion debt, twice its annual revenue. Moreover, as a moderate, she will have to make peace with her party's militant left wing. The last time the PT held São Paulo's city hall, its mayor wound up bolting the party because of intramural battles.

Should Suplicy throw her hat into the ring, she will have to compete for her party's nomination with Luiz Ignacio Lula da Silva, the PT's thrice-unsuccessful presidential candidate. Other presidential wanna-bes include Bahia Gov. Antonio Carlos Magalhaes (PFL), Central Bank Chairman Arminio Fraga (PFL), Ceará Gov. Tasso Jereissati, a Cardoso ally who belongs to the Brazilian Social Democracy Party (PSDB).

Despite its leftist rhetoric, the PT did well for several reasons. First, citizens have tired of the current administration's belt-tightening initiatives. Second, voters reacted against widespread urban violence, including a rash of cop killings that took the lives of 565 police officers since 1995. Just before the local elections, Cardoso cut short a tour of Germany to return home to deploy army troops to fight urban crime in Rio de Janeiro State. In early October, hundreds of law-enforcement officers held an unprecedented demonstration in Rio de Janeiro. They displayed a black banner in front of the municipal building, asking "Who will be the next?" Finally, the PT was enjoying a reputation for honesty at a time when corruption afflicted the Cardoso administration.

Voters also were reacting to a scandal publicized in mid-July, when the magazine *Istoé* announced that it had transcripts of 400 hours of wiretapped phone calls. In these transcripts, a fugitive judge implicated a former presidential aide, a cabinet member, and legislators in an unlawful patronage and influence-peddling scheme. These revelations, which the *Jornal do Brasil* called the most damning during Cardoso's six years in office, focused on a São Paulo courthouse, which—after a decade of delay and $150 million in government contracts—remained unfinished. The exposé prompted the Senate to expel one of its members for the first time in 170 years. Also on the firing line was Planning and Budget Minister Martus Tavares, who approved additional outlays on the project, even after reports of cost overruns surfaced. And Eduardo Jorge Caldas Pereira, Cardoso's chief of staff and campaign coordinator in 1998, had yet to explain why he received 117 phone calls from the renegade judge when the courthouse was under construction.

Economy. In September the *Financial Times* labeled Brazil the International Monetary Fund's (IMF's) "star pupil." This accolade sprang from Cardoso's having successfully pursued fiscal austerity following the 1999 devaluation of the real, the nation's currency. In the first half of 2000, for example, the nation recorded a $12 billion budget surplus, almost $4 billion above the target set by the IMF. This achievement was accompanied by declining interest rates, rising tax collections, and a 4% increase in gross domestic product (GDP).

High oil prices cut the trade surplus below $1 billion, as Brazil spent $253.7 million per month on petroleum imports. Still, the country, which has reduced its dependency on foreign petroleum from 36% of consumption in 1997 to 20% in 2000, aims for self-sufficiency by 2005.

Economists at the Getulio Vargas Foundation employed Transparency International's "Corruption Perceptions Index" to calculate the lost growth attributable to corruption. The economists concluded that if Brazil could lower its corruption rate to the world average, it would boost the country's per-capita income by 59% in 26 years.

Foreign Affairs. On August 31, President Cardoso hosted a two-day South American summit, which attracted a dozen heads of state to Brasília. Leaders discussed integrating the region's economies, fortifying democratic institutions, and improving education and technology. The meeting came on the heels of President Clinton's visit to Bogotá, Colombia, where he announced the $7.5 billion "Plan Colombia," designed to combat narco-trafficking and stabilize the guerrilla-infested Andean country. Consequently, Cardoso's guests also examined the possible spillover—into their countries—of the antidrug offensive in Colombia, as well as the possibility of U.S. military involvement in that nation. The White House issued a statement saying that "this is not Vietnam." Clinton also promised Colombia's neighbors that "the United States will not abandon them. We have funds that can be used to help other countries solve the problem."

For his part, Cardoso said that Brazil was concerned most about narco-traffickers using the Amazonian rain forest as a route for the shipment of chemicals required to process cocaine. He promised to deploy 6,000 soldiers along Brazil's 1,000-mi (1 600-km) border between Brazil and Colombia.

GEORGE W. GRAYSON
College of William & Mary

Bulgaria

The reformist government in Bulgaria continued to pursue a program of tough structural reforms while seeking to root out crime and corruption. On the international stage, Bulgaria made slow progress in its drive toward European Union (EU) membership, while voicing disappointment with the results of the EU-sponsored Stability Pact for South Eastern Europe.

Politics of Reform. The Union of Democratic Forces (UDF) government was criticized for its severe measures designed to restructure and revive the Bulgarian economy. The approval rating of Prime Minister Ivan Kostov reached a record low, as nearly 62% of citizens expressed disappointment with his performance. Sectors of society were unhappy with rising unemployment, low salaries, and widespread corruption. However, a vote of no confidence in the government, submitted in May by the oppositionist Bulgarian Socialist Party (BSP), failed to gain approval in parliament.

By the end of the year, the major political parties were gearing up for spring of 2001 parliamentary elections. The ruling UDF underscored its success in stabilizing the economy and the BSP focused attention on the social dislocations that had accompanied the economic reforms.

Crime Crusade. After several scandals within the administration, Kostov during the summer launched a major crackdown on organized crime and official corruption. Eight Yugoslav citizens and five Russian businessmen were expelled from Bulgaria for their alleged involvement in criminal syndicates.

President Petar Stoyanov urged Kostov to act decisively against corruption among senior officials. Alexander Bozhkov, the country's chief negotiator with the EU, resigned in a major corruption scandal, and government spokesman Mihail Mihailov left office after being accused of accepting bribes from businessmen. Meanwhile, former Interior Minister Bogomil Bonev, whom Kostov sacked in December 1999, accused the prime minister of failing to react to reports of graft among top officials.

Economic Indicators. Despite material hardships among Bulgarian workers, the International Monetary Fund (IMF) praised Bulgaria's "sound economic policy," and claimed the country was positioned for a solid recovery in 2001. Kostov announced that during its two-and-one-half years in office, the cabinet had privatized 70% of state assets and restored 95% of nationalized land. At the same time, Bulgaria's foreign debt dropped by almost $1 billion since the end of 1999, and totaled about $9 billion by the close of the year. The gross domestic product (GDP) was projected to grow by about 4.5% in 2000.

Progress Toward Europe. Despite macroeconomic progress, Bulgaria's accession to the EU was not expected until 2007 at the earliest, as the Union stalled its decision. The EU announced it would open talks with Bulgaria on just six of the 31 chapters of the *aquis communautaire*, the Union guidelines for membership. Nevertheless, the EU granted Bulgaria 250 million euros (U.S. $223 million) in 2000, to help the country achieve sustainable economic growth by implementing infrastructure projects.

Stability Pact Problems. Bulgarian authorities voiced strong dissatisfaction with the EU-sponsored Stability Pact for South Eastern Europe, launched in the summer of 1999 to promote Balkan reconstruction. Criticism centered around the lack of progress in securing Western investments in the region. Premier Kostov complained in particular about delays in starting the construction of the planned Vidin-Calafat bridge over the River Danube between Bulgaria and Romania. Bodo Hombach, the pact coordinator, visited Bulgaria in July and claimed the EU had committed itself to provide additional financing for projects in the Balkans.

JANUSZ BUGAJSKI
Center for Strategic and International Studies

BULGARIA • Information Highlights

Official Name: Republic of Bulgaria.
Location: Southeastern Europe.
Area: 42,823 sq mi (110 910 km²).
Population (2000 est.): 7,796,694.
Chief Cities (Dec. 31, 1996 est.): Sofia, the capital, 1,116,823; Plovdiv, 344,326; Varna, 301,421.
Government: *Head of state,* Petar Stoyanov, president (elected November 1996). *Head of government,* Ivan Kostov, prime minister (elected April 1997). *Legislature* (unicameral)—National Assembly.
Monetary Unit: Lev (2.2613 leva equal U.S.$1, Nov. 7, 2000).
Gross Domestic Product (1999 est. U.S.$): $34,900,000,000 (purchasing power parity).
Economic Index (1999, 1990 = 100): *Consumer Prices,* all items, 149,035.0; food, 152,828.0.
Foreign Trade (1999 U.S.$): *Imports,* $5,430,000,000; *exports,* $3,937,000,000.

Burma.   SEE MYANMAR.

Business and Corporate Affairs

Rarely in the past century has corporate leadership been presented with such a complexity of problems as in the year 2000. Companies old and new faced a barrage of challenges involving litigation, financing, profits, product quality, globalization, personnel, and other matters that tested seasoned executives and young entrepreneurs alike. It also was a year of great opportunities, a make-or-break year of big decisions. Many corporate leaders were unable to resolve problems, failed to seize opportunities, or took their companies down the wrong path and were replaced.

Largely unanticipated by management gurus and executive recruiters who tried to fill executive slots, retired chiefs were increasingly called upon by boards for their sure-handed experience and guidance. It was seen by some as a merging of old and new management philosophies, necessary and overdue as a corrective to the technologically bright, but sometimes erratic, young leaders. But just as many experienced managers were replaced, unable to guide their companies in a swiftly evolving business world. Good management, young or old, became more of a high priority than earlier in the expansion, and companies competed for talent with huge, and shareholder-criticized, financial packages based on stock options.

Corporate Troubles. The troubles of some companies, new and old, were unique to them. Coca-Cola's difficulties involved not just replacing executives, but European claims of unsanitary bottles, allegations of race bias at home, the threat of antitrust action in Mexico, and heightened competition from archrival PepsiCo. Defective tires led to allegations against Bridgestone/Firestone, and to a lesser degree against Ford Motor and Goodyear Tire & Rubber, for more than 100 fatalities. Sotheby's Holdings and Christie's, the world's most prominent fine-arts auction houses, were found guilty in federal court of having colluded in price-fixing schemes. Showing signs it had misread demand for its communications services, AT&T was forced to undo its string of acquisitions; the company then made plans to break into four parts.

With its U.S. operations losing money, DaimlerChrysler dismissed the head of its Chrysler unit and became almost fully controlled from Germany. Xerox, the world's largest copier company, suddenly found itself on the ropes late in the year and was forced to sell assets to survive. Owens Corning, beset by various legal issues involving breast implants, declared bankruptcy. Priceline, a so-called dot.com or on-line-sales company, earlier praised as revolutionary in allowing customers to name their price for travel tickets and other consumer products, failed to meet profit projections, saw its market value dwindle, and was forced to shrink operations.

A federal judge in June ordered that Microsoft, which had lost its antitrust case in November 1999, be broken into two companies—one for its Windows operating system, and one for its computer programs and Internet business. As expected, Microsoft appealed the ruling.

While many of the small companies seeking to sell products and services on the Internet failed at a growing rate as the year ended, many new-economy and most old-economy businesses thrived. The economic climate remained one of confidence, buoyed by wage increases, low inflation, solid if slowing profits, and continued belief in the future. Few companies exemplified success more so than the ageless General Electric (GE), an immense conglomeration of companies involved in everything from consumer credit to aircraft engines to innovative electronics. With the envy and admiration even of competitors, GE made the transition to the new economy while continuing to grow profits from the old. And no executive was hailed more for his success than GE's chairman, Jack Welch.

GE, A New- & Old-Economy Company. Facing retirement in April 2001 at GE's mandatory retirement age of 65, Welch spent several months preparing to name a successor and enjoying the praise and honors earned by an executive who in 20 years had built the company into first place in U.S. stock-market valuation. Welch was in vitally good mental and physical health, and it was clear he did not relish the prospect before him. Nonetheless, in late November, GE named Jeffrey R. Immelt, the 44-year-old head of GE Medical Systems, president and chairman-elect. He would share management responsibilities with Welch for one year. Only weeks earlier, Welch made an 11th-hour, $45 billion-plus bid for Honeywell, which the day before was pledged to merge with United Technologies. Honeywell, with holdings in aerospace, building controls, and other industries, agreed to the

Steve Chase (left), *chairman of America Online (AOL), and Gerald Levin, chairman of Time Warner, began 2000 with a dramatic announcement: Time Warner and AOL were joining together. The historic merger received approval early in 2001.*

offer, and United Technologies bowed out. Honeywell's chairman, Michael Bonsignore, was quoted as saying that Welch's promise to stay on through 2001—which was part of the negotiations—clinched the deal. Welch said the need to assure a smooth transition of Honeywell into GE left him no choice.

Though the reasons differed, GE was not the only company in which seasoned executives either stayed on or were rehired for their long and successful leadership. Paul Allaire returned to his chief-executive-officer (CEO) post at Xerox; former chief David Johnson returned as head of Campbell Soup; former chairman Henry Schacht rejoined Lucent Technologies as CEO; Procter & Gamble rehired former chairman John Pepper to the leadership post; and Apple Computer founder Steve Jobs became permanent CEO after assuming the role on an interim basis in 1997. Douglas Daft, who replaced M. Douglas Ivester in the top job at Coca-Cola, called in former president Donald Keough, 73, as an official adviser. These executive returns shared a common denominator: The challenge of leading a diversified company amid stiff competition in an evolving marketplace required initiative and innovation, to be sure, but experience, too.

Head of companies old and new often lacked one quality or another, and that led to numerous top-job changes. Edward DeGraan, a 32-year Gillette veteran, was named acting chief, replacing Michael Hawley. Dieter Zetsche was sent from Germany to Michigan to replace James Holden as Chrysler boss. John B. McCoy, longtime Bank One chairman, resigned under pressure. Notable retirements included the highly successful Charles Knight, Emerson Electric chief; Roger Enrico, PepsiCo chairman; and Sanford Litvack, Walt Disney vice-chairman. Commenting that "I have done what I set out to do here," Joel Klein, who won the court order to break up Microsoft, left his antitrust position at the U.S. Justice Department.

According to the Chicago-based outplacement firm Challenger, Gray & Christmas, the revolving executive door caused 350 chief executives in the United States to leave their jobs during the August-November period. The trend was forcing many companies to reconsider how they should fill their top spots and how they should groom future executives.

Vast Opportunities. This turnover and continued transition to a predominantly service economy, rapid economic growth, and the ever-changing demands of the technological age created vast opportunities. In growing numbers, women found slots at the highest levels of business, especially in technology, finance, and retailing. *Fortune* magazine listed Hewlett-Packard chief Carly Fiorina at the top of its Power 50, followed by Debby Hopkins, chief financial officer of Lucent; Meg Whitman, president and CEO of on-line auctioneer eBay; Donna Dubinsky, CEO of Handspring, producer of a handheld pocket-communications device; and Ellen Hancock, chairman of Exodus Communications. *Fortune* commented that four of the top five women "have husbands who don't work." While feminists continued to complain about a "glass ceiling" that limited progress of women executives, minorities also criticized what they viewed as corporate reluctance to promote them into top jobs. Nevertheless, the pace of assimilation intensified, greatly motivated by the growing need for talented leaders.

Perhaps the most notable appointment was that of E. Stanley O'Neal, who picked cotton as a youngster, to chief of brokerage operations at Merrill Lynch, a position viewed as a stepping-stone to the chief executive's office. But African-Americans lost a top slot as well with the resignation of Lloyd Ward, chairman and CEO of Maytag, an appliance maker in an industry where competition had reduced profits. Late in the year, W. James McNerney, Jr., who had been considered for GE's top position, was named chairman and CEO of Minnesota Mining & Manufacturing, and President-elect George W. Bush named Paul O'Neill, 65-year-old CEO of Alcoa, as his secretary of the treasury.

Huge Mergers. Big mergers contributed to the executive turnovers. Global-size companies seemed in constant search for new business combinations as either acquirer or target, often across national borders. It was a race for size. The Organization for Economic Co-operation and Development (OECD) reported that cross-border mergers and acquisitions rose fivefold among its 29 members in the decade through 1999.

Vivendi, a French conglomerate, acquired Seagram for $35 billion. PaineWebber, one of America's largest securities firms, was acquired by UBS, a Swiss bank, for about $12 billion. Another large securities firm—Donaldson, Lufkin & Jenrette—became part of Credit Suisse First Boston. Subject to regulatory scrutiny, the Anglo-Dutch Reed Elsevier and Canadian publisher Thomson planned to acquire U.S. publisher Harcourt General.

In spite of the recognized need for great size as markets became larger, antitrust and sometimes national interests blocked other mergers. Most notably, the year-old merger

plans of Burlington Northern Sante Fe and Canadian National Railway, to create North America's largest rail system, remained on hold due to a U.S. federal moratorium on rail mergers. Faced with antitrust scrutiny from the European Union (EU), Time Warner and Britain's EMI dropped a $20 billion joint-venture plan to expand their music businesses. And under regulatory pressure in the United States and Europe, telecommunications concerns WorldCom and Sprint dropped plans for a $129 billion joining of forces.

From a U.S. perspective, the most-notable merger plans were among domestic companies. The $135 billion planned merger of Time Warner and AOL received approval from the EU and the U.S. Federal Trade Commission (FTC), and from the U.S. Federal Communications Commission (FCC) in January 2001. In granting approval, however, the FCC laid down conditions to make AOL compatible with the systems of Internet rivals. The merger established the world's largest media business. In other merger news during 2000, General Mills agreed to acquire Pillsbury for $10.5 billion, and Philip Morris, which already owned Kraft Foods, agreed to buy Nabisco Holdings for $14.9 billion.

Chevron agreed to acquire Texaco for about $36 billion, creating the world's fourth-largest oil company. PepsiCo bought Quaker Oats, including its Gatorade soft-drink brand, for $13.4 billion. Kellogg agreed to acquire biscuit maker Keebler Foods. And, seemingly unable to adjust to the fast and less personal pace of modern banking, J.P. Morgan, founded by the legendary banker J. Pierpont Morgan, was taken over by Chase Manhattan, known for years as John D. Rockefeller's bank, in a $31 billion deal.

Throughout the world of finance, big became bigger. Citigroup, a banking-finance-insurance company, agreed to buy Associates First Capital, the nation's largest publicly traded consumer-finance company, for nearly $30 billion in stock. It was a good year for law firms involved in such transaction. *The American Lawyer* publication reported in midyear that the average income of lawyers in its top-100 firms was $753,000 in 1999, and that the firm of Skadden, Arps, Slate, Meagher & Flom had produced $1 billion-plus revenues, the first to do so.

See also THE U.S. ECONOMY—THE GREAT EXPANSION, page 38.

JOHN CUNNIFF, *Associated Press*

Cambodia

During 2000, Cambodia's Prime Minister Hun Sen oversaw the second year of relative peace after decades of internal strife and maintained economic stability as the country recovered from the 1997 regional financial crisis. Cambodia was less successful in attracting needed foreign investment, and floods damaged rice paddies.

Politics. The prime minister reaffirmed his political control after security forces defeated an insurgent attack on government buildings in November. Prince Ranariddh, head of the royalist party that shares power with the ruling Cambodian People's Party (CPP), was criticized by his party members and the opposition for cooperating too closely with Hun Sen. Senate President and CPP party leader Chea Sim, the prime minister's rival, suffered a minor stroke in October. Public concern about 78-year-old King Sihanouk's health prior to one of his trips to China for medical treatment played into an opposition-led debate over whether the National Assembly should prepare a more detailed succession law.

Opposition leader Sam Rainsy led several protests, including attempts to erect an unofficial memorial stupa to commemorate victims of a 1997 attack on an opposition rally. In October, Rainsy went on a hunger strike over alleged government mismanagement of aid distribution to flood victims. Newly organized labor unions were active, with garment workers demonstrating over working conditions, and farmers protesting against confiscation of their land.

At midyear, Cambodian leaders and representatives of the United Nations (UN) agreed on the framework for an international trial of former Khmer Rouge (KR) members for genocide, but by late in the year, Cambodian legislators still were deliberating over a draft law to support a tribunal.

The Economy. After the government made progress in addressing foreign-donor demands to contain illegal logging and initiate military demobilization plans, the Consultative Group in May pledged $548 million to finance the country's rebuilding effort. Foreign aid also helped when the worst flooding of the Mekong River in 70 years killed more than 300 Cambodians and destroyed farmland, producing food shortages. With international guidance, Phnon Penh contained inflation , but flood damage was expected to lower the Finance Ministry's projected 5.5% growth rate in the gross domestic product (GDP). Tourism remained one of the fastest-growing sectors of the economy.

Despite economic progress, new foreign-investment pledges through September fell by 15% compared with 1999. Cambodian competitiveness suffered from poor infrastructure, lack of skilled labor, corruption, and insufficient investor protection. The administration had revenue-collection problems and had yet to shift sufficient resources from defense to health, education, and rural-development programs.

Foreign Relations. As a new member of the Association of Southeast Asian Nations (ASEAN), Cambodia concentrated on ties with Asian neighbors and on building its reputation as a regional player. Hun Sen went on a nine-country tour of ASEAN capitals in August, and Cambodian officials made progress in talks on demarcating their contested borders.

Cambodian officials were host to then Prime Minister Keizo Obuchi, the first Japanese leader to visit in decades, and received the Thai prime minister and Vietnamese general-secretary. Chinese President Jiang Zemin's visit in November—the first by a Chinese leader since the 1960s—marked warmer ties between Cambodia and its former foe, which once backed the KR movement. While the U.S. Congress blocked new aid for Phnom Penh, U.S. officials helped mediate the stupa dispute and tried to bridge differences between Cambodia and the UN on a KR trial.

The UN refugee agency closed its last field offices in Cambodia. The government assumed responsibility for the final 46,000 of the more than 1 million refugees the UN had helped resettle.

CHRISTINE VAN ZANDT
U.S. Government Analyst on East Asian Affairs

CAMBODIA • Information Highlights

Official Name: Kingdom of Cambodia.
Location: Southeast Asia.
Area: 69,900 sq mi (181 040 km²).
Population (2000 est.): 12,212,306.
Chief City (1991 est.): Phnom Penh, the capital, 900,000.
Government: *Head of state,* Norodom Sihanouk, king (acceded Sept. 24, 1993). *Head of government,* Hun Sen, prime minister (named Sept. 24, 1993). *Legislature*—National Assembly and Senate.
Monetary Unit: Riel (3,870.00 riels equal U.S.$1, official rate, July 2000).
Gross Domestic Product (1999 est. U.S.$): $8,200,000,000 (purchasing power parity).
Foreign Trade (1999 est. U.S.$): *Imports,* $1,200,000,000; exports, $821,000,000.

Canada

In Canada the year 2000 saw the birth of a major political party and old-style power struggles over the disposal of an unaccustomed federal budget surplus. Pierre Elliott Trudeau, Canada's best-known former prime minister, died; so did the familiar ownership structures of Canada's media. Meanwhile, most Canadians grumbled about taxes and fuel prices, and wondered why another year of economic growth did so little for their own prosperity and contentment. And on November 27, Canadians voted in their 37th general election and returned Prime Minister Jean Chrétien and his Liberal Party to power.

Government. The year opened with allegations of scandal, when Canada's auditor general complained that Human Resources Development Canada (HRDC) had not properly accounted for C$1 billion in federal job-creation grants. Jane Stewart, the new HRDC minister, admitted to record-keeping problems but denied any improprieties. When questioned by members of Parliament (MPs), she was strongly defended by Prime Minister Chrétien.

Despite protests from Quebec separatists, the Chrétien government introduced its "clarity bill," a response to a 1998 Supreme Court ruling that required Canada to negotiate if a province got a clear majority on a clear question about secession. Bloc Québécois (BQ) MPs denounced the proposed legislation for interfering with "self-determination"; other critics were appalled that Canadians would debate the process for a national breakup. "One country makes sense," answered Stephane Dion, minister for intergovernmental affairs, "only if based on mutual consent."

Provincial governments demanded the C$4.2 billion for health and social welfare that Ottawa had cut in its deficit-chopping 1995 budget, this time without strings. Buoyed by surpluses since 1998, Ottawa agreed, but only if the money promoted home care and if provinces were more accountable. In Alberta the provincial-government bill allowing private clinics to operate as short-stay hospitals provoked bitter

In September 2000, people gathered outside Ottawa's Parliament Building to pay their respects to Pierre Elliott Trudeau, who had died at the age of 80. Canadian media had voted Trudeau, a member of the Liberal Party, the nation's greatest prime minister of the 20th century because of his strong personality and such achievements as Canada's 1982 Charter of Rights and Freedoms.

CANADA • Information Highlights

Official Name: Canada.
Location: Northern North America.
Area: 3,851,792 sq mi (9 976 140 km²).
Population (2000 est.): 31,281,092.
Chief Cities (May 1996 census [metro. areas]): Ottawa, the capital (incl. Hull),1,010,498; Toronto, 4,263,757; Montreal, 3,326,510; Vancouver, 1,831,665.
Government: *Head of state,* Elizabeth II, queen; represented by Adrienne Clarkson, governor-general (took office Oct. 4, 1999). *Head of government,* Jean Chrétien, prime minister (took office Nov. 4, 1993). *Legislature—* Parliament: Senate and House of Commons.
Monetary Unit: Canadian dollar (1.4991 dollars equal U.S.$1, Dec. 29, 2000).
Gross Domestic Product (1999 est. U.S.$): $722,300,000,000 (purchasing power parity).
Economic Indexes (1999, 1990 = 100): *Consumer Prices,* all items, 118.5; food, 115.6. *Industrial Production,* 129.8.
Foreign Trade (1999 U.S.$): *Imports,* $214,791,000,000; *exports,* $238,422,000,000.

debate between Conservatives and others who saw a challenge to the Canada-wide principles of fee-free Medicare. Quebec denounced any federal bid for accountability, and Ontario Premier Mike Harris' government became an ally. Ottawa yielded. In September the provinces won a promise of C$23.4 billion in health transfers over five years, while the provinces would design their own priorities and reporting. Ottawa also offered C$1 billion in medical equipment and large sums for information technology and primary care.

With voters in mind, Ottawa granted same-sex couples pension and other rights, but stopped short of recognizing same-sex marriages. The federal government offered C$305 million to cover a homelessness problem, signed an antipollution treaty with the United States, and threatened an Ontario government that was notably indifferent to its own major pollution sources.

Politics. In 1997 the Reform Party won 60 seats in the House of Commons, making it the main opposition party to Chrétien's ruling Liberal Party. But all of the Reform seats were from western Canada, and for Reform to be more than a regional protest movement, said party leader Preston Manning, it must gain seats from the east by merging with the right-wing Progressive Conservative (PC) Party.

On March 27, 2000, following a party referendum, the Reform Party voted itself out of existence and was replaced by the Canadian Alliance, a move that was attacked by the PC leadership. A campaign for the leadership of the new alliance then began, with Manning, Alberta Progressive Conservative Treasurer Stockwell Day (*see* SIDEBAR, page

169), Ontario Tory organizer Tom Long, and British Columbia MP Dr. Keith Martin, a social liberal, as candidates. Manning ranked highest in opinion polls, and Long had full backing from Conrad Black's *National Post,* but Day pulled ahead. He had an impeccable record as a social conservative.

On June 24, Day emerged from a national ballot in the lead, and won a runoff election for the leadership on July 8 with 63% of 114,000 votes cast. "This is a new century," declared Day, "and this is a new party." Day headed to Quebec to improve his French, recruited former *Le Devoir* editor Claude Ryan as an adviser, and persuaded two former BQ MPs with conservative leanings to support him. On September 11, Day won a safe parliamentary seat in Okanagan-Coquihalla, British Columbia.

In early October, anticipating that Chrétien would call for a November election, Day announced a Canadian Alliance platform that included C$66 billion in tax cuts over five years, a reduction of government debt, an increase in tax exemptions, and increased military spending. However, he abandoned his earlier call for a 17% flat-rate income tax.

Joe Clark, elected in 1999 to head the Progressive Conservatives, spent the year fighting a rearguard action against the Canadian Alliance. His party narrowly kept a Newfoundland seat but, while he won a safe Nova Scotia seat, three of his Quebec MPs defected to the Liberals, and the sole Ontario PC MP switched to the Alliance. So did scores of party officials, while Premiers Ralph Klein of Alberta and Mike Harris of Ontario became studiously neutral.

With the Tories crumbling, Prime Minister Chrétien began pressing for unity. Saskatchewan's New Democratic Party (NDP) Premier Roy Romanow announced his retirement in the fall amid rumors that he might become a high-profile Liberal. Romanow did not, but a Saskatchewan NDP MP switched, and the party feared mass voter defections to the Liberals to stop an Alliance victory. Saskatchewan's NDP scheduled a convention for January 2001 to select a new leader.

The Election. Buoyed by high poll standings and the emotions surrounding the funeral of former Liberal Prime Minister Trudeau, and worried that Stockwell Day could only grow in popularity, Chrétien ignored worried backbenchers and, on October 22, called an election for November 27, well short of the customary four-year term.

Though Liberals slumped as low as 39% in campaign opinion polls, Day's bland image did not survive his retreat from his more-sweeping tax-cut proposals and Liberal claims that the Alliance had a secret agenda that would undermine Canada's publicly funded health insurance and privatize the Canada Pension Plan. Hopes of an Alliance breakthrough in Ontario faded with evidence of Day's socially conservative and creationist views.

In retrospect, Chrétien's bold move in calling the election was a triumph. Despite constant media predictions of a minority government, the Liberals won more votes and seats than in 1993 or 1997. Chrétien became only the fourth Canadian party leader to pile up three successive majority governments. The Liberals won 172 seats in the House of Commons, up from 161 before the vote. The Canadian Alliance placed second with 66 seats, the BQ won 38, the NDP 13, and the PCs 12. Stockwell Day strengthened the Alliance hold on western Canada, leaving the Liberals only 14 seats in the four provinces. The Liberals took all three vast but underpopulated northern ridings.

All leaders held their own seats, and both Clark's Conservatives and Alexa McDonough's New Democrats elected enough members to retain official party status in Parliament.

Party Support, Before and After 37th Election

	Aug. 30, 2000.		On Nov. 27, 2000	
	Seats	Support	Seats	% Votes
Liberal*	159	55	172	41
Reform/CA	58	18	66	26
BQ*	44	8	38	11
NDP	20	7	13	9
PC	15	10	12	13

*(Recount on November 28 transferred Champlain from Liberal to BQ by 7 votes.)

Provincial Affairs. Only Nova Scotia and New Brunswick labored under deficits, and both provinces had new Conservative governments, poor populations, and big needs. Following a spring election, New Brunswick's Premier Bernard Lord boasted that he had kept 19 of his 20 election pledges within the promised 200 days, and that the 20th was met when he wiped out the controversial highway tolls that helped defeat his Liberal predecessor. Running for reelection, another Conservative, Prince Edward Island Premier Patrick Binns, persuaded voters with his "Let's Continue" slogan. Islanders gave the Conservatives 26 seats to one for the Liberals.

In Quebec, Premier Lucien Bouchard tried to divert impatient separatists with an estates general to review threats to the French language. In Ontario, Opposition critics tried to link the seven deaths and 2,000 sick in an *E. coli* outbreak at the little town of Walkerton to privatization of government water-testing laboratories. A judicial inquiry would distribute blame.

A ten-year high in oil and gas prices buoyed the "Alberta Advantage," allowing the province to boast of low unemployment and a C$300 rebate to each tax filer. Lacking oil or much else to sell to a still-depressed Asian Rim, British Columbia's new NDP premier, Ujjal Dosanjh, did well to announce a C$452 million surplus.

Economics, Business, and Labor. Canada's prosperity continued in 2000, but statistics for the previous decade suggested that the income of the richest 20% had risen from 41.9% of the total to 45.2%, while the income of the poorest fifth had dropped 0.7% to 3.1% of the total. In addition, real incomes for 60% of Canadians had dropped. The reasons included a drop in transfer payments to low-income earners, stagnant wages, a drop in private-sector unionism, and less-redistributive taxes.

Women's incomes had risen 14%, but they earned 72.5 cents for each dollar earned by a man—up from 66.1 cents in 1987. Business insisted on tax cuts to slow a brain drain of qualified young Canadians to the United States. Farmers did not share the prosperity. Record wheat crops inflated reserves and hurt prices, and Ottawa complained that it could not match the U.S.–European Union (EU) subsidy war.

Most Canadian banks combined record profits with continued layoffs. Air Canada digested its 1999 acquisition of Canadian Airlines and narrowly avoided a pilots' strike in August, but widespread complaints of poor service and fare gouging led to the appointment of a complaints commissioner.

Privatized since 1992, the Canadian National Railway Company (CN) had cut a third of its workforce and taken over the Illinois Central in 1999. In 2000, CN announced merger plans with the Burlington Northern Santa Fe, but regulators in the United States and Transport Canada killed the deal. Similarly, the EU scotched a merger of Montreal's Alcan, Zurich's Alusuisse Lonza, and Pechiney in Paris to create an aluminum giant. A French firm, Vivendi, bought Seagram, an alcoholic-beverage-and-entertainment conglomerate founded

©Andy Clark/Reuters/Archive Photos

STOCKWELL DAY

On July 8, 2000, Stockwell Day, who had held various posts in Alberta's provincial government, was elected leader of the new Canadian Alliance. After winning a by-election to the House of Parliament in September, Day led the Alliance into the federal election. Although the Alliance finished second to the Liberal Party in the voting on November 27, it became Canada's official oppositon party. Day easily retained his parliamentary seat.

Born Aug. 16, 1950, in Barrie, Ontario, Day was raised in the Maritimes, Ottawa, and Montreal. He attended the University of Victoria and subsequently worked in a variety of job, including time as a counselor and an assistant pastor. In 1986 he entered politics, winning a seat in the Alberta legislature, which he kept until 2000.

by the Samuel Bronfman family of Montreal 76 years before.

Canada's stock markets rationalized in 2000, with Calgary specializing in venture capital, Montreal in options and derivatives, and Toronto in managing large capitalizations. Angry at having to do deals for its Caisse de Dépôts et Placements—Quebec's largest pension-fund manager—through Toronto, Quebec's government organized a deal with Nasdaq to make the Montreal Stock Exchange a northern branch.

Mergers of media producers and carriers dominated the year. Bell Canada Enterprises (BCE), Canada's largest telecommunications company, spun off a 37% stake in its profitable Nortel Networks, offered C$9.6 billion for Teleglobe's worldwide fiber-optics network, and acquired CTV, Canada's oldest and largest private network, as well as three specialty cable channels, to add to Sympatico, the largest Internet server.

In February the Thomson Corporation announced that all its papers, except the *Toronto Globe and Mail*, were for sale. Four months later it was announced that Gannett, the largest U.S. newspaper owner, had purchased 21 of the newspapers, and Alabama-based Community Newspaper Holdings another 17. Television broadcaster CanWest Global Communications Corp. became Canada's biggest media conglomerate when it agreed to purchase 13 newspapers and other properties from Hollinger International, Canada's largest newspaper publisher, for C$3.5 billion.

In the spring, world gas and oil prices rose from about 40 cents to 70 cents a liter. Trapped in long-term contracts, truckers staged blockades to force Ottawa and provincial governments to cut taxes, which made up one-third or more of the price. Ontario asked customers to pay more, and most government promised to help low-income families with home-heating costs but avoided details.

Foreign Affairs and Defense. Canada's term on the United Nations (UN) Security Council proved painful when the Israeli-Palestinian conflict in October led to a resolution condemning Israel. Canada agreed to the measure, and Jewish voters protested. Foreign Minister Lloyd Axworthy rejected Canada's involvement in any U.S. nuclear-missile-defense system; Defense Minister Art Eggleton publicly disagreed, and Axworthy announced his early retirement from politics.

Canadian soldiers came home after five months in East Timor. A military inquiry failed to find a link between sick soldiers and their service in Croatia, but it described the soldiers' treatment as a "national disgrace." A judge said much the same when he awarded a potential $1 billion in compensation to disabled and mentally ill veterans of both World Wars I and II whose earnings and savings had simply been absorbed by the government over many years. On the other hand, the Chrétien government brought an Unknown Soldier of World War I from Vimy Ridge in France to an Ottawa memorial, promised $40 million for a new Canadian War Museum, and acquired the first of four former British submarines.

Canada also made plans to establish full diplomatic relations with North Korea and to normalize relations with Libya by reopening its embassy in Tripoli. And in December the government declared a debt-payment moratorium for 11 of the poorest African and Latin American nations.

Justice. Early in 2000, Beverly McLachlin succeeded Antonio Lamer as chief justice of the Supreme Court of Canada. She was the first woman to hold that position. Commentators claimed that she was more conservative than Lamer, even though her pro-rights record was the same (37%) as his. The Supreme Court struck down Ottawa's law requiring tobacco companies to put horrifying pictures on cigarette packages, compelled Prince Edward Island to provide a French school for 50 Francophone children at Summerside, and upheld Ottawa's firearms-registration law

Police reported the eighth consecutive drop in the nation's crime rate in 1999, with

On July 12, 2000, Matthew Coon Come (left), the 44-year-old former grand chief of the Cree Indians of northern Quebec, was elected head of the Assembly of First Nations.

youth crime down 7.2%. Alberta courts convicted environmental activist Wiebo Ludwig for sabotaging oil-company property, and a small-town doctor, Abraham Cooper, for killing a rival practitioner. David Milgaard, who had spent 23 years in prison for killing a Saskatoon nurse, was freed after DNA evidence caught the real killer.

Rival biker gangs have fought for years to control Montreal narcotics traffic. A truce between the Hell's Angels and the Rock Machine was brazenly concluded in a court building. Then an alleged biker hit man wounded police reporter Michel Auger. The bungler's body was found in a burned-out van, but Quebec media and politicians raged at Ottawa about its weak criminal laws. A lower court dismissed conspiracy charges against Hell's Angels leader Maurice "Mom" Boucher, largely because the evidence came from a man who had murdered

two prison guards. An appeals court reversed the judgment, and Boucher went back to jail.

Native Affairs. British Columbia's land-rights treaty with the Nisga'a nation—approved by Canada's House of Commons in December 1999 and by the Senate in April 2000—ended an 80-year battle and gave the Nisga'a 770 square miles (2 000 km^2) of land in the Nass Valley, C$2.3 billion in cash and benefits, and a form of self-government. In September 1999 the Supreme Court of Canada recognized a Micmac treaty right to subsistence fishing, but also ruled that the federal government could regulate that fishing. In reaction, some natives claimed total control of all land and resources, while non-natives reacted angrily.

Most native bands accepted the federal government's help in training and in buying boats, equipment, and licenses. But Micmac near the Burnt Church Reserve in New Brunswick denied Ottawa's regulatory authority, and confrontations occurred between Micmac, and nonnatives lobstermen in Miramichi Bay in August and September 2000. Newly elected Grand Chief Matthew Coon Come of the Assembly of First Nations, Mohawk warriors, and native militants across Canada backed the Micmac. Fisheries and Oceans Minister Herb Dhaliwal backed his local officers, and the Royal Canadian Mounted Police (RCMP) moved in to curb violence.

Dozens of native legal claims were filed against the Anglican Church and the United Church, Canada's largest Protestant denominations. The claims charged that natives had been abused by child-care workers and others at the residential schools once run by the churches for young natives.

Environment. The year 2000 featured a cooler-than-average summer in the east and dry weather in the west. Talk of global warming survived a chilly summer, thanks to reports of melting ice and open water near the North Pole.

At Pine Lake in central Alberta, a tornado wrecked a trailer camp and took 11 lives and injured more than 130. Toronto, Canada's largest city, voted to ship more than 1 million tons of garbage per year 360 miles (580 km) north to the huge Adams Mine near Kirkland Lake. Because the pit was filled with groundwater, locals wondered about the fate of their own drinking supply. Others welcomed jobs.

The *E. coli* outbreak at Walkerton in rural Ontario drew attention to the impact

CANADIAN PROVINCES AND TERRITORIES • Information Highlights

Province	Population (in millions)	Area (sq mi)	Area (km²)	Capital	Head of Government
Alberta	2.9	255,286	661 190	Edmonton	Lois E. Hole, lieutenant governor Ralph Klein, premier
British Columbia	4.0	365,946	947 800	Victoria	Garde Gardom, lieutenant governor Ujjal Dosanjh, premier
Manitoba	1.1	250,946	649 950	Winnipeg	Peter M. Liba, lieutenant governor Gary Doer, premier
New Brunswick	.75	28,355	73 440	Fredericton	Marilyn Trenholme Counsell, lieutenant governor Bernard Lord, premier
Newfoundland	.53	156,649	405 720	St. John's	Arthur Maxwell House, lieutenant governor Beaton Tulk, premier
Northwest Territories	.04	451,740	1 170 000	Yellowknife	Stephen Kakfwi, premier
Nova Scotia	.94	21,425	55 491	Halifax	Myra A. Freeman, lieutenant governor John F. Hamm, premier
Nunavut	.02	769,888	1 994 000	Iqaluit	Paul Okalik, premier
Ontario	11.6	412,580	1 068 580	Toronto	Hilary M. Weston, lieutenant governor Mike Harris, premier
Prince Edward Island	.13	2,185	5 660	Charlottetown	Gilbert R. Clements, lieutenant governor Patrick Binns, premier
Quebec	7.3	594,857	1 540 680	Quebec City	Lise Thibault, lieutenant governor Lucien Bouchard, premier*
Saskatchewan	1.0	251,865	652 330	Regina	Lynda M. Haverstock, lieutenant governor Roy Romanow, premier
Yukon	.03	186,660	483 450	Whitehorse	Pat Duncan, premier

*Announced resignation on Jan. 11, 2001

of mass livestock operations on rural water sources across Canada. Alberta's Livestock Alley, north of Lethbridge, where 900,000 cattle and hogs produce as much waste as a city of 8 million, had the province's highest incidence of intestinal disease.

Culture and Sports. Canadian professional teams in hockey, baseball, and basketball all finished out of the finals in 2000. Club owners and fans contrasted cross-border costs of recruiting star athletes with U.S. dollars and providing fully taxed facilities compared to taxpayer-funded American stadiums. They concluded that competition was hopeless. When Ottawa proposed help, however, the notion died in a week after a gust of outrage at millionaire athletes and club owners. Canadians expected franchises to pay their way.

Montrealers waited for their Expos baseball franchise to vanish southward, but no one warned them that Molson would put the Canadiens of the National Hockey League up for sale. Another brewer, Labatt, sold the Toronto Blue Jays.

Populism also battered the new president of the Canadian Broadcasting Corporation (CBC), Bob Rabinovitch, a former deputy minister and private-sector financial manager, when he proposed that the public-television network concentrate on quality production rather than local production. The Canadian Radio-television and Telecommunications Commission (CRTC), Canada's broadcast regulator, took its CBC license-renewal hearings to smaller cities and came back with demands that the CBC leave popular revenue-producing U.S. shows and sports to private networks, and feed whatev-

er audience remained with multicultural, feminist, and First Nations programming. Rabinovitch scorned the advice. Then regional protests, unions, Rabinovitch's own board savaged his plan to find $120 million for programming at the expense of local news programs.

At the XXVII Summer Olympics in Sydney, Canada's Olympic athletes fell below their 1996 Atlanta record—winning only 14 medals, including golds to triathlete Simon Whitfield and tennis pairs Sebastien Lareau and Daniel Nestor. Federal sports policies that favored mass amateur participation over a few well-paid, high-performance champions took the blame—or the credit.

Obituaries. Pierre Elliott Trudeau, prime minister from 1968 to 1984 (with a brief Tory interval in 1979–80), died of prostate cancer on September 28. Canadian media had voted him the greatest prime minister of the century because of his strong personality and achievements such as Canada's 1982 Charter of Rights and Freedoms. His death led to widespread grief, especially among newer Canadians, and what a reporter called "wistful liberals." Other Canadians, especially in Quebec and the West, were less admiring, and Chrétien's announcement that he would rename Canada's highest mountain in Trudeau's honor provoked much criticism. (*See also* OBITUARIES, page 388.)

Among the other notable deaths during the year were poet Anne Hébert, biographer Sandra Gwyn, and the Montreal Canadiens' great Maurice "Rocket" Richard.

DESMOND MORTON, *Director*
McGill Institute for the Study of Canada

Caribbean

For the most part, Caribbean nations entered the year 2000 with economic growth rates ranging from modest to good.

At one extreme, Jamaica had a negative rate of minus 0.4%, compared with minus 0.5% the previous year. At the other extreme was Trinidad and Tobago, with an almost 7% growth rate, driven by the performance of the petroleum sector. According to the annual report of the Caribbean Development Bank (CDB), hurricane damage in 1999 had created difficulties in Antigua and Barbuda (growth of 4.6%), the Bahamas (growth of 5%–6%), Dominica (0.4%), and St. Kitts and Nevis (2.8%), dampening economic performance.

In the tourism sector, growth in stay-over visitor arrivals to the Caribbean slowed to about 4% in 1999, down from 5%, while the cruise-passengers market generally had a disappointing year. Overall, it was another year of lackluster performance in Caribbean agriculture, with sugar production rising by a little more than 10% to an estimated 723,480 metric tons, but declining banana output in the major producing countries—except Belize (up 10.4%). Slowing demand and weak prices negatively affected the bauxite industry in both Jamaica and Guyana, with lower production levels reported in Jamaica, but output up 4.1% to 2.34 million tons in Guyana. The performance of the Caribbean manufacturing sector improved in 2000.

On the political front, Haiti's May parliamentary election was widely condemned as faulty, and its November presidential election was boycotted by opposition parties. Other elections produced new governments in the Dominican Republic, Suriname, and Dominica, while Prime Minister Denzil Douglas and his Labour Party held on to power in St. Kitts and Nevis in the March 6 poll, and in Trinidad and Tobago, Prime Minister Basdeo Panday won a Dec. 11, 2000, general election.

Caribbean Community heads of government pressed ahead with a plan to establish a Caribbean Court of Justice. The court would replace the Privy Council in Britain as the court of last resort for the region.

Offshore Banking. A blitz on the world's offshore banking centers in mid-2000 sent governments in the Caribbean scurrying to clean up their image and remove the impression that they had created a haven for money launderers and tax dodgers.

Suddenly new banking regulations were being passed and old ones were being amended. Watchdog bodies were being established, and businesses found guilty of breaking the law were being closed down. The frenetic action started after the Financial Action Task Force on Money Laundering, set up by the G-7 industrial nations in June, named 15 countries/territories as possible havens for money launderers. The 15 regions included the Bahamas, the Cayman Islands, Dominica, St. Kitts and Nevis, and St. Vincent and the Grenadines.

Also in June the Organization for Economic Cooperation and Development (OECD) listed 35 locales as unfair tax havens. Among them were the U.S. Virgin Islands, the British Virgin Islands, Barbados, Anguilla, and Aruba. The offending parties were told to reform their tax systems or face economic sanctions. For the most part, Caribbean governments rejected the G-7 and OECD claims as unsubstantiated and meant to weaken competition against the OECD's offshore-banking centers. Nevertheless, they were uneasy about the possibility of resulting economic losses, and moved swiftly to make adjustments.

Bahamas. The Bahamas in October announced formation of a new intelligence unit to investigate suspicious financial activity, including money laundering. Prime Minister Hubert Ingraham said that the Bahamas would have to improve the nation's offshore-banking laws to remove itself from the blacklist.

The Bahamas, seen as a gateway into the United States, continued to attract thousands of poor and often ill-fated Cuban and Haitian boat people seeking a better way of life. At least 14 Haitians died of dehydration in April when a group of more than 300 eventually reached the Bahamas in a rickety boat. Another 23 Haitians drowned after their crowded sailboat, with as many as 115 people on board, sank on October 10 following a collision in the Atlantic with a Bahamian mail boat during a storm.

Former Prime Minister Sir Lynden O. Pindling died on August 26 at age 70. Pindling had led the islands to independence from Britain in 1973, and was prime minister until his Progressive Liberal Party (PLP) lost power in 1992.

Dominica. Dominicans changed their government on Jan. 31, 2000, bringing to power socialist politician Roosevelt (Rosie) Douglas at the head of a Dominica Labour Party (DLP) / Dominica Freedom Party

(DFP) coalition. The coalition won 12 seats in parliament (the House of Assembly) to oust the United Workers Party (UWP) of former Prime Minister Edison James, which won the remaining nine seats. In September the new government went to parliament with a number of new laws and amendments to old legislation to strengthen the fight against money laundering. Douglas, 58, died on October 1, and was succeeded by the coalition's Pierre Charles.

Dominican Republic. Social Democrat Hipólito Mejía Dominguez won the Dominican Republic's May 16 presidential election, defeating 93-year-old former President Joaquín Balaguer of the Social Christian Reformist Party (PRSC) and Danilo Medina of the ruling Dominican Liberation Party. Mejía, the 59-year-old candidate for the center-left Dominican Revolutionary Party (PRD), campaigned on a platform of injecting more social justice into a booming economy. He took over on August 16 from President Leonel Fernández Reyna, whose liberalizing reforms gave the Caribbean nation of 8 million people an economic growth rate of more than 7% a year.

The country's human-rights record came under scrutiny in June following press reports that soldiers had machine-gunned a truck full of Haitians trying to cross the border into the Dominican Republic, killing six Haitians and the Dominican driver.

Guyana. After a period of political instability, Guyana settled down in 2000 and prepared for a general election on March 19, 2001—two years ahead of the constitutional deadline. The poll was part of a peace accord brokered by heads of government of the Caribbean Community and Common Market (CARICOM), following political unrest that erupted after the results of the December 1997 election were dismissed by the main opposition group, the People's National Congress (PNC), as fraudulent.

A long-standing border dispute with Suriname flared up in June when Surinamese gunboats ordered a Canadian oil-drilling team out of a disputed area of the Courantyne River that separates both South American countries. The Canadian firm CGX Energy had been exploring for oil under a ten-year concession granted by Guyana. Guyanese negotiators recommended sharing any oil discovered, but made little headway in talks with successive Surinamese administrations.

Haiti. Haiti's first national vote in more than three years was meant to take the impoverished country toward a stable democracy after decades of dictatorship. Instead, the May 21 legislative election marked another political controversy for the Caribbean nation. Electoral monitors, including the Organization of American States (OAS), charged that the Electoral Council had allowed ten senatorial candidates to take their seats in parliament despite complaints they did not win enough votes in the first round of the ballot and should have participated in a second-round runoff. The powerful Lavalas family party of former President Jean-Bertrand Aristide won nearly all of the 19 Senate seats up for grabs, as well as 26 of the 83 seats in the lower house of parliament, the Chamber of Deputies, and most of the mayoral and local posts at stake.

Because most of the opposition parties boycotted the November 26 presidential election, Aristide himself was virtually guaranteed a return to power. The provisional Electoral Council said Aristide had won 91.69% of the

Hipólito Mejía Dominguez (right) of the Dominican Revolutionary Party (PRD) and his running mate, Milagros Ortiz Bosch, gave a thumbs-up after being elected president and vice-president, respectively, of the Dominican Republic on May 16, 2000.

© John Riley/AP/Wide World Photos

As Haiti prepared for a presidential election, a campaign banner in French and Creole proclaimed that Jean Bertrand Aristide represents "security." On Nov. 26, 2000, voters returned Aristide to the presidency; most opposition parties boycotted the balloting.

vote. The council put the turnout for the election at 68%, but this figure and the conduct of the poll were rejected by opposition politicians, political observers, and diplomatic sources in Haiti.

Ahead of the election, the authorities had announced the trial of an array of former coup leaders and paramilitary officers for a massacre in a slum in 1994. Of the 58 defendants, 22 were being tried in absentia.

Jamaica. With 849 murders reported in 1999, and 600 reported by the first week of September 2000, the Jamaica government launched a new anticrime police unit to target people in organized crime, including gang leaders, extortionists, carjackers, and criminal deportees from the United States and elsewhere. But within weeks the police themselves faced allegations of illegally wiretapping the telephone lines of some prominent people, including Prime Minister Percival Patterson.

As the scandal broke, press reports stated that some police officers had been paid $2 million to guarantee the safe passage of $1 billion worth of Colombian drugs through Jamaica en route to the Bahamas and the United States.

Trinidad and Tobago. In September the oil company BP announced the largest oil and gas discovery in the history of Trinidad and Tobago—3 trillion cu ft (85 billion m³) of gas and 90 million barrels of associated oil condensate—off southeast Trinidad. The U.S.-based company Reema International Corporation also announced the start of engineering work in Trinidad and Tobago on the Western Hemisphere's first gas-to-liquids plant, to convert natural gas into diesel, jet fuels, naphtha, and other products.

Trinidad and Tobago held general elections on December 11. The United National Congress (UNC), headed by Prime Minister Basdeo Panday, was returned to power, winning 19 of the 36 seats at stake. The People's National Movement (PNM) of Patrick Manning, the main opposition party, won 16 seats, and the National Alliance for Reconstruction (NAR) took just one seat. Panday was sworn in as prime minister December 20. His cabinet took office on December 22. The PNM has gone to court to challenge the right of two UNC winners to be listed as candidates because one also held Canadian citizenship and the other also held American citizenship. One electoral law states that a person swearing allegiance to a foreign country is ineligible to run in a Trinidad and Tobago election. The challenge remained unresolved at year's end.

TREVOR YEARWOOD, *Chief Editor*
"Caribbean News Agency (CANA)"

Central America

For 175 years, varying combinations of Central American republics have sought to form a political union. The year 2000 brought a moderate shift in procedures—less talk of politics, but a great deal of cooperation in other directions. Help came from increasing Mexican leadership promoted by President-elect Vicente Fox, in a role traditionally taken by the United States. But much of the activity sprang from within Central America, as its people coped with terrible natural disasters and the need to catch up with the technical progress of industrialized nations.

After eight years of negotiating, Costa Rica, El Salvador, Guatemala, Honduras, and Nicaragua signed a free-trade agreement with Mexico. The same five, plus Panama, set up programs for the collective purchasing of oil, medications, and medical equipment—whose increasing costs had become burdensome to small purchasers. The assumption was that collective buying might drive down some of the prices. The private sector was encouraged to join the program. Other financial matters discussed in 2000 were a possible regional free-trade agreement with Canada and Brazil, and the elimination of a few persistently high tariffs still existing within Central America. The road to closer economic integration still was pocked with the problem of competing products, however. Newly welcomed was the emergence of Spain as a commercial partner and a major investor, apparently replacing the United States in that category. Increasingly, Spain used Central Americans as "guest workers."

A spokesman for the Central American Integration System (SICA) expressed renewed concern for the environment. Several states were vigorously establishing zones for environmental protection, but their cities were increasingly becoming polluted from the heavy importation of old electrical appliances and used cars.

Belize. Belize has been independent from Great Britain since 1981, yet boundary questions still disturbed the progress of the small state. Some Guatemalan officials claimed title to half of Belize by old treaty rights, while others wanted to expand Guatemalan limits by arbitrating the border. Belizeans felt the matter was settled by acts of diplomacy and not subject to new arbitration. Armed incursions took place even as talks were being held in Panama to settle the issues. In May, some new agreements were reached, but nothing very substantive. The discussions resumed in November in Washington, DC, in the wake of border violations and minor military threats. To most of the world, it is a minor matter, but the dispute caused much instability in Central America.

Violent weather attacked Belize, as Hurricane Keith brought torrential rains and fierce winds in October. No lives were lost, but thousands of homes were destroyed, and some towns were completely evacuated. The important banana crop was ruined for the season. In May, it was discovered that the hot, dry months had raised Caribbean water temperatures to record heights, destroying

In late August 2000, high-ranking Central American leaders gathered in Guatemala City, Guatemala, where Costa Rica, El Salvador, Guatemala, Honduras, and Nicaragua inked a free-trade agreement with Mexico that was more than eight years in the making.

ancient coral beds critical to both the fishing and tourist businesses.

In July the Organization for Economic Cooperation and Development (OECD) cited Belize among 35 nations operating as tax havens. The states were given one year to correct the problem. Belizean Prime Minister Said Musa officially declared there was a misunderstanding at hand that would be rapidly cleared up.

Belize sought to attract tourists to the country's many natural wonders, including its extensive rain forests. Belize participated in a new program, funded in part by German investors, the JANUS Foundation, and the Nature Conservancy. Forestland was bought up to prevent clear-cutting; farmers were assisted in finding new crops; and many tree species, including some nearly extinct, were introduced. The hope was to reduce pollution and save the rare timber, while creating a more diversified economy for Belize.

Costa Rica. For about 60 years, Costa Rica's electric and telecommunications systems had been state monopolies. Early in 2000 the Legislative Assembly enacted a measure opening those utilities to private investment. Public objection was great; in March, state employees went on strike, and 20,000 people marched in support of the strike. Major seaports and much industry were paralyzed. Schools and hospitals were forced to close. President Miguel Ángel Rodríguez proposed delays in implementation of the law to consider "dialogue." The president sought privatization to improve the power operations and to help finance health and education systems. A commission was set up for further study. For many years, environmental groups had charged the vast banana industry with contributing heavily to the nation's pollution. A new system was inaugurated by which growers were certified as meeting environmental and wage standards. By late 2000, about one-third of the Costa Rican production had met the requirements.

Costa Rica has a long tradition of safety for its citizens, as well as its many tourists. But in 2000, all types of crime and juvenile delinquency were on the increase. Kidnapping was up 500%. Most shocking was the murder of two U.S. coeds studying in Costa Rica. The nation was stunned by this new surge that could also affect the economy. About 20,000 U.S. citizens made their homes in Costa Rica in 2000, and the tourist trade was valued at about $1 billion a year. Government officials promised action, although some communities lacked resources to deal with much criminal activity. In August, 1 million people walked 19 m (30.6 km) from San José to the shrine of the Virgin in Cartago, most of them praying for an end to the violence. The suspect charged with the two murders was likely be tried in January.

In May, President Rodríguez visited with President Bill Clinton in Washington, and received promises of expanded trade benefits, including greater access to U.S. markets. A Christian Socialist, Rina Contreras, was elected president of the Costa Rican parliament—only the second time in history that a female has held the job.

Posters offered a reward for any information regarding the murders of two 19-year-old U.S. women who were found slain along a road in Costa Rica. With kidnapping up 500% in Costa Rica, many feared tourism, a big national industry, would suffer.

Colombia's civil war and terrible struggle with the drug trade had an impact on Costa Rica. Violence overflowed on occasion, and many Colombians fled their homes for the more peaceful Costa Rica. In October, Costa Rica hosted an international conference in San José. No new plans were adopt-

CENTRAL AMERICA • Information Highlights

Nation	Population (in millions)	Area (sq mi)	Area (km²)	Capital	Head of State and Government
Belize	0.3	8,865	22 960	Belmopan	Sir Colville Young, governor-general; Said Musa, prime minister
Costa Rica	3.6	19,730	51 100	San José	Miguel Angel Rodríguez, president
El Salvador	6.3	8,124	21 040	San Salvador	Francisco Flores Pérez, president
Guatemala	12.7	42,042	108 890	Guatemala City	Alfonso Portillo Cabrera, president
Honduras	6.1	43,278	112 090	Tegucigalpa	Carlos Flores Facusse, president
Nicaragua	5.1	49,998	129 494	Managua	Arnoldo Alemán Lacayo, president
Panama	2.9	30,193	78 200	Panama City	Mireya Moscoso de Grubar, president

ed; increased cooperation was promised, and the U.S. offer of greater military assistance frightened some delegates as much as assuring others.

El Salvador. Municipal and congressional elections in March indicated a strong resurgence of former leftist guerrillas who now were campaigning as the Farabundo Martí National Liberation Front (FMLN) party. Hector Silva was easily reelected mayor of San Salvador, the capital city. The party won 77 of 262 mayoral races, compared with 48 in 1997. FMLN won the greatest number of seats in the Legislative Assembly—31 out of 84. While this was not a majority, it was a victory over the National Republican Alliance (ARENA), which held on to 29. But votes of some smaller parties assured that the rightists will still control the government through ARENA. Going back to the 1992 peace accord, this was the first time that FMLN held the largest number of seats in the national congress.

Human-rights cases continued to disturb Salvadorans in 2000. In 1998, during the civil war, six Jesuits, their cook, and her daughter had been massacred. Nine military men were tried and convicted of the crimes, but were freed in 1999 under an amnesty law. Later, several senior officers were accused of ordering the deaths, but never were tried. In spite of pressure from the Catholic Church as well as Amnesty International, President Francisco Flores refused to conduct an investigation into allegations that the murders had been ordered by army officers. In October the Supreme Court ruled that further procedures did not fall in its hands, but should be conducted by a special peace court.

Human-rights activists were similarly distressed over the handling of the rape and murder of three U.S. nuns and a social worker in 1980. In 1984, five military men were convicted of the crime and sentenced to 30 years' imprisonment. The enlisted men, three of whom have already been released, have regularly contended that they had been ordered by higher officers to kill the women to frighten sympathizers for the leftists. Two generals, now living in Florida, were tried for ordering the murders. In October a federal jury in West Palm Beach acquitted the two men.

Health matters were also of concern in El Salvador in 2000. The death of six children and the illness of several hundred adults forced the health ministry to begin warfare against dengue fever, at epidemic levels in five provinces. More than 100 other people had died, presumably from drinking poisoned alcohol. It was unknown whether the poisoning was deliberate, but the legislature took steps to ban the sale of any suspicious alcohol.

Guatemala. In November 1999, Alfonso Portillo of the rightist Guatemalan Republican Front (FRG) had been elected president. One of his first acts in 2000 was a move to reform the army by retiring a number of hard-line generals, naming a politically moderate colonel temporary head of the army, and making plans to put all the military under civilian rule. This would take an act of Congress. The generals have been blamed for the vast majority of human-rights violations during the civil war that ended in 1996. They were also charged with genocide of the Maya.

In 1998, Bishop Juan Gerardi, a human-rights leader, was murdered. Many, including some military, were suspected of the assault, but in March the Rev. Mario Orantes, Gerardi's former assistant, was rearrested for the crime. Trials in the case have been delayed by the resignation of one of the judges. Bodies dating from the 1980s civil war continued to be disinterred; amid all the turbulence, evangelical Protestant churches were gaining membership rapidly from among Catholics.

Minor incidents along the Belize border took place throughout 2000 as some Guatemalans reiterated territorial claims. However, in November the two nations agreed to try to prevent such skirmishes in the future.

Guatemala received pledges from the international community of nearly $2 billion for repair of civil-war damages and for reform of the judicial system.

Most Guatemalans believed serious crime was on the rise. So many kidnappings took place that President Portillo even sent five of his relatives to Canada for safety, and extra precautions were taken to protect some justices. A liquor-fortune heiress was kidnapped and murdered; two men were sentenced to death for the crimes. A labor leader was assassinated in June. Overflowing orphanages and sloppy legislation instigated many adoptions, legal and otherwise. Most of the children were taken from Guatemala, prompting violent reactions from natives in small villages who felt their children were being stolen.

Guatemala continued to make grand new discoveries about its Maya past. A long-ignored site called Cancuén was explored in 2000, revealing an enormous community with a three-story palace of 170 rooms. Lacking pyramids, this southern Petén city probably was a commercial center for thousands of Maya from miles around, perhaps even from the more famous Tikal. Cancuén is about 2,500 years old, still covered by jungle. Archaeologists from Guatemala and the United States faced decades of study.

Honduras. In the year 2000 the Honduran National Congress passed a gender-equity bill that required political parties to reserve at least 30% of their candidate positions for women. It also states that in divorce cases, the woman shall retain half the couple's possessions and wealth. These measures suggested enormous changes in the position of Honduran women, who have traditionally been excluded from political life. All political positions are affected by the law.

Nearly two years after Hurricane Mitch ravaged the land, Honduras continued to dig its way out. Next to Haiti the poorest nation in Latin America, Honduras could not afford to restore homes, water, and roads. In addition, almost half its national budget was being used to pay the foreign debt of nearly $4 billion. Steps were being taken by the International Monetary Fund (IMF) and the World Bank to forgive their portion of the debt, amounting to about $2.4 billion of the total. To cope with the war on drugs, Honduras agreed to allow U.S. Coast Guard ships to patrol Honduran waters and board suspect ships. Although the vast majority of illegal migrants failed to reach

the United States, it was calculated that some 100,000 Hondurans were living in the United States illegally. In addition about 200,000 had legal status.

Nearly 75% of Hondurans were believed to be living below the poverty line. This terrible condition greatly added to the problems of crime and drugs. In April the legislature passed a stiff gun law that banned high-caliber and automatic weapons. Non-banned guns must be registered within a year; a provision existed for owners to trade their guns for food or cash. The United Nations (UN) sponsored the program and talked about providing cash for implementation. Very large cocaine seizures, trials of generals for embezzlement of public funds, and the breakup of a teenage prostitution ring all reflected the ghastly nature of Honduran crime.

International human-rights organizations accused Honduran police of the murder of "street children," perhaps 300 since 1998. Police admitted to only a few, and claimed they were accidental deaths or the result of gang wars. They labeled the children delinquents who added to the crime problem. Many of them had lost their parents in the bitter, drawn-out civil struggles of recent years. Following the decree of the International Council of Human Rights, an agency of the Organization of American States (OAS), Honduras paid nearly $2 million to the families of political activists killed in the 1980s by military or police. Claiming government failure to carry out a 1994 agreement to return lands to the Maya, the Indians staged demonstrations at various ruins, hoping that a disruption of the substantial tourist trade might force government action. The government contended that legislation had been passed setting aside funds for such reimbursement.

Nicaragua. Herty Lewites, the Sandinista candidate, won the important mayoralty election for the city of Managua in November 2000, defeating Wilfredo Navarro of the ruling Liberal Constitutionalist Party (PLC). The vote was about 43% to 29%. Conservative candidate William Baez received about 25% of the vote. President Arnoldo Alemán claimed that his PLC would easily win the majority of the nation's city elections, however. It led in some 60% of the municipalities. The vote seemed to indicate a modest resurgence of the Sandinistas, who had ruled Nicaragua from the 1979 revolution until 1989. Former President Daniel Ortega predicted he would

In November, Herty Lewites of the Sandinista National Liberation Front was chosen mayor of Managua, Nicaragua's capital. He captured approximately 43% of the vote in the important election.

again win the presidency in 2001. Vice-President Enrique Bolanos resigned in order to begin his campaign for the presidency. Both the municipal elections and the initial presidential campaigning were peaceful, the only problem being the disenfranchisement of a number of Indians near Puerto Cabezas who may have registered too late. They ultimately boycotted the voting. In June, Byron Jerez, head of the nation's tax-collection agency and a friend of President Alemán, resigned over charges of "gross violations" in procedures.

Relations with the United States were the best in several years. The United States gave Nicaragua certain benefits in migration quotas. In 2000, President Clinton proposed extending those benefits to the rest of Central America. In October, Nicaragua began permitting former banana workers to sue international banana corporations over the use of dangerous pesticides. The workers claimed 83 deaths and 22,000 people ill with fevers and bone troubles from the use of certain chemicals. Costa Rican workers had won similar suits in the 1980s. Following some gunfire exchanges in the Gulf of Fonseca, Nicaragua and Honduras seemed to have settled the question of boundaries in both the gulf and on the Caribbean side.

Hurricane Mitch in 1998 brought death and terrible destruction to Nicaragua. To help with reconstruction, international agencies awarded the nation some $2.6 billion, but much of the payment was delayed because some of the donors expressed concern over corruption and use of the money. Midyear consultations between agencies and Nicaragua helped. One major change resulted from agricultural programs to modernize methods and help restore the environment.

Panama. In September, President Mireya Moscoso, Panama's first female chief executive, celebrated one year in office. Still popular with many voters, President Moscoso faced criticism for the decline in the nation's economy. The slowdown could, of course, have been caused by the departure of U.S. armed forces during the year, but most Panamanians did not want to raise that issue. In spite of promises and intentions, the gross domestic product (GDP) sharply declined during 2000, and unemployment was on the increase.

In March, Panama hosted a Central American meeting to open a free-trade program of those nations. President Moscoso hoped the agreements being studied would create substantial new markets for Panamanian goods. As usual in the region, the economies are not very complementary. In October, cruise-ship passengers for the first time could stop and shop duty-free at Colón on the Caribbean, then travel overland to Panama City. The nation should benefit as new hotels are finished and tourists enjoy bargains and tours of the jungle.

The departure of the United States from the Canal Zone was accompanied by a reduction of U.S. influence in Panama. In August the United States made the last payment due from a canal-operating surplus. Panama still claimed that the United States should do more to clean up the former Canal Zone and remove dangerous ordnance. In November, Panama hosted another conference, this time an Ibero-American summit. Twenty-one Latin American states plus Portugal and Spain participated. The latter became a major trade partner, and probably replaced the United States as the region's major investor.

Panama continued to face the problem of the drug trade passing through its borders from Colombia—a problem that continues throughout Central America, and Mexico, and across the U.S. border. In November the Panamanian-U.S. drug-traffic pact was canceled over the matter of deployment of U.S. troops in Panama.

Thomas L. Karnes, *Southwestern University*

Chemistry

Developments in chemistry in 2000 included the creation of a neutral compound of argon; synthesis of the smallest carbon cage compound; confirmation that element 107 follows the general chemical behavior expected of its position in the periodic table; and a remarkable synthesis of a single molecule, using a molecular probe.

Argon Compound. When the elements located in the far-right column of the periodic table—helium, neon, argon, krypton, xenon, and radon—were first discovered, they were described as "inert gases," reflecting the observation that they did not appear to form chemical compounds. Therefore, chemists were quite excited in 1962 when a stable xenon compound was created. Later, compounds of krypton and radon were produced. The "inert gases" thus came to be called "noble gases." Still, until 2000, none of the three lightest elements in this group—helium, neon, and argon—could be coaxed to combine with other elements.

This changed in August, when chemists at the University of Helsinki in Finland announced they had synthesized argon fluorohydride, HArF. The Finnish team prepared this compound by shining ultraviolet light on a mixture of hydrogen fluoride in solid argon held at temperatures just a few degrees above absolute zero. HArF proved to be a fragile species, stable only at temperatures below $-246°C$ ($-475°F$). The argon compound was greeted as a "milestone," leaving only two stable elements in the periodic table lacking known compounds.

Smallest Cage Compound. In 1985, chemists were startled by the discovery of a new form of elemental carbon, consisting of 60 carbon atoms arranged in the form of a hollow, soccer-ball-shaped cage. The researchers who discovered this unusual species dubbed the molecule "buckminsterfullerene," in honor of the architect who designed cagelike geodesic domes. Workers quickly found other cage compounds consisting of various numbers of carbon atoms, and termed the resulting family of compounds "fullerenes."

In September 2000, a German team announced they had synthesized the smallest possible member of this family, a cage of just 20 carbon atoms arranged in the form of 12 pentagons. Creating this highly strained structure took strong chemistry. The compound dodecahedrane, consisting of a cage with 20 carbon atoms and 20 hydrogen atoms, had been synthesized in 1982, but pulling off the hydrogens represented a serious challenge.

The German workers eventually decided to replace the tightly bound hydrogens of dodecahedrane with bromine atoms, and to remove the less tightly bound bromines. To replace the hydrogens, they irradiated a solution of dodecahedrane in liquid bromine for three days in a pressurized flask. They then used a device called an electron-impact mass spectrometer to knock off the bromines. In addition to making the C_{20} cage, the team also synthesized a bowl-shaped form of C_{20}, consisting of a pentagon surrounded by five hexagons.

Element 107's Chemistry. Over the years, chemists have had success creating new elements beyond the 92 stable elements in the periodic table. To date, they have made more than 20 so-called "transuranium" elements using particle accelerators, which bombard one element with fast-moving nuclei from another element.

In September a team of scientists from Europe and the United States reported that they had created six atoms of element 107, also recognized by the name bohrium, and studied this element's chemical properties. The key here was to produce an isotope of bohrium, Bh-267, that lasts a relatively long 10–20 seconds, making it easier to study. Using rapid-fire techniques, the researchers tested Bh-267's chemistry and found that bohrium behaves like a typical member of group 7 of the periodic table. Some scientists speculated that because of relativistic effects, bohrium might deviate from such proper behavior.

Single-Molecule Chemistry. In September a team of German chemists announced they had reacted a pair of single molecules using a tool called a scanning tunneling microscope (STM). Normally an STM creates pictures of molecular surfaces by riding its fine tip over those surfaces. In these experiments, the German team injected electrons from the STM tip onto two iodobenzene molecules lying on a copper surface, causing the iodine atoms of the compounds to break off. The researchers then used the tip to nudge one of the altered benzenes over to the other, and injected another surge of electrons. Voilà! The benzene rings linked to form a biphenyl molecule. The experiment opened the door to a host of intriguing individual molecule reactions.

PAUL G. SEYBOLD
Wright State University

Chicago

During the year 2000, test scores in Chicago's beleaguered school system were up, while construction changed the face of many of the city's neighborhoods. Not since the Great Chicago Fire of 1871 had there been so much growth and economic activity, according to Mayor Richard M. Daley.

© Todd Buchanan/NYT Pictures

Sylvia Stamatoglou (above), an elementary-school principal in Chicago's Southwest Side, supported a new ordinance that permits Chicago police officers to arrest suspected gang members or drug dealers if they refuse to stop loitering in an area classified as a gang "hot spot."

Building Boom. The City of Big Shoulders would not see the world's tallest building rising in the downtown area, as announced during 1999 by a developer who planned a 112-story, 2,000-ft (610-m)-high structure. Unable to obtain financing, developer Scott Toberman returned the deed to the property to avoid foreclosure on his mortgage. But on a 26-acre (10.5-ha) golf course near the Loop, another developer moved forward with a $1.5 billion project of 4,550 luxury condominiums and townhouses. It could take a decade to complete the 12 towers planned in Lakeshore East—at Lake Shore and Wacker Drives—and make it the largest residential investment ever in the downtown area.

Meanwhile, Mayor Daley unveiled a program to assist owners of Chicago's 80,000 bungalows—most of them one-story brick homes on narrow lots—that line working-class neighborhoods across the city. The Historic Chicago Bungalow Initiative will give financial assistance to people who fix up and retain the historic look of the popular bungalows. The program could be politically popular for Daley, who grew up in a bungalow in the Bridgeport neighborhood. "We are Bungalow Belt U.S.A.," said James Capraro, director of a Southwest Side community organization.

On a larger scale, Daley announced a $3.2 billion renovation program for Chicago's busy O'Hare International Airport. The construction would take eight years and boost the number of boarding gates by 25%. A sixth terminal is planned, as well as a new parking garage and expansion of the people-mover system. Thomas Walker, the city aviation commissioner, said the World Gateway Program will reduce delays at O'Hare that affect airline travel nationwide.

Another big investment will be made by Ford Motor Co. in a $400 million expansion of its automotive assembly plant on Chicago's economically depressed Southeast Side. Close to $100 million in assistance will come from the city and the state of Illinois. "We will more than get our money back, as will the city," Gov. George Ryan said of the expansion.

Schools. Ten years of school reforms brought some improvement in test scores in Chicago's public schools, which had been called the worst in the nation in the 1980s. Gains were made by minority students, but remained far below the national average. A study by the Brookings Institution found that only one-third of elementary students read at grade level, and that about 45% did math at grade level. In short, the study said that Chicago schools have "a long way to go" to reach national norms.

Beetles. Chicago appeared to be winning its war against the tree-killing Asian long-horned beetle. The city lost 1,312 trees after the first beetle was discovered in July 1998. It cost $2.7 million to fight the invading pests and replace the trees, but City Forester Joseph McCarthy estimated that at least 90% of the beetles had been eliminated.

ROBERT ENSTAD
Formerly, "Chicago Tribune"

Chile

On Dec. 12, 1999, no candidate for the presidency of Chile had received the necessary majority to be elected. In accord with a new electoral system, this forced a runoff election for the first time in the nation's history. The rightist candidate, Joaquín Lavín, ran a strong campaign, appealing to what he called the voters' "real needs" in a highly populist and costly media blitz that featured the slogan "Long live change!" Ricardo Lagos Escobar (*see* SIDEBAR), candidate of the Concertación coalition, was saddled with the recent legacy of recession and voter frustration over the government's inability to reform the 1980 constitution and modify the economic system introduced by the military regime. The dilemma of "political reconciliation," a constant theme since transition from military to elected government in 1990, continued to frame national politics, as did the growing pressures for trials of military officers, including former dictator Gen. Augusto Pinochet.

The January 16 Elections. Lavín and Lagos attempted to skirt the Pinochet issue during the campaign, though both affirmed that it was a matter for Chile and Chileans—rather than British, Spanish, or other foreign authorities—to settle. Lagos shifted gears, promising voters jobs, housing, better health care, more police protection for their neighborhoods, improved educational opportunities, and a sports field and cultural center in every neighborhood. Critics said that Lagos had succumbed to populist promise making. If so, it worked. Lagos obtained 51.3% of the votes. Inaugurated as president in March, he declared that he would be "the president of all Chileans."

In March 2000, Chile's former dictator Gen. Augusto Pinochet returned to his homeland from Britain and encountered criminal accusations stemming from his years in power.

© Ricardo Mazalan/AP/Wide World Photos

Civil-Military Relations and the "Pinochet Case." Shortly before the January 16 runoff election, the British government announced that a team of doctors had found Pinochet medically unfit to stand trial. A week before Lagos' inauguration, the British government released Pinochet, allowing him to return to Chile. Received triumphantly by the armed forces, the former dictator almost immediately faced a legal challenge to the congressional immunity extended to him as a result of his position as "senator for life." The Santiago Appeals Court ruled against Pinochet, removing his immunity from prosecution; his lawyers immediately appealed to the Supreme Court. By mid-July, Pinochet faced more than 140 separate criminal actions. Human-rights movements and their lawyers were determined to ensure that history remembered him as a tyrant and a criminal. Inauguration of a monument to former President Salvador Allende further embittered Pinochet's supporters and those who blamed Allende for seeking to impose Marxism on the country in the early 1970s.

In July the "Mesa de Diálogo," convened by the government of Eduardo Frei Ruíz-Tagle to "solve" the problem of the "disappeared," reached a controversial agreement to rely on the military to provide information on the final disposition of the victims. Congress passed legislation protecting

---

CHILE • Information Highlights

Official Name: Republic of Chile.
Location: Southwestern coast of South America.
Area: 292,259 sq mi (756 950 km²).
Population (2000 est.): 15,153,797.
Chief Cities (June 30, 1997 est.): Santiago, the capital, 4,640,635; Concepción, 362,589; Viña del Mar, 330,736.
Government: *Head of state and government,* Ricardo Lagos, president (took office in March 2000). *Legislature*—National Congress: Senate and Chamber of Deputies.
Monetary Unit: Peso (570.250 pesos equal U.S.$1, Jan. 19, 2001).
Gross Domestic Product (1999 est. U.S.$): $185,100,000,000 (purchasing power parity).
Economic Indexes: *Consumer Prices* (Santiago, 1999, 1990 = 100): all items, 236.6; food, 231.2. *Industrial Production* (1999, 1990 = 100): 171.9.
Foreign Trade (1999 U.S.$): *Imports,* $15,137,000,000; *exports,* $15,616,000,000.

potential informants. As part of the agreement, the armed forces officially recognized that "agents of the state" had engaged in human-rights violations during the military government, and agreed that measures should be taken to prevent any recurrence.

Pinochet's lawyers went to the Supreme Court to appeal the Santiago Appeals Court decision to strip Pinochet of his congressional immunity. On August 8 the Supreme Court upheld the ruling of the Santiago Appeals Court, removing Pinochet's congressional immunity by a vote of 14 to 6. This decision cleared the way for possible prosecution in the "Caravan of Death" case, and maybe others, depending on Pinochet's medical condition. Military spokespeople warned that the decision against Pinochet would derail the agreement reached by the Mesa de Diálogo. Newly declassified U.S. government documents revealing details of involvement by the Central Intelligence Agency (CIA) in Chile in the 1960s and 1970s added to the drama. Civil-military relations and national political debate were influenced by ongoing prosecutions of armed-forces personnel and uncertainty regarding the legal fate of the aged Pinochet, increasingly infirm as he nears 86.

Economy. After 1999, in which the gross national product (GNP) shrank slightly and the country had a fiscal deficit for the first time in a decade, the economy returned to growth mode. Official projections estimated annual growth of gross domestic product (GDP) at about 5.8% for the year, and inflation at slightly more than 4%. Ministry of Finance estimates projected an increase in the value of exports to about $18.5 billion, 18% more than in 1999.

According to the Ministry of Finance, the government faced three critical challenges during 2000—the surge in oil prices (Chile imports almost all its oil); the decline in foreign investment; and high unemployment. To counter these trends, the Central Bank slightly lowered interest rates, and the government approved funding for backlogged public-works projects, a small one-time subsidy to targeted poor populations, and early refunds to almost 1 million taxpayers.

In late November, President Lagos visited Seattle and Silicon Valley in the United States, and signed an agreement with Microsoft to help modernize Chilean government information, health-care, and education systems.

BRIAN LOVEMAN
San Diego State University

RICARDO LAGOS ESCOBAR

Ricardo Lagos Escobar, elected as Chile's president on Jan. 16, 2000, was born in Santiago on March 2, 1938. An only child whose father died when he was 10, Lagos grew up in a middle-class household in the municipality of Nuñoa—a short distance from Chile's congress and its presidential palace, La Moneda, from which he would govern in 2000. Educated in local schools and the prestigious Instituto Nacional, Lagos entered law school at the University of Chile.

Lagos did his university thesis on "The Concentration of Economic Power in Chile." Published as a book, it went through five editions and resulted in a certain notoriety for the young scholar-politician, including an interview in *Time* magazine. Later, Lagos did postgraduate work in economics at Duke University.

After returning to Chile, Lagos directed the University of Chile's Instituto de Economía, the School of Political Science and Administration, and then returned to the law school as professor and researcher. During the government of Salvador Allende (1970–73), Lagos was executive secretary of FLACSO, a major social-science research institute that became a target after the military coup of 1973. He returned to teach at the University of North Carolina at Chapel Hill in 1974. After a 1975 stint with UNESCO in Buenos Aires, he was back in Santiago in 1978 as a functionary of the International Labor Organization (ILO).

During the next decade, Lagos was a leader in the "renovation" of the Chilean left and a founder in 1987 of the Party for Democracy (PPD). Lagos served as minister of education in the administration of Patricio Aylwin (1990–94) and as minister of public works during part of Eduardo Frei Ruíz-Tagle's administration (1994–2000).

BRIAN LOVEMAN

China

As is the custom, Premier Zhu Rongji took the occasion of his work report to the National People's Congress (NPC) in March 2000 to set out his priorities in the work of the Communist Party-state for the year. It proved to be a daunting list: promoting economic growth in the teeth of lingering deflation, encouraging the development of the country's backward Western region, completing the restructuring of loss-making state-owned enterprises and the reform of the banking system, providing a safety net for the growing ranks of the unemployed, coping with the effects on the domestic economy of China's pending entry into the World Trade Organization (WTO), managing the tense relationship with Taiwan through a presidential election and its aftermath, and, last but in no sense least, addressing the problem of corruption that was pervading every level of the Chinese Party-state.

Priming the Pump. While China's gross domestic product (GDP) grew at a respectable rate of just more than 7% in 1999, the consumer price index (CPI) registered a decline of close to 3%. Zhu proposed several measures to reverse this trend by "expanding domestic demand," as he put it. Pointing to the positive effect on the economy that has been exerted by $25 billion in government bonds for infrastructure projects over the previous two years, he promised an additional $12 billion for 2000. If past practice held, he said, the $12 billion would trigger some $24 billion in bank loans and equity capital, all of it to be spent on projects to develop the nation's transportation and communications networks, the power grid, and the water supply.

Three such infrastructure proposals were on the drawing boards. The first was a multibillion-dollar plan to divert water from the Changjiang (Yangtze River) in the south and pump it 1,000 mi (1 600 km) to supply the parched factories, fields, and homes in North China. The second proposal, equally ambitious, was for a natural-gas pipeline to connect the Tarim natural-gas fields in the far-western autonomous region of Xinjiang Uighur with the Shanghai metropolitan area. Natural gas, which was accounting for only about 2% of the country's energy consumption in 2000, is seen as a clean-burning alternative to soft coal, which accounts for nearly three-quarters of the energy consumed. The third project, which could cost up to $20 billion, was an 800-mi (1 287-km) high-speed rail link connecting Beijing and Shanghai.

To augment the desired effect on the economy of these massive projects, the premier also proposed some more-immediate steps in the form of salary increases for low- and middle-income urban workers, and the continued use of a carefully modulated government hand on the levers of taxation and price controls.

Manifest Destiny. The premier singled out the economic development of Western China as a particular target of his proposed infrastructure projects. The area—encompassing the provinces of Shaanxi, Qinghai, Gansu, Szechwan, Yunnan, and, Guizhou; the autonomous regions of Ningxia Huizu, Xinjiang Uighur, Tibet; and the municipality of Chongqing—accounts for nearly two-thirds of China's entire land area. While the region is home to less than one-quarter of the Chinese population, that quarter in-

© Adrian Bradshaw/Liaison Agency

Economic growth, regional development, banking reform, and help for the unemployed were among China's many goals in 2000 to improve life for Chinese citizens.

cludes four-fifths of the ethnic minorities of the country.

The region stands at a significant economic disadvantage to the rest of the country. Per capita GDP is only 40% of that in the coastal provinces; the area accounts for only 13% of consumer spending; and it has attracted only 3% of foreign direct investment. In his work report, Zhu described what came to be called the "Great Western Development Plan"—$12 billion for 70 projects over the next five years.

Skeptics questioned the wisdom of investing in the development of a region so lacking in resources, skills, and accessibility. Others saw a political motivation behind the plan, arguing that it was a transparent attempt to buy off the region's ethnic minorities, who have inclined in recent years toward ethnic separatism and have started to build links with Islamic fundamentalist organizations in neighboring countries. These issues came to international attention in March when Rebiya Kadeer, once touted as a model businesswoman, was sentenced to eight years in prison for "revealing state secrets." Arrested in August 1999, she was accused of providing a list of political prisoners in Xinjiang Uighur to a visiting U.S. congressional delegation. She also was accused of mailing newspaper clippings to her husband, Sidik Rouzi, an outspoken Uighur separatist residing in the United States and working for Radio Free Asia.

Ethnic unrest was also at issue in Tibet during the year, with the politically embarrassing flight into exile in January of the 14-year-old Karmapa Lama, who joined the Dalai Lama in Dharmsala, India. Chinese authorities responded by detaining the Karmapa Lama's parents, along with monks charged with security at the Tsurphu monastery from which he fled. Tibetans continued to take their grievances to the streets, culminating in the detonation of a bomb in the streets of Lhasa following the appointment of a new Communist Party secretary for Tibet in November.

Economic Restructuring. The year 2000 was the first year of a three-year plan announced in September 1999 to complete the restructuring of loss-making large and medium state-owned enterprises. By year's end, close to half of the 100,000 firms in the state sector had been closed, consolidated, or turned over to private or collective ownership. Of the 7,000 largest loss-making firms in the sector, half had begun to turn a profit for the first time in more than a decade, and

CHINA • Information Highlights

Official Name: People's Republic of China.
Location: Central-eastern Asia.
Area: 3,704,427 sq mi (9 596 960 km²).
Population (2000 est., including Hong Kong): 1,271,500,000.
Chief Cities (Dec. 31, 1990 est.): Beijing (Peking), the capital, 7,000,000; Shanghai, 7,830,000; Tianjin, 5,770,000.
Government: *Head of state,* Jiang Zemin, president (took office March 1993). *Head of government,* Zhu Rongji, premier (named March 17, 1998). *Legislature* (unicameral)—National People's Congress.
Monetary Unit: Renminbi (8.2774 renminbi equal U.S.$1, Nov. 29, 2000).
Gross Domestic Product (1999 est. U.S.$): $4,800,000,000,000 (purchasing power parity).
Foreign Trade (1999 U.S.$, including Hong Kong): *Imports,* $179,520,000,000; *exports,* $173,885,000,000.

profits for the sector as a whole were up substantially for the second year in a row. By late 2000 the state sector was accounting for 37% of GDP, the private sector 31%.

As a consequence of the restructuring, some 20 million employees were dismissed, pensioned, or "furloughed" from their once-secure positions in state-owned enterprises. Of these, only about half had found new employment by year's end, and many were not receiving their promised pensions or stipends. Protest demonstrations by victims of these hardships lent urgency to the party-state's expansion of its new social-security system. The 2000 budget included $4.3 billion for the system, three-quarters of it earmarked for pensions and stipends.

Progress was made in the reform of the banking system. However, as the year advanced, there were signs that the strict discipline of the debt-for-equity swap program announced in 1999 was beginning to slacken. In February, Zhu announced seven personnel changes at the top levels of the four major banks. The following month, he began a major overhaul of the 240 international trust and investment corporations nationwide, many of which were in serious financial jeopardy. Foreign investors stood to lose significantly in this process. The Guangdong International Trust and Investment Corporation, for example, was proposing to buy off its outstanding creditors at 23 cents to the dollar.

Meanwhile, the asset-management companies (AMCs) established by the four major banks in 1999 to carry out the debt-for-equity swaps were provided by the State Economic and Trade Commission with a list of 600 firms, selected from among 2,000 applicants. The AMCs would receive in excess of $50 billion in equity in these firms in exchange for their nonperforming loans held by the four banks. But problems remained. The assets acquired by the AMCs were calculated at book value, not at the far lower market value. Moreover, there were serious questions with respect to the ability of some of the 600 firms to make good on the promised 2.25% annual return on the bonds they have issued to the AMCs. Finally, despite the stern words of Zhu Rongji and Dai Xianglong, head of the People's Bank of China, local branch banks still were inclined to bail out the financially ailing, but politically well-connected, state-owned firms, thereby contributing to, rather than resolving, the problem.

The Chinese economy performed well in 2000. Economic growth exceeded 8% in the first nine months of the year, deflation was brought under control, consumer prices began to climb slightly, foreign trade was up nearly 40% in the first half of the year, and foreign direct investment was projected to increase by 25%.

The World Trade Organization (WTO). With a strong push from the premier, China moved through virtually all of the obstacles standing in the way of its joining the WTO (*see* U.S.-CHINA TRADE, page 189).

As China's membership drew close to being realized, some in China began to focus on its downside for the Chinese economy.

Farmers clearly had the most to lose. With protective tariffs significantly reduced, artificially elevated grain prices would drop to compete with world prices. As a result, farmers stood to lose close to $700 million in annual income, and as many as 10 million—out of an agricultural workforce of some 325 million—were likely to be put out of work. Farmers were joined in their opposition to WTO membership by an odd alliance of enterprise managers from the state sector and officials from state-security agencies. The former worried about the inability of their cumbersome old firms to compete in the global market; the latter saw WTO membership as yet another step away from socialist orthodoxy and as opening the Chinese economy to penetration by dangerous external forces.

Corruption. "Keeping the government strictly in line" was the way Premier Zhu referred to the daunting task of attacking political corruption. Although it was not the first task he listed in his report, it was clearly the most important, since pervasive corruption continued to emasculate the legitimacy of the Communist Party-state. Moreover, in his press conference following the NPC meetings, Zhu made it clear that he had staked his own reputation on his ability to reestablish honest government in China. The magnitude of the problem was suggested in a report from the auditor general,

Residents of Beijing were able to collect fish from puddles in a dried-up lake as rapid urbanization and industrialization development, as well as irrigated agriculture, have made water a scarce commodity in the areas near several of China's cities.

In Beijing in November 2000, Mary Robinson, UN high commissioner for human rights, and Chinese Vice Foreign Minister Wang Guangya (right) signed a memorandum of understanding on the development of human rights.

Province Foreign Trade Corporation. As the investigation was drawing to a close, however, the Web site of the State Council, China's cabinet, posted a notice exonerating Lin. This unexpected intervention at the highest government level was widely attributed to the fact that Lin's former husband, Jia Qinglin, a member of the party's Political Bureau, is a longtime crony of President and Party General Secretary Jiang Zemin.

Cross-Strait Relations. Zhu's report was delivered only days before the presidential election on Taiwan—an election that saw the opposition Democratic Progressive Party (DPP) candidate, Chen Shui-bian, as the victor—a result that could not have been less satisfying to Beijing. Zhu's remarks were firm but not inflammatory, though in his subsequent press conference he warned Taiwan voters against "acting on impulse," and reminded them sternly that "whoever pursues Taiwanese independence will not come to a good end." A month earlier the State Council had issued a white paper on Taiwan that met with an unexpectedly negative international reaction because it included the statement that a delay on Taiwan's part in committing to peaceful reunification would result in the use of force by China. Chinese spokesmen hastened to assert that the paper did not represent a change of policy, and foreign observers, upon reflection, concluded that the paper had much more to do with domestic politics than it did with cross-Strait or international relations. It was clear that the question of "Who lost Taiwan?" was not one that any Chinese politician was interested in being made to answer.

which stated that as much as $15 billion in government funds had been "stolen, misused, or wasted" over the past year. That figure amounted to more than 10% of the national government's expenditure budget for the year.

Zhu's approach in 2000 was to showcase the trials and subsequent executions of several very high-ranking offenders. Hu Changqing, a former vice-governor of Jiangxi, was executed in March, having been found guilty of taking some $650,000 in bribes between 1995 and 1999. He was the highest-ranking official to be executed since the founding of the People's Republic in 1949. Soon thereafter came the case of Cheng Kejie, a member of the party's Central Committee and former chairman of the southern autonomous region of Guangxi Zhuangzu. He was tried in July and found guilty of having accepted nearly $5 million in bribes while in office in Guangxi Zhuangzu. Cheng was sentenced to death, and in December his appeal of the sentence was rejected.

Not every case of high-level corruption was brought to a successful conclusion, however. A nationwide crackdown on smuggling in 1999 was so successful that it resulted in an 80% increase in customs revenue for the year. When the antismuggling campaign moved into the coastal city of Xiamen late in the year, it uncovered a ring that was said to be responsible for smuggling more than $10 billion in goods. More than 150 Xiamen officials were detained—including Lin Youfang, deputy president of the Fujian

In the end, there was no repetition of the attempt to intimidate Taiwanese voters with missile exercises, as had been the case in 1996. Although the official press studiously avoided printing Chen Shui-bian's name in its coverage of Taiwanese affairs, it also avoided escalating its threats of military action to coerce Taiwan into reunification. For his part, Chen's freedom to maneuver in his handling of the cross-Strait relationship was severely restricted by his own party's prior pro-independence stance and by the comparative weakness of his new government in the face of angry opposition from the large

In July 2000, U.S. Secretary of Defense William Cohen met in China with his China counterpart, Chi Haotian (right), and other Chinese leaders. Arms control, Taiwan, and the U.S. missile defense system were on the agenda.

and well-financed Kuomintang Nationalist Party (KMT)(*see* TAIWAN).

Foreign Relations. Chinese restraint in its handling of cross-Strait relations and approval by the U.S. Congress of permanent normal trade relations helped to mend somewhat the badly frayed relationship between Beijing and Washington that had reached a nadir of sorts in 1999 with the bombing of the Chinese Embassy in Belgrade, Yugoslavia. With that critical relationship on the mend, Beijing turned its attention during the summer to building its ties with Russia. Russian President Vladimir Putin visited Beijing in July and, with Jiang Zemin, took the occasion to denounce U.S. plans to develop a theater missile-defense system in Asia to protect Japan, South Korea, and Taiwan. While foreign observers noted that Sino-Russian political ties have "never been warmer" than they are now, the economic relationship between the two was dwarfed by China's economic ties with Japan and the United States.

Fence-mending was the first priority during Premier Zhu's visit to Tokyo in October. High-level exchanges in recent years have all been characterized by a Chinese proclivity for hectoring Japan about its wartime atrocities and the Japanese failure to adequately apologize for them. For their part, the Japanese pointed out that their government had contributed more than $20 billion to China's economic development over the previous 20 years, and that Japan has for many years been China's Number 1 trading partner—facts that are conspicuously absent from China's official press coverage of the relationship. Zhu appeared to have accomplished his conciliatory mission to Tokyo.

Hong Kong. The gradual process—excessively gradual, critics argued—of democratizing the new government of the Hong Kong Special Administrative Region advanced another step in the fall with the expansion from 20 to 24 of the number of seats on the 60-member Legislative Council filled by direct election. Participation in the election was down by 10% from 1995, with only 44% of eligible voters going to the polls. The Democratic Party, which had dominated the previous election, retained its 12 seats, but polled 170,000 fewer votes. Martin Lee, the party leader, drew the lesson from this outcome that the party needed to address more effectively Hong Kong citizens' "bread and butter issues," rather than focusing exclusively on the abstract questions of opposing Beijing and democratizing the Hong Kong government more rapidly.

The Hong Kong economy performed well during the year. Although the CPI—driven principally by a prolonged drop in the real-estate market—continued to decline, GDP growth in the first six months exceeded 13%. Despite this promising economic performance, the government acknowledged the problem of a growing gap between the wealthiest and the poorest of the region's citizens: 10% of the population have incomes of less than $600 per month.

An Afterthought. Interestingly absent from Zhu's ambitious March agenda was any mention of the government's campaign against the quasi-religious organization known as Falun Gong (Buddhist Law). This omission was perhaps the result of the premier's own low estimate of the threat to public order actually posed by the movement, or perhaps it was a manifestation of his chagrin over the party-state's utter failure to suppress its followers through intimidation. Throughout the year, groups of protesters staged protests—many of them in Tiananmen Square—were arrested, and returned to protest another day.

On balance, however, one must credit the party-state and its head of government for having made progress during the year toward a formidable set of policy goals.

JOHN BRYAN STARR, *Brown University*

U.S.-China Trade

In September 2000 the U. S. Congress completed the final step in its consideration of legislation granting China permanent normal trading relations (PNTR) status—a step mandated by the U.S.-Chinese trade agreement signed the previous November in a cliff-hanging conclusion to 13 years of negotiations. The bill, submitted by President Bill Clinton on March 8, was approved by the House of Representatives on May 24 by an unexpectedly large margin of 237 to 197. Approval by the Senate came on September 19 by a vote of 83 to 15.

Passage of the PNTR legislation ensured that the United States will enjoy the tariff reductions that will begin to be implemented when China joins the World Trade Organization (WTO), an event that likely would take place early in 2001.

U.S. Legislation. On the day President Clinton submitted the bill to Congress, he spoke in its support in an address at Johns Hopkins University. He described PNTR and WTO membership for China as opportunities that would bring about economic and political liberalization. The bill was strongly supported by the U.S. business community—particularly those corporations involved in trade with and investment in China. It also was supported by agricultural interests, which anticipated a large windfall of exports to China once WTO membership results in lowered tariff barriers for U.S. farm products.

Opposition to the bill came from several directions. Various trade unions opposed PNTR because they believed that it would result in the loss of U.S. jobs. Some human-rights organizations and their supporters in Congress opposed the bill on the grounds that relinquishing the annual renewal of what used to be called "most-favored-nation status" deprives Congress of a tool for influencing the Chinese Communist Party-state on human-rights matters. To assuage this latter group, a companion bill was introduced and passed establishing a commission on human rights in China that will issue an annual report on its findings.

Data and Background. The granting of PNTR came nearly 30 years after China and the United States reestablished informal political and economic ties in 1972. At that point, annual trade between the two amounted to a mere $5 million and was made up exclusively of U.S. imports from China. Two-way trade in 2000 was projected to approach $115 billion–$100 billion in Chinese goods exported to the United States, and only $15 billion in U.S. goods exported to China.

The growing Chinese trade surplus has been a persistent problem in the trade relationship between the two nations since the mid-1980s. In the early 1980s the United States enjoyed a modest annual trade surplus with China. The situation was reversed in 1983, when China realized a $68 million surplus in total two-way trade of just more than $4 billion. The 2000 surplus of nearly $85 billion, as calculated by the U.S. side, exceeded Japan's trade surplus for the first time. China and the United States differ in their methods of calculating trade figures: The United States counts goods from China transshipped through Hong Kong as imports from China; China counts them as domestic sales to the Hong Kong Special Administrative Region. Although other factors also are involved, the result is that U.S. trade data over the years have shown a surplus in China's favor

© Adrian Bradshaw/Liaison Agency

Such U.S. icons as Coca-Cola are well known in China. Now, newly enacted U.S. legislation granting China permanent normal trading relations will ensure reduced Chinese tariffs.

more than double the size of that surplus shown in Chinese trade data.

Another factor needs to be taken into account in considering China's trade surplus: As Taiwanese and Hong Kong manufacturers have relocated their production facilities to mainland China, goods produced in those facilities and exported to the United States count in U.S. trade statistics as exports from China, not from Taiwan or Hong Kong, and U.S. trade deficits with Taiwan and Hong Kong show a decrease as the one with China increases.

The problem of the surplus was not likely to go away in the immediate future. WTO membership would result in a reduction in Chinese tariffs over a five-year period from an average of about 25% to an average of about 10%. This would very substantially reduce the price of U.S. products for Chinese consumers able to afford them, and could result in an increase in U.S. exports. On the other hand, the Chinese pointed out that they are prevented by U.S. security regulations from expanding their importation of American goods that they are already eager to acquire. These regulations strictly limit the export of high-tech, "dual-use" equipment—items that have both a civilian and a military application.

China's Premier Zhu Rongji has put great store in his country's acquiring membership in the WTO. China had expected to be offered membership in the General Agreement on Tariffs and Trade (GATT) before that organization became the WTO in January 1995, since it was one of the original contracting parties to GATT in 1948, although the Nationalist government withdrew its membership four years later. Beijing began the application process in 1986, but was immediately confronted with objections arising from its policies protecting state-owned enterprises and its lack of transparency in trade and investment regulations.

Unresolved Issues. The difficult-to-conclude U.S.-Chinese trade agreement removed a major obstacle to China's acceptance, as did the trade agreement China signed with the European Union (EU) in May 2000. But there still remained a number of difficult issues to be resolved before the terms on which China joined the WTO could be finalized. Negotiations in Geneva in September were stalemated when the Chinese side appeared unwilling to grant any concessions—an intransigence perhaps brought on by opposition at home to the terms of WTO membership and their adverse effect on some sectors of the Chinese economy.

As negotiations reconvened in November, the Chinese delegation manifested a new flexibility, and the first two of some dozen agreements were signed. That was a major breakthrough after 14 years at the negotiating table. As the negotiations ended, WTO Deputy Director-General Paul-Henri Ravier commented, "China has clearly one foot in the place."

Negotiations resumed in December. If successful, China would likely join the WTO in the spring or early summer of 2001. A difficult-to-resolve issue on the table in the fall and winter was the question of Taiwan's entry into WTO. Although Taiwan applied for membership as a "customs territory" rather than a national economy, Beijing nonetheless insisted that the WTO acknowledge China's position that Taiwan falls under Chinese sovereignty. The WTO rejected that demand, and agreed that the two would be admitted simultaneously, thereby unintentionally delaying significantly the entry of Taiwan. (The latter had completed all the required agreements long in advance of Beijing.)

Another recurrent issue in the negotiations was China's apparent inability to protect intellectual property rights. The issue became a sticking point in U.S.-Chinese trade negotiations in the mid-1990s when, under intense pressure from the U.S. side, Chinese authorities began to crack down on producers of pirated compact discs (CDs) and software. But the problem has recurred as U.S. consumer products have become more widely available and sought after by Chinese consumers. Indeed, Procter & Gamble estimates that up to 20% of what appear to be its products on Chinese market shelves are actually counterfeits. A U.S. trade representative described the problem of counterfeit goods as "out of control."

Many observers view China's participation in the global economy as an "engine of change." They look at comparable cases—if considerably smaller in scale—of closed political systems that have opened their doors to trade and investment with the unintended consequence of initiating an inexorable political liberalization. In those instances, the entering wedge of political reform has been the legal reform necessitated by interaction with foreign corporations. Among those who hold this opinion are members of a loose collection of intellectuals and Communist Party members in China who have begun to refer to themselves as the "new left," and who fear globalization as a potentially fatal threat to socialism.

JOHN BRYAN STARR

Cities and Urban Affairs

As the United States entered the new millennium, its urban areas remained sites of considerable contrast. Some of its central cities were enjoying a renaissance; others were showing signs of a comeback. Suburbia, however, remained home to a majority of the nation's population, and continued to grow in terms of land area. New communities at the periphery drew residents from the older, inner suburbs and central cities.

Urban Sprawl. Although urban sprawl is no longer viewed as benignly as before, it continues largely unabated. Many states have tried to limit unimpeded growth of their large metropolitan areas, but adopted measures to protect open space have made little difference.

The phalanx of subdivisions spreading over farmland carries costs for existing urban residents. The entire area has to fund infrastructure for new communities, including roads, sewers, and water systems. Commuting distances and traffic congestion also increase apace. Despite these negative externalities, builders continue to build, home buyers look where the building is taking place, and new municipalities continue to incorporate with ease. U.S. urban areas remain highly fragmented, and a metropolitan approach to unlimited growth has remained difficult to achieve. Without sufficient teeth, measures to stem sprawl will do little while relative cost, racial fear, and school quality drive people farther and farther from the urban core.

New urbanists deplore the aesthetics of suburbia, the lack of community, and the automobile-centered lifestyle. Instead, they advocate smaller lots, homes that are closer to the street, the installations of sidewalks, and also a town center. The increasing concern over congested roadways may help the urbanists' case eventually. Port-land, OR, for example, has responded to some of the aesthetic concerns of new urbanists. The city outlawed homes that place their built-in garages front and center on the streetscape. The traditional central city actually fits the style advocated by new urbanists, but that is what migrants to suburbia often sought to avoid.

Central Cities. The strong economy of the late 1990s aided many central cities. Although population loss continued in some locations, other central cities reversed gears and added jobs, housing units, and residents. Strong mayoral leadership in Cleveland, Detroit, Chicago, and Philadelphia helped these cities make the most of the nation's plummeting unemployment and falling crime rates. Despite various paths to success, the stark inequalities within cities, and between cities and their suburbs, did not dissipate during 2000.

Cities capitalized on expanding one of the traditional roles of a metropolis. Mayors and civic leaders fostered the notion of the central city as the principal entertainment venue of the urban area. San Francisco, Detroit, and Houston all opened new baseball parks in the year 2000. Cincinnati, Pittsburgh, and Milwaukee would also follow suit. Except in Milwaukee, all of the new parks are located downtown. The new parks were expected to boost tourism, as well as patronage of hotels, restaurants, and shops.

The arts continue to be another means of attracting visitors to central cities. The resounding success of the New Jersey Performing Arts Center, which opened in the late 1990s in long-depressed Newark, has

© Bob Galbraith/AP/Wide World Photos

On May 24, 2000, Denver, CO, residents met to sign a petition aimed at fighting urban sprawl— the unimpeded growth and development of urban areas that threaten the surrounding natural landscape and compromise residents' quality of life.

inspired many cities. Newark now finds artists and writers moving to its nearby Ironbound neighborhood, which has begun to flourish. Ethnic restaurants attract new customers, and new dining spots are opening. Similarly, the Philadelphia Orchestra received a new home on that city's "Avenue of the Arts." Chicago continued to expand its theater district. Cultural tourism was an increased focus in many cities. Charlotte and Pittsburgh, among others, have begun to actively market themselves as artistic centers.

Housing Issues.   Housing, frequently geared to well-off young professionals, has been an important revitalization tool in core cities. Even Los Angeles, a city long synonymous with sprawl, is adding housing in its downtown area. In Chicago, increased prosperity pushed upper-middle-class housing development to the edge of the infamous Cabrini-Green housing project. In both Chicago and New York, residential and commercial development have taken place in historically neglected minority areas. However, cities that were revitalized also experienced a loss of affordable housing. San Francisco's working-class Mission District has experienced gentrification that neighborhood activists have decried.

Development. Creating a downtown that is alive after 5:30P.M. has been at the forefront of some city-redevelopment plans. In industrial cities, downtown housing, particularly loft apartments, remained a key to that goal. Denver made downtown housing its redevelopment cornerstone, having produced 20,000 units in the 1990s. New Orleans is planning 700 new homes near its convention center. It also planned to turn a historic building, the American Can factory, into an upscale 265-unit apartment complex, geared to young professionals and artists.

Hosting the 2000 Republican National Convention seemed to be a capstone to Philadelphia's comeback saga. In the four years prior to the convention, the city created 4,500 additional hotel rooms and spruced up its many historic treasures and entertainment sites. In addition, the city increased its investment in high technology by creating the University City Science Center Research Park near the University of Pennsylvania and Drexel University. Despite undeniable progress, Philadelphia could not escape other urban woes. In September the city contemplated a public-school teachers'

Despite great progress with city restorations, Philadelphia could not escape some urban problems: Several row-house buildings in low-income areas collapsed; others underwent inspection.

strike in an already troubled system. Then 25 abandoned row-house buildings in low-income areas collapsed. Philadelphia's comeback remained incomplete, as in other cities. Chicago's new housing, offices, and tourist destinations did not erase the hardcore poverty of the city's West Side. Detroit's new baseball stadium, Comerica Park—soon to be joined by Ford Field, the new home of the National Football League's Detroit Lions—represented the starkest contrast. Despite its new stadiums, Detroit is pockmarked with abandoned buildings and empty lots.

Downtown development is not always universally embraced, either. Pittsburgh's cultural district and Golden Triangle rebuilding have been models for other cities. Pittsburgh Mayor Thomas Murphy has proposed more-radical, additional development. He suggested razing or gutting 61 buildings in a timeworn shopping area, to erect trendy restaurants and shops, as well as additional parking. Preservationists and others criticized this strategy, reminiscent of the urban renewal of the 1950s.

U.S. cities are continuing their efforts to bring new or increased life to their core, and some have had notable success. Yet the struggle is not over. Cities for the most part go it alone. State help is often meager or unavailable, and state efforts to temper urban sprawl have been ineffectual. The rhetoric of the 2000 presidential campaign did not include a discussion of cities and urban problems, indicating few future initiatives for cities and urban areas from the federal government.

LANA STEIN
University of Missouri—St. Louis

Coins and Coin Collecting

Thanks to new designs on circulating coinage, the ranks of coin-collecting enthusiasts swelled in 2000.

State Quarters. The U.S. Mint estimated that more than 100 million adults were collecting its 50 state quarters, which honor each state in the order in which it ratified the Constitution or was admitted to the Union. Five new quarter issues—Massachusetts, portraying a minuteman; Maryland, highlighting its statehouse; South Carolina picturing key state symbols such as a palmetto tree, Carolina wren, and yellow jessamine; New Hampshire honoring the natural attraction "The Old Man of the Mountain"; and Virginia, featuring the ships *Godspeed, Discovery,* and *Susan Constant,* which brought the first English settlers to Jamestown almost 400 years ago—were added to the money supply in 2000, the second year of the ten-year program. With only 662,228,000 pieces struck, the New Jersey quarter had the lowest mintage of the 1999 releases, and topped the list of issues bringing premium prices at coin shops and shows.

Error Pieces and Other Commemoratives. Reports of several error pieces, including a "mule" of a Sacagawea dollar reverse with a Washington quarter obverse, sparked the interest of collectors. Several specimens were verified as official Mint products, and eBay, the on-line auction company, sold one for $41,395. Another error piece combined the obverse of a 1999 Lincoln cent with a Roosevelt dime reverse. On a related note, a Mint employee was charged with theft of government property for reportedly selling $80,000 worth of error coins illegally removed from the Philadelphia Mint.

For the first time ever, the United States joined another nation in producing a commemorative coin. A cooperative effort with Iceland honored the millennium of Leif Eriksson's discovery of the New World. Silver one-dollar and 1,000-krona coins were introduced on June 21.

The U.S. Mint unveiled its first gold-and-platinum bimetallic commemorative coin—a platinum core encircled by a gold outer ring. The $10 piece celebrated the Bicentennial of the Library of Congress (LC), and was complemented by a silver dollar.

Paper Money and the California Gold Group. Revised $10 and $5 bills continued the precedent of larger portraits, set off-center, with a watermark version at the right. The designs drew criticism for their lacklus-ter portraits and detail when compared to earlier series. Another redesign was planned for circulating currency in 2003, incorporating upgraded counterfeit deterrents.

In March the California Gold Marketing Group of Newport Beach began to market Gold Rush–era coins and assayers' gold bars recovered from the wreck of the ill-fated S.S. *Central America,* which sank off the Carolina coast in 1857. At a June Sotheby's auction, an .896 fine Justh and Hunter of San Francisco $12,091 gold bar brought a world-record price of $308,000. The group also prepared an exhibit of selected pieces and related historical items titled "Ship of Gold," which drew thousands of visitors to major U.S. coin shows.

MARILYN REBACK
American Numismatic Association

Colombia

National life improved slightly in Colombia during 2000. The guerrilla war continued with unabated ferocity, as the two main guerrilla groups became ever more daring in their attacks. However, the Colombian economy, which was in free fall during 1999, began a significant turnaround in 2000. In addition, a promised $1.3 billion from the United States, ostensibly designed to combat drug production, was approved by the U.S. Congress. The peace process, which was moribund during most of the year, did not die completely, as government and guerrilla negotiators continued to talk and even travel together through Scandinavia.

Municipal elections on October 29 were marred by the assassination of candidates for office by both guerrillas and right-wing paramilitary groups. Despite all the intimidation, candidates for office did present themselves, and the elections were carried out in a relatively calm atmosphere.

Politics. Colombia's ongoing insurgency problem continued throughout the year. Continuing efforts by President Andrés Pastrana to bring the two main guerrilla groups to the bargaining table were frustrated either by the guerrillas or by the actions of right-wing paramilitary organizations. The major guerrilla organization—the Revolutionary Armed Forces of Colombia (the Fuerzas Armadas Revolucionarias de Colombia or FARC)— refused an offer by the government in October that would have paid members of the FARC during peace talks. The FARC continued to control approximately one-fourth of Colombian real estate, mainly in less-populated areas in the Southeast. In the run-up to the October municipal and gubernatorial elections, both the FARC and the United Self-Defense Forces (Autodefensas Unidas de Colombia or AUC) were active either through assassinations of 36 candidates for office or through intimidation, which resulted in more than 100 candidates withdrawing from various contests. Nevertheless, the elections went off smoothly; even the abstention rate of 51% was slightly down from previous electoral contests.

The election, which was seen by most observers as a vote against the continuing civil war, produced some interesting results. First, the Conservative Party, with roots back to the 19th century, won no governorships and only two mayoral races, both in smaller cities. Liberals won 15 governorships; Independents took nine. Liberals won 13 mayoralties, and Independents won ten. One indicator of change in Colombian politics was the election of an Indian—Floro Tunubalá—as governor of the state of Cauca. Antanas Mockus, former mayor of Bogotá and sometime philosophy professor, was again elected mayor of Bogotá.

Economy. Estimates were for a 3.9% increase in economic growth for the year, compared with a 4.5% decrease in 1999. Industrial output rose 11.7% over 1999, industrial exports were up 17%, and petroleum exports increased by 45.5% for the first eight months of the year. Foreign investment dropped by more than 50% during the year, due mainly to profit repatriations by foreign-owned oil companies. Unemployment hovered at about 20%.

In Cali, Colombia, in October 2000, family members of those people kidnapped by the guerrilla group, the National Liberation Army (ELN), gathered to remember the captives.

Female unemployment was slightly higher at 24%, perhaps reflecting the fact that 55% of women were now in the workforce.

Colombia continued as a major exporter of illegal narcotics. Estimates of coca-leaf production showed Colombia with 65% of total production, followed by two other Latin nations–Peru and Bolivia.

Foreign Affairs. Visits in August by U.S. Drug Czar Barry McCaffrey and President Bill Clinton were designed to demonstrate continued U.S. support for the embattled Colombian government. Final approval of a $1.3 billion aid package—which included the sale of Black Hawk helicopters, designed for antiguerrilla combat—buoyed the spirits of the Colombian government. Ostensibly, the helicopters were not to be used in antiguerrilla operations, but on October 22, during combat between the FARC and an army unit, one of the helicopters was downed by guerrilla ground fire.

ERNEST A. DUFF
Randolph-Macon Woman's College

COLOMBIA • Information Highlights

Official Name: Republic of Colombia.
Location: Northwest South America.
Area: 439,734 sq mi (1 138 910 km²).
Population (2000 est.): 39,685,655.
Chief Cities (mid-1997 est.): Santa Fe de Bogotá, the capital, 6,004,782; Cali, 1,985,906; Medellín, 1,970,691; Barranquilla, 1,157,826.
Government: *Head of state and government,* Andrés Pastrana Arango, president (took office August 1998). *Legislature*—Congress: Senate and House of Representatives.
Monetary Unit: Peso (2,123.7500 pesos equal U.S.$1, Nov. 21, 2000).
Gross Domestic Product (1999 est. U.S.$): $245,100,000,000 (purchasing power parity).
Economic Indexes (1999, 1990 = 100): *Consumer Prices,* all items, 578.5; food, 491.1. *Industrial Production,* 135.2 (1998).
Foreign Trade (1999 U.S.$): *Imports,* $10,659,000,000; *exports,* $11,576,000,000.

Computers and Communications

The year 2000 began with a welcomed thud, as fears of a global Y2K computer crash failed to materialize. Few glitches were reported, in large part due to massive efforts to avoid a crisis. Subsequently other aspects of communications technologies, particularly the Internet boom, had a growing impact on society.

Internet Applications.   Stephen King called attention to the phenomenon of electronic books ("E-books"), and the ability to download and print books on demand, when he self-published a short story and, later, parts of a novel via the Internet. Napster's music-swapping service was at the center of the battle over copyright infringements caused by digital-music distribution. The Internet became critical in the political arena, with attractive, well-organized Web sites for political candidates. On-line voting had its debut in the Arizona Democratic primary, with almost 40,000 of the 90,000 voters casting ballots on-line.

Retail and business-to-business sales were hot Internet applications, but stock prices plunged and investors balked at continuing to finance unprofitable "dot-coms." As a result, hundreds of Internet companies, particularly those with poor business strategies and inflated expectations, closed or filed for bankruptcy protection. Meanwhile, traditional merchants, such as Wal-Mart, expanded onto the Internet. Analysts of the headline-making industry predicted that by 2006 most businesses would be "brick-and-click," offering both earthbound and cyberspace shopping options.

Electronic commerce ("E-commerce") became easier when the U.S. Congress and President Bill Clinton approved a bill giving electronic signatures the same legal status as signatures penned on paper. By supplying customers with contracts and other documents on-line, rather than with paper sent through the mail, companies could potentially save money, reduce paperwork, and complete transactions more speedily. Certain documents, such as mortgage-foreclosure, eviction, and insurance-cancellation notices, still must be in paper form. The bill hastened efforts to develop technologies for digital signatures.

In May, E-mail was transmitted to shore from the submarine USS *Dolphin*, while cruising off the California coast at a depth of 400 ft (122 m). It was the first time that a submerged and moving submarine communicated without giving away its position by surfacing or stopping to raise an antenna. The E-mail, including words and pictures, was sent using sound energy transmitted from an acoustic modem developed by Benthos. The modem encoded a message and sent it out as acoustic pulses—that is, an underwater sound wave. A buoy on the water's surface picked up the information and transmitted it to land via radio. The submarine could be up to 3 mi (4.86 km) from the relayer buoy at the time it sent or received E-mail. In addition to applications in the defense sector, the technology had potential uses in scientific and commercial underwater exploration.

The Internet Corporation for Assigned Names and Numbers (ICANN), which oversaw the Internet's address system, expanded the number of "homes" on the World Wide Web when it chose seven new top-level domains—the extensions at the end of Web addresses, such as .com, .gov, and .edu. The new domains were .aero (for airline Web sites), .biz (businesses), .coop (cooperatives), .info (any type of site), .museum (museums), .name (personal sites), and .pro (doctors, lawyers, and other professionals). It was anticipated that people would be able to begin registering Web sites with these domains by mid-2001.

Cybercrime. In February several people gained unauthorized access to computer systems at Yahoo.com and about a dozen other popular Web sites, knocking out service for hours. Visitors to the sites were greeted with blank screens until the companies fixed the problem. This type of attack is called "denial of service," since users are unable to use the Web sites' services. A 15-year-old boy in Montreal, Canada, was the first to be arrested and charged in the incidents.

The most destructive computer virus to date spread rapidly around the world in May. Attached to an E-mail message saying "ILOVEYOU," the virus jammed E-mail systems and destroyed data on thousands of computers. Investigators traced the virus, dubbed the "Love Bug", to a former student of Amable M. Aguiluz Computer College in the Philippines. The Philippines was unable to prosecute the student because it did not have laws governing the Internet or E-commerce; in June the Philippines passed a law making the theft or destruction of electronic data a crime punishable by imprisonment.

A variant of the "Love Bug" appeared several months later, targeting customers of the United Bank of Switzerland and stealing their account information. In September the first virus known to violate handheld computers appeared, deleting files on infected Palm devices.

In an effort to deter fraud, credit-card companies began offering cardholders one-time card numbers for purchases on-line. The numbers were linked to the cardholders' regular accounts, and any attempts to use the numbers more than once were rejected by the credit-card companies.

The Federal Bureau of Investigation (FBI) and the Justice Department's National White Collar Crime Center opened the Internet Fraud Complaint Center (IFCC). Consumers and businesses can report suspected cybercrimes to the IFCC, which will ensure that complaints are directed to the appropriate law-enforcement and regulatory agencies. The IFCC also will work to quantify Internet fraud patterns, allow for sharing of data, and offer training.

Mobile Communications. The convergence of technologies and the demand for mobility, particularly mobile access to the Internet, fueled interest in three new worldwide standards: Bluetooth, Wireless Application Protocol (WAP), and General Packet Radio System (GPRS). Long-term viability of all three was questioned in some quarters, due to concerns about security and other issues, but supporters of the standards moved ahead rapidly.

Bluetooth, invented by Sweden's telecom-giant Ericsson, is a specification for wireless communication of data and voice. It is a short-range radio-frequency technology that works on the 2.4GHz (gigahertz) frequency band and allows devices to communicate without cables over short distances, usually within 33 ft (10.1 m). Unlike IrDA infrared technology, Bluetooth does not need a line-of-sight connection. Also, because the transmitters use very little power, they can be about the size of a dime, making it easy to build them into devices from laptops to cell phones and wristwatches. The Bluetooth Special Interest Group, consisting of more than 2,000 companies, envisioned extensive applications for the future. For example, Panasonic displayed a concept for a Bluetooth headset accessory that would allow users to make and receive calls without requiring cables to connect it to a mobile phone, which could be carried in either a briefcase or handbag. TROY XCD demonstrated a wireless printing connection that allowed a laptop to communicate with a printer without cables. Toshiba introduced a Bluetooth card for laptops; by installing the card into two laptops, users can move files between the computers as easily as on a wired network.

WAP delivered an open specification for delivery of Internet content to mobile phones, pagers, two-way radios, personal digital assistants (PDAs), and other devices with small screens. Users can access a limited number of specially designed pages displaying such diverse information as stock quotes, sports scores, weather reports, and traffic alerts. Users select a menu item and press a button; the built-in WAP technology acts as a bridge between the mobile network and the Web. One drawback is that information retrieval is slow; in most cases, WAP content is carried over networks with a top speed of only 9.6 Kbps to 19.2 Kbps (kilobytes per second). GPRS, which supports high download speeds, became a superior platform for carrying WAP services, and vastly enhanced the Internet-browsing experience.

Despite concerns about health risks from radiation emitted by

© Bill Aron/PhotoEdit

As the number of handheld cell phones exploded in 2000, communities across the United States considered legislation prohibiting their use while driving. New York's Suffolk County was the first to enact such a law.

In 2000, Sony's PlayStation2 became the holiday-season's "must-have" item. People camped outside stores waiting to buy this 300 MHz video game as demand far exceeded production.

cell phones, use of these devices exploded. Nonusers often objected to the growing volume of phone chatter in restaurants, buses, and other public places. Of particular concern were people who spoke on cell phones while driving cars. In October, Suffolk County, NY, became the first county known to ban use of a handheld cell phone while driving. Several communities around the nation also banned the practice.

Palm Pilots were a fast-growing market during 2000. Palm, Microsoft, Hewlett-Packard, Compaq, and Casio introduced Palm software that could, in some cases, play music and video files, go on-line, and display E-books.

Operating Systems. Microsoft introduced Windows ME (Millennium Edition), an upgrade of Windows 98 that offered multimedia improvements and better protection from system crashes. Windows ME ran particularly well on newer PCs that lacked floppy disk drives and older accessories.

Offering growing competition to Windows were operating systems based on UNIX, a multiuser, multitasking operating system designed to run on a wide variety of computers, from PCs to mainframes. Leading the pack was Linux, created by Linus Torwalds in the early 1990s. It has a high reputation for stability; it is available free to anyone, and users are encouraged to make modifications as long as they share their changes with everyone else.

Apple Computer released a test version of its new Mac OS X. At its core is an operating system called Darwin that offers easy operability with UNIX systems and applications. The graphic user interface, called Aqua, includes buttons that indicate active or nonactive status by glowing and dimming, drop shadows that give windows greater depth, and other visual cues making user responses more intuitive.

In January, Transmeta introduced the Crusoe chip for laptop and notebook computers. The chip offered increased power, lower operating temperatures, and longer battery life; and enabled the computers to run all day on a single charge, as compared to the two to three hours possible with older chips. In May, Gateway and America Online (AOL) selected the Crusoe chip to power the new Internet appliances they were developing. In addition, Transmeta's Mobile Linux was chosen as the operating system for the products.

The race between Intel and Advanced Micro Devices (AMD) for the speediest chip in the PC market took a leap upward in March when AMD became the first company to mass-produce a PC chip with a speed of 1 GHz (more than 1 billion cycles per second). Intel soon followed with its own 1GHz Pentium III chip. In November, Intel introduced the Pentium 4 microprocessor, with initial available speeds of 1.4 GHz and 1.5 GHz. The high speeds supported the needs of the latest software developments, such as 3-D graphics and voice and video communications. Chips also drove numerous other electronic products. Eastman Kodak and Foveon came out with high-resolution chips for digital cameras.

Toshiba and Memtek announced the first computer drives that combined the recording functions of CD-R/RW with the read-functions of CD-ROM and DVD-ROM. The integration of technologies gave consumers a multimedia storage and playback solution in a single unit.

PC cards were used to add fax/modem, networking, memory, and storage capabilities to more than 99% of all notebook PCs, as well as to digital cameras, PDAs, and other devices. The new CardBay standard expanded PC cards to include real-time video capture. Matsushita Electric, SanDisk, and Toshiba jointly developed a small-size, high-speed, read/write memory card capable of providing a high level of copy protection for music and movie storage. Initially, this Secure Digital (SD) Memory Card was available in capacities of 32 MB (megabytes) and 64 MB, with 256 MB planned for 2002.

Video Gaming. PlayStation 2 (PS2), the highly anticipated sequel to Sony's original PlayStation, was released initially in Japan on March 4, then in the United States on October 26. In both countries, demand far surpassed production, with high prerelease orders, people camping out in front of stores for a chance to get one of the video-game consoles, and machines even popping up on on-line auction sites for more than several times their list price.

PS2 runs at 300 MHz (megahertz) with 32 MB of memory, versus the 200 MHz and 24 MB of its main competitor, Sega's Dreamcast, launched in 1999. Both consoles had 128-bit processors, but the PS2 offered superior graphics in terms of speed, sharpness, and color, providing gaming aficionados the most realistic play yet. PS2 also had a built-in DVD player, for both games and movies, and two ports for the addition of printers and other peripherals.

Microsoft showed game developers a prototype of the X-Box video-game console, which it expected to market in late 2001 at a price comparable to that of PS2. The X-Box basically is a Windows PC, with a 733MHz Intel processor, 64 MB of memory, and a video chip more than twice as fast as that in PS2. Experts pointed out that while the X-Box would be technologically superior to its competitors, its ultimate success would depend on the number of games available.

The violence and gore of video games made headlines following a September report, "Marketing Violent Entertainment to Children: A Review of Self-Regulation and Industry Practices in the Motion Picture, Music Recording & Electronic Game Industries," from the Federal Trade Commission (FTC). According to FTC Chairman Robert Pitofsky, the report illustrated that "companies in the entertainment industry routinely undercut their own rating restrictions by target marketing violent films, records, and video games to young audiences." Of the 118 electronic games with "mature" ratings for violence that the commission selected for its study, 83 (70%) targeted children under the age of 17. The marketing plans for 60 of these (51%) expressly included children under the age of 17 in the target audience.

Mergers and Breakups. The globalization and convergence of communications technology were a major reason for some of the year's most significant mergers, acquisitions, and joint ventures; few companies had the financial resources to be global players without joining forces with others in some way. A second important impetus was the desire to obtain needed technology or other expertise quickly—and hopefully more cheaply than developing it from scratch. In January, AOL, the world's largest Internet company, announced that it would buy Time Warner, one of the biggest media companies. If the Federal Communications Commission (FCC) approved the merger, it would be the largest ever. Of particular concern to the FCC was access by competitors to Time Warner's cable network; according to AOL and Time Warner, they would open up the cable system to competitors. In November, Time Warner agreed to allow EarthLink, the second-largest Internet service provider after AOL, to offer Internet access over the Time Warner system. In January 2001, the FCC approved the merger but imposed conditions meant to protect consumers and preserve the openness of the Internet. (*See also* BUSINESS AND CORPORATE AFFAIRS.)

Vodafone AirTouch of Britain acquired Mannesmann of Germany, making Vodafone the world's largest mobile-telephone company. Terra Networks, the Internet unit of the Spanish telephone company Telefónica, bought Lycos, creating Terra Lycos, an Internet network that was operating in 40 countries as the leading portal to Spanish- and Portuguese-speaking markets.

The FCC approved the merger of Bell Atlantic and GTE to create Verizon, the largest telephone company in the United States. In July a merger of WorldCom and Sprint was canceled in the face of opposition from U.S. and European regulators. In October, AT&T announced that it would split into four parts, with four publicly traded stocks, but all operating under the AT&T brand name. On the heels of the AT&T announcement, WorldCom announced a similar plan. Meanwhile, Microsoft's battle with the U.S. Justice Department, which sought to break the software giant into two parts, continued with no resolution in sight for the immediate future.

JENNY TESAR, *Author*
"The New Webster's Computer Handbook"

Congo, Democratic Republic of the

Congo's vicious civil war continued in 2000, despite the signing of a peace pact by the warring parties in 1999. The United Nations (UN) refused to send in more than a perfunctory number of observers.

Civil War. More than one year after a cease-fire was signed in Lusaka, Zambia, by the contending disputants in the Congo, none of the goals agreed to had been met. Nine other African nations remained active; Hutu *génocidaires* from Rwanda continued armed and dangerous; UN peacekeepers had not been deployed; and no national consensus on the country's future political structure was reached. For two days in May and a week in June, Uganda and Rwanda—who had been allied, although sponsoring competing rebel factions, in their effort to oust President Laurent Kabila from power—sent their armies against one another in Kisangani. Hundreds of civilians were killed and thousands were wounded while the city was ravaged. Both countries were perplexed by the outbreak and were unable to adequately address the causes. The fighting was halted only when UN Security Council representatives engaged in shuttle diplomacy between the two countries.

Thereafter, UN Secretary-General Kofi Annan demanded that Uganda and Rwanda withdraw their forces from the Congo. Although Annan had little leverage to enforce his injunction, Uganda withdrew half of its Congolese contingent and Rwanda pulled back 100 mi (160 km). Rwanda was cleaving to eastern Congo as a buffer zone to prevent exiled Rwandan Hutu from attacking its territory and Tutsi citizenry.

During the intense battles, civilians poured out of the immediate area, and relief agencies indicated that in eastern Congo

alone there were 750,000 refugees, almost four times the number of a year earlier. In northwest Congo, serious battles erupted in August between the forces of Kabila and those of Jean-Pierre Bemba, the rebel leader in Equateur Province. With weaponry supplied by Uganda, Bemba's forces routed government troops outside Dongo. Two weeks later, Kabila decreed the Lusaka pact invalid, only to reverse himself within two days. Never really committed to the cease-fire, Kabila was indifferent to the efforts of Botswana's former President Ketumile Masire to bring about a political dialogue of reconciliation. In October fighting broke out between Rwandan-backed rebels and government troops.

The United Nations. Because the Congolese war—also called Africa's First World War, since Uganda, Rwanda, Zimbabwe, Angola, Namibia, Zambia, the Central African Republic, Chad, and Burundi have become caught up in it—clearly was threatening international peace and security, the UN Security Council assented in February to deepen the commitment of the UN. The Security Council agreed that in addition to the 200 UN observers already in place, 537 military observers supported by 5,000 military personnel would be dispatched, but *only* to verify that rebel groups, militias, and outside forces have pulled back or withdrawn their armies. UN peacekeepers would enter the Congo only after some sort of peace had been established.

Social and Economic Disintegration. The International Rescue Committee found that by 2000 the two-year war, along with its accomplices—hunger and disease—had led to the deaths of almost 2 million people, and an equal number of casualties. Various diseases reached astonishing proportions. Unsafe drinking water and putrid sanitation facilities were commonplace. Schools and hospitals were largely nonfunctioning; most roads remained impassable; and local transport was virtually inoperative. Industry, manufacturing, banking, and agricultural production all but ceased functioning. More than 60% of the population was unemployed, and inflation was at a staggering 300%. In essence, the Congo's social edifice and its economic infrastructure were in overwhelming decay, while in the capital, Kinshasa, banners hung claiming that the people were "United Around Laurent Désiré Kabila to Achieve Prosperity."

PETER SCHWAB, *Purchase College, State University of New York*

CONGO • Information Highlights

Official Name: Democratic Republic of the Congo.
Location: Central equatorial Africa.
Area: 905,564 sq mi (2 345 410 km²).
Population (mid-2000 est.): 52,000,000.
Chief City (1984 est.): Kinshasa, the capital, 2,664,309.
Government: *Head of state and government,* Laurent Désiré Kabila, president (took office May 1997). *Legislature*—suspended.
Monetary Unit: Congolese franc (4.5 Congolese francs equal U.S.$1, January 2000).
Gross Domestic Product (1999 est. U.S.$): $35,700,000,000 (purchasing power parity).
Foreign Trade (1998 U.S.$): *Imports,* $460,000,000; *exports,* $530,000,000.

Consumer Affairs

The U.S. economy remained strong in 2000; the federal government modestly increased its consumer-assistance role; personal savings reached historic low levels; and the Internet continued to grow.

Information. The Federal Consumer Information Center (FCIC) was established in February following the merger of the Consumer Information Center (CIC) and the Federal Information Center (FIC). As a result, several information sources were combined into one comprehensive vehicle that is available by phone at 1-800-688-9889 or Internet at *www.pueblo.gsa.gov*.

In February, a series of consumer-education initiatives marked the second National Consumer Protection Week (NCPW). Organized by a coalition of federal, state, and private groups, and with "Armchair Armor: Shopping Safely from Home" as a theme, the week focused on consumer rights and responsibilities in E-commerce, telemarketing purchases, mail-order catalog sales, door-to-door sales, flea-market shopping, and yard-sale purchases.

The Internet. The Internet's growth continued to alter the way consumers interact with the marketplace. Consumers increasingly could purchase products and services from anywhere in the world. They also could get free, valuable information through thousands of Web sites. Such information previously was available only after exhaustive search. And the idea of shopping for the best price took electronic form as "shopping bots" promised to search the Internet to find the lowest price for a specific product.

According to Internet Fraud Watch (IFW), sponsored by the National Consumers League (NCL), complaints regarding on-line fraud increased rapidly, with fraudulent practices in auction sales far outpacing any other category.

E-Signature Law. The new U.S. Electronic Signatures in Global and National Commerce Act took effect on October 1. It specifies that no contract, signature, or record shall be denied legally binding status just because it is in electronic form. It also states that most electronic contracts and documents are legally enforceable only if they are capable of being retained and accurately reproduced for later reference.

Personal Savings. The U.S. personal-savings rate dropped to a negative 0.4% in August—its lowest level since such record keeping began in 1959. Some analysts attributed the decline in savings to the "wealth effect" that consumers felt because a booming economy allowed them to increase spending and feel comfortable saving little or no money. Others warned that, if the trend continued, a recession would result.

See also AUTOMOBILES—The Ford-Firestone Tire Story.

MEL J. ZELENAK
University of Missouri, Columbia

Credit-Card Skimming

Credit-card fraud has been a growing problem since credit cards were first used in the retail industry in the 1910s. In the late 1990s the problem was the stealing of credit-card numbers and information over the Internet. By 2000 a new type of fraud began occurring that, if left unchecked, had the potential to change the way the industry conducts business. The problem, known as "skimming" was the fastest-growing area of credit-card fraud, according to the U.S. Secret Service's Financial Crimes Division (FCD). Estimates of $125 million in losses were reported in 2000.

The scam begins with "skimmers" paying employees of credit-card accepting businesses—often waiters, retail clerks, and gasoline attendants—to steal information from cards by using a small, handheld "skimmer." The apparatus reads and stores, for later downloading into a computer, the cardholder's name and credit-card number as well as the encrypted card verification code, which previously had been known only to the credit-card company. Data then are mailed electronically to an outside source, often con artists, where cards are cloned.

The counterfeit cards are indistinguishable from legitimate ones by even the most advanced credit-card security systems. Cardholders often do not know of the fraudulent purchases until they receive their bills, sometimes 30 days or more after the skimming occurred.

In 2000, skimming was practiced primarily by organized-crime groups in Asia, Russia, Nigeria, and Latin America, but security officials predicted the practice would become more prevalent.

MEL J. ZELENAK

Crime

The number of serious crimes reported to police in the United States declined for the eighth consecutive year in 1999, dropping by 7%, and extending the longest-running reduction in crime on record, the Federal Bureau of Investigation (FBI) reported. The murder rate, at 5.7 per 100,000 residents—compared with 5.6 per 100,000 in 1966—was the lowest in 34 years.

The Falling Crime Rate. The overall violent-crime rate was at a 21–year low. The FBI reported there were 525 murders, rapes, robberies, and aggravated assaults reported per 100,000 residents, the lowest rate since 1978. The overall 1992–99 reduction in crime was almost three times as long as the previous longest decline, from 1982 through 1984, according to FBI records that date through 1960.

The Justice Department's Bureau of Justice Statistics, which measures crime differ-

ently, reported a 10.4% reduction in the violent-crime rate, the largest one-year drop since the bureau began its annual survey in 1973. The Justice Department report was based on interviews with people nationwide, and it collected data on crimes reported and not reported to police. The survey estimated that in 1999 there were 32.8 violent crimes for every 1,000 Americans over age 11, down from 36.6 in 1998.

According to the FBI report, the population-adjusted murder rate fell 8.5%, while robbery fell 8.4%, aggravated assault 6.2%, and rape 4.3%. Among property crimes, the burglary rate went down 10%, auto theft was down 7.7%, and larceny-theft dropped 5.7%. The number of crimes reported to police agencies was down 10% in the West, 7% in the Midwest and Northeast, and 5% in the South.

Analysts have cited a variety of reasons for crime reduction during the 1990s, including the aging of the baby boom generation, crime-reduction programs, and a lessening of the crack-cocaine epidemic. Attorney General Janet Reno credited "more police officers on the streets, more prosecutions and tougher sentences for violent offenders, prevention programs that work, a healthy economy, and a new approach to crime-fighting."

However, analysts believed the reductions might begin to taper. The FBI reported that cities with more than 1 million residents saw the smallest reduction in murder rate, down 4%, compared with reductions of more than 10% in most other categories of city population. "The big cities were the first to go up in the 1980s, the first to come down in the 1990s," said professor Alfred Blumstein of Carnegie Mellon University. "Now, having the lowest murder-rate decline suggests they'll be the first to stabilize."

In 1999 the number of people behind bars in the United States topped 2 million for the first time, according to the Bureau of Justice Statistics. There were 1,890,800 inmates in prisons and jails, and another 135,800 in juvenile, military,

On Mother's Day—May 14—2000, some 750,000 mothers and other gun-control advocates were in Washington, DC, for the "Million Mom March," asking for stricter federal gun-control legislation.

immigration, and other facilities. That translated to one of every 110 men and one of every 1,695 women in prison or jail. The growth rate slowed to 3.4%, from 4.7% in 1998. Even though crime rates had been dropping since the early 1990s, prison populations were driven up by longer sentences—particularly for drug and violent crimes. The last annual reduction in prison population was in 1972. The Sentencing Project, an organization that supports alternatives to incarceration, said the United States had the world's highest incarceration rate. (*See also* PRISONS.)

Government Action and Reports. A Justice Department report on domestic violence indicated that attacks and threats of violence toward women by intimate partners declined from 1993 to 1998, but women still were five times more likely than men to suffer such attacks. The report said 1.1 million women were attacked by husbands or boyfriends in 1993, a number that fell to 876,340 in 1998. Attacks on men by intimate partners remained stable at about 160,000 in both 1993 and 1998. Two-thirds of the domestic attacks were simple assaults.

The Bureau of Justice Statistics and the U.S. Education Department reported that the rate of students becoming victims of violent crime at school dropped from 48 crimes per 1,000 students in 1992 to 43 crimes per 1,000 students in 1998.

President Bill Clinton signed into law a sweeping crime bill that held states financially responsible if murderers, rapists, or child molesters released from prison went on to commit a similar crime in another state. The first state would lose enough federal funds to pay the prosecution and imprisonment costs in the state where the second crime was committed. The provision was named "Aimee's Law," after a college student murdered in suburban Philadelphia in 1996 by a man released from prison after serving time for another murder in Nevada. The crime measure also reauthorized the Violence Against Women Act, a law originally passed in 1994. The revision provided more than $3 billion over five years for programs aimed at preventing domestic violence and protecting its victims—more than double the amount provided in the 1994 law.

Legislation to expand the federal hate-crimes law to protect homosexuals and the disabled was dropped due to Republican opposition. The proposal, supported by President Clinton, would have treated crimes against homosexuals in much the same way as racially motivated crimes. It would have added crimes motivated by sexual orientation, gender, or disability to the offenses covered under a 1968 law, and would have allowed federal prosecutors to pursue a hate-crime case if local authorities refused to press charges. In New York, Gov. George Pataki signed a hate-crime law in July, stiffening penalties for crimes motivated by bias against a victim's race, religion, sex, sexual orientation, disability, or age.

Gun Control. A Justice Department report said background checks stopped 204,000 of about 8.6 million gun-purchase applications in 1999. The Bureau of Justice Statistics said a total of 536,000 of almost 22.3 million prospective gun purchases had been rejected since background checks were begun in 1994 under the Brady Handgun Violence Prevention Act.

The U.S. Department of Education said the number of school students expelled for taking firearms to class dropped to 3,523 during the 1998–99 school year, down 4% from 3,658 the previous year. More than half of the expulsions occurred in high schools, but about 350 elementary-school students were expelled for having a firearm at school. Texas had the largest number of expulsions

© Gail Burton/AP/Wide World Photos

In 2000, Maryland became the first state to require that a gun's ballistic fingerprint be filed with the state police whenever a new handgun is sold. State Police firearms examiner Joseph Kopera, right, points to the area on the bullet that will be used to help identify the gun that a bullet is fired from.

with 294, followed by California with 290, Georgia with 208, and New York with 206. Seven states—Vermont, North Dakota, Rhode Island, Hawaii, Maine, South Dakota, and Delaware—had fewer than ten expulsions.

Smith & Wesson, the nation's largest gun maker, announced an agreement with the federal government in April, promising to install gun locks on all weapons it sold, to introduce "smart gun" technology within three years, and to bar sales of its weapons at gun shows without a background check. In exchange, Smith & Wesson, and any other gun maker that agreed to the plan, would be given preferential

School violence remained an issue in 2000. U.S. Senate Minority Leader Tom Daschle, right, listened as Patty Nielson, a Columbine High School teacher, told her story of surviving the April 1999 shooting incident at the Littleton, CO, school.

© Larry Downing/Reuters/Corbis

treatment in gun purchases by law-enforcement agencies. At least 500 communities signed on to the plan, but seven other gun makers sued the federal government and a number of cities, saying the agreement was an illegal restraint of trade.

In October, Maryland began requiring the manufacturer of every new handgun sold in the state to give state police a spent shell casing with the gun's ballistic fingerprint. The first-in-the-nation law required the casings to be entered into a database that police could check against bullet casings found at crime scenes. The law also required all new handguns to be sold with a trigger lock. A New York State law signed in August required background checks on gun buyers at gun shows in the state. Starting in 2001, New York also planned to require test firings of new guns to provide ballistic fingerprints to police. In June, New York also became the first state to sue the firearms industry, under a state public-nuisance law, in an effort to force the industry to change the way it sold guns.

Major Crimes. Young people with guns continued making crime headlines. A 6-year-old boy was alleged to have killed first-grade classmate Kayla Rolland in Flint, MI, with a gun the shooter found at home. The boy was not charged after prosecutors said he was too young to be held responsible. A man who lived with the boy, in what prosecutors called a flophouse, pleaded no contest to involuntary manslaughter for allowing the boy access to the gun. Another man who lived in the house pleaded guilty to

possessing the gun. Thirteen-year-old honor student Nathaniel Brazill was arrested in Lake Worth, FL, in May, and charged with first-degree murder in the shooting death of his English teacher, Barry Grunow. Police said the boy took the gun from his grandfather's dresser and shot his teacher on the last day of school. In January a Michigan boy who shot a man when the shooter was 11 was sent to a juvenile detention center until he turned 21. Nathaniel Abraham was convicted in 1999 of second-degree murder for shooting 18-year-old Ronnie Greene, Jr., in 1997, with a stolen rifle. Abraham was in sixth grade at the time.

In Golden, CO, the sheriff's department released a report on the April 1999 Columbine High School massacre, in which 12 students and a teacher were killed by teenage gunmen Eric Harris and Dylan Klebold, who also killed themselves. The report, which gave a minute-by-minute account of the attack, said the 12 students were dead within the first 16 minutes of the attack. In February, ten months after the attack, Columbine students Stephanie Hart Grizzell and Nick Kunselman were found dead after a shooting at a sandwich shop near the school. Police released composite drawings of a suspect.

Among crimes involving adults, five people were killed in a Pittsburgh-area shooting spree in April that police said was motivated by racial hatred. Richard Baumhammers was charged with killing a Jewish woman, an Indian man, two Asian men, and a black man. In September he was ruled mentally competent to stand trial. Two men were charged with killing five employees during a robbery at a Wendy's restaurant in New York City in May. Prosecutors said John Taylor and Craig Godineaux took the victims into a large freezer and shot each of them in the head.

The community activist formerly known as H. Rap Brown was arrested in Georgia and charged with shooting Fulton County sheriff's deputy Ricky Kinchen to death in March. Brown, now known as Jamil Abdullah Al-Amin, was an Atlanta community leader and, in the 1960s, a leader of the Student Nonviolent Coordinating Committee (SNCC). Former mob hit man Salvatore "Sammy the Bull" Gravano was charged in Arizona with conspiring to sell the drug "ecstasy." Gravano, who once admitted killing 19 people while part of the Gambino crime organization, and who lived for a time in the federal Witness Security Program, was charged in March, along with 44 other people, including three members of his family.

In some instances, police officers were accused of violating the law. Four white New York City officers were acquitted in February of murder charges in the shooting death of Amadou Diallo, an African immigrant who was unarmed when officers fired 41 bullets at him. The police said they mistook the wallet Diallo pulled from his pocket for a gun. In a separate incident, three white New York City officers were convicted of either aiding or covering up the torture of Haitian immigrant Abner Louima in a police-station rest room. A fourth officer pleaded guilty to carrying out the attack.

In Los Angeles, a police-misconduct scandal continued to make headlines. Officers in the Ramparts Division, in a heavily minority neighborhood, were accused of shooting, beating, and planting evidence on innocent people. More than 100 convictions were thrown out, and 20 officers left active duty. (*See also* POLICING—A PROBLEMATIC ENTERPRISE page 66.)

Former Sen. John Danforth (R-MO), appointed by Attorney General Janet Reno to investigate the government's role in the 1993 fire that killed about 80 people at the Branch Davidian compound in Waco, TX, concluded that cult leader David Koresh—and not the government—was to blame. "There are no doubts in my mind," Danforth said in July. The former senator said he determined that federal agents did not start the fire or shoot at cult members, but he added that the government had fueled spec-

ulation by failing to disclose all of its actions. Also in July a civil-trial jury in Waco ruled for the government in a wrongful-death lawsuit filed by surviving cult members and relatives of those who had died.

In nonviolent crime, a political supporter of Vice-President Al Gore was convicted in March in Washington, DC, of arranging illegal donations during the 1996 presidential campaign. Maria Hsia was convicted of five felony charges. In July the former head of the U.S. military's antidrug operation in Colombia was sentenced to five months in prison for trying to launder money his wife had received in a scheme to smuggle cocaine and heroin to the United States. Col. James Hiett admitted he tried to get rid of the money by paying bills in cash and depositing the money in bank accounts. His wife, Laurie Hiett, received a five-year sentence on her guilty plea to drug conspiracy.

Several high-profile crimes from past decades were in the news. In May, two former Ku Klux Klansmen were charged with murder in the 1963 bombing of a Birmingham, AL, church that killed four black girls. Those charged—Thomas E. Blanton, Jr., of Birmingham, and Bobby Frank Cherry of Mabank, TX—for years had denied any role in the Sunday-morning bombing of the Sixteenth Street Baptist Church. Former Klan member Robert Edward Chambliss had been convicted of the bombing in 1977 and died in prison.

A Justice Department investigation of the 1968 assassination of civil-rights leader Martin Luther King, Jr., found no reliable evidence to support allegations that conspirators framed James Earl Ray. Ray had pleaded guilty to killing King, but afterward insisted he had been framed by a man named Raoul. The June report said, "We found nothing to disturb the 1969 judicial determination that James Earl Ray murdered Dr. King."

An Ohio jury ruled against an effort by the son of Dr. Sam Sheppard to have the doctor declared innocent of the 1954 beating death of his wife, Marilyn. Sam Reese Sheppard filed a wrongful-imprisonment lawsuit against the state of Ohio, but the jury decided in April that he had not proved his father was innocent. The doctor was convicted of murdering his wife, and spent nearly a decade in prison, but the verdict was overturned and he later was acquitted in a second trial. Sheppard died in 1970.

Laurie ASSÉO
Legal Affairs Journalist, Washington, DC

Capital Punishment

Nearly a quarter-century after capital punishment was reinstituted in the United States, doubts about the way the death penalty is administered, whether it is imposed fairly, and whether it is an effective method of combating crime were growing, even among supporters.

The Debate. The intensity of the debate over capital punishment was dramatized by several factors in 2000. For example, the governor of Illinois temporarily halted executions amid concern about possible errors, while New Hampshire's governor vetoed a bill that would have repealed that state's death penalty. Members of Congress, including Senate Judiciary Committee Chairman Orrin Hatch (R-UT) and Sen. Patrick Leahy (D-VT), proposed legislation to provide DNA testing to inmates seeking to establish their innocence. "We are in a better position than ever before to ensure that only the guilty are executed," said Hatch. In addition, the American Bar Association (ABA) renewed its 1997 call for a nationwide moratorium on capital punishment until "questions about its fairness" could be resolved.

Despite the increased debate about capital punishment, it was not a major issue during the presidential campaign. Both nominees, Democrat Al Gore and Republican George W. Bush, supported the death penalty. Bush had presided over more than 130 executions during his tenure as governor of Texas. In June, for the first time, he granted a 30-day reprieve to allow DNA testing. The testing, however, confirmed Ricky McGinn's guilt, and he was put to death in September.

Meanwhile, public support for capital punishment remained high, although lower than in previous years. The Gallup Organization reported that 67% of those polled in August and September backed the death penalty. From 1985 until 1999, support for the death penalty ranged from 70% to a high of 80% in 1994, according to Gallup.

State and Federal News. Thirty-eight states had laws in 2000 allowing capital punishment. Nationwide, more than 670 people had been executed since the Supreme Court in 1976 allowed states to restore capital punishment. Of those, more than 230 were executed in Texas, and five were women. Tennessee had its first execution in 40 years, putting Robert Glen Coe to death in April for killing an 8-year-old girl.

On the legislative front, Florida lawmakers voted in January to give death-row inmates the choice of lethal injection, ending the state's policy of using just the electric chair. During a 1999 electrocution in Florida, blood had flowed from an inmate's nose, and flames had shot up from a man's head as he was being executed two years earlier. New Hampshire Gov. Jeanne Shaheen, a Democrat, vetoed legislation in May that would have repealed the state's death penalty. She said some crimes were so heinous that "the death penalty is the only appropriate penalty." Meanwhile, Illinois Gov. George Ryan, a Republican, temporarily halted executions on January 31, saying the death-penalty system was "fraught with error," and that state officials would study and revise it.

Virginia death-row inmate Earl Washington, Jr., was pardoned by Gov. James Gilmore III in October after DNA tests cleared him of the 1982 killing of a woman. Later that month, a federal appeals court reinstated the conviction of death-row inmate Calvin Jerold Burdine, whose case gained notoriety because his court-appointed lawyer had slept during parts of his trial. The Texas-based appeals court said Burdine did not show that his lawyer had slept through crucial parts of his trial.

No federal inmate had been executed since 1963, and two prisoners were seeking to avoid becoming the first. Juan Raul Garza succeeded in having his execution postponed while the Justice Department prepared new guidelines for presidential clemency. David Paul Hammer sought to show that his trial was unfair.

Studies. In June, Columbia University law professor James Liebman released a study that said that the capital-punishment system was "collapsing under the weight of its own mistakes," with two-thirds of death sentences nationwide thrown out on appeal. The study examined 4,578 death-penalty cases that had been through at least one round of appeal between 1973 and 1995.

A U.S. Justice Department study of the federal death-penalty system between 1995 and July 2000 showed that 80% of the 20 people sentenced to death were minorities. Attorney General Janet Reno called the figures troubling, but said they were caused by overall societal injustice.

LAURIE ASSÉO

Croatia

Croatia made significant strides toward democratic rule in 2000, following both parliamentary and presidential elections. The new coalition government committed itself to implementing far-reaching political and economic reform, and to stabilizing its relations with neighboring states.

Democratic Breakthrough. Following the death of President Franjo Tudjman in December 1999, Croatia held new presidential elections in January. The ballot was won by Stjepan Mesic, a former prime minister and Tudjman opponent. In the parliamentary elections the same month, a multiparty democratic coalition won the vote for the bicameral Assembly, or Sabor, defeating Tudjman's nationalist party, the Croatian Democratic Union (CDU). Ivica Racan, the head of the Social Democratic Party (SDP), became the new prime minister.

The two elections signaled the end of the CDU era and the beginning of a democratic administration. Top on the government's domestic political agenda was the constitutional reduction of presidential powers, and the combating of widespread official corruption in the privatization process. By November the Sabor approved changes in the constitution that redefined Croatia as a parliamentary democracy.

CROATIA • Information Highlights

Official Name: Republic of Croatia.
Location: Southeastern Europe.
Area: 21,829 sq mi (56 538 km²).
Population (2000 est.): 4,282,216.
Chief Cities (1991 census): Zagreb, the capital, 706,770; Split, 189,388; Rijeka, 167,964; Osijek, 104,761.
Government: *Head of state,* Stjepan Mesic, president (took office February 2000). *Head of government,* Ivica Racan, prime minister (took office January 2000). *Legislature*—Assembly: House of Counties and House of Representatives.
Monetary Unit: Kuna (8.8213 kuna equal U.S.$1, Nov. 15, 2000).
Gross Domestic Product (1999 est. U.S.$): $23,900,000,000 (purchasing power parity).
Economic Indexes (1999, 1990 = 100): *Consumer Prices,* all items, 67,258.4; food, 62,293.5. *Industrial Production,* 63.2.
Foreign Trade (1999 U.S.$): *Imports,* $7,777,000,000; *exports,* $4,280,000,000.

The authorities also launched a crackdown on former officials and businessmen who had embezzled millions of dollars from the state. Several individuals were arrested and tried during the year.

Economic Pains. Increasing budgetary discipline by the new government, in order to ensure macroeconomic stability, led to protests by workers. Meanwhile, the closure of loss-making companies increased unemployment to an estimated 20% of the workforce. Croatia's gross domestic product (GDP) was projected to remain stagnant for the year.

Foreign Progress. Unlike the Tudjman administration, the new Croatian government seemed determined to cooperate fully with the Hague-based International War Crimes Tribunal. The government turned over documents dealing with the Croatian army's campaigns against rebel Serbs in 1995, and supported the prosecution of indicted Croatian war criminals. Zagreb also committed itself to resettling more than 16,000 Serbian refugees who had fled the country during the 1995 war.

In May, Croatia became the newest member of NATO's Partnership for Peace program, and of the Euro-Atlantic Partnership Council. It also became a member of the World Trade Organization (WTO), and was on track for an association agreement with the European Union (EU).

JANUSZ BUGAJSKI, *Center for Strategic and International Studies*

Stjepan Mesic, a 65-year-old former prime minister, was elected president of Croatia in January following the death of President Franjo Tudjman in December 1999. The election was the beginning of a process which redefined the nation as a parliamentary democracy.

© Wade Goddard/Corbis-Sygma

Cuba

In 2000, Cuba continued to improve economically, attracting increased foreign investment and business. Despite this, the number of Cubans leaving the island topped 1999 figures, highlighted by the dramatic saga of Elián González (*see* SPECIAL REPORT, page 209).

The Economy. Officials predicted economic growth between 4.5% and 5% for 2000. The improvement, although modest, was seen by President Fidel Castro as a vindication of his decision to maintain a socialist regime and a quasi-Chinese model. While foreign visitors witnessed an increase in the Cubans' standard of living, economic conditions were not back to the level prior to the collapse of the Soviet Union a decade earlier. Still, Havana and provincial towns boasted smaller lines for rationed products, more available food, and better transportation. The U.S. dollar was the country's main currency, and almost any foreign products could be bought in special dollar stores. The 1-to-21 exchange ratio between the dollar and the Cuban peso held steady for the third consecutive year, indicating the peso's relative stability.

Having to do it alone, Cuba has changed the focus of its economy from exports of sugar (currently an inexpensive commodity) to the promotion of tourism, exports of minerals and high-priced cigars, and courting foreign investments. Dollar remittances by Cubans living abroad accounted for well more than $1 billion in 2000, practically as much as the value of exported sugar. Oil production—500,000 tons in 1995—was expected to reach 2.8 million tons in 2000, one-third of the country's consumption. Various foreign companies were exploring offshore areas in the Gulf of Mexico for oil and gas.

Of more immediate economic importance was an agreement, signed in October by Castro and Venezuelan President Hugo Chávez, stating that over the next five years, Venezuela would provide Cuba one-third of its oil needs—53,000 barrels a day—at cut-rate prices. The $3 billion deal was to be paid over 15 years at a 2% interest rate.

In March, Leisure Canada, a Vancouver development company, broke ground for a 370-room hotel on a 2-sq-mi (5.2–km^2) beachfront property in the tourist resort of Varadero, 70 mi (113 km) east of Havana. Before starting construction, Leisure Canada—partly owned by U.S. interests—investigated the provenance of the property, so as not to run afoul of the 1996 Helms-Burton Act, which prohibits U.S. companies from doing business on properties confiscated by the Cuban government from U.S. citizens. While U.S. corporations were prohibited from investing or operating in Cuba, other Western companies continued to fill the gap.

Despite trade restrictions, BellSouth and AT&T continued to receive revenues for telephone calls made to Cuba through wholly owned subsidiaries or affiliated companies in nine European and Latin American countries. In July the Cuban and U.S. Olympic Committees signed the first Cuban-U.S. agreement in 40 years, establishing cooperation in various sports activities.

U.S.-Cuba Relations. Pressure to open U.S.-Cuba trade, applied principally by the U.S.

© José Goitia/AP/Wiide World

Cuba's President Fidel Castro and Venezuela's President Hugo Chávez (right) conferred in Caracas in October 2000. The two leaders signed an agreement that allowed Cuba to buy Venezuelan oil at reduced prices.

Chamber of Commerce as well as by various farm organizations and members of Congress, increased in 2000. The principal reason for the U.S. private sector's interest in doing business in Cuba was that, according to recent studies, a free Cuba trade could generate $20 billion in annual commercial exchanges, mostly in exports of U.S. goods and services, and in the utilization of the well-trained and inexpensive Cuban labor force. In October—for the first time in almost 40 years—the U.S. Congress, in its agriculture-appropriations bill, allowed the sale of U.S. food and medicines to Cuba. But the new legislation prohibited U.S. banks from financing the exports, thus requiring Cuba to pay in cash or make financial arrangements with foreign banks for the purchase of U.S. goods. Even though some legal experts questioned the constitutionality of the legislation, the law prohibited the president from expanding U.S. travel to Cuba. The Castro government denounced the law as discriminatory, and said Cuba would not buy American food products or medicines.

Despite restrictions, close to 200,000 U.S. citizens—twice the 1998 total—visited Cuba in 2000, either legally licensed by the Treasury Department, or illegally. They included senior members of Congress, businesspeople, religious groups, sports teams, and high-school students. Many U.S. citizens traveled to Cuba without a permit through Mexico, Canada, or the Bahamas. Cuban authorities did not stamp their passports, making it difficult for the Treasury Department Office of Foreign Assets Control to charge the travelers with violating travel restrictions. Cuban-Americans, who can visit their families on the island once a year without a license, continued to fly there. In all, more than 2 million foreigners visited Cuba in 2000, about 6% more than in 1999.

While public-opinion polls indicated that about 70% of U.S. citizens favor the reestablishment of relations with Cuba, Castro did not expect that to happen soon. In October, while visiting Venezuela, he stated it did not matter who became the next U.S. president, as the two principal candidates pledged to continue the Cuban economic embargo to please what Castro called a "Cuban-American mafia in Miami." Having neutralized most of the already weak internal opposition by mobilizing the country's youth around the pro–Elián González banner (dissidents also supported the Cuban government's posture on Elián), Castro frequently excoriated Miami's Cuban exiles.

CUBA • Information Highlights

Official Name: Republic of Cuba.
Location: Caribbean.
Area: 42,803 sq mi (110 860 km²).
Population (2000 est.): 11,141,997.
Chief Cities (Dec. 31, 1995 est.): Havana, the capital, 2,184,990; Santiago de Cuba, 432,396; Camagüey, 296,601; Holguín, 243,240.
Government: *Head of state and government,* Fidel Castro Ruz, president (took office under a new constitution, December 1976). *Legislature* (unicameral)—National Assembly of People's Power.
Monetary Unit: Peso (1.0000 pesos equal U.S.$1, Dec. 11, 2000).
Gross Domestic Product (1999 est. U.S.$): $18,600,000,000 (purchasing power parity).
Foreign Trade (1999 est. U.S.$): *Imports,* $3,200,000,000; *exports,* $1,400,000,000.

The Clinton administration's policy toward Cuba remained contradictory. While the administration relaxed travel controls and did not hinder cultural and sports exchanges, it continued to support appropriations of tens of millions of dollars for the exile-run Radio and TV Marti, for exile groups that supposedly help anti-Castro opposition in Cuba.

Internationally, only Israel and the Marshall Islands joined with the United States in voting against a United Nations resolution in November that called for the "end to the economic, commercial, and financial U.S. blockade of Cuba." At the same time, Cuba and Russia were reestablishing ties that had languished after the collapse of the Soviet Union. According to Moscow, the December visit of President Vladimir Putin to Cuba would "consolidate the two countries' political wills to develop relations."

Leaving Cuba. The number of Cubans who abandoned the island grew in 2000. This was principally due to the growth of Miami's contraband industry. According to the U.S. Coast Guard, 80% of the 2,048 Cubans who arrived by boats in south Florida in 1999—the number was expected to reach 2,500 in 2000—came paying up to $4,000 each to contraband operators, who are seldom caught or prosecuted. The majority of the escapees reach U.S. soil, are immediately set free, and become eligible for U.S.-resident status in one year. Ironically, real dissidents—without wealthy relatives to pay the smugglers—who flee the island on makeshift rafts or small boats, are routinely apprehended by the Coast Guard before they reach Florida, and are immediately returned to Cuba.

GEORGE VOLSKY
North-South Center, University of Miami

The Saga of Elián González

The ocean rescue of Elián González, whose mother had died fleeing Cuba with him, and the subsequent custody case made international news. Cuban-Americans, above, demanded that the boy be allowed to remain with relatives in the United States.

On Thanksgiving Day, Nov. 25, 1999, two men fishing in the Atlantic Ocean a few miles off Fort Lauderdale, FL, spotted an inner tube floating nearby with a small boy clinging to it. The boy, then two weeks shy of his sixth birthday, and later identified as Elián González, was rushed to the Joe DiMaggio Children's Hospital in Hollywood, south of Fort Lauderdale, where he was listed in stable condition. Almost immediately, Elián's Miami relatives—his great-uncle, Lazaro González, and Lazaro's daughter, Marisleysis—came to the hospital to claim him.

Lazaro González had learned from his kin in Cuba that three days earlier, the boy; his divorced mother, Elizabet Brotons Rodriguez; and 12 others had escaped Cárdenas, their hometown on Cuba's north coast. Trying to reach Florida aboard a 17-ft (5-m) aluminum boat, they had kept their departure secret from Elián's father, Juan Miguel González. Almost instantly, the story of the boy's rescue became a major international news item. Pictures of the boy on a stretcher being wheeled to an ambulance were published and distributed widely.

Elián was released from the hospital the next day and placed by the U.S. Immigration and Naturalization Service (INS) into the custody of Lazaro González. The INS action, without first contacting the boy's father, began a bitter, seven-month-long feud that ended June 28 when the father and son returned to Cuba.

A Long Feud. The battle lines were drawn very quickly. On November 27, Cuba asked the United States to return Elián to his 31-year-old father, stating that the boy was being held illegally in Miami. At the same time, the U.S. State Department declared that the courts would decide the child's future. The Cuban American National Foundation (CANF), an influential and wealthy Miami exile group, entered the fray and offered financial support to Elián's working-class Miami family.

Turning a family custody dispute into a political contest, the foundation printed thousands of posters showing Elián on the stretcher with an anti-Castro message. CANF sent the posters to Seattle, where, as an unfounded Miami rumor had it, Cuban President Fidel Castro was to attend a meeting of the World Trade Organization (WTO).

Elián became a miracle child for many Miami exiles who came to believe that only a divine hand, and possibly friendly dolphins, had kept the boy alive in the inner tube for more than two days. The reality of his survival is puzzling in the absence of a fully credible explanation. The only two other survivors of what the U.S. Coast Guard believed was a Cárdenas-Miami smuggling operation came ashore on Key Biscayne, some 30 mi (48 km) south of Fort Lauderdale. Giving only scant details, the survivors told the authorities that the aluminum boat had capsized at night on November 22, which meant that they and Elián had spent more than 50 hours in the water. Blisters on their faces indicated that they could have been in the sea for more than a day. But the physician who examined Elián shortly after his arrival at the hospital opined, in a statement revealed in May, that the boy, who had no discernible signs of prolonged exposure to the sun and salty waves, had been in the water much less than 24 hours.

© José Luis Magana/AP/Wide World Photos

In Cuba, too, the custody dispute surrounding Elián González drew national attention. Billboards, such as the one above, called for his release from the United States. Elián returned to Cuba, with his father, on June 28, seven months after he was found clinging to an inner tube in the Atlantic Ocean.

Practically overnight, with the foundation's help, Lazaro González acquired a spokesperson and a legal team that eventually grew to a dozen lawyers. The 21-year-old Marisleysis took a leave from her bank position and became Elián's full-time caretaker. Their two-bedroom home became a shrine of sorts, visited by hundreds of cheering, Cuban-flag-waving exiles. Elián was put on display daily by his relatives; his activities were filmed by scores of TV cameramen and photographers.

On January 5, after U.S. officials met twice in Cuba with the boy's father to ascertain his paternity and his desire to have his son back, INS Commissioner Doris Meissner declared that Juan Miguel González was the only person who could speak for Elián. She announced that arrangements for Elián's January 14 return to Cuba were being made, and asked Lazaro González to turn over the boy to the INS. Great-Uncle Lazaro rejected the commissioner's request, and said he wanted his day in court. In an action applauded by a large segment of Miami's Cuban community, Lazaro's lawyers asked a Miami family judge to declare him the boy's legal guardian. On January 10, Circuit

Court Judge Rosa Rodriguez granted Lazaro emergency custody. Even before that ruling was overturned by another state judge, Attorney General Janet Reno, supported by President Bill Clinton, declared that as an undocumented minor alien, Elián was subject to federal jurisdiction. But Reno suspended the boy's January 14 return date. Lazaro's lawyers then petitioned the Miami U.S. District Court to order the INS to hold an asylum hearing for the boy.

Elián's case was no longer local. It had turned into a national political issue as Republican and Democratic legislators proposed plans to keep him in the United States. One plan, to make the six-year-old boy a permanent U.S. resident, was endorsed by the eventual presidential nominees, Texas Gov. George W. Bush and Vice-President Al Gore. Both were accused of pandering to Miami's Cuban voters. Elián became a household name worldwide.

Late in January, Elián's two Cuban grandmothers, who believed he should be returned to Cuba, arrived in Miami. They were able to see him only briefly, and the meeting exacerbated the hostility between the two branches of the extended González family. On March 21, Lazaro González was dealt his first judicial setback. In strong language, U.S. District Court Judge K. Michael Moore ruled that Elián was too young to request asylum, and that he should be placed in his father's custody. Lazaro's lawyers immediately appealed to the U.S. Court of

Appeals for the 11th Circuit in Atlanta. Two weeks later, Juan Miguel González—with his second wife and an infant son, Elián's half brother—flew to Washington, DC, to reunite with his son. But Lazaro, who had said he would turn the child over to Juan Miguel if he came to the United States, declared he would not do so because Elián was afraid of the father. Elián's great-uncle stated that if the INS wanted the boy, it would have to take him by force.

On April 12, Attorney General Reno went to Miami and tried unsuccessfully to persuade Lazaro and his legal and political advisers to surrender the boy peacefully. The following day, Lazaro released what looked like a staged video interview in which Elián said he did not want to return to Cuba. At the same time, Lazaro's house was surrounded daily by militant exiles who proclaimed they would prevent the boy from being taken by federal agents. Miami–Dade County Mayor Alex Penelas declared that if the INS came to seize Elián, Penelas would not allow the county's police to assist federal officials, and he would hold the president and the attorney general responsible if blood were shed.

At dawn on April 22, armed INS agents forcefully entered the house of Lazaro González, seized Elián, and flew him to his father in Maryland. Two photographs—one of the frightened Elián looking at a heavily armed INS agent in Miami, and the other of the smiling Elián in the arms of his father several hours later—epitomized the story. As the news of the raid spread in Miami, angry Cuban exiles gave vent to their frustration. For more than 24 hours, about 100,000 protesters blocked streets in many parts of the city, clashed with the police, burned tires, and overturned trash bins. About 200 people were arrested, but there were only minor casualties. Television viewers nationwide watched acts of vandalism on Miami streets awash with Cuban flags. They also saw demonstrators burning a few U.S. flags, or flying them upside down. Two days later, thousands of U.S.-flag-waving residents staged a counterrally in the non-Cuban districts of the city.

The battle for Elián's custody then moved from Miami to Atlanta. On June 1, three judges of the 11th Circuit Court of Appeals upheld Judge Moore's ruling. Lazaro's attorneys asked that all of the court's judges review the case. On June 23, the entire Court of Appeals confirmed the opinion of its three members. But the court ordered the boy to stay in the United States pending an appeal to the Supreme Court of the United States. On June 28, the Supreme Court declined to review the case, and Elián González and his father left the United States and flew back home to Cuba (*photo, left*).

President Castro was not at the airport. After a brief ceremony, the González family was driven to an undisclosed location. Kept out of public view while readjusting to his previous life, Elián appeared briefly on Cuban television on September 1, when, with other boys and girls, he went back to his refurbished Cárdenas elementary school.

Aftermath. In Miami, the fight over young Elián left deep scars. Many Cuban exiles felt betrayed by the Clinton administration and the U.S. courts. However, many other local residents and the majority of Americans who favored the boy-father reunification believed that the Miami Cubans had failed to comprehend the U.S. judicial system, and that, irrationally, the Miami Cubans looked at any issue concerning Cuba through the prism of their visceral enmity toward President Castro.

A *New York Times* editorial noted:"The image of the Cuban-American community in Miami, however, suffered because of its belligerence in disrupting family ties between father and son. The posturing by Miami's elected leaders in refusing to aid federal authorities was unsupportable. The Miami city politics have become more divisive than ever." Another consequence of the Elián incident was a diminution of the influence of the once-strong anti-Castro exile lobby. In October, Congress passed the first relaxation of the 38-year-old U.S. economic embargo of Cuba, and more such actions were expected in 2001. As for Lazaro González and his family, they moved into obscurity.

GEORGE VOLSKY

Cyprus

Cyprus remained divided into two parts in 2000, just as it had been since a 1974 Turkish invasion left the island de facto split into Greek Cypriot and Turkish Cypriot.

The Turkish Republic of Northern Cyprus, a political entity proclaimed in 1983, continued to function with the septuagenarian Rauf Denktash as president; but except for Turkey, this state was not recognized internationally. The internationally recognized government of the Republic of Cyprus controlled the southern part of the island and was headed by President Glafcos Clerides, a Greek Cypriot octogenarian. The United Nations (UN) maintained forces in a buffer zone on the island to keep the peace between the majority Greek Cypriots and the minority Turkish Cypriots. In addition, Great Britain retained two sovereign bases on the island. In the north the Turkish government stationed about 25,000 Turkish troops; in the south, there were fewer troops from Greece.

For more than 25 years, all attempts to find a solution to the island's division had failed, even though the UN had often tried to mediate. Basically, Clerides' Greek Cypriot government favored a solution that would leave Cyprus a unitary state composed of a bicommunal and bizonal federation. This was in line with what the UN had pressed for previously. Denktash was in favor of splitting the island into two independent states, plus what he called a confederation with a very loose central administration. Clearly, the two points of view could not easily be reconciled. Another major issue was the fact that 200,000 Greek Cypriots had been forced from their homes in the north in 1974 and never allowed to return, and it did not seem that Denktash would permit this soon.

Proximity Talks. Under the aegis of the UN, proximity talks between Greek Cypriots and Turkish Cypriots were held at intervals during the year. Though Clerides and Denktash were involved, they never met together, only through UN intermediaries. In September, Clerides publicly voiced strong disapproval of a statement by UN Secretary General Kofi Annan that seemed to treat both sides as equals, something the Greek Cypriots never have accepted. In November, Denktash emphasized that he would discontinue negotiations if his state were not recognized internationally and if the European Union (EU) accepted

CYPRUS • Information Highlights

Official Name: Republic of Cyprus.
Location: Eastern Mediterranean.
Area: 3,571 sq mi (9 250 km²).
Population (mid-2000 est.): 900,000.
Chief Cities (Dec. 31, 1997 est.): Nicosia, the capital, 194,100; Limassol, 152,900.
Government: *Head of state and government*, Glafkos Clerides, president (took office March 1, 1993). *Legislature* (unicameral)—House of Representatives.
Monetary Unit: Pound (0.6183 pound equals U.S.$1, Dec. 29, 2000).
Gross Domestic Product (1999 est. U.S.$): $9,000,000,000 (purchasing power parity).
Economic Indexes (1999, 1990 = 100): *Consumer Prices* all items, 139.7;(1999, 1998 = 100): food, 100.8. *Industrial Production*, 104.0.
Foreign Trade (1999 U.S.$): *Imports*, $3,618,000,000; *exports*, $997,000,000.

Cyprus' membership before Turkey was accepted as an EU member. Despite the acrimonious exchanges, talks were scheduled to restart in January 2001.

Although Denktash made clear his opposition to Cypriot entry into the EU before Turkey joined, the Clerides government placed a priority in its negotiations for the accession of Cyprus. In November the EU, at the instigation of Greece, presented Turkey with an accession plan, including references to the Cyprus problem as well as to the continuing Greek-Turkish dispute over Aegean Sea control. Turkey responded angrily and sharply, but by early December the wording had been softened, and Turkey was mollified.

Military Exercises. Just a week before the final round of 2000's proximity talks, the Greek Cypriot National Guard held military exercises that included Greek warplanes. Turkish planes buzzed the Greek planes, and the Turkish government criticized the maneuvers. The Greek and Greek Cypriot governments said they needed to be able to defend themselves against the potential threat from the Turkish troops stationed in the northern Turkish-controlled territory.

Turkish Cypriot Demonstrations. With Turkey's support, Denktash's position seemed secure as he was elected to a fourth consecutive term as president of Turkish Cyprus in April. However, there was evidence of unrest against him among some Turkish Cypriots. Apparently, they feared that the area was becoming too dependent on Turkey, and that Turkey was not fostering indigenous economic growth. The outbursts by Turkish Cypriots in their own area showed the contrast between the north, where the economy was very weak, and the south, which had a thriving, continuously growing economy and a much higher standard of living.

GEORGE J. MARCOPOULOS, *Tufts University*

Czech Republic

The Czech government of Miloš Zeman remained in office in 2000. In January the minority Social Democratic (CSSD) government renewed its opposition agreement with Václav Klaus' Civic Democratic Party (ODS), the main party of the opposition. The opposition agreement, which allowed the minority government to remain in office, continued to be controversial. Public-opinion polls demonstrated that the public was skeptical of the arrangement.

Domestic Affairs. The CSSD experienced internal strife. Deputy Petra Buzkova, targeted by activists in the party who attempted to ruin her reputation, resigned as party vice chair in protest of the opposition agreement. Prime Minister Zeman reiterated his pledge to resign as CSSD leader at the next party congress.

Klaus' ODS emerged as the winner in the regional elections held in November with 27.8% of the vote. The opposition four-party coalition came in second with 22.9%, and the Communist Party third with 21%. The governing CSSD received 14.7% of the vote. Voter turnout was relatively low—only a third of the electorate voted. CSSD also fared badly in the November Senate elections, winning only one of 26 seats. The four-party coalition won 16 seats; ODS won eight; and an independent won a seat. The results of the Senate elections cost CSSD and ODS their majority in the Senate.

Low voter turnout reflected popular dissatisfaction with national politics. In late October, public-opinion polls indicated that 66% of those surveyed were dissatisfied with the political situation.

Several important pieces of legislation were passed in 2000. In November the government proposed a law that would set up an ethnic-minorities council, as required by the European Union (EU) of aspirants for membership. In October, Parliament overrode President Václav Havel's veto of a law extending lustration until EU accession. The lustration law forbids officials of the former communist regime from holding civil-service positions. President Havel's veto stemmed from his concern that extending the law would complicate reform of the civil-service and state-administration system.

The Czech economy continued its recovery in 2000. Industrial output increased 5.8% in the first eight months. Gross domestic product (GDP) was expected to grow by 2.7%. Inflation was expected to remain at 4%. Unemployment averaged approximately 9% throughout the year.

The government continued its campaign to attract foreign investment to the Czech Republic. In October the government proposed a plan to privatize utilities. Czech truckers protested increased fuel prices in September, and Czech teachers protested to call attention to their difficult situation and the low levels of funding for education.

Foreign Affairs. In October, EU officials gave a positive assessment of Czech measures to prepare for accession to the EU. They also identified the judicial system and the system of state administration as areas in need of further reform.

Czech leaders cooperated with others in the Visegrad grouping. Officials maintained warm relations with the Slovak government headed by Mikuláŝ Dzurinda. They also welcomed the government of Vojislav Kostunica, which ousted Slobodan Milosevic in Yugoslavia in October.

Czech relations with Austria were strained by the results of the Austrian elections and also by the Czech government's decision to open the Temelin nuclear-power plant in October. The Austrian government threatened to block EU accession talks with the Czech Republic over the issue of the Temelin plant. Czech leaders refused to meet with their Austrian counterparts to discuss the issues until protests stopped.

SHARON WOLCHIK
George Washington University

CZECH REPUBLIC • Information Highlights

Official Name: Czech Republic.
Location: East-central Europe.
Area: 30,450 sq mi (78 866 km²).
Population (2000 est.): 10,272,179.
Chief Cities (Jan. 1, 1999 est.): Prague, the capital, 1,193,270; Brno, 384,727; Ostrava, 322,111.
Government: *Head of state,* Václav Havel, president (took office Jan. 1, 1993). *Head of government,* Miloš Zeman, prime minister (appointed July 17, 1998). *Legislature*—Parliament: Senate and Chamber of Deputies.
Monetary Unit: Koruna (37.2750 koruny equal U.S.$1, Dec. 29, 2000).
Gross Domestic Product (1999 est. U.S.$): $120,800,000,000.
Economic Indexes (1999, 1990 = 100): *Consumer Prices,* all items, 336.7; food, 258.0. *Industrial Production,* 80.9.
Foreign Trade (1999 U.S.$): *Imports,* $28,781,000,000; *exports,* $26,831,000,000.

Dance

Dance in the year 2000 was filled with more contrast than usual. Experimental troupes such as H. Art Chaos from Japan offered provocative images and new idioms. Established U.S. choreographers remained true to their signature styles.

There were other extremes: A new company was formed and a venerable one shut down. Twyla Tharp founded a modern-dance troupe after 12 years of freelance choreography. Meanwhile, a faction of the board of the Martha Graham Dance Company ceased the company's operations during a power struggle with Ron Protas, Graham's longtime associate—to whom she willed the rights to her works.

Ballet. The New York City Ballet, founded by George Balanchine and Lincoln Kirstein, is the major repository of Balanchine ballets. But they also are performed throughout the world. In 2000 the two-week Balanchine Celebration at the John F. Kennedy Center for the Performing Arts presented a highly successful showcase illustrating the breadth of this influence. A group from the Bolshoi Ballet in Moscow and five U.S. companies—Miami City Ballet, Joffrey Ballet of Chicago, San Francisco Ballet, Suzanne Farrell Ballet, and the Pennsylvania Ballet—performed a range of Balanchine ballets. The event represented a milestone, an unprecedented concentration of different companies focused on the works of one choreographer.

The New York City Ballet's own blockbuster presentation was its fourth Diamond Project since 1992. This showcase for new choreography has left few lasting works but has developed new talent. One obvious example was Christopher Wheeldon, whose *Mercurial Manoeuvres* wittily deployed a large cast to dazzling effect. The Diamond Project produced two other major premieres—Helgi Tomasson's *Prism* and Peter Martins' *Harmonielehre*, named after its score by John Adams and striking in its mysterious images. Martins, the City Ballet's artistic director, also created two lighter pieces, *Slonimsky's Earbox* and *Todo Buenos Aires*.

Other premieres in the project were *Tributary*, choreographed by Robert La Fosse and Robert Garland in tribute to Arthur Mitchell, director of Dance Theatre of Harlem; *Triptych* by Christopher d'Amboise; *Swerve Poems* by Kevin O'Day; and *Appalachia Waltz* by Miriam Mandaviani.

Earlier in the year, Twyla Tharp choreographed *The Beethoven Seventh* for the company. Opinions were divided about her use of Beethoven's *Seventh Symphony*, but the ballet was one of her most classical works and was highlighted by a strong and poignant duet.

American Ballet Theatre (ABT) also presented a Tharp premiere, *The Brahms-Haydn Variations*, an intricate, plotless piece. The company's major production was *Swan Lake*, staged straightforwardly by ABT's artistic director, Kevin McKenzie. John Cranko's *The Taming of the Shrew*, new to the troupe, presented impressively strong, comic performances.

Weren't We Fools?, Christian Holder's romantic ballet tribute to the music of George Gershwin, and *Jabula*, a ritualistic piece by Australian choreographer Natalie Weir, also premiered.

Eliot Feld created two offbeat novelties for his company, Ballet Tech—*Nodrog Doggo*, about an urban gang, and *Coup de Couperin*, a witty stylization of Baroque dances. Augustus van Heerden created the allegorical *Memento Mori* for Dance Theatre of Harlem.

Outside New York City, the Joffrey Ballet of Chicago came to national prominence again with splendid new stagings of 20th-century classics. In 1995 the Joffrey Ballet had moved from New York and reorganized in Chicago, where it found new financial and civic support. The 2000 season included a Copland tribute with a sensitive staging of Martha Graham's *Appalachian Spring* with Protas' blessing. Elsewhere, the Houston Ballet presented Ben Stevenson's new *Cleopatra*. Boston Ballet did a staging of the 19th-century classic, *La Bayadère*, and presented Wheeldon's ballet to Vivaldi—*The Four Seasons*.

Modern Dance. American companies had little in common except that some choreographers explored a staccato way of moving. This was especially evident in premieres for the Alvin Ailey American Dance Theatre—Judith Jamison's *Double Exposure*, Alonzo King's *Following the Subtle Current Upstream*, and Dwight Rhoden's *Chocolate Sessions*. By contrast, Carmen de Lavallade, Ailey's partner in the 1940s and 1950s, used the flowing mainstream idiom of an earlier modern-dance era to great success in a romantic duet, *Sweet Bitter Love*.

An example of slow-moving flow came from Eiko and Koma, who were faithful to their usual theme of catastrophe and rebirth

*Dancers Adam Hendrickson and Edward Liang perform in Peter Martins'
symphonic ballet "Harmonielehre," presented in 2000 as part of the New
York City Ballet's fourth Diamond Project for new choreography.*

in *When Nights Were Dark*. Using a mobile shiplike set festooned with mosslike hangings, the husband-and-wife team offered a spectacular and primeval image of human instincts. Another innovative production, Ralph Lemon's *Tree*, experimented with concepts of contrast and convergence, using performers from China, Africa, and the United States.

Among established names, Paul Taylor's joyous *Dandelion Wine* stood out in addition to two acclaimed elegant pieces, *Arabesque* and *Cascade*. Merce Cunningham's *Interscape (2000)* at the Kennedy Center was enhanced by Robert Rauschenberg's stunning front curtain and backdrop, with smudged postmarks and Victorian design. Former Cunningham disciples who had major seasons were Lucinda Childs in a polished series of minimalist pieces, *Parcours*, and Trisha Brown, with *Five Part Weather Invention* and the suave *Rapture to Leon James*. A remarkable performance came from Bill T. Jones in a conceptional solo, *The Breathing Show*.

Mark Morris choreographed *Pecadillos*, a solo, and John Jasperse created *See Through Knot* for Mikhail Baryshnikov's White Oak Dance Project. Yvonne Rainer, a leader of the 1960s' avant-garde that once rejected stars and Establishment theaters, appeared with Baryshnikov in the collage of excerpts she called *After Many a Summer Dies a Swan*.

Tharp's troupe, Twyla Tharp Dance, made its debut at the American Dance Festival in Durham, NC, with *Mozart Clarinet Quintet K.581*, which integrated ballet and modern dance in a plotless piece, and with *Surfer at the River Styx*, which hinted murkily at a story of redemption.

Foreign Companies. The Bolshoi Ballet, absent from New York for ten years, returned with "Giselle" and a Balanchine ballet, *Symphony in C.* At the Kennedy Center and on tour, the company concentrated on two signature pieces, *Don Quixote* and *Romeo and Juliet.* The old male bravura was absent, but new talent included Maria Alexandrova, Galina Stepanenko, and Svetlana Lunkina. Boris Akimov replaced Alexander Fadeyechev as ballet director.

The Eifman Ballet of St. Petersburg presented Boris Eifman's *Russian Hamlet*, and visitors included the Stuttgart and the Royal Birmingham Ballets.

Experimental troupes were more interesting as seen in Sakiko Oshima's *Secret Club...Floating Angels 2000*, a social critique for H. Art Chaos. Innovative work came from Mathilde Monnier of France; Vicento Saez of Spain; Susanne Linke from Germany; and Lin Hwai-Min of Taiwan.

Awards and Obituaries. Mikhail Baryshnikov was a recipient of the Kennedy Center Honors. Also in 2000, the Samuel H. Scripps-American Dance Festival Award went to Pilobolus Dance Theater, and Paul Taylor received the Capezio Award.

Major figures who died in 2000 were the modern-dance choreographer Anna Sokolow; the ballerina Tatiana Riabouchinska, one of Balanchine's "baby ballerinas"; two early stars of the New York City Ballet, Janet Reed and Tanaquil Le Clercq; and Lucia Dlugoszewski, the avant-garde composer who married Erick Hawkins and directed his company after his death.

ANNA KISSELGOFF, *"The New York Times"*

Denmark

In a referendum held on Sept. 28, 2000, a majority of Danes (53%) voted against joining the European Union's (EU's) single currency, the euro. There were no immediate economic or political repercussions to the vote, however, and Denmark was to maintain close links to the euro. The Faeroe Islands scheduled a referendum on the issue of full independence from Denmark for 2001. In November, Danes mourned the death of Queen Mother Ingrid, the 90-year-old widow of King Frederik IX and mother of the current queen, Margrethe.

Politics and European Affairs. Social Democratic Prime Minister Poul Nyrup Rasmussen reshuffled his government in February, prior to calling the September 28 popular vote on the euro. Among the new ministers was former member of the European Commission Ritt Bjerregaard. A comfortable lead in the polls of 8% to 10% rapidly dissipated when sovereignty, rather than economics—as both the government and the "yes" side had planned for—became the dominant campaign issue.

Denmark joined in imposing sanctions against the new Austrian government, protesting the presence of the right-wing Freedom Party of Jörg Haider. However, the decision in favor of sanctions split the "yes" side on the euro issue, as the Liberal and Conservative parties dissented openly. Polls showed that a clear majority of Danes opposed the sanctions as a violation of Austrian sovereignty. The "no" side trumpeted the sanctions as proof that the EU is turning into a political union, and Austria was successfully designated a proxy for Danish sovereignty. The right-wing Danish People's Party, led by Pia Kjaersgaard, launched its "no" campaign on April 9, recalling the Nazi invasion of Denmark that began on that same date in 1940.

The government published a report in June listing the alleged economic benefits of Danish participation in the euro, including increased Danish influence on EU economic policies, board membership on the European Central Bank, complete elimination of currency uncertainty, and a smaller interest-rate differential to the German mark and the euro. The bottom line for the "yes" side was that the euro represented higher growth and lower unemployment. Sovereignty remained the key issue throughout the campaign, however, and it developed that Danes voted "no" to further EU political integration rather than "no" to the euro. Almost one-third of Liberal and Conservative voters rejected the euro. Polls showed that party political preferences did not shift on the euro. Likewise, the parliamentary situation did not change.

Economy. Fears that a "no" to the euro would trigger an economic downturn proved unfounded. In fact, the Danish stock market and economy performed better than expected, both before and after the referendum. Unemployment hit a new low of 5.2% in August, and strong exports sustained a growth rate of more than 2%.

The Oresund Bridge, linking Denmark and Sweden, opened in July. Traffic was below expectations during the bridge's initial months of operation.

Faeroe Islands. The government of the autonomous Faeroe Islands decided to call a referendum on independence from Denmark in 2001. Located in the North Atlantic, the islands have a population of 43,000. Rasmussen's government said that the 18 rocky islands would give up Danish subsidies within four years if they voted in favor of total independence. Islanders had voted against independence in 1906 and 1946.

LEIF BECK FALLESEN, *Editor in Chief*
"Boersen," Copenhagen

DENMARK • Information Highlights

Official Name: Kingdom of Denmark.
Location: Northwest Europe.
Area: 16,638 sq mi (43 094 km²).
Population (2000 est.): 5,336,394.
Chief Cities (Jan. 1, 1999 est.): Copenhagen, the capital, 491,082; Århus, 216,564; Odense, 144,940.
Government: *Head of state,* Margrethe II, queen (acceded Jan. 1972). *Head of government,* Poul Nyrup Rasmussen, prime minister (took office Jan. 1993). *Legislature* (unicameral)—Folketing.
Monetary Unit: Krone (7.9534 kroner equal U.S.$1, Jan. 17, 2001).
Gross Domestic Product (1999 est. U.S.$): $127,700,000,000 (purchasing power parity).
Economic Indexes (1999, 1990 = 100): *Consumer Prices,* all items, 120.1; food, 116.8. *Industrial Production,* 129.2.
Foreign Trade (1999 U.S.$): *Imports,* $44,068,000,000; *exports,* $48,446,000,000.

Drugs and Alcohol

The importation and use of illicit drugs as well as the abuse of alcohol, especially among young people, continued to be significant problems in the United States in 2000.

Drugs. Although the nation's 29-year "war on drugs" was a nonissue during the presidential campaign, voters in Alaska,

Colorado, California, and Nevada paid attention to one aspect of drug use—legalizing marijuana—on Election Day, November 7. In Alaska, an initiative that would have eliminated penalties for marijuana possession, use, cultivation, and sale was defeated, with 61% of voters rejecting it. Voters in Colorado and Nevada approved amendments to their states' constitutions to authorize the medical use of marijuana for cancer, AIDS, and other serious diseases. In California, voters approved a statewide ballot allowing first- and second-time, nonviolent drug offenders to enter drug-treatment programs instead of going to prison. Also in California, a measure that permitted citizens to grow up to 25 marijuana plants for personal use was passed in Mendocino County.

On June 14, Hawaii Gov. Ben Cayetano signed into law a bill that legalized the use of marijuana in that state as a medical treatment. That marked the first time a state used legislation—rather than a ballot initiative—to legalize the possession and use of marijuana for medical purposes. On August 29 the U.S. Supreme Court ruled that an Oakland, CA, clinic could not legally distribute marijuana for medicinal purposes. That decision, however, did not overturn California's 1996 medical-marijuana law, and local governments throughout the state continued to allow medical use of the drug.

A study released in March indicated, for the first time, a link between marijuana use and heart attacks. The study, presented to an American Heart Association conference, found the risk of heart attacks among middle-aged marijuana users increased drastically in the first hour after smoking the drug. Marijuana smoking caused heart rates and blood pressure to rise significantly, the study found.

Surveys released during the year reported a mixed picture on drug use among young people. Marijuana and cocaine use by high-school students increased significantly from 1991–99, according to a June 9 report by the federal Centers for Disease Control and Prevention (CDC). The number of high-school students who said they used marijuana increased from 14.7% in 1991 to 26.7% in 1999, the "Youth Risk Behavior Surveillance System" survey found. For cocaine, the percentages increased from 1.7% to 4% in the 1991–99 time period.

On the other hand, a survey by the Partnership for a Drug-Free America, released November 25, and the federal government's annual National Household Survey on Drug Abuse, released August 31, reported decreases in the number of American teenagers who smoked marijuana. The government survey reported a 26% drop in marijuana use among teenagers in that same period. Drug use among the 18- to 25-year-old cohort, though, rose from 14.7% in 1997 to 18.8% in 1999.

The U.S. Customs Service reported record seizures of ecstasy—which is largely manufactured in Belgium and the Netherlands. In the first ten months of fiscal year 2000, the Customs Service seized some 8 million doses of the drug, which was controlled for the first time by organized drug-smuggling traffickers. Other developments in the nation's drug-importation fight in 2000 included the 17-day Operation Conquistador, during which a group of international agencies, led by the U.S. Drug Enforcement Agency (DEA), arrested a record 2,331 suspects in March in the Caribbean, Central America, and South America. The operation included the eradication of coca fields, the destruction of cocaine laboratories, and large seizures of cocaine and heroin. About half of the arrests were in the Dominican Republic, the main conduit for cocaine from Colombia to the United States.

DEA and FBI agents broke up a multimillion-dollar heroin ring in Mexico in June. The approximately 200 suspects arrested were responsible, DEA said, for distributing heroin in 22 U.S. cities. In August, a team of drug agents from 12 countries broke up a large international cocaine-trafficking operation in Colombia, confiscating some 25 tons of cocaine.

Alcohol. Half of all 12- to 17-year-olds interviewed said that they had at least one drink of alcohol in the previous 30 days in 1999, according to a CDC survey. The survey also reported that in 1999, some 32% of young people said that they had taken part in "binge drinking," imbibing five or more drinks in one night, in the month preceding the survey.

The National Highway Traffic Safety Administration reported that alcohol-related traffic fatalities declined in 1999 to the lowest figure since those statistics were first tabulated in 1975. Alcohol was involved in nearly 15,800 traffic deaths, compared with some 15,900 in 1998, the agency reported in April. On October 23, President Clinton signed into law a bill that set a new, tougher national standard—a 0.085% blood-alcohol level—for drunken driving.

MARC LEEPSON, *Freelance Writer*

Ecuador

Ecuador began the new century with a bang, undergoing the first military coup in Latin America since the region made a return to the politics of democracy (*see* LATIN AMERICA).

Economic Turmoil. Facing a collapse of the banking system in 1999, President Jamil Mahuad's government froze bank accounts and funneled scarce resources to failing banks. Ecuador became the first country to default on its Brady bonds, and national currency lost 60% of its value during the year. The economy shrank 7.3% in 1999, and the impoverished Indian population, in the mountainous regions surrounding the capital city of Quito, was hardest hit. In January 2000, President Mahuad, with his popularity sinking, made a last-ditch effort to salvage the economy, announcing he would replace Ecuador's currency with the U.S. dollar.

Military Coup. Only 27% of Quito residents supported dollarization—the complete replacement of the Ecuadorian sucre with U.S. dollars—and the announcement fueled calls for Mahuad's resignation. Several thousand Indians marched on the capital to protest dollarization, and further plans for privatization of the telephone and electric companies. Protesters gathered in front of the Congress building, joined by military officers and cadets, who had lost confidence in the government. The uniformed presence in the crowd inspired the congressional guards to surrender the building without a fight, and within hours the protesters also captured the Supreme Court building. On January 21, they took over the presidential palace and boldly declared a new governing triumvirate. The coup government lasted mere hours before senior military officers swiftly replaced the triumvirate's military representative, and then withdrew their support entirely.

New Leadership. Under heavy international pressure, the armed forces swore in Vice-President Gustavo Noboa Bejarano as the new president, thereby averting economic sanctions. Deposed President Mahuad refused to resign, but he recognized Noboa as president, and later moved abroad.

Noboa, a former university professor, was viewed as honest and less beholden to the Popular Democracy party (DP) and its funders than was Mahuad. Noboa was from the coastal province of Guayas, where citizens were so disenchanted with Quito's governance that, just two days after the coup, they voted for fiscal autonomy in a nonbinding referendum. Although Noboa could not count on the support of the coast's Social Christian Party (PSC), his coastal origins bought him time and a measure of tolerance to work with.

Shift to Dollarization. In a bold decision, Noboa declared he would proceed with dollarization and privatization. The leading Indian organization, the Confederation of Indigenous Nationalities of Ecuador (CONAIE), remained opposed to those policies, and gave him six months to respond to their demands or face renewed protests.

In March, despite widespread skepticism about his government's prospects for survival, Noboa pushed through omnibus legislation to enable privatization and other unpopular economic reforms. By the time the six months were up and CONAIE called a protest, the turnout was low, suggesting that the social dynamics behind the coup no longer threatened the government's stability. When dollarization was completed on September 9, inflation had fallen from 14.3% in January to 1.4% in August. Fifty-five percent of Quito residents said they felt dollarization was helping the economy, and business confidence levels were rising apace. With oil prices high, the economy was expected to register positive growth in 2000.

Significant problems hampered the political sphere, where partisan politics caused a constitutional crisis in August, after the Congress split in a feud over who should reign as president of the legislature. Under the fourth president of the republic in as many years, Ecuador's future remained uncertain. Nonetheless, President Noboa had proven an able pinch hitter, surviving the odds to start Ecuador toward economic recovery.

SHELLEY A. MCCONNELL, *Emory University*

ECUADOR • Information Highlights

Official Name: Republic of Ecuador.
Location: Northwest South America.
Area: 109,483 sq mi (283 560 km²).
Population (2000 est.): 12,920,092.
Chief Cities (mid-1997 est.): Quito, the capital, 1,444,363 (mid-1996); Guayaquil, 1,973,880; Cuenca, 255,028.
Government: *Head of state and government,* Gustavo Noboa Bejarano, president (took office Jan. 2000). *Legislature* (unicameral)—National Congress.
Monetary Unit: Sucre (25,000.00 sucres equal U.S.$1, Nov. 2, 2000).
Gross Domestic Product (1999 est. U.S.$): $54,500,000,000 (purchasing power parity).
Economic Index (1998, 1990 = 100): *Consumer Prices,* all items, 1,153.1; food, 1,146.4.
Foreign Trade (1999 U.S.$): *Imports,* $3,017,000,000; *exports,* $4,451,000,000.

Education

While the U.S. presidential candidates argued in 2000 over who would do the most for failing schools, educators debated the growing use of state achievement tests to decide which students will be promoted. Most surveys during the year showed test scores increasing and schools becoming more challenging, but many experts worried about low minority achievement and mediocre teaching.

Pupil Assessment and Testing. On January 7, U.S. District Judge Edward C. Prado ruled that using the Texas Assessment of Academic Skills (TAAS) tests to determine high-school graduation did not violate the constitutional and civil rights of black and Hispanic students. Lawyers for the Mexican American Legal Defense and Educational Fund (MALDEF) argued it was unfair to deny diplomas to students who had passed their courses but could not pass the state test. Antitesting educators said the ruling was a blow to their efforts to curtail a decade-long national trend to use tests to stop the promotion of ill-prepared students and identify schools that need changes in programs and personnel.

In his seventh and last State of American Education speech, on February 22, U.S. Secretary of Education Richard W. Riley responded to critics of the standards movement—and its focus on tests—by suggesting a "midcourse review" of the growing demands on students. "Setting high expectations does not mean setting them so high that they are unreachable except for a very few," he said.

The National Reading Panel, after assessing 100,000 published studies, issued a long-awaited report in April supporting the renewed emphasis on phonics instruction—making certain that students understand how the sounds of spoken language reflect written letters. The panel also recommended that reading be taught in a "vibrant, imaginative, and entertaining fashion," with specific attention to the needs of individual students.

In May, President Bill Clinton issued an executive order requiring federal education officials to extend extra help to low-performing schools and to release an annual report on their progress. The presidential initiative fit with a proposal by Vice-President Al Gore to create a $500 million accountability plan allowing states and districts to identify and fix failing schools.

An outbreak of reports in June on cheating by teachers and administrators supervising state tests led to increased debate over lax security and the sometimes subtle difference between intense teaching and improper coaching. The Montgomery County, MD, school district suspended a teacher and accepted the resignation of a principal after students were allegedly helped during a state test at the Potomac Elementary School, which serves a high-income area. There were reports of improper test practices by educators in Virginia, California, New York, Illinois, Florida, and Ohio.

A report by the Brookings Institution in Washington, DC, said the federal Blue Ribbon Schools Program, the most important government award for school quality, put too little emphasis on academic achievement. Only 19 of 70 recent Blue Ribbon schools in seven states had achievement levels equal to the top 10% of schools with similar demographic characteristics, according to the study.

© Karen Tam/AP/Wide World Photos

In his final State of American Education address, U.S. Secretary of Education Richard W. Riley suggested that, among other things, teaching should be an 11-month job and that teachers should be compensated accordingly.

New national SAT results released in August showed the highest average mathematics scores in 30 years. College Board officials credited this to more high-school students taking challenging courses.

Teacher Quality. President Clinton, in January's State of the Union address, announced a $1 billion initiative to improve teacher quality. He proposed increases in after-school grants; funds for the preschool program Head Start; and changes in the Title I grants to schools with many low-income students, so that educators would have to document improvements.

In his State of American Education speech in February, Education Secretary Riley suggested making teaching a year-round profession, with substantial pay raises in exchange for working 11 months instead of the usual nine months a year. The extra time, he said, could be devoted to training and professional development, as well as to parent meetings and additional attention for struggling students.

The National Council for Accreditation of Teacher Education (NCATE) announced in May that education schools, beginning in 2001, will have to provide more information on their students' teaching skills and knowledge of subject matter before the schools become accredited. A study released in October said teachers who received certification from the National Board for Professional Teaching Standards performed several classroom exercises better than similarly experienced and motivated teachers who failed to be certified.

Summer School and the School Calendar. More students attended summer school in 2000 than ever before. Many urban districts told students scoring low on state tests that they would have to return to class in June and July, or risk repeating a grade. In New York City, 250,000 students—a quarter of the total enrollment—were told to attend summer sessions. Broward County, FL, which includes Fort Lauderdale, had 65,000 students in summer classes, and Detroit had 36,000. A 1998 federal study estimated that 27% of school districts had mandatory summer programs, but experts said that percentage was increasing. By the end of the summer, Chicago reported major increases in the number of students who met grade-promotion standards; New Orleans students did poorly; and results in New York City were mixed.

In July the Rochester, NY, school board approved a plan by Superintendent Clifford

B. Janey which allows students to complete high school a year early, or even take an extra year to graduate, depending on their educational needs.

Vouchers. A Wisconsin state review of the Milwaukee voucher program reported in February that the tuition grants for private schools had been used by low-income families as intended, and had not hurt public-school funding. Voucher supporters welcomed the report, while critics of the 8,000-student program said the study had not addressed the impact of vouchers on individual school demographics and special-education students.

A March conference on vouchers, sponsored by the University of Pennsylvania's Annenberg Public Policy Center, failed to develop any areas of significant compromise between supporters and critics of the idea. "It's unfortunate how toxic this debate has become," White House education-policy adviser Andrew Rotherham told Mark Walsh of the newspaper *Education Week*. Rotherham said publicly financed charter schools were a better option than encouraging students to go to private schools.

On March 14, L. Ralph Smith, a circuit-court judge in Leon County, FL, ruled invalid the nation's only statewide voucher program. His decision was overturned by an appeals court in October, leaving the program intact while voucher opponents appealed the ruling.

In August, new studies released regarding private-scholarship programs in New York City; Washington, DC; Dayton, OH; and Charlotte, NC; showed that black students who transferred to private schools improved more on mathematics and reading tests, after one or two years, than their counterparts in public schools. Several antivoucher groups attacked the studies as biased.

Charter Schools. On February 1, Maryland's state school board became the first in the country to seize control of local schools for the purpose of turning them over to for-profit managers. The board voted 10–2 to take over three elementary schools in Baltimore that had failed to improve dismal scores on the state achievement tests. "No child should have to attend a failing school by accident of where he or she lives," said State School Superintendent Nancy S. Grasmick. In March the school board awarded the contract for managing the schools to New York–based Edison Schools Inc.

A report by the U.S. Education Department, released in February, revealed the

Two years after voters approved plans to abolish bilingual education in California, higher test scores were seen in many schools, including the Ravenswood City Elementary District in Menlo Park, where Maria Ibarra, above, taught Cesar Jimenez in the fourth grade.

still significantly below those of non-Hispanic whites. High-school-graduation rates for African-Americans increased from 68% in 1977 to 75% in 1997, and for Hispanics from 55% to 62%, the report said. The college-graduation rate for blacks increased from 7% to 13% in that 20-year period, and from 6% to 10% for Hispanics.

The school board in North Carolina's Wake County decided in April to become one of the first districts in the country to integrate its schools by academic achievement and family income instead of race.

number of charter schools—public schools that operate independently of school-district rules and supervision—had grown to about 1,700, serving 250,000 students. Michael Mintrom, a political scientist at Michigan State University, said in February that his survey of 272 principals of both charter and regular high schools in the state showed the innovative practices in the charter schools were not very different from those found in many regular public schools.

Affirmative Action. In February the University of Texas at Austin said minority enrollment had increased slightly, despite the ending of special preferences for black and Hispanic applicants. In the fall of 1999, the university reported that 4% of the campus's freshmen (286 students) identified themselves as African-American, compared with 3% (190 students) in 1997. Fourteen percent of the freshmen (976 students) said they were Hispanic, compared with 13% (892 students) in 1997.

University officials said the numbers showed the new policy of admitting any students in the top 10% of their high-school class was opening the door to qualified minorities without giving them an advantage because of their ethnicity. The university had been ordered to drop its race-based admissions policy by a federal appeals court in the 1996 decision *Hopwood v. Texas.*

The American Council on Education (ACE) reported in February that more minorities were completing high school and college, but that their graduation rates were

Several civil-rights organizations chose the 46th anniversary of the landmark desegregation decision *Brown v. Board of Education* to sue the state of California for alleged failure to provide basic educational necessities in many low-income-area schools. The suit said many schools were full of vermin, lacked textbooks, and in some cases were so short of space that pupils were assigned to the wrong grade so that they would at least have a seat.

In June, civil-rights leaders attending a conference in Washington, DC, heard that while annual suspension rates for all students between 1974 to 1998 rose from 3.7% to 6.9%, suspension rates were much higher for blacks and Hispanics. The greatest disparity was found in the suspension rates of African-Americans, who accounted for 17% of all suspensions in 1998, and for 33% of suspensions for misbehavior.

In August, advocates of Proposition 227, the 1998 California initiative that abolished bilingual education—except for students whose parents asked for it—said new, improved state test results proved they were right to support teaching in English for everyone. Supporters of California's previous effort to gradually introduce 1.5 million limited-English students to all-English instruction said the improved scores proved nothing. They said there was no data to show if those students responded any differently than others to overall academic improvements, such as smaller class sizes.

Technology. A U.S. Department of Education study released in February showed school Internet connections were almost universal, with 95% of schools having at least one hookup. But the percentage of classrooms connected in low-income schools was only 39%, compared with 74% in high-income schools.

In early March the Bill & Melinda Gates Foundation—supported by the fortune of Microsoft Corporation cofounder Bill Gates—announced a $350 million gift to finance four programs designed to improve public and private K–12 schools. The money was to pay for professional development for principals, superintendents, and teachers, as well as for awards to schools and districts for unusual achievements.

The National Education Association (NEA) reported in May that fixing and modernizing the nation's schools, including adding new technology, would cost $322 billion. The association's estimate was far above the $112 billion price tag calculated by the U.S. General Accounting Office (GAO) in 1995. NEA officials said they had done a more comprehensive, state-by-state analysis than the GAO.

Latest Studies and Statistics. In February the Rural School and Community Trust, a nonprofit education and advocacy group in Washington, DC, said their study of 13,600 public schools in four states showed that smaller schools were significantly more successful in raising achievement for low-income students.

A study released in February by the Manpower Demonstration Research Corporation in New York showed that career academies—programs within high schools that focus on preparing students for jobs—did not raise test scores above those of similar students not in the academies, but increased the chances that the low-income students would graduate.

The Washington, DC–based Justice Policy Institute reported in April that public fear of school shootings had not abated despite a decline in the number of violent school-related crimes. The number of violent deaths associated with schools dropped from 43 in 1998 to 26 in 1999, the institute said, while opinion polls showed that 71% of Americans thought it was likely a school shooting could happen in their communities.

An April study released by the National Center for Education Statistics showed that girls are doing as well as or better than boys in school, although girls still trail boys in math and science. Once enrolled in college, the report said, freshman women are more likely to graduate in five years than their male classmates.

The U.S. Education Department reported in June that the percentage of high-school students taking difficult science and mathematics courses had increased. The percentage taking higher-level math had grown from 25.2% in 1982 to 41.4% in 1998, and the portion taking tougher science courses increased from 4.8% to 7.3%.

Major Legislation and Politics. In early February the Clinton administration asked for $40.1 billion in discretionary funding for the Department of Education. This was a nearly 13% increase. The effort to reduce class sizes by recruiting more teachers with federal money would receive $1.75 billion under the proposal, up from $1.3 billion. But department officials cautioned that congressional approval for such a large increase—the greatest boost in discretionary spending in the department's history—was in doubt. By early December, there was no resolution since legislators were still at odds with the White House over several spending bills for the forthcoming fiscal year.

In the presidential campaign, both major-party candidates said that as president they planned to make significant changes in the way federal funds are spent on the neediest schools. Democratic candidate Al Gore said bad schools that failed to improve would, if their state wanted to maintain normal federal funding, have to be closed and replaced with public charter schools or at least have new staffs. Republican candidate George W. Bush said those schools would have to let parents take shares of their federal funding as vouchers that could be used to transfer their children to private schools. Both candidates supported the movement to raise education standards, and ignored objections from parents and teachers to the increasing use of state tests in promotion and graduation decisions.

Court Decisions. In July the U.S. Supreme Court ruled in *Santa Fe Independent School District v. Doe* that prayers spoken over a loudspeaker at a high-school football game were unconstitutional, despite being initiated by students and not administrators. In *Mitchell v. Helms* the court said computer and library books bought with tax dollars could be given to religious schools.

JAY MATHEWS
Education Reporter and Columnist
The Washington Post

Egypt

Egypt continued its role as the leading Arab state during 2000, as President Hosni Mubarak convened a Cairo summit of Arab heads of state and acted as an intermediary in the conflict between Israel and the Palestinians. In November elections for parliament, parties opposed to the government's National Democratic Party (NDP) won a significant number of seats for the first time since 1987, as a result of intervention by the constitutional court.

Domestic Issues. In January, clashes erupted in southern Egypt between Muslims and Coptic Christians. Several thousand Muslims looted and burned Coptic shops in el-Kusheh and in neighboring villages. Gun battles between the contending factions resulted in dozens of deaths. Economic problems were among the causes of Muslim-Coptic tension, according to local authorities. Copts made up approximately 10% of Egypt's 68 million population and owned 22% of the country's wealth. However, Copts held only 1.5% of official positions in Egypt. In February the Coptic weekly *Watani* and the liberal daily *al-Wafd* published a statement that was signed by 100 prominent Muslims and Christians, calling on all Egyptians to help eliminate tensions between the two communities.

In February, Pope John Paul II made the first visit by a modern pontiff to Egypt, with back-to-back calls on the Coptic pope, Shenouda III, and the sheikh of al-Azhar, Muhammad Sayed Tantawi, the highest Egyptian authority of Sunni Islam. The pope was warmly received by leaders of all faiths in Egypt. Warning that "there is no time to lose," he called for new dialogue with Coptic leaders, with a view to ending "painful divisions" within Christianity. In the first papal Mass ever held in Egypt, he addressed a crowd of 20,000 with a plea for "dialogue and reconciliation" to resolve problems "that still impede full communion." In a visit to the Greek Orthodox monastery at Mount Sinai, where tradition says Moses once stood, John Paul II called himself a pilgrim "in the footsteps of God."

In the summer the government acknowledged that Egypt faced a severe liquidity crisis when the Central Bank devalued the national pound from about 3.4 to 3.65 per dollar, squeezing the purchasing power of most Egyptians. Several NDP members of parliament were convicted in high-profile corruption cases throughout the year. One deputy was charged with selling permits to Mecca, and 28 others were jailed for exploiting connections with the Nile Bank to receive illegal loans totaling $1.5 billion. The link between the Nile Bank scandal and the nation's liquidity crisis angered many middle-class Egyptians, whose average income is about $3,000 per year.

In January, parliament voted to grant women the right to divorce their husbands

© Menahem Kahana/AFP/Corbis

After clashes between Israeli and Palestinian forces heated up in the fall, Egypt's President Mubarak (right) U.S. President Clinton, and Palestinian leader Arafat (left) met at Sharm el-Sheikh. Israel's Prime Minister Barak and other leaders also attended the emergency summit.

without first having to prove to judges that they were mistreated. Despite the new law, divorce could still be complicated for women, who are faced with two choices: to use the existing system, which requires a wife to present family-court judges with witnesses of bad treatment; or to argue simple incompatibility, a procedure taking several months. Even if a woman obtained a divorce, she would still have to return all money, gifts, and property received in the marriage, and forgo alimony.

EGYPT • Information Highlights

Official Name: Arab Republic of Egypt.
Location: Northeastern Africa.
Area: 386,660 sq mi (1 001 450 km²).
Population (2000 est.): 68,359,979.
Chief Cities (December 1996 census): Cairo, the capital, 6,800,992; Giza, 4,779,865; Alexandria, 3,339,076.
Government: *Head of state,* Mohammed Hosni Mubarak, president (took office October 1981). *Head of government,* Atef Ebeid, prime minister (took office October 1999). *Legislature*—People's Assembly.
Monetary Unit: Pound (3.880 pounds equal U.S.$1, Jan. 4, 2001).
Gross Domestic Product (1999 est. U.S.$): $200,000,000,000 (purchasing power parity).
Economic Index (1998, 1990 = 100): *Consumer Prices,* all items, 207.5; food, 190.9.
Foreign Trade (1999 U.S.$): *Imports,* $16,022,000,000; *exports,* $3,559,000,000.

In July, Dr. Saad Eddin Ibrahim, a prominent Egyptian-rights activist and sociology professor at the American University in Cairo (AUC), who holds both Egyptian and U.S. citizenship, was imprisoned for allegedly collaborating with foreign parties on projects to harm Egypt. Other arrests included Ali Salem, a prominent satirist who was charged with threatening national security and harming the national interest for encouraging Egyptians to vote their conscience and for criticizing the government.

In May, *al-Shaab,* the newspaper of the al-Amal (Labor) Party was closed down after launching a campaign protesting the Ministry of Culture's approval of a book deemed offensive to Islam. The protest was followed by huge demonstrations at al-Azhar University, which authorities construed as an attempt by the Muslim Brotherhood to raise its profile prior to November parliamentary elections. Even though the Brotherhood was banned from parliamentary elections, dozens of its members said that they would run as independents.

Although the Egyptian 1971 constitution calls for judges of the Supreme Constitutional Court to supervise balloting, civil servants had overseen past voting in many small polling places where election fraud had occurred. Meeting demands from opposition parties, the court decided to take on supervision in the 2000 election. Because the 6,000 judges were not enough for the 18,000 polling places, the court decided to carry out the election in three stages to ensure proper supervision everywhere. In July the court also dissolved parliamentary assemblies elected in 1985 and 1987 for discriminating against independent candidates. Election procedures in 1990 and 1995 were also ruled unconstitutional.

As the election progressed, it became evident that the new procedures resulted in a decline of seats won by the government's NDP. In the 1995 election, only 14 of the 444 seats went to the opposition. In 2000, representatives of the outlawed Muslim Brotherhood made an unexpectedly strong showing. Violent clashes broke out between NDP and opposition supporters during the third round of voting in November, resulting in several deaths. When the three stages of voting were completed, however, the NDP had won an overwhelming majority in the People's Assembly. Although Mubarak's governing NDP controlled 87% of the seats in the 454-member parliament compared with 94% in 1995, the election was seen as a tentative step toward democracy.

Foreign Affairs. President Mubarak met several times throughout the year with Palestinian, Israeli, and U.S. officials, with proposals to the Middle East peace negotiations. In January, Egyptian and Israeli foreign ministers met in Moscow to discuss arms control and regional security. In his annual visit to Washington, DC, in March, Mubarak met with President Clinton in connection with the stalled Israeli-Syrian and Palestinian peace talks. A meeting of Egyptian, Israeli, Jordanian, Palestinian, and U.S. leaders at Sharm el-Sheikh in mid-October sought to end the violent conflict between Israel and the Palestinians, but the struggle continued. In October, the Arab League held a summit in Cairo, and focused on the fighting in Israel-Palestine. Although Mubarak joined in signing a statement condemning Israel's use of force, he was a moderating influence, and opposed breaking relations with Jerusalem for the time being. In late November, however, following Israel's intense bombing of the Gaza Strip, Egypt recalled its Tel Aviv ambassador to protest what the Arab world called a disproportionate response to a Palestinian terrorist attack. Israel officials expressed regret and sadness at Egypt's actions. (*See also* MIDDLE EAST.)

DON PERETZ
State University of New York at Binghamton

Energy

A sudden rise in oil prices dominated the energy picture in 2000, as the price of crude oil rose to its highest level since the 1990 Persian Gulf crisis. The spike in oil prices, which peaked at about $37 a barrel in Octo-

On Sept. 22, 2000, U.S. Secretary of Energy Bill Richardson announced the Clinton administration's decision to release 30 billlion barrels of oil from the Strategic Petroleum Reserve in an effort to combat rising fuel prices.

avert an energy crisis and economic downturn in consuming countries, OPEC boosted members' production quotas four times during the year, including a 500,000-barrel-per-day increase at the end of October.

That increase was largely symbolic, however, as members were already pumping oil at maximum capacity, more than at any time in the previous two decades. Further, the organization's ability to manipulate oil prices by adjusting output was limited by the fact that non-OPEC producers—including Britain, Norway, and Russia—controlled 60% of global oil production. By late November, despite OPEC's production increases, oil prices still exceeded $34 a barrel.

For this reason, industrial countries were disappointed when OPEC ministers rebuffed their requests for relief from high oil prices and declared, in early November, that member countries would not increase their output of oil through the end of the year. OPEC's decision appeared to be justified by mid-December, when oil prices fell once again, to less than $22 a barrel, before rising to about $28 by year's end.

A brutal reminder of the industrial world's dependence on Middle Eastern oil came on November 17, when a car bomb exploded in Riyadh, Saudi Arabia, on the opening day of a global oil conference there. Although no group claimed immediate responsibility for the bombing, which killed a British citizen, it came amid mounting calls by Arab militants throughout the Middle East for oil exporters to take a tougher stance against the United States for its support of Israel in ongoing hostilities between Israelis and Palestinians.

ber, was equivalent to the tripling of oil prices during the energy crises of the mid-1970s, and came as a shock to consumers who had bought gas-guzzling sport-utility vehicles (SUVs) with the expectation that affordable gas would flow indefinitely (*see* SIDEBAR, PAGE 227). But fears that high energy prices would cripple the U.S. economy proved premature.

Oil. The price rise came as a result of efforts by the 11-member Organization of Petroleum Exporting Countries (OPEC) to curb oil production as a way to raise the price of oil from its December 1998 low of about $10 a barrel. The increase also resulted from a shortfall in capacity at U.S. and European refineries, where oil is turned into gasoline and heating oil. When economic recovery in Asia boosted demand for petroleum products early in 2000, there were not enough supplies of crude and refined petroleum to go around; prices took off.

Throughout the year, OPEC ministers repeated their goal of adjusting oil production to achieve a steady price between $22 and $28 a barrel, a level they and most consuming-country officials agreed would both ensure producers' economic health and provide affordable energy to industrial countries. Indeed, an energy-driven recession in the industrial world also posed a threat to OPEC countries, which had heavily invested their petrodollar oil revenues in U.S. and European stock markets. In an effort to

Caspian Sea Reserves. In July, oil companies reported that exploratory underwater drilling in the Caspian Sea had turned up at least one significant deposit of oil and natural gas. The discovery bolstered prospects for construction of a controversial oil pipeline connecting oil fields in and around the Caspian to Western ports. The $2.4 billion, 1,080-mi (1 737-km) pipeline would pass from the Caspian port of Baku, the capital of Azerbaijan, through Georgia, and terminate at the Mediterranean port of Ceyhan, Turkey.

The Clinton administration strongly backed this route as a safer alternative to existing pipelines that passed through Russia and Iran. The Turkish government also supported the project because it would reduce the already heavy tanker traffic through the environmentally vulnerable Bosporus. Before the new oil and gas discoveries, BP Amoco and the seven other oil companies that would actually build the pipeline balked at the $2.4 billion construction cost. In November, however, they agreed to begin initial studies in preparation for construction, which was expected to take about three years.

U.S. Concerns.   The immediate impact of the oil-price hike was felt at the gasoline pump, where prices averaged $1.66 by the end of June, up from $1.11 a year earlier, and approached $2.50 in parts of the Midwest, before settling at around $1.50 toward year's end.

The price hike had surprisingly little immediate impact on the U.S. economy. Despite the rapid rise in gas prices, consumers did not cut back on their driving during the summer months, and continued to buy SUVs and other popular, but energy-inefficient, vehicles. Government reports in late fall showed steady increases in U.S. citizens' incomes and continued low inflation. Despite a slowing of U.S. economic growth to a 2.7% annual rate in the third quarter, those trends suggested the economy was resilient enough to absorb the year's energy-price spike without significant damage.

As the year's winter heating season approached, however, officials feared that tight supplies might drive up energy costs in the Northeast, where oil is widely used for residential heating, leaving many lower-income residents without sufficient heat. The combination of higher fuel prices and short supplies, together with a predicted cold spell, prompted the U.S. Department of Energy to predict that home heating costs would rise by an average $200 for the winter of 2000–2001, with families using oil to heat their homes bearing the heaviest burden.

To reduce that risk, President Clinton in September released 30 million barrels of oil from the Strategic Petroleum Reserve, a 570-million-barrel reserve created in the 1970s to use in national energy emergencies. Republican lawmakers criticized the move as an election-year ploy. Democrats, in turn, blamed the Republican-controlled Congress for placing the country at risk by failing to reauthorize the reserve, which expired in March. On November 9, President Clinton signed a law reauthorizing the program and creating a 2-million-barrel home-heating-oil reserve to be used in case of shortages or price hikes.

During the presidential-election campaign, both major-party candidates emphasized the need to reduce U.S. dependence on foreign oil, but their prescriptions for energy independence differed widely. Texas Gov. George W. Bush, the Republican presidential candidate, called for opening Alaska's Arctic National Wildlife Refuge to oil drilling. The refuge, which may contain enough oil to produce a million barrels a day for 20 years, had been kept off limits to oil drilling because of its fragile ecosystem. Vice-President Al Gore, the Democratic nominee, opposed drilling in the refuge, and called instead for greater federal support of alternative energy sources. The vice-president also supported the president's decision to temporarily release oil from the Strategic Petroleum Reserve, a move Governor Bush denounced as politically motivated.

The reliability of U.S. oil supplies was called into question by reports that the 23-year-old Trans-Alaska Pipeline linking the North Slope oil fields—the largest single source of domestic oil—to the tanker terminal in Valdez was in danger of failing. Accidents and breakdowns at the terminal forced the Alyeska Pipeline Service Company, the consortium of oil companies that operates the system, to close off one of the main loading docks in October. Regulators warned that similar maintenance problems plagued other domestic oil-production and -distribution systems, left unattended in the wake of oil price drops in the mid-1990s and a series of mergers in the industry.

The rise in energy prices was a windfall for the nation's three largest oil companies, which reported a record $7 billion in profits for the third quarter alone. Exxon Mobil Corporation, the world's largest publicly held energy firm, earned $4.3 billion, the largest quarterly profit ever for a U.S. corporation. The domestic oil industry continued to experience mergers and acquisitions. Texaco and Chevron Corp., the second- and third-largest U.S. oil companies, respectively, in October announced plans to merge, a deal that would create the world's fourth-largest oil firm. In November, OAO Lukoil Holdings, Russia's largest oil company, announced plans to buy Getty Petroleum Marketing, a gas-station chain that was part of the late oil magnate J. Paul Getty's holdings. The sale would be the first Russian acquisition of a publicly traded U.S. company.

Gas Prices

The tripling of oil prices, from $10 a barrel of crude in December 1998 to almost $30 by June 2000, hit U.S. drivers at the pump, where the price for a gallon of regular-unleaded gasoline rose from 98 cents to $1.62 over the same period. In parts of the Midwest, gas prices exceeded $2.50 in early June, before settling at about $1.50 as the year came to an end. The sudden increase in gasoline prices recalled fears of the gas shortages and endless lines at the pump of the 1970s—the last time oil prices tripled. By year's end, however, that nightmare scenario remained a thing of the past.

Although gasoline prices remained higher than in 1999, the increases in 2000 had little impact on drivers' habits. A record number of people hit the road over the July 4 holiday weekend, when prices neared their peak. Sales of popular sport-utility vehicles (SUVs) and other gas-guzzlers grew. Only the largest SUVs, such as the Chevrolet Suburban, experienced any decline in sales, which was not clearly linked to energy prices. Indeed, gasoline consumption appeared likely to exceed 1999's record level.

A number of factors helped explain why U.S. consumers remained relatively unfazed by rising gas prices. For one thing, even though gas prices had risen steadily for almost two years, they never reached levels seen during the energy crises of the 1970s, when adjusted for inflation. Rising incomes also had reduced the average driver's sensitivity to gas-price fluctuations. In 1980, gas and other fuel consumed 6% of U.S. citizens' after-tax income; by 2000, fuels accounted for less than 3% of after-tax income.

There were pockets of unrest, especially in the Chicago and Milwaukee metropolitan areas, where a combination of rising oil prices, a pipeline outage, and a federal clean-air regulation—which mandated the use of expensive, reformulated gasoline—pushed gas prices well over the $2 mark. Amid public charges of price gouging by oil companies, the governors of Illinois and Indiana moved to temporarily reduce state fuel taxes. A move to suspend the 18.4–cent-per-gallon federal gas tax fizzled, however, as the Senate overwhelmingly rejected the proposal in July.

While U.S. consumers took rising gas prices in stride, the same trend sparked widespread protests in Europe. Picketers in Britain so intimidated fuel-truck drivers that they dared not deliver their cargo to gas stations. As the pumps went dry in early September, motorists were stranded, bringing parts of the country to a halt, and prompting Prime Minister Tony Blair to warn oil companies to keep the gas pumps running or face government sanctions. Bowing to the demands of truckers and other protesters, the French government cut fuel taxes by 15%.

High fuel taxes helped explain why European drivers took to the streets over gas prices while their U.S. counterparts remained relatively indifferent. Gas cost about $4.50 a gallon in Britain, some $3.30 of which was tax; of the $1.50 that U.S. citizens paid for gas, federal and state fuel taxes accounted for only about 40 cents. European officials justified their high fuel taxes as a way to encourage fuel efficiency, reduce traffic congestion, and curb emissions of harmful pollutants. Fuel taxes also were an important source of government revenues.

Although energy prices remained a touchy issue across Europe, fears that the September protests would spread to other parts of the continent waned by late fall. In mid-November, efforts to reorganize protests in London over gasoline taxes were largely ignored.

MARY H. COOPER

© Scott Olson/Archive Photos

Natural Gas.   As prices of petroleum products jumped, so did prices for natural gas, which doubled from 1999 levels to more than $5 per million British thermal units (BTU), the highest level in 15 years. The price surge prompted the Energy Department to estimate that consumers in the Midwest, where natural gas was the leading fuel for home heating, would face a 44% rise in heating costs over the winter.

There was little flexibility in the market for natural gas to ease upward pressure on prices. Domestic reserves had been in decline for years, even among the richest remaining reserves under the Gulf of Mexico. Because natural gas was expensive to transport over long distances, most gas consumed in the United States came from domestic wells, with imports limited mainly to supplies from Canada. Rising demand by electric utilities for gas, a cleaner-burning fuel than coal, placed further pressure on prices. Increasing production to ease that pressure was hampered by the fact that gas-drilling companies, like oil-drilling companies, had cut back on exploration for new deposits during the price drop of 1998–99.

Alternative Sources.   The Clinton administration added a new incentive for companies that make alternative fuels from farm crops—such as ethanol and biodiesel—by offering them subsidies to buy corn, soybeans, and other crops. The two-year program would subsidize up to 40% of the cost of the crops. Production of ethanol, a gasoline additive that accounted for 7% of the total corn crop grown in 2000, was already subsidized by a 5.4-cent-per-gallon federal tax break, but the new program provided the first such incentive for biodiesel production from soybeans. The Agriculture Department also announced it would launch pilot projects that would use vegetation harvested from farmland, taken out of regular crop production, to produce gas or liquid fuels.

Hybrid Cars.   Two new mass-market, alternative-fuel automobiles became available to consumers in the United States during 2000 with the unveiling of the Honda Insight and the Toyota Prius. The hybrid vehicles run on a gasoline engine and an electric motor, providing exceptional mileage (40 to 50 mi per gallon) and low emissions at a competitive selling price of around $20,000. Unlike all-electric vehicles, which require time-consuming recharges, the hybrid cars' batteries self-charge.

Despite their advantages, new hybrid cars were expected to account for only about 0.1% of the 17 million vehicles sold during 2000. Meanwhile, General Motors (GM) stopped production of its all-electric car, the EV1, after it failed to achieve expected sales levels. Despite the continuing development by a number of automakers of prototypes powered by hydrogen fuel cells, GM's actions cast doubt on California's ability to meet its stated goal of having zero-emission—meaning electric—cars account for 10% of all new auto sales by 2003.

Electricity Deregulation.   California's traditional role as an energy-policy pacesetter for the rest of the nation came into question as federal regulators investigated the state's innovative program to deregulate the electricity market. After angry consumers protested when their electricity bills tripled amid a wave of brownouts over the summer, the Federal Energy Regulatory Commission called the state's deregulation regime "seriously flawed" and called for construction of more power plants and transmission lines to help meet growing demand for electric power. The problems in California's deregulation program, set in motion by a landmark 1996 law, appeared likely to slow the move toward deregulation of electricity markets in other states, where similar trends have emerged as consumer demand for power has outstripped the supply of electricity.

Los Alamos Tapes.   The mystery of the missing nuclear-weapons data from Los Alamos National Laboratory continued despite the settlement of the criminal case in September, when former Los Alamos scientist Wen Ho Lee (*see* BIOGRAPHY) pleaded guilty to a single felony count of mishandling classified information. The case had erupted in 1999, when Lee was fired from the nuclear-weapons lab, an agency of the Energy Department, and arrested on charges of downloading 400,000 pages of classified information onto computer tapes. The case sparked protests from Asian-Americans who charged that Lee, a 60-year-old naturalized U.S. citizen born in Taiwan, had been unfairly targeted.

Under a plea-bargain agreement, government prosecutors dropped the 58 other counts against Lee in exchange for his promise to tell Federal Bureau of Investigation agents why he had made the tapes and what he had done with them. Seven of the tapes were still missing. Lee was sentenced in November to the nine months in prison that he had served while awaiting trial.

MARY H. COOPER
"The CQ [Congressional Quarterly] Researcher"

Engineering, Civil

Among the civil-engineering highlights of the year 2000 were the completion of major bridges in South Korea and the United States and the opening of a unique stadium/arena/concert hall outside of Tokyo.

Award-winning Projects. The Cape Hatteras Light Station Relocation Project in North Carolina won the 2000 Outstanding Civil Engineering Achievement Award (OCEA) from the American Society of Civil Engineers (ASCE). The lighthouse would have been swallowed by the Atlantic Ocean within a decade had it not been moved about half a mile inland in 1999. OCEA awards also were given to the Colville River Pipeline Crossing on the North Slope in Alaska and to the Eastside Reservoir Project in southern California. The Colville River Pipeline Crossing used Horizontal Directional Drilling (HDD), a technique that had never before been tried in an Arctic setting, to protect fragile permafrost. The $1.9 billion Eastside Reservoir Project almost doubled southern California's surface-water storage capacity.

Bridges. The Seohae Grand Bridge—one of the largest cable-stayed bridges in the world, with a main span of 2,884 ft (879 m)—opened in South Korea. The first cast-in-place segmental concrete-arch bridge in the United States was completed across the Crooked River Gorge in central Oregon. The sheer 295-ft (90-m)-high cliff walls made construction of a different type of bridge virtually impossible.

Sporting Arenas. The Saitama Super Arena in Japan opened in September 2000. Unique in the world, this "smart" arena easily converts from a 5,000-seat concert hall to a 27,000-seat arena for basketball, hockey, or tennis to a 36,500-seat stadium for soccer and American football. The complexity of moving 15,000 tons of structure is compounded by the need to allow building elements to move during seismic events without major structural failures, while still having safely enclosed exits.

In San Francisco, the $306 million Pac Bell Park opened for the 2000 baseball season. The ballpark was the first privately funded ballpark built for Major League Baseball since Dodger Stadium opened in 1962. In Houston, Enron Field opened and replaced the Astrodome as the home of the Houston Astros. The $250 million project has a retractable roof and follows the trend of retro-styled sporting areas. Tiger fans, meanwhile, welcomed the $300 million Comerica Park in downtown Detroit.

Unique Projects. In Seattle, the $240 million Experience Music Project opened. The project's complex design by world-renowned architect Frank Gehry led to many innovations in construction, including direct fabrication of large building components from the 3-D computer-aided-design (CAD) model. The Walt Disney Company continued construction on its new theme park, Disney's California Adventure, next to Disneyland in Anaheim, CA. The park features the world's longest roller coaster. In Dubai, the world's tallest hotel opened. The 1,053-ft (321-m)-tall building with its sail profile quickly became one of the signature buildings in the world.

Transportation. A one-of-a-kind, dual-use railroad tunnel was completed in Alaska. The tunnel allows alternating train and road service to the isolated town of Whittier. In Manila, the Philippines, the $645 million Line 3 of the light-rail system opened in June. A significant challenge of the project was to build it within the 39-ft (12 -m)-wide median of a major avenue.

The new $800 million, 2,475,780-sq-ft (230 000 m²) San Francisco International Terminal was completed. Curving trusses that form the roofline are the building's trademark. Officials required that the new terminal not only be able to survive an earthquake but remain operating afterward. Designers separated the terminal from its foundation by a base-isolation system resting on 267 stainless-steel sliders that sit in giant, concave dishes. During an earthquake, the building will roll around on the dishes—up to 20 inches (51 cm) in any direction.

Industrial Projects. Dow Chemical completed a $720 million refinery plant in Bahia Blanca, Argentina. Engineering for the project was done in the United States, the Netherlands, and the Philippines, with all the design-and construction-materials information linked through a large 3-D CAD model. Pemex, the Mexican oil company, completed the world's largest and quietest nitrogen-production center amid a fragile environment on the Atasta peninsula. The Alliance Pipeline, the longest pipeline in North America, entered service. The 1,858-mi (2 988-km)-long, $3 billion pipeline delivers 1.3 billion cu ft (37.5 million m³) of natural gas per day from northeastern British Columbia and Alberta to the Chicago area.

MARTIN FISCHER
Terman Engineering Center, Stanford University

Environment

The worst wildfire season in half a century (*see* SIDEBAR) and a push by Washington lawmakers to fund local conservation programs made 2000 an important year for environmental stewardship. Issues such as forest management, protection of open spaces, water quality, and restoration of Florida's Everglades dominated public debate, despite continued disagreement between the U.S. Congress and the Bill Clinton administration over the scope and purpose of environmental laws. Environmental issues also played a part in the 2000 presidential election.

Conservation and Reinvestment. Congressional Republicans and Democrats were divided on forest stewardship, but a broad bipartisan coalition formed around efforts to use offshore oil and gas royalties to fund local environmental programs. The action centered on the Conservation and Reinvestment Act (CARA), a giant environmental bill, that, as initially proposed, would have guaranteed about $3 billion annually to a host of federal and state conservation efforts, mostly in coastal states. The oil and gas royalties have been deposited in the U.S. Treasury, where they are used for such purposes as paying down the national debt.

CARA supporters argued that rapid urban growth and suburban sprawl created the need for measures preserving open space, creating parks, and improving coastal areas. Backers included House Resources Committee Chairman Don Young (R-AK) and Rep. George Miller (D-CA), usually political opposites on environmental issues, as well as a grassroots coalition of nearly 5,000 recreation and conservation groups. Republican lawmakers from some interior Western states opposed the measure—in particular the annual authorization of $900 million for federal and state purchases of environmentally sensitive tracts. The lawmakers said the purchases could continue Clinton administration policies of securing large tracts of land and restricting mining, grazing, and other uses. Many of the opponents came from states where the federal government already owned more than 50% of the land.

While Clinton had vowed to make passage of CARA a priority in his final budget negotiations with the Republican-led Congress, growing opposition led him to back down somewhat. In the end, the White House opted for a scaled-back six-year, $12 billion discretionary fund for public-land programs under its Lands Legacy Initiative. CARA supporters, such as Sen. Mary L. Landrieu (D-LA) and Senate Majority Leader Trent Lott (R-MS), managed to get priority funding through the normal congressional appropriations process for some local projects that would have been assured funding under the broader bill.

Everglades Restoration. One local environmental initiative receiving special attention in 2000 was an ambitious effort to restore the Everglades ecosystem in south Florida. A plan agreed upon by federal and state officials, American Indian tribes, and agricultural interests called for spending $7.8 billion over 35 years to restore flows to threatened estuaries, improve water quality, and deliver water to agricultural and urban interests. The project was billed as the largest ecosystem restoration ever.

The Everglades have been in decline since 1948, when the Army Corps of Engineers began draining south Florida wetlands to accommodate urban growth. The ecosystem has shrunk by nearly half since then, threatening as many as 68 plant and animal species. That project also unintentionally had the effect of flushing about 1.7 billion gallons of freshwater each day into the Atlantic Ocean, contributing to pollution from agricultural runoff and altering the salinity of Florida Bay and other waterways.

The new plan, approved as part of the $7 billion congressional water-resources bill, will create storage facilities to catch and redistribute rainwater into the Everglades' canals and estuaries. A total of $1.4 billion to start the project was to be released in 2000. The Army Corps was given two years to develop restoration rules and goals that are acceptable to both Florida and the federal Department of the Interior. Changes could be made to the plan as state and federal officials proceed and learn what strategies work the best. An unusual aspect of the project was the 50-50 cost-sharing arrangement between the federal government and Florida. This arrangement was in recognition of the federal government's role in destroying the ecosystem. Also unusual was the diverse collection of supporters, including the Clinton administration, congressional Republicans, Vice-President Al Gore, and Republican Gov. Jeb Bush of Florida and his brother, presidential candidate and Texas Gov. George W. Bush.

Antiquities Act. One land-stewardship issue that divided Republicans and Demo-

Earth Day at 30

On April 22, 2000, ceremonies were held in more than 180 countries around the world to mark Earth Day 2000, the 30th anniversary of the first Earth Day.

At the National Mall in Washington, DC, *photo, below left,* politicians, celebrities, and activists joined together in a festive atmosphere to view a multimedia stage presentation and exhibits promoting nonpolluting energy sources. "Clean Energy Now" was the theme of the various Mall events.

Across the globe, schoolchildren in New Delhi, India, held a rally on behalf of the environmental cause, *photo, right*, and Chinese families in Beijing buried a rock as they planted new trees, *photo, below right*. "Car-free" days were held in Korea; a renewable-

© Ricardo Watson/UPI/Presslink

energy fair was staged in the African nation of Burkina Faso; Russians in the city of Voronezh protested importing nuclear waste; and Ecuadorians in Guayaquil sought to conserve nearby Santay Island.

Since the first Earth Day, heroic environmental efforts have been made. The quality of the waterways has improved; millions of acres of wilderness have been protected; and air pollution has been reduced. However, environmentalists warned that serious problems still remain. Worldwide, during the past 30 years, there were increases in greenhouse gases; additional pressure was put on biodiversity; and significant population growth occurred.

U.S. President Bill Clinton responded to Earth Day 2000 by requiring federal agencies to reduce, by 20% over five years, the amount of gasoline their vehicles consume. He also announced a program that allows federal workers to set aside up to $65 tax free every month if they use public transportation to get to work.

© Ajit Kumar/AP/Wide World Photos

© AFP/Corbis

crats—and, in some cases, federal and local officials—was the Clinton administration's continued effort to designate national monuments under the Antiquities Act of 1906. The designations restrict the development of public land and prevent such activities as mining, logging, and off-road-vehicle use in environmentally fragile or historically significant tracts. The practice has been decried as a "land grab" by property-rights advocates as well as by resource industries and their mostly Republican allies, who argue the designations usurp local governmental authority and are being made without public input.

Clinton designated ten monuments in 2000, continuing his four-year effort to end-run the Republican Congress. The effort began when he created the 1.7 million-acre (689 259 ha) Grand Staircase-Escalante National Monument in Utah. New monuments included 197,000 acres (79 757 ha) of the Hanford Reach in Washington State, the last undeveloped stretch of the Columbia River, and more than 300,000 acres (121 457 ha) of redwood forest in California. Monument designations can be overridden by Congress, but cannot be reversed by a new presidential administration.

While more tracts were being considered for monument designations before Clinton left office, the issue was dividing voters in some states. The White House sought to minimize political fallout by delaying future announcements until after Election Day. In Montana, for example, a plan to designate a 149-mi (240-km) stretch of the upper Missouri River traversed by the explorers Lewis and Clark ran into opposition from ranching interests, who contended they are the best stewards of the land.

Clean Water. Another controversial initiative attempted to address what the Clinton administration viewed as the biggest remaining threat to clean water—agricultural and urban runoff that carries pollution into lakes, streams, and aquifers. This phenomenon is known as "non-point-source" pollution. New water-quality regulations issued by the Environmental Protection Agency (EPA) on July 11 required states to compile a list of polluted waterways within four years, then gave the states 15 years to establish plans to clean up the waterways. If a state did not make adequate progress, the regulations gave the EPA new authority to order remedial measures. The rules were based on a section of the 1972 Clean Water Act dealing with "total maximum daily load," a measurement of how much pollu-

tion waterways can absorb and still meet minimum clear-water standards.

Farm, business, and labor groups opposed the rules, saying they usurped states' authority to police water quality and enter into voluntary programs with industrial and agricultural interests. The groups feared the rules were excessively broad and applied to everything from animal waste and pesticides at agricultural plants to runoff and sediment from construction sites. Some predicted the new rules would result only in numerous lawsuits. Industries expected to feel the most-dramatic effects were the forestry and paper industries. Logging activities previously exempt from Clear Water Act rules could be subject to new regulations if a state decides such moves are necessary to implement a cleanup plan. Congress attempted to block the rules, but succeeded only in delaying their effective date to 2001.

Supreme Court Case. The EPA also came under fire in a significant clean-air case heard by the U.S. Supreme Court in November. At issue were standards the agency developed in 1997 to reduce vehicle emissions of ozone and particulate matter thought to be responsible for killing thousands of people annually. The American Trucking Associations, the U.S. Chamber of Commerce, and other business groups claimed the EPA had overstepped its mandate by devising excessively broad rules that infringed on Congress' power to make new laws. The case, *Browner v. American Trucking Associations*, also took up the secondary issue of whether agencies, such as the EPA, must consider the costs any new standards impose on affected industries. The court was expected to rule by mid-2001.

The Political Campaign. The environment became a potent issue in the 2000 presidential campaign. Vice-President Gore assailed Republican challenger George W. Bush's environmental record as governor of Texas, charging that Texas had become home to some of the worst pollution in the nation, and pointing, in particular, to pervasive smog problems in Houston. Gore also took Bush to task for favoring oil exploration in protected portions of Alaska and opposing a ban on logging in roadless areas of national forests. Bush's campaign countered Gore's criticisms, stating that Texas had become the Number 1 state in eliminating toxic pollution and had made major strides in reducing air pollution during the governor's tenure.

ADRIEL BETTELHEIM, *"CQ Researcher"*

Wildfires

The most dramatic environmental development of 2000 was a spate of nearly 85,000 wildfires that charred a total of 6.97 million acres (2.82 million ha), mostly in Western states. Low moisture along the Southern portion of the United States brought about by the weather pattern known as "La Niña" led to a combination of dry vegetation and hot, windy weather, creating tinderbox conditions in many areas. The National Interagency Fire Center in Boise, ID, estimated total fire-suppression costs from January to October reached $877.8 million. Federal officials said wildfire conditions were the worst the government had recorded in 50 years.

The season's first major blaze was caused by a prescribed fire set by the National Park Service (NPS) on May 4 to reduce thick brush and rehabilitate the landscape on the Bandelier National Monument near Los Alamos, NM. Flames, driven by strong, erratic winds, jumped across control lines and spread to the neighboring town and the perimeter of Los Alamos National Laboratory, home of the nation's top-secret nuclear-weapons program. By the time the blaze was controlled, more than 47,000 acres (19 035 ha) had been scorched and 235 homes destroyed.

Continued dry conditions and summertime thunderstorms played havoc with fire-fighting efforts. By late July, major wildland fires were burning in 11 Western states and Texas, stretching the government's resources. Fighting the largest fire—in the Clear Creek area of Salmon-Challis National Forest in central Idaho—required help from Canadian firefighters, army troops, and 500 marines. Wildfires also menaced Mesa Verde National Park in southwest Colorado, a large archaeological preserve that is home to famed Anasazi cliff dwellings. By late August an estimated 30,000 people were manning fire lines or flying sorties in aerial tankers. Conditions finally abated when cooler temperatures and higher humidity moved into portions of the West in early September, bringing heavy showers to hardest-hit areas in Idaho and Montana.

In the nation's capital, the fires rekindled a long-running debate between Western lawmakers and the Clinton administration over forest management. Republicans intensified criticism of practices they said allowed dense, dry underbrush to accumulate on forest floors. Congressional critics said federal-land managers should rely on more logging to remove small trees and flammable brush. Conservation groups and many Democrats worried that political fallout from the blazes would provide the opening that timber interests were seeking to expand logging operations in national forests and on other public lands. The Department of the Interior, parent agency of the NPS, halted its policy of "prescribed burns," and said it would revise policies and training to avoid incidents similar to what happened in Los Alamos (*photo left*).

© Michael Caulfield/AP/Wide World Photos

Forestry experts generally agreed that the problems were exacerbated by a century of fire suppression that disregarded the buildup of small trees and other "ladder fuels" that can carry fire into larger, older trees. As federal officials contemplated new fire-prevention techniques, the U.S. Congress approved $1.1 billion in a fiscal-2001 agriculture-spending bill to cover the costs of battling the summer's blazes.

ADRIEL BETTELHEIM

Ethiopia

Drought and famine struck Ethiopia once again in 2000. Not since the years 1983–86, when more than 1 million Ethiopians died, had famine so afflicted the country. At least 8 million Ethiopians faced food shortages, largely in the Ogaden region. Foreign nations and aid agencies became caught up in a political imbroglio as they demanded that Ethiopia stop spending moneys on its war with Eritrea if emergency food aid was to be sent (*see* SIDEBAR).

Drought and Famine. In April the United Nations and independent relief agencies informed the world that Ethiopia was menaced with a devastating famine that threatened to engulf 8 million of its people. The primary cause was a three-year lack of rainfall, complicated by Ethiopia's two-year war with Eritrea. With focus directed toward the war effort, Ethiopia was spending $1 million daily on war matériel and troop support, while in 1999 it had spent $480 million on arms. Little attention was directed toward resolving the effects of the drought.

Centered in the Ogaden, domestic and foreign relief agencies reported that scores of people, mostly children, were dying daily. In the villages of Gode and Denan, where international relief organizations had set up feeding centers, tens of thousands of refugees were encamped, and hundreds had died of malnutrition by April. With cows, goats, and camels also perishing, milk and meat vanished; people fled the smaller villages and towns; land was left fallow; and the crisis intensified. Untold and uncounted, Ethiopians were perishing in the smaller towns and villages of the Ogaden.

Although Ethiopia purchased 100,000 tons of grain from abroad in the first three months of the year, Prime Minister Meles Zenawi refused to reallocate funds from the war to the famine. He argued that "you do not wait until you have a full tummy to protect your sovereignty." With most attention and resources directed to the military, Ethiopia fully expected that the West would come to its rescue.

Food Aid. Claire Short, Great Britain's minister for international development, maintained that "I do not believe that anyone in the U.K. believes we should be providing long-term assistance to a country which is increasing its spending on arms, year on year." That position was matched by the United States, which, in coordination with the nations of Europe, temporarily suspended $1 billion in development aid. But as the extent of the crisis became evident, along with the fear that it would spread to Ethiopia's heartland—the highlands—the West relented. By the end of April, the European Union (EU) pledged 430,000 tons of food; the United States agreed to contribute an additional 432,000 tons. The feeding centers of relief agencies were designated as distribution points.

By early May, as Ethiopia was on the verge of attacking Eritrea, Prime Minister Meles expressed the belief that with the arrival of international food aid, the risk of starvation had greatly diminished. Ironically, the imminent appearance of the food supplies may very well have enabled Ethiopia to believe it could strike at Eritrea and not have to be concerned with a spreading famine. Finally, in late September, the World Bank and the International Monetary Fund (IMF), meeting in Prague, the Czech Republic, with the approval of the Group of Seven (G-7) nations, pledged debt relief of $1.3 billion to Ethiopia, which amounts to 23% of its outstanding foreign debt.

Politics. In October, Prime Minister Meles was reelected by acclamation by the lower house of Parliament. In May the governing Ethiopian People's Revolutionary Democratic Front (EPRDF) had won 90% of the seats in elections for the lower house. Opposition candidates were harshly intimidated. . . . In November the remains of former Emperor Haile Selassie I were entombed in Addis Ababa. He died under mysterious circumstances in 1975, one year after being deposed.

PETER SCHWAB, *Purchase College State University of New York*

ETHIOPIA • Information Highlights

Official Name: Federal Democratic Republic of Ethiopia.
Location: Eastern Africa.
Area: 435,184 sq mi (1 127 127 km²).
Population (mid-2000 est.): 64,100,000.
Chief Cities (October 1994 census): Addis Ababa, the capital, 2,112,737; Dire Dawa, 164,851; Harar, 131,139.
Government: *Head of state,* Negasso Ghidada, president (took office May 1995). *Head of government,* Meles Zenawi, prime minister (took office May 1995). *Legislature*—Parliament: House of Federation and House of People's Representatives.
Monetary Unit: Birr (8.1614 birr equal U.S.$1, Nov. 5, 2000).
Gross Domestic Product (1999 est. U.S. $): $33,300,000,000 (purchasing power parity).
Economic Index (1998, 1997 = 100): *Consumer Prices,* all items, 100.9; food, 101.8.
Foreign Trade (1998 U.S.$): *Imports,* $1,250,000,000; *exports,* $420,000,000.

Ethiopia-Eritrea War

© Roger LeMoyne/Liaison Agency Inc.

The war between Ethiopia and Eritrea that began May 6, 1998, came to an end in June 2000, concluding two years of fierce fighting. Heavy battles had erupted once again in May 2000 when Ethiopia launched an explosive attack in and beyond the Yiagra Triangle, the 160-sq-mi (414-km^2) austere wasteland separating the two countries. Both nations claimed sovereignty over that region, and it was the center of the dispute.

The Ethiopian Blitzkrieg. In the midst of an extraordinary famine affecting 8 million Ethiopians and 800,000 Eritreans, and under increasing pressure from the United Nations (UN) to terminate a war that had resulted in the deaths of some 70,000 soldiers on both sides, Ethiopia launched a massive attack against Eritrean troops in the Triangle on May 12. Storming the region along three fronts, Ethiopia's 350,000 troops moved from west to east, capturing the Badme Plain; Tsorona and Zalambessa in the central zone; and Bure in the eastern area, south of the port of Aseb.

Eritrean soldiers, above, take a break from heavy fighting near the village of Adi Keshi in late May. A cease-fire halting the two-year Ethiopia-Eritrea border war was signed in June. The bitter hostilities took the lives of some 70,000 soldiers on both sides.

With lightning speed, Ethiopian ground troops and tank battalions moved through the Yiagra Triangle and within days penetrated 65 mi (105 km) deep into Eritrea, capturing scores of towns in the southern part of the country—including Barentu, the regional capital, 43 mi (69 km) north of the Ethiopian border. The Ethiopian Air Force engaged in comprehensive bombing of Eritrea, including its main airport in the capital, Asmara; military targets in Aseb and Mendefera; and installations near Massawa, Eritrea's primary port. Within days, 500,000 Eritrean civilians were routed from their homes and fled north. They were joined by some of Eritrea's 300,000 troops, seeking to escape the Ethiopian onslaught. Tens of thousands of Eritrean soldiers were captured, and thousands were killed.

The concentrated assault exacerbated the effects of the famine that had been ravaging Eritrea for three years. Beset by misery, military defeat, and humiliation, Eritrea indicated it was prepared to accept a cease-fire under Ethiopia's terms.

Cease-Fire. The agreement officially halting the war was signed in Algiers on June 18, and was brokered by the Organization of African Unity (OAU), the United Nations, the United States, and Algeria. But the reality was that the bloody conflict was brought to an end only by Ethiopia's military success on the battlefield. Previous international efforts to conclude the war had failed because of the intransigence of Ethiopia and Eritrea.

The cease-fire accord called for a 15.5-mi (25-km) buffer zone along the border within Eritrea. In effect, that acknowledged Ethiopia's military success and Eritrea's responsibility for the war due to its initial aggression in 1998. The agreement also called for UN peacekeepers to patrol the main areas of the Yiagra Triangle and the demarcation of the border between the two nations that would be decided by UN cartographers using the colonial treaties of 1900, 1902, and 1908 that were signed by Ethiopia and Italy.

A few days after the cease-fire signing, Ethiopian troops withdrew from captured Eritrean territory. In July, UN liaison officers traveled to Ethiopia and Eritrea to determine the country of origin and scope of responsibility of the 4,200-strong UN peacekeeping force that began to move into place by November.

PETER SCHWAB

Ethnic Groups

Voting returns across the United States in 2000 showed a continued success in mobilizing minority voters in urban areas. Large minority turnouts in major cities helped presidential candidate Al Gore rack up large majorities that carried such key swing states as Michigan, Pennsylvania, and Wisconsin in the contested presidential race. More important, the voter-registration and get-out-the-vote efforts of civil-rights and community-activist groups helped to reinvest minorities in the political process, continuing a trend from the 1998 elections. Also revealing was the growing strength, diversity, and unpredictability of the Hispanic vote, with Cuban-Americans continuing to favor Republican candidates. Mexican-Americans and other citizens from Central and South American backgrounds tended to give Democrats their votes but also supported candidates who spoke to their needs in education, health care, and law-and-order issues, regardless of party affiliation.

Such voting patterns reflected a much-reviewed June poll of likely Hispanic voters conducted by Knight-Ridder Newspapers that found one-third of the Latinos polled considered themselves conservative, less than a third moderate, and only slightly more than a quarter liberal but also found such Latino voters were issue-oriented rather than loyal to particular parties, and were generally feeling better about themselves than in 1996. Still, "persistent racism" stirred Hispanic and other minority voters to action. Defining racial categories, though, was more problematic as the Census Bureau for the first time allowed respondents to claim one or more of 14 racial/ethnic identities in the 2000 count, which will change the way civil-rights cases are enforced and discrimination is measured.

Persistent racism was a fundamental problem in the United States, as reported in the first analysis of U.S. compliance with the United Nations International Convention on the Elimination of All Forms of Racial Discrimination, released in September. The report concluded that despite continued "vigorous" efforts to end racial discrimination over the past 30 years, racism has endured because many Americans' racial attitudes and American culture remain trapped in "a legacy of segregation, ignorance, stereotyping, [and] discrimination" toward minorities and because of poor enforcement of antidiscrimination laws, rollbacks of affirmative-action policies, racial biases hindering minorities' employment and job advancement, lack of equal access to capital and credit markets and technology, economic disadvantage, and unequal opportunities due to residential segregation and poor public schools. The report also noted that racial profiling (the practice by police of stopping and searching suspects on the basis of race), high incarceration rates, and biases against minorities in the criminal-justice system further proved the existence of racism and explained its persistence.

Meanwhile, access to education and affirmative-action policies at public universities continued to be hot topics in 2000 (*see also* EDUCATION).

Racial Profiling. Racial profiling, much in the news in 1999, continued to generate protests and investigation in 2000. In January the Justice Department closed a three-year investigation into racial profiling by Montgomery County, MD, police by working out an agreement with officials to institute a tracking system of all stops police make for traffic violations as a way to monitor complaints. The agreement followed a similar one approved by a federal judge for New Jersey state police on Dec. 31, 1999, and ones already in place in San Jose and San Diego, CA. In New Jersey a state review panel examined issues of racial profiling, as the nation watched the trial of state troopers accused of racial profiling and shooting blacks in a van the police had stopped. At the same time, in June the U.S. Commission on Civil Rights reported that New York City's police department had engaged in illegal racial profiling of blacks and Hispanics. The New York City report was especially significant in the public mind because of high-profile trials of New York City police officers in attacking and killing blacks suspected of crimes.

Racial profiling also was an issue in customs searches, as noted by a U.S. General Accounting Office report in April, which found that U.S. Customs officials strip-searched or used X-ray examinations of African-American women more often than for other passengers. With numerous lawsuits charging abusive searches over the past two years hanging over its head, the Customs Service altered its procedures for checking passengers for drugs. Racial profiling also affected Asian-Americans. A six-month study by the U.S. Energy Department, released in January, reported racial profiling and an "atmosphere of distrust and suspicion" toward Asian-Americans at nuclear-weapons and defense laboratories due largely, though not wholly, to concerns about alleged Chinese espionage.

In the private sector, lawsuits and boycotts pointed to patterns of "retail racism," a form of racial profiling of customers. Early in the year, Washington, DC, civil-rights groups brought suit against KB Toys, charging the national chain with refusing to let customers in predominantly black neighborhoods write checks for purchases. In March the Adam's Mark hotel chain agreed to implement nondiscriminatory policies, attract more minority customers, and pay $8 million in monetary relief

© Ric Feld/AP/Wide World Photos

Workplace discrimination remained a hot topic during 2000, especially at Coca-Cola, where approximately 2,000 current and former black workers alleged pay and promotion discrimination and in November won a $192 million settlement.

under an agreement with the Justice Department. The agreement settled two suits alleging that the hotel chain had engaged in discrimination against its guests. In June, American General Life and Accident Insurance Company agreed to pay $206 million to settle claims that companies it had acquired had for years charged blacks more than whites for burial insurance.

Race and Criminal Justice. Racial bias in the criminal-justice system further attested to persistent racism in the United States. In April, Building Blocks for Youth, a coalition of groups working for juvenile justice, released a major federally funded study, "And Justice for Some," showing that racial and ethnic minorities were treated different-

ly than whites "at every stage of the adjudication process." According to the study, black and Hispanic youths charged with drug offenses, robbery, rape, or murder were disproportionately tried, sentenced, and jailed as adults, and received longer sentences than whites charged with similar crimes. In May the Leadership Conference on Civil Rights issued its own report, "Justice on Trial: Racial Disparities in the American Criminal Justice System," on racial and ethnic bias in arrests and sentencing for drug crimes, noting that although the rate of drug use for blacks and whites was roughly the same between 1985 and 1995, blacks made up more than one-third of those arrested for drug offenses and 59% of those convicted, and that federal prison sentences for blacks were almost 50% longer than for whites. The report also noted that the number of Hispanics jailed has doubled and the number of Asians jailed has quadrupled during the same period. The report warned that such patterns not only suggest institutional bias in handling drug offenders, but also invite institutional bias by creating stereotypes of minorities as drug offenders.

Also in April, the Youth Law Center released a study by the National Council on Crime and Delinquency that found that between 1990 and 1998 a black youth was six times more likely than a white youth to be jailed for a drug offense, even when charged with a similar crime and when neither black nor white had a prior record. Black youths charged with drug offenses also were disproportionately tried in adult courts and sent to adult prisons. The report attributed the discrepancies to racial profiling and stereotyping, among causes of discrimination. *(See also* CRIME—Capital Punishment; PRISONS.)

Employment. Job discrimination remained part of "the persistent racism" problem in 2000. According to the Bureau of Justice Statistics, reported in January, private lawsuits alleging discrimination in the workplace more than tripled during the 1990s, in part due to new federal laws making such suits possible. In February, Amtrak settled a racial-discrimination lawsuit filed by black workers in 1998 charging Amtrak with tolerating a "racially hostile environment." As safeguards against future bias, Amtrak agreed to pay a $16 million settlement and to keep detailed records of applications for jobs and advancement and of disciplinary actions against workers. In November, Coca-Cola agreed to a $192 million settlement with roughly 2,000 black workers who had alleged discrimination in salary and promotions. The settlement was the largest of its kind, and provided for direct payments to the victims, salary adjustments, and new oversight procedures of Coca-Cola's employment practices.

States also initiated efforts to improve the workplace. In May the U.S. Supreme Court let stand a California judge's order barring supervisors at Avis Rent A Car from using "derogatory racial and ethnic epithets" against Latino employees. The 8–1 court ruling did not apply nationally, but by upholding the California prohibition on racial slurs in the workplace, the court implicitly endorsed similar efforts to limit such speech elsewhere.

Disparities in income and wealth also persisted, with Hispanics and Native Americans lagging behind.(*See* SOCIAL WELFARE).

Stereotyping. Believing that stereotyping in mass media affects race relations, employment, and the quality of life generally, a coalition of Asian, Hispanic, and Native American civil-rights groups joined the National Association for the Advancement of Colored People (NAACP) in threatening lawsuits and boycotts of the major television networks unless they opened up hiring to minorities. In January, NBC and ABC signed broad agreements with the NAACP to identify and recruit more minority writers, directors, and producers, and in February, Fox and CBS followed suit. None of the agreements set specific diversity goals. In May the NAACP echoed its concern about the lack of minorities in prominent roles on prime-time network programs, and in a report issued by the Screen Actors Guild in May, two-thirds of the 1,200 Latino actors surveyed complained of ethnic stereotyping and the lack of on-screen opportunities for dark-skinned Hispanics. In November the NAACP and its civil-rights allies reported satisfactory progress in networks meeting their hiring on and behind the camera and presenting minorities on screen.

Native Americans. In 2000, Native Americans continued to seek recovery of land and artifacts due them under treaty provisions. In January, as part of a deal to clean up uranium waste along the Colorado River, the U.S. government agreed to return 84,000 acres (34 000 ha) to the Northern Ute tribe in Utah in one of the largest "givebacks" of Indian lands in history. Under the deal, the Ute can open the land to oil and gas drilling, an arrangement that made environmental groups uneasy. The Clinton administration used the Antiquities Act of 1906, intended to protect Native American sacred and historic landmarks and sites, to preserve open land in the West.

While Native American groups were ambivalent about the use of the Antiquities Act in such a manner, they did not hesitate to insist on compliance with treaties and laws guaranteeing repatriation of Indian relics and objects. In February the Clackamas tribe in Oregon sued to get a meteorite that had hit the Earth 10,000 years ago returned to them from the Museum of Natural History in New York City, claiming the meteorite, which is the centerpiece of the museum's new planetarium, was a holy tribal object. In June the museum and the tribe signed an agreement of joint custody of the 16-ton "Willamette Meteorite." In September the U.S. Department of the Interior ordered the return of the 9,000-year-old Kennewick Man bones, found in the Columbia River, to five Native American tribes who claimed him as an ancestor and wanted to bury the bones; the Interior Department did so over the protests of scientists who had sued for the right to study the bones.

Who owned what sacred relics divided Native Americans, too. In October the Narragansett Indians of Rhode Island disputed the claims of the Wampanoag Indians of Massachusetts to glass and shell beads, brass kettles, and a glass bottle that Harvard University's Peabody Museum proposed to return to the Wampanoag. The dispute grew out of the museum's response to an Interior Department request in 1998 to inventory its vast collection of funerary artifacts and human remains as part of a major repatriation plan. Land ownership also was contested in 2000. In August the Miami tribe, with its reservation in Oklahoma, filed suit to recover 2.6 million acres (1.05 million ha) of farmland in Illinois, under terms of an 1805 treaty granting them the land.

RANDALL M. MILLER
St. Joseph's University, Philadelphia

Europe

Throughout 2000, two unrelated issues dominated policy making within the European Union (EU). The first was: What could or should be done about the declining value of the euro, the new common currency adopted by 11 EU members on Jan. 1, 1999? The second issue was: What steps should be taken to expedite the admission to the EU of the 13 countries that had posed their official candidacy and to complete the constitutional reforms of the EU needed before new members are admitted?

The Declining Euro. In spite of the absence from the euro zone of Britain, Denmark, and Sweden, which had decided not to join, and Greece, which had not met the criteria for participation, the introduction of the euro at an exchange rate of $1.17 by the other 11 members had gone smoothly. But almost immediately the new currency began to slip in value. In spite of a very occasional and brief upswing, the currency declined every month; by October 2000 it was worth only 83 cents, a decline of 30% from its original value.

The acceptance of Greece into the renamed Euro Group—which originally had been known as the Euro-11—in 2000, far from strengthening the euro, had raised further doubts about its stability. This was due to the fact that in spite of Greece's greatly improved fiscal and budgetary situation, doubts remained about its long-term economic health. The continent-wide protests against high fuel prices, which had paralyzed many of Europe's major cities and highways in September, had not only shown again the EU's dangerous dependence on increasingly expensive overseas oil and the widespread resentment at the burden of high taxes on both the transportation industry and the average consumer, but had further weakened the euro. Moreover, the rise in oil prices and the increasing cost of imports due to the fall in the euro brought back the specter of inflation, which had risen from only 0.8% in early 1999 to 2.4% by July 2000, well above the European Central Bank's target of 2.0%.

Supporters of the euro hoped that a positive vote in the Danish referendum on September 28 on Denmark's membership in the Euro Group might lead Sweden and even Britain to reconsider membership. But the failure of a surprise intervention in the currency markets by the European Central Bank, several European national banks, and the U.S. Federal Reserve to boost the euro for more than a few days further discouraged the Danish voters, who already were deeply concerned that the EU was threatening their cherished welfare state. By a decisive margin of 53% to 47%, the Danes rejected adoption of the euro, and Sweden postponed holding a similar referendum.

Some blame for the lackluster performance of the euro was leveled against the European Central Bank, with its inadequate statistical services and its lack of a clearly expressed, or even thought-out, monetary philosophy. More important, both corporate and individual investors seemed convinced that the European governments lacked the will to carry out necessary changes in loosening labor markets and capital flows and in reducing the tax burden on employers, particularly on those willing to find jobs for new workers. Investment in the United States, both in government bonds—made attractive by higher interests rates than those in Europe—and in companies participating in the frantic U.S. economic boom—which had given the United States a growth rate at least two percentage points higher than the European rate—caused a huge outflow of capital from the euro area.

The embattled supporters of the euro argued, however, that the currency markets were ignoring the growing strength of the European economies. The countries on the EU periphery—such as Ireland, Finland, and Spain—were far exceeding the U.S. growth rate. The larger economies—such as Germany and France—were advancing, too, to pull the overall growth rate of the euro area to above 4% by midyear. Moreover, many saw the creation of the euro as a major reason for this progress. The weak euro had made European exports more competitive. Freedom from currency fluctuations among its members had increased capital mobility, and mergers of companies across national borders, often as a result of hostile takeovers, had doubled. The labor markets had become more flexible, as governments relaxed their controls over short-term or part-time employment. The unemployment rate had dropped substantially to less than 8%. The higher growth had even produced government surpluses in many countries. In turn, these countries—led by Germany—had used their surplus to lower tax rates and thus further encourage expansion. If the U.S. economy were to falter in 2001, it was expected that the euro would finally stabilize and perhaps even advance.

Expanding the EU. At the EU summit of heads of state and government in Helsinki in December 1999, the leaders had invited six applicants—Bulgaria, Latvia, Lithuania, Malta, Romania, and Slovakia— to open membership negotiations in 2000, joining six other applicants—Cyprus, Czech Republic, Estonia, Hungary, Poland, and Slovenia— with whom negotiations had begun in 1998. In addition, the EU leaders even informed Turkey, a Muslim country whose political and human-rights record was held to need improvement, that it also would be recognized as an official applicant. The overture was so grudging, however, and the date for entry so far in the future, that Javier Solana, EU's new representative for foreign and security policy, had to make a trip to Turkey to soften that country's resentment.

Some progress was made in 2000 on settling the trickiest difficulties posed by the new entrants. They would not be immediately eligible for a full share in the vast subsidies available under the common agricultural policy—which already was costing $50 billion, half the EU's budget—since payments to new members would probably reduce payments to existing members. The new members also would probably be permitted free movement of their labor into the EU in only a restricted way for up to ten years. Judgments on individual countries varied. Those most prepared for early entry into the highly competitive EU market were found to be Cyprus, whose Greek section, it had been decided, could be admitted without its Turkish segment; the Czech Republic; Hungary; Malta; and Slovenia. Poland was less prepared, but because of strong German support would probably be admitted anyway. Latvia and Slovakia would be admitted at a later date. The lack of economic progress in Bulgaria and Romania was a major obstacle to their admission. Negotiations with Turkey had not even begun. The Executive Commission's report in November on the progress of the applicants thus caused considerable surprise when it predicted that most of the applicants would be ready for membership by the end of 2002.

Constitutional Reform. The EU's government heads seemed unlikely to act on the commission's findings, partly because the transitional concessions asked by the new members were becoming exorbitant and because the revision of the EU constitution necessary to handle the increase in membership would have to be written, approved, and made functional first. The constitutional conference assigned the task of writing the new rules opened in February, and was faced with the task of presenting a new treaty to the summit meeting in France in December. Two basic problems faced the conference—to restrict the number of commission members in order to prevent the paralysis of the union's principal executive body, and to increase the number of areas of union decision making where unanimity of the EU members would not be required. At issue was the vitally important problem of the relative strength of small and large states in the running of the EU. The original six members had made great efforts to reassure the small. For example, Luxembourg, with 430,000 inhabitants, had one commissioner and two votes in the Council of Ministers; Germany, with 82 million people, had two commissioners and ten votes. Suggestions by Germany and France that the small states rotate their right to name a commissioner were frightening both to the present small member states and to the large numbers of small states that would join. For example, Malta has a population of less than 400,000.

Such fears were magnified in February when the other 14 members of the EU ended bilateral diplomatic relations—but not their relations in the EU—with Austria because that nation's far-right Freedom Party had been admitted to a new coalition government. For the first time, EU members had not only criticized the morality of a small member government, but had implicitly attempted to intervene in the internal politics of a smaller member. The issue became so divisive that the sanctions were dropped, before Austria could paralyze the December summit in Nice, which increased the voting strength of the big states in the Council of Ministers, raised Germany's leverage by requiring all decisions to be supported by states with at least 62% of EU's population, and increased the number of areas where decisions would not require unanimity. Eight or more countries would be permitted to pursue increased measures of integration without participation of the other members. Creation of an EU 60,000 person defense force was approved. But the decisions failed to achieve the full constitutional reforms needed before admission of new members, and it was agreed that a new treaty would be negotiated by 2004.

F. ROY WILLIS
University of California, Davis

Family

Concerns over money, child care, and children's safety continued in 2000.

Money Matters. When adjusted for inflation, the cost of raising a middle-class child to age 17 has risen only 13% since 1960. However, where that money is spent has changed significantly, according to the U.S. Department of Agriculture's annual report "Expenditures on Children by Families." Of the total cost of $160,140, for example, child care and education—which was not a separate category in 1960—accounted for 10% in 1999. Health care rose from 4% to 7%; clothing remained relatively constant at 7%; and housing was the largest expense at 33%.

The percentage of households living in poverty—with incomes for a household of four below $17,029—dropped to its lowest point in more than two decades, according to the U.S. Census Bureau. Middle-class families continued to struggle as their income languished and their workload grew. Since 1989, middle-class workers added the equivalent of 3.4 weeks of work to their schedule, while median income rose only about $2,000, to $40,816. The number of children living in poverty continued its recent decline but, at 13 million, was still about 3 million more than in 1979.

Marriage, Cohabitation, and Divorce. As the percentage of unmarried couples grew sharply from 1.5% in 1977 to 4.8% in 1997, so did research on the effects of such a lifestyle. Studies found, for example, that cohabiting couples tended to have more conflict and less satisfaction with their relationships than married couples; less stable marriages; and, if children are born to the unmarried couple, less paternal involvement after the relationship ends.

The effect of divorce on children continued to be controversial, especially following the publication of sociologist Judith Wallerstein's book *The Unexpected Legacy of Divorce: A 25 Year Landmark Study*. Wallerstein found that, contrary to popular belief, children do not overcome the divorce of their parents. They suffer from the lack of a role model, are less likely to get paternal help paying for college, are likely to have difficult stepfamily relationships, are more likely to have substance-abuse problems, and tend to be less socially competent, she said. Meanwhile, efforts to decrease the divorce rate—nearly half of all marriages now end in divorce—continued across the United States. Various states, including Florida, have proposed or enacted laws requiring premarital education.

Protecting Children. The well-being of children in the United States continued to rise in most areas. Due in part to blunt sex-education classes and abstinence campaigns, the birthrate among teens 15 to 19 years old dropped to a 60-year low in 1999—with only 49.6 births per 1,000. Teenage motor-vehicle deaths dropped by 36% over the past 20 years, while the percent of juveniles involved in crimes—as either perpetrators or victims—also dropped. Less encouraging were increases in the percentage of high-school students who used illicit drugs in the previous month (about 26% of seniors in 1999), and the 31% of high-school seniors who had five or more alcoholic drinks in a row in the previous two weeks.

Rights for Newborns and Parents. As newborn-abandonment cases grew—from 65 in 1991 to 105 in 1998—a number of states took measures to protect the babies and give women an opportunity to "safely" abandon unwanted children. By requiring that such action be positively considered in any legal action, a Texas law, for example, encouraged mothers to bring unwanted babies to hospitals and firehouses.

Grandparents, meanwhile, can be legally prevented from interfering with the way their grandchildren are raised. A June U.S. Supreme Court ruling, which stated that parents make the determination on who can visit their child, was seen as a significant reinforcement to parental rights.

Work and Family. Even decades after a substantial number of women entered the full-time workforce, debate over who should care for the kids—and how having kids affects workplace success—continued. A study by Catalyst, a research organization, found that while 74% of men who have risen within three levels of chief executive officer have children, only 49% of women do.

With child care an increasingly large percentage of a young family's budget, cities such as Seattle, San Francisco, and Denver were trying to ease the burden by raising the salaries of child-care workers and funding other related programs. Additionally, 42 states had prekindergarten initiatives. In an effort to ease child-care costs and guilt, a growing number of parents were working from home. A study by IDC showed that of the 37.8 million households with children, 11.6 million have at least one parent who works from home.

KRISTI VAUGHAN

The Fatherhood Movement

The Elián González custody case (*see* CUBA/SPECIAL REPORT, page 209) brought the fatherhood movement to the forefront in 2000. It was Juan Manuel González' tireless pursuit of being reunited with his son that helped reinforce a message that has been gaining momentum since the early 1990s: Fathers matter.

In essence the fatherhood movement attempts to advance the idea that fathers make unique and irreplaceable contributions to the well-being of children.

The Beginnings. Although isolated fatherhood programs—such as the National Institute for Responsible Fatherhood and Family Revitalization in Cleveland, OH—were operating prior to the 1990s, attention to the issue of fatherlessness was given new impetus by an article titled "Dan Quayle Was Right" by social historian Barbara Dafoe Whitehead in the April 1993 issue of *Atlantic Monthly*. The central theme of Whitehead's article was that fatherless children, on average, have worse outcomes than children reared with the positive involvement of both a mother and a father. Other articles and books—including *Life Without Father* by David Popenoe (1996), *Fatherless America* by David Blankenhorn (1995), and "The Coming White Underclass" by Charles Murray in *The Wall Street Journal* in October 1993—refined and expanded Whitehead's theme.

These writings, in turn, sparked a new interest in programmatic activity on the fatherhood issue, including skill-building programs, outreach programs for unwed fathers, the development of public-service announcements, and legislative advocacy. At the same time, such gatherings as the Million Man March, organized by Nation of Islam leader Louis Farrakhan in October 1995, and the Stand in the Gap rally, convened by the Promise Keepers in October 1997, spurred an increased interest in fatherhood. In March 1994 the National Fatherhood Initiative (NFI) had been formed. This group,

© Camille Tokerud/Photo Researchers, Inc.

which promotes men's active involvement in children's lives, hosted the first National Summit on Fatherhood in Dallas, TX, in October 1994. Other meetings, including an Interfaith Summit on Fatherhood and a number of statewide, governor-sponsored fatherhood conferences, followed. In June 1997 more than 50 of the nation's leading fatherhood advocates issued "A Call to Fatherhood," a statement of principles for the emerging fatherhood movement.

Today. With a large percentage of mothers working outside the home and with divorce prevalent, many of today's fathers are determined to do a better job helping to raise their children. In fact, there now are about 2 million fathers who are the primary caregiver, staying home with their children. There are 2,000 grassroots groups, on both the national and local levels, advocating on behalf of fatherhood. Thousands more provide local support, encouragement, and skill-building programs. The common theme that binds these efforts is a commitment to the idea that every child deserves the love, support, and nurturance of a legally and morally responsible father. In June, *dad's* magazine, devoted to fathers, was launched. Dozens of Web sites provide helpful parenting—and fathering—information. In addition, books on fatherhood abound.

The fatherhood movement functions through a broad array of organizations, such as the NFI, the National Center on Fathers and Families, the National Center for Fathering, and the National Practitioners Network for Fathers and Families (NPNFF). The movement's central message—that positive father involvement matters to the well-being of children—rapidly is becoming mainstream. An important, unresolved issue is the degree to which the fatherhood movement should promote married fatherhood as the ideal.

WADE F. HORN
President, National Fatherhood Initiative

Fashion

E-commerce made a huge leap in many industries in 2000, and fashion was no exception. Selling clothes and accessories over the Internet even has overshadowed the continued consolidation among design houses and luxury-goods companies.

The Web Influence. In 1995, selling fashion on-line was practically unknown. In 2000, hundreds of fashion Web sites offered everything from lipsticks to expensive clothes. Most major department stores, such as Neiman Marcus, have developed their own sites. Individual designers also have created their own pages on the Web—some to keep their name in front of the public, others to sell merchandise. LVMH Moet Hennessey Louis Vuitton, one of the pioneers in the luxury-goods conglomerate movement, has established a site for expensive fashions. Other Web sites—for example, *DesignerOutlet.com*—were emphasizing markdowns, much as stores run sales.

Will the selling of fashion switch from what are called conventional "brick and mortar" stores to more-ephemeral computer listings? There are those who believe that the act of shopping at a mall or store is an integral part of the fashion business, arguing that buyers want to feel the material, examine the construction, and, most important, try on the merchandise. Others observe that consumers are already familiar with shopping by catalog and mail order. The computer is merely the next step, they say.

Those who tested sales over the Internet generally agreed that merchandise returns were high. They also pointed out that costs generally were higher than some anticipated, with employees needed to pick out the styles, pack them, and ship them.

Nancy Evans, who founded *iVillage.com* in the mid-1990s, was enthusiastic about fashion E-commerce. When she started her business, less than 9% of women used computers. By 2000, more than 60% did. She considers the Internet "another household appliance." Debby Koster, who founded *nystyle.com*, about the same time as Evans, said that when she started, hardly anyone knew what the Web was all about. Now, with the explosion of ads in newspapers, magazines, and television, that is no longer a problem.

But what kind of styles will sell best over the Web? Designers said they must be pretty basic to appeal to a wide range of possible customers. The designer Mary McFadden planned to stockpile select styles so they could be shipped immediately. Adri was considering concentrating on making clothes with a loose fit so she did not have to worry too much about returns. While it was not yet known whether E-commerce would represent a major change in fashion itself or in marketing, fashion was "entering a new era," according to Koster.

Many fashion retailers were turning to the Internet during 2000 as a new way of marketing and selling their clothes. At the upscale Neiman Marcus site, *below,* buyers could make their selections based on designer or category of merchandise.

Courtesy, Neiman Marcus Direct

The Latest Look. That era may possibly be quite different from the one that dominated the past few years—when casual clothes ruled, and a T-shirt and jeans could be worn almost everywhere. Reflecting a time of prosperity—and a time for change—femininity and luxury were the new fashion catchwords. Femininity took the form of clothes with a snugger fit and the use of more-decorative fabrics, such as sequin-studded blouses and pants. And blouses themselves were part of the new order, with ruffly necklines and softer sleeves. A new breed of suits was made available, minus big shoulder pads and equipped with either a skirt or pants.

Television host Regis Philbin popularized a new look for men in 2000—dark ties with similar colored shirts.

One of the hottest themes of the season was color—all sorts of different ones, and used in all sorts of ways. Even men's clothes were included in the rush to color, primarily in shirts and sweaters. Patterns—such as plaids, checks, florals, and geometrics—made a popular comeback with both men and women. An exception was the dark tie matched to a dark shirt, inspired by the clothes worn by Regis Philbin on his television shows.

There was much enthusiasm for leather, in skirts and pants as well as in the more familiar jackets and coats. The new leathers were a far cry from the tough styles associated with motorcyclists. They were treated to a soft finish and appear in many colors, including pastels. When paired with chiffon blouses, leather could be considered part of the new femininity trend.

Casual Fridays have expanded into other days of the week. Sweaters, sport shirts, and casual jackets were being worn increasingly to work. When suits were required, men tended to stash away their ties and leave their shirts open at the neck.

In Hollywood, actresses flauted their femininity with exposure—wide, plunging necklines on award-show gowns, and trousers and shirts worn at hipbone level, baring a good deal of midriff.

Vintage style gained popularity. From Ossie Clark–inspired bias-cut dresses in print chiffons and torso-hugging snakeskin jackets to off-the-shoulder "boyfriend" sweaters and silk blouses with ascot-tie necklines, a resurgence of energy and sex appeal was under way. The feeling was the 1980s at its best. Big hair, faux fur, synthetic suede, and chain belts reemerged, but in more tasteful moderation than in the 1980s, when women were excessive—with makeup, accessories, color, and cleavage.

Accessories got a new lease on life. Instead of dour black nylon handbags, women were carrying boldly colored printed styles. Jewelry started making an occasional appearance in wide, gold-colored bracelets; big belt buckles; and even necklaces.

It Is More Than Just Clothes. For designers, fashion is about originality and personality, and this was evident in many different ways in 2000. Two American designers, Tara

Supermodel Paulina Porizkova attended the Vivienne Tam Spring 2001 "7th on Sixth" fashion show in New York City in September. Economic prosperity helped to bring a new femininity and luxury to women's fashions.

Subkoff and Matt Damhave, introduced their collection in a funeral home in New York City; Alexander McQueen showed his clothes in a garage dump near the Thames River in London, decorated to suggest a funeral home.

On the runways, designers showed their flair. Oscar de la Renta presented his "girlie" spring collection, which included tangerine spangled pants and bouffant party skirts. Marc Jacobs featured peplum jackets, taffeta knicker suits, and plastic brooches in colors ranging from fuchsia and aqua to yellow and royal blue.

To enhance their following, designers aggressively added beauty and bath products, articles for the home, and accessories such as shoes and handbags. There was an attempt to push designer names with initials (for example, LV for Louis Vuitton) worked into the design, and distinctive patterns, such as Burberry's plaids. While these trends had a certain amount of success, designers' names did not have the appeal they had in the 1980s.

© Mitch Jacobson/AP Wide World Photos

© Jonathan Barth/
Liaison Agency, Inc.

© Stuart Ramson/
AP/Wide World
Photos

Designers did not carry as much weight as they had in the 1980s, but the time-honored tradition of seasonal fashion shows continued. The model, above right, demonstrated Tommy Hilfiger's plaid and high-boot look. Renata, above, modeled a relaxed, silk shirt dress during the spring 2001 Sully Bonnelly women's fashion show, and an irregular striped halter dress, left, was shown at the Vivienne Tam show.

Attempts to revive the fortune of Halston and to continue the house of Bill Blass after the designer himself retired failed to stir enthusiasm. A new conglomerate in New York, headed by Stephen L. Ruzow, was trying to spur interest in designers. The group included the young designer Miguel Adrover, who attracted attention with his first two collections; Pamela Dennis, who has dressed Hollywood personalities; and Judith Leiber, who makes jeweled handbags. The aim was to continue in the United States the move by LVMH Moet Hennessy Louis Vuitton in Paris, and Prada and Gucci in Italy, to bind together different designers to increase their effect on worldwide markets.

BERNADINE MORRIS, *Fashion Journalist*

Fiji

In May 2000, just one year after a government dominated by ethnic Indians was elected to power in Fiji, dissident ethnic Fijians took hostage the nation's first ethnic Indian prime minister during an attempted coup. Two months of turmoil followed the attempted coup, including rioting by indigenous Fijians, the takeover of the government by the military, the imposition of martial law, and a decline in the economy of the small Pacific island nation.

Background to the Crisis. Fiji's population of just more than 800,000 includes a small majority of indigenous Fijians (51%) and also a large minority of ethnic Indians (44%). The Indians are the descendants of laborers brought by the British to Fiji, beginning in the late 1800s, when both India and Fiji were British colonies. There have long been serious tensions between the two ethnic groups.

By the time Fiji won independence from Britain in 1970, ethnic Indians dominated the economy. Then, in the 1987 elections, the Indians won control of the government. But an army officer, Sitiveni Rabuka, quickly seized the reins and, in 1990, a new constitution gave the ethnic Fijians permanent control of the government. Most of the Indians' political rights were restored in 1997. Then, in the May 1999 elections, the Indian-dominated Fiji Labour Party and its allies won a majority of seats in the legislature. Mahen-

dra Chaudhry was named prime minister, becoming the first ethnic Indian to hold that government post.

Attempted Coup and Martial Law. The coup attempt, on May 19, 2000, was led by George Speight, a part-Fijian businessman who purportedly represented the interests of ethnic Fijians. Speight and his armed followers seized the parliament building in Suva, the capital, and took hostage Prime Minister Chaudhry and about 40 others, including cabinet members and President Kamisese Mara's daughter. On May 29, in response, the Fijian military took control of the government, declared martial law, and forced President Mara to step down. The military negotiated with Speight, and on July 13, Chaudhry and 17 other hostages were released. The other hostages had been released earlier.

The Crisis Ends. Speight had demanded amnesty for himself and his followers, a role in selecting a new government, and a new constitution that would again leave ethnic Indians without political legitimacy. At first, it seemed the military government

©STR/Reuters/Archive Photos

Taken prisoner during an attempted coup in May 2000, deposed Fijian Prime Minister Mahendra Chaudhry smiles as he is surrounded by supporters and well-wishers after being freed July 13.

would accede. The Fijian Great Council of Chiefs elected Ratu Josefa Iloilo, a former vice-president and the choice of George Speight, as president. And the military appointed Laisenia Qarase as prime minister of an interim government. But on July 26, Speight and hundreds of his supporters were arrested. Two days later, it was announced that the interim government had been sworn in, and that it included only one ethnic Indian. On August 11, Speight was charged with treason. The turmoil that ensued after Fiji's attempted coup had brought the nation's economy to a standstill.

WILLIAM SHAPIRO
Freelance Writer and Editor

Finland

In February 2000, former Foreign Minister Tarja Halonen, the Social Democratic candidate, was elected president of Finland, defeating the Center Party candidate. Meanwhile, economic growth remained strong, but looming labor shortages posed serious threats to technology-led growth industries. In foreign relations, Finland developed closer ties with Russia.

Politics and Foreign Affairs. Halonen, the Social Democratic candidate with 25 years of political experience, won the decisive second round for the Finnish presidency, defeating Esko Aho, the Center Party candidate, with 51.6% of the popular vote. A constitutional change, effective in March, limits the power of the presidency in the conduct of foreign policy. Power now would be shared by both the government and the president, but the presidency retained the strongest influence on relations with countries outside the European Union (EU). Halonen opposed Finnish membership in the North Atlantic Treaty Organization (NATO), but was a strong supporter of enlargement of the EU—with Central and Eastern European countries. Halonen, however, stated that if the Baltic countries join NATO—which they aspire to do—both Finland and Sweden must reconsider. An October poll showed that 83% of Finnish voters rated Halonen's performance as "good" or "very good," up from 73% in June. She was especially popular with women and young voters, and faithfully pursued her campaign issue of a strong Nordic welfare state.

Finland intensified its cooperation with Russia directly following the election of Russian President Vladimir Putin. In September, Finnish Prime Minister Paavo Lipponen met his Russian counterpart at a border checkpoint to symbolize the long-awaited end of territorial disputes. In October, Finland agreed to help Russia destroy stockpiles of chemical weapons. In November, Russia announced that new customs posts would open along the Finnish border to help promote cross-border trade. Finland declared its interest in developing closer links with the estranged Russian Kaliningrad region, enclosed by Lithuania and Poland.

The Budget and the Economy. The 2001 budget planned for income-tax reductions of about 6.4 billion markkaa (U.S.$930 million), or about 1.3%. The International Monetary Fund (IMF) and the Organization for Economic Cooperation and Development (OECD) voiced concerns that high Finnish taxes reduced the supply of labor to the market. The cuts were criticized for being too marginal, given the size of the Finnish general government surplus of 4.5% of gross domestic product (GDP).

Finland's economy grew at more than 5% in 2000, and was expected to continue at this strong rate in 2001. Unemployment fell to 9.6% in 2000—high by Nordic standards—but was reduced from its high point in the 1990s. But growth was heavily skewed. The high-tech sector—the new economy—yielded high growth rates. Nokia, a global leader in mobile phones, was dominating the Helsinki Stock Exchange; its market recoil in 2000 led global markets lower. The government privatized Sonera, the former state telephone monopoly, and dominant national customer of Nokia.

LEIF BECK FALLESEN
Editor in Chief, "Boersen," Copenhagen

FINLAND • Information Highlights

Official Name: Republic of Finland.
Location: Northern Europe.
Area: 130,127 sq mi (337 030 km²).
Population (2000 est.): 5,167,486.
Chief Cities (Dec. 31, 1998 est.): Helsinki, the capital, 546,317; Espoo, 204,962; Tampere, 191,254.
Government: *Head of state,* Tarja Halonen, president (took office March 1, 2000). *Head of government,* Paavo Lipponen, prime minister (took office April 13, 1995). *Legislature* (unicameral)—Eduskunta.
Monetary Unit: Markka (6.4956 markkaa equal U.S.$1, Dec. 21, 2000).
Gross Domestic Product (1999 est. U.S.$): $108,600,000,000 (purchasing power parity).
Economic Indexes (1999, 1990 = 100): *Consumer Prices,* all items, 116.9; food, 95.6. *Industrial Production,* 147.4.
Foreign Trade (1999 U.S.$): *Imports,* $30,727,000,000; *exports,* $40,666,000,000.

Food

Major food issues in 2000 included food safety, genetically modified food or foods containing genetically modified organisms, GMOs (*see* SPECIAL REPORT), adequacy of global food supplies, and the task of reducing malnutrition in the world's poorest nations. Adverse weather in several countries slowed the growth in world food production to less than the population growth. While global supplies remained adequate for current needs, reserve supplies of wheat dropped to a record-low percentage of use by the end of the marketing year. Low stocks reflected the world's decreased capacity to adjust to back-to-back years of widespread adverse weather, which, for instance, made food less affordable in several African nations. Meanwhile, favorable weather brought increased U.S. supplies of most major fruits and vegetables.

Food Safety. Food safety was an important issue in the United States, due to several recalls of ground beef contaminated with *E. coli* bacteria. U.S. government agencies took immediate action to withdraw these products from the market and reduce the incidence of such problems. While some irradiated meat products were test marketed as one means of reducing such problems, many U.S. consumers remained skeptical of irradiated meat.

The issue of food manufactured from transgenic crops also came to the forefront. Late in the year, U.S. agencies reviewed an application to sell GMO fish. In the European Union (EU), consumers expressed a desire for meat produced from animals fed non-GMO feeds. GMO labeling for animal feeds was being considered in the EU.

Malnutrition and Demand. To reduce malnutrition in the developing nations, the United States introduced a global school-lunch program late in the year. The program was patterned after one used domestically, in which government subsidies reduce the cost of nutritionally formulated lunches for schoolchildren.

A major U.S. and global fast-food restaurant indicated it will require U.S. egg suppliers to provide more cage space per chicken than is typical of the egg industry. The standards being required were based on those used in the EU.

U.S. consumer demand for beef and pork rose sharply. The beef industry offered easy-to-prepare consumer products to compete with other meats. In the United States, more eggs were consumed, reversing a long-term downward trend. Cheese consumption expanded with the popularity of fast-food products that include cheese.

With passage of the bill providing permanent normal trade status for China, the U.S. meat industry positioned itself for entry into China's meat market. The industry anticipated that significant U.S. meat exports to upscale restaurants and hotels in China would occur soon. (*See also* CHINA—Special Report, page 189.)

Despite adverse weather and rising prices for farm supplies, the food industry continued to provide abundant supplies of high-quality food, except in lower-income developing nations. Ongoing research set the stage for future increases in quantity, quality, and varied future food supplies.

ROBERT WISNER, *Iowa State University*

The safety of genetically modified foods was a concern in 2000. Protesters, right, representing the DC Real Food Campaign, Community Harvest, and Friends of the Earth, urged more testing and full-labeling.

Genetically Modified Foods

Genetically modified foods became increasingly controversial in 2000. These foods, housing genetically modified organisms (GMOs), are produced by inserting a gene from an unrelated life-form into a plant, to create desirable features, most commonly resistance to pests and herbicides. Despite arguments in favor of producing GMO crops, questions arose regarding environmental impact and food safety, specifically whether governmental-approval processes adequately determined the long-term safety of such foods.

Arguing in Favor of GMOs. Advocates of genetically modified crops lauded potential gains for developing nations if crops could be grown to enhance the quality of food or to survive droughts and floods. A Swiss scientist, for example, developed genetically engineered rice that contained beta-carotene, a building block for vitamin A.

Initially, the concept of genetically engineered food came in reaction to world population growth. The grain demand, for both human consumption and animal feed, was expected to grow by 50% in the next 20 years.

Dominant Crops. Two dominant types of GMO crops in the limelight were Roundup Ready (RR) soybeans and Bt corn. They accounted for 54% and 18%, respectively, of the U.S. land designated to grow these crops in 2000. RR soybeans contain a gene that gives resistance to the herbicide Roundup. Roundup kills nearly all plants it contacts, making RR soybeans attractive to farmers. Bt corn contains DNA from a soil fungus called *Bacillus thuringiensis* (Bt), a bacterium producing a protein toxic to the European corn borer (ECB). These insects damage corn plants, thereby reducing yields.

During the year 2000, GMO foods also included genetically engineered potatoes, while plant breeders and geneticists indicated GMO wheat would be commercially available within two years.

Environmental Impact. Environmentalists expressed concern over the potential of superweeds, which is one possible result of a herbicide being used repeatedly, year after year—or when commercial crops crossbreed with closely related wild varieties. Other environmental issues centered around the safety of insects and species that feed on GMO crops; the inherent risks to the genetic base if GMO crops cross with wild varieties; and the patented ownership of these life-forms by a handful of large global companies. The latter raised concerns about future impacts on farmers, the structure and control of farming, and possible implications for future food prices.

Labeling. Several European countries required food labeling according to the genetic origin of ingredients. Japan and South Korea were to begin labeling programs in 2001, and a number of other Asian countries planned to follow suit. In the United States, polls by Harris and *USA Today* in February and June 2000 indicated 86% and 79% of consumers, respectively, want a GMO-labeling program. However, the U.S. food industry said such a program would be costly, and therefore unlikely.

Late in the year a blue-ribbon technology committee composed of representatives from the United States and the EU recommended that GMO foods have "content-based mandatory labeling for finished products containing novel genetic material." It was uncertain, however, how much weight the recommendation would carry and whether the recommendation was, in fact, different from what the Food and Drug Administration (FDA) already required.

Several food companies marketing in the United States said they were shifting to non-GMO ingredients in some or all of their products, and one large fast-food chain in the United States indicated it would not use GMO potatoes for french fries.

Food Contamination. The GMO issue received increased attention in late 2000, when the StarLink Bt corn was found in food products. StarLink had been approved only for livestock feed and nonfood processing in the United States, and was prohibited from being exported. The discovery occurred during harvest, after some GMO StarLink corn had been commingled with approved varieties. In fact, several food manufacturers and chain stores announced nationwide recalls of taco shells after discovering GMO corn in their products. StarLink concerns, which seriously limited U.S. corn exports in the last quarter of the year, had the potential to bring changes to the U.S. approval system, and to encourage increased GMO labeling in world markets.

ROBERT WISNER

France

For France, the year 2000 began with a sensational fireworks display at the Eiffel Tower that was seen on television around the world. The famous steel monument, engulfed in smoke and light, appeared to take off like a rocket ship, an appropriate metaphor at the start of a new year for the country's booming economy and newfound confidence after years of crisis and doubt. But as 2000 came to an end, the French had become disenchanted with their political leaders, whom they perceived as being far removed from their everyday problems.

The year also saw the possible end of Concorde flights, an enduring symbol of French technological prowess, after one of the delta-wing planes crashed on takeoff from Charles de Gaulle Airport on July 25, killing 113 people.

Environment. The first days of 2000 brought scenes of destruction and desolation, both natural and human-made, across France. Two violent storms, with winds of more than 120 mi (193 km) per hour, crisscrossed the country during the last week of 1999, killing more than 80 people, bringing down power lines, and damaging or destroying some 250 million trees. The cost of the two storms on December 26 and 27 was estimated at more than 53 billion francs ($7 billion), and experts said it would take a generation before the forests that dot the country would fully recover. The tempest caused indiscriminate damage, tearing off roofs from homes, churches, and cathedrals; overturning thousands of automobiles; depriving more than 2 million homes of electricity for various periods; and causing heavy damage to the gardens at the Palace of Versailles

and to dozens of monuments, including the famous Notre Dame Cathedral.

A second ecological catastrophe was human-made. On Dec. 12, 1999, the *Erika*, a giant oil tanker leased by the French petroleum company TotalFina, sank 90 mi (145 km) off the Brittany coast, spilling 19,000 tons of oil into the sea. For weeks the French watched helplessly as blankets of heavy petroleum, carried along by the strong winter winds, soiled 500 mi (805 km) of craggy coastline, ruined oyster farms, and infected more than 300,000 birds. TotalFina, which initially reacted with silence to the ecological catastrophe, eventually agreed to pay for much of the cleanup, and during the summer of 2000, the company emptied the remaining 400,000 tons of oil still in the sunken vessel. Adding insult to injury, Total-Fina announced a 47.8% increase in after-tax profits from the previous year. For many French people, the entire affair was just one more example of capitalism gone haywire. On October 31, yet another transport vessel, the *Ievoli Sun*, sank off the Brittany coast in heavy seas with 6,000 tons of chemical products aboard, including 4,000 tons of styrene.

Also in late October, a new crisis centered around "mad-cow" disease emerged as more cases were discovered despite strict controls. Many school districts forbade serving red meat to students in canteens, and the government banned the use in animal feed of meat and bonemeal, which already is banned for cattle but is used as a protein supplement for other animals. The new crisis emerged when the random testing of animals already slaughtered turned up cases not previously detected.

Politics. The year 2000 was one most French politicians would like to forget. The country entered its fourth year of power sharing between a conservative president and a Socialist government and prime minister, and by the fall, both camps had declared open war on each other. Although most of the year went by uneventfully, things suddenly fell apart for France's political class as summer ended. A referendum reducing the president's term from seven to five years— one of the most significant changes ever made to the Fifth Republic's Constitution since its adoption in 1958—was approved by 73% of the voters. The real news, however, was the almost 71% abstention rate. The result was that instead of being perceived as a major step toward modernizing French political life, as its proponents claimed, the referendum became the symbol of the

---

FRANCE • Information Highlights

Official Name: French Republic.
Location: Western Europe.
Area: 211,208 sq mi (547 030 km²).
Population (2000 est.): 59,329,691.
Chief Cities (1999 census): Paris, the capital, 2,115,757; Marseilles, 797,700; Lyons, 416,263.
Government: *Head of state,* Jacques Chirac, president (took office May 1995). *Head of government,* Lionel Jospin, prime minister (took office June 1997). *Legislature*—Parliament: Senate and National Assembly.
Monetary Unit: Franc (6.9827 francs equal U.S.$1, Jan. 23, 2001).
Gross Domestic Product (1999 est. U.S.$): $1,373,000,000,000 (purchasing power parity).
Economic Indexes (1998, 1990 = 100): *Consumer Prices,* all items, 116.0; food, 110.7. *Industrial Production,* 108.3.
Foreign Trade (1999 U.S.$): *Imports,* $289,925,000,000; *exports,* $300,161,000,000.

High oil prices and the resignations of popular cabinet ministers, including Labor Minister Martine Aubry made 2000 a difficult year for France's Prime Minister Lionel Jospin (right). *Justice Minister Elisabeth Guigou* (below, left) *took over as labor minister.*

© Patrick Gardin/AP/Wide World Photos

© Daniel Janin/AFP/Corbis

increasingly wide chasm separating the French people from their political leaders. President Jacques Chirac, who until June had adamantly opposed reducing the chief executive's term of office, changed his mind for what many saw as politically motivated reasons. The president apparently decided that given his age, 68, it would be easier to stand for reelection to a five-year rather than a seven-year term in the scheduled 2002 presidential race.

Chirac agreed to the reduction in the presidential term only on condition that there be no further reforms in the Fifth Republic's Constitution, but most political observers said adoption of the reform likely would lead to other changes, such as reducing the nine-year term enjoyed by senators. Even more important, the correlation between the president's mandate and that of the National Assembly is likely to result in increased powers for the latter and a diminished role for the chief executive. The referendum did not help Prime Minister Lionel Jospin despite the fact that he, like the vast majority of the French people, always had backed such a move. Unfortunately for the prime minister, the campaign for the referendum came as truckers, farmers, and taxi and ambulance drivers took to the streets to demand lower gasoline prices in the wake of the surge in oil prices. The government gave in to the demands, causing tensions within the Greens, a political party that forms part of the Leftist ruling coalition, leading Jospin's popularity to plummet for the first time since he came to power in June 1997. His long honeymoon with the French people appeared to be over, but Jospin had recovered most of his losses in the polls by November.

The referendum and the high oil prices, however, marked only the beginning of the ordeal for France's ruling elite. In its September 21 edition, the newspaper *Le Monde* sent shock waves through the political establishment by publishing the transcript of a taped interview in which Jean-Claude Méry, a political operator who died in 1999, claimed he had collected and distributed between 35 million and 40 million francs ($4.6 million and $5.3 million) to finance political parties of both the right and left. Even worse, he claimed to have given 5 million francs ($666,000) in 1986 to Chirac's Rally for the Republic (RPR) Party in the presence of the president himself when the latter was prime minister. Chirac quickly denied the accusations but refused to testify on the matter or to explain himself publicly.

Méry's revelations capped a year of scandals surrounding the RPR and Paris Mayor Jean Tiberi, who was placed under formal judicial investigation for allegedly tampering with voting lists in the capital's Fifth District. Tiberi forcefully denied the accusations and indirectly threatened to implicate Chirac in the scandal. The RPR, however, sensing that it would lose the Paris mayoralty in municipal elections in March 2001 for the first time since the office became elective in 1977 if it nominated Tiberi, chose a right-wing maverick, Philippe Seguin, as its candidate. On October 12, the RPR formally expelled Tiberi from the party. The danger for Chirac, who served as Paris mayor from 1977 until his election to the presidency in 1995, was that he would be implicated and indicted once he leaves office for his alleged role in the illegal financing of the RPR. As the year ended, Michel Roussin, Chirac's cabinet chief when the president was mayor of Paris, also was indicted and briefly jailed.

The revelations in the Méry tapes did not leave the Socialist Party unscathed. Just a few days after *Le Monde* dropped its bombshell, it turned out that former Finance Minister Dominique Strauss-Kahn, who had been forced to resign from the government in 1999 as a result of another scandal, had been given the original copy of the videotape many months before it became public. Strauss-Kahn, who was the Socialists' leading candidate for the Paris mayoralty before his forced resignation, had curiously failed to turn over the tape to the appropriate judicial authorities. Chirac backers quickly charged that the Socialists had manipulated the whole matter in order to embarrass the president. With the French proclaiming themselves disgusted with their political leaders, there was talk that perhaps the two main candidates in the scheduled 2002 presidential election should not be Chirac and Jospin after all. Chirac, whose political and moral leadership clearly suffered from the scandals, was certain to face a challenge from within his own ranks unless he restored confidence in his presidency. Jospin, for his part, seemed to be entering a more dangerous and difficult phase in his quest for the presidency. As the year ended, it even seemed possible that Chirac would be forced to call early presidential elections.

Jospin faced serious divisions within his ruling coalition during the year, with the resignations of a number of important ministers forcing him to renew his cabinet on two different occasions. In March, Jospin brought two of his rivals within the Socialist Party, Jack Lang and Laurent Fabius, into the government. Lang replaced Education Minister Claude Allègre, who resigned when he failed to push through his proposed reforms in the face of widespread opposition from the powerful teaching establishment. As finance minister, Fabius became the second-most-important figure in the government, and quickly made it clear he would be his own man by forcing Jospin to agree to his massive tax cuts. In October, Jospin was forced to replace Labor Minister Martine Aubry, who had instituted the 35-hour workweek and was one of the most popular and respected politicians in France. Aubry insisted on leaving the government to run for mayor of Lille in northern France in the 2001 municipal elections. Her replacement was Justice Minister Elisabeth Guigou, who along with Aubry, is considered a leading candidate to become prime minister should Jospin become president.

The most spectacular resignation of 2000, however, was that of Interior Minister Jean-Pierre Chevènement, a close personal friend of Jospin. Chevènement resigned because of the Mediterranean island of Corsica. Following months of negotiations, the central government of France and representatives of the Corsican political parties, including those favoring independence for the beautiful but troubled island, reached an agreement on Corsica's future status. The plan, announced in July, called for handing over substantially increased powers to the local government in the areas of education, transporta-

© François Liccia/APF/Corbis

On the French-controlled island of Corsica in August 2000, mourners paid tribute to Jean-Michel Rossi, the founder of the Corsican National Liberation Front. He and his bodyguard had been murdered.

tion, the environment, culture, and the economy. More significant, however, was the intention to eventually allow the Corsican legislature to adapt national laws to the island's specific needs, a first in highly centralized France. Critics charged that Jospin had made major concessions to the nationalists without extracting a promise to end the violence that has plagued the island for 25 years. Others said it meant the beginning of the end of a unified France—and indeed, it did not take long for independent-minded groups in regions such as Brittany and the Basque country to demand the same degree of autonomy promised the Cor-

© Christophe Ena/AP/Wide World Photos

To protest the highest fuel prices in France since the Persian Gulf War, truckers blocked fuel depots and oil refineries leaving many gas stations empty. The lack of gas and its high price caused various hardship for the typical citizen.

sicans. In fact, the proposed agreement, which must be approved by the National Assembly, did not stop the violence on the island. Politically motivated killings continued during the summer. Jospin appeared to backtrack somewhat in the final months of the year as many French and important segments of the press expressed serious reservations about the agreement, and by year's end, the so-called Corsican peace process appeared on hold.

Economy. The French economy continued to churn along during the year despite the highest petroleum prices since the Persian Gulf War, an increasingly weak euro (which did help exports), a decline in consumer spending, and higher-than-expected inflation. The economy grew by about 3.2% in 2000, significantly lower than the 4% growth some experts had expected, but still better than the 2.9% growth registered in 1999. The sharp rise in petroleum prices reduced household spending power, while inflation was at 2.3% in the 12-month period ending in November, significantly higher than the 1.1% expected before the oil-price rise and above the 2% ceiling set by the European Central Bank. The major beneficiaries from the continuing strong growth, in addition to the job market, were French companies. During the first six months of the year, the country's 20 biggest industrial and commercial groups registered profits equivalent to those for all of 1999. Domestic consumption was the locomotive that pushed the economy, with sales of automobiles, for example, growing by more than

17% during the first six months of the year compared with the same period in 1999.

The best economic news for the average Frenchman in 2000 was the continuing decline in the unemployment rate, which dropped below 10% in April to its lowest level since 1991. By the end of October, unemployment stood at 9.4%, a 16.9% drop from the previous year. While the government claimed the steady decline in the number of jobless was due to the introduction of the 35-hour workweek and the creation of thousands of public-service jobs for young people, the business community insisted the decline was the result of worldwide economic growth. Whatever the reason, the high corporate profits, a sharp increase in the sales-tax revenues due to increased consumption, and added revenue from the special tax on the largest personal fortunes resulted in a budget surplus estimated at more than 80 billion francs ($10.6 billion). The surplus became an embarrassment to the government, which at first tried to deny the extent of the windfall so as not to increase pressure for a much-needed tax cut. But the matter was so badly mishandled that Jospin was forced to fire Finance Minister Christian Sautter after only three months in office and replace him with Fabius, who quickly announced tax cuts totaling 120 billion francs (16 billion dollars) over three years. The cuts included the elimination of an unpopular annual tax paid by all car owners, lower taxes on corporations, and income-tax reductions for even the wealthiest individuals.

EDUARDO CUE, *Freelance Writer, Paris, France*

Gardening and Horticulture

The estimated 70 million households that garden in the United States found a multitude of award-winning plant introductions for the year 2001.

All-America Selections Awards for 2001. The All-America Selections (AAS) committee, a nonprofit organization that evaluates new seed-grown plant varieties for home-garden use, announced two flowers, three bedding plants, and four vegetable winners for 2001.

Zinnia " Profusion White," a disease-tolerant, compact, early bloomer from seed with 2- to $2^1/_2$-inch (5- to 6.35-cm) white, single, daisylike flowers from Sakata Seed Corporation, Japan, won the Gold Medal Award for a breeding breakthrough. The honoree also captured the Gold Medal of Fleuroselect, the international association of flower-seed breeders and distributors that evaluates performance of new seed-grown flowers. Sunflower "Ring of Fire," the other AAS flower winner, produces 5-inch (12.7-cm) blossoms with petals that have a golden edge with an inner ring of red and a chocolate-brown center.

The bedding-plant AAS award winners included Portulaca "Margarita Rosita," with dark pink, semidouble blooms on compact mounds spreading to 14 inches (35.6 cm); Nicotiana "Avalon Bright Pink," with a profusion of colorful blossoms on a compact plant bred by Floranova Ltd, United Kingdom; and Eustoma "Forever Blue" (Lisianthus), which, whether grown in patio pots or as bedding plants, provides gardeners with their favorite blue color.

Vegetable winners included "Giant Marconi," an F1 hybrid, 6- to 8-inch (15.2- to 20.3-cm)-long Italian grilling pepper; Onion F1 "Super Star," an improved, day-length neutral sweet onion that is white and weighs 1 lb (0.45 kg) or more; Sweet Corn "Honey Select" F1 hybrid with a delicious sweet honey flavor; and Tomato F1 "Jolly," a new pink, $1^1/_2$-oz (42.5-g) peach-size fruit produced on indeterminate vines.

All-America Rose Selections. Gardeners and rose connoisseurs were treated to the introduction of three All-America Rose Selections (AARS) award winners. "Glowing Peace" is a round, bushy grandiflora growing to 4 ft (1.2 m) tall by 3 ft (0.9 m) wide with 3-inch (7.6-cm) blossoms of golden yellow and cantaloupe-orange-blended petals. "Marmalade Skies" is a floribunda that produces clusters of five to eight brilliant tangerine-orange blossoms—with a complete bouquet on each stem. Both "Glowing Peace" and "Marmalade-Skies" were hybridized by the French house of Meilland and introduced in the United States by Conard-Pyle Company. The third AARS award went to "Sun Sprinkles," an upright, rounded miniature that has blazing yellow blossoms and grows to 24 inches (61 cm). "Sun Sprinkles" was hybridized by John Walden and introduced by Bear Creek Gardens, Inc., Medford, OR. AARS winners were evaluated for 15 traits, including disease resistance, hardiness, color, and novelty, for two years.

"Marmalade Skies"

"Glowing Peace"

Courtesy, All-America Rose Selections, Inc.

Other Honorees. *Calamagrostis acutiflora* " Karl Foerster," feather reed grass, was selected as the perennial plant of the year by the Perennial Plant Association. It plumes to 4 ft (1.2 m) tall on plants 2 ft (0.6 m) wide and is hardy in most U.S. Department of Agriculture (USDA) hardiness zones. The American Ivy Society, Inc., of Naples, FL, selected *Hedera helix* "Lady Frances," a miniature ivy with small, variegated leaves of gray and white, highly asymmetrical, about 1 inch (2.5 cm) long and as wide, as the very first "Ivy of the Year." Hardy in USDA Zone 5, "Lady Frances" was discovered by Mo Halawi of Weidners' Gardens, Encinitas, CA.

RALPH L. SNODSMITH
Ornamental Horticulturalist

Genetics

During the latter months of 1999 and in 2000, plant-flowering genes were discovered that respond to specific environmental cues; rotifer species were found that have reproduced asexually for abnormally long periods of time; ribozymes were shown to act as enzymes in protein synthesis; and aging was determined to be a result of cumulative errors in the cell-division process. In addition, headline-making developments occurred in the Human Genome Project (HGP)(*see* SIDEBAR).

Flowering in Plants. Depending on the species, plants will form flowers in response to various environmental conditions. The mustard plant *Arabidopsis thaliana* normally flowers when the duration of daylight in the spring exceeds a certain critical length. In the absence of a daylight stimulus, it will flower in response to a drop in temperature. Should neither type of stimulus be present, when flowering occurs is determined by the age of the plant.

A group led by A. Samach at the John Innes Centre (JIC), Norwich, England, reported on the *A. thaliana* genes called *CONSTANS* (*CO*) and *FLOWERING LOCUS C* (*FLC*). These genes were found to have antagonistic effects on other genes that directly induce the active growing point of the plant (apical meristem) to form flowers rather than stem and leaves. It was found that *CO* activity depends on length of daylight, whereas *FLC* activity is sensitive to temperature change. It remained to be discovered how environmental changes detected by the plant are integrated in determining its response.

Long-Term Asexuality. Of the planet's 2 million identified species, only about 2,000 appear to reproduce solely by asexual means. The shortcoming of long-term asexual reproduction appears to lie in the gradual buildup of mutations, most of which prove to be deleterious, in the genomes of such organisms. This would be expected to result in the extinction of any totally asexual species within a period of 5 million to 10 million years after the species has formed.

D.M. Welch and M.S. Meselson at Harvard University analyzed the genomes of four species of small multicellular freshwater animals belonging to the phylum Rotifera. The species are totally asexual in their reproduction. Based on fossil evidence, the species date back at least 40 million years. The scientists found a tremendous number of mutations in the genomes of individual animals belonging to each of the four species. The amount of mutants was significantly greater than that found in any sexually reproducing rotifer species. This surprising finding raises the need to investigate how these rotifers have been able to survive the buildup of mutations over these many millions of years.

Ribozymes and Protein Synthesis. Any RNA molecule that functions as an enzyme in a chemical reaction is called a ribozyme. The term indicates that it was one of the RNA units of a ribosome that was the first RNA molecule found to have catalytic properties. Ribosomes, which are composed of a number of both RNA and protein molecules, are the cell structures on which newly formed proteins are produced.

A group led by T.A. Steitz at Yale University reported on their investigation of the ribosomes of the bacterium *Haloarcula marismortui*. They found that one of the RNA molecules in each ribosome acts as a ribozyme in forming the peptide bond that joins consecutive amino acids together in protein synthesis. In most organisms, humans included, it is a protein enzyme that forms the peptide bonds. The discovery that a ribozyme is the catalyst of protein synthesis in this bacterium lends support to the theory that an RNA was the original enzymatic molecule that subsequently was replaced in most evolutionary lines by protein enzymes.

Old Though Young. A genetic disease called Hutchinson-Gilford Progeria syndrome (HGPS) causes an individual to age prematurely, resulting in death at an average age of 13, usually from heart problems. A team led by R. Lerner and P. Schultz of the Scripps Research Institute in La Jolla, CA, analyzed the number of chromosomes in actively dividing cells obtained from young, middle-aged, elderly, and HGPS individuals. The scientists found that with aging, there are an increasing number of errors in the cell-division process, resulting in cells with abnormal numbers of chromosomes, and sometimes even with multiple nuclei. However, elderly and HGPS individuals had a similar proportion of cells with abnormal numbers of chromosomes and nuclei. The scientists believe that the chromosomal, hence DNA, imbalances that occur in the cells of both elderly and HGPS individuals lead to changes in gene activity that cause the aging process.

LOUIS LEVINE, *City College of New York*

Human Genome Project

On June 26, 2000, Dr. Francis S. Collins, director of the U.S. National Human Genome Research Institute (NHGRI) at the National Institutes of Health (NIH), and Dr. J. Craig Venter, the chief executive of Celera Genomics, a private company, joined with President Bill Clinton at the White House in announcing that their two groups had independently achieved a "working draft" of the human genome. Namely, each had determined between 85% and 90% of the sequence of the units (nucleotides) that make up the genes (DNA) of the human hereditary constitution. The White House meeting was a landmark occasion for this project, begun in 1990, to determine the sequence of the estimated 3.1 billion pairs of nucleotides that constitute the human genome. When this is accom-

© Rick Bowmer/AP/Wide World Photos

In June 2000, Dr. Francis S. Collins (right) of the National Institutes of Health and Dr. J. Craig Venter of Celera Genomics announced that the two teams had independently completed "a working draft" of the human genome.

plished in about 2003, the exact chromosomal location of the approximately 40,000 to 60,000 human genes, plus regulatory elements, also will be established.

A Cooperative Effort. Although initiated and largely maintained by the United States, the Human Genome Project (HGP) has become a worldwide effort, involving a consortium of governmental laboratories from Great Britain, France, Germany, China, and Japan. In addition, a number of private companies independently began to map the human genome. The companies plan to sell subscriptions to their databases to biotechnology and pharmaceutical companies that have need of such information in their development of medically oriented

products and procedures. By contrast, the DNA information gathered daily by the international consortium is made available, without charge, nightly on the Internet. Rivalry between the international consortium and the private companies has proved beneficial in speeding up the analysis of the human genome. The most successful company has been Celera.

Most of the consortium's DNA comes from a single male, but 12 other individuals of both genders and of various ethnic backgrounds also have contributed DNA. Celera's DNA also comes from a single male, but with contributions from five other people. The use of more than one individual is necessary because of the various differences in nucleotide sequences among human beings. The use of a male is required in order to take into account the Y chromosome that is found in males (XY) but not in females (XX).

The Effects and the Future. Although progress in sequencing the human genome has been achieved, neither group of investigators could state by late 2000 the genome's full size or exact number of genes. In addition, there was need to learn more about many of the genes, including how they interact with other genes. However, it was possible to make use of the information that was available. For example, in the case of certain cancers, it is known that a particular type of treatment (medicines, surgery, chemotherapy, radiation) is not equally effective for all patients. The difference in response to treatment often appears to depend on the specific genetic change (mutation) that caused the cancer. It should now become possible, in an ever-increasing number of cases, to match type of treatment with a patient's particular cancer.

As knowledge of the human genome increases, human diseases will be diagnosed not by the physical or physiological condition of the patient, but rather by the DNA nucleotide sequence of the person. In addition, early detection of potential problems will become commonplace, and appropriate procedures will be applied. However, much time and effort will be required for this to be realized.

LOUIS LEVINE

Geology

In 2000 the field of geology was highlighted by the stirring discovery of a fossilized dinosaur heart, along with new indications that the Earth's solid-iron core rotates. Meanwhile a dinosaur named "Sue" was attracting large crowds to Chicago's Field Museum (*see* SIDEBAR, page 259).

Earth's Core and Mantle. A new analysis of nuclear-test explosions strengthened one side of the long-standing debate over whether the Earth's inner core rotates. Telltale anomalies in the inner core—a solid-iron sphere—disrupt the speed of vibrations as they travel through the Earth. Seismic readings showed that these anomalies migrated slightly between the time of one nuclear blast in 1971 and another in 1974. Based on this movement, researchers calculated that the inner core spins roughly once every 2,400 years, relative to the rest of the planet. A spinning inner core might influence the magnetic fields generated by the flow of liquid iron in the outer core.

Extraterrestrial donations may not be necessary to explain the unexpected abundance of iron-loving metals in the mantle. This abundance was a surprise to researchers because more than 99% of these metals, including gold and platinum, sank to the Earth's iron core when the Earth first formed. The most popular explanation for this irregularity was that the extra metal arrived inside chondritic meteorites that bombarded the planet later on. But a team of Australian researchers found that the ordinary melting of rocks in the upper mantle had actually concentrated high levels of these metals inside certain sulfide minerals, leaving others depleted. The mixing of these enriched and depleted sulfides just happened to result in the same abundance patterns of iron-loving metals as were contained in chondritic meteorites.

Earth's Crust. An ancient crater buried in Western Australia could be a vestige of cosmic destruction. A rock sample pulled up from 620 ft (189 m) deep contained minerals shocked by the fiery temperatures and enormous pressures characteristic of a collision; gravity maps of the area revealed a multiring structure some 75 mi (120 km) wide. The crater is second in size only to Mexico's Chicxulub crater—the site of the impact famous for having doomed the dinosaurs. The Australian impact could have had similar consequences: The precise date of the event is unclear, but the region showed signs of having experienced extreme heat between 250 million and 280 million years ago. That was near the end of the Permian—the time of the planet's greatest mass extinction—when more than 90% of all life in the oceans disappeared.

A new study of volcanoes submerged in the Pacific Ocean reinvigorated the controversial idea that the Earth's surface can roll rapidly with respect to its magnetic poles. Magnetic minerals in volcanic rocks indicated that the whole planet rotated as much as 20° in only 2 million years—about 84 million years ago. That twist—ten times more rapid than the motion of tectonic plates—correlated in time with a reversal of the Earth's magnetic field and a reorganization of the continents. Our spinning globe is more stable when massive objects—such as ice-covered continents—are at the equator, farthest from the spin axis.

Paleontology. An April report about a fossilized dinosaur heart strengthened the argument that dinosaurs were warm-blooded. Computerized tomography (CT) scans of the animal's chest cavity revealed an organ more closely resembling that of a bird or mammal than of a modern reptile. The images outlined a four-chambered heart—like that of birds and mammals—that probably delivered fully oxygenated blood to the body and thus fueled a fast metabolism. Living reptiles tend to be sluggish, in contrast, because their simpler heart structures transfer less oxygen. The surprisingly complex heart belonged to a two-legged dinosaur called a *thescelosaur*. Experts estimated the *thescelosaur* to be 13 ft (4 m) long.

The process of moving on two legs—long thought by scientists to be an invention of the dinosaurs—actually appeared 80 million years before the first thunder lizard stormed the scene. Researchers reported in November that a tiny 290-million-year-old reptile called *Eudibamus cursoris* had the body of a biped: Its hind limbs were 64% longer than its forelimbs, and its knee and ankle joints were specialized like those of modern animals that sprint on their back legs. The *Eudibamus*' teeth have the shape of a plant eater's, suggesting that it used its speed to escape predators.

Two separate studies suggested that a single catastrophic event probably caused the greatest mass extinction of all time, at the end of the Permian period about 250 million years ago. Previous studies had narrowed the time of the disaster—in which more than 90% of all life in the oceans died out—to a 500,000-year window. But a detailed census of 333 marine species in a Permian rock outcrop in China showed that all the creatures—from fish to algae—could have died in a sudden event 251.4 million years ago. In a second study, Permian fossils from a particular spot in the Austrian Alps disappeared across a layer only 2.6 ft (0.8 m) thick. Based on known rates of sedimentation, researchers calculated that the extinction took place in 8,000 years or less.

Earthquakes. Indonesia suffered the biggest and deadliest earthquakes of the year. On May 4, a magnitude-7.6 earthquake in Sulawesi killed at least 46 people and injured 264 others. Dozens of houses in the island's Luwuk area toppled, and a fire destroyed a local market. Nearby islands also suffered extensive damage and power outages. On Banggai, 80% of the buildings were damaged or destroyed. A local tsunami with estimated wave heights up to 19.6 ft (6 m) was responsible for much of the damage east of Luwuk.

One month later, on June 4, a magnitude-7.9 earthquake rocked southern Sumatra, killing 103 people and injuring 2,174. Hardest hit was the city of Bengkulu, which also experienced destruction from resulting landslides. A magnitude-6.7 aftershock rattled the area 11 minutes later, and more than 50 smaller aftershocks caused telephone and power outages. The original tremor reached as far as Singapore and Jakarta—each about 400 m (640 km) away. People in Bengkulu, Jakarta, and Padang-panjang felt another big quake, which jarred the South Indian Ocean on June 18. The magnitude-7.8 event knocked small items from shelves and generated a local tsunami near the Cocos Islands.

Earthquakes of magnitude 6.5 or greater also hit Tonga, Vanuatu, Sakhalin Island in Russia, two regions of Argentina, and three islands of Japan. The most destructive of these events struck Honshu, Japan—about 375 mi (604.8 km) west of Tokyo—on October 6. The magnitude-6.7 quake injured at least 130 people and destroyed more than 2,300 homes and other buildings in the Tottori-Yonago-Sakaiminato area. Landslides near the epicenter blocked many roads. Previously the most recent earthquake to devastate Japan was in Kobe, the port city southwest of Tokyo, where a 7.1-magnitude earthquake in January 1995 took nearly 6,000 lives and destroyed approximately 250,000 homes. Japan is one of the most seismically active areas on Earth, where frequent tremors and earthquakes are generated by the merging of tectonic plates.

California's wine country experienced a magnitude-5.2 earthquake in September; the disturbance fell along a previously undiscovered fault line and surprised seismologists. The quake's epicenter was 3 mi (4.8 km) southwest of Yountville, CA, below Mount Veeders, the highest peak in the area. "This does not put it on any known fault, making it a totally new event," said Pat Jorgensen, spokesperson for the U.S. Geological Survey. "It's unusual because with all today's technology we really feel we have most of the faults located. But then something like this happens and we go, 'Oops, I'll be darned.'"

Volcanoes. In February military troops helped evacuate some 15,000 people in southeastern Luzon, Philippines, when the Mount Mayon volcano spewed fiery debris the size of refrigerators and sent a river of lava down the mountain's flank. On March 31, more than 2,000 people escaped from the foot of Mount Usu on Hokkaido, Japan's northernmost main island, when the mountain shot debris and smoke plumes streaked with blue lightning as high as 10,500 ft (3 201 m) into the air. Area residents felt more than 600 earthquakes in the days leading up to the explosion, and some 10,000 people left the area early in response to emergency bulletins—the first official warnings the Japanese government had ever issued before a volcanic eruption.

Flying rocks killed two Indonesian scientists and injured five other visitors at Semeru, Java's tallest volcano, when the group climbed within meters of the crater rim just as an explosion occurred on July 27. That same day a new crater formed on New Zealand's White Island volcano during its largest eruption in 20 years. On August 23, pyroclastic flows on Arenal volcano in Costa Rica killed two people and injured another. Heavy ashfalls forced the evacuation of 3,750 residents of New Britain Island, Papua New Guinea, when the Ulawun volcano erupted on September 29.

Just before Christmas 2000, Popocatepetl volcano, outside Mexico City, Mexico, spewed a fountain of ash and rock in its most spectacular explosion in 1,200 years. Residents of towns within 6 mi (10 km) of the volcano were forced to evacuate. Mexico's newly inaugurated president, Vicente Fox, went to the region to reassure evacuees.

SARAH SIMPSON
Editor, "Scientific American"

"Sue"—The World's Largest T. rex

© Charlie Bennett/AP/Wide World Photos

A dinosaur named "Sue," the largest, most complete, and best-preserved skeleton of a "Tyrannosaurus rex" ever found, made its public debut in the main hall of the Field Museum of Natural History in Chicago on May 17, 2000.

Ten years after fossil hunter Sue Hendrickson discovered some giant bones eroding out of a cliff in the Badlands of South Dakota, the Tyrannosaurus rex (T. rex) that was given her name made its public debut—to a raving audience. Daily attendance at the Field Museum of Natural History in Chicago doubled after it unveiled the famous dinosaur named "Sue" on May 17, 2000.

Sue's celebrity status is not surprising if the immense popularity of the British Broadcasting Corporation's (BBC's) documentary *Walking with Dinosaurs,* which attracted a U.S. television audience of some 36 million when it was viewed on the Discovery Channel, is any indication of how dinosaurs have gripped public imagination. Dinophiles who seek an experience more visceral than television need only to witness Sue's towering skeleton—13 ft (4 m) high at the hips and 42 ft (12.8 m) long from nose to tail—standing center stage in the Field Museum's main hall. The dino's dynamic pose shows off the largest, most complete, and best preserved of the 22 T. rex specimens discovered to date. One three-clawed foot rests just ahead of the other, and the massive tail extends horizontally for balance. Head cocked slightly, the 7-ton beast appears to be looking up from a meal, perhaps hearing a noise in the distance, just as it might have done in life 67 million years ago.

The more than 200 bones in Sue's displayed skeleton are the real things. Only the head is a cast replica. At 600 lbs (272 kg), it was too heavy to mount on the steel armature that holds the bones together. The real skull, bearing serrated teeth a foot long, is displayed on a balcony overlooking the main hall. There, visitors can also explore the story behind Sue, such as the fact that it took seven workers 3,500 hours to clean and repair the skull alone.

The exquisite preservation of the bones has paid off scientifically. Detailed impressions of muscle attachments are enabling paleontologists to re-create the dinosaur's muscular system from hip to tail. The skeleton also includes the first furcula, or wishbone, ever found in a T. rex—one of several clues indicating that birds may have evolved from dinosaurs. High-resolution X-ray scans of Sue's skull revealed large olfactory bulbs, which suggest that T. rex had a keen sense of smell. Such research would not end now that Sue is in the public eye: Hinged brackets in the armature make each bone removable for study.

For the first five years after Sue's discovery in 1990, it looked like the skeleton might not be available for research or public viewing. In the end, a judge decided that the rancher who owned Sue's burial site would choose its fate—public auction. With contributions from McDonald's, Walt Disney World Resort, and private individuals, the Field Museum won the bidding war for $8.4 million—the most money ever paid for a fossil.

For dinophiles who cannot make it to Chicago to see the new permanent exhibit at the Field Museum, two life-size Sue replicas would tour some 20 U.S. cities through the fall of 2003. A third replica is displayed permanently at Walt Disney World Resort in Florida.

SARAH SIMPSON

Georgia

Georgia experienced little improvement in 2000. There was no progress regarding secessionist disputes in Abkhazia and South Ossetia, despite United Nations (UN) and Organization for Security and Co-operation in Europe (OSCE) involvement. The April presidential election was the most fraudulent since independence, and the economy stagnated under the weight of uncontrollable corruption. Relations with Turkey, Azerbaijan, and the West improved, but tensions with Russia persisted.

Domestic Politics. The first four months of the year in Georgia were dominated by the presidential election, which took place April 9. Political struggles focused on changes in the electoral laws. The most significant charge concerned the staffing and control of electoral commissions. Amendments to electoral legislation, introduced to increase the weight of the opposition in the commissions, were enacted so late that the new opposition representatives were unable to participate effectively. The official turnout in the election was 75.9%. President Eduard Shevardnadze gained 79.8% of the vote; his main opponent, Dzhumber Patiashvili, garnered only 16.7% of the vote.

After the election, Shevardnadze forced his cabinet to resign, but subsequently rehired almost all of them. Continuing economic decline and growing political cynicism undermined the authority of the president's party, the Citizen's Union of Georgia (CUG). It began to fracture as conservatives fought reformers over legal and economic reforms. The CUG maintained its majority, but had little political coherence or popular support. Demonstrations and social dissatisfaction over the lack of salaries and pensions, combined with pressure from Western governments, led Shevardnadze to launch an anticorruption campaign in the fall.

The region of Achara (Adjaria) under the leadership of Aslan Abashidze continued to enhance its autonomy, and proclaimed a new constitution in June without consulting leaders at the capital.

The Economy. Georgia's gross domestic product (GDP) growth in 2000 was 3%. Georgia joined the World Trade Organization (WTO) in April, but negative economic signs predominated. Georgia experienced a trade deficit with 70 trade-partner countries and a surplus with only 18. A drought threw agriculture into crisis, and insufficient revenues—due to the massive black market

and corruption—forced major cutbacks in budget expenditures. In June the International Monetary Fund (IMF) temporarily withheld assistance, blaming the Georgian government's failure to reduce poverty, lower spending, and fight corruption.

Foreign Policy. Relations with Russia remained tense. Russia accused Georgia of sheltering Chechen soldiers, and reluctantly closed down its base in Vaziani, just outside Georgia's capital of Tbilisi. Russia unilaterally announced its intention to introduce a visa regime for Georgians, and saw Georgia's active role in GUUAM—a regional grouping consisting of Georgia, Ukraine, Uzbekistan, Azerbaijan, and Moldova—as an unwelcome assertion of Georgia's foreign-policy independence. Georgia maintained its pro-Western line, signed agreements on military aid with Turkey, and participated actively in Partnership for Peace exercises in the Caucasus.

STEPHEN F. JONES, *Mount Holyoke College*

Germany

In 2000, Germans celebrated the tenth anniversary of Germany's unification. Contrary to the fears of some of its neighbors, unified Germany continued to be a model citizen in the heart of an integrating Europe. But a rash of right-wing violence against immigrants and Jews; a major political scandal; and the continued economic, social, and cultural divide between East and West sectors were disturbing reminders of the challenges still facing the unified nation.

Politics. The year 2000 was a good one for the ruling Social Democrats (SPD)–Green government of Chancellor Gerhard Schröder. A reviving economy, a scandal-plagued opposition, and the willingness of traditionalists in Schröder's SPD to accept probusiness tax and spending policies all contributed to the good fortune of the government.

The high point of the year for the Schröder government came in July when he skillfully guided a major tax-reform package through both houses of parliament—the Federal Assembly (Bundestag) and the Federal Council (Bundesrat). Under the new law, the most significant since World War II, the top corporate tax rate would drop from about 52% to 39% by 2005. Individual rates would also be cut from a current high of 51% to 42%, while the bottom rate would go from 22.9% to 15%. The government hoped that lower taxes coupled with cuts in social programs would lead to increased investment and more jobs.

In October 2000, Germans gathered in front of the Reichstag building in Berlin to mark the tenth anniversary of German reunification. The East Germans began to enjoy a higher standard of living during the 1990s and into 2000, but still lagged behind West Germans.

The scandal involving former Chancellor Helmut Kohl, which broke into the news in late 1999, was a major problem for the Christian Democrats (CDU) throughout the year. In mid-January, following further revelations of illegal donations and secret slush funds, Kohl resigned as honorary chairman of the CDU. He refused to make public the names of the anonymous donors to his secret funds. Several weeks later, prosecutors revealed that during Kohl's administration, more than $70 million was illegally paid in kickbacks to middlemen on the sale of tanks and an oil refinery. One former second-ranking official in the Defense Ministry, reputed to have received more than $2 million in kickbacks, went into hiding. Kohl adamantly denied any knowledge of these illegal payments.

The scandal took a tragic turn in January when a finance officer of the CDU's parliamentary organization committed suicide. He left behind a note indicating that he had embezzled party funds. His activity seemed to be independent of the larger scandal.

In February the CDU was hit with the biggest fine ($21 million) for breaking campaign-finance laws in the history of the Federal Republic. Some observers and commentators feared that the scandal could threaten the party's survival and create a power opening for the extreme right.

By February the scandal had spread to Kohl's successor as CDU leader, Wolfgang Schäuble, who admitted that he also had received campaign contributions from the same German-Canadian arms dealer under investigation in the Kohl case. Schäuble resigned under heavy pressure from CDU members of parliament.

The CDU's sister party, the Bavarian Christian Social Union (CSU), managed to avoid the scandal, and its leader, Bavarian Minister President Edmund Stoiber, emerged as a possible candidate for chancellor in the 2002 federal election. Bavaria under Stoiber has become one of Germany's most prosperous states. While conservative on social issues, including abortion and immigration, Stoiber has embraced the new high-tech economy. To become the CDU's national candidate, however, he must overcome the traditional reluctance in the rest of Germany to support someone from Catholic Bavaria.

The Christian Democrats hoped to make voters forget about the Kohl scandal by seizing on the issue of immigration. In Novem-

In July, German Chancellor Gerhard Schröder (right) and Finance Minister Hans Eichel celebrated after guiding a major tax-reform package through both houses of parliament.

ber, several leaders of the party proclaimed that foreigners settling in Germany should accept the "defining German culture." That same month the CDU accused the Social Democrats of having a "distorted" relationship to the nation and to patriotism. In an emotional parliamentary debate, Chancellor Schröder swiftly counterattacked. He reminded the CDU that Social Democrats were being murdered in concentration camps long after the conservatives had caved in to the Nazis.

Women in 2000 continued to enter the upper echelons of German politics. Two political parties appointed females—both from the former East Germany—to top posts. In April, Angela Merkel became the national chairperson of the CDU after Schäuble resigned in the wake of the finance scandal. Merkel became the first female to lead a major German political party. She also became a prime contender to oppose Chancellor Schröder in the next national election in 2002.

In October the Party of Democratic Socialism (PDS), the former ruling communist party in East Germany, selected Gabriele Zimmer as its new leader. Zimmer, a former French and Russian teacher, was a mid-level communist party official in the former East German regime.

Elections. At the two state elections held in 2000, Schleswig-Holstein and North Rhine–Westphalia, the SPD-Green governments were reelected, thus strengthening the national coalition. In both states, the Christian Democrats appeared poised for victory until the financial scandal engulfed the party. In North Rhine-Westphalia, Ger-

many's most populous state, the CDU's anti-immigration message, expressed in the slogan "*Kinder statt Inder*" ("[Our own] Children Instead of Indians [immigrants]"), clearly backfired.

In addition to Chancellor Schröder's Social Democrats, the small Free Democratic Party (FDP) benefited from the CDU's electoral problems. After doubling their vote in the May election in North Rhine-Westphalia, the Free Democrats challenged the Social Democrats to abandon their coalition with the Greens and align with them. During the year the environmentalist Greens were a source of frustration for Schröder and the SPD. The Greens wanted all the country's nuclear-power plants phased out as quickly as possible, while the Social Democrats preferred a gradual phaseout over as much as 20 years.

Right-Wing Violence. The year 2000 saw an increase in neo-Nazi hate crimes, including vandalism, beatings, murder, and the display of Nazi symbols. A disproportionate amount of radical right-wing activity took place among young people in the East. The relatively few foreigners in the Eastern regions make them ideal targets for skinheads and other radical-right groups. Immigrants from the nations of Asia and Africa, whose skin color easily distinguished them from Germans, were routinely insulted, harassed, and physically attacked by roving gangs of skinheads. Many East Germans were passive and indifferent, thus giving some legitimacy to the violence.

But West Germany was not immune from xenophobic attacks. In July, nine immigrants were wounded by a bomb in Düsseldorf; six of the victims were Jewish. With the end of the Cold War, Germany's Jewish community, largely through immigration from the former Soviet Union, more than tripled to about 100,000. Governmental support for Jewish immigration was based on the conviction that the Nazi past requires the country to be open to Jewish refugees. Among some ordinary Germans, however, there was a latent resentment about what is termed "Jewish blackmail."

Responding to the problem, the Schröder government, joined by several states, proposed a ban on the radical-right National Democratic Party (NPD), which many believe serves as a cover for the illegal neo-Nazi groups. Such a ban is permitted by the constitution, but it must be issued by the Federal Constitutional Court. Critics of the ban argued that it would focus more attention on the party, which was electorally weak, and drive it underground.

The great majority of the public condemned the outbreaks of rightist violence. In November, on the 52d anniversary of *Kristallnacht* ("Night of Broken Glass")—when synagogues and Jewish businesses across Germany were attacked in a Nazi-orchestrated campaign and many Jews were sent to concentration camps—demonstrations were held throughout the country. In Berlin, 200,000 people, including Chancellor Schröder, marched through the capital in protest against right-wing violence. The leaders of Germany's Jewish community lashed out at conservative politicians for whipping up a national debate on immigration and for suggesting that minorities had to adopt German culture.

Ten Years of Unity. The celebration in October of the tenth anniversary of unification, held in Dresden, was muted by the right-wing violence and the absence of the "unity chancellor," Helmut Kohl. Miffed that he had not been invited to speak, Kohl attended an alternate celebration sponsored by a foundation in close association with the Christian Democrats.

After a decade of unity and the transfer of almost $100 billion from West to East, the

Former Chancellor Helmut Kohl (below) was under investigation in 2000, forced to testify over accusations of illegal fundraising activities within the Christian Democrats.

© Michael Urban/Reuters NewMedia Inc./Corbis

record was mixed. While East Germans enjoyed a far higher standard of living than they did under communism—and more opportunities—they still lagged behind West Germans. Many East Germans also resented their continued dependence on financial help from the West, and felt that powerful Western interests were deliberately keeping them down for fear of competition. Nonetheless, the great majority of Easterners, according to the many public-opinion polls taken throughout the anniversary year, thought that unification was a positive step, and they had no regrets.

The Economy. In spite of high energy prices, the economy in 2000 grew at a real rate of 3%, the best performance since unification in 1990. The weak euro and strong demand from the recovering Asian markets boosted exports by 13%, as compared with only a 5% gain in 1999. Unemployment dropped a full percent to 9.6%, while inflation climbed to 2%—largely due to the increased price of oil.

For the former East Germany, the economic picture in 2000 was not as bright. For the fourth consecutive year, economic growth in the region lagged behind that of West Germany, while unemployment remained high at about 18%.

International Role and Foreign Policy. Germany in 2000 sent out conflicting signals about its future international role. The nation continued to contribute more than its share in manpower and money to the peace-keeping operations of the European Union (EU) in Kosovo. Berlin was also a major supporter of the EU's planned rapid-deployment force, a multinational, high-tech army of 60,000 troops.

But in May the Schröder government announced a $9 billion cut in defense spending and a planned reduction of 100,000 troops, or about 20%, from Germany's armed forces over the next five years. The goal of the troop reductions would be a more professional army that could react quickly to distant crises rather then focusing on territorial defense. In the opinion of many experts, however, such an army will require increased expenditures for high-tech training and equipment. The planned reductions were criticized by U.S. Defense Secretary William S. Cohen and by President Clinton during a June visit to Berlin. German military spending dropped to only 1.5% of its gross domestic product (GDP)—among the lowest in Europe, and only half of the U.S. defense effort.

In June, Vladimir V. Putin paid his first official visit to Germany as Russia's president. Putin was no stranger to the country, having served for several years as a KGB officer in Dresden. Speaking in fluent German, Putin asked for some relief from Russia's $90 billion debt to German banks, and for more investments in his country. He also encouraged the Schröder government to show more independence from the United States. The Russian leader praised Germany's ambivalence over a proposed U.S. missile-defense system, and reiterated Moscow's view that the program would violate the 1972 Anti-Ballistic Missile Treaty. With the end of the Cold War, Germany has more room to reach out to Moscow without damaging its ties to the Western Alliance. At the conclusion of the visit, the president and chancellor agreed to restructure some of Russia's debt and to begin joint ventures for oil and gas development in Russia.

In May, Foreign Minister Joschka Fischer proposed major reforms in the governance of the EU. He called for a European federal state with a directly elected two-house parliament and possibly a directly elected president. Fischer also suggested that some countries within the EU may want to move ahead toward an even closer union.

During a June visit to Berlin, French President Jacques Chirac also proposed a fast track to European unity by a core group of countries led by France and Germany. Like Foreign Minister Fischer, he endorsed the drafting of a European constitution. But in his speech at the Bundestag, the first there by a foreign head of state since its renovation, Chirac declared that he hoped for a united Europe of states rather than a United States of Europe. He also did not endorse Fischer's proposal for a directly elected president of the EU.

Miscellaneous Headlines. The discovery in November of the first case of mad-cow disease in Germany prompted a nationwide ban on the use of feed ground from the carcasses and entrails of cattle or sheep. Processed into pellets, this type of feed was widely used as a dietary supplement for livestock. It is believed that mad-cow disease is transmitted to cattle through these feed pellets, and then to humans. By December, no cases involving humans had been reported. Following the news, beef consumption dropped by 50%, and the minister of agriculture was in danger of losing his job and being replaced.

In July, following several attacks on humans by pit-bull dogs, authorities moved to aggressively enforce national bans on the pit bull and the American Staffordshire terrier breeds. Several state governments banned additional breeds. Dog owners responded with protests, including a demonstration of 10,000 dog owners in Düsseldorf. Some owners reported that they had been physically and verbally abused while walking their pets. Fighting or attack dogs, however, were favorites of skinheads, youth gangs, and drug dealers. German police were reluctant to go into urban areas where the offenders lived simply to enforce dog laws. At year's end the Schröder government was planning additional legislation requiring character tests for certain breeds.

Near Paris in July, an Air France Concorde with 96 German tourists aboard crashed shortly after takeoff. The passengers were en route to New York, where they were to board a luxury ocean liner, the MS *Deutschland*, for a two-week cruise. The crash interrupted the start of the traditional summer-vacation season. French President Chirac and Chancellor Schröder attended memorial services to honor the victims.

Finally, from June through the end of October, the city of Hanover hosted Expo 2000, the first full-scale world's fair since 1992. More than 180 nations presented exhibits around the themes of nature and technology. Most notable by its absence was the United States. Nonetheless, with some 18 million visitors, the fair was called a modest success by its organizers. (*See also* PEOPLE, PLACES, AND THINGS, page 400.)

DAVID P. CONRADT
East Carolina University

GERMANY • Information Highlights

Official Name: Federal Republic of Germany.
Location: North-central Europe.
Area: 137,846 sq mi (357 021 km²).
Population (2000 est.): 82,797,408.
Chief Cities (June 30, 1997 est.): Berlin, the capital, 3,446,600; Hamburg, 1,706,800; Munich, 1,216,500.
Government: *Head of state,* Johannes Rau, president (took office July 1999). *Head of government,* Gerhard Schröder, chancellor (inaugurated November 1998). *Legislature*—parliament: Federal Assembly (Bundestag) and Federal Council (Bundesrat).
Monetary Unit: Deutsche mark (2.0765 D. marks equal U.S.$1, Dec. 29, 2000).
Gross Domestic Product (1999 est. U.S.$): $1,864,000,000,000 (purchasing power parity).
Economic Indexes (1999): *Consumer Prices* all items (1990 = 100): 120.4; food (1995 = 100): 101.7. *Industrial Production* (1995 = 100): 110.2.
Foreign Trade (1999 U.S.$): *Imports,* $472,171,000,000; *exports,* $541,090,000,000.

Great Britain

In 2000, after three years in power, the political fortunes of Great Britain's Prime Minister Tony Blair and his Labour government began a downturn. The opposition Conservative Party attempted to recover support among middle-class voters. The Northern Ireland peace process suffered a series of setbacks. The British economy remained strong, enabling Prime Minister Blair's chancellor of the exchequer to order substantial increases in state spending on health and welfare.

Domestic Politics. Early in the year, Blair's personal-popularity ratings, which had remained remarkably high, dipped sharply, heralding a series of problems for the Labour government. Having promised to be "tough on crime and the causes of crime," the government had to concede that recorded crime rates had risen for the first time in six years. After undertaking to make drastic improvements in the National Health Service (NHS), there were lengthening waiting lists for surgery and a shortage of doctors and hospital nurses. Blair was criticized—and at one point openly jeered—by his own supporters for attempting to block the candidacy of a populist left-winger, Ken Livingstone, for London's mayoralty. Blair's embarrassment deepened when Livingstone subsequently won the post. Alun Michael, whom Blair in 1999 had handpicked to be first minister in a devolved Welsh Assembly, resigned ahead of an expected no-confidence vote. In Scotland, the Labour Party suffered a serious setback when Donald Dewar, first minister in the

Britain's Prime Minister Tony Blair and his wife, Cherie, above, became parents again in May 2000. Their son, Leo, was the first child born to a sitting prime minister in 152 years.

© Mary McCartney/AP/Wide World Photos

devolved Scottish Parliament, died in October. Minister Dewar was succeeded by Henry McLeish.

Taking advantage of the new situation, the opposition Conservative Party and its leader, William Hague, began to pursue foreign and domestic policies calculated to appeal to middle-class voters who had deserted the Tories in the general election. Aware that opinion polls showed as much as two-thirds of the electorate opposed to Britain joining a single European currency, Hague hardened his opposition to the euro. He proposed greater use of the private sector for health care, demanded a clampdown on welfare fraud, attacked a government plan that he claimed would permit the promotion of homosexuality in schools, and pledged that a Conservative government would cut taxes.

On May 20, Blair received a much-needed popularity boost when his wife, Cherie (*see* BIOGRAPHY), gave birth to a son, Leo—the first child born to residents of 10 Downing Street in 152 years. Soon afterward, however, the

© Adrian Dennis/AFP/Corbis

Ken Livingstone, an Independent, above, became the first elected mayor of London in May. Livingstone won despite not having the support of Prime Minister Tony Blair.

When gasoline prices soared during 2000, British farmers and truck drivers, above, protested by blocking traffic in London and picketing at oil refineries and fuel depots.

prime minister suffered embarrassment when his teenage son was arrested for drunkenness in a central London square.

Until the early summer, Blair was able to deflect most of the Conservative criticisms, but new problems continued to arise. The number of asylum seekers from Asia and Eastern Europe arriving in Britain rose sharply, evoking protests from citizens that the newcomers were a burden on local authorities that had to house them. Hague called on the government to imprison and deport asylum seekers found begging in the streets. Blair instituted a fast-track system for processing asylum applications.

Results of local-authority elections in May indicated that Hague's attacks on the government were hitting home. Labour lost 600 council seats in England, recording its lowest share of votes in 23 years. Days afterward, an ICM opinion poll showed that Blair's net approval rating had fallen from +34 a year earlier to +1. A series of government briefing documents leaked to newspapers from inside Blair's private office revealed that the prime minister was worried about the drift in the government's fortunes.

An increasingly common interpretation of Blair's difficulties pinpointed his dependence on so-called "spin doctors" to publicize government policies. According to *The Guardian* newspaper, "their activities had the effect of raising public expectations higher than the government's ability to fulfill its own promises."

Blair's difficulties continued into the fall. In early September, facing the highest gasoline prices in Europe, British farmers and truck drivers blockaded fuel refineries and depots. As pumps across the nation ran dry amid panic buying, Blair castigated the protesters for "trying to bring the country to a halt." The blockades intensified as the protesters, pointing to strong public support, noted that 72% of motor-fuel prices consisted of government taxes. The farmers and haulers were persuaded to call off their protest, but threatened to renew it if fuel duties were not heavily reduced within 60 days. Blair's initial hard-line response to the fuel protest served to further undermine his own and his government's popularity. Four opinion surveys in mid-September showed Labour's lead over the Conservatives had disappeared. A Gallup poll showed Labour five points behind. Labour spokesmen portrayed the figures as a temporary "blip."

As the 60-day deadline approached, the government at first responded by training 1,000 soldiers to drive fuel trucks. But in early November, it announced a series of measures aimed at helping road haulers, including a two-year standstill in fuel duty. The Conservatives said that, if elected, they would make significant cuts in the fuel duty.

By then, Blair faced another embarrassment that had been building up throughout the year. On January 1, London's Millennium Dome, which the prime minister described as "the first line in Labour's reelection manifesto," had opened amid much fanfare and forecasts that it would attract 12 million visitors during the year. Soon it became clear that the forecasts were seriously astray, and the government was forced to provide huge injections of cash to

GREAT BRITAIN • Information Highlights

Official Name: United Kingdom of Great Britain and Northern Ireland.
Location: Island, western Europe.
Area: 94,525 sq mi (244 820 km²).
Population (2000 est.): 59,511,464.
Chief Cities (mid-1998 est.): London, the capital, 7,187,300; Birmingham, 1,013,400; Leeds, 727,400; Glasgow, 619,700; Sheffield, 531,100.
Government: *Head of state,* Elizabeth II, queen (acceded Feb. 1952). *Head of government,* Tony Blair, prime minister and First Lord of the Treasury (took office May 1997). *Legislature*—Parliament: House of Lords and House of Commons.
Monetary Unit: Pound (0.6784 pound equals U.S.$1, Dec. 14, 2000).
Gross Domestic Product (1999 est. U.S.$): $1,290,000,000,000 (purchasing power parity).
Economic Indexes (1999, 1990 = 100): *Consumer Prices,* all items, 131.2; food, 120.4. *Industrial Production,* 109.9.
Foreign Trade (1999 U.S.$): *Imports,* $317,958,000,000; exports, $268,254,000,000.

prevent the project from going bankrupt. In the summer, the Japanese bank Nomura withdrew an offer to purchase the Dome, and soon afterward government auditors disclosed that visitors would total a bare 5 million, and that 628 million pounds (c. $900 million) of National Lottery money had been spent to avoid the Dome's premature closure. Hague called on Blair to sack Lord Falconer, the minister responsible for the Dome and a friend of Blair's.

In October, Betty Boothroyd, speaker of the House of Commons, retired. She was succeeded by Michael Martin, also a Labour member of parliament (MP). One commentator described Martin as "amiable but undistinguished." He was elected speaker by a majority of Labour MPs against the wishes of Blair, who had supported a Conservative Party candidate. In another political development, Charles Kennedy succeeded Paddy Ashdown as leader of the centrist Liberal Democratic Party.

In late November, as predictions of a general election in 2001 became widespread, Blair's popularity ratings began to recover. Those of Hague and the Conservatives continued to languish.

Economy. While the fortunes of the government faltered, the British economy flourished. Inflation and unemployment levels remained low during the year. The pound sterling was strong against the euro and other Continental currencies.

In March, Gordon Brown, chancellor of the exchequer, forecasting a government surplus of 16.5 billion pounds (c. $23.6 billion), insisted that his own "prudent" policies were the reason for the economy's "good health." He announced spending of 2 billion pounds (c. $2.8 billion) on the NHS over four years, new measures to help parents on low pay, a special "winter fuel payment" increase for pensioners, and a cut in capital-gains tax. A Conservative opposition economic spokesman attacked the measures as "long-term electioneering." In July, Brown showed further evidence of his confidence by announcing a rise in government spending of 6.7%—the biggest increase in 26 years.

Brown was assisted in his budgetary calculations by unexpectedly high proceeds from the auction in April of licenses for the third generation of mobile telephones, which yielded 22 billion pounds (c. $31.4 billion) to the Exchequer.

Throughout the year, Chancellor Brown, like other senior government ministers, wrestled with the issue of a single European currency. The government's official policy remained in favor of joining the euro, but only when a series of economic criteria could be met. Meanwhile, the euro continued to lose ground against other world currencies, fueling Conservative Party criti-

QUEEN ELIZABETH THE QUEEN MOTHER

Great Britain's Queen Elizabeth the Queen Mother celebrated her 100th birthday on Aug. 4, 2000, amid a national outpouring of affection. The celebrations began in June with a party at Windsor Castle and continued through August when, after receiving a hand-delivered birthday card from her daughter "Lilibet," she rode alongside Prince Charles in a horsedrawn carriage to Buckingham Palace to greet well-wishers.

The "Queen Mum" is, arguably, the most popular member of the royal family. Her ever-present smile, reputation as a steadying influence on the royal family, and touch of the common person won the hearts of Britons, particularly during World War II. It was at this time, when touring the ruins of a section of Buckingham Palace that had been bombed, she was quoted as saying, "I'm glad we have been bombed. It makes me feel I can look the East End [where bombing had been heavy] in the face."

As the eighth child of the 14th Earl of Strathmore, Elizabeth Angela Marguerite Bowes-Lyon was born into a long line of Scottish nobility. She met her future husband, Albert, at a dance in 1920 and wed him in 1923 when he was Duke of York. Following the abdication of Edward VIII in 1936, Albert was crowned King George VI and she became Queen Consort. Following the death of King George in 1952, she assumed the role of Queen Mother.

cisms that Britain would be foolish to abandon the pound. Exporters, however, complained that the strength of sterling was pricing them out of European markets.

In a prebudget statement in November, Brown revised his estimate of Britain's surplus upward from 12 billion pounds (c. $17 billion) to 16.6 billion pounds (c. $23.6 billion). In a package of measures worth 5 billion pounds (c. $7 billion) he announced an above-inflation increase in the old-age pension as well as other payments aimed at meeting complaints that the government had been stingy toward senior citizens. *The Times* (London) welcomed Brown's statement, but said the chancellor was attempting to "buy Labour out of trouble."

Northern Ireland.   The year 2000 witnessed deepening problems for the government and its attempts to implement the 1998 Good Friday Agreement in Northern Ireland. In January, Peter Mandelson, the Northern Ireland secretary, announced plans to reform the province's 92% Protestant Royal Ulster Constabulary (RUC) by renaming it the Police Force of Northern Ireland and, crucially, requiring it to recruit many more Roman Catholic officers. David Trimble, leader of the Ulster Unionist Party (UUP) and first minister in the province's power-sharing Executive, called the plan "an insult." Catholic nationalists broadly welcomed it. Trimble, under pressure from Unionists and members of the Protestant Orange Order opposed to the agreement, renewed demands that the Irish Republican Army (IRA) decommission its weapons in line with the Good Friday peace process. The IRA refused to respond, and in mid-February, the British government suspended the Executive.

On May 6, in an apparent breakthrough, the IRA announced that it was willing to allow international inspectors to examine some of its arms dumps. Cyril Ramaphosa, a leading figure in the African National Congress (ANC), and Martti Ahtisaari, a former president of Finland, agreed to carry out the inspections and Northern Ireland's devolved government resumed work on May 31. By then, however, the IRA; the political wing of the IRA, Sinn Fein; and moderate nationalists were expressing fears that the British government was preparing to water down reforms to the RUC in a bid to placate the Unionists. The latter were insisting that inspections of IRA arms dumps had to be followed by actual decommissioning of weapons.

Problems in Northern Ireland continued with home rule reinstated by Secretary of State for Northern Ireland Peter Mandelson, above, only after Ulster Unionists backed power sharing.

An uneasy standoff continued. In further pursuit of the Good Friday Agreement, the last releases of paramilitary prisoners held on terrorism charges took place in July. Meanwhile, violence arose between two rival Loyalist paramilitary groups, apparently as a result of "turf wars" over control of Protestant areas. Johnny Adair, a prominent member of one of the groups, who had recently been released under the agreement, was ordered returned to prison by Mandelson who accused him of involvement in terrorist violence.

In September the fragility of Trimble's position in the UUP was further exposed when, in a by-election for the House of Commons in London, a candidate for the rival Democratic Unionist Party (DUP), which opposes the agreement, defeated the UUP candidate. With his position as leader under challenge by a senior UUP member, Trimble on October 28 faced his party's ruling council knowing that he must put renewed pressure on the IRA to decommission its weapons and explosives. Trimble narrowly survived a vote of confidence, but only after he had promised to suspend a section of the agreement requiring ministers from the Northern Ireland Executive and the government of the Irish Republic to meet and discuss cross-border issues. The Dublin government attacked the move and agreed to a meeting anyway with a Sinn Fein minister of the Executive.

Near year-end, the IRA agreed to a further inspection of its arms dumps, but showed no readiness to decommission its weapons. Gerry Adams, Sinn Fein president, claimed to have done "everything possible" to further the peace process. Prime Minister Blair called for "renewed efforts by all parties" to keep the peace process alive. Marjorie (Mo) Mowlam, an architect of the Good Friday Agreement, announced her retirement from politics. U.S. President Bill Clinton visited Northern Ireland for the third time in December amid hopes he could keep the peace process alive.

Foreign Affairs. The 17-month detention in London of Gen. Augusto Pinochet ended on March 2 when the former Chilean dictator was allowed to fly home. Jack Straw, Britain's home secretary, said he had made the decision on medical grounds, following appeals by Pinochet's lawyers. Human-rights campaigners, who were seeking Pinochet's extradition to Spain on charges of torture and other crimes while in office, claimed Straw had acted politically. Straw insisted that Pinochet, 84, was unfit to stand trial, but the home secretary conceded the halt to extradition proceedings meant "he will probably not be tried anywhere."

When it took office, the Blair government undertook to use the British military as "a force for good" in the world as part of an "ethical foreign policy." In May, it put the concept into practice in the West African state of Sierra Leone, dispatching 1,000 paratroopers and marines and seven warships on a "humanitarian mission" to secure the capital, Freetown, against attacks by rebels. Although providing indirect help to a United Nations peacekeeping force, Britain declined to place its force under UN control. Within weeks, Britain withdrew all but a small number of its troops who remained behind to train Sierra Leone's own forces.

In August, 11 British servicemen were seized by a dissident rebel group, although five were quickly released. One British soldier and 25 rebels were killed in a successful attempt to free the prisoners. Despite Conservative Party criticism of British involvement in Sierra Leone, the Blair government continued its training mission. In October, the government sent a 100-man brigade headquarters to Freetown. Military analysts said the task force would effectively take control of Sierra Leone's army. British forces later staged training exercises off the coast of Sierra Leone. In addition, a 5,000-strong British rapid-reaction force was put at the disposal of the UN, should it be needed. These decisions appeared to commit British forces to Sierra Leone for the foreseeable future.

Throughout the year, Prime Minister Blair and Foreign Secretary Robin Cook continued to argue that the government was pro-Europe, despite its hesitation over adopting the euro. Pressure meanwhile mounted on Britain to accept closer European integration. Joschka Fischer, Germany's foreign minister, called for rapid moves toward a federal Europe. Jacques Chirac, the French president, proposed that France and Germany should spearhead a group of "pioneer states" that would set their own pace toward political integration.

On October 6, speaking in the Polish capital, Warsaw, Blair urged Europe to become a "superpower but not a superstate," and pressed for early enlargement of the EU by the addition of East European applicants. "The most important challenge for Europe is to wake up to the new reality," Blair said. "Europe is widening and deepening simultaneously. There will be more of us in the future, trying to do more." Analysts saw the speech as Blair's first serious attempt to sketch a British vision of Europe's future. Lord Hurd, the former Conservative foreign secretary, said Blair, "not before time," had "entered the real debate on the future of the European Union." That debate, Hurd said, was "not about how to abolish the national state, but how to get the nations to work together effectively where needed." At year-end, Prime Minister Blair and Foreign Secretary Cook made a series of speeches arguing that support for British membership of the EU was "patriotic." Senior government ministers conceded, however, that joining the euro was probably a long way off. At a summit of the EU in Nice, France, in December, Blair successfully defended Britain's right of veto over EU policy on tax, social security, and defense.

Other News. The Tate Modern, a new art museum, drew huge crowds, but the Blade of Light, a new, high-tech bridge across the River Thames to the museum was closed because it swayed dangerously. . . . A fatal train accident near London triggered urgent track repairs to hundreds of miles of Britain's privatized rail network. . . . Surgeons in Manchester separated Siamese twins, knowing that one of them was certain to die. . . . The European Convention on Human Rights was incorporated into British law, making it unnecessary for United Kingdom citizens to resort to a court in Strasbourg to defend their liberties.

ALEXANDER MACLEOD
"The Christian Science Monitor"

Greece

During 2000, Greece staged presidential and parliamentary elections. Improved relations with Turkey seemed to worsen as the year progressed. Finally, Greece was accepted into the European Union's Economic and Monetary Union (EMU), signaling the eventual end of the Greek drachma.

Politics. On February 8, the Greek Parliament elected Costis Stephanopoulos, 74, to his second five-year presidential term. His election—he garnered 269 of the 300 votes—was assured through the strong support of deputies from the ruling Panhellenic Socialist Movement (PASOK) party as well as from deputies of the leading opposition party, New Democracy (ND)

Prime Minister Costas Simitis and PASOK won April's general parliamentary elections by an incredibly slim margin, receiving 43.79% of the votes; Konstantine Karamanlis' ND took 42.73%. Still, Greece's proportional representation system gave PASOK control of Parliament with 157 seats to ND's 126.

Court Decision. In late November the European Court of Human Rights in Strasbourg supported the claims of former King Constantine II, his sister, Princess Irene, and his aunt, Princess Katherine, that the Greek government had taken their personal property, consisting of three estates, in violation of the European Convention of Human Rights. The court withheld judgment on compensation, and the Greek government claimed that taxes owed on the property exceeded its total value. Earlier, in June, the European Union (EU) Court of Justice had fined Greece for not following a 1992 judgment on environmental pollution.

Economy. Bolstered by winning the April general elections, the Simitis government emphasized the strength of Greece's developing economy, pushing for more privatization and foreign investments. In June, Greece was accepted as the 12th member of the EMU, with formal entry into the "Eurozone" set for Jan. 1, 2001. This meant that on Jan. 1, 2002, the euro would replace the Greek currency, the drachma. Greece's acceptance into the EMU was generally seen as something that would have an enormous impact on the economy.

Foreign Relations. In October, Greece was part of the North Atlantic Treaty Organization's (NATO's) war games in the Aegean Sea, which brought Greek troops onto Turkish soil for the first time in almost 80 years. Turkey subsequently took a stand that Greece could not fly over two Greek islands near Turkey, claiming that they were demilitarized. Greece disagreed that international pacts related to such demilitarization, and pulled all its armed forces from the exercise three days before it ended. Despite this controversy, the two countries appeared to seek a friendly connection, and within a short time the foreign ministers of both announced together that they would agree to "confidence-building measures" to improve relations. Disagreements relating to the island of Cyprus and rights in the Aegean Sea clearly made real rapprochement difficult. (*See* CYPRUS).

The Greek government continued to express concern about Yugoslavia's President Slobodan Milosevic's harsh, repressive policies. In September, Foreign Minister George Papandreou visited Belgrade, despite U.S. opposition, and urged Milosevic to hold fair, free elections. After Milosevic lost power in October, Papandreou was the first EU or NATO minister—Greece is a member of both—to go to Belgrade, arriving just hours before the inauguration of the new president, Vojislav Kostunica.

Greece remained friendly with Romania and Bulgaria. Although Greece continued to call its neighbor, Macedonia, the Former Yugoslav Republic of Macedonia (FYROM)—instead of just Macedonia—relations between the two countries were stable. Greek-Albanian relations were strained, particularly over Greek accusations that Albania had deliberately restricted the voting rights of its Greek Orthodox minority in local elections.

See also RELIGION—Orthodox Eastern.

GEORGE J. MARCOPOULOS, *Tufts University*

GREECE • Information Highlights

Official Name: Hellenic Republic.
Location: Southeastern Europe.
Area: 50,942 sq mi (131 940 km²).
Population (2000 est.): 10,601,527.
Chief Cities (1991 census): Athens, the capital, 772,072; Salonika, 383,967; Piraeus, 182,671.
Government: *Head of state,* Costis Stephanopoulos, president (took office March 1995). *Head of government,* Costas Simitis, prime minister (took office January 1996). *Legislature* (unicameral)—Parliament.
Monetary Unit: Drachma (366.6200 drachmas equal U.S.$1, Dec, 26, 2000).
Gross Domestic Product (1999 est. U.S.$): $149,200,000,000 (purchasing power parity).
Economic Indexes: *Consumer Prices* (1999, 1990 = 100): all items, 235.0; food, 211.6. *Industrial Production* (1999, 1990 = 100): 112.3.
Foreign Trade (1998 est. U.S.$): *Imports,* $27,700,000,000; *exports,* $12,400,000,000.

Housing

The level of activity in U.S. housing markets was well maintained in 2000 as a whole, although the pace of home sales and housing production dwindled to some degree as the year progressed. Interest-rate increases by the U.S. central bank (the Federal Reserve), along with the sapped strength of the U.S. economy, provoked year-end slides in major segments of the housing market. Despite this pattern, the rate of increase in single-family-house prices accelerated during the year and the home-ownership rate climbed to a new record.

On the international scene, economic recovery in several major regions supported stronger housing markets. The glaring exception was Japan, where production levels continued to languish.

Market Segments. Interest rates on home mortgages rose at the start of the year, reflecting a monetary tightening process begun by the Federal Reserve (the Fed) during the latter part of 1999. Despite rising costs for fixed-rate and adjustable-rate loans, the volume of activity in single-family housing markets rose at the start of 2000 as income and employment growth, along with unusually good weather conditions, spurred buyer demand. However, the Fed tightened early in 2000, driving yields on fixed-rate mortgages to 8.65% and pushing yields on one-year adjustable-rate loans to 7.25%. This monetary tightening took a toll on economic growth and housing demand as the year progressed, even though the Fed moved to the sidelines and mortgage rates subsided over the balance of the year.

For the year as a whole, sales of both new and previously occupied, conventionally built, single-family homes (excluding mobile homes) amounted to 5.86 million, down about 4% from the record set in 1999. In addition, about 375,000 custom homes were built on lots already owned by the occupants, including a sizable number of secondary residences or vacation homes. In total, builders started 1.26 million single-family homes in 2000, down about 6% from 1999. The year ended with roughly 320,000 unsold units in the hands of the builders, about the same as 1999.

The mobile-home market contracted dramatically, following a tough 1999. Shipments of mobile-home units from factories to dealers declined by nearly 30% in 2000, to a level of about 250,000 units, as the market remained glutted by overproduction during the 1996–98 period. Despite production cutbacks, the number of units on dealers' lots exceeded 100,000 by year's end.

The production of apartment units in multifamily structures (containing two or more units) surged to an annual rate of 395,000 units in the first quarter of 2000, but then contracted substantially. For the year as a whole, builders started about 330,000 multifamily units. Nearly 80% of the units built in 2000 were for the rental market, about the same proportion as in 1999, while the rest were built for sale as condominium or cooperative units. The overall rental-vacancy rate held around 8.1% in 2000, while the vacancy rate for large apartment buildings (having five or more units) edged above 9%.

Outlays for residential remodeling reached another record in 2000, rising to an estimated $152 billion. Owner-occupants continued to account for more than 75% of residential remodeling, as spending for remodeling of renter-occupied units remained below earlier highs.

Characteristics. The size of conventionally built single-family homes experienced an upward trend, as the median size of new units climbed to about 2,060 sq ft (191 m²) and the average size reached 2,280 sq ft (212 m²) by late in the year. More than 33% of new homes had at least four bedrooms; more than 50% had at least two- and one-half bathrooms; more than 80% had garages for two or more cars; 86% had central air conditioning; and about 75% of new homes had one or more fireplaces.

Mobile homes continued to increase in size and market value, despite the demand-supply imbalances that limited the volume of new production. The average size of new units was about 1,500 sq ft (139 m²). About 90% of the units had three or more bedrooms. The average price of new units was about $46,300, excluding site costs, compared with an average price of about $203,400 for new, conventionally built, single-family homes situated on lots.

The average size of apartments in new multifamily structures was about 1,100 sq ft (110 m²) in 2000, up from about 1,000 sq ft (93 m²) in 1990. Two-thirds of new units had at least two bedrooms, and more than 50% had two or more bathrooms—about the same proportions as during the late 1990s. Nearly 90% of all new apartment units were in buildings having three or fewer floors and the rest were in high-rise buildings.

Consumer Preferences. The National Association of Home Builders (NAHB) conducted an extensive survey of households to find out what prospective buyers wanted in new homes. The survey showed that consumers wanted a lot of bedrooms, but not necessarily for sleeping. Furthermore, the traditional living room fell out of favor, while traditional dining rooms made a comeback in people's preferences. Higher ceilings were in vogue, and 66% of respondents wanted ceiling heights of at least 9 ft (3 m) on the first floor. Laundry rooms, linen closets, and walk-in pantries ranked high with prospective home buyers. With respect to garages, 25% of survey respondents wanted garages capable of holding three or more cars. It was clear, however, that demand for this much space normally was for storage rather than for vehicles.

In NAHB's survey, many respondents said that amenities such as park areas, walking/jogging trails, lakes, playgrounds, and outdoor swimming pools would attract them to new communities, and a substantial share of respondents wanted to live in gated communities as well. In fact, an emerging trend was to include community facilities within new developments in the United States, which necessitated the formation of community associations to maintain and operate the facilities. Among owners living in homes built in 1997 or later, nearly 33% were members of community associations, compared with only 7% for all occupants of single-family homes.

Prices, Ownership Patterns, and Policy. House prices appreciated across the United States in 2000, rising at a much faster pace than overall inflation in goods and services, and generating sizable increases in the real value of homeowner equity. By the third quarter of the year, the national average of house prices had risen at a year-over-year rate of 7.3%. Prices were up substantially across the nation. At the state level, Massachusetts, New Hampshire, Rhode Island, California, and Colorado led the pack, while the weakest price performance was recorded in Alaska, North Dakota, and Utah. No state experienced actual price declines.

Falling interest rates and growing homeowner equity both encouraged a strong wave of mortgage refinancings late in 2000. Indeed, refinancings approached 50% of all home mortgages applied for near year's end, as homeowners sought to lower their mortgage rates and convert some of their accumulated housing equity into cash.

The U.S. home-ownership rate rose to a record 67.7% by the third quarter of 2000.

This dramatic success reflected gains in home ownership for most racial, ethnic, and economic groups—although not all the numbers glowed. While the home-ownership rate for white households exceeded 71% in the third quarter, the rates for both blacks and Hispanics were below 46%. Furthermore, home ownership among families with below-median incomes was only 52%, compared with nearly 82% for families at or above the median incomes in their areas. These home-ownership differentials, as well as the persistence of affordability issues facing lower-income rental households, left serious housing-policy issues for the incoming administration of George W. Bush.

The U.S. housing-policy structure was improved at the end of 2000 when legislation was passed and signed to increase volume caps and install inflation indexing for two key programs—the low-income housing tax credit, and tax-exempt financing for affordable rental housing and moderate-income home ownership.

The housing-policy platforms of both political parties were quite positive during the 2000 presidential campaigns. Neither side proposed weakening housing-policy pillars, such as the tax deductibility of interest on home mortgages, and both sides proposed policies to bolster home ownership and assist low-income renters.

International Comparisons. Major industrialized countries generally posted good economic performances in 2000, with the notable exception of Japan. Furthermore, large parts of the developing world turned upward after slipping into recession during 1998–99, particularly in Asia and Latin America. These strengthening economic foundations bolstered housing markets across many parts of the globe.

In Japan, economic growth remained below 2% in 2000, following recession conditions in 1998–99, and housing starts held around 1.20 million units—quite low by historical standards. The real value of residential construction expenditures by the Japanese private sector grew by less than 1%.

Residential investment grew throughout Western Europe, especially in France and Italy. Housing starts in Canada reached an estimated 155,000 units in 2000—the highest level in more than a decade. Private residential investment grew by an estimated 3.2%, down from an exceedingly strong pace in 1999, but still good by historical standards.

DAVID F. SEIDERS
National Association of Home Builders

Human Rights

The global movement for human rights gained in 2000 through various initiatives.

UN Global Compact. At the invitation of United Nations (UN) Secretary-General Kofi Annan, business, labor, and civic leaders met at UN headquarters on July 26 to commit their organizations to implement and promote a "Global Compact" on human rights, labor standards, and environmental practices as formulated in nine basic principles drawn from the Universal Declaration of Human Rights and other UN documents. Annan said the chief executive officers (CEOs) from nearly 50 multinational corporations had a key role "to ensure that the global market is embedded in broadly shared values and practices that reflect global social needs, and that all the world's people share the benefits of globalization." In establishing a UN Global Compact Office, Annan, who heads a UN system that is predominantly governmental, signaled the importance that private-sector leadership has in making progress on human rights.

Russia and China. At its spring meeting in Geneva, the UN Commission on Human Rights, with representatives of 53 governments, took the unusual step of rebuking a permanent member of the UN Security Council, Russia. By a 25-to-7 vote, with 19 abstentions, the commission criticized Russian atrocities committed in Chechnya. "It shows that no one is immune from scrutiny," said Joanna Weschler, UN representative of Human Rights Watch (HRW).

During the same meeting, however, efforts to censure another Security Council member, China, eluded the commission for the tenth straight year. By a 22-to-18 vote, with 12 abstentions, the body decided not to discuss a U.S. resolution criticizing China's human-rights violations, despite Madeleine Albright's appearance before the commission—the first by a U.S. secretary of state—to plead for the resolution's adoption.

Globalization. In August the UN commission's Subcommission on the Promotion and Protection of Human Rights adopted a report, *Globalization and Its Impact on the Full Enjoyment of Human Rights*, charging that the World Trade Organization (WTO), the World Bank (WB), and the International Monetary Fund (IMF) pursue "grossly unfair and even prejudiced" policies harmful to poor countries. Sixteen of the subcommission's 26 members are from developing countries, The report, which would be presented to the parent Human Rights Commission at its 2001 session, calls for "a radical review of the whole system of trade liberalization," rejects linking trade to human rights, and urges, instead, that "human-rights principles are integrated into the rule-making process" from the outset.

Punishing Traffickers. Bringing women and children across borders and forcing them into prostitution or sweatshop labor—"trafficking"— is a worldwide human-rights problem, according to testimony before a U.S. congressional committee. Estimates of the number of victims vary tremendously, with a high of 2 million. In October, U.S. federal legislation was enacted to penalize, by up to 20 years' to life imprisonment, people who smuggle women and children into the United States for involuntary servitude.

A top U.N. anticrime official, Pino Arlacchi, earlier in the year had called trafficking the fastest-growing business of organized crime, involving mostly victims from Southeast Asia, Eastern Europe, and the former Soviet Union.

Judicial Outreach. U.S. courts increasingly were agreeing to hear lawsuits involving human-rights violations occurring outside U.S. territory. In a case filed in May, several thousand Chinese men, whom Mitsubishi and other Japanese companies had used as forced laborers during World War II, were suing for compensation and an apology. Their class-action suit came under a 1999 California law permitting claims, even by foreigners, for forced-labor violations committed by foreign corporations with subsidiaries in the United States. The group hopes to repeat the successful settlement of U.S. lawsuits brought by Holocaust survivors against Swiss banks and European businesses accused of profiting from the Holocaust.

Saudi Arabia. Amnesty International's annual campaign focusing on one country was dedicated to raising awareness about arbitrary arrest, torture, amputations, and other gross human-rights violations in Saudi Arabia. The suffering of the Saudi people, Amnesty charged, "is perpetuated and hidden by a system based on secrecy and fear, and is largely ignored by the world's governments." According to Amnesty officials, even the UN Human Rights Commission has failed to criticize Saudi Arabia because oil-dependent nations such as the United States do not want to offend the kingdom's rulers.

ROBERT A. SENSER
Editor, Human Rights for Workers

Hungary

In 2000, the nation celebrated 1,000 years of statehood by moving the historic Holy Crown of Hungary's founder and first king, Saint Stephen, from the National Museum to parliament; electing a new president; continuing to make steady economic progress; and remaining on track for European Union (EU) membership.

Political Developments. In June, Ferenc Madl, a law professor and former culture minister under Jozsef Antall, was elected by parliament as the country's new president. He replaced Arpád Goncz.

Prime Minister Viktor Orban had to deal with several different scandals among government officials. The environmental minister resigned in June after being criticized for alleged financial wrongdoings and a lack of professionalism as the head of the ministry. Investigations also continued into alleged police corruption, organized-criminal involvement, and also high-level political links to illicit oil deals during the previous few years. The oppositionist Socialist Party submitted a petition for an extraordinary parliamentary session to examine the affair. Nonetheless, the government's popularity remained steady throughout the year.

The ruling coalition was criticized at home and abroad for establishing broadcast-media supervisory boards that were made up only of government-nominated members. The leading coalition party, FIDESZ, blamed opposition parties for fail-

HUNGARY • Information Highlights

Official Name: Republic of Hungary.
Location: East-central Europe.
Area: 35,919 sq mi (93 030 km²).
Population (2000 est.): 10,138,844.
Chief Cities (Jan. 1, 1999 est.): Budapest, the capital, 1,838,753; Debrecen, 205,032; Miskolc, 176,629.
Government: *Head of state,* Ferenc Madl, president (elected June 6, 2000). *Head of government,* Viktor Orban, prime minister (took office July 1998). *Legislature* (unicameral)—National Assembly.
Monetary Unit: Forint (289.04 forints equal U.S.$1, Dec. 21, 2000).
Gross Domestic Product (1999 est. U.S.$): $79,400,000,000 (purchasing power parity).
Economic Indexes (1999, 1990 = 100): *Consumer Prices,* all items, 569.5; food, 493.7. *Industrial Production,* 125.2.
Foreign Trade (1999 U.S.$): *Imports,* $27,920,000,000; *exports,* $24,947,000,000.

ing to propose their own candidates to the boards. Meanwhile, the Socialist Party, trade unions, and several nongovernmental organizations demanded an independent supervisory board for the broadcast media.

Economic Progress. Hungary's economic performance continued to be very impressive. Gross domestic product (GDP) was projected to grow by about 5.5% for the year, and the country remained the top recipient of direct foreign investment. Under an ambitious new plan presented by Economics Minister Gyorgy Matolcsy, $1.6 billion would be allotted for a major highway project to promote tourism and trade as well as to construct 35,000–40,000 new homes each year. The government also approved a National Employment Action Plan aimed at creating full employment. The plan included infrastructure projects, investment incentives, and job-creation subsidies, and gave priority to employment opportunities for Romanies (Gypsies), the long-term unemployed, and the disabled.

In a move toward European Union (EU) integration, the Hungarian currency was pegged to the euro. According to an annual report of the United Nations Conference on Trade and Development (UNCTAD), Hungary's economy was by far the most open among all the Central and East European countries.

©Attila Kisbenedek/AFP/Corbis

In January 2000, then Hungarian President Arpád Goncz and his wife admired the Holy Crown of Hungary's first king, St. Stephen, as it is moved to parliament from the National Museum.

According to EU Commissioner for Enlargement Günter Verheugen, negotiations with Budapest on EU accession seemed to be proceeding successfully with Hungary. It was expected to be among the first to join the Union, with a planned accession date of Jan. 1, 2003. The country met most of the political and economic criteria for EU membership, but it still needed reforms in environmental protection, health insurance, transport, justice, internal security, and agriculture to fully qualify.

Environmental Disputes. Hungarian authorities sought major compensation for the leakage of large quantities of cyanide from a Romanian mine into the Somes and Tisza rivers. Hungary initiated lawsuits against the Australian-Romanian joint venture Aurul as well as against its Australian co-owner, Esmeralda, claiming extensive ecological and economic damage along Hungary's second-largest river network.

JANUSZ BUGAJSKI
Center for Strategic and International Studies

Iceland

Iceland's economy slowed in 2000, in response to tighter fiscal and monetary policies. Export growth was expected to be negative in 2001, as lower government quotas restricted quantities of fish available to the fishing industry, pulling the nation's gross domestic product (GDP) expansion down. A Foreign Ministry study of Iceland and the European Union (EU) stated that Iceland would retain control of its fisheries policy if the country joined the EU, but a membership application was not on the agenda.

Politics. Alliance, the left-of-center electoral coalition consisting of the Social Dem-

ocratic Party, the People's Alliance, the Women's List, and remnants of the dissolved People's Movement merged in May. The People's Movement re-formed under the same name, with Ossur Skarphedinsson as its leader. The party is expected to move toward the center of Icelandic politics. Meanwhile, Foreign Minister Halldór Ásgrímsson's Progressive Party—formed to challenge Prime Minister Davíd Oddsson's Independence Party—made little headway in the polls. One major challenge to the government remained the engineering of a soft landing in the Icelandic economy, rather than a full stop.

Economy. In October, the unemployment rate fell to a nine-year low of 0.9%, which is one of the world's lowest recorded rates. It signaled that the Icelandic economy was still overheating, an assessment that was supported by an inflation rate above 5%. Fiscal and monetary tightening were expected to slow the economy from about 4% in 2000 to 2.5% in 2001.

Private consumption was expected to stagnate, and the fisheries sector was expected to contract by 7%, due to lower fish quotas. In a potential blockbuster agreement, Landsbanki Islands and Bunadarbanki Islands initiated merger talks to create Iceland's largest bank.

Foreign Policy. In 2000, Foreign Minister Ásgrímsson's Progressive Party organized a working committee to study Icelandic membership in the EU. Depending on the findings of the report, the party could be the first from Iceland to recommend membership. The fishing sector accounts for more than half of Iceland's gross domestic product (GDP), and would be a priority in any negotiation with the EU. Accordingly, a Foreign Ministry study concluded that Iceland, as an EU member, should keep control of its fisheries policy. That suggestion eliminated the major economic argument of opponents of EU membership, including Prime Minister Oddsson.

Iceland protested that the British government's promises to reduce the number of discharges of radioactive material into the sea—from the Sellafield nuclear-reprocessing plant—were just not enough to prevent damage to the fishing stock. Iceland wanted the plant closed down. The British government refused to do this, and insisted discharges would be slashed to almost zero over a period of two decades.

LEIF BECK FALLESEN, *Editor in Chief "Boersen," Copenhagen*

ICELAND • Information Highlights

Official Name: Republic of Iceland.
Location: North Atlantic Ocean.
Area: 39,768 sq mi (103 000 km²).
Population (2000 est.): 276,365.
Chief City (December 1, 1998): Reykjavík, the capital, 108,351.
Government: *Head of state,* Ólafur Ragnar Grímsson, president (took office August 1996). *Head of government,* David Oddsson, prime minister (took office April 1991). *Legislature* (unicameral)—Althing.
Monetary Unit: Króna (87.095 krónur equal U.S.$1, Dec. 21, 2000).
Gross Domestic Product (1999 est. U.S.$): $6,420,000,000.
Economic Index (1999, 1990 = 100): *Consumer Prices,* all items, 130.3; food, 121.1.
Foreign Trade (1999 U.S.$): *Imports,* $2,502,000,000; *exports,* $2,013,000,000.

India

Three new states were created in India during 2000. The government and courts stepped up efforts against corruption, as three top political leaders were convicted. Drought and floods contributed to an economic slowdown. And for several weeks in July, the country was caught up in winning the release of a retired film star, kidnapped by an infamous bandit.

New States. Three new states—Chhatisgarh, Jharkhand, and Uttaranchal—were created, bringing the total to 28. Chhatisgarh was carved out of tribal areas of Madhya Pradesh state in central India; Jharkhand consisted of the tribal areas of Bihar state; and Uttaranchal was made up of the hill areas of Uttar Pradesh state. Each of these territories had seen strong movements to win autonomy since 1990. Under the Indian constitution, the creation of a new state requires approval by the legislature of the state from which the new state is to be created, along with parliamentary consent. Although Madhya Pradesh, Bihar, and Uttar Pradesh had all given approval in the past, parliamentary consent was given only in 2000. There were fears in the new tribal states that violence might erupt if indigenous people retaliated against "foreigners," who dominated the economic and political life of the areas and were seen as exploiters. In both Chhatisgarh and Jharkhand states, security forces were brought in to keep the peace. The Bharatiya Janata Party (BJP) and its allies formed the governments of Jharkhand and Uttaranchal, while the Congress Party took over in Chhatisgarh.

Chhatisgarh and Jharkhand began with a strong chance to improve the well-being of their people, as both states were deemed rich in natural resources. Chhatisgarh boasts diamond and gold mines, potential forest products, and other minerals. It is one of a few areas of India with a surplus of electricity. Jharkhand contains 30% of the country's mineral wealth, including the only source of its nuclear-grade uranium. Uttaranchal's future depends heavily on tourism and the possibility of further developing hydroelectric power. Agroforestry also could provide income for its people, but would require considerable investments in reforestation of large sections of the Himalayas. Uttaranchal is the poorest state and least populated of the three.

The Parties. The BJP-dominated National Democratic Alliance (NDA) endured four major cabinet reshuffles during 2000. Partially these were due to attempts to keep the coalition intact by incorporating members of the smaller parties. The Telegu Desam of the south, Shivsena of Maharashtra, and the Trinamool Congress of Bengal showed signs of breaking away. Each of these parties had met with the Nationalist Congress Party (NCP) about possible future legislative and electoral alliances.

Perhaps more important, internal problems and public-image concerns pushed the BJP to try and sideline its own religious fundamentalists—particularly the Rashtriya Swayamsevak Sangh (RSS) wing. Faced with election losses in traditional strongholds such as Uttar Pradesh, splits in state parties along RSS and non-RSS lines, and a lack of strong electoral support in other states outside the Hindi-speaking north, the BJP tried to overcome its "saffron" Hindu-only image. In November several old-time party stalwarts were replaced by younger members known for broader outlooks and subject-matter expertise. Party leaders continued to call for the creation of a new, inclusive character to bring in low-caste Hindus and Muslims. Instead of the push for Hindutva, the party talked of Indian nationalism. It stated there was no intention of forcing beliefs and practices on minority groups. Prime Minister Atal Bihari Vajpayee went further to state that his government accepted and respected the diversity of India. The one exception was to change Christian divorce laws to give women the same rights and grounds in seeking divorce as men—a move supported by Protestant and women's groups, but opposed by the

---

INDIA • Information Highlights

Official Name: Republic of India.
Location: South Asia.
Area: 1,269,340 sq mi (3 287 590 km²).
Population (2000 est.): 1,014,003,817.
Chief Cities (1991 census): New Delhi, the capital, 301,297; Mumbai (Bombay), 9,925,891; Delhi, 7,206,704; Calcutta, 4,399,819.
Government: *Head of state,* Kocheril Raman Narayanan, president (elected July 1997). *Head of government,* Atal Bihari Vajpayee, prime minister (sworn in on March 19, 1998). *Legislature*—Sansad (Parliament): Rajya Sabha (Council of States) and Lok Sabha (People's Assembly).
Monetary Unit: Rupee (46.7038 rupees equal U.S.$1, Dec. 27, 2000).
Gross Domestic Product (1999 est. U.S.$): $1,805,000,000,000 (purchasing power parity).
Economic Indexes (1999, 1990 = 100): *Consumer Prices,* all items, 228.0; food, 232.5. *Industrial Production,* 168.5.
Foreign Trade (1999 U.S.$): *Imports,* $44,889,000,000; *exports,* $36,310,000,000.

In New Delhi in March 2000, U.S. President Bill Clinton and his daughter Chelsea were greeted by India's Prime Minister Atal Bihari Vajpayee. India's development of nuclear weapons, trade, and Kashmir were major issues between the two nations.

NDA together. After months of rumors about cancer and other possible ailments, his doctors announced he suffered from arthritic knees and had undergone a knee-replacement operation in October.

The Congress Party continued to struggle with its political identity and leadership. After its poor showing in the 1999 elections, members debated over programs and electoral alliances. In the spring, several party leaders criticized the BJP's tactics and performance in the 1999 armed conflict with Pakistan, in the Kargil sector of Kashmir. They accused the BJP of a lack of training and resources for India's troops. Later in the fall, Sonia Gandhi, the Congress Party president, surprised observers by criticizing the government for proceeding too rapidly with economic liberalization. Specifically, she objected to the potential opening up of the insurance industry to international investment, privatization of state-owned enterprises, and import-tariff removal on a range of consumer goods—all, she said, would harm the overall national interests of India.

A small but revealing challenge to her party presidency emerged in the fall's party elections. Although Gandhi was reelected handily, the candidacy of Jitendra Prasada from Uttar Pradesh was the first challenge to the Nehru-Gandhi family in the party's history. In view of the continued machinations within the ruling NDA, any challenges to the Gandhi leadership were of interest in the event of an NDA split.

Leftist parties attempted to redefine their role and ideology in the wake of the decline of Marxist parties worldwide. Younger Marxists appeared more comfortable with some forms of liberalization, especially if deregulation could lower bureaucratic corruption.

Corruption. It was a watershed year in the government's fight against corruption. Former Congress Prime Minister P.V. Narasimha Rao, former Congress cabinet member Buta Singh, and former Chief Ministers Laloo Prasad Yadav and Jayalalitha Jayaram were all convicted on various grounds of corruption. The charges were

Indian-Catholic religious hierarchy. The BJP/NDA alliance also promised to pursue the issue of women's representation in Parliament—another controversial issue with conservatives—stating it would introduce a bill during the winter 2001 session of the legislature. Prior to the introduction of any proposed bill, Prime Minister Vajpayee promised to convene a multiparty group to reach a consensus on the issue.

Parliamentary opposition members maintained accusations of the communal tendencies of the BJP. For three days in early December, the Lok Sabha was in an uproar over members' calls for the resignation of three BJP leaders—including Home Minister L.K. Advani—who were felt to have supported and perhaps instigated the destruction of the mosque at Ayodhya in 1992. There was a pending court case that implicated Advani, Human Resources Development Minister Murli Manohar Joshi, and Sports Minister Uma Bharati in the mosque's destruction. Plans continued on the part of several fundamentalist groups to build a Hindu temple on the same site. Prime Minister Vajpayee contended the construction of a temple was an expression of "nationalist sentiment," which alarmed opposition members. He reiterated, however, that neither he nor BJP leadership supported the destruction of the mosque.

Prime Minister Vajpayee's health concerned coalition members and observers alike, due to his critical role in keeping the largely related to bribes and kickbacks from several official programs. Rao, Singh, and Jayaram received sentences of three years imprisonment each. In late 2000, all remained free on bail pending appeals.

Observers felt that while these convictions illustrated the government's commitment to cleaning up politics, there remained a lot more to be done; namely, the attack on bureaucratic corruption. Reports of police corruption—long prevalent in many jurisdictions—led the New Delhi police commissioner to alert his officers and constables that no brutality or corruption would be tolerated. India's Supreme Court ruled in September that any member of the police forces could be prosecuted and convicted if torture were used against suspected criminals or prisoners. Previously there had been a six-month limit for complaints to be filed, but the ruling struck down the time limitation in torture-related cases.

In a melodrama befitting the best of India's film industry, a retired Indian film star, Rajkumar, was kidnapped by a famous bandit, Veerappan, in late July. Protests and demonstrations were held by fans throughout the south, where the governments of Tamil Nadu tried to negotiate Rajkumar's release over the next several months. Veerappan's main demand was the release of his jailed gang members in both states, along with other prisoners considered part of the Tamil Tigers, involved in a separatist movement in Sri Lanka. The states agreed to the terms but were blocked by the Indian Supreme Court. Rajkumar, however, was set free in November without gaining anyone's release. Veerappan, wanted in at least 100 murder cases, has expressed sympathy for Tamil nationalists and makes a living by elephant poaching and sandalwood smuggling.

Religious and Caste Violence. Church bombings and violent attacks on Christian clergy marred the religious landscape. Christian leaders blamed the central government for creating an atmosphere in which religious fanatics could attack other groups with impunity. In October, during the 75th-anniversary celebrations of the fundamentalist RSS, group leaders openly criticized Muslims and Christians for having given up their Hindu heritage, questioned their loyalties to India, and forcibly converted low-caste and poor people. Foreign pressure—including U.S. accusations that the BJP was linked to Hindu extremist groups—forced the government to deny the charges. It also renewed the hunt for those responsible for

violent attacks. Twenty-three people were apprehended by October.

Perhaps feeling intense pressure from the BJP's new secular initiatives, members of two other Hindu fundamentalist groups—the Vishwa Hindu Parishad (VHP) and the Bajrang Dal—in November marched on one of India's most famous Islamic historic sites, the Qutab Minar complex in New Delhi. The groups insisted on praying to Hindu deities whose archaeological remains were buried under the existing mosques. Although police kept them away, demonstrators vowed to return monthly to try again to pray.

In June, violence escalated in the state of Bihar. Retaliating against higher-caste Hindus for killing low-caste farmers, a group of approximately 50 men killed at least 11 people. Maoist rebel groups had worked for several decades organizing the poor, low-caste, rural population against perceived exploitation by upper-caste landowners and mine operators. Sporadic violence continued throughout the year.

Environment and Climate. In October, India's Supreme Court ruled that work should continue on the controversial Sardar Sarovar dam, spanning the Narmada River in Gujarat state. Environmentalists had demonstrated and used legal action to halt the construction of what they felt was a project with a destructive impact on the area's ecology. The court ruled that the potential benefits, including increased food production through irrigation, outweighed the ecological impacts, further noting that sufficient safeguards existed to protect the environment from harm.

In another controversial ruling in January, the Supreme Court ordered thousands of polluting industrial units closed or moved out of Delhi. Known as one of the more polluted cities in the world, Delhi had experienced an enormous rise in respiratory diseases and cancer over the past several decades. As city officials moved in November to enforce the decision, millions of demonstrators turned out in protest. The city, caught between the law and political reality, retreated from making owners evacuate immediately.

In a year of extraordinary natural disasters, India faced both drought and extensive flooding. While the western states reeled under a second year of water shortages, the east faced a devastating monsoon. In Calcutta alone, more than 55,000 people were left homeless. Between Bangladesh and

Drought, including in the state of Rajasthan (above), as well as floods contributed to India's economic downturn in 2000. Economic growth fell below the projected 7% range.

eastern India, more than 11 million were estimated to have been marooned by flood waters. Thousands of acres of crops, accompanying livestock, and millions of houses were damaged or destroyed. The state governments involved, as well as the central government, came under attack by opposition groups for not predicting these disasters or responding more effectively.

The Economy.   Contrary to optimistic forecasts, the Indian economy showed clear signs of a slowdown by year's end. Instead of a projected growth of between 6% and 7%, economists predicted growth of perhaps less than 5%. Both climate and increased oil prices were culprits, while some observers thumbed slow progress on the liberalization front.

The agricultural economy showed sluggishness due only partially to the climate. Without increased irrigated acreage, spread of the hybrid varieties was impossible. The continuing increased consumption of freshwater, however, raised the specter of severe future shortages. Some felt the answer lay in the dissemination of genetically modified (GM) varieties of grains that could boost production and nutrition. Massive political protests against GM crops, particularly in central and southern areas of the countries, indicated their acceptance remains far off.

Kashmir.   After 1999's bloody fighting in the Kargil sector of Kashmir, 2000 began with cautious optimism about new peace talks between Pakistan and India. The Hizbul Mujaheddin, a local Kashmiri insurgent group seeking independence, called for a cease-fire in July, and began meetings with Indian officials. Hopes faded shortly thereafter as Pakistan-based guerrilla groups wanting to incorporate Kashmir into Pakistan denounced the peace initiatives and renewed violent attacks. India insisted that Pakistan must stop supporting insurgent groups and curb their activities before any further meaningful dialogue could occur. Late in the year, India called for a truce during the Muslim holy month of Ramadan. The truce was welcomed by the Hizbul faction but opposed by several Pakistan-based groups, and violence continued in the province. In December, however, India and Pakistan announced steps to reduce tensions along the border in Kashmir. Prime Minister Vajpayee told Parliament he would extend a unilateral cease-fire in Kashmir into 2001, for at least a month, and begin "exploratory steps" to pursue peace talks with Pakistan. Then Pakistan's army announced a partial withdrawal of troops along the border, indicating that peace might not be an impossible goal.

International Affairs.   Landmark visits by U.S. President Clinton to India in March and by Prime Minister Vajpayee to Washington in October ushered in what many hoped would be a new era of cordial relations between India and the United States. The development of nuclear weapons, trade liberalization, and Kashmir remained issues. Clinton stressed the necessity for peaceful relations on the subcontinent, while recognizing, though, that there was little the outside world could do unless India and Pakistan reached agreement.

There was an increase in sentiments in Nepal, Sri Lanka, and Bangladesh that India was using its overwhelming economic power to negotiate trade-liberalization agreements within the auspices of the South Asian Association for Regional Cooperation (SAARC) to its own advantage. The Indian government's decision to invite Gen. Maung Aye of Myanmar's ruling military junta as a state guest in November raised consternation in India and among its neighbors.

ARUNA NAYYAR MICHIE
Kansas State University

Indonesia

Indonesia's new democratic government experienced a stormy 2000. Little progress was made toward achieving political stability or economic recovery.

Politics. There was no honeymoon period for Abdurrahman Wahid, who became president in 1999. His government's responses to the multiple political, economic, and security challenges facing Indonesia were largely ineffective. As a result, the government's authority and President Wahid's personal popularity steadily eroded. Indonesia's political disarray acted as a brake on economic recovery, which in turn spurred further political conflict. Wahid's problems were compounded by questions of his fitness for office. Eccentric and careless policy statements by Wahid, who is blind and stroke-weakened, as well as allegations of new corruption scandals undermined his credibility with the people.

Democracy advocates accused the government of lagging in its pursuit of fundamental reform. To his detractors, Wahid's failure was symbolized by the collapse of the prosecution of former President Suharto for corruption. After months of legal wrangling, and the defendant's failure to appear in court, the presiding judge dismissed the case in September because of the former president's age and health. Wahid had promised to pardon Suharto if he were convicted.

The People's Consultative Assembly (MPR), Indonesia's highest legislative body, met in August amid calls for Wahid's removal from office. MPR Speaker Amien Rais was Wahid's fiercest critic. Wahid sought to mollify his parliamentary critics by reorganizing his government and promising to delegate real day-to-day authority to Vice-President Megawati Sukarnoputri. She leads the Indonesian Democratic Party-Struggle (PDI-P), the largest party in the parliament. Many of Wahid's opponents thought that Megawati should have been president. President Wahid's actions after the MPR adjourned made clear his reluctance to share power in any meaningful way with the vice-president. The cabinet was reshuffled on August 23. By locking out the PDI-P and the second-largest party, Golkar, the president increased his political isolation from the legislature, promising continuing political strife.

The political struggle in Jakarta took place against the background of a nationwide breakdown of law and order, ethnic violence, and threatened secessions. In the rebellious Aceh province, a humanitarian cease-fire between the government and the Free Aceh Movement (GAM) was signed in June and extended for three months in September. Continued killings punctuated the cease-fire. Even as new talks between GAM and the government were scheduled for Geneva in November, nearly 400,000 Acehnese, a tenth of the province's population, massed in Aceh's capital to demand an independence referendum. Pro-Indonesian militias controlled West Timor's border with United Nations (UN)-administered East Timor and terrorized the East Timor refugee population. The government seemed unwilling or incapable of halting the disintegration of the nation's social and political integrity, further undermining its standing at home and abroad.

At the end of the first year of Wahid's constitutional five-year term, his opponents threatened renewed efforts to impeach or force him from office. With characteristic insouciance, the president shrugged off the criticism as an indication that a healthy, lively democracy was taking root in Indonesia.

Economy. The economy of Indonesia remained the worst in Southeast Asia. The pace of its recovery from the "Crash of '97" badly lagged behind the rest of the region. Real growth of the gross domestic product (GDP) was barely at 4%, less than half that of Malaysia. The GDP growth figure was not really indicative, since it was driven in part by high global oil prices. The Indonesian currency lost a quarter of its value over the year, and the stock market dropped 40%. Investor confidence continued to be shaken by political instability and spreading ethnic violence. The bombing of the Jakarta

---

INDONESIA • Information Highlights

Official Name: Republic of Indonesia.
Location: Southeast Asia.
Area: 741,097 sq mi (1 919 440 km²).
Population (2000 est.): 224,784,210.
Chief Cities (Dec. 31, 1996, est.): Jakarta, the capital, 9,341,400; Surabaya, 2,743,400; Bandung, 2,429,000; Medan, 1,942,000.
Government: *Head of state and government,* Abdurrahman Wahid, president (appointed October 1999). *Legislature* (unicameral)—House of Representatives.
Monetary Unit: Rupiah (9,490.0 rupiahs equal U.S.$1, Dec. 27, 2000).
Gross Domestic Product (1999 est. U.S.$): $610,000,000,000 (purchasing power parity).
Economic Indexes (1999, 1998 = 100): *Consumer Prices* all items, 120.5; food, 125.0. *Industrial Production* (1998, 1990 = 100): 112.8.
Foreign Trade (1999 U.S.$): *Imports,* $24,004,000,000; *exports,* $48,665,000,000.

The struggle between the Indonesia government and the rebellious Aceh province continued during 2000. In June, Acehnese protested outside parliament, demanding an independence referendum and the resignations of all Acehnese from the legislature.

Stock Exchange in September was symptomatic. The August cabinet reshuffle brought in a new economic team. But a Wahid crony—who had previously failed a "fit and proper" test to head Bank Indonesia—was brought on as minister of finance; the appointment was not the hoped-for signal that a substantive improvement in managing recovery and growth could be expected.

Looming over the economy was a huge debt burden. Indonesia's external debt was nearly $120 billion. The country spent nearly 6% of its GDP to service the debt. Chafing under International Monetary Fund (IMF) oversight, the government sent confusing and ambiguous signals regarding its commitment to the macroeconomic and monetary-policy reforms imposed as a condition of external assistance. In October the international consortium of Indonesia's major donor institutions and nations, the Consultative Group for Indonesia (CGI), met in Tokyo. The CGI pledged $4.8 billion in new loans to Indonesia. This would support the nearly $6 billion deficit in the 2001 budget. This also was the irony of the Indonesian debt trap: New borrowing pays for old borrowing, and the debt overhang increases.

Foreign Policy. In his first year in office, President Wahid visited 50 countries. Australia was one country he did not visit. Scheduled visits by the president and members of his cabinet were postponed as deliberate snubs. The coolness stemmed from continuing anger in Jakarta about Australia's role in East Timor, and from suspicions about Australia's intentions in West Papua. Although widely criticized at home for his extensive travels, Wahid defended his itineraries in terms of mobilizing support and keeping Indonesia visible on the international scene. The wrong kind of visibility dominated, however. Ethnic cleansing in the Moluccas and the terrorism against East Timorese refugees in West Timor by uncontrolled militia groups outraged the international community. Indonesia, in turn, warned against intervention. The dismal record was capped in September by the brutal killings of three UN aid workers by militia elements in Atambua, West Timor.

U.S.-Indonesian relations deteriorated during 2000. Relatively outspoken comments by the U.S. ambassador on human rights, corruption, and the pace of reform brought Indonesian charges of meddling in domestic affairs. Indonesia's new minister of defense launched a media attack against the envoy. The situation worsened in the aftermath of the breakdown of the Middle East peace process. Indonesian Muslim groups attacked the United States for support of Israel. In late October, the U.S. embassy closed down for two weeks because of threats, and the U.S. State Department issued warnings against travel to Indonesia.

DONALD E. WEATHERBEE
University of South Carolina

Industrial Production

U.S. industrial production grew strongly in 2000, benefiting from technological advances that, with the exception of energy, allowed mines, factories, and utilities to stay within capacity and cost limitations. Production gains moderated in the second half of the year, however, as the pace of economic expansion slowed to what was widely foreseen as a soft landing. Still, production late in the year averaged more than 5.7% higher than 1999. The greatest early strength was in the manufacturing sector, especially production of business equipment.

It was hardly a year without challenges. The ability of utilities to supply energy to a decade-long economic expansion was tested, especially late in the fall, when winter oil supplies ran low and natural-gas suppliers had an unexpected increase in demand. Defense and space-equipment production remained in a slump, 40% below 1990.

Innovation, a characteristic of the high-tech age, was especially evident in the development of clean energy. Billions of dollars were spent researching and developing alternative fuels, most significantly fuel-cell technology, a method of producing energy with little residue through noncombustible chemical action. Some of the largest companies—including General Electric (GE), United Technologies, and automakers—were involved in the quest, amid predictions that within the decade, such energy sources would be used to power automobiles and to heat and cool homes and large commercial structures. Innovation was just as evident in managing industrial operations. The use of outsourcing, or contract manufacturing, grew among companies seeking to benefit from the expertise of particular specialists while avoiding expensive investments in plant and equipment.

New concepts, methods, and engineering were readily accepted in manufacturing. While manufacturing employment of 18,363,000 in September was slightly lower than a year earlier, production in the sector was averaging nearly 5% higher. The contrast was even greater when measured from 1991; with employment remaining essentially the same, production had soared more than 60%.

The major contribution to the performance came from the manufacture of electrical machinery, indicative of the speed with which new concepts were accepted by individuals and assimilated into the production process. By fall the level at which such products were produced and used ran 25% higher than in January, and the Federal Reserve's measurement of electrical-machinery production was more than five times the level of 1992.

Energy Strains. At times the demands for power in a continuing economic boom and the slow process of bringing new production facilities on-line led to serious shortages and threats of shortages. Some blamed deregulation of the industry, others the hot summer, and still others the lack of tankers to move crude oil. Many Americans blamed production restraints of the Organization of Petroleum Exporting Countries (OPEC), the international oil cartel, and critics in the industry put the onus on environmentalists who opposed construction of new plants. Some simply attributed the strains to population growth. But all agreed that the long economic expansion, primarily in the United States but to a lesser extent in other industrial nations, was a primary factor in the shortages, and in the price of oil remaining more than $30 a barrel. The American Petroleum Institute reported in October that U.S. demand for petroleum products rose to 20.5 million barrels a day, a 3.3% jump over October 1999. With world demand limiting imports, the domestic

INDUSTRIAL PRODUCTION—MAJOR MARKET GROUPS

(1992 = 100; monthly data seasonally adjusted)			
	1990	1995	2000*
Consumer Goods			
Total	97.3	110.8	120.1
Durable	98.0	128.4	155.3
Nondurable	97.1	106.5	111.8
Equipment			
Total	103.2	112.8	161.8
Business	98.2	119.4	190.3
Defense and space			
equipment	115.9	84.0	67.5
Intermediate Products			
Total	101.9	108.1	123.4
Construction	102.9	112.5	135.9
Business supplies	101.4	105.4	115.9
Materials			
Total	97.2	120.3	169.9
Energy	100.6	102.4	102.5
Primary Metals			
Total	104.0	116.2	129.5
Iron and steel	106.4	116.5	126.6
Fabricated Metal			
Products	101.2	116.4	130.7
Industrial Machinery			
and Equipment	100.1	143.7	272.2
Electrical Machinery	87.7	165.7	565.7
Transportation Equipment			
Total	102.3	106.7	117.4
Motor vehicles and parts	95.3	133.2	150.1
Lumber and Products	101.6	107.9	114.8
Nondurable Manufactures			
Apparel products	97.2	107.1	84.5
Printing and publishing	103.1	101.3	105.7
Chemicals and products	97.3	107.4	122.3
Food	97.0	105.8	111.0

*September preliminary

Source: Board of Governors of the Federal Reserve System

industry raised the number of rotary rigs seeking oil to 223 in November from 130 at the same time in 1999, according to Smith International, an industry-research firm. It reported the number of natural gas rigs rose to 711 from 512 in the prior period. Seeking to lessen the strain, President Clinton ordered 30 million barrels of crude to be released from the nation's Strategic Petroleum Reserve. Though criticized for security reasons, the release amounted to less than two days of domestic consumption.

Meanwhile, industry figures showed that coal production grew only slightly, if at all. Through early November the industry had produced 1.1 million tons for the year, almost all bituminous and lignite, and had loaded 6.8 million railroad cars. But coal, essential to power plants, was rarely used in homes anymore. The Energy Department forecast that consumers would pay 44% more than a year before to heat their homes with gas, and 25% more for heating oil. The industry's image was not helped when the three largest U.S. oil producers reported record-high profits in the third quarter.

Nevertheless, heavy-industry production was sluggish in many areas, explained, at least in part, by the continued transition to a service economy. Construction was an exception. Benefiting at times from benign weather, new spending rose to an estimated $819.3 billion in the 12 months through September from $764 billion in the year 1999, based on Commerce Department figures. And the American Iron and Steel Institute reported that the steel industry, though operating below capacity, had produced 92.9 million net tons for the year through early October, compared with 83 million tons in the earlier period. Consumers showed a marked preference for durable items, products lasting several years, a contrast to the general impression of wasteful and reckless spending. The production of consumer goods rose little over the preceding few years, but not because of disinterest in electronic communications devices and games. Sony Corporation could not supply enough PlayStation 2 video-game consoles for the Christmas season, and Palm, originator of a handheld computer whose sales exploded in 2000, was plagued by parts shortages.

By year's end, indications of a production slowdown—long anticipated and long delayed—became more numerous. Such a slowdown was especially noticeable in manufacturing, where the National Association of Purchasing Management said in November that its manufacturing index had declined for the fourth straight month. The year's output of passenger cars and light trucks was still projected to exceed 17 million units, but October sales fell for most major automakers. Ford Motor Company reported sharply lower profits, which it attributed to the recall of 6.5 million Firestone tires, many of which were original equipment on its Ford Explorers. Despite high, postmerger hopes, DaimlerChrysler reported a more than $500 million loss in the third quarter. Factory orders turned erratic in midsummer, and while they bounced back with strong demand for electronics and aircraft—Boeing reported a surge of orders late in the year—economists saw the pattern as indicative of an economic slowdown. Some wage and basic price levels crept higher. And while new construction seemed to hold its own for the time being, the Federal Deposit Insurance Corporation (FDIC) warned that overbuilding of commercial structures in 13 major cities posed the danger of a glut of office and retail space. Moreover, analysts speculated that some large companies, anticipating almost endlessly growing demand, may have overspent on capital expansions.

JOHN CUNNIFF, *Business News Analyst*
Associated Press

INDUSTRIAL PRODUCTION

Major Industrial Countries
1992 = 100 (seasonally adjusted)

	Canada	France	Germany	Great Britain	Italy	Japan	United States
1990	102.9	101.3	99.9	103.1	101.7	104.1	98.9
1991	98.9	101.1	102.3	99.7	101.3	106.1	97.0
1992	100.0	100.0	100.0	100.0	100.0	100.0	100.0
1993	104.5	96.3	92.4	102.2	97.9	96.5	103.4
1994	111.3	100.1	95.6	107.7	103.9	97.7	109.1
1995	116.3	102.6	96.8	109.5	109.2	100.9	114.4
1996	117.9	103.5	97.4	110.7	107.1	103.2	119.4
1997	123.1	107.3	100.8	111.8	111.1	107.0	127.1
1998	126.0	112.8	105.0	112.7	112.3	99.9	132.4
1999*	131.6	115.2	106.7	113.3	112.3	100.7	137.1
2000**	141.1	120.3	116.5	116.4	117.9	109.9ʳ	145.6ʳ

*Preliminary   **August preliminary   ʳRevised

Source: National data as reported by U.S. Department of Commerce

Interior Design

The millennial year was the year in which interior design stylishly combined the comforts of the past with the harbingers of the future. Interior design continued to converge with fashion—both Giorgio Armani and Joseph Abboud introduced home collections—and even technology—the iMac color palette was extended to home appliances and accessories both great and small. In fact, the resurgence of interior design made such a splash that *Time* magazine devoted a special issue to the subject.

Information Explosion. Numerous new magazines featuring different ideas about interior design were launched, including *Real Simple*, *Room*, and *dwell*. Style and design publications called "magalogues"— for example, IKEA'S quarterly *Space* (called *Room* outside the United States)—which combine the editorial vision of a magazine with the selling function of a catalog, also proliferated. Even the Pottery Barn catalog offered the equivalent of decorating advice in the room settings it puts together to promote its products for the home. Interior design also exploded on the Web, where various sites—*homeportfolio.com*, *eZiba.com*, and *eLUXURY.com*, to name just three— offered information and products. Designers and manufacturers also put up Web sites in unprecedented numbers.

Cable television provided yet another outlet through which design information reached an ever-curious public. Cable offerings included the long-running *This Old House* (and a magazine by the same name); the resident upstart HGTV, the cable channel with house-and-garden programs around the clock; *Trading Spaces*, a so-called reality-based show, debuting on The Learning Channel, where neighbors make over one room in each other's houses with a limited budget ($1,000) and limited time (48 hours); and *Cribs*, a new show on MTV that offers inside views of rock stars' homes. Moreover, there never was such a boom time in the quantities of books published

As interior design and fashion continued to intertwine in 2000, fashion designer Joseph Abboud introduced his collection for the home, featuring various textiles and an assortment of hues.

Photos, Courtesy, Jill Glover Creative Services for Joseph Abboud House

about interior design, decorating styles, and designers.

The Trends. Apart from the information explosion, the healthy U.S. economy sparked an all-time high of new-home starts, and expansions and renovations to existing residences. Decorators mixed antiques of all periods with classic modern pieces from the 1940s through the 1970s, and then tossed a fur throw here, a flokati rug there, and placed a precious bibelot in a position of casual importance. While a nostalgia for mid-20th-century modern design still provided designers with considerable inspiration, primarily for younger clients in urban centers, designers also parlayed their trained knowledge of historical styles to create traditional interiors with a look, or at least elements, of luxury.

The Midas touch resurfaced in both interiors and objects: Metallic finishes, gilding, and reflective materials came back into vogue. So did saturated colors. And so did transparent and translucent materials, especially plastics: clear plastic furniture that blows up like beach balls (a relic from the 1970s), a transparent Swingline stapler, colored plastic telephones, Karim Rashid's clear and frosted plastic wastebaskets and chairs, and Philippe Starck's collection for Target, among others.

JUDITH NASATIR
Freelance Design Journalist and Editor

International Trade and Finance

The 21st century began on a relatively positive note for the global economy. A decade of strong, steady economic growth in the United States served as locomotive to much of the rest of the world, as American consumers continued to purchase imported goods, thus stimulating the economies that produced them. However, during 2000, doubts about the management of international trade and finance exploded into street protests; the momentum in technology investments began to slow; and a sudden rise in energy prices threatened to darken the prospects for continued improvements in global welfare.

In its annual report issued in September, the International Monetary Fund (IMF) projected a healthy 4.7% growth in the global economy for 2000, up from 3.3% in 1999 and the strongest in more than a decade. But although almost every region of the world shared in the general prosperity, the agency reported, one person in five continued to live in poverty, subsisting on less than a dollar a day.

Globalization Controversy. The leading institutions tasked with promoting stability in the global economy came under an unprecedented degree of criticism. Thousands of protesters took to the streets to denounce the role of institutions furthering globalization—a trend the protesters saw as forcing weak countries to accept the goals of rich countries and multinational corporations, threatening the environment and deepening the divide between global haves and have-nots. The protests—attracting a coalition of environmentalists, anticorporate activists, and other critics of free-market policies—had begun in November 1999 in Seattle, where riots had broken out near the site of a meeting of the World Trade Organization (WTO), the Geneva-based multilateral organization that oversees international trade. Protesters reiterated their message in April 2000 in Washington, DC, on the occasion of a meeting of the IMF and the World Bank. In September they reappeared in Prague, Czech Republic, for the joint annual meeting of the IMF and the World Bank.

Criticism of multilateral lending practices, trade policies, and the globalization of free-market policies was not limited to the streets, as mainstream economists also raised doubts about the impact of unfettered capitalism on the world economy. A United Nations (UN) report issued in October concluded that both the IMF and the World Bank used overly optimistic assumptions on international economic growth in designing their jointly administered debt-relief program. Without additional money, the UN Conference on Trade and Development (UNCTAD) concluded, the program would fall short of helping the world's poorest countries, most of them in Africa.

Some mainstream economists agreed that the two institutions' policies were flawed. The IMF works for economic stability by lending money to countries with temporary economic troubles, while the bank provides development assistance to poor countries, but the two institutions had combined their Third World lending programs in recent years. In exchange for low-interest loans, recipient countries usually agreed to privatize industries, reduce government bureaucracies, and take other belt-tightening steps to improve economic stability and promote long-term growth. But such steps often benefited the wealthy while leaving the poor behind. In one controversial study in the fall, William Easterly, a World Bank economist, concluded that poor people in some developing countries that had accepted IMF and World Bank loans fared worse than the poor in some other countries, such as China and India, that had not.

Multilateral lending and foreign aid also failed to live up to expectations in Russia and other formerly communist countries that had received billions of dollars in loans and aid to help ease their transition into the global-market economy. In one study on the subject, the General Accounting Office (GAO) concluded in November that lending conditions imposed on Russia had hastened that country's economic decline and had opened the door to widespread corruption. Indeed, the IMF suspended a scheduled $4.5 billion loan to Russia amid charges that some of the approximately $20 billion in loans to the country since 1992 had been wasted as a result of money laundering and poor economic policies.

Acknowledging the growing criticism, World Bank President James D. Wolfensohn promised that the institution would adapt to the changing global economic environment. Another indication that the message of the antiglobalization protesters had begun to influence economic-policy decisions came in October, when Congress approved a $14.9 billion foreign-aid bill that included a provision requested by President Bill Clinton to

In Bangkok in June 2000, Horst Kohler (left), *managing director of the International Monetary Fund (IMF), discussed critical issues facing the global economy with Prime Minister Chuan Leekpai* (center) *and other Thai officials.*

forgive the debts held by the poorest developing countries. The $435 million debt-relief measure covered the U.S. share of an IMF initiative to forgive the debts of about 30 countries whose debt burdens prevented economic growth. The bill also included $300 million to help control and fight an AIDS epidemic in Africa, and lifted long-standing restrictions on $425 million in aid for family-planning groups that lobby for abortion services overseas.

International Mergers. One trend in the global economy the protesters failed to halt was the growing clout of multinational corporations. As globalization continued to break down national barriers to trade and financial markets, some of the world's biggest companies crossed boundaries to merge with foreign counterparts to take advantage of emerging market opportunities. UNCTAD reported that the value of international mergers and acquisitions reached $720 billion in 1999, a figure that seemed all but certain to be repeated or even surpassed in 2000.

Most of the merger activity took place in the United States and Europe. In October, the 15-nation European Union's (EU's) executive commission approved a controversial $183 billion mergher between America Online and Time Warner after the two U.S. behemoths agreed to sever ties with a number of large European music, publishing, and media firms. The EU's administrative branch had earlier opposed other mergers involving U.S. firms with business in Europe, prompting U.S. lawmakers to charge the European authorities with yield-ing to protectionist sentiments.

A major European financial-market merger failed to materialize in September, when the London Stock Exchange pulled out of its planned merger with Germany's Deutsche Boerse, a deal that would have created a Europe-wide market for technology stocks.

Stock and Financial Markets. After several years of unprecedented growth, the world's leading stock markets stumbled as investors pulled back from the fast-growing high-technology sector. Investor jitters first cropped up in the United States, the world's leader in high-tech products. After reaching an all-time high on March 10, the technology-heavy Nasdaq Composite Index plummeted, falling 39.3% for the year. The Dow Jones Industrial Average also stalled, falling by 6.2% over the same period. Many analysts attributed the slowdown to a long-awaited injection of prudence on the part of investors whose enthusiasm for start-up ventures, especially in the high-tech sector, had fueled the stock-market surge of the previous decade.

With the growing interdependence of the world economy, it came as no surprise when investors' skittishness spread to other parts of the world. In Asia, financial markets suffered setbacks just as the region was pulling out of a severe recession that had begun in 1997. European markets also faltered, as the euro—the European single currency adopted in January 1999 by 11 of the EU's 15-member nations—steadily lost value against the dollar and other currencies. Worried that the euro's weakening might undermine the global economy, the European Central Bank in November intervened for the seventh time in foreign-exchange markets to shore up the beleaguered currency. The moves failed to reverse the fall of the euro, which stood at a third of its initial value against the dollar by the end of November.

Following on the currency's poor performance, Danish voters rejected membership in the euro in a September 28 referendum.

Energy Prices. World oil prices surged in the first half of the year as a result of production cutbacks by the 11-member Organization of Petroleum Exporting Countries (OPEC) and a global shortfall in refining capacity at a time of continuing high demand by the United States, Europe, and Asia. In November, representatives of 50 consumer and producer nations met in Riyadh, Saudi Arabia, and released a grim prognosis of the impact of oil prices on the global economy: Unless prices could be stabilized, they agreed, rising demand for oil among developing countries would likely spark serious energy crises in the absence of significant new reserves. Ironically, the analysts' pessimistic outlook stemmed from a positive trend: signs of burgeoning economic growth in the developing world that had long been left at the margins of the global economy. Third World auto sales—as many as 170 million in China alone by 2020—were expected to spur oil consumption from 2000's 76 million barrels a day to 115 million within two decades.

The most dangerous aspect of oil prices, the experts agreed, was their volatility, demonstrated by 2000's price rise to $37 a barrel, up from just $10 a barrel two years earlier. That low price, seemingly a boon to consumers at the time, discouraged oil companies from investing in the kind of new exploration and equipment required to meet the growing demand for oil.

U.S. Trade Deficit. For the United States, the expansion of trade was accompanied by a rapidly growing trade deficit, as Americans imported far more goods from overseas than they exported. Through September the deficit had reached a record $360 billion, much higher than the previous record of $265 billion set in 1999.

Despite a slowdown in U.S. economic growth, imports reached record levels, buoyed by industrial purchases of foreign computer chips, civilian aircraft, and telecommunications equipment, and by consumer imports of clothing, automobiles, and other goods. U.S. exports, however, led by organic chemicals, computer chips, and civilian aircraft—were dampened by a fall in overseas sales of American automobiles and automobile parts, as well as soybeans, fish, and several other agricultural products.

Reflecting China's growing role in world trade, the U.S. trade deficit with that country reached a record $61.1 billion in the first nine months of the year, for the first time exceeding the deficit with Japan. The trade deficits with Canada, $4.7 billion, and Mexico, $2.7 billion, also were records.

Experts disagreed over the causes of the growing U.S. trade deficit. The U.S. Trade Deficit Review Commission, set up by Congress to examine the issue, came to two different and largely partisan conclusions in November. Members of the Republican Party attributed the imbalance to the fact that the U.S. economy was growing much faster than the rest of the world, drawing in more goods than it could export. Democrats tended to blame other countries' trade barriers for the problem. Both camps worried that the deficit and the stagnation of America's basic-manufacturing industries might spark a new wave of protectionist sentiment in the United States.

Indeed, tensions between the United States and the EU flared over long-standing bilateral trade disputes. On November 14, Congress repealed controversial income-tax breaks for U.S. exporters. The EU had complained that the breaks amounted to unfair export subsidies, and the WTO had ruled them illegal. But trade negotiators were unable to resolve differences involving U.S. complaints about European discrimination against Central American bananas sold by U.S. companies and hormone-treated beef sold by U.S. ranchers. In November, both sides agreed that they would refrain from imposing trade-crippling sanctions pending the outcome of ongoing negotiations to resolve the disputes.

New Trade Agreements. In July the Clinton administration signed a trade agreement with Vietnam reducing tariffs on imports from the communist country. The pact still had to be ratified by both nations, however. President Clinton reiterated his support for broader trade ties with Vietnam during a visit to the country in November.

The visit and the call for open markets were an apt conclusion to the presidency of Bill Clinton, who had spent much of his two terms in the White House in support of broader trade ties. On Sept. 19, 2000, the Senate approved a Clinton-supported agreement extending permanent normal trade relations to China—a prerequisite for the world's largest country to join the WTO. (*See also* U.S.-China Trade.)

MARY H. COOPER
*"The CQ [Congressional
Quarterly] Researcher"*

Iran

During 2000 the main theme of Iranian politics was the conflict between the rigid clerical regime and its opponents. With no serious attempt to undo the basic nature of the regime, there persisted an Islamic framework that reformists accepted without question. Still, there was an entirely real strife that gave rise to incidents throughout the year. Each side in the struggle had in its ranks a considerable range of opinion: On one side stood the hard-line clerics, on the other those who wished to make Iran more tolerant and flexible.

If the reformers' aims appeared modest, they had great and ultimately unforeseeable results. Such steps would entail an opening toward the West, and particularly toward the United States, "the great Satan." Economically the steps would entail replacing—as the goal—virtual autarky with willing participation in the world economy. As amply demonstrated, the reformist side had substantial majority support, shown in the overwhelming and surprising victory of Mohammed Khatami in the 1997 presidential election. Though a cleric in good standing, Khatami was a moderate reformer. Support for the reformers was shown even more convincingly in the 2000 elections to the Majlis (parliament).

Given the fact that the majority of the Iranian population was under 20 years old in 2000, future victory for the reformers seemed inevitable. Conservative forces in Iran made it clear that they were prepared to resist the reformers tooth and nail, and they eventually did so successfully in 2000. The optimism that prevailed at the beginning of the year—the comfortable assumption that Iran was setting toward reform—was not sustained by year's end. The issue was still in doubt.

The champions of the *status quo* had the commanding institutional heights. Supreme spiritual leader Ayatollah Ali Khamenei was superior in both status and power to the elected President Khatami. Khamenei commanded the armed forces. His vast clerical network had powers of oversight over the Council of Guardians (which could veto candidates for the Majlis and overturn election results), the official media, the judiciary, and the great foundations (in possession of nearly a third of the nation's economy).

The Election: A Conservative Defeat. The February 18 general election attracted great interest and participation: About 5,000 candidates ran for the 290 seats in the Majlis, and some 80% of those eligible to vote did so. The reformers won control of approximately 200 seats. Former President Hashemi Rafsanjami, whom some had envisaged as a bridge between the two sides, lost his seat. (Later, after a dubious recount victory, he resigned.) In Tehran and Mashad, the two largest cities, the conservatives did not win any seats. More women and fewer clerics were elected to the Majlis. The run-off elections in May, and intervention by the Council of Guardians, made no substantial difference in the results.

The Counterattack. Conservative forces on the defensive responded with vigor. The counterattack took two main forms—the banning of reformist publications, and attacks on individual reformers. The latter mostly took the form of arresting reformers on various charges, alleging disloyalty to the regime, with subsequent trials. There also were, however, acts of violence committed by some extremists on the right. On March 12, a leading reformist politician and newspaper editor Saeed Hajjarian, who had received death threats, was seriously wounded on a Tehran street when shot by a would-be assassin riding a motorcycle. On April 20, Khamenei made a speech complaining bitterly about the role of the reformist press.

In April, various Iranian politicians, journalists, and intellectuals attended a Berlin conference on Iranian reforms. They were questioned by police upon their return, and some were imprisoned. In November, 16 who attended the conference were put on trial—after months of imprisonment. Among them were Akbar Ganji, Iran's leading investigative journalist, whose defiant attitude in court attracted much publicity,

---

IRAN • Information Highlights

Official Name: Islamic Republic of Iran.
Location: Southwest Asia.
Area: 636,293 sq mi (1 648 000 km²).
Population (2000 est.): 65,619,636.
Chief Cities (1996 census): Tehran, the capital, 6,758,845; Mashad, 1,887,405; Esfahan, 1,266,072; Tabriz, 1,191,043.
Government: *Head of state and government,* Mohammed Khatami, president (elected May 1997). *Legislature* (unicameral)—Islamic Consultative Assembly (Majlis).
Monetary Unit: Rial (1,752.50 rials equal U.S.$1, Jan. 16, 2001).
Gross Domestic Product (1999 est. U.S.$): $347,600,000,000 (purchasing power parity).
Economic Index (1999, 1990 = 100): *Consumer Prices,* all items, 770.6; food, 855.6.
Foreign Trade (1998 est. U.S.$): *Imports,* $13,800,000,000; *exports,* $12,200,000,000.

A special edition of the Iranian newspaper Sobhe Emrooz *reported the assassination attempt against its editor, Saeed Hajjarian, a leading reformist in Iran.*

cannot be praised." He commented that he was sometimes powerless to protect press freedoms outlined in the constitution. During the summer, Khatami voiced his intention of running again in the next presidential election, due in May 2001. However, toward the end of the year he voiced doubts about whether he should or would run.

and Jamileh Kadivar, Iran's most popular female politician. The main charge was "undermining Iran's security" by attending the conference. In January 2001, Ganji was sentenced to ten years in prison.

Since about 1998, there had been a remarkable efflorescence of new reformist newspapers and journals—thanks in part to Ataollah Mohajerani at the culture ministry. But in April, 12 major newspapers and liberal magazines were ordered closed by the judiciary. Two more newspapers were suppressed later in the month. By the middle of August, 22 publications had been closed. This assault on the freedom of the press evoked demonstrations in universities and in the city streets. Neither President Khatami nor his brother Mohammed Reza Khatami, head of the Mosherakat political grouping—the most important reformist political group—wanted any out-and-out clash, and publicly urged restraint.

Likewise, Ali Khamenei was far from the most extreme on his side, as he had sometimes supported Khatami in tricky situations. However, after the Majlis met on May 27, and turned to the framing of a new press law that would have vastly improved the situation of the press, the assembly received a peremptory order from Khamenei to desist from consideration of any such measure.

The closure of publications was publicly and ruefully deplored by President Khatami in a broadcast television interview seen on August 21. The interview marked the third anniversary of his presidency. He said, "I support legal action against any kind of violations, but the mass closure of newspapers

In January 2001, something of a truce between the opposing forces in Iran seemed to have been reached when the Majlis approved the appointment of five new ministers to Khatami's cabinet. Two of the five—including Ahmed Jamei, who replaced Ataollah Mohajerani at the culture ministry—were considered conservative; three were liberals.

Convicted Spies. In Shiraz, a long trial before a revolutionary court ended on July 1 with the conviction and sentencing of ten Iranian Jews convicted of spying for Israel. None were sentenced to death, though it had been a possibility. Two Muslims also were convicted. Three Jewish defendants and two Muslims were acquitted. The trial had been closed to the public and conducted without a jury.

The trial attracted widespread international attention—and condemnation. U.S. President Clinton called on Iran to overturn the sentences. Israel denied that the accused were connected with Mossad, the Israeli secret service. However, the outrage became muted after September 21, when, on appeal, all the sentences were substantially reduced.

Foreign Relations. In March, President Clinton extended a 1995 executive order that banned oil contracts with Iran. However, Secretary of State Madeleine Albright announced the lifting of import bans on Iranian carpets, caviar, and pistachios. The secretary also said that there would be more concessions if Iran showed "a desire and a commitment" to better relations with the United States.

Iran seemed to be edging closer to a reconciliation with Iraq, after fighting an eight-year war in the 1980s. In May, Iran released a total of 2,479 Iraqi prisoners of war (POWs) as a "humanitarian gesture."

February and March witnessed mortar attacks on Tehran that killed one person and wounded eight. These were said to be the work of an Iranian dissident group based across the border in Iraq.

ARTHUR CAMPBELL TURNER
University of California, Riverside

Iraq

Aug. 2, 2000, marked the tenth anniversary of the swift invasion and conquest of Kuwait by Iraq under the leadership of President Saddam Hussein. February 2001 would be the tenth anniversary of the Gulf War, in which a U.S.-led military coalition of many nations defeated Iraq, freed Kuwait, and reestablished the status quo. Later in 1991, a sanctions regime that imposed restrictions on Iraq's trade was put in place, while air traffic was virtually prohibited. The objective was to oblige Iraq to dismantle its manufacturing of weapons of mass destruction and chemical warfare and to destroy all existing stocks. Sanctions were to remain in place until these requirements had been carried out, and an international inspection team was to monitor the situation.

During the Gulf War, antigovernment uprisings erupted in the Kurdish north of Iraq and in the south, largely Shiite. The rumblings were suppressed savagely and successfully by forces of President Hussein, but in order to provide protection to these regions, "no-fly zones" were decreed to the north and south, where no Iraqi aircraft were allowed to fly.

An Unsatisfactory Decade. As 2000 ended, the no-fly zones were still maintained, and much of the machinery of restraint or coercion was still in place, especially in theory, although much had changed externally. Internally, there was very little change in Iraq in 2000—no crises and no changes in the regime of Hussein, who had been president since 1979. Externally, there was a steadily improved foreign-relations status. Taken together, no dictator could wish for more. Sheer determination, persistence, delay, and prevarication had enabled Hussein not only to stay in power, but to enhance his situation.

An international humanitarian reaction favored modifying or abandoning sanctions, which bore most heavily on the poorest part of the Iraqi population. In fact, those regarded as faithful supporters of the Hussein regime were essentially exempt from hardship and doing very well.

A Crumbling Coalition. The cohesion of the diplomatic and military coalition of 1991 steadily crumbled through the 1990s. France,

International flights from at least ten countries, including a Syrian Airbus-320 with humanitarian aid (below), began to arrive at Baghdad's Saddam Hussein International Airport following its reopening in August 2000. The airport had been closed for ten years.

IRAQ • Information Highlights

Official Name: Republic of Iraq.
Location: Southwest Asia.
Area: 168,754 sq mi (437 072 km²).
Population (2000 est.): 22,675,617.
Chief City (1987 census): Baghdad, the capital, 3,844,608.
Government: *Head of state and government,* Saddam Hussein, president (took office July 1979). *Legislature* (unicameral)—National Assembly.
Monetary Unit: Dinar (0.3125 dinar equals U.S.$1, Jan. 16, 2001).
Gross Domestic Product (1999 est. U.S. $): $59,900,000,000 (purchasing power parity).
Foreign Trade (1999 U.S.$): *Imports,* 8,900,000,000; *exports,* 12,700,000,000

Russia, and China—permanent members of the United Nations (UN) Security Council—were more interested in reestablishing economic links with Iraq than putting pressure on Hussein. The inspection team designated to monitor Iraq's disarmament, the United Nations Special Commission on Iraq (UNSCOM), was virtually expelled soon after August 1998 when Iraq alleged that it had disarmed. During 1999, U.S. influence in the Security Council was weakened by a revelation that the United States had made some use of UNSCOM members for intelligence gathering. In December 1999, a new offer was made to Iraq: a temporary lifting of sanctions in return for Iraq's permitting a new inspection group to work within its borders. This new inspection team was to be called UNMOVIC (United Nations Monitoring, Verification, and Inspection Commission). Iraq refused to accept the offer, and there was little doubt that Iraq continued to develop and manufacture prohibited weapons.

Sanctions Eased. The sanctions regime had been modified progressively in Iraq's favor, with the beginning of the oil-for-food program in 1996. The program—which allows Iraq to make limited sales of oil to purchase humanitarian supplies, mainly food, for the Iraqi people—had been renewed at six-month intervals; the British desired yearly intervals, but could not persuade the Security Council. At the December 2000 renewal, Iraq was given new leeway in spending the billions of dollars generated from the program. A provision, pushed by France and others, permitted the release to Iraq of $525 million at each six-month interval to be spent on repairing and maintaining the Iraqi oil industry. The list of goods permitted for import also was extended. The UN, however, had some control over how the money was spent. Annoyed at the

refusal to permit a surcharge (directly payable to Iraq) on oil sales, Iraq suspended all oil sales from December 2 to 13, but the effect on the oil market was minimal.

Equally important to Iraq was the vast amount of smuggling—most notably of oil exports on ships out of the Persian Gulf, exported from Basra—being carried out. The territorial waters of Iran offered a safe route that was protected from U.S. naval patrols for much of the way. In February a Russian tanker that neglected this precaution was intercepted by U.S. forces. The U.S. State Department estimated that Iraq doubled its illegal oil exports since 1999. The smuggling of oil (in trucks) and goods, and the importation of luxury items, largely took place across Iraq's land frontiers with Turkey, Jordan, and Syria.

Hussein made great strides in reestablishing Iraq's international legitimacy. In addition to sympathizers on the Security Council, even the United Arab Emirates, Qatar, and Bahrain restored diplomatic ties to Iraq. It seemed likely that Turkey would do so in the near future. However, U.S. policy, while supported firmly only by Britain, remained basically unchanged. It also seemed unlikely that any change would come with a new administration. In his first public statement after being named secretary of state in the forthcoming Bush administration, retired Gen. Colin Powell vowed to "reenergize" sanctions.

Airport Reopened. On August 17, Iraq officially reopened Saddam Hussein International Airport in Baghdad, which had been closed for ten years. Over the remaining months of the year, international flights from at least ten countries arrived at the airport, which highlighted different opinions from the various powers. The U.S. and British view was that passenger flights were banned, though humanitarian flights could receive UN permission to land. France and Russia held that the trade ban was not relevant to passenger flights. On September 17 and 23, Russian flights carried medical supplies, business executives, and other passengers. A French flight on September 22 was called a "a blatant violation of UN sanctions resolutions" by a U.S. State Department spokesman. This appeared to be even more the case when a French flight on December 2 carried the French foreign minister and more than 100 politicians, members of the clergy, and officials.

ARTHUR CAMPBELL TURNER
University of California, Riverside

Ireland

In Ireland in 2000, the Fianna Fáil government sustained remarkably little damage from the embarrassing Flood Tribunal revelations of corruption and influence peddling on the part of its former leader and prime minister, Charles J. Haughey. Despite the evidence of payoffs and interest-free loans—including Haughey's undeclared and untaxed receipt of more than 8 million Irish pounds ($7.2 million) from rich businessmen between 1979 and 1996—there were no convictions for wrongdoing. During the summer, Haughey's lawyer announced that his client suffered from terminal prostate cancer, and that further appearances at the tribunal would jeopardize his health. Another public inquiry dug up proof that a prominent Fianna Fáil member had secretly lodged large sums of money in an offshore account. Such disclosures generated more public disquiet and cynicism toward politics and politicians.

In May critics of the government protested the appointment of Hugh O'Flaherty, a former judge of the Supreme Court, to the vice-presidency of the European Investment Bank (EIB). In 1999 he had stepped down from the Supreme Court under the serious charges of undue interference in the case of a prominent Dubliner who had killed a woman with his car. O'Flaherty had approved this driver's early release from prison. However, Prime Minister Bertie Ahern stoutly defended his choice for the EIB position.

At the United Nations (UN) on October 10, Ireland won one of ten nonpermanent seats on the Security Council. The two-year term was effective on Jan. 1, 2001.

The Economy and Labor Strife. The robust performance of the Irish economy during 1999, when the gross national product (GNP) grew by almost 8%, enabled consumers to spend more money on necessities and luxuries. While profits spiraled upward, so, too, did the price of housing in the Dublin area, where houses had doubled in value since 1995. Fortified by a projected budget surplus of 2% of the gross national product (GNP), the government agreed on February 9 to offer union workers a 16% increase in pay over the next three years. At the same time, the economic boom sowed seeds of discontent in the form of mounting industrial strife.

Inflationary trends triggered a number of work stoppages in the fall that threatened to undermine the labor compact or "social partnership" between the government and the trade unions. Rising fuel and housing prices caused inflation to reach 6.8% by October, which far exceeded the target figure of 2% set by the European Union (EU). However, the economic boom enabled Finance Minister Charlie McGreevy to cut income taxes by 2% and increase child benefit payments in his "giveaway" budget of December 6.

Although a gallon of gasoline cost an average of $3.13 in Ireland—including a tax of 58.1%—this was lower than Britain's rate (where taxes amounted to 72%). Ahern's negotiations with the leaders of various unions spared Ireland the truckers' blockades seen elsewhere.

Security Matters. On January 4, the high court in Dublin stopped an order to extradite to Northern Ireland a former member of the Irish Republican Army (IRA), Angelo Fusco, who was convicted in 1981 of murdering a British officer working undercover for the Special Air Service (SAS). The court order came through only hours before Fusco was to be taken north. Although Fusco was denied bail, he was assured that the extradition order would be reviewed by an Irish court. On May 26, police arrested seven members of the Real IRA, a dissident group opposed to peace in the North and linked to the explosion in Omagh that had killed 29 men, women, and children on Aug. 15, 1998.

In Dublin and Dundalk on December 12, President Clinton met with Prime Minister Ahern and President Mary McAleese and urged the Irish people to embrace the peace process in Northern Ireland.

L. PERRY CURTIS, *Brown University*

IRELAND • Information Highlights

Official Name: Ireland.
Location: Island in the eastern North Atlantic Ocean.
Area: 27,135 sq mi (70 280 km²).
Population (2000 est.): 3,797,257.
Chief Cities (1996 census [incl. suburbs]): Dublin, the capital, 952,700; Cork, 180,000; Limerick, 79,100.
Government: *Head of state,* Mary McAleese, president (took office Nov. 11, 1997). *Head of government,* Bertie Ahern, prime minister (elected June 26, 1997). *Legislature*—Parliament (Oireachtas): Senate (Seanad Eireann) and House of Representatives (Dail Eireann).
Monetary Unit: Pound (1.1963 pounds equal U.S.$1, Dec. 31, 2000).
Gross Domestic Product (1999 est. U.S.$): $73,700,000,000 (purchasing power parity).
Economic Indexes (1999, 1990 = 100): *Consumer Prices,* all items, 121.6; food, 123.1. *Industrial Production,* 228.2 (1998).
Foreign Trade (1999 U.S.$): *Imports,* $46,535,000,000; *exports,* $70,544,000,000.

Israel

Within months of Ehud Barak's May 1999 election as prime minister, the One Israel government was threatened by both domestic and foreign-policy crises. What followed was a series of debacles. Barak's efforts to conclude peace agreements with Syria and the Palestinians were unsuccessful. Relations with Yasir Arafat's Palestinian National Authority deteriorated into a low-intensity war, and clashes between Israeli police and the country's Palestine Arab citizens erupted into a large-scale uprising. Ultimately, Barak's lack of success in the peace process and failure to deliver on domestic election promises in 2000 led to the collapse of his coalition government, threats of a parliamentary vote of no-confidence, his resignation, and a new election scheduled for February 2001.

Domestic Affairs. Only weeks after forming a coalition cabinet of seven diverse political factions, disputes broke out between the left-of-center Meretz party and the ultra-Orthodox Shas. Meretz Minister of Education Yossi Sarid threatened to withhold funds from the Shas religious-school system because of poor conditions of the schools. He demanded a series of reforms, including closure of schools with low enrollment. Shas spiritual mentor, former Sephardi Chief Rabbi Ovadia Yosef, accused Sarid of being "a bitter enemy of Judaism. . . . the devil. . . . God will extirpate him," Yosef threatened.

The dispute between Sarid and Rabbi Yosef was symptomatic of the deep ideological divide within the cabinet. Shas, Israel's third-largest party with 17 Knesset seats in 2000, largely represents Jews of Middle East origin who were marginalized, many of them from development towns and urban areas with poor housing, inadequate schools and social services, higher unemployment rates, and lower income than the Ashkenazi, or European, Jewish sector of society.

Meretz, the fourth-largest party with ten seats in 2000, represents the more Western-educated Ashkenazi middle class, considered left of the Labor Party because of its dovish approach to peace and support for welfare programs. Meretz was Barak's strongest ally during his peace initiatives.

Prime Minister Barak was faced with the choice of supporting Shas demands for funding its educational and social-welfare institutions, or backing recommendations of his Meretz ministers. Since Shas agreed not to block the government's peace efforts, Barak gave in to its fiscal demands in June, and Meretz cabinet members subsequently resigned their posts.

A month later, Shas, the National Religious Party (NRP), and Yisra'el Ba'Aliya—a party of Russian immigrants—also quit in protest against expected concessions to the Palestinians in peace negotiations. On July 10, the day that Barak left Israel for the United States to participate in the Camp David peace negotiations with the Palestinians, he faced a no-confidence motion of 54 to 52, seven short of the majority required to topple his government.

When Barak returned from Camp David, he shifted emphasis from the peace process to plans for major "civic" reform and adoption of Israel's first constitution. Barak's plans included abolition of the Religious Affairs Ministry; legitimizing civil marriage, now the prerogative of the clergy; removing ethnic classifications from identity cards; and imposing English, math, and citizenship studies on the entire school system, including the ultra-Orthodox schools that now focus on religious texts. This scheme seemed intended to rally support from the various

© Elizabeth Dalziel/AP/Wide World Photos

Following a turbulent year, Ehud Barak resigned as prime minister of Israel on December 9. Under a special law, elections only for the position of prime minister would be held within 60 days.

nonreligious parties, including the opposition nationalist Likud. By declaring "time out" in the peace process, Barak hoped to form a coalition of secular-oriented groups, including those opposing his peace efforts.

Despite Barak's 1999 victory in the election for prime minister, both One Israel and Likud suffered major losses while a plethora of 13 other parties won Knesset seats. This made coalition building extremely difficult; therefore, Barak aimed to form a wall-to-wall "national emergency" government. By summer, Barak began negotiations with Ariel Sharon, leader of the Likud opposition. Sharon, however, resisted Barak's advances.

Political turmoil in Israel was exacerbated by a series of scandals. Early in the year, police questioned Barak and Cabinet Secretary Isaac Herzog on suspicion of violating the Party Funding Law. Former Prime Minister Benjamin Netanyahu was accused of obstructing justice, bribery, fraud, and breach of trust, but was not prosecuted. The attorney general said that he dropped the case against Netanyahu because there was not enough evidence to convict. Transportation Minister Yitzhak Mordechai was investigated for alleged sexual misconduct, and resigned from the cabinet and as leader of the Center Party. President Ezer Weizman was probed for receiving funds from a millionaire friend; he, too, resigned.

Israeli security men guard opposition leader Ariel Sharon (center) as he leaves the Temple Mount, a site in Jerusalem's Old City that is sacred to Jews and Muslims. The visit precipitated increased violence between Israelis and Palestinians.

Weizman's resignation led directly to the Knesset's election of a new president on July 31, an upset for Barak and the Labor Party. Labor's candidate, former Prime Minister Shimon Peres, was unexpectedly defeated by the Likud's Iranian-born Moshe Katsav. Katsav, who emigrated from Iran in 1951, previously served as minister of labor, transportation, and tourism; his election was seen as a victory for the "second Israel,"— that is, the underprivileged Sephardi Jewish community.

In November a national poll showed that two-thirds of those surveyed distrusted Barak's leadership, and believed peace with Arafat impossible. By the end of the year, both Barak and Sharon fell behind former Prime Minister Benjamin Netanyahu in public opinion. Although Netanyahu had resigned from politics after his defeat in 1999, there were indications that he intended to again seek the prime minister's office and Likud leadership.

To save his government from defeat in the Knesset, Barak finally made a deal with Shas to support its fiscal demands in return for a promise not to vote against him for at least the last weeks of 2000. Shas, however, did not rejoin the coalition. The outcry for Barak's removal intensified, and in late November the prime minister caved. In response to a blistering, raucous Parliament attack aimed at his leadership abilities, Barak made it clear he was not blind. "I say to you: 'You want elections? I'm prepared,'" he said. "I've won every election I've ever run in to date."

ISRAEL • Information Highlights

Official Name: State of Israel.
Location: Southwest Asia.
Area: 8,019 sq mi (20 770 km²).
Population (2000 est.): 5,842,454.
Chief Cities (Dec. 31, 1998, est.): Jerusalem, the capital, 613,700 (including East Jerusalem); Tel Aviv–Jaffa, 348,100; Haifa, 265,700.
Government: *Head of state,* Moshe Katzav, president (elected July 31, 2000). *Head of government,* Ehud Barak, prime minister (sworn in July 6, 1999). *Legislature* (unicameral)—Knesset.
Monetary Unit: Shekel (4.0827 shekels equal U.S.$1, Jan. 6, 2001).
Gross Domestic Product (1999 est. U.S.$): $105,400,000,000 (purchasing power parity).
Economic Indexes (1999, 1990 = 100): *Consumer Prices* all items, 245.8;(1998, 1990 = 100): food, 203.9. *Industrial Production* 160.6.
Foreign Trade (1999 U.S.$): *Imports,* $33,160,000,000; *exports,* $25,794,000,000.

Then, come December, in a surprise move, Barak suddenly resigned as prime minister. A new election for the post was scheduled for February 2001. Late in the month, however, Parliament voted against disbanding, meaning that Israel would elect only a prime minister. As a result, Netanyahu indicated he would drop out of the race—he said he would not run if Parliament would not dissolve itself, claiming it would be impossible to govern.

Foreign Affairs. The year began with expectations for peaceful resolution of the conflict between Israel and its Arab neighbors. In January, negotiations resumed between Israel and Syria in Shepherdstown, WV, under U.S. auspices. Talks between Prime Minister Barak and Syrian Foreign Minister Farouk al-Shara' focused on borders and water issues. Negotiations were suspended indefinitely just weeks later because of border disagreements.

Barak and Palestinian National Authority leader Arafat met several times early in the year with little progress toward a settlement. President Clinton attempted to break the deadlock in July when he convened an "open-ended" summit at Camp David, MD. The meeting, lasting more than two weeks, ended inconclusively. Press reports indicated that progress was made on some issues, including borders, distribution of water resources, and security concerns. But no final treaty was signed, primarily because of disagreement over Jerusalem and the "right of return" for Palestinian refugees. Arafat insisted on the return of all Arab East Jerusalem that was seized by Israel in the June 1967 war.

Barak was believed to have offered more than any previous Israeli prime minister in exchange for a final settlement; his offer included return to Arab control of more than 90% of the occupied West Bank and Gaza seized during 1967, joint Israeli and Palestinian administration in parts of Jerusalem's walled Old City, and some concessions on the Palestinian refugee "right of return."

Following failure of the Camp David summit, relations between Israel and the Palestinians rapidly deteriorated. Palestinian impatience with lack of progress erupted in violence during September, sparked by Sharon's visit to the Temple Mount/Haram al- Sharif. Sharon, accompanied by a retinue of fellow Likud leaders and some 1,000 armed Israeli police, asserted Jewish rights to the site, considered holy by both Jews and Muslims. The Temple Mount adjoins the Wailing, or Western, Wall, considered by Jews as the last remnant of their ancient temple. Muslims revere a mosque in the immediate area where the Prophet Muhammad is believed to have ascended to visit heaven.

Palestinian demonstrations against Sharon's visit quickly developed into an uprising, with violence escalating into a war between Israeli troops and Palestinian guerrilla forces. As the number of shooting incidents continued to mount, Israel used tanks and helicopter gunships in an unsuccessful effort to quell the uprising. By December, casualties included more than 250 killed and several thousand wounded, mostly Palestinian civilians.

In May, Barak kept his election promise to withdraw Israel's troops from the "security zone" it had established in southern Lebanon. Most Israelis supported the move because of mounting casualties and what many considered the futility of maintaining an armed force in hostile territory. Although clashes between Israeli and Lebanese Shiite guerrillas ended, tensions continued between the Israeli army and civilians across the border.

Relations with the United States were strained early in the year because of Israel's proposed sale to China of the $250 million Falcon surveillance aircraft. The United States feared that China might use the Falcon against its Pacific ally, Taiwan. After a bitter dispute, Israel agreed not to supply China with the advanced radar system.

Pope John Paul II visited Israel and the Palestinian areas during March. The pontiff's pilgrimage in Israel included visits to the Yad Vashem Holocaust memorial in Jerusalem and various sites in the life of Jesus such as Nazareth and Lake Tiberias (the Sea of Galilee).

See also MIDDLE EAST.

DON PERETZ
State University of New York at Binghamton

Italy

The Kosovo crisis that rattled Europe and Italy during 1999 abated during 2000, as politics and economics returned to the fore. Italian political parties geared up for the 2001 general elections. Meanwhile, the center-left coalition that won the 1996 parliamentary elections remained in power, but it became increasingly fractious as a new prime minister took office once again.

On April 26, 2000, Italy's President Carlo Azeglio Ciampo (right) congratulated Giuliano Amato, the head of a newly installed center-left government. Amato, a former socialist, had served as prime minister (June 1992–April 1993).

Politics. Prime Minister Massimo D'Alema had reshuffled his cabinet in December 1999, but the new government proved weaker than the previous. In part, D'Alema was the victim of opponents within his own ruling coalition; they feared he would be named the standard-bearer for the center-left during the 2001 elections. The end came with the regional elections held on April 17. D'Alema campaigned hard, but the center-left was defeated. The results gave eight regions with 32 million people to Silvio Berlusconi's center-right "Pole," and seven regions, with only half that population, to the center-left. The Pole captured the prosperous North and Rome's Lazio region.

Following the elections, D'Alema announced that he intended to resign. The prime minister rejected Berlusconi's call for early national elections and insisted upon a May referendum. This referendum—which would have been canceled if early elections had been called—would ask voters whether to implement a national "winner-take-all" voting system for Parliament by eliminating the vestiges of proportional representation. D'Alema resigned on April 19. That same month, after a brief crisis, President Carlo Azeglio Ciampi swore in a new center-left cabinet headed by Giuliano Amato. It marked Italy's 56th postwar government.

Nicknamed "Dr. Subtle" and known as a shrewd political calculator, Amato, a professor of constitutional law, came to political prominence during the government of Betti-no Craxi, longtime secretary of the defunct Italian Socialist Party. Amato continued on the course set by the previous government. He campaigned for passage of the May 21 referendum opposed by Berlusconi and his Forza Italia party.

Berlusconi favored the German system of proportional voting over the pure majoritarian system that the referendum instituted. He maintained that the German method, which required a minimum 5% vote for representation in parliament, would bring Italy greater stability. In preparation for the referendum and for the 2001 voting, Berlusconi allied with Northern League leader Umberto Bossi. Bossi had called for secession of the northern regions, but, unable to get his way, favored institution of a federal system. The Pole sought to defeat the referendum by encouraging voters not to go to the polls on May 21. Italian law requires a 50% turnout for a referendum to be valid. Fewer than 33% of voters participated, and the proposed reform was defeated.

Pre-Electoral Maneuvering. Following the defeat, Amato appealed to Berlusconi for a pact on electoral reform, declaring that he was ready to negotiate on the German system. Berlusconi, riding high in the polls, demanded an agreement within a month and requested early elections, but was refused by the center-left. The campaign for the 2001 national elections swung into high gear, and some observers questioned the solidity of the Berlusconi-Bossi alliance. In 1994, Berlusconi had come to power after winning an election with Bossi's support, but Bossi abandoned him and helped bring down his government. Bossi remained a doubtful ally, but by 2000 the center-left and the League had been quarreling for some time, and Bossi had nowhere else to go. Historically, when the Pole consisted of Forza Italia, Bossi's League, and Gianfranco Fini's National Alliance (AN), it garnered 60% of the vote. This calculation induced Berlusconi to come to terms with Bossi despite the 1994 unpleasantness.

Berlusconi's personal position strengthened during the year. In May, for the fourth time, he was acquitted on appeal of corruption charges that he maintained were politically motivated. He attempted to resolve the conflict-of-interest issue that had dogged him, one that his opponents had utilized against him. Parliament debated a law setting up a "blind trust," then sought to make it more rigid by inserting clauses that would have disqualified Berlusconi from office unless he got rid of his economic interests. The attempt went nowhere, and Berlusconi announced that if a law were not passed, he would put his assets in a blind trust on the U.S. and European models.

Meanwhile, the center-left attempted to strengthen its own political position. Amato presented a budget that, for the first time in years, did not contain tax increases. Amato also lowered taxes on fuel. The government, however, could not avoid a weakening of the economy due to price increases. Higher prices made Italian imports more expensive and, because oil had to be paid for in appreciating dollars, increased the outflow of U.S. currency. The government was embarrassed regarding the poor performance of the Universal Mobile Telecommunications System (UMTS). Like Britain, Germany, and other countries, Italy held an auction to sell off UMTS licenses. The government expected a good result, and hoped the income would help pay off some of the Italy's high debt, estimated at more than 112% of its gross domestic product (GDP). The auction, however, brought in just 12.2 billion euros ($11.4 billion), compared with 50.2 billion euros ($46.9 billion) and 38 billion euros ($35.5 billion) raised by the German and British auctions, respectively. The government found it necessary to halt the auction when one group withdrew, leaving so few contenders as to make bidding pointless. Government handling of the auction led to charges of incompetence and renewed calls from center-right opponents for resignation and early elections.

In the meantime, competition developed in the ruling coalition to name a candidate who would become premier in case of a center-left victory in 2001. There was general agreement that the nominee should not come from the largest party, the former Communists. The two major rivals were Amato and Francesco Rutelli, the Green Party member and mayor of Rome. Rutelli was attractive, articulate, and young, but inexperienced. In September, Amato withdrew from the contest, stating that the center-left was too split. He pledged to remain as prime minister while Rutelli ran the campaign. Officially christened standard-bearer of the center-left in October, Rutelli pledged to reinvigorate the coalition and bring victory, but the polls still indicated the center-right was significantly ahead in the race.

Economics. Economic optimism marked the beginning of 2001. The Milan stock market ended 1999 with a 20% increase, the best showing in Europe. D'Alema declared that the country was in a full economic recovery, and Amato predicted that the gross domestic product (GDP) would grow at a 2.5% rate in 2000, instead of the previously announced 2.2%, bringing Italy in line with the large European Union (EU) countries. Official statistics revealed that the nation had added 700,000 jobs since 1997. Adding to the good news, the "New Economy" sector added 50,000 jobs. Moreover, the EU promised to provide significant development funds for the South under its program favoring disadvantaged areas.

Unfortunately, major oil-price hikes hit resource-poor Italy especially hard. Inflation resumed an upward curve. Even if the rise was not dramatic, it threatened to slow the progress Italy had made in confronting its financial problems. EU and International Monetary Fund (IMF) officials remained wary about the high Italian deficit, and criticized Italy for its high taxes on business that slowed employment growth. More bad news appeared on the trade front as the Italian trade surplus shrank. The rising cost of imports caused by rising oil prices was partly offset by the euro's drop in value, which made Italian goods cheaper and stimulated exports. It was a different story in the EU, where Italy's large surplus turned into a significant deficit. This indicated that the country had difficulty in adjusting to the new

---

ITALY • Information Highlights

Official Name: Italian Republic.
Location: Southern Europe.
Area: 116,305 sq mi (301 230 km²).
Population (2000 est.): 57,634,327.
Chief Cities (Dec. 31, 1998): Rome, the capital, 2,646,408; Milan, 1,307,785; Naples, 1,020,120.
Government: *Head of state,* Carlo Azeglio Ciampi, president (sworn in May 18, 1999). *Head of government,* Giuliano Amato, prime minister (sworn in April 26, 2000). *Legislature*—Parliament: Senate and Chamber of Deputies.
Monetary Unit: Lira (2,021.1587 lire equal U.S.$1, Jan.. 6, 2001).
Gross Domestic Product (1999 est. U.S.$): $1,212,000,000,000.
Economic Indexes: *Consumer Prices* (1999, 1990 = 100): all items, 140.3; food, 132.9. *Industrial Production* 111.7.
Foreign Trade (1999 U.S.$): *Imports,* $216,626,000,000; *exports,* $230,199,000,000.

euro trading area. On the other hand, tax revenues increased more than 6%, despite lower fuel taxes.

The weakened economic picture brought criticism from the center-right. Berlusconi called for less government interference in the economy and for more-flexible work rules. Privatization continued apace with the closing of the Institute for Industrial Reconstruction (IRI), the giant state holding company, 67 years after its founding by the Fascist government. IRI was credited with helping pull Italy out of the Great Depression and being a major contributor to the country's impressive modernization following World War II. There was general agreement, however, that IRI was not compatible with Italy's membership in the EU and the liberalized economic climate.

Foreign Affairs. Foreign affairs became embroiled with domestic questions when the EU imposed diplomatic sanctions on Austria for allowing Jörg Haider's Freedom Party to join the government. German Chancellor Gerhard Schröder stated that the EU would intervene in Italy should the National Alliance (AN) ever become part of a cabinet. AN, a member of the center-right Pole, had Fascist antecedents, but years earlier had professed to moving away from its origins and accepting the democratic system. In 1994, AN became part of the short-lived Berlusconi government, and since then had been treated as a normal fixture of the Italian political scene. Schröder's remarks brought a rare display of solidarity among all Italian political forces. Prime Minister D'Alema ordered the Italian ambassador in Berlin to lodge a protest, and remarked that Schröder had a "limited understanding" of Italian reality. In a strongly worded statement, D'Alema declared that "None of the political forces belonging to the opposition Pole professes a nondemocratic, neo-fascist ideology," nor did they have anything to do with Haider's ideas.

This intervention quieted the German storm; but during a trip to Italy, Haider attempted to link up with the Pole, which ignored him. Haider caused further consternation when he suggested that, because of their economic affinity, his province of Carinthia in southern Austria could link up with a northern Italian region and become a sort of "super-province" within the EU. Haider's assertions brought a stiff response from Foreign Minister Lamberto Dini, who asked the Austrian government to discourage future visits by Haider.

Besides Austria, Kosovo retained some power to disturb the Italian political scene. The commander of the Italian contingent and second in command of Kosovo Forces (KFOR) criticized the government for its lack of support for the Italian peacekeeping effort. He maintained that Italy did not have the weight in the area that its peacekeeping role entitled it to have, and criticized U.S. arrogance. As a result of his comments, the government replaced him. In a possibly related development, Parliament adopted legislation that would gradually do away with conscription and create a professional army. As part of this program, the Italian armed forces would be reduced in number, but transformed into a much more agile organization. Italy's peacekeeping forces serving under United Nations (UN) auspices were second in number only to those of the United States.

In another development perhaps signaling a more independent foreign policy, Italy broke with its EU partners and abstained on a UN motion condemning Israel for the excessive use of force against the Palestinians in the riots that shook the Middle East during the latter part of the year. The Italians objected because Arab extremists were not condemned as well.

Social Issues. The problem of illegal immigration continued to escalate during 2000, with thousands of desperate people landing on the Adriatic coast of southern Italy from Asia. The government took a hard line, promising to ship the immigrants back to their homelands, but many of them remained in Italian reception centers, found jobs in Italy, or moved on to other countries in the EU.

Government attempts during recent years to stabilize the declining birthrate had some effect, even if it was too early to confirm results statistically. Reports from different parts of the country indicated an increase in the birthrate. The country's national statistical agency published a study of the Italian family that focused on its changing nature. Between 1988 and 1998 the number of families increased, but average family size decreased from 2.9 to 2.7 individuals. Households composed of single persons and of childless couples increased. The study revealed that 71.3% of families had only three members, 21.4% had four, and only 7.7% contained five or more. Stepfamilies also increased.

SPENCER M. DI SCALA
University of Massachusetts, Boston

Japan

Viewed from outside, Japan's government during early 2000 seemed to devote all energies in domestic and foreign affairs to a July summit meeting of eight leading industrial nations (Group of Eight, or G-8). Both Prime Minister Keizo Obuchi, before he died in May, and his protégé, Prime Minister Yoshiro Mori, saw the conference as a progressive step in rescuing the nation from a stubborn recession. They deliberately chose Okinawa, the country's southern island, for the main meeting. The island had suffered in World War II, and been neglected since. It also housed the greatest concentration of U.S. peacekeeping forces based in Japan. As a result, U.S.-Japan relations were involved in preparing for and mounting the summit.

Domestic Affairs.

Since 1952 the Liberal Democratic Party (LDP)—with two brief exceptions—has dominated Japanese politics. In 1993, splinter groups weakened the LDP, and for the first time in 38 years, it failed to form a government. In 1994 the party returned to power, forming a coalition with minor parties. In fact, during the 1990s the LDP has never captured a simple majority in any election—in 1990, 1993, and 1996—for the (lower) House of Representatives.

Party Politics. When the 147th ordinary Diet convened on January 20, distribution of strength in the 500-seat lower house was: LDP 271, Democratic Party of Japan (DPJ) 95, New Komeito 47, Japanese Communist Party (JCP) 26, Conservative Party (CP) 18, Liberal Party (LP) 18, Social Democratic Party (SDP) 14, and minor parties 11. The LDP had only 105 seats in the 252-seat (upper) House of Councillors. On January 28, when Prime Minister Obuchi presented his keynote address to the Diet, he spoke to vacant opposition benches. It was the first time in modern history that a policy speech was partially boycotted.

Opposition parties—the DPJ, the SDP, and the JCP—were protesting the governing coalition's railroading of a bill through the lower house the day before. The legislation abolished 20 lower-house seats, all in the proportional-representation sector of votes (where opposition forces tended to be stronger). Approval was won with support by the governing bloc—the LDP, the LP, and the New Komeito—and in the upper house, February 2.

A second issue soon split the parties. In January a controversial move created a Constitutional Review Council, with a panel in each house of the Diet. It was the first time a formal review of the organic law, adopted in 1947, had been proposed. Most sensitive was Chapter II, Article 9, which denied the nation "land, sea, and air forces" or "other war potential" and named the document the Peace Constitution. The council was not to submit legislation for change, but to devote five years to preliminary debate, and three to revision.

On February 16 the first study session began in the upper house. A number of conservatives in the ruling coalition (the LDP and the Liberals) insisted the process must lead to alteration of the constitution. One party in the coalition (New Komeito) and one in the opposition (the DPJ) agreed only to "discuss" change. Others in the opposition camp (the SDP and the JCP) were adamantly against any charter revision.

Between April and June the LDP suffered a number of political blows. On April 1, Ichiro Ozawa, who years before had left the LDP to form the DPJ, took this party out of the governing coalition. On April 2, Prime Minister Obuchi was hospitalized for exhaustion. A little more than 24 hours later, it was announced he had suffered a

In April 2000, Yoshiro Mori, above, of Japan's dominant Liberal Democratic Party, succeeded the hospitalized Keizo Obuchi as prime minister. Obuchi died on May 14.

stroke, and was temporarily relieved of duties. Chief Cabinet Secretary Mikio Aoki was named acting prime minister. As usual, maneuvers to identify a leader of the LDP, and a prime minister, were screened from the press and the public "behind the clouds" (*kumogakurei*). On April 5 the Diet approved the LDP nomination of Yoshiro Mori to be prime minister (*see also* BIOGRAPHY). The new installed leader promptly reappointed the entire cabinet, including members of New Komeito, which remained in the coalition.

Former Prime Minister Obuchi died May 14. Later in May, Mori made an apology for a series of public gaffes and, facing declining public support, dissolved the lower house on June 2, and called for a national election on June 25. After the June 25 poll, party strength in the lower house was: LDP 233, DPJ 127, New Komeito 31, JCP 20, New Conservative Party (NCP) 7, LP 22, SDP 19, minor parties 21 (for a new total of 480). The governing coalition finished with 271 seats. Opposition Democrats made dramatic gains, advancing from 95 to 127 seats in the new house. On July 4, Yoshiro Mori was reconfirmed as prime minister, and the next day formed a cabinet with holdovers in the Ministries of Finance and Foreign Affairs. But in November he barely survived a no-confidence vote in the lower house. LDP members were among those opposed to the coalition government. Observers predicted that Mori's tenure would be brief.

During the year, precedent was defied in two local elections. On February 6, Fusae Ota became the first woman in Japan to be selected governor, in Osaka Prefecture (the second-largest metropolis). On April 18, Yoshiko Shiotani, backed by the LDP, became the second, in the gubernatorial poll in Kumamoto Prefecture.

The Economy.   Despite the lingering domestic recession, Japan remained prominent among economic powers abroad. The Finance Ministry announced that, as of the end of January, the nation's foreign-currency reserves hit a record high of $293 billion. But, in 1999 the trade surplus fell 11.7% year-over-year to $123 billion. It was the first fall in three years, as a stronger yen undermined Japanese exports by boosting prices of products sold overseas.

On January 28 the government took an unorthodox approach to the domestic financial situation. To meet local government obligations, money was to be borrowed from banks, instead of raised through public

---

JAPAN • Information Highlights

Official Name: Japan.
Location: East Asia.
Area: 145,882 sq mi (377 835 km²).
Population (2000 est.): 126,549,976.
Chief Cities (Oct. 1, 1995 census, metropolitan areas): Tokyo, the capital (city proper), 7,967,614; Yokohama, 3,307,136; Osaka, 2,602,421; Nagoya, 2,152,184.
Government: *Head of state,* Akihito, emperor (acceded Jan. 9, 1989). *Head of government,* Yoshiro Mori, prime minister (took office April 7, 2000). *Legislature*— Diet: House of Councillors and House of Representatives.
Monetary Unit: Yen (110.635 yen equal U.S.$1, Dec. 7, 2000).
Gross Domestic Product (1999 est. U.S.$): $2,950,000,000,000 (purchasing power parity).
Economic Indexes (1999, 1990 = 100): *Consumer Prices,* all items, 109.4; food, 108.9. *Industrial Production,* 95.3.
Foreign Trade (1999 U.S.$): *Imports,* $310,012,000,000; *exports,* $417,623,000,000.

---

bonds. The size of the shortfall, 8 trillion yen ($76 billion), stunned economists. It exceeded the total the government had injected into troubled banks in 1999. Some predicted the gross public debt might surpass gross domestic product (GDP) by the end of the fiscal year (March 2001).

Of course, Metropolitan Tokyo Prefecture was not immune to the problems. In February the flamboyant Shintaro Ishihara, a former LDP minister elected as an independent to be governor of Tokyo, proposed a tax on major banks with headquarters in the city. Beginning in fiscal 2000, the levy would bring in $1 billion per year for five years. Since Tokyo, like other local regimes, regularly received subsidies from the central government, it was vulnerable to pressure from national ministries.

By March 17 the government passed a budget through both houses of the Diet. At $850 billion, it was the largest debt-dependent fiscal plan in Japan's history. The new budget was labeled the "final push" to full recovery.

Economic evaluations were mixed. One survey showed that, in the final three months of 1999, the GDP shrank at an annualized rate of -5.6%. It recovered to +2.4% (quarterly rate, January–March), owing to growth in personal consumption. On June 19 the Economic Planning Agency (EPA) declared that the economy had entered a "trough," 25 months after the down cycle began. The agency predicted a growth rate of 1.6% for fiscal 2000. Gov. Masaru Hayami of the Bank of Japan was more cautious, but on August 14 he implemented a rise in the short-term interest rate, the first in 18 months. The overnight call rate rose to 0.25% from 0%. In the third quarter, ended Sept. 30, the economy grew at only 0.2%, or about 1% for the year.

Inflation was not a serious matter. Coming into 2000, the consumer price index stood at 102.2 (1995=100). The unemployment rate was modest, too (but the Japanese did not think so). In January, jobless numbered 4.7% of the labor force, the highest number in 47 years of record keeping. (At the time the U.S. rate was 4.2%.)

Society. A grimmer set of statistics articulated the prevalence of suicides. In the 12 months to the end of March, the number hit a record 33,048. Health problems accounted for half; economic hardship, another fifth, with 92% of the latter involving men whose companies had abandoned the tradition of lifetime employment.

In July, three former leaders of a doomsday sect were sentenced to death by hanging. Toru Toyoda and Kenichi Hirose belonged to the Aum Shinrikyo, which in 1995 carried out a nerve-gas attack during rush hour in Tokyo's subway system. Satoru Hashimoto also was sentenced for use of sarin gas, and for the murder of a lawyer investigating the band. In February the sect reemerged under a new name, Aleph, and distanced itself from founder Shoko Asahara, on trial for masterminding the attacks.

Foreign Affairs.

Until the end of July, Japan's leaders and local government officials, particularly in the southern islands, were preoccupied with plans for a world conference. Three previous meetings of the leaders of the leading economic powers had been held in Japan—the fifth (1979), the 12th (1986) and the 19th (1993)—and were assembled in the capital and thus were called Tokyo Summits. In 2000 the 26th was the first hosted by Japan outside of Tokyo, and was named the Kyushu-Okinawa Summit. It welcomed delegates of seven nations (the G-7—Japan, Italy, France, Germany, Great Britain, Canada, and the United States)—and Russia (making the G-8).

Kyushu-Okinawa Summit. The summit met in three phases. The finance ministers' meeting was held in Fukuoka, northern Kyushu, on July 8. It dealt with the impact of the revolution in information technology, and called for reform of the international financial system. The foreign ministers' sessions were held July 12–13 in Miyazaki, southern Kyushu. Devoted to the prevention of regional conflicts, the diplomats considered reform of the United Nations (UN), especially of the Security Council. All reports were then sent to the assembly of

© Tom Hanson/AP/Wide World Photos

Leaders of the G-8, the leading industrial nations, met in Japan in July 2000 to discuss financial, technological, and diplomatic matters. The leaders, above, from left, were: Great Britain's Prime Minister Tony Blair; U.S. President Bill Clinton, Canada's Prime Minister Jean Chrétien, Germany's Chancellor Gerhard Schroder, Japan's Prime Minister Yoshiro Mori, Russia's President Vladimir Putin, European Commission President Romano Prodi, Italy's Prime Minister Giuliano Amato, and France's President Jacques Chirac.

heads of state, which met July 21–23 in Nago on Okinawa. Japan contributed to the final "Okinawa 2000" communiqué by suggesting establishment of a digital opportunity task-force to bridge the "digital divide" between developed and developing nations.

U.S. Relations. Relations between Tokyo and Washington centered on Okinawa in 2000. Two-thirds of the 47,000 U.S. troops in Japan were based on this tiny island with less than 1% of Japan's total area. Indeed, in 1996 the United States had signed an agree-ment to reduce its military presence in Oki-nawa and, specifically, to close the base at Futenma, providing Japan found an alterna-tive site. In 1999, Prime Minister Obuchi, facing protests against "base pollution," decided to match two objectives. He chose the coastal city of Nago for the summit, and agreed that a planned U.S. heliport be locat-ed offshore. In return, the United States offered $1 billion for reconstruction of Nago and preparations to build the air base.

U.S. President Bill Clinton arrived in Okinawa for the G-8 summit on July 21. It was the first visit by a U.S. president since the island reverted to Japan in 1972. Clinton went first to a memorial devoted to more than 200,000 Okinawan civilians, Japanese soldiers, and U.S. servicemen who died in 1945. Meanwhile, Tokyo and Washington had been engaged in ongoing trade disputes. In January, the U.S. Commerce Department imposed punitive dumping duties on certain Japanese steel products, claiming they were being exported at prices below cost of pro-duction. On March 22 in Tokyo, two trade delegations remained deadlocked in negoti-ations over deregulation of Japan's telecom-munications. The dispute involved Nippon Telegraph & Telephone (NTT), a former state monopoly that still controlled 99% of local phone traffic. On July 19 in Tokyo, the two sides agreed to reduce hookup fees by 40%. The U.S. case had been supported by private Japanese firms, such as Sony.

Russian Relations. In May, when Prime Minister Mori made his grand tour to brief leaders on the upcoming summit, he natu-rally sought out Russia's newly elected pres-ident, Vladimir V. Putin. They met first in St. Petersburg on April 29, not under auspi-cious circumstances. Eight days before, a Russian patrol boat had fired on and seized a Japanese fishing vessel in waters just north of Hokkaido. The incident occurred near a string of small islands claimed by Japan but occupied by Russia since the end of World War II. What the Japanese called the

"Northern Territories" dispute had blocked a peace treaty with Russia. The two leaders promised to settle the matter and to aim for a treaty by the end of the year.

China Relations. The Japanese were star-tled when several of their large companies were sued by individuals in China. For ex-ample, Canon Inc. was taken to task for cir-culating, on the mainland, a disc implying that China, Hong Kong, and Taiwan were three separate countries. In fact, Tokyo, like Washington, has recognized only one China. Another suit charged Toshiba Corporation with treating Chinese consumers like sec-ond-class customers.

Despite strengthening trade ties many Chinese still harbored long-simmering resentment toward the Japanese. The Chi-nese further pointed to joint U.S.-Japan poli-cy, which pledged defense of "areas sur-rounding Japan," and concluded that the areas include Taiwan.

The Two Koreas and Southeast Asia. Japan has faced a similar dilemma in formu-lating policy toward the Korean peninsula. On March 7 the government announced plans for talks with delegates from the Democratic People's Republic of Korea (North Korea), the first formal contact in 22 years. To aid with the famine in the North, Tokyo released 100,000 tons of rice by way of a UN program. On April 8, negotiations to normalize relations opened in Pyongyang, but soon stalled over the demand that Japan compensate for its colo-nial domination of Korea from 1910 to 1945. The two sides did agree to meet again in Tokyo, but on August 23 a two-day session reached a dead end. North Korea continued to insist on reparations, and Japan countered with a demand for information on ten of its citizens believed to have been kidnapped and taken to the north.

Meanwhile, formal relations with the Republic of Korea (South Korea) were fur-ther enhanced by a boom in travel between Japan and the peninsula, via the door-city of Fukuoka. After the thaw in relations be-tween Pyongyang and Seoul, President Kim Dae Jung visited Prime Minister Mori in the resort of Atami in September. Kim urged Japan to normalize ties with North Korea.

In January, Prime Minister Obuchi made a six-day visit to Thailand, Cambodia, and Laos. It marked an effort to intensify dia-logue between members of the Association of Southeast Asian Nations (ASEAN) and the G-8 nations.

Ardath W. BURKS, *Rutgers University*

Jordan

When Jordan's King Hussein died on Feb. 7, 1999, his eldest son, Abdullah II, acceded to the throne. By the end of 2000, the new king had completed nearly two years as monarch. While it was too early to make a definitive assessment of Abdullah's success as a ruler, the early impressions were favorable. Any ruler of Jordan is certain to have problems and difficult policy decisions to make. Jordan is a fairly small country, much of it desert, with limited natural resources and chronic economic troubles. In 2000, poverty was widespread, and Jordan's foreign debt amounted to about $7 billion. Jordan has frontiers with six other states—one of the limitrophe countries being Israel, and another Iraq—so King Abdullah had to step warily in terms of foreign policy, as King Hussein did throughout his long reign, with an occasional sacrifice of consistency sometimes necessary.

As ruler, King Abdullah II has been energetic, adroit, and, with some qualifications, effective. If no great breakthroughs were achieved during his first full year as king, neither were there any crises.

Toward Economic Development. King Abdullah placed high priority on economic development, making it the primary objective of his policies. It was clearer perhaps than during Hussein's reign that Jordan was simply not possessed of the power to shape major regional developments in the foreign policy arena—though a good deal was achieved by Hussein through example and influence based on his maturity and long experience. Abdullah's foreign policy has been quite active, and primarily motivated by economic concerns and hopes. Such considerations indeed permeated the whole of his domestic and external policies.

Internally, the king worked to free commerce and development from the host of restrictions and bureaucratic impediments—including corruption, cronyism, and old-boy solidarity—that had hampered it. In this ongoing effort, the king was moderately successful, though clearly he felt obliged to proceed slowly so as not to disturb the opposition. Desirable technical changes in such matters as trademarks, copyrights, patents, and the general investment climate were carried through. Economic reforms insisted upon by the International Monetary Fund (IMF)—deficit reduction and the curbing of inflation—were carried out, though they were often unpopular.

It was a somewhat controversial step that was taken when Jordan became a member of the World Trade Organization (WTO) on May 11. Approval of Jordan's pending application should have occurred late in 1999 at the WTO meeting in Seattle, but the disruption there delayed the decision. Only six other Arab countries were members of the WTO in 2000.

Economics and Diplomacy. An agreement with Iraq enabled Jordan to receive oil from Iraq, its only source, at less than market prices. This annual pact—permitted by the United Nations (UN) as an exception to the sanctions imposed after the Gulf War—was renewed by Jordan and Iraq on January 22, with improved terms for Jordan. The new agreement envisaged Jordanian-Iraqi trade at a level of $300 million per year, an increase of 50%. In the first major privatization of a state-owned industry, the Jordanian

In April 2000, King Abdullah II (left) made his first visit to Israel as Jordan's monarch, meeting with Israeli Prime Minister Ehud Barak in the Red Sea resort of Eilat.

government on January 23 approved the sale of 40% of the network Jordan Telecommunications to France Telecom. The latter undertook to invest $400 million in modernizing the facilities over the next several years. On April 23, the king met Israel's Prime Minister Ehud Barak. The two leaders sought to better economic links between Jordan and Israel. The 1994 peace with Israel had not brought to Jordan much of the hoped-for economic advantages. They also discussed Israeli relations with the Palestinians. On April 25, the king met with Palestinian leader Yasir Arafat. Also in April, Abdullah launched a project for a low-tax economic zone at Jordan's port of Aqaba. This, it was hoped, would stimulate foreign investment, especially in tourism and technology, and eventually create as many as 70,000 jobs.

In June the king visited President Bill Clinton in Washington, DC, and they agreed to open talks on creating mutual free trade. U.S.-Jordanian trade was amounting to some $300 million per year. On July 19, in Damascus, Abdullah and the new ruler of Syria, Bashar al-Assad, agreed on plans to bolster economic relations between their countries. Syria also undertook to supply Jordan with much-needed water.

Other Developments. In March 1999, when the king appointed Abdel Rauf Rawabdeh prime minister, he publicly directed the new premier to proceed with "fundamental reforms" in fighting corruption and unemployment, as well as advancing democracy. The prime minister undertook to do so, but was very slow in executing reforms. Something of a rivalry developed between Rawabdeh and the newly appointed chief of the royal court, Abdul Karim Kabariti, who was more liberal in the poli-

© AP/Wide World Photos

Jordan's Queen Rania (left)—at 29 the world's youngest queen in 2000—realizes that she represents "women in the Arab world" and shares their "hopes and aspirations."

cies he advocated. The rivalry was not entirely productive, but it was a surprise in January when Kabariti was dismissed. Also in January the prime minister's son, Issam, was accused of corruption. The charge later was held groundless by a parliamentary investigation. However, in June the king dismissed Rawabdeh and appointed Ali Abul al-Ragheb, a former businessman and reformer, as prime minister.

In March, Pope John Paul II journeyed to the Holy Land and made a stop in Jordan, where he was welcomed by the king and the entire royal family.

Demonstrations and Violence. In October, violence between Israel and the Palestinians evoked widespread protests in the Middle East. In Amman, a group of Palestinians demonstrated outside the Israeli embassy, demanding its closure, and were fired on by troops. One young Palestinian was killed, though Jordanian authorities claimed not by the troops. During an October meeting of the Arab League in Cairo, Jordan signed a joint document that accused Israel of committing atrocities; Jordan undertook to keep relations with Israel to a low minimum.

In July an attempted hijacking of a Royal Jordanian Airlines jet en route from Amman to Damascus was thwarted when security agents aboard shot and killed the would-be hijacker. However, he threw a grenade that wounded 15 passengers. Finally, two employees of the Israeli embassy in Amman were wounded in separate gunshot attacks in November and December.

ARTHUR CAMPBELL TURNER
University of California, Riverside

JORDAN • Information Highlights

Official Name: Hashemite Kingdom of Jordan.
Location: Southwest Asia.
Area: 34,445 sq mi (89 213 km²).
Population (2000 est.): 4,998,564.
Chief Cities (Dec. 31, 1991 est.): Amman, the capital, 965,000; Zarqa, 359,000; Irbid, 216,000.
Government: Head of state, Abdullah II, king (acceded Feb. 7, 1999). Head of government, Ali Abu al-Ragheb, prime minister (took office June 19, 2000).
   Legislature—National Assembly: Senate and House of Representatives.
Monetary Unit: Dinar (0.7110 dinar equals U.S.$1, Dec. 31, 2000).
Gross Domestic Product (1999 est. U.S.$): $16,000,000,000 (purchasing power parity).
Economic Indexes (1999, 1990 = 100): Consumer Prices, all items, 140.1; food, 148.5. Industrial Production, 136.7.
Foreign Trade (1999 U.S.$): Imports, $3,728,000,000; exports, $1,782,000,000.

Kenya

During 2000, Kenya's politics continued to be dominated by question of President Daniel arap Moi's succession, and deep division over the path that constitutional reform should take. The nation's economy, hard hit by continuing drought conditions, worsened despite the resumption of financial aid from the International Monetary Fund (IMF) and the World Bank (WB).

Politics. Division over the nation's political future characterized the ruling Kenya African National Union (KANU) and the main opposition parties. The constitutional-reform process remained split between those calling for parliamentary control and those advocating the inclusion of civic society. Among the former was President Moi, and the National Assembly passed legislation creating a select committee to lead the process. Most opposition politicians and religious leaders championed a more inclusive process, led by the People's Commission of Kenya, where the views of ordinary citizens will be incorporated in constitutional changes. In September, the formation of a new pressure group, *Muungano wa Mageuzi* (Movement for Change), mobilized support from ordinary Kenyans.

Deep discontent surfaced as a result of Kenya's poor economic performance. In July the resumption of IMF and World Bank aid was first hailed by the Moi government as a great victory; when that resumption was marked by extremely tough conditions, dissatisfaction emerged among the public. This was particularly the case with the government's attempts to reduce its workforce. Retrenchment was met with much hostility directed toward the government, and donor agencies were perceived to be pushing the government to send thousands of employees to an early retirement.

The Economy. The Kenyan economy faced huge difficulties in 2000, with some commentators citing the worst economic crisis in the nation's history. Gross domestic product (GDP) growth had slowed to 1.4% in 1999, and Central Bank projections for 2000 pointed to a growth rate of less than 1%. Drought produced a food shortage, necessitating imports of maize and government appeals for food aid. Even so, a September report indicated that more than 3 million Kenyans still faced starvation. Power rationing negatively influenced industry and urban households. Indications that the 2000 short rains would be a failure in several parts of the country pointed to further food shortages in 2001. Water was in short supply in many urban areas.

Tea production fell in 2000; coffee production rose, but drought and poor husbandry undermined quality. While tourism earnings had grown in 1999, the sector, hard hit by power cuts and reports of increased crime, experienced a difficult 2000. Horticulture-export earnings showed significant growth. Inflation was increased by the drought and food shortages. The rise in oil prices also boosted inflation and caused further depreciation of the shilling, which reached 78 to U.S. $1.00 in late November. The negative economic impact of the HIV/AIDS epidemic continued to be felt.

The resumption of lending by the IMF and WB provided some assistance to the ailing economy, but was accompanied by strict conditions. Donor institutions gained oversight over much of the government's economic activities. While the IMF eased the conditions in October, donors exerted pressure on the government to effectively combat corruption, speed up the privatization of state-owned firms, and reduce its payroll. The latter led the government to issue more than 25,000 termination notices to state employees in August and September.

Foreign Affairs. Kenya signed a treaty to join Uganda and Tanzania in formation of the East African Community (EAC), which aims to unite the three nations through trade, customs, and East African law. It was agreed in October that each member state would have nine representatives in the community's Legislative Assembly. The EAC inauguration was set for November 2000.

See also AFRICA: A CONTINENT OF PROBLEMS, page 44.

ROBERT M. MAXON, *West Virginia University*

KENYA • Information Highlights

Official Name: Republic of Kenya.
Location: East coast of Africa.
Area: 224,961 sq mi (582 650 km²).
Population (2000 est.): 30,339,770.
Chief Cities (1990 est.): Nairobi, the capital, 1,505,000; Mombasa, 537,000.
Government: *Head of state and government,* Daniel T. arap Moi, president (took office Oct. 1978). *Legislature* (unicameral)—National Assembly.
Monetary Unit: Kenya shilling (77.95 shillings equal U.S.$1, Nov. 21, 2000).
Gross Domestic Product (1999 est. U.S.$): $45,100,000,000 (purchasing power parity).
Economic Index (1998, 1990 = 100): *Consumer Prices,* all items, 377.8; food, 401.6.
Foreign Trade (1999 U.S.$): *Imports,* $2,833,000,000; *exports,* $1,759,000,000.

Korea

Significant political changes in both South Korea and North Korea evolved in the wake of June's epoch-making inter-Korean summit (*see* THE KOREAS: A RAP-PROCHEMENT, page 54). Subsequent to President Kim Dae Jung's bold diplomatic initiative, Seoul became more conciliatory and tolerant toward Pyongyang, but the president's partisan opponents at home raised questions about the pace and conditions of the détente. In April's general elections, a field of veteran politicians were defeated by younger challengers, possibly suggesting the rise of a new generation of political professionals in South Korea. In the North, Chairman Kim Jong Il cautiously maneuvered his country toward more-open contact with the outside world, including the United States, without loosening Pyongyang's tightly authoritarian social order. However, North Korea's economic performance remained lackluster, requiring foreign assistance to feed its population.

Republic of Korea (South Korea)

Politics and Government. In January, Prime Minister Kim Jong Pil, leader of the United Liberal Democrats (ULD), the minority partner in the ruling coalition, resigned in protest of President Kim's reluctance to introduce the cabinet system and share power with the prime minister. Park Tae Jun, former head of Pohang Iron & Steel Co., became the new prime minister, but lasted only five months, plagued by an alleged bribery scandal. Lee Han Dong, a colleague of Kim Jong Pil, became the third prime minister for the year.

Equally uncertain were the tenures of other cabinet ministers. In January, nine ministers, including those in charge of foreign and inter-Korean affairs, were replaced, perhaps in anticipation of the upcoming diplomatic démarche toward North Korea. In August those in charge of economic affairs were replaced, which reflected the rising concern over the economic health of the nation.

The persistent specter of bribery, influence peddling, and other acts of official misconduct loomed heavily over the cabinet-level reshuffling. In the last week of 1999, the minister of justice was arrested in connection with the so-called "furgate" scandal—alleged bribes of expensive clothes and furs that were given to the wives of cabinet ministers, while the director of the National Intelligence Service—the South's powerful spy agency—resigned for his complicity in illicit political fund-raising. Charges of influence peddling and bribery forced a close confidant of President Kim and the minister of tourism to resign abruptly in August. This crisis was followed by the November suicide of a ranking official in a financial-oversight agency.

On April 13, South Korean voters went to the polls to elect their representatives to the National Assembly. The election campaign was particularly fierce for two reasons. First, an electoral-law change enacted just prior to the election reduced the number of electoral districts by 26 to 237 and heightened the competition for a seat. Secondly, both the ruling party, the Millennium Democratic Party (MDP), and the main opposition party, the Grand National Party (GNP), refused to endorse some of their senior party colleagues, thereby creating ill will within the organization and spawning a brand-new Democratic People's Party (DPP) that consisted of the spurned veteran politicians. Moreover, for the first time, a coalition of civic groups waged an active campaign to defeat scores of candidates, including many well-known power brokers in the ruling and opposition parties.

The GNP won the plurality (133, up by 2); the MDP came in second (115, a gain of 10); the ULD lost more than 66% of its Assembly seats (down to only 17); and the DPP secured only two seats, as several of its big-name candidates suffered humiliating defeats. The ULD's disaster was judged by some as a reflection of the declining political clout of its founder, Kim Jong Pil. Then,

---

SOUTH KOREA • Information Highlights

Official Name: Republic of Korea.
Location: Northeastern Asia.
Area: 38,023 sq mi (98 480 km²).
Population (2000 est.): 47,470,969.
Chief Cities (1995 census): Seoul, the capital, 10,231,217; Pusan, 3,814,325; Taegu, 2,449,420; Inchon, 2,308,188.
Government: *Head of state,* Kim Dae Jung, president (formally inaugurated Feb. 25, 1998). *Head of government,* Lee Han Dong, prime minister (appointed June 2000). *Legislature* (unicameral)—National Assembly.
Monetary Unit: Won (1,202.5 won equal U.S.$1, Dec. 14, 2000).
Gross Domestic Product (1999 est. U.S.$): $625,700,000,000.
Economic Indexes (1999, 1990 = 100): *Consumer Prices,* all items, 160.5; food, 168.9. *Industrial Production,* 198.6.
Foreign Trade (1999 U.S.$): *Imports,* $119,750,000,000; *exports,* $144,745,000,000.

simultaneously, the ruling MDP's failure to capitalize significantly on the surprise announcement of the impending inter-Korean summit—only three days before the election—seemed to underscore the continuing strength of the opposition. Legislative gridlock was frequent and prolonged as the result.

In the fall, MDP lawmakers blocked a GNP-sponsored impeachment vote against the prosecutors who were charged with partisan bias in investigation of opposition candidates; the GNP boycotted the legislative session for 45 days. Despite President Kim Dae Jung's enhanced political stature in the aftermath of the Pyongyang summit, South Korea's political scene in 2000 showed serious splits and discord among the ruling and opposition camps.

Prior to a historic summit with South Korea's President Kim Dae Jung in June 2000, North Korea's Chairman Kim Jong Il (left) traveled secretly to Beijing where he met with Chinese President Jiang Zemin (right). China encouraged the reconciliation of the two Koreas.

Society and Economy. The euphoria of the June summit lasted for months, as reassuring words of goodwill and cooperation poured forth from high officials of both sides, and as family members who had been separated for half a century were reunited. A conciliatory tone replaced the strident anti-North rhetoric, much to the discomfort of some conservatives who held to the old confrontational views on Pyongyang. As the momentum for rapprochement began to wane in late fall, however, the general mood in the South appeared to swing away from emotional highs to a more sober reassessment of the situation.

Apart from the headline-grabbing events in inter-Korean relations, South Koreans had little to cheer about. Many tales of bribery, influence peddling, and illegal business and financial practices appeared in the media almost ad nauseam throughout the year. Popular cynicism could be inferred from the 57.2% voter-turnout rate (the lowest ever) in the April elections.

The rising wave of strikes that affected large numbers of wage earners and their employers was more direct evidence of social unrest. By early July, 146 labor disputes were reported, a 35% increase from 1999. The long-standing dispute between doctors and pharmacists over the doctor's right to dispense, as well as prescribe, drugs resulted in repeated, serious disruptions in medical care. Thousands of doctors all across the country went on strike in June and August, in protest against the government's plan to change the age-old practice. By late November a compromise was being negotiated to avert a catastrophic collapse of health services.

Wage and job security were the major demands when Lotte Hotel employees confronted riot police in June; bank employees took similar actions. In November, workers at Daewoo Motor struck for 20 days to stop a projected layoff of nearly 4,000 workers, which the creditor banks demanded of the cash-starved, Number 3 Korean automaker. Also that month, the union at the Korea Electric Power Corporation (KEPCO) threatened to walk out, jeopardizing the country's crucial energy supply, but accepted a last-minute compromise. As December approached, more rumblings on the labor front were clearly audible, as political and economic pressures for corporate restructuring grew ever more intense.

Labor unrest echoed the financial hardships that threatened many businesses, including some of the largest *chaebol* groups.

A list of 18 large companies that faced insolvency—together with scores more that were under financial duress—was made public in early November. Perhaps the most shocking was the cash-flow crisis looming over Hyundai Engineering & Construction Company (HDEC), the original flagship unit of the Hyundai Group, and the largest construction company in Korea.

Despite these tales of woe, South Korea managed to show continued gains in macroeconomic statistics. Buoyed by a record trade surplus of $24.5 billion in 1999, the first and the second quarters of 2000 showed higher-than-expected gross domestic product (GDP) growth rates of 12% and 11%, respectively. However, the trade surplus for the first quarter was only $4.2 billion, while the estimate for the year was set at $9.7 billion. Nevertheless, Seoul announced in early October that it planned to repay the remaining $6 billion of the 1998 International Monetary Fund (IMF) loan.

Foreign Relations. South Korea's diplomacy toward its allies and neighbors continued to focus on relations with North Korea. Seoul informed and consulted with both Washington and Tokyo at every major step of its dealings with Pyongyang, and encouraged them to improve their relations with North Korea. South Korea solicited and received China's help in arranging the Pyongyang summit. Russia was approached for the same purpose. President Kim Dae Jung had opportunities to engage in unofficial talks with his counterparts when he attended the June Asia-Pacific Economic Cooperation (APEC) meeting in Japan, and the November meeting of the Association of Southeast Asian Nations (ASEAN). He also paid state visits to Italy, Germany, and France in March, and to Singapore and Indonesia in late November.

In bilateral relations with the United States, Seoul initiated negotiations for revising the Status of Forces Agreement (SOFA) and held sessions in July and August, in order to secure greater control over legal disputes involving U.S. servicemen, but no final accord was reached. Simultaneously, news that U.S. aircraft mistakenly had fired on civilian targets during training exercises in Maehyang-ni and that U.S. Army personnel had dumped a toxic substance into the municipal sewage system in Seoul added fuel to the latent anti-U.S. sentiment. The investigation into the alleged machine-gun attack on refugees in 1950 continued in 2000 but without resolution.

Seoul's decision to open its doors to Japanese pop culture was welcomed by Tokyo, but the Korean effort to persuade Japan to grant limited voting rights to Korean nationals who were longtime residents of Japan produced no result. A new convention center in Seoul was the venue for a third Asia-Europe Meeting (ASEM) in October, when leaders from 26 nations adopted a "Seoul Declaration," endorsing the process of détente in inter-Korean relations.

Democratic People's Republic of Korea (North Korea)

Ideology and Leadership. The *Rodong Sinmun*, official organ of the ruling Korean Workers' Party (KWP), declared on January 1 that ideology, guns, and scientific know-how were the three pillars for a strong and prosperous state—a familiar refrain coming out of North Korea for years. There was no suggestion of the momentous departure in the North's policy toward the outside world that was to unfold later in the year. Nor was there any hint that the absolute rule of Kim Jong Il would change. Indeed, Kim, chairman of the all-powerful National Defense Commission, managed Pyongyang's dramatic diplomatic about-face without any immediate discernible relaxation of his personal control that was rooted in the demigod status of his father, Kim Il Sung. The 31st volume of the *Collected Works of Kim Il Sung* was published in July, and this latest addition to the monumental collection covered a period in 1963; more than three decades are left yet to be included!

In October the ruling KWP celebrated the 55th anniversary of its founding with a military parade and a mass rally of "1 million persons." Immediately preceding the festivities, an extensive personnel change of military leadership was announced, including the promotion of 44 generals in the 1.2 million–member Korean People's Army (KPA). A few days later, all major KPA unit commanders signed a public pledge of loyalty to Chairman Kim. Another potentially significant personnel change in Pyongyang's leadership involved the replacement of the finance minister and the president of the central bank, which some analysts saw as a preparation for closer economic interactions with South Korea.

Economy. In June the Bank of Korea in Seoul estimated that the North Korean economy had finally bottomed out in 1999; the GDP grew 6.2% for the first time since

1989, although it was only 75% of the corresponding figure ten years earlier. The same South Korean source calculated North Korea's gross national income (GNI) for 1999 as 18.74 trillion won ($15.7 billion), or less than one-twenty-fifth of the South's GNI. The per-capita income was estimated to be 849,000 won ($713), or about one-twelfth of the South's figure. The *Rodong Sinmun* itself admitted at the beginning of 2000 that economic conditions in the North were still difficult.

Crops and livestock suffered once again from drought and heat, and the United Nations (UN) urged its members to donate $332 million in 2000 alone. But such appeals for food aid no longer carried the tone of urgency they used to. At the same time, fragmentary evidence seemed to suggest that Pyongyang was becoming more aware of the need to change its economic policies. When Kim Yong Sun, the senior party secretary in charge of inter-Korean affairs, visited the South in September, his itinerary included a visit to the giant Pohang steel mill. Chairman Kim Jong Il himself paid a visit to a computer-manufacturing plant during his short trip to China in May. In the same month, Pyongyang formally joined the International Chamber of Commerce.

Working-level preparations for North-South joint ventures and the South's investment in the North started with promise. The press reported on plans to construct industrial parks near the border cities of Kaesong and Haeju, to expand the resort facilities in the Mt. Kumgang area, and to construct a less-expensive, faster-to-build thermal-power plant. However, these efforts seemed to be in the preliminary stages at year's end.

In the meantime, inter-Korean trade rose more than 50% in 1999 to reach $334 million. While tens of thousands of Southern tourists visit the famed Mt. Kumgang resort in the North, marine and farm products from the North became part of normal merchandise selections in some of the large supermarkets in the Southern cities.

Foreign Relations. The year 2000 opened wide Pyongyang's diplomatic doors to the outside world, beginning with Italy in early January. By early November, eight other nations—Australia, the Philippines, Canada, Britain, Germany, the Netherlands, Spain, and Belgium—either established or publicly announced the intention to establish diplomatic relations with North Korea.

Nevertheless, for North Korea, the most important diplomatic objectives still concerned the United States and Japan. The momentum created by Vice-Marshal Jo Myong-rok's visit to Washington brought about Secretary of State Madeleine Albright's trip to North Korea in October. However, it stopped short of bringing about President Clinton's widely rumored stopover in Pyongyang on his way home from Southeast Asia in November. Pyongyang's hopes for a complete lifting of U.S. economic sanctions and the removal of its name from the U.S. list of terrorist states were dashed, at least for the time being.

North Korea was no more successful in its negotiations with Japan. Pyongyang's persistent and urgent demand for Tokyo's apology and also for compensation for the latter's colonial record in Korea, and Japan's counterdemand for return of Japanese citizens allegedly abducted by North Korea and also for the discussion of missile tests produced serious debates, but yielded no agreement, in spite of Japan's offer of half a million tons of grain. However, more meetings were promised.

As if to compensate for these difficulties, North Korea stepped up its efforts to strengthen its traditional ties with Russia and China. In July, Russian President Vladimir Putin became the first Russian or Soviet head of state to visit Pyongyang, where he signed a new treaty of friendship and cooperation to replace the defunct military alliance of the Cold War era. China continued to stress its military tie with North Korea by sending its defense chief, Gen. Chi Haodien, to Pyongyang in October. At the same time, China also continued to play the role of an honest broker in encouraging the two Koreas to reconcile—a very delicate maneuver with high stakes.

HAN-KYO KIM, *University of Cincinnati*

NORTH KOREA • Information Highlights

Official Name: Democratic People's Republic of Korea.
Location: Northeastern Asia.
Area: 46,540 sq mi (120 540 km²).
Population (2000 est.): 21,687,550.
Chief Cities (1993 census): Pyongyang, the capital, 2,741,260; Hamhung, 709,730.
Government: *Supreme leader,* Kim Jong Il, chairman of the National Defense Commission and General Secretary of the Workers' Party of Korea (Communist Party). *Nominal head of state,* Kim Yong-nam, president of the Presidium of the Supreme People's Assembly. *Legislature* (unicameral)—Supreme People's Assembly.
Gross Domestic Product (1999 est. U.S.$): $22,600,000,000.
Foreign Trade (1998 est. U.S.$): *Imports,* $954,000,000; exports, $680,000,000.

Labor

The U.S. economy slowed down somewhat during the third quarter of 2000, but still continued to be strong. By December the labor force had increased by 1.4 million compared with December 1999, while the number of unemployed remained essentially unchanged. Inflation for the 12-month period ending October 2000 totaled 3.6%, as compared with 2.7% during the previous year. Worker productivity experienced a second-quarter increase of 6.1%, then dipped to 3.3% during the third quarter.

Unemployment in other industrialized countries, though substantially higher than in the United States, showed improvement over 1999. Japan, Sweden, and Great Britain reported the lowest unemployment rates. Britain reported the highest inflation rate (3.2%), while Japan experienced a 0.7% price decline in the third quarter of 2000.

United States.

Employment. In December, U.S. employment was up by 1.4 million—to 135,800,000—over 1999. The number of unemployed workers remained at 5.4 million—4.0% of the labor force. Unemployment rates improved for teenagers to 13.1% from 13.8% in November 1999, to 7.6% from 7.9% for African-Americans, and to 3.4% from 3.6% for women. Unemployment rates for white workers remained unchanged at 3.5%, rose from 3.3% to 3.4% for adult men, and dropped to 5.7% from 6.0% for Hispanic workers.

Settlements. One of the largest white-collar strikes in years, lasting almost six weeks, was settled by the Society of Professional Engineering Employees in Aerospace and the Boeing Company. The strike affected some 15,000 workers, delayed jet deliveries, and sent Boeing's stock price tumbling. National union leaders saw the settlement as a crucial sign of their ability to organize professional employees. The three-year contract provided average wage increases of 8% to engineers in 2000, and 4.5% increases for 2001 and 2002, plus cash bonuses of up to $2,500. Boeing agreed to extend health coverage to workers' domestic partners, and withdrew a demand that workers contribute toward their health-insurance coverage. Boeing secured the ability to control discretion over which employees would receive about half of the overall wage increases; many workers had opposed merit increases,

not trusting Boeing to distribute raises fairly. Boeing depicted the pact as a compromise, but many analysts viewed it as a victory for the union. Union membership among the 20,000 employees in the bargaining unit jumped from about 40% to nearly 65% after the settlement.

Verizon Communications, the nation's largest telecommunications employer, and its two unions—the Communications Workers of America (CWA) and the International Brotherhood of Electrical Workers (IBEW)—reached a contract agreement after a 15-day strike by 86,000 telephone workers. The strike affected 12 states from Maine to Virginia and the District of Columbia. Another 35,000 CWA members in several mid-Atlantic states settled their strike days later. The agreements provided a 12% wage increase over three years, benefit increases, stock options, greater job security, and more flexibility for the unions to organize in Verizon's fast-growing wireless division. Negotiations were closely watched by the high-technology industry because they involved issues that extended beyond traditional wage and benefits concerns. Verizon promised that union telephone workers would be given the opportunity to do more work in fast-growing areas, such as the installation of high-speed Internet lines, for which the company had tended to use nonunion contractors. Verizon was under pressure to settle the strike, which came at the busiest time of the year—in August, when many students were about to return to college and would require new telephone and Internet service.

In October a six-month strike by thousands of actors who appear in television commercials was settled by the Screen Actors Guild (SAG), the American Federation of Television and Radio Artists (AFTRA), and a coalition of advertisers and agencies represented by the Joint Policy Committee on Broadcast Talent Union Relations. Companies affected by the strike included Anheuser-Busch, Coca-Cola, Burger King, and Procter & Gamble. During the walkout the companies involved were forced to rely on reruns of old commercials, the use of nonunion talent, and foreign shoots. Among the issues settled by the parties were a near doubling, over three years, of the maximum flat fees paid to actors in commercials on cable television. The advertisers also dropped their resistance to recognizing the jurisdiction of the unions for commercials run on the Internet.

Actor Joe Bologna (right) addresses members of the Screen Actors Guild (SAG) and the American Federation of Television and Radio Artists (AFTRA) at an AT&T shareholders' meeting in Chicago. The unions were at odds over AT&T's use of nonunion actors in its ads. Union members (below) also gathered at SAG headquarters in Los Angeles, CA, to show their displeasure with the advertising industry.

© Stephen J. Carrera/AP/Wide World Photos

© Lucy Nicholson/AFP Photo/Corbis

The World Umpires Association, which defeated the Major League Umpires Association in an election conducted by the National Labor Relations Board (NLRB), negotiated a five-year contract with baseball owners. Under the new agreement, salaries in the year 2000 ranged from $81,704 for new umpires to $260,345 for those with 26 or more years' experience. Salaries in the fifth year of the contract would range from $85,716 to $340,505. The establishment of the neutral fact-finder was less than the union's demand for impartial arbitration. It gives an umpire who is fired, suspended for more than seven days, or fined more than $2,000 recourse to appeal to a neutral fact-finder. Findings on dismissals will go to the Commissioner of Major League Baseball, while findings on lesser penalties will be resolved by the executive vice-president for baseball operations. The agreement also provided for the creation of a joint union-management system for training and evaluating umpires in the major leagues.

Unionization. Union membership increased by 265,000 in 1999, to a total of 16.5 million, reflecting increases in both the private and public sectors of the economy. The increase—the largest in ten years—was due to a significant increase in union funds invested in organizing, and also increased hiring by unionized employers. At the end of 1999, unions represented 13.9% of the labor force, about the same as in 1998. Union membership in the private sector was 9.4 million, representing 9.4% of private employment, and 7.1 million public employees—37.3% of employees at all levels of the government.

In the most ambitious organizing drive ever undertaken in the high-technology sector, three unions mounted a campaign to unionize Amazon.com, a leader in electronic retailing. CWA tried to recruit some 400 customer-service representatives in Seattle, Amazon's home base. The United Food and Commercial Workers Union and the Prewitt Organizing Fund, an independent group, sought to unionize 5,000 workers at Amazon's eight distribution centers across the country. The unionization drive gained momentum because workers were upset about layoffs at Amazon and the sharp dip in the value of their stock options. Amazon resisted unionization by providing its supervisors with antiunion material on its Web site to pass on to employees. The company charged that unions mean strife and possible strikes, charge expensive dues, and cannot guarantee improved wages or benefits. The Web site advised managers on warning signs that a union is trying to organize workers. It told supervisors what they could do to oppose a union and what actions violate laws barring retaliation against workers who support unionization. Union leaders admitted that their organizing drive was going somewhat worse than anticipated because of the aggressiveness of Amazon's antiunion efforts. These included meetings for customer-service workers in Seattle where managers argued that unions are bad for workers and customers. The Web site told supervisors: "A union promises and thrives upon problems between supervisors and employees. Frontline supervisors who deal effectively with associate problems avoid associates believing they need a union."

The NLRB ruled for the first time that graduate students who work as research and teaching assistants at private universities have a right to form unions to negotiate wages, benefits, and other conditions of employment. The ruling in a case involving 1,700 graduate-student assistants at New York University (NYU) reversed an NLRB position made in the mid-1970s. Graduate assistants in public universities, who were covered by state laws, already were unionized in several states, including Wisconsin, Michigan, California, and New York.

Officials at Yale University, Columbia University, the Massachusetts Institute of Technology (MIT), and Stanford University supported NYU's position opposing unionization of graduate assistants. By late 2000, NYU had not decided whether to appeal the NLRB decision to the courts. One university president said that "the decision reverses a long-standing precedent that has served this country well and helped to ensure that our system of higher education remains the world's very best."

The three-member labor-board decision was unanimous. It rejected the argument that graduate assistants were predominately students and could not also be employees. It found that the assistants perform services under the control and direction of the employer and that they are compensated by the employer. Despite the new policy, there was no guarantee that the United Automobile Workers (UAW), the union that brought the case to the NLRB, actually would be recognized as the representative of the NYU graduate assistants. That would depend on the outcome of an election in which 1,500 students voted in the spring on whether they wished to be represented by the UAW. The ballots remained to be counted, pending the NLRB decision.

Obituaries.   Two widely known labor activists died in 2000.

Solomon Barkin, 92, served as director of research for the Textile Workers Union 1937–63), after which he held a number of labor-related posts in U.S. and international organizations, taught economics, and wrote widely in academic and popular journals.

Donald F. Ephlin, 74, vice president of the United Auto Workers from 1985–88, was best known for negotiating the innovative agreement between the UAW and the Saturn Division of General Motors.

International

Canada.   Two of the biggest labor organizations in Canada—the Canadian Auto Workers (CAW) and the Canadian Labour Congress (CLC)—were engaged in a power struggle that promised to have a significant impact on that nation's labor movement. CAW, with 220,000 members, is the largest private-sector union in Canada. It split from the U.S. UAW in 1985. The CLC is an umbrella federation representing 2.4 million members, two-thirds of all unionized workers in Canada.

The Congress said that the rift was a result of a blatant grab for members and power by CAW. Workers claimed that their union fought for workers' democratic rights, including the right to break away from foreign-controlled unions. The dispute involved an attempt by some 30,000 Canadian members of the Service Employees International Union (SEIU) to leave its Washington-based parent to join CAW. The CLC charged that CAW had raided the service employees' local unions. The CLC imposed sanctions against CAW, which prevented their officers from speaking or voting at Congress meetings. Buzz Hargrove, president of CAW, denied the charge on the ground that the union did not initiate recruitment of service employees, but that it was approached by service-employee-union leaders. If the CAW forms a rival coalition

---

U.S. EMPLOYMENT AND UNEMPLOYMENT

	(Armed forces excluded)	
	Nov. 1999	Nov. 2000
Labor Force	139,827,000	140,800,000
Participation Rate	67.0%	67.0%
Employed	134,085,000	135,100,000
Unemployed	5,743,000	5,700,000
Unemployment Rate	4.1%	4.0%
Adult Men	3.3%	3.5%
Adult Women	3.6%	3.4%
Teenagers	14.1%	13.1%
White	3.5%	3.5%
African Americans	8.1%	7.4%
Hispanic	6.0%	6.1%

Source: U.S. Bureau of Labor Statistics

to the CLC, there could be a noticeable increase in labor militancy, which could affect labor negotiations in Canada.

Japan. Japan's unemployment rate remained at 4.7% in the year 2000—more than double the rate in the 1980s and early 1990s. This led the Japan Federation of Employers' Associations (Nikkeiren) to urge companies to create jobs by investing in growth-potential areas and to spare no effort to maintain employment levels. Maintaining employment was regarded as a "natural duty," and dismissal of employees before mandatory retirement was "an act of perfidy, " according to Nikkeiren.

The unemployment situation influenced spring wage negotiations; both management and labor emphasized job security over wage increases. As a result, wage increases in 220 major companies averaged 1.97%—17% below 1999, when the wage level rose by 2.14%. The 1.97% increase was the lowest since 1956. An unusual aspect of negotiations in the year 2000 was a joint appeal issued by Nikkeiren and the Japanese Trade Union Confederation (RENGO) on the building of a society friendly to childbearing and child care. Employers and unions were urged to redouble efforts to improve the environment for bearing and rearing children through measures that promote combining a work career with family life.

Ireland. After more than a decade of cordial industrial relations, Irish labor unions returned to the picket lines in November with a series of intermittent one-day strikes by railroad and hospital workers, airline pilots, and journalists. The most serious threat to Ireland's 13-year-old "social partnership" model of industrial relations was posed by the teachers' union. Some 16,000 high-school teachers, members of the Association of Secondary Teachers, joined a growing number of unions that threatened to pull out of a national agreement—called the Programme for Prosperity and Fairness—that sets an annual level of wage increases for three years, if the unions' demands for more pay are not met. The unions contended that rising prices—Ireland's inflation rate of 7% was more than double the European average—made the 5.5% wage increases called for by the national agreement meaningless. The government insisted that the terms of the agreement were not negotiable.

In recent years, the supply and demand for workers have shifted toward flexible and high-paying, private-sector jobs, thanks in large part to the influence of U.S. corporations. Union membership of 500,000, out of a workforce of 1.7 million, fell because most new jobs were in nonunionized areas.

Argentina. The Argentine Senate passed a reform bill intended to lower the 14% unemployment rate by reducing labor costs for business and curtailing the power of labor. The lower house, the Chamber of Deputies—controlled by President Fernando de la Rúa's coalition—passed a slightly different version of the bill. The legislation was designed to replace a rigid labor code set up in the 1950s by President Juan Domingo Perón. As enacted, the new law, encouraged businesses to hire more workers at lower cost. Large companies would be allowed to increase the 30-day probationary period for new hires to six months, and small businesses to one year, after which workers can be dismissed without benefits. Payroll taxes on new hires would be reduced to 12% from 17.5%. Unions opposed the new law and vowed to punish senators who supported the bill by voting against them in elections in 2001.

Venezuela. Voters in Venezuela decisively approved a referendum that ousted the leaders of the country's labor unions who were sympathetic to opposition parties. Fewer than a quarter of eligible voters voted in the referendum, which was boycotted by local labor groups. Leaders of the Venezuelan Workers' Confederation, which represented more than 1.7 million workers who belong to some 200 unions, described the vote as illegitimate. However, in order to avoid a confrontation with President Hugo Chávez, leaders of the country's main labor union federation "temporarily" resigned. A rival pro-Chávez labor movement planned to call a national assembly in February 2001 to create an entirely new union structure.

President Chávez was seeking to consolidate the union movement, which consistently has fought him since his election in 1998, into a single state-controlled entity to be called the Bolivarian Labor Force. The national constitution says that unions cannot be subjected to government intervention, suspension, or administrative dissolution. One editorial stated that industrialists would negotiate directly with the government, instead of with the unions, which could be reduced to a decorative role. As a result of the referendum, Venezuela faced the prospect of international ostracism and possible trade sanctions.

JACK STEIBER, *Michigan State Universit*

Laos

As the Communist Party marked its 25th anniversary since taking power, the Laotian government faced unprecedented challenges in 2000.

Politics. The ruling Lao People's Revolutionary Party was said to be divided, and struggled to contain a deteriorating security situation. At least seven unsolved bomb incidents plagued the capital, insurgent activity intensified, and growing corruption problems generated unrest. Lao dissidents abroad were outspoken after a Laotian prince, linked to the last Lao king, announced plans to replace—through nonviolent means—the one-party system with a constitutional monarchy.

Economy. The government's preoccupation with security, overshadowing economic reform, slowed recovery from the 1997 regional financial crisis. Vientiane announced gross domestic product (GDP) growth of 5.9% for 1999–2000. Tighter monetary policies helped stabilize the Lao kip, which had lost much of its value since 1997. Inflation fell from triple- to double-digit figures. Critical foreign investment, however, slowed considerably, including from neighboring Thailand, traditionally a top investor and trade partner.

Foreign Policy. Faced with less foreign assistance, Vientiane strengthened relations with communist allies Vietnam and China. Vietnam began construction of a military hospital in central Laos, and initiated a joint venture to create a more stable Lao banking system. Beijing financed a cultural center in the capital, and provided low-interest loans for infrastructure building.

Relations with Thailand were strained after Lao rebels crossed the Thai border to stage attacks in Laos. Still active in multilateral groups, including the Association of Southeast Asian Nations, Lao diplomats agreed to host a European Union (EU)–ASEAN meeting in December.

In October the Laotian government announced that it had given the United States the remains of four U.S. citizens listed as missing in action during the Vietnam war.

CHRISTINE VAN ZANDT
U.S. Government Analyst on East Asian Affairs

Latin America

The year 2000 brought economic recovery but weakened democracy to many Latin American nations.

Economic Recovery. As the region overcame the external shocks from Asian and Russian crises, a healthy U.S. economy helped increase Latin American exports. Gross domestic product (GDP) grew 4%, inflation remained manageable at 10%, and some countries relaxed monetary policy. The current-account deficit remained steady at about 3% of GDP. Driven by rebounds in bank lending and intermittently high bond issues, external capital flows were expected to rise to 3.5% of GDP. The employment rate rose slightly. Pay losses slowed in Brazil, while wage gains were felt in the other large economies, including Mexico, Colombia, and Chile. Moderate increases in commodity prices for bananas, shrimp, aluminum, copper, tin, zinc, soybeans, and cotton helped, and the oil-producing countries of Mexico, Venezuela, Colombia, and Ecuador benefited from a steep rise in petroleum prices.

Mexico and Central America. In the July elections, the Institutional Revolutionary Party (PRI) lost the Mexican presidency for the first time in 71 years. Vicente Fox Quesada (*see* BIOGRAPHY) was the winning candidate for the National Action Party (PAN), a business-based party with links to the Catholic Church and a stronghold in the northern states. Fox was expected to dismantle corporatist power networks, further aligning Mexico with neoliberal economic trends; he also promised antipoverty reforms and peace with the Zapatista rebels in Chiapas.

Central America enjoyed good economic growth, but faced a panoply of social problems that polarized politics. Guatemala had elected Alfonso Portillo to the presidency in December 1999, despite his party's links to coup leader Gen. Rios Montt, hoping Portillo could curb soaring crime rates. Hon-

---

LAOS • Information Highlights

Official Name: Lao People's Democratic Republic.
Location: Southeast Asia.
Area: 91,430 sq mi (236 800 km²).
Population (2000 est.): 5,497,459.
Chief City (mid-1995 census): Vientiane, the capital, 531,800.
Government: *Head of state,* Khamtai Siphandon, president (appointed Feb. 24, 1998). *Head of government,* Sisavath Keobounphan, prime minister (named Feb. 24, 1998). *Legislature* (unicameral)—National Assembly.
Monetary Unit: New kip (7,527.1802 new kips equal U.S.$1, Nov. 6, 2000).
Gross Domestic Product (1999 est. U.S.$): $7,000,000,000.
Foreign Trade (1999 est. U.S.$): *Imports,* $525,000,000; *exports,* $311,000,000.

duran authorities barred the most promising opposition candidate from running in primary elections. In Nicaragua, the governing Liberal Constitutionalist Party (PLC) and opposition Sandinista National Liberal Front (FSLN) colluded to pack the Supreme Court, comptroller, and Supreme Electoral Council, and implemented legislation that made it prohibitively difficult for other parties to participate in elections. Municipal elections in November boosted the left-wing Sandinistas' control of key towns, including the capital of Managua.

Troubled Andean Democracies. On January 21, Ecuador experienced a military coup, the first in Latin America since the region returned to democratic government. Under pressure from the United States, Vice-President Gustavo Noboa was sworn in as president. He proceeded with dollarization, which reduced inflation. Nonetheless, in August, two rival legislatures claimed authority and paralyzed politics. Ecuador considered fiscal and administrative decentralization. In December, Ecuador's consitutional tribunal ruled important elements of the country's privatization law invalid, leaving the country again at odds with the International Monetary Fund (IMF).

Peruvian President Alberto Fujimori ran for a third term—having fired the three magistrates of the Supreme Court who had judged his candidacy unconstitutional—and brought the electoral authorities and media under his control through the military-intelligence service. The campaign fell short of international standards for free and fair elections. Second-place finisher Alejandro Toledo withdrew from the runoff after the Organization of American States (OAS) declared the election system nontransparent. President Fujimori won the May 28 runoff election, but resigned on November 20 after revelations that his shadowy intelligence chief, Vladimiro Montesinos, had bribed legislators and run guns to the Revolutionary Armed Forces of Colombia (FARC). Peru's interim government planned a major housecleaning to prepare for new elections in April 2001, but the military demanded an amnesty.

Colombia continued to fight a guerrilla war with the FARC and National Liberation Army (ELN). In 2000, it became the major beneficiary of a controversial $1.3 billion aid package to the Andean region. Critics argued the aid would strengthen Colombia's military without improving its poor human-rights reputation, and did nothing to end right-wing militia violence. Meanwhile, the illegal drug trade continued to pervade Colombia's economy.

Bolivia was slated to receive $25 million to continue eradication and crop-substitution policies, which halved coca production under the Hugo Banzer government. Structural adjustment cut government subsidies and social-welfare plans, shrank the public sector, froze wages, and privatized key services. More than 100 civilians were killed or wounded in protests over economic policy. A 27% reduction in debt servicing offered by donor countries in April 2000 helped South America's poorest country service its estimated $6.2 billion foreign debt.

Meanwhile, populist President Hugo Chávez transformed Venezuela's democracy in an authoritarian direction. A constitutional reform passed in a referendum in December 1999, forcing Venezuela to hold "megaelections" for all posts in May 2000. The elections were postponed at the 11th hour due to technical problems, but Chávez won reelection handily in July, effectively extending his term. Meanwhile, Chávez centralized power by appointing leaders in the judicial and electoral branches, and ignoring his own constitution's provisions for citizen input in selection of the attorney general and ombudsman. The legislature awarded him power of decree to regulate the constitution.

Southern Cone Incoherence. The Southern Cone Common Market (Mercosur) was shaken when Chile declined full membership in order to avoid increasing its tariffs to match Mercosur's standard, preferring to seek trade integration through the Free Trade Area of the Americas (FTAA). In October, President Ricardo Lagos' Concertación won the local elections with 52.1% of the vote. In December, Chile announced it intended to buy ten F-16s to modernize its air force. Some feared the purchase could potentially alter the level of force in the region and spark an arms race.

Argentina's President Fernando de la Rúa's first year in office included five strikes, three cabinet shuffles, and a major scandal in which members of his cabinet stood accused of bribing senators to vote for a labor-reform bill. In October, Vice-President Carlos "Chacho" Alvarez resigned, endangering the governing alliance. The government negotiated an agreement with opposition governors and obtained fresh funding from the IMF, but this victory was soured by a two-day labor stoppage.

SHELLEY MCCONNELL, *The Carter Center*

Law

The 1999–2000 term of the Supreme Court of the United States was one of the most politically explosive in recent memory, as the justices took on some of America's most difficult social and legal issues— including school prayer, abortion, homosexual Boy Scouts, grandparents' rights, and police procedures. The court upheld its famous *Miranda* ruling, which requires police to warn criminal suspects of their rights before questioning them, and let the Boy Scouts ban homosexual troop leaders. The justices dramatically limited states' power to ban "partial-birth abortions," banned organized prayer at public high-school football games, and limited states' power to give grandparents the right to see their grandchildren against the parents' wishes. The justices also continued what some observers have called a states' rights revolution, tipping the federal-state balance of governmental power toward the states. They barred rape victims from suing their attackers in federal courts, and ruled that state employees cannot go into federal court to sue over on-the-job age discrimination.

The justices handed down 73 signed decisions, the fewest since the 1950s. Twenty of those rulings were reached by 5–4 votes, the highest percentage of one-vote outcomes in more than a decade, underscoring for many observers the importance of the November presidential election in determining the court's future direction. The nine justices had been together since 1994, when Justice Stephen G. Breyer joined the court.

Justice Sandra Day O'Connor continued as the court's ideological center, casting only four dissenting votes. Chief Justice William H. Rehnquist and Justice Anthony M. Kennedy dissented nine times each, while Justice Clarence Thomas dissented ten times. Justice John Paul Stevens dissented 28 times, more than any other justice. Many of the 5–4 votes featured the court's most common lineup of Rehnquist, O'Connor, Kennedy, Thomas, and Antonin Scalia on the conservative side, with Stevens, Breyer, David H. Souter, and Ruth Bader Ginsburg on the more liberal side.

In the lower courts, a federal judge ruled that Microsoft Corp. illegally tried to maintain its monopoly, and in June ordered the giant computer software firm split into two companies. Among cases involving the tobacco industry, a Florida jury in July awarded $145 billion in punitive damages to ill smokers in that state. In Washington, DC, a federal judge in September let the federal government pursue racketeering charges against cigarette makers for allegedly concealing the dangers of smoking but dismissed other government claims to recover the Medicare cost of treating sick smokers.

In 2000 the U.S. Supreme Court included (l-r): Chief Justice William H. Rehnquist and Justices Stevens, O'Connor, Scalia, Kennedy, Souter, Thomas, Ginsburg, and Breyer. The court had remained unchanged since 1994.

In international law, the Yugoslav war-crimes tribunal handed down a major ruling in July that broadened the definition of rape as a war crime, making it punishable as an act of torture. The five judges who compose the tribunal's court of last resort upheld a 1998 decision against Anto Furundzija, a Bosnian Croat paramilitary commander during the 1992–95 Bosnian war. Furundzija had been sentenced to ten years in prison for allowing a subordinate to rape a woman prisoner; his appeal claimed the prison term was excessive because the woman had not been killed.

United States

U.S. Supreme Court. The landmark 1966 *Miranda* ruling by the Supreme Court of the United States required police to warn suspects, before questioning them, of their "right to remain silent" and of their right to a lawyer's help. In June 2000 the justices upheld that ruling, 7–2, with Rehnquist writing for the majority that "*Miranda* has become embedded in routine police practice to the point where the warnings have become part of our national culture." The warnings were familiar to generations of Americans through movies and television. A federal appeals court had put the future of those warnings in doubt, ruling that the U.S. Congress in effect overruled the *Miranda* decision when it enacted a 1968 law—long ignored by administrations of both political parties—that said such warnings were not necessarily required. But Rehnquist wrote in *Dickerson v. United States* that Congress could not supersede a constitutional ruling.

Rehnquist again wrote the majority opinion in the court's June ruling that the Boy Scouts of America (BSA) could ban homosexuals from serving as troop leaders. The 5–4 ruling said forcing the scouts to accept gay troop leaders would violate the organization's right of "expressive association" under the Constitution's 1st Amendment, and force the BSA "to send a message, both to the youth members and the world, that the Boy Scouts accepts homosexual conduct as a legitimate form of behavior." Some observers believed the ruling (*Boy Scouts of America v. Dale*) also could allow the scouts to reject homosexual boys as members.

The justices struck down Nebraska's ban on "partial-birth abortion" as an undue burden on women's rights in a 5–4 decision (*Stenberg v. Carhart*) that jeopardized similar laws in 30 other states. The court said the Nebraska law could criminalize more types of abortion procedures than the one at which it was aimed, and the state law lacked an exception to protect women's health. Abortion was legalized nationwide in the court's landmark 1973 *Roe v. Wade* decision, a ruling reaffirmed by the justices in 1992. After the Nebraska law ruling, President Bill Clinton said the right to abortion was "very much in the balance," depending on who won the November presidential election. The court also gave states more leeway to restrict antiabortion demonstrations outside health clinics in a 6–3 ruling (*Hill v. Colorado*) upholding Colorado's limit on "sidewalk counseling."

School-prayer supporters suffered a defeat when the justices ruled that students cannot lead stadium crowds in prayer before public high-school football games. The 6–3 decision (*Santa Fe Independent School District v. Doe*) said such prayers would violate the constitutionally mandated separation of government and religion. A Texas school district had allowed student-elected representatives to give a "message or invocation" over the loudspeaker before football games, but the justices said government could not sponsor the "particular religious practice of prayer." In contrast, another 6–3 ruling (*Mitchell v. Helms*) allowed use of taxpayer money to buy computers and other instructional materials for religious schools.

Underlining parents' right to rear their children free from government interference, the justices ruled on June 5 that Washington State had gone too far in letting grandparents get court-ordered visitation with their grandchildren over the parents' objections. The ruling (*Troxel v. Granville*) did not give parents absolute veto power over who gets to see their children, and did not directly endanger grandparent-visitation laws in the 49 other states, but it did say that states normally should not interfere when parents are adequately caring for their children.

The justices threw out the Clinton administration's main antismoking initiative, ruling 5–4 that the Food and Drug Administration (FDA) lacked authority to regulate tobacco as an addictive drug. The ruling (*FDA v. Brown & Williamson Tobacco Corporation*) invalidated FDA rules that required stores to require identification from anyone under age 27 seeking to buy tobacco products; limited vending-machine cigarette sales to adults-only locations; and limited cigarette advertising.

Continuing the court's states' rights trend, the justices threw out a key provision of the federal Violence Against Women Act, ruling that rape victims cannot sue their attackers in federal court. It is up to the states to provide remedies to women victimized by violence, the 5–4 ruling (*United States v. Morrison*) said.

In criminal cases, the court ruled that an anonymous tip generally is not enough to justify a police officer's stopping and frisking someone (*Florida v. J.L.*), but the court also said that officers often can stop and question someone who runs at the sight of police (*Illinois v. Wardlow*). In two rulings benefiting defendants, the justices said that juries, not judges, must decide whether someone can be given a higher maximum sentence for a hate crime (*Apprendi v. New Jersey*), and that a jury must decide whether people deserve extra punishment for using a machine gun during a crime (*Castillo v. United States*). In the machine-gun case, the justices set aside long prison sentences given to five members of the Branch Davidians.

Local Law. The Justice Department came out on top, perhaps only temporarily, in its antitrust war with Microsoft Corp. U.S. District Judge Thomas Penfield Jackson ruled in April that the giant computer-software company had unlawfully tried to maintain its monopoly over the operating systems that run personal computers, and that Microsoft had tied its Web browser to its Windows operating system. In June the judge ordered the company broken in two pieces—one to sell the Windows operating system, and the other to sell software such as the "Word" program and Internet browser. The Justice Department asked the Supreme Court to take direct review of Microsoft's appeal, but the justices granted Microsoft's request to delay a final decision by having a federal appeals court hear the case first.

The music-recording industry squared off against Napster Inc. over whether the Internet music-sharing service was helping its users violate federal copyright law. In late October, Napster agreed to charge a fee for its service, giving a portion of the income as royalties to record companies. The agreement was intended to settle a lawsuit.

Lawsuits against the tobacco industry were being pursued in numerous courts by smokers, the federal government, cigarette wholesalers, and tobacco growers. After a two-year trial, a Florida jury decided in July that the tobacco industry should pay a record $145 billion in punitive damages to ill smokers in that state. Spectators in the courtroom gasped when the first dollar figure was read, and industry lawyers said the award, if upheld on appeal, would break the industry. In Washington, DC, a federal judge let the Clinton administration seek billions of dollars in damages from the industry for allegedly concealing the dangers of smoking, but dismissed the government's bid to recover the Medicare cost of treating ill smokers. U.S. District Judge Gladys Kessler said the government could pursue racketeering claims in an effort to force the industry to give up profits dating back to the 1950s. Lawsuits also were filed against the industry in February by cigarette wholesalers, who accused cigarette makers of price-fixing, and by tobacco farmers, who said the industry misled them into helping stop federal legislation in 1998 that would have given growers $28 billion.

After fighting a sex-discrimination lawsuit for 23 years, the federal government agreed to pay $508 million to women who had been denied jobs with the U.S. Information Agency (USIA), which disseminates U.S. news and information overseas. It was the largest settlement of a federal sex-discrimination case since the Civil Rights Act became law in 1964. The women had applied for jobs as international radio broadcasters, radio-broadcast or electronic technicians, writers and editors, and production specialists at USIA and the Voice of America (VOA) between 1974 and 1984.

A federal judge awarded former hostage Terry Anderson and his family $341 million from Iran for his treatment during nearly seven years of captivity in Beirut. Anderson, the former chief Middle East correspondent for the Associated Press (AP), was the longest-held American hostage. He was abducted at gunpoint in March 1985 and released in December 1991. U.S. District Judge Thomas Penfield Jackson said evidence was conclusive that Anderson was kidnapped and imprisoned by agents of the Islamic Republic of Iran. Anderson said it was uncertain whether he would ever receive the money.

A federal judge approved New York State's agreement to pay $8 million to former Attica Correctional Facility inmates over the deadly retaking of the prison during a 1971 riot in which 32 inmates and 11 correction officers died, and hundreds more were wounded.

LAURIE ASSÉO
Legal Affair Journalist, Washington, DC

International Law

During 2000 the International Criminal Tribunal for Rwanda and the International Criminal Tribunal for the former Yugoslavia issued a number of indictments and further sought the prosecution of individuals responsible for genocide and other war crimes against humanity.

Rwanda Tribunal. The International Criminal Tribunal for Rwanda (ICTR) was established in Arusha, Tanzania, on Nov. 8, 1994, in response to the genocide that occurred in Rwanda during 1994. The ICTR was established by a resolution of the United Nations (UN) Security Council to ensure the prosecution of individuals responsible for genocide and other violations of international humanitarian law. The ICTR also was mandated to deal with Rwandan citizens who had committed similar acts in neighboring states during the same period. The domestic courts of Rwanda heard charges of genocide and crimes against humanity brought by the Rwandan government against approximately 80,000 individuals.

By late 2000, there were 43 detainees being held in the UN Detention Facility in Arusha. Those in custody included former military commanders, political leaders, journalists, and senior cabinet members from the interim government of Rwanda in 1994, as well as a number of businessmen. Eight detainees—including Jean Kambanda, former prime minister of Rwanda—were convicted by the ICTR.

In 2000, two detainees were convicted and sentenced. On June 1, Georges Ruggiu, a journalist, was sentenced to 12 years in prison for direct and public incitement to commit genocide and crimes against humanity. On January 27, detainee Alfred Musema was sentenced to life in prison for complicity in genocide. The trial of Ignace Bagilishema, former mayor of Mabanza, was completed in October, though a verdict was not immediately issued. Bagilishema had stood accused of genocide, complicity in genocide, crimes against humanity, and serious violations of Article 3 common to the Geneva Conventions of 1949. The appeal of Omar Serushago, a former businessman, was dismissed on February 2. Serushago had been convicted of genocide and crimes against humanity on Feb. 5, 1999. In addition, there were six ongoing trials that had not been completed as 2000 drew to an end.

Yugoslav Tribunal. The International Criminal Tribunal for the former Yugoslavia (ICTY) was established by UN Security Council Resolution 827 in May 1993. Located in The Hague, the Netherlands, the mandate of the ICTY is "to prosecute and try persons responsible for serious violations of international humanitarian law committed on the territory of the former Yugoslavia since 1991." The ICTY has authorization to try four categories of offenses—grave breaches of the Geneva Conventions of 1949, violations of customs or laws of war, genocide, and crimes against humanity.

In 2000 the president of the ICTY was Claude Jorda of France, and the vice-president was Florence Ndepele Mwachande Mumba of Zambia. There were three presiding judges, and Carla del Ponte of Switzerland was serving as chief prosecutor. Tribunal personnel included 1,200 staff members from 75 countries.

From the inception of the tribunal until late 2000, 96 people had been publicly indicted. Eighteen had charges dropped; eight died; four were transferred to serve their sentences; and one was acquitted, leaving 65 outstanding indictments. Of these 65 indictees, 38 of the accused were currently engaged in proceedings; 34 were detained at the Detention Unit in The Hague; four were provisionally released; and 27 of the accused—including Gen. Ratko Mladic, who was indicted for genocide in Bosnia, and former Yugoslav President Slobodan Milosevic, who was indicted for crimes against humanity in Kosovo—were still at large.

Of the judgments in progress, four were on appeal, and 12 were on trial. Thirty-seven of the indictments included grave breaches of the Geneva Conventions, 67 were accused of violating the laws or customs of war, nine were accused of genocide, 60 were charges with crimes against humanity, and 19 were indicted for sexual offenses.

The Bosnian government continued to pursue a case against the Federal Republic of Yugoslavia before the International Court of Justice. Bosnia alleged that forces under the control of the Yugoslav government had carried out a plan of genocide against the people of Bosnia, and that the government of Yugoslavia must be held accountable for these acts. A similar case was filed by Croatia against Yugoslavia. In Kosovo, the UN Mission in Kosovo undertook domestic prosecutions of indicted war criminals before tribunals consisting of Kosovar judges and international judges. No decisions were rendered in these cases.

PAUL R. WILLIAMS, *American University*

Lebanon

The politics of Lebanon are bizarre and convoluted. In 2000 the basic fact, which affected and warped everything else, was that Lebanon had been essentially a satellite of Syria, its larger and more powerful neighbor, for about a decade.

Since the foundation of Israel in 1948, both Syria and Israel have been deeply involved in the affairs of Lebanon, which often functioned as the battleground of their interests. Israel invaded Lebanon in 1982, with the objective of crushing Palestinian guerrilla strongholds. Israel completed a withdrawal from most of Lebanon by 1985, but left some troops in a "security zone" some 6.2 mi (10 km) wide just north of the border, where they cooperated with a friendly Christian, pro-Israeli militia, the South Lebanese Army (SLA). The Lebanese civil war (1975–90) ended when Syria moved in troops that enforced a peace embodied in the Taif agreement. A treaty of friendship and cooperation between Syria and Lebanon was concluded in 1991 that essentially gave Syria control of Lebanese affairs, especially in foreign relations.

Nevertheless, Lebanon experienced substantial changes in 2000. At the beginning of the year, there was explicit Syrian control, in the cautious but ruthless hands of Syrian President Hafiz al-Assad, 30 years in power.

But by midyear, though Syrian control persisted, Hafiz al-Assad was dead, and power was in the hands of his son, President Bashar al-Assad. The Israeli occupation of any part of Lebanon was at an end.

The January Insurrection. The first important happening of the year was an armed insurrection—it was centered on the Dinniya Plateau area, about 30 mi (45 km) northeast of Tripoli. There was also violence in Beirut. The rebellion, though easily crushed in a week, was the most serious internal disturbance since the civil war. It began on Dec. 31, 1999, when an army patrol was ambushed by Sunni militants outside the village of Assun. The insurrection spread, but the Lebanese army quickly moved in force with 3,000 men, and the defeated rebels disintegrated into small groups that quickly disappeared. Rumor assigned responsibility to scapegoats ranging from the Israelis to the universal bogey, Osama bin Laden.

Hezbollah and Israel. The main episodes of violence in 2000, however, stemmed from the fraying away of the 1996 truce between Israel and the militant Islamic group Hezbollah, which over the years had become a sort of controlling force in south Lebanon. There can be little doubt that the cumulative casualties suffered by Israeli forces, though seldom amounting to large numbers at any one time, were the principal

In May 2000, residents of the Israeli-occupied territories in southern Lebanon welcomed fighters from the militant Islamic group Hezbollah after Israeli forces completed their withdrawal from the area. Lebanon remained essentially a satellite of Syria in 2000.

reason for Israel's withdrawal—but that did not end them. Peace negotiations between Israel and Syria were suspended in January. Hezbollah then mounted a series of successful guerrilla attacks against Israeli and SLA forces. Five Israeli soldiers and two SLA men were killed. In February, Israel retaliated by bombing several power stations in Lebanon, reducing much of the country to darkness. There were other attacks by planes and artillery on March 13–14.

The Arab world found the Israeli attacks deeply offensive. President Hosni Mubarak of Egypt visited Lebanon in February, and issued a joint statement with President Emile Lahoud of Lebanon that endorsed Hezbollah's actions and condemned Israel's. The statement demanded that Israel withdraw from the Golan Heights. Similarly, visiting Crown Prince Abdullah of Saudi Arabia underlined Arab solidarity. In March the Arab League issued a pronouncement that supported Lebanon and condemned Israel's "continued aggressions."

The Israeli Withdrawal. In 1999, Premier Ehud Barak of Israel had indicated that he intended to withdraw Israeli forces from Lebanon within a year, with or without a peace pact with Syria. On March 5, 2000, the Israeli cabinet unanimously agreed that Israel should withdraw its troops by July 7. This unconditional undertaking curiously evoked from Lebanon not the welcome one might have expected, but something close to dismay. It held no promise to Lebanon of liberation from Syrian supervision.

In any event, Israel's SLA allies collapsed with unforeseen speed, and the Israeli pullout was totally completed by May 24—six weeks ahead of schedule. Israel had announced in late May that it would grant immigrant status to all SLA members and families who fled to Israel, even though they were not Jewish. Some 3,000 or more did so. In the second half of the year, however, the Lebanese authorities arrested 40 or more Lebanese citizens who were charged with assisting Israel during the occupation; many were given prison sentences.

Lebanon was extremely reluctant to acknowledge that the Israeli withdrawal had actually happened, though under international pressure to do so. On June 15, United Nations (UN) Secretary-General Kofi Annan announced at UN headquarters that the Israeli withdrawal was complete; but Lebanon's Premier Salim al-Hoss retorted that Israel had not yet withdrawn from all Lebanese territory. There were, he said, several Israeli military outposts inside the Lebanese border. Late in May the UN agreed to double—from some 4,500—the existing UN Interim Force in Lebanon (UNIFIL). It was not, however, until August—weeks after the Israeli withdrawal—that Lebanese military and security forces—to the number of about 1,000—began to arrive in south Lebanon. They were not stationed along the border, leaving security to the UN and Hezbollah—which meant, effectively, to the latter. Even after the UN and the Lebanese government had formally accepted the Israeli withdrawal, Hezbollah, virulently anti-Israeli, continued to regard it as incomplete.

Domestic Politics. After the accession of Bashar Assad to the Syrian presidency, voices in Lebanon questioning the nation's dependence on Syria and the presence of 35,000 Syrian troops began to be more daringly raised—though to little practical effect. In these activities the Druze leader Walid Jumblatt played a notable, risky part. In early November the Lebanese parliament ventured to spend five days debating Syria's continued military presence despite the Israeli withdrawal.

A general election for the Lebanese parliament was held in stages in late summer. Former Prime Minister Rafik al-Hariri and his supporters scored a resounding success. He, however, was accepted as prime minister-designate only reluctantly by President Lahoud on October 22; shortly after, Hariri and his new cabinet were given a resounding vote of confidence in the legislature. The new prime minister had always been on the best of terms with Syria, and the composition of his cabinet confirmed that particular relationship would be one of the main planks of his policy.

ARTHUR CAMPBELL TURNER
University of California, Riverside

LEBANON • Information Highlights

Official Name: Lebanese Republic.
Location: Southwest Asia.
Area: 4,015 sq mi (10 400 km²).
Population (2000 est.): 3,578,036.
Chief Cities (1982 est.): Beirut, the capital, 509,000; Tripoli, 198,000.
Government: *Head of state,* Emile Lahoud, president (took office November 1998). *Head of government,* Rafik al-Hariri, prime minister (appointed Oct. 23, 2000). *Legislature* (unicameral)—National Assembly.
Monetary Unit: Lebanese pound (1,507.0 pounds equal U.S.$1, Dec. 27, 2000).
Gross Domestic Product (1999 est. U.S.$): $16,200,000,000 (purchasing power parity).
Foreign Trade (1999 est. U.S.$): *Imports,* $5,700,000,000; *exports,* $866,000,000.

Libraries

In 2000, U.S. libraries were playing an essential role in offering technology to those who could not afford it. A 2000 survey by the U.S. National Commission on Libraries and Information Science found that 94.5% of public libraries offered Internet access to the public and 62.3% provide Internet training. Many libraries had been able to launch these services since 1998 because of discounted phone charges provided by the universal-service programs of the Federal Communications Commission (FCC), funding from the federal Library Services and Technology Act, and computer hardware and software purchased through grants from the Bill & Melinda Gates Foundation.

New Thinking. In the 21st century, literacy encompasses the need for information literacy—the ability to obtain, interpret, and use information from print sources, computers, and other media. This larger definition demands that libraries—public, school, and academic—become influential, relevant community centers where children, parents, and grandparents can develop the skills they need to live, learn, work, and govern in a society transformed by technology. In order to stay vital in an increasingly digital world, libraries have had to offer new services to attract a new generation of users. Some of the ways public libraries have been doing this include: computer-activated pickup lockers for book delivery; interlibrary loan requests through the Web; new library branches in gymnasiums, day-care centers, and malls; Saturday-night Generation-X socials; 24/7 reference service by E-mail; Internet connections for patrons with laptops; Web access for people with various disabilities; video-game competitions; Web scavenger hunts; and interactive media exhibits on community history.

Even the Library of Congress (LC), which celebrated its bicentennial in 2000 (*see* SIDEBAR), has had to rethink its mission and goals. A 2000 report by the National Research Council (NRC) recommended that the LC must continue not only to handle artifacts in traditional media—such as the printed book—but also to collect and preserve electronic books, newspaper Web sites, digital music, and other forms of electronic information. It will be important to preserve materials that lack a print equivalent.

The Freedom to Read. Librarians have been in the front lines in preserving the right of each citizen to choose what to read. In 1995 the number of reported challenges to library materials reached a high of 762, but by 1999 had declined to 472. This decline was likely due to an increased focus away from books to Web sites. Seventy-one percent of the challenges in the past ten years were to materials in schools or school libraries; another 26% were to materials in public libraries. Topping the list of most-frequently challenged books is *Scary Stories*, a series by Alvin Schwartz that was accused of "being too scary" and "unsuited to age group," followed by Michael Willhoite's *Daddy's Roommate*, accused of "promoting homosexuality as a normal lifestyle."

Associations. The American Library Association's (ALA's) 119th annual conference, held July 6–12 in Chicago, IL, drew 24,913 librarians and library supporters. Presiding over the event was ALA President Sarah Ann Long; its theme, "Libraries Build Community," focused on the core values of the profession. Nancy Kranich, associate dean of libraries at New York University, became the ALA's new president.

The Special Libraries Association (SLA), the second-largest library association in North America, held its 91st annual conference June 10–15 in Philadelphia. There are at least 152 national, regional, and state library associations in the United States, with a total membership of about 228,000.

GEORGE M. EBERHART
"American Libraries" magazine, Chicago, IL

Beta Phi Mu Award for distinguished service to education for librarianship: Shirley A. Fitzgibbons, Graduate School of Library and Information Science, Indiana University
Caldecott Medal for the most distinguished picture book for children: Simms Taback, for *Joseph Had a Little Overcoat*, published by Viking
Melvil Dewey Medal for recent creative professional achievement in the tools and techniques of librarianship: Paul Sybrowsky, president, LibraryPlace.com.
Grolier Foundation Award for unique contributions to the stimulation and guidance of reading by children and young people: Michael Cart, writer and consultant
Joseph W. Lippincott Award for distinguished service to the profession of librarianship: John Y. Cole, founding director, Center for the Book, Library of Congress
Newbery Medal for the most distinguished contribution to literature for children: Christopher Paul Curtis, for *Bud, Not Buddy*, published by Delacorte

---

INTERNET LINKS

American Library Association: http://www.ala.org
Special Libraries Association: http://www.sla.org
700+ Great Sites for Kids:
  http://www.ala.org/parentspage/greatsites/
Teen Hoopla: An Internet Guide for Teens:
  http://www.ala.org/teenhoopla
12 Ways Libraries Are Good for the Country:
  http://www.ala.org/alonline/news/12ways.html
100 Most Frequently Challenged Books of 1990–1999:
  http://www.ala.org/alaorg/oif/top100bannedbooks.html

The Library of Congress is 200

On April 24, 2000, the Library of Congress (LC), located in Washington, DC, celebrated its bicentennial with a daylong series of events, kicked off by ceremonies marking the issuance of a commemorative stamp and two coins. It also launched a new Web site, *americaslibrary.gov*, designed especially for children and their families.

On April 24, 1800, President John Adams had authorized $5,000 to purchase books for a library that the U.S. Congress could use in the new capital city of Washington, DC. The books, ordered from London, arrived in 1801 and were kept in the Capitol building. Thirteen years later, during the War of 1812, the British invaded Washington and burned down the Capitol and its library. To replace this tragic loss, Thomas Jefferson sold his private library—the best collection in the country—to Congress in 1815. Those 6,487 books blossomed into what is now the largest and most prestigious library in the world, with nearly 119 million items on approximately 530 mi (853 km) of bookshelves. Today the library's collections include some 18 million books, 2 million recordings, 12 million photographs, 4 million maps, and 53 million manuscripts.

The Library of Congress is unique among the libraries of the world. Though technically it is not the national library of the United States, it operates—in conjunction with the National Agricultural Library, the National Library of Medicine, and the Smithsonian Institution—in the same way as national libraries in other countries.

In addition to its primary function as the legislative library of the U.S. Congress, this national treasure also is: the U.S. copyright agency, a research library for scholars, a public library serving readers in 22 reading rooms, a government library for members of the executive and judicial branches, a national library for the blind and physically disabled, a world-class law library, a provider of cataloging and other

© Gerard Rancinan/Liaison Agency

The Library of Congress, which celebrated its bicentennial in 2000, is the world's largest and most prestigious library. The Main Reading Room, with its ornately designed dome, above, is at the heart of the library's primary building, the Thomas Jefferson Building, named for the president who sold his personal library to Congress in 1815.

bibliographic products to other libraries, a musical-performance center, the home of the U.S. poet laureate, and a showcase for the nation's cultural heritage. The library's on-line catalog is available at *lcweb.loc.gov/catalog/*, while other information can be found at *loc.gov/help/*.

GEORGE M. EBERHART

Libya

The trial of two alleged Libyan intelligence agents charged with bombing Pan Am flight 103 over Scotland in 1988 opened in the Netherlands in May 2000. Following Libya's agreement to surrender the suspects, international sanctions that had isolated the country for almost a decade were lifted, enabling Libya to seek international investments to shore up its faltering economy. In an effort to enhance its image abroad, Libya played an important role in securing the release of hostages held by Muslim guerrillas in the Philippines.

The Lockerbie Trial. Abdel Basset Ali al-Megrahi and Lamen Khalifa Fhimah, the Lockerbie suspects, pleaded not guilty in February, clearing the way for their trial to open in May. Conducted in accordance with Scottish law and presided over by a Scottish judge, the trial continued throughout the year at Camp Zeist, a former military base in the Netherlands. Even before the trial started, relatives of the victims expressed suspicion that United Nations (UN) Secretary-General Kofi Annan, with the approval of the British and U.S. governments, had promised Libyan leader Muammar el-Qaddafi personal immunity in return for handing over Megrahi and Fhimah. All the parties involved, however, denied the existence of such an arrangement.

The defendants' lawyers began their case by challenging the prosecution's assertion that the bombing had been a Libyan operation, attempting instead to incriminate extremist Palestinian groups acting on behalf of Iran. In June a former Iranian intelligence official publicly lent credence to that assertion, but the Iranian government dismissed the allegation.

Ending Isolation. The lifting of UN sanctions drew business from around the world to Libya, which was anxious to attract international investments to an economy damaged by years of isolation and—except for its oil sector—critically underdeveloped. During the European Union (EU)–Africa summit in April, Qaddafi encouraged the renewal of economic and political ties. Simultaneously, he made clear Libya's intention to use its improved international position to promote African causes. Libya contributed personnel to a UN mission in the Democratic Republic of the Congo, marking its first participation in such an international endeavor in more than a decade. Qaddafi also hosted a series of mul-

LIBYA • Information Highlights

Official Name: Socialist People's Libyan Arab Jamahiriya ("state of the masses").
Location: North Africa.
Area: 679,359 sq mi (1 759 540 km²).
Population (2000 est.): 5,115,450.
Chief Cities (1988 est.): Tripoli, the capital, 591,062; Benghazi, 446,250.
Government: *Head of state,* Muammar el-Qaddafi (took office 1969). *Head of government,* Mubarak al-Shamikh, Sec. Gen. People's Committee (since Mar. 2, 2000). *Legislature* (unicameral)—General People's Congress.
Monetary Unit: Dinar (0.50 dinar equals U.S. $1, July 2000).
Gross Domestic Product (1999 est. U.S.$): $39,300,000,000 (purchasing power parity).
Foreign Trade (1998 est. U.S.$): *Imports,* $7,000,000,000; *exports,* $6,600,000,000.

tilateral meetings, seeking a solution to the Congo war. In the spring a sharp increase in oil prices fueled the revival of Western commercial interest in Libya.

U.S.-Libyan relations improved in 2000. In February a Libyan UN official attended an international conference in Washington, DC, marking the first time since the severing of relations in 1981 that a Libyan diplomat was permitted to travel outside New York City. In April a State Department delegation charged with reevaluating a ban on travel to Libya concluded that U.S. citizens faced "no imminent danger" there. U.S. participation in Libya's economic boom was facilitated in June when Congress loosened sanctions imposed in 1986. This legislation allowed the export of food and medicines to Libya, along with other previously blacklisted states, and was expected to generate several billion dollars in sales.

Libya and the Filipino Muslims. In late summer, Libya brokered the release of more than a dozen hostages held by a Muslim guerrilla organization in the southern Philippines. Libya agreed to pay some $12 million in ransom to the Abu Sayyaf movement, as well as to provide an additional $25 million in economic-development funds to the impoverished Muslim regions of the country. Libya's links to Filipino-Muslim groups are almost three decades old, and are rooted in its support for the first stirrings of opposition to the national government by the Moro National Liberation Front. In 1996, Libya had mediated a peace treaty between the Front and the government, but the latter's failure to uphold its commitments sparked the emergence of radical groups, including Abu Sayyaf.

KENNETH J. PERKINS
University of South Carolina

Literature

Overview

A Chinese author was awarded the Nobel Prize in literature in 2000, but there was no celebrating in that country, as the books of Gao Xingjian have been banned there for 13 years. . . .*The Wonderful Wizard of Oz,* by L. Frank Baum, celebrated its 100th birthday in 2000 amid just as much popularity as it had in the early part of the 20th century. . . .Several former Pulitzer Prize finalists finally won the prize, and Susan Sontag, 67, won her first National Book Award for the fiction title *In America.*

Nobel Prize. In awarding the Nobel literature prize to Gao Xingjian, 60, the Swedish Academy cited him for "bitter insights and linguistic ingenuity" in writing about the "struggle for individuality in mass culture." Gao, an author and playwright, left China for Paris in 1987. He denounced the Communist Party after the spring 1989 Tiananmen Square demonstrations.

Although many people, including some in the U.S. literary community, had never heard of Gao prior to the Nobel announcement, he had years of attention from the Chinese government. During the Cultural Revolution of the 1960s, when the government punished intellectuals for their learning, Gao burned much of his early work. He left China so that he could express himself without fear of repercussion. The Chinese Foreign Ministry denounced the award, saying it was being used "for political purposes with ulterior motives."

© Michel Lipchitz/AP/Wide World Photos

Gao Xingjian

Gao's writings have been described as a hodgepodge of styles. His plays mix modernistic techniques with elements of traditional Chinese theater. His most celebrated play, *Bus Stop*, was published in 1983, and was condemned by Communist Party officials as "the most pernicious piece of writing since the foundation of the People's Republic." His best-known book, *Soul Mountain* (1989), uses a variety of literary styles and techniques to trace a ten-month walking tour along the Chang (Yangtze) River. It was the political play *Fugitives*, which is set against the backdrop of the Tiananmen Square massacre, that caused his books to be banned in China.

Other Honorees. Four writers who previously were finalists for Pulitzer Prizes finally received the coveted award in 2000. Donald Margulies won the drama prize for his off-Broadway play *Dinner With Friends*. David M. Kennedy was presented the history award for *Freedom from Fear: The American People in Depression and War, 1929–1945*. C.K. Williams took the poetry prize for *Repair*. And Stacy Schiff was honored for the biography *Vera (Mrs. Vladimir Nabokov)*.

Other winners of 2000 National Book Awards included, for nonfiction: Nathaniel Philbrick, *In the Heart of the Sea: The Tragedy of the Whaleship Essex*; for poetry, Lucille Clifton, *Blessing the Boats: New and Selected Poems 1988–2000*; and, in young-people's, Gloria Whelan, *Homeless Bird*.

Poet Laureate. At the age of 95, Stanley Kunitz, whose first poem appeared in 1930, was named the tenth poet laureate of the United States. He succeeded Robert Pinsky, who had held the position since 1997. Kunitz, who has taught at Columbia University and other institutions, is a founder of the Fine Arts Work Center in Provincetown, MA. He has won just about every poetry prize available. His 12th book of poetry was published late in 2000.

KRISTI VAUGHAN

© Cris Yarborough/AP/Wide World Photos

Stanley Kunitz

American Literature

The year 2000 arrived, and somehow the world did not end. The Y2K bug did not render all the world's computers inoperable and bring about the end of civilization, nor did a biblical apocalypse descend upon the New Year's revelers. Denied catastrophe, American writers instead looked back in consideration of the departing century, summing up its achievements and missteps, reevaluating historical and literary figures in the light of current notions and perspectives. Acknowledging the lessons of the past, writers attempted to understand what the future would bring their nation and culture through examining human connections; in 2000, authors of every variety attempted to redefine what exactly American culture is and what it is becoming. Concern for the future was heightened further by the competitive U.S. presidential race.

Novels. Novels were true to the retrospective quality of the year in at least two ways. Among the most lauded books were those published by authors whose careers had spanned many years, including

Courtesy, Viking/Penguin Putnam

such writers as John Updike, Joyce Carol Oates, Susan Sontag, Philip Roth, E.L. Doctorow, Charles Baxter, and Saul Bellow. At the same time, a number of novels published in 2000 reevaluated the ghosts of times past by focusing upon legendary figures. Joyce Carol Oates sought to lend a new voice to Marilyn Monroe in *Blonde*, and Kathryn Stern described the effect that one date with Elvis Presley had upon a woman's life in *Another Song About the King*. Historian and social critic Richard Slotkin painted the portrait of a more historically significant personage in *Abe*, a book that chronicles in fictional form the first 23 years of Lincoln's life. Jody Shields breathed life into Sigmund Freud's famous patient with a vivid characterization of Dora in *The Fig Eater*, and Gloria Emerson told of a woman obsessed with the literary legacy of the British author in *Loving Graham Greene*.

Lydia Millet placed a darkly humorous spin on obsession in *George Bush, Dark Prince of Love: A Presidential Romance*, her timely story about a love-struck political junkie and stalker. John Updike advanced the concept of reconsidering historical (or in this case fictitious) personalities a step further in his novel concerning Hamlet's usurping uncle and possibly complicitous mother in *Gertrude and Claudius*.

© Dominique Nabokov/Courtesy, Viking/Penguin Putnam

Several important novels published in 2000 were about academic characters or involved academic settings, perhaps indicating the evolving nature of the relationship between serious literature and the modern American university. Francine Prose's *Blue Angel* tells of a college professor navigating the midlife minefields brought about by a challenging woman student and the heightened political sensitivity of his professional world. Denis Johnson's *The Name of the World* is about a former senatorial aide turned history professor who seeks to overcome the profound grief that besets him after having lost his wife and child.

Saul Bellow's *Ravelstein* is a thinly veiled, expansive portrait of the late academic and cultural critic Allan Bloom. Philip Roth's *The Human Stain* renders a complex study of race consciousness and self-creation in its story of how the author's often-used alter ego, Nathan Zuckerman, discovers that a longtime associate (another professor) is actually of African descent despite his having passed for a number of years as Jewish.

Novels that tried to come to terms with the realities of America's past, present, and future include Susan Sontag's experimental *In America*, the tale of a formidable Polish actress who emigrates to the United States. Sontag won her first National Book Award for this effort. In *The Barbarians Are Coming*, David Wong Louie described the Chinese-American experience through this story about a second-generation son who wants to avoid his family's ambitious medical-school plans and become a chef. E.L. Doctorow's metafictional, experimental *City of God* offers a complex portrait of modern faith; similarly, Charles Baxter's equally experimental *The Feast of Love* describes a similar consideration of love and togetherness through examining several characters and their relationships with those closest to them. Catherine Ryan Hyde's popular *Pay It Forward* portrays a young boy's quest to battle back the chaotic world through acts of human kindness. Tony Earley's *Jim the Boy* looks back to the earlier time of the 1930s with unabashed nostalgia and asks whether the American people can ever regain the lost innocence of their childhood.

Short Fiction. Short-story collections in 2000 reflected many of the same thematic interests as their longer counterparts. Collections of short fiction continued to give new writers a voice in an incredibly competitive market, and many of the best collections of the year were by first-time authors. Tim Parrish's *Red Stick Men* uses Baton Rogue, LA, as a setting to examine the relationships between brothers, the lingering effects of the Vietnam war on our culture, and the difficulty of coming of age in modern America. David Means' *Assorted Fire Events: Stories* portrays how haves and have-nots face differing battles for survival as they are battered by the vagaries of life. F.X. Toole's collection *Rope Burns: Stories from the Corner* is ostensibly centered around boxing, but delves much deeper into questions of empowerment and control. The various stories in *The Green Suit* by Dwight Allen all center around the misadventures of one self-interested, wandering protagonist.

Stories in Amy Bloom's *A Blind Man Can See How Much I Love You* show characters sidetracked by circumstance and situations beyond their control who must learn to rely on the human heart. Sherman Alexie continued to describe the experience of modern Native Americans and other dispossessed people of all varieties in his collec-

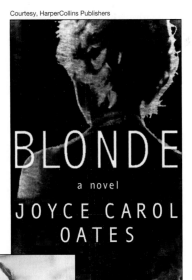

Courtesy, HarperCollins Publishers

BLONDE
a novel
JOYCE CAROL OATES

© Marion Ettlinger/Courtesy, HarperCollins Publishers

tion *The Toughest Indian in the World*, and Tom Paine showed how individuals can be caught up in the sweeping changes of faceless, indifferent politics in *Scar Vegas: And Other Stories*. Russell Banks also dealt with issues of the individual and his role in larger society in *The Angel on the Roof: The Stories of Russell Banks*. George Saunders gave both modern and near-future America sidelong, furtive glances in his equally humorous and sad, as well as experimental, *Pastoralia*. In stark contrast, Alabama writer Helen Norris wrote delicate stories of softly considered relations, family duties, and traditional obligations in her collection *One Day in the Life of a Born Again Loser*.

Poetry. Two of the most important occurrences in poetry in 2000 were not focused so much on current poets as upon those who preceded them. The Library of America released its inclusive two-volume *American Poetry: The Twentieth Century* anthology, containing a vast amount of poems selected by such well-known poets as Robert Haas and Carolyn Kizer, among others. Karen V. Kukil edited the release of *The Unabridged Journals of Sylvia Plath, 1950-1962*, offering insight into the troubled soul and mind of the late poet. Stanley Kunitz, 95, was named poet laureate in 2000, an act commemorated by the publication of *The Collected Poems*.

Narrative poetry prevailed as a popular form in 2000; Kim Addonizio's *Tell Me* uses the narrative form to examine the manifold faces of love. In *Atomic Field: Two Poems*, Nicholas Christopher's entire book is made up of two long narrative ruminations on both high science and the calamities of everyday life. David Kirby related biographical "memory" poems about growing up in Louisiana and a life in letters in *The House of Blue Light: Poems*. Wyatt Prunty also made use of his experiences to show that our lives are equal parts comedy and tragedy in his *Unarmed and Dangerous: New and Selected Poems*. In *Blessing the Boats: New and Selected Poems 1988-2000*, the

NOVELS

Adams, Alice, *After the War*
Allen, Jeffery Renard, *Rails Under My Back*
Antrim, Donald, *The Verificationist*
Baxter, Charles, *The Feast of Love*
Bender, Aimee, *An Invisible Sign of My Own*
Bingham, Robert, *Lightning on the Sun*
Brown, Larry, *Fay*
Bushnell, Candace, *Four Blondes*
Butler, Robert Olen, *Mr. Spaceman*
Danielewski, Mark Z., *House of Leaves*
D'Erasmo, Stacey, *Tea*
Fowler, Connie May, *Remembering Blue*
Goldberg, Myla, *Bee Season*
Harrigan, Stephen, *The Gates of the Alamo*
Hegi, Ursula, *The Vision of Emma Blau*
Heller, Ted, *Slab Rat: A Novel*
Humphreys, Josephine, *Nowhere Else on Earth*
Johnson, Diane, *Le Mariage*
Kafka, Kimberly, *True North*
Kingsolver, Barbara, *Prodigal Summer*
Lent, Jeffrey, *In the Fall*
Lightman, Alan P., *The Diagnosis*
Livesey, Margot, *The Missing World*
Majors, Inman, *Swimming in Sky*
Martin, Gregory, *Mountain City*
Morris, Mary, *Acts of God*
Nixon, Cornelia, *Angels Go Naked*
Oates, Joyce Carol, *Blonde*
Prose, Francine, *Blue Angel*
Shand, Rosa, *The Gravity of Sunlight*
Smith, April, *Be the One*
Sontag, Susan, *In America*
Wheeler, Kate, *When Mountains Walked*
Williams, Joy, *The Quick and the Dead*

SHORT FICTION

Alexie, Sherman, *The Toughest Indian in the World*
Allen, Dwight, *The Green Suit*
Banks, Russell, *The Angel on the Roof: The Stories of Russell Banks*
Berry, R.M., *Dictionary of Modern Anguish: Fictions*
Bloom, Amy, *A Blind Man Can See How Much I Love You*
Carter, Emily, *Glory Goes and Gets Some*
Davies, Peter Ho, *Equal Love*
Harrison, Jim, *The Beast God Forgot to Invent*
Honig, Lucy, *The Truly Needy: And Other Stories*
Means, David, *Assorted Fire Events*
Morgan, Robert, *The Balm of Gilead Tree: New and Selected Stories*
Norris, Helen, *One Day in the Life of a Born Again Loser and Other Stories*
Paine, Tom, *Scar Vegas and Other Stories*
Parrish, Tim, *Red Stick Men*
Remnick, David, and Susan Choi, editors, *Wonderful Town: New York Stories from The New Yorker*
Rodburg, Maxine, *The Law of Return*
Saunders, George, *Pastoralia*
Toole, F.X., *Rope Burns: Stories from the Corner*
Updike, John, *Licks of Love*
Vonnegut, Kurt, *God Bless You, Dr. Kevorkian*
Wolfe, Tom, *Hooking Up*

MEMOIR, CRITICISM, AND LITERARY BIOGRAPHY

Acocella, Joan, *Willa Cather and the Politics of Criticism*
Atlas, James, *Bellow: A Biography*
Bass, Rick, *Colter: The True Story of the Best Dog I Ever Had*
Boyd, Brian, *Nabokov's Pale Fire: The Magic of Artistic Discovery*
Frazier, Ian, *On the Rez*
Gelb, Arthur and Barbara, *O'Neill: Life with Monte Cristo*
Johnson, Kurt, and Steven L. Coates, *Nabokov's Blues: The Scientific Odyssey of a Literary Genius*
Karr, Mary, *Cherry*
King, Stephen, *On Writing: A Memoir of the Craft*
Kumin, Maxine, *Always Beginning: Essays on a Life in Poetry*
Matthiessen, Peter, *Tigers in the Snow*
McGuane, Thomas, *The Longest Silence: A Life in Fishing*

Nordan, Lewis, *Boy with Loaded Gun: A Memoir*
Norman, Geoffrey, *Two for the Summit: My Daughter, the Mountains, and Me*
Rich, Frank, *Ghost Light: A Memoir*
Waitzkin, Fred, *The Last Marlin: The Story of a Family at Sea*

SOCIETY, HISTORY, AND BIOGRAPHY

Armstrong, Karen, *The Battle for God*
Auchincloss, Louis, *Woodrow Wilson*
Barzun, Jacques, *From Dawn to Decadence: 500 Years of Western Cultural Life, 1500 to the Present*
Cahill, Thomas, *Desire of the Everlasting Hills: The World Before and After Jesus*
Carville, James, *Stickin': The Case for Loyalty*
Costas, Bob, *Fair Ball: A Fan's Case for Baseball*
Fraser, Caroline, *God's Perfect Child: Living and Dying in the Christian Science Church*
Gathorne-Hardy, Jonathan, *Sex the Measure of All Things: A Life of Alfred C. Kinsey*
Gordon, Mary, *Joan of Arc*
Gross, Michael, *My Generation: Fifty Years of Sex, Drugs, Rock, Revolution, Glamour, Greed, Valor, Faith, and Silicon Chips*
hooks, bell, *All About Love: New Visions*
Ivins, Molly, and Lou Dubose, *Shrub: The Short but Happy Political Life of George W. Bush*
Kaplan, Alice Yaeger, *The Collaborator: The Trial and Execution of Robert Brasillach*
Lewis, David Levering, *W.E.B. Du Bois: The Fight for Equality and the American Century, 1919-1963*
Morris, Dick, *Vote.com*
Nasaw, David, *The Chief: The Life of William Randolph Hearst*
Philbrick, Nathaniel, *In the Heart of the Sea: The Tragedy of the Whaleship Essex*
Safire, William, *Scandalmonger: A Novel*
Schlesinger, Jr., Arthur M., *A Life in the 20th Century: Innocent Beginnings, 1917-1950*
Simpson, Brooks D., *Ulysses S. Grant: Triumph Over Adversity, 1822-1865*
Snyder, Jack L., *From Voting to Violence: Democratization and Nationalist Conflict*
Spence, Jonathan D., *Mao Zedong*
Thornhill, Randy, Craig T. Palmer, and Margo Wilson, *A Natural History of Rape: Biological Bases of Sexual Coercion*
Tierney, Patrick, *Darkness in El Dorado: How Scientists and Journalists Devastated the Amazon*
Tosches, Nick, *The Devil and Sonny Liston*
Woodward, Bob, *Maestro: Alan Greenspan's Fed and the American Economic Boom*

POETRY

Addonizio, Kim, *Tell Me*
Christopher, Nicholas, *Atomic Field: Two Poems*
Clifton, Lucille, *Blessing the Boats: New and Selected Poems 1988-2000*
Dings, Fred, *Eulogy for a Private Man*
Galassi, Jonathan, *North Street*
Graham, Jorie, *Swarm*
Gunn, Thom, *Boss Cupid*
Howe, Fanny, *Selected Poems*
Ignatow, David, and Virginia Terris, *Living Is What I Wanted: Last Poems*
Kinnell, Galway, *A New Selected Poems*
Kirby, David, *The House of Blue Light*
Koch, Kenneth, *New Addresses*
Kunitz, Stanley, *The Collected Poems*
Lehman, David, *The Daily Mirror: A Journal in Poetry*
Macklin, Elizabeth, *You've Just Been Told*
McHugh, Heather, *The Father of the Predicaments*
Mitchell, Susan, *Erotikon*
Pinsky, Robert, *Jersey Rain*
Prunty, Wyatt, *Unarmed and Dangerous: New and Selected Poems*
Raab, Lawrence, *The Probable World*
Rich, Adrienne, *Midnight Salvage: Poems 1995-1998*
Schnackenberg, Gjertrud, *The Throne of Labdacus*
Seidel, Frederick, *The Cosmos Poems*
Smith, Bruce, *The Other Lover*
Wilbur, Richard, *Mayflies: New Poems and Translations*

winner of the National Book Award for poetry for 2000, Lucille Clifton addressed the race consciousness of American culture.

The Daily Mirror: A Journal in Poetry, by David Lehman, manages to consider both the whimsical and tragic sides of life without dismissing either; similarly, Vermont poet Galway Kinnell's *A New Selected Poems* shows how he has been able to view the mundane world through fresh new eyes again and again over the years. Well-known poets and former poet laureates Richard Wilbur and Robert Pinsky both published books in 2000; Wilbur's *Mayflies: New Poems and Translations* shows his mastery of classical forms and how he transforms them into his own verse stylings, and Pinsky's *Jersey Rain* describes a densely lyrical picture of everyday life in New Jersey.

The Memoir, Criticism, and Literary Biography. Many vital and interesting biographies and critical studies were published in 2000; a number of them were made doubly interesting because they not only focused on living writers but also on authors who released widely scrutinized books in 2000. William H. Pritchard made a defense of John Updike's artistry in *Updike: America's Man of Letters*. Carl Rollyson and Lisa Paddock argued that Susan Sontag's first creation was of her public image in *Susan Sontag: The Making of an Icon*. James Atlas published his exhaustively researched critical biography of Nobel novelist Saul Bellow, *Bellow: A Biography*.

Harold Bloom again contributed to his immense critical legacy with his reader-friendly book *How to Read and*

© Annie Leibovitz/Courtesy, Farrar, Straus and Giroux

Courtesy, Farrar, Straus and Giroux

© Felix Candelaria/MTA New York City Transit/Courtesy, Houghton Mifflin

GALWAY KINNELL

A NEW
SELECTED POEMS

Courtesy, Houghton Mifflin

Why. The Beat writers were fixed beneath the critical microscope once again in 2000; James Grauerholz edited *Last Words: The Final Journals of William S. Burroughs*, and Joyce Johnson published her letters with Jack Kerouac in *Door Wide Open: A Beat Love Affair in Letters, 1957-1958*. The New York of old came under further investigation in David Laskin's *Partisans: Marriage, Politics, and Betrayal Among the New York Intellectuals*, an examination of the soap-opera-like atmosphere that clung to members of the *Partisan Review* crowd, including Edmund Wilson, Mary McCarthy, and Robert Lowell. Also, a number of books were published in honor of the 75th anniversary of *The New Yorker*, including Ben Yagoda's *About Town: The New Yorker and the World It Made*, and *Life Stories: Profiles from The New Yorker*, edited by David Remnick.

Just as the tendency in history in 2000 was to tear the myths away and deconstruct legends of old, so, too, did literary biographies attempt to set the record straight with their subjects. In *James Dickey: The World as a Lie*, Henry Hart tried to show the apocryphal nature of the extravagant stories surrounding the poet's life. Frances Kiernan's *Seeing Mary Plain: A Life of Mary McCarthy* probes to the heart of the stories that have sprung up about the notoriously acerbic writer.

Several excellent memoirs were published in 2000. Dave Eggers' *A Heartbreaking Work of Staggering Genius* tells in a whimsical, postmodern fashion the story of a young man who loses both parents to cancer in a month and must become his young brother's guardian. Michael Paterniti wrote about his bizarre journey through the heartland in *Driving Mr. Albert: A Trip Across America with Einstein's Brain*. *A Walk Toward Oregon: A Memoir* by Alvin M. Josephy, Jr., looks back over the life experiences of a long-lived political journalist.

Society, History, and Biography. Much of the nonfiction written in 2000 was not only retrospective but also revisionist; historical figures and events were reconsidered in the cold glare of the encroaching century. In *Arming America: The Origins of a National Gun Culture*, Michael A. Bellesiles argued that the belief that most Americans owned private firearms at the time of the Revolutionary War is a myth. David Roberts deconstructed frontier mythology in *A Newer World: Kit Carson, John C. Frémont, and the Claiming of the American West*. Evan Thomas attempted to tear down the legends that cling to the more recent legend of Robert F. Kennedy in *Robert Kennedy: His Life*. Two books that reversed the deconstructive trend were Stephen E. Ambrose's *Nothing Like It in the World: The Men Who Built the Transcontinental Railroad, 1863-1869*, and James Bradley and Ron Powers' *Flags of Our Fathers*, about the sacrifice of American troops in the Pacific theater during World War II.

A number of books had a political agenda in mind. Al Gore's lack of free will in determining his destiny was the focus of both Bill Turque's *Inventing Al Gore: A Biography* and *The Prince of Tennessee: The Rise of Al Gore*, by David Maraniss and Ellen Nakashima. George W. Bush was subjected to similar scrutiny in Elizabeth Mitchell's *W: Revenge of the Bush Dynasty*.

Questions of race in America in the 20th century and the approaching 21st were at the heart of a number of books published in 2000. David Levering Lewis' portrayal of the activist in *W.E.B. Du Bois: The Fight for Equality and the American Century, 1919-1963* depicted the earliest days of the civil-rights struggle; David J. Dent tried to discern the true threads of African-American culture in the United States in his book *In Search of Black America: Discovering the African-American Dream*. Scott Malcomson offered commentary on the past and present of race consciousness in *One Drop of Blood: the American Misadventure of Race*.

SCOTT YARBROUGH
Charleston Southern University

Children's Literature

The year 2000 belonged to the sequel in children's literature. Most of the excitement centered around the latest installment in J.K. Rowling's Harry Potter series and the last in Philip Pullman's trilogy, *His Dark Materials*.

Harry Potter and the Goblet of Fire, the fourth in a projected series of seven, was, at 734 pages, almost twice as long as the three previous books. This did not deter legions of readers worldwide, who waited in July to get a copy of the book. It contains a mix of high adventure and evocative storytelling, with a hint of teen angst.

The Amber Spyglass by Philip Pullman follows *The Golden Compass* (1996) and *The Subtle Knife* (1997) and brings to an end the saga of Lyra Belacqua, who has traveled to different worlds to find the source and the meaning of the mysterious Dust, which is causing havoc in the universe. Both books engendered controversy: *Harry Potter and the Goblet of Fire* with its focus on witchcraft and wizardry, and *The Amber Spyglass* because of its antireligion stance. (*See also* BIOGRAPHY—Rowling, J[oanne] K[athleen].)

Illustration by Mary GrandPre
© 2000/Warner Bros. By permission of Scholastic Inc.

The Harry Potter series also was partly responsible for a decision by editors at the *New York Times Book Review* to publish a separate best-seller list for children's books beginning in July. At that time, Harry Potter books had been on the combined list for more than a year and a half.

In award news during 2000, the desired Newbery Award went to *Bud, Not Buddy* by Christopher Paul Curtis, the story of an African-American orphan who goes on the run during the Depression. Simms Taback was presented the prestigious Caldecott Medal for *Joseph Had a Little Overcoat*, which was adapted from a Yiddish song and uses mixed media and collage for its lively illustrations. A new prize, the Michael L. Printz Award—cosponsored by the Young Adult Library Services Association (YALSA), a division of the American Library Association (ALA), and the ALA's review journal, *Booklist*—

was given to *Monster* by Walter Dean Myers.

Picture Books. It was a quiet year for young children's picture books. More interesting were illustrated books aimed at an older audience. *So You Want to Be President*, written by Judith St. George and illustrated by David Small, featured sharp and amusing pictures in the style of political cartoons. In *Michelangelo*, Diane Stanley scanned images of Michelangelo's works into her own paintings. Terry Widener evoked the 1920s in *America's Champion Swimmer: Gertrude Ederle*, a picture biography written by David A. Adler.

Middle Grades. Series books have almost disappeared, but Scholastic's *Dear America* series was popular. The historical fiction books tell the stories of girls during different times in America's history. They are inspired by real letters and diaries from girls who lived in extraordinary circumstances.

Young Adult. The year saw a large number of exceedingly strong young-adult books. Well-known writers such as Gary Paulsen (*The Beet Fields: Memories of a Sixteenth Summer*) and Richard Peck (*A Year*

2000 Newbery Award Winner

2000 Caldecott Medal Winner

SELECTED BOOKS FOR CHILDREN

Picture Books

Chorao, Kay, *Pig and Crow*
Falconer, Ian, *Olivia*
Hamilton, Virginia, *The Girl Who Spun Gold*
Henkes, Kevin, *Wemberly Worried*
Hooper, Meredith, *River Story*
Johnson, Donald B., *Henry Hikes to Fitchburg*
Kellogg, Steven, *The Missing Mitten Mystery*
Lasky, Kathryn, *Vision of Beauty*
Lindbergh, Reeve, *In Every Tiny Grain of Sand: A Child's Book of Prayers and Praise*
Osborne, Mary Pope, *Kate and the Beanstalk*

The Middle Grades

Bishop, Nic, *Digging for Bird-Dinosaurs: An Expedition to Madagascar*
Creech, Sharon, *The Wanderer*
Gantos, Jack, *Joey Pigza Loses Control*
Giblin, James Cross, *The Amazing Life of Benjamin Franklin*
Giff, Patricia Reilly, *Nory Ryan's Song*
Jarvis, Robin, *The Dark Portal*
Konigsburg, E.L., *Silent to the Bone*
Lisle, Janet Taylor, *The Art of Keeping Cool*
Lynch, Chris, *Gold Dust*
Staples, Suzanne Fisher, *Shiva's Fire*

Young Adults

Almond, David, *Kit's Wilderness*
Dessen, Sarah, *Dreamland: A Novel*
Ferris, Jean, *Eight Seconds*
Fradin, Judith Bloom, *Ida B. Wells: Mother of the Civil Rights Movement*
Heneghan, James, *The Grave*
Levine, Ellen, *Darkness Over Denmark: The Danish Resistance and the Rescue of the Jews*
Lowry, Lois, *Gathering Blue*
Spinelli, Jerry, *Stargirl*
Whelan, Gloria, *Homeless Bird*
Wittlinger, Ellen, *What's in a Name*

Down Yonder) did some of their best work. New voices also were heard. Among the best was Terry Trueman, whose *Stuck in Neutral* is about a boy with cerebral palsy whose father may be trying to kill him.

Celebrity Books Publishers in 2000 sought to capitalize on well-known names when they published a number of books written by celebrities. The advantage to publishers was instant name recognition for their authors. The advantage to the celebrity authors often was recognition that they could do more than just act, sing, or play a sport. Among the celebrities publishing children's books in 2000 were newscaster Katie Couric, singer Carly Simon, actress Julie Andrews Edwards, actor John Lithgow, and talk-show host Laura Schlessinger. One of the most successful celebrity authors was actress Jamie Lee Curtis whose four books published since 1993 have sold 1.5 million copies.

ILENE COOPER
Children's Book Editor, "Booklist Magazine"

English Literature

During 2000 the wealth of English literary talent commanded attention not only in the novel but in nonfiction and poetry as well. The coveted Booker Prize for fiction was awarded to Margaret Atwood for *The Blind Assassin*. Atwood's tenth novel tells of the reminiscences of an elderly woman living out her life in a small Canadian town.

Fiction. In Doris May Lessing's new novel, *Ben, In the World: The Sequel to the Fifth Child*, the author continues her penchant for writing tales underscored with fundamental questions of identity and morality as the titular hero seeks meaning for his life. Amit Chadhuri's latest novel, *A New World*, focuses on the life of a Bengali family in Calcutta, a portrait that conveys more the nuance of its fiber than the action of its reality. In contrast, Amitav Ghosh's *The Glass Palace* has an epic sweep of multiple and intertwined stories about an Indian family whose allotted time, character, and development are poised against the fate of Burma from the British conquest of Mandalay in 1886 to the Japanese invasion of 1941. Jaishree Misra, in her first novel, *Ancient Promises*, displays an instinct for writing a good tale centered in lost loves, divided loyalties, and, finally, a bittersweet resolution.

New from Michael Ondaatje, author of the much-acclaimed *The English Patient*, was *Anil's Ghost*, which frequently uses devices of the detective novel to explore character and the scene of his native Sri Lanka. In *Easter*, a liturgically based novel, Michael Arditti ably uses a cyclical narrative pattern to infuse character interest and aesthetically offset the inevitable moral ending. Muriel Spark compounds the plots of two dark tales in *Aiding and Abetting* to rouse the expectation and further the delight of readers of her 21st novel.

Diamond Dust: Stories, Anita Desai's new book of stories, reveals the depth of longing that girds the double lives led by so many family members of the vast Indian diaspora. James Meek's *The Museum of Doubt* shows international urbanity in 14 short stories, half of which focus on one character, a device that unifies and compounds the intensity earned through the short-story medium. And *Liam O'Flaherty: The Collected Stories*, edited in three volumes by A.A. Kelly and published in 1999, provides rich narrative perspective, nuance of character, and amplification of theme in a new setting.

In addition to the winner, fiction that was honored by being included on the Booker Prize shortlist included *Hiding Place* by Trezza Azzopardi, Michael Collins' *Keepers of Truth*, *When We Were Orphans* by Kazuo Ishiguro, Matthew Kneale's *English Passengers*, and *The Deposition of Father McGreevy* by Brian O'Doherty.

Nonfiction. Among the most compelling letters of 2000 were *The Letters of Charlotte Brontë, Volume Two, 1848–1851*, edited by Margaret Smith, bringing the lone Brontë voice vividly to life. *The Letters of Kingsley Amis*, edited by Zachary Leader, appeared in a thick, 1,208-page single volume, and enhances the high regard in which Amis is held. Its publication coincided with that of the autobiographical *Experience: A Memoir*, by Martin Amis, his son. In *Hungry for Home: Leaving the Blaskets: A Journey from the Edge of Ireland*, Cole Moreton traces emigration from a small community on one of the isolated, remote islands of Ireland.

Also in 2000, John Boardman's *Persia and the West: An Archaeological Investigation of the Genesis of Archaemenid Persian Art* examines the imperial art and palatial architecture of ancient Persia, set in contrast, particularly, to the democratically inspired Athenian Parthenon. Among the best books of 2000 in natural history was Richard Fortey's well-written *Trilobite! Eyewitness to Evolution*, which covers thoroughly the now-fossilized arthropod from 540 million years ago. Since no field of study has been untouched by the influence of literary criticism, Volume 7 of *The Cambridge History of Literary Criticism*—edited by A. Walton Litz, Louis Menand, and Lawrence Rainey—was welcomed. This work looks at Modernism and New Criticism.

Poetry. Douglas Dunn's poem, *The Donkey's Ears, Politovsky's Letters Home*, narrates epiclike scenes centered around preparations for the 1905 sea battle between Russia and Japan. The new *Collected Poems* by Derek Mahon firmly establishes his reputation as master poet of the life and passion of the modern urban world. *Weather Permitting*, the fifth book of poems by Dennis O'Driscoll, winner of the 1999 Lannan Award, displays delight in the day-to-day. *The Complete Poems of William Empson*, edited by John Haffenden, with illuminating notes by the poet and the editor, offers an assist to the erudite complexity that infuses so much of the Empson's poetry.

DONALD JENNERMAN
Indiana State University

World Literature

The literary stars rose primarily in the East in the year 2000, with the largest number emerging from Eastern Europe and East Asia. The single brightest literary work of all, however, came out of South America, and flashes of incandescent brilliance appeared in other areas of the world as well.

Latin America. With *La Fiesta del Chivo* ("The Goat's Party"), Peru's Mario Vargas Llosa produced what many readers consider his finest novel ever, perhaps even Latin America's finest ever. Interweaving three separate narratives in a series of alternating

© Martin Mejía/AP/Wide World Photos

Mario Vargas Llosa

chapters, Vargas Llosa both re-creates and examines the 30-year reign and ultimate demise of Dominican Republic dictator Rafael Leónidas Trujillo, also known as El Jefe (The Boss) or El Chivo (The Billy Goat). The author also evokes the chaos and confusion that followed Trujillo's assassination in 1961. The novel is a powerful denunciation of both the private and the public figure of Trujillo and of all such tyrants. But, as one critic astutely pointed out, it also "subtly explores the moral confusion that a dictatorship provokes in the dictator himself as well as in his subjects."

The 1992 Nobel Prize winner Derek Walcott of St. Lucia took up a Caribbean theme as well in his new book-length poem, *Tiepolo's Hound*. The volume's dual narrative examines two lives: that of the noted St. Thomas–born impressionist painter Camille Pissarro, and that of the painter-poet-wanderer Walcott himself. The work finds in the careers of the two artists a shared experience of exile, artistic achievement, and a cer-

tain division in each man between the cultural influences of Europe and those of the West Indies. The power of Walcott's lyricism and his linguistic range more than compensate for any failure to sustain psychological tension throughout his attempted epic.

Russia and East Europe. The gifted and original young Russian author Victor Pelevin led a banner year in East European fiction with his wildly imaginative novel *Buddha's Little Finger*, a hallucinatory recasting of the life of the legendary Bolshevik commander Vasilli Chapaev as told by a time-traveling asylum inmate named Pyotr Void. The result is a surprisingly readable work of postmodern pop art that both satirizes Soviet mythmaking and hero worship and captures the social chaos and psychological disorientation sparked by the disintegration of the Soviet Union. The older superstar author Vassily Aksyonov weighed in with *The New Sweet Style*, a modern picaresque tale of a displaced Russian who wanders the United States, providing a rich panorama of what is ordinary and what is eccentric in the life of a new emigrant. Irina Ratushinskaya's satiric and yet compassionate second novel, *Fictions and Lies*, depicts the close, complex relationship between the old Soviet Union's literary elite and the KGB as it tracks the secret-police investigation into the allegedly slanderous final work by the celebrated late author Pavel Pulin and its imminent publication in the West. Ratushinskaya is able to blend a great variety of tones, ranging from the comical and mocking to the wise, poetic, and forgiving. She manages to humanize and three-dimensionalize the characters on both sides of the ideological divide. The work produces KGB operatives who are not irredeemably vile, and artist-dissidents who are not entirely free of vanity, ambition, and intolerance.

The acclaimed Hungarian author György (George) Konrád brought out *Stonedial* in 2000. The striking new work combines elements of the intellectual teaser and whodunit with the more expansive tapestry of a historical novel covering the years from World War II through the early 1990s. Through the personal story of a famous but world-weary writer returning to visit hometown friends for the first time in years, Konrád limns the turbulent history of a Central European country over more than half a century. He explores such familiar themes as guilt, greed, eroticism, political rivalries, and the responsibilities and burdens of fame. In Polish writer Antoni Libera's new novel,

Madame, a teenage boy in Poland of the 1960s falls obsessively and fatefully in love with his glamorous, charismatic French teacher. The satire of the youth's romantic impulse mixes with tantalizing psychological and sociopolitical intrigue in an epic fantasy that is at once deeply satisfying, heartbreaking, and enthralling. And in *S: A Novel About the Balkans*, the Croatian journalist and writer Slavenka Drakulic documents one of the many horrors perpetrated in the Serbian-run internment camps during the 1990s Balkan conflict: the systematic rape of Muslim and Croatian women and girls in the camps' so-called women's rooms. Too programmatic and illustrative to be deemed a true literary success, the work nevertheless manages to present a fictional study of mass sexual violence and victimization that is both harrowing and effective.

Asia. Mainland Chinese novelist Mo Yan, famed for the scathing satire and historical sweep of such works as *Red Sorghum* and *The Garlic Ballads*, celebrated the year 2000 with an even more stunning novel, the savage and hallucinatory farce *The Republic of Wine*. Alarming reports of widespread corruption and infanticidal cannibalism in the province of Liquorland prompt Communist Party officials to dispatch a special investigator, but he himself soon falls prey to debauchery and mental breakdown, and fails to survive the province's insidiously pervasive (and wildly funny) destructive tendencies. In one of many ancillary story lines, Mo Yan himself appears as a character, a well-known author who carries on a spirited correspondence with a local hack writer and doctoral candidate on matters both literary and nonliterary.

Another of China's "bad boy" novelists, Wang Shuo, produced in *Please Don't Call Me Human* a timely and wickedly inventive satire centered around the 2000 Summer Olympics—awarded some years ago to Sydney, Australia, rather than to Beijing in a decision that caused China a tremendous loss of face internationally. In Wang's novel, we find a version of the Olympics where nations compete not on the basis of athletic prowess but on their citizens' capacity for humiliation. When the thuggish slacker cabdriver from Beijing who is representing China at the Games ultimately triumphs for the motherland by literally ripping off his own face to take the gold, the message is clear: China is the country willing to lose face completely in its obsessive need to win at all costs.

Japan's popular and best-selling Banana Yoshimoto came out with yet another spare, luminous new work in 2000, *Asleep*, a collection of three novellas. Each is narrated by a young Japanese woman who recently has been physically or psychologically paralyzed by some devastating trauma (the death of a beloved brother, the end of a painful affair). All three narrators ultimately manage to work their way back (to health, to sanity, to renewed hope), primarily through the close, regenerative, therapeutic relationships developed with other young women and the narrators' realization of the importance of this female connection.

The Sri Lankan–born writer Michael Ondaatje followed up the huge international success of *The English Patient* with a superb new novel, *Anil's Ghost*, set in his native country during its vicious civil war of the mid-1980s. The politically tinged murder mystery that dominates the main plot line is never resolved fully, but the novel succeeds beautifully in all other aspects, conveying the essence of a people and their history via individual stories etched against a background of natural beauty and human brutality. More broadly still, it illuminates the human condition through the evocation of pity and terror. Many were calling the work the finest of Ondaatje's career to date.

Pakistan's Tariq Ali brought out *The Stone Woman* in 2000, the third novel in his "Islam Quartet"—following *Shadows of the Pomegranate Tree* and *The Book of Saladin*. In the summer of 1899, the family of the retired Ottoman notable Iskender Pasha has retreated to their summer palace overlooking the Sea of Marmara, in full realization that the last great Islamic empire is in serious decline even as they themselves continue to enjoy the advantages accrued through five centuries of unwavering loyalty and service. The end is all too clear in the attitude of a new generation, deeply hostile to the half-truths and myths of the "golden days" of so long ago.

And in the gripping novel *In Search of Walid Masoud*, the Arab author Jabra Ibrahim Jabra tracks the disappearance of a Palestinian intellectual who had been living in Baghdad, Iraq, since the Israeli war of 1948. Since Masoud was a member of an organization engaged in the armed struggle against Israel, the suspicion arises that he has gone underground as part of some political operation.

WILLIAM RIGGAN
"World Literature Today"

Los Angeles

Overall in Los Angeles in 2000, crime was down; the economy was up; housing prices had returned to pre-1990-recession highs; and, by most accounts, racial polarization was quiet. An exodus of residents had reversed, with Los Angeles County leading the nation with a net population gain of 106,182 in the 1990s.

The city saw its new downtown arena, the Staples Center, become the backdrop to two major events. In August, the city—and the center in particular— hosted the Democratic National Convention. Some 40,000-plus delegates, and even more journalists and protesters, were in town for the convention. Many helped to inaugurate a new multibillion-dollar Red Line extension of the city's growing subway system. Earlier, in June, a revamped Los Angeles Lakers basketball team, under new coach Phil Jackson and playing in the new center, won its first National Basketball Association (NBA) championship title in 12 years. The win brought new confidence to a city that lacked a major football franchise. However there were complaints from Staples Center's neighbors about the traffic jams the new arena was causing.

A Negative View. The city was mired in a police-corruption probe that was called the largest scandal in Los Angeles history. It had begun in September 1999, and unfolded in almost daily legal proceedings throughout 2000. The testimony of a rogue police officer implicated dozens of fellow officers accused of shooting suspects, falsifying testimony, and routinely planting evidence to obtain convictions. More than 100 convictions were overturned, and analysts predicted damage settlements could reach $500 million. In mid-November, in the first case to go to court, three officers were convicted of framing gang members. A court-appointed federal monitor was overseeing the Los Angeles Police Department (LAPD). (*See also* POLICING—A PROBLEMATIC ENTERPRISE, page 66.)

Two other developments fed a negative view of the city. In March the city's major civic-boosting entity, the *Los Angeles Times*, was purchased by Tribune Company, owner of the *Chicago Tribune*. And the last Fortune 500 company headquartered in downtown Los Angeles, ARCO—which also had been a leading monetary supporter of culture, education, and other social causes—merged into BP Amoco, with headquarters in London. Both developments were seen as possible harbingers of a loss of local control over important economic and cultural entities.

Labor Unrest and the School District. Three key citywide strikes also commanded headlines. In April, after days of marching in the streets, 8,500 janitors and service-working members of Service Employees International Union (SEIU) Local 1877 won raises. In October, 4,300 striking bus and rail operators stranded 450,000 workers without public transit for nearly a month. And the longest actors' strike in Hollywood history was settled after six months.

At year-end, former Colorado Gov. Roy Romer, the new head of the nation's second-largest school district—with 711,000 students, 70% of whom are Hispanic—was trying to stave off a breakup of the system with plans to create minidistricts.

DANIEL B. WOOD, *Los Angeles Bureau Chief*
"The Christian Science Monitor"

© Patrick Liotta/AP/Wide World Photos

Picketing Los Angeles transit workers shut down the second-largest U.S. bus system and stranded 450,000 commuters and other daily mass-transit riders for nearly a month. The strike was one of three which disrupted city life in 2000.

Macedonia

Macedonia maintained its multiethnic coalition government in 2000, although local-election results indicated that many voters sought change in order to remedy economic and ethnic turbulence.

Politics. Public support for the coalition government, which combined the Internal Macedonian Revolutionary Organization (VMRO) and the largest Albanian party, sagged during 2000. In September's local elections, the opposition Social Democratic Party gained control of 37% of district and municipal seats, winning approximately the same number of posts as the ruling centrist party and the major Albanian organizations. Opposition leaders tried to force the government into early general elections by claiming that authorities failed to deliver on their economic promises.

During the local-election campaign, VMRO Prime Minister Ljupco Georgievski pledged that if support for his coalition fell by more than ten percentage points, he would call early parliamentary elections. The Social Democrats did not gain the needed balloting advantage.

Ethnic Issues. Albanian representatives complained about both insufficient minority inclusion in various public institutions and alleged police harassment of Albanian activists. In July the Macedonian parliament approved measures sponsored by the Organization for Security and Co-operation in Europe (OSCE) to legalize the underground Albanian-language university in Tetovo, establishing it as an accredited private institution.

Economy. Macedonia experienced economic difficulties as a result of several factors, including the long-term impact of the 1999 North Atlantic Treaty Organization (NATO) war over Kosovo and limited foreign investment. The unemployment rate reached about 35% of the working population, while the growth in the gross domestic product (GDP) was projected to be under 3% for 2000. Macedonian officials were eager to promote economic relations with more-developed countries; in May they initialed a trade agreement with the four-member European Free Trade Association (EFTA) in Geneva.

Foreign Relations. In March talks in Skopje focused on creating an agreement to expand relations and trade between Macedonia and the European Union (EU). By year's end, Macedonia appeared ready to sign an agreement with Brussels. In September the EU announced plans to establish a large free-trade zone for industrial and agricultural products from several Balkan states, including Macedonia, Bosnia and Herzegovina, and Albania.

In February officials from Macedonia, Albania, Bosnia and Herzegovina, Bulgaria, Croatia, and Romania agreed to organize a program to encourage free trade and transportation across borders. The EU, the United States, and the World Bank planned to provide financial aid for the upgrading of border crossings, customs administration, and enhancing the Internet infrastructure in order to increase the flow of information among those countries.

JANUSZ BUGAJSKI
Center for Strategic and International Studies

Malaysia

Malaysian Prime Minister Mahathir bin Mohamad clung to power in 2000, but his Malay-based United Malays National Organization (UMNO) reeled from losses in the November 1999 national elections.

Politics. UMNO's chief rival, Parti Islam Semalaysia (PAS), controlled 19 seats in the national Parliament along with two state governments—Trengganu and Kelantan. Mahathir faced open criticism from his own party, yet deftly protected his political position. The prime minister suggested that it would be his final term in office; in May he tapped his deputy, Abdullah Ahmad Badawi, as his successor. The question was whether UMNO and the Barisan Nasional (BN) governing coalition could wait.

In January the government arrested two opposition politicians—Parti Keadilan Vice-

President Marina Yusoff and Karpal Singh, deputy chairman of the Democratic Action Party (DAP)—along with Zulkifli Sulong, editor of the PAS newspaper *Harakah*, on charges of sedition. Yusoff and Singh were linked to Mahathir's rival and former Deputy Prime Minister Anwar Ibrahim, who was convicted of sodomy in August and sentenced to nine years in prison.

In May, UMNO party leadership reappointed Mahathir party president without contest, in a move aimed at building unity and preventing infighting. The UMNO then elected three party vice-presidents—all insiders and supporters of the prime minister. The party did little to regain the backing of its Malay supporters and of the UMNO Youth membership lost to the opposition because of Mahathir's treatment of Anwar.

The BN was shocked when it lost December's Lunas by-election to Parti Keadilan in Mahathir's Kedah state. The BN was hit by a massive defection of Chinese voters. Mahathir retaliated by having nine opposition politicians arrested, including Ezam Mohamad Noor and Azmin Ali. Both are members of Keadilan leadership council.

Defense and Foreign Policy. In response to threats at home and missions abroad, Malaysia planned a fivefold increase in its Territorial Army—from 47,000 to 240,000 by 2020. On July 2 the Islamic fundamentalist group Al-Ma'unah tricked soldiers at two army posts in Perak state into handing over a store of weapons. Although the 27-man group surrendered on July 6, government officials were shocked at the ease with which the operation succeeded. On April 23 the Philippine-based Abu Sayyaf kidnapped 21 tourists from an island resort in East Malaysia. Some proposed expanding Malaysia's 80,000-man army outside the country for possible peacekeeping missions, especially in East Timor.

Economy. The Malaysian economy grew by about 8.5% in 2000, with unemployment at 3% and inflation around 2%. In an effort to encourage foreign investment, the government lifted the 10% exit tax on some portfolio-investment profits. It also eased restrictions on foreign ownership in strategic industries, and planned to allow equity partnerships in the country's crown jewels—Malaysian Airlines and the Proton automobile project. Foreign investment appeared to be headed downward, and money flowed out of the Kuala Lumpur Stock Exchange.

Malaysian Deputy Prime Minister Badawi identified the "New Malay Dilemma" as the fundamental problem confronting the Malaysian economy. In short, how far should the government go to benefit the Malay majority over the Chinese minority? Mahathir initiated the New Economic Policy (NEP) in 1971. It was an affirmative-action program that gave Malays a chance to advance economically through a series of privileges, quotas, and preferences. The NEP succeeded, and officially ended in 1990. However, Badawi acknowledged that the affirmative-action program had been replaced by a de facto system of cronyism, which protected wealthy Malays with UMNO connections. The Malaysian Chinese Election Appeals Committee suggested that all Malaysians, regardless of their ethnic origin, should be helped.

Environment and Society. Air quality in the nation's capital, Kuala Lumpur, was relatively good. All chlorofluorocarbons (CFCs) were to be phased out of manufacturing by 2001. However, only about 25% of the country's waterways were suitable as freshwater sources. Land degradation was a serious problem. In October the government placed a temporary freeze on all development projects in Malaysia's highland areas. Land clearing and logging in the Cameron Highlands caused severe problems of downstream silt buildup.

Malaysian society was pulled in different directions by two different forces. Islamization was evident on university campuses, where there was a growing presence of religious activists and ideologues, by the recent ban on video arcades, increased controls on television content, and the growing strength of Parti Islam.

PATRICK M. MAYERCHAK
Virginia Military Institute

MALAYSIA • Information Highlights

Official Name: Malaysia.
Location: Southeast Asia.
Area: 127,317 sq mi (329 750 km²).
Population (2000 est.): 21,793,293.
Chief Cities (1991 census): Kuala Lumpur, the capital, 1,145,342; Ipoh, 382,853; Johor Baharu, 328,436.
Government: *Head of state,* Sultan Salahuddin Abdul Aziz Shah, king (installed September 1999). *Head of government,* Mahathir bin Mohamad, prime minister (took office July 1981). *Legislature*—Parliament: Senate and House of Representatives.
Monetary Unit: Ringgit (Malaysian dollar) (3.8000 ringgits equal U.S.$1, Jan. 2, 2001).
Gross Domestic Product (1999 est. U.S.$): $229,100,000,000 (purchasing power parity).
Economic Indexes: *Consumer Prices* (1999, 1990 = 100): all items, 139.5; food, 158.3. *Industrial Production* 209.2.
Foreign Trade (1999 U.S.$): *Imports,* $64,962,000,000; *exports,* $84,451,000,000.

Medicine and Health

The government reported in 2000 that life expectancy in the United States reached a record high of 76.7 years. Other statistics revealed that breast-cancer death rates fell approximately 25%, teenage births fell to a 60-year low, and the number of cigarettes smoked annually per person declined 42% between 1990 and 1999. Counterbalancing this upbeat news were reports of alarming increases in diseases such as asthma, diabetes, and untreated tooth decay. Worldwide during 2000, diseases of poverty continued to extract an enormous toll, and an estimated 5.3 million people became infected with AIDS, with the continent of Africa particularly affected (*see* AFRICA: A CONTINENT OF PROBLEMS, page 44).

A World Health Organization (WHO) study of the health systems of its 191 member nations found the best health systems in Europe—France, Italy, San Marino, Andorra, and Malta—ranked one through five. The United States, which spends more money per capita than any other nation on health care, was ranked 37, scoring poorly on its ability to deliver good health care to a large percentage of its population.

Elimination of health disparities among population groups is a primary goal of Healthy People 2010, an initiative with 467 specific objectives to improve the health of U.S. citizens by 2010. These objectives range from improved access to prenatal care to increased physical activity among adolescents and adults. The initiative is under the direction of the U.S. Department of Health and Human Services.

Also in the United States, greater public attention was focused on the quality of health-care services and on Parkinson's disease. Meanwhile the rising cost of prescription drugs caused concern, and a late-1999 report by the surgeon general drew interest in mental-health circles. In the field of bioethics, new debate occurred on the extent to which genes can be patented.

Overview

Cardiovascular Disease. Chest pain has long been considered the characteristic sign of a heart attack, but a study led by John G. Canto of the University of Alabama found that about 33% of heart-attack patients experienced no chest pain. These patients arrived at the hospital three hours later than those suffering chest pain, and were less

© Donna Day/STONE

Dietary habits, including among American youngsters who tend to prefer "junk" food, remained a prime concern in health circles. The National Institutes of Health reported in 2000 that, for the first time, a majority of Americans were clinically overweight.

likely to be diagnosed with a heart attack at the time of admission. Perhaps as a result of these factors, the patients were more than twice as likely to die in the hospital compared to heart-attack patients that suffered chest pain.

A study led by Janice Williams, while at the University of North Carolina, followed nearly 13,000 adults for six years. It found that people who are most anger-prone are nearly three times more likely to have a heart attack than people who rank low in anger-proneness. Researchers at Ohio State University reported that people with high levels of hostility show increased levels of homocysteine, a blood chemical strongly associated with coronary heart disease.

Brief interruptions of blood flow to the brain cause ministrokes, or transient ischemic attacks (TIAs), that last anywhere from a few seconds to 24 hours. Symptoms, such as weakness or numbness, are variable and sometimes ignored by patients. TIAs seldom cause permanent damage, but often presage a major stroke. Researchers at the Mayo Clinic estimated that some 500,000 TIAs occur in the United States annually.

Evidence has shown that aspirin interferes with the formation of blood clots. Giving a stroke patient an aspirin immediately upon arrival at the hospital, and continuing aspirin therapy in the days and months following the stroke, significantly reduces the risk of recurrent stroke, according to an analysis of studies involving 40,000 stroke patients. "Early aspirin therapy should be used much more widely," said lead author Zheng Ming Chen of the University of Oxford in England.

A study from the Massachusetts General Hospital reported that aspirin use in patients with coronary heart disease—the cause of heart attacks and angina, and the United States' single-largest killer—also was low: 26% in 1996 (the latest statistics available). "A substantial number of patients are at higher-than-necessary risk of developing future heart problems because they are not taking aspirin," commented the study's author, Randall Stafford.

New research confirmed the relationship between diet and cardiovascular disease. A group led by Frank Sacks of Harvard University Medical School showed that a diet low in salt and high in fruits and vegetables can be as effective as medication in reducing hypertension. Tetsuji Yokoyama of the Tokyo Medical and Dental University in Japan found that people with high blood levels of vitamin C have a significantly reduced risk of stroke. During the 20-year period of the study, said Yokoyama, risk of stroke was 70% higher in the quarter of the individuals with the lowest vitamin-C level than in the quarter with the highest level.

Cancer. The National Institute for Environmental Health Sciences added 14 substances to the list of known causes of cancer, including alcoholic beverages, excessive sunshine, sunlamps, silica dust, and secondhand tobacco smoke. The drug tamoxifen, widely used to treat and help prevent breast cancer in women at high risk for the disease, also made the list because it can increase the risk of ovarian cancer. The report pointed out, however, that tamoxifen's benefits can outweigh the risks.

Women with breast cancer who have high blood levels of the hormone insulin are at increased risk of developing a recurrence and dying of the disease, according to a Canadian study headed by Pamela J. Goodwin of the University of Toronto. The study followed 535 women with newly diagnosed breast cancer for up to ten years. Of the women with the highest insulin levels, 70% were alive after seven years, as compared with 95% of the women with the lowest insulin levels.

A team headed by Janet Stanford at the Fred Hutchinson Cancer Research Center in Seattle collected data that highlighted the profound effect that removing a cancerous prostate can have on a man's quality of life. The survey of 1,291 men found that nearly 60% were rendered impotent by the surgery, and more than 8% experienced bladder-control problems.

Two screening exams for colon cancer—sigmoidoscopy and colonoscopy—use a fiber-optic device inserted through the rectum into the colon. Sigmoidoscopy, the more commonly used procedure, examines only the lower part of the colon, while colonoscopy looks at the organ's full length. Two studies reported that sigmoidoscopy is likely to miss precancerous growths. They found that half the patients with precancerous lesions in the upper colon had no abnormalities in the lower region.

The Pap test has been used since the 1940s to detect cervical cancer and precancerous changes in the cervix. A new test may be more effective. Called the HPV test, it looks for the presence of the human papillomavirus (HPV), a sexually transmitted microorganism responsible for almost all cervical cancer. In a South African study, the HPV test detected 84% of cancers and precancerous growths versus only 68% identified by the Pap test. Similar results were obtained in a Costa Rican study.

Asthma. The prevalence of asthma, a chronic inflammation of the lungs, increased dramatically, particularly among children, since 1980. About 14 million U.S. citizens have asthma. It is the most common chronic disease among children, the leading medical cause of school absenteeism, and the main reason for emergency-room visits. A study released by the Centers for Disease Control and Prevention (CDC) during the year showed that most states lack systems to track and monitor people with asthma.

The root cause of asthma is unknown, but a variety of factors, including bronchial diseases and atmospheric pollution, can set off attacks. Sufferers who regularly use steroid inhalers to ease breathing problems also decrease their risk of dying from the disease, according to a large study headed by Samy Suissa of McGill University in Canada. In August the Food and Drug Administration (FDA) approved the use of a corticosteroid inhalant for use by asthmatic children as young as 1 year.

Researchers at the University of Arizona College of Medicine reported that children exposed at an early age to other children in day-care centers suffered more sniffles and ear infections than toddlers kept at home. But it appeared that fewer of the day-care children developed asthma. Furthermore, those who did develop asthma experienced fewer attacks than asthmatic children not as exposed to other children. The findings suggest that early infections and exposure to other children protect against the development of asthma and allergies.

Colds, Flu, and Pneumonia. In November the FDA warned that PPA (phenylpropanolamine), an ingredient in hundreds of over-the-counter cold remedies and diet pills, is unsafe and would be banned. The action came after a five-year study at Yale University showed that PPA increases the risk of stroke in young women. Manufacturers of affected products pulled PPA-containing versions from store shelves, and began offering reformulated versions.

In 1999 the FDA approved two new influenza drugs, Tamiflu (oseltamivir) and Relenza (zanamivir). The drugs promised to reduce the period of severe flu symptoms by a day or two, and demand for them grew. Early in 2000, however, the FDA warned that physicians might be relying too heavily on the drugs. Apparently, some patients had been treated solely with these drugs, even though they had developed bacterial infections, against which the drugs are ineffective.

The FDA approved Zyvox (linezolid), the first entirely new kind of antibiotic in 35 years. Zyvox is designed to attack deadly bacteria that cause pneumonia and other infections commonly found in hospitals and nursing homes, killing some 80,000 U.S. citizens annually. Experts stressed that Zyvox should be used only for the worst infections and for those suspected of being resistant to older antibiotics; otherwise, bacteria will soon develop a resistance to it, too.

Gynecology. During menopause, levels of the hormone estrogen in a woman's body drop dramatically. For years, hormone-replacement therapy (HRT)—estrogen or estrogen combined with progestin—was widely recommended for postmenopausal women. A great deal of research indicated

multiple benefits from HRT, including protection against heart disease. However, studies reported in 2000 produced contradictory evidence. A study led by David Herrington of Wake Forest University Baptist Medical Center followed 309 older women who suffered heart disease. The study found no indication that HRT slowed the progression of their disease. Herrington noted that HRT "did lower cholesterol, but these changes didn't translate into a measurable benefit in the arteries of the heart." Early data from the Women's Health Initiative, a federal study involving 25,000 women, suggested that HRT slightly increased the risk of heart attacks, strokes, and blood clots. (This study will be completed about 2006.)

Sixteen years after U.S. clinical trials began, and more than a decade after the drug became available in Europe, mifepristone, or RU-486, was approved by the FDA. Mifepristone blocks the action of the hormone progesterone, thereby preventing implantation of a fertilized egg in the lining of the uterus. Its use is followed by a dose of the previously approved drug misoprostol, which induces contractions that expel the embryo. This regimen, an alternative to surgical abortion, is effective only during the first seven weeks of pregnancy.

Since the mid-1980s the United States has experienced a steady increase in the proportion of low-birth-weight babies, those weighing less than 5.5 lb (2.5 kg). A federal report attributed most of the increase to the use of fertility aids, such as in-vitro fertilization, and drugs that increase ovulation. These techniques often produce multiple births, with babies more likely than single babies to be premature and tiny. Twin births rose more than 50% from 1980 to 1997, and the number of triplet births quadrupled.

At the time of birth, about 4% of babies are in the breech position, ready to come out rear end first, rather than headfirst. A British study involving 2,083 pregnant women in 26 countries, who all carried babies in the breech position, found that cesarean sections (C-sections) were three times safer than vaginal deliveries in this situation, and greatly reduced the infant's risk of dying or being severely handicapped.

Approximately 294,000 C-sections done in the United States each year are performed because of lack of progress in labor. Researchers at RAND and two universities found that up to 24% of these C-sections may be performed too early, before the cervix is dilated to 1.6 inches (4 cm) or

Medical Mistakes

During the year 2000, greater public attention was focused on the quality of health-care services and especially the safety of health care in the United States.

Incidence and Definitions. The issue of safe or proper health care came to the foreground largely as a result of an Institute of Medicine (IOM) report, *To Err Is Human: Building a Safer Health System*. The report, which was issued in late 1999, built on other IOM quality-oriented work in 1997. The 1999 report focused on adverse events in which an injury was caused by medical management. Such events occur among 3% to 4% of hospitalized patients, and result in about one death in ten.

Health-care researchers have known for years that the U.S. system of care has suffered from a variety of limitations that result in avoidable human injury and death. Medical errors cause an estimated 44,000 to 98,000 deaths in U.S. hospitals annually. The estimates exceed annual deaths from breast cancer, AIDS, or motor-vehicle accidents.

Further, there is reason to believe that half of those deaths are preventable. Some believe that the estimated number of deaths is exaggerated; however, the committee's estimates included no deaths arising from care delivered outside hospital settings, within doctors' offices or clinics. The data within the system are of such poor quality that precise numbers are unavailable, but the number is significant enough to spur action.

In discussing the quality of health care, the committee was careful in its definitions. *Error* is defined as a failure of a planned action to be completed as intended (an error of execution), or the use of a wrong plan to achieve an aim (an error of planning). *Patient safety* is freedom from accidental injury. An *adverse event* is an injury caused by medical management rather than by the underlying disease or condition of the patient. A *preventable adverse event* is an adverse event attributable to error.

Errors are estimated to cost between $17 billion and $29 billion annually. Errors occur because of system failures, and the solution will be found in designing safer systems of care. Many factors—including event reporting, education, information systems with decision support, clearer drug labeling and dosing, and improved policy—require attention.

Recommendations. The IOM report recommended a four-part strategy to reduce errors by at least 50% in five years. First, a national center for patient safety is needed to offer leadership and research. The center would set safety goals, track progress, make periodic reports, and support relevant research. Such a center may be forthcoming within the Agency for Healthcare Research and Quality (AHRQ).

Second, reporting systems are needed to identify errors. The committee recommended a mandatory, nationwide, state-based reporting program for all serious injuries and deaths. The objective is to standardize, not centralize, reporting. Near misses need to be reported voluntarily within each care system. The reporting system will produce firm data that will lead to appropriate changes. The system should help clinical providers acknowledge and discuss errors rather than downplay them. Finally, such structures should assure the public that the care system is committed to continuous quality improvement. It is anticipated that some data would be made public, but protections for the confidentiality of certain information is envisioned. A robust health-information infrastructure will assure the public a more active role in the health-care process. Reporting systems should involve all entities, including purchasers, accreditors, and professional groups.

Third, the needed safety standards should involve all related organizations. Regulators and accreditors should make patient safety a prime component of their evaluations. Licensing and certifying organizations should implement periodic reviews of doctors, nurses, and other key providers. The U.S. Food and Drug Administration (FDA) should be more concerned with public safety. Similar-sounding names for drugs and confusing drug labeling and packaging should be eliminated.

Fourth, health-care organizations must implement safety strategies and provide the leadership to prevent, detect, and minimize hazards. Where feasible, standardized, simplified work will allow teams to be more effective and anticipate the unexpected. Substantial progress is possible through the creation of learning environments designed for continuing improvement, close study of near misses, and system recovery when lapses do occur.

DON E. DETMER, M.D

more, as recommended by the American College of Obstetricians and Gynecologists.

Nutrition and Diets. For the first time in history, the majority of U.S. citizens—an estimated 55%—are clinically overweight, reported the National Institutes of Health (NIH), putting them at increased risk for heart disease, cancer, diabetes, osteoarthritis, and other diseases. A surprising 78% of respondents to a survey commissioned by the American Institute for Cancer Research (AICR) said that eating certain kinds of food while avoiding others was more important for managing their weight than eating less food. They concentrated on cutting fat or going on fad diets, strategies that often fail to address the issues of good nutrition and total calories consumed. Only 12% of respondents referred to recommended serving size on nutrition labels. "People are eating more and wondering why they're getting fatter," said Melanie Polk, director of nutrition education at the AICR.

New dietary guidelines from the American Heart Association for the first time stressed the importance of preventing obesity. The guidelines encouraged people to focus on their overall eating patterns rather than percentages of dietary fat and other nutrients, recommending a diet rich in fruits, vegetables, low-fat dairy products, poultry, lean meats, and fish—including two weekly servings of fatty fish, such as tuna or salmon. For obese individuals, the guidelines recommended a gradual weight loss of 1 to 2 lb (0.45 to 0.91 kg) per week. "Simply put, to lose weight, you must eat fewer calories than you burn, and you must increase physical activity, such as brisk walking, to at least 30 minutes daily," said Ronald M. Krauss of the Lawrence Berkeley National Laboratory at the University of California and the principal author of the guidelines.

Researchers at Johns Hopkins reported that eating a well-balanced diet rich in fruits and vegetables and low in saturated fat reduces blood levels of homocysteine. More than a dozen studies have linked elevated homocysteine levels to health problems.

Two studies financed by the National Cancer Institute, one of which tracked 88,757 women for 16 years, found no evidence that a high-fiber diet reduces the risk of colorectal cancer. This contradicts a long-held belief that is supported by animal and biochemical data. Health experts noted, however, that dietary fiber has other benefits, including a proven ability to reduce the risk of heart disease.

Diabetes. Diabetes is a disease in which the body cannot regulate blood sugar (glucose). It is a leading cause of blindness, kidney failure, heart disease, and limb amputations, and annually kills 180,000 Americans. The CDC reported that the number of Americans with diabetes increased 33% from 1990 to 1998, from 4.9% to 6.5% of the population. Among people age 30 to 39, prevalence jumped 76%, from 2.1% to 3.7%. Some 13 million Americans have been diagnosed with diabetes, and an additional 5 million are believed to have the disease without knowing it.

Almost all diabetics have type 2 diabetes, which is associated with obesity. It once was known as adult-onset diabetes because it was typically found among older people. But an American Diabetes Association panel reported that the percentage of childhood type 2 diabetes rose from fewer than 4% in 1990 to approximately 20%, and that 85% of these children were obese.

A Finnish study that focused on 523 adults, average age 55, with impaired glucose tolerance—a state between "normal" and "diabetic"—demonstrated that changes in eating and exercise habits can prevent type 2 diabetes. "Our intervention was relatively inexpensive compared to the high costs of having diabetes," said Jaakko Tuomilehto of Finland's National Public Health Institute. "It showed that a modest weight loss of less than 10 lb [4.55 kg], combined with a healthy diet and regular, moderate exercise can produce major benefits in people with impaired glucose tolerance."

The FDA withdrew the drug Rezulin (troglitazone) from the market. Approved in 1997 for treating type 2 diabetes, and used by about 500,000 Americans in early 2000, Rezulin was linked to 90 cases of liver failure, 63 of which resulted in death. Physicians warned that patients taking two related drugs, Avandia and Actos, approved in 1999, also should be monitored carefully for signs of liver problems.

Researchers at the University of Alberta in Canada reported that they had transplanted insulin-producing cells into eight patients with severe type 1 diabetes, in which the body produces little or no insulin. The procedure was at least initially successful in all eight patients. At the time of the report, the patients had been free of symptoms of the disease for up to 14 months, and no longer needed insulin injections to regulate their blood sugar.

JENNY TESAR

Parkinson's Disease

The departure of actor Michael J. Fox from television's popular situation comedy *Spin City* in May 2000 focused attention on Parkinson's disease (PD). The 38-year-old actor is one of a group of famous people who are afflicted with the slowly progressive disease of the brain that affects 1 million Americans. The number of new patients diagnosed with PD each year is 50,000. The peak age of onset is 50–70 years. Approximately I5% of those afflicted develop the disease before age 50.

Symptoms, Pathology, and Cause. The disease's major symptoms are slowness of movements (bradykinesia); rigidity of the arms, legs, and trunk; poor balance; stooped posture; and tremor. Despite the perception of an invariable association of tremor and PD, 30% of patients have no tremor. The tremor, when present, involves muscles when they are relaxed, hence the term, resting tremor. Other signs—called motor symptoms—include loss of facial expression, decreased blinking of the eye, changed handwriting (micrographia), a low and monotonous voice, and difficulty walking. In most patients the symptoms start on one side of the body and later involve the other side. Nonmotor symptoms, such as depression and intellectual decline, occur in 30% of patients.

Microscopic examination of the patient's brain shows a loss of darkly pigmented nerve cells in the midbrain. This loss is associated with the presence, inside the cells, of round inclusions called Lewy bodies. Their presence is essential for diagnosing PD.

Although the exact cause of PD is unknown, there is evidence linking it to environmental and genetic agents. A study of twins showed that the frequency of PD is higher among identical twins (with identical genes) than fraternal twins—if the disease begins before age 50. This suggests a genetic origin for the disease. However, the frequency of PD was the same in identical and fraternal twins—if the disease strikes after age 50. As identical and fraternal twins share the same environment, this suggests an environmental cause. In 15% of patients, there is a family history of the disease.

Diagnosis. PD can be diagnosed if a patient has two or more of the prime symptoms, one of which is resting tremor or bradykinesia. Resting tremor by itself is enough to diagnose PD. However, one must be careful to differentiate PD from Parkinson-like diseases. For example, essential tremor is frequently confused with PD. Within two to five years of diagnosis, the Parkinson-like disorders develop features that distinguish them from PD. In addition, the Parkinson-like disorders do not respond to levodopa, a drug for the treatment of PD. Microscopically, the absence of Lewy bodies distinguishes the Parkinson-like disorders from PD.

Treatment. Most Parkinson symptoms result from a deficiency of a specific chemical, dopamine. Most anti-Parkinson drugs either restore dopamine, or mimic or sustain its effects. Although currently there is no medicine

© Ken Lambert/"Washington Times" via Newsmakers/Liaison Agency

Actor Michael J. Fox, above, has become a leading spokesperson in behalf of increased funding for Parkinson's research.

that halts PD's progression, the following drugs treat the disease's symptoms:

• *Levodopa/carbidopa (or Sinemet)*. The levodopa enters the brain and is changed to and restores dopamine. The carbidopa helps the levodopa enter the brain.

• *Dopamine agonists (Mirapex, Permax, and Requip)*. They mimic the actions of dopamine.

• *Selegiline, entacapone, and tolcapone*. This group blocks enzymes that break down dopamine. They sustain levodopa's effects.

In addition, surgical treatments are reserved for patients with advanced stages of the disease when drug treatment is no longer satisfactory. Such surgery includes:

• *Thalamotomy and pallidotomy*. Operations that destroy overactive parts of the brain.

• *Deep brain stimulation (DBS)*. Operations that stimulate parts of the brain.

• *Transplantation*. Operations that transplant new sources of dopamine-producing cells.

ALIREZA MINAGAR, M.D. and
ABRAHAM LIEBERMAN, M.D.

Health Care

During 2000, the U.S. Congress and President Bill Clinton debated health-care issues on many fronts. But the 106th Congress ended in December much as it began nearly two years earlier—with much agreement on the health-care problems faced by the United States, but precious little consensus on how to solve those problems, and minimal legislation that actually addresses any long-standing issues.

The list of issues that Congress failed to address was far longer than its accomplishments. Congress debated but did not resolve issues that played a major role in the 2000 presidential campaign—most notably a prescription-drug benefit for the federal Medicare program and a so-called "patients' bill of rights" for those Americans enrolled in health-maintenance organizations (HMOs) and other types of managed-care plans. Congress also failed to reach resolution on a score of minor health-care issues, including how to develop an equitable distribution system for the scarce supply of human organs for transplants, and how to protect the confidentiality of various types of medical information.

Meanwhile, the number of Americans without health insurance declined for the first time since 1988. While this does represent good news, at 43.6 million people, the uninsured level nevertheless remained stubbornly high after eight years of a booming economy, and more than a decade after the issue came to the political forefront.

New Measures. Congress and the president did enact a new law that allows states to provide Medicaid coverage to uninsured women diagnosed with breast or cervical cancer through a federally funded screening program. The measure sought to solve a fundamental problem with the 1990 Breast and Cervical Cancer Early Detection Program, which provided free mammograms and Pap tests to low-income, uninsured women: If such a woman actually was found to have cancer, she was unlikely to be in a position to pay for her care. While the measure passed the House 421 to 1 in May, conservatives blocked it in the Senate for several months. The president signed the measure into law in October.

Congress and the president also agreed to provide about $35 billion in additional funding for various Medicare providers who claimed that reductions imposed by the 1997 Balanced Budget Act went deeper than Congress intended, and jeopardized the ability to provide care to the program's 39 million elderly and disabled beneficiaries. Hospitals, managed-care plans, nursing homes, home-health agencies, hospices, and others launched aggressive advertising and lobbying campaigns, even as objective analysts suggested that the problems were not as dire as many providers claimed—or were not the result of federal cutbacks. Nevertheless, as part of the bill that wrapped up the work of the 106th Congress, lawmakers provided the funding, along with some new benefits earmarked for preventive care for Medicare beneficiaries.

Disagreements. But on most other health-policy issues, Congress agreed to disagree. While both the House and Senate in 1999 passed a "patients' bill of rights," they were unable to resolve differences between the two bills, and in the end, nothing was enacted. The most hotly contested question involved in the bill-of-rights issue was whether patients injured or killed as a result of being denied care should be able to sue health plans for damages in state court. The House bill said they should, while the Senate bill, heeding complaints from insurance and business groups that lawsuits would merely drive up costs, did not.

Almost equally contentious was whether the protections to be conferred by the new law—such as guaranteeing patients the right to seek treatment in the nearest emergency room or the ability to see specialists without prior approval from their health plan—should apply to all Americans or just those who could not be reached by state insurance laws. The House bill would have protected every American with private insurance coverage, while the Senate version would have applied only to the roughly 55 million people in plans exempt from state regulations.

Congress and the president came no closer to resolution on how to provide outpatient prescription-drug coverage to Medicare. While just about everyone agreed that the program's failure to pay for medications was a major failing, the immense cost and technical complexity of the subject proved too difficult on a substantive level, while different philosophies proved politically problematic. Republicans for the most part wanted to use the private sector to provide prescription coverage, as a stepping stone to a more privatized Medicare program in general, while Democrats wanted to make drugs a core Medicare benefit provided via the government.

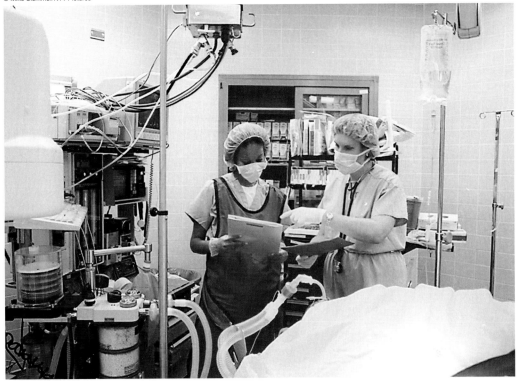

The high cost of medical care has been an important factor in the development of new nursing specialties that, in some cases, perform tasks long restricted to physicians. In some hospitals, for example, nurse anesthetists (above) work as part of an operating-room team, administering sedation and otherwise monitoring a patient's pain-sensation level during surgery.

On December 26, the Clinton administration killed a congressional program to allow imports of low-cost prescription drugs from Canada and elsewhere overseas. The administration said the import plan would not be safe and would not save money for the consumer.

Another source of continuing disagreement was the Clinton administration's efforts to change the way human organs were allocated for transplants. The private organization that ran the nation's organ transplant network had for years distributed organs based on the proximity of a patient to that organ—whether or not a sicker patient who needed the organ more urgently but was located farther away was still near enough to benefit. But rules requiring the network to take a patient's medical need more into account were met with cries of outrage from states that would lose precious organs to other states. Congress stepped in, and in April the House passed a bill that would have overturned the rules. The Senate, led by Tennessee Republican Bill Frist, a physician and a former heart-lung transplant surgeon, worked out a compromise. Senators from states that opposed changing the system blocked it, however. In the end

no bill was passed, and the new regulations took effect.

Medical Records. One health-care-related issue that Congress gave up on entirely was finding a plausible and effective way to protect the confidentiality of medical records. In 1996, Congress ordered itself to pass such a bill by 1999. If it failed, the law said, President Clinton would be required to issue rules himself.

Congress foundered over questions of how to balance the privacy rights of patients against the needs for an ever-automating health-care industry to share and distribute medical information and diagnostic data for treatment, payment, and research purposes. So in the end it was left to President Clinton. On December 20, the president issued a sweeping set of regulations giving patients new rights to see and correct their own records, and requiring new responsibilities of health-care providers and payers to protect patients' privacy—including doctors and hospitals being required to gain consent from patients before releasing records. Those who violated the new rules, which were to take effect by 2002, could be subject to fines of up to $250,000.

JULIE ROVNER, *Health-Policy Writer*

Prescription Drugs

The disparity between the ability of modern prescription drugs to treat and cure our most dreaded diseases and the inability of many Americans to pay for those medications burst onto the political agenda in 2000.

The Problem. The problem quietly grew during the 1990s—much of it spurred, perhaps unintentionally, by Congress itself. Huge annual increases given by Congress for biomedical research through the National Institutes of Health (NIH), coupled with a 1992 bill that allowed drugmakers to pay "user fees" to speed the

© Corbis

notoriously slow drug-approval process by the U.S. Food and Drug Administration (FDA), combined to make available new drugs to treat everything from life-threatening diseases—such as AIDS and diabetes—to such common maladies as heartburn and arthritis.

But those new drugs came at a price—often quite a steep one. Spending on prescription drugs doubled between 1990 and 1998; from 1997 to 1998 alone, spending rose by 15%. Spending increases were due to more than simply price increases for existing drugs. More important factors were the increase in the number of prescriptions filled by Americans, and the switch from older and cheaper to newer and more expensive medications.

Drug spending in 1999 accounted for 40% of premium increases, and rising drug spending drove increases in health-insurance premiums into double digits. Most Americans with insurance felt little of that increase. With a continuing tight labor market, employers largely absorbed the increases instead of passing them on to workers. But for those without insurance, particularly those on Medicare, which did not offer outpatient prescription coverage as part of its basic package of benefits, the rising cost of drugs became a more serious problem. An estimated 31% of Medicare beneficiaries lacked any coverage for prescription drugs in 1996 (the most recent available statistics), and of those who had insurance, only 53% were covered for a full year. That problem was complicated by the fact that sources of drug coverage for most seniors—plans provided by a former employer and Medicare health-maintenance organizations (HMOs)—were cut back in 2000, largely in response to the skyrocketing drug costs.

Proposals and Action. Congress considered but failed to pass legislation to add a prescription-drug benefit to Medicare. Both Vice-President Al Gore, the Democratic candidate for president, and his Republican opponent, Texas Gov. George W. Bush, offered very different plans to provide drug coverage. Gore and President Bill Clinton wanted to add a voluntary prescription-drug benefit directly to Medicare; President-elect Bush and House and Senate Republicans proposed to combine drug coverage with a broader overhaul of Medicare and to allow private insurance plans to compete to offer it.

Congress did pass one bill that addressed drug prices, but it was unclear the effect it would have. The measure—part of the annual spending bill for the FDA—relaxed the 1988 ban on importing U.S.-made prescription drugs from other countries into the United States. Because other countries imposed price controls on prescription drugs, many Americans found it economical to travel to Canada or Mexico to buy their medications. Lawmakers, some of whom sponsored and even led drug-buying bus or plane trips, wanted to make international prices available to those in the United States. The drug industry vigorously opposed the proposal. The final bill eased the ban on "reimportation" of drugs, but only from countries with strict handling and drug-approval procedures. That list included Canada and most European countries, but not Mexico. President Clinton signed the bill into law in October, but noted that it was not the proposal he preferred.

JULIE ROVNER

Bioethics

It was a staggering year of discovery and debate in the world of medicine and science. In many cases, bioethics generated hotly contested questions. More than a dozen major issues were debated in U.S. state and national administrative law, but the most important discussions about the ethics of medicine took place in broad context.

Genetics. In the world of genetics, new debate focused on the extent to which genes can be patented. Heated discussion swarmed around reports that the United States and Britain had discussed a joint plan to allow patents on genetic information, and that Iceland would potentially allow a U.S. company to sell genetic information about its people on the open market—experts were concerned by precedents being set in unexplored territory. Meanwhile, families in Chicago sued a hospital and its research staff for using their children's genetic information to file a patent, without sharing profits. Patenting of genetics raised fundamental ethical and constitutional questions about whether or not genetic material is a device or a part of nature, and about human control and ownership of bodies and body parts.

In March, British Prime Minister Tony Blair and U.S. President Bill Clinton asserted that patenting genetics is a dangerous area of intellectual property. These declarations by the two national leaders sparked an immediate loss of 20% to 30% of the total value of biotechnology shares on the U.S. stock markets, which was not regained by the end of the year.

While little new information was announced in the world of human cloning, there was significant legal action with regard to the patenting of human embryonic stem cells, and in funding research on those cells, which are sometimes derived from nuclear transfer of the cell type that would be used to make a clone.

Research Ethics. The debate about human-subjects research continued in the United States and abroad, with a renewed focus on international research ethics. In particular, revisions to the important Helsinki and World Health Organization (WHO) codes of ethics and other institutional treatises raised new questions about the use of placebos in research; the use of lower-than-therapeutic doses in research on subjects who are ill; and research on entire communities. Discussion focused on a revolutionary new study of cannibalism in Venezuela; international toxicology research using known pollutants; and research about transplantation in Russia and India. In the United States, an important lawsuit against the University of Pennsylvania centered on the death of a young man in a trial of gene-therapy research, and raised questions about whether research in genetics should be conducted. This study was also the first prominent lawsuit—although not the first such action—in which an ethicist, Arthur Caplan, was named as codefendant.

Internet Issues. With the growth of Internet health information, many began to publish codes of ethics aimed at governing the dissemination of health information on the Web. Several codes of ethics rose to prominence, but there was dissent as to the effectiveness of industry-designed codes of ethics not backed by research.

In the United States, biomedical industry of all kinds began to seek in earnest the assistance of ethicists. For example, the DuPont Company initiated an effort to create a code of ethics for genetic engineering of food, while stem-cell engineering firms Geron and Advanced Cell Technology established their own ethics boards. The development of corporate ethics, and the lawsuit against Caplan, spawned a major international debate about the proper role of ethics in consulting relationships.

The End of Life. Finally, health care at the end of life—debated in the U.S. presidential elections in the form of a proposed drug plan to be added to Medicare—was subject to a variety of challenges in the courts, legislative arena, and business. Vice-President Al Gore and President-elect George W. Bush vied to see who could promise the more attractive supplement to Medicare; each attacked their opponent's proposal for Social Security reform on grounds that seniors would be harmed. Some political analysts feared that the chaos of the 2000 presidential election could doom immediate reform of Medicare, which was a powder-keg political problem before the election.

The U.S. Food and Drug Administration's (FDA's) challenge to the Oregon law allowing assisted suicide was upheld in several federal courts. Although the imprisonment of Jack Kevorkian brought physician-assisted suicide and euthanasia out of the limelight, the FDA's derailment of Oregon's law promised an important new battle about how life ends in the United States.

GLENN MCGEE
Center for Bioethics, University of Pennsylvania

Mental Health

In 2000 some significant advances were made in the field of mental health. A new report by the surgeon general on the subject was analyzed, and important studies were conducted on drinking and depression, children's and women's mental health, and schizophrenia.

A Report of the Surgeon General. A range of effective, well-documented treatments exist for most mental disorders, yet nearly half of all Americans with severe mental illness fail to seek treatment, according to the first-ever report of the surgeon general on mental health, *Mental Health: A Report of the Surgeon General*, which was released in December 1999. The report focused on the connection between mental and physical health, barriers to receiving mental-health treatment, and the specific mental-health issues of children, adults, and the elderly.

The report provided a long-needed baseline of the mental-health-care system in the United States. It noted that disorders such as depression, schizophrenia, and eating disorders are real illnesses that, if untreated, can be as disabling and serious as cancer and heart disease, in terms of premature death and lost productivity. One in five Americans suffers from a mental illness in his or her lifetime. But the report stressed that quality of life is positively impacted when a mental disorder or mental-health problem is diagnosed early and treated appropriately.

About 15% of the U.S. adult population use some form of mental-health service in any given year. But the complexity of mental-health services, financial barriers, and stigma serve as deterrents to the receipt of appropriate and necessary care. These factors result in a gap between what research has shown to be optimally effective treatments and what many people receive in actual practice settings.

Related to the findings of the report of the surgeon general, three national surveys described in the July issue of *American Psychologist* indicated that the percentage of Americans who report feelings of a "nervous breakdown" has increased in the previ-

ous 40 years. The surveys—administered in 1957, 1976, and 1996—were designed to measure the past and current profile of the public's view of their own mental health.

In 1957, 19% of participants reported ever feeling they were going to have a nervous breakdown; in 1976 the number rose to

© Dennis Cook/AP/Wide World

Courtesy, U.S. Department of Health and Human Services

In late 1999, U.S. Surgeon General David Satcher, above, issued "Mental Health: A Report of the Surgeon General." The report noted that 15% of the U.S. population receive some form of mental-health services in any year.

21%; and in 1996 the number climbed to 26%. During the 40-year period, the major changes in people's responses to the feelings of having a nervous breakdown included an increased dependency on friends and family, a decline in seeking physician's assistance, and an increased reliance on nonmedical mental-health professionals. In 1996 events most frequently related to impending nervous breakdowns were divorce, marital strains and separation, and troubles with members of the opposite sex.

Problem Drinking. Depression, loneliness, and certain kinds of coping strategies go hand in hand with adults' drinking behavior. But the type of drinking behavior one turns to under different circumstances may depend on age, noted researchers in the June issue of *Psychology of Addictive Behaviors*.

Both depression and coping style were found to be the strongest predictors of problem-drinking behaviors. Among the other findings from the study was that lonely women tended to drink to intoxication more frequently than did lonely men. Younger individuals were found more likely to cope with depression through binge drinking and intoxication, while older adults were more likely to turn to consuming several alcoholic beverages quickly, in order to get a fast high. Older adults reported less binge drinking overall, and tended to drink more when avoiding stressful situations, or when seeking support from others when under stress.

Children and Mental Health.

Violence in Video Games. Playing violent video games can increase a person's aggressive thoughts, feelings, and behavior, both in laboratory settings and in actual life. Studies in the April issue of the *Journal of Personality and Social Psychology* examined this issue. The studies found that violent video games may be more harmful than violent television and movies, because they are interactive, and often require the player to identify with the aggressor.

One study involved 227 college students who completed a measure of trait aggressiveness, and described both their actual aggressive behaviors in the recent past, and their video-game playing habits. The researchers said that students who played more-violent video games in junior high and high school engaged in more-aggressive behavior. The amount of time spent playing video games in the past was also found to be associated with lower academic grades in college.

Number of Children and Birth Order Not Directly Related to IQ. Having more children born into a family does not necessarily result in lower-IQ offspring, according to a study published in the June issue of the *American Psychologist.* The research found that neither birth order nor family size has any effect on a child's IQ. Parents' IQ, however, was found to be an important causal source of the relationship between family size and children's IQ, because low-IQ parents have been having relatively larger families in the United States than high-IQ parents. The researchers found that family environment and genetic heritage also may play roles in both family size and children's intelligence.

Adverse Effects in Sleep-Deprived Children. Children in the sixth grade were found to suffer adverse cognitive, behavioral, and emotional consequences due to an increased risk of being chronically sleep-deprived. The study, published in the May issue of *Developmental Psychology*, discovered that children in sixth grade experienced a subjectively lesser quality of sleep and spent less overall time sleeping than children in second grade. The sixth-grade children reported significantly higher levels of morning drowsiness and daytime sleepiness than their second-grade counterparts. The researchers suggested that, based upon their study's data, preteen children may not be getting enough sleep to meet their daily physical and mental needs. The study also found that the best predictors of sleep quality were the parents' education, and family stress, suggesting that parents of higher education, and families that had less measurable stress, resulted in higher-quality sleep.

Schizophrenia-Related Gene Site Reported. In the April 28 issue of *Science*, researchers reported on their discovery of evidence for the existence of a gene on Chromosome 1 that appears to confer vulnerability to schizophrenia. The evidence suggests that several genes on different chromosomes interact with environmental factors to cause schizophrenia.

The study reported a strong statistical connection between a specific location on Chromosome 1 and the occurrence of schizophrenia in 22 large, affected families of German and Celtic descent in Eastern Canada. DNA from 288 subjects, spanning at least a few generations, was analyzed. The statistical power of the linkage was the highest reported in a dozen years.

Women and Mental Health. Women who suffer from depression as they enter the early stages of menopause (also called "perimenopause") may find estrogen to be an alternative to traditional antidepressants, according to an August *American Journal of Obstetrics and Gynecology* study.

The researchers studied 34 women, ages 44–55, who experienced onset of depression coinciding with perimenopause. The researchers confirmed that estrogen significantly boosted mood in 80% of the depressed women, independent of hot flashes. The level and time to relief were found to be comparable to antidepressant-drug treatments. Depression symptoms that improved with the hormone were early-morning awakening, loss of enjoyment, sadness, and irritability.

JOHN M. GROHOL
Psychologist, HelpHorizons.com

Meteorology

Scientists continued to refine the observational picture of the Earth's changing climate and launched major new satellite systems to provide better information across a wide range of weather-climate time and space scales.

Warmer—and Not. The year 1999 was the fifth warmest on record for the Earth's surface, although, as a La Niña year, it normally would have been cooler. Outside the band between 20°N to 20°S latitude, 1999 was the second-warmest year of the 20th century, just behind 1998. Researchers believed there was only a one-in-20 chance that the string of record-high temperatures in 1997–98 was nothing more than an unusual event. The Earth's surface temperature rose about 0.7°–1.4°F (0.4°–0.8°C) in the past century, and half of that occurred in the 25-year period beginning in the mid-1970s.

Meanwhile, 50 years of balloon-based observations and 20 years of satellite observations of the troposphere, the atmosphere extending up to about 5 mi (8 km) above the Earth's surface, indicated little, if any, warming. A major review panel concluded that the surface and upper-air data sets are consistent with each other. In other words, while a combination of human activities and natural causes contributed to rising surface temperatures, other human and natural forces counteracted warming in the upper atmosphere. Cooling effects included volcanic eruptions, the production of aerosols through burning coal and oil, and depletion of stratospheric ozone. When these variables were accounted for in atmospheric models, the various data were reproduced more exactly than in earlier versions.

These refinements were considered an important step in building confidence in the ability of computer models to estimate more accurately the future state of the Earth's climate. The latest estimates projected a warming of 3.6°–9°F (2°–5°C) during the 21st century. Researchers expected impacts such as heavier precipitation and increased drought to vary widely from region to region; believed that some natural ecosystems could disappear entirely and others could be severely disrupted; forecasted that changes in rain and snowfall patterns could affect the availability of fresh water; and estimated that crop productivity could rise nationally, although specific regional cropping patterns could change significantly.

Another important part of the global energy cycle is the variability of the heat content (mean temperature) of the Earth's oceans. The initial survey from the surface through 10,000-ft (3 000-m) depth for the period 1948–96 showed that the Atlantic and Pacific Oceans have warmed since the 1950s, and the Indian Ocean since the 1960s. The warming patterns of the Pacific and Indian Oceans were similar, suggesting that the same phenomenon was causing changes in both the oceans.

Burying CO_2. In efforts to contain the negative impact of humans on the climate, the 1997 United Nations (UN) convention in Kyoto, Japan, established targets for the emission of greenhouse gases by each nation. Most approaches focused on reducing emissions, but the alternative of geologic disposal received serious discussion. Geologic disposal would be achieved by injecting the carbon dioxide, in semiliquid form, deep underground into deep coal seams, depleted oil and gas fields, large voids and cavities, and unusable (saline) aquifers. The geologic-disposal approach has been tested

A Geneva County agent surveys the effects of a severe ten-month drought in Alabama that prompted officials to declare some counties disaster areas, June 2000.

A dazed survivor of the February 14 tornado that touched down near Camilla, GA, contemplates the damage and what belongings can be salvaged. Considered the deadliest tornado to hit the state of Georgia in 50 years, it took 18 lives.

in selected North Sea oil fields and Queensland, Australia.

Global Climate Patterns. The La Niña phase of the El Niño/Southern Oscillation (ENSO) pattern across the tropical Pacific Ocean persisted for an unusual second straight year, fading in late summer. The ENSO usually has significant effects that extend well beyond the Pacific, so long-range forecasters made somewhat more-confident forecasts than in a non-ENSO year. However, researchers were hot on the trail of two other large-scale patterns, the Pacific Decadal Oscillation and the North Atlantic Oscillation. The former is related to previously observed fluctuations in North Pacific Ocean surface temperatures that vary over 20 to 30 years. The latter tends to favor one atmospheric-flow pattern for up to a decade—perhaps even much longer—before switching to the opposite pattern, but the physical mechanism is not that well understood. Researchers expected that a better understanding of the two patterns could significantly improve weather forecasts a few seasons ahead.

Stratospheric Ozone Loss. In mid-September the Antarctic ozone hole covered a record area three times the size of the United States. The depletion peaked and then started returning to normal relatively early, compared to previous years. Such fluctuations were expected, although the severity of 2000's hole surprised researchers. Partly because of the size of such natural fluctuations, scientists estimated it could take as much as 15 to 45 years before statistically significant improvements in total stratospheric ozone would be detected, even assuming full compliance with the Montreal Protocol, which governs chemicals known to damage the stratospheric ozone.

Meanwhile, researchers converged on the Arctic in the middle of winter to conduct the SAGE III (a satellite program) Ozone Loss and Validation Experiment (SOLVE). Compared to the relatively simple situation over Antarctica, the continually changing flow patterns over the Arctic put a premium on correctly understanding the complex interactions among solar radiation, temperature, water, chlorofluorocarbons, aerosol particles, and polar stratospheric clouds (PSCs), in order to predict ozone loss in the Northern Hemisphere. The field program showed that an unusually cold winter pattern promoted the formation of PSCs, accelerating the destruction of ozone, with up to 60% reduction at 60,000 ft (20 km). The total polar ozone for the first two weeks of March was 16% lower than scientists had observed during the same period in the early 1980s.

Satellites. Forty years after the first meteorologic satellite was launched, a direct descendant, the National Oceanic and At-

Torrential rainfall left many parts of Great Britain underwater in the fall. In the town of Bewdley on the Severn River, left, submerged signposts clearly indicated how high the flood waters had reached.

© Alastair Grant/AP/Wide World Photos

mospheric Administration-16 (NOAA-16), was lifted into low-Earth orbit in September. A more distant cousin, the Geostationary Operational Environmental Satellite 11 (GOES-11), was launched into geostationary orbit in mid-May. A third milestone had been the launch of Terra in December 1999. This National Aeronautics and Space Administration (NASA) satellite was the first of the major Earth Observing System (EOS) series, intended to provide long-term monitoring of the Earth's environment. Finally, Canada's RADARSAT provided scientists with their first comprehensive look at the thickness of sea ice.

One relatively new focus of satellite research was developing techniques for relating satellite data to various ecological and disease events. For example, it was possible to infer from satellite data the "blooms" of the tiny plankton that harbor the cholera bacteria. Other diseases studied were malaria, Lyme disease, and Rift Valley fever.

Weather Highlights. In the United States drought and heat across the South, Southwest, and West during the summer attracted the most attention in 2000. The summer saw hundreds of daily maximum-temperature records and dozens of monthly or even all-time records across the Gulf states and Texas, along with many records for low rainfall over the South and West. Dallas–Ft. Worth, TX, lacked measurable rain during an 84-day span that surpassed the record 1934 and 1950 drought years. Dry conditions helped promote a wildfire season, focused in Nevada, Idaho, and Montana, that charred 130% more acres than in an average year (*see* ENVIRONMENT—Wildfires). Meanwhile, the Midwest, Middle Atlantic, and New England

saw a wet, cool summer. Averaged over the entire country, the first half of 2000 was the warmest on record for many different periods and areas. The fall cooling over much of the country prevented more-extreme records for the year on the whole. In fact, December saw two severe ice storms across Texas and Arkansas, with record snows across the Great Lakes. In all, temperatures for November and December were the coldest ever for the two-month period.

Overall, the nation saw much less storminess than in recent years. A major East Coast snowstorm in late January dumped 4 to 20 inches (10 to 51 cm) of snow from the Carolinas to New England, shutting down metropolitan areas from Washington, DC, to New York City for several days. Fewer than 900 tornadoes occurred in 2000, about two-thirds of the average over the previous three years. There were 27 associated fatalities, less than one-third of the recent average. In mid-February, 18 died in the deadly tornadoes around Camilla, GA. The Atlantic hurricane season was above average, with 14 named storms, eight hurricanes, and three "intense" hurricanes. In September, Hurricane Gordon and Tropical Storm Helene broke the drought in the Southeast. The precursor to Tropical Storm Leslie followed suit, drenching south Florida with upward of 15 inches (38 cm) of rain in October.

Drought was a major story internationally, particularly in eastern and southeastern Europe, sub-Saharan Africa, and southeastern and central Asia. Three storms initiated massive flooding in Mozambique (*see* AFRICA—Mozambique) and southeastern Africa that prompted large-scale international relief efforts. Other notable floods occurred in the Australia outback in February, across eastern Argentina in March, central Chile in June, and the Po River valley in northern Italy in October. Central Asia suffered the most severe winter in 30 years, with deep snows hampering travel and preventing grazing by livestock.

GEORGE J. HUFFMAN,
NASA/Science Systems and Applications, Inc.

Mexico

Vicente Fox Quesada (*see* BIOGRAPHY) broke the 71-year hammerlock on power of the Institutional Revolutionary Party (PRI) when he captured the presidency of Mexico in midyear 2000. Outgoing President Ernesto Zedillo, who had earned international praise for his deft economic management and commitment to democracy, immediately recognized Fox's triumph on election night and took pains to ensure a peaceful changing of the guard. Fox would have to recruit new allies—business leaders and governors—to overcome congressional hostility to his ambitious reform agenda.

Politics. Two years of barnstorming the country paid off for Fox on July 2, when he tallied 42.5% of the vote to defeat Francisco Labastida Ochoa (36.1%), the PRI's standard-bearer; Cuauhtémoc Cárdenas (17%), candidate of the leftist-nationalist Party of the Democratic Revolution (PRD); and two minor-party candidates. Fox carried the banner for the "Alliance for Change," a coalition composed of his center-right National Action Party (PAN) and the local Greens.

During a hard-hitting campaign, Fox astutely portrayed himself as the "only option" to the PRI and its corrupt, ineffi-

cient, and poverty-producing governance. The tall, dynamic former governor of Guanajuato State also organized "Amigos de Fox" to encourage the PAN to give him its nomination; to raise money; and to attract women, young people, and independents to his cause. Fox found another powerful ally in the Roman Catholic Church. Although Mexico City's Cardinal Norberto Rivera and other church notables declaimed their neutrality, Mexico's bishops issued a pastoral letter in late March that condemned corruption, neoliberalism, abortion, and corporatist organizations. Six weeks later, the bishops specified qualities they believed desirable in the next chief executive. The clergy's specific job description seemed tailor-made for Fox.

In addition, Fox drew the backing of disaffected leftists and *priístas* (members of the PRI), enabling him to assert that he could work with people across the political spectrum. Postelection polls showed him garnering strong support from young people, women, university graduates, the business community, urban dwellers, the middle class, and northerners. In contrast, the PRI scored better with older voters, blue-collar workers, small farmers, and residents of the southern part of the country.

With a distinct campaign style, Vicente Fox Quesada, 58-year-old former governor of Guanajuato State, led a coalition of his National Action Party (PAN) and local Greens to historic victory in Mexico's presidential race on July 2, 2000.

Fox's coattails were not long enough to achieve majorities in Congress. The PRI (211 seats) and the PRD (51 seats) won more than half the seats in the 500-member Chamber of Deputies, where the PAN (207 seats) and its Green partner held 223 seats. In the 128-member Senate, the PRI had 60 seats, the PAN 46, the PRD 15, and the Greens five.

The PRD began excoriating Fox's legislative agenda even before his December inauguration. Thus, Mexico's new president would have to hammer out deals with the PRI if he was to deliver on promises to create jobs, combat poverty, curb corruption, devolve more power to states and municipalities, reform the tax system, and improve educational and health-care facilities. Fox's first bill focused on bringing a lasting peace to Chiapas, Mexico's southernmost state, where the Zapatista guerrillas launched a short-lived uprising in early 1994.

To help advance his legislation, Fox must recruit effective allies from the business community. Even more important, the nation's new chief executive needs to activate the nation's governors, who may determine the fate of his six-year rule. With a handful of exceptions, these men evince far more pragmatism than deputies and senators. For instance, they should be willing to assist Fox in opening the country's electricity sector, which needed $50 billion over the next six years to avoid brownouts and blackouts. In most cases, governors wield substantial clout with their states' congressional delegations. First, the 20 PRI governors had an important voice in selecting their party's nominees for the 200 deputies and 32 senators selected by proportional representation. Second, the constitution forbids lawmakers from seeking immediate reelection, which makes state governments an attractive postlegislative employer—especially for deputies, who serve but three years. Finally, governors can furnish grossly understaffed federal solons with aides, secretaries, research assistance, vehicles, airline tickets, and other perks that U.S. congressmen take for granted.

Partisan differences aside, state leaders have a strong incentive to lend Fox a hand. These men occupy the front line in fighting poverty, promoting social services, boosting production, stimulating exports, and creating employment. Thus, they are vigorously courting new industries, whose profitability will hinge on the effectiveness of the federal government. Fox's commerce ministry can

---

MEXICO • Information Highlights

Official Name: United Mexican States.
Location: Southern North America.
Area: 761,602 sq mi (1 972 550 km²).
Population (2000 est.): 100,349.766.
Chief Cities (November 1995 census): Mexico City (Federal District and surrounding municipalities), the capital, 16,387,087; Guadalajara, 1,633,216; Nezahualcóyotl, 1,233,868; Puebla, 1,122,569; Monterrey, 1,088,143; León, 1,042,132; Ciudad Juárez, 1,011,786.
Government: *Head of state and government,* Vicente Fox Quesada, president (took office Dec. 1, 2000). *Legislature*—National Congress: Senate and Federal Chamber of Deputies.
Monetary Unit: Peso (9.4286 pesos equal U.S.$1, Dec. 7, 2000).
Gross Domestic Product (1999 est. U.S.$): $865,500,000,000 (purchasing power parity).
Economic Indexes (1999, 1990 = 100): *Consumer Prices,* all items, 491.9; food, 473.6. *Industrial Production,* 138.7.
Foreign Trade (1999 est. U.S.$): *Imports,* $136,800,000,000; *exports,* $142,100,000,000.

---

direct prospective investors to the states of cooperative governors; the finance and communications and transport ministries can guarantee the infrastructure required for their projects; and various ministries can slash the mind-numbing quantity of regulations confronting entrepreneurs.

Unlike lawmakers in Mexico City, governors spend more time wrestling with day-to-day problems. Fox, himself governor of Guanajuato from 1995 to 1999, realizes the pivotal role that state officials can play. Thus, he invited half a dozen governors to travel to Central America during his early-September visit to the area. Fox's encounters with several presidents sparked the concept of a development zone stretching from Panama to Puebla, a Maryland-sized state that lies just to the southeast of Mexico City. (*See* CENTRAL AMERICA.)

The PRI emerged from the July election with a discredited leadership, a mountainous debt, and a lack of direction. Tabasco Gov. Roberto Madrazo blamed Labastida, Zedillo, and neoliberal policies for the party's debacle. Most observers assumed that Madrazo—aided by fellow governors and grassroots activists—would grasp the party's reins. Yet the PRI's loss of the Chiapas statehouse in mid-August—followed by a narrow victory for Madrazo's protégé in Tabasco's gubernatorial contest—sparked concerns among PRI officials about Madrazo's ability to unite and invigorate their reeling party. The party's National Political Council postponed the selection of a new president until the spring of 2001. In the absence of a strong, legitimate leader, the PRI had no one who could serve as an effective interlocutor with Fox. Although the PRD lost ground in the presidential and legislative contests, its candidate, Andrés Manuel López Obrador, nosed out the PAN's contender to win the mayoralty of Mexico City.

Economy. Surging oil prices and President Zedillo's careful stewardship powered a 7% growth in national income, up from 3.7% in 1999, as the inflation rate fell from 12.3% to 8.9%, and unemployment declined. Mexico's foreign-exchange holdings rose to a record $31.9 billion. Zedillo was determined to turn over power to Fox without the economic crises that had plagued the previous four changes of administration. To "shield" the economy against such a calamity, he negotiated contingency credits of more than $20 billion with the International Monetary Fund (IMF) and other international lenders.

The influx of $4 billion in additional oil revenues kept the current-account deficit to 3.1% of gross domestic product (GDP). However, in late October, Central Bank President Guillermo Ortiz—whose term runs until 2003—castigated the government for spending all of the petroleum-generated windfall. He warned that the economy was growing "too fast"—with demand outstripping production increases. While denying any desire to dictate fiscal policy, Ortiz did raise the reserve requirements of banks in hopes of bringing the inflation rate down to 6.5% in 2001, 4.5% in 2002, and 3% in 2003.

Fox's financial team, headed by highly esteemed Treasury Secretary Francisco Díaz Gil favored a balanced budget complemented by higher outlays on education, social programs, and initiatives to assist small businesses and microbusinesses. Meanwhile, Fox proposed raising Mexico's oil production above the current level of 3 million barrels per day. If such a boost takes place, and if prices remain high—two big "ifs"—Fox would have more money to spend by 2003.

Mexico's new president, though, stressed the need for fiscal reform to raise additional resources. High on his priority list were incentives to encourage small businesses—now operating in the informal economy—to come above ground. PRI, PRD, and other legislators urged that Fox postpone any move to overhaul the country's antiquated tax regime until a fair replacement can be found. They lambasted as a "blow to poor people" the Fox team's idea that the sales tax be extended to food and medicine. Opposition lawmakers, who were spoiling for a fight with the new administration, ignored the second part of the proposal, under which rebates would be provided to low-income families and the overall tax rate would be reduced from 15% to 12%. To encourage tax payments, Fox vowed during his first 100 days in office to mobilize his cabinet for a "crusade against [the] corruption," which pervades the nation's bureaucracy. "The only thing that I am going to do," the newly elected president said, "is to clean our house . . . [by] prosecuting and punishing every corrupt and illegal act."

Foreign Affairs. During the run-up to the July 2 election, the Alliance for Change nominee made several trips abroad to embellish his international credentials, expand his foreign contacts, drum up support among expatriated Mexicans, and cultivate the U.S. and European media. Always eager for a close race, the press in the United States appeared fascinated by the iconoclastic, boot-wearing candidate. He spoke English well, exuded confidence, offered a stark contrast to the colorless Labastida, and promised sweeping changes in the political system.

After winning the presidential race, Fox underlined his intent to chart a new course in foreign affairs. During a late-August visit to Ottawa, New York, and Washington, DC, he stated his belief that partners in the North American Free Trade Agreement (NAFTA) should embrace elements of the European Union (EU)—specifically, creating a financial mechanism for transferring funds from Canada and the United States to Mexico, and moving toward open borders throughout the continent. Canada's Prime Minister Jean Chrétien wasted no time before throwing cold water on these proposals, and, while more diplomatic, U.S. presidential candidates George W. Bush and Al Gore showed little interest in Fox's "vision."

Mexico's new chief executive called for a "more formal, more proactive integration" with Central and South America. As a result, he championed the negotiation of a free-trade agreement between Mexico and Mercosur (the Southern Cone Common Market). Fox also voiced his desire to strengthen ties with the EU, with which Mexico has entered into a free-trade agreement. Secretary of State Madeleine Albright led the U.S. delegation to Fox's inauguration on December 1, which also attracted Cuba's President Fidel Castro.

GEORGE W. GRAYSON
College of William and Mary

Microbiology

For microbiology, late 1999 and the year 2000 were noted for the discoveries of a bacterial species that thrives in an extreme acid environment, a bacterial infection that results in a change in host mating behavior, and the mechanical infection of a plant by a fungus. The year also brought a warning of possible epidemics of antibiotic-resistant bacteria.

Life at pH of 0. The degree of acidity or alkalinity of a solution or body of water is indicated by its pH. A pH of 0 signifies extreme acidity; a pH of 7 indicates neutrality (pure water); and a pH of 14 signifies extreme alkalinity. Very few organisms can live in environments, such as bogs or lakes rich in decaying vegetation, that have a pH as low as 1. The organisms that can do so are bacteria that belong to the primitive microbial kingdom Archaea.

K. Edwards of the Woods Hole Oceanographic Institution (WHOI) in Massachusetts and her colleagues reported on their study of the drainage system of an abandoned mine in Iron Mountain, CA. They found that the drainage water had a pH of 0. They also found that living successfully in this drainage system was a hitherto-unknown species of Archaea, which they named *Ferroplasma acidarmanus*. This discovery marks the most extreme acidic environment to which any organism has been able to adapt.

Varied Effects of Infection. Bacteria belonging to the genus *Wolbachia* are known to infect about 20% of arthropod species. They are transmitted from one generation to the next through the eggs of infected females. In wasps the bacteria cause unfertilized eggs to develop parthenogenetically into viable and fertile females. In wood lice the bacteria cause normally produced genetic males to develop female bodies.

An unusual effect of infection by *Wolbachia* on its host was described by F.M. Jiggins of the University of Cambridge in England. Studying the sub-Saharan butterfly, *Acraea encedon*, it was found that the bacteria destroy eggs that would have hatched into males, thereby depleting the male population of the next generation. In these male-depleted populations, the females form groups (leks) that display themselves to the few available males. This is a reversal of the normal mating pattern in which males form leks that display themselves to females. This is the first reported instance in which a bacterial infection has resulted in a reversal of a species mating-behavior.

Mechanical Infection of a Plant. According to estimates, microbial plant pathogens cause a reduction in yield of almost 20% in food crops worldwide. Those microbes that gain access to the tissues of the plant through the leaves have the problem of penetrating the nonliving tough outer layer (cuticle) of the leaf. Some pathogens circumvent this problem by entering the pores (stomata) of the leaf epidermis. Others have enzymes that dissolve the cuticle at the point of infection.

A study of the cereal pathogen *Colletotrichum graminicola* by C. Bechinger at the University of Konstanz, Germany, and others found that this fungus produces specialized infection structures called appressoria that adhere tightly to the leaf cuticle, thereby exerting pressure on it. In addition, each appressorium produces a penetration peg that pierces the cuticle. The scientists measured the pressure generated by the appressoria and found it more than sufficient to rupture the cuticle, thereby permitting the pathogen to invade the underlying leaf cell through the penetration peg. This is the first direct evidence of the mechanical infection of a plant by a fungus.

Antibiotic Resistance. In the 1950s and 1960s, it appeared that an array of antibiotics would eliminate most, if not all, of the infectious bacterial-caused diseases. In fact, it became customary to administer antibiotics to patients suffering from viral diseases, against which the antibiotics were ineffective, in order to prevent possible secondary bacterial infections. Unfortunately, the indiscriminate overuse of antibiotics resulted in the unintended survival and spread of those bacteria that happened to be resistant to the particular antibiotic. As a result, antibiotic-resistant strains of bacteria became prevalent, and infections that were once treatable have become incurable.

In 2000 the World Health Organization (WHO) issued the report "Overcoming Antimicrobial Resistance." The report pointed out that the world's biggest killers— pneumonia (3.5 million people per year), tuberculosis (2 million people per year), and malaria (1.1 million people per year)—have become progressively more difficult to treat, and that the world may be facing major epidemics of these and other bacterial-caused diseases unless there are severe restrictions placed on the use of antibiotics.

LOUIS LEVINE, *City College of New York*

Middle East

If one were to try to frame some brief generalization about the course of events in the Middle East in the year 2000, it would be tempting just to offer the French saying *Plus ça change, plus c'est la même chose*—"the more things change, the more they are the same." There would be a strong case for such an attitude. A considerable number of the region's rulers—King Hussein of Jordan, Morocco's King Hassan II, the Sheikh Isa bin Salman Al Khalifa of Bahrain, and Syria's President Hafiz al-Assad—had died in 1999 and 2000. Yet, the advent of new rulers brought extraordinarily little change in the policies, domestic or external, of these four states. The same old problems persisted. Prime Minister Ehud Barak of Israel, who swept to power in 1999 on his promise to create peace with both Syria and Palestine, achieved neither goal and faced an election challenge early in 2001.

The innumerable conferences and meetings concerned with relations between Israel and the Palestinians—more, probably, than in any other year—failed to produce solutions. Palestinians and Israelis exchanged hostilities—and killings—early in the year. By year's end, they were still doing so, in larger numbers. Peace between Israel and Syria, which seemed a possibility as 2000 began, was not achieved.

The most substantial change, in territorial terms, was the complete withdrawal of Israel from Lebanon in late May. This put an end to a situation that had existed since 1982, though latterly it was merely a matter of the "security zone" north of the border held by Israel and its Lebanese allies. The withdrawal, however, did little to improve Israeli relations with Syria or Lebanon. Occasional trans-border attacks or forays by Hezbollah partisans breached Israeli security.

Farther east, Saddam Hussein of Iraq, ten years after the Gulf War, was not seriously threatened, and well on his way to regaining international legitimacy.

Yet, the apparent stability masked real dangers. Situated at the crossroads of Asia, Africa, and Europe, the Middle East is a volatile place, and moreover it is the one region whose volatility is a major concern to other parts of the world. In 2000 there were deep passions of hostility stirred in the Arab masses toward not just Israel, but the West in general, and particularly the United States. This was less true of the rulers of the Arabs—Saddam Hussein was an exception, and even Col. Muammar el-Qaddafi of Libya showed signs of mellowing during the year. There was a perceptible tendency for the Arab masses to become discontented with their rulers for not being sufficiently anti-Israeli. Demonstrations took place in several countries in October. Considering how dependent on Middle East oil the United States, Europe, and Japan are, the threats of some general conflagration, which could all too easily happen, were ominous.

Israeli-Palestinian Relations. The quest to advance the "peace process" that had been going on since the Oslo agreements of 1993 led to an extraordinary number of meetings during 2000—all of which ended in general failure. Barak and Arafat each crossed the Atlantic, in pilgrimages to Washington, innumerable times. The two typically met face to face or one-on-one with U.S. President Bill Clinton.

During the first half of the year, Barak pursued a "two-track" diplomacy, and concentrated his attention on attempted peace

© David Silverman/Newsmakers/Online/Liaison Agency

An elderly Palestinian argued with Israeli soldiers, who refused him entry into the West Bank town of Bethlehem, amid increased violence between Israelis and Palestinians in the fall of 2000.

with Syria. That attempt failed; it was pretty clear that it would, following the fiasco of the one-day meeting between Clinton and Hafiz al-Assad in Geneva on March 26. When the younger Assad, Bashar, succeeded his father in June, he failed to modify his father's absolute insistence on the total return of the Golan Heights.

In Israeli-Palestinian relations, the next step was supposed to be the implementation of the Wye River Memorandum from the fall of 1998. But Barak procrastinated on carrying out the third of the agreed Israeli withdrawals from pieces of the West Bank territory. Barak and Arafat had a "difficult" meeting at Gaza on February 3. Arafat was exasperated by Barak's suggestion that the target date for the final status agreement should be postponed from September 2000 to June 2001, and also by the map showing the areas that the Israeli prime minister proposed to hand over in the third transfer. In the West Bank, Palestinian-inhabited areas and Jewish settlements were almost inextricably dotted about; it was hard to imagine a satisfactory division.

Negotiations were temporarily suspended. Arafat's hand was possibly strengthened by the agreement between the Holy See and the Palestine Liberation Organization (PLO), which was signed in Rome on February 15. It protects freedom of religion and the legal status of Christian churches and recognizes the "inalienable national legitimate rights and aspirations of the Palestinian people." Some of the agreement's expressions were interpreted as pro-Palestinian. The Vatican had established diplomatic relations with Israel in 1993, and formally recognized the PLO in 1994. Pope John Paul II visited the Middle East in March. Although the pontiff avoided all political pitfalls that had been foreseen, his trip did not reduce Arab-Israeli hostility.

On April 11, Prime Minister Barak met with President Clinton in Washington. On April 20, Arafat did the same. On April 30, Israeli and Palestinian negotiators met at Eilat on the Gulf of Aqaba in an attempt to round off the final status draft, with U.S. negotiator Dennis Ross in attendance after May 3. Arafat was not enchanted by the Israeli proposal to transfer three villages on the outskirts of Jerusalem to the Palestinian Authority. He was less pleased by the Israelis' floating of the trial balloon of the "three canton solution"—the idea of transferring to Palestinian control not one solid block of contiguous territory, but three discrete areas separated from one another. Arafat retaliated by voicing his intention of proclaiming Palestine an independent sovereign state in September.

Palestinian rioting and Israeli reprisals reached a high point in the West Bank city of Ramallah, above, in late October. Numerous efforts to produce a peace agreement in 2000 failed.

© Ami Vitale/Newsmakers/Online/Liaison Agency

All through the year's wearing negotiations, President Clinton was the main external force trying to push the two sides into an agreement. He was anxious to achieve results during his final year in office. The exclusive role of the United States in Middle East intervention was even more notable than in previous years, which testified to the unprecedented status of the United States in the world. At the same time, failure would demonstrate the limitations of what even a superpower can achieve. Only once in 2000 did Russia—formerly a major player in the region—intervene. In late November, Russian President Vladimir Putin persuaded Arafat and Barak to speak to one another on the phone—something they had not done all month.

Clinton's major, though not last, attempt to achieve peace was the Camp David summit that occupied the second half of July. During these meetings, Barak went far beyond the concessions offered by previous Israeli negotiators. His plan amounted to a readiness to concede to the Palestinians somewhere around 90% of the West Bank, and share control of the holy places in

Jerusalem. Beyond expressing discontent, Arafat essentially did not reply to these efforts. He unsuccessfully solicited aid from various Arab courts (presumably to put pressure on Israel for even more concessions), and then embarked on a world tour.

Things took a darker turn on September 28 when Ariel Sharon, former Israeli general and defense minister, chose to visit the Temple Mount in Jerusalem. The Temple Mount—known to the Arabs as al-Haram al-Sharif, the holiest of places—was both the site of the First and Second Temples, and a holy shrine to the Muslims, who believed it to be the mountain from which Mohammed was transported to heaven. It had been under Israeli sovereignty since 1967, but in practice the Arabs were allowed to administer it. In theory, there was no reason why any Israeli should not visit the site. However, Palestinians and Arabs generally chose to regard Sharon's visit as a gratuitous insult, and deliberatively provocative. The immediate result was the beginning of a violent Palestinian protest, sometimes called the second *intifada* (uprising)—the first having begun in 1986. It lasted through the end of the year, and then began to abate somewhat. There were attacks on Israeli settlers and police. Many incidents occurred, typically with stone-throwing youths being combatted by Israeli soldiers. Palestinian young people were killed, but there was also a Palestinian attack on an Israeli school bus that killed schoolchildren. Selective killings were committed by both sides.

These events evoked enormous hostility throughout the Arab world. In Israel, public opinion turned quickly against Barak, whose attempts at peacemaking had come to naught. In December, he announced his resignation and called for early elections; from then on he was no more than a caretaker prime minister. Sharon emerged as his opponent in the election for prime minister, to be held on Feb. 6, 2001; and Sharon was favored in the polls. (*See* ISRAEL.) By mid-January 2001, the three and one-half months of violence had resulted in 365 deaths—314 Palestinians, 13 Arab Israelis, 37 other Israelis, and one German doctor.

All during the uprising, President Clinton continued his efforts to push the two sides into agreement, and indeed off-and-on negotiations continued into January 2001. Arguing that no peace could be achieved without important concessions from both sides, President Clinton unveiled in December what he considered to be a reasonable framework. The main points were that a portion of Jerusalem should be ceded to the new Palestinian state and that Arafat should largely give up the "right of return" of Palestinian refugees. Barak said he was prepared to consider such terms if Arafat would; but Arafat did not concur. Negotiations in various forms continued even into Clinton's last week in office. They were conducted at that point in Jerusalem by Arafat and former Israeli Prime Minister Shimon Peres. However, by that time, the talks only had the modest aim of summing up gains made so far for use as a basis and guideline for whenever talks might be resumed.

Barak had conceded so much at Camp David in July that commentators questioned whether Arafat in fact sought peace with Israel as a long-term goal or whether all negotiations were merely tactical moves and that his long-term goal was simply Israel's destruction. There was a distressing volume of evidence to support this interpretation. It was to be found in his public pronouncements in Arabic, in radio and television broadcasts, and school textbooks authorized by his embryo government—all full of pure denunciation of Israel's existence. Arafat had been offered by Barak about 95% of what he demanded, but he was insisting on 100%. He had made this sort of mistake earlier in his career—it had led to the expulsion of him and his movement from Jordan, then Lebanon. The two great areas of difference remained the status of Jerusalem (*see* SIDEBAR, page 360) and Palestinian refugees.

Palestinian Refugees. The refugees were those Palestinians who had left the region—voluntarily or involuntarily, versions differ—when Israel was founded. Historically, the Arabs and the United Nations (UN) have spoken of their "right of return." The refugees number somewhere between 3.5 million and 4.5 million. The original refugees had left in 1948, and presumably many of them were dead by 2000. What, therefore, is talked about are descendants of the original refugees, now running into the third generation. In the neighboring Arab countries where the original refugees went, descendants were kept deliberately separate and not allowed to settle down. For Israel to admit those original refugees still living as well as their descendants into their nation would be sheer demographic suicide. Israel has a total population of about 6.5 million, including 1.5 million Israeli Arabs.

ARTHUR CAMPBELL TURNER
University of California, Riverside

Jerusalem—The Focus of Dispute

© Lefteris Pitarakis/AP/Wide World Photos

Jerusalem, the capital of Israel and a key point of difference preventing a peace agreement between the Israelis and the Palestinians, is in the unique situation of being a sacred place to the three great religions of Judaism, Christianity, and Islam. This extraordinary, unparalleled situation, pregnant with danger and competitiveness, can only be explained historically. The Jewish connection is certainly the oldest of the three. It dates from 1,000 years before Christianity, 1,600 from the beginning of Islam.

A very old city—occupied as early as several thousand years B.C.—Jerusalem was captured by King David around 1000 B.C. He walled the city. King Solomon built the (First) Temple, and made the city the administrative capital and religious center it remained. It was captured and held by the Babylonians for several decades in the 6th century B.C. When the city was regained, the (Second) Temple was built to replace the destroyed one. Captured by the Romans under Pompey, Jerusalem initially was ruled by the Herod dynasty under the Roman aegis, and later ruled directly from Rome. After a rebellion in A.D. 70, Emperor Titus stormed the city and destroyed the Temple, and many Jews fled abroad—the beginning of the *diaspora* (dispersal).

Islamic forces wrested the city, and the region, from Byzantium in 637 A.D. The forces of the First Crusade took Jerusalem in 1099 and restored it to Christian rule, but it was lost to Saladin in 1187. Jerusalem remained under Muslim control—in the later centuries, that of the Ottoman Turks—until taken by British forces under Gen. Edmond Allenby in 1917. In the 19th century, many Jews had returned to settle in Palestine, and by 1900 the city had a Jewish majority. Jerusalem was the capital of Palestine under the Mandate until the establishment of the Jewish state in 1948. That year, Jordanian forces captured Old Jerusalem, but nascent Israel held New Jerusalem and made it the capital of the restored state. The Israelis gained the whole city in 1967.

Jerusalem is intimately associated with the life and death of Jesus Christ. Under Constantine, the Roman Empire became Christian, and a number of shrines were created that became holy places to Christians. For Muslims, from the 7th century, Jerusalem was revered as the place from which Muhammad ascended to heaven—and the third holiest place of all, ranking behind Mecca and Medina. But for devout Jews and devout Christians, there is no rival city.

Geographically, Jerusalem consists of the walled city, Old Jerusalem, which houses all the shrines except for the Garden of Gethsemane and the Mount of Olives, located just beyond the eastern edge of the walled city; and New Jerusalem, lying to the west and southwest. West Jerusalem was largely the creation of the 19th and 20th centuries, and much larger than the old city.

The old city is roughly quadrangular in shape, and divided into four: The Muslim Quarter, the largest, is to the northeast; the Jewish Quarter southeast; the Armenian quarter southwest; and the Christian Quarter northwest. Under Israeli rule, the Jewish population of the whole of Jerusalem has more than doubled since 1967, and now amounts to almost 500,000. Muslims number 182,000, and Christians (a diminishing minority) 14,000. However, areas to the north, east, and south of the walled city are largely Muslim.

ARTHUR CAMPBELL TURNER

Military Affairs

As the year 2000 began, the two largest nuclear-weapons states, the United States and Russia, posted a joint watch to ensure that a Y2K glitch did not mistakenly trigger a missile launch via computer malfunction. As it turned out, the Center for Year 2000 Strategic Stability, located at the U.S. Space Command in Colorado Springs, CO, quietly disbanded two weeks after New Year's Day, when it was deemed safe to disperse U.S. and Russian team members. Subsequently, relations between the United States and Moscow became strained when the two nations wrangled over a new ballistic-missile-defense program under development by the United States. Moscow also charged that the United States was not seriously interested in disarmament, mainly because the U.S. Senate refused to ratify the Comprehensive Nuclear Test-Ban Treaty. Later in the year, both nations lost sailors when an accident sank a Russian submarine with all hands on board, and a terrorist bomb killed 17 U.S. sailors on a destroyer in the port of Aden, Yemen. Late in the fall, U.S. Secretary of State Madeleine Albright visited the North Korean capital of Pyongyang—as the highest-ranking U.S. official to visit that reclusive communist nation—and returned with what appeared to be a substantial breakthrough on arms control.

National Missile Defense. In September, President Bill Clinton announced his decision that the technology to deploy a ballistic-missile defense was not yet available to the United States. This ended a complex debate that intertwined science and engineering on the one hand, and politics on the other. In tests conducted high above the Pacific Ocean, a missile designed to hit a dummy warhead and destroy it on impact failed. Part of the problem was that a decoy accompanied the dummy warhead and confused the missile. Beyond Washington, a number of defense experts voiced opposition

to the missile-defense program. They argued, as did North Atlantic Treaty Organization (NATO) allies, that deployment would stimulate both Russia and China to seek means to penetrate the U.S. missile shield, thus reopening the arms competition dampened in recent years by several major disarmament treaties.

Support for the National Missile Defense (NMD) system was manifold. First, there was the argument that the so-called "rogue" states, renamed "states of concern" at midyear—Iran, Iraq, and North Korea—were moving toward deployment of long-range missiles capable of carrying nuclear warheads. Some speculated this looming threat to the United States could be blunted with NMD. It also was noted that the United States could be protected against accidental launches of ballistic missiles by either Russia or China—if small in number—by NMD. Lastly, some advocates of NMD believed the system was necessary to protect Japan and Taiwan, and ultimately the United States, from the slowly increasing arsenal of intercontinental ballistic missiles (ICBMs) being deployed by China. At year's end, it was generally believed by defense experts that Beijing had approximately 20 ICBMs.

The NMD debate was complicated. Essentially, the system under discussion violated restrictions on the deployment of antiballistic missiles contained in the Anti-Ballistic Missile (ABM) Treaty of 1972. In an effort to resolve this impediment, the U.S. government suggested that the Russians work with Washington to amend the treaty to permit the deployment of 100

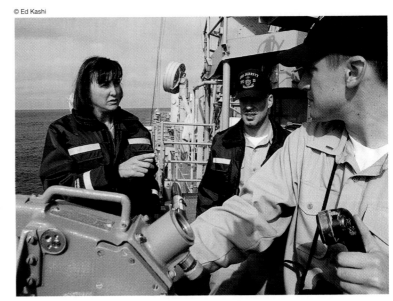

© Ed Kashi

During 2000, Cmdr. Kathleen McGrath, right, a 47-year-old mother of two small children, became the first American woman to command a warship at sea.

antiballistic missiles in Alaska by 2005. Initially, new Russian President Vladimir Putin balked at the plan because it could provide an advantage to the United States. However, as the year ended, it appeared the Russians might be willing to accept amendments in the treaty to permit the U.S. NMD deployment if Washington agreed to substantial cuts in offensive missiles.

Others outside the United States protested the proposed missile-defense plan. In Beijing, the Chinese echoed Russian fears that the small system would serve as a building block for a larger system that would negate China's nuclear deterrent. There was further concern in Beijing that the U.S. system could be modified to protect Taiwan, which China claimed as a legitimate part of China. Some Republicans suggested scrapping the ABM Treaty completely, freeing the United States to consider resurrecting a much larger missile-defense plan—along the lines of the Strategic Defense Initiative (SDI) suggested by President Ronald Reagan in 1983. That plan was rejected, first by the George Bush administration and later by the Clinton administration, because of severe technological difficulties.

Disarmament and Arms Control. In April, Russia's President Putin succeeded in persuading both houses of the Russian Federal Assembly (parliament) to ratify an agreement negotiated with the United States in 1993, known as START (Strategic Arms Reduction Treaty) II. The treaty calls for both sides to reduce nuclear warheads to no more than 3,500 by 2007. It bans the large, multiple-warhead Russian SS-18 and the U.S. MX. The nongovernmental Arms Control Association estimated that the United States had 7,763 warheads and Russia 6,472. Washington and Moscow disagreed on the next step in the disarming process, called START III. The Russians wanted the next round of cuts to reduce warheads to 1,500 each. U.S. negotiators preferred reductions to 2,500, or possibly 2,000. It generally was believed the Russians support a lower figure because of budgetary constraints, while the U.S. government desired a larger force for security purposes. President Putin warned that Russia's support for the treaty would evaporate should the United States unilaterally modify the ABM Treaty to permit deployment of its NMD system.

The North Korean Missile Threat. Late in October, Secretary Albright made an unprecedented visit to Pyongyang. She met with the reclusive communist leader Kim Jong Il and discussed means to resolve the dispute over Washington's objections to North Korea's missile-development program. Problems arose in the late 1990s when North Korea tested a Taepodong missile and claimed it was designed to place a small satellite into orbit. This meant that the communist nation had the technology to hurl a warhead, possibly a nuclear one, across the Pacific at the United States. Compounding the disagreement was the belief by U.S. officials that North Korea was selling missiles and related technology to nations such as Libya and Iran.

According to Secretary Albright, Kim Jong Il agreed to discussions with U.S. negotiators that could lead to the suppression of the North Korean missile research-and-development program, and an end to missile exports. The United States would need to meet certain conditions, such as assisting North Korea in launching nonmilitary satellites. Previously, the North Korean government had stated it would cease missile development only in exchange for large sums of money, viewed in Washington as blackmail. As the year ended, U.S. and North Korean officials were working to fill in details of the Albright-Kim discussions. Should the North Koreans shut down their missile program, a major justification for building the U.S. antiballistic missile shield would be removed. From the U.S. perspective, any deal would have to include means to verify North Korean compliance.

The Chinese Military Buildup. Accompanied at times by bellicose rhetoric regarding the physical unification of Taiwan with mainland China, Beijing continued the slow expansion of its military establishment, often with purchases of modern naval and missile equipment from Russia. Periodically, the Chinese conducted military exercises along their coast and in waters opposite Taiwan. However, few U.S. defense experts felt the Chinese possessed the military capability to invade Taiwan should the United States oppose such action. On the other hand, many believed China would acquire such capability, but well into the future. Washington's strategy included working for a peaceful solution to the problem.

Terrorism. Four years after a truck bomb destroyed Saudi Arabian barracks housing U.S. Air Force personnel, and two years after the bombing of two U.S. embassies in East Africa, terrorists struck U.S. forces again. This time the target was the guided-

The Sinking of the "Kursk"

Russia's government and military suffered harsh criticism following the sinking of its modern attack sub, the "Kursk," above, and 118 sailors in August 2000. The accident led military experts to reconsider the role of the submarine in the post-Cold War era.

Already plagued by low morale and lack of funding, the Russian military suffered another blow on Aug. 12, 2000, when a pair of explosions sent the *Kursk*, one of the most modern attack submarines in Russia's Northern Fleet, 350 ft (107 m) to the bottom of the Barents Sea. For many in Russia, the loss of the *Kursk* was a metaphor for everything that has gone wrong in Russia since the collapse of the Soviet Union in 1991—loss of empire, loss of pride, loss of technological excellence, and loss of military competence once thought on par with the United States.

The *Kursk* was participating in a naval exercise off the northwest coast of Russia when, according to U.S. intelligence, a small blast in the forward torpedo room caused a catastrophic explosion minutes later that destroyed part of the submarine's first two compartments. The U.S. explanation for the accident was that a new type of torpedo exploded, setting off the fatal detonation. The Russian explanation was that the *Kursk* suffered a collision with a foreign submarine.

Intense criticism of the government developed as word spread that the Russian Navy had been slow in asking for help from other nations to mount a rescue operation for the crew of the *Kursk*; it was also learned that Russian President Vladimir Putin failed to terminate his summer vacation when told of the accident. Officials asked forgiveness for the loss of the 118 sailors of the *Kursk*, and President Putin ordered the amount of aid given to grieving families to be tripled to the equivalent of $450.

In late October, Russian and Norwegian divers finally cut holes in the outer and inner hulls of the *Kursk* and retrieved four bodies. It was then announced that at least 23 of the *Kursk*'s crew had survived for some time in the aft turbine room. This information was contained in a note found in the pocket of Lt. Capt. Dimitri Kolesnikov. The Russian officer had written, apparently in the dark: "There are 23 of us here. We have made this decision as a result of the accident. None of us can get out." The discovery of that note reopened criticism of the government for its failure to move more swiftly in rescue operations, and for stating that all crew members died almost immediately. After retrieving eight more bodies, the Russians announced in early November that the recovery operation would cease due to the danger faced by divers attempting to crawl through the shattered compartments of the *Kursk*.

The tragedy of the *Kursk* served to remind the world that while the Cold War ended a decade ago, both Russia and the United States continue to deploy submarines in the world's oceans as part of their naval operations. During the 1950s the United States had invested heavily in submarine technology to counter a vast Soviet submarine force, and added nuclear-powered submarines to their arsenal. Today the undersea craft continue to conduct a number of missions. They are prepared to sink enemy ships with torpedoes, launch strikes with nuclear-tipped ballistic missiles, and conduct a variety of intelligence-gathering tasks.

ROBERT M. LAWRENCE

missile destroyer USS *Cole*, refueling in the Yemeni port of Aden. At approximately 9:45 A.M. on October 12, a small boat, believed to have carried two suicide bombers, motored alongside the *Cole*, and a powerful explosion blew a 40-sq-ft (3.7 m²) hole in the side of the ship, killing 17 sailors, two of whom were women, and injuring 37 more.

Determining who was ultimately responsible for the attack proved daunting. Initially, U.S. military and personnel from the Federal Bureau of Investigation (FBI) flew to Aden to seek physical evidence and reported complete cooperation by Yemen authorities. However, several weeks after the attack, the United States complained its investigators were encountering difficulty interviewing potential Yemeni witnesses and suspects. Problems arose when Yemeni President Ali Abdullah Saleh objected to U.S. officials directly questioning Yemeni citizens, on the basis that it violated Yemeni sovereignty. In mid-December the Yemini government announced that as many as six Yemenis could go on trial for the bombing. Although no "smoking gun" was found, many believed the attack would eventually be traced to Saudi millionaire Osama bin Laden, who stated his intent to drive U.S. forces from the Middle East. It also was generally thought that bin Laden was continuing to live in Afghanistan under the protection of the Taliban government. As the year ended, the *Cole* had been brought back to the United States to be repaired (*See also* TERRORISM.)

Sexual Harassment in the Military. In June the U.S. Army's highest-ranking woman officer, Lt. Gen. Claudia Kennedy, retired after 31 years in the military. Two months later, Maj. Gen. Larry Smith, accused earlier by General Kennedy of sexual harassment, also retired, after 34 years in the army, with a reprimand for "conduct unbecoming an officer and a gentleman." For his part, General Smith said he was "deeply disappointed" with the army's action. It marked the end to an episode in which, for the first time, one general had accused another of sexual harassment. Previously, General Kennedy alleged General Smith had kissed her against her will, and had touched her inappropriately.

In 1999, General Smith had been selected by the army to be its deputy inspector general, a job that could have required he deal with allegations of sexual harassment and other improper activities by senior officers. Several months later, General Kenne-

© Tom Callan/AP/Wide World Photos

In June 2000, Lt. Gen. Claudia Kennedy, above, retired as the highest-ranking woman in the U.S. Army, after filling a sexual-harassment complaint against another Army general.

dy, then the army's chief of intelligence, protested the appointment, and mentioned General Smith's unwanted approaches three years earlier.

Philosophic Considerations. In the aftermath of the air war that forced Yugoslav President Slobodan Milosevic to withdraw his army and special police from Kosovo, U.S. military planners wrestled with the political implications of the "risk avoidance" strategy. The problem, as seen by many U.S. military leaders, is that the low casualty figures associated with the Bosnian and Kosovo operations (no combat deaths in either one) could develop a false sense of security, and unrealistic expectations on the part of politicians and the public that future combat situations could be won without the loss of life. It was suggested that a United States perceived as reluctant to run the risk of casualties might serve as a temptation to violence for "rogue states."

Another area of concern in the military establishment was whether regular combat troops—such as those from the 82d Airborne Division, patrolling to keep peace among Kosovar Albanians and Serbs—were adequately trained to serve as peacekeepers. As a result of instances where it appeared U.S. troops used unnecessary force in Kosovo, some military observers suggested the Pentagon consider creating a constabulary force with special training for crowd control, civilian searches, and interrogation, apart from the units in which the "warrior instinct" is instilled.

ROBERT M. LAWRENCE
Colorado State University

Morocco

In 2000, King Mohamed VI sought to improve the image of Morocco and the monarchy. While strengthening his power, he worked to project an image of a reformist in contrast to the more conservative approach of his father, the late King Hassan II.

In regional and political affairs, the Moroccan monarchy faced difficulties in dealing with the Western Sahara conflict while the Islamist movement continued to gain strength. The economy was characterized by a persistent drought and by the discovery of oil.

Government. Morocco underwent a cabinet reshuffle in response to criticism that the administration was difficult to manage given its size and the number of parties involved within the governing coalition. The reshuffle led to a streamlined cabinet of 33 departments, down from 46. The new cabinet was the result of intense negotiations led by Prime Minister Abderrahmane Youssoufi and involving coalition parties. New faces in the executive included the veteran politician and head of the nationalist party Istiqlal, Abbas el-Fassi, who was appointed to head the difficult Employment and Solidarity Ministry. Abbas el-Fassi is Youssoufi's rival within the governing Koutla coalition composed of left-wing political parties.

In the area of human rights, the monarchy released the Islamist opposition leader Sheikh Abdeslam Yassine, who had spent ten years under house arrest. Abraham Serfaty, a Jewish Marxist opposition figure, returned from exile in France and was appointed to a key senior position in the petroleum and mining authority. Other exiled dissidents returned to Morocco as well.

To improve Moroccco's human-rights image, the monarchy approved the inception of a special commission to investigate the 5,819 cases of missing persons. By late 2000, however, only 68 such cases had been settled with financial compensations for victms' relatives.

Economy. While Morocco's five-year economic plan that began in 2000 targeted a real growth in gross domestic product (GDP) of 5% annually, growth in 2000 was only slightly above 3%, given the damaging effect of drought. However, Morocco succeeded in keeping inflation down (about 1.5%) in spite of a slight increase because of the persistent drought.

The most important economic news was the oil discovery at Talsinnt, an area some 500 mi (800 km) southeast of the capital, Rabat. The finding was made by the Moroccan-American company Lone Star Energy. According to Lone Star, Talsinnt could contain 10 billion to 15 billion barrels of oil equivalent. Such a quantity would fulfill domestic demand for decades. Since Morocco is an importer of oil, this discovery could be a key factor in lowering the nation's energy-import bill and reducing the trade deficit. Morocco has been importing up to $1.5 billion worth of petroleum products. This amount accounts for more than 10% of the nation's entire import bill.

In the area of trade, Morocco's competitiveness in the European market declined due to a weak euro against the U.S. dollar. Pressure from exporters and manufacturers on the government to devalue the local currency, the dirham, increased considerably, but authorities refused devaluation.

Regional Affairs. The Western Sahara dispute escalated and threatened to turn into an armed conflict. Morocco, which continued to insist that the territory formerly occupied by Spain be annexed, was opposing the independence group, the Polisario Front. This conflict remained a major hurdle to improved relations between Morocco and its neighbor, Algeria, which always has backed the Polisario Front in seeking independence. A series of meetings among the feuding parties failed to produce an agreement, and a referendum proposed by the United Nations (UN) was not expected to be approved.

ROSE RYAN, *Executive Editor*
"The North Africa Journal"

MOROCCO • Information Highlights

Official Name: Kingdom of Morocco.
Location: Northwest Africa.
Area: 172,413 sq mi (446 550 km²).
Population (2000 est.): 30,122,350.
Chief Cities (1994 census): Rabat, the capital (incl. Salé), 1,385,872; Casablanca, 2,940,623; Fez, 774,754; Marrakech, 745,541.
Government: *Head of state,* Mohamed VI, king (acceded 1999). *Head of government,* Abderrahmane Youssoufi, prime minister (appointed November 1997). *Legislature* (bicameral)—Chamber of Councillors and House of Representatives.
Monetary Unit: Dirham (10.7778 dirhams equal U.S.$1, Dec. 21, 2000).
Gross Domestic Product (1999 est. U.S.$): $108,000,000,000 (purchasing power parity).
Economic Indexes (1999): *Consumer Prices* (1990 = 100): all items, 144.3; food, 145.1. *Industrial Production* 125.5.
Foreign Trade (1999 U.S.$): *Imports,* $9,925,000,000; *exports,* $7,367,000,000.

Hardly surprising in an election year, Hollywood was pelted with attacks for the level of violence and other objectionable material in its products. Leading the fray were Democratic and Republican candidates who charged studios with targeting children in the marketing of R-rated films. Amid congressional hearings, threats of government action against the studios, and counterwarnings that free speech could be violated, Hollywood executives—such as Jack Valenti, president of the Motion Picture Association of America (MPAA)—pledged not to target children inappropriately when films had violent content.

Major Achievements. The year 2000 was not a banner one for great works from American filmmakers, but, despite disappointments, there were enough domestic and imported films to provide extensive, worthwhile, and entertaining moviegoing. Many of the better films were driven by impressive performances.

Oscar honors for the previous year's films included an award for Kevin Spacey as best actor for *American Beauty*, the major winner, and one for Hilary Swank as leading actress in *Boys Don't Cry*. As for the next round of Oscars, *Erin Brockovich*, one of 2000's early releases, provided a strong vehicle for Julia Roberts, who was immediately projected as a potential nominee for her feisty portrait of the real person who fought against alleged polluters. The film, while vigorous in its social comment, was highly entertaining. It also had potential as an award candidate, as did Albert Finney for his supporting performance as a lawyer.

Toward year's end, another striking film was *Pollock*, in which Ed Harris, who also directed, gave a powerful performance as the volatile and troubled artist Jackson Pollock. There also was award-caliber acting by actress Marcia Gay Harden as Pollock's devoted wife, artist Lee Krasner. In *The Contender*, Joan Allen was memorable as a U.S. senator who, after being tapped to take over a sudden vice-presidential vacancy, was subjected to a barrage of dirty politics. Jeff Bridges was tops as the canny chief executive who appoints her. Also earning high marks was Richard Gere as a gynecologist in Robert Altman's zippy Texas satire *Dr. T and the Women*.

Denzel Washington turned in yet another superb performance, this time as an African-American football coach who steps into a racially charged situation in *Remember the Titans*, based on a true story. Newcomer Michelle Rodriguez made a striking debut as a troubled teenager who finds herself by learning the sport of boxing in *Girlfight*, which also marked the strong debut of Karyn Kusama as writer-director. The satirical *American Psycho*, based on Bret Easton Ellis' controversial novel, was not for everyone, but Christian Bale was powerful in the demented leading role. Jamie Bell gave a winsome performance in the title role of *Billy Elliot*, an unusual import about a teenage boy in a British mining town who yearns to become a dancer. Ralph Fiennes gave a tour de force acting turn playing men from three generations of a Hungarian Jewish family in director Istvan Szabo's drama set against changing historical background. Icelandic singing star Björk was haunting in the role of a young woman hanged for murder in Lars von Trier's odd musical drama *Dancer in the Dark*, a Cannes Film Festival winner subsequently showcased by the New York Film Festival and known for dividing audiences into those who loved or hated it.

The New York and Toronto Film Festivals presented the phenomenal Swedish film *Faithless*, astutely directed by Liv Ullmann from a script by Ingmar Bergman. The film mercilessly explored explosive relationships and contained a magnificent performance by Lena Endre. Patrick Fugit scored as a teenager aspiring to write for *Rolling Stone*, while Kate Hudson was touching as a groupie in Cameron Crowe's *Almost Famous*, an autobiographical reflection on the world of rock 'n' roll. Russell Crowe, fresh from 1999's triumph in *The Insider*, was the dominating force in the massive action film *Gladiator*, a high-grossing epic directed by Ridley Scott and crammed with high-tech special effects that re-create ancient Rome and its Colosseum. Two of the most entertainingly bizarre acting turns were contributed in *Shadow of the Vampire*: John Malkovich was the silent-film director F.W. Murnau, obsessed with making a great vampire film, and a heavily made-up Willem Dafoe was his comically fearsome, neck-biting star.

Strictly for Laughs. Robert De Niro's expertise at character acting was delightfully evident in *Meet the Parents*, a funny comedy about an overpossessive father who makes life miserable for the suitor (Ben Stiller) his daughter brings home. Woody Allen was on track with his hilarious *Small Time Crooks*, co-starring himself with a very funny Tracey

Ullman. They played a conniving couple whose aborted crime plan takes an unexpected turn.

In *Me, Myself & Irene*, Jim Carrey was at his slapstick best as a Rhode Island state trooper with a dual personality. Although Renee Zellweger was engaging as Carrey's love interest, she really came into her own in the gallows-humor comedy *Nurse Betty*, where she was a dreamer infatuated with a soap-opera hero. *East Is East*, a 1999 British import based on a play by Ayub Khan-Din, starred noted Indian actor Om Puri as a stern father who tries to raise his children in the Pakistani tradition as they are trying to assimilate to English life. The film, often uproariously funny, made telling points about cultural conflict. Bruce Willis starred in the offbeat *The Whole Nine Yards*, a comedy about hit men and those who hire them. *Best in Show* was a send-up of dog shows in

what has come to be known as the "mockumentary" category.

What would a year be without a grossout, youth-oriented film? *Road Trip* mined humor from college students desperately trying to retrieve an incriminating video that accidentally had been mailed. Eddie Murphy had multiple roles in *Nutty Professor II: The Klumps*, and Martin Lawrence provided comedy in *Big Momma's House*.

Films for Thought. Among films with something special to say, *Pay It Forward* involved a boy (Haley Joel Osment) leading the way toward hope and a better life for two adults—his mother (Helen Hunt), who has been struggling with alcoholism, and his burn-victim teacher (Kevin Spacey). *Wonder Boys* gave special acting opportunities to Michael Douglas as a professor and Tobey Maguire as an unusual student in a story about sorting out goals and values. There also were strong parts for Frances McDormand and Robert Downey, Jr. Billy Crudup, who is increasingly viewed as an important actor, starred in *Waking the Dead*, which measured idealism against political practicality in a story about an activist (Jennifer Connelly) killed in a car bombing. Or was she?

The most daring message attempt was by Spike Lee in *Bamboozled*, in which he used the racist minstrel form and assorted stereotypes in a satire aimed at spotlighting prejudice against African-Americans. The British import *Ratcatcher* creatively examined the grim life of a working-class neighborhood in Glasgow. Problematic ethics in the world of gambling and payoffs were at the core of *Croupier*, a slick contemporary film noir from Britain, with a dynamic lead performance by Clive Owen. *George Washington*, a first feature by David Gordon Green, honed in on youngsters struggling to exist in a difficult environment. Denys Arcand's Canadian import *Stardom* skewered the celebrity world of high-priced models.

Broad Menu. There was the customary helping of action pictures aimed at hefty box-office results. Apart from *Gladiator*, major movies of the genre included *X-Men*, stemming from comic-book lore; the sequel *Mission: Impossible*

© Universal/Everett Collection

Julia Roberts, above, won accolades for her portrayal of a lawyer's feisty assistant who battles polluters in the true-life story of "Erin Brockovich." The film also featured Albert Finney as the crusty lawyer.

2; and *Shaft*, this time with Samuel L. Jackson as the supercool detective. America's Revolutionary War was the setting for *The Patriot*, a bloody, not-very-credible saga with Mel Gibson as a reluctant warrior. Action at sea was the keynote of *The Perfect Storm*, in which George Clooney, playing a fisherman in Wolfgang Petersen's version of Sebastian Junger's book about a true story, battles an unusual conflux of ocean storms. With a nod to seniors, *Space Cowboys* featured aging astronauts in orbit, with direction by Clint Eastwood, who also starred. One of the strangest action flicks was *Crouching Tiger, Hidden Dragon*, a romantic martial-arts story filmed in China by Ang Lee and featuring special effects that allowed combatants to soar over rooftops and treetops.

Family-oriented films attempted to fill a perennial void. The animated *Chicken Run* was rich in humor and amusing ideas. Disney's *The Kid* cast Bruce Willis as an image consultant who gets in touch with himself as a youngster in a fantasy tale. Spencer Breslin played the younger version. Disney also unveiled *102 Dalmatians*, an outgrowth of its previous gold mine.

Many films were scheduled for year-end release, including Robert Redford's *The Legend of Bagger Vance*, a fable involving golfers; *What Women Want*, with Mel Gibson as a male chauvinist who hears women's voices; *Cast Away*, with Tom Hanks trying to survive on a remote island; *Quills*, starring Geoffrey Rush as the infamous Marquis de Sade; *Before Night Falls*, a dramatization of the persecution of Cuban homosexual and dissenting writer Reinaldo Arenas; *State and Main*, David Mamet's satire on a film company shooting in a small town; and *Book of Shadows: Blair Witch 2*, a spin-off of the previous box-office success.

An outstanding documentary was *The Life and Times of Hank Greenberg*, in which filmmaker Aviva Kempner portrayed the celebrated 1930s and 1940s baseball player in the context of his time. An irreverent, entertaining approach to film biography was taken in *The Eyes of Tammy Faye*, which satirically yet sometimes sympathetically looked at the world of Tammy Faye Bakker.

Foreign-Language Films. Many filmgoers did not see some of the best movies made because they were in a foreign language and got comparatively limited distribution. Despite censorship problems, Iran has been a fertile source of creative works expressing aspects of life in that country. *Two Women* was a searing look at the problems of women in a repressive, male-oriented society, and *The Circle* dramatically covered similar ground. *The Color of Paradise* wrenchingly told of a blind boy whose father has pressures that interfere with doing right by his needy son.

France continued to make an impact with *East-West*, an expansive story about Russians who, lured back from abroad after World War II, find life filled with repression and terror; *La Bûche*, a colorful, lively family drama set in the Christmas season; *An Affair of Love*, teaming Nathalie Baye and Sergi Lopez as two people who intend to meet for pure eroticism and find their humanity taking over; *Venus Beauty Institute*, also starring Baye as one of the women who work in a beauty salon searching for Mr. Right; *Human Resources*, a thoughtful film about individuals caught between labor and management; *Humanité*, a chilling drama about the investigation of a murder; and *The Gleaners and I*, a creative documentary by veteran filmmaker Agnes Varda.

China, another important film source, was the setting for *Shower*, which told of the clash between those whose lives revolve around a bathhouse and plans for revamping the neighborhood.

From Israel came the controversial *Kadosh*, telling of problems women face in rigidly Orthodox communities.

Business Affairs. The Hollywood scene was gripped by strike worries in advance of possible conflicts in mid-2001. In preparation, the studios were planning schedules so that films could be completed without getting caught in a job action. Key issues involved union jurisdiction over earnings from the Internet and other technologies. As the result of a six-month-long strike by the Screen Actors Guild (SAG) and the American Federation of Television and Radio Artists (AFTRA), actors made gains for a greater share of return on their TV advertising work.

At the box office, some movies counted upon to be blockbusters did not meet expectations. Still, by early October, Paramount's *Mission: Impossible 2* had taken in more than $215 million domestically and more than $350 million abroad; DreamWorks' *Gladiator* tallied more than $186 million at home and nearly $254 million abroad; and *The Perfect Storm* reached more than $180 million and $135 million at home and abroad, respectively.

WILLIAM WOLF
New York University

Motion Pictures • 2000

ALMOST FAMOUS. Written and directed by Cameron Crowe. With Billy Crudup, Frances McDormand, Kate Hudson, Anna Paquin, and Patrick Fugit.

AMERICAN PSYCHO. Director, Mary Harron; screenplay by Harron and Guinevere Turner, based on the novel by Bret Easton Ellis. With Christian Bale, Willem Dafoe, Jared Leto, and Chloe Sevigny.

BAMBOOZLED. Written and directed by Spike Lee. With Damon Wayans, Michael Rapaport, Savion Glover, Tommy Davidson, and Jada Pinkett Smith.

BEDAZZLED. Director, Harold Ramis; screenplay by Larry Gelbart, Harold Ramis, and Peter Tolan. With Brendan Fraser, Elizabeth Hurley, and Frances O'Connor.

BEFORE NIGHT FALLS. Director, Julian Schnabel; screenplay by Cunningham O'Keefe, Julian Schnabel, and Lazaro Gomez Carriles. With Andrea Di Stefano, Javier Bardem, Johnny Depp, Olivier Martinez, and Sean Penn.

BEST IN SHOW. Director, Christopher Guest; screenplay by Guest and Eugene Levy. With Guest, Jennifer Coolidge, John Michael Higgins, Michael Hitchcock, and Parker Posey.

THE BIG KAHUNA. Director, John Swanbeck; screenplay by Roger Rueff. With Danny DeVito, Kevin Spacey, and Peter Facinelli.

BIG MOMMA'S HOUSE. Director, Raja Gosnell; screenplay by Darryl Quarles and Don Rhymer, based on a story by Quarles. With Martin Lawrence, Nia Long, Paul Giamatti, and Ella Mitchell.

BILLY ELLIOT. Director, Stephen Daldry; screenplay by Lee Hall. With Jamie Bell, Julie Walters, Jamie Draven, and Gary Lewis.

BLESS THE CHILD. Director, Chuck Russell; screenplay by Tom Rickman, Clifford G\reen, and Ellen Green, based on the novel by Cathy Cash Spellman. With Kim Basinger, Jimmy Smits, Christina Ricci, and Ian Holm.

BOESMAN AND LENA. Written and directed by John Berry, based on the play by Athol Fugard. With Danny Glover, Angela Bassett, and Willie Jonah.

BOUNCE. Written and directed by Don Roos. With Ben Affleck, Gwyneth Paltrow, Joe Morton, Johnny Galecki, and Jennifer Gray.

CAST AWAY. Director, Robert Zemeckis; screenplay by William Broyles, Jr. With Tom Hanks, Helen Hunt, and Nick Searcy.

THE CELL. Director, Tarsem Singh; screenplay by Mark Protosevich. With Jennifer Lopez, Vince Vaughn, Vincent D'Onofrio, and Marianne Jean-Baptiste.

CHARLIE'S ANGELS. Director, McG; screenplay by Ryan Rowe, Ed Solomon, and John August. With Cameron Diaz, Lucy Liu, and Drew Barrymore.

© Giles Keyte/2000 Universal Studios/Photofest

"Billy Elliot," starring newcomer Jamie Bell, is the story of a young boy growing up in an impoverished English mining town who finds hope and refuge in ballet dancing.

CHICKEN RUN. Written and directed by Peter Lord and Nick Park. With Phil Daniels, Lynn Ferguson, Mel Gibson, Tony Hayart, and Jane Horrocks.

CHOCOLAT. Director, Lasse Hallstrom; screenplay by Joanne Harris and Robert Nelson, based on Harris's novel. With Juliette Binoche, Johnny Depp, and Alfred Molina.

THE CLAIM. Director, Michael Winterbottom; screenplay by Frank Cottrell Boyce, based on Thomas Hardy's novel *The Mayor of Casterbridge.* With Peter Mullan, Nastassja Kinski, Wes Bentley, Milla Jovovich, and Sarah Polley.

THE CONTENDER. Director, Rod Lurie; screenplay by Lurie and Denis Maloney. With Joan Allen, Christian Slater, Jeff Bridges, Gary Oldman, and William Petersen.

CROUCHING TIGER, HIDDEN DRAGON. Director, Ang Lee; screenplay by James Schamus, Kuo-Rong Tsai, and Wang Hui Ling. With Chang Zheng, Chow Yun Fat, Michelle Yeoh, Zhang Zi-Yi, and Zheng Pei-Pei.

DANCER IN THE DARK. Written and directed by Lars von Trier. With Bjork, Catherine Deneuve, Peter Stomare, David Morse, and Joel Grey.

DR. SEUSS' HOW THE GRINCH STOLE CHRISTMAS. Director, Ron Howard; screenplay by Jeffrey Price and Peter S. Seaman. With Jim Carrey, Christine Baranski, Molly Shannon, and Bill Irwin. Narrated by Anthony Hopkins.

DR. T & THE WOMEN. Director, Robert Altman; screenplay by Anne Rapp. With Richard Gere, Helen Hunt, Farrah Fawcett, Shelley Long, and Laura Dern.

DUETS. Director, Bruce Paltrow; screenplay by John Byrum. With Gwyneth Paltrow, Andre Braugher, and Huey Lewis.

EAST IS EAST. Director, Damien O'Donnell; screenplay by Ayub Khan-Din, based on his play. With Om Puri, Linda Basset, Jordan Routledge, and Archie Panjabi.

EAST-WEST. Director, Regis Wargnier. Screenplay by Roustam Ibraguimbek, Sergei Bodrov, Louis Gardel, and Wargnier. With Sandrine Bonnaire, Oleg Mecikov, and Catherine Deneuve.

ERIN BROCKOVICH. Director, Steven Soderbergh; screenplay by Susannah Grant. With Julia Roberts, Albert Finney, Aaron Eckhart, and Peter Coyote.

FANTASIA 2000. Directors, James Algar, Gaeten Brizzi, Paul Brizzi, Hendel Butoy, Francis Glebas, Eric Goldberg, Don Hahn, and Pixote Hunt; screenplay by Carl Fallburg, Irene Mecchi, Perce Pearce, and David Reynolds, based, in part, on Hans Christian Anderson's *The Steadfast Tin Soldier.* With Steve Martin, James Levine, Quincy Jones, Bette Midler, James Earl Jones, and Angela Lansbury.

FINDING FORRESTER. Director, Gus Van Sant; screenplay by Mike Rich. With Sean Connery, F. Murray Abraham, Anna Paquin, Busta Rhymes, and Rob Brown.

GEORGE WASHINGTON. Written and directed by David Gordon Green. With Candace Evanofski, Donald Holden, and Curtis Cotton III.

David Lee/© 2000 New Line Cinema/ Kobal Collection

"Bamboozled," featuring Tommy Davidson and Savion Glover, is director and writer Spike Lee's controversial satire about racism and race relations in contemporary culture.

© Phillip V. Caruso/ SMPSP/ Everett Collection

"Meet the Parents" stars Ben Stiller as a neurotic suitor who must win the approval of his girlfriend's protective father, a former CIA operative played by Robert DeNiro.

THE GIFT. Director, Sam Rami; screenplay by Billy Bob Thornton and Tom Epperson. With Cate Blanchett, Hilary Swank, and Keanu Reeves.

GIRLFIGHT. Written and directed by Karyn Kusama. With Michelle Rodriguez, Jamie Tirelli, Paul Calderon, Santiago Douglas, and Elisa Bocanegra.

GLADIATOR. Director, Ridley Scott; screenplay by David Franzoni, John Logan, and William Nicholson, based on a story by Franzoni. With Russell Crowe, Joaquin Phoenix, Connie Nielson, and Oliver Reed.

GROOVE. Written and directed by Greg Harrison. With Lola Glaudini, Hamish Linklater, Ari Gold, and Elizabeth Sun.

HAMLET. Written and directed by Michael Almereyda, based on Almereyda's adaptation of a play by William Shakespeare. With Ethan Hawke, Kyle MacLachlan, Julia Stiles, Bill Murray, and Liev Schreiber.

HANGING UP. Director, Diane Keaton; screenplay by Delia and Nora Ephron, based on the book by Nora Ephron. With Keaton, Meg Ryan, Lisa Kudrow, Walter Matthau, and Cloris Leachman.

HIGH FIDELITY. Directors, Stephen Frears and Seamus McGarvey; screenplay by Nick Hornby, D.V. DeVincentis, John Cusack, Scott Rosenberg, and Steve Pink. With John Cusack, Iben Hjejle, Jack Black, Lisa Bonet, and Tim Robbins.

THE HOUSE OF MIRTH. Written and directed by Terence Davis. With Gillian Anderson, Dan Aykroyd, Anthony LaPaglia, Elizabeth McGovern, and Eric Stoltz.

I DREAMED OF AFRICA. Director, Hugh Hudson; screenplay by Paula Milne and Susan Shilliday, based on the book by Kuki Gallmann. With Kim Basinger, Vincent Perez, Eva Marie Saint, and Liam Aiken.

JOE GOULD'S SECRET. Director, Stanley Tucci; screenplay by Howard A. Rothman, based on *Professor Sea Gull* and *Joe Gould's Secret* by Joseph Mitchell. With Sir Ian Holm, Tucci, Hope Davis, and Susan Sarandon.

JUDY BERLIN. Written and directed by Eric Mendelsohn. With Barbara Barrie, Bob Dishy, Anne Meara, and Madeline Kahn.

KEEPING THE FAITH. Director, Edward Norton; screenplay by Stuart Blumberg. With Ben Stiller, Edward Norton, and Jenna Elfman.

LA BÛCHE. Director, Daniele Thompson; screenplay by Thompson and Christopher Thompson. With Sabine Azema, Emmanuelle Beart, Charlotte Gainsbourg, Claude Rich, Christopher Thompson, and Jean-Pierre Darroussin.

THE LADIES MAN. Director, Reginald Hudlin; screenplay by Andrew Steele, Dennis McNicholas, and Tim Meadows. With Meadows, Will Ferrell, Tiffani-Amber Thiessen, Billy Dee Williams, and Lee Evans.

LITTLE NICKY. Director, Steven Brill; screenplay by Tim Herlihy, Adam Sandler, and Brill. With Sandler, Patricia Arquette, Harvey Keitel, and Rodney Dangerfield.

"Pay it Forward" stars Kevin Spacey as a teacher who challenges his class to think of a way to change the world. Haley Joel Osment is the young student roused to take action. Helen Hunt plays Osment's mother.

THE LITTLE VAMPIRE. Director, Uli Edel; screenplay by Karey Kirkpatrick and Larry Wilson. With Jonathan Lipnicki, Richard E. Grant, Jim Carter, Rollo Weeks, John Wood, and Dean Cook.

LOST SOULS. Director, Janusz Kaminski and Mauro Fiore; screenplay by Betsy Stahl and Pierce Gardner. With Winona Ryder, Ben Chaplin, John Hurt, Philip Baker Hall, and Elias Koteas.

LOVE AND BASKETBALL. Written and directed by Gina Prince-Bythewood. With Sanaa Lathan, Omar Epps, Dennis Haysbert, and Debbi Morgan.

LOVE'S LABOUR'S LOST. Written and directed by Kenneth Branagh, based on a play by William Shakespeare. With Branagh, Richard Briers, and Nathan Lane.

LUCKY NUMBERS. Director, Nora Ephron; screenplay by Adam Resnick. With John Travolta, Lisa Kudrow, and Bill Pullman.

ME, MYSELF AND IRENE. Directors, Bobby Farrelly and Peter Farrelly; screenplay by Peter Farrelly, Mike Cerrone, and Bobby Farrelly. With Jim Carrey, Renee Zellweger, and Anthony Anderson.

MEET THE PARENTS. Director, Jay Roach; screenplay by Jim Herzfeld and John Hamburg. With Robert DeNiro, Ben Stiller, Blythe Danner, Teri Polo, and Owen Wilson.

MEN OF HONOR. Director, George Tillman, Jr; screenplay by Scott Marshall Smith. With Robert DeNiro, Cuba Gooding, Jr., Hal Holbrook, and Charlize Theron.

MISS CONGENIALITY. Director, Donald Petrie; screenplay by Marc Lawrence. With Sandra Bullock, Michael Caine, Benjamin Bratt, and Candice Bergen.

MISSION TO MARS. Director, Brian DePalma; written by Jim Thomas, John Thomas, and Graham Yost, based on a story by Lowell Cannon and Jim and John Thomas. With Gary Sinise, Tim Robbins, Don Cheadle, and Kim Delaney.

THE NINTH GATE. Director, Roman Polanski; screenplay by Enrique Urbizu, Polanski, and John Borwonjohn, based on the novel *El Club Sunas* by Arturo Perez-Reverte. With Johnny Depp, Frank Langella, and Lena Olin.

NURSE BETTY. Director, Neil La Bute; screenplay by John C. Richards and James Flamberg, based on a story by Richards. With Renee Zellweger, Morgan Freeman, Chris Rock, and Greg Kinnear.

NUTTY PROFESSOR II: THE KLUMPS. Director, Peter Segal; screenplay by Barry Blaustein, David Sheffield, and Chris Weitz, based on a story by Steve Oedekerk, Blaustein, and Sheffield. With Eddie Murphy.

O BROTHER, WHERE ART THOU? Director, Joel Coen; screenplay by Ethan Coen and Joel Coen. With Tim Blake Nelson, George Clooney, John Goodman, John Turturro, and Holly Hunter.

102 DALMATIANS. Director, Kevin Lima; screenplay by Kristen Buckley, Brian Regan, Bob Tzudiker, and Noni White. With Glenn Close, Joan Grufudd, Alice Evans, Tim McInnerny, and Gerard Depardieu.

THE ORIGINAL KINGS OF COMEDY. Director, Spike Lee. With Steve Harvey, D. L. Hughley, Cedric the Entertainer, and Bernie Mac.

THE PATRIOT. Director, Roland Emmerich; screenplay by Robert Rodat. With Mel Gibson, Heath Ledger, and Joely Richardson.

PAY IT FORWARD. Director, Mimi Leder; screenplay by Leslie Dixon, based on a novel by Catherine Ryan Hyde. With Kevin Spacey, Helen Hunt, Haley Joel Osment, and Jay Mohr.

THE PERFECT STORM. Director, Wolfgang Petersen; screenplay by William D Wittliff, based on the book by Sebastian Junger. With George Clooney, Mark Wahlberg, Diane Lane, and Mary Elizabeth Mastrantonio.

POLLOCK. Director, Ed Harris; screenplay by Barbara Turner and Susan Emshwiller. With Harris, Marcia Gay Harden, Amy Madigan, Jeffrey Tambor, and Jennifer Connelly.

Everett Collection

© Andrew Cooper; SMPSP/ Everett Collection

"The Patriot" is an epic revenge adventure about an unassuming man, Benjamin Martin (portrayed by Mel Gibson), who is forced to join the American Revolution after a British colonel murders one of his sons and takes another son captive.

PROOF OF LIFE. Director, Taylor Hackford; screenplay by Tony Gilroy. With Meg Ryan, Russell Crowe, David Morse, Pamela Reed, and David Caruso.

QUILLS. Director, Philip Kaufman; screenplay by Doug Wright, based on his play. With Geoffrey Rush, Kate Winslet, Joaquin Phoenix, and Michael Caine.

RED PLANET. Director, Anthony Hoffman; screenplay by Chuck Pfarrer and Jonathan Lemkin. With Val Kilmer, Carrie-Anne Moss, and Tom Sizemore.

REINDEER GAMES. Director, John Frankenheimer; screenplay by Ehren Kruger. With Ben Affleck, Gary Sinise, and Charlize Theron.

REMEMBER THE TITANS. Director, Boaz Yakin; screenplay by Gregory Allen Howard. With Denzel Washington, Will Patton, Donald Faison, Wood Harris, and Ryan Hurst.

THE REPLACEMENTS. Director, Howard Deutch; screenplay by Vince McKewin. With Keannu Reeves, Gene Hackman, Orlando Jones, and Jack Warden.

REQUIEM FOR A DREAM. Director, Darren Aronofsky; screenplay by Aronofsky and Hubert Selby Jr. With Ellen Burstyn, Jared Leto, Jennifer Connelly, Marlon Wayans, and Keith David.

RETURN TO ME. Director, Bonnie Hunt; screenplay by Hunt, Andrew Stern, and Don Lake. With Hunt, David Duchovny, Minnie Driver, Carroll O'Connor, and Robert Loggia.

THE ROAD TO EL DORADO. Directors, Will Finn, Bibo Bergeron, Don Paul, and Eric Bergeron; screenplay by Ted Elliott and Terry Rossio. With Armand Assante, Edward James Olmos, Kenneth Branagh, Kevin Kline, and Rosie Perez.

ROAD TRIP. Director, Todd Phillips; screenplay by Phillips and Scot Armstrong. With Breckin Meyer, Seann William Scott, Amy Smart, and Tom Green.

RULES OF ENGAGEMENT. Director, William Friedkin; screenplay by James Webb. With Tommy Lee Jones and Samuel L. Jackson.

SAVING GRACE. Director, Nigel Cole; screenplay by Craig Ferguson and Mark Crowdy, based on a story by Crowdy. With Brenda Blethyn, Ferguson, and Matthew Clunes.

THE 6TH DAY. Director, Robert Spottiswoode; screenplay by Cormac Wibberley and Marianne Wibberley. With Arnold Schwarzenegger, Michael Rapaport, Tony Goldwyn, and Robert Duvall.

SHADOW OF THE VAMPIRE. Director, E. Elias Merhige; screenplay by Steven Katz. With John Malkovich, Willem Dafoe, Cary Elwes, Catherine McCormack, and Udo Kier.

SMALL TIME CROOKS. Written and directed by Woody Allen. With Allen, Tracey Ullman, Tony Darrow, Hugh Grant, Elaine May, and Jon Lovitz.

SPACE COWBOYS. Director, Clint Eastwood; screenplay by Ken Kaufman and Howard Klausner. With Eastwood, Tommy Lee Jones, Donald Sutherland, and James Garner.

STARDOM. Director, Denys Arcand; screenplay by Arcand and J. Jacob Potashnik. With Jessica Pare, Dan Aykroyd, Charles Berling, and Frank Langella.

STATE AND MAIN. Written and directed by David Mamet. With Alec Baldwin, Charles Durning, Clark Gregg, William H. Macy, and Sarah Jessica Parker.

STEAL THIS MOVIE! Director, Robert Greenwald; screenplay by Bruce Graham, based on books by Abbie and Anita Hoffman and Marty Jezer. With Vincent D'Onofrio, Janeane Garofalo, Jeanne Tripplehorn, and Kevin Pollak.

SUNSHINE. Director, Istvan Szabo; screenplay by Szabo and Israel Horovitz. With Ralph Fiennes, Rosemary Harris, Rachel Weisz, and Jennifer Ehle.

THIRTEEN DAYS. Director, Roger Donaldson; screenplay by David Self. With Kevin Costner, Bruce Greenwood, Steven Culp, and Dylan Baker.

TIMECODE. Directed and written by Mike Figgis. With Saffron Burrows, Salma Hayek, and Jeanne Tripplehorn.

TRAFFIC. Director, Steven Soderbergh; screenplay by Stephen Gaghan. With Catherine Zeta-Jones, Dennis Quaid, Erika Christensen, Michael Douglas, and Salma Hayek.

28 DAYS. Director, Betty Thomas; screenplay by Susanna Grant. With Sandra Bullock, Viggo Mortensen, and Dominic West.

U-571. Written and directed by Jonathan Mostow; screenplay by Sam Montgomery and David Ayer. With Matthew McConaughey, Bill Paxton, Harvey Keitel, and Jon Bon Jovi.

UNBREAKABLE. Written and directed by M. Night Shyamalan. With Bruce Willis, Samuel L. Jackson, and Robin Wright Penn.

UP AT THE VILLA. Director, Philip Haas; screenplay by Belinda Haas, based on the novella by W. Somerset Maugham. With Kristin Scott Thomas, Sean Penn, and Anne Bancroft.

VENUS BEAUTY INSTITUTE. Written and directed by Tonie Marshall. With Nathalie Baye, Bulle Ogier, Audrey Tautou, Samuel Le Bihan, and Jacques Bonnaffe.

WAKING THE DEAD. Director, Keith Gordon; screenplay by Robert Dillon, based on the novel by Scott Spencer. With Billy Crudup, Jennifer Connelly, Molly Parker, and Hal Holbrook.

WHAT LIES BENEATH. Director, Robert Zemeckis; screenplay by Sarah Kernochan and Clark Gregg. With Harrison Ford and Michelle Pfeiffer.

WHAT WOMEN WANT. Director, Nancy Meyers; screenplay by Nancy Meyers, Diane Drake, Josh Goldsmith, and Cathy Yuspa. With Mel Gibson, Helen Hunt, Marisa Tomei, Lauren Holly, and Alan Alda.

WHAT'S COOKING? Director, Gurinder Chadha; screenplay by Chadha and Paul Mayeda Berges. With Alfre Woodard, Joan Chen, Mercedes Ruehl, and Kyra Sedgwick.

WHERE THE HEART IS. Director, Matt Williams; screenplay by Lowell Ganz and Babaloo Mandel. With Ashley Judd, Natalie Portman, Stockard Channing, and Joan Cusack.

THE WHOLE NINE YARDS. Director, Jonathan Lynn; screenplay by Mitchell Kapner. With Bruce Willis, Matthew Perry, Rosanna Arquette, and Michael Clark Duncan.

WOMAN ON TOP. Director, Fina Torres and Thierry Arbogast; screenplay by Vera Blasi. With Penelope Cruz, Murilo Benicio, Harold Perrineau Jr., Mark Feuerstein, and John DeLancie.

WONDER BOYS. Director, Curtis Hanson; screenplay by Steve Kloves. With Michael Douglas, Tobey Maguire, Frances McDormand, Katie Holmes, and Robert Downey Jr.

WONDERLAND. Director, Michael Winterbottom; screenplay by Lawrence Coriat. With Kika Markham, Jack Shepherd, Gina McKee, Shirley Henderson, and Molly Parker.

X-MEN. Director, Bryan Singer; screenplay by David Hayter, based on a story by Tom DeSanto and Singer. With Hugh Jackman, Patrick Stewart, Halle Berry, and Anna Paquin.

THE YARDS. Director, James Gray; screenplay by Gray and Matt Reeves. With Mark Wahlberg, Joaquin Phoenix, Charlize Theron, James Caan, and Faye Dunaway.

YOU CAN COUNT ON ME. Written and directed by Kenneth Lonergan. With Jon Tenney, Laura Linney, Mark Ruffalo, Matthew Broderick, and Rory Culkin.

© Michael Dwyer/AP/Wide World Photos

Boston Symphony Orchestra's music director Seiji Ozawa compliments the acoustics and architecture of Boston's Symphony Hall, which celebrated its 100th birthday in 2000 much the way it opened—a performance of Beethoven's "Missa Solemnis."

Overview

For the first time in 19 years, pianist Martha Argerich of Argentina gave a solo performance in the United States. She did so at New York City's Carnegie Hall in March 2000, playing works by Bach, Chopin, and Profokiev—the composer with whom she is most associated. The Pulitzer Prize for music went to Lewis Spratlan for his opera *Life is a Dream, Opera in Three Acts: Act II, Concert Version*, which premiered Jan. 28, 2000, in Amherst, MA. French composer and champion of 20th century music Pierre Boulez won the Grawemeyer Award for *Sur Incises*, a 40-minute chamber work. Symphony Hall in Boston turned 100. The centennial of Aaron Copland and the 80th birthday of Isaac Stern were causes for celebrations. Tenor Plácido Domingo was among those honored by the John F. Kennedy Center for the Performing Arts.

The music industry encountered a new dilemma in 2000: Napster—a computer program developed by a 19-year-old that facilitates swapping music files over the Internet.

Such teen pop singers as Britney Spears and 'N Sync dominated a hit-song market. Rap remained popular, and nobody caused more stir than a white rapper named Eminem.

The Grammy Awards in popular music were dominated by Santana, and *Stravinsky: Firebird; The Rite of Spring; Perséphone*, with Michael Tilson Thomas conducting, took the Grammy as top classical album. Saxophonist James Carter emerged as a bright new jazz star.

Classical

Crossroads. Symphony Hall in Boston celebrated its 100th birthday in 2000. Its acoustics rank with those of the greatest concert halls in Europe; along with New York's Carnegie Hall, Symphony Hall remains an international symbol for traditional music-making in America. The birthday was celebrated with a repeat of the opening program, Ludwig van Beethoven's *Missa Solemnis*, and with a season's worth of festivities, including the premiere of John

Corigliano's *Symphony No. 2*, commissioned in honor of the occasion.

There were milestones in other famous buildings as well: A successful $37.5 million renovation was completed in Severance Hall, home to the Cleveland Orchestra; and a major renovation plan was under development for New York's Lincoln Center.

While traditions were being celebrated, some traditions came under duress in some circumstances. The distinguished composer Gunther Schuller, who celebrated his 75th birthday, observed that "The worse the music business gets, the more people there are to fight against it or even absent themselves from it altogether. All across this country, in every nook and cranny, there are people trying to do things on a basis of total artistic integrity, people who are not concerning themselves with how much of a career they can make. . . .At the same time, one has to worry what is going to happen to such people in the midst of a culture that does nothing to support them."

The nation's conservatories and other centers of musical training continued to turn out idealistic musicians of the highest calibre, but they could not produce an audience and support system, too, so virtually every performing-arts organization in the country developed educational initiatives to try to replace what was lost in the public-education system and mass media.

Many avenues of access that brought classical music to older listeners have been narrowed or closed down. Nationwide, classical-music stations on FM radio have followed commercially successful formulas, rather than clearing new and artistically adventurous pathways. The classical-record business endured a state of upheaval, and RCA/BMG, one of the proudest names in the history of recording, virtually closed down its classical divisions, canceling the contracts of its exclusive artists, including longtime moneymakers like James Galway.

On the other hand, record companies that identified and concentrated on niche markets continued to flourish. Britain's Hyperion label finished its great survey of Franz Schubert, coordinated by collaborative pianist Graham Johnson; Harmonia Mundi continued its superb series of early-music performances, recorded both in the United States and in Europe. Nonesuch focused on such high-profiles performers as John Adams and on such adventurous performers as Dawn Upshaw. The Metropolitan Opera's Saturday-afternoon broadcasts—the longest-running program in radio history—continued to have trouble in many markets, mainly because stations were unwilling to commit the time and potential revenue to opera; this season the broadcasts began streaming through several sites on the Internet, where specialized programming of every kind became increasingly available.

Orchestras. With several premieres, Augusta Read Thomas was the most prominent U.S. composer of the year. The Chicago Symphony Orchestra, where she is composer-in-residence, opened 2000 with her *Ceremonial*, and later premiered a work for piano and orchestra, *Aurora*. She also delivered two chamber music pieces, *Invocations* and *Fugitive Star*, as well as a choral work, *Ring Out, Wild Bells, To the Wild Sky* (Choral Arts Society, Washington, DC.). *Song in Sorrow*, premiered by the Cleveland Orchestra at the Blossom Festival, was a memorial to the tragedy of the Kent State University students gunned down a few miles away from Blossom during an anti-Vietnam War demonstration in 1970. Other noteworthy new works included Lowell Lieberman's *Dorian Gray: A Symphonic Portrait*, based on his opera; Philip Glass' *Tympani Concerto* and the multicultural *Fifth Symphony*; Bright Sheng's *Red Silk Dance* for piano and orchestra (Emanuel

In September 2000 at New York City's Carnegie Hall, violinist Isaac Stern received applause from an adoring audience during the conclusion of a concert celebrating his 80th birthday.

Ax and the Boston Symphony); Steven Mackey's *Tuck and Roll* for electric guitar and orchestra (New World Symphony); and Einojuhani Rautavaara's *Eighth Symphony* (Philadelphia Orchestra). John Corigliano's long-awaited *Symphony No. 2* was an effective revision for string orchestra of the String Quartet he wrote in 1995 for the farewell tour of the Cleveland Quartet. It was premiered by the Boston Symphony under Seiji Ozawa. Corigliano's first symphony, *Of Rage and Remembrance*—the so-called "AIDS"—symphony, was the most frequently performed new American symphony of the last 50 years.

Carnegie Hall's programming of festivals continued to attract praise. Among the central figures of 2000 were Daniel Barenboim and Pierre Boulez. Ursula Oppens played the premiere of ten stunning original piano pieces assembled as the Carnegie Hall Millennium Piano Book.

Opera. The most prominent operatic premieres of the year were Jake Heggie's *Dead Man Walking* in San Francisco and Carlisle Floyd's *Cold Sassy Tree* in Houston.

Heggie's opera proved a local favorite. The subject of capital punishment was topical. Playwright Terrence McNally adapted his stage-worthy libretto from the story of Sister Helen Prejean, familiar both from her book and from the acclaimed 1995 film. Heggie's own story is full of human interest. He was the first employee of the press office at the San Francisco Opera to write an opera, and many prominent singers have taken his attractive songs into their repertoires. One of them, Frederica von Stade, accepted a role in the opera. Susan Graham took the key role of the nun. John Packard sang the death-row prisoner. Most observers found the music awkwardly orchestrated though attractively sung, but otherwise unmemorable.

Floyd announced that *Cold Sassy Tree* would be his last opera, closing a distinguished career that began 45 years before. Based on Olive Ann Burns' novel set in rural Georgia, Floyd's latest work followed familiar patterns, some of them ones that he created. The principal roles were taken by Patricia Racette and Dean Patterson.

Other new operas of the year were Minoru Miki's *Tale of Genji* (St. Louis); Hans Werner Henze's *Venus and Adonis* (American premiere at Santa Fe); Mark Antony Turnage's *Blood on the Floor* (American premiere under Sir Simon Rattle at the Ojai Festival); and Louis Andriessen's *Writing to Vermeer* (American premiere by the Netherlands Opera during the Lincoln Center Festival). John Adams' *El Nino*, an oratorio on the subject of the Nativity, had its premiere in Paris in mid-December. William Bolcom's Chicago Opera *A View From the Bridge* planned a 2001 exchange to the Met; the composer had already added two new arias to the work.

The Pulitzer Prize for music went to an opera that had not yet been staged, Lewis Spratlan's *Life is a Dream*. Spratlan wrote the opera between 1975 and 1977 for the New Haven Opera Theatre, which closed before it could present the work. Eager to hear at least some of the music, Spratlan raised $72,000 to put on concert performances of Act II of his opera in Amherst, MA, where he teaches, and in Boston. The music is written in a profoundly unfashionable mandarin style, but in concert performance the work seemed vividly theatrical.

Major revivals were Philip Glass' *Akhnaten* (Boston and Chicago); Scott Joplin's *Treemonisha* (St. Louis); and a real "sleeper," John Philip Sousa's *The Glass-Blowers* (Glimmerglass Opera). Major attention went to the first performances in more than a half a century of Kurt Weill's largest work, the Biblical pageant *The Eternal Road* (presented at the Brooklyn Academy under the direction of John Mauceri).

In more mainstream opera, Renée Fleming consolidated her position as America's favorite soprano in performances of *Der Rosenkavalier*, *Don Giovanni*, as well as in recordings of Jules Massenet's *Thais*, George Frederick Handel's *Alcina*, and a program of opera arias. Soprano Lauren Flanigan continued as queen of the New York City Opera by taking on one of the roles most closely associated with her predecessor, Beverly Sills, Elizabeth I in Gaetano Donizetti's *Roberto Devereux*. Some operas that have been popular with the public for 150 years, like Giuseppe Verdi's *Il Trovatore*, proved difficult to cast and conform to contemporary trends in staging. The Met's new production was vociferously booed.

The most controversial figure in opera in 2000 was the Italian crossover superstar, the blind tenor Andrea Bocelli, who released an album of Verdi arias and a complete recording of Giacomo Puccini's *La Bohème* that left many connoisseurs angry and troubled, but kept the cash registers busy and introduced a new public to Italian opera. While not every operatic expert was dismayed by Bocelli, there is the opinion that he sings

Theresa Hamm-Smith (left) and Susan Graham (right) perform during a dress rehearsal of the San Francisco Opera's much-anticipated world premiere of "Dead Man Walking" in October.

© George Nikitin/AP/Wide World Photos

music ill-suited to his light, lyric voice, and that he sounds better amplified than without electronic reinforcement. Nevertheless, Bocelli is several cuts above the crossover competition, including such phenomena as Izzy; Filippa Giordano; Michael Jordan, who made an opera album; and the young Charlotte Church. Bocelli's voice is steadier than that of his *Bohème* costar, the much-heralded soprano Barbara Frittoli. And, he can sometimes sing with distinction of phrase and style and considerable technical aplomb. Each of the Three Tenors of the previous generation—Luciano Pavarotti, Plácido Domingo, and José Carreras—has said that he came to opera through the films and recordings of a previous crossover tenor, Mario Lanza, so the consequences of Bocelli's popularity remain to be charted.

Conductors. In his 75th year, Pierre Boulez won the $200,000 University of Louisville Grawemeyer Award for his 40-minute *Sur incises*, strikingly scored for three pianos, three harps, and three percussionists. Cellist Yo-Yo Ma announced *Silk Road Project*, that will involve concerts and festivals in many cities and several countries, and planned to present new-works composers from nations along the ancient Silk Road that connected Europe to China, along with cross-cultural works like Gustav Mahler's *Das Lied von der Erde*.

Celebrations of the centennial of Aaron Copland continued across the country. Conductor Michael Tilson Thomas made some spectacular new Copland recordings in San Francisco, and programmed a fascinating 12-concert festival of American Mavericks from Charles Ives to Frank Zappa. The New York Philharmonic played Copland's complete orchestral music, and the Tanglewood Festival programmed everything else. Three major U.S. orchestras continued their search for music directors: New York (publicly turned down by Riccardo Muti), Boston,

and Philadelphia. Controversy, charisma, and accomplishment of the kind represented for decades by Leonard Bernstein were in short supply, a fact underlined by the New York Philharmonic's superb reissue of live Bernstein performances.

Meanwhile Hans Graf took over the Houston Symphony, Robert Spano the Atlanta Symphony (with Donald Runnicles as principal guest conductor), and Paavo Jarvi the Cincinnati Symphony. Violinist Itzhak Perlman enjoyed his experiments in conducting so much that he accepted the position of principal guest conductor in Detroit. Grant Llewellyn accepted the music directorship of the Handel & Haydn Society in Boston.

Conductor John Crosby retired from the Santa Fe Opera, which he founded in 1957; his successor would be his longtime associate Richard Gaddes. The beloved mezzo-soprano Marilyn Horne announced her retirement from the recital platform. Conductor Gerard Schwarz announced he would leave New York's Mostly Mozart after 17 years; and Nicolas McGegan was leaving the Philharmonia Baroque after 16 years. Meanwhile violinist Isaac Stern turned 80 and returned to performance after a hiatus due to hand problems, and pianist Earl Wild celebrated his 85th birthday with a New York recital and a solo recording featuring what he hopes is the first piano sonata of the 21st-century—performed only by himself.

RICHARD DYER, *Chief Classical Music Critic*
"The Boston Globe"

Popular and Jazz

The most influential personality in the world of popular music in 2000 was young enough to be in a boy band but was not known for singing, playing an instrument, or rapping in rhymes. Shawn Fanning, 19, instead shook up the pop world by creating Napster, a computer program that facilitates swapping music files over the Internet.

Napster—The Latest Hit. Computer-savvy music fans already had been downloading music files encoded in the MP3 format, but Napster made the process of trading MP3 files both simpler and far more popular. By

© Dan Loh/AP/Wide World Photos

Shawn Fanning, 19, made recording history when he created Napster, a computer program that allows users to exchange music files via the Internet. The program was under fire from record companies and artists for copyright infringement.

mid-2000, more than 20 million people had downloaded the software to use the Napster service.

The explosive growth of Napster prompted the record industry and individual performers, such as Metallica and Dr. Dre, to cry foul. The performers declared that the unauthorized distribution of music files over the Internet cheated both record labels and creative artists. Universal Music won a copyright lawsuit against the company promot-

ing MP3, the digital format that first facilitated the trading of music files. But where the MP3 site actually stores musical files, Napster is a "peer-to-peer," or "P2P," software. That means that Napster.com does not actually contain copyrighted music, but rather, an index that guides the music seeker to the computer of another Napster user that contains the desired music.

The future of an ongoing lawsuit against Napster by the major record companies was uncertain at year end as Napster, in late October, reached an agreement with one of the record companies, Bertelsman, to charge a fee for its service and pay royalties to record companies.

Some wonder whether the genie is already out of the bottle. The Napster model already has spawned similar software to facilitate the digital exchange of films and videos, though limited consumer bandwidths make such transfers slow and laborious. Still, with programs such as Gnutella and Freenet following Napster's lead, creative artists and the companies that market them are extremely concerned about controlling the distribution of their product.

The Napster phenomenon has quickened the pace of the record industry's own efforts to exploit the Internet. Companies have begun or have announced plans to let consumers pay to download music, but the exact future remains unclear. Options under discussion have consumers making a single payment to copy a piece of music, paying for each track, as in a jukebox, or subscribing to Internet-delivered music services that would mimic the business model of cable TV.

Another legal battle pitted artists against record companies after the U.S. Congress passed legislation that included a provision that defined recordings as "works-for-hire." A broad coalition of recording artists argued that this designation made it all but impossible to retain the copyright of their own work. By year's end, Congress was poised to reinstate the original language.

Teenage Pop. Teen pop singers continued to thrive in a market driven more by individual hit songs than by album-oriented artists. That is why the MTV program *Total Request Live*, or *TRL*, has become a pathway up the pop charts, as viewer votes determine the day's top-ten videos and thereby help to get these lavishly promoted acts valuable radio exposure.

Among the teen sensations riding the *TRL* wave were Britney Spears, who followed her 9-million-selling debut with a col-

The rap artist Eminem benefited from the popularity of rap with the teens. Although the lyrics of his second album, "The Marshall Mathers LP" faced criticism , it led the charts in 2000.

lection called *Oops! . . . I Did It Again*, and the boy group 'N Sync, whose *No Strings Attached* sold a record-breaking 2.4 million copies during its first week.

The teen market has embraced these highly manicured pop acts and the unruly bands who have ridden to fame combining elements of rap with hard rock and heavy metal. Over the past few years, albums by acts such as Limp Bizkit (*Significant Other*), Korn (*Issues*), Kid Rock (*Devil Without a Cause*), Rage Against the Machine (*The Battle of Los Angeles*), and Blink-182 (*Enema of the State*) have sold in the millions. Meanwhile, Smashing Pumpkins, one of the last surviving bands to rise to fame in the grunge-rock era of the early 1990s, disbanded after lackluster sales of its latest album, *Machina/The Machines of God*.

Rap continued to be hugely popular with the young and nobody caused more stir in 2000 than a white rapper named Eminem. His second album, *The Marshall Mathers LP*, titled after his real name, topped album charts and drew criticism for lyrics insulting to women and the gay community. Eminem claimed that he was not necessarily the char-

acter he portrayed in his songs, but in fact, while fans appreciated Eminem's rhythmic patter, his appeal owed as much to the production provided by Dr. Dre, who is credited with being a primary architect of "gangsta rap" in the 1990s, and who continues to be the most influential producer in rap. Dr. Dre's latest album, *Dr. Dre 2001*, sold more than 4 million copies and featured guest appearances by a number of other stars, including Eminem.

Traditional rock and roll was not completely dead. The extraordinary comeback of Carlos Santana (*see also* BIOGRAPHY) with the Grammy-winning *Supernatural* was one of the year's big stories. The Red Hot Chili Peppers enjoyed a long chart run with *Californication*, while U2 received glowing reviews for its late-2000 release, *All That You Can't Leave Behind*. But a number of critically lauded records, including the Jayhawks' *Smile* and the reformed Steely Dan's *Two Against Nature,* were seen as commercial disappointments.

Creative marketing was key for a number of artists. The career of singer-songwriter Aimee Mann, who had been dropped by her record label, got a boost when director P.T. Anderson used her songs in the movie *Magnolia*. Sting's *Brand New Day* won the Grammy for best pop album, but integral to the success of its hit single, "Desert Rose," was the singer and his song's appearance in a television commercial for Jaguar. The dance-oriented producer-musician Moby went further in marketing his hit album *Play*, with its 18 tracks licensed for use in commercials and sound tracks.

The oddest success of such an ancillary marketing strategy occurred when Nick Drake's "Pink Moon" was used in a Volkswagen ad, spurring sales of albums recorded in the early 1970s; the sudden interest in the obscure British singer-songwriter came a quarter century after he died. Happier circumstances found seminal blues singer and guitarist B.B. King celebrating his 75th birthday with the biggest album of his career, a collaboration with British guitarist Eric Clapton called *Riding With the King*.

Barbra Streisand marked the millennium by singing for high rollers at the MGM Grand in Las Vegas. Then, concurrent with the release of a live album documenting those shows, she announced her retirement from the concert stage following farewell concerts in Los Angeles and New York.

Rhythm & Blues. While such rap stars as Nas, Q-Tip, Nelly, and DMX shot to the top of the black-music charts, performers from a more traditional mold continued to find an audience. D'Angelo, whose music reflects artists as varied as Stevie Wonder and Prince, scored commercially and critically with his second album, *Voodoo*. Similarly, Mary J. Blige's *Mary* confirmed she is one of the best female singers of her generation. Perhaps the year's most interesting new artist was Macy Gray, whose debut album, *On How Life Is*, was a savvy mix of rock and rhythm and blues (R & B) that reflected the influence of everybody from Sly and the Family Stone to Parliament-Funkadelic.

Destiny's Child sold more than 3 million copies of its debut album, *The Writing's On the Wall*, and confirmed the enduring appeal of a trio of stylishly appointed female singers. Indeed, fans hardly seemed to notice when group members were replaced. This was not quite the case with what was to be one of the year's biggest concert tours—a reunion of the classic female trio, the Supremes. But when lead singer Diana Ross balked at the fiscal demands of her old colleagues, she instead chose to perform with singers who sang with the Supremes after Ross had left for her solo career. The resulting "Return to Love" tour resulted in less-than-sellout business and ultimately was canceled before its scheduled ending.

Country. Country singers long have been tempted by the idea of crossing over to the much larger pop audience, especially since the huge success of such pop-friendly singer-songwriters as Garth Brooks and Shania Twain. Faith Hill's *Breathe* used the Shania strategy—pop-oriented songs promoted by sexy videos—to great commercial success. The Dixie Chicks' hugely popular *Fly* succeeded with more-traditional fare; the trio is known for using such "traditional" instruments as banjo and mandolin. Though cheered by the success of the Chicks, critics continued to complain about the tendency for mainstream country artists to tailor their music to the increasingly conservative tastes of country radio.

Veteran country artists can be forgotten in Nashville's search for the next young star. *Cold Hard Truth* was George Jones' best album in years, but it found little success on country radio. Shortly after Merle Haggard was celebrated by the country community in a television special, he released his latest album, *If I Could Only Fly*, on a record label best known for its punk-rock bands. Haggard hoped that his new label would be better equipped to market his music to both

fans of traditional country and those of a genre of bands and singer-songwriters known as "Americana."

The Americana audience includes music fans who grew up listening to rock and roll, but who now are drawn to the fringes of country music, or so-called "alternative country." Shelby Lynne ended up hating the music she made in Nashville; working with a more sympathetic producer, her *I Am Shelby Lynne* turned out to be one of the best-reviewed pop-rock albums of the year. Emmylou Harris, regarded as the grande dame of alternative country music, also got good reviews for her *Red Dirt Girl*.

Jazz. One of the year's biggest jazz events was not scheduled to occur until 2001. Ken Burns, the documentary filmmaker who had produced monumental studies of the Civil War and baseball, finished production on a 19-hour history of jazz. The jazz business long has celebrated its past with a steady stream of reissues by such giants as Louis Armstrong, Duke Ellington, Charlie Parker, Miles Davis, and John Coltrane. The Burns documentary prompted another reissue flood. Some critics bemoaned the fact that current jazz often is ignored over vintage sounds, while others suggested that the documentary is another step by which jazz has been recognized as a core component of American culture.

Saxophonist James Carter emerged as one of the year's brightest new jazz stars. Carter released two albums simultaneously—the groove-oriented *Layin' in the Cut* and *Chasin' the Gypsy*, an album of music by, and inspired by, the legendary guitarist Django Reinhardt. Carter won praise for the range and intensity of his playing. The success of Cuba's Buena Vista Social Club continued, with solo albums by Ibrahim Ferrer, Compay Segundo, Eliades Ochoa, Rubén González, and Omara Portuondo. The ensemble, which has toured the world in various permutations since the unexpected success of its self-titled 1998 album, also played its first official concert in Cuba.

Rock and Roll Lives On. The story of how rock and roll got started is the theme of the Experience Music Project, a Seattle-based interactive museum that opened in June (*see also* ARCHITECTURE). While the museum originally was intended to be a tribute to Jimi Hendrix, it contains 85,000 items, including Hendrix' "Electric Ladyland" lyrics notebook, an 18th-century Italian guitar, and Kurt Cobain artifacts.

JOHN MILWARD, *Freelance Writer and Critic*

Myanmar

Many of the factors that have made the Myanmar government among the least successful and most repressive regimes in the world continued in 2000. Ever since the military took control in a bloody 1988 coup, and then refused to hand over power following defeat in the 1990 elections, democracy has been an elusive goal.

In 2000, this country of 42 million was considered an international pariah because of its human-rights abuses. It was also an economic basket case. Still, there were signs that the ruling State Peace and Development Council may consolidate its position because the council endured so many sanctions designed to unseat it. Some governments reevaluated their policies toward Myanmar, and distanced themselves from the regime, even as splits surfaced in the opposition National League for Democracy (NLD) after the stalemate.

The NLD, led by Aung San Suu Kyi, the 55-year-old Nobel Peace Prizewinner, continued its role as the opposition party. The government has kept Suu Kyi under various forms of house arrest since 1990. Her efforts to drive beyond Yangon resulted in her being confined to her car for days. And each time the government stopped her as she left the city, its human-rights records were publicized worldwide.

For much of the previous 12 years, the universities were closed because they were seen as opposition strongholds. In July, for the first time since 1996, the universities reopened, and more than 60,000 students were receiving long-delayed training.

Economy. The government claimed economic sanctions by the European Union (EU) and the United States have not hurt the country, but this resource-rich nation's economy was in shambles. Per capita income was $300 a year, despite the nation's relatively high literacy rate. Foreign reserves were desperately low. Tourism was essentially a nonentity, and Myanmar's airline was bankrupt. The World Health Organization (WHO) ranked Myanmar as 190th out of 191 countries in health services.

Foreign investment largely pulled out except for a joint natural-gas venture. In fact, foreign investment stood at $29 million in 2000, as opposed to $777.4 million in 1998. The U.S. Supreme Court determined in June that states could not forbid companies in their jurisdiction from doing business in a particular country. Only the federal government had that power. The United States had banned new investment in Myanmar.

Myanmar was second only to Afghanistan in production of heroin and opium for underground export abroad. The minority Wa area on the Thai border has become infamous for methamphetamine production.

Foreign Policy. It was hoped that admitting Myanmar into the Association of Southeast Asian Nations (ASEAN) in 1997 would encourage better behavior by the regime. That hope has died. Thailand, which supported Myanmar's admission, contemplated surgical strikes on the Myanmar border to stop the flood of illegal narcotics and refugees into Thailand. That would be a violation of ASEAN's policy of noninterference in member nations, but Thailand was becoming desperate. More than 100,000 refugees crossed into Thailand, and efforts to forcibly return them prompted Myanmar to threaten violence against returnees.

China remained Myanmar's only ally. Chinese influence, coupled with their establishment of a naval base in the Bay of Bengal, prompted India to reconsider its opposition to the regime.

In October the United Nations (UN) special envoy to Myanmar, Razali Ismail, vainly sought to negotiate a way out of the political standoff between the NLD and the government. His mandate came from a December 1999 General Assembly resolution urging Myanmar to stop human-rights abuses and restore democracy. The public was warned in advance of the UN envoy's visit that any political outburst would be considered treasonous. Democracy and human rights remained a mirage in Myanmar throughout 2000.

LINDA K. RICHTER
Kansas State University

MYANMAR • Information Highlights

Official Name: Union of Myanmar.
Location: Southeast Asia.
Area: 261,969 sq mi (678 500 km²).
Population (2000 est.): 41,734,853.
Chief Cities (1983 census): Yangon (Rangoon), the capital, 2,513,023; Mandalay, 532,949.
Government: *Head of state and government,* Gen. Than Shwe (took power April 23, 1992). *Legislature* (unicameral)—People's Assembly.
Monetary Unit: Kyat (6.3500 kyats equal U.S.$1, Nov. 14, 2000).
Gross Domestic Product (1999 est. U.S.$): $59,400,000,000 (purchasing power parity).
Economic Index (1999, 1990 = 100): *Consumer Prices,* all items, 893.4; food, 997.0.
Foreign Trade (1999 U.S.$): *Imports,* $2,301,000,000; *exports,* $1,125,000,000.

Netherlands

With 2000 being a quiet year in the Netherlands, legislation granting full marital rights to lesbians and homosexuals proved the most notable development.

Marriage for Gays. In 1998 same-sex partners were granted the right to register as partners and claim inheritances, social security, and pensions. A new bill, passed by the lower house and expected to become law in 2001, permitted regular marriages at city halls and the adoption of Dutch children. Divorce, as for heterosexual couples, would be handled through the courts. The legislation grants to Dutch gays rights not found in other countries.

All parties in the governing coalition— the left-of-center Labor Party (PvdA), the right-leaning Liberal Party, and the Democrats '66 —backed the measure. Some members of the opposition Christian Democratic Appeal (CDA) were supportive, although the few representatives from the Reformed Political Party were not. The final vote in the lower house, after three days of debate, was overwhelming, 109–33. This result reflected the continuing decline of influence of the traditional Protestant and Roman Catholic churches, which do not recognize gay marriage. Two small splinter religious groups, the Remonstrant Brotherhood (Protestant) and the Old Catholics, support gay rights.

Transportation Concerns. Traffic jams are an increasing plague. Changes seem needed, but consensus on these is elusive. Transport Minister Tineke Netelenbos called for a "pay-as-you-drive" system, but both industry and associations of private automobile owners view such a system as potentially disastrous. They instead proposed construction of additional bus lanes on existing highways, encouragement of off-hours deliveries for industry, and expansion of public-transport systems. Meanwhile, sales of motorcycles increased significantly as commuters appreciated their superiority over cars for moving through traffic.

In September, truckers angry over the high price of petroleum products blockaded roads in Rotterdam and in the east of the country. At the time, the Dutch were paying $4.02 per gallon, with 64.9% of that sum going to taxes. The effect of their demonstration was not as great as that of similar protests in other countries. Demands for a reduction in gasoline taxes were resisted by the government. Fuel taxes are a key source of revenue and are believed to reduce production of greenhouse gases, a matter of concern to ecologically oriented citizens.

Employment. Anglo-Dutch Unilever PLC, the world's largest producer of consumer goods, announced in February that it would downsize to increase profits. The plan called for the elimination of 25,000 jobs, representing 10% of the company's workforce, and the closing of 100 factories.

The Netherlands provides the most part-time jobs within Europe, as 38% of Dutch employees work part-time. Thus, the average Dutch workweek is the shortest in Europe, 32.3 hours. More than half of the adult women in the country hold paid jobs.

Other Developments. The first-ever shooting at a Dutch school—in December 1999, when a 17-year-old wounded four students and a teacher—led to an arms amnesty. Some 3,500 illegal weapons, including grenades and swords as well as revolvers and shotguns, were handed in to police in such cities as Utrecht, The Hague, Rotterdam, and Amsterdam.

In late November, the lower house of parliament voted to allow doctors to assist in ending the lives of severly ill patients who have asked to die. The bill, which likely would become law in 2001, would make the Netherlands the first nation to legalize mercy killing.

A May explosion at a fireworks depot in Enschede killed 18, injured more than 900, and demolished hundreds of homes. Two company directors were arrested for alleged breaches of safety codes.

The nation took pride in its representatives at the Sydney Olympics, where Dutch athletes and teams won a total of 25 medals.

JONATHAN E. HELMREICH, *Allegheny College*

NETHERLANDS • Information Highlights

Official Name: Kingdom of the Netherlands.
Location: Northwestern Europe.
Area: 16,036 sq mi (41 532 km²).
Population (2000 est.): 15,892,237.
Chief Cities (Jan. 1, 1999 est.): Amsterdam, the capital, 727,053; Rotterdam, 592,665; The Hague, the seat of government, 440,743.
Government: *Head of state,* Beatrix, queen (acceded April 30, 1980). *Head of government,* Willem Kok, prime minister (took office Aug. 22, 1994). *Legislature*—States General: First Chamber and Second Chamber.
Monetary Unit: Guilder (2.5943 guilders equal U.S.$1, Nov. 20, 2000).
Gross Domestic Product (1999 est. U.S.$): $365,100,000,000 (purchasing power parity).
Economic Indexes (1999, 1990 = 100): *Consumer Prices,* all items, 124.2; food, 116.2. *Industrial Production,* 116.8.
Foreign Trade (1999 U.S.$): *Imports,* $187,529,000,000; *exports,* $200,290,000,000.

New York City

In 2000 a booming economy raised New York City's spirits and its rents. Almost 37 million tourists, many entranced by a redeveloped Times Square, helped the city displace Las Vegas as the nation's second-most-popular destination. The city was saddened by the death of Cardinal John O'Connor (*see* OBITUARIES), the influential Roman Catholic archbishop, and welcomed his successor, Archbishop Edward M. Egan (*see* BIOGRAPHY). New York City went solidly for Vice-President Al Gore in both the Democratic presidential primary and the November 7 election. In a tough, unpredictable, and big-spending race to replace retiring U.S. Sen. Daniel Patrick Moynihan (D), First Lady Hillary Rodham Clinton prevailed over U.S. Rep. Rick Lazio. The city's mayor, Rudolph W. Giuliani, had made a strong early push for the Republican U.S. Senate nomination, but withdrew after he was diagnosed with prostate cancer.

Economy and Real Estate. Driven by growth in financial services, new technology, and the Internet, the real-estate market soared. Landmark skyscrapers traded hands for hundreds of millions of dollars. With office vacancy rates at historic lows, demand strongly outstripped supply, driving midtown rents up 30% and threatening the city's ability to attract new business and retain established ones. Residential rents also spiked, with one-bedroom apartments in Manhattan renting for a monthly average of $3,000.

Crime. Crime rates reached 30-year lows, but several murder cases caught the public eye. A grifter mother-and-son team, Kenneth and Sante Kimes, were charged in the death of an Upper East Side socialite who had disappeared in 1998. A plastic surgeon, Robert Bierenbaum, was accused of murdering his wife in 1985 and dumping her body into the ocean. Each case ended in conviction, despite the absence of a body.

And in one of the city's most horrific crimes, two men were charged with the execution-style slayings of five workers at a Wendy's restaurant in Queens. White-collar crime was also in evidence, as Christie's and Sotheby's, the city's premier auction houses, became embroiled in charges of price-fixing.

The police force was scrutinized after an officer shot and killed an unarmed, off-duty black security guard named Patrick Dorismond. Police were also criticized for failing to take aggressive action after a group of men overtook a corner of Central Park after the annual National Puerto Rican Day Parade and sexually assaulted dozens of women. Early in the year the trial and acquittal of four New York City policemen who had mistakenly killed an unarmed man with an array of 41 bullets in February 1999 drew national attention (*see* POLICING—A PROBLEMATIC ENTERPRISE, page 66).

Education and Health. A new schools chancellor, Harold O. Levy, grappled with contract negotiations with teachers, a shortage of certified teachers, the Board of Education's bureaucracy, and one of the largest summer-school enrollments in the nation.

The West Nile virus returned. Officials of the city responded with a spraying program that prompted environmental complaints as well as accusations of overreaction. About a dozen New Yorkers caught the virus, which is carried by birds and spread by mosquitoes and can cause encephalitis; one person died

ANDREA KANNAPELL
"The New York Times"

© Monika Graff/UPI/Presslink

The Radio City Music Hall Rockettes performed at a rally in New York's Bryant Park to help celebrate the city's first Subway World Series since 1956. The Yankees defeated the Mets in five games.

New Zealand

The honeymoon for New Zealand's Labour-Alliance government, which took office in December 1999, proved short-lived, with looming economic decline constituting its most demanding challenge.

Politics. Until mid-2000 the coalition government enjoyed huge popular support. The Labour Party led the National Party in the polls by two-to-one; Prime Minister Helen Clark of the Labour Party headed the preferred-leader table by nearly four-to-one; and 65% believed New Zealand was in good hands. Among the most important issues, the economy ranked behind education, unemployment, and health.

Opinion—fed partly by an embarrassing sacking of a cabinet minister and the enactment of radical labor-relations legislation—veered quite rapidly. However, the change in political sentiment was attributable mainly to a worsening economic downturn. By October the National Party was actually outpolling Labour by 44% to 40%, with the minor parties barely registering. Although Clark was still the preferred leader, approval of the government's performance was slipping, and pessimists exceeded optimists as regards the country's future, with no general election due until 2002.

The Economy. The early signs of economic strength were followed by negative movements among the main indicators. Gross domestic product (GDP) grew by 4.4% in the fiscal year ending March 31, and by August, unemployment of 6.1% dropped to a three-year low. Otherwise, though, the news was overwhelmingly discouraging. A current-account deficit of 7.1% of GDP was reported; the New Zealand Stock Exchange lost 4.7% on a single day's trading in April; gasoline prices rose 25% in nine months; and inflation trended above the critical 3% benchmark.

Against the U.S. dollar, the Kiwi dollar exhibited serious weakness. From NZ $1.00 equals U.S. $0.49 in January, it repeatedly recorded all-time lows, reaching U.S. $0.39 in October. While this induced a primary-exports boom, its impact on all imported goods and services was becoming severe. Business confidence slumped, reaching a 16-year low in July. The World Economic Forum's analysis of growth rates relegated New Zealand to 20th from 13th.

Minister of Finance Michael Cullen proceeded cautiously in his first budget. There were boosts for health, Maori initiatives, and

a return to regional-development subsidies, but little left-wing ideology. Limits on spending were forecast to ensure a $1 billion surplus, the general verdict being that prudence and patience had triumphed over substance and stimulation.

Foreign Relations. New Zealand troops continued to be part of the United Nations (UN) peacekeeping force in East Timor, with a New Zealand soldier in July becoming the first battle casualty. Fiji's midyear coup saw New Zealand's high commissioner recalled, and New Zealand-Fiji defense and sporting ties were temporarily suspended.

Continuing civil disorder in the Solomon Islands saw a New Zealand frigate being sent as a truce-talks venue. The government agreed to dispatch unarmed personnel to monitor progress toward the restoration of normality.

A major defense review heavily favored the army, with the upgrading of surveillance aircraft rejected and an air-force base scheduled for closure. Earlier, the proposed purchase of secondhand U.S. F–16 jet fighters was scrapped.

Prime Minister Clark addressed the UN Millennium Summit in September, when she also signed a number of international treaties. In Sydney for the Olympic Games, she discussed defense and closer economic relations with Australia's Prime Minister John Howard.

GRAHAM BUSH, *University of Auckland*

Nigeria

Difficulties within both the executive and legislative branches and an upswing of traditional cleavages prompted de facto parti-tioning of the multiethnic Nigerian state, which celebrated its 40th anniversary in 2000. Yet a sharp jump in international oil prices and peaceful relations with Western governments aided the government of President Olusegun Obasanjo.

Domestic Politics. President Obasanjo retained his popularity, but a number of Nigerians felt he appeared overly interested in foreign affairs while disregarding domestic problems. The government's delivery of basic services improved only marginally as long lines at gas stations reappeared and power supplies were irregular. Problems existed before Obasanjo's rule, which began in May 1999, but the new government appeared incapable of quickly solving them.

The president and National Assembly disagreed over division of power and responsibilities. Parliamentarians often considered former General Obasanjo too authoritarian, while he regarded the Assembly as prone to attaching divisive amendments to proposed legislation, and inclined toward personal graft. Obasanjo was often unable to rely on support from his People's Democratic Party (PDP). The Alliance for Democracy (AD), a leading opposition party, split in two during 2000. The National Assembly had institutional problems. The Senate saw its first two presidents impeached for corruption, and the House of Representatives also removed its speaker.

An interrelated combination of subnational divisions (ethnic, regional, and religious) sparked violence. Starting in Zamfara state in 1999, some eight northern states announced plans to institute the Muslim *sharia* legal system, which can provide for the amputation of limbs and decapitation for criminals. This produced a series of killings

and a hardening of long-standing divisions between Nigeria's different regions. February riots in Kaduna and slayings in Aba in March forced the government to send troops into several cities to establish order. Most states decided not to implement *sharia*, given the violent reaction.

The *sharia* controversy and the subsequent killings increased subnational allegiances and renewed speculation of secession, most probably by the north. Subnational—mostly ethnic—militias grew, sparked partly by *sharia* and by anger over inequitable revenue redistribution.

President Obasanjo was hoping to "reprofessionalize" his military, which has suffered from decades of corruption and lowering of military capabilities. Obasanjo removed more than 250 officers and accepted advice and training from several countries. The United States dispatched several hundred Special Forces (Green Berets) to Nigeria, where they began training five Nigerian battalions in combat skills for possible combat in Sierra Leone.

The Economy. Despite tremendous oil and gas supplies, Nigeria has remained a lower-tier country as measured by per capita income; the World Bank ranked Nigeria 179th out of 206 countries. Yet the Nigerian economy saw strong growth, especially during the latter half of 2000.

The world's demand for oil supplied a necessary windfall that allowed the government to reduce its deficit spending. Nigeria produced near its maximum of 2 million barrels of oil daily during the latter half of 2000. The price per barrel of oil jumped to about $30 during the second half of 2000. Foreign reserves by late October stood at $8 billion, versus $5.85 billion in January. Obasanjo's 2001 budget predicted economic growth at 5% for 2001, compared with 3% for 2000. Inflation lessened to 5% in 2000.

In June the Nigerian Labor Congress staged a weeklong strike against a government-proposed 50% hike of oil prices, pushing the authorities to reduce the hike to 10%. Economic expansion was further hurt by the fact that domestic oil deliveries remained irregular, and Transparency International labeled Nigeria as the most corrupt country in which to do business in 2000.

Privatization of state-owned corporations continued, and foreign aid increased under the Obasanjo government. The United States, for example, provided only $7 million in 1998, but supplied about $165 million for fiscal year 2000.

NIGERIA • Information Highlights

Official Name: Federal Republic of Nigeria.
Location: West Africa.
Area: 356,668 sq mi (923 770 km²).
Population (2000 est.): 123,337,822.
Chief City (1993 unofficial est.): Abuja, the capital, 250,000.
Government: *Head of state and government,* Olusegun Obasanjo, president (sworn in May 29, 1999). *Legislature*—National Assembly: Senate and House of Representatives.
Monetary Unit: Naira (116.0 naira equal U.S.$1, Dec. 3, 2000).
Gross Domestic Product (1999 est. U.S.$): $110,500,000,000 (purchasing power parity).
Economic Index (1998, 1990 = 100): *Consumer Prices,* all items, 1,075.5; food, 984.6.
Foreign Trade (1999 U.S.$): *Imports,* $14,142,000,000; *exports,* $12,082,000,000.

Foreign Policy. Obasanjo spent a lot of time pursuing an international agenda. He sought debt relief for Nigeria, which had a foreign debt of $28–$34 billion. Meanwhile, Nigerian troops remained one of the largest outfits in the United Nations (UN) peacekeeping force in Sierra Leone. U.S. President Bill Clinton visited Nigeria in late August, and granted Nigerian exports greater access to the U.S. market.

HERBERT M. HOWE
School of Foreign Service
Georgetown University

Norway

In 2000, Jens Stoltenberg's minority Labour (Social Democratic) government replaced Kjell Magne Bondevik's minority center government. Also, right-wing Progress Party surged ahead in the polls.

Politics and Foreign Policy. At 41, Stoltenberg became Norway's youngest-ever prime minister when he formed a minority Labour (Social Democratic) government in March, controlling only 65 of the 165 seats in Norway's parliament, the Storting. The new government replaced Bondevik's minority center coalition that had controlled only 42 seats. Bondevik had resigned after an opposition majority voted to construct new power stations fired by natural gas, which he insisted would be environmentally destructive.

Stoltenberg is a strong supporter of Norwegian membership in the European Union (EU), although the issue was not on the political agenda in 2000. A Labour Party congress in November stipulated that no application for EU membership be made before 2005. Stoltenberg's first budget was fiscally neutral, increasing business payroll taxes by 6.4 billion kroner (U.S.$710 million), despite a budget surplus rising to 192 billion kroner ($24 billion). The government refused to increase spending, claiming it might overheat the economy.

Wealth taxes and aid to developing countries were scheduled to be increased, giving the budget a strong left-of-center hallmark. The fate of the budget was uncertain, as parties positioned themselves for the mandatory September 2001 elections. The strongest critic of the budget was the populist, right-wing Progress Party of Carl I. Hagen, which wanted to spend oil revenues on simultaneous tax cuts and increases in public services, especially health care. The Labour Party slumped to 22% in a September poll, against 35% in the 1997 election. The Progress Party—albeit prone to volatile poll support—hit 34%, more than doubling its election support.

Norway offered to contribute 3,500 troops to the planned EU rapid-reaction force. In September, Russian Prime Minister Mikhail M. Kasyanov visited Norway, and the two nations agreed to expand cooperation in nuclear and military spheres. Russian President Vladimir Putin accepted an invitation to visit Norway in 2002. In August, Putin paid homage to Norway for its aid in the *Kursk* submarine-rescue effort.

Economy. Norway's economy grew at 3.4% in 2000, more than three times the rate of 1999, and was forecast to slow only moderately in 2001. With unemployment estimated at 3.2% in 2000, labor shortages hampered growth. Wage costs were expected to increase, and consumer-price inflation was one of the highest in Western Europe. In October, interest rates rose to 9% for Central Bank overnight loans, almost twice the euro price. Political control of business was liberalized. The much-disputed telecommunication merger of Norway's Telenor and Sweden's Telia did not occur, but Telenor did acquire 53% of Denmark's Sonofon, the remainder being held by the U.S. company BellSouth. The sale of Christiana Bank to Nordic Baltic Holding (Nordea), the Nordic region's largest bank, was accepted. The Labour Party congress accepted the prime minister's proposal that the state-owned oil company, Statoil, should be partially privatized in 2001.

LEIF BECK FALLESEN, *Editor in Chief*
"Boersen," Copenhagen

NORWAY • Information Highlights

Official Name: Kingdom of Norway.
Location: Northern Europe.
Area: 125,182 sq mi (324 220 km²).
Population (2000 est.): 4,481,162.
Chief Cities (Jan. 1, 1998 est.): Oslo, the capital, 750,404; Bergen, 200,243; Trondheim, 138,008; Stavanger, 108,802.
Government: *Head of state,* Harald V, king (acceded January 1991). *Head of government,* Jens Stoltenberg, prime minister (took office March 2000). *Legislature—* Storting.
Monetary Unit: Krone (9.2198 kroner equal U.S.$1, Dec. 3, 2000).
Gross Domestic Product (1999 est. U.S.$): $111,300,000,000 (purchasing power parity).
Economic Indexes (1999, 1990 = 100): *Consumer Prices,* all items, 122.3; food, 118.8. *Industrial Production,* 137.5.
Foreign Trade (1999 U.S.$): *Imports,* $34,047,000,000; *exports,* $44,892,000,000.

Obituaries

O'CONNOR, John Joseph

Roman Catholic archbishop of New York since 1984: b. Philadelphia, PA, Jan. 15, 1920; d. New York City, May 3, 2000.

There was a two-minute standing ovation in New York's St. Patrick's Cathedral at the funeral Mass for Cardinal John J. O'Connor on May 8, 2000, when Boston's Cardinal Bernard F. Law said in the homily: "What a great legacy he has left us in his constant reminder that the church must always be

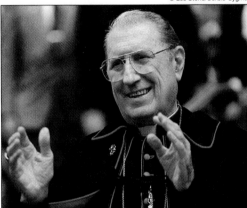

Cardinal John J. O'Connor

unambiguously pro-life." Even pro-choice politicians, among them President Bill Clinton, in the throng of more than 3,000 people were moved to stand.

After being appointed archbishop of New York on Jan. 31, 1984, the future cardinal immediately announced that efforts on behalf of the unborn would be his "Number 1 priority." But it became apparent that Cardinal O'Connor's commitment was to the sacredness and dignity of all life, as he worked for racial justice, for the rights of labor and immigrants, for the care of the elderly and people with disabilities, for support of the poor, and for justice and peace throughout the world.

Cardinal O'Connor's commitment to the unborn included his pledge to support any woman of any religion with a problem pregnancy who chose not to have an abortion. He founded the Sisters of Life, whose work includes a shelter for single pregnant women. He chaired the U.S. bishops' Committee for Pro-Life Activities. His preaching against racial prejudice was underlined by Cardinal O'Connor's gift of his Social Security check to the education of African-American youngsters and his commitment to keeping open inner-city Catholic schools.

The cardinal pleaded for peace and justice in Ireland. He joined rallies of Jews in New York, and was instrumental in the Vatican's granting diplomatic recognition to Israel. He went on diplomatic missions to Cuba and other Latin American countries. To raise awareness of the famine in Ethiopia, he was photographed there holding dying babies.

For all his international influence, Cardinal O'Connor remained primarily a priest, the shepherd of his flock—the sprawling archdiocese of New York. He rarely missed celebrating Sunday Mass in the cathedral. He met personally with men who were thinking about studying for the priesthood; became a superstar to youths and teenagers; and, although he enunciated the church's position against homosexual activity, he met with people of homosexual orientation.

Background. John Joseph O'Connor was born on Jan. 15, 1920, in Philadelphia, and was ordained a priest of the archdiocese of Philadelphia on Dec. 15, 1945. He taught high school, was a parish priest, and began a ministry to mentally retarded children. In 1952, during the Korean War, he became a military chaplain, distinguishing himself on the combat lines with U.S. Marines. He became chaplain at the U.S. Naval Academy in Annapolis, and rose to be chief of navy chaplains with the rank of rear admiral. After serving in Vietnam and earning a doctorate, he retired from the navy in 1979 after 27 years. He was promptly ordained a bishop on May 27, 1979, by Pope John Paul II in Rome, became vicar-general of the Military Vicariate, and was named bishop of Scranton, PA, in May 1983.

On May 25, 1985, Archbishop O'Connor was elevated to the rank of cardinal. At the age of 75, he submitted the required letter of resignation and was pleased that the pope asked him to remain in his post. In August 1999 he had surgery for a small tumor on the surface of his brain. Cardinal O'Connor was the author of several books.

ANNE M. BUCKLEY

GIELGUD, Sir John

British stage, motion-picture, and television actor, director, and author: b. London, England, April 14, 1904; d. near Aylesbury, England, May 21, 2000.

John Gielgud was the last of the British 20th-century theatrical knights. For much of that century, the triumvirate of Gielgud, Laurence Olivier, and Ralph Richardson dominated the British stage, creating a golden age of classical theater. Gielgud was especially celebrated for his Shakespearean roles, though he excelled equally in plays by Wilde, Chekhov, Coward, Shaw, Sheridan, and Ibsen. He performed Hamlet more than 500 times and appeared as Prospero and Lear on five occasions. Assessed by some as a limited actor, Gielgud truly had a talent for diverse character impersonation, proven conclusively in the contemporary theater of the late 1960s and 1970s.

Though noted for his delicate and lyrical voice and his aristocratic bearing, Gielgud transcended classification with disarming versatility and simplicity. To the popular culture, he will be remembered more for his appearance in some 130 films and television productions,

Sir John Gielgud

mostly after he turned 75. Often in mediocre fare, he nonetheless made notable appearances in such films as *Julius Caesar* (1953), *Richard III* (1955), *Becket* (1964), *Chimes at Midnight* (1966), *The Charge of the Light Brigade* (1968), *Providence* (1977), *The Elephant Man* (1980), *Arthur* (1981), *Gandhi* (1982), and *Prospero's Books* (1991). He was awarded an Oscar as best supporting actor for portraying the butler in *Arthur*. Gielgud was working on his final film, Samuel Beckett's *Catastrophe,* a month prior to his death.

A demanding stage director, he also was a graceful writer, producing notable memoirs—*Early Stages* (1939), *An Actor and His Time* (1979), and *Backward Glances* (1989). His collections of essays and observations on theatrical matters include *Stage Directions* (1963), *Distinguished Company* (1973),

Shakespeare—Hit or Miss (1991), and *Notes from the Gods* (1994).

Background. The third of four children, Arthur John Gielgud was a great-nephew of actress Ellen Terry and a cousin of designer Edward Gordon Craig. He studied at the Royal Academy of Dramatic Art, making his professional stage debut in 1921 and his film debut in 1924. His Broadway debut was in 1928; he returned there frequently, for the final time in Harold Pinter's *No Man's Land* (1976). His first *Hamlet* was in 1930 (New York production in 1936), yet it was Gielgud's portrayal of Richard II in *Richard of Bordeaux* (1933) that made him a star. He directed and starred in a famous production of *Romeo and Juliet* in 1935. His reputation as a great classical stage actor of the world continued through the next three decades, with sporadic film work and visits to the United States (notably in 1951 with Christopher Fry's *The Lady's Not for Burning* and his one-man show, *The Ages of Man,* which was presented in 1958).

Gielgud's diverse acting career shifted more to modern roles and daring productions, in Albee's *Tiny Alice* (1964), Peter Brook's production of Seneca's *Oedipus* (1968), David Storey's *Home* (1970), Pinter's *No Man's Land* (1975), and Alain Resnais' experimental film *Providence* (1977). During the following decades, Gielgud's film and television appearances increased, culminating in his Emmy-winning, best-actor performance in the 1990 miniseries *Summer's Lease.* His final stage appearance was as a museum curator in Hugh Whitemore's *The Best of Friends* (1988).

Knighted in 1953, he was appointed Companion of Honour in 1977 and received the Order of Merit in 1996. In 1994, London's Globe Theatre was renamed the Gielgud Theatre. In 1976 he moved to the country with his companion of 40 years, Martin Hensler (d. 1999). Sir John's favorite pastimes were reading, gardening, and watching television.

DON B. WILMETH

ASSAD, Hafiz al-

Absolute leader of Syria from 1970: b. Qardaha, Syria, Oct. 6, 1930; d. Damascus, Syria, June 10, 2000.

One of the Middle East rulers longest in power, Hafiz al-Assad maintained absolute control over Syria for 30 years. He was a loner who kept his own counsel, made his own decisions, and acquiesced to no persuasions. Western leaders found him obdurate and infuriating; in the Arab world, he was respected as an unrivaled champion of the Arab cause, but not greatly liked. He often took a line that differentiated him from other Arab leaders.

Assad was a man of cold calculation. His changes of policy, when they occurred, were in response to changes in circumstances rather than the result of altered convictions. It might be claimed that his rule was less brutal than that of Iraq's Saddam Hussein. Assad's preferred methods were cronyism and corruption, but he could on occasion be responsible for acts of great violence. Assad had limited knowledge of the Western world. He traveled reluctantly, and never visited the United States. The lodestar of his policy was an adamant hostility to the very existence of Israel—modified, perhaps only nominally, in his very last years.

Assad's gift to Syria was 30 years of stability, which followed almost continuous turmoil after independence in 1946. Some economic development took place in the 30 years, but it was unimpressive, especially considering that oil had been discovered in moderate amounts.

Background. Hafiz al-Assad, one of 11 children, was the son of a small landowner. The family adhered to the minor, secretive Alawi sect of Shia Islam, regarded by many Muslims as heretical. He was the first of his family to attend high school, in Latakia Province, and quickly became interested in politics. He joined the new Arab Baath Socialist Party. Like many leaders in the Middle East, Assad rose to power through the military.

After attending Syria's air-force college, he entered the air force in 1955 and advanced rapidly through the ranks. He served briefly in Egypt during the short-lived union of Egypt and Syria (the United Arab Republic, 1958–61). In Cairo he found a congenial group of fellow Syrian officers, and they seized power in Syria in 1966. He was minister of defense during the disas-trous war with Israel in 1967, and he became Syria's premier after a bloodless coup in September 1970. The following year, under a new constitution, Assad became president and remained such until his death.

In 1973 he joined with Anwar el-Sadat of Egypt in an unprovoked attack on Israel, which after initial successes again resulted in an Arab defeat. Assad was appalled when some subtle change took place in Arab atti-

© George Ashi/Reuters/Archive Photos

Hafiz al-Assad

tudes toward Israel that made acceptance of the Jewish state's existence tolerable to some Arab countries, leading to an Egyptian-Israeli peace treaty in 1979, later to peace between Israel and Jordan (1994), and serious tentatives of peace between Israel and the Palestinians. But Assad's conflict with Israel now was by proxy, in the battleground of Lebanon, using guerrilla groups that he indirectly supported. Assad's Syria was alone among Arab states in favoring Iran in the Iran-Iraq war (1980–88).

Assad enjoyed playing the United States off against the Soviet Union, and he derived economic and military aid from both. This game came to an end with the disintegration of the Soviet Union. He joined in the anti-Iraqi coalition that ousted Iraq from its conquest of Kuwait in 1991. By the late 1990s, it appeared that, in his book, negotiations with Israel had to be preceded by an Israeli readiness to return the whole of the Golan Heights. He reiterated that position when meeting with U.S. President Bill Clinton in Geneva in March 2000 (*see* MIDDLE EAST).

President Assad was survived by his son and designated political heir, Bashar, and three other children.

ARTHUR CAMPBELL TURNER

TRUDEAU, Pierre Elliott

Former prime minister of Canada: b. Montreal, Quebec, Canada, Oct. 18, 1919; d. Montreal, Sept. 28, 2000.

The death of Canada's charismatic and enigmatic former prime minister, Pierre Elliott Trudeau, recalled a political career that bedazzled and confounded Canadians through parts of three decades. His style—fresh, breezy, and unorthodox—appealed to many even while, increasingly, offending others. And despite Trudeau's undoubtedly profound impact on the country's development, his legacy remains both complicated and controversial.

Trudeau led the Liberal Party to victory in four of five federal elections, beginning in 1968. His hold on power was interrupted for only one brief interlude of Conservative rule (June 1979–March 1980). As prime minister, Trudeau dominated the Canadian political landscape with panache and flair, wit and wisdom, and a fondness for pranks that Canadian citizens initially found charming but eventually tired of. He retired from politics in June 1984.

Background. Joseph Philippe Pierre Yves Elliott Trudeau was born of a wealthy, bicultural French- and English-speaking Montreal family. He received a Catholic, Jesuit-style school education, then studied at institutions of higher learning in Montreal, the United States, France, and England. He was called to the Quebec bar in 1944, and later lectured on civil liberties and constitutional law at the University of Montreal.

First elected to Parliament in 1965, Trudeau was immediately drafted into Lester Pearson's cabinet, rising quickly to the most-senior cabinet ranks. When Pearson retired as Liberal leader and prime minister in 1968, Trudeau won a bitterly fought contest to succeed him. Three days after being sworn in as prime minister on April 20, and riding a razzle-dazzle wave of "Trudeaumania," the dashing bachelor

© Paul Chiasson/Liaison Agency

Pierre Elliott Trudeau

prime minister dissolved Parliament and called an election, which he handily won.

In office, however, contradictions soon began to surface. Though an avowed champion of civil liberties, he invoked the harsh War Measures Act—a form of martial law—to quell a limited outbreak of separatist terrorism in predominantly French-speaking Quebec in 1970. Hundreds were rounded up and thrown into jail for varying periods, without ever being charged. Though a self-proclaimed crusader for national unity, Trudeau in 1982 brought home the Canadian Constitution from Britain—complete with an amending formula and a groundbreaking Charter of Rights and Freedoms—with the consent of all ten provinces, except Quebec. National unity is still bleeding from that action. A more unambiguous contribution to unity was the Official Languages Act, which designated English and French as official languages of Canada. The latter act made it fashionable for English-speaking Canadians to speak French.

Trudeau expanded social-welfare programs and the role of government. In the process, he saddled Canadians with a succession of budgetary deficits—the consequences of which he left future governments to deal with. Internationally, the prime minister's most important initiative was Canadian recognition of Communist China in 1970. Other Western and pro-Western countries followed his lead, creating the conditions for Beijing's admission to the United Nations in 1971.

Trudeau had three sons by his wife, Margaret Sinclair, a "flower child," whom he married in 1971 when he was 51, she 22. They were divorced in 1984. Their youngest son, Michel, was killed in an avalanche in British Columbia in 1998 at age 22. Trudeau's survivors also included a daughter, Sarah.

A state funeral in Montreal on October 3 ended five days of national mourning for the former prime minister.

JOHN BEST

The following is a selected list of prominent persons who died during 2000.
Articles on major figures appear in the preceding pages.

Albert, Carl (91), U.S. congressman (D-OK, 1947–77); served as House majority whip (1955–62), majority leader (1962–71), and speaker (1971–77): d. McAlester, OK, February 4.

Allen, Lewis (94); film and TV director; after working on stage productions in New York and London, he directed his first film, *The Uninvited*, in 1944. This ghost story is still celebrated for its excellent acting and haunting atmosphere. He later worked on films with such stars as Frank Sinatra, Burt Lancaster, and Sean Connery, and directed episodes of *Bonanza*, *Route 66*, and *Mission: Impossible* for television: d. Santa Monica, CA, May 3.

Carl Albert

Allen, Steve (78); songwriter and comedian; in more than 50 years in show business, he composed more than 5,000 songs, including "This Could Be the Start of Something Big" and "Gravy Waltz." He pioneered late-night television talk shows as host of the *Tonight* show (1953–57), preceding Johnny Carson. He later hosted *The Steve Allen Show*, and was a perennial guest on *I've Got a Secret*, and *What's My Line?*: d. Los Angeles, October 30.

Anhalt, Edward (86); screenwriter; a graduate of Columbia University, he worked as a writer during the very early days of television in the 1930s and 1940s before turning to films. He won a screenwriting Oscar in 1950 for *Panic in the Streets*, and became known for his adaptations of works by other authors. He won a second Academy Award in 1964 for his adaptation of the Jean Anouilh play, *Becket*. He cowrote the 1972 Robert Redford film, *Jeremiah Johnson*: d. Pacific Palisades, CA, September 3.

Bandaranaike, Sirimavo (84), Sri Lankan prime minister; she became the world's first female prime minister in

Steve Allen

1960, after her husband, S.R.W.D. Bandaranaike, was assassinated in 1959. She lost the 1965 elections but returned to power in 1970. In 1980 she was expelled from Parliament for "abusing her powers" and was suspended from holding office for seven years. Narrowly losing the presidential election in 1988, she served as her daughter's prime minister from November 1994 until ill health forced her to resign in August 2000: d. Colombo, Sri Lanka, October 10.

Barks, Carl (99); comic-book illustrator; from 1942 to 1966 he drew comic books under license to the Walt Disney Company, in the process creating the character of Scrooge McDuck, who first appeared in 1947. He also created the Beagle Boys, Gladstone Gander, and the inventor Gyro Gearloose: d. Grants Pass, OR, August 25.

Bartel, Paul (61); actor and filmmaker; after serving his Hollywood apprenticeship in such B-films as *Death Race 2000*, he wrote, directed, and costarred in *Eating Raoul*, a 1982 black comedy that quickly became a cult favorite: d. New York City, May 13.

Barty, Billy (born William Bertanzetti) (76); actor and activist; a 3′ 10″ (1.17 m) dwarf, he performed in movies, radio, and on Broadway. He portrayed a wizard in the 1988 fantasy film *Willow*, and appeared in the TV sitcom *Frasier*. In 1957 he founded Little People of America, an advocacy group for others with dwarfism: d. Glendale, CA, December 23.

Bloch, Konrad (88); German-born biochemist; he was awarded the Nobel Prize in Medicine or Physiology in 1964, for his work on how cholesterol is made in the body: d. Burlington, MA, October 15

Borge, Victor (born Borge Rosenbaum) (91); musical humorist; trained in his native Denmark as a concert pianist, he preferred adding comedy to his music and working in nightclubs and the theater. Emigrating to the United States during World War II, he worked at NBC Radio, and in 1953 opened

his one-man *Comedy in Music* show on Broadway; it set a record by running 849 performances. Afterward, he took the show on tour, and he continued to perform internationally past the age of 90: d. Greenwich, CT, December 23.

Bourguiba, Habib (96); Tunisian leader; a lawyer by training, he led the fight for the independence of Tunisia, then a French colony, from 1934–54. He was elected prime minister of independent Tunisia in 1956 and then chosen president in 1957, a post he held for 30 years, governing as a modernizer and a supporter of women's rights: d. Monastir, Tunisia, April 6.

Brooks, Gwendolyn (83); African-American poet; her first poetry anthology, *A Street in Bronzeville*, published in 1945, explored the South Side of Chicago where she grew up. It earned her a Guggenheim Fellowship. She won the 1950 Pulitzer Prize for her second collection, *Annie Allen*, which utilized an experimental form she called the "sonnet-ballad." In the late 1960s she ran a poetry workshop in her home that included the younger poets Nikki Giovanni and Sonia Sanchez, along with members of the Blackstone Rangers, a Chicago street gang. In 1995 she received the National Medal of Arts award: d. Chicago, December 3.

Brower, David (88); militant environmentalist; as executive director of the Sierra Club conservation group from 1952 to 1969, he increased its membership from 7,000 to 77,000 and its assets to $3 million. He was a force in preventing the construction of two government dams in the Grand Canyon during the 1960s, a fight that lost the Club its tax-exempt status. After leaving the Sierra Club he founded Friends of the Earth, where he was chairman until dismissed in 1984 amid complaints about his uncompromising attitudes. He rejoined the Sierra Club board in 1982, remaining until spring 2000, when he resigned: d. Berkeley, CA, November 5.

Bullaty, Sonja (76); Czech-born photographer; an Auschwitz survivor, she arrived in the United States in 1947. In 1951 she married fellow photographer Angelo Lomeo, and over five decades they collaborated on a large body of work, including books on Provence, Tuscany, Venice, and Vermont. She was known for her strong use of color and light and her intricate compositions: d. New York City, October 5.

Bundy, William P. (83); presidential adviser; born into a family with a tradition of government service, he was an important figure in the making of Vietnam policy during the Eisenhower, Kennedy, and Johnson administrations, although unlike his brother McGeorge he never reached the highest levels of power. After leaving government in 1969 he taught at MIT and Princeton, and edited the magazine *Foreign Affairs*: d. Princeton, NJ, October 6.

Burr, Robert (78); actor; hired to understudy Richard Burton in a 1964 Broadway production of *Hamlet*, he gave a brilliant performance when Burton took sick, and later the same year played the role to great acclaim at the Delacorte Theater in New York City's Central Park. He returned many times to Shakespeare in Central Park, finishing as Claudius in a 1975 production of *Hamlet*. He also worked in film and television: d. Los Angeles, CA, May 13

Barbara Cartland

Canby, Vincent (76); film and theater critic; as film critic at *The New York Times* (1965–93), he covered the French New Wave, the rise of the great U.S. directors of the 1970s, and the return of the big-budget Hollywood blockbuster. In 1993 he became a theater critic for *The Times*: d. New York City, October 15.

Carnahan, Mel (66); Democratic governor of Missouri; a lifelong politician, he served as Missouri's treasurer and lieutenant governor before being elected governor in 1993. He pushed through a controversial $315 million tax increase for public schools in his first term, and in 1999 commuted the death sentence of a murderer after an appeal from Pope John Paul II. He was running for the U.S. Senate when he died in a plane crash; under state law his name remained on the ballot, and he won the election. His wife Jean was appointed to serve in his place: d. St. Louis, MO, October 16.

Cartland, Barbara (98); English-born writer; author of 723 romance novels since 1922, with a billion copies printed in 36 languages, she often produced 23 titles a year, dictating 7,000 words a day to secretaries and tape recorders. She used her profits to move into a 19th century palace, and in 1990 was made a Dame of the British Empire for her charity work: d. Hatfield, England, May 21.

Casey, Robert P. (68); Democratic governor of Pennsylvania (1987–95); a Roman Catholic with strong feelings against abortion, he signed a bill in 1989 that imposed a 24-hour waiting period for abortions in

Victor Borge

Pennsylvania; after a suit by Planned Parenthood, the U.S. Supreme Court upheld the waiting period in 1992: d. Scranton, PA, May 30.

Cassidy, Frederic (92), Jamaican-born lexicographer; as editor of the *Dictionary of American Regional English*, he spent nearly four decades exploring the folk language of the United States. He carried a 40-lb (18.2–kg) tape recorder around Jamaica in the 1950s and 1960s to research a dictionary of Jamaican English and Creole: d. Madison, WI, June 14.

Chapman, Leonard F., Jr. (86), U.S. Marine Corps general; As commandant of the Marines, Chapman oversaw the corps' last-remaining combat forces withdraw from Vietnam in 1971. After his military retirement, Chapman became head of the U.S. Immigration and Naturalization Service: d. Fairfax, VA, January 6.

Cirker, Hayward (82), paperback publisher; he started Dover Publishing in 1941 as a mail-order business for remaindered books, and then in 1945 began reprinting out-of-print volumes. While other paperback houses of the 1950s concentrated on detective novels and pulp romances, Dover specialized in more-interesting and practical books, including a reprint of one of Albert Einstein's theoretical works: d. Roslyn, NY, March 8.

Claiborne, Craig (79), food journalist; emerged from the Mississippi Delta to become the nation's preeminent food critic. He once savored a $4,000 dinner in Paris, and regularly informed and entertained *The New York Times* readers on the ranging delights of a deli sandwich to haute cuisine: d. New York City, January 22.

Coggan, Frederick (90), British churchman; as Archbishop of Canterbury (1974–80), he proposed the ordination of women, in spite of fierce opposition. A progressive, he denounced racial intolerance and sought to improve relations between Christians and Jews: d. southern England, May 17.

Cohen, Alexander H. (79), theater and television producer; starting in the early 1950s he produced 101 shows on Broadway and London's West End, including *The Homecoming*, *Little Murders*, and Richard Burton's *Hamlet*. He also produced 20 television specials as well as the first 20 Tony Award telecasts: d. New York City, April 22.

Comfort, Alex (80), British writer; author of the 1972 best-seller, *The Joy of Sex*, which sold more than 12 million copies, as well as novels, poetry, plays, and books on science and philosophy: d. Banbury, England, March 26.

Corallo, Anthony (87), Mafia boss known as "Tony Ducks"; born in East Harlem, New York City, he rose through the ranks of the Lucchese crime family to become the group's boss in the early 1970s. During his reign the family concentrated on labor racketeering in the trash-hauling and construction industries. After government agents planted a listening device inside his automobile and recorded his conversations detailing the mob's control over the construction business, he was sentenced to 100 years in federal prison: d. Springfield, MO, August 23.

Cormier, Robert E. (75), author; beginning as a newspaper journalist, he began writing novels for young adults in 1960. His 1963 book *A Little Raw on Monday Mornings* won critical praise, but it was *The Chocolate War* in 1974 that gained him popular success. He also wrote *I Am the Cheese* (1977). He was frequently attacked for his realistic portrayals of teenage life: d. Leominster, MA, November 2.

Coverdell, Paul (61), Republican senator from Georgia; a conservative and close ally of majority leader Sen. Trent Lott, he was the fourth-ranking Republican in the Senate, and helped shape the party's positions on education, taxes, Social Security, defense, and drug control: d. Atlanta, GA, July 18.

Cranston, Alan (86), former U.S. senator; as Democratic senator from California (1969-73), he supported an end to the war in Vietnam and the development of the B-1 bomber. He made a failed bid for the presidential nomination in 1984. In 1991 he was formally rebuked by the Senate Ethics Committee for his involvement in the Charles Keating savings-and-loan scandal. After leaving the Senate he had helped run a nonprofit group seeking to abolish nuclear weapons: d. Los Altos Hills, CA, December 31.

Craxi, Bettino (65), Italian Socialist politician; he served as Italy's prime minister (1983–87), an era of unprecedented economic growth. His image was hurt in the early 1990s, however, when corruption investigations revealed bribery, nepotism, and kickbacks in his administration: d. Tunisia, Jan. 19.

Curtis, Carl (94), former U.S. senator; a Republican from Nebraska, Curtis spent more than 40 years in Congress and remained loyal to President Richard M. Nixon during the final moments of Watergate. Following his political career, Curtis returned to his beloved Nebraska: d. Lincoln, NE, January 24.

Daniel, (Elbert) Clifton, Jr. (87), journalist; joined *The New York Times* in 1944 to cover World War II and later served as its managing editor (1964–69) and chief of the Washington Bureau (1973–76). He was married to Margaret Truman, President Harry Truman's only child: d. New York City, February 21.

Davies, Donald (75), computer pioneer; renowned for his invention of "packet-switching", a rapid message-switching technique that helped make the Internet possible. Davies' later work concentrated on data security: d. London, May 28.

© NYT Pictures

Clifton Daniel, Jr.

Davis, James H. (Jimmie) (101), Louisiana governor and songwriter; the son of sharecroppers, he served two terms as Louisiana's Governor (1944–48 and 1960–64). He also wrote songs for the likes of Gene Autry and Bing Crosby, including the hit "You Are My Sunshine": d. Baton Rouge, LA, November 5.

Day, Robin (76), British television journalist; during the 1960s, when television news interviews in England were sedate and deferential, he pioneered a hard-edge method of probing and relentless questioning that earned him the nickname "Grand Inquisitor." His cut-and-thrust style soon became the norm in British broadcasting. He retired in 1989: d. London, August 6.

de Camp, L. Sprague (92), science-fiction and fantasy writer; author of more than 100 novels and numerous short stories, he was an important figure in the "Golden Age" of science fiction during the 1930s and 1940s. He toned down the heroism of his main characters and placed his stories in recognizable futures that were based on scientific projections. He was an early recipient of the Grand Master Award given by the Science Fiction and Fantasy Writers of America. He also wrote a number of historical novels and nonfiction books: d. Plano, TX, November 6.

Devine, Annie (88), civil-rights leader; a native of Mississippi, she began organizing voter-registration drives in her native state in the early 1960s, at a time when white control of the process prevented blacks from voting. A founder of the Mississippi Freedom Democratic Party, she attended the 1964 Democratic National Convention in a failed attempt to unseat Mississippi's all-white delegation. In January 1965 she led hundreds of protesters to Washington, DC, where they demanded that Congress deny membership to the Mississippi representatives: d. Ridgeland, MS, August 22.

Dewar, Donald (63), Scottish politician; born in Glasgow, he was elected as a Labour Party member to London's House of Commons in 1966. After Labour won the 1997 general election he was appointed secretary of state for Scotland, from which position he pushed for creation of the first Scottish Parliament since the 17th century. He became first minister when the new Parliament opened in 1999: d. Edinburgh, Scotland, October 11.

Douglas, Roosevelt (58), prime minister of Dominica; a leader of the black-power movement in the Caribbean, he worked for the independence of Dominica from Great Britain, a freedom the island won in 1978. He took control of the country's Labour Party in 1992, and became prime minister in January 2000: d. Portsmouth, Dominica, October 1.

Drury, Ian (57), rock singer; his 1976 hit *Sex & Drugs & Rock & Roll* became an anthem for punk rockers the world over. Besides recording and touring with his band, the Blockheads, he acted in television and films. He had polio as a child, and performed at many benefits to raise awareness about the disease: d. London, March 27.

Dyk, Ruth (born Ruth Belcher) (99), suffragist; born into a family that descended from the Mayflower colonists, she worked as a psychiatric social worker and was a member of the woman's suffrage movement to gain the right to vote. Shortly before her death she voted in the 2000 national election. She coauthored three books on psychology and anthropology: d. Rochester, NY, November 18.

Egan, Daniel (84), priest who ministered to drug addicts; a Franciscan Friar of the Atonement since 1937, his work rehabilitating drug addicts earned him the nickname "the Junkie Priest." He was a certified drug- and alcohol-abuse counselor and chaplain of Narcotics Anonymous. In 1962 he founded Village Haven, a halfway house for women addicts in New York City's Greenwich Village; eight years later he set up New Hope Manor for addicted teenage girls. In addition to his drug work, he ministered to people with AIDS: d. Peekskill, NY, February 10.

Egerton, John (85), sixth duke of Sutherland, Scotland; descended from one of the richest men of the 19th century, he inherited the dukedom in 1963. The inheritance included a collection of some 500 old master paintings, including works by Rembrandt, Raphael, and Titian. He was captured during World War II after parachuting into Crete and spent several years in prison camps: d. St. Boswells, Scotland, September 21.

Erwin, Lee (92), organist and composer; he was fascinated by silent films, and composed scores for more than 70 of them, including comedies by Chaplin and Keaton and such epics as the 1925 *Ben Hur*: d. New York City, September 21.

Fairbanks, Douglas, Jr. (90), actor; son of silent-movie superstar Douglas Fairbanks, he forged a career of his own in film and television from 1925 to 1981. He starred in *The Prisoner of Zenda*, *Gunga Din*, and *Sinbad the Sailor*, among other movies, and hosted and performed in a television anthology show, *Douglas Fairbanks Presents*, in the 1950s. He served as an officer with British commandos during World War II: d. New York City, May 7.

Farnsworth, Richard (80), actor; a stuntman in Hollywood Westerns for more than 30 years, he turned to acting at the age of 57, appearing in *The Grey Fox*, *The Natural*, and other films. He received two Academy Award acting nominations for *Comes a Horseman* and *The Straight Story*: d. Lincoln, NM, October 6.

Fears, Tom (76), pro-football player; former Los Angeles Rams wideout (1948-56) whose precise buttonhook routes made him one of the game's best receivers. Fears was enshrined in the Pro Football Hall of Fame in 1970: d. Seminole, FL, January 4.

Fein, Nat (86), news photographer; a staff photographer for three decades with the *New York Herald Tribune*, he won a Pulitzer Prize for his poignant image of the dying Babe Ruth being honored at Yankee Stadium in 1948. He remained with the *Herald Tribune* until it went out of business in 1966: d. Westwood, NJ, September 26.

Fitzgerald, Penelope (83), British novelist; a graduate of Oxford, she published her first novel, *The Golden Child*, in 1977 at age 60, then went on to win the Booker Prize in 1979 and the National Book Critics Circle Award in 1998. Her novels are short, understated, and written in vibrant prose: d. London, April 28.

Flusser, David (83), Austrian-born biblical scholar; a professor of comparative religion at Hebrew University of Jerusalem, he popularized the idea that Jesus Christ was a faithful Jew who never intended to found a new religion. He presented his ideas in the 1965 book, *Jesus*. An Orthodox Jew, he was awarded the Israel Prize in 1980: d. Jerusalem, September 15.

Fowler, Henry H. (91), former U.S. treasury secretary; he presided over "guns and butter" economic policies and expanded social programs while serving in Lyndon Johnson's administration (1965–68): d. Falls Church, VA, January 3.

Freund, Gisele (91), German-born photographer; after moving to Paris, she became famous for her portraits of European writers, including James Joyce, Virginia Woolf, Boris Pasternak, and André Malraux. She was a founding member of Magnum Photo Agency: d. Paris, March 31.

Gassman, Vittorio (77), Italian actor; a popular movie star in films of the 1950s and 1960s, including *Big Deal on Madonna Street*, and *War and Peace*, he was also a critically praised stage actor. He used his film money to finance his own theater company, which toured Italy using a portable stage: d. Rome, Italy, June 29.

Gennaro, Peter (80), dancer and choreographer; after nearly a decade dancing on Broadway in such musicals as *Kiss Me, Kate*, *Guys and Dolls*, and *The Pajama Game*, he gained notice for his work with Jerome Robbins choreographing *West Side Story* in 1957, and went on to create dances for a number of Broadway hits in the 1960s. From 1960 to 1963 he was on television's *Perry Como Show* leading the Peter Gennaro Dancers. He won a Tony Award for his choreography of the 1977 hit musical *Annie*: d. New York City, September 28.

Gertz, Elmer (93), leading Chicago lawyer; in a career that spanned seven decades, his clients included thrill killer Nathan Leopold, author Henry Miller, and Jack Ruby, who shot President Kennedy's alleged assassin Lee Harvey Oswald. He was an important legal figure in the civil-rights movement and argued many cases for fairness in Chicago housing during the 1940s and 1950s: d. Chicago, IL, April 27.

Giacomelli, Mario (75), Italian photographer; a self-taught photographer, he is best known for his 1962 pictures of priests frolicking in the snow, their black cassocks set off against the brilliant white of the landscape. Although many of his photos are near-abstractions of fields and buildings, he also worked in a documentary style, photographing for two years in an impoverished country town and in an old-age home (1954–83): d. Senigallia, Italy, November 25.

Gifford, Don (81), James Joyce scholar; professor of English and U.S. studies at Williams College (1951–84), he coauthored *Ulysses Annotated*, a major work of scholarship on Joyce. He also wrote short stories and poems: d. North Adams, MA, May 22.

Gilliam, Joe (49), pro-football player; he was the first black quarterback to start a National Football League (NFL) game, leading the Pittsburgh Steelers to a 4–1–1 record in 1974 before he was replaced by Terry Bradshaw. Trouble with cocaine and heroin led to his benching, and he spent time in several drug-rehab centers after leaving the Steelers, eventually becoming a drug counselor himself. He opened a youth-football camp in Tennessee where he promoted drug and alcohol abstinence: d. Nashville, TN, December 25.

Gilruth, Robert (86), project manager at the National Aeronautics and Space Administration (NASA); as head of NASA's Space Task Group, he supervised the design and development of the Mercury space capsule, and assigned which astronauts to fly in it. He then ran the Manned Space Center in Houston during the Gemini flights and the Apollo moon landings, retiring in 1972: d. Charlottesville, VA, August 17.

Gillespie, Gregory (64), artist; his paintings mixed realism, surrealism, and expressionism in a search for a reality beyond the ordinary. Although his work is represented in the collections of the Metropolitan and Whitney Museums, among others, he remained an outsider in the art world: d. Belchertown, MA, April 26.

Glasier, Phillip (84), British falconer and author; he almost single-handedly helped revive the sport of falconry, and wrote the book many consider the subject's bible, *Falconry and Hawking*, in 1979. In 1967 he established the Falconry Center to protect and breed hunting birds; now called the National Birds of Prey Center in Britain, it houses more than 300 birds from 80 species: d. Gloucestershire, England, September 11.

Gonzalez, Henry (84) U.S. congressman; a Democrat, served in the U.S. House of Representatives (1961-99). Was a member of the House Banking Committee for 35 years and its chairman (1989-95): d. San Antonio, TX, Nov. 28.

Gorey, Edward (75), artist and author noted for his blending of the comic and the macabre; he wrote and illustrated more than 100 books, including *The Doubtful Guest* (1958), which features a penguin who wears a long scarf and tennis shoes, and *Amphigorey* (1972). He also created the animated film that serves as prelude to the public-television series, *Mystery*: d. Hyannis, MA, April 15.

Greco, Jose (82), Italian-born dancer in the Spanish style; raised in Brooklyn, NY, he started his dancing career as a teenager performing on stage and in nightclubs. In 1942 he began partnering with the famous Spanish dancer La Argentinita, and founded his own company five years later. Although his repertoire ranged widely, in the 1960s he became especially identified with flamenco dancing. He was appreciated for his spectacular footwork: d. Lancaster, PA, December 31.

Gross, Al (82), Toronto-born inventor; a wizard of wireless communication, he invented the circuitry behind cell phones, cordless phones, paging systems, garage-door openers, and walkie-talkies. A man who was truly ahead of his time, he never became rich off his inventions because the patents expired before the devices became popular. He received the Lemelson-MIT Lifetime Achievement Award for Invention: d. Sun City, AZ, December 21.

Groza, Lou (76), pro-football player; as offensive tackle and place-kicker for the Cleveland Browns from 1946–67, he amassed 1,608 career points, which is still a Browns record, and was named National Football League (NFL) player of the year in 1954. He is best known to fans for his last-second kick on Christmas Eve 1950, which beat the Los Angeles Rams 30–28 and won the NFL title for the Browns: d. Middleburgh Heights, OH, November 29.

Guinness, Sir Alec (86), British actor; after working on stage in the 1930s, he began acting in films, first as Herbert Pocket in *Great Expectations*, then as Fagin in *Oliver Twist*. He delighted audiences by starring in a series of hilarious English comedies, including *Kind Hearts and Coronets* and *The Lavender Hill Mob*. He won the Academy Award for Best Actor in 1957 for *The Bridge on the River Kwai*. In 1977 he enchanted a whole new generation, playing Obi-Wan Kenobi in *Star Wars*: d. West Sussex, England, August 5.

© AP/Wide World Photos

Sir Alec Guinness

Halberstam, Shlomo (92), Grand rabbi of the Bobov Hasidic sect; for about 50 years he was the spiritual leader of the Bobover lineage of ultra-Orthodox Jews centered in the Borough Park neighborhood of Brooklyn. After the rest of his family was killed in Europe by the Nazis, he and his oldest son arrived in New York in the late 1940s. For a time he shaved his beard and went through a severe crisis of faith, but then took up his duties as rabbi again and helped nurture the rebirth of the Bobov group: d. New York City, August 2.

Hall, Gus (90), Communist Party leader; joining the American Communist Party in 1927 (his father had joined in 1919), he remained unwavering in his support of its ideology through seven decades, even after the fall of the Soviet Union. He was in federal prison from 1949–57 on a charge of conspiracy to overthrow the government. He became general secretary of the party in 1959, by which time its membership was a mere 3,000. He was unable to forge an alliance with the far more popular New Left movement of the 1960s, leaving the Communist Party isolated and marginal. After the fall of the Soviet Union in 1991 he switched his support to North Korea: d. New York City, October 13.

Hamilton, William (63), evolutionary biologist; while still a graduate student at Cambridge University he proposed an original way of understanding the genetic basis of altruism among living beings in terms of kin selection. He was a major contributor to the modern synthesis of Darwinian natural selection and Mendelian genetics: d. Oxford, England, March 7.

Harsanyi, John C. (80), Hungarian-born economist; he escaped to the West from Communist Hungary in 1950, and taught at a number of universities in Australia and the United States before settling at Berkeley in 1964. He won the 1994 Nobel Prize in Economics for his work in fine-tuning the principles of game theory, which uses mathematics to predict the outcome of such "games" as price wars, hostile takeovers, and other economic conflicts: d. Berkeley, CA, August 9.

Hartshorne, Charles (103), philosopher and theologian; a major proponent of "process theology," a concept derived from the philosopher Alfred North Whitehead, he wrote more than 20 books and 100 articles. His lifelong goal was to prove that God exists, and that God is dynamic rather than static, a partner in cosmic evolution rather than its omnipotent overlord, and a being who suffers along with humankind: d. Austin, TX, October 10.

Haza, Ofra (41), Israeli pop singer; a Sephardic Jew of Yemenite descent, she merged traditional Middle Eastern and Arabic music with pop tunes and dance rhythms to become a world star, with hits in Asia, Europe, and the United States. Her 1985 album *Fifty Gates of Wisdom* was an international success: d. Tel Aviv, Israel, February 23.

Hearst, Randolph A. (85), newspaper publisher; son of legendary newspaper owner William Randolph Hearst, he was chief executive of Hearst Publishing and ran his father's flagship paper, the *San Francisco Examiner*. In 1974 his 19-year-old daughter Patricia was kidnapped for more than a year by a radical political group calling itself the Symbionese Liberation Army. *Forbes* magazine estimated his worth in 1999 at $1.6 billion: d. New York City, December 18.

Heitz, Joseph (81), wine maker; as founder of Heitz Cellars he helped make the Napa Valley area of California famous as a source of fine wines: d. St. Helena, CA, December 16.

Hemingway, Jack (77), conservationist and author; son of author Ernest, he was the father of actresses Margaux and Mariel. An avid sport fisherman, he served as Idaho Fish and Game Commissioner (1971–77), and was a noted conservationist: d. New York City, December 1.

Henning, Doug (52), Canadian-born magician; a master illusionist, he appeared in three Broadway shows and in television specials: d. Los Angeles, February 7.

Herling, Gustaw (81), Polish-born prisoner and author; captured by Russian troops in the early days of World War II, he was sentenced to hard labor in a Soviet prison camp near the Arctic Circle. He escaped in 1942 and joined a Polish military force that eventually took part in the Allied assault on Italy in 1943. After the war, he moved to England, where he wrote *World Apart*, a well-received memoir of his time in the Gulag: d. Naples, Italy, July 4.

Hernandez, Amalia (83), Mexican choreographer; she founded the Ballet Folklorico de Mexico in 1952, guiding its popularity first in Mexico and then around the world. The group specialized in Mexican folk dance: d. Mexico City, November 4.

Hinton, Milt (90), jazz bassist; for seven decades he was a noted jazz musician, working with such figures as Louis Armstrong, Count Basie, Duke Ellington, Frank Sinatra, and Barbra Streisand. He also turned his photography hobby into a second career, documenting jazz life and the societal changes he had lived through: d. New York City, December 19.

Hovhaness, Alan (born Alan Chakmakjian) (89), composer; prolific creator of some 500 works, including operas, ballets, religious choral pieces, and nearly 70 symphonies. Trained at the New England Conservatory, he was strongly influenced by Indian, East Asian, and Armenian music. Strong elements of Christian and nature mysticism run through his works: d. Seattle, WA, June 21.

Irons, Evelyn (99), British journalist; best known for her coverage of World War II for the *London Standard* newspaper, she accompanied the First French Army through Germany and Austria, becoming the first woman war-correspondent to win the Croix de Guerre. She later was New York bureau chief for the *London Sunday Times*: d. Brewster, NY, April 3.

Isaksson, Ulla (born Ulla Lundberg) (83), Swedish writer; although primarily a novelist, she is probably best known for two motion-picture screenplays she wrote for director Ingmar Bergman, *Brink of Life* and *The Virgin Spring*: d. Stockholm, Sweden, April 20.

Jones, Robert Trent (93) golf-course architect; he designed or rebuilt more than 400 golf courses in 43 states and 34 countries during a career that spanned seven decades. Known for his challenging course designs, Jones' work played a role in the sport's major events: d. Fort Lauderdale, FL, June 14.

Kane, Gil (born Eli Katz) (73), Latvian-born comic-book artist; self taught, he made himself into a superb figure-drawer and was known for the kinetic quality of his work, with action that burst out of the standard boxes. He gave dynamism to such characters as the Hulk, Spider-Man, Conan, and Green Lantern while working for DC Comics and Marvel: d. Miami, FL, January 31.

Karski, Jan (86), member of the Polish Underground and university professor; as an officer in the Polish Underground during World War II, he infiltrated the Jewish Ghetto in Warsaw in 1942, and later gained entry, for a day, into a concentration camp in Izbica where Jews were being killed. He escaped to the West, where he reported to the British and U.S. governments. He taught history at Georgetown University from the mid-1950s until 1984: d. Washington, DC, July 13.

Kedrova, Lila (82), Russian-born actress; best known for her Oscar-winning performance in the film, *Zorba the Greek*. After her family fled from the Russian Revolution to Paris, she became a successful stage actress in France and England: d. Sault St. Marie, Ontario, February 16.

Kelly, Fred (83), dancer and choreographer; younger brother of actor/dancer Gene Kelly, he began his show-business career as one of the Five Dancing Kellys, then went on to direct television shows and choreograph for the Ice Capades and the Latin Quarter nightclub. Legend has it he created the cha-cha: d. Tucson, AZ, March 15.

Kennedy, Florynce (Flo) (84), civil-rights advocate and feminist; a 1951 graduate of Columbia University Law School and the only black woman in her class, she went on to represent civil-rights leader H. Rap Brown and the Black Panthers in the 1960: d. New York City, December 21.

Kety, Seymour S. (84), psychobiologist; as the first director of the National Institute of Mental Health, he shifted the direction of psychiatric research in the 1950s by emphasizing the biological basis of mental illness. His work on the importance of heredity in schizophrenia showed there was a physical basis to the disease: d. Westwood, MA, May 25.

Kieser, Ellwood (71), Catholic priest and film producer; an imposing 6′ 7″ (2 m) clergyman, he founded the nonprofit Paulist Productions (named after his religious order) in 1968 in order to make socially oriented, religiously committed films. The company produced *Insight*, a public-service television series that won six Emmy Awards over 23 years. He produced the feature films *Romero*, about the assassination of an El Salvadorian archbishop, and *Entertaining Angels*, a biography of the Catholic lay-activist Dorothy Day. He established the Humanitas Prize in 1974 to honor screenwriters who promoted human values: d. Los Angeles, September 16.

Kleindienst, Richard (76), former U.S. attorney general; as President Nixon's attorney general, he served (1972–73) during the Watergate scandal. When he learned of the break-in shortly after it occurred, Kleindienst rejected suggestions that presidential aides involved be protected from prosecution: d. Prescott, AZ, February 4.

Klemperer, Werner (80), German-born actor; son of the famous German classical conductor Otto Klemperer, he pursued an eclectic career in films, stage, and television, but was best known for portraying the bumbling Nazi prisoner-of-war camp commander Col. Klink on the TV sitcom *Hogan's Heroes*. On stage he appeared in *Uncle Vanya* and a revival of *Cabaret*, he played the role of Adolf Eichmann in the film *Operation Eichmann*: d. New York City, December 6.

© Photofest

Knipling, Edward (90), scientist, National Medal of Science-winning researcher who developed pesticide-free ways of controlling the insect population bugs via sterilization: d. Arlington, VA, March 17.

Kray, Reggie (66), British gangster; with his identical-twin brother Ronnie and older brother Charlie, he ran East London's underworld in the 1950s and 1960s. Although the brothers projected images as dapper Robin Hood types, their control of protection and extortion rackets was based on the use of ferocious violence. Ronnie and Charlie both died in prison; Reggie had been granted parole August 26 after serving 32 years for murder. The twin brothers were immortalized as the Piranha Brothers in a Monty Python skit: d. Norwich, England, October 1.

Kujau, Konrad (62), German swindler; in 1983 he sold 60 volumes of the supposed *Hitler Diaries* to *Stern* magazine for $4.8 million; the diaries were also published in the *Times of London*. Soon after, however, chemical tests showed the diaries were fake, and he was arrested and sentenced in 1985 to four-and-a-half years in prison; he served three years. He ran unsuccessfully for mayor of Stuttgart in 1996: d. Stuttgart, Germany, September 12.

Hedy Lamarr

Kung, Pin-Mai (98), Chinese-born Roman Catholic clergyman; was named bishop of Shanghai in 1949. He was created a cardinal by Pope John Paul II in 1979, while serving a life sentence in isolation in China; the nomination that was kept secret until 1991. Had been exiled to the United States in 1988: d. Stamford, CT, March 12.

Lamarr, Hedy (born Hedwig Eva Marie Kiesler) (86), actress; she epitomized sultry glamour during a string of 1930s and 1940s films, playing the female lead to such legends as Clark Gable, Charles Boyer, and Spencer Tracy: d. Altamonte, FL, January 19.

Landry, Tom (75), pro-football coaching legend; as the heart and soul of the Dallas Cowboys, Landry built "America's Team" from scratch in 1960, and coached it for three decades, including 20 consecutive winning seasons (1966-85), 18 playoff appearances, 13 division championships, and five Super Bowls—winning two: d. Dallas, TX, February 12.

© Ron Heflin/AP/Wide World Photos

Lardner, Ring, Jr. (85), blacklisted screenwriter; as a member of the Hollywood 10, he was blacklisted for nearly two decades from working in films, and served nine months in federal prison, because he refused to cooperate with the House Un-American Activities Committee's investigation of communism in 1950. Son of humorist and short-story writer Ring Lardner, he shared an Academy Award in 1942 for the screenplay of *Woman of the Year*, and won a second Oscar in 1970 for *M*A*S*H*. During the 1950s and 1960s he used a variety of pen names to conceal his identity. He also wrote two memoirs and novels: d. New York City, October 31.

Tom Landry

Laurin, Lucien (88), horse trainer; he was the remarkable Hall of Fame trainer who won six Triple Crown races with Riva Ridge and Secretariat from 1972–73: d. Miami, June 26.

Lawrence, Jacob (82), painter; a leading modern figurative painter, he was also a passionate visual chronicler of black life in America. A series of works in the 1950s and 1960s explored the themes of racial discrimination, intermarriage, and the civil-rights movement. He designed a 72-ft (22-m) mosaic scheduled to be placed in New York City's Times Square subway station in 2001: d. Seattle, WA, June 9.

Lemon, Bob (79), major-league baseball pitcher; as a Hall of Fame ace for the Cleveland Indians, Lemon was a 20–game winner seven times. He later managed the New York Yankees, guiding them to victory in the 1978 World Series: d. Long Beach, CA, January 11.

Levi, Ed (88), former U.S. attorney general; former President Gerald Ford labeled Levi a gifted and principled man. As attorney general, Levi was largely credited with rebuilding a Justice Department crippled by Watergate: d. Chicago, March 7.

Levitt, Alfred (105), painter and photographer; beginning as a realist painter, he adapted the Cubist style to American themes and played an important role in the development of American modernism during the 1940s: d. New York City, May 25.

Liebowitz, Jack (100), comics publisher; through his two publishing lines, Detective Comics and Action Comics, he revolutionized the comic-book industry in America, introducing *Superman* in 1938 and *Batman* a year later. He successfully sued rival Fawcett Publications in the 1940s to close down publication of *Captain Marvel*, claiming copyright infringement: d. Great Neck, NY, December 11.

Lindsay, John V. (79), mayor of New York City; as a liberal Republican he served three terms in the U.S. House of Representatives before becoming New York City mayor (1965–73). From the beginning it was a troubled administration as the city was paralyzed by a subway strike during his first 13 days in office. In 1968 a teachers' strike closed most of the city's schools for nearly two months. He oversaw a long-needed reorganization of the police department, and encouraged creative use of parks and other city spaces. Switching to the Democratic Party, he ran unsuccessfully for president in 1972 and U.S. Senate in 1980: d. Hilton Head, SC, December 19.

Linville, Larry (60), actor, was known for his portrayal of Maj. Frank Burns on television's *M*A*S*H*: d. New York City, April 10.

Lockley, Ronald (96), Welsh naturalist and writer; author of *Watership Down*, a fictional tale about a wandering group of rabbits, he also wrote the well-received nonfiction study, *The Private Life of the Rabbit*. A born naturalist, he founded Britain's first bird observatory: d. Auckland, New Zealand, April 12.

© Photofest

Julie London

London, Julie (born Julie Peck) (74), actress and singer; she was best known to audiences as nurse Dixie McCall on the 1970s television hospital drama *Emergency!*. This sultry-voiced actress had a hit record with the 1950s song "Cry Me a River": d. Los Angeles, October 18.

MacArthur, Jean (101), widow of Gen. Douglas MacArthur; she won admirers around the globe for her charm. Following her husband's death in 1964, she continued with social and civic duties related to his position: d. New York City, January 22.

MacNelly, Jeff (52), newspaper cartoonist; three-time winner of the Pulitzer Prize for editorial cartooning (1972, 1978, 1985), he also created the syndicated cartoon *Shoe*. He joined the staff of the *Chicago Tribune* in 1982: d. Baltimore, MD, June 8.

Maggio, Michael (49), theater director; an active talent in the Chicago theater community and associate artistic director of the nonprofit Goodman Theater since 1987, he directed a wide range of works, from Shakespeare to Beckett to Tom Stoppard, helping to make Chicago an active theatrical rival to New York. Born with cystic fibrosis, he was six months from death when he received a double-lung transplant in 1991: d. Chicago, August 19.

Marchand, Nancy (71), actress; she was critically praised during her career, which lasted five decades, as a character actress in plays by O'Casey, Shakespeare, Genet, and Chekhov. She won four Emmy awards for her television work as the publisher Mrs. Pynchon on *Lou Grant* and later portrayed the malevolent mother of a mob boss in the TV show *The Sopranos*: d. Stratford, CT, June 18.

Martin, Don (68), cartoonist; he sold his first cartoon to *Mad* magazine in 1956, eventually earning the title "Mad's maddest artist." He left *Mad* in 1987 for a rival magazine, *Cracked*, because of disagreements over reprint rights. Paperback collections of his cartoons have sold more than 7 million copies: d. Miami, FL, January 6.

Matthau, Walter (born Walter Matuschanskayasky) (79), actor; starting as a theater actor in the 1940s, he became a star playing the character of grouchy, rumpled Oscar Madison in the stage and film versions of *The Odd Couple*. He went on to make dozens of movies, costarring with Barbra Streisand in *Hello, Dolly*, George Burns in *The Sunshine Boys*, and Jack Lemmon in *Grumpy Old Men*. He won the 1966 Academy Award for Best Supporting Actor for his role as a crooked lawyer in *The Fortune Cookie*: d. Santa Monica, CA, July 1.

Maxwell, William (91), author and editor; as fiction editor at *The New Yorker* magazine, he became legendary for his work with such authors as John Updike, John Cheever, J.D. Salinger, and Eudora Welty. Along with his talent for polishing manuscripts, he was known for his tact in dealing with demonstrative writers. Among his own works were three

© Anthony Neste/HBO/Photofest

Nancy Marchand

collections of short stories, a memoir, and six novels, including *Time Will Darken It* and *So Long, See You Tomorrow*: d. New York City, July 31.

McAllister, Wayne (92), architect; he designed flamboyant commercial structures that redefined the landscapes of southern California and Las Vegas. His work ranged from neon-lit drive-ins, such as Simons in Los Angeles, to the Sands Hotel in Las Vegas: d. Arcadia, CA, March 22.

McCurdy, Ed (81), folk musician and actor; after a start singing in burlesque shows, he turned to folk music in the 1940s and became well known during the folk revival of the 1950s and early 1960s. He also was an actor and announcer on children's television shows, and after moving to Canada in 1984 he forged a new career as a TV character actor: d. Halifax, Nova Scotia, March 23.

Merrick, David (born David Margulois) (88), theatrical producer; from the 1950s until 1980 he dominated the Broadway theater, often producing six or more plays or musicals a season, and helping to launch careers for both Woody Allen and Barbra Streisand. His productions included *Gypsy*, *Hello, Dolly*, *Look Back in Anger*, *Rosencrantz and Guildenstern Are Dead*, and *42nd Street*: d. London, April 26.

Meyer, Michael (79), British translator of Ibsen; working with the British Broadcasting Company, he translated all 16 of Ibsen's major plays, as well as 18 plays by Strindberg. In 1971 he published a well-received biography of Ibsen, followed by one of Strindberg in 1985: d. London, August 3.

Mielke, Erich (92), East German spymaster; as minister for state security in East Germany, he built up and ran the secret agency called the "Stasi." He served four years in jail after German reunification in 1990: d. Berlin, May 21.

Miller, Merton H. (77), winner of the 1990 Nobel Prize in Economics for his analysis of ways to judge the value of corporations. His ideas, first presented in 1958 and developed in 1961, helped ease investors' fears of corporate borrowing, and led to the popularity of junk bonds and arbitrage: d. Chicago, June 3.

Mitchell, Stephen A. (54), psychoanalytic theorist; a leader of the relational approach in psychoanalysis, he reached a wide professional and popular audience through his books and lectures: d. New York City, December 21.

Montgomery, George (born George Letz) (84), film and television actor; after a short career boxing, he appeared as a stuntman in dozens of low-budget Westerns from 1935–40, when he switched to acting. His most notable performance was as detective Philip Marlowe in *The Brasher Doubloon* in 1947. In the late 1950s he appeared on television, and was a regular on the series *Cimarron City*. He later became a successful furniture-maker and sculptor: d. Rancho Mirage, CA, December 12.

Moyes, Patricia (77), British mystery writer; creator of Detective Chief Superintendent Harry Tibbet and his wife, Emmy, Moyes was known for her cozy, civilized, meticulously plotted mysteries. She wrote 19 novels, including *Dead Men Don't Ski* and *Many Deadly Returns*, which won an Edgar Allan Poe Special Award from the Mystery Writers of America. Her stories appeared in *Alfred Hitchcock* and *Ellery Queen* magazines: d. Virgin Gorda, British Virgin Islands, August 2.

Mulligan, Richard (67), actor; during a 40-year career in films, theater, and television, he won Emmy Awards in 1980 and 1989 for his work on the TV sitcoms *Soap* and *Empty Nest*. His film work included portrayals of a Hollywood producer in *S.O.B.* and of George Armstrong Custer in *Little Big Man*: d. Los Angeles, September 28.

Nagako (97), dowager empress of Japan; daughter of a Japanese prince, she married Crown Prince Hirohito in 1924, becoming empress of Japan two years later. She is the mother of the present emperor, Akihito. A talented artist, she published three collections of paintings: d. Tokyo, June 16.

Nash, N. Richard (87), playwright and novelist; after writing a number of moderately successful plays in the 1940s, he achieved fame in 1954 with *The Rainmaker*, a romantic fable about a naive farm girl and a charming con man: d. New York City, December 11.

Nelson, Lars-Erik (59), newspaper columnist; after ten years as an international correspondent with the news agency Reuters, he joined the *New York Daily News* in 1979 and remained with the paper—except for two years as a columnist for *Newsday*: d. Bethesda, MD, November 20.

Nicholas, Harold (79), dancer; younger member of the tap-dancing act The Nicholas Brothers. Beginning in the early 1930s, he and his brother Fayard dazzled audiences with dance routines that combined jazz, tap, acrobatics, and ballet. They performed at the Cotton Club in New York, on Broadway, and in the movies, where they broke the color bar against blacks dancing with whites by performing with Gene Kelly in the 1948 film *The Pirate*: d. New York City, July 3.

© Photofest

David Merrick

© Julie Markes/AP/Wide World Photos

Walter Matthau

Nitzsche, Jack (63), musician; beginning in 1962 he was music arranger for record producer Phil Spector, creating the thunderous Wall of Sound that was a staple of such hits as *He's a Rebel* and *River Deep, Mountain High*. Was studio keyboardist and arranger for such groups and stars as the Rolling Stones, Buffalo Springfield, Neil Young, the Monkees, and others. With Sonny Bono he cowrote the pop hit *Needles and Pins*, and he won the Academy Award for Best Song in 1982 for *Up Where We Belong*, cowritten with his wife, singer Buffy Sainte-Marie: d. Los Angeles, August 25.

Obuchi, Keizo (62), Japanese politician; a shrewd consensus-builder known for his lack of charisma and strong personal beliefs, he became prime minister of Japan on July 30, 1998, and served until he suffered a stroke in April 2000: d. Tokyo, May 14.

Oppenheimer, Harry (91), billionaire tycoon and philanthropist; he ran the world's largest diamond and gold mines and used his fortunes to vocally oppose apartheid in his South African homeland: d. Johannesburg, South Africa, August 19.

Padilla, Heberto (68), Cuban poet and exile; a friend since boyhood of Fidel Castro, he supported the 1959 Cuban Revolution and was a correspondent for the Communist Party newspaper, *Granma*. Falling out of favor with Castro, he was jailed in 1971. After leaving Cuba in 1980 he lived and taught literature in the United States: d. Auburn, AL, September 25.

Pais, Abraham (82), Dutch-born physicist and historian of science; he survived being captured by the Gestapo in 1945, and afterward went to the United States to do research at Princeton and Rockefeller Universities. In the 1950s he helped build the foundations of the modern theory of elementary particles, but he is best known to the public for his 1982 biography of Albert Einstein, *Subtle Is the Lord*: d. Copenhagen, Denmark, July 28.

Pastore, John (93), politician; a power in Rhode Island and national politics for three decades, he was the first Italian-American to be elected a governor, serving from 1945–50, and the first to become a U.S. senator. A liberal Democrat and chairman of the Joint Committee on Atomic Energy, he provided key support in 1963 for President John Kennedy's treaty with the Soviet Union banning nuclear tests above ground: d. North Kingstown, RI, July 15.

Patterson, Frank (61), Irish singer; called "Ireland's Golden Tenor" by his fans, he was best known for a repertoire that balanced light-classical songs with sentimental ballads, although he also sang Berlioz, Bach, and Schubert: d. New York City, June 10.

Peters, Jean (73), film actress; a contract player with 20th Century Fox, she appeared in costume epics, comedies, and Westerns of the late 1940s and early 1950s. In 1957 she secretly married reclusive billionaire Howard Hughes; the marriage ended in divorce in 1971: d. Carlsbad, CA, October 13.

Petty, Lee (86), stock-car racer; he began racing professionally in 1949, and by his retirement in 1964 had won 54 NASCAR races (including the first Daytona 500) and three national championships. Forefather of three generations of NASCAR/Winston Cup racers: d. Greensboro, NC, April 5.

Pham Van Dong (94), prime minister of North Vietnam and, later, Vietnam (1954–87); he joined with Ho Chi Minh beginning in the 1920s with the aim of bringing about a Marxist revolution in Vietnam. As a leader of the communist Viet Minh, he helped defeat both the French colonial regime in 1954 and the U.S.-supported government in South Vietnam in 1975: d. Hanoi, Vietnam, April 29.

Powell, Anthony (94), English novelist; he is best known for a 12-volume work collectively titled *A Dance to the Music of Time*, which follows the lives of a group of schoolmates from youth and World War I to old age in the Britain of the 1970s: d. Frome, England, March 28.

Puente, Ernest (Tito) (77), Latin musician; legendary percussionist and band leader, he popularized mambo music and helped fuse Latin rhythms with jazz after forming his own band in 1948. Known as "El Rey" (The King), he recorded 118 albums and CDs and won five Grammy Awards: d. New York City, May 31.

© Hayden Roger Celestin/Corbis-Sygma

Tito Puente

Purdy, Al (81), Canadian poet; author of 33 books of verse, beginning with *The Enchanted Echo* in 1944, he was considered one of Canada's greatest English-language poet. He won the Governor General's Award for Poetry in 1965 and 1986: d. Sidney, British Columbia, April 21.

Quine, Willard Van Orman (92), philosopher; developed a system of truth and knowledge based on radi-cal empiricism. He taught philosophy at Harvard beginning in 1936: d. Boston, MA, December 25.

© Mark Wilson/Reuters/Archive Photos

Leah Rabin

Rabin, Leah (72), wife of slain Israeli Prime Minister Yitzhak Rabin; a homemaker turned peace activist, she enthusiastically advocated Israeli-Arab relations, and counted many world leaders among her friends. She also endured harsh detractors, who accused her of being controversial and divisive: d. Tel Aviv, November 12.

Rampal, Jean-Pierre (78), classical musician; he almost single-handedly brought the flute back to prominence as a solo instrument, playing and recording jazz, folk tunes, Indian music, and his favorite, Baroque music, in a career that began after World War II: d. Paris, May 20.

Reeves, Steve (74), actor and bodybuilder; after winning the Mr. America and Mr. Universe bodybuilding titles, he starred in a low-budget Italian film about Hercules that became a surprise hit when it was dubbed into English and released in the United States in 1959, giving rise to a decade of sword-and-sandal epics: d. Escondido, CA, May 1.

Reisner, Marc (51), environmental writer; in 1986 he wrote *Cadillac Desert*, a scathing indictment of the environmental costs of water projects in the American West. The book was chosen in 1999 as one of the 100 best English-language nonfiction books of the 20th century, and was the basis for a PBS documentary in 1997. He lectured widely on environmental topics: d. San Anselmo, CA, July 21.

Richard, Maurice (78), Canadian-born hockey star; known to fans as the "Rocket," he was an overpowering scorer for the Montreal Canadiens in the 1940s and 1950s. In an 18-year career, he scored 544 regular-season goals, 82 play-off goals (in 133 games), was the first player to score 50 goals in a season, and led the league in goals five times: d. Montreal, Quebec, May 27.

Robards, Jason (78), stage and film actor; son of actor Jason Robards, Sr., he electrified the theater world in 1956 with his performance as Hickey in an off-Broadway production of Eugene O'Neill's *The Iceman Cometh*, and went on to become O'Neill's foremost interpreter in productions of *Long Day's Journey Into Night* and *A Touch of the*

© Warner Brothers/AP/Wide World Photos

Jason Robards

Poet. He also made his mark in Hollywood, winning back-to-back Oscars for his performances in *All the President's Men* (1976) and *Julia* (1977). His last film was *Magnolia*, which he did while severely ill with cancer: d. Bridgeport, CT, December 26.

Robinson, Vicki Sue (46), pop singer; her 1976 dance hit, *Turn the Beat Around*, was an anthem of the disco era. She began her career as a folk singer, then performed on Broadway in the musicals *Hair* and *Jesus Christ Superstar*. In 1999 she had a successful off-Broadway show, *Vicki Sue Robinson: Behind the Beat*: d. Wilton, CT, April 27.

Rowan, Carl (75), journalist; after serving in World War II as one of the first African-American commissioned naval officers, he studied journalism under the G.I. Bill. As a young reporter, he covered civil-rights battles in the South, which prompted President John Kennedy to appoint him a deputy assistant secretary of state. Returning to journalism in 1965, he became a nationally syndicated columnist and a television commentator on *Inside Washington*: d. Washington, DC, September 23.

Ruff, Charles (61), White House counsel; he became familiar to millions of Americans for his defense of President Clinton during the Senate impeachment trial of January 1999. In a wide-ranging career, he defended many public figures. After contracting an unknown virus in Africa, where he had gone to teach law in the 1960s, he used a wheelchair for the rest of his life: d. Washington, DC, November 19.

Runcie, Lord Robert (78), British churchman; Archbishop of Canterbury and spiritual leader of the Anglican Church (1980–91), he was a reformer who favored the ordination of women and reconciliation with the Roman Catholic Church. He fell out with the Conservative government of Prime Minister Margaret Thatcher. In 1981 he presided over the marriage of Prince Charles and Diana Spencer: d. St. Albans, England, July 11.

Runciman, Sir Steven (97), British historian; a specialist in Byzantine history and culture, he won praise for his three-volume *History of the Crusades* in the 1950s, and for *The Fall of Constantinople* in 1965. He also wrote on the Balkans and Borneo: d. Radway, England, November 1.

Schindler, Alexander M. (75), German-born Reform rabbi; he was a leader of the Reform movement in American Judaism as president of the Union of American Hebrew Congregations (1973–96). Supported the ordination of women as rabbis: d. Westport, CT, November 15.

Schulz, Charles M. (77), creator of the Peanuts comic strip: d. Santa Rosa, CA, Feb. 12 2000. (*See* THE LIFE AND LEGACY OF CHARLES M. SCHULZ, page 78).

Sealy, Malik (30), basketball player; a college star as a guard at St. John's University, he was picked 14th in the 1992 National Basketball Association draft by the Indiana Pacers. He joined the Minnesota Timberwolves in 1999, and averaged 11.3 points a game: d. Minneapolis, MN, May 20.

Segal, George (75), sculptor; a major representative of the pop-art school; his sculptures were based on full-body casts of ordinary people, which he placed in carefully assembled environments of chairs, beds, brick walls, and even a subway car. He was awarded a National Medal of the Arts in 1999: d. South Brunswick, NJ, June 9.

Shapiro, Karl (86), poet; won the 1945 Pulitzer Prize in poetry for his book *V-Letter and Other Poems*, written while he was a soldier in the Pacific during World War II: d. New York City, May 24.

Shuker, Gregory B. (67), documentary filmmaker; he was one of the early developers of the cinema vérité documentary style, which sought to capture unrehearsed, unscripted events. His films include *The Chair*, about the legal struggle to prevent a prisoner's execution, and *Crisis*, which covered the Kennedy administration's struggle over desegregation: d. Bronx, NY, March 29.

Simon, William E. (72), financial investor and cabinet member; a successful bond trader on Wall Street, he was appointed secretary of the treasury by President Richard Nixon in 1974, as such he dealt with a lingering recession and the aftereffects of the Arab oil embargo: d. Santa Barbara, CA, June 3.

Staples, Roebuck "Pops" (85), gospel and soul singer; as a teenager, he began singing with a local gospel group in his native Mississippi. After moving to Chicago, he formed the Staples Singers in 1948 with his wife and two of his children. The group allied itself with the civil-rights movement in the 1960s, and in the 1970s turned to singing soul music. In the 1990s the group was inducted into the Rock and Roll Hall of Fame: d. Dolton, IL, December 19.

Stevens, Craig (born Gail Shikles Jr.) (81), actor; best known for playing the tough but debonair private detective Peter Gunn in the television series (1958–61). He also acted on Broadway and in films: d. Los Angeles, May 10.

Stewart, Nick (90), actor; he was the voice of Br'er Bear in the 1946 Disney animated film *Song of the South*, but probably was best known as Lightnin', the janitor on television's all-black *Amos 'n' Andy* show in the early 1950s. He used his television money to found the Ebony Showcase Theater in Los Angeles, which provided training and experience for numerous black performers (1950–96): d. Los Angeles, December 18.

Takeshita, Noboru (76), Japanese politician; a legendary kingmaker in postwar Japanese politics, he was prime minister from 1987 until forced to resign two years later in the midst of a financial scandal. He retained his influence within the dominant Liberal Democratic Party, however, and handpicked a succession of prime ministers: d. Tokyo, June 19.

Thomas, Derrick (33), pro-football player; one of the game's most dominant linebackers, he was an All-American at Alabama, and became a star as a pass-rushing specialist for the Kansas City Chiefs after being taken in the first round of the 1989 draft. He was an All-Pro in his first nine seasons and recorded an astounding 126$\frac{1}{2}$ sacks during his career. He set the single-game sack record of seven against Seattle in 1990: d. Miami, FL, February 8.

Titov, Gherman Stepanovich (65), Soviet cosmonaut; after training as a fighter pilot, he was drafted into Russia's top-secret man-in-space program, and in August 1961 became the second man to orbit the Earth when he spent 25 hours in space. Afterward, he joined the design department of the space program, where he helped create a Soviet version of the U.S. space shuttle. After the fall of the Soviet Union, he was elected to parliament as a Communist Party representative: d. Moscow, September 20.

Trevor, Claire (born Claire Wemlinger) (91), actress; known for playing hard-boiled but warmhearted career girls in Hollywood films of the 1930s and 1940s, she won the Academy Award for Best Supporting Actress for *Key Largo* (1948). She also worked in radio, theater, and television: d. Newport Beach, CA, April 8.

Trout, Robert (91), broadcast journalist; over a career that lasted nearly 70 years, he covered Franklin Roosevelt's inauguration, the D-Day invasion of France, and the funerals of both Roosevelt and Winston Churchill. One of the elite group of reporters called "Murrow's Boys," because they had been hired by legendary newsman Edward R. Murrow, he began work in the CBS news department in the early 1930s and was still delivering occasional reports in the 1990s: d. New York City, November 14.

Turrentine, Stanley (66), jazz tenor saxophonist; he played in a blues- and gospel-influenced style that made him popular beyond the limits of the jazz world. He began his career as a teenager in a band that included the young Ray Charles on piano. His 1970 album *Sugar*, made with George Benson, was his biggest hit, setting the stage for what became known as smooth jazz: d. New York City, September 12.

Ulam, Adam B. (77), Polish-born historian; a longtime professor at Harvard, he was best known for his insights into the Soviet Union: d. Cambridge, MA, March 28.

van Vogt, A.E. (87), Canadian-born science-fiction writer; a leading writer of the "Golden Age" of science fiction, which lasted from 1939 to 1951, he was known for his fast-moving, even visceral, tales of confrontations between humans and aliens. His novels include *Slan*, *The World of Null-A*, and *The Weapon Shops of Isher*: d. Los Angeles, February 2.

Verdon, Gwen (75), dancer and actress; regarded by many as Broadway's finest dancer, she began performing at the age of 3, but was 28 when she became a star in the 1953 musical *Can-Can*. With *Damn Yankees* in 1955 her career became linked with that of choreographer Bob Fosse. They worked on *New Girl in Town*, *Redhead*, *Sweet Charity*, and *Chicago*. She won four Tony Awards, and also appeared in films and on television: d. Woodstock, VT, October 18.

Wechsler, Herbert (90), legal scholar; as a professor at Columbia University Law School, his work on criminal and constitutional law was a major influence on the U.S. legal system in the 1960s and 1970s. His arguments influenced the 1964 Supreme Court decision on *The New York Times v. Sullivan*, a major case concerning freedom of the press: d. New York City, April 26.

Werner, Ruth (born Ursula Kuczynski) (93), German-born Soviet spy; during 20 years as an intelligence operative for the Soviet Union in China, Poland, Switzerland, and England, she helped set up numerous spy rings and passed on important atomic bomb data to Moscow during World War II. She settled in East Germany in the 1950s: d. Berlin, July 7.

Gwen Verdon

© Bob De Stolfe/The Kobal Collection, Ltd.

Wills, Frank (52), foiled Watergate break-in; in 1972, as a security guard in Washington's Watergate office complex, he called police after twice finding tape over a basement door lock. Five men were arrested that night for breaking into the sixth-floor headquarters of the Democratic National Committee; the arrests eventually led to the resignation of President Richard Nixon in 1974: d. North Augusta, SC, September 27.

Wilson, Robert R. (85), nuclear physicist; he led the Manhattan Project and served as director of the National Accelerator Laboratory (Fermilab): d. Ithaca, NY, January 16.

Whyte, William F. (86), sociologist; an academic with a passion for reform, he spent over a year living in Boston's North End to gather material on street-gang life, which became the best-selling book, *Street Corner Society*, published in 1943. Calling his research method "participatory action research," he expanded his ideas in a research textbook called *Learning from the Field*: d. Ithaca, NY, July 16.

Williams, Hosea (74), civil-rights leader; the chief organizer of Martin Luther King's civil-rights marches in the 1960s, he was at the Memphis motel when King was shot in 1968. He was executive director of the Southern Christian Leadership Council until ousted in 1979, and served in the Georgia General Assembly from 1974–84. He continued to lead drives for improved housing and working conditions for black people: d. Atlanta, GA, November 16.

© Corbis-Bettmann

Loretta Young

Windsor, Marie (born Emily Bertelsen) (80), actress; as star of dozens of low-budget films in the 1940s and 1950s, she earned the informal title "Queen of the Bs." She later appeared in more than 100 television shows: d. Beverly Hills, CA, December 10.

Yohe, Thomas (63), creator of "Schoolhouse Rock"; while working at an advertising agency in New York, he created a song about the number three in order to help a colleague's child learn multiplication. The song, with added animation, became the basis for ABC's educational children's show, *Schoolhouse Rock*, produced from 1973 through 1985: d. Norwalk, CT, December 20.

Young, Loretta (born Gretchen Young) (87), actress; a Hollywood star of the 1930s and 1940s, she made the transition to television in the 1950s, enchanting a new generation of admirers with *The Loretta Young Show*. She first appeared on screen at the age of four, and by 1928 was a leading lady. She won the Academy Award for Best Actress for *The Farmer's Daughter* in 1947; in 1953 she won the first of three television Emmys, making her the first actress to win both an Oscar and an Emmy: d. Los Angeles, August 12.

Zatopek, Emil (78), Olympic track champion; he was a four-time Olympic champion who set 18 world records on the track, and was the first ever to run the 10 000–m race in under 29 minutes. Zatopek enjoyed cult status in his Czech homeland: d. Prague, November 21.

Zumwalt, Elmo (79), former chief of U.S. naval operation; he was appointed by President Nixon in 1970 to oversee the U.S. Navy, and was best known for his efforts to modernize the service and for ordering the spraying of Agent Orange in Vietnam: d. Durham, NC, January 2.

Oceanography

U.S. congressional involvement in oceanography surged in 2000. A highlight was August 7, when President Bill Clinton signed into law PL 106–256, setting up a 16-member commission to review federal ocean policies and make recommendations to Congress for changes. Sen. Ernest F. Hollings (D-SC) had introduced the bill.

Earlier, in July, congressional leaders of the new House of Representatives Oceans Caucus joined forces with scientists and ocean advocates during an all-day conference titled "Oceans for the New Millennium: Developing and Implementing Ocean Policy." Hosted by the American Geophysical Union (AGU) and the American Association for the Advancement of Science (AAAS), the conference included keynote presentations and four panel discussions on themes identified by the caucus as critical to the ocean community—biology, pollution, security, and governance.

The 50-member bipartisan caucus—chaired by Representatives Sam Farr (D-CA), Curt Weldon (R-PA), Thomas Allen (D-ME), and James Greenwood (R-PA)—was to craft a legislative agenda to spur action in the 107th Congress, which would open in January 2001. Representative Greenwood introduced HR 2090, the Exploration of the Seas Act, which would initiate extensive research and exploration into the oceans. The proposed legislation was placed on the Senate legislative calendar in mid-September.

In May, Rep. Curt Weldon (R-PA) and Rep. James Saxton (R-NJ) held a joint hearing on the National Ocean Research Leadership Council Report, "An Integrated Ocean Observing System." According to the report, appropriate policy modifications, relatively modest increases in funding, and implementation of a management structure are essential to the development of a U.S. Ocean Observing System. Such a system could become a reality within ten years, and result in significant economic and environmental benefits to the United States.

To track the involvement of Congress in ocean-related activity, there are two sites on the Internet: http://thomas.loc.gov and www.legislative.noaa.gov.

Sustained Ocean Observing System for Climate. One of the first steps in achieving both a national and international Ocean Observing System was announced at a National Press Club briefing on Sept. 19, 2000. Plans were announced for the deployment of more than 1,000 drifting buoys for sea-surface temperature, pressure, and current measurements (installed by 2003); the deployment of 3,000 Argo floats for upper-ocean temperature and salinity profiling (by 2004); the deployment of 106 tropical moorings for measurements of the ocean, atmosphere, and ocean/atmosphere exchanges (by 2005); the establishment of 86 tide gauges for altimeter-drift calibration and documenting long-term trends in sea-level change (by 2006); as well as new coastal moorings, including calibration points and fixed sites, and additional volunteer observing ship lines.

When completed, this composite system will deliver continuous, long-term, climate-quality global data sets. The following suite of routine analyses of the ocean also will be offered:

- For the global ocean, four-times-daily analyses of sea-surface pressure, sea-surface wind, and marine weather and sea-state conditions.
- For the global tropics, weekly analyses of upper-ocean temperature and salinity, sea-surface temperature, and sea level.
- For the global ocean, weekly analyses of upper-ocean temperature and salinity, sea-surface temperature, and sea level.
- For the global ocean, an ocean carbon inventory once every ten years, and seasonal (four-times-yearly) analyses of the variability of ocean-atmosphere carbon exchanges.

Pew Oceans Commission. Late May 2000 saw the launch of the Pew Oceans Commission, a two-year initiative to assess, gauge potential economic impacts, and identify solutions to sustain biodiversity in U.S. seas. Established by the Pew Charitable Trusts, the commission assembled a 17-member panel, with New Jersey Gov. Christine Todd Whitman as chair and former White House Chief of Staff Leon Panetta as vice-chair. The Pew Oceans Commission is an independent group of distinguished Americans conducting a national dialogue on the policies needed to restore and protect living marine resources in U.S. waters. The commission identified six primary areas of inquiry—coastal development, unintended consequences of fishing, pollution, climate change, aquaculture, and invasive species. The commission's Web site is http://www.pewoceans.org.

JOHN KERMOND
National Oceanic and Atmospheric Administration (NOAA)

Pakistan

During 2000, Pakistan's fourth military regime, which had seized power on Oct. 12, 1999, was accorded legitimacy by the Supreme Court. The court, however, mandated a deadline of three years to return the country to civilian hands. Gen. Pervez Musharraf, self-designated chief executive of the regime, continued to give mixed signals. The political and economic record of his government's first year in control also was mixed, while both external- and internal-security issues remained problematic.

Political Scene. In Pakistan's cyclical political history, each return of the military to power has brought new experiences, along with a degree of déjà vu. While the regime that was in power in 2000 was unique for not having declared martial law, and for some of its reformist rhetoric, the effects were much the same.

In January the government ordered all judges to pledge loyalty to Musharraf and the Provisional Constitutional Order (PCO). The chief justice and five Supreme Court judges refused to do so, and were replaced. Nine justices of the four provincial high courts also lost their positions. In May the reconstituted Supreme Court validated the military takeover, but asked the government to restore civil rule within three years from the date of the coup. Chief Justice Irshad Hasan Khan argued that the overthrow of the civilian government of Mian Mohammad Nawaz Sharif had been justified by the "doctrine of necessity." The terms of the 2002 deadline appeared to have been negotiated with the government, and to have been outlined to persuade external powers that present military rule is only a temporary interlude in Pakistan's lurching progress toward a viable democratic system.

The government's ability to meet the deadline was not certain. It set an ambitious agenda of reform, including revival of the economy, rooting out of corruption, and establishment of an extensive local-government structure, reminiscent of Ayub Khan's "Basic Democracies" system. The 1973 constitution remained in effect, except where superseded by the PCO, and newspapers were free to criticize the government.

Musharraf himself articulated secular and liberal democratic goals for the country, but government actions and inactions on several fronts stirred speculation that real power lay with more conservative and fundamentalist generals. At one point, Musharraf announced that the draconian Blasphemy Law, by which people can be jailed or put to death for anti-Islamic statements, would be moderated, but he backed down in the face of fundamentalist pressures. Similarly, it was announced that the country would be "deweaponized" to restore civil order and public safety, but no subsequent steps were taken to implement that goal. To do so would have meant confronting heavily armed militant groups, and the thousands of *madrasas* (Islamic religious schools) training young people for holy war in Kashmir or elsewhere. On September 1, Musharraf reshuffled a number of senior generals. These and some other changes were interpreted as reducing fundamentalist influence in the ruling junta.

The local-government plan, announced March 23, was Musharraf's most-far-reaching program. It was intended to generate a bottom-up transformation of society. The plan entailed establishing new governmental

© K.M.Chaudary/AP/Wide World Photos

Pakistan's deposed Prime Minister Nawaz Sharif remained a focus of attention as he was sentenced to life imprisonment in April 2000. He later was sentenced to 14 years of hard labor and disqualified from politics for 21 years.

PAKISTAN • Information Highlights

Official Name: Islamic Republic of Pakistan.
Location: South Asia.
Area: 310,402 sq mi (803 940 km²).
Population (2000 est.): 141,553,775.
Chief Cities (1998 census): Islamabad, the capital, 204,364 (1981); Karachi, 9,269,000.
Government: *Head of state and government,* Gen. Pervez Musharraf, leader under martial law (took power October 1999). *Legislature*—suspended.
Monetary Unit: Rupee (58.15 rupees equal U.S.$1, Dec. 29, 2000).
Gross Domestic Product (1999 est. U.S.$): $282,000,000,000 (purchasing power parity).
Economic Index (1999, 1990 = 100): *Consumer Prices,* all items, 231.1; food, 237.9.
Foreign Trade (1999 U.S.$): *Imports,* $10,159,000,000; exports, $8,383,000,000.

structures at local, subdistrict *(tehsil)*, and district levels. The goal was to build a more civic culture in Pakistan by providing more people opportunities for participation and leadership. The plan had the enthusiastic support of such external organizations as the United Nations Development Program (UNDP) and the Asia Society. Critics questioned whether the program would simply entrench already-powerful local elites and destabilize Pakistan's shaky federal system by undermining the importance of provincial and national government. The system was also criticized for being too expensive and complex—some felt it would take up to three years to implement.

The government brought several cases against deposed Prime Minister Nawaz Sharif. It sought to impose the death penalty for his alleged attempt to kill Musharraf and others at the time of the coup. The court, instead, awarded Sharif two life sentences. In a later anticorruption trial, a special Accountability Court sentenced Sharif to 14 years of hard labor, banned him from politics for 21 years, and fined him 20 million rupees (about U.S.$3. 6 million).

Pakistan's two major political parties—Nawaz Sharif's Pakistan Muslim League (PML) and Benazir Bhutto's Pakistan People's Party (PPP)—were largely immobilized, with Sharif in jail and Bhutto in exile in London. Some PML politicians, including Ejaz ul-Haq, son of former President Muhammad Zia ul-Haq, sought to open dialogue with the military. Those close to deposed Prime Minister Sharif, including his wife Kulsoom, remained outspoken in their opposition. For much of the year the parties were prohibited from open political activity. Modified in August, the local government plan clarified that the elections would be held on nonpartisan basis. As the gap between the military government and the politicians widened, various political parties undertook to bridge earlier differences, and to form a common movement for the early restoration of democracy.

Economy. Revival of the Pakistani economy, devastated in turn by the former civilian governments of Bhutto and Sharif, had been one of the seven key goals announced by Musharraf following the October coup. Certainly there were some successes. Debts were rescheduled with several donor countries. The Karachi Stock Exchange rose more than 70% in the six months following the coup. The economy also was helped by a good agricultural year. However, major roadblocks were encountered in mid-2000. In an attempt to expand the tax base, the government announced that traders would need to document their economic activities. Widespread protests, including strikes and demonstrations, arose. One prominent businessman in Islamabad committed suicide in a government office, according to official reports, over the documentation issue.

In July, Finance Minister Shaukat Aziz presented a budget of 700 billion rupees (about U.S.$12.5 billion), focused on relief and investment. The budget increased development allocations by more than 19%. Debt servicing was expected to constitute 44% of the entire budget for the coming year.

The annual *Economic Survey*, released in June, projected Pakistan's economy to grow by 4.5% during the fiscal year ending June 30. Agriculture showed a 5.5% growth, and exports and imports grew by about 10% during the first ten months of the fiscal year. However, a later *Economic Review*, released in August, stressed the deterioration the country's economy had suffered during the previous three years. An average fiscal deficit of 6.6% during that period, aggravated by economic sanctions imposed after India's and Pakistan's nuclear tests in 1998, resulted in a real gross domestic product (GDP) growth of only 3.1%, barely above the country's population growth. These problems were not new. What remained uncertain was whether the regime in power could effect significant change.

The nation's economic survival hinged on the willingness of donor countries and agencies such as the International Monetary Fund (IMF) to provide further support. Such support came in late November when the IMF approved a $596 million loan which will help the country avoid defaulting on $36 billion owed foreign lenders.

International. Kashmir and Indo-Pakistani enmities continued to be the major security concerns of the region. A December 1999 hijacking of an Indian Airlines flight by Kashmiri militants brought Indian accusations of Pakistani involvement, and, in response, official Pakistani denials.

U.S. President Bill Clinton's visit to South Asia in March demonstrated both the intractability of long-standing regional problems and Pakistan's secondary status in the equation. Inclusion of Pakistan on the president's itinerary—at all—was controversial, given that it could be seen as endorsing the military's 1999 coup. After a four-day stay in India, President Clinton spent only a few hours in Islamabad on March 25, and offered the Pakistani generals more criticism and advice than support.

WILLIAM L. RICHTER
Kansas State University

Paraguay

In Paraguay, 2000 was a year of turmoil, filled with widespread protests over projected state reforms. Unrest in the armed forces led to another coup attempt.

Politics and Government. The Authentic Radical Liberal Party (PLRA) quit President Luis González Macchi's all-party coalition in February, having failed in its quest for the vice-presidency and 40% of public-sector posts. PLRA's defection left the governing coalition of the Colorado and National Encounter parties without a majority in the lower house of Congress.

Then, on May 18, cavalry and armored units—along with some police sympathetic to the fugitive former Gen. Lino Oviedo—

conspired to topple an unpopular government. The rebels shelled the legislative building and dropped grenades on the presidential palace. Order was restored in five hours, with support from neighboring nations as well as from the United States. González Macchi was granted extraordinary powers for 30 days to deal with the upheaval. From a hideaway in Brazil, Oviedo denied involvement in the coup attempt once it had failed. Authorities in both Paraguay and Brazil agreed that Oviedo should be detained, and he was taken to Brasília in June. He was held pending extradition to Paraguay, or to be placed on trial in Brazil for drug and money-laundering offenses.

In a closely watched contest on August 13 for the vacant vice-presidency, Julio César "Yoyito" Franco of the opposition PLRA finished slightly ahead of the Colorado party's Felix Argaña, son of the former vice-president. Luis María Argaña had been slain in March 1999.

Economy. At the center of urban and rural unrest was the government's privatization scheme, which embraced state companies functioning in the areas of railways, water, and telephones. In January, public and peasant organizations demanded the resignation of President González Macchi, questioning his ability to rule the country. In May the senate proceeded to approve the administration's privatization bill, as some 3,000 protesters demonstrated outside.

Foreign Affairs. President González Macchi paid a state visit to Europe in October. He attempted to interest investors in Spain and Germany in opportunities presented by ongoing privatizations and in other private investment activities available in Paraguay.

Cuba and Paraguay restored diplomatic relations after 39 years on October 19. Paraguay expected that the new level of relations with Cuba would help commercial exchanges. Following reestablishment of consular relations in 1996, the number of Paraguayan students attending medical school on the island increased. More than 50 Cuban doctors were working in Paraguay with the approval of public-health authorities in both countries.

Following a confrontation with its bigger partners in the Southern Cone Common Market (Mercosur), Paraguay was granted a 23% tariff on imported autos, rather than the prevailing 35%.

LARRY L. PIPPIN, *University of the Pacific*

PARAGUAY • Information Highlights

Official Name: Republic of Paraguay.
Location: Central South America.
Area: 157,046 sq mi (406 750 km²).
Population (2000 est.): 5,585,828.
Chief Cities (1992 census): Asunción, the capital, 550,060 (1997); Ciudad del Este, 133,881; San Lorenzo, 133,395.
Government: *Head of state and government,* Luis González Macchi, president (sworn in March 28, 1999). *Legislature*—Congress: Chamber of Senators and Chamber of Deputies.
Monetary Unit: Guaraní (3,510.0000 guaraníes equal U.S.$1, Nov. 6, 2000).
Gross Domestic Product (1999 est. U.S.$): $19,900,000,000 (purchasing power parity).
Economic Index (Asunción, 1998, 1990 = 100): *Consumer Prices,* all items, 303.1; food, 275.1.
Foreign Trade (1997 U.S.$): *Imports,* $3,403,000,000; *exports,* $1,089,000,000.

People, Places, and Things

The following four pages recount the stories behind a selection of people, places, and things that may not have made the headlines in 2000 but that drew attention and created interest.

The Confederate submarine "H.L. Hunley," above, the first sub to sink an enemy vessel, was raised by crane at the former Charleston Naval Base, Charleston, SC, during the summer 2000. The "Hunley," with an eight-man crew, had sunk on Feb. 17, 1864, after ramming a harpoonlike torpedo into the side of the USS "Housatonic," a Union blockade ship, during a Civil War battle. The cause of the sub's sinking has been a mystery, but the vessel itself was a prototype for those that followed. A team hired by novelist Clive Cussler had located the sub in 1995. It was expected to take at least seven years of preservation efforts before the sub could go on museum display. More current technology was the focus at the science branch of the German Pavilion at Expo 2000, a world's fair, in Hanover, Germany, right. For the first time in the 149-year history of world's fairs, the United States did not participate. Some 180 countries and organizations were represented, however.

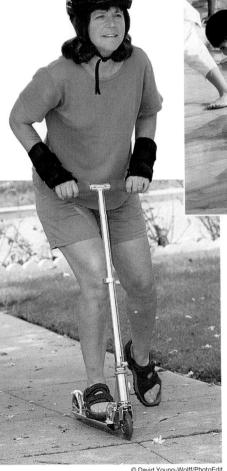

Jonathan G. Lebed, a 15-year-old from Cedar Grove, NJ, flanked by friends, top left, successfully made $272,826 in illegal stock-market profits by dealing in penny stocks on the Internet and then using chat rooms to push up the value of those stocks. The boy settled the case with regulators by returning his profits, plus $12,174 in interest, without admitting wrongdoing. Author Stephen King and his publisher, Simon & Schuster, also were using the Internet for profit as King's book, "Riding the Bullet," top right, was published electronically as an eBook. Kids had their own trends, especially in sports where classes in karate, above, and other martial arts, for those under 12 were growing at the annual rate of 15%. The scooter craze, left, which began in Japan and moved to the U.S. mainland in late 1999, hit various ages. More than 2 million scooters were expected to be sold in the United States in 2000. They would be used for transportation as well as for fun. Parents, however, became concerned as scooter injuries among children increased visits to hospital emergency rooms.

For fun art, it was the year of the animal. Accordingly, a 43-ft- (13-m-) tall topiary sculpture of a West Highland terrier graced New York City's Rockefeller Center during the summer. "Puppy," above, featured some 70,000 fresh flowers—including marigolds, impatiens, petunias, and begonias. It was the work of artist Jeff Koons, a New Yorker who previously had displayed the sculpture in Germany and Australia and has another version on permanent view at the Guggenheim Museum in Bilbao, Spain. Koons said he had imagined Louis XIV telling his staff that he wanted "to see a floral puppy in the garden." Meanwhile, fiberglass statues of animals—be it pigs in Cincinnati or moose in Toronto—were popular attractions in various locales. In New York City, more than 500 life-size cows decorated parks and traffic islands, right. The new art trend had begun in Zurich, Switzerland, in 1998.

Doris Haddock, left, of Dublin, NH, completed a 14-month, 3,200-mi (5 150-km) walk across the United States to push for campaign-finance reform. The 90-year-old "Granny D" had begun the walk at the Rose Bowl in Pasadena, CA, on Jan. 1, 1999, and concluded it on Feb. 29, 2000, with a rally on the steps of the U.S. Capitol in Washington, DC. Also reaching a milestone was Iranian singer Googoosh, center, who on July 29 performed in her first concert in 21 years in Toronto. The "queen of Persian pop" had shot to fame as a child star, but she has been prohibited from performing in Iran since 1979 when the pro-Western Shah was ousted and Islamic ayatollahs declared that female voices corrupted men. The bright stars of the universe came down to earth again in February when the rebuilt Hayden Planetarium at New York City's American Museum of Natural History, bottom, was reopened.

© Aurelio Hernandez/Liaison Agency, Inc.

© Peter Jones/
Reuters/Archive
Photos

© Chris Hondros/Liaison Agency, Inc.

Peru

The year 2000 was turbulent in Peru. For many months, it appeared as if the increasingly authoritarian government of Alberto Fujimori, which had been in power since 1990, would withstand the opposition's challenge. In the final quarter of the year, however, the opposition prevailed, and Peru was on the road to democracy.

Politics. Early in the year, Fujimori's political coalition, Perú 2000, and nine opposition parties campaigned for April 9 elections. As a result of the decimation of two insurgencies, the conquest of hyperinflation, and food and public-works programs for the very poor, the Fujimori government continued to enjoy some popular support. However, this support had eroded considerably from the mid-1990s. The economy was stagnant; unemployment was severe; and political harassment was common. Most educated Peruvians believed that a third consecutive term for Fujimori was unconstitutional.

Fearing defeat, the Fujimori government tilted the electoral playing field. Although this strategy risked criticism from domestic and international election monitors, for several months it appeared to work. Two leading opposition candidates were unable to counter Perú 2000's dirty tricks, and their campaigns fell apart. In March, however, a third opposition candidate, Alejandro Toledo of Perú Posible (Peru is Possible), began to rise in the polls. Although Toledo's political experience was scant and Perú Posible

PERU • Information Highlights

Official Name: Republic of Peru.
Location: West coast of South America.
Area: 496,224 sq mi (1 285 220 km²).
Population (2000 est.): 27,012,899.
Chief Cities (1993 census): Lima, the capital, 6,321,173 (metropolitan area); Arequipa, 642,478; Trujillo, 588,638; Chiclayo, 566,027.
Government: *Head of state,* Valentín Paniagua, interim president (took office Nov. 22, 2000). *Head of government,* Javier Pérez de Cúellar, prime minister (took office November, 2000). *Legislature* (unicameral)— Democratic Constituent Congress.
Monetary Unit: New sol (3.51 new sols equal U.S.$1, Dec. 20, 2000).
Gross Domestic Product (1999 est. U.S.$): $116,000,000,000 (purchasing power parity).
Economic Indexes: *Consumer Prices* (Lima, 1999; 1990 = 100): all items, 2,426.9; food, 1,917.7. *Industrial Production* (1999, 1990 = 100): 148.6.
Foreign Trade (1999 U.S.$): *Imports,* $6,728,000,000; *exports,* $6,116,000,000.

was a personal political vehicle, Toledo's life story was appealing: Despite humble origins and indigenous ethnicity, he had earned a doctorate from Stanford University and had become a business-school professor and an international-development consultant. Promising democracy and jobs, Toledo proved effective on the stump, and he rallied most of the opposition behind him.

On April 9, the balloting went smoothly, but the counting did not. Exit polls and quick counts indicated that Fujimori was short of the 50%-plus-one-vote threshold necessary for a first-round victory. Yet for several days, election officials reported tallies hovering at the threshold, and it appeared that Perú 2000 might claim victory. Finally, however, international and domestic pressure led to the announcement that there would be a runoff on May 28.

In the wake of the first round, election monitors doubted the integrity of Peru's electoral institutions. In mid-May, when new computer software was introduced, the Organization of American States (OAS) delegation requested a postponement of the runoff so that it could review the program. Then, Toledo announced that he would boycott the runoff if it were not postponed. The requests for a delay were rejected; Toledo and all election monitors withdrew. The official result was 51% of the ballots for

© Noboru Hashimoto/Corbis-Sygma

Plagued by political turmoil, a stagnant economy, and serious scandals, Peru's President Alberto Fujimori (far left) *tendered his resignation from Japan, the country of his parents' birth, on Nov. 20, 2000.*

Fujimori, 31% null or blank, and 18% for Toledo (despite his boycott).

The international community was ambivalent. The election monitors' conclusions were clear: Peru's elections did not meet international standards for freedom and fairness. However, for years, Fujimori and his intelligence chief, Vladimiro Montesinos, had cooperated with U.S. officials on a spectrum of issues. By contrast, the United States did not trust Toledo. Ultimately, the Clinton administration decided not to repudiate the elections or to reduce bilateral aid to Peru. Despite opposition protest, Fujimori was inaugurated on July 28.

Within six weeks, twin scandals suddenly shook the political landscape. First, Montesinos was tied to the smuggling of guns from Peru to Colombia's guerrillas—severely alienating his military and intelligence colleagues in both Peru and the United States. Second, a videotape showing Montesinos bribing an opposition congressman was leaked and broadcast on Peruvian television. Peruvians were enraged. On September 16, Fujimori announced that he would disband Montesinos's intelligence service and that he would step down in July 2001, after new elections had been held. Montesinos left for Panama.

Peru's opposition, however, doubted that Fujimori had truly put Peru back on the democratic road. Soon, foreign-bank accounts worth more than $50 million were found in Montesinos's name; at such amounts, the possibility that Fujimori was not complicit in his colleague's corruption was remote. Unable to govern and fearing prosecution, Fujimori departed for Asia; on November 20, he faxed his resignation from Japan, the country of his parents' birth.

As both vice-presidents had also resigned, Peru's next president became Valentín Paniagua, the newly elected speaker of congress. A politically experienced constitutional lawyer from the moderate opposition party, Popular Action, Paniagua seemed an excellent choice for the leadership of an interim government. Peru's political instability had battered the economy, and a steady hand at the helm was important. Paniagua's other key responsibilities were to cleanse sullied political institutions and orchestrate free and fair elections on April 9, 2001. The immediate front-runner for the presidency was Toledo, but as many as ten candidates were likely to run.

CYNTHIA MCCLINTOCK
The George Washington University

Philippines

The year 2000 was generally a disturbing one for the Philippines. Natural disasters, crimes, and economic and political scandals again derailed hopes for prosperity. President Joseph Estrada was disgraced by charges that he took more than $10 million in illegal gambling kickbacks and tobacco revenues. His potential impeachment, street demonstrations, and a wave of violent kidnappings shook investor confidence and threatened political stability.

Disasters. Filipinos faced an unusual mix of challenges in 2000. The Mount Mayon volcano erupted in February, displacing thousands. In April an Air Philippines flight crashed, killing all 131 aboard; it was the Philippines' worst air crash. In July, back-to-back hurricanes savaged the islands, killing at least 16 and leaving 400,000 homeless. Torrential rains destabilized a mountain of garbage in Manila called "Promised Land." Eight-hundred shanties built upon trash were destroyed, and at least 218 were killed in the avalanche of waste.

In October a major blackout knocked out power to the chief island, Luzon. It disrupted the economy and recalled the blackouts of the early 1990s. This one was attributed to an enormous school of jellyfish!

Crime turned bizarre in 2000. In May a hijacker robbed 291 passengers and then jumped to his death. The same month, a powerful computer virus known as "Love Bug" triggered massive worldwide disruption, costing businesses more than $2 billion before it was controlled. The virus was traced to a Manila student, but the young man was not tried because the Philippines lacked cybercrime law.

Insurgencies. In February a wave of bombings shook the southern island of Mindanao. Busses and radio stations were targeted. Forty-five died and 27 were injured in total. Blame was placed on the Muslim Islamic Liberation Front (MILF), which had broken off talks with President Estrada. The MILF, which calls for independence of Muslim areas of the Philippines, is a breakaway faction of the Muslim National Liberation Front (MNLF), which has struggled for Muslim autonomy since 1972. The MNLF has achieved a modest measure of regional autonomy, but its lack of tangible development has encouraged MILF, and a more extreme group, Abu Sayyaf, to use violence.

Abu Sayyaf provoked a wave of terror, torturing priests, beheading two teachers, and engaging in a series of opportunistic kidnappings. On April 23, Abu Sayyaf seized 21 hostages from a Malaysian resort island. The international hostages were forced to swim to a boat that spirited them off to the Philippines. They were held in the jungles under ghastly conditions. Eventually, a few were released after enormous ransoms were paid. Most endured more than six months of captivity. Others continued to be kidnapped and ransomed. Abu Sayyaf membership soared to more than 5,000, as its extortionist activities continued.

President Estrada was forced in the fall to order the bombing of the group's suspected jungle hideouts. The military action killed some hostages, but most succeeded in escaping or were released. Abu Sayyaf suffered a rapid decline in membership from desertion, death, and surrender, and by late in the year was estimated to have no more than 300 members.

Politics. The Estrada presidency came under attack when specific evidence of corruption was linked to the president himself. Luis Singson, governor of Illocos Sur, charged that Estrada personally accepted $8.6 million in illegal gambling kickbacks and $2.8 million in provincial tobacco revenues. Singson had ledgers and tapes as evidence. He accused the president when Estrada decided to ban illegal gambling and develop a state-run gambling game, with the kickbacks going to Singson's rival. Singson protested, and there was an assassination attempt on his life. Estrada denied the charges, but 41 House members sought his impeachment. More than the required one-third of the House recommended impeachment to the Senate. Two-thirds of the 23-member Senate are needed for conviction.

Both Houses were controlled by Estrada's Party of the Filipino Masses (LAMP), but many party defections followed media reports of still other corrupt activities allegedly involving the president.

On December 7, the impeachment trial finally began. The senators stressed the need to solve political scandal through lawful means. "This is just a wake-up call for me," Estrada said. "I leave my fate to God and to the sense of fairness and justice of the senators." As the impeachment trial continued into the new year, 2001, Estrada was forced to give up the presidency on January 20, amid increasing protests. He was barred from leaving the country and his bank accounts were frozen. Vice-President Gloria Macapagal Arroyo was sworn in as the new president. Prosecutors called on President Arroyo to establish an independent counsel to oversee a criminal case against Estrada.

Economy. The bombings, kidnappings, corruption, and impeachment prospects severely hurt the economy. The Philippine peso was at an historic low against the dollar, and the stock market plunged repeatedly. Tourism was down, and consumer and investor confidence sank. World Bank and International Monetary Fund (IMF) officials warned the government that failure to curb corruption was crippling the economy. An estimated one-third of the economy was in the underground black market, further eroding the nation's tiny tax base. Foreign direct investment dropped 40% in 2000, following a 1999 drop of 39%.

Foreign Policy. Relations with the United States and China dominated foreign policy in 2000. President Estrada visited the United States in May, seeking help in modernizing his army and controlling piracy. His visit followed joint-military maneuvers in February, which were part of the Visiting Forces Agreement concluded in 1999. These measures were designed to shore up Philippine defenses, which proved quite vulnerable since the United States was forced from its 23 installations in the Philippines in 1992.

The Chinese have heightened tensions in the waters of the Spratly Islands by building a barracks and landing strip on Mischief Reef, 800 mi (1 287 km) off the Chinese mainland. Six nations, including China and the Philippines, claim the Spratlys, which are on sea lanes through which one-third of world shipping passes and are estimated to be rich in gas and oil deposits. President Estrada visited China in June.

LINDA K. RICHTER, *Kansas State University*

PHILIPPINES • Information Highlights

Official Name: Republic of the Philippines.
Location: Southeast Asia.
Area: 115,830 sq mi (300 000 km²).
Population (2000 est.): 81,159,644.
Chief Cities (1995 census): Manila, the capital, 1,654,761; Quezon, 1,989,419; Caloocan, 1,023,159; Davao, 1,006,840.
Government: *Head of state and government,* Gloria Macapagal Arroyo, president (sworn in Jan. 20, 2001). *Legislature*—Congress: Senate and House of Representatives.
Monetary Unit: Peso (51`.60 pesos equal U.S. $1, Jan. 13, 2001).
Gross Domestic Product (1999 est. U.S.$): $282,000,000,000 (purchasing power parity).
Economic Index: *Consumer Prices* (1999, 1990 = 100): all items, 217.6; food, 200.8.
Foreign Trade (1999 U.S.$): *Imports,* $32,547,000,000; *exports,* $36,576,000,000.

Photography

The year 2000 was good for traditional film-based and digital photography. With consumer interest in digital cameras spiking sharply upward, one might think that significant new film-based camera introductions would be tapering off, but they did not.

Film-Based Equipment. Canon again updated its flagship 35mm single-lens reflex (SLR), this time as the EOS-1V. New features include incorporation of the 45-point Area autofocusing (AF) system, proven in the EOS-3; 72 body seams and interfaces that are sealed against dust and moisture; and a personal-computer (PC) connection to facilitate wide-ranging data-management functions and camera-function customizing. When equipped with the optional PB-E2 Power Drive Booster, the camera can shoot continuously at up to ten frames per second (fps) in One-Shot AF mode, something formerly possible only in cameras with a fixed (nonmoving), semisilvered pellicle mirror, such as the EOS-1N RS.

For the second year in a row, the biggest surprise came from Contax. In 1999 the company introduced the autofocus Contax 645, its first medium-format camera. In 2000, it was the Contax N1, the company's first 35mm autofocus SLR, featuring a new series of N-mount Zeiss lenses. (Previous manual-focus lenses are not compatible.) A nice touch was the Dual Focus Mechanism, which instantly disengages the AF system when the lens' manual focusing ring is moved, allowing precise "touch-up" focus on-the-fly. Another innovation was the optional FE-1 LCD Viewfinder, a 1.5-inch (3.8-cm) display screen similar to those in digital cameras, which permits remote viewing of the image for studio or wildlife photography. Many cameras can auto-bracket the exposure, but the N1 can auto-bracket the focus point slightly, as sharpness insurance with fast-moving subjects.

Even the darkroom scene showed movement. Ilford expanded its selection of variable-contrast black-and-white papers with the addition of Multigrade RC Cooltone, which complements the neutral- and warm-tone papers.

Two new 6x7cm format, high-tech enlargers from Germany stirred further interest. The Kaiser VME 7005 AF overcame major previous limitations of autofocus enlargers: factory calibration to one lens or the necessity of lens-matched focusing cams, and the inability to employ lens and negative stage movements for distortion correction because the lens calibration would be lost. The Kaiser enlarger has a baseboard electronic AF control unit so the user can calibrate any suitable lens to the enlarger and reestablish calibration after tilting the lens or negative stage.

The Dunco Vario Split was made to make prints quickly from many negatives of varying quality. After a probe on the baseboard control unit—which is factory-programmed for all brands of variable-contrast papers—determines exposure and contrast, the required exposure time and filtration are set automatically. The dichroic variable-contrast head employs a "split-filtration" technique using two separate exposures through pure-magenta and pure-yellow filters, a system many printers feel produces a superior tonal range.

Digital Cameras. Three companies introduced digital SLRs based on existing 35mm camera bodies and lens/accessory systems. All represented a combination of quality, versatility, and price that professionals and advanced amateurs have been waiting for. The three cameras range from $3,500 to $5,000 in price — one-third to one-quarter the cost of previous digital SLRs of comparable performance.

First was the Nikon D1. Based on Nikon's rugged F100 body, it features a 2.74-megapixel RGB CCD image sensor; AF or manual focus; ISO equivalents 200 to 1600; 1/16,000 sec. top shutter speed; flash sync at 1/500; three compressed, three uncompressed, and monochrome modes; 4.5-fps capture rate in continuous mode, up to ten or 21 frames depending on compression; PC/Mac connectibility with high-speed interface; CompactFlash storage media; and choice of more than 80 Nikkor lenses.

Fuji's FinePix S1 Pro also is based on a Nikon body (N60) and lens system. The S1 features Fuji's proprietary Super CCD sensor. Its unique interwoven pattern of octagonal photodiodes and pixels is claimed to provide superior resolution and dynamic range; the 3.4 million sensing elements deliver performance equivalent to 6.1 million conventional pixels. ISO equivalents are 320 to 1600; 1.5-fps capture rate, up to five frames; 1/2,000 sec. top shutter speed; three resolutions in three file formats; compatible with SmartMedia, CompactFlash, and IBM Microdrive storage media.

Canon joined the fray with the EOS D30, allowing current Canon EOS users to utilize their existing EF lens inventory.

Cultural Scene. Fans of French photographer Eugène Atget (1856–1927) could view a significant collection of his photographs from the turn of the 20th century at the J. Paul Getty Museum in Los Angeles. Atget was an enigmatic individual, and the bulk of his work would have been lost if not for the U.S. photographer Berenice Abbott, who gained custody of Atget's glass-plate negatives after his death. Abbott subsequently printed, exhibited, and published the images. Atget had a passion for recording Paris street scenes; many of his photos were taken just ahead of a city renovation project that would demolish large tracts of unique and historic architecture. Other Atget exhibits were held later at the Museum of the City of New York and the International Center of Photography (ICP), also in New York City.

One of the year's notable photographic exhibits was "Reflections in Black: A History of Black Photography, 1840 to the Present." With Deborah Willis, above, as curator, the exhibit opened at the Smithsonian Institution and then toured.

Coincident with the Getty's Atget exhibit was a presentation by Los Angeles photographer Gerald M. Panter, who has rephotographed a large number of still-existing Atget scenes. Many depict very little change, while others display varying degrees of architectural evolution.

"Reflections in Black: A History of Black Photographers, 1840 to the Present" gathered the works of some 80 African-American photographers and represented a wide variety of style and subject. Beginning with daguerreotypist Jules Lion in the 1840s, African-Americans used photography as a means to document their struggles, present their culture in a hostile environment, and interpret their personal stories. The show was seen at the Smithsonian Institution from February through June. It then began a three-year tour.

By any accounting, though, the year's major photographic exhibit was the stark revelation in photos of one of America's darkest, unacknowledged secrets, the large number of lynchings of blacks in the South during the first quarter of the 20th century. An assemblage of 150 photographs and postcards, the *Without Sanctuary* collection, co-owned by James Allen and John Littlefield, was begun by Allen in 1985. Ferreted out one-by-one from largely underground sources, the images depict incomprehensible atrocities by one race of people against another, underscored by the unbelievable callousness of the people who were glad to let photographers take their pictures posing with the corpses. These macabre images were distributed widely as souvenirs and postcards at the time. The collection was published in book form, *Without Sanctuary: Lynching Photography in America* (Twin Palms Publishers, Santa Fe, NM), and was on exhibit at the Roth Horowitz Gallery in New York City and later at the New York Historical Society. The collection is on permanent loan to Emory University in Atlanta, with international tours planned. An on-line magazine, *Journal E*, displays many of the images in an interactive environment.

Those interested in photographic history will benefit from the announced alliance between the George Eastman House in Rochester, NY, with its 5 million object photographic collection, and the International Center of Photography (ICP). Public exposure to the Eastman archives will be greatly increased via the ICP's widely accessible venue, and regular exchanges of exhibits and programs are planned.

DAVE HOWARD
Freelance Writer and Photographer

Physics

The gravitational constant, the tau neutrino, and the Higgs boson made the headlines in physics in 2000.

New Gravitational Constant. Physicists at the University of Washington in Seattle, led by Jens Gundlach, designed an experiment to measure the universal gravitational constant, also known as "Big G." Scientists use G in calculating the force of gravitational attraction between masses. The new value measured by Gundlach's team is ten times more accurate than the previous one.

Because G is a very small number, it always has been difficult to measure accurately. Lab results are easily affected by the presence of other nearby masses, as well as vibrations from outside sources. Henry Cavendish, an 18th-century English experimenter, was the first to successfully determine G by experiment. He began by measuring how far a dumbbell-shaped pendulum hung by wire twisted in response to the presence of nearby masses. Engineering advances led to improved experiments, but they still suffered from the same basic sensitivity problems. Then physicists realized in 1995 that the pendulum wires were not perfectly elastic, which added more experimental error. In the end, scientists were forced to admit that the then-current value of G was much bigger than it should have been—12 times too big, in fact.

Gundlach's team mounted their dumbbell-pendulum stand on a rotating turntable. As the ends of the dumbbell swung close to the attracting masses and the pendulum began to twist, a sensor triggered a switch that sped up the turntable and counteracted the twisting. The attractor masses also rotated in the opposite direction, which made the measured signal periodic and easy to subtract out, removing the influence of any outside gravitational influences.

Shy Particle Steps Out. Physicists now have direct evidence of the existence of the tau neutrino, one of the rarest members of particle physics' so-called Standard Model. Byron Lundberg, leader of the Direct Observation of the Nu Tau (DONUT) experimental group at the Fermi National Accelerator Laboratory (Fermilab) outside Chicago, IL, announced the groundbreaking result in July. The tau neutrino is nearly massless and seldom interacts with matter. Until the DONUT experiment, this coy particle had been seen only indirectly, by studying the particles created in high-energy collisions within particle accelerators. Although the tau neutrino is difficult to observe, it decays into a series of other particles that are much easier to detect. The presence of these decay products suggested the existence of the tau neutrino in mid-1970s experiments by physicist Martin Perl.

The DONUT experiment used Fermilab's Tevatron accelerator to speed protons to 800 GeV and shatter them against a tungsten target. (Particle masses are measured in electron volts, or eVs. One eV is the amount of energy an electron gains as it is accelerated across a voltage difference of one volt in a vacuum. One GeV equals 1 billion eV.) Each high energy collision produced a shower of particles that traveled through detectors built from dense lead sheets. Physicists calculate that about one tau neutrino in a trillion interacted with the nucleus of the metal to produce tau particles that are easily detected and measured.

A Peek at the Higgs Boson?. By late 2000, physicists at the European Laboratory for Particle Physics (CERN) in Geneva, Switzerland, were crossing their fingers that four events observed in the Large Electron Positron (LEP) collider would prove the first experimental evidence for the mysterious Higgs boson, the missing link between the Standard Model of particle physics and supersymmetry theories that merge gravity with the strong and electroweak forces.

The LEP results showed particles associated with the presence of the Higgs boson, but the results occurred at the lower edge of the Higgs' expected energy regime. With only four events to work from, the data could also be explained statistically by proposing other particles as candidates. Scientists needed more evidence before they could celebrate an actual discovery.

The LEP accelerator was scheduled to be shut down in the fall to make way for a more powerful device, the Large Hadron Collider (LHC). Although the LHC will have more than enough energy to produce the Higgs, the new collider will not be on-line until 2005. CERN researchers extended the LEP experiment another month in hopes of finding more-conclusive data, but were unsuccessful. Rival Fermilab could reap the glory when it starts its own search for the Higgs boson in 2001. The Higgs is named for British physicist Peter Higgs, who postulated its existence in the mid-1960s. Theory holds that the Higgs gives the other fundamental particles their masses.

CHARLENE BRUSSO, *Freelance Science Writer*

Poland

Both economically and politically, Poland was a leader among postcommunist countries in 2000, though developmental disparities reinforced some political divisions.

Economy. The economy continued its strong postcommunist performance with annual growth of about 5% and record levels of new foreign investment—estimated at 50% above the 1999 level of $8 billion. However, inflation (between 11% and 12%) and unemployment (almost 14%) persisted. There was increasing imbalance between surging imports and exports. Foreign travel to Poland continued to expand substantially.

In an important measure that linked Poland's economy to the West, the National Bank said in April it would allow Polish currency to float freely on the national and international exchange markets, against the euro and other currencies. This was viewed as a necessary prelude to Polish integration into the European Union (EU).

Polish farmers—approximately one-quarter of the labor force—suffered the bulging price gap between the agricultural and nonagricultural sector. Late in the year, nonagricultural prices rose faster than farm prices, at a disparate rate of almost 25%. The prospect of still-lower rewards—the result of unrestricted imports from the EU—buffered opposition to European integration among Polish agriculturalists.

Government and Politics. During the summer of 2000, Poland faced a government crisis. On June 6 the Freedom Union (UW), led by Finance Minister and famed free-marketeer Leszek Balcerowicz, pulled out of the coalition cabinet dominated by the Solidarity Election Action (Akcja Wyborcza Solidarnosc), or AWS, of Prime Minister Jerzy Buzek. The crisis brewed over the failure of many AWS deputies to support government policy measures needed for Poland's eventual entry into the EU. These measures promoted painful austerity, such as cutting down on agricultural and welfare subsidies, maintaining a balanced budget, and curbing inflation. To some, they appeared to be sacrificing Poland's social safety nets to appease West Europeans.

The AWS attempt to replace Jerzy Buzek as premier with its party chief, Marian Krzaklewski, proved unacceptable to the UW. The coalition split after a nearly three-year existence. New legislative elections were scheduled for fall 2001.

Five ministers from the defecting Freedom Union quit Buzek's cabinet. With the party's departure, the ruling coalition ostensibly controlled only 186 out of 460 seats in the Sejm. The prime minister directed a new minority coalition with ad hoc support from various factions represented in parliament.

In mid-August, both Aleksander Kwasniewski, the sitting president, and former President Lech Walesa were cleared by a Warsaw court of charges that they had been spies for Poland's communist secret police. Under a 1997 law, candidates who had collaborated with the secret police, and lied about it, were banned from seeking elective office for a period of ten years.

In the presidential elections, held October 8, President Kwasniewski, a 46-year-old former communist, and now Social Democrat, handily won reelection to a five-year term. Kwasniewski was opposed by 11 other candidates, but managed to garner the support of 54% of Polish voters, thereby avoid-

© Alik Keplicz/AP/Wide World Photos

President Aleksander Kwasniewski, a Social Democrat, was congratulated by his wife Jolanta, after easily winning reelection on Oct. 8, 2000. President Kwasniewski sympathized with Poles struggling in the transition to a market economy

ing a runoff. Kwasniewski cultivated the image of being sympathetic to Poles who were experiencing privations and frustrations in Poland's successful but, for many, painful transition to a market economy. The president's victory was foreshadowed by public-opinion polls, and seemed to have been aided by divisions among his more conservative or right-wing opponents. Krzaklewski drew the support of about 16% of the electorate; independent economist Andrzej Olechowski won 17% of the vote; and Walesa, running under the banner of the Christian Democratics, a small party, received less than 1%—an astoundingly small percentage given Walesa's heroic popularity as leader of the Solidarity movement in the 1980s.

Church and Religion. In late August the bishops of the Catholic Church issued a letter to the faithful asking forgiveness for the sin of anti-Semitism. The letter was to be read by clergy at Sunday Masses throughout Poland. It attributed anti-Semitism to wrong interpretations of church teachings and to racist and nationalist conceptions. Forgiveness was asked from all who "did not find understanding, or met with rejection, or suffered because Christians forgot the basic truth that we are all children of God." Nevertheless, the declaration also "equally" condemned the anti-Polish attitudes of some Jewish groups. Although the Jewish population of Poland was currently statistically insignificant, the controversies of anti-Semitism continued. Also in August, coinciding with the 20th anniversary of the Solidarity movement's birth in Gdansk, Pope John Paul II issued a statement appealing for renewed unity among its former and current members. This call was echoed by Cardinal Jozef Glemp, head of the Polish Church. Such pleas seemed ineffective.

Foreign Relations. The most important aims in Poland's foreign policy continued to be closer relations with the West and membership in the EU. There were no dramatic breakthroughs in these areas, but there was a compensatory chill in relations with Russia. On January 20, in a development symbolic of the continuing tensions since the dissolution of the old Soviet empire, Poland ordered the expulsion of nine Russian diplomats. Espionage was the alleged cause. Within 24 hours, Russia retaliated by expelling nine Polish diplomats from Moscow on analogous charges.

On March 1 the Polish ambassador to Yemen, Krzysztof Suprowicz, was kid-

POLAND • Information Highlights

Official Name: Republic of Poland.
Location: Eastern Europe.
Area: 120,728 sq mi (312 683 km²).
Population (2000 est.): 38,646,023.
Chief Cities (Dec. 31, 1996, est.): Warsaw, the capital, 1,628,500; Lodz, 818,000; Kraków, 740,700; Wroclaw, 640,600; Poznań 580,800.
Government: *Head of state,* Aleksander Kwasniewski, president (took office December 1995). *Head of government,* Jerzy Buzek, prime minister (named Oct. 17, 1997). *Legislature*—National Assembly: Senat and Sejm.
Monetary Unit: Zloty (4.15 zlotys equal U.S.$1, Dec. 29, 2000).
Gross Domestic Product (1999 est. U.S.$): $276,500,000,000 (purchasing power parity).
Economic Indexes (1999, 1990 = 100): *Consumer Prices,* all items, 986.0; food, 102.0. *Industrial Production,* 165.3.
Foreign Trade (1999 U.S.$): *Imports,* $45,903,000,000; *exports,* $27,397,000,000.

napped by armed tribesmen who sought to exchange him for one of their own jailed compatriots. He was released through the intervention of Yemen's military on March 5. On April 4 a Polish peacekeeper was injured in a clash also involving some U.S. military in Kosovo.

At the end of June, representatives of 107 countries met in Warsaw to support the promotion and maintenance of political democracy around the globe. Following a two-day meeting, the participating delegates agreed on the so-called Warsaw Declaration, promising to work for the "expansion of the frontiers of freedom," and to ensure that "wherever democracy has taken root, it would not be reversed."

Other Developments. On April 14 the Sejm voted, 257 to 117, with 33 abstentions, to authorize President Kwasniewski to sign the European Human Rights Convention, banning the death penalty in Poland.

Beginning in mid-May, considerable public attention focused on the trial of Gen. Czeslaw Kiszczak, the interior minister in Poland's last communist government. The general was charged with having ordered security forces to fire on demonstrators following the imposition of martial law on Dec. 13, 1981. This measure was linked by the prosecution to the deaths of nine coal miners and injuries to 25 others in southern Poland. Within a few sessions, the defendant's ill health led to a postponement of proceedings.

In early June, thousands of Poles paid their respects to Stanislaw Mikolajczyk, prime minister of the Polish government in exile in London during World War II. Between 1945 and 1947, he had led the democratic opposition to the communists within Poland. Initially interred in the United States in 1966, his body was later returned for burial in his native Poznan. On July 15, a notable figure in the Polish resistance movement in World War II, Jan Karski, died in Washington, DC, at age 86. In 1942 and 1943, Karski (originally Kozielewski) briefed top Allied leaders, from personal observations, about Nazi extermination of Jews on Polish territory. His reports were met with incredulity and indifference in the West. In 1994, Karski was made an honorary citizen of Israel.

Alexander J. GROTH
University of California, Davis

Polar Research

The Arctic and Antarctic polar regions continued to play important roles in understanding and predicting future weather patterns and global climate changes.

Changing Environments. The ozone hole over Antarctica, which typically grows in late September, reached a record size in 2000, about 11 million sq mi (28.5 km^2)—approximately three times the size of the United States. For two days, September 9–10, this hole covered the city of Punta Arenas in Chile, exposing residents to dangerously high levels of ultraviolet radiation.

Meanwhile, in the Arctic, more than 60% of the ozone in the Arctic stratosphere was destroyed during the winter of 1999–2000. The growing depletion zone reinforced concerns of continued decline despite reductions in stratospheric chlorine levels.

An aerial survey by the National Aeronautics and Space Administration (NASA) showed that more than 11 cubic miles of ice —or the equivalent of 50 billion tons of water—disappears from the Greenland ice sheet annually. This increases the risk of coastal flooding around the world and is responsible for about 7% of the annual rise in global sea level.

A Canadian vessel, the *Nadon*, navigated the Northwest Passage in the Arctic in a record-breaking nine-week voyage. The ease and speed of the passage—the first in clear water all the way—increased speculation that commercial ships could use the passage to cut 5,000 mi (8 046 km) off the trip between Europe and Japan.

Open water at the North Pole, at least part of the time, was viewed by many scientists as a sign that global warming, as caused by the release of heat-trapping gases from industrial society, was a real phenomenon and not just a natural climatic fluctuation. The polar ice cap is last known to have melted more than 50 million years ago during the Eocene geological period.

Icebergs. Concerns about navigation in the Antarctic grew, with an increase in the number of icebergs breaking off, or calving, from the Ross and Ronne Ice Shelves. The largest iceberg, B-15, is about 158 nautical miles long and 20 nautical miles wide. It calved from the Ross Ice Shelf. B-15 is the equivalent of about 80% of the total annual snowfall on Antarctica. Another, iceberg, B-20, measuring 345 sq mi (894 km^2), calved from the Ross Ice Shelf in September.

Scientific Space Laboratory. The Antarctic has proven to be a handy testing ground for space exploration. In 2000, for the first time on Earth, the technologies of search and classification were successfully applied by a robot to the kind of tasks that missions to the planets hope to achieve. This happened when the robot, *Nomad*, from Carnegie Mellon University, found, without human assistance, meteorites in the trans-Antarctic mountains.

Other News. A boom of sorts occurred in auction prices for Antarctic memorabilia, with a record $148,159 paid for the 1912 journal of surgeon Murray Levick of Captain Scott's expedition. A very rare copy of *Aurora Australis*, the hand-published book of articles, poems, and sketches produced by Sir Ernest Shackleton's British Antarctic Expedition at Cape Evans in winter 1908, sold for $59,295. The sextant that had belonged to Shackleton sold for $59,295.

Californian professional surfer Chris Molloy was believed to have became the first person to surf Antarctica. He caught a small reef break left-hander at Elephant Island in the bay where Sir Ernest Shackleton's party sought shelter in 1916.

The autobiography of Dr. Jerri Nielsen, 47, who self-diagnosed and treated breast cancer while isolated at the South Pole in 1999, was to be published in January 2001. *Ice Bound: A Doctor's Incredible Battle for Survival at the South Pole* would bring the experience of living in Antarctica to a wider public. Geochemist Lois Jones, who helped break the gender barrier against American women scientists in Antarctica, died at the age of 65. Jones had led a 1969 all-female expedition to study Lake Vanda in the Dry Valleys near McMurdo Base.

DAVID W. H. WALTON, *British Antarctic Survey*

Portugal

Prime Minister António Guterres raised Portugal's international profile, even while a slowdown of the nation's buoyant economy diminished the Socialist leader's popularity. A malaise, embodied by an increased disenchantment with the domestic policies pursued by the Socialist government, beset the Portuguese public.

Politics. Growing abstentionism revealed a widening cleavage between politicians and the electorate, as well as the decline of such traditional institutions as the Roman Catholic Church, the military, labor unions, and political parties. For years after the overthrow of the country's dictatorship, citizens stood stoically in line to vote. In 1998, however, only 32% of eligible voters—too few to enact reforms—cast ballots in a referendum on liberalizing the nation's strict abortion laws. Five months later the participation rate in a national vote on creating regional assemblies also failed to attain the required 50% approval. And in October 1999 low turnout contributed to the failure of the Socialist Party (PS) to win an absolute majority of seats in the 230-member Assembly of the Republic.

In light of these outcomes, Guterres abandoned plans to hold a plebiscite on his nation's further integration with the European Union (EU). President Jorge Sampãio, who will stand for reelection in 2001, suggested that the issues presented to the electorate were too esoteric. "They want to hear about jobs, schools, courts, the drug problem, traffic, and transport," the PS leader said. "That is what they deal with every day."

Former Prime Minister Francisco Pinto Balsemão argued that hierarchical organizations—such as political parties—were in crisis because "helped by mobile phones and the Internet, horizontal networks are becoming more and more important."

Economics. Portugal's gross domestic product (GDP) grew 3%, just below the rates achieved in 1999 (3.3%) and 1998 (3.5%). Soaring energy costs took Prime Minister Guterres by surprise. To combat inflation, he cut gasoline taxes and froze fuel prices between March and December. These initiatives enabled him to hold the inflation rate to 2.7%, up from 2% in 1999. Productivity and per-capita wage gains hovered around 3.5%, with the unemployment level holding steady at 4.5%.

Still, the rival Social Democratic Party (PSD) lambasted the government for boosting spending and indebtedness without preparing the country for soaring oil prices and higher interest rates. The prime minister said he would rather "die by the sword" than cave in to PSD demands.

Failure to obtain support from at least one opposition deputy—the PS holds 115 seats—would spark an election in May 2001. This prospect heartened José Manuel Durão Barroso, head of the center-right PSD, who said that a crisis that helped solve national problems would be better than "the stability of an impasse." According to the *Financial Times*, the president of the Confederation of Portuguese Industry, the main employers' organization, excoriated the budget as so flawed that it should be defeated, even at the risk of holding early elections. "There is no alternative to cutting state spending and taxes" if Portugal wants to "recover competitiveness inside" the EU, he said.

Foreign Policy. In January, Portugal assumed the presidency of the EU for six months. Guterres took advantage of this bully pulpit to open discussions with African nations—including former Portuguese territories—about economic and diplomatic concerns of mutual interest.

In early May, Guterres flew to Moscow, where he discussed the Chechnya conflict and economic cooperation with Russian leader Vladimir Putin. Later in the month, U.S. President Bill Clinton became the first U.S. chief executive to visit Portugal since Ronald Reagan, in 1985. Although opponents of a missile-defense system splashed "Clinton Go Home" slogans on a wall in Lisbon, the U.S. president lauded his hosts for their hospitality.

GEORGE W. GRAYSON
College of William & Mary

PORTUGAL • Information Highlights

Official Name: Portuguese Republic.
Location: Southwestern Europe.
Area: 35,672 sq mi (92 391 km²).
Population (2000 est.): 10,048,232.
Chief Cities (1991 census): Lisbon, the capital, 681,063; Oporto, 309,485; Vila Nova de Gaia, 247,499.
Government: *Head of state,* Jorge Sampãio, president (took office March 1996). *Head of government,* António Guterres, prime minister (took office October 1995). *Legislature* (unicameral)—Assembly of the Republic.
Monetary Unit: Escudo (230.957 escudos equal U.S.$1, Nov. 30, 2000).
Gross Domestic Product (1999 est. U.S.$): $151,400,000,000 (purchasing power parity).
Economic Indexes (1999): *Consumer Prices* (1990 = 100): all items, 156.7; food, 143.5. *Industrial Production* (1990 = 100): 120.2.
Foreign Trade (1999 U.S.$): *Imports,* $38,461,000,000; *exports,* $23,864,000,000.

Prisons

The number of people held behind bars as well as those on probation and parole in the United States rose to all-time highs in 2000, although the rate of increase was slowing down. In fact, the 3.4% increase was well below the average rate of 6.5% per year since 1990.

Prison Population. U.S. Justice Department figures released in August 2000 showed a record-high prison population in 1999—1,284,894 inmates in state and federal prisons, and 605,943 adults in local jails. If military and juvenile facilities were included, the total would surpass 2 million for the first time in U.S. history. Over the past 20 years, the number of people imprisoned for drug offenses increased more than eightfold. Jason Ziedenberg of the Justice Policy Institute, a research-and-development organization promoting changes in the U.S. justice system, noted that the United States has "about 5% of the world population but close to 25% of the world's prison population." He attributed the disproportionately large prison population to a policy of using severe prison sentences to combat drugs, homelessness, and mental illness.

No country has a larger prison count, either in terms of raw numbers or in the proportion of citizens locked away. With more than 4 million on probation and parole, the number of adults under penal supervision at federal, state, and local levels exceeded 6 million. Almost all states were continuing to build more prisons, toughening sentencing standards, and putting more people under correctional supervision. California, previously the state with the largest prison system in the United States, with 163,067 prisoners, was replaced by Texas, with 163,190 inmates. The federal prison system was third, with 135,246.

All incarceration facilities—from the most secure federal prison to the smallest town jail—count their prisoners every day, several times a day. Originally designed to assure that no one escaped, these figures eventually are forwarded to Washington, DC, where each year the Justice Department's Bureau of Justice Statistics issues an annual report. These figures are among the most accurate issued by any federal agency. From one perspective, however, they contain a basic flaw that seriously understates the number of people incarcerated in a given year. The numbers published are for one day—for example, the last day of the previous year. Although many inmates in the nation's prisons have sentences ranging from 15 years to life, the average sentence, while continuing to rise over the past decade, was 28 months in 2000. This means that hundreds of thousands of inmates are moving into and out of U.S. prisons in just a year's time. Statistically, if the average sentence is 28 months, the nation's prisons empty themselves, and are refilled with new bodies, in just over two years' time. The number of people who experience imprisonment in a given year is much higher—a conservative estimate would be at least 25%—than bare statistics reveal. In addition to the costs of building and staffing U.S. prisons, there are also vast sums spent by other agencies to care for the families, especially children, of those in prison.

Minorities in Prison. For decades, black men have been incarcerated at almost ten times the rate of white men, and this has been especially true for drug offenses. While five times as many whites use drugs as blacks, the majority (62%) of drug offenders sent to prison are black. In June, Human Rights Watch, a nongovernmental organization that monitors human-rights conditions in more than 70 countries around the world, issued a report, "Punishment and Prejudice: Racial Disparities in the War on Drugs." The report detailed the state-by-state practice of sending black drug offenders to prison at far higher rates than whites. Illinois has the worst racial disparity in the country, with black males being sent to prison at 57 times the rate of white males. More than 90% of all drug admissions are blacks—the highest percentage in the country. Other states with particularly high disparities include Wisconsin, Minnesota, Maine, Iowa, and Maryland. One factor contributing to the disparity might be the techniques used to enforce drug laws—including massive street sweeps; "buy and bust" operations; and other policies focused on street-level, retail drug transactions in minority neighborhoods.

While the actual number of women in prison is far less than men, the percentage has grown steadily—650% over the past 20 years. Of the 149,000 women behind bars, 70% have at least one child under the age of 18. By 2000, there were almost 1.5 million children with a parent in prison, and studies indicated that half of the children would commit a crime before they turn 18.

See also CRIME—Capital Punishment.

DONALD GOODMAN
John Jay College of Criminal Justice

Prizes and Awards

NOBEL PRIZES [1]

Chemistry: Alan J. Heeger, University of California at Santa Barbara; Alan MacDiarmid, The University of Pennsylvania; Hideki Shirakawa, University of Tsukuba, Japan, for creating a plastic that conducts electricity like a metal.

Economics: James J. Heckman, University of Chicago, and Daniel L. McFadden, University of California at Berkeley, for work that has helped to explain complex behavior, like why some working mothers earn more than those with fewer children and why one route for a new highway is favored over another.

Literature: Gao Xingjian, a novelist and playwright from China, "for an oeuvre of universal validity, bitter insights and linguistic ingenuity, which has opened new paths for the Chinese novel and drama." (LITERATURE—Overview.)

Peace: Kim Dae Jung, president of South Korea, for his work for democracy and human rights in South Korea and East Asia in general, and for peace and reconciliation with North Korea in particular. (*See* page 60.)

Physics (shared): Jack S. Kilby, retired engineer for Texas Instruments, Dallas, for his part in the invention of the integrated circuit, the miniaturized electronic chip that drives computers; Zhores I. Alferov, director of A.F. Ioffe Physico-Technical Institute, St. Petersburg, Russia, and Herbert Kroemer, University of California at Santa Barbara, for independently developing electronic components that turned small, solid-state lasers into practical devices and greatly accelerated communications circuitry.

Physiology or Medicine: Paul Greengard, Rockefeller University; Eric Kandel, Columbia University; and Arvid Carlsson, University of Gothenberg, Sweden. Each recipient has made many important contributions to understanding the brain at a molecular level, in particular in working out the changes that occur inside a neuron after it has received a signal from another neuron.

[1] approx. $960,000 in each category

ART

American Academy and Institute of Arts and Letters Awards

Academy-Institute Awards: architecture—Will Bruder, Jesse Reiser and Nanako Umemoto; art—Ellen Gallagher, James Siena, Honoré Sharrer, Trevor Winkfield, Steve Wolfe; literature—David Bromwich, Jonathan Galassi, Lorrie Moore, David St. John, Ellen Douglas, Craig Lucas, Brian Morton, Ellen Bryant Voight; music—Sebastian Currier, David Rakowski, Libby Larsen, Melinda Wagner

Award for Distinguished Service to the Arts: Schuyler Chapin

Arnold W. Brunner Memorial Prize in Architecture: Toyo Ito

Jimmy Ernst Award in Art: Charles Garabedian

Award of Merit for Painting: Pat Passlof

Walter Hinrichsen Award: Susan Forrest Harding

Charles Ives Fellowship in Music: Carlos Sanchez-Gutierrez and Gregory T. S. Walker

Charles Ives Scholarships in Music: Christiana Haisung Ahn, Sara Doncaster, John Kaefer, Marcus Karl Maroney, Eli Marshall, and Laurie San Martin

Wladimir and Rhoda Lakond Award in Music: Robert Livingston Aldridge

Goddard Lieberson Fellowships in Music: Kenneth Frazelle and Richard Wargo

Willard L. Metcalf Award in Art: Steve DeFrank

Richard and Hinda Rosenthal Foundation Awards: **Art:** Alex Brown; **Literature:** Matthre Stadler, *Allan Stein*

Canada Council Molson Prize for the Arts ($50,000): Kiawak Ashoona

Capezio Dance Award ($10,000): David Randolph White

Dorothy and Lillian Gish Prize for outstanding contribution to the arts ($250,000): Merce Cunningham

John F. Kennedy Center Honors for career achievement in the performing arts: Mikhail Baryshnikov, Plácido Domingo, Angela Lansbury, Chuck Berry, Clint Eastwood

John F. Kennedy Center Humor Award: Carl Reiner

National Academy of Recording Arts and Sciences Grammy Awards for excellence in phonograph records

Album of the year: Santana, *Supernatural*

Classical album: *Stravinsky: Firebird; The Rite of Spring; Perséphone*, Michael Tilson Thomas, conductor

Classical vocal performance: Thomas Quasthoff, baritone; Anne Sofie von Otter, mezzo soprano, *Mahler: Des Knaben Wunderhorn*

Country album: Dixie Chicks, *Fly*

Country song (songwriter(s) award): Robert John Mutt Lange, Shania Twain, "Come On Over"

Country vocal performance: (female)— Shania Twain, "Man! I Feel Like a Woman!"; (male)— George Jones, "Choices"; (group or duo)— Dixie Chicks, "Ready to Run"

Jazz instrumental performance: Gary Burton, Chick Corea, Pat Metheny, Roy Haynes, Dave Holland, *Like Minds*

Jazz instrumental solo: Wayne Shorter, "In Walked Wayne"

Jazz vocal performance: Diana Krall, *When I Look in Your Eyes*

New artist: Christina Aguilera

Pop album: Sting, *Brand New Day*

Pop vocal performance: (female)—Sarah McLachlan, "I Will Remember You"; (male)—Sting, "Brand New Day"; (group or duo)—Santana, "Maria Maria"

Rap album: Eminem, *The Slim Shady LP*

Rap duo or group performance: The Roots, featuring Erykah Badu, "You Got Me"

Rap solo performance: Eminem, "My Name Is"

Record of the year: Santana, featuring Rob Thomas, "Smooth"

Rhythm-and-blues album: TLC, *Fanmail*

Rhythm-and-blues song (songwriter(s) award): Kevin Shekspere Briggs, Kandi Burruss, Tameka Cottle, "No Scrubs"

Rhythm-and-blues vocal performance: (female)—Whitney Houston, "It's Not Right But It's Okay"; (male)—Barry White, "Staying Power"; (group or duo)— TLC, "No Scrubs"

Rock album: Santana, *Supernatural*

Rock song (songwriter(s) award) Flea, John Frusciante, Anthony Kiedis, Chad Smith, "Scar Tissue"

Rock vocal performance: (female)—Sheryl Crow, "Sweet Child O' Mine"; (male)—Lenny Kravitz, "American Woman"; (group or duo)—Santana, featuring Everlast, "Put Your Lights On"

Song of the year (songwriter(s) award) Itaal Shur and Rob Thomas, "Smooth"

National Humanities Medal: Robert N. Bellah, Will D. Campbell, Judy Crichton, David C. Driskell, Ernest J. Gaines, Herman T. Guerrero, Quincy Jones, Barbara Kingsolver, Edmund S. Morgan, Toni Morrison, Earl Shorris, Virginia Driving Hawk Sneve

National Medal of Arts: Maya Angelou, Eddy Arnold, Mikhail Baryshnikov, Benny Carter, Chuck Close, Horton Foote, Lewis Manilow, National Public Radio's Cultural Programming Division, Claes Oldenburg, Itzhak Perlman, Harold Prince, Barbra Streisand

Praemium Imperiale for lifetime achievement in the arts ($150,000 ea.): Richard Rogers, Great Britain (architecture); Hans Werner Henze, Germany (music); Ellsworth Kelly, United States (painting); Niki de Saint Phalle, France (sculpture); Stephen Sondheim, United States (theater and film)

Pritzker Architecture Prize ($100,000): Rem Koolhaas

Pulitzer Prize for Music: Lewis Spratlan, *Life is a Dream, Opera in Three Acts: Act II, Concert Version*

Samuel H. Scripps/American Dance Festival Award ($35,000): Pilobolus Dance Theatre

JOURNALISM

Maria Moors Cabot Prizes ($1,500 ea.): Eloy O. Aguilar, Chief of Bureaus, Associated Press, Mexico, D.F.; Paul Knox, International Affairs reporter, *The Globe and Mail*, Toronto, Canada; Ricardo Uceda, Chief of the Investigative Unit, Peru; **special citations:** Francisco Santos, columnist *El Tiempo*, Columbia; Lloyd Williams, Senior Associate Editor, *The Gleaner Newspapers*, Sacramento, CA

National Magazine Awards

Design: *Fast Company*

Essays: *The Sciences*

Feature writing: *Sports Illustrated*

Fiction: *The New Yorker*

General excellence: *National Geographic, The New Yorker, Saveur, Nest*

General excellence in new media: *Business Week Online*

Personal service: *PC Computing*

Profiles: *Sports Illustrated*

Photography: *Vanity Fair*

Public interest: *The New Yorker*

Reporting: *Vanity Fair*

Reviews and criticism: Esquire

Special interest: *I.D. Magazine*

Overseas Press Club Awards

Whitman Bassow Award (for best foreign environmental reporting in any medium): David Talbot, *Boston Herald*

Robert Spears Benjamin Award (for best reporting in any medium from Latin America): Sebastian Rotella, *Los Angeles Times*

Hal Boyle Award (for best newspaper or wire service reporting from abroad):

Nobel Prize in Economics

James J. Heckman

Daniel L. McFadden

David Filipov, *The Boston Globe*

Eric and Amy Burger Award (for best foreign reporting on human rights for broadcast): Diane Sawyer and Catherine Harrington, *20/20*, ABC News

Robert Capa Gold Medal (for photographic reporting from abroad requiring exceptional courage and enterprise): John Stanmeyer, *SABA for Time*

Bob Considine Award (for best newspaper or wire service interpretation of international affairs): Mark Schoofs, *The Village Voice*

Ed Cunningham Memorial Award (for best magazine reporting from abroad): Rod Nordland, *Newsweek*

Joe and Laurie Dine Award (for best reporting in a print medium dealing with human rights): Charles M. Madigan, Executive Editor, and Colin McMahon, Moscow correspondent, *Chicago Tribune*

John Faber Award (for best photographic reporting from abroad in newspapers or wire services): Yannis Behrakis, Reuters

Malcolm Forbes Award (for best business reporting from abroad in newspapers or wire services): Anita Raghavan and *The Wall Street Journal* staff, *The Wall Street Journal*

Morton Frank Award (for best business reporting from abroad in magazines): John Colmey, David Liebhold and *TIME Asia* staff

David Kaplan Award (for best TV spot news reporting from abroad): Ron Allen, Bob Faw, Martin Fletcher, Dana Lewis, Kerry Sanders, *NBC Nightly News*

Edward R. Murrow Award (for best interpretation or documentary on foreign affairs): Sherry Jones, David Fanning, Michael Sullivan, Washington Media Associates for *Frontline/WGBH Boston*

Thomas Nast Award (for best cartoons on foreign affairs): Rob Rogers, *Pittsburgh Post-Gazette*

Olivier Rebbot Award (for best photographic reporting from abroad for magazines or books): Gille Peress, Gille Peress/Magnum for *The New Yorker*

Madeline Dane Ross Award (for best foreign reporting in any medium showing a concern for the human condition): Sang-Hun Choe, Charles J. Hanley, Martha Mendoza, Randy Herschaft, Associated Press

Cornelius Ryan Award (for best nonfiction book on foreign affairs): Thomas L. Friedman, *The Lexus and the Olive Tree: Understanding Globalization*

Carl Spielvogel Award (for best foreign business reporting for broadcast): Jocelyn Ford, J.J. Yore, *Report from a Tokyo Barstool*

Lowell Thomas Award (for best radio news or interpretation of foreign affairs): NPR News, *National Public Radio*

George Polk Memorial Awards

Career award: Studs Terkel

Criminal-justice reporting: Ken Armstrong and Steve Mills, *Chicago Tribune*

Editorial writing: *The New York Daily News*

Financial reporting: Ellen E. Schultz, *The Wall Street Journal*

Foreign reporting: Paul Watson, *Los Angeles Times*

International reporting: Charles J. Hanley, Martha Mendoza, Sang-hun Choe, and Randy Herschaft, Associated Press

Local reporting: Kevin Carmody, *The Daily Southtown*

Medical reporting: Andrea Gerlin, *The Philadelphia Inquirer*

National reporting: Jason DeParle, *The New York Times*

Regional reporting: Todd Richissin (reporter) and Andre Chung (photographer), *The Baltimore Sun*

Special award: National Security Archive

Television reporting (local): WWOR-TV, Secaucus, NJ

Television reporting (foreign): Olenka Frenkiel (reporter), Giselle Portenier (photographer), and Fiona Murch (executive producer), British Broadcasting Corporation

Pulitzer Prizes

Beat reporting: George Dohrmann, *St. Paul Pioneer Press*

Breaking news reporting: Staff of *The Denver Post*

Commentary: Paul A. Gigot, *The Wall Street Journal*, for "informative and insightful columns on politics and government"

Criticism: Henry Allen, *The Washington Post*

Editorial cartooning: Joel Pett, *Lexington* (Ky.) *Herald-Leader*

Editorial writing: John C. Bersia, *The Orlando Sentinel*

Explanatory reporting: Eric Newhouse, *Great Falls* (Mont.) *Tribune*

Feature photography: Carol Guzy, Michael Williamson and Lucian Perkins, *The Washington Post*

Feature writing: J.R. Moehringer, *Los Angeles Times*

International reporting: Mark Schoofs, *The Village Voice*

Investigative reporting: San-Hun Choe, Charles J. Hanley and Martha Mendoza, Associated Press

National reporting: Staff of *The Wall Street Journal*

Public service: *The Washington Post*

Breaking news photography: Photo staff of *The Denver Rocky Mountain News*

LITERATURE

American Academy and Institute of Arts and Letters Awards

Academy Award in Literature: Lorrie Moore

New Foreign Honorary Member: Michael Ondaatje

Witter Bynner Prize for Poetry: Dana Levin

E.M. Forster Award in Literature: Carol Ann Duffy

Gold Medal for Biography: R. W. B. Lewis

Gold Medal for Music: Lukas Foss

Sue Kaufman Prize for First Fiction: Nathan Englander, *Relief of Unbearable Urges*

Addison M. Metcalf Award in Literature: Jhumpa Lahiri, *Interpreter of Maladies*

William Dean Howells Medal: Don DeLillo, *Underworld*

Rome Fellowship in Literature: Sigrid Nunez

Richard and Hinda Rosenthal Foundation Award: Edison Tak-Bun Liu, M.D.

Harold D. Vursell Memorial Award: Richard Powers

Morton Dauwen Zabel Award: Edward W. Said

Bancroft Prize in American history ($4,000): John W. Dower, *Embracing Defeat: Japan in the Wake of World War II*; Linda Gordon, *The Great Arizona Orphan Abduction*; James H. Merrell, *Into the American Woods: Negotiators on the Pennsylvania Frontier*

Booker Prize: Margaret Atwood, *The Blind Assassin*

Canada's Governor-General Literary Awards ($10,000 ea.)

English-language awards

Children's: Marie-Louise Gay, *Yuck, a Love Story*

Drama: Timothy Findley, *Elizabeth Rex*

Fiction: Michael Ondaatje, *Anil's Ghost*

Nonfiction: Nega Mezlekia, *Notes From the Hyena's Belly*

Poetry: Don McKay, *Another Gravity*

Translation: Robert Majzels, *Just Fine*

French-language awards

Children's: Anne Villeneuve, *L'Écharpe rouge*

Drama: Wajdi Mouawad, *Littoral*

Fiction: Jean Marc Dalpé, *Un vent se lève qui éparlille*

Nonfiction: Gérard Bouchard, *Genése des nations et cultures du Noveau Monde*

Poetry: Normand de Bellefeuille, *La March de l'aveugle sans son chien*

Translation: Lori Saint-Martin and Paul Gagné, *Un parfum de cèdre*

Lincoln Prize ($20,000 shared): Allen C. Guelzo, *Abraham Lincoln: Redeemer President*; John Hope Franklin and Loren Schweninger, *Runaway Slaves: Rebels on the Plantation*

Mystery Writers of America/Edgar Allan Poe Awards

Critical or biographical work: Daniel Stashower, *The Life of Arthur Conan Doyle*

Fact crime: James B. Stewart, *Blind Eye*

First novel: Eliot Pattison, *The Skull Mantra*

Grandmaster award: Mary Higgins Clark

Juvenile: Elizabeth McDavid Jones, *The Night Flyers*

Novel: Jan Burke, *Bones*

Original paperback: Ruth Birmingham, *Fulton County Blues*

Play: Joe Di Pietro, *The Art of Murder*

Short story: Anne Perry, *Heroes*

Television Episode: Rene Balcer, *Law and Order: Refuge, Part 2*

Television Feature/Mini-Series: Steven Schachter and William H. Macy, *A Slight Case of Murder*

Young Adult: Vivian Vande Velde, *Never Trust A Dead Man*

National Book Awards ($10,000 ea.)

Medal for distinguished contribution to American letters: Ray Bradbury

Fiction: Susan Sontag, *In America*

Nonfiction: Nathaniel Philbrick, *In the Heart of the Sea: The Tragedy of the Whaleship Essex*

Poetry: Lucille Clifton, *Blessing the Boats: New and Selected Poems 1988-2000*

Young people's literature: Gloria Whelan, *Homeless Bird*

National Book Critics Circle Awards

Biography/autobiography: Henry Wiencek, *The Hairstons: An American Family in Black and White*

Criticism: Jorge Luis Borges, *Selected Non-Fictions*

Fiction: Jonathan Lethem, *Motherless Brooklyn*

Nonfiction: Jonathan Weiner, *Time, Love, Memory: A Great Biologist and His Quest for the Origins of Behavior*

Poetry: Ruth Stone, *Ordinary Words*

Nona Balakian Citation for Excellence in Reviewing: Benjamin Schwarz

PEN Literary Awards

PEN/Nabokov Award (celebrating the accomplishments of a living author whose work, either written or translated into English, represents achievement in a variety of literary genres, $20,000): William Gass

PEN/Laura Pels Foundation Awards for Drama: master American dramatist: Horton Foote; American playwright in mid-career: Suzan-Lori Parks

PEN/Voelcker Award for Poetry ($5,000): Heather McHugh

Margaret Atwood

© Alastair Grant/AP/Wide World Photos

PEN/Ralph Manheim Medal for Translation: Edmund Keeley

PEN/Architectural Digest Award for Literary Writing on the Visual Arts ($10,000): Anne Hollander, *Feeding the Eye*

PEN/Spielvogel-Diamonstein Award for the Art of the Essay ($5,000): Annie Dillard, *For the Time Being*

PEN/Martha Albrand Award for First Nonfiction ($1,000): Eileen Welsome, *The Plutonium Files*

PEN/Martha Albrand Award for the Art of the Memoir ($1,000): Jeffery Smith, *Where the Roots Reach for Water*

PEN/Book-of-the-Month Club Translation Prize ($3,000): Richard Sieburth, translator of *Selected Writings* by Gerard De Nerval

PEN/Poetry in Translation Award ($3,000): James Brasfield & Oleh Lysheha for their joint translation of *The Selected Poems of Oleh Lysheha*

PEN/Amazon.com Short Story Award ($10,000): Marlene Reed Wetzel, *A Map of Tripoli, 1967*

Renato Poggioli Translation Award ($3,000): Wendell Ricketts, for his translation of *La segretaria* and other one-act plays of Natalia Ginzburg

PEN/Faulkner Award for fiction ($15,000): Ha Jin, *Waiting*

Pulitzer Prizes

Biography: Stacy Schiff, *Vera*

Fiction: Jhumpa Lahiri, *Interpreter of Maladies*

General nonfiction: John W. Dower, *Embracing Defeat: Japan in the Wake of World War II*

History: David M. Kennedy, *Freedom From Fear: The American People in Depression*

Poetry: C. K. Williams, *Repair*

Kingsley Tufts Poetry Award ($50,000): Robert Wrigley, *Reign of Snakes*

Whitbread Book of the Year Award ($34,000): Seamus Heaney, for his reworking of the Old English epic poem *Beowulf*

Whiting Awards ($35,000): Fiction writers: Colson Whitehead, Robert Cohen, Samantha Gillison, Lily King and John McManus; poets Albert Mobilio, James Thomas Stevens and Claude Wilkinson; nonfiction writer Andrew X. Pham; and playwright Kelly Stuart

MOTION PICTURES

Academy of Motion Pictures Arts and Sciences ("Oscar") Awards

Actor—leading: Kevin Spacey, *American Beauty*

Actor—supporting: Michael Caine, *The Cider House Rules*

Actress—leading: Hilary Swank, *Boys Don't Cry*

Actress—supporting: Angelina Jolie, *Girl, Interrupted*

Cinematography: Conrad L. Hall, *American Beauty*

Costume design: Lindy Hemming, *Topsy-Turvy*

Director: Sam Mendes, *American Beauty*

Documentary feature: *One Day in September*

Film: *American Beauty*

Foreign-language film: *All About My Mother* (Spain)

Original score: John Corigliano, *The Red Violin*

Original song: "You'll Be In My Heart,"*Tarzan,* music and lyrics by Phil Collins

Screenplay—original: Alan Ball, *American Beauty*

Screenplay—adaptation: John Irving, *The Cider House Rules*

American Film Institute's Life Achievement Award: Harrison Ford

Cannes Film Festival Awards

Palme d'Or (best film): Lars von Trier, *Dancer in the Dark* (Denmark)

Caméra d'Or (first-time feature direction) shared : Hassan Yektapanah, *Djomeh* (Iran); Bahman Ghobadi, *The Time for Drunken Horses* (Iran)

Grand Prize: Jiang Wen, *Devils on the Doorstep* (Japan)

Jury Prize (shared): Samira Makhmalbaf, *Blackboards* (Iran); Roy Anderson, *Songs from the Second Floor* (Sweden)

Best actor: Tony Leung, *In the Mood for Love* (Japan)

Best actress: Bjork, *Dancer in the Dark* (Denmark)

Best director: Edward Yang, *Yi Yi* (Taiwan)

Best screenplay: Neil LaBute, *Nurse Betty* (USA)

Directors Guild of America Awards

Documentary: Nanette Burstein and Brett Morgen, *On the Ropes*

Feature film: Sam Mendes, *American Beauty*

Golden Globe Awards

Actor—drama: Denzel Washington, *The Hurricane*

Actress—drama: Hilary Swank, *Boys*

Michael Caine

Don't Cry

Actor—musical or comedy: Jim Carrey, *Man on the Moon*

Actress—musical or comedy: Janet McTeer, *Tumbleweeds*

Cecil B. De Mille Award (for outstanding contribution to the entertainment field): Barbra Streisand

Director: Sam Mendes, *American Beauty*

Drama: *American Beauty*

Musical or comedy: *Toy Story 2*

Screenplay: Alan Ball, *American Beauty*

Supporting actor: Tom Cruise, *Magnolia*

Supporting actress: Angelina Jolie, *Girl, Interrupted*

PUBLIC SERVICE

Charles A. Dana Foundation Distinguished Achievement Award:

Heinz Awards:

Arts and the Humanities: Peter Matthiessen

Environment: Paul Gorman

Human Condition: Robert Moses

Public Policy: Edward Zigler

Technology, the Economy, and Employment: Mary Good

Sidney Hillman Foundation Awards for pursuit of social justice and public policy for the common good:

General awards ($2,000 ea.): (book)—Katherine S. Newman, *No Shame in My Game: The Working Poor in the Inner City*; (newspaper reporting)—Maya Bell, "Young and Deadly: Why Children Kill,"*The Orlando Sentinel,* Orlando, FL; (magazine feature)—Barbara Ehrenreich, "Nickel-and-Dimed," *Harper's*; (television/radio)—Brian Lamb, C-span

Officers' UNITE Award for Public Service: Studs Terkel

American Institute for Public Service Jefferson Awards

Benefiting the Disadvantaged: Benjamin Carson

Elected or Appointed Official: John Glenn

Private Citizen: Elayne Bennett

Citizen 35 or Younger: Faith Hill

John F. Kennedy Profile in Courage Award ($25,000): California State Sen. Hilda Solis, for efforts in passing a law which helps protect minority neighborhoods from being exposed to pollution from waste sites and factories

Ronald Reagan Freedom Award: Billy Graham

Eleanor Roosevelt Human Rights Award (presented by President Bill Clinton on Dec. 6, 2000): Tillie Black Bear, Frederick Charles Cuny, Norman Dorsen, Elaine R. Jones, Archbishop Theodore McCarrick

Franklin D. Roosevelt Four Freedoms Medal:

Freedom of Speech and Expression: Bronislaw Geremek

Freedom of Religion: Dame Cicely Saunders

Freedom from Want: Monkombu S. Swaminathan

Freedom from Fear: Louise Arbour

Four Freedoms Award: Martti Ahtisaari

Templeton Prize for Progress in Religion ($948,000): Freeman J. Dyson, physicist and ethicist

U.S. Congressional Gold Medal: Cardinal John O'Connor, Ronald and Nancy Reagan, Pope John Paul II, Charles Schulz, U.S. Sen. Richard Lugar

U.S. Congressional Medal of Honor (presented by President Clinton on Feb. 8, 2000): Alfred Rascon

U.S. Presidential Medal of Freedom (presented by President Clinton on Aug. 9, 2000): James Edward Burke, Sen. John Chafee, Gen. Wesley K. Clark, Adm. William Crowe, Marian Wright Edelman, John Kenneth Galbraith, Msgr. George G. Higgins, The Rev. Jesse Jackson, Mildred McWilliams Jeffrey, Dr. Mathilde Krim, George McGovern, Sen. Daniel Patrick Moyni-

U.S. Presidential Medal of Freedom

The Rev. Jesse Jackson   Msgr. George G. Higgins   John Kenneth Galbraith

han, Cruz Reynoso, The Rev. Gardner C. Taylor, Simon Wiesenthal; presented by President Clinton on Dec. 6, 2000, Aung San Suu Kyi

SCIENCE

King Faisal International Prize for Medicine ($200,000): Cynthia Kenyon, University of California, San Francisco, California
King Faisal International Prize for Science ($200,000 (shared)): Edward Osborne Wilson and Dr. John Craig Ventor
Albert Lasker Medical Research Awards
   Basic Research ($10,000 ea.): Aaron Ciechanover and Avram Hershko of the Technion-Israel Institute of Technology; Alexander Varshavsky, California Institute of Technology
   Clinical Research ($25,000 shared): Harvey Alter, National Institutes of Health; Michael Houghton of the Chiron Corporation
   Special Achievement in Medical Science ($25,000): Sydney Brenner, Molecular Sciences Institute
National Medal of Science: Willis Lamb, Jr.
National Medal of Technology: Douglas C. Englebart and Dean Kamen, *individual medals*; Donald B. Keck, Robert D. Maurer, and Peter C. Schultz, *team medal*; IBM Corporation and Louis V. Gerstner, *company medal*
Wolf Prizes ($100,000 each):
   Agriculture: Gurdev S. Khush, International Rice Institute, Philippines
   Chemistry: Frank Albert Cotton, Texas A&M University
   Mathematics: Raoul Bott, Harvard University
   Medicine: not awarded
   Physics: Raymond Davis, Jr., University of Pennsylvania
   Arts (Music): Pierre Boulez, Institut de recherche et coordination acoustique/musique (IRCAM)

TELEVISION AND RADIO

Academy of Television Arts and Sciences ("Emmy") Awards
Actor—comedy series: Michael J. Fox, *Spin City* (ABC)
Actor—drama series: James Gandolfini, *The Sopranos* (HBO)
Actor—miniseries or movie: Jack Lemmon, *Oprah Winfrey Presents: Tuesdays with Morrie* (ABC)
Actress—comedy series: Patricia Heaton, *Everybody Loves Raymond* (CBS)
Actress—drama series: Sela Ward, *Once and Again* (ABC)
Actress—miniseries or movie: Vanessa Redgrave, *If These Walls Could Talk 2* (HBO)
Comedy series: *Late Show With David Letterman*, (CBS)
Directing—comedy series: Todd Holland, *Malcolm in the Middle* (Fox)
Directing—drama series: Thomas Schlamme, *The West Wing: Pilot* (NBC)
Directing—miniseries or movie: Charles S. Dutton, *The Corner* (HBO)
Directing—variety or music program: Louis J. Horvitz, *72nd Annual Academy Awards* (ABC)
Drama series: *The West Wing* (NBC)
Individual performance—variety or music program: Eddie Izzard, *Eddie Izzard: Dress to Kill* (HBO)
Miniseries or a special: *The Corner* (HBO)
Movie made for television: *Oprah Winfrey Presents: Tuesdays With Morrie* , (ABC)
Supporting actor—comedy series: Sean Hayes, *Will and Grace* (NBC)
Supporting actor—drama series: Richard Schiff, *The West Wing* (NBC)
Supporting actor—miniseries or movie: Hank Azaria, *Oprah Winfrey Presents: 'Tuesdays With Morrie'* (ABC)
Supporting actress—comedy series: Meghan Mullally, *Will and Grace* (NBC)
Supporting actress—drama series: Allison Janney, *The West Wing* (NBC)
Supporting actress—miniseries or movie: Vanessa Redgrave, *If These Walls Could Talk 2* (HBO)
Variety, music, or comedy series: *Late Show With David Letterman* (CBS)
Variety, music, or comedy special: *Saturday Night Live: The 25th Anniversary Special* (NBC)
Writing—comedy series: Linwood Boomer, *Malcolm in the Middle: Pilot* (Fox)
Writing—drama series: Aaron Sorkin and Rick Cleveland, *The West Wing: In Excelsis Deo* (NBC)
Writing—miniseries or movie: David Simon and David Mills, *The Corner* (HBO)
Writing—variety or music program: Eddie Izzard, *Eddie Izzard: Dress to Kill* (HBO)
Golden Globe Awards
Actor—comedy series: Michael J. Fox, *Spin City* (ABC)
Actress—comedy series: Sarah Jessica Parker, *Sex and the City* (HBO)
Actor—drama series: James Gandolfini, *The Sopranos* (HBO)
Actress—drama series: Edie Falco, *The Sopranos* (HBO)
Actor—miniseries or TV movie: Jack Lemmon, *Inherit the Wind* (Showtime)
Actress—miniseries or TV movie: Halle Berry, *Introducing Dorothy Dandridge* (HBO)
Drama series: *The Sopranos* (HBO)
Miniseries or TV movie: *RKO 281* (HBO)
Musical or comedy series: *Sex and the City* (HBO)
Humanitas Prizes
Feature film ($25,000): Eric Roth and Michael Mann, *The Insider*
Cable- or public-television production ($25,000): Ann Peacock, *A Lesson Before Dying* (HBO)

Children's animated television production ($10,000): Harvey Fierstein, *Happily Ever After* (HBO)
Children's live-action television production ($10,000): Paris Qualles, *The Color of Friendship* (Disney Channel)
Network television production (90-minute or longer) ($25,000): Tom Rickman, *Tuesdays With Morrie* (ABC)
Network television production (60-minute) ($15,000): Lawrence O'Donnell, Jr., Paul Redford, and Aaron Sorkin, *The West Wing* (NBC)
Network television production (30-minute) ($15,000): Jay Kogen, *Frasier* (NBC)
George Foster Peabody Awards
Radio: *Lost and Found Sound*, National Public Radio and the Kitchen Sisters; *The Mississippi: River of Song*, Smithsonian Productions, presented on Public Radio International; *Morning Edition with Bob Edwards*, National Public Radio
Television: *ABC 2000*, ABC News and anchor Peter Jennings; Bob Simon, for international reporting for CBS News; *Singled Out*, WAGA-TV, Atlanta; *Stadium Investigation*, WCPO-TV, Cincinnati; investigative reporting by GMA Network, Manila, Philippines; *20/20*, "Those Were Our Children," ABC News; *BIOrhythm*, MTV Networks; *Playing the China Card*, Brook Lapping Productions for Channel 4, London, presented on PBS by WGBH-TV, Boston; *Facing the Truth with Bill Moyers*, Public Affairs Television, presented on PBS by Thirteen/WNET; *The Second World War in Colour*, a TWI/Carlton coproduction for TV, London, The History Channel; *ESPN SportsCentury*, ESPN; *Not for Ourselves Alone: The Story of Elizabeth Cady Stanton and Susan B. Anthony*, Florentine Films in association with WETA-TV, Washington, DC, presented on PBS; *Frontline*, "The Lost Children of Rockdale County," a *Frontline* coproduction with 10/20 Productions, presented on PBS; *Dare to Compete: The Struggle of Women in Sports*, HBO Sports; *Arguing the World*, Riverside Films, New York, presented on PBS; *The Valley*, a Mentorn Barraclough Carey production for Channel 4, London; *Fists of Freedom: The Story of the '68 Summer Games*, HBO Sports in association with Black Canyon Productions; *Murder in Purdah*, BBC News, London; *I'll Make Me a World: A Century of African-American Arts*, Blackside, Inc., in association with Thirteen/WNET, presented on PBS; *The Life of Birds by David Attenborough*, BBC in association with PBS; *Goodnight Moon & Other Sleepytime Tales*, HBO; *Annie*, ABC, Storyline Entertainment, Columbia-Tristar Television, Inc., and Chris Montan Productions in association with Walt Disney Television; *VH1 Save the Music Campaign*, VH1 Public Affairs, MTV Networks; *The Sopranos*, HBO and Brillstein-Gray Entertainment; *Having Our Say: The Delany Sisters' First 100 Years*, CBS, Televest, Columbia-Tristar Television in association with Cosby & James Productions; *Strange Justice*, Showtime and Haft Entertainment; *ExxonMobil Masterpiece Theatre: Lost for Words*, a Yorkshire Television Production, presented on PBS by WGBH-TV, Boston; *A Lesson Before Dying*, HBO, a Spanky Pictures Production in association with Ellen M. Krass Productions; *City Life*, Thirteen/WNET; *ExxonMobil Masterpiece Theatre: A Rather English Marriage*, Wall to Wall Television, Ltd., BBC, Carlton Television, presented on PBS by WGBH-TV, Boston; *The West Wing*, NBC, John Wells Productions in association with Warner Bros. Television; *American Presidents: Life Portraits*, C-SPAN, Washington, DC; Sheila Nevins, HBO, personal award

THEATER

New York Drama Critics Circle Awards
   Best foreign play: *Copenhagen*
   Best musical: *James Joyce's The Dead*
   Best play: *Jitney*
Outer Critics Circle Awards
   Actor—play: Derek Jacobi, *Uncle Vanya*
   Actor—musical: Brian Stokes Mitchell, *Kiss Me, Kate*
   Actress—play: Eileen Heckart, *The Waverly Gallery*
   Actress—musical: Marin Mazzie, *Kiss Me, Kate*
   Choreography: Susan Stroman, *Contact* and *The Music Man*
   Director—play: Daniel Sullivan, *A Moon for the Misbegotten* and *Dinner With Friends*
   Director musical: Susan Stroman, *Contact* and *The Music Man*
   Musical: *Contact*
   Play: *Copenhagen*
   Revival—play: *A Moon for the Misbegotten*
   Revival—musical: *Kiss Me, Kate*
Antoinette Perry ("Tony") Awards
   Actor—play: Stephen Dillane, *The Real Thing*
   Actor—musical: Brian Stokes Mitchell, *Kiss Me, Kate*
   Actress—play: Jennifer Ehle, *The Real Thing*
   Actress—musical: Heather Headley, *Aida*
   Choreography: Susan Stroman, *Contact*
   Director—play: Michael Blakemore, *Copenhagen*
   Director—musical: Michael Blakemore, *Kiss Me, Kate*
   Featured actor—play: Roy Dotrice, *A Moon for the Misbegotten*
   Featured actor—musical: Boyd Gaines, *Contact*
   Featured actress—play: Blair Brown, *Copenhagen*
   Featured actress—musical: Karen Ziemba, *Contact*
   Musical: Contact Producers, *Contact*
   Musical—book: Richard Nelson, *James Joyce's The Dead*
   Musical—score: Elton John, Tim Rice, *Aida*
   Play: Copenhagen Producers, *Copenhagen*
   Revival of a musical: Kiss Me, Kate Producers, *Kiss Me, Kate*
   Revival of a play: The Real Thing Producers, *The Real Thing*
   Scenic Design: Bob Crowley, *Aida*
Pulitzer Prize for Drama: Donald Margulies, *Dinner With Friends*

Publishing

As 2000 unfolded, the publishing industries celebrated unusually durable good times, amid often-plush profits and some-times-soaring sales. The popularity of Harry Potter books grabbed headlines around the world, and unprecedented acquisition activity hit the newspaper industry. The planned merger of America Online (AOL) and Time Warner, which includes many popular magazine titles, seemed likely to accelerate the trend of increased synergy between the industries and new technology.

Books. The Book Industry Study Group projected total sales would grow by 5.2% in 2000, to an estimated $24.71 billion, outpacing 1999's 4.3% growth. The greatest increase took place in children's books, helped by sales of Potter titles from Scholastic.

Investment bankers Veronis, Suhler & Associates predicted that during the next five years, spending on consumer titles would grow at a 4.3% compound annual rate. Unit sales were expected to increase by 2% annually. Management-consulting firm PricewaterhouseCoopers foresaw rapid growth in electronic books. These include E-Books, which are read at a computer screen or similar device; print-on-demand titles; and downloaded material from the Internet. PricewaterhouseCoopers predicted that such books would account for 26% of all unit sales by 2004. Spending on them would hit $5.4 billion annually, the firm said, up from $367 million in 2000.

In this regard, Barnes & Noble started an on-line E-Book store, and Amazon.com announced plans to do so. Each involved cooperative arrangements with Microsoft, which provides E-Book technology. Shortly after the merger plans between AOL and Time Warner were announced, Time Warner Trade Publishing said it was setting up iPublish.com, an in-house on-line venture. It would appear early in 2001 and would bring print books to the Web, as well as featuring original E-Books. Some observers predicted that within five or ten years, all books would be available in both digital and print formats. Technology also made possible a trend toward increased self-publishing by authors, who often do so in an effort to earn larger royalties. For example, Stephen King made a manuscript, *The Plant*, available in segments on the Internet.

Acquisition activity grew slightly in 2000. During the summer, McGraw-Hill Companies acquired the Tribune Company's educational-publishing unit for about $635 million, plus $45 million estimated adjustments. In the wake of its purchase of the Times Mirror Company, the Tribune Company is focusing on newspapers and broadcasting. In June, Scholastic Inc. acquired Grolier Inc., publisher of *Encyclopedia Americana*, from French conglomerate Lagardere for $400 million. During the spring, Random House became the first large trade house to purchase a major stake in an electronic publisher. It bought 49% of Xlibris. In October, Reed Elsevier and the Thomson Corporation agreed to buy Harcourt General for $4.4 billion in cash and the assumption of $1.2 bilion of debt. During the summer, Barnes&Noble.com agreed to buy Fatbrain.com for an estimated $64 million in stock and cash.

Large bookstore chains continued to grow in importance. For the year ending in January, total revenues for the four largest rose by 11%. This far outpaced the 3.7% growth among all bookstores. It raised the chains' market share to 50% of retail-bookstore sales. During the first half of 2000, sales at the big four—Barnes & Noble, Borders, Books-A-Million, and Crown—grew by another 8.9%. Losses had continued to mount during 1999 at on-line bookstores Amazon.com and Barnes&Noble.com, but both expressed hopes that profitability soon would occur.

In July, J.K. Rowling's fourth Potter title, *Harry Potter and the Goblet of Fire*, became the fastest-selling title in print history. During the weekend of its initial U.S. release, nearly 3 million copies were sold. Worldwide, the Potter series has sold more than 35 million copies. (*See also* LITERATURE—Children's Literature.)

Magazines. In some ways, 2000 had all the markings of a banner year for magazines. Nonetheless, publishers worried about planned postal-rate increases and possible and actual losses of advertising and human talent to the Internet. During the first six months, advertising pages rose 14% and revenues 17% for consumer magazines, compared with the same period in 1999, according to the Publishers Information Bureau (PIB). For 1999, ad revenues rose 12.8% and pages 5.2%. The circulation picture was a bit more mixed, however.

Merger and acquisition activity continued. In December 1999, Chicago-based equity firm Willis Stein & Partners agreed to buy Ziff-Davis Publishing from Softbank Corp. for $780 million in cash. Ziff-Davis publishes *PC Magazine* and other influential technology titles. In February, Microsoft cofounder Paul Allen bought *The Sporting News*, the nation's oldest sports publication, from Times Mirror. The Tribune Company, which acquired Times Mirror in June, announced plans to sell its magazine properties. Times Mirror publishes *Golf Magazine*, *Field & Stream*, and *Popular Science*.

The biggest merger news involved America Online's proposed $183 billion acquisition of Time Warner. If approved by the regulators, the deal would join the world's largest Internet provider with its biggest media and entertainment company. Observers expressed uncertainty about what the potentially huge impact on magazines might be. Time Warner owns numerous popular titles, including *Time*, *People*, *Sports Illustrated*, and *Entertainment Weekly*. Shortly after merger plans were announced, Time Inc. closed *Life* with the May issue. It kept the title alive on the Web and via planned commemorative issues, however. An inadequate advertising base was blamed. Time Warner also created *Real Simple*, designed to show relatively affluent working mothers how to ease their often-harried lives. The launch was seen as a possible test of synergy between AOL, serving in this case in a promotional role, and the entertainment giant. Based upon early indications, *Real Simple* was a hit, despite receiving some ridicule within the industry.

Even more successful was *O, The Oprah Magazine*, named for founder and editorial director Oprah Winfrey. It appeared in the spring as a coventure of Hearst Magazines and HARPO Entertainment Group. Marketed as a women's personal-growth guide, its initial issue sold more than 1.6 million copies. By the early fall, many media executives and advertisers considered it the most successful new magazine in decades. In September, *Details* reappeared as a general-interest men's magazine. It had closed in March. Rodale folded *New Woman* after its January issue. Slumping retail sales were blamed. Among titles being redesigned was circulation leader *Modern Maturity*, published by the American Association of Retired Persons (AARP). Two versions—one for readers 55–65, and another for those 65 and older—were planned. AARP also announced plans for a new title, *My Generation*, designed to help aging baby boomers lead a fuller life.

Some publishers feared mounting losses of tobacco advertising after Philip Morris said it was suspending cigarette ads in 42 titles with youth readership. Observers said magazines could lose more than $130 million in revenue. The suspension had the most impact on *Sports Illustrated*, *People*, *TV Guide*, and *Entertainment Weekly*. There was no indication that other tobacco companies would do likewise, however.

Newspapers. The short-term outlook for newspapers looked exceptionally bright during 2000. Publishers seemed slightly nervous about the longer-term prospects, however, in the face of technological innovation and declines in circulation and readership. Veronis, Suhler & Associates projected an 8.4% increase in daily-newspaper ad spending for 2000. The firm also predicted that such spending would increase to $63 billion by 2004. Industry observers viewed the projection as very favorable. For 1999, daily ad spending had reached $46.3 billion, a 5.4% increase from 1998.

The number of dailies continued to fall slightly during 1999, to 1,483. Total circulation decreased somewhat, from about 56.2 million in 1998 to 55.97 million. Daily read-

Talk show host Oprah Winfrey, below, launched "O, The Oprah Magazine" as a women's personal-growth guide. The initial issue sold more than 1.6 million copies.

ership also fell. Sunday circulation declined as well, from about 60.1 million to about 59.9 million. In 2000, *USA Today*, became the circulation leader with about 1.777 million, closely followed by its circulation rival *The Wall Street Journal* at 1.762 million. *The New York Times* and the *Los Angeles Times* followed. According to the Newspaper Association of America (NAA), about 8,138 nondailies, with total circulation of about 74.45 million, were being published in 1999. At the end of May, the last daily issue of *The Journal of Commerce*, a newspaper devoted to international trade and transportation, appeared. In June, *JoC Week*, a weekly newsmagazine, debuted in its place.

Record merger and acquisition activity occurred. In June, the Tribune Company completed the largest U.S. newspaper merger ever with its $8 billion purchase of the Times Mirror Company, publisher of the *Los Angeles Times*, *Newsday*, and *Popular Science* magazine. The Tribune Company, publisher of the *Chicago Tribune*, became the third-largest U.S. newspaper company. The deal alone exceeded the previous annual record total of $6.2 billion in such activity among all U.S. newspapers, set in 1997. In August, Gannett Co. completed the $2.6 billion purchase of Central Newspapers, publishers of *The Arizona Republic* of Phoenix, *The Indianapolis Star*, and several other dailies. The deal was the second largest in U.S. newspaper history. In July, Gannett acquired 19 small dailies from Thomson Corporation, which sold all of its U.S. newspaper holdings to focus on Internet-related business. Community Newspaper Holdings, Inc. and Media General, Inc. also purchased Thomson papers, which sold for a reported total of $2.44 billion. In July, following a federal antitrust trial, the Hearst Corporation completed its $660 million purchase of the *San Francisco Chronicle* and its sale of the *San Francisco Examiner*. The Fang family, publishers of a free community paper, obtained the *Examiner* for $100 and received $66 million from Hearst to keep it running for three years. The deal ended a joint-operating agreement in which the business operations, but not the newsrooms, of the two newspapers were merged. In early 2000, a group of investors purchased *The Village Voice* and other alternative titles from Stern Publishing. The investors formed Village Voice Media.

In March, *The Seattle Times* changed to morning circulation, putting it in direct competition with the *Seattle Post-Intelligencer*.

Never before have two morning newspapers competed within a joint-operating agreement. A 1970 law legalized these agreements in an effort to save failing newspapers and preserve competition in what otherwise might be one-newspaper cities. As of early 2000, only 13 such arrangements remained. A joint-operating agreement was proposed between two other morning newspapers, *The Denver Post* and the *Denver Rocky Mountain News*. In September, U.S. Justice Department antitrust regulators said the *News* met the legal definition of a financially failing newspaper and would not survive without the deal. In recent years, the two newspapers had engaged in circulation and advertising wars in which papers at times were sold for a penny per issue.

The four-month suspension of *Boston Globe* columnist Jeff Jacoby for failing to indicate that one of his columns contained previously published materials raised controversy. Critics described the penalty given the conservative columnist as excessive for a minor incident. In a September editorial, *The New York Times* criticized its own coverage of Wen Ho Lee's nuclear-secrets case. The editorial questioned the propriety of singling out Lee, a former Los Alamos scientist, as the prime suspect. (*See also* BIOGRAPHY—Wen Ho Lee.)

Among the titles undergoing a redesign were *The Boston Globe* and *USA Today*. *The Wall Street Journal* announced plans to use more color. Many papers shifted to a narrower page size to save newsprint costs. In the wake of its acquisition, the *Los Angeles Times* ceased publication of 14 "Our Times" community-news sections. Cartoonists Charles Schulz and Jeff MacNelly died. Some newspapers continued to run old editions of Schulz' exceptionally popular "Peanuts" strip. (*See also* CARTOONING: THE COMICS ARE HERE TO STAY, page 74.)

In early summer, the U.S. Circuit Court of Appeals in Washington reversed a National Labor Relations Board (NLRB) ruling that unfair labor practices by management caused the Detroit newspaper strike that began in 1995. The NLRB had ordered the *Detroit Free Press* and *The Detroit News* to rehire all former strikers who had not returned to work. Late in the year, various newspapers were under fire for printing the winner of the tight presidential race before the election was actually decided (*see* U.S. ELECTION SECTION, pages 22–35).

DAVID K. PERRY
The University of Alabama

Refugees and Immigration

The beginning of the 21st century did not end the conflicts and persecution that force people to seek refuge either in their own countries or abroad. To the contrary, millions of displaced people in Africa, Asia, the Balkans, and the Caucasus ushered in the new millennium in refugee camps awaiting the day they could safely return home. At the same time, organized-crime syndicates were using ever-more-sophisticated methods to smuggle Third World immigrants into Western Europe and North America. At year-end, the U.S. Congress and the Clinton administration wrestled over new immigration legislation.

Growing Numbers of Displaced People. During 2000, there were approximately 30 conflicts under way in different regions of the world, the large majority being civil wars within states. Among those uprooted from their homes as a result were Serbs and Roma from Kosovo, several hundred thousand ethnic Chechens who ran for their lives from a brutal Russian onslaught early in the year, hundreds of thousands more who were displaced in the Horn of Africa by fighting on the Ethiopia-Eritrea border, and large numbers of refugees and internally displaced who were uprooted in renewed fighting in Sierra Leone, Angola, and the Democratic Republic of the Congo. Hundreds of thousands of people were pushed off their lands by an insurgency and a counterinsurgency mixed with the drug trade in Colombia, and masses of Afghans fled their homes as a result of continued fighting between the Taliban and opposing forces. Millions of refugees and displaced people began the new millennium living in conditions similar to those existing several centuries earlier: in primitive living conditions, effectively unprotected by the rule of law. The killings of three United Nations High Commissioner for Refugees (UNHCR) staff members in West Timor by rampaging Indonesian militiamen in September underscored the insecurity of international-aid workers in conflict situations. Since 1992, 50 internationally recruited civilians and 148 local United Nations (UN) employees—30 of whom worked for UNHCR—have been killed in the line of duty.

In 2000, internal population displacement was numerically two or three times greater than the global refugee problem. There were around 25 million internally displaced people, and their numbers were increasing more rapidly than refugees. To a great extent, such displacement is a hidden humanitarian problem, harder to identify and more difficult to address than refugees. Contrary to refugees, internally displaced populations are often not in camps, receive little media attention, and have no designated international agency to represent them. To try to improve the international response to this major humanitarian problem, the UN took steps to give more attention to this burgeoning global problem during the year. In January the UN Security Council set up an interagency mechanism, involving the Red Cross and nongovernmental organizations, with all UN agencies to mobilize a more effective response.

Smuggling of Migrants. In an effort to reduce the number of asylum applications, the United States and the European Union (EU) states continued to develop newer border-control measures, contributing to a cycle of more-and-more-restrictive measures. However, it was questionable whether these actions only deterred genuine asylum seekers, merely shifted refugee flows to other countries, or resulted in an expansion of migrant trafficking, illegal immigration, and organized crime in industrialized states. Some experts believed that greater controls meant more people simply "went underground" and entered countries illegally. In other words, the restrictive asylum practices introduced by Western states converted what had been a visible flow of asylum seekers into a covert movement of irregular migrants. In the year 2000, irregular migration represented one-quarter of the total yearly inflow into the United States and as much as one-half of that in Europe. At the global level, some $7 billion was channeled during the year into human trafficking.

Migrant trafficking almost inevitably meant that international criminal syndicates got involved, making huge profits on the stealing and forging of travel documents, passports, and work and residence permits. The migrants themselves were subjected to constant physical insecurity and financial exploitation. In June 2000, British customs officers at the port of Dover discovered 54 dead Chinese men and women who had suffocated in a sealed container truck in their failed attempt to secretly enter Great Britain. The more fortunate migrants often found that they had to turn to crime to pay off their debts to traffickers. Increasingly, illegal migrants were forced to transport or

The aftereffects of the conflict of the early 1990s between Armenia and Azerbaijan remained as hundreds of Azerbaijani refugees, including small children, continued to live in squalor in self-constructed pits or "graves" in the ground in south-central Azerbaijan.

sell drugs for criminal organizations or to engage in prostitution or other criminal activities. Thus, an unintended consequence of the restrictive measures of EU and North American states was to further expand the marginalized, excluded, and criminalized underclass in Western societies. The association with organized crime also made it more difficult for some refugee groups to seek asylum in the West.

U.S. Immigration Debate. Anti-immigration sentiment in the United States has decreased since the early 1990s, when immigration was attacked by politicians and anti-immigration groups as a threat to the economic security of Americans. The nation's low unemployment rate coupled with the need for skilled foreigners to keep the high-technology revolution in gear have been largely responsible for this change of sentiment.

In October the United States enacted legislation to increase the number of visas for highly skilled foreign workers to fill specialized jobs, largely in the high-technology industry. Under the new measure, the Immigration and Naturalization Service (INS) is permitted to issue 195,000 visas a year for each of the next three years, up from the existing limit of 115,000. This action spurred controversy, especially with Hispanic advocacy groups who saw it as a contradiction to hard-line policies on illegal immigration. Late in the year, Democrats and Republicans became embroiled in election-year tensions over broader immigration issues. Congressional Democrats pushed hard for granting amnesty to some 1 million long-term illegal aliens, and for addressing the status of immigrants from Central America. Most Republicans opposed such an amnesty, offering instead more-limited legislation designed to make it easier for as many as 400,000 immigrants to become permanent U.S. residents. A final bill created a new type of temporary visa to allow spouses and children of permanent legal residents or citizens to remain in the United States. A proposal to allow legal immigrants to remain in the United States during the residency application process was included instead on the conference report on the fiscal 2001 spending bill, enacted in December. However, the amnesty for illegal immigrants that the Democrats had wanted was not included in either piece of legislation.

See also CUBA—The Saga of Elián González.

GIL LOESCHER
University of Notre Dame

Religion

Pope John Paul II blesses the crowd after celebrating Mass at Korazim near the Sea of Galilee in Israel on March 24, 2000. The pope was on a six-day visit to the Holy Land where he visited places Jesus had lived and died.

Overview

One of the most significant religious events of the year 2000 was Pope John Paul II's pilgrimage to the Holy Land in March. The trip had three purposes—reconciliation among the Jewish, Christian, and Islamic faiths; peacemaking; and spiritual fulfillment. The pope visited Jordan, Israel, as well as the Palestinian-administered territories, conferring with Jordan's King Abdullah II, Israel's President Ezer Weizman and Prime Minister Ehud Barak, and Palestinian leader Yasir Arafat. On March 23 the pope paid a somber visit to Israel's Yad Vashem Holocaust memorial.

Improved relationships also were on the minds of hundreds of religious leaders who attended the Millennium World Peace Summit of Religious and Spiritual Leaders in New York in early September.

Religion stepped into U.S. politics when Sen. Joseph Lieberman of Connecticut became the first Jew to be nominated to the presidential ticket of a major party. Politics and religion also crossed paths in the U.S. House of Representatives during selection of a new House chaplain. Accusations of anti-Catholic bias ended in March with the swearing-in of the Rev. Daniel Coughlin of Chicago—the first Roman Catholic priest to hold the post. The initial selection of a Protestant minister over another Roman Catholic for the post had fueled the controversy. The Rev. James D. Ford, a Lutheran who had been House chaplain since 1979, retired.

Growth in the Mormon Church was marked in April by the opening of a new Conference Center to replace the Mormon Tabernacle as a site for semiannual church conferences. The church now has nearly 11 million members. A shortage of prospective ministers, priests, and rabbis crossed faith lines.

Templeton Prize The 2000 Templeton Prize for Progress in Religion was awarded to an English-born physicist Freeman J. Dyson. Dyson, a 77-year-old professor emeritus at the Institute for Advanced Study in Princeton, NJ, has challenged humanity to reconcile technology and social justice and has become concerned about the potential for abuse in genetic research.

Far Eastern

Among the biggest news of the year 2000 in Buddhism, Hinduism, and the other Far Eastern religions was the escape of a high-ranking lama from Tibet.

Buddhism, the Dalai Lama, and an Escape. The daring escape of Ugyen Trinley Dorje, 14, from Chinese-controlled Tibet to India occurred during the last week of 1999 and first week of 2000. The boy had been endorsed as the 17th incarnation of the Karmapa, one of Tibetan Buddhism's holiest figures. Details of the Karmapa's escape were sketchy, but he apparently fled, with the aid of others, by horseback, foot, and a four-wheel-drive vehicle across the mountains of Nepal to Dharamsala—the home of the Tibetan government in exile and the Dalai Lama. The Dalai Lama, who is the spiritual and temporal head of Tibetan Buddhists, had made a similar escape 41 years earlier, but was unaware of the Karmapa's escape until the boy's journey was complete.

The Karmapa fled after he was repeatedly denied requests to visit India for religious studies and his Indian-based religious tutor, Tai Situ Rinpoche, was prevented from visiting him in Tibet. Chinese leaders had hoped that Ugyen Trinley Dorje would remain in China, and thereby counter the political power of the exiled Dalai Lama.

Falun Gong Sect. A year after the Chinese government banned the Falun Gong meditation sect, the government acknowledged the fight against the group would be long-lasting. The Chinese government has jailed thousands of Falun Gong members and has launched media smear campaigns to try and get rid of the sect. Despite arrests, harassment, and political campaigns, the Falun Gong remained a strong force in China. The group has been challenging Communist rule in that country, and has attracted millions of followers.

World Hindu Conference. Hindus from around the world gathered on the Caribbean island of Trinidad in August to demonstrate the universality of their religion. The World Hindu Conference focused on the relevance of Hinduism in modern times, and sought to demonstrate that the Hindu religion is not confined to the Indian subcontinent. Conference organizers claimed there were about 1 billion Hindus practicing in 75 countries.

Sikhs Killed. For the first time in recent history, Sikhs were killed in Kashmir, the site of a long conflict between Pakistan and India. Kashmir is the only Muslim-majority territory in Hindu-dominated India, and the Sikhs have been neutral during the dispute. At least 35 Sikhs were killed in a brutal attack while U.S. President Bill Clinton was visiting India in March. One of Clinton's objectives in visiting the region was to reduce tensions between India and Pakistan.

KRISTI VAUGHAN

Islam

Employing new tactics in their continuing insurrection, Muslim groups in the southern Philippine Islands seized hostages and held them for ransom in 2000. When negotiations failed to resolve the ensuing crisis, the army attacked the rebels' strongholds. In Nigeria the introduction of Islamic Shariah law in several predominantly Muslim states precipitated serious demonstrations. Conservative Muslim political parties in Iran lost control of parliament to more moderate groups, sparking hopes for a liberalization of Iranian society. The year also saw adaptations of some traditional practices to contemporary Muslims' needs.

Insurrection in the Philippines. An insurgency spearheaded by the Moro Islamic Liberation Front (MILF) and the smaller, more radical, group, Abu Sayyaf, intensified in the southern Philippines, where most of the country's 5 million Muslims live. The rebels faulted the government for failing to meet obligations from a 1996 peace accord with the Moro National Liberation Front (MNLF), of which the MILF and Abu Sayyaf are splinter groups. Angered by the lack of economic development in their impoverished region and the absence of a viable power-sharing arrangement, the MILF and Abu Sayyaf demanded establishment of an independent Muslim state. To pressure the government, they began attacking army installations and taking civilian hostages. In April, Abu Sayyaf guerrillas kidnapped 21 people, including tourists, from a neighboring Malaysian resort.

When government negotiators refused to meet the kidnappers' demands, some hostages were killed, but a few Malaysians and Filipinos also were released in the following months. The crisis came to a head in August and September, with Libya securing the freedom of most of the Western victims by paying a ransom exceeding $10 million. In return, Libya anticipated an amelioration of its isolation within the international community. But when an Abu Sayyaf faction violated a pledge not to seize additional hostages, President Joseph Estrada ordered a full-scale military assault intended to destroy guerrilla camps, free the remaining hostages, and quell the uprising.

Nigeria and Iran. Muslims and Christians each comprise roughly half of Nigeria's population. The 1999 accession of the country's first Christian president in more than 20 years weakened the political and economic influence of northern Muslim leaders. Hopeful of solidifying the Islamic identity of their followers, they pressed for the expansion of Islamic law, already in effect for civil matters, to criminal cases as well. In January, Zamfara State did impose the Shariah, but only on its Muslim citizens. As other states considered similar actions, riots erupted in Kaduna in February, causing hundreds of deaths and the destruction of mosques, churches, and other buildings. Shortly thereafter, President Olusegun Obasanjo prevailed upon northern leaders to suspend the enforcement of the Shariah. Nevertheless, renewed rioting broke out in Kaduna in May, leading to hundreds of additional fatalities. Although the violence manifested itself along sectarian lines, the core issue at stake was access to political and economic power.

February's parliamentary elections in Iran resulted in the first victory since the Islamic Revolution in 1979 of reformist parties advocating tolerance of diversity and protection of civil rights. Conservative politicians resisted their rivals' triumph—questioning election results, attempting to prevent new deputies from taking their seats, and, in extreme instances, even resorting to assassinations. In April the government closure of most liberal newspapers further impeded the reformers from advancing their agenda. In May, however, Ayatollah Khamenei, the country's supreme leader, ordered the acceptance of the electoral results, paving the way for the convening of the most moderate legislative body in modern Iranian history.

Innovations and Healing a U.S. Rift. Two unrelated events during the year highlighted the magnitude and range of innovations affecting the daily lives of many Muslims. In January, Egypt enacted a law allowing women to sue for divorce, thereby becoming one of very few Muslim-majority states permitting a divergence from traditional interpretations of Islamic law, according to which only men are empowered to initiate divorce except in a few carefully delineated circum-stances. In a quite different sort of change, a financial Web site, begun in March, was the first electronic service of its kind geared specifically to Muslims' needs. The site offers banking, finance, and insurance products and services that comply with Islamic legal requirements.

In the United States, Louis Farrakhan, head of the Nation of Islam, renounced beliefs most Muslims regarded as incompatible with their faith. Farrakhan and leaders of the two largest Muslim organizations in the country—W. Deen Muhammad of the Muslim American Society and Sayyid Syeed of the Islamic Society of North America—appeared together in February, beginning the process of healing a more-than-20-year rift between Farrakhan's group and mainstream American Muslims.

KENNETH J. PERKINS
University of South Carolina

Judaism

Although Orthodox Judaism constituted a minority in Israel and made up less than 10% of American Jewry in 2000, its steadily growing importance within Judaism achieved unprecedented recognition during the year. The widely reviewed book *Jew Vs. Jew*, by Columbia University journalism professor Samuel Freedman, argued convincingly, based on interviews with Jews around the United States, that the religious seriousness of Orthodox Jews was quickly becoming the model for Jews of all persuasions who were determined to preserve the Jewishness of their families. A census of Jewish all-day schools in the United States, conducted by the Avi Chai Foundation, seemed to corroborate this point, showing a large growth in the establishment of day schools under both Orthodox and non-Orthodox auspices.

The Lieberman Candidacy. Freedman's book came out just as Sen. Joseph I. Lieberman of Connecticut (*see also* BIOGRAPHY), an Orthodox Jew, made history by being nominated for vice-president by the Democratic Party, the first Jew ever named to a major party's national ticket. Not only did the U.S. public receive a quick education, via the media, in the principles and practices of Orthodox Judaism, but Lieberman himself became something of a role model for Orthodox and other Jews who sought to maintain their faith undiluted, while at the same time engaging fully in the secular

Campaign signs appeared in Hebrew after Sen. Joseph Lieberman (D-CT) became the first Jew to be nominated to a major party's national ticket.

© AFP/Corbis

U.S. Reform Rabbinate and the Conservative Movement. The U.S. Reform rabbinate resolved a long-standing internal debate in March when the Central Conference of American Rabbis (CCAR) overwhelmingly approved a resolution stating that "the relationship of a Jewish, same-gender couple is worthy of affirmation through appropriate Jewish ritual." To assuage the concerns of traditionalists, the resolution avoided the words "marriage" and "wedding," did not impute holiness to same-gender relationships, and expressed support for the decisions of those rabbis who opted not to officiate at such unions.

Continued strains within the American Conservative movement over religious standards were evident in reaction to the January announcement of new requirements for acceptance into the movement's Ramah summer camps: Only children of Jewish mothers or individuals who had converted would be admitted. This excluded "patrilineal" Jews, whose fathers were Jewish but whose mothers were not, people whose Jewishness was affirmed by Reform. Many Conservative Jews felt the restriction sent an unduly negative message of exclusion.

Jewish Identification. Concern over the erosion of Jewish identification among the young led to two initiatives in 2000. A program called Birthright Israel, conceived and funded by American Jewish philanthropists with help from the Israeli government, sent hundreds of Jewish college students for free ten-day trips to Israel. After their return in January, local federations were so impressed with the newfound Jewish enthusiasm of the participants that, in June, the federations collectively committed more than $50 million to expand the program.

Then, in September, three Jewish philanthropists hosted a meeting in Chicago for Jewish leaders that launched Project STAR (Synagogue Transformation and Renewal). Grounded in the assumption that many young Jews were bored by synagogues, STAR's sponsors pledged $18 million to develop innovative approaches to worship services, education, leadership, and membership activities of the American synagogue.

LAWRENCE GROSSMAN
"The American Jewish Year Book"

world. The simple fact that Lieberman would not campaign on the Jewish Sabbath—and apparently was respected for it by non-Jews—tended to validate the sacrifices that observant Jews long had made to preserve their way of life. And the lift that Lieberman seemed to give the Democratic ticket challenged the assumption, prevalent among many Jews, that anti-Semitism was still a serious national problem.

Yeshiva University and Modernity. Developments at Yeshiva University, the flagship academic institution of American Orthodoxy, also showed a renewed commitment to addressing the challenges of modernity, particularly the religious status of women. In February, 11 members of the rabbinical faculty called on all rabbis to insist on use of a prenuptial agreement at weddings that would, it was hoped, prevent unscrupulous husbands from withholding Jewish divorces from their wives. That same month the university announced the opening of an unprecedented two-year graduate program for women in Talmud—serious study the university previously had confined to men.

But modern Orthodoxy of this sort was hardly the sole voice of Orthodox Judaism, whose spokesmen in Israel tended to be far more insular and antagonistic to modernity. The very week in August that Lieberman was named to the Democratic ticket, Rabbi Ovadia Yosef, a former Sephardic chief rabbi and now the spiritual adviser to Israel's Shas Party, announced that the victims of the Nazi Holocaust had suffered because they carried the reincarnated souls of sinners who had not been adequately punished in their own lifetimes, and declared that Arabs were "snakes."

Orthodox Eastern

Canonizations made news in Orthodox Eastern churches during 2000.

Canonizations. Raphael Hawaweeny, the first Orthodox bishop consecrated on American soil, in 1903, was added to the saints of the Orthodox Church at ceremonies in St. Tikhon's Monastery in South Canaan, PA, May 28–29, 2000. The bishop's canonization was an act of the Orthodox Church in America headed by Metropolitan Theodosius of Washington, DC.

In Moscow in August, the Russian Orthodox Church canonized as saints more than 865 believers who perished during the Bolshevik period. Those canonized included Czar Nicholas II; his wife, the Empress Alexandra; their children; and royal relatives. The canonization ceremonies, which were headed by Patriarch Aleksy II, occurred at the Cathedral of Christ the Savior, which had been rebuilt exactly as it was before being destroyed by the communists.

Issues, Recognition, and Transition. Archbishop Demetrios of the Greek Orthodox Archdiocese of America spent his first year as primate healing wounds from the divisive three-year leadership of his predecessor, Archbishop Spyridon. Demetrios also confirmed the election of the Rev. Nicholas Triantafilou as president of Hellenic College and Holy Cross Greek Orthodox School of Theology in Brookline, MA.

Ecumenical Patriarch Bartholomew of Constantinople, known as "the green patriarch" for his worldwide efforts to support the environment, was not welcome to bring his ecological activities to Russia because of new conflicts with the Moscow Patriarchate over church leadership in Estonia. The Russian Church claimed that Bartholomew was unfaithful to a 1996 agreement to have a bishop of the Moscow Patriarchate in Estonia along with a hierarch appointed by Constantinople, thus giving Orthodox believers in the country a choice of ecclesiastical allegiance. Communion between the churches was retained, but relations were strained.

The Serbian Orthodox Church rejoiced in the downfall of Yugoslavia's President Slobodan Milosevic and welcomed the newly elected government as the devastated church continued to rebuild. Patriarch Maxim of the Orthodox Church in Bulgaria retained recognition by other Orthodox churches, while a rival patriarch named Pimen led a schismatic group that continued to receive the support of the Bulgarian government. Patriarch Teoctist, 87, of the Romanian Orthodox Church asked forgiveness of his church and nation for cooperating with the Nicolae Ceauşescu regime, which "made a great number of the faithful suffer." Archbishop Anastasios of Tirana, who continued the reconstruction of the Orthodox Church in Albania, was acclaimed for philanthropic service during the conflict in Kosovo. The Orthodox Church of Greece, led by Archbishop Christodoulos of Athens, fought against government plans to remove the religious-affiliation entry from state identification cards.

Archbishop Nikolai of Prešov, Slovakia, was elected to succeed the deceased Metropolitan Dorotej of Prague as primate of the Orthodox Church in the Czech Republic and Slovakia. Bishop Daniel (Nushiro) was elected primate of the Japanese Orthodox Church to succeed the deceased Metropolitan Theodosius of Tokyo after the first elected successor, Bishop Peter (Arihara), died of cancer before being enthroned.

Ecumenism. Pope John Paul II met with Orthodox leaders during his March visit to the Holy Land. Common declarations were made about peace and the need to safeguard access to sacred sites in the Holy Land for all religious believers. The Joint International Commission for Theological Dialogue between the Roman Catholic Church and the Orthodox Church met for the first time in its 20-year history in North America in July. Those gathered in Emmitsburg, MD, failed for the first time to make a common statement because of bitter division over the issue of "uniatism" (papal authority).

THE REV. THOMAS HOPKO, *Dean, St. Vladimir's Orthodox Theological Seminary*

Protestantism

For Protestants in 2000, the long debate over questions of homosexuality focused on the emotionally charged issue of whether churches should bless same-sex unions. There also were continuing struggles over the role of women in at least two Protestant denominations. And Lutherans and Episcopalians took a historic step forward on the path of ecumenism.

Social Issues. In the most tumultuous meeting of a year filled with denominational drama, delegates to the 8.5-million-member United Methodist Church's (UMC's) quadrennial General Conference watched as dozens of protesters, including two bishops, were arrested on the convention floor and a woman teetered on a balcony rail screaming of her gayness. Despite it all, 992 delegates voted 2–1 to retain language in the church's Book of Discipline that says that "homosexual practice is incompatible with Christian teaching," and that no self-avowed sexually active homosexual can be ordained to the ministry or given a pastoral appointment. By a similar ratio, they voted to maintain prohibitions against the blessing of same-sex unions. During the votes, protesters who were part of a coalition of United Methodist organizations supporting gay rights stood silently on the floor in keeping with an agreement not to disrupt the conference. But afterward, they moved onto the dais and began singing the civil-rights anthem "We Shall Overcome." Police removed the demonstrators and charged them with disrupting a lawful meeting. Among those arrested were Bishop Joseph Sprague of Chicago and Bishop Susan Morrison of Albany, NY. The Rev. Gregory Dell of Chicago, who had been suspended from the ministry in 1999 for blessing a same-sex union a year earlier, also was arrested.

The General Assembly of the Presbyterian Church (U.S.A.), meeting in sunny Long Beach, CA, also held the line on homosexual relationships. After wrenching hearings, commissioners voted 268–251 (51% to 48%) to send a constitutional amendment to the country's 173 presbyteries that would explicitly prohibit performance of same-sex unions in the denomination's churches or by its clergy. The amendment would add a section to the Directory of Worship that calls for people to live in fidelity within heterosexual marriage or in singleness, and continues, "Church property shall not be used for, and church officers shall not take part in conducting, any ceremony or event that pronounces blessing or gives approval of the church or invokes the blessing of God" on any other relationship. The assembly rejected, 453–71, an overture that would have declared an "irreconcilable impasse" in the denomination over issues such as biblical authority, salvation, and the nature of the church. Instead, the assembly voted to send a letter to members of the denomination saying, "We choose to see differences positively and believe that differences in fact have the potential to make our unity in Christ even stronger."

The Episcopal Church's General Convention, meeting in Denver in July, stopped

In Cincinnati, OH, July 11, 2000, the Rev. Vashti McKenzie, above, became the first woman to be consecrated as a bishop of the 2.5-million member African Episcopal Church.

just short of creating a rite that could be used by same-sex couples in commitment ceremonies. Both the House of Deputies and the House of Bishops of the 1.5-million-member denomination overwhelmingly passed a resolution recognizing that some people in the church live in "lifelong committed relationships" outside heterosexual marriage. But both groups failed to ask for development of a liturgy "by means of which the church may express" support of committed relationships outside the sacrament of marriage.

Southern Baptists, meeting in Orlando, adopted a revised statement of faith that removes room for interpretation of Scriptures and specifically prohibits women pastors, gay relationships, abortion, and racism. Conservative leaders in the 15-million-member denomination regarded the overwhelming vote for the new Baptist Faith and Message as the culmination of a two-decade-long battle for the Bible. Although Southern Baptists emphasized that the statement is not a creed, the six seminaries and six national agencies of the convention will use it as a standard. Preconvention publicity centered on the question of whether women should be pastors, but debate on the floor focused on the theological issue of the relationship between Jesus and Scripture. Specifically, the most significant debate was whether to restore language from the 1963 version of the document that said, "The criterion by which the Bible is to be interpreted is Jesus Christ." Efforts to replace the wording failed. In other action, the Southern Baptist Convention approved a resolution supporting use of the death penalty "as a legitimate form of punishment for those guilty of murder or treasonous acts that result in death," but only when there is "clear and overwhelming evidence of guilt." In the months following the June meeting, several churches left the convention, citing the new Faith and Message. Former President Jimmy Carter severed ties with his lifelong denomination, saying it had become "increasingly rigid." The Baptist General Convention of Texas also voted later in the year to cut back $5 million in support for the denomination.

Members and supporters of Soulforce—an ecumenical gay-rights group headed by the Rev. Mel White, a former ghostwriter for several leading conservative Christians—were arrested in choreographed demonstrations at various conventions and meetings.

Ecumenical Efforts. In a symbolic exchange of chalices, the presiding bishops of the Episcopal Church and the 5.2-million-member Evangelical Lutheran Church in America (ELCA) symbolically sealed their churches' full-communion agreement in July. The historic event took place at the triennial meeting of the Episcopal Church's General Convention in Denver after Episcopalians approved an agreement, "Called to Common Mission," that was passed by the ELCA in 1999.

The country's two largest ecumenical organizations—the National Council of Churches (NCC) and the National Association of Evangelicals (NAE)—seemed to be breaking down barriers that have divided American Christians into separate camps. In 2000 the more conservative NAE removed its rule excluding from membership churches that also belong to the NCC. The NCC, meanwhile, is beginning an initiative to work with Evangelicals, Roman Catholics, and Pentecostals when possible.

An effort to merge two historically black denominations stalled in 2000. Delegates to the convention of the 1.3-million-member African Methodist Episcopal (A.M.E.) Zion Church delayed plans to merge with the 719,000-member Christian Methodist Episcopal (C.M.E.) Church until at least 2008. Leaders of the two groups had hoped the convention would approve a plan that called for a merger in 2004. The A.M.E. Zion Church, founded in New York in 1796, and the C.M.E. Church, founded in 1870 with roots in the South, share similar theology and have a record of working together.

New Leadership. The Rev. Vashti McKenzie, pastor of Payne Memorial African Episcopal Church in Baltimore, became the first woman elected as a bishop in her 2.5-million member denomination. McKenzie, 53, a journalist before entering the ministry, referred to her elevation as "breaking the stained-glass ceiling." The election came at the denomination's meeting on July 11 at the Cincinnati Convention Center. Hours later, four male bishops formally consecrated her. McKenzie was assigned to head the 18th Episcopal District in southern Africa.

The Rev. James Merritt, pastor of First Baptist Church in Snellville, GA, was elected president of the Southern Baptist Convention at its annual meeting in Orlando. The Presbyterian Church (U.S.A.) elected a Korean refugee, the Rev. Syngman Rhee, as its moderator. Rhee, 69, is a professor of mission and evangelism at Union Theological Seminary in Richmond, VA. The assembly also reelected the Rev. Clifton Kirkpatrick as its stated clerk.

GAYLE WHITE, *Religion Writer*
"The Atlanta Journal-Constitution"

Roman Catholicism

Roman Catholics around the world celebrated 2000 as a Year of Jubilee, commemorating the 2,000th anniversary of the birth of Christ. For Catholics, the special year started not on January 1 but on Dec. 24, 1999, when Pope John Paul II opened the bronze "Holy Door" of St. Peter's Basilica in Rome. That door had been sealed since the end of the last Holy Year in 1984. It was the signal for the entrance of the first of what would be millions of pilgrims who would visit Rome before the door would shut on Christmas Eve 2000.

Pope John Paul II. The pope, too, became a pilgrim through the March 20–26 visit to the Holy Land, which saw stops in Jordan, Israel, and the Palestinian territories. It was John Paul's 91st foreign trip as pope. The previous week, during a St. Peter's Basilica Lenten liturgy, the pope led Vatican officials in asking for forgiveness for Christian sins throughout history, including persecution of Jews, intolerance for other religions, and marginalization of women. Similar apologies were echoed by bishops worldwide.

Pope John Paul II was greeted by some 2 million Catholic youth from around the world during World Youth Day celebrations in Saint Peter's Square in mid-August 2000.

In the spring, the Vatican published the text of the third secret of Fátima, revealing that the prophecy referred to the 1981 assassination attempt against Pope John Paul II. The pontiff visited the Fátima shrine in May.

John Paul turned 80 on May 18, and his physical condition continued to deteriorate, especially from the effects of what is presumed to be Parkinson's disease.

Canonizations and Beatifications. On October 1, Mother Katharine Drexel (1858–1955), a Philadelphia heiress who became a nun and spent $20 million caring for African-Americans and Native Americans, was the second U.S.-born person to be canonized. On the same day, against the opposition of the People's Republic of China, 87 Chinese Christians and 33 European missionaries to China who had been slain over the years also were canonized. It was the contention of the Chinese government that many of these men and women were not martyrs but traitors killed during the Opium Wars and the Boxer Rebellion. At the same time, the pope also canonized Josephine Bakhita, a former slave from the Sudan, and María Josefa, a Spanish nun who founded a religious order.

Earlier, the September 3 beatification—the final step before canonization—of two previous popes had engendered controversy. Few, if any, disagreed with John Paul II's beatification of John XXIII (1881–1963), the highly regarded architect of Vatican Council II. However, the similar honor accorded to the convener of Vatican Council I in the 19th century, Pius IX (1792–1878), was opposed by many Catholics who considered him reactionary, and by Jews who charged him with anti-Semitism.

Relations with China and other Religions. Strained relations between the Vatican and China also were exacerbated by the Vatican's refusal to cut diplomatic ties with Taiwan, and by China's perceived persecution of Catholics who are not members of the government-sanctioned Chinese Patriotic Catholic Association. The latter is not permitted to have ties with the Holy See.

In September, relations between Catholicism and other religions became further strained by the issuance of *Dominus Iesus*, a Vatican document signed by Cardinal Joseph Ratzinger of the Congregation for the Doctrine of the Faith. While the document acknowledged that others could be saved it said the Church of Christ "continues to exist fully only in the Catholic Church." Vatican officials contended that the purpose of the document was to combat relativism, the belief that one religion is as good as another. On September 27, at an interreligious meeting in Rome, John Paul II tried to soothe ruffled feelings when he urged further steps in dialogue with other religions, saying the difference between religions "does not cancel the common condition of being pilgrims."

Transition. On May 3, American Catholics lost their best-known prelate, Cardinal John J. O'Connor, archbishop of New York, who died of cancer at age 80 (*see* OBITUARIES). Edward M. Egan (*see* BIOGRAPHY), 68, the bishop of Bridgeport, CT, was named to the New York post. On November 21, Pope John Paul II accepted the resignation of Cardinal James A. Hickey, 80, the archbishop of Washington, DC. Theodore E. McCarrick, 70, archbishop of Newark for 14 years, was named as Hickey's successor. Archbishop McCarrick had served as head of various U.S. bishops' committees.

Before year-end, the number of cardinals under age 80 and eligible to vote for a pope would slip to under 100. In the year 2000 the Vatican estimated the number of Catholics around the globe was more than 1 billion, representing 17.4% of the world's population. The U.S. figures stood at almost 62.4 million, or 23% of the national total.

LOUIS BALDWIN
Reporter, "Catholic Standard and Times"

Retailing

The year 2000 was a roller-coaster ride for the U.S. retail industry. On the one hand, the economy was robust for most of the year. Consumer confidence remained high, inflation and unemployment were low, and consumers continued to spend through much of the year. Conversely, interest rates rose, fuel prices skyrocketed, and some analysts predicted a 2001 recession. Additionally, by November, the Standard & Poor's (S&P) 500 stock index lost 8% of its value since Jan. 1, 2000, and the S&P Retailing Industry Index was down 30% during the same period.

E-Commerce (Internet Shopping). There was a shakeout of Internet companies in 2000. Many went out of business, others had their stock prices plunge 80% or more, and others totally revamped their Web sites and committed enormous amounts of capital to better compete in the burgeoning market. Despite complications, E-commerce gained widespread acceptance among consumers, businesses, and government.

According to Jupiter Communications, an Internet-research company, on-line projections of spending during the November–December holidays would exceed $12 billion in 2000, up from $3.1 billion and $7 billion during the same time period in 1998 and 1999, respectively. Jupiter further estimated that 48 million U.S. shoppers made purchases on the Internet in 2000, up from 33 million in 1999. Total on-line commerce for 2000, including business-to-business transactions, approached $132 billion. That total was expected to reach $283 billion in 2001 and $533 billion by 2002.

"E-wallets" and auction sites became popular in 2000. Shopping "bots" (short for robots) purport to find the cheapest prices on products and services available on-line, and search for those bargains automatically in a matter of seconds. The E-wallet software was designed to securely store a person's credit-card number, mailing address, and other information, and transmit it safely and efficiently to on-line merchants. On-line auctions expanded, despite fraud and capitalization problems. The world's largest on-line auction site, eBay, announced that its third-quarter profits rose 13-fold, and its third-quarter site traffic more than doubled to 18.9 million; eBay also had massive expansion plans for 2001.

A further indication of the E-retailing trend was the substantial commitment that major traditional retailers—such as Wal-Mart, Target, Costco, Sears, JCPenney, and Kmart—made in this milieu. All focused on developing their Internet business, although it was evident that they were taking a slow, cautious approach to on-line selling.

The U.S. Commerce Department released its first E-commerce sales report in March. It reported that Internet sales accounted for a small portion of total retail sales, only 0.63%, in the fourth quarter of 1999. By the second quarter, however, sales rose to 0.68%, and preliminary third-quarter data reported that retail Internet sales increased to 0.78%, as total E-commerce sales rose to $6.37 billion.

Retail Leaders. Wal-Mart Stores, the world's largest retailer, announced late in the year that it would embark on an aggressive expansion plan that involved building at least 365 stores, supercenters, warehouse clubs, and separate grocery stores beginning in February 2001. When completed, the retailer would have 4,465 stores. Although Wal-Mart had a successful year in 2000, its sales growth was slowed down; and the company had problems with its presence on the Internet as its on-line shopping site was closed and revamped in October. Meanwhile, Kmart, the second largest retailer, had a difficult year, reporting a third-quarter loss of $67 million. On December 28, Montgomery Ward ended 128 years in business, filing for bankruptcy.

Consumer Credit. By year's end, consumer debt was up 8%—approaching $1.5 trillion—according to the Federal Reserve. Credit-card debt, which accounted for $501 billion of consumer debt, increased by 10% over 1999. The average household credit-card balance approached $8,000. At 18%, annual interest costs on that amount totaled about $1,400. Nonetheless, it appeared that many consumers had learned how to use credit cards wisely by avoiding the revolving-credit trap. According to CardWeb, 44% of cardholders paid their bills in full every month, up from 29% in 1990.

Toys. Every year has its "toy of the moment." For example, Tickle Me Elmo (1996); Sing & Snore Ernie (1997); Furby (1998); and Pokémon (1999) generated wild hype. The most popular toy in 2000 was Poo-Chi, Sega's interactive robotic dog. PlayStation 2, another "must have" game gift, had supply problems, and consumer demand was restricted until after the holidays.

MEL J. ZELENAK
University of Missouri-Columbia

Romania

During 2000, Romania confronted a series of domestic problems, including political turmoil within the governing coalition, stalled economic reforms, and mounting social unrest.

Political Turmoil. Romania's ruling coalition was torn by conflicts during the year. The National Peasants' Christian and Democratic Party (PNTCD) leadership elected a new secretary-general, replacing former Prime Minister Radu Vasile, who was expelled from the party. He had been succeeded as prime minister by Mugur Isarescu in December 1999. In local elections in June, the governing parties performed poorly. The oppositionist Party of Social Democracy in Romania (PDSR) scored a major victory over the ruling coalition, the Democratic Convention of Romania (CDR), which came in fifth in mayoral elections.

In the parliamentary elections in November, the PDSR gained a majority, and its leader, Ion Iliescu, gained 37% of the vote in the presidential race. Iliescu, who had been president (1990–96), faced Corneliu Vadim Tudor of the Greater Romanian Party (PRM) in a December 10 runoff. Tudor had surprised analysts by winning 27% of the vote in the first round. In the second round on December 10, Iliescu triumphed with 67% of the vote to Tudor's 33% after the country's democratic forces decided to support Iliescu's candidacy.

Economic Turbulence. The collapse in public support for the reformist government of President Emil Constantinescu was the result of a combination of factors, including economic hardship and corruption. Inflation exceeded 50% for the year, and the gross domestic product (GDP) was projected to grow by only 1.3%. Prime Minister Isarescu asserted that the economic strategy for 2000–2004 would need to be painful, involving large cuts in the civil service and the closure of unproductive state enterprises.

President Constantinescu claimed that a "mafia-type system with links to official institutions" was dominating the country's economic and political structures. He asserted that competition among parties and individuals had "deteriorated into a blind struggle for power-seeking personal and group interests." Meanwhile, a U.S.-funded study published in August showed that Romania's "bureaucratic maze" smothered free enterprise and fueled official corruption.

In June police arrested five top bankers involved in the collapse of the National Investment Fund. The government suspended the executive board of the country's capital-market regulatory agency, which had administered the fund. More than 1,000 people who had invested in the collapsed fund clashed with riot police outside the government's headquarters in Bucharest as they staged a protest to demand that the government return their money.

The International Monetary Fund (IMF) was critical of Romania's economic performance. The government was moving too slowly in privatizing state-owned companies, had failed in its pledge to curb inflation, and had made little progress in reducing debts in state-owned companies. The European Parliament's report on Romania's progress toward membership in the European Union (EU) concluded that Bucharest had a long way to go before it was ready for accession. The report pointed to serious environmental problems, corruption, and the growth of crime as well as the urgent need to reform the legal system.

Balkan Initiatives. Romania continued to promote Balkan reconstruction. Officials from Romania, Albania, Bosnia and Herzegovina, Bulgaria, Croatia, Hungary, and Macedonia agreed in February to establish a program to encourage free trade and transportation across their borders. The EU, the United States, and the World Bank pledged to provide financial aid for the upgrading of border crossings, customs administration, and enhancing the Internet infrastructure in order to increase the flow of information among those countries.

JANUSZ BUGAJSKI
Center for Strategic and International Studies

ROMANIA • Information Highlights

Official Name: Romania.
Location: Southeastern Europe.
Area: 91,699 sq mi (237 500 km²).
Population (2000 est.): 22,411,121.
Chief Cities (July 1, 1997 est.): Bucharest, the capital, 2,027,512; Iaşi, 348,399; Constanţa, 344,876.
Government: *Head of state,* Ion Iliescu, president (elected December 2000). *Head of government,* Mugur Isarescu, prime minister (named December 1999). *Legislature*—Parliament: Senate and Chamber of Deputies.
Monetary Unit: Leu (25,653 lei equal U.S.$1, Dec. 21, 2000).
Gross Domestic Product (1999 est. U.S.$): $87,400,000,000 (purchasing power parity).
Economic Indexes: *Consumer Prices* (1999, 1991 = 100): all items, 28,394.4; food, 23,789.2. *Industrial Production* (1999, 1990 = 100): 48.9.
Foreign Trade (1999 U.S.$): *Imports,* $10,392,000,000; *exports,* $8,505,000,000.

Russia

The year 2000, President Vladimir Putin's first year in office, was a successful period for Russia politically and economically and in foreign affairs. Politically, Russia completed its first constitutional transfer of power, with Putin's election followed by a spate of political and legal reforms. On the economic front, the country enjoyed its best year since the 1991 breakup of the USSR. In foreign affairs, Putin displayed considerable talent at diplomacy and statesmanship on the world stage. (*See* BIOGRAPHY—Putin, Vladimir Vladimirovich.)

Political Developments. President Boris Yeltsin's surprise resignation on Dec. 31, 1999, transferred power to Prime Minister Putin, who became acting president under the Russian Constitution, pending a special presidential election. The campaign got under way in early January, with Putin the heavy favorite in a field of 11 candidates. As a campaigner, Putin concentrated on appearing presidential, combining a U.S.-style "Rose Garden" strategy with a number of high-profile and popular public actions: He boosted pensions, announced help for orphans, found money to keep the space station *Mir* flying, engaged in a photo session with frontline Russian troops fighting in Chechnya, and published a campaign autobiography. In the March 26 election, turnout was high at 69%, and Putin coasted to victo-

ry with 52.94% of the vote. Putin's percentage avoided the necessity of a runoff election. A distant second was Gennady Zyuganov, leader of the Russian Communist Party, with 29.21%. Putin's victory was broad-based, as he carried 83 of the 89 regions of the Russian Federation. Although allegations of vote fraud later surfaced, even the Communists conceded that Putin would have won a two-candidate runoff if he had failed to receive more than 50% of the vote in the first round.

Even during the election campaign, Putin set about his long-term strategy of strengthening the Russian state to make it more effective at home and abroad. Yeltsin had endured constant policy conflict with the majority Communist Party opposition in the State Duma, the lower house of parliament. Acting President Putin was presented with the opportunity of working with a new Duma, elected in December 1999. The party that Putin had backed, Unity, came in a close second to the Communist Party. Thus, Unity—combined with other centrist parties friendly toward the Kremlin—was able to unseat the Communists as the long-dominant faction in the Duma. However, to soften Communist opposition, Putin, behind the scenes, engineered a deal by which Unity and the Communists divided a majority of the most important committee chairmanships. The deal infuriated the other four parties in the Duma, but ensured a Kremlin-

In early June 2000, President Bill Clinton visited Moscow and hoped to illustrate the positives behind U.S. construction of an antimissile shield. Despite two days of detailed talks, President Vladimir Putin was not persuaded.

friendly lower house through which long-blocked reform initiatives might now pass.

Following his inauguration as Russia's second president on May 7, Putin proceeded with his state-strengthening program on several domestic fronts—by installing a prorefom prime minister, curbing the heavy political influence of "big business," and reasserting strong federal control over Russia's numerous runaway provincial governments. To serve as prime minister, President Putin nominated Mikhail Kasyanov, a 43-year-old liberal economist who had served as Putin's first deputy prime minister. Kasyanov was quickly confirmed by the Duma, and began the process of setting up a government or cabinet. Simultaneously, Putin launched his offensive against the oligarchs who dominated the business world and wielded inordinate influence over public policy. All of the half a dozen or so major oligarchs were potentially vulnerable to legal action. They had acquired their great wealth during the Yeltsin years through buccaneering practices. Nevertheless, Putin was selective in his assault on the business-politics nexus. He primarily singled out the two most prominent figures—Vladimir Gusinsky and Boris Berezovsky. In May the police made a dramatic midday raid on Gusinsky's corporate offices in Moscow, carting off large quantities of files to be sifted through by criminal investigators. A month later, Gusinsky was arrested and temporarily jailed on a charge of embezzlement. The attack on Gusinsky had a chilling effect on the big-business community. Berezovsky, a self-proclaimed kingmaker who had been close to the Yeltsin family, was next to experience the Kremlin's displeasure. By the end of the year, both men were in self-imposed exile abroad to excape prosecution. The remaining oligarchs took notice and trimmed their sails.

The reformation continued with Putin's radical reconfiguration of the power relationship between Moscow's central government and the 89 subnational governments, organized mainly as regions or ethnic republics. Continuous legislative-executive infighting during Yeltsin's tenure had allowed these governments to gain considerable leverage over the center. As elite groups in Moscow bid for support, the situation became quite abnormal. In fact, a majority of the 21 republic constitutions were at variance with the Russian Constitution. Moreover, an estimated 50,000 legal acts by regional governments conflicted

---

RUSSIA • Information Highlights

Official Name: Russian Federation.
Location: Eastern Europe and northern Asia.
Area: 6,592,772 sq mi (17 075 200 km²).
Population (2000 est.): 146,001,176.
Chief Cities (July 1, 1995, est.): Moscow, the capital, 8,368,449; St. Petersburg, 4,232,105; Nizhniy Novgorod (Gorky), 1,375,570; Novosibirsk, 1,367,596; Yekaterinburg (Sverdlovsk), 1,276,659.
Government: *Head of state,* Vladimir V. Putin, president (took office May 7, 2000). *Head of government,* Mikhail M. Kasyanov, prime minister (appointed May 2000). *Legislature*—Federal Assembly: Federation Council and State Duma.
Monetary Unit: Ruble (27.8840 rubles equal U.S.$1, Dec. 20, 2000).
Gross Domestic Product (1999 est. U.S.$): $620,300,000,000 (purchasing power parity).
Economic Indexes: *Consumer Prices* (1999, 1991 = 100): all items, 773,814.0; food, 810,254.0. *Industrial Production* (1998, 1990 = 100): 45.4.
Foreign Trade (1999 U.S.$): *Imports,* $40,429,000,000; *exports,* $74,663,000,000.

---

with federal legislation, subnational entities shortchanged the national treasury on collected tax revenue, and many of the powerful governors and republic presidents ignored presidential decrees. Putin, along with most of the national elite, found the situation intolerable, and a factor contributing to the fiscal and administrative weakness of the Russian state.

Putin's plan for reigning in the provinces involved three steps. First, by means of presidential decree, Putin divided the Russian federal system into seven superadministrative districts. This corresponded with the country's seven military districts, and, similarly, the new districts subsumed the 89 regions and republics. As administrators of the new districts, Putin appointed a cadre of five military and police generals along with two politicians to serve as superpresidential representatives, accountable to the president. Armed with extensive federal powers, the instructions of the new viceroys were to ensure that local laws, charters, and constitutions were in compliance with federal legal acts, and to oversee the implementation of federal legislation.

The next two steps required new laws proposed by the Putin administration and eventually passed in the Duma. The first converted the Federation Council, the upper house of parliament, from a part-time body to a professional legislature, to which full-time legislators would be sent from each constituent unit of the federation. This bill was bitterly opposed by a majority of the existing Federation Council for two main reasons: The former senators as full-time subnational executives would lose their

© Efrem Lukatsky/AP/Wide World Photos

The Russian military continued their bitter struggle with rebels from Chechnya who were seeking independence from Russia, forcing numerous Chechen refugees to live in bleak tent camps and subsist on distributed food.

leverage in the national political process, as well as their access to the president; and the governors and presidents as former senators would lose their legislative immunity from criminal prosecution. Both concerns were brushed aside by the Duma, which mustered the necessary supermajority to override the Federation Council's veto and pass the bill along to Putin, who signed it into law. As a conciliatory gesture, however, Putin created a consultative body, the State Council, in which the 89 political executives were invited to participate. Chaired by the president, the State Council's steering committee of seven executives planned to meet monthly, while the full council scheduled quarterly gatherings. The initial meetings were in November.

The remaining law to complete Putin's federal reform package allows the president to remove from office, subject to court review, any governor found to be systematically violating federal law. While the elective principle remained in place at the subnational level of government, this law gave the Kremlin significant leverage over any regional executive who might presume to withhold federal-tax revenue or disregard parliamentary legislation or presidential decrees.

August proved to be a fateful month for Putin. On August 12 the pride of the Russian fleet, the submarine *Kursk*, sank in the Barents Sea while taking part in maneuvers. Explosions aboard the *Kursk* were recorded by other vessels. The Russian Navy launched a valiant but futile effort to rescue those sailors still alive in the downed vessel. The

sad spectacle was played out over the following week on national television; families of the doomed men gathered on the northern shores, only to see their hopes dashed in the end. The fallout from this tragedy took several forms. The bungled rescue attempt highlighted the funding crisis of the Russian armed forces—the navy had previously rented out its essential deep-sea diving equipment to private oil-drilling companies. The admirals' immediate reaction, blaming foreign submarines in the area, was an echo of Cold War thinking when it was readily apparent that the explosions were internal to the *Kursk*. The government's slow response to foreign offers of assistance reflected lingering illusions about lost superpower capabilities; by the time the Norwegians—with the right gear—were called in, it was too late. Finally, President Putin was on vacation when the accident occurred, and his initial reaction was insufficiently sensitive to the political and human dimensions of the crisis, forcing him to play catch-up by belatedly rushing to the scene and apologizing to the families of the crew. Casting a further pall, just two weeks later an electrical fire broke out in Moscow's Ostankino Television Tower, the world's second-tallest structure; four people were killed, and television and telecommunications in the Moscow region were knocked out. Firefighters had great difficulty fighting the blaze, once again calling into public question the condition of Russia's infrastructure and the state's capabilities in coping with such problems. Compounding the impression was the image of the Russian military sinking deeper into the quagmire of the ongoing second war against the Chechen guerrillas. Perhaps the only good news at the end of summer in Russia, at least for the faithful, was the canonization of Czar Nicholas II and his family by the Orthodox Church.

Economy. Russia had a banner year economically, by far the best to date of its post-Soviet experience. While many of the positive trends had been under way in the latter half of 1999—and President Putin could not necessarily claim credit—he was surely a beneficiary of better times. Nearly all international financial agencies raised their estimates of Russia's economic prospects for the year, although Russian economists worried that the post–August 1998 recovery might be waning, especially if world oil prices, a main driver of Russia's economy, softened. While 1999 had finished strong—with a 3.2% increase in the gross domestic product (GDP), the fastest growth since the 1980s—the first quarter of 2000 came in with a GDP growth rate of 7.8%. Other economic positives for the quarter included substantial increases in the average monthly wage, industrial production, capital inflows, and the trade surplus, along with notable decreases in the consumer-price index and unemployment. By late spring, several international bond-and debt-rating services had upgraded Russia.

The boom in the industrial economy continued through the second and third quarters. For the first nine months, GDP growth stood at 7.3% year to year; industrial production was up 9.8%; foreign investment increased by 22%; and unemployment continued to decline, down by 18% from September 1999. Other favorable indicators included rising consumer spending, consecutive monthly budget surpluses, soaring foreign-currency reserves, and a very positive balance of payments due to expanding exports and slowing imports. On the negative side, inflation, while reduced by half from 1999, was running at 16.5% by the fourth quarter. Meanwhile, foreign investment was still largely concentrated in Russia's extractive industries, as foreign investors shunned the manufacturing sector; and oil and natural gas, potentially subject to commodity price fluctuations, continued to dominate exports. Another familiar problem, the off-the-books shadow economy, continued to affect the Russian economic scene. A consensus estimate of 25% shadow transactions effectively meant that 25 kopecks of every ruble were diverted from the economic mainstream and the tax-revenue base.

While industry drove the economy, Russian agriculture remained in a catastrophic state, with only a marginal increase in needed equipment. For instance, a shortage of combine harvesters cost 10 million tons of grain during the summer and fall harvests. Still, in spite of these losses and a chilly sowing season in the spring, the grain harvest came in at 72 million tons by late fall—an increase of 13 million tons over 1999. Finally, long-sought tax reform moved steadily through the legislative process. The second part of the new tax-law code was completed by summer, thanks to the realigning parliamentary election of December 1999, which had installed a centrist, pro-economic-reform majority in the Duma. Most notable of the tax-law changes was the introduction of a 13% flat income tax.

Foreign Affairs. President Putin left his mark, not only on the Russian polity and society, but on the world at large, as he skillfully reasserted Russia's influence in the international scene. Traveling extensively, Putin earned the praise of Western leaders and the applause of his various interlocutors. In February, during his acting presidency, Russia successfully persuaded the London Club of creditor banks to write off 36.5% of the $32 billion Soviet-era debt and to reschedule payments on the balance. Then, in March, shortly before the presidential election, Putin received his first visit from a Western leader. British Prime Minister Tony Blair made clear in Moscow that Great Britain was prepared to work with Russia on a range of issues, without letting the war in Chechnya become an obstacle. The Parliamentary Assembly of the Council of Europe, however, was less accommodat-

© Peter Blakely/SABA

Russia's economy roared to its finest post-Soviet performance, thanks in part to a rise in consumer spending—at this department store, for example.

ing, voting to suspend Russia's voting rights over the Russian armed forces' human-rights violations in Chechnya.

After his election as president, Putin began to move quickly on the foreign-affairs front. On the president-elect's initiative, the Duma, which had for years rejected START (Strategic Arms Reduction Treaty) II, ratified the document by a comfortable margin as the first major indication of the new centrist majority. In mid-April, President Putin was off on his first postelection trip. Stopping first in Minsk, Belarus, to dis-

© AFP/Corbis

During a whirlwind first year in office, President Putin nominated Mikhail Kasyanov (left), a 43-year-old economist who had been his first deputy prime minister, as prime minister and championed a stronger Russian state—domestically and internationally.

cuss the Russian-Belarusan Union, Putin made his way west to London to reciprocate Prime Minister Blair's visit to Russia. Well briefed and very upbeat in his first Western appearance as Russian head of state, Putin clearly hit it off with Tony Blair, who later in the year spoke of a special relationship between Britain and Russia.

In June, Putin had further successes, first hosting U.S. President Bill Clinton in Moscow and then paying a state visit to Germany. Clinton arrived with a very clear agenda—to persuade the Russians to allow the United States to build an antimissile shield in modification of the Soviet-U.S. Anti-Ballistic Missile (ABM) Treaty of 1972. Although Clinton argued that the shield was intended to protect U.S. cities from possible attack by rogue states such as North Korea, Putin was not persuaded. To paper over their strategic differences, the two leaders found several minor agreements to sign, and ended their meeting in amity. A week later, Putin—who speaks fluent German—traveled to Germany, Russia's major creditor, where he was exceptionally well received by Chancellor Gerhard Schröder. By far the high point of Putin's first 100 days as Russia's premier statesman was his participation in the July G-8 summit in Japan, on the island of Okinawa. This was Putin's first appearance as a coequal with the leaders of the major industrial democracies, and he performed to rave reviews from his peers. In particular, he presented a report on North Korea where, en route to the G-8, he

had persuaded the leadership to suspend its nuclear-missile program, a report that Chancellor Schröder termed "brilliant."

Putin continued his foreign travels during the fall, visiting India, France, and Cuba, and representing Russia at the Asia-Pacific Economic Cooperation (APEC) conference in Brunei in November. In addition, under his aegis, Russia endorsed the September victory of Vojislav Kostunica in Yugoslavia's presidential election and encouraged incumbent President Slobodan Milosevic to step down peacefully. Those actions helped to ease a potential crisis. Putin's efforts to help end the Israeli-Palestinian fighting were constructive, although less successful. At the same time, Putin also reached out to Russia's erstwhile Soviet allies, including Iraq, Libya, Angola, and Cuba. For much of the year, Russia kept its relations with the United States on hold—due not only to differences on certain issues, but also because of the U.S. presidential campaign. The Russian leadership knew it would be negotiating with a different U.S. leader in 2001. Still, in an expressly friendly gesture to the United States, Putin pardoned an U.S. retired naval officer and businessman, Edmond Pope, who had been convicted in December of trying to buy secret Russian military technology. The court verdict and subsequent presidential pardon occurred within a week, indicating how highly Russia continued to value its relationship with the United States.

ROBERT SHARLET
Union College

Saudi Arabia

A remarkable increase in the price of oil dominated Saudi Arabian affairs in 2000.

Economy. Saudi Arabia's oil price changed from a low of about $10 per barrel in December 1998 to a ten-year high of $37.80 in September 2000. While prices fluctuated throughout 1999 and 2000, they tended to rise in response to increased worldwide demand and shortages in available refined gasoline in the United States.

In 1999, as prices gradually increased, Saudi petroleum production averaged approximately 8.5 million barrels per day. By February 2000, prices per barrel were at about $30, prompting Saudi Arabia to seek both greater production quotas and a more stable pricing mechanism at March's Organization of Petroleum Exporting Countries (OPEC) conference in Vienna. Saudi Petroleum and Mineral Resources Minister Ali al-Naimi, on March 29, said "We want a stable market..." and a price range of between $21 and $26 per barrel, as he successfully urged other OPEC countries to increase overall production by 1.7 million barrels per day. From January through June, Saudi oil averaged about $25 per barrel, as production was about 8.2 million barrels per day.

Refining and distribution problems in the United States helped increase world prices for oil to above $30 per barrel by June. The United States pressured Saudi Arabia, its ally, to increase production in order to reduce prices. Although OPEC increased Saudi Arabia's production quota by about 225,000 barrels per day at its June conference, prices remained stubbornly high. On July 3, Saudi officials hinted that they would defy the OPEC limit and unilaterally raise production by as much as 500,000 more barrels per day, unless the high oil prices fell below $30 per barrel.

On September 5, Crown Prince Abdullah said that "Saudi Arabia will continue to make every effort to ensure equilibrium in the oil markets and to stabilize prices." He also urged oil-importing countries to reduce taxes on gasoline so that consumer prices could be cut. U.S. President Bill Clinton advised Abdullah in advance concerning the planned release of oil from the U.S. Strategic Petroleum Reserves so as to lower domestic prices. Nevertheless, late in September, prices reached a peak of $37.80 per barrel, despite a further increase in OPEC oil quotas. While attending the September OPEC summit in Caracas, Venezuela, Prince Abdullah voiced concern that the high oil prices might unavoidably tip the world economy into a decline. When heightened Palestinian-Israeli tensions helped maintain high prices, Saudi Arabia once again hinted, on October 16, that it would boost future production, so as to try and stabilize world oil prices. (*See also* ENERGY.)

Domestic Affairs. The Saudi government profited from the unexpected bonanza resulting from higher oil prices. In 1999 the national budget experienced a $9 billion deficit; the new budget, announced on December 21, also called for a deficit, with expenditures of $49.3 billion and income of $41.9 billion. However, actual revenues were much higher, creating increased spending, but also allowing for the paying off of debts incurred in earlier years and the building up financial reserves for the future.

Saudi Arabia's Seventh Develop-

© Andres Leighton/AP/Wide World Photos

During 2000, Saudi Arabia's King Fahd delegated more administrative control to Crown Prince Abdullah. Venezuela's President Hugo Chávez (left) welcomed Abdullah to Caracas for an OPEC meeting.

SAUDI ARABIA • Information Highlights

Official Name: Kingdom of Saudi Arabia.
Location: Arabian peninsula in southwest Asia.
Area: 756,981 sq mi (1 960 582 km²).
Population (2000 est.): 22,023,506.
Chief City (1993 est.): Riyadh, the capital, 3,000,000.
Government: *Head of state and government,* Fahd bin Abd al-Aziz Al Sa'ud, king and prime minister (acceded June 1982). *Legislature*—consultative council.
Monetary Unit: Riyal (3.7502 riyals equal U.S.$1, Jan. 4, 2001).
Gross Domestic Product (1999 est. U.S.$): $191,000,000,000 (purchasing power parity).
Economic Index (1999, 1990 = 100): *Consumer Prices,* all items, 109.9; food, 114.0.
Foreign Trade (1999 U.S.$): *Imports,* $28,032,000,000; *exports,* $48,000,000,000.

Plan (2000-2005) was approved by the Saudi cabinet on August 28. The plan emphasized spending on human resources, training, education, and health measures.

Saudi Arabia continued to pursue membership in the World Trade Organization (WTO), opening the economy to foreign investment and privatization of government-run enterprises. On April 10, the cabinet authorized a new law making it easier for foreigners to invest and to own real estate in Saudi Arabia; meanwhile, the government pursued talks with international companies that could lead to natural-gas-processing investments.

King Fahd continued to delegate real administrative control to Crown Prince Abdullah, who maintained the general policies of government along traditional, religiously sanctioned lines, despite the harsh criticism received from abroad. Public executions of criminals had numbered at least 99 in 1999, and increased in frequency in 2000, reaching 103 executions by late September. Amnesty International issued a critical report on Saudi Arabia in March, citing a pattern of alleged judicial abuses. Saudi authorities, on April 6, responded to the allegations by pledging to create a human-rights commission. On May 7, the Majlis al-Shura (Consultative Council) agreed to Saudi adherence to the United Nations Convention on the Elimination of All Forms of Discrimination against Women.

International Relations. The international economy was the center of attention for Saudi leaders. For example, trade and economic cooperation with China continued to increase. During the first nine months of 2000, Sino-Saudi trade totaled $2.1 billion—a 77% increase compared with the same period in 1999. Other international issues for Saudi Arabia included relations with Iraq, the Arab-Israeli dispute, and peace and terrorism in the Middle East.

Even though the leaders of Saudi Arabia were enemies of President Saddam Hussein of Iraq, the kingdom welcomed UN Security Council authorization in December 1999 of a partial lifting of the ban on air flights to Iraq, permitting humanitarian assistance for Iraqis and pilgrimage traffic to Mecca. However, the United States continued to operate air patrols over southern Iraq, with U.S. airplanes based on Saudi territory.

U.S. Secretary of State Madeleine Albright had visited Saudi Arabia in December 1999 and secured government approval of new U.S. plans to bring about peace between Palestinians and Israelis. The collapse of these plans led Crown Prince Abdullah to announce on Sept. 14, 2000, that he favored Palestinian claims to Jerusalem, which he said was "something on which there can be no compromise."

In June, King Fahd and Yemeni President Ali Abdullah Saleh announced in Jidda that they had settled a long dispute about the common border between their two countries, reaching as far as Najran. Following the resumption of talks by the Yemeni-Saudi Coordination Council, which had been suspended due to Yemen's support of Iraq during the Gulf War, Yemen and Saudi Arabia signed nine agreements of mutual cooperation in December. Discussions regarding the rescheduling of the debt owed by Yemen to Saudi Arabia were to follow.

The internal peace of Saudi Arabia, however, was disturbed by two airplane hijackings. On September 14, a Qatar Airways plane was taken over and forced to land in Saudi Arabia at Ha'il. On October 14, a Saudi Arabian Airlines plane that had been hijacked in Jidda, with 103 passengers and crew, and had landed in Baghdad, was permitted to return to Riyadh.

WILLIAM OCHSENWALD,
Virginia Polytechnic Institute and State University

Singapore

In 2000, Singapore experienced solid economic performance and a calm political environment engineered by Senior Minister Lee Kuan Yew. With the media under control, and the ability to sue, threaten, or jail the opposition, the People's Action Party (PAP) remained in firm control. Still, there were signs that "Big Brother" was loosening up a bit. Internationally, Singapore challenged the business-as-usual agenda of the Association of Southeast Asian Nations (ASEAN). The ministate remained a well-run meritocracy, with a forward-looking view of the region and the world.

Society.   In 2000, the government attempted to convince people that free speech truly existed in Singapore. On September 21, a new "speakers' corner" was dedicated in Singapore City's Hong Lim Park. Speakers were permitted to talk on any subject, provided they do not incite racial or religious division, commit slander, run afoul of the Sedition Act, the Religious Harmony Act, or the penal code. Police kept records of all speakers, and foreigners could not participate.

In November, Defense Minister Tony Tan suggested that the government would take a more hands-off policy toward the Internet. Forty-two percent of all Singapore homes had Internet access. This strategy was necessary if the government was to realize its goal of transforming Singapore into Asia's information-technology capital.

In an environment of national apathy toward politics, the PAP had difficulty recruiting the next generation of leaders. The problem was a lack of substantive public debates, struggles, or causes to fight for, and even if there were, the PAP's intolerance to dissent was enough to dissuade most. This inability to inspire citizens to national service led to a pragmatic solution: The base pay for a junior minister was elevated to $556,000 per year. With a 13% raise, Prime Minister Goh Chok Tong was earning $1.1 million annually.

Singapore's other perennial problem, a low-population growth rate, became a front-page item. The fertility rate for Singapore's women of childbearing age dropped to 1.5 (2.1 is considered adequate to maintain a stable population). A $5,000 bonus for a second child and $10,000 for a third had little effect. To offset the shortfall, Singapore imports some 15,000 foreigners yearly.

Economy. Singapore's economy was predicted to grow by 8.5% in 2000. Unemployment hovered around 2.5%. As a result, the contribution of employers to the Central Provident Fun (CPF)—Singapore's mandatory, national retirement plan for all workers—was to be raised to 16%. The CPF has helped to establish the nation's upwardly mobile middle class. At the same time, recent data indicated that the gap between the rich and the poor was increasing, with a growing number of destitute citizens living on an average of $75.81 per month. This situation has only been encouraged by Singapore's policy of importing cheap labor in order to maintain competitiveness. By law, Singapore requires working adults to take care of their elders, but many elderly fall through the cracks.

Foreign Relations. Singapore became disillusioned over ASEAN's loss of credibility and lack of resolve to achieve a regional free-trade area. This frustration broke into the open at November's ASEAN summit in Singapore City. Prime Minister Goh stated that those nations that can run faster in terms of trade had the right to do so. In line with this, Singapore had concluded new bilateral trade agreements with Australia, Canada, Chile, Japan, Mexico, New Zealand, South Korea, and the United States. This policy went against the ASEAN plan to first establish a regional free-trade agreement and negotiate as a bloc with nonmember countries on the issue of trade.

Malaysia and Indonesia especially took exception to Singapore's new strategy. Indonesia also was irritated by Singapore's rejection of Jakarta's call for the inclusion of Papua New Guinea and East Timor into ASEAN. Improving relations with Malaysia and resolution of ongoing issues, including Singapore's reliance on Malaysia for fresh water and access to Malaysian air space for the Singapore Air Force, could be on hold.

In October, Singapore celebrated ten years of normal, if somewhat unprofitable, bilateral economic ties with China. Beijing officially encouraged Singapore to participate in the development of its western provinces. Singapore remained one of India's top-ten foreign investors.

PATRICK M. MAYERCHAK
Virginia Military Institute

SINGAPORE • Information Highlights

Official Name: Republic of Singapore.
Location: Southeast Asia.
Area: 250 sq mi (647.5 km²).
Population (2000 est.): 4,151,264.
Chief City: Singapore City, the capital.
Government: *Head of state,* S.R. Nathan, president (took office Sept. 1, 1999). *Head of government,* Goh Chok Tong, prime minister (took office November 1990). *Legislature* (unicameral)—Parliament.
Monetary Unit: Singapore dollar (1.7355 S. dollars equal U.S. $1, Jan. 4, 2001).
Gross Domestic Product (1999 est. U.S.$): $98,000,000,000 (purchasing power parity).
Economic Index (1999, 1990 = 100): *Consumer Prices,* all items, 117.1; food, 115.7.
Foreign Trade (1999 U.S.$): *Imports,* $111,062,000,000; *exports,* $114,691,000,000.

Slovakia

In 2000, Slovakia's coalition government headed by Prime Minister Mikulas Dzurinda survived several obstacles. The Party of the Democratic Left and the Hungarian Party remained in the coalition, despite threats to leave. Minister of Justice Jan Carnogursky survived a no-confidence vote in September.

Politics. Investigations of the officials involved in the 1995 kidnapping of the son of former President Michal Kovač contin-

© Sean Gallup/Newsmakers/Liaison Agency

Leaders of the "Visegrad-Four" — (l-r) Prime Ministers Jerzy Buzek of Poland, Milos Zeman of the Czech Republic, Viktor Orban of Hungary, and Mikulas Dzurinda of Slovakia — gathered in the Czech Republic in mid-October 2000 for an update regarding membership in the European Union. All four nations desire EU admission.

ued. Ivan Lexa, the former director of the intelligence services, fled the country after parliament stripped his immunity. In April police forcibly removed former Premier Vladīmir Mečiar from his house when he would not be served with a subpoena.

On November 11, the opposition Movement for a Democratic Slovakia succeeded in getting enough signatures on petitions to hold a referendum on early elections. The governing coalition urged citizens to boycott the referendum. Slovak law required a 50% voter turnout for a referendum to be valid; only 20.3% of voters participated.

Slovak leaders passed measures to improve the situation of the Roma. Sporadic violence against Roma, including the death of a Roma woman who was beaten in August, continued. Roma leaders proposed that Roma be allowed to use their own language in areas where they account for more than 20% of the population, a provision available to other minorities. In October, 14 Roma political parties and 29 nongovernmental organizations agreed to support a common program in the next parliamentary elections. Numerous Roma attempted to gain asylum in other European countries.

The legislature passed a freedom of information law in May. In October the government adopted a law against money laundering that also abolished anonymous bank accounts.

Economy. The government continued economic reform, despite growing discontent with economic developments. The price of utilities and transportation increased substantially in January. Gross domestic product (GDP) rose 1.9% in the second quarter, while exports increased 18% in the first half. Most exports were directed to the countries of West European and the Central European Free Trade Agreement (CEFTA). Unemployment was 20% in the second half of the year. The government continued to encourage foreign investment with tax breaks and other incentives. U.S. Steel's decision to buy the country's largest steel works was a positive step in this area.

Foreign Relations. Slovak leaders took steps to further their goal of joining the European Union (EU) and the North Atlantic Treaty Organization (NATO). Negotiations

---

SLOVAKIA • Information Highlights

Official Name: Slovak Republic.
Location: East-central Europe.
Area: 18,859 sq mi (48 845 km²).
Population (2000 est.): 5,407,956.
Chief Cities (Dec. 31, 1998 est.): Bratislava, the capital, 449,547; Košice, 241,941.
Government: *Head of state,* Rudolf Schuster, president (elected May 29, 1999). *Head of government,* Mikulás Dzurinda, prime minister (sworn in October 1998). *Legislature* (unicameral) — National Council of the Slovak Republic.
Monetary Unit: Koruna (47.5695 koruny equal U.S.$1, Dec. 28, 2000).
Gross Domestic Product (1999 est. U.S.$): $45,900,000,000 (purchasing power parity).
Economic Indexes (1999): *Consumer Prices* (1990 = 100): all items, 223.5; food, 116.5. *Industrial Production* (1990 = 100): 83.8.
Foreign Trade (1999 U.S.$): *Imports,* $11,110,000,000; *exports,* $10,031,000,000.

with the EU on eight chapters opened in March. EU officials were positive about Slovakia's progress. They identified additional economic reforms and steps to reduce unemployment as areas where further work was needed. NATO officials visited Bratislava in October, and commented favorably on Slovakia's preparations for membership. Slovakia was invited to become a member of the Organization for Economic Co-operation and Development (OECD) in July.

President Rudolf Schuster visited Israel in February, where he apologized for the actions of the Slovak government in the Holocaust. Slovak leaders also supported steps to increase cooperation with Slovakia's neighbors. Relations with Hungary were strained as the result of a disagreement over plans for administrative reform in Slovakia.

SHARON WOLCHIK
George Washington University

Slovenia

Slovenia faced a prolonged government crisis in 2000, culminating in a breakup of the center-left coalition between the Liberal Democratic Party and the People's Party. The Liberal Democrats won the parliamentary elections in October. Despite this political turbulence, Slovenia maintained strong economic growth and remained on track for European Union (EU) membership.

Political Volatility. After months of dispute within the governing coalition, amid various public scandals and official resignations, the Liberal-People's Party government collapsed in mid-April, and a transitional government was formed. Social Democrats signed an agreement with the People's Party and the Christian Democrats. Subsequently, the Social Democrats gained a majority in parliament, and elected Andrej Bajuk as prime minister in May.

However, the new coalition was unable to hold together because of personality and policy conflicts. The more-coherent and better-organized Liberal Democrats regained public support during the summer under the leadership of Janez Drnovsek, who had served as the country's prime minister for most of the 1990s. The Liberal Democrats gained 36% of the vote in the October general elections. The nearest challenger, the Social Democrats, only managed to muster 16% of the vote. In November, Drnovsek returned to the prime ministership as head of a new coalition government.

SLOVENIA • Information Highlights

Official Name: Republic of Slovenia.
Location: Southeastern Europe.
Area: 7,821 sq mi (20 256 km²).
Population (2000 est.): 1,927,593.
Chief Cities (Dec. 31, 1994 est.): Ljubljana, the capital, 269,972; Maribor, 103,113.
Government: *Head of state,* Milan Kucan, president (took office April 22, 1990). *Head of government,* Janez Drnovsek, prime minister (took office November 2000). *Legislature* (unicameral)—National Assembly.
Monetary Unit: Tolar (230.73 tolars equal U.S.$1, Dec. 28, 2000).
Gross Domestic Product (1999 est. U.S.$): $21,000,000,000 (purchasing power parity).
Economic Indexes (1999, 1990 = 100): *Consumer Prices,* all items, 1,642.7; food, 1,559.6. *Industrial Production,* 84.4.
Foreign Trade (1999 U.S. $): *Imports,* $9,952,000,000; *exports,* $8,604,000,000.

Economic Progress. Slovenia displayed consistent economic progress. It had the highest gross domestic product (GDP) per capita of the transitioning economies in Central Europe, and GDP was projected to grow by 4.7% in 2000. Exports to the EU, Slovenia's leading export market, continued to climb, and the government pursued its privatization program in banking, telecommunications, and the public-utility sectors. The country's priority was to further liberalize the economy, in order to attract greater foreign investment over the coming two years.

Foreign Priorities. There was a broad consensus across the political spectrum on the most important foreign policy issues: gaining membership in the EU and the North Atlantic Treaty Organization (NATO). During the year, Slovenian authorities had one major goal: to harmonize Slovenian laws with those of the EU. In the early part of the year, the country had fallen behind in its schedule of enacting legislation necessary to help meet admission requirements. The new government was determined to adopt several new laws and speed up its privatization program, in order to avoid losing its chance of joining the EU in the first round of enlargement, tentatively scheduled for 2003.

Slovenia remained a strong candidate for NATO accession, and made significant preparations through the Membership Action Plan (MAP) in restructuring its armed forces. The government expected to be issued an invitation to join NATO at the 2001 summit. Slovenia also looked poised to settle maritime border disputes with Croatia.

JANUSZ BUGAJSKI
Center for Strategic and International Studies

Social Welfare

The strength of the U.S. economy in 2000—with continued low unemployment and low inflation—had a positive impact on the economic conditions of the nation's poor. The national poverty rate dropped in 1999 to 11.8%, the lowest in two decades, according to statistics released September 26 by the U.S. Bureau of the Census. At the same time, the bureau reported that real median household income reached $40,816—the fifth consecutive annual increase—and the highest level since such statistics were first recorded in 1967.

"Every racial and ethnic group experienced a drop in both the number of poor and the percent in poverty, as did children, the elderly, and people ages 25 to 44," said Daniel Weinberg, the head of the Census Bureau's Housing and Household Economic Statistics Division. The declines in poverty, Weinberg said, were concentrated in metropolitan areas, primarily large cities.

That annual Census Bureau survey of family income and poverty reported that some 32.3 million U.S. citizens lived below the poverty line in 1999—defined as a total income of $17,029 for a family of four, and $13,290 for a family of three. Some 2.2 million fewer people were living in poverty in 1999 than in 1998.

Some 23.6% of African-Americans—about 8.4 million people—lived below the poverty line in 1999, the lowest African-American poverty percentage since the government began tabulating such data in 1959. Some 7.4 million Hispanic-Americans lived below the poverty line in 1999, the survey found. At 22.8%, Hispanic-Americans had the lowest poverty rate since 1979. The poverty rate for non-Hispanic whites stood at 7.7% (14.9 million people).

The survey found that the poverty rates for all families declined in 1999 to 20-year lows. The poverty rate for married-couple families stood at 4.8%; for those families headed by single mothers, the poverty rate was 27.8%. Median household income, the survey also reported, rose for the fifth consecutive year to a record high of $40,816, a 2.7% increase over 1998. The 1999 median income figures were the highest ever recorded for non-Hispanic white households ($44,366), African-American households ($27,910), and Hispanic households ($30,735). The figure for Asian and Pacific Islander households was $51,205, about the same as it was in 1998.

Other reports issued in 2000 buttressed the generally positive nature of the Census Bureau findings. The annual report of the White House Council of Economic Advisers, issued February 11, for example, said that real income for the nation's poorest families reversed a 20-year downward trend in 1993. Beginning in that year, the incomes of poor families rose an average of 2.7% annually through 1998, the last year complete statistics were available. That compared with a 0.8% annual decline in real wages for the lowest-earning 20% of families from 1973 to 1993.

A study issued July 13 by the Federal Interagency Forum on Child and Family Statistics reported the lowest rates of child poverty, child mortality, teenage pregnancy, and juvenile violence in 20 years. The agency's fourth annual report looked at the social welfare of the nation's 70.2 million children under age 18. The report—which President Bill Clinton called "very good news"—took into consideration more than two dozen economic, health, behavior, education, and social-environment factors.

More generally good news came with a study released August 10 by the National Center for Children in Poverty, a Columbia University nonpartisan research center. The study found that child poverty rates improved in most states from 1993 to 1999, and that nine states reduced their child poverty rates by one-third or more during that time period. Still, the report noted, the number of American children living in poverty in 1999—13.3 million—increased from 10.3 million in 1979.

Advocates for the disadvantaged pointed out that the booming economic conditions prevalent in the United States still left more than 32 million Americans living in poverty. Many of the working poor toiled in low-paying jobs that provided no or few benefits. That situation affected Hispanic families disproportionately.

A survey issued July 5 by the National Council of La Raza, a Latino civil-rights group, reported that in 1997 some 21% of Hispanic married couples with children lived below the poverty line. That compared with 6% of white families with children, and 9% of black households. "You need two or three jobs per family to make ends meet," La Raza's president, Raul Yzaguirre, said. "Even then, many Hispanic families are unable to get beyond poverty."

Homelessness continued to be a serious national problem in 2000. A February analysis by the Urban Institute in Washington, DC, reported that at least 2.3 million U.S. adults and children—nearly 1% of the population—were likely to become homeless at least once during 2000. "Housing costs are on the rise in metropolitan areas, while extreme poverty and other vulnerabilities are facts of life for millions of people, homeless and otherwise," the report said. "Preventing homelessness in a booming economy is an ongoing challenge."

Welfare Reform. Aug. 22, 2000, marked the fourth anniversary of President Clinton's signing into law a far-reaching welfare-reform bill. That measure turned the national welfare program over to the states, thereby ending the federal government's six-decade guarantee of open-ended cash assistance to needy families. The new welfare-reform law went into effect Oct. 1, 1996. It was designed to encourage welfare recipients to find jobs (and get off the wel-

© Gary Rings/"Tampa Tribune"

Across the United States, volunteers, such as the ones above, at the "Cinderella Project" collect thousands of slightly-worn prom dresses and accessories and donate them to high-school students who otherwise would not be able to afford to outfit themselves for their proms. Under various names, such programs have sprung up in many of the nation's major cities.

fare rolls) by restricting how long families could receive benefits, most often to two years, and by creating a lifetime five-year limit on benefits.

The federal Department of Health and Human Services reported in August 2000 that some 2.4 million American families were receiving welfare benefits at the end of 1999. That compared with some 4.6 million welfare families in August 1996, when the sweeping reform law was passed. The report also said that in 1999 some 38.3% of welfare recipients were working or were in government-subsidized work-training programs, compared with 35.4% of welfare recipients in such programs in 1998.

Advocates of sweeping welfare changes praised the large drop in welfare recipients, and the increasing number of welfare recipients who were employed. Others pointed out that many of those who had left the welfare system still lived in poverty, and that many working welfare recipients—particularly single-parent females—were mired in low-paying service jobs. Many of those jobs paid wages so low that workers could not afford to provide adequate food for their families, or to pay rent. The average annual salary for working welfare recipients in 1999, according to the Health and Human Services report, was $7,200.

A February study looked at single mothers who moved from welfare to work, and estimated that about 1 million of their children were in child care—much of it low quality. The study—by Bruce Fuller of the University of California, Berkeley, and Sharon Lynn Kagan of Yale University—extrapolated from data gleaned from nearly 1,000 single mothers whose children were between 1 and $3\frac{1}{2}$ years old, in California, Connecticut, and Florida. The study found "early warning signals of a child-care problem that's going to get worse as the work requirements of the welfare laws ramp up from 30% to 50% of the women getting assistance," Fuller said.

As large numbers of people moved off welfare, many families lost Medicaid health coverage. That was the conclusion of a study released in June by Families USA, a non-profit consumer group. The study estimated that nearly 1 million low-income parents had lost their Medicaid coverage since 1996. "Most parents moving from welfare to work are in jobs that provide no health coverage, but they are losing the Medicaid lifeline," Families USA executive director Ronald F. Pollack pointed out.

Another change in the social fabric, as a result of the sweeping welfare-law changes in 1996, was a concentration of welfare recipients in the nation's largest cities. Nearly 60% of those on welfare lived in the 100 largest U.S. cities in 1999, cited a July report by the Brookings Institution, a Washington, DC–based group. Those cities contained about one-third of the national population. Richmond, for example, which had less than 3% of Virginia's population, was home to 11% of the state's welfare cases. The report stated that African-Americans and Hispanic-Americans accounted for a large and growing proportion of welfare recipients living in the large cities.

The 1996 welfare-reform law also ended eligibility for federal food stamps to most legal immigrants who were not U.S. citizens, and restricted childless adults aged 18 to 50 to three months of food stamps over three years. The result was a large drop in the number of U.S. citizens receiving food stamps. In 1996 an average of some 25.5 million individuals received food stamps. That number dropped to about 16.9 million people (in more than 7.2 million families) in July 2000, according to U.S. Department of Agriculture statistics. Total food-stamp benefits dropped from about $24.3 billion in fiscal year 1996 to $21.5 billion in fiscal 1997, $18.9 billion in fiscal 1998, and $17.7 billion in fiscal 1999. The average monthly food-stamp allotments in 2000 were $72 per person and $167.52 per household.

International Social Conditions. U.S. social problems were dwarfed once again in 2000 by the severe poverty, malnutrition, serious threats of famine, and social dislocation faced by hundreds of millions of people in developing countries around the world. Some 2.8 billion people, about half of the world's population, lived on less than $2 a day, and about 1.2 billion—some 24% of the population—had incomes of less than $1 a day, according to the World Development Report 2000/2001, an analysis released by the World Bank in September. The report on global poverty also found that more than 5% of children in the world's poorest countries died before reaching 5 years of age. That compared with fewer than one child per 100 in high-income countries. The report found that progress in reducing poverty varied greatly around the world. In East Asia, for example, the number of people living on less than $1 a day declined from approximately 420 million in 1987 to 280 million in 1998, the last year complete statistics were available. In Eastern Europe and Central Asia, though, the number of those living in poverty rose 20-fold.

Some 50 million children in Eastern Europe and the former Soviet Union were living in poverty, according to a report issued in October by the European Children's Trust, a London-based nonprofit advocacy group. Hunger and poverty in the former Soviet Union, the report said, "are now at levels approaching those in the developing world and...the situation threatens to reach crisis proportions."

As in previous years, social conditions were particularly dire in South Asia and in sub-Saharan Africa. Thirty of the 35 countries at the bottom of the United Nations Development Programme's (UNDP's) annual Human Development Report index were in sub-Saharan Africa. The report, released in July, took into consideration factors such as educational opportunities, literacy, life expectancy, medical care, and sanitary conditions to come up with its "Human Development Index" of nations. Sierra Leone, where 66% of the population lacked access to clean water, was ranked last in the index. The other African nations at the bottom of the index were Niger, Burkina Faso, Ethiopia, Burundi, Guinea-Bissau, Mozambique, Chad, the Central African Republic, and Mali.

Social conditions were particularly bad in the six nations on the Horn of Africa—Sudan, Eritrea, Djibouti, Ethiopia, Somalia, and Kenya—where the continued combination of drought and civil warfare brought the threat of famine to some 16 million people early in 2000. Spring and summer rains in the northern section of the Horn, along with an enormous shipment of food assistance from April to August, much of it from the United States, appeared to avert famine in the area. In Kenya, however, where the rains did not come, officials estimated that some 3.3 million people were in danger of starvation during the summer.

In the Democratic Republic of the Congo (formerly Zaire), in Central Africa, some 1.7 million people had died since 1999 as a result of fighting involving a rebellion against the government. The fighting involved several African nations and caused hundreds of thousands of people to flee their home areas. Many died of hunger and malaria.

See also AFRICA: A CONTINENT OF PROBLEMS, page 44.

MARC LEEPSON, *Freelance Writer*

South Africa

Considerable national and international attention was focused during 2000 on South Africa's President Thabo Mbeki's controversial views on the connection between AIDS and HIV. Crime remained a major problem in South Africa, and bombings by an extremist Muslim organization in the Western Cape province were a cause of concern. Two parliamentary opposition parties—the Democratic Party (DP) and the New National Party (NNP)—merged. Early in December the country went to the polls in critical local elections.

Politics. In June the official opposition in the South African Parliament—the DP and the NNP—joined to form the Democratic Alliance (DA). The new party would be led for two years by the leader of the DP, Tony Leon; the leader of the NNP, Marthinus van Schalkwyk, would be deputy leader. While the membership of both parties is mainly white, the NNP has substantial support from the coloured population in the Western Cape province. The NNP had been known as the National Party until 1998, when it renamed itself the NNP in an effort to change its image as the party that had ruled South Africa during the apartheid era. In the 1999 general elections, the DP won 9% of the votes cast, the NNP won 6.8%, and the ruling African National Congress (ANC) received 66% of the votes. In late 2000, DA had 66 seats in the 400-member Parliament, while the ANC had 266.

In July, 2000 members of the national general council of the ANC met in Port Elizabeth for four days to assess the goals and achievements of the party since it came into power in 1994. Among the concerns discussed were black unemployment and poverty. Mbeki pledged to continue the government's commitment to market-friendly policies. While acknowledging the need for social and economic reform, he claimed that the government's policy for growth, employment,

and redistribution (GEAR) was necessary if South Africa was to be part of the world economy. He discouraged trade-union leaders and activists from engaging in strikes because of their negative effects on investment. While there was no overt criticism of Mbeki from the ANC allies, the Congress of South African Trade Unions (COSATU) and the South African Communist Party (SACP), were increasingly marginalized within the ANC, and some commentators believed that the alliance was under considerable strain.

In September the controversial Promotion of Equality and Prevention of Unfair Discrimination Act, which was passed by the South African Parliament in January, was signed into law by Mbeki. Opposition parties and many legal experts criticized the act, which created equality courts and, in some instances, required those accused of discrimination to prove their innocence. The government stressed its belief that the act could help redress the inequities of the apartheid era by prohibiting hate speech, racial harassment, and discrimination on grounds of race, gender, or disability. It covered the workplace, education, health services, housing, goods and services, sports, and insurance services.

In December local-government elections, only about 9 million—out of 18.5 million registered voters—cast votes for 30,000 candidates running for 8,900 seats. Apart from trouble at two polling stations near Johannesburg, the elections were free of violence and intimidation. The ANC won overwhelmingly in rural areas, and the DA made substantial gains in the urban areas. Many observers considered that votes were essen-

© Thembe Hadebe/AP/Wide World Photos

A Johannesburg woman casts her ballot during South Africa's local-government elections in December 2000. Despite the peaceful atmosphere, voter turnout was below 50%.

tially cast along ethnic lines, with the DA receiving the majority of white, coloured, and Indian votes, although it made limited inroads in some African townships. While the ANC won a decisive victory, a clear result of the election was the emergence of the DA as a major opposition party; the ANC received 59.7% of the votes, the DA 22.7%, and the Inkatha Freedom Party 9.1%. The ANC now controlled most of the 284 municipalities and eight of the country's nine provinces.

In the Cape Town metro election, the DA received a decisive 53.6% of the vote against 38.4% for the ANC. The DA won 17 municipal councils, mostly in the Western Cape province. President Mbeki responded to the DA success by suggesting that they were supported by people who wanted to return to a racist society. Others believed that large numbers of ANC voters stayed away from the polls out of apathy or because they believed that little progress had been made in delivering needed social programs or in fighting unemployment, poverty, and crime.

President Mbeki also established a new cabinet committee to coordinate and monitor all issues related to national security. It was expected that the interministerial committee would deal quickly with security threats, natural disasters, regional conflicts, and internal instability. In addition to Mbeki and Deputy President Jacob Zuma, the ministers of safety and security, defense, intelligence, foreign affairs, home affairs, justice, and finance were appointed ex officio—and other ministers would be called on depending on the crisis.

Former ANC Secretary General Alfred Nzo died in January at age 74. He served as ANC secretary general from 1961 to 1991. In 1994, Nelson Mandela appointed him foreign minister. When Mbeki became president, Nzo was dropped from the cabinet.

Economics. In February, Finance Minister Trevor Manuel introduced a national budget that aimed at stimulating growth, creating jobs, and reducing inequalities. It also set as a goal the reduction of the prevailing inflation rate of 7.7% to between 3% and 6%. The budget introduced tax reforms and the liberalization of exchange-control regulations, and promised increased fiscal discipline. Capital-gains tax and a residence-based tax system were introduced as part of the budget. According to Finance Director-General Maria Ramos, these moves were aimed at inspiring foreign investors.

At the end of October the government set up an international marketing council composed of government officials and business leaders in order to address negative perceptions of South Africa due to crime, AIDS, and economic instability in the region. In 2000 the rand lost more than 20% of its value against the U.S. dollar, and dropped in value against other currencies. Presidential Minister Essop Pahad summed up the importance of the new council when he underscored that it was essential for South Africa "to attract quality investment."

In October, Mbeki issued a statement that condemned the occupation of white-owned commercial farms in Zimbabwe. He was pressured to do so because it was feared that unless he strongly condemned the illegal takeovers, foreign investors might assume the same could take place in South Africa. At the end of October, Finance Minister Manuel announced that because of the Zimbabwe crisis, the low price of gold, and the dramatic increase in the price of oil, South Africa's estimated growth forecast of 3.6% would be reduced to 2.6%.

Crime. In a measured response to South Africa's alarming crime rate, a new law was introduced in October that gave police extensive powers to search suspects and seize firearms. South Africa, nevertheless, continued to have one of the highest rates of murder and rape in the world. Government estimates indicated that there were 3.5 million licensed weapons in the country and at least 500,000 illegal ones. In another move, the South African Police Service decided not to publish crime statistics for 2000 because of potential damage to foreign perceptions of the country.

SOUTH AFRICA • Information Highlights

Official Name: Republic of South Africa.
Location: Southern tip of Africa.
Area: 471,008 sq mi (1 219 912 km²).
Population (2000 est.): 43,421,021.
Chief Cities (1991 census, city proper): Pretoria, the administrative capital, 525,583; Cape Town, the legislative capital, 854,616; Durban, 715,669; Johannesburg, 712,507.
Government: *Head of state and government,* Thabo Mbeki, president (took office June 16, 1999). *Legislature*—Parliament: National Assembly and National Council of Provinces.
Monetary Unit: Rand (7.5787 rands equal U.S.$1, Jan. 1, 2001).
Gross Domestic Product (1999 est. U.S.$): $296,100,000,000 (purchasing power parity).
Economic Indexes (1999, 1990 = 100): *Consumer Prices* all items, 223.7; (1998, 1990 = 100): food, 244.2. *Industrial Production* 104.3.
Foreign Trade (1999 U.S.$): *Imports,* $25,890,000,000; *exports,* including exports of gold, $25,901,000,000.

In December 2000, during the closing weeks of the Clinton administration, U.S. Secretary of State Madeleine Albright traveled to South Africa for meetings with President Thabo Mbeki and Foreign Minister Nkosazana Dlamini-Zuma (right).

President Thabo Mbeki expressed doubts that HIV is the cause of AIDS. More than 4 million people in South Africa, close to 10% of the population, were said to be infected by AIDS. Unlike the controversial U.S. scientists Mbeki invited to advise him on AIDS, the president never officially stated that HIV did not cause AIDS. However, many experts maintained that Mbeki impeded attempts to address the severity of the AIDS problem in South Africa by engaging in discussions with discredited medical researchers and by delaying programs for prevention and care.

On May 12, former antiapartheid leader the Rev. Allan Boesak was sentenced in the Supreme Court of Appeal to a three-year prison term after being found guilty of fraud and theft involving $200,000. Boesak, who had been leader of the World Alliance of Reformed Churches and leader of the ANC in the Western Cape, was found guilty of misusing a Swedish grant, and stealing from funds donated by the musician and composer Paul Simon.

Cape Town was menaced by bombings that killed three people and injured more than 100. The violence included more than a dozen car and garbage-can bombs. Among targets were a police station, a magistrates' court, restaurants, bars, and a synagogue. There was also the murder of a policeman investigating the Muslim vigilante group People Against Gangsterism and Drugs (PAGAD), which the government blamed for the bombings. It also held PAGAD responsible for the September assassination of a prominent antiterror magistrate, Pieter Theron, 50, who had presided over a case involving PAGAD; he was shot several times in the head and chest as he got out of his car. In a second September attack, PAGAD attempted to assassinate Western Cape's top politician, Prime Minister Gerald Morkel. The bomb, which injured seven people, was placed on a tree between a mosque and a community center where Morkel was to attend a political rally in the suburb of Gatesville. As the year drew to a close, further bombings took place near a restaurant in the suburb of Bellville and a shopping center in Kenilworth.

Durban AIDS Conference. In the opening of the 13th International AIDS Conference,

Former President Nelson Mandela ended the AIDS conference on a more hopeful and realistic note. In his closing address, he said that "the challenge is to move from rhetoric to action, and action at an unprecedented intensity and scale." Mandela emphasized that it was essential to reduce mother-to-child transmission of AIDS. The South African government had failed to implement a national program to prevent transmission of AIDS to babies at birth through short courses of antiviral drugs to mothers and newborns. AIDS activists were pleased that, in contrast to President Mbeki, Mandela mentioned abstinence, safe sex, and condom use as necessary steps "about which there can be no dispute" in the prevention of AIDS. By the end of October, Mbeki was keeping a lower profile on the AIDS issue because of the negative publicity it generated. (*See also* AFRICA: A CONTINENT OF PROBLEMS, page 44.)

Oil Spill. An oil spill in the coastal waters around Cape Town threatened the lives of 60,000 penguins after an ore carrier sank. Thousands of penguins were evacuated from Robben Island and Dassen Island by boat and helicopter for cleaning and protection. Valli Moosa, the conservation minister, asked the cabinet to send in soldiers to help relocate the penguins, saying the spill had put 40% of all African penguins at risk.

PATRICK O'MEARA, *Indiana University*

Space Exploration

The first live-in crew boarding the International Space Station (ISS), exciting new evidence suggesting liquid water may exist on Mars, and dramatic close-up images of an asteroid captured by the Near Earth Asteroid Rendezvous (NEAR) spacecraft were among the high points in space exploration during 2000. The U.S.-built Mars craft suffered back-to-back failures in late 1999, prompting a major overhaul of U.S. Mars exploration plans in 2000. Russia struggled to keep its *Mir* space station working in orbit, and decided to reenter the huge complex later in 2001.

During the year, five U.S. space-shuttle flights were completed; all but one were tasked with assembly of the ISS. One shuttle flight served as an Earth observatory, toting a special radar to map the topography of the planet. Meanwhile, the National Aeronautics and Space Administration's (NASA's) orbiting Hubble Space Telescope and Chandra X-ray Observatory scanned the heavens, relaying impressive and unprecedented views of the cosmos. Otherwise, Europe's launch-for-hire Arianespace had a spotless record of lofting numbers of satellites with its Ariane rocket, and the commercial space business suffered numerous setbacks.

Human Spaceflight. In February the *Endeavour* shuttle carried out the Shuttle Radar Topography Mission (SRTM), considered a breakthrough in the science of remote sensing. Mounted in the shuttle's cargo bay, a high-powered radar scanned the Earth from orbit. Topographic maps of Earth, 30 times more precise than the best global maps, were produced. During its 11-day mission, *Endeavour* radar covered 99.98% of the planned mapping area. Data collected on 300 digital tapes will enable the production of 3-D maps of Earth.

In May, shuttle *Atlantis* docked with the previously launched Russian Zarya module, a key element of the ISS. The crew delivered logistics and supplies, and prepared the station for the arrival of the Russian-built Zvezda Service Module. *Atlantis* revisited the site of ISS construction in September. Both astronauts and cosmonauts worked to move supplies from the shuttle into the station, and during the 11-day flight, spacewalking crew members connected power, data, and communications cables to the newly arrived Zvezda.

Shuttle *Discovery* docked to the ISS in October. The crew installed a truss (exterior framework that holds solar arrays for power generation), a pressurized mating adapter, communications gear, and a set of gyros on the growing cluster of station hardware. Four space walks were organized to complete outside work.

The December flight of shuttle *Endeavour* lasted ten days. Spacewalking astronauts installed the first of four pairs of massive U.S. solar arrays on the space station. Subsequent pairs of arrays were scheduled to be delivered on shuttle flights slated for 2002, 2003, and 2006. Batteries, radiators, support structure, supplies, and other hardware were also delivered to the orbiting outpost. Work completed by the shuttle crew set the stage for the installation of the station's next major component, the U.S. Destiny Laboratory Module, in early 2001. For the first time, shuttle crew members visited the station's initial occupants, who had arrived there via a Russian Soyuz booster on November 2.

The steadily growing ISS took center stage as the premier space activity throughout 2000. As the largest structure ever to be built in space, the ISS is a product of the scientific and technological expertise of 16 cooperating nations.

More than four times as large as the Russian *Mir* space station, the completed ISS will comprise six state-of-the-art laboratories, housing up to seven people. When completed in 2006, total cost for the facility was estimated to be upwards of $37 billion.

Called the Expedition One crew—cosmonauts Yuri Gidzenko, Sergei Krikalev, and U.S. astronaut Bill Shepherd—rocketed skyward October 31 in their *Soyuz TM-31* spacecraft from the Baikonur Cosmodrome in Kazakhstan. Linking up with the ISS two days later, the space travelers were the first batch expected to permanently inhabit the orbiting outpost for many years to come.

Russia's 14-year-old *Mir* space station continued to circle Earth. The core of *Mir* was launched in February 1986, and the space station continued to show its age. A two-person crew of cosmonauts was lofted to the empty *Mir* on April 4, docking with the complex after a 50-hour voyage. Inside maintenance of *Mir* and space walks by the cosmonauts permitted an up-close inspection of the overall health of the Russian station. The twosome returned to Earth on June 16. The mission to *Mir* was partly financed by a Western company, MirCorp, with the intention to lease the Russian space station for potential commercial use. MirCorp's hope was to make the *Mir* available

In November, a crew of two Russians and one American (left) became the first of what is hoped to be a continuous series of International Space Station (ISS) residents. In December, the first of four sets of solar panels (above) was deployed on the ISS.

for operations ranging from space tourism and in-orbit advertising to industrial production and scientific experimentation. MirCorp signed up Dennis Tito, a former aerospace engineer turned money manager, to the tune of approximately $20 million, to fly to *Mir* in early 2001. In addition, the producer of the top-rated reality television show *Survivor* began planning a similar show, called *Destination Mir*, where the winner would be rewarded with a trip to the Russian space station. *Mir*'s worsening health, however, became apparent in late December. Ground controllers ran into communication problems with the huge, ailing station. That situation further fueled an earlier decision to crash the *Mir* into the Pacific east of Australia in 2001. MirCorp also found itself short of private-investor moneys to keep the station alive.

Applications Satellites. Navstar 51, a new addition to the U.S. Global Positioning System (GPS) of navigation satellites, was rocked into orbit by a Delta 2 rocket May 11. The 24-satellite fleet was completed in 1994, but the latest Navstar addition re-

placed a failing member. GPS navigational location had been at 328-ft (100-m) accuracy for civilian-use signals, and at 66-ft (20-m) accuracy for military-use signals. Navstar 48 was lofted July 16, and Navstar 49 flew into space on November 10. As of May 1 the U.S. Defense Department voided the intentional degradation of the accuracy for civilian use, and made it on a par with the military accuracy. Still, the military retained the prerogative to degrade the accuracy at selected locations when needed.

On October 30 and again on December 20, China placed the Beidou navigational spacecraft into orbit. The two-satellite system was designed to provide positional information for highway, railway, and marine transportation.

A Russian search-and-relay spacecraft, intended to locate ships or aircraft in distress, was boosted into orbit on June 28 atop a Cosmos-3M rocket from the Plesetsk launch site. The Nadezhda (meaning "Hope") satellite joined the international Cospas-Sarsat fleet of such satellites.

The U.S. GOES 11 meteorologic spacecraft was launched atop an Atlas IIA Centaur rocket on May 3. The satellite, which was operated by the National Oceanic and

Atmospheric Administration (NOAA), carried a transponder for search-and-recovery activities. NOAA-16, a U.S. weather-monitoring satellite, was launched September 21. It was outfitted with sensors to study land, sea, clouds, high-altitude water vapor, and to profile ozone.

On September 1, China orbited the Zhangguo Ziyuan 2 (meaning "China Resource 2") using its Long March 4B booster from the Taiyuan launch center. It planned to monitor crop yields and natural disasters, and simplify urban planning.

NASA's Earth Observing mission 1 (EO-1) was hurled into space by a Delta 2 rocket on November 21. This high-tech satellite carried advanced sensors to image Earth's surface in numerous wavelength bands. It was expected to provide better crop estimates and better mineral-resource areas than were being provided by NASA's Landsat 7, which was launched in 1999. Among the new technology toted by EO-1, an X-band phased-array antenna will transmit data at extremely high speeds.

On the same rocket that boosted the EO-1, the SAC-C satellite was placed into orbit. The international SAC-C involved Argentina, the United States, France, Italy, Denmark, and Brazil. It also toted instruments to remotely sense vegetation, wetlands, and ecosystems, as well as carry out a whale-tracking experiment. The orbital paths taken by EO-1 and SAC-C were such that they were to fly in formation with NASA's Landsat 7 and the Terra spacecraft. By flying in formation, a given site on Earth can be visited successively by each spacecraft, and different suites of sensors, within an hour of each other.

There was bad news for the commercial Quickbird 1 remote-sensing satellite. The U.S. spacecraft took off from the Plesetsk Cosmodrome on a Cosmos-3M rocket on November 20, but could not be sighted or commanded after the first orbit. It reentered the atmosphere the next day.

Israel's Earth Resources Observation Satellite (EROS A1) was boosted by a START 1 rocket from a new launch site at Svobodni in Siberia on December 5.

Communications Satellites. Described as one of the most spectacular business failures ever, Motorola's $5 billion Iridium satellite system filed for bankruptcy protection in the summer. Consumer interest in using the global-satellite-phone system waned due to high usage cost, and handheld phones that were too bulky and unable to operate indoors, among other problems. The U.S. Defense Department, however, found the system was of value to support military operations in far-flung areas. It agreed in late November to pay the new Iridium owners $72 million over two years for the satellite-phone service.

In February, another commercial U.S. satellite provider and Iridium competitor, Globalstar, launched the final members of a 52-satellite constellation—48 primary and four reserve spacecraft. The fleet enabled relay of data and voice communications from or to mobile or remote telephones located almost anywhere in the world.

The French company Arianespace completed the year with a 100% launch log of 12 flights of the Ariane-class booster. Four of those flights involved the heavy-lift Ariane 5 booster. Satellites for many nations—including Canada, Japan, Brazil, India, and the United States—were orbited via Ariane.

Other significant events in the satellite-telecommunications industry included the loss of the first ICO Global Communications satellite. It was destroyed March 12 when a Ukrainian Zenit rocket en route to orbit failed after liftoff from Boeing's Sea Launch Odyssey platform in the Pacific Ocean. After multiple delays, the first Lockheed Martin Atlas IIIA rocketed into orbit on May 24, making use of Russian rocket-engine technology. It delivered the Eutelsat W4, a geosynchronous satellite.

The year's roster of successfully orbited satellites included: Hispasat 1C, a Spanish communications spacecraft, orbited by an Atlas launcher on February 3; Indonesia's Garuda 1 by Proton rocket on February 12; the first Advanced Tracking and Data Relay Satellite for NASA by an Atlas booster on June 30; a U.S. EchoStar VI on July 14 using an Atlas; a U.S. GE-6 boosted by a Proton rocket; and the Thuraya, a United Arab Emirates satellite, by a Zenit launcher on October 21. The latter took off from a floating Sea Launch platform in the Pacific.

June, September, and November Proton launches placed U.S. Sirius digital-radio satellites into geosynchronous orbit. The three-satellite system relayed music, news, and entertainment directly to special radios, or into upscale automobiles preequipped with the receiver.

Space Science. Double failures of a Mars orbiter and lander in late 1999 rippled through NASA, sparking an overhaul of future plans to explore the Red Planet. Early in 2000, hopes were raised that weak signals from the missing-in-action Mars Polar Lander had been detected by Stanford University radio scientists. This prospect was later discounted, and the lander mission was chalked off as a total loss. A Mars Program Independent Assessment Team concluded in March that the lander likely had crashed due to a premature shutdown of its descent engine. Computer software on board the lander was thought to have misread a signal indicating the probe had touched down on the Martian surface, turning off the descent engine far too high above Mars.

NASA restructured its Mars-exploration program throughout the year. A 2001 lander was dropped, but a go-ahead was given to launch an orbiter, later given the name 2001 Mars Odyssey. In August the space agency announced plans to launch two large scientific rovers to the Red Planet in 2003. Two months later, NASA agreed to launch a powerful Mars Reconnaissance Orbiter in 2005. It would be capable of taking ultradetailed pictures of the Martian landscape. Also, perhaps as early as 2007, a long-range, long-duration mobile science lab would be flown to Mars, a stepping-stone to gathering Martian rocks and other surface materials.

Mars scientists said in June that liquid water may exist near the Martian surface and might be the cause of gullylike features spotted by the orbiting Mars Global Surveyor. In December the same Mars circling probe took pictures of possible layers of sedimentary rock. That find spurred researchers to suggest that Mars once had numerous lakes and shallow seas. These possible findings, and the link to possible life—past or present—were exciting revelations that unveiled Mars as a planet ripe for future exploration.

Japan's ASTRO-E X-ray astronomy satellite lifted off on February 10. However, the vehicle strayed off course, leading to its destruction as it plunged to Earth.

Starting February 14 the U.S. NEAR began orbiting asteroid Eros. The probe maneuvered itself over the giant space rock at low and high altitudes. During the passes, NEAR transmitted a variety of images and other data. Months of observations created a photo album of more than 150,000 pictures. Elated scientists were able to discern on the huge space rock myriad craters, lengthy groves, huge fields of boulders, and a surface covering of rock and dirt. Preparations were under way to carry out a controlled descent of NEAR onto the surface of Eros in early 2001.

The pockmarked surface of the Eros was photographed by the NEAR Shoemaker probe, which was expected to descend onto the asteroid early in 2001.

The NASA Imager for Magnetopause-to-Aurora Global Exploration (IMAGE) science spacecraft was launched on March 25 on a Delta rocket. Being readied for a July launch, the High Energy Solar Spectroscopic Imager (HESSI) spacecraft was shaken ten times stronger than originally planned during a test at the Jet Propulsion Laboratory (JPL) on March 21. Two of four HESSI solar panels were damaged, delaying the satellite's launch into 2001.

Gyroscope problems aboard the Compton Gamma Ray Observatory (CGRO) forced NASA to purposely deorbit the science satellite on June 4. The controlled reentry nixed any chance that debris leftovers from reentry might damage property or people. Chunks of the massive satellite impacted in the Pacific southeast of Hawaii. Lobbed into orbit on October 9, the High Energy Transient Explorer (HETE-2) began measuring gamma rays and X rays.

Circling Jupiter since late 1995, the U.S. Galileo spacecraft continued to perform beyond its planned mission lifetime. It zipped by Io, the volcanic moon of Jupiter, on February 22. During the year, Galileo gathered convincing evidence that salty oceans may exist beneath the icy facade of Europa, as well as two other moons of Jupiter—Ganymede and Callisto. In late December, both Galileo and the Cassini spacecraft doubled up on Jupiter, carrying out tandem observations of the giant planet's complex atmosphere. Cassini was making a fleeting flyby of Jupiter to augment its speed in order to reach Saturn in 2004.

LEONARD DAVID
Space Data Resources & Information

Spain

Spain's Prime Minister José María Aznar's center-right Popular Party (PP) captured a legislative majority in 2000, which gave impetus to free-market reforms long resisted by the Left and organized labor. This victory constituted not only a body blow to the reeling Spanish Socialist Workers Party (PSOE), but also bucked a trend toward moderate left-wing rule in Europe. A contagion of killings by the Basque Fatherland and Liberty (ETA) terrorists prompted Aznar to seek aid from France in combating the armed separatists who operate along the Franco-Spanish frontier.

Politics. The Popular Party (PP) scored a landslide victory in the March national elections. As a result, Aznar will no longer have to depend on regional-party support to pass legislation. His vibrant PP captured 183 seats in the 350-member Cortes. These gains came at the expense of the Socialists, who lost 16 seats to finish second. Meanwhile, the communist United Left (IU) saw its seats reduced from 21 to eight, seven fewer than those held by the Catalan nationalists.

The Popular Party's success sprang from Aznar's deft handling of the economy, his resolute stance against offering concessions to Basque radicals, and his avoidance of the scandals that have plagued the PSOE. As journalist Elizabeth Nash expressed it: "Borne gently upon the pillow of prosperity, Spaniards seem to have floated free from ideas to pursue pragmatic parcels of individual pleasures and personal advancement."

The Socialists lost ground because Aznar successfully portrayed them as corrupt, political mummies. The voters also penalized the PSOE for forging a left-left coalition with the Communists. The deal angered both moderate leftists and hard-line Marxists. PSOE General Secretary Joaquín Alumia resigned in the wake of the debacle, and the party's shocked leadership vowed to implement root-and-branch changes.

Aznar made good on his promise to "promote women" to high positions of public trust. He supported Luisa Fernada Rudi as president of the Congress of Deputies, and Esperanza Aguirre as the Senate's presiding officer.

Economy. Robust manufacturing output, surging exports, and lower taxes powered growth in the nation's gross domestic product (GDP), which increased 4.2%, up from 3.7% in 1999, and 4% in 1998. At the same time, rising oil prices combined with a weak-

ened euro to boost the inflation rate to approximately 4% from 1999's level of 2.3%.

Aznar, who enjoys a reputation as Europe's top job creator, cut the unemployment level from 22% to 14% during his four years in office—with further reductions expected in 2001. Finance Minister Cristóbal Montoro stated his intention to spur job creation, and emphasized his determination to slice the budget deficit as a percentage of national income to 0.3 in 2000. In another action to curb rising prices, he stressed the need both to open up the oil, gas, electricity and the telecommunications markets, and to limit the dominance of formerly state-controlled operators.

Foreign Policy. Madrid moved to improve bilateral relations with Chile, following the tension that surrounded Spanish efforts to prosecute former dictator Augusto Pinochet. Aznar met with Chile's President Ricardo Lagos during the UN Millennium Summit in September. They vowed to strengthen economic ties, and Spain agreed to support a Chilean–European Union (EU) free-trade agreement.

Spain played an ever more active role in the EU. Former Foreign Minister Javier Solana was serving as head of the EU's agency for security policy, and Lt. Gen. Juan Ortuño of Spain took command of the peacekeeping forces in Bosnia and Kosovo. In addition, the Spanish prime minister welcomed Russian President Vladimir Putin to Madrid. Aznar impressed upon his guest the urgency of reaching a political resolution of the Chechnya conflict.

GEORGE W. GRAYSON
College of William & Mary

SPAIN • Information Highlights

Official Name: Kingdom of Spain.
Location: Iberian Peninsula in southwestern Europe.
Area: 194,898 sq mi (504 782 km²).
Population (2000 est.): 39,996,671.
Chief Cities (Jan. 1, 1998 est., metropolitan areas): Madrid, the capital, 2,881,506; Barcelona, 1,505,581; Valencia, 739,412; Zaragoza, 603,367; Málaga, 528,079.
Government: *Head of state,* Juan Carlos I, king (took office Nov. 1975). *Head of government,* José María Aznar, president of the government (took office May 5, 1996). *Legislature*—Cortes Generales: Senate and Congress of Deputies.
Monetary Unit: Peseta (197.2801 pesetas equal U.S.$1, Nov. 30, 2000).
Gross Domestic Product (1999 est. U.S.$): $677,500,000,000 (purchasing power parity).
Economic Indexes (1999, 1990 = 100): *Consumer Prices,* all items, 141.6; food, 130.2. *Industrial Production,* 112.9.
Foreign Trade (1999 U.S.$): *Imports,* $144,438,000,000; *exports,* $109,966,000,000.

Sports

There was standing room only at San Francisco's new and well-received Pac Bell Park, above, as the Giants finished the 2000 regular season with the best record in Major League Baseball. New ballparks also opened in Detroit and Houston.

Overview

Tiger Woods, the 24-year-old golf phenomenon, was *the* name in sports for the year 2000. Pete Sampras made tennis history by winning his 13th Grand Slam title at Wimbledon, but was completely overpowered by a 20-year-old Russian, Marat Safin, in his quest for a 14th at the U.S. Open. Two sisters—Venus and Serena Williams—let it be known that they now were the powers on the women's side of the net. The St. Louis Rams, the Los Angeles Lakers, the New Jersey Devils, and the New York Yankees captured football's Super Bowl, the National Basketball Association (NBA) championship, hockey's Stanley Cup, and baseball's World Series, respectively, in 2000.

For a second consecutive year, Lance Armstrong won cycling's Tour de France, and Doug Swingley of Lincoln, MT, finished first in the Iditarod Trail Sled Dog Race.

Team New Zealand retained yachting's America's Cup early in the year. New Olympic heroes, including Cathy Freeman of Australia, were crowned in Sydney in September. Lemon Drop Kid, Fusaichi Pegasus, and others battled for top billing in horse racing. Salilyn 'N Erin's Shameless, an English springer spaniel, was judged best in show at the Westminster Kennel Club Dog Show, and Pajean's Wild Thang, a blue-and-white Persian, was similarly honored at the International Cat Show.

In increasing numbers, pro athletes were finding themselves in trouble with the law. Daughters of famous boxers were seeking to make female boxing a marquee sport. The conduct of legendary basketball coach Bobby Knight led to his dismissal at Indiana University. New baseball stadiums debuted in Detroit, Houston, and San Francisco. Quarterback Steve Young was among those who said farewell to pro sports.

Escalating Ticket Prices

Even before Washington Redskins' owner Dan Snyder decided in the summer of 2000 that he would be the first National Football League (NFL) owner to charge fans to attend team practices, the average family of four attending a Redskins game in 1999 spent an estimated $391.11, including concessions and parking, for the afternoon's entertainment. Sadly, neither the Redskins nor the NFL were alone in raising the cost of attendance at live sporting events.

The stadium-building boom of the 1990s, together with rising incomes and America's growing fascination with spectator sports, fueled an escalation in ticket prices that has challenged the claim of the NFL, the National Basketball Association (NBA), the National Hockey League (NHL), and Major League Baseball (MLB) to being mass pastimes.

The Situation. Average ticket prices in baseball increased from $8.64 in 1991 to $16.65 in 2000—an increase of 92.7%. In basketball, they rose from $22.52 in 1991–92 to $48.37 in 1999–2000—an increase of 114.8%. In football, ticket prices were $25.21 in 1991 and $45.63 in 1999—an increase of 81%; and, in hockey, prices rose from $33.49 in 1994–95 to $45.70 in 1999–00—a 36% jump.

High as these prices are, they do not include the amenities charges that are paid for luxury suites and club seats. Ticket prices in premium seating areas are averaged in as the highest-price box seat. Thus, for example, the highest-price box seat at New York City's Yankee Stadium is $50, but the cost of a seat in a $225,000-per-year luxury suite averages $174 per game. The amenities premium, or $124 per game, is the difference. Only the $50, not the $124, enters into the calculation of average-ticket prices. Similarly, most of the $1,500 that Spike Lee pays for his courtside club seat at a New York Knicks game is an amenities charge. As the number of luxury suites rises into the hundreds in new facilities, and the number of club seats into the thousands, the average-ticket price becomes more and more of an underestimate of what it actually costs to attend a game.

Baseball continues to offer the most accessibly priced tickets of the four major sports. The reason for this is that baseball stadiums average about 50,000 in capacity, and each team plays 81 regular-season home games per year. Thus, the average baseball team has about 4 million tickets to sell annually. This quantity represents a greater supply of tickets

Average Ticket Prices, 1991–2000

Sport	1991–92	1994–95	1999–2000	Increase since 1991
MLB	$8.64	$10.67	$16.65	92.7%
NBA	$22.52	$28.63	$48.37	114.8%
NHL	NA	$33.49	$45.70	–
NFL	$25.21	$33.63	$45.63	81.0%

than is available in basketball or hockey—41 games and roughly 18,000 capacity, or 738,000 seats per year—or in football—ten games, including preseason, and roughly 70,000 capacity, or 700,000 seats per year. The greater supply relative to demand for tickets accounts for the lower ticket prices in baseball.

The Reasons. Many owners and journalists blame the high ticket prices on escalating player salaries. Such a claim has little basis in economics. A profit-maximizing owner will set his or her ticket prices in order to maximize revenue, and that price will be determined by fans' demand for tickets, not by player salaries. The source for rising prices lies with the fan. It is the fan who encourages politicians to offer hundreds of millions of dollars in public subsidies to build new ballparks. These new parks usually are funded out of sales tax or lottery revenues that fall more heavily on lower-income individuals. Yet these parks cater to higher-income and corporate personnel. With more-comfortable seats, better sight lines, and more amenities, fan demand and ticket prices go up. Since the teams can generate more revenue at the new parks—with higher prices as well as more attendance, initially at least—generally they can hire better players and make the team more competitive. Better teams, in turn, lead to more demand and support still-higher ticket prices.

The facilities-construction boom that began about 1990 is near its end. Most teams in the major sports will have a new or renovated stadium by 2005. A new construction cycle probably will not begin before 2020. Without a stream of new stadiums and arenas, and with a likely cooling of U.S. economic growth, the principal propellants of higher ticket prices should be less active in the coming decade.

ANDREW ZIMBALIST

Editor's Note. Andrew Zimbalist is the Robert A. Woods Professor of Economics at Smith College in Northampton, MA. He has written about and consulted extensively in the sports industry. His book, *Unpaid Professionals: Commercialism and Conflict in Big-Time College Sports,* is being published by Princeton University Press in February 2001.

Auto Racing

Germany's Michael Schumacher won his third Formula One championship, clinching the title by winning the Japanese Grand Prix in the next-to-last race of the season. Schumacher then won the Malaysian Grand Prix for his ninth triumph of 2000.

Schumacher finished the season with 108 points to 89 for Finnish runner-up Mika Hakkinen. Schumacher's victories for Ferrari included the U.S. Grand Prix, which returned to the schedule for the first time in nine years.

Texas' Bobby Labonte captured the Winston Cup championship for stock cars, clinching the title with one race left on the schedule. Labonte wrapped up the crown by finishing fourth in the Pennzoil 400 at Homestead, FL. Labonte and his brother, Terry, the Winston Cup champion in 1984 and 1996, became the first brothers to win championships.

© Jean-Marc Loubat/Agence Vandystadt/Allsport

With a victory at the Japanese Grand Prix, Germany's Michael Schumacher captured his third Formula One championship. It was Ferrari's first driving title since 1979.

Auto Racing

Major Race Winners, 2000
Indianapolis 500: Juan Montoya, Colombia
Daytona 500: Dale Jarrett, United States
U.S. Grand Prix: Michael Schumacher, Germany
Brickyard 400: Bobby Labonte, United States

2000 Champions
Formula One: Michael Schumacher, Germany
Winston Cup: Bobby Labonte, United States
CART: Gil de Ferran, Brazil
Indy Racing League: Buddy Lazier, United States

Grand Prix for Formula One Cars, 2000
Australian: Michael Schumacher, Germany
Brazilian: Schumacher
San Marino: Schumacher
Monaco: David Coulthard, Great Britain
Spanish: Mika Hakkinen, Finland
Canadian: Schumacher
French: Coulthard
British: David Coulthard, Great Britain
Austrian: Hakkinen
German: Rubens Barrichello, Brazil
Hungarian: Hakkinen
Belgian: Hakkinen
Italian: Schumacher
European: Schumacher
Japanese: Schumacher
Malaysian: Schumacher

Stock car racing's showcase event, the Daytona 500, was won by Dale Jarrett for the third time. The Championship Auto Racing Teams (CART) series was one of the most competitive in its 22 years, as eleven drivers captured victories. Brazil's Gil de Ferran won the season championship, finishing with 168 points to 158 for runner-up Adrian Fernandez. CART regular Juan Montoya won the Indianapolis 500, which is sanctioned by the Indy Racing League. The IRL season champion was Buddy Lazier.

Two Winston Cup drivers, Adam Petty and Kenny Irwin Jr., died in separate crashes in Loudon, NH.

STAN SUTTON, *Freelance Sportswriter*

Baseball

Baseball fans learned in 2000 that the more things change, the more they stay the same.

Although the New York Yankees won their third straight World Championship during the 2000 campaign, they defeated their third different opponent. Like the Yankees, the Atlanta Braves earned a return trip to the postseason, winning a record ninth consecutive divisional crown, before bowing in the first round. The only other repeat play-off team was the New York Mets, whose second consecutive postseason appearance was a club record. The other five 2000 play-off participants were newcomers: the St. Louis Cardinals and San Francisco Giants from the National League (NL), and the Chicago White Sox, Seattle Mariners,

The Colorado Rockies' season left something to be desired in 2000, but first baseman Todd Helton was a high-octane machine, batting .372, with 42 homers, 216 hits, and 147 RBI.

© Brian Bahr/Allsport

and Oakland Athletics from the American League (AL).

The AL's best pitcher and best hitter of 1999, teammates Pedro Martinez and Nomar Garciaparra of the Boston Red Sox, kept their titles, but the National League's did not. Nobody hit more than 50 home runs, pitched a no-hitter, or fired a manager during the season (the first time that happened since 1942).

Play-offs and World Series. Although the San Francisco Giants, champions of the NL West, had baseball's best record (97–65) and biggest margin of victory (11 games), neither they nor the Chicago White Sox, whose 95–67 mark led the American League, got past the first round. Neither did the Atlanta Braves, who lost a Division Series for the first time.

The Giants won their first game against the New York Mets, 5–1, but then lost a pair of extra-inning games, 5–4 (ten innings) and 3–2 (13 innings), before Bobby J. Jones pitched a one-hitter to win the finale of the best-of-five series, 4–0. He was perfect in eight of the nine innings.

When the St. Louis Cardinals, NL Central champions by ten games, swept the heavily favored Braves, 7–5, 10–4, and 7–1, the Mets breathed a sigh of relief. The elimination of the NL East champions helped clear the way for the wild-card Mets, who had finished one game behind Atlanta in a

grueling divisional-title chase, to win their first pennant since 1986. There were still the Cardinals to deal with, however. Winning the first two games, both in St. Louis, helped. The Mets won, 6–2 and 6–5, dropped an 8–2 verdict in Game 3 at home, then wrapped up the best-of-seven National League Championship Series (NLCS) in five games by winning 10-6 and 7-0. First-year Met pitcher Mike Hampton, who won the first and last games, was named most valuable player (MVP) of the series.

Like the Mets, the American League's wild-card winner also survived longer than expected. The Seattle Mariners, who finished one-half game behind the Oakland Athletics in the AL West, swept the White Sox, 7–4 (ten innings), 5–2, and 2–1.

Seattle's opponent in the second round remained to be determined. It would be either the upstart Athletics, who had knocked the Mariners out of first place on the final weekend, or the Yankees, who came into the play–offs with a seven-game losing streak, 15 losses in 18 games, and the worst record of any of the eight play-off teams (87–74).

Although Oakland got off to a good start against New York, it did not last. After winning the Division Series opener, 5–3, the A's lost, 4–0 and 4–2, before evening the series with an 11–1 win at Yankee Stadium in Game 4. That forced a decisive fifth game, won by the Yankees in Oakland, 7–5, on the strength of a six-run first inning.

Facing Seattle in postseason play—for the first time since the Mariners beat them in the last inning of the 1995 Division Series—the Yankees were out for revenge. After losing the opener, 2–0, they won three in a row, 7–1, 8–2, and 5–0, to grab a commanding lead in the best-of-seven affair. A 6–2 Seattle win sent the series back to the

Bronx, where the Yankees won Game 6, 9–7, on a three-run home run by midseason acquisition David Justice, later named MVP of the American League Championship Series (ALCS).

That created baseball's first Subway Series involving New York teams since the Yankees played the Brooklyn Dodgers in 1956. The Yankees won the first game, 4–3 in 12 innings, after tying the score in the bottom of the ninth against Mets closer Armando Benitez. They also won the second, 6–5, though the Mets scored all of their runs in the ninth inning after Yankee starter Roger Clemens had thrown eight shutout innings. Both games made history: the first because it was the longest in World Series annals, and the second because Clemens was fined $50,000 for throwing a jagged broken bat in the general direction of Mets slugger Mike Piazza in the first inning.

There was less controversy in World Series Game 3, won by the Mets, 4–2, in their own ballpark. Strong work by the Yankee bullpen helped them win the fourth and fifth games, 3–2 and 4–2, respectively, to wrap up the series in five games. Yankee shortstop Derek Jeter, also the most valuable player of the 2000 All-Star Game, was named World Series MVP.

The win made the Yankees the first team since the 1972–74 Oakland Athletics to win three straight World Series (and four in five years). The Game 3 win by the Mets ended the Yankees' record winning streak at 14 World Series games.

Regular Season. The opening of new ballparks in San Francisco (Pac Bell Park) and Houston (Enron Field) had opposite results. The Giants sold out every seat at every game, throve in their new surroundings, and tied the Mets for the best home record in the National League. The Astros, on the other hand, ended a string of three straight division titles by finishing nine games under .500, despite an NL-record 249 home runs.

After two consecutive seasons as runner-up to St. Louis' Mark McGwire in the National League's home-run race, Sammy Sosa of the Chicago Cubs finally won his first crown, leading the majors with 50.

With Pac Bell Park to his liking, San Francisco's Jeff Kent hit .334 with 33 homers and 125 runs batted in (RBIs) to win the National League MVP, and solidify himself as one of the game's best offensive second basemen. His 475 RBIs from 1997–2000 broke Rogers Hornsby's 75-year-old record for most at the position over such a span. Kent topped teammate Barry Bonds and Mike Piazza of the Mets in MVP voting. Giants manager Dusty Baker stated that Kent—a proven clutch hitter—would have gotten his MVP vote, not Bonds. Had Todd Helton's Colorado team been in contention, the first baseman of the Rockies might have won the award. He led the majors with 147 RBIs and a .372 batting average.

Nomar Garciaparra won his second consecutive AL batting title with a .372 average, making him the first right-handed hitter since Joe DiMaggio to win consecutive AL hitting crowns. The star shortstop was the league's first repeat champion since Wade Boggs won four straight for the 1985–88 Red Sox.

American League MVP honors went to Oakland's Jason Giambi, who led the majors with a .476 on-base percentage and 137 walks. Giambi hit .333 with 43 homers and 137 RBIs. Darin Erstad of the Anaheim Angels led the majors with 240 hits, while Jeff Bagwell of the Houston Astros topped both leagues in runs with 152.

New York Yankees' superstar Derek Jeter, left, was named MVP of the All-Star Game in July, and World Series MVP in October. Jeter hit .409 in the Series, leading the Yankees to their third consecutive championship.

© Al Bello/Allsport

BASEBALL

Professional—Major Leagues
Final Standings, 2000

AMERICAN LEAGUE

Eastern Division

	W	L	Pct.
New York	87	74	.540
Boston	85	77	.525
Toronto	83	79	.512
Baltimore	74	88	.457
Tampa Bay	69	92	.429

Central Division

	W	L	Pct.
Chicago	95	67	.586
Cleveland	90	72	.556
Detroit	79	83	.488
Kansas City	77	85	.475
Minnesota	69	93	.426

Western Division

	W	L	Pct.
Oakland	91	70	.565
Seattle*	91	71	.562
Anaheim	82	80	.506
Texas	71	91	.438

NATIONAL LEAGUE

Eastern Division

	W	L	Pct.
Atlanta	95	67	.586
New York *	94	68	.580
Florida	79	82	.491
Montreal	67	95	.414
Philadelphia	65	97	.401

Central Division

	W	L	Pct.
St. Louis	95	67	.586
Cincinnati	85	77	.525
Milwaukee	73	89	.451
Houston	72	90	.444
Pittsburgh	69	93	.426
Chicago	65	97	.401

Western Division

	W	L	Pct.
San Francisco	97	65	.599
Los Angeles	86	76	.531
Arizona	85	77	.525
Colorado	82	80	.506
San Diego	76	86	.469

*Play-off wild-card team

Play-offs—American League: Division Series—New York Yankees defeated Oakland, 3 games to 2; Seattle defeated Chicago White Sox, 3 games to 0. Championship Series—New York defeated Seattle, 4 games to 2. National League: Division Series—New York Mets defeated San Francisco, 3 games to 1; St. Louis defeated Atlanta, 3 games to 0. Championship Series—New York defeated St. Louis, 4 games to 1.

World Series—New York Yankees defeated New York Mets, 4 games to 1. First Game (Yankee Stadium, New York, October 21, attendance 51,913): New York Yankees 4, New York Mets 3, 13 innings; Second Game (Yankee Stadium, New York, October 22, attendance 56,059): New York Yankees 6, New York Mets 5; Third Game (Shea Stadium, New York, October 24, attendance 55,299): New York Mets 4, New York Yankees 2; Fourth Game (Shea Stadium, October 25, attendance 55,290): New York Yankees 3, New York Mets 2; Fifth Game (Shea Stadium, October 26, attendance 55,292): New York Yankees 4, New York Mets 2.

All-Star Game—(Turner Field, Atlanta, July 11, attendance 51,323): American League 6, National League 3.

Most Valuable Players—American League: Jason Giambi, Oakland; National League: Jeff Kent, San Francisco.

Cy Young Memorial Awards—(outstanding pitchers)—American League: Pedro Martinez, Boston; National League: Randy Johnson, Arizona.

Managers of the Year—American League: Jerry Manuel, Chicago; National League: Dusty Baker, San Francisco.

Rookies of the Year—American League: Kazuhiro Sasaki; National League: Rafael Furcal, Atlanta.

Leading Hitters—(Percentage) American League: Nomar Garciaparra, Boston, .372; National League: Todd Helton, Colorado, .372. (Runs Batted In) American League: Edgar Martinez, Seattle, 145; National League: Todd Helton, 147. (Home Runs) American League: Troy Glaus, Anaheim, 47; National League: Sammy Sosa, Chicago, 50. (Hits) American League: Darin Erstad, Anaheim, 240; National League: Todd Helton, 216. (Runs) American League: Johnny Damon, Kansas City, 136; National League: Jeff Bagwell, Houston, 152. (Slugging Percentage) American League: Manny Ramirez, .697; National League: Todd Helton, 698.

Leading Pitchers—(Earned Run Average) American League: Pedro Martinez, Boston, 1.74; National League: Kevin Brown, Los Angeles, 2.58. (Victories) American League: Tim Hudson, Oakland; David Wells, Toronto 20; National League: Tom Glavine, Atlanta 21. (Strikeouts) American League: Pedro Martinez, 284; National League: Randy Johnson, 347. (Shutouts) American League: Pedro Martinez, 4; National League: Randy Johnson; Greg Maddux, Atlanta, 3. (Saves) American League: Todd Jones, Detroit; Derek Lowe, Boston, 42; National League: Antonio Alfonseca, Florida, 45. (Innings) American League: Mike Mussina, Baltimore, 237.2; National League: Jon Lieber, Chicago, 250.

Professional—Minor Leagues, Class AAA
International League: Indianapolis
Mexican League: Tigres
Pacific Coast League: Memphis

Amateur
NCAA: Louisiana State University
Little League World Series: Canada

Rifle-armed Atlanta shortstop Rafael Furcal made a strong first impression. The youngest man in the majors at age 19, he jumped from the Class A level in 1999 to National League rookie of the year after hitting .295 with 40 stolen bases. The AL's top newcomer was Seattle closer Kazuhiro Sasaki, who arrived from the Japanese leagues to save a rookie-record 37 games, one more than Todd Worrell in 1986.

Pedro Martinez won his second straight American League Cy Young Award with a 1.74 earned run average (ERA), the league's best. Martinez fanned 284 men, leading the AL for the second year in a row, while finishing with an 18–6 record and seven complete games, including an AL-best four shutouts. He has now won three ERA titles and three Cy Young Awards.

Like Martinez, Randy Johnson rode the strikeout title to his consecutive Cy Young, and third of his career. The towering left-hander of the Arizona Diamondbacks led the majors in whiffs for the seventh time, with 347, and reached double digits 23 times for the second successive summer, tying Nolan Ryan's 1973 record. Atlanta's Tom Glavine led the majors in victories, recording the fifth 20-win season of his career with a 21–9 mark.

There was yet another milestone for Cal Ripken, Jr. of the Baltimore Orioles. On April 15, he became the 24th man in baseball history to reach 3,000 hits, with a single against Minnesota's Hector Carrasco. Seven of the 24 players, including Ripken, have also hit 400 home runs.

The American League was a 6–3 winner in the All-Star Game, played July 11 at Atlanta's Turner Field. Twelve days later, five men were inducted into the Baseball Hall of Fame in Cooperstown, NY. They were catcher Carlton Fisk; first baseman Tony Perez; manager Sparky Anderson; Negro Leagues star Norm (Turkey) Stearnes; and 19th-century standout Bid McPhee, the last position player who did not use a glove.

Baseball finished the season with a record attendance of 72,748,970. A record ten teams drew more than 3 million fans.

In September, Team USA surprised Cuba, 4–0, to win the gold-medal finale of the Olympic Games in Sydney, Australia. The team, made up of retired major leaguers and promising prospects, was managed by Hall of Famer Tommy Lasorda, the former skipper of the Los Angeles Dodgers.

DAN SCHLOSSBERG, *Baseball Writer*

Basketball

The Los Angeles Lakers, riding the play of center Shaquille O'Neal and the coaching of Phil Jackson, won the 1999–2000 National Basketball Association (NBA) title by defeating the Indiana Pacers in six games of the best-of-seven championship series. It was the Lakers' first title since 1988.

The Houston Comets once again dominated the Women's National Basketball Association (WNBA), sweeping their playoff opponents to win their fourth consecutive championship.

In college basketball, the Michigan State Spartans used their experience and superior shooting ability to defeat Florida, 89–76, and win the men's Division I National Collegiate Athletic Association (NCAA) championship. The Connecticut Huskies proved far too powerful for perennial power Tennessee, overwhelming the Lady Vols, 71–52, to capture the women's NCAA championship.

In September, Indiana University fired its highly successful coach Bobby Knight for violating a "zero tolerance policy" that the university had imposed on the coach in May as the result of a "pattern of inappropriate behavior." Knight had a 661–240 record, including three national championships, during his 29 years at Indiana.

Shaquille O'Neal led the Los Angeles Lakers to the NBA title in June 2000. He was the regular season's most valuable player and MVP of the championship round of the play-offs.

Professional

Regular Season. The 1999–2000 NBA season began with the return of one familiar figure, former Chicago Bulls coach Phil Jackson (*see* BIOGRAPHY), and was highlighted in midseason by the return of another, former Bull star Michael Jordan. Jackson, who had been out of the game for one season after winning six NBA titles during his tenure in Chicago, took over as head coach of the Lakers. Jordan, who had retired after the Bulls had won their last title, finishing the greatest career in NBA history, became part-owner and president of basketball operations for the Washington Wizards, one of the league's weakest teams. Abe Pollin, the longtime owner of the Wizards, hoped that Jordan's presence could transform his franchise into a winner.

Other milestones became season headlines. San Antonio forward Sean Elliott, who had undergone kidney-transplant surgery, surprised even himself by resuming his career with the Spurs. Charles Barkley, one of the game's most memorable players and a perennial all-star, hurt a knee and then announced his retirement. Two players, Bobby Phills of the Charlotte Hornets and Malik Sealy of the Minnesota Timberwolves, died in car accidents. In August, all-star Penny Hardaway was traded from the Orlando Magic to the Phoenix Suns before the season started. Hall of Famer Jerry West announced his retirement as head of basketball operations for the Lakers.

Jackson's presence in Los Angeles immediately put the spotlight on this talented but previously underachieving team. The biggest question entering the season centered around whether Jackson could transform the Lakers into champions, just as he had built the Bulls into the league's best team. To bring out the best in Los Angeles, he had to maximize the performance of his two superstars, Shaquille O'Neal and young Kobe Bryant. Standing in the Lakers' way was defending champion San Antonio and its two stars, David Robinson and Tim Duncan, along with the Indiana Pacers, New York Knicks, and Miami Heat.

The Spurs had high hopes to repeat as champions but the absence of Elliott for most of the season, as he recovered from the kidney transplant, and injuries to both Robinson and Duncan never allowed San

MEN'S PROFESSIONAL BASKETBALL

National Basketball Association
(Final Standings, 1999–2000)

Eastern Conference

Atlantic Division	W	L	Pct.	Games Behind
*Miami	52	30	.634	—
*New York	50	32	.610	2
*Philadelphia	49	33	.598	3
Orlando	41	41	.500	11
Boston	35	47	.427	17
New Jersey	31	51	.378	21
Washington	29	53	.354	23

Central Division				
*Indiana	56	26	.683	—
*Charlotte	49	33	.598	7
*Toronto	45	37	.549	11
*Detroit	42	40	.512	14
*Milwaukee	42	40	.512	14
Cleveland	32	50	.390	24
Atlanta	28	54	.341	28
Chicago	17	65	.207	39

Western Conference

Midwest Division	W	L	Pct.	Games Behind
*Utah	55	27	.671	—
*San Antonio	53	29	.646	2
*Minnesota	50	32	.610	5
Dallas	40	42	.488	15
Denver	35	47	.427	20
Houston	34	48	.415	21
Vancouver	22	60	.268	33

Pacific Division				
*Los Angeles Lakers	67	15	.817	—
*Portland	59	23	.720	8
*Phoenix	53	29	.646	14
*Seattle	45	37	.549	22
*Sacramento	44	38	.537	23
Golden State	19	63	.232	48
Los Angeles Clippers	15	67	.183	52

*In play-offs

Play-offs

Eastern Conference

First Round	Indiana	3 games	Milwaukee	2
	Miami	3 games	Detroit	0
	New York	3 games	Toronto	0
	Philadelphia	3 games	Charlotte	1
Second Round	Indiana	4 games	Philadelphia	2
	New York	4 games	Miami	3
Finals	Indiana	4 games	New York	2

Western Conference

First Round	L.A. Lakers	3 games	Sacramento	2
	Phoenix	3 games	San Antonio	1
	Portland	3 games	Minnesota	1
	Utah	3 games	Seattle	2
Second Round	L.A. Lakers	4 games	Phoenix	1
	Portland	4 games	Utah	1
Finals	L.A. Lakers	4 games	Portland	3
Championship	L.A. Lakers	4 games	Indiana	2
All-Star game	West 137		East	126

Individual Honors

Most Valuable Player: Shaquille O'Neal, Los Angeles Lakers
Most Valuable Player (championship): Shaquille O'Neal
Rookie of the Year: Elton Brand, Chicago, Steve Francis, Houston (tied)
Coach of the Year: Glenn (Doc) Rivers, Orlando
Defensive Player of the Year: Alonzo Mourning, Miami
Sixth-Man Award: Rodney Rogers, Phoenix
Most Improved Player: Jalen Rose, Indiana
Executive of the Year: John Gabriel, Orlando
J. Walter Kennedy Citizenship Award: Vlade Divac, Sacramento Kings
Leader in Scoring: Shaquille O'Neal
Leader in Assists: Jason Kidd, Phoenix
Leader in Rebounds: Dikembe Mutombo, Atlanta
Leader in Field-Goal Percentage: Shaquille O'Neal
Leader in Three-Point-Shooting Percentage: Hubert Davis, Dallas
Leader in Free-Throw Percentage: Jeff Hornacek, Utah
Leader in Steals: Eddie Jones, Charlotte
Leader in Blocked Shots: Alonzo Mourning

Antonio to rise to the level of their 1998–99 play. Instead, the Western Conference race came down to the Lakers, who quickly adapted to Jackson's coaching methods, and the Portland Trail Blazers, one of the league's deepest teams. The Trail Blazers were led by yet another former Bull, Scottie Pippen. The Trail Blazers pushed the Lakers hard, but ultimately did not have enough talent to prevent Los Angeles from winning the Pacific Division title with a 67–15 record, which tied the Lakers for the fifth-best record in NBA history. The Spurs also finished second to Midwest Division winner Utah Jazz, led one more year by Karl Malone and John Stockton. Young Minnesota vaulted among the league's best teams behind star Kevin Garnett.

In the Eastern Conference, old rivals Miami and New York once again battled furiously for the Atlantic Division title. Miami, despite an injury to point guard Tim Hardaway, was able to hold off the Knicks, winning the division by two games. Philadelphia, with standout guard Allen Iverson providing the bulk of the offense, finished a surprising third—only three games out. Orlando was another surprise; despite depleting its roster of most of its best players, the Magic still managed a 41–41 record behind the stellar coaching of Doc Rivers. But no team in the East could top the record of Indiana, which won the conference and the Central Division title due to the play of Reggie Miller and Jalen Rose. Charlotte and improving Toronto emerged among the better teams.

Toronto's Vince Carter combined his great jumping ability with a fine jump shot to emerge as perhaps the league's most exciting new player. Carter stole the All-Star Game with an impressive performance, and his on-court charisma reminded many of Michael Jordan. But the 1999–2000 season really belonged to O'Neal, the massive Lakers center whose game took on a new maturity under the guidance of Jackson. O'Neal became the league's dominant player. He won the scoring title, averaging 29.7 points, beating out Iverson (28.4). He was second in rebounding (13.6 per game) to Dikembe Mutombo of the Atlanta Hawks (14.1). He finished first in field-goal percentage (57.4%); Mutombo was second (56.2%). In most-valuable-player balloting, O'Neal got all but one first-place vote, which went to Iverson, to win the award. Kevin Garnett was second in the voting, and Alonzo Mourning was third.

© Al Tielemans/"Sports Illustrated"/TimePix

The University of Connecticut defeated arch-rival Tennessee, 71–52, to capture the NCAA championship. The Huskies' Shea Ralph (33) was judged MVP of the tournament's Final Four.

The assist leader was Jason Kidd of the Phoenix Suns (10.1 per game), while Eddie Jones of Charlotte led in steals (2.67 per game). Mourning was first in blocks (3.72 per game). The best rookies were Elton Brand of the Chicago Bulls and Steve Francis of the Houston Rockets. They were joined on the all-rookie team by Andre Miller of Cleveland, Lamar Odom of the Los Angeles Clippers, and Wally Szczerbiak of Minnesota. Rodney Rogers of the Suns was selected the best sixth man, while the all-defensive team included Gary Payton of Seattle, Kobe Bryant, Mourning, Garnett, and Duncan. Doc Rivers was coach of the year. The league's best players were Kidd, Payton, O'Neal, Garnett, and Duncan. Bryant, Mourning, Iverson, Detroit's Grant Hill, and Malone also were outstanding. After the season, Detroit's Hill signed as a free agent to play with the Orlando Magic.

Among the coaches who either retired or were fired during the season or after its end were veteran Lenny Wilkens of the Hawks, Gar Heard of the Wizards, P.J. Carlesimo of Golden State, Alvin Gentry of the Pistons, Chris Ford of the Clippers, Don Casey of the Nets, Butch Carter of Toronto, Brian Hill of Vancouver, and Danny Ainge of Phoenix. Larry Bird retired from the Pacers once the play-offs ended. Wilkens quickly was hired by Toronto as its new coach, while Leonard Hamilton became the Wizards' coach; George Irvine assumed the Pistons' coaching role; Lon Kruger was hired by the Hawks; Dave Cowens took over in Golden State; Byron Scott was hired by the Nets;

and Sidney Lowe, Isiah Thomas, Scott Skiles, and Alvin Gentry were appointed by Vancouver, Indiana, Phoenix, and the Clippers, respectively.

The Play-offs. Although the Lakers had the league's best record, there still were questions about their ability to sustain a run to a championship. Their road to that title turned out to be as difficult as anticipated. They had problems from the very first round, barely holding off the tough Kings, winning the five-game series—three games to two. After breezing past the Suns, the Lakers played the Trail Blazers in the conference final. The series came down to the seventh game, when Portland led by 13 to start the fourth quarter. But O'Neal and Bryant rallied the Lakers as Portland suddenly could not make a basket. The Lakers wound up winning, 89–84, to advance to the championship round.

They were joined in the championships by Indiana. The Pacers had defeated both the Bucks and the 76ers to advance to the conference-title round against the Knicks, who had to survive a difficult play-off series against the Heat. Indeed, the two teams played seven games in that series, with the Knicks pulling out the victory, 83–82, in the final minutes. New York did not have enough energy left to hold up against the fresher Pacers, who romped to the champi-

WOMEN'S PROFESSIONAL BASKETBALL

Women's National Basketball Association
(Final Standings, 2000)

Eastern Conference	W	L	Pct.	Games Behind
*New York	20	12	.625	—
*Cleveland	17	15	.531	3
*Orlando	16	16	.500	4
*Washington	14	18	.438	6
Detroit	14	18	.438	6
Miami	13	19	.406	7
Indiana	9	23	.281	11
Charlotte	8	24	.250	12
Western Conference				
*Los Angeles	28	4	.875	—
*Houston	27	5	.844	1
*Sacramento	21	11	.656	7
*Phoenix	20	12	.625	8
Utah	18	14	.563	10
Minnesota	15	17	.469	13
Portland	10	22	.313	18
Seattle	6	26	.188	22
*In play-offs				

Play-offs

Eastern Conference

First Round	Cleveland	2 games	Orlando	1
	New York	2 games	Washington	0
Finals	New York	2 games	Cleveland	1

Western Conference

First Round	Houston	2 games	Sacramento	0
	Los Angeles	2 games	Phoenix	0
Finals	Houston	2 games	Los Angeles	0
Championship	Houston	2 games	New York	0
All-Star game	West 73		East	61

onship in six games behind the scoring of Reggie Miller.

In the finals, the Lakers were heavily favored to win, mostly because the Pacers lacked anyone who could cover O'Neal. Indiana's concerns proved correct in the first game. O'Neal got the ball inside almost at will and came away with 43 points and 19 rebounds as the Lakers won easily, 104–87. In Game 2, the Pacers got a break when Bryant hobbled off the court in the first quarter with an injured ankle, but Glen Rice and Ron Harper each scored 21 points, and the Lakers won again, 111–104. The series returned to Indiana, where the Pacers were revitalized by the home fans. Reggie Miller scored 33 points as Indiana got its first victory, 100–91. Bryant played in Game 4 despite his bad ankle, and his performance turned the series toward the Lakers. In overtime, with O'Neal having fouled out, Bryant scored six of his 28 points, and the Lakers held on for a 120–118 triumph. Jalen Rose took over Game 5 and sent the series back to Los Angeles by scoring 32 points. That meant the Lakers would be able to win the series on their home court, which they did. In Game 6, O'Neal had 41 points and Bryant added 26 to clinch the victory.

WNBA. The WNBA was expanded from 12 to 16 teams for its fourth season. In the Eastern Conference, the Cleveland Rockers, the New York Liberty, the Orlando Miracle, and the Washington Mystics made it to the play-offs. In the Western Conference, the Houston Comets, the Los Angeles Sparks, the Phoenix Mercury, and the Sacramento Monarchs were play-off bound. Houston forward Sheryl Swoopes was judged the season's most valuable player as well as the year's best defensive player. Betty Lennox of the Minnesota Lynx and Michael Cooper of Los Angeles were named top rookie and coach of the year, respectively.

For a fourth consecutive time, the Comets captured the WNBA championship. Houston swept the New York Liberty in two games in the championship round. They had defeated Sacramento and Los Angeles in the Western Conference play-offs. In the championship game, Houston was led by Swoopes and Cynthia Cooper, who said that she would retire after the play-offs.

College

Regular Season. The 1999–2000 collegiate-basketball season became one of the more open in recent history, with no team

In NCAA title-game action, Florida's Udonis Haslem tries to stop Michigan State's Mateen Cleaves from scoring two. The Spartans took their first NCAA crown since 1979, 89–76.

emerging as a dominant power or as a heavy favorite to win the NCAA tournament. Entering the season, Connecticut was favored to repeat as champion. The Huskies' stiffest opposition was supposed to come from Cincinnati, Michigan State, Auburn, Ohio State, and North Carolina. But Connecticut never lived up to expectations and quickly fell out of the top spot. Cincinnati took over as Number 1 and seemed to be improving every week, only to lose Kenyon Martin, its best player, who wrecked a knee in March.

By season's end, the top teams in the nation included Duke, Michigan State, Stanford, and Arizona, along with Cincinnati, Iowa State, St. John's, and Temple. Michigan State won the Big Ten Conference, while Duke was the best in the Atlantic Coast Conference. Arizona and Stanford emerged in the Pacific-10, and Syracuse and St. John's were the Big East elite.

Despite his knee injury, Kenyon Martin was chosen the top player in the country. Martin, who also was the Conference USA player of the year, averaged 18.9 points and 9.7 rebounds. His closest competition was forward Marcus Fizer of Iowa State. Fizer, the Big 12 player of the year, led Iowa State to its first league title since 1945. He was the school's first All-America since 1957. Other first-team All-Americas included A.J. Guyton of Indiana, the Big Ten player of the year; Texas center Chris Mihm; and Notre Dame forward Troy Murphy. Other standouts included Chris Carrawell and Shane Battier of Duke, Mateen Cleaves and Morris Peterson of Michigan State, Courtney Alexander of Virginia, Scoonie Penn of Ohio State, Pepe Sanchez of Temple, Mark Madsen of Stanford, Eduardo Najera of Oklahoma, and Stromile Swift of LSU. Fitzer, Mihm, and Swift were among those who decided to pass up their remaining college eligibility and join the NBA.

The NCAA Tournament. Arizona, Duke, Michigan State, and Stanford were the top-seeded teams in the NCAA tournament. There was no clear-cut favorite, although Michigan State, which was mostly a veteran team, seemed to have the best chance. Stanford was the first to fall, losing to North Carolina, which barely got into the tournament. Both Arizona and Duke could not make it to the regional finals—losing to Wisconsin and Florida, respectively. That left Michigan State, which racked up victories against Valparaiso, Utah, Syracuse, and Iowa State, as the only Number 1 seed to make it to the Final Four. The Spartans were joined in Indianapolis by Florida, which beat Oklahoma State in the East Regional final; North Carolina, which downed Tulsa in the South Regional; and Wisconsin, which overcame Purdue in the West Regional final.

In the Final Four, Big Ten rivals Wisconsin and Michigan State played for the fourth time this season. And the Spartans won for the fourth time, overcoming a physical game by the Badgers. In the other semifinal game, Florida got its fast-break offense going and overwhelmed North Carolina. That set up a Michigan State–Florida contest for the championship. Seniors Mateen Cleaves, Morris Peterson, and A.J. Granger combined for 58 points, and the Spartans outscored Florida, 27–4, on fast breaks to coast to an easy victory over the young Gators. It was the most points given up all season by Florida, which decided not to use its full-court press against Michigan State. But even with this change of strategy, the Spartans still were able to force an up-tempo game that proved too quick for the Gators. Michigan State had last won the NCAA title in 1979.

Women's Tournament. Connecticut was the dominant women's team during the

COLLEGE BASKETBALL

Men's Division I Conference Champions

America East: Hofstra [r,t]
Atlantic Coast: Duke [r,t]
Atlantic 10: Temple (East) , Dayton (West) [r]; Temple [t]
Big East: Syracuse and Miami (tied) [r]; St. John's [t]
Big Sky: Montana and Eastern Washington [r]; Northern Arizona [t]
Big South: Radford [r]; Winthrop [t]
Big 12: Iowa State [r,t]
Big Ten: Ohio State and Michigan State (tied) [r]; Michigan State [t]
Big West: Utah State (East), Long Beach State (West) [r]; Utah State [t]
Colonial Athletic: James Madison and George Mason [r]; UNC–Wilmington [t]
Conference USA: Cincinnati (American) [r], Tulane and South Florida (tied, National) [r]; Saint Louis [t]
Ivy League: Pennsylvania
Metro Atlantic Athletic: Siena [r]; Iona [t]
Mid-American: Bowling Green (East) [r], Ball State and Toledo (tied, West) [r]; Ball State [t]
Mid-Continent: Oakland [r]; Valparaiso [t]
Mid-Eastern Athletic: South Carolina State [r,t]
Midwestern Collegiate: Butler [r,t]
Missouri Valley: Indiana State [r]; Creighton [t]
Northeast: Central Connecticut State [r,t]
Ohio Valley: Murray State and Southeast Missouri (tied) [r]; Southeast Missouri [t]
Pacific-10: Arizona and Stanford (tied)
Patriot League: Lafayette and Navy (tied) [r]; Lafayette [t]
Southeastern: Florida, Kentucky, Tennessee (tied, East) [r], Louisiana State (West) [r]; Arkansas[t]
Southern: Appalachian State (North) [r], College of Charleston (South) [r]; Appalachian State [t]
Southland: Sam Houston State [r]; Lamar [t]
Southwestern Athletic: Alcorn State [r]; Jackson State [t]
Sun Belt: Louisiana–Lafayette and South Alabama (tied) [r]; Louisiana–Lafayette [t]
Trans America Athletic: Troy State and Georgia State (tied) [r]; Samford [t]
West Coast: Pepperdine[r]; Gonzaga [t]
Western Athletic: Tulsa [r]; Fresno State [t]

[r] regular-season winner
[t] conference-tournament winner

Men's Tournaments

NCAA Division I: Michigan State
NCAA Division II: Metro State
NCAA Division III: Calvin
NAIA Division I: Life University
NIT: Wake Forest

Women's Tournaments

NCAA Division I: Connecticut
NCAA Division II: Northern Kentucky
NCAA Division III: Washington (MO)
NAIA Division I: Oklahoma City

1999–2000 season, and the outcome of the NCAA tournament proved no different. The Huskies were just too strong for the rest of the field, including usually powerful Tennessee, which ultimately could not match Connecticut's firepower. To reach the final, Connecticut had to defeat Penn State in the semifinals, while Tennessee downed Rutgers. Connecticut's only loss of the season had come at the hands of Tennessee, so it was anticipated that the final would be close. But the Huskies were strong from the start. They led by 15 just 12 minutes into the game and breezed to a 71–52 triumph. All-Americas Shea Ralph and Svetlana Abrosimova led the Huskies in scoring, with 15 and 14 points, respectively. Connecticut had won the 1995 championship. Tennessee did produce the player of the year, Tamika Catchings, who joined teammate Semeka Randall on the All-America team.

PAUL ATTNER, *"The Sporting News"*

Boxing

Wherever heavyweight boxer Mike Tyson went in 2000, controversy followed. Meanwhile, Evander Holyfield captured the World Boxing Association (WBA) heavyweight title.

Heavyweights. Despite protest from women's groups and some politicians, Tyson was allowed into Manchester, England, to fight Julius Francis on January 29. Francis was knocked down five times before the fight was stopped in the second round. In June, there was further outcry when Tyson was allowed to fight Lou Savarese in Glasgow, Scotland. Savarese, knocked to the mat by a left hook to the head only 12 seconds into the bout, appeared badly hurt when referee John Coyle stopped the match. Tyson then elbowed the referee aside and attacked Savarese but was pulled away before he could land a punch. He was fined $187,500, but not suspended by the British Boxing Board of Control.

Tyson's final fight of the year, in October, also had a controversial ending: Andrew Golota quit after the second round in the Palace of Auburn Hills, MI. Golota, a native of Poland living in Chicago, was admitted to the hospital the day after the fight with what a doctor said was a concussion, fractured left cheekbone, and herniated disc in his neck.

Controversy also touched Lennox Lewis, who had become the undisputed heavyweight champion by outpointing Evander Holyfield in 1999. He lost the WBA title when a federal judge ruled that he had breached a contract by signing to fight Michael Grant instead of signing to fight the leading WBA contender. Lewis kept the World Boxing Council (WBC) and the International Boxing Federation (IBF) titles by stopping both Grant and Francois Botha in the second round and scoring a one-sided decision over David Tua.

Holyfield became the WBA champion by winning a close, but unanimous decision over John Ruiz. The 37-year-old Holyfield was the first man to win pieces of the heavyweight title four times.

Lighter Divisions. Felix Trinidad and Shane Mosley became major players in boxing. The unbeaten Trinidad, a former welterweight champion from Puerto Rico, won the WBA junior-middleweight title by beating David Reid. Trinidad then won the IBF junior-middleweight championship by stopping Fernando Vargas in the 12th round of a brawl. Mosley, a former lightweight champion, who remained unbeaten, won the WBC welterweight title by scoring a split decision over Oscar De La Hoya. He defended the title once.

Roy Jones, Jr., the undisputed light-heavyweight champion, made three successful title defenses. His unanimous decision over David Telesco on January 15 was featured on the first boxing show ever held in New York City's Radio City Music Hall.

Women. Almost all attention attracted by women's boxing was focused on the daughters of former heavyweight champions, especially Muhammad Ali's 23-year-old daughter, Laila, and Jacqui Frazier-Lyde, the 39-year-old daughter of Smokin' Joe Frazier. Ali won all seven of her bouts, while Frazier-Lyde went unbeaten in five matches.

Freda George Foreman, the 24-year-old daughter of George Foreman, won both of her bouts, but Ingemar Johansson's 35-year-old daughter, Maria, lost both of hers. Irichile del Carmen Duran, 24, whose father Roberto won titles from lightweight through middleweight, split two bouts.

ED SCHUYLER, JR., *Boxing Writer*

WORLD BOXING CHAMPIONS

Heavyweight: World Boxing Council (WBC)—Lennox Lewis, Britain, 1997; World Boxing Association (WBA)—Evander Holyfield, United States, 2000; International Boxing Federation (IBF)—Lewis, 1999.

Cruiserweight: WBC—Juan Carlos Gomez, Cuba-Germany, 1998; WBA—Virgil Hill, United States, 2000; IBF—Vassily Jirov, Kazakhstan–United States, 1999.

Light Heavyweight: WBC—Roy Jones, Jr., United States, 1997; WBA—Jones, 1998; IBF—Jones, 1999.

Super Middleweight: WBC—Davey Hilton, Canada, 2000; WBA—Bruno Girard, France, 2000; IBF—Sven Ottke, Germany, 1998.

Middleweight: WBC—Keith Holmes, United States, 1999; WBA—William Joppy, United States, 1998; IBF—Bernard Hopkins, United States, 1995.

Junior Middleweight: WBC—Francisco J. Castillejo, Spain, 1999; WBA—Felix Trinidad, Puerto Rico, 2000; IBF—Trinidad, 2000.

Welterweight: WBC—Shane Mosley, United States, 2000; WBA—vacant; IBF—vacant.

Junior Welterweight: WBC—Konstantin Tszyu, Russia-Australia, 1999; WBA—Sharmba Mitchell, United States, 1998; IBF—Zab Judah, United States, 2000.

Lightweight: WBC—José Luis Castillo, Mexico, 1999; WBA—Takanori Hatakeyama, Japan, 2000; IBF—Paul Spadafora, United States, 1999.

Junior Lightweight: WBC—Floyd Mayweather, United States, 1998; WBA—Joel Casamayor, Cuba-United States, 2000; IBF—vacant.

Featherweight: WBC—Guty Espadas, Mexico, 2000; WBA—Derrick Gainer, United States, 2000; IBF—Mbulelo Botile, South Africa, 2000.

Junior Featherweight: WBC—Guillermo Jorrin, United States, 2000; WBA—Clarence Adams, United States, 2000; IBF—Benedict Ledwaba, South Africa, 2000.

Bantamweight: WBC—Veerapohl Nakhonluang, Thailand, 1998; WBA—Paulie Ayala, United States, 1999; IBF—Tim Austin, United States, 1998.

Junior Bantamweight: WBC—Masamori Tokuyama, Japan, 2000; WBA—Leo Gamez, Venezuela, 2000; IBF—Felix Machado, Venezuela, 2000.

Flyweight: WBC—Malcolm Tunacao, Philippines, 2000; WBA—Eric Morel, Puerto Rico, 2000; IBF—Irene Pacheco, Colombia, 1999.

Junior Flyweight: WBC—Yosam Choi, South Korea, 1999; WBA—Beibis Mendoza, Colombia, 2000; IBF—Ricardo Lopez, Mexico, 1999.

Strawweight: WBC—José Antonio Aguirre, Mexico, 2000; WBA—Keitaro Hoshino, Japan, 2000; IBF—vacant.

Football

The National Football League's (NFL's) 2000-2001 championship game matched the Baltimore Ravens against the New York Giants. It was the first time the Ravens, who had been in Baltimore for five years after relocating from Cleveland, had been in the Super Bowl. The Giants had not played in a Super Bowl since the 1990-1991 season. The Ravens, led by one of the best defenses in the history of the league, overwhelmed the Giants, 34–7, in Super Bowl XXXV.

In college football, undefeated Oklahoma upset Florida State, 13–2, in the Orange Bowl to win the national championship. The game was the third under a system designed to produce a legitimate national winner, although calls for a formal play-off system were rejected. Quarterback Chris Weinke of Florida State won the Heisman Memorial Trophy, as college football's best player.

Professional

Regular Season. The NFL continued a trend of unpredictability during the 2000 season. Teams that were expected to excel flopped, while franchises that had been struggling turned into winners. It was also a season played without two outstanding quarterbacks—Dan Marino of the Miami Dolphins and Steve Young of the San Francisco 49ers. Both men retired after the 1999 season because of lingering injury problems.

The league underwent some public-relations problems, too. Two of its players—Carolina wide-receiver Rae Carruth and Baltimore linebacker Ray Lewis—were accused of murder. The murder charges against Lewis, stemming from an incident outside a bar after Super Bowl XXXIV in Atlanta in which two men were killed, eventually were dropped near the end of his trial. He pleaded guilty to one charge of obstruction of justice. Carruth, accused in the murder of his pregnant girlfriend, was found guilty of three felony charges but innocent of first-degree murder. On Jan. 22, 2001, a judge sentenced Carruth to up to 24 years and four months in prison. In February, linebacker Derrick Thomas of the Kansas Chiefs died of cardiac arrest 16 days after being involved in a car accident. Safety Eric Turner, who played for Cleveland, Baltimore, and Oakland, died of complications from abdominal cancer on May 28.

A number of teams also underwent coaching changes prior to the start of the season. Dave Campo replaced Chan Gailey in Dallas; Jim Haslett replaced Mike Ditka in New Orleans; Mike Martz replaced the retired Dick Vermeil in St. Louis; Mike Sherman replaced Ray Rhodes in Green Bay; Dave Wannstedt replaced Jimmy Johnson in Miami; Al Groh replaced Bill Parcells in New York; and Bill Belichick replaced Pete Carroll in New England. Parcells' retirement from the Jets created a strange sequence of events. Parcells, who also ran the team's football operations, picked Belichick, his defensive coordinator, to replace him. But after accepting, Belichick then changed his mind and quit. He wound up in New England and Parcells turned to Groh, who was also one of his assistant coaches. Vermeil stepped down a few weeks after winning Super Bowl XXXIV as coach of the St. Louis Rams. The new Houston

© Stephen Dunn/Allsport

The Baltimore Ravens colossal defense—characterized by a Duane Starks (22) interception during the AFC Championship, (left)—was possibly as dominating as any in NFL history and was a major factor in the Ravens win over the Giants in Super Bowl XXXV.

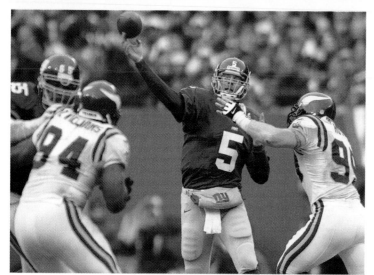

The New York Giants were championed by the consistent—if not commanding—play of revitalized quarterback Kerry Collins, who orchestrated a 41–0 magic show against the Minnesota Vikings in the NFC Championship.

PROFESSIONAL FOOTBALL

Final Standings, 2000

AMERICAN CONFERENCE

Eastern Division	W	L	T	Pct.	Points For	Points Against
Miami	11	5	0	.688	323	226
Indianapolis	10	6	0	.625	429	326
N.Y. Jets	9	7	0	.563	321	321
Buffalo	8	8	0	.500	315	350
New England	5	11	0	.313	276	338
Central Division						
Tennessee	13	3	0	.813	346	191
Baltimore	12	4	0	.750	333	165
Pittsburgh	9	7	0	.563	321	255
Jacksonville	7	9	0	.438	367	327
Cincinnati	4	12	0	.250	185	359
Cleveland	3	13	0	.188	161	419
Western Division						
Oakland	12	4	0	.750	479	299
Denver	11	5	0	.688	485	369
Kansas City	7	9	0	.438	355	354
Seattle	6	10	0	.375	320	405
San Diego	1	15	0	.062	269	440

PLAY-OFFS

Miami 23, Indianapolis 17
Baltimore 21, Denver 3
Oakland 27, Miami 0
Baltimore 24, Tennessee 10
Baltimore 16, Oakland 3

NATIONAL CONFERENCE

Eastern Division	W	L	T	Pct.	Points For	Points Against
N.Y. Giants	12	4	0	.750	328	246
Philadelphia	11	5	0	.688	351	245
Washington	8	8	0	.500	281	269
Dallas	5	11	0	.313	294	361
Arizona	3	13	0	.188	210	443
Central Division						
Minnesota	11	5	0	.688	397	371
Tampa Bay	10	6	0	.625	388	269
Green Bay	9	7	0	.563	353	323
Detroit	9	7	0	.563	307	307
Chicago	5	11	0	.313	216	355
Western Division						
New Orleans	10	6	0	.625	354	305
St. Louis	10	6	0	.625	540	471
Carolina	7	9	0	.438	310	310
San Francisco	6	10	0	.375	388	422
Atlanta	4	12	0	.250	252	413

PLAY-OFFS

New Orleans 31, St. Louis 28
Philadelphia 21, Tampa Bay 3
Minnesota 34, New Orleans 16
New York Giants 20, Philadelphia 10
New York Giants 41, Minnesota 0

SUPER BOWL XXXV: Baltimore 34, New York Giants 7

franchise, which will begin play in 2002, received a nicknamed "Texans" and hired Charley Casserly as general manager. Arizona voters approved a new stadium for the Cardinals. The Cincinnati Bengals began play in their new stadium while the Denver Broncos' new stadium would open prior to the 2001 season.

The season began with the Tennessee Titans, Indianapolis Colts, and Oakland Raiders as the favorites to compete for the American Football Conference (AFC) title, and the St. Louis Rams, Washington Redskins, and Tampa Bay Buccaneers as the favorites in the National Football Conference (NFC). A number of those teams wound up struggling.

Tennessee withstood a difficult schedule to win the AFC Central crown and compile the best record (13–3) in the AFC. They were challenged all season by the Ravens, who were the only team to beat the Titans in Tennessee. The Ravens finished second in the division but qualified for the play-offs. The Colts—heavy favorites to win the AFC East—hit a late-season slump and barely made it into the play-offs. That division was won instead by the Miami Dolphins, who overcame the retirement of coach Jimmy Johnson and relied on a strong defense. Quarterback Jay Fiedler played decently in place of the retired Marino. The New York Jets, after a quick start, fell back in December and were eliminated from the play-offs. In the AFC West, the Raiders got unexpected strong play from quarterback Rich Gannon. Oakland was pressed hard by the Denver Broncos, even though the Broncos lost star running back Terrell Davis to injury for the bulk of the season.

In the NFC, the Washington Redskins spent $100 million in salaries and bonuses in the off-season to build a Super Bowl contender. But the Redskins played poorly the final half of the season and missed the play-offs. Their coach, Norv Turner, was fired by owner Daniel Snyder with three games remaining. The Tampa Bay Bucs qualified for the play-offs, but never played as consistently as expected, finishing second behind the Minnesota Vikings in the NFC Central. The St. Louis Rams could not defend their NFL championship. Injuries to quarterback Kurt Warner and halfback Marshall Faulk limited their effectiveness, and they squeezed into the play-offs as a wild card. The NFC West instead was won by the surprising New Orleans Saints, who rallied behind new coach Jim Haslett and the late-season play of quarterback Aaron Brooks. The NFC East went to another surprise team, the New York Giants, who rallied behind head-coach Jim Fassel's guarantee that they would make the play-offs.

Arizona fired head-coach Vince Tobin before the end of the campaign; he was replaced by Dave McGinnis. The Bengals replaced coach Bruce Coslett before the end of the season, giving the job to Dick LeBeau. Once the season ended, Chris Palmer was fired in Cleveland, Wade Phillips in Buffalo, and Gunther Cunningham in Kansas City. Al Groh left the Jets to take the head-coaching job at the University of Virginia. Bobby Ross quit his head-coaching job with the Lions during the season and was replaced by Gary Moeller.

Play-offs. In the AFC, Miami eliminated the Colts in overtime at home. The Ravens used stout defense to subdue the Broncos. In the semifinals, Miami was overwhelmed by the Raiders, while the Ravens traveled to Tennessee and beat the Titans 24–10, despite scoring only one offensive touchdown.

In the NFC, the upstart Saints knocked out the Rams and Philadelphia eliminated Tampa Bay in the wild-card. In the semifinal round, the Giants were too good for the Eagles, 20–10. The Saints were no match for the Vikings, losing in Minnesota, 34–16.

Even though they were playing at home, the Giants were underdogs to the Vikings in the NFC title game. But quarterback Kerry Collins threw for five touchdown passes, the Giant defense shut down the Vikings powerful offense, and New York romped, 41–0. In the AFC, the Raiders were favored to beat the Ravens. But the Baltimore defense—which set league records for fewest points allowed, fewest rushing yardage allowed over a 16-game schedule, and was considered one of the best ever—limited Oakland to one field goal, 16–3.

Super Bowl. The Baltimore Ravens bragged openly about their dominating defense, and for good reason. In the season's biggest game, Super Bowl XXXV, played before 71,921 fans at Raymond James Stadi-

um in Tampa, FL, on Jan. 28, 2001, they simply terminated the New York Giants, 34–7, intercepting Giants quarterback Kerry Collins four times and limiting New York to 152 total yards. The Ravens led 10–0 at half-time and special-teams phenom Jermaine Lewis ultimately broke New York's spirit in the third quarter, returning a kickoff 84 yards for a score and the 24–7 lead. Baltimore's offense, led by quarterback Trent Dilfer and running-back Jamal Lewis, was efficient, but Ravens middle linebacker Ray Lewis was all over the field and was named the game's most valuable player.

Individual Performances. Running back Marshall Faulk of the Rams set records for his versatility and was named the league's most valuable player—he beat out quarterback Donovan McNabb of Philadelphia. Daunte Culpepper of the Vikings had an outstanding season, as did quarterback Peyton Manning (*see* BIOGRAPHY) of the Colts; quarterback Rich Gannon of the Raiders; running back Eddie George of the Titans; running back Edgerrin James of the Colts, who led the league in rushing with 1,709 yards; running back Robert Smith of the Vikings; receiver Muhsin Muhammad of Carolina, who tied with Marvin Harrison of the Colts for most receptions (102); Rams

Florida State quarterback Chris Weinke took an unusual route to the college football mountaintop, but collected a national championship in 1999 and the Heisman Trophy in 2000.

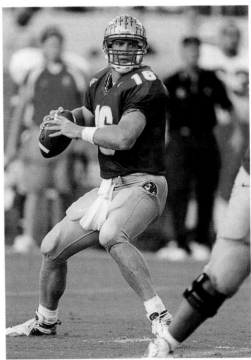

receiver Torry Holt; receivers Rod Smith and Ed McCaffrey of Denver, who had 101 and 100 catches respectively; and defensive lineman La'Roi Glover of the Saints with 17 sacks.

Ray Lewis was selected defensive player of the year and Jim Haslett of New Orleans and Andy Reid of Philadelphia were honored by different organizations as coach of the year. Linebacker Brian Urlacher of the Bears was picked as rookie of the year.

Grey Cup. In the Canadian Football League (CFL), the British Columbia Lions won their second Grey Cup in six years as they foiled a potential tying two-point conversion with 44 seconds to play, for a 28–26 victory over the Montreal Alouettes.

COLLEGE FOOTBALL

Conference Champions
Conference Champions
Atlantic Coast—Florida State
Big Ten—Michigan, Northwestern, Purdue (tied)
Big 12—Kansas State (North); Oklahoma (South)
Big West—Boise State
Pacific Ten—Oregon St., Washington, Oregon (tied)
Southeastern—Florida (East); Auburn (West)
Western Athletic Conference—Texas Christian, Texas-El Paso (tied)

NCAA Champions
Division I-AA—Georgia Southern
Division II—Delta State
Division III—Mount Union

NAIA Champion: Georgetown

Individual Honors
Heisman Trophy—Chris Weinke, Florida State
Lombardi Award—Jamal Reynolds, Florida State
Outland Trophy—John Henderson, Tennessee

MAJOR BOWL GAMES
Alamo Bowl (San Antonio, TX, Dec. 30)—Nebraska 66, Northwestern 17
Aloha Bowl (Honolulu, HI, Dec. 25)—Boston College 31, Arizona State 17
Blue-Gray Classic (Montgomery, AL, Dec. 25)—Gray 40, Blue 37
Citrus Bowl (Orlando, FL, Jan. 2)—Michigan 31, Auburn 28
Cotton Bowl (Dallas, TX, Jan. 2)—Kansas State 35, Tennessee 21
Fiesta Bowl (Tempe, AZ, Jan. 2)—Oregon State 41, Notre Dame 9
Galleryfurniture.com Bowl (Houston, TX, Dec. 27)—East Carolina 40, Texas Tech 27
Gator Bowl (Jacksonville, FL, Jan. 1)—Virginia Tech 41, Clemson 20
Heritage Bowl (Atlanta, GA, Dec. 26)—Southern 28, Bethune-Cookman 2
Holiday Bowl (San Diego, CA, Dec. 29)—Oregon 35, Texas 30
Humanitarian Bowl (Boise, ID, Dec. 29)—Boise State 38, UTEP 23
Independence Bowl (Shreveport, LA, Dec. 31)—Mississippi State 43, Texas A&M 41
Insight.com Bowl (Phoenix, AZ, Dec. 28)—Iowa State 37, Pittsburgh 29
Las Vegas Bowl (Las Vegas, NV, Dec. 21)—UNLV 31, Arkansas 14
Liberty Bowl (Memphis, TN, Dec. 29)—Colorado State 22, Louisville 17
MicronPC.com Bowl (Miami, FL, Dec. 29)—NC State 38, Minnesota 30
Mobile Alabama (Mobile, AL, Dec. 20)—Southern Miss 28, TCU 21
Motor City Bowl (Pontiac, MI, Dec. 29)—Marshall 25, Cincinnati 14
Music City Bowl (Nashville, TN, Dec. 28)—West Virginia 49, Mississippi 38
Oahu Bowl (Honolulu, HI, Dec. 24)—Georgia 37, Virginia 14
Orange Bowl (Miami, FL, Jan. 3)—Oklahoma 13, Florida State 2
Outback Bowl (Tampa Bay, FL, Jan. 1)—South Carolina 24, Ohio State 7
Peach Bowl (Atlanta, GA, Dec. 29)—LSU 28, Georgia Tech 14
Rose Bowl (Pasadena, CA, Jan. 1)—Washington 34, Purdue 24
Silicon Valley Classic (San Jose, CA, Jan. 1)—Air Force 37, Fresno State 34
Sugar Bowl (New Orleans, LA, Jan. 2)—Miami 37, Florida 20
Sun Bowl (El Paso, TX, Dec. 29)—Wisconsin 21, UCLA 20

College

The Season. Under the Bowl Championship Series (BCS), Florida State and undefeated Oklahoma met in the Orange Bowl, the game chosen to host the title contest at the end of the 2000 season. The BCS format relies on a combination of newspaper and coaches' polls, computer rankings, and strength-of-schedule determinations. It is surrounded by controversy.

Entering the season, Florida State, Florida, Miami, Nebraska, Alabama, Wisconsin, Kansas State, and Texas were considered the strongest teams. Florida State was the defending national champion, but the biggest shock was Oklahoma, which emerged under coach Bob Stoops. The Sooners finished undefeated as the Number 1 team in the country.

Bowl Games. In the Orange Bowl matchup between Oklahoma and highly favored Florida State, most of the focus centered on quarterbacks Chris Weinke and Josh Heupel. Weinke, who played minor-league baseball before enrolling at Florida State, was a "senior citizen" of college football; Heupel was a lightly regarded player prior to the 2000 season, yet emerged as one of the game's top performers. In this showdown, though, only Heupel lived up to his billing. He was just efficient enough on offense to help the Sooners score 13 points in what otherwise was a disappointing offensive demonstration by both teams. It was Oklahoma's seventh national title, but first under Stoops.

Miami made a case for being the nation's best team by trouncing Florida, 37–20, in the Sugar Bowl. Washington likewise finished strongly by subduing Purdue, 34–24, in the Rose Bowl; Virginia Tech trounced Clemson, 41–20, in the Gator Bowl; and Oregon State ran over Notre Dame, 41–9, in the Fiesta Bowl.

The Best Players. Weinke, who led the nation in passing with 4,167 yards, and threw for 33 touchdowns, won the Heisman Trophy in very close voting over Heupel, who threw for 3,392 yards and 20 touchdowns. Michael Vick was outstanding at quarterback, as was Drew Brees of Purdue. LaDainian Tomlinson of TCU was the nation's best running back. He gained 2,158 yards and finished fourth all-time on the major-college rushing list. Miami linebacker Dan Morgan was chosen as best linebacker and defensive player in the nation.

PAUL ATTNER, *The Sporting News*

Golf

Karrie Webb and Larry Nelson enjoyed banner years on their respective professional golf tours in 2000. Phil Mickelson also was outstanding on his tour. But all players' achievements were obscured by Tiger Woods, who rolled what would be a glittering career for most players into one outstanding season.

Woods won three of the world's four major championships, plus six other tournaments on the Professional Golfers' Association (PGA) Tour. His nine victories were the most since Sam Snead's 11 in 1950, and the fifth-highest total ever. He won a PGA Tour record $9,188,321, making him the all-time career money leader with $20,503,450 after only four years and four months as a professional golfer. He set an adjusted scoring record of 67.79, and his pure scoring average of 68.17 beat Byron Nelson's 1945 record of 68.33. Woods was named the Associated Press Male Athlete of the Year for the third time—only basketball's Michael Jordan has matched that. Woods also was chosen Sportsman of the Year by *Sports Illustrated* magazine for the second time—another first. He was, in short, phenomenal.

So was Webb on the Ladies Professional Golf Association (LPGA) Tour, with seven victories, including two majors. Larry Nelson, in his third full year on the Senior PGA Tour, erupted onto the scene with six victories and the money title. Woods, Webb, and Nelson were each voted Player of the Year by their golfing peers and by the Golf Writers Association of America.

PGA Tour. Woods also won a tournament on the European PGA Tour; teamed with David Duval to win the EMC World Cup; and won the unofficial PGA Grand Slam of Golf. His worldwide earnings were $11,034,530. He won the U.S. Open at Pebble Beach by a record 15 strokes, and trashed the field by eight strokes in the British Open at St. Andrews. His only close call came in the PGA Championship at Valhalla in Louisville, KY, where he needed a play-off to beat Bob May. He became the first player since Ben Hogan in 1953 to win three professional majors in one year, and became the fifth and youngest player to win the career Grand Slam.

Mickelson's four victories and $4,746,457 in winnings—a brilliant year by any measure—paled in comparison to Woods' feats. Mickelson won the season-ending Tour Championship by two strokes over Woods, but still had never won a major.

The other major—the Masters Tournament—went to Vijay Singh, by three strokes over Ernie Els. Paul Azinger, whose victory in Hawaii was his first since overcoming cancer in the mid-1990s, was named Comeback Player of the Year; and Michael Clark, winner of the John Deere Classic, won top rookie honors in 2000.

The U.S. professionals captured the President's Cup with a 21 $\frac{1}{2}$–10 $\frac{1}{2}$ rout over the International team.

Senior PGA Tour. Nelson's near-record $2,708,005 in earnings led the money list on the Senior PGA Tour, but Bruce Fleisher and Hale Irwin, each with four victories, both topped the $2 million mark. Irwin won his second U.S. Senior Open, and his four victories during the year tied him with Lee Trevino at 29 all-time senior wins.

Doug Tewell won the PGA Seniors' Championship and two other tournaments to earn Rookie of the Year honors. Raymond

© Stephen Dunn/Allsport

Karrie Webb, the LPGA Player of the Year in 1999 and 2000, soared to $6 million in earnings faster than any golfer in association history—all at the tender age of 25. Her flowering career bears a striking resemblance to that of another young phenom: Tiger Woods.

GOLF

PGA Tour

Mercedes Championships: Tiger Woods (276)
SONY Open in Hawaii: Paul Azinger (261)
Bob Hope Chrysler Classic: Jesper Parnevik (331)
Phoenix Open: Tom Lehman (270)
AT&T Pebble Beach National Pro-Am: Tiger Woods (273)
Buick Invitational: Phil Mickelson (270)
Nissan Open: Kirk Triplett (272)
World Golf Championships (Anderson Consulting Match Play):
    Darren Clarke
Touchstone Energy Tucson Open: Jim Carter (269)
Doral-Ryder Open: Jim Furyk (265)
Honda Classic: Dudley Hart (269)
Bay Hill Invitational presented by Cooper Tires: Tiger Woods (270)
THE PLAYERS Championship: Hal Sutton (278)
BellSouth Classic: Phil Mickelson (205)
The Masters: Vijay Singh (278)
MCI Classic: Stewart Cink (270)
Greater Greensboro Chrysler Classic: Hal Sutton (274)
Shell Houston Open: Robert Allenby (275)
Compaq Classic of New Orleans: Carlos Franco (270)
GTE Byron Nelson Classic: Jesper Parnevik (269)
MasterCard Colonial: Phil Mickelson (268)
Memorial Tournament: Tiger Woods (269)
Kemper Open: Tom Scherrer (271)
Buick Classic: Dennis Paulson (276)
U.S. Open: Tiger Woods (272)
FedEx St. Jude Classic: Notah Begay III (271)
Canon Greater Hartford Open: Notah Begay III (260)
Advil Western Open: Robert Allenby (274)
Greater Milwaukee Open: Loren Roberts (260)
British Open: Tiger Woods (269)
B.C. Open: Brad Faxon (270)
John Deere Classic: Michael Clark II (265)
The International presented by Qwest: Ernie Els (48 points)
Buick Open: Rocco Mediate (268)
PGA Championship: Tiger Woods (270)
World Golf Championships-NEC Invitational: Tiger Woods (259)
Reno-Tahoe Open: Scott Verplank (275)
Air Canada Championship: Rory Sabbatini (268)
Bell Canadian Open: Tiger Woods (266)
SEI Pennsylvania Classic: Chris DiMarco (270)
Westin Texas Open at LaCantera: Justin Leonard (261)
Buick Challenge: David Duval (269)
Michelob Championship at Kingsmill: David Toms (271)
Invensys Classic at Las Vegas: Billy Andrade (332)
Tampa Bay Classic: John Huston (271)
National Car Rental Classic: Duffy Waldorf (262)
THE TOUR Championship presented by Southern Company:
    Phil Mickelson (267)
Southern Farm Bureau Classic: Steve Lowery (266)
World Golf Championships (American Express Championship):
    Mike Weir (277)
World Golf Championships (EMC World Cup): David Duval/Tiger
    Woods, USA (254)

Senior PGA Tour

MasterCard Championship: George Archer (207)
Royal Caribbean Classic: Bruce Fleisher (30 points)
ACE Group Classic: Lanny Wadkins (202)
GTE Classic: Bruce Fleisher (200)
LiquidGolf.com Invitational: Tom Wargo (202)
Toshiba Senior Classic: Allen Doyle (136)
Audi Senior Classic: Hubert Green (197)
Liberty Mutual Legends of Golf: Jim Colbert/Andy North (191)
Emerald Coast Classic: Gil Morgan (197)
The Countrywide Tradition: Tom Kite (280)
PGA Seniors' Championship: Doug Tewell (201)
Las Vegas Senior Classic: Larry Nelson (197)
Bruno's Memorial Classic: John Jacobs (203)
Home Depot Invitational: Bruce Fleisher (203)
Nationwide Championship: Hale Irwin (207)
TD Waterhouse Championship: Dana Quigley (198)
Boone Valley Classic: Larry Nelson (200)
BellSouth Senior Classic at Opryland: Hale Irwin (198)
SBC Senior Open: Tom Kite (207)
SBC Championship: Doug Tewell (274)
Cadillac NFL Golf Classic: Lee Trevino (202)
U.S. Senior Open: Hale Irwin (267)
State Farm Senior Classic: Leonard Thompson (205)
FORD SENIOR PLAYERS Championship: Raymond Floyd (273)
Instinet Classic: Gil Morgan (199)
Lightpath Long Island Classic: Bruce Fleisher (198)
Coldwell Banker Burnet Classic: Ed Dougherty (197)
AT&T Canada Senior Open: Tom Jenkins (274)
Novell Utah Showdown: Doug Tewell (199)
FleetBoston Classic: Larry Nelson (203)
Foremost Insurance Championship: Larry Nelson (198)
Comfort Classic: Gil Morgan (131)
Kroger Senior Classic: Hubert Green (200)
Bank One Championship: Larry Nelson (203)
Vantage Championship: Larry Nelson (198)
The Transamerica: Jim Thorpe (198)
Gold Rush Classic: Jim Thorpe (195)

EMC Kaanapali Classic: Hale Irwin (198)
SBC Senior Classic: Joe Inman (198)
SENIOR TOUR Championship: Tom Watson (270)

LPGA Tour

The Office Depot: Karrie Webb (281)
Subaru Memorial of Naples: Nancy Scranton (275)
Los Angeles Women's Championship: Laura Davies (211)
Hawaiian Ladies Open: Betsy King (204)
Australian Ladies Masters: Karrie Webb (274)
LPGA Takefuji Classic: Karrie Webb (207)
Welch's/Circle K Championship: Annika Sorenstam (269)
Standard Register PING: Charlotta Sorenstam (276)
Nabisco Championship: Karrie Webb (274)
Longs Drugs Challenge: Juli Inkster (275)
Chick-fil-A Charity Championship: Sophie Gustafson (206)
The Philips Invitational Honoring Harvey Penick: Laura Davies
    (275)
Electrolux USA Championship: Pat Hurst (275)
Firstar LPGA Classic: Annika Sorenstam (197)
LPGA Corning Classic: Betsy King (276)
Kathy Ireland Greens.com LPGA Classic: Grace Park (274)
Wegmans Rochester International: Meg Mallon (280)
Evian Masters: Annika Sorenstam (276)
McDonald's LPGA Championship: Juli Inkster (281)
ShopRite LPGA Classic: Janice Moodie (203)
Jamie Farr Kroger Classic: Annika Sorenstam (274)
Japan Airlines Big Apple Classic: Annika Sorenstam (206)
U.S. Women's Open: Karrie Webb (282)
Giant Eagle LPGA Classic: Dorothy Delasin (205)
Michelob Light Classic: Lorie Kane (205)
du Maurier Classic: Meg Mallon (282)
Weetabix Women's British Open: Sophie Gustafson (282)
Oldsmobile Classic: Karrie Webb (268)
State Farm Rail Classic: Laurel Kean (198)
First Union Betsy King Classic: Michele Redman (202)
The Safeway LPGA Golf Championship: Mi Hyun Kim (215)
New Albany Golf Classic: Lorie Kane (277)
Samsung World Championship: Juli Inkster (274)
AFLAC Champions presented by Southern Living: Karrie Webb
    (273)
Cisco World Ladies Challenge: Japan
Mizuno Classic: Lorie Kane (204)
Arch Tour Championship: Dottie Pepper (279)
Women's World Cup Golf: Karrie Webb, Rachel Hetherington,
    Australia (275)

Other Tournaments

Presidents Cup: United States 21$^1/_2$, International 10$^1/_2$
The Solheim Cup: Europe 14$^1/_2$, USA 11$^1/_2$
Curtis Cup: United States 10, Great Britain/Ireland 8
U.S. Women's Amateur Public Links: Catherine Cartwright
U.S. Amateur Public Links: D.J. Trahan
U.S. Junior Amateur: Matthew Rosenfeld
U.S. Girls' Junior: Lisa Ferrero
U.S. Women's Amateur: Marcy Newton
U.S. Amateur: Jeff Quinney
U.S. Mid-Amateur: Greg Puga
USGA Senior Women's Amateur: Carol Semple Thompson
USGA Senior Amateur: Bill Shean Jr.
U.S. Women's Mid-Amateur: Ellen Port
NCAA Women: Team—Arizona (1,175); Individual—Jenna
    Daniels, Arizona (287)
NCAA Men: Team—Oklahoma State (1,116); Individual—Charles
    Howell, OklahomaState (265)
World Amateur Team Championship: Team—United States
    (841); Individual—Bryce Molder, U.S. (273)
Women's World Amateur Team Championship: Team—France
    (580); Individual—Suzann Petersen, Norway (285)
Senior British Open: Christy O'Connor (275)
British Amateur: Mikko Ilonen
British Mid-Amateur: Andrew Farmer
PGA TOUR Qualifying Tournament: Stephen Allan (400)
SENIOR PGA TOUR National Qualifying Tournament: Bob Gilder
    (269)
Cisco World Match Play: Lee Westwood
Dunhill Cup: Spain
Chrysler Senior Match Play Challenge: Vicente Fernandez
Certain Teed Hall of Fame Golf Challenge: Johnny Miller/Beth
    Daniel (196)
Franklin Templeton Shootout: Brad Faxon/Scott McCarron (190)
PGA Grand Slam of Golf: Tiger Woods (139)
Sun Microsystems Par-3 Challenge: Dottie Pepper 51
Skins Game: Collin Montgomerie
Senior Skins Game: Gary Player
Nedbank Golf Challenge: Ernie Els (268)
Williams World Challenge: Davis Love III (266)
Our Lucaya Senior Slam: Hale Irwin (135)
Office Depot Father/Son Challenge: Raymond-Robert Floyd
    (122)
Hyundai Team Matches: PGA Tour—Tom Lehman/Duffy Wal-
    dorf; SENIOR PGA TOUR—Jack Nicklaus/Tom Watson; LPGA
    Tour—Dottie Pepper/Juli Inkster
Wendy's Three-Tour Challenge: PGA Tour

Floyd won the Ford Seniors Players Championship and was voted Comeback Player of the Year. It was Floyd's fourth major title on the circuit, and 14th overall.

LPGA Tour. At the age of 25, Webb swept Player of the Year honors; won the money title with a record $1,876,853; and won the Vare Trophy with a scoring average of 70.5—all for the second year in a row. She became the fastest player in LPGA history to reach the $5 million and $6 million marks. She won the Nabisco Championship and the U.S. Women's Open.

Annika Sorenstam won five tournaments and was second on the money list with $1.4 million and second to Webb in scoring average and Player of the Year voting. Dorothy Delasin, with $339,112 in winnings, was voted Rookie of the Year.

In the Solheim Cup, Europe upset the U.S. team, 14 1/2–11 1/2.

LARRY DENNIS, *Creative Communications*

Horse Racing

Tiznow, who did not win his first horse race until May 2000, was the surprise winner of the $4,296,040 Breeders' Cup Classic on November 4. The 3-year-old Tiznow, ridden by Chris McCarron, narrowly edged European standout Giant's Causeway. Favored Fusaichi Pegasus finished sixth.

The Breeders' Cup Turf, which carried a $2,271,680 purse, was won by Kalanisi, who emerged from a slow pace to beat Quiet Resolve in a time of 2:26.96 over 1.5 mi (2.43 km). The Breeders Cup Distaff saw two fillies trained by D. Wayne Lukas finish first and second. The winner was Spain, a 55–1 long shot ridden by Victor Espinoza, who beat Surfide, with Pat Day aboard.

Caressing's victory in the Juvenile Fillies came against 47–1 odds. She was the first horse that owner Carl Pollard or trainer David Vance had entered in a Breeders' Cup event. The victory margin was half a length over Platinum Tiara. The Breeders' Cup Juvenile saw Macho Uno cover the 1 1/16-mi (1.72 km) course in 1:42.05 under the ride of Jerry Bailey.

War Chant won the Breeders' Cup Mile on the same track where he had suffered a hairline shoulder fracture in the Kentucky Derby. The horse did not return to the track until about a month before the Cup races. The winner of the Breeders' Cup Sprint was Kona Gold. Perfect Sting won the Breeders' Cup Filly and Mare Turf.

HORSE RACING

Major U.S. Thoroughbred Races

Arkansas Derby: Graeme Hall, $500,000 (total purse)
Arlington Million: Chester House, $2 million
Belmont Stakes: Commendable, $1 million
Blue Grass Stakes: High Yield, $750,000
Breeders' Cup Classic: Tiznow, $4,296,040
Breeders' Cup Turf: Kalanisi, $2,271,680
Breeders' Cup Juvenile: Macho Uno, $980,120
Breeders' Cup Juvenile Fillies: Caressing, $1,025,920
Breeders' Cup Mile: War Chant, $1,071,720
Breeders' Cup Distaff: Spain, $2,161,760
Breeders' Cup Sprint: Kona Gold, $916,000
Breeders' Cup Filly and Mare Turf: Perfect Sting, $1,108,360
Flamingo Stakes: Trippi, 4250,000
Florida Derby: Hal's Hope, $750,000
Haskell Invitational Handicap: Menifee, $1 million
Hollywood Gold Cup: Early Pioneer, $1 million
Illinois Derby: Gilt Trip, $100,000
Kentucky Derby: Fusaichi Pegasus, $1,188,400
Louisiana Derby: Mighty, $750,000
Metropolitan Handicap: Yankee Victor, $750,000
Pacific Classic: Skimming, $1 million
Preakness Stakes: Red Bullett, $1 million
Santa Anita Derby: The Deputy, $1 million
Santa Anita Handicap: General Challenge, $1 million
Suburban Handicap: Lemon Drop Kid, $500,000
Swaps Stakes: Cat Thief, $500,000
Travers Stakes: Unshaded, $1 million
Wood Memorial: Fusaichi Pegasus, $750,000

Major North American Harness Races

Breeders Crown Open Pace: Western Ideal, $440,000
Breeders Crown Open Trot: Magician, $1 million
Breeders Crown Mare Pace: Ron's Girl, $332,500
Cane Pace: Blissful Hall, $377,934
Hambletonian: Yankee Peco, $1 million
Little Brown Jug: Astreos, $547,972
Meadowlands Pace: Gallo Blue Chip, $1,150,000
Peter Haughton Memorial: Yankee Mustang, $460,400
Sweetheart Pace: Hawaiian Jenna, $433,800
Woodrow Wilson Pace: Whitefish Falls, $703,000

Each year since 1997, a 3-year-old had entered the Belmont Stakes with a chance to win the Triple Crown, only to come up short. But when Fusaichi Pegasus overwhelmed the Kentucky Derby field in 2000, he looked like a strong bet to pull off the sport's most heralded achievement. Fusaichi Pegasus was the first favorite to win the Derby since Spectacular Bid in 1979, but he finished second to Red Bullet in the Preakness Stakes. Red Bullet had skipped the Derby and won the Preakness on a muddy track. Fusaichi Pegasus then missed the Belmont with a minor hoof injury. Red Bullet also was kept out of the 1.5-mi (2.43-km) race to better prepare for the Breeders' Cup, which left 19–1 Commendable to win the Belmont. Lemon Drop Kid, a 4-year-old, won the Suburban Handicap, the Brooklyn Handicap, and the Whitney Handicap in succession.

Harness Racing In harness racing, T. J. Ritchie drove Yankee Peco to victory in The Hambletonian at the Meadowlands in East Rutherford, NJ. Credit Winner was second and Ambro Trick third. The Little Brown Jug at Delaware, OH, was won by Astreos, with Gallo Blue Chip second and George Scooter third. The $1 million Breeders Crown Open Trot was taken by Magician.

STAN SUTTON

Ice Hockey

In a storybook ending, the New Jersey Devils won the 1999–2000 National Hockey League (NHL) title for their octogenarian owner John McMullen, who sold the club at the end of the season. In a twist, Devils general manager Lou Lamoriello fired his coach, Robbie Ftorek, with eight games to go in the regular season and gave the job to Ftorek's popular assistant, Larry Robinson. The players rallied around Robinson, a Hall of Fame defenseman in his days with the Montreal Canadiens in the 1970s and 1980s, and won the club's second Stanley Cup. No team ever had won the league title after making a coaching change so late in the regular season, but New Jersey beat Philadelphia in a thrilling Eastern Conference final after being down three games to one. During the series, Flyer captain Eric Lindros suffered a concussion in a sickening open-ice hit by New Jersey captain Scott Stevens. It was Lindros' third concussion in a year that threatened to end his great career.

After getting by the favored Flyers, the Devils dethroned the reigning champion Dallas Stars. It was the first time in 16 years that a champion had been knocked off in the Stanley Cup finals the following year. In 1984 the Wayne Gretzky–led Edmonton Oilers had ended the New York Islanders' four-year run as champions.

NHL Regular Season. The Philadelphia Flyers were the most compelling team story of the year. Their likable coach, Roger Neilson, got bone-marrow cancer in December; their anthem singer was struck with non-Hodgkin's lymphoma; their longest-serving player, Rod Brind'Amour, was traded; and their captain suffered concussions. Through all the adversity, Philadelphia still had the most points, 105, in the Eastern Conference. The St. Louis Blues were the flip side, a team of overachievers, who led the entire league in points, 114, even though they had only one player, Pavol Demitra, in the top 15 in league scoring.

For the first time since 1968, when Stan Mikita won the scoring title with 87 points, nobody got 100 points. Jaromir Jagr won his third straight scoring title with 96, playing in only 63 of Pittsburgh's 82 games because of leg injuries. He beat Florida's flashy Pavel Bure, who had 94. Philadelphia winger Mark Recchi was the only other player to exceed 90 points. He had 91. The league's best rookie, New Jersey forward Scott Gomez, had an impressive 70. Bure was the only player to score 50 or more goals. He had 58. San Jose winger Owen Nolan was next with 44.

Anaheim winger Teemu Selanne, who had the most goals in the 1998–99 season with 47, slumped to 33. On the whole, scoring was anemic. The Blues lost only 20 of 82 games, but scored only 248 goals, barely three a game. The Detroit Red Wings led with 278 goals, and New Jersey was the only other team that had more than 250 goals (251).

New Jersey captain Scott Stevens led the Devils to Stanley Cup victory with his exceptional defensive play as he continually shut down the opposing teams' offensive stars. He was awarded the Conn Smythe Trophy as the most valuable player of the play-offs.

There were a couple of nice milestones, however. Brett Hull tied his legendary father, Bobby, in career goals with 610. Detroit winger Pat Verbeek reached the 500-goal plateau; defenseman Paul Coffey, playing for the Carolina Hurricanes, moved past one of the game's all-time greats, Mario Lemieux, in total points; and legendary Boston captain Ray Bourque, who had spent his entire 21-year career with the Bruins, was traded to Colorado late in the season. Blues goalie Roman Turek had the most shutouts (seven) and the best goals-against average of anybody playing at least 40 games (1.95).

The Blues won the Central Division with 114 points—six more than Detroit, who had the second-most points in the entire league. Dallas took the Pacific with 102, eight more than Los Angeles, and Colorado was first in the Northwest with 96, eight clear of Edmonton. The Flyers nosed out New Jersey (105–103) to take the Atlantic Division; Toronto won the Northeast with 100, five up on Ottawa; and Washington squeezed past Florida (102–98) in the Southeast. Under a new rule, the category regulation ties (RT) was added to the official standings. A team earns one point for a tie in regulation play, even if it is defeated in overtime.

Play-offs. In a shocking upset, the eighth-seeded San Jose Sharks beat the Blues in seven games in round one (the quarterfinals) of the Western Conference play-offs. After that, the Western quarterfinals went according to form. Dallas beat Edmonton in five games; the Red Wings silenced Los Angeles in a four-game sweep; and Colorado got by Phoenix in five. In the Eastern Conference's quarterfinals, the only upset was Pittsburgh, the seventh seed, rolling over Washington in five games. The Flyers blew out Buffalo in five; New Jersey swept Florida in four; and Toronto outlasted Ottawa in six.

In the second round (the semifinals), the Penguins and Flyers played the third-longest overtime in NHL history in Game 4, going 12 minutes into the fifth overtime period before the Flyers' Keith Primeau beat Ron Tugnutt for a 2–1 win. The Penguins, up two games to none in the series, never recovered from the overtime setback as Philadelphia won the next four. New Jersey beat the Maple Leafs in six games, holding Toronto to a play-off record six shots over 60 minutes in the final game. In the semifinals in the West, Colorado thumped the favored Red Wings in five games, mark-

ICE HOCKEY

National Hockey League
(Final Standings, 1999–2000)

Eastern Conference

Atlantic Division	W	L	T	RT**	Pts.	Goals For	Against
*Philadelphia	45	25	12	3	105	237	179
*New Jersey	45	29	8	5	103	251	203
*Pittsburgh	37	37	8	6	88	241	236
N.Y. Rangers	29	41	12	3	73	218	246
N.Y. Islanders	24	49	9	1	58	194	275
Northeast Division							
*Toronto	45	30	7	3	100	246	222
*Ottawa	41	30	11	2	95	244	210
*Buffalo	35	36	11	4	85	213	204
Montreal	35	38	9	4	83	196	194
Boston	24	39	19	6	73	210	248
Southeast Division							
*Washington	44	26	12	2	102	227	194
*Florida	43	33	6	6	98	244	209
Carolina	37	35	10	0	84	217	216
Tampa Bay	19	54	9	7	54	204	310
Atlanta	14	61	7	4	39	170	313

Western Conference

Central Division	W	L	T	RT	Pts.	Goals For	Against
*St. Louis	51	20	11	1	114	248	165
*Detroit	48	24	10	2	108	278	210
Chicago	33	39	10	2	78	242	245
Nashville	28	47	7	7	70	199	240
Northwest Division							
*Colorado	42	29	11	1	96	233	201
*Edmonton	32	34	16	8	88	226	212
Vancouver	30	37	15	8	83	227	237
Calgary	31	41	10	5	77	211	256
Pacific Division							
*Dallas	43	29	10	6	102	211	184
*Los Angeles	39	31	12	4	94	245	228
*Phoenix	39	35	8	4	90	232	228
*San Jose	35	37	10	7	87	225	214
Anaheim	34	36	12	3	83	217	227

*In play-offs
**Regulation ties

Stanley Cup Play-offs

Eastern Conference

Quarterfinals	New Jersey	4 games	Florida	0
	Philadelphia	4 games	Buffalo	1
	Pittsburgh	4 games	Washington	1
	Toronto	4 games	Ottawa	2
Semifinals	New Jersey	4 games	Toronto	2
	Philadelphia	4 games	Pittsburgh	2
Finals	New Jersey	4 games	Philadelphia	3

Western Conference

Quarterfinals	Colorado	4 games	Phoenix	1
	Dallas	4 games	Edmonton	1
	Detroit	4 games	Los Angeles	0
	San Jose	4 games	St. Louis	3
Semifinals	Colorado	4 games	Detroit	1
	Dallas	4 games	San Jose	1
Finals	Dallas	4 games	Colorado	3

Stanley Cup Finals

New Jersey	4 games	Dallas	2

Individual Honors

Hart Memorial Trophy (most valuable player): Chris Pronger, St. Louis
Art Ross Trophy (leading scorer): Jaromir Jagr, Pittsburgh
Maurice Richard Trophy (most goals): Pavel Blure, Florida
Vezina Trophy (top goaltender): Olaf Kolzig, Washington
William M. Jennings Trophy (fewest goals allowed): Roman Turek, St. Louis
James Norris Memorial Trophy (best defenseman): Chris Pronger
Frank J. Selke Trophy (best defensive forward): Steve Yzerman, Detroit
Calder Memorial Trophy (rookie of the year): Scott Gomez, New Jersey
Lady Byng Memorial Trophy (most gentlemanly player): Pavol Demitra, St. Louis
Conn Smythe Trophy (most valuable in play-offs): Scott Stevens, New Jersey
Jack Adams Award (coach of the year): Joel Quenneville, St. Louis
King Clancy Memorial Trophy (leadership and humanitarian service): Curtis Joseph, Toronto
Bill Masterton Memorial Trophy (perseverance, sportsmanship, and dedication): Ken Daneyko, New Jersey
Lester B. Pearson Award (outstanding player, voted by the players): Jaromir Jagr

ing the second straight year that Detroit did not made it past the second round. Dallas rolled over the emotionally spent Sharks in five games as the Stars held San Jose to seven goals.

In the conference finals, the Flyers, behind rookie goalie Brian Boucher, roared to a 3–1 game lead over New Jersey, but let it slip away. Patrik Elias had both goals in a 2–1 series clincher. In the West, Dallas ended Bourque's attempt to get back to the Stanley Cup finals for the first time in ten years, when the Stars beat the Avalanche, 3–2, in Game 7.

Stanley Cup Finals. In the opener of the Stanley Cup finals, Jason Arnott and his linemate Petr Sykora and Elias combined for four goals and seven assists as New Jersey blew out Dallas, 7–3. Goalie Ed Belfour had his shakiest performance in years; he was pulled after giving up six goals in an 18-shot span. Belfour bounced back in Game 2 in New Jersey, however, as Dallas won, 2–1. The Devils shocked the Stars, who had been nearly unbeatable at home over the previous two play-off years, by winning the third and fourth games in Dallas. In Game 3, New Jersey overcame some sparkling goaltending by Belfour to win, 2–1. In Game 4, the Devils scored three goals in the third period, including a shorthanded marker by John Madden, to win, 3–1. The Stars hung in in Game 5, as Mike Modano scored in the third overtime on a tip of a Hull shot. In Game 6, New Jersey won, 2–1, on Arnott's overtime shot on Belfour in the second extra period.

Personnel Changes. When Neilson got sick, his assistant, Craig Ramsay, took over and was hired as head man when the season ended. Chicago fired coach Lorne Molleken in May and appointed Finnish-born Alpo Suhonen, who had been an assistant in Toronto, as head coach. In June, Pittsburgh hired Ivan Hlinka, the coach of the Czech Republic's 1998 Olympic team, as head man. In a sweeping housecleaning, the New York Rangers fired general manager Neil Smith and coach John Muckler on May 28. They were replaced by longtime Oiler manager Glen Sather and Edmonton coach Ron Low, respectively. In other moves, Gretzky became a minority owner of the Phoenix Coyotes, and Don Hay was named head coach of the Calgary Flames.

NCAA. North Dakota defeated Boston College, 4–2, in the championship game of the National Collegiate Athletic Association (NCAA) tournament in Providence, RI, in April. North Dakota's senior Lee Goren was named the tournament's most valuable player. Mike Mottau, a senior defenseman at Boston College, captured the Hobey Baker Award as the year's outstanding player in college hockey.

JIM MATHESON, *"The Edmonton Journal"*

Ice Skating

Michelle Kwan was the dominant name in figure skating in 2000. Gianni Romme of the Netherlands and Germany's Claudia Pechstein captured the men's and women's overall titles at the World Speed Skating Championships.

Figure Skating. Michelle Kwan, a 19-year-old student at UCLA, finished first at both the World and U.S. Figure Skating Championships. It was her third world title and her fourth U.S. crown. At the World Championships, Russia's Irina Slutskaya, the winner of the European Championships in 2000, took the silver medal, and 1999's victor, Russia's Maria Butyrskaya, was awarded the bronze. At the U.S. competition in Cleveland in February, two young skaters with bright futures—Sasha Cohen, 15, and Sarah Hughes, 14—won the silver and bronze medals, respectively.

On the men's side, Michael Weiss repeated as U.S. champion and was third at the World Championships. Russia's Alexei Yagudin skated to his third consecutive World crown. Canada's Elvis Stojko finished second.

ICE SKATING

World Figure Skating Championships
Men: Alexei Yagudin, Russia
Women: Michelle Kwan, United States
Pairs: Maria Petrova and Alexei Tikhonov, Russia
Dance: Marina Anissina and Gwendal Peizerat, France

U.S. National Figure Skating Championships
Men: Michael Weiss, United States
Women: Michelle Kwan
Pairs: Kyoko Ina and John Zimmerman, United States
Dance: Naomi Lang and Peter Tchernyshev, United States

European Figure Skating Championships
Men: Evgeni Plushenko, Russia
Women: Irina Slutskaya, Russia
Pairs: Yelena Berezhnaya and Anton Sikharulidze, Russia
Dance: Marina Anissina and Gwendal Peizerat

Speed Skating World Cup—Final Points
Men's 500 meters: Jeremy Wotherspoon, Canada
Men's 1,000 meters: Jeremy Wotherspoon
Men's 1,500 meters: Adne Sondral, Norway
Men's 5,000 meters/10,000 meters: Gianni Romme, Netherlands
Women's 500 meters: Monique Garbrecht, Germany
Women's 1,000 meters: Monique Garbrecht
Women's 1,500 meters: Gunda Niemann-Stirnemann, Germany
Women's 3,000 meters/5,000 meters: Gunda Niemann-Stirnemann

World Speed Skating Championships
Men's Overall: Gianni Romme
Women's Overall: Claudia Pechstein, Germany

The XXVII Summer Olympic Games opened in Sydney, Australia, on Sept. 15, 2000, with Cathy Freeman, an Aborigine, lighting the flame, below. *They concluded on October 1 with a dramatic fireworks display,* above, *over the city's famous opera house.*

The XXVII Summer Games

The XXVII Summer Olympic Games, hosted by Sydney, Australia, from Sept. 15 to Oct. 1, 2000, were an extraordinary mixture of national spirit, joyous atmosphere, breathtaking setting, and intense competition that produced many exemplary athletic accomplishments.

The Australians, who surprised the world in 1993 by beating out Beijing, China, to win the opportunity to host these Olympic Games, put on a wonderful show (*see also* AUSTRALIA—Sydney: An Olympic City). The Games were upbeat and positive, despite the constant shadows created by alleged high-volume drug usage by many of the registered athletes. This was a far less

commercial Olympics compared to the 1996 Games in Atlanta, which were highly criticized by International Olympic Committee (IOC) officials for selling out to corporate interests, in order to raise enough money to put on the two-week event.

In contrast, the Sydney Games had very few glitches, including no security or transportation problems—two of the most controversial elements of any modern Olympic Games, and particularly so in Atlanta. Besides, the weather cooperated beautifully, producing picture-perfect days for the competitors and the record number of spectators who attended.

In all, a record 11,084 athletes from 200 countries were in Australia; 38% of the competitors were women, also a record. In the parade of nations during the opening ceremonies, North and South Korea marched in together, a dramatic and an unprecedented display of a new relationship.

The United States, as expected, emerged as the dominant athletic power. It won the most gold medals, 40, and the most overall medals, 97. Russia was second in both categories, with 32 gold and 88 overall. Host Australia, which had never been among the most successful nations in the Summer Olympics, delighted its home fans by winning 16 gold medals and 58 overall, good enough for fourth place, one medal behind China. If you included all the former members of the Soviet Union, however, those 13 countries combined for 163 medals, including 48 gold.

But for many other countries lacking the quantity of great athletes to compete against the larger nations, there still were many memorable moments. Five countries—Barbados, Kuwait, Kyrgyzstan, Saudi Arabia, and Vietnam—won their first medals of any kind, while six others—Azerbaijan, Cameroon, Colombia, Latvia, Mozambique, and Slovenia—won their first gold medals.

The proper spirit for these Games was set during the opening ceremonies when Australian track star Cathy Freeman, an Aborigine and the first of her race to win an Olympic medal, lit the Olympic torch. This emotional moment featured a member of a minority race that, at one point in the history of the country, had been considered outcasts. Now Freeman's presence was symbolic not only of an attempt at Australian unity, but of desired unity in the world.

Track and Field. Beyond her role in the opening ceremonies, Cathy Freeman provided the track-and-field venue with its most touching moment, too. The defending world champion in the 400 m, she was a favorite to win that event in Sydney. Before the race, it seemed as if all of Australia paused to watch. Despite incredible pressure, she produced a magnificent performance, overwhelming the field and cruising to victory. When she was done, Freeman knelt on the track, overcome with emotion and relief.

Her triumph vied for exposure with the feats of American sprinter Marion Jones (*see also* BIOGRAPHY), who came to the Games vowing to win five track-and-field gold medals, an unprecedented accomplishment. She began her quest with strong efforts both in the 100-m and 200-m sprints. She won both by near-record distances, swamping fields of talented competitors in the process. But her attempt to win a long-jump gold failed. Heike Drechsler of Germany, the defending champion, won again with a jump of 22′ 11″ (6.99 m). Jones, fouling on most of her attempts, including her last, finished third with a jump of 22′1/2″ (6.92 m). She also was a member of the U.S. 4x100 relay team that finished third. But Jones picked up a third gold medal as a member of the winning 4x400 relay team. Her total of five medals—three gold and two bronze—tied her with swimmers Ian Thorpe of Australia and Dara Torres of the United States for the second-highest total in the Games. Russian gymnast Alexei Nemov took six.

Michael Johnson of the United States, who won gold medals in 1996 in the 200-m and 400-m races, returned to defend his 400-m championship. He did so in dominant fashion. He also anchored the winning 4x400 relay team. He did not compete in the 200 m; in the American Olympic trials, Johnson had pulled up lame, as had sprinter Maurice Greene, who rebounded to take the 100 m in Sydney, and then anchored the winning 4x100 relay team. The biggest upset in track and field was registered by another men's sprinter, Konstantinos Kenteris of Greece, who took advantage of the absence of Johnson and Greene to win the 200 m.

Erki Nool of Estonia took the men's decathlon, and now could boast of being the world's greatest athlete. Denise Lewis of Britain won the women's heptathlon. The women's pole vault was held for the first time in Olympic competition, and the gold went to Stacy Dragila of the United States.

The track-and-field competition was not without controversy. C.J. Hunter, husband of Marion Jones and a world-class shot-putter, had withdrawn from the Games in early September because of knee problems. But during the Games, it was announced that he had failed a series of drug tests, thus making him ineligible for the competition. Hunter

© Adam Pretty/Allsport

Stacy Dragila, a 29-year-old resident of Pocatello, ID, left, cleared 15′ 1″ to win the gold medal in the women's pole vault—an event that made its Olympics debut at Sydney.

© Thomas Kienzle/AP/Wide World Photos

Cathy Freeman wore a hooded bodysuit as she captured the 400-m track race in 49.11 seconds. "I could feel the crowd around me, all over me," Australia's newest hero said.

heatedly denied the allegations, and Jones said the reports did not hinder her performances.

Basketball. The latest version of the U.S. Dream Team in basketball was not nearly as impressive as in past Games. A field of improving competition resulted in a lackluster win for the United States.

The U.S. team was led by Vince Carter of the Toronto Raptors and Alonzo Mourning of the Miami Heat. Mourning endured a complicated Games. His wife gave birth to their second child during the middle of the Games, and he flew home to Miami in time for the birth before returning to play in the remaining games. The original Dream Team, which played in the 1992 Olympics, won by an average margin of 43.8 points. This latest team won by a margin of 22 points, and was challenged strongly by both Lithuania and France in the medal round. The Americans beat Lithuania by two points in the semifinals, and then defeated France in the gold-medal game, 85-75, behind 13 points each from Carter and Ray Allen of the Milwaukee Bucks. Other standouts included Kevin Garnett of the Minnesota Timberwolves, Tim Hardaway of the Miami Heat, and Jason Kidd of the Phoenix Suns.

The U.S. women hoopsters also won the gold medal, in much more impressive fashion. The veteran team, with a nucleus that had played together in international competition for years, got stronger with every game in Sydney, saving their best effort for the medal-round games. In the finals, the Americans trounced Australia, 76-54, in front of a highly partisan Aussie crowd, to finish undefeated. Standout players for the Americans included Lisa Leslie, Nikki McCray, and Sheryl Swoopes.

Baseball. In one of the biggest upsets of the Games, the United States beat Cuba in the gold-medal baseball game to complete an extraordinary performance in Sydney. The Cubans were a veteran team that had lost just a few international games over the past decade, and they were heavily favored to win in these Games, just as they had done in Atlanta. But the young American team, consisting mostly of minor-league players with a sprinkling of aging, former major leaguers, got solid pitching and clutch hitting throughout the baseball tournament.

The U.S. team was managed by Tommy Lasorda, the former manager of the Los Angeles Dodgers. In the gold-medal game, the United States won, 4-0, behind the strong pitching of Ben Sheets.

Gymnastics. Marred by drug controversies and the mediocre showing of the United States, gymnastics did not fill its usual niche as the glamour sport of the Summer Games. The dominant story became the disqualification of Romania's Andreea Raducan, who failed a drug test because she took an over-the-counter medicine to treat a cold. She

Russia's Aleksei Nemov, 24, was the gymnastic star of the men at Sydney—winning gold in the horizontal bar, left, and the all-around and four other medals.

© Amy Sancetta/
AP/Wide World Photos

© Amy Sancetta/AP/Wide World

The trampoline was another event to be introduced at the 2000 Summer Olympics. Russia's Irina Karavaeva, above, somersaulted, pirouetted, and jumped high for a gold medal.

had won the women's all-around title, but lost her gold medal.

The gymnastics star was supposed to be Svetlana Khorkina of Russia, a 5'5" (1.65 m) competitor who towered over her fellow athletes. But she lost any hope for the all-around title when she flubbed her vaults. It later was determined that the vault height had been set incorrectly, creating a series of falls and bad vaults. The affected competitors were given the option of redoing their vaults, but Khorkina was too upset over doing poorly in the uneven bars, and it was too late for her to catch up for the gold. She did win the individual gold in the uneven bars, and finished second in the floor exercise to teammate Yelena Zamolodtchikova, who also took the gold in the vault. Romania beat out Russia for the gold in the team competition. The U.S. women, who had finished first in the team competition in 1996, ended up fourth this time, a disappointment.

The Russian men did almost as poorly, finishing third behind China and Ukraine. However, Russia's Aleksei Nemov proved the most durable of the all the gymnasts. He won the all-around and the horizontal bars, finished second in the floor, and was third in the pommel horse and parallel bars. Nemov also was a member of Russia's bronze-winning team.

Soccer. In one of the Games' more stunning upsets, the U.S. women's soccer team lost the gold medal to Norway, 3-2. The United States, the defending world champion, was favored to win in Sydney, making its way through a very difficult bracket to advance to the medal round. After defeating Brazil in the semifinals, the Americans had some defensive lapses against Norway,

FINAL MEDAL STANDINGS

Country	Gold	Silver	Bronze	Total
United States	40	24	33	97
Russia	32	28	28	88
China	28	16	15	59
Australia	16	25	17	58
Germany	13	17	26	56
France	13	14	11	38
Italy	13	8	13	34
Netherlands	12	9	4	25
Cuba	11	11	7	29
Great Britain	11	10	7	28
Romania	11	6	9	26
South Korea	8	9	11	28
Hungary	8	6	3	17
Poland	6	5	3	14
Japan	5	8	5	18
Bulgaria	5	6	2	13
Greece	4	6	3	13
Sweden	4	5	3	12
Norway	4	3	3	10
Ethiopia	4	1	3	8
Ukraine	3	10	10	23
Kazakhstan	3	4	0	7
Belarus	3	3	11	17
Canada	3	3	8	14
Spain	3	3	5	11
Iran	3	0	1	4
Turkey	3	0	1	4
Czech Republic	2	3	3	8
Kenya	2	3	2	7
Denmark	2	3	1	6
Finland	2	1	1	4
Austria	2	1	0	3
Lithuania	2	0	3	5
Azerbaijan	2	0	1	3
Slovenia	2	0	0	2
Switzerland	1	6	2	9
Indonesia	1	3	2	6
Slovakia	1	3	1	5
Mexico	1	2	3	6
Algeria	1	1	3	5
Uzbekistan	1	1	2	4
Latvia	1	1	1	3
Yugoslavia	1	1	1	3
Bahamas	1	1	0	2
New Zealand	1	0	3	4
Estonia	1	0	2	3
Thailand	1	0	2	3
Croatia	1	0	1	2
Cameroon	1	0	0	1
Colombia	1	0	0	1
Mozambique	1	0	0	1
Brazil	0	6	6	12
Jamaica	0	4	3	7
Nigeria	0	3	0	3
Belgium	0	2	3	5
South Africa	0	2	3	5
Argentina	0	2	2	4
Morocco	0	1	4	5
Taiwan	0	1	4	5
North Korea	0	1	3	4
Saudi Arabia	0	1	1	2
Moldova	0	1	1	2
Trinidad and Tobago	0	1	1	2
Ireland	0	1	0	1
Uruguay	0	1	0	1
Vietnam	0	1	0	1
Georgia	0	0	6	6
Costa Rica	0	0	2	2
Portugal	0	0	2	2
Armenia	0	0	1	1
Barbados	0	0	1	1
Chile	0	0	1	1
India	0	0	1	1
Iceland	0	0	1	1
Israel	0	0	1	1
Kyrgyzstan	0	0	1	1
Kuwait	0	0	1	1
Macedonia	0	0	1	1
Qatar	0	0	1	1
Sri Lanka	0	0	1	1

XXVII SUMMER OLYMPICS—Gold Medalists

ARCHERY
Men's Individual: Simon Fairweather, Australia
Men's Team: South Korea
Women's Individual: Yun Mi Jin, South Korea
Women's Team: South Korea

BADMINTON
Men's Singles: Ji Xinpeng, China
Men's Doubles: Tony Gunawan and Candra Wijaya, Indonesia
Women's Singles: Gong Zhichao, China
Women's Doubles: Gu Jun, Ge Fei, China
Mixed Doubles: Zhang Jun, Gao Ling, China

BASEBALL

Men: United States

BASKETBALL

Men: United States
Women: United States

BEACH VOLLEYBALL

Men: Dain Blanton and Eric Fonoimoana, United States
Women: Natalie Cook and Kerri Pottharst, Australia

BOXING

Light Flyweight: Brahim Asloum, France
Flyweight: Wijan Ponlid, Thailand
Bantamweight: Guillermo Rigondeaux Ortiz, Cuba
Featherweight: Bekzat Sattarkhanov, Kazakhstan
Lightweight: Mario Kindelan, Cuba
Light Welterweight: Mahamadkadyz Abdullaev, Uzbekistan
Welterweight: Oleg Saitov, Russia
Light Middleweight: Yermakhan Ibraimov, Kazakhstan
Middleweight: Jorge Gutierrez, Cuba
Light Heavyweight: Aleksandr Lebziak, Russia
Heavyweight: Félix Savón, Cuba
Super Heavyweight: Audley Harrison, Great Britain

CANOEING

Men's 500-m Canoe Singles: Gyorgy Kolonics, Hungary
Men's 1,000-m Canoe Singles: Andreas Dittmer, Germany
Men's 500-m Canoe Doubles: Hungary
Men's 1,000-m Canoe Doubles: Romania
Men's Canoe Slalom Singles: Tony Estanguet, France
Men's Canoe Slalom Doubles: Slovakia
Men's 500-m Kayak Singles: Knut Holmann, Norway
Men's 500-m Kayak Doubles: Hungary
Men's 1,000-m Kayak Singles: Knut Holmann, Norway
Men's 1,000-m Kayak Doubles: Italy
Men's 1,000-m Kayak Fours: Hungary
Men's Kayak Slalom Singles: Thomas Schmidt, Germany
Women's 500-m Kayak Singles: Josefa Idem Guerrini, Italy
Women's 500-m Kayak Doubles: Germany
Women's 500-m Kayak Fours: Germany
Women's Kayak Slalom Singles: Stepanka Hilgertova, Czech
  Republic

CYCLING

Men's Keirin: Florian Rousseau, France
Men's Madison: Australia
Men's Pursuit: Robert Bartko, Germany
Men's Points Race: Juan Llaneras, Spain
Men's Individual Time Trial: Vyacheslav Yekimov, Russia
Men's 1-km Time Trial: Jason Queally, Great Britain
Men's Road Race: Jan Ullrich, Germany
Men's Sprint: Marty Nothstein, United States
Men's Olympic Sprint: France
Men's Mountain Bike: Miguel Martinez, France
Men's Team Pursuit: Germany
Women's Pursuit: Leontien Zijlaard, Netherlands
Women's Points Race: Antonella Belluti, Italy
Women's 500-m Time Trial: Felicia Ballanger, France
Women's Sprint: Felicia Ballanger, France
Women's Road Race: Leontien Zijlaard, Netherlands
Women's Individual Time Trial: Leontien Zijlaard, Netherlands
Women's Mountain Bike: Paola Pezzo, Italy

EQUESTRIAN

3-Day Event: David O'Connor, United States
Team 3-Day Event: Australia
Dressage: Anky van Grunsven, Netherlands
Team Dressage: Germany
Jumping: Jeroen Dubbeldam, Netherlands
Team Jumping: Germany

FENCING

Men's Epée: Pavel Kolobkov, Russia
Men's Team Epée: Italy
Men's Foil: Kim Young Ho, South Korea
Men's Team Foil: France
Men's Individual Saber: Mihai Claudiu Covaliu, Romania
Men's Team Saber: Russia
Women's Epée: Timea Nagy, Hungary
Women's Team Epée: Russia
Women's Foil: Valentina Vezzali, Italy
Women's Team Foil: Italy

FIELD HOCKEY

Men: Netherlands
Women: Australia

GYMNASTICS

Men's All-Around: Aleksei Nemov, Russia
Men's Floor Exercise: Igors Vihrovs, Latvia
Men's Horizontal Bar: Aleksei Nemov, Russia
Men's Parallel Bars: Li Xiaopeng, China
Men's Pommel Horse: Marius Urzica, Romania
Men's Rings: Szilveszter Csollany, Hungary
Men's Vault: Gervasio Deferr, Spain
Men's Team: China
Men Trampoline: Aleksandr Moskalenko, Russia
Women's All-Around: Simona Amanar, Romania
Women's Balance Beam: Liu Xuan, China

Women's Floor Exercise: Yelena Zamolodtchikova, Russia
Women's Uneven Parallel Bars: Svetlana Khorkina, Russia
Women's Vault: Yelena Zamolodtchikova, Russia
Women's Team: Romania
Women Trampoline: Irina Karavaeva, Russia

HANDBALL

Men: Russia
Women: Denmark

JUDO

Men's Extra Lightweight: Tadahiro Nomura, Japan
Men's Half-Lightweight: Huseyin Ozkan, Turkey
Men's Lightweight: Giuseppe Maddaloni, Italy
Men's Half-Middleweight: Makoto Takimoto, Japan
Men's Middleweight: Mark Huizinga, Netherlands
Men's Half-Heavyweight: Kosei Inoue, Japan
Men's Heavyweight: David Douillet, France
Women's Extra Lightweight: Ryoko Tamura, Japan
Women's Half-Lightweight: Legna Verdecia, Cuba
Women's Lightweight: Isabel Fernandez, Spain
Women's Half-Middleweight: Severine Vandenhende, France
Women's Middleweight: Sibelis Veranes, Cuba
Women's Half-Heavyweight: Tang Lin, China
Women's Heavyweight: Yuan Hua, China

MODERN PENTATHLON

Men: Dmitri Svatkovsky, Russia
Women: Stephanie Cook, Great Britain

RHYTHMIC GYMNASTICS

Women's Individual All-Around: Yulia Barsukova, Russia
Women's Group All-Around: Russia

ROWING

Men's Single Sculls: Rob Waddell, New Zealand
Men's Double Sculls: Slovenia
Men's Quadruple Sculls: Italy
Men's Pairs Without Coxswain: France
Men's Fours Without Coxswain: Great Britain
Men's Lightweight Double Sculls: Poland
Men's Lightweight Four Without Coxswain: France
Men's Eights: Great Britain
Women's Single Sculls: Ekaterina Karsten, Belarus
Women's Double Sculls: Germany
Women's Quadruple Sculls: Germany
Women's Pairs Without Coxswain: Romania
Women's Lightweight Double Sculls: Romania
Women's Eights: Romania

SHOOTING

Men's Air Pistol: Franck Dumoulin, France
Men's Free Pistol: Tanyu Kiriakov, Bulgaria
Men's Rapid-Fire Pistol: Sergei Alifirenko, Russia
Men's Running Game Target: Yang Ling, China
Men's Air Rifle: Yalin Cai, China
Men's Rifle, 3 Positions: Rajmond Debevec, Slovenia
Men's Rifle, Prone: Jonas Edman, Sweden
Men's Open Skeet: Mykola Milchev, Ukraine

© Katsumi Kasahara/AP/Wide World

Rulon Gardner, right, a 29-year-old farmer from Wyoming, sent shock waves through the Olympics as he defeated Russia's Alexander Karelin in heavyweight Greco-Roman wrestling.

Men's Open Trap: Michael Diamond, Australia
Men's Double Trap: Richard Faulds, Great Britain
Women's 10m Air Pistol: Tao Luna, China
Women's Sport Pistol: Maria Grozdeva, Bulgaria
Women's Air Rifle: Nancy Johnson, United States
Women's Rifle, 3 Positions: Renata Mauer-Rozanska, Poland
Women's Skeet: Zemfira Meftakhetdinova, Azerbaijan
Women's Trap: Daina Gudzineviciute, Lithuania
Women's Double Trap: Pia Hansen, Sweden

SOCCER

Men: Cameroon
Women: Norway

SOFTBALL

Women: United States

SWIMMING AND DIVING

Men's 100-m Backstroke: Lenny Krayzelburg, United States
Men's 200-m Backstroke: Lenny Krayzelburg, United States
Men's 100-m Breaststroke: Domenico Fioravanti, Italy
Men's 200-m Breaststroke: Domenico Fioravanti, Italy
Men's 100-m Butterfly: Lars Froelander, Sweden
Men's 200-m Butterfly: Tom Malchow, United States
Men's 50-m Freestyle: Anthony Ervin and Gary Hall, Jr., United States
Men's 100-m Freestyle: Pieter van den Hoogenband, Netherlands
Men's 200-m Freestyle: Pieter van den Hoogenband, Netherlands
Men's 400-m Freestyle: Ian Thorpe, Australia
Men's 1,500-m Freestyle: Grant Hackett, Australia
Men's 4x100-m Freestyle Relay: Australia
Men's 4x200-m Freestyle Relay: Australia
Men's 200-m Individual Medley: Massimiliano Rosolino, Italy
Men's 400-m Individual Medley: Tom Dolan, United States
Men's 4x100-m Medley Relay: United States
Men's Platform Diving: Tian Liang, China
Men's Springboard Diving: Xiong Ni, China
Men's Synchronized Platform Diving: Russia
Men's Synchronized Springboard Diving:China

Women's 100-m Backstroke: Diana Mocanu, Romania
Women's 200-m Backstroke: Diana Mocanu, Romania
Women's 100-m Breaststroke: Megan Quann, United States
Women's 200-m Breaststroke: Agnes Kovacs, Hungary
Women's 100-m Butterfly: Inge de Bruijn, Netherlands
Women's 200-m Butterfly: Misty Hyman, United States
Women's 50-m Freestyle: Inge de Bruijn, Netherlands
Women's 100-m Freestyle: Inge de Bruijn, Netherlands
Women's 200-m Freestyle: Susie O'Neill, Australia
Women's 400-m Freestyle: Brooke Bennett, United States
Women's 800-m Freestyle: Brooke Bennett, United States
Women's 4x100-m Freestyle Relay: United States
Women's 4x200-m Freestyle Relay: United States
Women's 200-m Individual Medley: Yana Klochkova, Ukraine
Women's 400-m Individual Medley: Yana Klochkova, Ukraine
Women's 400-m Medley Relay: United States
Women's Platform Diving: Laura Wilkinson, United States
Women's Springboard Diving: Fu Mingxia, China
Women's Synchronized Platform Diving: China
Women's Synchronized Springboard Diving: Russia

SYNCHRONIZED SWIMMING

Duet: Russia
Team: Russia

TABLE TENNIS

Men's Singles: Kong Linghui, China
Men's Doubles: Wang Liqin and Yan Sen, China
Women's Singles: Wang Nan, China
Women's Doubles: Li Ju and Wang Nan, China

TAE KWON DO

Men's 58–kg: Michail Mouroutsos, Greece
Men's 68–kg: Steven Lopez, United States
Men's 80–kg:Angel Valodia Matos Fuentes, Cuba
Men's 80–kg plus: Kim Kyong Hun, South Korea
Women's 49–kg: Lauren Burns, Australia
Women's 57–kg: Jung Jae Eun, South Korea
Women's 67–kg: Lee Sun Hee, South Korea
Women's 67 kg plus: Chen Zhong, China

TENNIS

Men's Singles: Yevgeny Kafelnikov, Russia
Men's Doubles: Daniel Nestor and Sebastien Lareau, Canada
Women's Singles: Venus Williams, United States
Women's Doubles: Serena Williams and Venus Williams, United States

TRACK AND FIELD

Men's 100-m: Maurice Greene, United States
Men's 200-m: Konstantinos Kenteris, Greece
Men's 400-m: Michael Johnson, United States
Men's 4x100-m Relay: United States
Men's 800-m: Nils Schumann, Germany
Men's 1,500-m: Noah Ngeny, Kenya
Men's 4x400-m Relay: United States
Men's 5,000-m: Millon Wolde, Ethiopia
Men's 10,000-m: Haile Gebrselassie, Ethiopia

Men's 20-km Walk: Robert Korzeniowski, Poland
Men's 50-km Walk: Robert Korzeniowski, Poland
Men's 110-m Hurdles: Anier Garcia, Cuba
Men's 400-m Hurdles: Angelo Taylor, United States
Men's 3,000-m Steeplechase: Reuben Kosgei, Kenya
Men's Marathon: Gezahgne Abera, Ethiopia
Men's Decathlon: Erki Nool, Estonia
Men's Discus: Virgilijus Alekna, Lithuania
Men's Hammer Throw: Szymon Ziolkowski, Poland
Men's High Jump: Sergei Kliugin, Russia
Men's Javelin: Jan Zelezny, Czech Republic
Men's Long Jump: Ivan Pedroso, Cuba
Men's Pole Vault: Nick Hysong, United States
Men's Shot Put: Arsi Harju, Finland
Men's Triple Jump: Jonathan Edwards, Great Britain
Women's 100-m: Marion Jones, United States
Women's 200-m: Marion Jones, United States
Women's 400-m: Cathy Freeman, Australia
Women's 400x100-m Relay: Bahamas
Women's 800-m: Maria Mutola, Mozambique
Women's 4x400-m Relay: United States
Women's 1,500-m: Nouria Merah-Benida, Algeria
Women's 5,000-m: Gabriela Szabo, Romania
Women's 10,000-m: Derartu Tulu, Ethiopia
Women's 20-km Walk: Wang Liping, China
Women's 100-m Hurdles: Olga Shishigina, Kazakhstan
Women's 400-m Hurdles:Irina Privalova, Russia
Women's Marathon: Naoko Takahashi, Japan
Women's Heptathlon: Denise Lewis, Great Britain
Women's Discus: Ellina Zvereva, Belarus
Women's Hammer Throw: Kamila Skolimowska, Poland
Women's High Jump: Yelena Yelesina, Russia
Women's Javelin: Trine Hattestad, Norway
Women's Long Jump: Heike Drechsler, Germany
Women's Shot Put: Yanina Korolchik, Belarus
Women's Triple Jump: Tereza Marinova, Bulgaria
Women's Pole Vault: Stacy Dragila, United States

TRIATHLON

Men: Simon Whitfield, Canada
Women: Brigitte McMahon, Switzerland

VOLLEYBALL

Men: Yugoslavia
Women: Cuba

WATER POLO

Men: Hungary
Women: Australia

WEIGHT LIFTING

Men's 56–kg: Halil Mutlu, Turkey
Men's 62–kg: Nikolay Pechalov, Croatia
Men's 69–kg: Galabin Boevski, Bulgaria
Men's 77–kg: Zhan Xugang, China
Men's 85–kg: Pyrros Dimas, Greece
Men's 94–kg: Akakios Kakiasvilis, Greece
Men's 105–kg: Hossein Tavakoli, Iran
Men's 105–kg plus: Hossein Rezazadeh, Iran
Women's 48–kg: Tara Nott, United States
Women's 53–kg: Yang Xia, China
Women's 58–kg: Soraya Jimenez Mendivil, Mexico
Women's 63–kg: Chen Xiaomin, China
Women's 69–kg: Lin Weining, China
Women's 75–kg: Maria Isabel Urrutia, Columbia
Women's 75–kg plus: Ding Meiyuan, China

WRESTLING, FREESTYLE

Men's 54–kg: Namig Adbullayev, Azerbaijan
Men's 58–kg: Alireza Dabir, Iran
Men's 63–kg: Mourad Oumakhanov, Russia
Men's 69–kg: Daniel Igali, Canada
Men's 76–kg: Brandon Slay, United States
Men's 85–kg: Adam Saitiev, Russia
Men's 97–kg: Saghid Mourtasaliyev, Russia
Men's 130–kg: David Moussoulbes, Russia

WRESTLING, GRECO-ROMAN

Men's 54–kg: Sim Kwon Ho, South Korea
Men's 58–kg: Armen Nazarian, Bulgaria
Men's 63–kg: Varteres Samourgachev, Russia
Men's 69–kg: Filiberto Azcuy, Cuba
Men's 76–kg: Mourat Kardanov, Russia
Men's 85–kg: Hamza Yerlikaya, Turkey
Men's 97–kg: Mikael Ljungberg, Sweden
Men's 130–kg: Rulon Gardner, United States

YACHTING

Open Laser: Ben Ainslie, Great Britain
Open Soling: Denmark
Open Star: United States
Open Tornado: Austria
Open 49ers: Finland
Men's Finn: Iain Percy, Great Britain
Men's Mistral: Christoph Sieber, Austria
Men's 470: Australia
Women's Europe: Shirley Robertson, Great Britain
Women's Mistral: Alessandra Sensini, Italy
Women's 470: Australia

© Doug Mills/AP/Wide World Photos

U.S. swimmer Lenny Krayzelburg, above, dominated the 100-m and 200-m backstroke, and Australia's Ian Thorpe, right, set a world record in the 400-m freestyle.

© Thomas Kienzle/AP/Wide World Photos

which kept the game close. Then, in overtime, Norway's Dagny Mellgren scored the winning goal. It was a devastating loss for the U.S. team, whose international triumphs had advanced the game of women's soccer in the United States.

The U.S. men did not make it to the gold-medal game, but their first presence in the medal round was a major development in the soccer world. The young U.S. team displayed great teamwork and strong scoring to survive as one of the last four teams. Then they lost to Chile, 2-0, to finish fourth, by far the country's best showing. Cameroon won the gold medal by defeating Spain.

Swimming and Diving. The swimming competition was billed as a showdown between the Australians and the U.S. team, particularly with the men. The Aussies' main hope was young Ian Thorpe, who had dominated the world sprinting competition entering the Olympics. Thorpe got off to a great start by setting a world record in the 400-m freestyle, but then could win only one more individual medal, a silver in the 200 m. He did take two golds and a silver in the relays. He was eclipsed in the individual spotlight by Pieter van den Hoogenband of the Netherlands, who won both the 100-m and 200-m freestyle races and finished third in the 50 m, behind Americans Gary Hall, Jr., and Anthony Ervin, in a rare tie for first. Lenny Krayzelburg of the United States won both the 100-m and 200-m backstroke, while Domenico Fioravanti of Italy took the 100-m and 200-m breaststrokes. Tom Dolan of the United States repeated as gold medalist in the 400-m individual medley.

In the women's events, the United States dominated, although individual honors went to Inge de Bruijn of the Netherlands. She won gold in the 50-m and 100-m freestyle in world-record times, and in the 100-m butterfly. Veteran swimmer Jenny Thompson of the United States failed in her quest to win her first individual goal medal, but still picked up three golds in relays, and a bronze in the 100-m freestyle, where she tied fellow American Dara Torres for third. Torres also finished third in the 50-m freestyle and 100-m butterfly, and was on two gold-medal relay teams. Torres joined Marion Jones as the only American women to win five medals at one Olympic Games.

Three of the four individual diving medals were won by Chinese athletes. Fu Mingxia repeated her gold in the women's springboard, and Xiong Ni did the same in the men's springboard. Laura Wilkinson of the United States took the women's platform competition—a major upset.

Other Sports. The most sensational and surprising victory of the Olympics was pulled off by U.S. Greco-Roman wrestler Rulon Gardner. Gardner was an unknown on the international wrestling scene, but was able to defeat the legendary Alexander Karelin of Russia, the most famous Greco-Roman wrestler in history. Karelin had not lost in 13 years, but Gardner went ahead 1-0 in the match, and then hung on to win the gold medal in the heavyweight division.

The United States had hoped to make some inroads against Cuba in boxing, but could not win any gold medals. The Cubans left with four. . . . In tennis, Venus Williams of the United States won the gold medal in women's singles, and teamed with her sister, Serena, to win the doubles. Yevgeny Kafelnikov of Russia won the men's singles, and Sebastien Lareau and Daniel Nestor of Canada took the doubles. . . . The U.S. women's softball team had to win five straight games to win the gold.

Overall. Even Australian citizens had doubts that their country could produce a memorable Olympic Games. But they were surprised and pleased, as was the rest of the world, with these Games. The 2004 Summer Games will be held in Athens, Greece.

PAUL ATTNER

Skiing

In the 2000 Alpine World Cup, the men's overall championship went to Austria's Hermann Maier, who dominated competition with victories in the downhill, giant slalom, and super-giant slalom. Renate Goetschl, also of Austria, earned the women's overall title, marked by her triumph in the super-giant slalom. Regina Haeusl captured the women's downhill.

© Tor Richardsen/ AP/Wide World Photos

Austria's Hermann Maier electrified the skiing community with his overall championship in the 2000 Alpine World Cup.

The Nordic World Championships—last dominated by Finland in 1999—was to take place in Lahti, Finland, in February 2001.

SKIING

Alpine World Cup
Men's Downhill: Hermann Maier, Austria
Men's Slalom: Kjetil-Andre Aamodt, Norway
Men's Giant Slalom: Hermann Maier, Austria
Men's Super-Giant Slalom: Hermann Maier, Austria
Men's Overall: Hermann Maier, Austria
Women's Downhill: Regina Haeusl, Germany
Women's Slalom: Spela Pretnar, Slovenia
Women's Giant Slalom: Michaela Dorfmeister, Austria
Women's Super-Giant Slalom: Renate Goetschl, Austria
Women's Overall: Renate Goetschl, Austria

U.S. Alpine Championships
Men's Downhill: Chris Puckett, United States
Men's Slalom: Erik Schlopy, United States
Men's Giant Slalom: Casey Puckett, United States
Men's Super-Giant Slalom: Daron Rahlves, United States
Men's Combined: Casey Puckett, United States
Women's Downhill: Kirsten Clark, United States
Women's Slalom: Caroline Lalive, United States
Women's Giant Slalom: (cancelled due to weather)
Women's Super-Giant Slalom: Kirsten Clark, United States
Women's Combined: Caroline Lalive, United States

NCAA Alpine Championships
Men's and Women's Team: Denver University

The University of Denver upset defending champion the University of Colorado (CU) to win the 2000 National Collegiate Men's and Women's Skiing Championships by a net score of 720 to 621. It was Denver's first collegiate skiing championship in 29 years, but their 15th overall, tying CU for the most in sport.

Soccer

The year 2000 was one of firsts in soccer, both in the United States and internationally. It marked the first time a reigning world champion also won the European Championship, with France performing that feat. For the first time, too, nations from Africa won back-to-back gold medals at the Olympic Games, with Cameroon winning gold in Sydney, as Nigeria had done in Atlanta in 1996. The first player, male or female, in history reached the 200-game milestone for a national team when midfielder Kristine Lilly of the United States set the record.

Off the field, there were two major controversies. The first centered around the selection of Germany over South Africa for the right to stage the 2006 World Cup, on a fractious 12–11 vote, with one abstention. The second concerned the right of players to move freely from team to team, without their new club having to pay their former club a transfer fee. The debate continued late in the year.

U.S. Developments. Both U.S. national teams had an eventful year, with the women winning the silver medal at the Sydney Olympics, and the men winning their tournament, the U.S. Cup, over Ireland, Mexico, and South Africa. The Olympic competition was the only event the U.S. women entered and did not win in 2000. They won five international tournaments, including the prestigious Algarve Cup in Portugal for the first time.

Major League Soccer (MLS) completed its fifth season, with the Kansas City Wizards earning their first championship. They defeated the Chicago Fire, 1–0, in the title game at Robert F. Kennedy Stadium in Washington, DC. Kansas City goalkeeper Tony Meola completed a hat trick of awards by being named MLS player of the year, goalkeeper of the year, and championship-game most valuable player (MVP).

Year 2000 witnessed the formation of the Women's United Soccer Association

(WUSA), the first professional league for women in the United States. Teams were formed in eight cities, with play set to begin in April 2001.

April Heinrichs, captain of the U.S. team that won the first women's world championship, in China in 1991, was named coach of the U.S. team in January, replacing former coach Tony DiCicco.

On the college level, the University of Connecticut won its first National Collegiate Athletic Association (NCAA) title since 1981—and only its second ever—defeating Creighton, 2–0, in the men's final. The University of North Carolina won its 16th national championship in 19 years with a 2–1 comeback victory over the University of California at Los Angeles (UCLA) in the women's final.

The International Scene. On the international level, 2000 saw the beginning of qualifying play for the 2002 World Cup, which will be cohosted by Japan and South Korea. A record 198 countries, including the United States, entered the quadrennial tournament.

Meanwhile, four continental championships were played in 2000. Cameroon won the African Nations Cup, defeating host Nigeria, 4–3, in the final. The Gold Cup saw Canada emerge as a surprise winner, defeating Colombia, 2–0, in the final. The European Championship went to France, which beat Italy in overtime, 3–2, in the final. Japan became Asia's new champion by defeating Saudi Arabia, 1–0, in the final.

On the club level, Real Madrid of Spain earned its record eighth European Champions Cup when it beat another Spanish club, Valencia, 3–0, at the Stade de France in Saint-Denis. The Union of European Football Association's EUFA Cup was won by Galatasaray of Turkey, which defeated Arsenal of England, 4–1, on penalty kicks after a 0–0 tie in the final, in Copenhagen, Denmark. Boca Juniors of Argentina won the Copa Libertadores, the South American club championship, defeating Palmeiras of Brazil, 4–2, on penalty kicks.

France's Zinedine Zidane was chosen the International Federation of Association Football (FIFA) world player of the year, which he also won in 1998. Brazil's Pele and Argentina's Diego Armando Maradona were selected as the players of the century, while China's Sun Wen and the United States' Michelle Akers were named women's players of the century.

GRAHAME L. JONES
Soccer Columnist, "Los Angeles Times"

Swimming

Swimming consistently made the headlines in 2000, as world records fell with astonishing regularity, and controversy grew over the issues of illegal drugs and new, high-tech bodysuits.

Assault on the Record Books. In all, some 20 long-course world marks were shattered, along with 21 short-course records. The record breaking reached a peak at the Olympic Games in Sydney. Perhaps the most impressive swimmer was the Netherlands' Inge de Bruijn, who lowered 11 world records in four events between May and September. The "Flying Dutchwoman" went on to capture three gold medals at the Sydney Olympics—the 50-m and 100-m freestyle and the 100-m butterfly—setting world marks in all three.

World Swimming Records Set in 2000

Men—50-m Pools (Long Course)
50-m freestyle: Alexandre Popov, Russia, 0:21.64
100-m freestyle: Pieter van den Hoogenband, Netherlands, 0:47.84
200-m freestyle: Pieter van den Hoogenband, 1:45.35
400-m freestyle: Ian Thorpe, Australia, 3:40.59
100-m breaststroke: Roman Sludnov, Russia, 1:00.36
50-m butterfly: Geoff Huegill, Australia, 023.60
200-m butterfly: Tom Malchow, United States, 1:55.18
400-m individual medley: Tom Dolan, United States, 4:11.76
400-m medley relay: U.S. Olympic Team, 3:33.73
400-m freestyle relay: Australia Olympic Team, 3:13.67
800-m freestyle relay: Australia Olympic Team, 7:07.05

Women—50-m Pool
50-m freestyle: Inge de Bruijn, Netherlands, 0:24.13
100-m freestyle: Inge de Bruijn, 0:53.77
50-m backstroke: Sandra Volker, Germany, 0:28.25
50-m butterfly: Inge de Bruijn, 0:25.64
100-m butterfly: Inge de Bruijn, 0:56.61
200 m butterfly: Susan O'Neill, Australia, 2:05.81
400-m individual medley: Yana Klochkova , Ukraine, 4:33.59
400-m medley relay: U.S. Olympic Team, 3:58.30
400-m freestyle relay: U.S. Olympic Team, 3:36.61

Men—25-m Pool
50-m freestyle: Anthony Ervin, United States, 0:21.21
200-m freestyle: Ian Thorpe, Australia, 1:41.10
50-m backstroke: Neil Walker, United States, 0:23.42
100-m backstroke: Neil Walker, , 0:50.75
200-m backstroke: Matt Welsh, Australia, 1:51.61
100-m breaststroke : Ed Moses, United States, 0:57.66
200-m breaststroke : Ed Moses, 2:06.40
50-m butterfly: Lars Frolander, Sweden, 0:23.19
100-m butterfly: Lars Frolander, 0:50.44
100-m individual medley: Neil Walker, 0:52.79
200-m individual medley: Attila Czene, Hungary, 1:54.65
400-m freestyle relay: Sweden National Team, , 3:09.57
800-m freestyle relay: U.S. National Team, 7:01.33

Women—25-m Pool
50-m freestyle: Therese Alshammar, Sweden, 0:23.59
100-m freestyle: Therese Alshammar, , 0:52.17
50-m backstroke: Haley Cope, Unites States, 0:27.25
100-m butterfly: Jenny Thompson, United States, 0:56.56
200-m butterfly: Susan O'Neill, Australia, 2:04.16
400-m medley relay: University of Georgia, United States, 3:57.46
800-m freestyle relay: Great Britain National Team, 7:49.11

Pieter van den Hoogenband, de Bruijn's teammate at the Eindhoven Swim Club in the Netherlands, was a giant killer in Sydney. The Dutchman captured the 100-m freestyle and beat Australian superstar Ian Thorpe in the 200-m freestyle, setting world records in both events.

Neil Walker of the United States and Sweden's Therese Alshammar were the outstanding swimmers at the World Short Course Championships, held in Athens in March. Walker won three individual events—the 50-m backstroke (23.42), 100-m backstroke (50.75), and 100-m individual medley (52.79)—all in world-record time. The smooth-stroking Alshammar set global standards in winning the 50-m (23.59) and 100-m freestyle (52.17). Sweden's Lars Frolander was the other standout in Athens. Frolander set world records in the 50-m (23.19) and 100-m butterfly (50.44).

NCAA Competition. In the United States, the National Collegiate Athletic Association (NCAA) Championships were held for the first time ever in a 25-m (short-course) format. Five world records resulted. The University of Virginia's Ed Moses smashed global standards in the 100-m and 200-m breaststroke, clocking 57.66 for the 100-m and 2:06.40 for the 200-m. Unheralded University of California freshman Anthony Ervin swam 21.21 for the 50-m freestyle, setting another world mark.

The other world records set at the NCAA Championships fell to Attila Czene, a Hungarian swimming for Arizona State University, who equaled the record in the 200-m individual medley (1:54.65), and the Georgia Lady Bulldogs, who clocked 3:57.46 in the 400-m medley relay.

Substance Scandals and Bodysuits. In July the International Swimming Federation (FINA) announced that China's Wu Yanyan, the world-record holder in the women's 200-m individual medley, had tested positive for steroids and would be banned for four years. Wu said she would appeal. Then, just before the Sydney Games, China cut 27 athletes, including six swimmers, from its Olympic team after they returned positive doping tests. Other doping scandals involved swimmers from Romania and Italy.

The new high-tech bodysuits introduced by several major swimsuit manufacturers led to another controversy. The manufacturers claimed the suits reduced water resistance significantly, though such performance enhancement is strictly prohibited under FINA rules. Nonetheless, FINA approved the suits for competition. A statistical study indicated that the suits apparently confer no advantage to swimmers wearing them.

PHILLIP WHITTEN, *"Swimming World"*

Tennis

Venus Williams, the tall and powerful 20-year-old American, was the tennis player of the year 2000. She won a pair of majors (Wimbledon and the U.S. Open), Olympic gold in singles and doubles, and orchestrated a 35-match singles winning streak.

The Men. Although Pete Sampras was hampered by injuries, he won a seventh Wimbledon title, his 13th career major, surpassing the 33-year-old men's singles record of Australian Roy Emerson. By beating Australia's Patrick Rafter—6–7 (10–12), 7–6 (7–5), 6–4, 6–2—in the Wimbledon final, Sampras caught up with Britain's Willie Renshaw, who won seven Wimbledon titles from 1881–89. However, in the U.S. Open final, Sampras was overwhelmed by a startling young strongman, 20-year-old Marat

---

TENNIS

Davis Cup: Spain
Federation Cup: United States

Major Tournaments

Australian Open—men's singles: Andre Agassi; men's doubles: Ellis Ferreira (South Africa) and Rick Leach; women's singles: Lindsay Davenport; women's doubles: Lisa Raymond and Rennae Stubbs (Australia); mixed doubles: Jared Palmer and Rennae Stubbs (Australia).

French Open—men's singles: Gustavo Kuerten (Brazil); men's doubles: Todd Woodbridge (Australia) and Mark Woodforde (Australia); women's singles: Mary Pierce (France); women's doubles: Martina Hingis (Switzerland) and Mary Pierce (France); mixed doubles: David Adams (South Africa) and Mariaan de Swardt (South Africa).

Wimbledon—men's singles: Pete Sampras; men's doubles: Todd Woodbridge (Australia) and Mark Woodforde (Australia); women's singles: Venus Williams; women's doubles: Serena Williams and Venus Williams; mixed doubles: Donald Johnson and Kimberly Po.

U.S. Open—men's singles: Marat Safin (Russia); men's doubles: Lleyton Hewitt (Australia) and Max Mirnyi (Belarus); women's singles: Venus Williams; women's doubles: Julie Halard-Decugis (France) and Ai Sugiyama (Japan); mixed doubles: Arantxa Sanchez-Vicario (Spain) and Jared Palmer.

Other Tournaments

Indian Wells—men's singles: Alex Corretja (Spain); women's singles: Lindsay Davenport.

Ericsson Open—men's singles: Pete Sampras; men's doubles: Todd Woodbridge (Australia) and Mark Woodforde (Australia); women's singles: Martina Hingis (Switzerland); women's doubles: Julie Halard-Decugis (France) and Ai Sugiyama (Japan).

Italian Open—men's singles: Magnus Norman (Sweden); men's doubles: Martin Damm (Czech Republic) and Dominik Hrbaty (Slovakia); women's singles: Monica Seles; women's doubles: Lisa Raymond and Rennae Stubbs (Australia)

German Open men's singles: Gustavo Kuerten (Brazil); women's singles: Conchita Martinez (Spain).

Masters Cup—singles: Gustavo Kuerten (Brazil).

NCAA (Division I)—men's singles: Alex Kim, Stanford; men's doubles: Graydon Oliver and Cary Franklin, Illinois; men's team: Illinois; women's singles: Laura Granville, Stanford; women's doubles: Amy Jensen and Claire Curran, California; women's team: Georgia.

N.B. All players are from the United States unless otherwise noted.

Women's tennis was championed by Venus Williams (above) and her younger sister Serena; the men's scene witnessed the emergence of Russian strongman Marat Safin (right), a 20-year-old fireball who defeated Pete Sampras in the U.S. Open final.

© Dylan Martinez/Reuters/Archive Photos

© Michelle V. Agins/NYT Pictures

Wimbledon and U.S. titles, both of which she won over Number 2, compatriot Lindsay Davenport—6–3, 7–6 (7–3) at London, and 6–4, 7–5, at New York. Davenport took the Australian Open over Hingis, 6–1, 7–5. Paris rejoiced at the 6–2, 7–5, triumph of Mary Pierce over Spaniard Conchita Martinez. Pierce was the first French citizen to win the French title since Françoise Durr in 1967.

The Olympics and Federation and Davis Cups. Olympic gold medals belonged to Venus Williams as she beat Russian Elena Dementieva—6–2, 6–4,—in the singles, and then joined her 19-year-old sister, Serena, in a 6–1, 6–1, crushing of Netherlands' Kristie Boogert and Miriam Oremans, the most one-sided of all Olympic finals. In Sydney, Kafelnikov won the men's gold over German Tommy Haas. In their farewell together, the favored Australian "Woodies"—Mark Woodforde and Todd Woodbridge—were upset in the doubles final by Canada's first tennis medalists, Daniel Nestor and Sebastien Lareau.

Davenport and Monica Seles were unbeaten in singles to win a 17th Federation Cup for the United States, 5–0 over Spain in the title round. Still, Spain won the Davis Cup in a momentous 3–1 victory over the defenders, Australia, on indoor clay in Barcelona. Rookie Juan Carlos Ferrero, 20, won both of his singles matches, stopping Lleyton Hewitt in the clincher to give Spain the Davis Cup. Spain became the tenth nation to hold the Cup. In December, Patrick McEnroe was named to succeed his brother John as captain of the U.S. Davis Cup team.

BUD COLLINS, *"The Boston Globe"/NBC*

Safin—6–4, 6–3, 6–3. Safin was the first Russian to win a U.S. title.

At the climactic playoffs of the Masters Series, the Masters Cup in Lisbon, Safin—who won a season-high seven titles—entered at Number 1. But in a stunning finish, Brazil's Gustavo Kuerten became the first Latin American to make it to the top by beating 1999's Number 1, Andre Agassi—6–4, 6–4, 6–4—in the 3,012th match of the campaign. Beaten by Agassi in the semis, Safin lost his chance in the closest contested race ever to the pinnacle, falling to Number 2. Kuerten, who had won the French Open over Sweden's Magnus Norman, seized Number 1 by knocking off Number 3 Sampras and Number 6 Agassi consecutively. Agassi had started impressively, winning the Australian Open over Russian Yevgeny Kafelnikov, but he slumped as the season went on.

The Women. Although unable to win a major, Switzerland's Martina Hingis, 20, finished at Number 1 for a second consecutive year on a high-performance campaign of nine tournament victories. Venus Williams, ranked Number 3, and winner of six of ten tourneys, beat Hingis on the way to her

Track and Field

While most of the world's top track athletes focused on the Olympic Games in Sydney during 2000, that did not stop them from producing a great season of action on ovals from Adelaide to Zurich.

New Records. In stark contrast to 1999's record barrage, the Olympic year brought no official world records in men's events. The only "bests" that occurred came in rarely run, unofficial events. Michael Johnson clipped 300 m in 30.85, and British hurdler Chris Rawlinson went over 300 m of hurdles in 34.59. The dearth of "real" world records had never happened before in the sport's modern history. Rather than a sign of decline, the drought was more likely due to the athletes' emphasis on winning Olympic medals. In the running events especially, world records increasingly have been the result of competitions with prearranged pacing and designated pacesetters, or "rabbits."

The women broke records, as Stacy Dragila of the United States set three pole-vault marks, including 15'2.25" (4.63 m), to win the Olympic Trials. Trine Hattestad of Norway set two records in the javelin, topped by a 227'11" (69.48 m). The women's 4x200-m relay standard fell when a U.S. team ran 1:27.46 at the Penn Relays.

The Golden League. The seven-meet Golden League, in conjunction with the Grand Prix, highlighted summer action. At its conclusion, five undefeated athletes—U.S. hurdler Gail Devers, Algerian miler Hicham El Guerrouj, U.S. sprinter Maurice Greene, Norwegian javelin thrower Trine Hattestad, and Russian long jumper Tatyana Kotova—remained in contention for the prize of 110 lb (50 kg) of gold. The deadlock was broken a week after the Olympics, at the Grand Prix Final in Doha, Qatar. The venue drew scant crowds, and athletes complained that it was too far to go after the very long season. In fact, Greene and El Guerrouj skipped the meet.

Devers, the year's fastest hurdler with a U.S.-record 12.33 at the Olympic Trials, won in Doha. The gold, however, went to Hattestad, who topped the Grand Prix rankings, despite finishing second in the finale. The men's Grand Prix crown went to U.S. 400-m hurdler Angelo Taylor.

Notable Marathons. Josephat Kiprono of Kenya won the January 1 Rome race in 2:08:27, as Tegla Loroupe clocked 2:32:03. Lidia Simon of Romania won Osaka in 2:22:54, while in Tokyo a week later, Japhet Kosgei of Kenya led six men under 2:10 with his 2:07:15. Another major Japanese race, Nagoya, saw Naoko Takahashi run 2:22:19 in March. Antonio Pinto of Portugal won London in 2:06:36, with Loroupe taking the women's race in 2:24:33. At Rotterdam, Kenneth Cheruiyot of Kenya (2:08:22) and Ana Isabel Alonso of Spain (2:30:21) won. On April 17 in Boston, two Kenyans—Elijah Lagat (2:09:47) and Catherine Ndereba (2:26:11)—emerged victorious.

The major fall races proved just as exciting. Berlin featured wins by Kenya's Simon Biwott (2:07:42) and Japan's Kazumi Matsuo (2:26:15). Naturalized U.S. citizen Khalid Khannouchi won Chicago in a U.S.-record 2:07:01, while Ndereba stunned with a world-leading 2:21:33. Finally, in New York, Abdelkhader El Mouaziz of Morocco won in 2:10:08, with Russia's Ludmila Petrova taking the women's race in 2:25:45.

JEFF HOLLOBAUGH
Track Columnist, ESPN.com

Yachting

In the world of sailing, the clear highlight of 2000 was the dominant defense of the America's Cup by Team New Zealand (TNZ) in the challenging waters off Auckland. In a series that showcased the overall superiority of TNZ—in yacht design, tactics, and boat handling—the Kiwis dispatched the Prada Challenge from Italy by a score of 5–0 in the best-of-nine Cup finals.

America's Cup. Prada, the $55 million challenge skippered by Francesco de Angelis and bankrolled by fashion magnate Patrizio Bertelli, earned the right to face TNZ after winning the Louis Vuitton Cup (LVC), the five-month-long elimination tournament to determine the challenger, which began in October 1999.

In a back-and-forth series, Prada outlasted AmericaOne, the San Francisco–based challenge captained by Paul Cayard, in a 5–4 victory in the LVC finals. The ensuing Prada-TNZ duel marked the first time in the event's 149-year history that a U.S. boat did not compete for the America's Cup.

By virtue of their gusty performance versus AmericaOne, the Italians were perceived as a serious threat to the Kiwis at the outset of the regatta, in mid-February. But TNZ, with Cup veterans Russell Coutts at the wheel and Brad Butterworth calling tactics, was untouchable. With Coutts driving, the Kiwis built a 4–0 lead. Counting his five straight wins in the Kiwis' triumphant 1995 effort in San Diego, the TNZ helmsman tied the record of nine consecutive Cup victories, originally set by the legendary Charlie Barr at the turn of the 20th century.

In a move that showcased the depth of the New Zealand team, however, Coutts

In February 2000, Team New Zealand (TNZ) (left) and Italy's Prada Challenge (right) battled for position during the America's Cup in Auckland, New Zealand—won ultimately, and decisively, by the remarkable Kiwi forces.

ran out of wind and took first-to-finish-line honors with a passage of just under four days. On handicap, the slow pace favored the smaller boats, and *Restless*, a Rhodes 41, won the prestigious Lighthouse Trophy for first overall on corrected time.

The quadrennial Single-handed Transatlantic Race—from Plymouth, England, to Newport, RI—also featured some surprises. The multihull victor was unsponsored Frenchman Francis Joyon, who won with a time just under ten days. In the radical Open 60 class, with 20 entries, the winner was 23-year-old newcomer Ellen MacArthur from England, who bested a star-studded field after a voyage just shy of 15 days. MacArthur's stunning victory made her a prohibitive favorite for the gruelling Vendée Globe nonstop race around the world, which started from France on November 9.

Speed Sailing and the Olympics. The summer saw several attempts on the transatlantic speed record, held by the French yacht *Jet Services V* with a time of seven days, nine hours. American Steve Fossett tried twice aboard his wild 105-ft (32-m) catamaran *PlayStation*. But Fossett was unable to topple the mark, with a best time still four hours shy of the record.

stepped off the boat and handed the wheel to his understudy, Dean Barker, for the decisive fifth race in early March. It was the first time the Cup had ever been successfully defended outside the United States. The Kiwis led around every mark of every race.

Two months after the Cup finals, Coutts, Butterworth, and five other members of the winning crew quit TNZ to join a new challenge for 2003. It would be funded by Swiss pharmaceutical billionaire Ernesto Bertarelli. Soon after, U.S. technology billionaires Craig McCaw and Larry Ellison also announced inaugural Cup challenges. Ellison bought the assets of AmericaOne and hired Paul Cayard for his afterguard.

Offshore Racing. In offshore racing, the classic 635-mi (1 022-km) Newport Bermuda Race, which started in early June, began in a solid breeze that vanished as the fleet approached the Atlantic outpost. After a record early pace, Larry Ellison's *Sayonara*

In September the world's best dinghy sailors gathered in Sydney, Australia, for the Olympic regatta in the 2000 Summer Games. Racing took place in 11 classes over six courses, four of which were laid out in beautiful Sydney Harbour. Great Britain posted outstanding results in the two-week event, with Finn sailor Iain Percy, Europe sailor Shirley Robertson, and Laser sailor Ben Ainslie all winning gold medals. The Brits also scored silver in the 49er and Star classes. After a dismal showing at the 1996 Games, the U.S. team rebounded with a gold by Mark Reynolds and Magnus Liljedahl in the Star; silvers from J. J. Isler and Pease Glaser and from Paul Foerster and Bob Merrick in the respective women's and men's 470; and bronze from brothers Jonathan and Charlie McKee in the 49er.

HERB MCCORMICK
Editor, "Cruising World"

SPORTS SUMMARIES[1]

ARCHERY—U.S. Target Champions: men's Olympic bow: Richard Johnson, Woodstock, CT; women's Olympic bow: Karen Scavotto, Enfield, CT; men's compound bow: Dave Cousins, Westbrooke, ME; women's compound bow: Christie Bisco, Raymond, ME.

BEACH VOLLEYBALL—Association of Volleyball Professionals (AVP) Championship: King of the Beach: Mike Whitemarsh, San Diego, CA; Queen of the Beach: Barbara Fontana, Manhattan Beach, CA.

BIATHLON—World Champions: men: 10k: Frode Andresen, Norway; 20k: Wolfgang Rottmann, Austria; 4x7.5k relay: Russia; women: 7.5k: Liv Greteskjelbreid, Norway; 15k: Olena Zubrilova, Ukraine; 4x7.5k relay: Russia.

BILLIARDS—World Champions: men: 9-ball: Fong-Pang Chao, Taiwan; 3-Cushion: Dick Jaspers, Netherlands; Snooker: Mark Williams; women: 9-ball: Julie Kelly, Ireland; Snooker: Kelly Fisher, England; **U.S Champions:** 3-Cushion: Sang Chun Lee, New York City; Snooker: Ajaya Prabhakar.

BOWLING—Professional Bowlers Association (PBA) Tour: Tournament of Champions: Jason Couch, Clermont, FL; PBA National Championship: Norm Duke, Clermont, FL; PBA Senior Championship: Bob Glass, Lawrence, KS. **Professional Women's Bowlers Association (PWBA):** Sam's Town Invitational: Dede Davidson, Las Vegas, NV; Women's International Bowling Congress Queens: Wendy MacPherson, Henderson, NV; Hammer Players Championship: Tennelle Grijalva, Orange, CA; Brunswick Women's World Open: Cara Honeychurch, Australia. **American Bowling Congress (ABC):** singles: Garran Hein, Brea, CA; doubles: Billy Seprodi, Indianapolis, IN, and Jim O'Connor, Greenwood, IN; all events: Roy Daniels, El Paso, TX; regular team: Team 8 Ball, Medford, OR; team all events: Linds Limited, Milwaukee, WI; Masters Tournament: Mika Koivunierni, Finland; Brunswick/ABC World Team Challenge: Sunset Lanes/Hammer West, Las Vegas, NV; senior masters: Dave Soutar, Bradenton, FL; Queen's Tournament: Wendy MacPherson; Senior Queen's Tournament: Rose Smith, Las Vegas, NV

CRICKET—World Champion: Australia.

CYCLING—Road Races: Tour de France: Lance Armstrong, Austin, TX; Tour de Flandres: Andrei Tchmil, Belgium; Amstel Gold: Erik Zabel, Germany; Tour of Spain: Roberto Heras, Spain; U.S. Pro: Henk Vogels, Team Mercury.

DARTS—Men's World Match Play: Phil Taylor, England; **North American Open:** men: Louis Martinez, Texas; women: Stacy Bromberg, Las Vegas, NV; **U.S. National Champions:** men: Louis Martinez; women: Stacy Bromberg.

EQUESTRIAN—U.S. Champions: State Line Tack United States Equestrian Team (USET); Grand Prix Dressage Champion: Flim Flam, Sue Blinks, Wellington, FL; Rolex USET Show Jumping Champion: Liberty, Laura Kraut, Oconomowoc, WI; State Line Tack USET Intermediate Champion: Ricardo, Jan Ebeling, Moorpark, CA; Rolex USET Three-Day Event Four Star Championship: Rattle N Hum, David O'Connor, The Plains, VA; Cosequin/USET Three-Day Event Fall Champion: Sir Nicholas, Gayle Molander, Upperco, MD.

FENCING—U.S. Championships: men: foil: Cliff Bayer, New York City; épée: Chris O'Loughlin, New York City; saber: Akhnaten Spencer-El, New York City; women: foil: Felicia Zimmermann, Rochester, NY; épée: Stephanie Eim, State College, PA; saber: Christina Crane, Atlanta, GA. **NCAA:** team: Penn State; men: foil: Felix Reichling, Stanford; épée: Daniel Landgren, Penn State; saber: Gabor Szelle, Notre Dame; women: foil: Eva Petschnigg, Princeton; épée: Jessica Burke, Penn State; saber: Caroline Purcell, MIT.

FIELD HOCKEY—NCAA: women: Division I: Old Dominion. **World:** Men's Champions Trophy: Netherlands; Women's Champions Trophy: Netherlands.

GYMNASTICS—U.S. Men's Championships: all-around: Blaine Wilson, Columbus, OH; floor: Blaine Wilson; pommel horse: John Roethlisberger, Falcon Heights, MN; still rings: Blaine Wilson; vault: Blaine Wilson; parallel bars: Trent Wells, Keizer, OR; high bar: (tie) Jamie Natalie, Wilmington, DE, and Trent Wells. **U.S. Women's Championships:** all-around: Elise Ray, Columbia, MD; vault: Kristen Maloney, Pen Argyl, PA; uneven bars: Elise Ray; balance beam: Alyssa Beckerman, Cincinnati, OH; floor: Kristen Maloney. NCAA men: all-around: Jamie Natalie, Ohio State; team: Penn State. NCAA women: all-around: (tie) Mohini Bhardwaj, UCLA, and Heather Brink, Nebraska; team: UCLA.

JUDO—U.S. International: 56 kg: Mickey Matsumoto, United States; 60 kg: Daniel G. Simmard, Canada; 66 kg: Stephane Chrétien, Canada; 73 kg: Orlando Fuentes, United States; 81 kg: Dominique Hischier, Switzerland; 90 kg: Gavin Kelly, Australia; 100 kg: Alto Hand, United States; 100 kg plus: Martin Boonzaayer, United States; open: Jamie McDowell, Great

Britain. women: 44 kg: Stephanie Hata, United States; 48 kg: Tomoe Makabe, Japan; 52 kg: Yuki Yokozawa, Japan; 57 kg: Ayako Okkazaki, Japan; 63 kg: Kellie Roberts, Great Britain; 70 kg: Amanda Costello, Great Britain; 78 kg: Amy Cotton, Canada; 78 kg plus: Misuzu Yanagihana, Japan; Open: Miyuki Kurihara, Japan.

RODEO—Professional Rodeo Cowboys Association: World Champion All-Around Cowboy: Joe Beaver, Huntsville, TX.

ROWING—Men's World Championships: lightweight single sculls: Czech Republic; pair with coxswain: United States; lightweight pair: Canada; lightweight quadruple sculls: Japan; four with coxswain: Great Britain; lightweight eight: United States. **Women's World Championships:** lightweight single scull: Finland; lightweight pair: Great Britain; lightweight quadruple scull: Germany; four: Belarus. **International Rowing Association (IRA) Regatta:** men's varsity eight: California; men's lightweight varsity eight: Yale; women's lightweight varsity eight: Princeton.

RUGBY—International Champions: Tri Nations: Australia; Six Nations: England; Pacific Rim: Western Samoa; Super 12: Canterbury; Bledisloe Cup: Australia.

SHOOTING—U.S. Champions: running target 30 plus 30: Adam Saathoff, Hereford, AZ; **Rifle:** women's air rifle: Melissa Mulloy, Middleton, MD; women's 50 m three-position rifle: Jean Foster, Bozeman, MT; men's air rifle: Jason Parker, Omaha, NE; men's 50 m three-position rifle: Glenn Dubis, Bethel Park, MD; men's prone: Eric Uptagrafft, Spokane, WA; **Pistol:** men's 50 m free pistol: Daryl Szarenski, Saginaw, MI; men's rapid fire pistol: Terry Anderson, Dallas, TX; men's air pistol: Michael Douglass, Beach Park, IL; women's air pistol: Rebecca Snyder, Grand Junction, CO; women's 25 m sport pistol: Janine Bowman, Woonsocket, RI; **Shotgun:** men's trap: Lance Bade, Ridgefield, WA; men's double trap: Glenn Eller, Katy, TX; women's trap: Cindy Gentry, Stone Mountain, GA; women's double trap: Kim Rhode, El Monte, CA; men's skeet: Scott Schroeder, McMinnville, OR.

SOFTBALL—Amateur Softball Association (ASA): men's major fast pitch: Meierhoffer, St. Joseph, MO; super slow pitch: Team TPS, Louisville, KY; major slow pitch: Long Haul/TPS, Albertville, MN; women's major fast pitch: Phoenix Storm, Phoenix, AZ; women's major slow pitch: Premier Sports, Pittsboro, NC. **NCAA:** Division I: Oklahoma.

SUMO— New Year Grand Sumo: Musoyami; Spring Grand Sumo: Takatoriki; Summer Grand Sumo: Kaio; Autumn Grand Sumo: Musashimaru; Nagoya Grand Sumo: Akebono; Kyushu Grand Sumo: Akebono.

TRIATHLON—World Champions: men: Olivier Marceau, France; women: Nicole Hackett, Australia. Ironman Men: Peter Reid, Canada; Ironman Women: Natascha Badmann, Switzerland. **U.S. Champions:** men: Marcel Vifian, Boulder, CO; women: Joanna Zeiger, Baltimore, MD.

VOLLEYBALL—International Champions: Men's World League: Italy; Women's Grand Prix: Cuba; **U.S. Open Champions:** men: Team Paul Mitchell; women: Dominican Dream Team. **NCAA:** men: UCLA; Division I women: Nebraska.

WEIGHT LIFTING—U.S. men: 56 kg: Shelton Gilyard; 62 kg: Legrand H. Sakamaki; 69 kg: Scott E. Dibert; 77 kg: Oscar Chaplin III, Savannah, GA; 85 kg: Corey J. Wilkes; 94 kg: Thomas W. Gough; 105 kg: Andrew C. Tysz; 105 kg plus: Shane Hamman, Mustang, OK. **U.S. Women:** 48 kg: Tara Nott, Stilwell, KS; 53 kg: Carrie Boudreau; 58 kg: Melanie Kosoff-Roach, Auburn, WA; 63 kg: Danice Rue; 69 kg: Stacie M Blaskowski; 75 kg: Cara M. Heads-Lane; 75 kg plus: Cheryl Haworth, Savannah, GA.

WRESTLING—Women's World Championships: 46 kg: Irina Melnik, Ukraine; 51 kg: Hitomi Sakamoto, Japan; 56 kg: Seiko Yamamoto, Japan; 62 kg: Nikola Hartmann, Austria; 69 kg: Kristie Marano, United States; 75 kg: Christine Nordhagen-Vierling, Canada. **U.S. Men's Freestyle:** 54 kg: Sammie Henson, Norman, OK; 58 kg: Kerry Boumans, Colorado Springs, CO; 63 kg: Cary Kolat, Morgantown, WV; 69 kg: Lincoln McIlravy, Iowa City, IO; 76 kg: Brandon Slay, Colorado Springs, CO; 85 kg: Les Gutches, Colorado Springs, CO; 97 kg: Melvin Douglas, Mesa, AZ; 130 kg: Kerry McCoy, State College, PA. U.S. Men's Greco-Roman: 54 kg: Brandon Paulson, Golden Valley, MN; 58 kg: Dennis Hall, Plover, WI; 63 kg: Kevin Bracken, Colorado Springs, CO; 69 kg: Heath Sims, Huntington Beach, CA; 76 kg: Matt Lindland, Lincoln, NE; 85 kg: Quincey Clark, New Brighton, MN; 97 kg: Jason Gleasman, Colorado Springs, CO; 130 kg: Rulon Gardner, Colorado Springs, CO. **U.S. Women:** 46 kg: Tricia Saunders, Phoenix, AZ; 51 kg: Stephanie Murata, Williamsburg, KY; 56 kg: Mabel Fonseca, San Juan, Puerto Rico; 62 kg: Sara McMann, Lock Haven, PA; 69 kg: Sandy Bacher, San Jose, CA; 75 kg: Iris Smith, Colorado Springs, CO.

[1]Sports for which articles do not appear in pages 455–89.

Sri Lanka

Events in Sri Lanka continued to be dominated by civil war during 2000.

The War. After handily winning the presidential election in December 1999, Chandrika Kumaratunga began immediate discussions with the opposition, the United National Party (UNP), to forge a wide consensus on peace terms within the Sinhalese parties. Kumaratunga favored constitutional devolution of powers to the states, which was opposed by the UNP and other smaller parties. A brief lull in fighting lasted until April 22, when the Liberation Tigers of Tamil Eelam (LTTE) overran Elephant Pass, the main road link between Jaffna and the rest of the country. Fearful for the safety of Sinhalese troops, the Sri Lankan government asked India to intervene militarily to help evacuate the troops; India was reluctant. In May the Sri Lankan government put the country on a full war footing and after months of fighting established some control again over parts of Jaffna. By year's end, the war had taken more than 60,000 lives.

The economic consequences of the war were severe for Sri Lanka, as its budget deficit rose to more than 8% of its gross domestic product (GDP). In May, Sri Lanka passed a Public Security Ordinance with a long list of new measures: All reports of the war in the Sri Lankan and foreign media had to be submitted to censors; any public meeting, marches, or demonstrations could be banned if they might "promote disaffection"; and the government was given powers to requisition property, vehicles, and even personnel for the war effort.

Frustration with the war's stalemate and cost led to talks between LTTE and the government. Several months of work led to a proposed settlement by LTTE. The year ended with LTTE announcing a monthlong cease-fire and with the government halting military operations.

Elections. Sri Lanka held parliamentary elections in October. The main rivals were Kumaratunga's seven-party People's Alliance (PA) and the opposition leaders of the UNP. War and the economy were the main issues: The PA backed a plan to amend the constitution to devolve powers to Sri Lanka's regions, in an attempt to provide more autonomy to Tamil areas. The UNP opposed this and criticized the government for its economic policies. More than 5,400 candidates competed for 225 parliamentary seats. The election was marred by violence, including the deaths of several candidates. Still, an estimated 75% of the electorate turned out. On October 18, the PA and its allies—holding 107 seats to the UNP's 89—formed a new government short of a majority. The UNP called on the PA for a common front to tackle war issues and political and economic reforms. Failure to appease the UNP could result in a government stalemate and early elections in 2001 or 2002.

Foreign Relations. The war dominated foreign relations. Sri Lanka sought financial and diplomatic support from its neighbors, including India and the West. Sri Lanka chaired the South Asia Association for Regional Cooperation (SAARC), and suggested postponement of the annual heads-of-state meeting. At issue were strained relations between India and Pakistan, which Sri Lanka maintained would make any meaningful dialogue impossible.

Sirimavo Bandaranaike. Sirimavo Bandaranaike, who holds the distinction of being the world's first female prime minister, died of a heart attack on October 9. Bandaranaike became Sri Lanka's prime minister in 1960, after her husband's assassination in 1959 propelled her to the leadership of the Sri Lanka Freedom Party. She lost the 1965 elections but returned to power in 1970. In 1980 she was expelled from Parliament for "abusing her powers" and was suspended from holding office for seven years. Narrowly losing the presidential election in 1988, she served as her daughter's prime minister from November 1994 until ill health forced her to resign in August 2000.

ARUNA NAYYAR MICHIE
Kansas State University

SRI LANKA • Information Highlights

Official Name: Democratic Socialist Republic of Sri Lanka.

Location: South Asia.

Area: 25,332 sq mi (65 610 km²).

Population (2000 est.): 19,238,575.

Chief Cities (mid-1990 est.): Colombo, the capital, 615,000; Dehiwala–Mount Lavinia, 196,000; Moratuwa, 170,000.

Government: *Head of state,* C.B. Kumaratunga, president (took office November 1994). *Head of government,* Ratnasiri Wickramanayake, prime minister (took office Aug. 10, 2000). *Legislature* (unicameral)—Parliament.

Monetary Unit: Rupee (82.7650 rupees equal U.S.$1, Dec. 20, 2000).

Gross Domestic Product (1999 est. U.S.$): $50,500,000,000 (purchasing power parity).

Economic Index (Colombo, 1999; 1990 = 100): *Consumer Prices,* all items, 237.2; food, 247.1.

Foreign Trade (1999 U.S.$): *Imports,* $5,884,000,000; *exports,* $4,593,000,000.

Stamps and Stamp Collecting

In 2000 the United States Postal Service (USPS) issued 141 postage stamps, including its first stamps containing holographic images.

USPS Stamp Issues. The four holograms were part of a set of 15 stamps with space-exploration themes issued to salute World Stamp Expo 2000, an international philatelic exhibition in Anaheim, CA. The holograms showed the Earth, a lunar lander, and the International Space Station. This set also included the first U.S. circular and pentagon-shaped stamps.

USPS issued a "commemorative prestige booklet" containing text and photos in addition to the stamps, five historic submarines. Several sheets containing multiple varieties helped boost the total number of stamps issued. Two of these sheets displayed 20 historic American flags and honored 20 Legends of Baseball. The Celebrate the Century series concluded with two 15-stamp sheets honoring the events, personalities, and culture of the 1980s and 1990s.

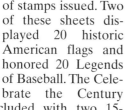

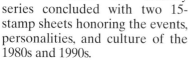

USPS always looks for stamp subjects that appeal to young people. In 2000 these included a block of four, Stampin' the Future, showing whimsical visions of the future, with artwork by children. A stamp for Wile E. Coyote and Road Runner continued the series picturing Warner Bros. Studios' Looney Tunes characters. Four Youth Team Sports stamps featured basketball, football, soccer, and baseball, and five stamps depicted deep-sea creatures. A sheet, showing a scene from a Pacific Coast rain forest—with ten wildlife stamps that could be punched out—was the second in the Nature of America series.

In other ongoing series, the 2000 Black Heritage and Legends of Hollywood stamps honored former cabinet officer Patricia Roberts Harris and Edward G. Robinson, respectively. The Lunar New Year stamp celebrated the Year of the Dragon, and author Thomas Wolfe was the Literary Arts series subject.

International Issues. Canada Post allowed customers to submit photos and create their own personalized stamps, bearing pictures of their children, pets, or themselves. Other countries—including Great Britain, Ireland, and Australia—offered personalized tabs attached to actual stamps.

Many nations issued stamps saluting the 2000 Olympic Games in Sydney, Australia. The host country produced unprecedented "instant stamp" souvenir sheets, featuring gold-medal Australian athletes or teams, which went on sale within 24 hours of a victory. Switzerland, which is well known for its embroidery, issued the world's first embroidered stamp, made of polyester thread at a textile factory.

Dominica and St. Vincent and the Grenadines each issued stamps featuring the British comedy troupe Monty Python. Fiji and the Cayman Islands postally honored *Sesame Street* characters.

GEORGE AMICK
Author, "Linn's U.S. Stamp Yearbook"

SELECTED U.S. STAMPS FOR 2000

Subject	Denomination	Date
Year of the Dragon	33¢	Jan. 6
Celebrate the Century 1980s	33¢	Jan. 12
Grand Canyon	60¢	Jan. 20
Patricia Roberts Harris	33¢	Jan. 27
U.S. Navy Submarines	22¢, 33¢, 55¢, 60¢, $3.20	March 27
Pacific Coast Rain Forest	33¢	March 29
Louise Nevelson	33¢	April 6
Edwin Powell Hubble	33¢	April 10
American Samoa	33¢	April 17
Library of Congress	33¢	April 24
Wile E. Coyote and Road Runner	33¢	April 26
Celebrate the Century 1990s	33¢	May 2
Distinguished Soldiers	33¢	May 3
Summer Sports	33¢	May 5
Adoption Awareness	33¢	May 10
Youth Team Sports	33¢	May 27
The Stars and Stripes	33¢	June 14
Legends of Baseball	33¢	July 6
Space Exploration	60¢, $1, $3.20, $11.75	July 7–11
Stampin' the Future	33¢	July 13
Joseph W. Stilwell	10¢	Aug. 24
Claude Pepper	33¢	Sept. 7
California Statehood	33¢	Sept. 8
Deep Sea Creatures	33¢	Oct. 2
Thomas Wolfe	33¢	Oct. 3
White House	33¢	Oct. 18
Edward G. Robinson	33¢	Oct. 24

On Nov. 7, 2000, the residents of the 50 U.S. states and the District of Columbia went to the polls to elect a president and vice-president, 34 of the 100 members of the U.S. Senate, all 435 members of the U.S. House of Representatives, 11 state governors, and other state officials. They also indicated their approval or disapproval of the various amendments, propositions, and initiatives. In one of the closest and most-disputed presidential elections in U.S. history, Texas Republican Gov. George W. Bush defeated Democratic Vice-President Al Gore. Gore won 20 states and the District of Columbia, for a total of 266 electoral votes, and received 539,947 more popular votes than Bush. But Bush won 30 states with a total of 271 electoral votes—one vote more than necessary—and the presidency. (See THE 2000 U.S. PRESIDENTIAL ELECTION, page 22.)

On the economic front, the good times continued in early 2000, with federal budget-surplus predictions rising and unemployment falling. But later in the year, rising oil prices and plunging stock-market prices did not bode well for a continuation of the unprecedented U.S. economic boom.

Other noteworthy events of the year were the rash of wildfires that ravaged the West during the summer months (see ENVIRONMENT—Wildfires, the 22d decennial census (see UNITED STATES—The 22d U.S. Census), and fierce ice storms and snowstorms that battered the Midwest and Northeast just before the end of the year.

ALABAMA. New legislation, the presidential election, and a string of devastating tornadoes were among the top news stories in Alabama in 2000.

Legislation. Education funding and teacher pay raises were major accomplishments of the 2000 legislative session. The legislature also approved tougher penalties for drunken driving, domestic abuse, and animal cruelty. Motorists were required to have liability insurance as of June 1, 2001. The legislature approved advertisements featuring photos of the state's worst deadbeat parents in state newspapers. A "Safe Place for Babies" act allows mothers to drop off an unwanted newborn at a hospital without being prosecuted for abandonment. Other new laws made women who seduce boys subject to rape laws, banned open containers of alcohol in motor vehicles, increased drunken-driving penalties, and allowed adult adoptees to see their original birth certificates.

Elections. In November 7 balloting, Alabama voters delivered a majority to Republican George W. Bush in the presidential race, reelected five Republicans and two Democrats to the U.S. House, and elected Roy Moore, who displayed a copy of the Ten Commandments in his circuit courtroom, to the Alabama Supreme Court. Voters also abolished a ban on interracial marriage that was contained in the 1901 state constitution, but was unenforceable.

Race Relations. The city of Selma, where violent reactions to the civil rights marches of 1965 took place, elected James Perkins, Jr., as its first African-American mayor. Two men—Bobby Frank Cherry and Thomas E. Blanton, Jr.—were charged with the 1963 bombing of a Birmingham church that killed four African-American girls.

Other News. Voters on March 21 approved a simpler and higher corporate income tax to replace a franchise tax struck down by the courts. Alabama football coach Mike DuBose announced in November that he would resign at the end of the season, ending a disappointing four-year run. In mid-December, an outbreak of vicious tornadoes pummeled communities in Tuscaloosa, Geneva, Etowah, and Limestone counties, killing 12 people, injuring at least 50, and destroying or damaging hundreds of homes and businesses.

ELAINE STUART

ALASKA. The Alaskan legislature met its goal of reducing spending by $250 million in five years. Republican majority leaders said they had cut the state's budget while still maintaining support for public safety, education, and transportation.

Legislation. The 2000 session also passed legislation establishing an endowment to subsidize high power costs for rural areas. Alaska authorized pilot programs allowing local Native American organizations to run their own welfare-reform programs with state and federal funds. Legislation recognizing the principle of restorative justice in sentencing for certain crimes allows for community-based sentencing. The law stressed accountability, restitution, and reconciliation. A new law helped law-enforcement agencies prosecute those who commit crimes through the use of computers and high technology.

Elections. In November 7 elections, Republicans kept their majority in the state House. Voters defeated a ballot initiative to legalize use of marijuana by adults and proposals to limit property taxes, and to limit the power of initiatives over wildlife issues. Republican presidential candidate Bush won the state's electoral-college votes, but the state's voters gave Green Party candidate Ralph Nader his strongest showing—10% of the vote.

ELAINE STUART

ARIZONA. Arizona legislators in December sharply reduced subsidies for alternative-fuel vehicles. More than 15,000 state residents had filed to take advantage of the tax rebate on up to half the cost of any vehicle that would burn alternative fuels. At an average cost of $20,000 or more per vehicle, the state estimated it would have been forced to pay out $500 million or more. In response, Gov. Jane Dee Hull had called the legislature into session in October to place a one-year moratorium on the giveaway. The governor said no one closely considered the legislation that was rushed through at the end of the regular session in April. House Speaker Jeff Groscost, a Republican, was blamed for devising the tax break and, as a result, in the November 7 election he lost his bid for a Senate seat to his Democratic opponent. With that loss, Republicans lost control of the state Senate, resulting in a 15-15 split between Republicans and Democrats.

Legislation. Legislation passed in the regular spring session allows patients to sue their health maintenance organizations (HMOs) for denying or delaying treatment. The legislature also funded a new state mental hospital and authorized $20 million for teacher pay raises amounting to $500 a year for each teacher. To help the state shift to a new economy, the session approved $17 million in job training funds as well as tax credits for businesses to provide workers with technology training. A new law required insurance coverage of routine care for cancer patients in clinical drug trials. Passengers in vehicles could no longer drink alcohol. A cybercrime bill targeted Internet fraud, identity theft, computer hacking, and on-line sex offenses. Shooting a gun in the air—a common New Year's practice—became illegal. The state required grade-school children to recite daily the passage from the Declaration of Independence that "all men are created equal."

Politics. Although unsuccessful, U.S. Sen. John McCain's campaign for the Republican presidential nomination drew much attention. The Republican Party's (GOP's) nominee, George W. Bush, carried the state in November, and Republican Sen. Jon Kyl won reelection with no Democratic opposition. The Republicans picked up one U.S. House seat. Voters statewide approved an initiative to end bilingual education in the state—even though one of every eight public school students is not a native speaker of English.

Other News. In April a wildfire burned more than 5,370 acres (2 175 ha) in the Tonto National Forest. On November 7, Maricopa County voted to build a new $331 million stadium for the pro football Arizona Cardinals in the Phoenix area. The money would come from taxes on hotel rooms and rental cars.

ELAINE STUART

ARKANSAS. In the November election, Governor Bush gained Arkansas' electoral votes. Two devastating ice storms struck the state in December, leaving more than 500,000 people without electricity. Gov. Mike Huckabee declared 29 counties disaster areas.

Politics. In a major victory for the Democrats, Mike Ross, a state senator who began his political career as a driver for then-governor Bill Clinton, defeated fourterm Republican incumbent Jay Dickey for the U.S. House seat in President Clinton's home district. A heavy turnout among African-Americans helped Ross win the race. Incumbents won easily in the state's other three House races.

In July the Committee on Professional Conduct of the Arkansas Supreme Court recommended that President Clinton lose his license to practice law in the state as a punishment for his false testimony in the Paula Jones sexual-harassment case. The president filed a response in August. Prior to leaving the White House on January 20, the president and the prosecutors reached an agreement under which the president would surrender his Arkansas law license for five years and pay a $25,000 fine. In turn, Clinton would not be indicted once he left office.

Plans to construct Clinton's presidential library in Little Rock moved ahead after a judge ruled the city had properly laid claim to a 3-acre (1.2-ha) tract whose owner refused to sell. The $25-million library and museum complex, scheduled to open in 2003, will fill 28 acres (11.3 ha) along the Arkansas River.

Race Relations. At a two-day conference in Little Rock, historians opened a public examination of a violent racial incident that took place in the town of Elaine in 1919. Following the shooting death of a white deputy sheriff, white mobs attacked black farmers in the area, killing at least a dozen and perhaps as many as 200 people. Army troops were called in to restore order. Historians at the conference hoped a search of military records would provide more evidence about the riot.

Death Penalty. Christina Marie Riggs, 28, was executed by lethal injection on May 2, making her the first woman to be executed in Arkansas in 150 years. She had been convicted of killing her two children.

JIM ANDERSON

CALIFORNIA. California took center stage in the "marijuana as medicine" debate when the U.S. Supreme Court in late 2000 decided to review the concept of "medical necessity" as an exception to the illegality of marijuana. Earlier in the year, a successful budget, a new national monument, a strengthening of Democratic power in Congress, and police corruption made headlines in the state.

Legislature. For the second year in a row, California succeeded in having its state budget in place by the beginning of the fiscal year on July 1. The $99.4 billion budget, which was 18% higher than the 1999–2000 budget, included $1.4 billion in tax cuts. The state expected to spend $30.8 million on public schools.

In September, Gov. Gray Davis signed a bill giving free tuition at any state public university to any high school senior in the state with a B average and a household income of less than $64,000 for a family of four.

Environment and Energy Crisis. President Clinton in April created the Giant Sequoia National Monument. In creating the 328,000-acre (133 000-ha) monument in Sierra Nevada, Clinton banned timber harvesting and the use of off-road vehicles there. A record summer heat wave created a major power emergency.

California's two-year experiment with electricity deregulation created problems: By year's end, utilities neared bankruptcy, electric rates were rising, and a lack of new power plants created power shortages.

Elections. Vice-President Gore easily won the November 7 presidential contest in California, carrying 53% of the vote. Also easily winning was incumbent U.S. Sen. Dianne Feinstein. In races for the U.S. House, Democrats took four seats from the Republicans. Rep. Julian Dixon (D) of the 32d District died of an apparent heart attack on December 8. Earlier in the year, former Democratic Rep. Norman Mineta was named secretary of commerce in the Clinton administration; after the presidential election, President-elect Bush nominated Mineta as secretary of transportation.

Police and Crime. As allegations of police corruption and misconduct continued to surface in Los Angeles (*see* POLICING—A PROBLEMATIC ENTERPRISE, page 66), six police officers were charged in July with misconduct in connection with a 1996 shooting and subsequent cover-up. In an unrelated incident, another police officer was charged with attempting to murder a gang member during a 1996 stakeout.

A Justice Policy Institute study, released in February, showed that minority youths in California were 6.2 times more likely to be tried as adults by the courts than were white youths. The minority youths also were seven times more likely to be sent to prison if they were tried as adults.

KRISTI VAUGHAN

THE U.S. STATES

	Population * (in millions)	Area (sq mi)		Capital (km²)	Governor**
Alabama	4.4	52,423	135 776	Montgomery	Donald Siegelman (D)
Alaska	.6	656,424	1 700 130	Juneau	Tony Knowles (D)
Arizona	5.1	114,006	295 276	Phoenix	Jane Dee Hull (R)
Arkansas	2.7	53,182	137 741	Little Rock	Mike Huckabee (R)
California	33.9	163,707	424 001	Sacramento	Gray Davis (D)
Colorado	4.3	104,100	269 619	Denver	Bill Owens (R)
Connecticut	3.4	5,544	14 359	Hartford	John Rowland (R)
Delaware	.8	2,489	6 447	Dover	Ruth Ann Minner (D)
Florida	15.9	65,758	170 313	Tallahassee	Jeb Bush (R)
Georgia	8.2	59,441	153 952	Atlanta	Roy Barnes (D)
Hawaii	1.2	10,932	28 314	Honolulu	Benjamin J. Cayetano (D)
Idaho	1.3	83,574	216 457	Boise	Dirk Kempthorne (R)
Illinois	12.4	57,918	150 008	Springfield	George Ryan (R)
Indiana	6.0	36,420	94 328	Indianapolis	Frank O'Bannon (D)
Iowa	2.9	56,276	145 755	Des Moines	Tom Vilsack (D)
Kansas	2.7	82,282	213 110	Topeka	Bill Graves (R)
Kentucky	4.0	40,411	104 664	Frankfort	Paul Patton (D)
Louisiana	4.5	51,843	134 273	Baton Rouge	Mike Foster (R)
Maine	1.3	35,387	91 652	Augusta	Angus King, Jr. (I)
Maryland	5.3	12,407	32 134	Annapolis	Parris N. Glendening (D)
Massachusetts	6.3	10,555	27 337	Boston	Paul Cellucci (R)
Michigan	9.9	96,705	250 466	Lansing	John Engler (R)
Minnesota	4.9	86,943	225 182	St. Paul	Jesse Ventura (Reform)
Mississippi	2.8	48,434	125 444	Jackson	Ronnie Musgrove (D)
Missouri	5.6	69,709	180 546	Jefferson City	Bob Holden (D)
Montana	.9	147,046	380 849	Helena	Judy Martz (R)
Nebraska	1.7	77,358	200 357	Lincoln	Mike Johanns (R)
Nevada	2.0	110,567	286 369	Carson City	Kenny Guinn (R)
New Hampshire	1.2	9,351	24 219	Concord	Jeanne Shaheen (D)
New Jersey	8.4	8,722	22 590	Trenton	Christine Todd Whitman (R)***
New Mexico	1.8	121,598	314 939	Santa Fe	Gary Johnson (R)
New York	18.9	54,556	141 300	Albany	George Pataki (R)
North Carolina	8.0	53,821	139 396	Raleigh	Mike Easley (D)
North Dakota	.6	70,704	183 123	Bismarck	John Hoeven (R)
Ohio	11.3	44,828	116 105	Columbus	Bob Taft (R)
Oklahoma	3.5	69,903	181 049	Oklahoma City	Frank Keating (R)
Oregon	3.4	98,386	254 820	Salem	John Kitzhaber (D)
Pennsylvania	12.3	46,058	119 290	Harrisburg	Tom Ridge (R)
Rhode Island	1.0	1,545	4 002	Providence	Lincoln Almond (R)
South Carolina	4.0	32,008	82 901	Columbia	Jim Hodges (D)
South Dakota	.7	77,121	199 743	Pierre	William Janklow (R)
Tennessee	5.7	42,146	109 158	Nashville	Donald Sundquist (R)
Texas	20.8	268,601	695 673	Austin	Rick Perry (R)
Utah	2.2	84,904	219 901	Salt Lake City	Michael O. Leavitt (R)
Vermont	.6	9,615	24,903	Montpelier	Howard Dean (D)
Virginia	7.0	42,777	110 792	Richmond	James S. Gilmore III (R)
Washington	5.9	71,302	184 672	Olympia	Gary Locke (D)
West Virginia	1.8	24,231	62 758	Charleston	Bob Wise (D)
Wisconsin	5.3	65,499	169 642	Madison	Tommy G. Thompson (R)***
Wyoming	.5	97,818	253 349	Cheyenne	Jim Geringer (R)

*2000 Census   **As of January 2001   ***Named to incoming Bush administration

COLORADO. The Colorado legislature enacted tax cuts and Republican Gov. Bill Owens' education package. The new education legislation assigns letter grades to public schools based on how well their students perform on standardized achievement tests. Schools that test the best or show the most improvement will be allocated more money. Those schools failing after three years could be revamped as charter schools. The Colorado Education Association organized rallies to oppose the new law. The state set aside $190 million over the next decade for construction and repairs for the state's neediest schools.

Legislation. The legislature passed $210 million in permanent tax reductions, including an income-tax reduction from 4.75% to 4.63%, a state-sales tax from 3% to 2.9%, and temporary reductions of $175 million. Businesses will receive their share of a personal property-tax refund totaling $100 million. A 20% cut in the amount employers pay on unemployment insurance will save employers $52 million annually.

In response to the late-night murders of two teenagers at a Jefferson County sandwich shop in February, the legislature increased penalties for employers who violate child-labor laws that restrict the hours young people can work. The legislature also reinstated the state's instant background check for gun purchasers, but did not pass the other gun measures that responded to the 1999 massacre at Columbine High School.

Elections. In November 7 elections, Colorado voted for Governor Bush. Voters reelected incumbents to all six of the state's seats in the U.S. House. Voters approved a ballot measure requiring background checks of buyers at gun shows and a measure to permit the medical use of marijuana. Voters rejected a 24-hour waiting period for a woman to obtain an abortion. Democrats won control of the state Senate for the first time in 40 years. Democrat Stan Matsunaka, the new Senate president, became the first lawmaker of Asian descent in the Colorado leadership.

Other News. Summer wildfires destroyed dozens of homes and burned hundreds of acres of forests near Denver and Boulder. Nathan Hall, 21, was convicted of criminally negligent homicide for causing the 1997 accidental death of another skier at Vail.

ELAINE STUART

CONNECTICUT. Late in the year, residents of Connecticut waited with the rest of the nation to learn whether Joseph Lieberman would remain the state's junior U.S. senator or become Al Gore's vice-president.

Elections. Connecticut had more than a passing interest in the outcome of the disputed presidential election because a win by the Gore-Lieberman ticket meant Gov. John Rowland would have the opportunity to appoint a new senator and thus move the seat from Democratic to Republican control. Lieberman had been in the unusual position of running simultaneously for U.S. Senate and vice-president. As a senatorial candidate, he won 64% of the vote. The Gore-Lieberman ticket captured 56% of the state's vote, but not enough electoral votes nationwide to win the White House.

Democrats suffered a blow when Robert Simmons narrowly defeated incumbent U.S. Rep. Sam Gejdenson for the 2d District seat. Incumbents held onto their seats in the other five districts.

Crime and Tragedy. Michael Skakel, a nephew of Ethel Kennedy, was charged with the 1975 Greenwich murder of 15-year-old Martha Moxley; he turned himself in to the police. At year's end, a court ruling was still awaited on whether Skakel would be tried as an adult or a juvenile.

The suicide of two young boys, ages 13 and 15, shook the state in May. The boys had called friends on a cell phone to say good-bye and then drove a truck owned by one of the boys' fathers into a tree.

Newspaper Ownership. The ownership of several of the state's major newspapers changed hands in 2000. The *Hartford Courant* and *The Advocate* of Stamford were sold to the Tribune Company, and in July the *Connecticut Post* was sold, along with five community newspapers, to the MediaNews Group.

Census News. Statistics from the U.S. Census Bureau showed that almost 9% of state residents and 15% of children in the state lived in poverty in 1997. The highest poverty level was in New Haven County.

Population estimates released in November by the Census Bureau showed that Hispanics were rapidly becoming the state's largest minority and that Hispanics outnumbered non-Hispanic blacks in five of the state's eight counties.

Legislation. Responding in part to the 1999 corruption case in which Paul J. Silvester, whom Governor Rowland had appointed treasurer, pleaded guilty to charges of money laundering and racketeering, the state legislature passed a bill limiting the treasurer's role in investment decisions. The legislature also made the Martin Luther King, Jr., holiday an official state holiday thus requiring municipalities to observe it. The town of Wallingford had been the only town in the state refusing to give town workers a paid day off. Rowland also approved spending $455 million in state money for the $771 million Adriaen's Landing riverfront project in Hartford.

KRISTI VAUGHAN

DELAWARE. On November 7, voters elected Ruth Ann Minner, the Democratic lieutenant governor, the state's first female governor. Also, U.S. Sen. William Roth, Jr., five-term Republican incumbent, lost his battle for reelection to the state's popular Democratic governor, Thomas Carper. Democratic presidential nominee Gore carried the state.

Legislation. The state legislature passed Governor Carper's education accountability plan for teachers, after failing twice to do so in 1999. The law established a professional standards board. Another new law stiffened penalties for school truancy and subjects parents of truants to fines and imprisonment.

New environmental laws ensured long-term water supplies, put in place nutrient management initiatives to protect waterways, and increased statewide recycling efforts. Other new laws allowed state residents to select their electricity provider, enhanced early childhood education, set safety rules for personal watercraft, and provided pay raises for state employees. Several other new laws were enacted. One allowed lawsuits against owners, landlords, managers, or tenants of buildings habitually used by drug dealers or drug users. Another required that telephone calls to publicly listed state agencies be answered by a person.

ELAINE STUART

FLORIDA. For much of the year 2000 the state was in the headlines, as observers at home and abroad followed the Elián González drama (*see* CUBA—The Saga of Elián González) and later the legal and political efforts to win Florida's 25 electoral votes and the presidency (*see* THE 2000 U.S. PRESIDENTIAL ELECTION, page 22).

Elections. Longtime Florida politician Bill Nelson, a Democrat, defeated Republican Representative Bill McCollum for the Senate seat vacated by the retirement of Republican Connie Mack. Nelson has won 11 different elections in the state since the start of his career in 1972. As a U.S. congressman he rode a space shuttle into orbit in 1985.

Florida voters also approved a state constitutional amendment ordering the construction of a high-speed train linking Florida's five largest cities. Construction was mandated to begin no later than Nov. 1, 2003. The amendment left it up to state legislators to decide how to pay for the system, whose cost was estimated at a minimum of $5.6 billion.

Weather. A severe drought struck Florida and much of the country in late spring and summer, giving rise to a series of brushfires. Relief came in September, when Hurricane Gordon dropped more than 4 inches (10 cm) of rain. Just two weeks later, more than 18 inches (46 cm) of rain fell during a two-day tropical downpour, flooding many areas, cutting off power, and prompting Gov. Jeb Bush to declare a state of emergency.

© Roberto Borea/AP/Wide World Photos

In November 2000, Delaware voters chose Ruth Ann Minner (left) the state's first female governor. Elected to the Delaware House of Representatives in 1974, and named the state's Woman of the Year in 1985, she had been an active environmentalist.

On Dec. 11, 2000, President Bill Clinton signed legislation allocating $7.8 billion for a joint federal-state project to restore the Everglades—the vast wetland in southern Florida that is home to a wide variety of endangered species, both plants and animals. The measure received bipartisan support in both houses of Congress.

Courts. In the first smokers' class-action suit to go to trial, a six-member jury in July awarded $145 billion in punitive damages against the five largest cigarette companies. The jury found the companies guilty of conspiracy, fraud, and misrepresentation. A circuit-court judge upheld the record-breaking award in November, rejecting claims that such an enormous sum would bankrupt the tobacco industry. A long appeals process in state courts was expected.

JIM ANDERSON

GEORGIA. Republican U.S. Sen. Paul Coverdell died on July 18, 2000, and Gov. Roy Barnes appointed Zell Miller, the state's Democratic former governor, to succeed him on an interim basis. Tornadoes hit southwest Georgia on February 14, killing 18 people and injuring more than 100.

Elections. Senator Miller won a special election on November 7 to fill out the four years remaining in the term of Senator Coverdell. The state gave its electoral votes to Texas Governor Bush. Following the November 7 elections, majority Democrats in the Georgia House selected Tom Murphy, 76, as speaker for the 27th and 28th years. Murphy is the longest actively serving speaker in the nation.

Legislation. The legislature passed most of Governor Barnes' education-reform proposals. The measures, which took effect on July 1, called for state control of any schools that fail to perform well for two consecutive years. Reforms also rewarded schools that score well on standardized tests by giving teacher bonuses. Teachers must be tested for competency in using computers, and the state eliminated job protections for teachers hired after July 1. The reforms were opposed by the state's largest teachers union, which in response backed Republicans in state-legislative races in November. The $14.4 billion state budget included pay raises for teachers and other state employees, property-tax breaks for homeowners, and $5.4 billion for public schools.

The legislature approved spending $62 million of the state's first $150 million of the state tobacco settlement on promoting rural development and $15.8 million on smoking prevention. Spurred by the death of a 5-year-old Atlanta boy in 1998, the legislature made improvements in the child-protection system, including giving doctors authority to take into protective custody children believed to be in imminent danger of abuse or neglect. Other new legislation provided $30 million to 40 fast-growing counties to protect green space and wetlands and allowed for execution by lethal injection rather than the electric chair for those newly convicted of a capital crime.

ELAINE STUART

HAWAII. In November 7 elections, Hawaii's voters gave a majority to the Gore ticket and to incumbent Sen. Daniel Akaka, as well as to its two Democratic U.S. House incumbents.

Legislation. The 2000 Hawaii legislature became the first state-lawmaking body to allow use of marijuana as a medical treatment. The Hawaii legislature also passed 24 measures to lure technology-driven, knowledge-based firms. Three of the measures gave tax breaks to high-tech firms, allowed investment of state-pension funds in high-tech ventures, and conferred legal status on electronic records and signatures.

The legislature increased funds for education and provided $45 million for school repairs and $2.6 million to reduce class sizes in lower grades. Another law provides for new rules to hold teachers and schools accountable for student learning. Other laws require minors riding in the back seats of vehicles to wear seat belts, and bicyclists under age 16 to wear helmets.

Social Services. The state began offering its Children's Health Insurance Program on July 1 to children from low-income families. Gov. Ben Cayetano announced in August that the state would institute a program whereby long-term care insurance is offered to public employees and their relatives.

Environment. President Clinton directed the Commerce and Interior Departments to develop a plan to protect the magnificent coral reefs of the northwest Hawaiian Islands. Governor Cayetano declared a state of emergency for the entire Big Island in the wake of catastrophic flooding that caused an estimated $20 million in damages in November.

ELAINE STUART

IDAHO. Idaho's electoral votes went to the GOP in November 2000. The Aryan Nations white supremacist group lost a multimillion dollar court case. Huge wildfires destroyed 700,000 acres (283 500 ha) of forest throughout the state.

Elections. Republican "Butch" Otter, a popular four-term lieutenant governor, easily beat Moscow City Councilwoman Linda Pall in the race for the congressional seat vacated by retiring Rep. Helen Chenoweth-Hage. Republican incumbent Mike Simpson also won handily in his congressional race against businessman Craig Williams.

Legal. A jury in Coeur d'Alene returned a $6.3 million civil judgment in September against the white supremacist group Aryan Nations and its founder, Richard Butler. The suit had been brought by civil-rights lawyer Morris Dees of the Southern Poverty Law Center, on behalf of Victoria Keenan and her son, Jason. In 1998, after their car backfired, the Keenans had been chased and beaten by guards at the Aryan Nations compound in Hayden Lake. The jury found that the Aryan Nations was negligent in the operation of its security force.

A judge denied a new trial for the group in October, clearing the way for Dees and the Keenans to take control of the 20-acre (8-ha) Aryan Nations compound and church. A few days later Butler and two dozen followers marched through downtown Coeur d'Alene; Butler announced plans to open a new church in the town of Hayden.

Fires. A hot, dry summer led to 26 major forest fires, covering 700,000 acres (283 500 ha). The largest destroyed 180,000 acres (72 900 ha) of the Salmon-Challis National Forest near the Montana state line. Fires in the Frank Church-River of No Return Wilderness forced the U.S. Forest Service to close the popular Middle Fork of the Salmon River.

JIM ANDERSON

ILLINOIS. Gov. George Ryan took several decisive actions in 2000, including calling a special legislative session to suspend the state's gas sales tax because gas prices were getting too high, and declaring a moratorium on executions in the state because the system was "fraught with errors."

Elections. Vice-President Gore defeated Governor Bush in Illinois by a margin of 55% to 43%. Incumbent Democrats won ten of the state's 20 races for the U.S. House of Representatives, while incumbent Republicans held onto eight seats. In the heavily Democratic 10th District, Lauren Gash, a Democrat, was defeated by Republican Mark Kirk. Timothy V. Johnson (R) was the other newly elected House member following his win in the 15th District.

Native Americans. Native Americans who objected to the use of Indians as school mascots gained ground in Illinois in 2000 when the school board overseeing Niles West High School voted to drop "Indians" as a school nickname. The school board joined others

around the country that had changed mascots. Various groups of activists continued their efforts to get the University of Illinois to join the trend and get rid of its mascot, Chief Illinewek.

The attorney general and legislature, meanwhile, took steps to help 15 landowners in the Wabash River Watershed area fight a suit by the Miami tribe of Oklahoma. The tribe claimed that 2.6 million acres (1 million ha) of land rightfully belonged to them.

Courts and the Death Penalty. The Illinois Supreme Court in August ordered hearings held on claims that two men on death row were tortured into confessing by a former Chicago police commander and others. Governor Ryan halted executions in the state on January 31, claiming that he could not allow executions to continue until he was certain innocent people were not being put to death.

In September a Cook County judge dismissed claims by the city of Chicago that the gun industry should be liable for the costs resulting from the violence caused by their product.

KRISTI VAUGHAN

INDIANA. The 2000 Indiana General Assembly agreed to spend $110 million of its share of the multistate tobacco settlement on public health, including $35 million on smoking prevention. About half the state's annual share of money will be placed in a trust fund to finance future public-health needs. The legislative session also increased benefits for workers' compensation and unemployment. Gov. Frank O'Bannon suspended the state's 5% tax on gasoline from July 1 to September 30 in an attempt to hold down prices at the pump.

The Courts. A legislative measure calling for posting the Ten Commandments and other religious and historic documents in public buildings was in limbo pending a final court ruling. In July the U.S. District Court in New Albany, IN, enjoined the state from placing a monument with the Ten Commandments on the statehouse grounds.

A Marion County Superior Court voided Indiana's ban on Medicaid-funded abortions on October 18. Similar bans have been voided by lower courts in other states. A U.S. District Court in Indianapolis on October 11 gave the city the right to proceed with an ordinance banning minors from playing violent and sexually explicit video games without parental permission.

The Indiana Court of Appeals struck down the state's random drug testing in schools on August 21, saying schools can only impose tests on students suspected of using drugs.

Elections. In November 7 elections, the state's electoral vote went to Bush, and U.S. Sen. Richard Lugar, also of the GOP, easily captured a fifth term. Governor O'Bannon, a Democrat, also won reelection by a convincing margin.

Bobby Knight. In September, Indiana University basketball coach Bob Knight was dismissed by the university president for violating a school policy against temper outbursts. Knight won three national championships and 11 Big Ten titles in his 29 years as coach of the Hoosiers.

ELAINE STUART

IOWA. The state legislature approved the spending of an additional $78.6 million on schools in fiscal year 2002. Much of the new money would be earmarked to go into teachers' salaries.

Legislation. The legislature also passed a measure to allow elderly people to stay in their homes rather than go to nursing homes. In a move to encourage food-processing businesses, the legislature allowed such companies additional tax relief. The state also approved lifting the sales tax on clothing and shoe sales for two days at the start of each school year.

A "Vision Iowa" program called for giving up to $300 million in state grants to local communities for recreational and tourism projects. New legislation provided tuition assistance for career education, as well as funds to market Iowa-produced products, to assist welfare recipients and people with disabilities in entering the workforce, and for technology improvements. The legislature allocated $55 million of the state's share of the multistate tobacco settlement to smoking cessation programs and expanding Iowans' access to health care.

Elections. Iowa's five incumbent U.S. House members were reelected on November 7, and the state delivered its electoral vote to Gore. The vice-president's margin was just more than 4,000 votes.

Other News. Gov. Tom Vilsack asked for federal disaster assistance for counties suffering extreme drought conditions in the summer. Many of the state's grain elevators found traces of genetically altered Starlink corn in their bins and shipments. Food products using genetically altered corn were recalled from store shelves nationwide in October.

ELAINE STUART

KANSAS. The Kansas legislature passed a tight budget in light of a revenue shortfall of some $60 million. In a cost-cutting measure, the legislature eliminated planned spending for the state's April presidential primary and adopted a bill to cancel the primary.

Elections. In November 7 elections, Governor Bush carried the state. The one Democratic and three Republican incumbents were returned to the U.S. House of Representatives. Voters also authorized investment of state-pension funds in the stock market.

Legislation. A new law calls for the state to pay up to $1,200 a year toward a qualifying resident's prescription drugs. It would cover people who are at least 67 years old with incomes of less than $12,500. Another new law provided health insurance for employees who make less than $16,700 annually. To discourage infanticide, the state will permit parents to abandon babies up to 45 days old at hospitals, health clinics, and fire stations. A $60 million program for building facilities for juvenile offenders was approved.

Other News. In August voters in Kansas rejected the reelection bids of two of the three state education leaders who in 1999 voted to de-emphasize teaching of evolution in the public schools. In August 1999, the two had joined in a 6-4 decision by the Kansas Board of Education to allow biblical theories of creation to be taught and tested.

ELAINE STUART

KENTUCKY. In 2000, the two-party system came into play for the first time in more than a century in Kentucky's legislature. With Republican numbers increased by legislators switching parties, the GOP took control of the state Senate, 20-18. That set the stage for a battle between the Senate and the Democratic House and Democratic governor. As the first reelected Kentucky governor in two centuries, Paul Patton had an ambitious agenda, which had to be scaled back in the face of Republican opposition.

Legislation. The legislature passed a $14 billion two-year budget. It approved much of the governor's $56 million proposal for early-childhood health and education programs. A new law lowered the threshold for drunken driving to 0.08% blood-alcohol levels. Another law made it a crime to leave a child under 8 years old unattended in a vehicle during dangerously hot weath-

er. Still other new legislation makes identity theft a crime and requires colleges to keep crime logs. The legislature agreed to give counties dependent on tobacco 35% of agriculture's share of the tobacco settlement and give the rest to a statewide board to distribute. The legislature also adopted a resolution that allowed posting of the Ten Commandments in public buildings and required the state to post a monument depicting the Commandments on capitol grounds.

Environment. In October a coal company impoundment of slurry collapsed, causing a massive spill of liquid coal waste in eastern Kentucky. The spill, estimated at 250 million gallons, caused an environmental disaster and had an estimated cleanup cost of $16.5 million. The U.S. Congress approved more than $100 million for cleanup and worker health testing at a uranium plant in Paducah, in the western part of the state.

Elections. On November 7, the six incumbents—five of them Republicans—retained their U.S. House seats, and Republican Bush won the state's electoral votes. Voters also approved a ballot measure calling for annual sessions of the state legislature.

ELAINE STUART

LOUISIANA. The legislature met in three sessions in 2000. In a spring special session, the legislature tackled the state's budget deficit by renewing expiring sales taxes on food and utilities. In the April to June regular session, lawmakers raised the sales tax on food and utilities by 1% to generate $110 million, and increased the cigarette tax from 20 cents to 24 cents a pack. The session also reduced income-tax breaks given to people with young children. In a third session that ended in August, lawmakers passed a $13.9 billion state budget. They also raised tuition by $250 a year at state colleges, and increased fees for hunting and fishing licenses. Lawmakers also cut the number of state employees by 4% and cut spending in most state departments. A new law permits parents to safely abandon newborns without fear of prosecution.

Elections. On November 7, five Republican and two Democratic members of the U.S. House were reelected, and Governor Bush took the state's electoral votes. Voters rejected a measure on the ballot to increase state-income taxes to fund education and to end state-sales tax on food and utilities. Following the election, Gov. Mike Foster warned that teachers might strike and public-health programs might be shut down as a result of the voter defeat of his proposal to raise funds with higher income taxes.

Other News. The National D-Day Museum, which pays tribute to the June 6, 1944, invasion of Normandy by the Allies during World War II, opened in New Orleans in June. A jury in May convicted former Louisiana Gov. Edwin Edwards on 17 counts of violating federal racketeering and fraud laws. Jimmie Davis, a songwriter and singer who penned "You Are My Sunshine" and who was twice elected governor, died in November at age 101.

ELAINE STUART

MAINE. Maine assumed a leading role in 2000 in the growing national debate over how to best help senior citizens and other Americans pay for the rising cost of prescription drugs.

Health. Maine's answer to the prescription-drug debate, which quickly was challenged by drug companies, was to establish price controls. This first-of-a-kind program was set to begin on Jan. 1, 2001. Under the program, the state would first use its position as a bulk purchaser to obtain lower prices for drugs and then, by 2003, if prices were not significantly lower, impose price controls on drug companies doing business in Maine. The drug companies argued that the program was unconstitutional because it regulated transactions between manufacturers and out-of-state wholesalers.

Elections. Maine's seats in both the U.S. Senate and House remained in the hands of incumbents. Republican Sen. Olympia J. Snowe easily won reelection, as did U.S. Democratic Reps. Tom Allen and John Baldacci. Democrat Al Gore won the presidential election in Maine. Voters defeated proposals to allow doctor-assisted suicides and to outlaw discrimination against gays and lesbians.

Environment. Maine's fisheries and blueberry businesses suffered a substantial blow during 2000 when the wild Atlantic salmon was placed on the endangered species list. According to Gov. Angus King, who objected to the designation, the listing meant regulations on the use of rivers where salmon spawn for irrigation, thus affecting blueberry growers and restrictions on the types of salmon that can be raised in Maine's aquaculture farms. Governor King feared the loss of jobs. Researchers in Maine, meanwhile, were trying to find an edible use for the European green crab that had wreaked havoc on Maine's shellfish industry for decades.

KRISTI VAUGHAN

MARYLAND. Gov. Parris N. Glendening convinced the 2000 legislature to mandate built-in locks on new handguns, effective in 2003. Until then, handguns must be sold with external trigger locks. Gun-safety legislation also required ballistic fingerprinting of guns to help police investigate gun crime, a safety course for new handgun owners, and mandatory sentencing for criminals caught with guns.

Legislation. The legislature enacted other initiatives pushed by the governor, including pay increases for state workers and new environmental proposals. The legislature also spent the state's $1 billion surplus in approving a $19.5 billion budget that allocated money for building improvements in public schools, juvenile-justice programs, and higher education. The session allocated funds for textbooks for private schools and raises for school teachers, as well as scholarships for college students who plan to teach.

Maryland was to spend its $4 billion share of the tobacco settlement on education initiatives and anti-smoking efforts. State-funded health-insurance coverage was extended to an additional 19,000 children of working families without insurance. To discourage underage smoking, the state banned most cigarette-vending machines that accept coins. The legislature also required more testing of children for lead poisoning, following reports of widespread poisoning in some Baltimore neighborhoods.

Elections. Vice-President Gore won the state's electoral votes. Democratic U.S. Sen. Paul Sarbanes won reelection, as did the eight incumbent House members.

ELAINE STUART

MASSACHUSETTS. It was a good year and a bad year for budgets in Massachusetts, as voters approved the biggest tax cut in the state's history, but cost overruns grew on the nation's largest highway project.

The Big Dig. The cost of the nation's largest road project—designed to ease traffic congestion in downtown Boston—continued to rise in 2000 amid questions about whether project managers misled the federal government about costs. The so-called "Big Dig," a 7.5-mi (12-km) stretch of roadway that when complete would include a ten-lane underground highway, two new bridges, and an extension of the Massachusetts Turnpike, began in 1993 at an estimated cost of $2.6 billion. By the end of 2000, the estimated cost was more than $12 billion. In May, after the federal government said it would deny the state further money unless a bailout plan was created, Gov. Paul Celucci signed a bill covering $1.9 billion in cost overruns and $500 million in funding for construction on other state roads and bridges.

Politics. The dreaded nickname "Taxachusetts" became a thing of the past when voters on November 7 approved the biggest tax cut in the state's history, reducing the income tax from 5.85% to 5% by 2003. This dropped Massachusetts to the Number 10 spot on the list of states with the highest tax burden.

In the presidential race, voters in Massachusetts chose Gore by a margin of 60% to 33% for Bush. Green Party candidate Ralph Nader received 6% of the vote. Also overwhelmingly supported was Democrat Edward M. Kennedy, who was returned for a seventh full-term in the U.S. Senate. All ten of the state's incumbent members of the U.S. House were reelected.

Crime. Organized crime leader James "Whitey" Bulger, who had been on the Federal Bureau of Investigation's (FBI's) Ten Most Wanted List since 1999, was arrested in September on charges that he and an associate were responsible for a "reign of intimidation and murder that spanned some 25 years."

A single father of four was beaten to death in July by the father of another boy with whom his son was playing hockey. Thomas Junta, who was charged with manslaughter in the beating, said he was acting in self-defense and that a fight started after he became concerned about rough hockey play. Michael Costin, who was killed, was supervising the play. In December, Michael McDermott, a software tester, shot and killed seven of his coworkers at a Wakefield Internet consulting company.

In April, Massachusetts began enforcing the nation's strictest gun-safety laws by banning gun makers and dealers from selling handguns in the state that do not have tamper-proof serial numbers, trigger locks, and a mechanism for letting the user know whether or not the gun is loaded.

KRISTI VAUGHAN

MICHIGAN. Debbie Stabenow upset incumbent Spencer Abraham to capture a U.S. Senate seat for the Democrats. Voters gave Michigan's electoral votes to Vice-President Gore and by a two-to-one margin defeated a school-voucher proposal. A 6-year-old boy killed a classmate in first grade.

Politics. By less than 40,000 votes out of more than 3.7 million cast, Debbie Stabenow eased past Republican Spencer Abraham to become the first woman from Michigan to be elected to the U.S. Senate. Although heavily outspent by Abraham, Stabenow, who served two terms in the U.S. House of Representatives, had firm support from organized labor, and performed strongly during the debates. Abraham later was nominated as secretary of energy by President-elect Bush. In another tight race, Republican Mike Rogers squeaked past Democrat Dianne Byrum to win Stabenow's old House seat.

Michigan voters soundly defeated a proposal to give $3,300 vouchers to parents whose children were enrolled in poorly performing school districts. The proposal was backed by the Roman Catholic Church in Michigan and financed by conservative millionaire Richard DeVos, Jr., but Republican Gov. John Engler declined to support it. State teachers' unions spent $6 million in opposition. According to exit polls, a majority of black voters in the state were against the measure.

Former Michigan Gov. James Blanchard offered his views on the state's proposal to give $3,300 vouchers to parents whose children were attending poorly performing schools. Michigan voters rejected the plan by a large margin on Election Day.

Crime. In February a 6-year-old boy shot a female classmate to death in front of their first-grade class in Mount Morris Township, a Flint suburb. The child had been living with an uncle in a house neighbors said was full of drugs and guns. In July the uncle, Sirmarcus Winfrey, pleaded guilty to possessing the stolen .32-caliber handgun that was used. The boy told investigators he just wanted to scare the girl and the shooting had been an accident.

In a case that drew attention to the date-rape drug GHB, four young men from the Detroit suburbs were sentenced to jail terms of up to 15 years for the accidental death of a 15-year-old girl. The four, aged 18 to 26, had put a fatal quantity of the drug in the girl's drink at a party.

JIM ANDERSON

MINNESOTA. In February 2000, Minnesota Gov. Jesse Ventura disaffiliated from the national Reform Party and declared himself an Independent.

Legislation and the Budget. In a unique solution to potentially divisive politics, Minnesota's Republican-controlled House and the Senate, controlled by the Democratic Farmer-Labor Party, decided to divide up the annual surplus—estimated at $569 million. The House allocated its one-third share to income-tax cuts; the Senate used its portion for education funding; and the governor supported a reduction in vehicle-license-registration fees. The agreement came after a month-long deadlock that Ventura said showed why his proposal for a unicameral legislature was a good idea. However, the legislature refused to place a constitutional amendment calling for a one-house legislature on the ballot.

Before ending its session in May, the legislature enacted a $1 billion-plus tax cut that included a $640 million sales-tax rebate, average income-tax cuts of

2.8%, and vehicle-registration-fee reductions. It also approved spending $596 million for transportation projects and $583 million on capital projects, including ones for higher education and public schools. A new law allows parents to drop off unwanted newborns at hospitals without fear of prosecution.

Elections. On Election Day, November 7, Democrat Gore won the state's ten electoral votes. Democrats also won a Senate seat when Mark Dayton defeated incumbent Republican Rod Grams.

Other News. A twister that hit near Granite Falls in July killed one person and left 14 others injured. A national report—the annual Kids Count survey by the Annie E. Casey Foundation—found Minnesota the best place for children because of its low poverty rate and success in keeping teens in school.

ELAINE STUART

MISSISSIPPI. The first order of business for the 2000 legislative session was to choose the state's new governor. With none of the four candidates in the November 1999 election securing a majority vote, the state House of Representatives, under the state constitution, chose between the top two vote-getters, selecting Ronnie Musgrove, the Democratic lieutenant governor.

Legislature. The most important achievement of the session was a six-year $338 million teacher-pay plan, which provided a 30% salary increase to the state's 30,000 teachers. Funds for the pay raises were included in the state's new $3.6 billion budget. In other action, the legislature mandated that drivers carry liability insurance, joining 46 other states with this mandate. Lawmakers also banned tobacco use in schools, even for teachers.

A debate flared up in the regular session over the design of the state flag, which has a Confederate emblem on it. This resulted in the state Supreme Court considering the flag issue and, in a surprise ruling in May, holding that the state did not have an official flag. The governor then created a commission to consider a new design for the flag. The commission was to report by the end of 2000.

After adjourning its regular session in May, the legislature met again in August to pass the governor's new economic-development plan. The "Advantage Mississippi Initiative" offered tax incentives to industries to locate in the state. Legislators approved a $295 million incentive package to attract Nissan Motor Co. to build a plant employing 4,000 autoworkers.

Elections. On November 7, voters returned all the state's incumbent representatives to Congress, including Republican U.S. Sen. Trent Lott, the majority leader, and gave Mississippi's electoral votes to Bush.

ELAINE STUART

MISSOURI. Gov. Mel Carnahan died suddenly while campaigning for the U.S. Senate. A Democrat also won the statehouse. Missouri outlawed racial profiling by its police force.

Politics. Carnahan, a Democrat, died October 16 in a small plane crash while campaigning against incumbent Sen. John Ashcroft. Under Missouri law, Carnahan's name could not be removed from the ballot, so acting Gov. Roger Wilson, who had been Carnahan's lieutenant governor, said if Carnahan won the Senate race he would appoint his widow, Jean Carnahan, to the post. Carnahan beat Ashcroft by two percentage points, and Jean Carnahan was to serve as senator for two years until a special election is held. Subsequently, Ashcroft was nominated as U.S. attorney general by President-elect Bush, who had captured Missouri's electoral vote.

In October, a memorial service was held at the Missouri Capitol for Gov. Mel Carnahan (D), who died in a plane crash while campaigning against incumbent Sen. John Ashcroft (R). After Ashcroft lost to Carnahan, acting Gov. Roger Wilson appointed Carnahan's widow, Jean Carnahan, to the Senate seat. President-elect Bush named Ashcroft U.S. attorney general.

In the race for governor, Democratic State Treasurer Bob Holden edged Republican Rep. Jim Talent by fewer than 22,000 votes. In House races, Republican Jo Ann Emerson, who was first elected in a special contest to succeed her husband, won reelection, as did Democratic Minority Leader Richard Gephardt. Democrat William Lacy Clay, Jr., succeeded his father, William L. Clay, in the 1st District, a seat the elder Clay—Missouri's first black congressman—won in 1968.

Law and Order. In June, Governor Carnahan signed into law a bill outlawing racial profiling by police, making Missouri the fifth state to ban the practice. The law required that police record the race, sex, and age of all drivers stopped, then review the data to see if a disproportionate number of stops involved minorities.

Missouri prison inmates who had been sent to privately run Texas jails because of overcrowding won $2.2 million in a class-action lawsuit that featured videotapes of Texas guards beating, kicking, and shaking down prisoners. The 2,100 inmates in the suit were to share $1.12 million, with the balance covering attorney fees and legal costs.

JIM ANDERSON

MONTANA. Republicans remained in power on the state and federal level, in spite of three strong Democratic challenges. Massive wildfires destroyed hundreds of thousands of acres of woodlands during the summer. Snow, ice, and record-low temperatures hit four northern counties in November.

Elections. In spite of Democratic hopes to the contrary, Montana voted solidly Republican in the November national elections. Lt. Gov. Judy Martz edged State Auditor Mark O'Keefe for the governor's seat, which Republican Marc Racicot had to surrender due to term limits. Conrad Burns was reelected to a third term as U.S. senator, defeating Democratic challenger Brian Schweitzer. Schweitzer, a farmer who had never held

elected office, focused his campaign on the high cost of prescription medicine. Even though Schweitzer led for most of the summer and fall, Burns, with millions more to spend, managed to pull out a narrow victory. In another strongly contested race, former GOP Lt. Gov. Dennis Rehberg won Montana's sole House seat over Democratic State Superintendent of Public Instruction Nancy Keenan. Montana's three electoral votes went to Governor Bush.

Environment. A hot, dry summer set the stage for dozens of lightning-caused wildfires that destroyed nearly 650,000 acres (263 000 ha) throughout the state in July and August. More than 10,000 firefighters—including federal troops and convicts—were called up to fight the blazes, and at one point Governor Racicot declared the entire state a disaster area. A single fire in the Bitterroot Valley covered nearly 250,000 acres (101 250 ha) and destroyed 70 homes.

In November, ice storms and snowstorms lasting more than a week stranded thousands of cattle and cut electricity in four counties along the Canadian border.

JIM ANDERSON

NEBRASKA. The unicameral, nonpartisan state legislature met in a session limited to 60 working days in 2000, adjourning April 12.

Legislation. Under a new law, state residents will be able to save for their children's higher education by contributing to a new state fund. They will be able to deduct up to $1,000 from their taxable income, and their contributions will grow tax free. The legislature also eliminated the last responsibility of the state-tax board by giving its power to set the variable tax on gasoline to the state Department of Roads.

In a move to get Nebraska off the National Humane Society blacklist, the legislature required commercial dog and cat breeders to be licensed and inspected. Drivers with out-of-state drunken-driving convictions

Montana's Republican Lt. Gov. Judy Martz, a former Olympic speed skater, made history on Nov. 7, 2000, by becoming the first woman to be elected governor of the state.

would have them counted against them under a new law. The legislature allocated more funds to study the fairness of the death penalty in the state. Salaries of state constitutional officers would increase, effective Jan. 9, 2003, under a measure enacted by the legislature over the governor's veto. The governor's salary was increased to $85,000 from $65,000.

Elections. Voters on November 7 gave a majority to Republican presidential candidate Bush, but elected Democrat Ben Nelson, a former governor, to the U.S. Senate seat being vacated by Democrat Bob Kerrey. Republicans won the state's open congressional seat as University of Nebraska's football coach Tom Osborne scored a big election victory. Voters also endorsed limiting state senators to two consecutive terms. They also approved a ban on same-sex marriages in the state.

ELAINE STUART

In May, New Hampshire Sen. Burt Cohen (right) introduced a bill in the State Senate to repeal the state's death penalty. The bill passed but was vetoed by Gov. Jeanne Shaheen. In November the state's Democratic chief executive won a third term.

NEVADA. The state legislature did not meet in 2000, but was scheduled to convene in February 2001.

Executive Actions. In October, Republican Gov. Kenny Guinn postponed electric deregulation in the state, citing the need for safeguards against price hikes for residential customers. In another executive action, the governor in July announced a 7% hike in Medicaid payments to nursing homes in the state. The governor said the hike was needed to protect the health-care industry in the state. Nevada already had the nation's second-highest rate of bankrupt nursing homes.

Elections. Republicans picked up an open seat for the U.S. Senate with the election of former Rep. John Ensign. The one Republican and one Democratic incumbent in the U.S. House won reelection. Governor Bush won the state's electoral votes. State voters approved a ban on same-sex marriages and endorsed a proposal allowing doctors to prescribe marijuana to patients in need.

Other News. A jury in May convicted Sandy Murphy, a former topless dancer, and her lover, Rick Tabish, of killing Ted Binion, a wealthy gambling figure, in September 1998. In November the Centers for Disease Control and Prevention (CDC) announced that Nevada held the dubious distinction of having the highest smoking rate in the nation. The CDC estimated that nearly one third of the state's residents smoke. And in December, the Census Bureau reported that Nevada's population of just under 2 million represented a 66.3% increase over 1990, making it the nation's fastest growing state.

ELAINE STUART

NEW HAMPSHIRE. A law passed by the legislature makes it easier for workers denied equal pay for equal work because of their gender to seek redress through a state administrative hearing. Democratic Gov. Jeanne Shaheen vetoed the legislature's attempts to repeal both the death penalty and the state inheritance tax. With the state facing a $250 million deficit in its 2002–03 budget, the governor named a commission of business leaders and economists to come up with revenue-raising proposals.

The governor in May imposed a hiring freeze on most state jobs until June 30, 2001. She cited the need to fill a budget gap created by a school-funding law passed in 1999. The New Hampshire House of Repre-

sentatives impeached state Supreme Court Justice David Brock, alleging misconduct, but the Senate failed to find enough evidence to convict.

Elections. In November 7 balloting, Shaheen won her third two-year term as governor, defeating former U.S. Sen. Gordon Humphrey. New Hampshire's four electoral votes went to Bush, and two Republican incumbents won reelection to the U.S. House.

ELAINE STUART

NEW JERSEY. President-elect Bush nominated New Jersey Gov. Christine Todd Whitman as administrator of the federal Environmental Protection Agency (EPA). Assuming her nomination received approval by the U.S. Senate, Republican State Senate President Donald DiFrancesco would complete Whitman's term as governor.

Elections. In the November election, Vice-President Gore won 56% of New Jersey's popular vote and the state's 15 electoral votes. In the race for the U.S. Senate, Democrat Jon Corzine edged past Republican Rep. Bob Franks by three percentage points. Corzine, a former Wall Street banker, spent nearly $62 million to win the race, ten times what his opponent spent and double the previous record for a Senate candidate. Corzine succeeded Democratic Sen. Frank Lautenberg, who had retired after three terms.

© Charles Rex Arbogast/AP/Wide World Photos

In New Jersey, Democrat Jon Corzine (above) was joined by his daughter Jennifer as he campaigned for the U.S. Senate seat being vacated by Sen. Frank Lautenberg. In defeating Rep. Bob Franks in a tight race, Corzine spent nearly $62 million—ten times more than his opponent.

Three weeks after the election was held, Republican challenger Dick Zimmer conceded defeat to incumbent Democrat Rush Holt in the race for the U.S. House seat for the 12th District. After a number of recounts it became clear that Holt had won the election by about 750 votes. Zimmer had held the central New Jersey seat for six years before stepping down to make a failed Senate run in 1996.

Police. Documents released by the state attorney general's office in November showed that more than 80% of the stops made by state troopers on the New Jersey Turnpike were on vehicles driven by blacks or Hispanics. Attorney General John Farmer said the practice of singling out drivers of color came about during the antidrug war of the 1980s. Although the actions had some success as a crime-fighting tool, he added, they were a "disaster" in terms of social policy.

In December five police officers from the city of Orange were convicted of beating and pepper-spraying Earl Faison, who then died in police custody. The officers, who had been investigating the killing of a policewoman, mistakenly believed that Faison had shot her.

Tragedy. An early morning fire in a dormitory at Seton Hall University in South Orange killed three students and injured more than 50 others. The six-story building did not have a sprinkler system, and many residents ignored the fire alarm. The cause of the January fire was not determined.

JIM ANDERSON

NEW MEXICO. Wildfires that ravaged much of the West in 2000 did not spare New Mexico, as the worst fire in the state's history burned 48,000 acres (19 440 ha). And New Mexico added to the confusion over who won the presidential election by not declaring a winner until Nov. 28, 2000.

Elections. New Mexico gained national attention when it was one of several states with disputed presidential votes. Vice-President Gore appeared to be the winner by a narrow 5,000 vote margin on election night, but the lead vanished when a computer glitch was discovered and votes were declared missing. A recount gave New Mexico's electoral votes to Al Gore by a 366-vote margin.

In the U.S. Senate race, Democratic incumbent Jeff Bingaman easily won reelection. Only one U.S. House race was close, with Republican incumbent Heather Wilson (R) narrowly defeating challenger John Kelly, a former U.S. attorney in New Mexico. Incumbent Representatives Joe Skeen, a Republican, and Democrat Thomas Udall easily won reelection.

Disasters. A Los Alamos wildfire began as a prescribed burn by the National Park Service set at the nearby Bandelier National Monument. It quickly grew out of control, burning for more than a week and reaching the Los Alamos National Laboratory, one of the nation's nuclear-weapons-research centers. In addition to destroying homes and forcing the evacuation of more than 18,000 people, the fire caused about $300 million in damage to the nuclear-weapons facility. Several scientists also lost important research when computer hardware was damaged. As a result of the fire, Park Service officials were revamping their procedures for controlled burns.

A natural gas explosion at a Carlsbad campsite killed 12 people from two families camping about 500 ft (153 m) from the pipeline.

KRISTI VAUGHAN

NEW YORK. In one of the nation's most closely watched contests, First Lady Hillary Rodham Clinton defeated Republican U.S. Rep. Rick Lazio to win the U.S. Senate seat being vacated by retiring Sen. Daniel Moynihan (*see* THE FIRST LADY BECOMES SENATOR-ELECT, page 37). The Environmental Protection Agency (EPA) announced its plan to clean up chemical contamination in the Hudson River.

Elections. Democratic presidential candidate Gore easily captured New York's 33 electoral votes. U.S. congressional incumbents won their 29 races. Democrat Steve Israel took over Rick Lazio's U.S. House seat in eastern Long Island by soundly defeating Joan Johnson, one of the few black Republican women running for office. In the other open seat, in the 1st District, Brookhaven Supervisor Felix Grucci (R) defeated Regina Seltzer, an environmental lawyer.

Environment. After decades of controversy, the EPA in December issued its plan to clean up PCB (polychlorinated biphenyl) contamination in the Hudson River. More than a million pounds of PCBs—a highly carcinogenic chemical that passes to humans who eat Hudson River fish—were legally released into the river between 1946 and 1977 from two upstate factories owned by General Electric (GE). The PCBs, a by-product of the manufacture of electric capacitors, are in the form of a heavy oil that lies on the Hudson's floor. The EPA plan called for dredging the PCBs off the bottom along a 40-mi (64-km) stretch of river, with the $490 million cost to be picked up by GE. The company, which already had spent more than $200 million voluntarily to clean the Hudson, was strongly opposed to the plan, but their case was not helped when Republican Gov. George Pataki came out in favor of dredging. The EPA's final order was expected in June 2001.

Other News. Nearly 4,000 Buffalo teachers went on strike for two days in September, after working without a contract since June 1999. Although they won a new contract with pay raises, the teachers later were fined $1,000 each for their action.

Novelist Kurt Vonnegut was named state author for New York in November. Vonnegut, 78, has written more than two dozen books, including *Player Piano*, *Cat's Cradle*, and *Slaughterhouse Five*. He spent much of his life in upstate New York.

JIM ANDERSON

NORTH CAROLINA. In November 7 balloting, the Democrats kept control of North Carolina's governor's mansion, but the state's 14 electoral votes went to Governor Bush.

Elections. Democratic Attorney General Mike Easley won the governor's seat being vacated by term-limited Democratic Gov. James B. Hunt, Jr. Voters returned all 12 incumbents to the U.S. House—seven Republicans and five Democrats. Voters also approved $3.1 billion in bonds for higher education, the biggest bond issue in the state's history.

Legislation. In 2000, the North Carolina legislature raised teacher pay and provided funding to "Smart Start," which provides child care, health care, and family support for preschool children. Other education measures funded a statewide report card for schools, scholarships for child-care teachers, school technology, and programs to boost student performance.

The legislature set aside $1.7 million to preserve open space in the form of farmland and increased funding for clean water to $100 million annually. The legislature also approved ways to use the state's $4.6 billion from the tobacco settlement—dividing the money between helping tobacco-dependent communities, farmers and displaced tobacco workers, and health and anti-smoking programs. A new law sought to protect tobacco companies by limiting to $25 million the amount of punitive damages out-of-state courts can force the companies to pay. To avoid losing federal highway funds, the state made it illegal for passengers in a car to drink beer or wine.

Other News. A pedestrian bridge at Lowe's Motor Speedway collapsed in May, injuring 100 people who were exiting following the conclusion of a NASCAR race. Officials said that bad grout used in manufacturing the concrete slabs had corroded the steel cables in the five-year-old span.

ELAINE STUART

NORTH DAKOTA. In November, Republicans held on to the governor's mansion; George W. Bush took the state's three electoral votes; and incumbent Democrats won their races for the U.S. House and Senate. Severe snowstorms cut power lines and stranded cattle.

Elections. Republican banker John Hoeven easily defeated Democratic state Attorney General Heidi Heitkamp for governor. Hoeven succeeded outgoing Republican Edward Schafer. During the contest, Heitkamp was diagnosed with breast cancer and underwent an operation in September, but returned to the campaign nine days later.

Incumbent Democratic Sen. Kent Conrad beat out challenger Duane Sand. Sand, recently retired from the U.S. Navy, had won the Republican nomination by campaigning on foot across 346 mi (557 km) of the state in January, braving snow and frigid temperatures.

Weather. Thousands of cattle were stranded in snowdrifts up to 8 ft (2 m) high after two ice and snowstorms pelted the Canadian border region in November. Record-cold temperatures followed the storms, which also snapped hundreds of electrical poles, cutting power in the area.

An Honored Student. A high-school science project won student Jordan Sand the Lemelson-Massachusetts Institute of Technology (MIT) High School Invention Apprenticeship for 2000. The MIT award honors young inventors. Sand, whose parents own a farm near Ellendale, devised a way to make quality newsprint and packing paper from the corn, straw, and cattails that filled the fields around his house.

JIM ANDERSON

© Karen Tam/AP/Wide World Photos

North Carolina legislators—including (left to right) Rep. Howard Hunter, Sen. Jeanne Lucas, and Rep. Mickey Michaux—considered a wide range of education programs in 2000. Several measures were enacted.

OHIO. U.S. Sen. Michael DeWine and other incumbents were returned to office in the November 2000 elections. In the courts, a jury refused to clear the name of Dr. Sam Sheppard.

Elections. Republican presidential candidate Bush won the state's 21 electoral votes. Republican Sen. Mike DeWine easily defeated a challenge by real-estate broker Theodore Celeste, brother of former Gov. Richard Celeste. In House races, 18 incumbents won reelection. In the campaign for the only open seat, state Rep. Patrick Tiberi (R) beat Democratic Columbus City Councilwoman Maryellen O'Shaughnessy.

Courts and Crime. Reviewing the case that was the basis for the TV show *The Fugitive*, a Cleveland civil jury in April rejected an attempt by Sam Reese Sheppard to prove the innocence of his father, Dr. Sam Sheppard. Dr. Sheppard was convicted in 1954 of beating his wife to death, and served ten years in prison. His case was overturned by the U.S. Supreme Court in 1966 because of the pretrial publicity. Dr. Sheppard, who died in 1970, had contended that an intruder killed his wife, and his son presented DNA evidence to support this. After a two-month trial, however, the jury deliberated less than two hours before finding against the younger Sheppard.

Jason Wagner, who pleaded guilty to kidnapping a 3-year-old neighbor and imprisoning her in his attic, was strangled in his prison cell in November. Wagner was serving 44 years to life at the Warren Correctional Institution in Lebanon. Police would not identify Wagner's cell mate or say whether or not the cell mate was a suspect.

Other News. Police barricaded parts of downtown Cincinnati and arrested 35 protesters during a three-day demonstration against the Transatlantic Business Dialogue, a meeting of corporate executives and international-trade officials. Protest leaders said the aim of the conference was to weaken rules protecting workers and the environment.

The school district in Blue Ash, a city northeast of Cincinnati, ended its two-year experiment of closing schools on the Jewish holy days of Rosh Hashanah and Yom Kippur. The district had been sued by the American Civil Liberties Union, although district officials said the decision to close during the holidays was religiously neutral, and based solely on an anticipated high absentee rate.

JIM ANDERSON

OKLAHOMA. Five incumbent U.S. congressmen won reelection. In the only open House race, Democrat Brad Carson defeated Republican Andy Ewing in the 2d District. Oklahoma's eight electoral votes went to Governor Bush.

Oklahoma City. On April 19 at 9:01 A.M. the people of Oklahoma City observed a moment of silence to mark the fifth anniversary of the bombing of the Murrah Federal Building that killed 168 people, including 19 children. Shortly afterward, President Bill Clinton led the dedication of the $29.1 million Oklahoma City National Monument on the grounds of the building. The field within the monument holds 168 stone chairs, each engraved with the name of a victim; on one side of the field is a reflecting pool.

Tulsa Race Riot. A state commission in February recommended reparations be given to 80 aged survivors of one of the nation's bloodiest race riots, which occurred in Tulsa in 1921. Forty deaths were documented, but records and interviews indicated the death toll could have been 300. The riot began when a white mob attempted to lynch a black man falsely accused of attempted rape by a white woman. The Ku Klux Klan

made an appearance, and more than 1,200 buildings were burned in the city's black Greenwood section. The commission's preliminary report recommended that $12 million be divided among the survivors.

Ice Storm. A brutal ice storm struck the state in late December, leaving 120,000 people without electricity. Gov. Frank Keating declared the state a disaster area.

JIM ANDERSON

OREGON. In a year when electing a president proved to be difficult, Oregon added to the confusion by being the only state to require voters to mail in their ballots rather than go to the polls on November 7. The positive result was an apparent increase in voter participation. But it took much longer to count the ballots, and a winner—Al Gore—was not certified until November 28. All five incumbent members of the U.S. House were reelected by significant margins.

Foster Care and Adoption. Oregon's foster care system apparently was more efficient than in other states, according to a U.S. Department of Health and Human Services report, which found that 80% of Oregon children in foster care did not return to the system after they leave, 15% better than the national average.

Responding to an issue affecting adoptees and birth mothers nationwide, Oregon voters in 1998 became the first to allow all adult adoptees access to their birth records. Birth mothers objected and challenged the law, but, in May 2000, the U.S. Supreme Court rejected an emergency request delaying the law. More than 2,200 adoptees had requested information.

Assisted Suicide. Oregon continued to be the only state with a law allowing assisted suicide. In 1999, 27 terminally ill people, mostly cancer patients, took advantage of the law and ended their lives through the use of lethal drugs. This was a significant increase from the 16 legally assisted suicides recorded in 1998.

Environment. In June, President Clinton signed a decree making a 52,000-acre (21 000-ha) site in south-central Oregon a national monument. The designation of the Cascade-Siskiyou National Monument was intended to block environmentally harmful activities such as development and mining.

Efforts also were being made to restore endangered salmon populations. Gov. John A. Kitzhaber proposed breaching four federal dams on the Snake River to better allow the salmon to complete their annual upriver trip to their spawning grounds. Previous efforts such as fish ladders failed to stop the decline in salmon numbers. Farmers and others who rely on electricity produced by the dams opposed the proposal.

KRISTI VAUGHAN

PENNSYLVANIA. The Republican Party held its 2000 National Convention in Philadelphia. Teachers in the city decided against a strike.

Politics. The Republican Party held its convention in Philadelphia from July 31 to August 3. While George W. Bush and Richard Cheney were being nominated inside, thousands of demonstrators protested outside. Most were peaceful, but 15 police officers were injured during an August 1 outburst. By the end of the convention, police had arrested 369 people; most charges were eventually dropped.

Vice-President Al Gore captured Pennsylvania's 23 electoral votes. Republican Sen. Rick Santorum easily won reelection over challenger Rep. Ron Klink, who never gained statewide Democratic support for his campaign. Republicans also triumphed in the race for Klink's House seat, with state Sen. Melissa Hart (R) taking nearly 60% of the vote over state Rep. Terry Van Horne. Todd Platts (R) captured the House seat vacated by the retirement of a fellow Republican, Rep. William Goodling.

Education. Philadelphia school teachers reached a last-minute contract agreement on October 30, allowing classes to continue for 210,000 students in the nation's seventh-largest school district. The teachers' union had opposed contract concessions, including a pay-for-performance teacher rating system.

Police and Crime. A TV news helicopter captured videotape of an African-American suspect being beaten and kicked by a cluster of Philadelphia police officers in July. The man, Thomas Jones, had allegedly stolen a car, led police on a high-speed car chase through the city, and then opened fire on officers before they were finally able to handcuff him. City officials rejected comparisons with the 1991 videotaped police beating of Rodney King in Los Angeles. Philadelphia's black leaders agreed that the incident seemed to be free of racial overtones.

In December, in what was believed to be a drug-related crime, four gunmen killed seven people in a West Philadelphia house.

JIM ANDERSON

RHODE ISLAND. In the presidential election, Rhode Island voters went for Al Gore by a margin of 61% to 32% for George W. Bush. State prison guards staged a strike for the first time in 30 years.

Elections. Lincoln C. Chafee, a Republican and son of the late U.S. Sen. John H. Chafee, was elected to the U.S. Senate by a vote of 57% to 42% over his opponent, former U.S. Rep. Robert Weygand. Chafee had filled the seat since his father's death in 1999. State Secretary of State James Langevin (D) was elected to the U.S. House of Representatives from the 2d District. He had been injured 20 years ago when he was a police cadet and a police officer showing off a new gun, unaware that there was a bullet in the chamber, fired. The bullet ricocheted and hit Langevin. U.S. Rep. Patrick Kennedy (D) was reelected easily in the 1st District to a fourth term in Congress.

Political Corruption. Rosemary Glancy, 47, Providence's deputy tax assessor and the last of six people arrested in a City Hall bribery scheme, was found guilty on seven counts, including attempted extortion, conspiracy to commit extortion, and mail fraud. She was sentenced to three years in a federal prison in Texas but was released in October following a diagnosis of liver failure.

Prison Strike. Prison guards at the state's only prison, the Adult Correctional Institutions in Cranston, walked off the job for one day before being ordered back by a Superior Court judge. The guards had not received a raise for five years and were working without a contract.

Health. Rhode Island became the first state to use federal Medicaid funds to finance lead removal. Under a program that took two years to develop, Medicaid funds were to be combined with other funds to finance the replacement of windows contaminated with lead paint. This was considered to be the most common source of lead dust in homes.

KRISTI VAUGHAN

SOUTH CAROLINA. Incumbents won easily in South Carolina in the November 2000 elections. The Confederate battle flag was lowered from the statehouse for the last time. A Confederate Navy submarine was raised after 136 years on the sea floor.

Elections. Republican presidential nominee Bush won South Carolina's eight electoral votes. Republican Rep. Floyd Spence, who was first elected to the U.S.

The Confederate Stars and Bars battle flag was removed from South Carolina's state Capitol building in Columbia after a long and bitter conflict over the flag's symbolic representation of both slavery and, to its supporters, Southern heritage.

House in 1970, won another term by defeating Democrat Jane Frederick. Rep. John Spratt, a fiscally conservative Democrat, was reelected over Republican challenger Carl Gullick. Voters approved a state initiative backed by Gov. Jim Hodges to create a state lottery that would generate up to $150 million to pay for classroom equipment, college scholarships, and free tuition for teachers working toward a master's degree.

Confederate Flag. After 38 years atop the state Capitol building in Columbia, the Confederate Stars and Bars battle flag was finally removed on July 1. As part of a legislative compromise worked out in May, a smaller flag was raised near a Confederate memorial in front of the statehouse. The flag had been the center of controversy between those who saw it as a banner of racism, and defenders who claimed it symbolized the Southern heritage and honored Confederate war dead.

Hunley Raised. As canons boomed along the shore, divers in August raised the Confederate submarine *H.L. Hunley* from 30 ft (9 m) of water outside Charleston harbor. The *Hunley* sank with eight crew members after sinking the Union blockade ship *Housatonic* in February 1864. The hand-cranked sub will remain in a conservation lab for seven years before going on display at the Charleston Museum. (*See also* PEOPLE, PLACES, AND THINGS.)

King Holiday. Governor Hodges signed a bill on May 1 making South Carolina the last state to recognize the Martin Luther King, Jr. holiday. The bill also created a permanent holiday, May 10, honoring Confederate Memorial Day.

JIM ANDERSON

Houston's Enron Field, christened by Major League Baseball's Houston Astros during an exhibition game against the New York Yankees on March, 30, 2000, was one of the latest in the recent wave of downtown ballparks to sweep the nation. The $250 million facility boasts a retractable roof, retail shops, and a running train—which many fans, incidentally, found rather annoying.

SOUTH DAKOTA. The forest fires that ravaged much of the West during the summer of 2000 did not spare South Dakota. And voters there continued to cast their ballot for the GOP.

Forest Fires. A total of 83,000 acres (33 615 ha) in the Black Hills burned during the summer as part of a string of forest fires in the West. A Wyoming woman was accused of setting the South Dakota fire.

Elections. As they have done for nearly four decades, the voters of South Dakota overwhelmingly cast their ballots for the Republican presidential candidate. Bush defeated Gore by a margin of 60% to 38%. In the one other race, incumbent U.S. Rep. John Thune, a Republican, easily won reelection to his third term. Thune is South Dakota's lone representative in the House.

Disasters. An evening gas explosion in mid-November destroyed a school building in Plankinton, injuring three people. School officials had smelled gas about two hours before the explosion and evacuated wrestlers from the gym. One person was killed and another injured when a train carrying corn derailed in Brookings in August.

Other News. The U.S. Supreme Court refused to hear a 1995 lawsuit brought by a group of Oglala Sioux girls who had claimed racial and sexual bias as the result of being required to prove their gender before playing in a 1995 basketball tournament in Rapid City.

KRISTI VAUGHAN

TENNESSEE. Tennessee continued its trend of returning incumbents to office, but did not give Vice-President Al Gore, a native son, its electoral votes.

Elections. Tennessee's nine incumbent members of the U.S. House of Representatives easily won reelection, as did U.S. Sen. Bill Frist, a Republican. Republicans succeeded in convincing independent Tennessee

voters that Gore was no longer as conservative as he was when he represented Tennessee in the U.S. House. George W. Bush took the state by a 51% to 47% vote.

Crimes and Tragedy. Frederick Williams, an off-duty firefighter, shot and killed two fellow firefighters responding to a blaze at his house in March. Williams confessed to earlier killing his wife and then setting their house on fire. The mayor of Lebanon was investigating why police mistakenly burst into the wrong home during a drug raid and shot John Adams to death. Five children were injured and two killed when their school bus was hit by a freight train at an ungated railroad crossing.

Courts. The Tennessee Supreme Court ruled in September that parts of the state's abortion law were unconstitutional because they were burdensome to women. These provisions included a two-day waiting period, mandatory counseling, and a requirement that second trimester abortions be performed in hospitals.

KRISTI VAUGHAN

TEXAS. Republican Gov. George W. Bush easily won his state's 32 electoral votes in the November 7 presidential election. He resigned as governor of Texas on December 21, and was succeeded by Republican Lt. Gov. Rick Perry. Drought and high temperatures cost Texas agricultural producers an estimated $850 million in losses. Dallas experienced 84 days without rain until September 23. Rains in October and November offered hope for farmers.

Elections. Republican U.S. Sen. Kay Bailey Hutchison won her race for reelection. The state's delegation to the U.S. House remained split—17 Democrats to 13 Republicans—with 29 incumbents, including Republican Majority Leader Dick Armey, being reelected. Attorney John Culberson (R) captured the U.S. House seat that was vacated by the retirement of Ways and

Means Chairman Bill Archer in the 7th District. Democrats kept control of the state House of Representatives, but Republicans maintained control of the state Senate. Also on November 7, San Antonio voted to add fluoride to its water.

Capital Punishment. As of November 15, Texas had executed 37 death-row inmates during the year. The U.S. Supreme Court granted a stay on November 16 to the scheduled execution of a mentally retarded inmate, Johnny Paul Penry. Governor Bush granted his first temporary stay of execution in June to a death-row inmate seeking DNA testing for a 1993 rape and murder. However, the inmate was executed in September after the DNA test failed to exonerate him. (*See also* CRIME—Capital Punishment.)

Courts. A federal appeals court gave Texas more time to fix long-standing problems in providing health care to poor children, saying the public would be better served by the delay. U.S. District Judge William Wayne Justice had given state officials an October 13 deadline to come up with a plan to fix problems in providing medical and dental care for children under Medicaid.

The wrongful death lawsuit brought by surviving members of the Branch Davidian sect was dismissed by a federal judge in September. The judge ruled that sect members and not the federal government were responsible for the 1993 deaths at Waco. About 80 members of the sect died in a fire at their compound, while in a standoff with FBI agents.

Escaped Inmates. On December 13, seven inmates broke out of the maximum-security Connally Unit prison in Kenedy, TX, southeast of San Antonio. It supposedly was the largest escape from a Texas state prison in modern history. After bluffing their way out of jail, the convicts gathered an arsenal of weapons, and gunned down a policeman, Officer Aubrey Hawkins, during the Christmas Eve robbery of a sporting-goods store. Hawkins was shot 11 times and run over by a vehicle. On Jan. 22, 2001, four of the escaped convicts were captured near a mobile-home park in Woodland, CO, where they had stayed for up to three weeks; police described the capture as peaceful. Investigators were unsure how the men got the motor home; possibly with some of the $70,000 stolen from the sporting-goods store. A fifth escapee killed himself. The last two fugitives surrendered to authorities outside a hotel in Colorado Springs, CO, on January 24.

A&M Bonfire. Texas A&M University marked the one-year anniversary of the collapse of the student bonfire structure that killed 12 persons in November 1999. A&M president Ray Bowen in June decided to postpone the 90-year bonfire tradition until 2002 and to make changes in its size and student involvement.

ELAINE STUART

UTAH. Republican Gov. Michael Leavitt won a third term in the November 7 elections, and Republican U.S. Sen. Orrin G. Hatch won a fifth term. Democrat Jim Matheson, the son of a former governor, won election to the U.S. House in a race in which the National Republican Congressional Committee spent nearly $1 million in a failed attempt to defeat him. Matheson outpolled Derek Smith, a Republican who had ousted the incumbent Republican in the primary. Republican incumbents held onto the state's other two U.S. House seats. In the presidential election, Governor Bush captured the state's five electoral votes.

Voters endorsed an initiative that makes English the official language for state business. They also approved a measure that bans police seizure of property involved in a crime when the owner does not participate in the crime. Supporters said law-enforcement agencies rou-

tinely seize property just to fatten their budgets. Voters agreed to create a trust fund for half the state's $26 million tobacco settlement and spend the rest on health and antismoking programs.

Legislation. Education was the overriding issue of the 2000 session. Legislators increased school funding by 7% and gave teachers pay raises. In the wake of two shootings by mentally ill people in Salt Lake City in 1999, the legislature enacted a law to keep the mentally ill from buying guns. The legislature also approved more funds for special courts to rule on drug offenders and passed stricter measures against drunk driving.

ELAINE STUART

VERMONT. In April 2000, Gov. Howard Dean signed the nation's first law that recognizes legal unions between same-sex couples. And the law was an obvious concern of voters in November.

Legislation. The legislature passed the gay-union law after the Vermont Supreme Court had ruled in December 1999 that the state constitution required that gay couples have legal rights. In addition to debating the gay-rights measure, the legislature also debated prescription-drug pricing, but failed to agree on price regulations. The 2000 session adjourned May 16, but the turmoil over the civil unions law continued throughout the campaign season. The legislature also allowed students a choice of public high schools in their area, enacted a safe schools law, and banned weapons from schools. The state also increased income-tax credits for low-income workers and increased the state minimum wage by 50 cents to $6.25 an hour. A new law makes Internet fraud a crime.

Elections. Democrat Al Gore won a majority of the state's presidential vote, while Green Party candidate Ralph Nader picked up 7%. Voters reelected Gov. Howard Dean, the Democrat who signed the new gay-union law, but rejected some legislators who supported the law. As a result, Republicans gained a majority in the state House for the first time in 14 years. Demo-

© Rick Bowmer/AP/Wide World Photos

In a big win for the GOP, Virginia's former Gov. George Allen, the son of former professional football coach George Allen, defeated two-term incumbent U.S. Sen. Charles Robb, the son-in-law of former President Lyndon B. Johnson.

crats retained their control of the state Senate. Voters reelected Republican U.S. Sen. James M. Jeffords and U.S. Rep. Bernard Sanders, an Independent.

ELAINE STUART

VIRGINIA. Virginia was the site of one of the Republicans' biggest victories when former Gov. George Allen defeated incumbent Sen. Charles Robb, a Democrat. New school prayer rules and the use of DNA evidence also captured headlines in 2000.

Elections. The U.S. Senate seat held by Charles Robb was seen as vulnerable by both the Republican and Democratic parties. As such, a great deal of money and effort was focused there, with sharp lines drawn between the candidates on issues such as abortion and gun control. In the end, Allen captured 52% of the vote. In the presidential race, Governor Bush captured 53% of the vote, and Republicans gained one seat in the U.S. House of Representatives when Edward Schrock defeated Jody Wagner in the 2d District. Amendments authorizing a state lottery and establishing a right to hunt and fish were approved.

School Prayer. A mandatory minute of silence, which went into effect in Virginia's schools in July, passed its first court test when the Fourth U.S. Circuit Court of Appeals refused to block students from praying on the first day of school. Further court tests were expected as ten students working with the American Civil Liberties Union said they felt pressured to participate in prayer.

DNA and Death Row. DNA evidence played a critical role in two death-row cases during 2000. In the case of Earl Washington, Jr., a mentally-retarded farmhand imprisoned for 17 years for a 1982 rape and murder, DNA evidence raised the possibility that someone else had committed the crime. Gov. James S. Gilmore III pardoned Washington in October. In September, Derek R. Barnebei was executed for the rape and murder of a college student in 1993 after DNA tests confirmed his guilt.

Environment. A study by the University of Virginia's Department of Environmental Studies found that the state's streams were continuing to be degraded by acid rain. Samples taken in 2000 and compared with those taken in 1987 showed a slowing of the degradation but an increase in the number of acidic streams.

River Dispute. The U.S. Supreme Court agreed to hear arguments in a lawsuit brought by Virginia against Maryland over jurisdiction of the Potomac River, which separates the two states. At issue was Virginia's right to extend a drinking water intake pipe halfway across the river without getting Maryland's approval.

KRISTI VAUGHAN

WASHINGTON. Voters awaiting word in late November on the outcome of its U.S. Senate race could not get their news from the major Seattle dailies, as workers at both papers went on strike. Elsewhere, the year was one for buildings, as new landmarks were erected and old ones brought tumbling down.

Elections. Washington was one of several states where hotly contested congressional races took several days to decide. The Senate race between Republican incumbent Slade Gorton and Democratic challenger Maria Cantwell, a dot-com millionaire who financed her own campaign, was not decided until December 1. A recount confirmed Cantwell's victory. In the presidential race, Vice-President Gore won Washington's 11 electoral votes.

Seattle's Buildings. One Seattle landmark, the Kingdome sports stadium, crashed to the ground in a planned implosion in early 2000. A new landmark was

In Washington state, the U.S. Senate race mirrored the drama of the Bush-Gore contest, as Democrat Maria Cantwell, a dot-com millionaire, beat incumbent Slade Gorton. It took until December 1 before her victory was officially declared.

established with the opening of the Experience Music Project (EMP), and a third, the Space Needle, received a $20 million renovation. The Kingdome, home to the Mariners, Seahawks, and SuperSonics, was demolished to make way for a new $430 million football and soccer stadium. The Seattle Mariners had opened a $517 million baseball park in 1999. The $240 million EMP was the creation of Microsoft cofounder Paul Allen, who originally had planned a simple gallery to show off his collection of Jimi Hendrix paraphernalia (*see also* ARCHITECTURE).

Disasters. A wildfire burned across three waste sites at the Hanford Nuclear Reservation in July, but state and federal officials said they detected no radioactive releases. The fire destroyed more than 25 houses and forced the evacuation of some 7,000 people.

Environment. A 200,000-acre (81 000-ha) stretch of the Columbia River known as the Hanford Reach was designated a national monument by President Clinton. The designation protects the land from development. Plum Creek Timber Co. became the largest private timberland owner in July when it agreed to acquire Timber Co., an operating group of Georgia Pacific.

KRISTI VAUGHAN

WEST VIRGINIA. The state's five presidential electoral votes went to the GOP on November 7, but voters turned out Republican Gov. Cecil Underwood, in favor of Democrat Robert Wise, Jr., a U.S. representative. At 78, Underwood was the nation's oldest governor. Wise received support from U.S. Sen. Robert C. Byrd, a Democrat, who was reelected. A Republican state legislator won the congressional seat that Wise vacated for the governorship. In the gubernatorial race, independent Denise Giardina won enough votes to form a new Mountain Party in the state, which will gain an automatic ballot spot in 2004.

Legislation. The legislature required special colored driver's licenses for drivers under age 18, to make it easier for store clerks to tell if a person is old enough to buy tobacco or liquor. Another new law provides for graduated licenses for young drivers, requiring them to drive under supervision before earning full driving rights. Higher-education reforms seek to make the state's governance of colleges more effective and accountable. Racing-car fans will be able to obtain special issue NASCAR state license plates. A new law bans recognition of same-sex marriages in the state. Over the vehement objections of a number of environmental groups, a tax break was given to companies that mine coal from thin-seamed resources.

ELAINE STUART

The Democratic Party picked up one governorship on Nov. 7, 2000. In West Virginia, voters went for the younger candidate, ousting Republican Gov. Cecil Underwood, 78, in favor of U.S. Rep. Robert Wise, Jr., 52. The winning Democrat had been a member of the U.S. House since January 1983.

© Bob Bird/AP/Wide World Photos

WISCONSIN. The late campaign efforts of Vice-President Gore paid off as he narrowly defeated his Republican challenger in Wisconsin.

Politics. The Wisconsin presidential race was particularly difficult for Gore, because Green Party candidate Ralph Nader won 4% of the vote. The vice-president topped Bush by fewer than 6,000 votes. Republican Gov. Tommy G. Thompson had campaigned extensively for the Bush-Cheney ticket—and was rewarded by being nominated secretary of health and human resources by the president-elect. (Thompson's nomination was ultimately approved by the U.S. Senate in January 2001.) With Thompson's departure, Lt. Gov. Scott McCallum, a Republican, would be sworn in as Wisconsin's new governor.

Incumbents were returned to office in the state's nine U.S. House Districts, and incumbent Democrat Herbert Kohl was reelected to his U.S. Senate seat.

Schools. In July the Wisconsin Supreme Court upheld the state's school-aid formula, which had been challenged by more than 100 school districts. The school districts claimed the formula favored students in districts with higher property tax revenues.

Scandal and Crime. Four-term Milwaukee Mayor John O. Norquist announced in December that he had had an affair with a woman who worked for him for five years. Norquist, who was married, said the affair was consensual. The woman, Marilyn Figueroa, disagreed, and accused the mayor of sexual harassment and racial discrimination.

A large marijuana bust resulted in the arrest of two brothers, ages 74 and 80, accused of growing marijuana on the farm of one of the brothers. Police seized about 500 plants and nearly 100 lbs (45 kg) of marijuana.

Archaeological Find. An amateur archaeologist revealed that two years earlier he had found an Indian cave in southeastern Wisconsin containing drawings of Indian hunters that date back more than 1,000 years.

KRISTI VAUGHAN

WYOMING. Wildfires and budget woes plagued Wyoming in 2000, as Gov. Jim Geringer attempted to tackle such long-term issues as increased school costs, an aging population, and uncertain revenues from the mineral industry.

Elections. The home state of Republican vice-presidential candidate Dick Cheney was solidly behind the GOP ticket, giving 69% of its popular vote to the Bush-Cheney ticket, as well as the state's three electoral-college votes. U.S. Sen. Craig Thomas, a Republican, easily won reelection, as did incumbent Rep. Barbara Cubin, also a Republican.

Sacred Cows. University of Wyoming law professor Debra Donohue learned just how much residents of Wyoming value the state's livestock industry when she published a book that argued that livestock should be banned from grazing on arid federal land because the practice could harm native vegetation and wildlife, degrade water quality, and allow for invasions of exotic plant species. Infuriated livestock interests immediately demanded—though unsuccessfully—that the law school be closed.

Environment. Hunters were warned of a fatal brain disease, similar to mad cow disease, that had been found in elk and deer in Wyoming and Colorado. Although there was no evidence that the disease, chronic wasting disease (CWD), could be transmitted to humans, hunters were advised to use rubber gloves when cutting up carcasses and to avoid animals obviously suffering from CWD.

Devils Tower National Monument was closed over the Labor Day holiday weekend as the result of a wildfire that plagued the area. Low-risk inmates from the Wyoming Department of Corrections were among those who had been called upon to volunteer to fight the summer's wildfires in Wyoming, South Dakota, and other nearby states.

KRISTI VAUGHAN

Stocks and Bonds

The runaway bull market for U.S. stocks screeched to a halt in 2000. Computer and telecommunications stocks with big stakes in the Internet led the market indexes lower, ending a string of five consecutive two-digit annual gains.

The sell-off was attributed to many influences, ranging from rising energy prices to the uncertainties of a presidential election. But in simplest terms, analysts said a Federal Reserve campaign, dating back to mid-1999, to restrain economic growth helped chill the high spirits that had prevailed on Wall Street since the mid-1990s.

The Dow Jones average of 30 industrials dropped 6.2% from its 1999 close to l0,786.85. Standard & Poor's 500-stock composite index fell 10.1% to 1,320.28. The declines of those two broad indicators were modest, however, by comparison with the composite index of the Nasdaq market, home to many "technology" stocks, which tumbled 39.3%. After setting record highs above 5,000 in early March, the Nasdaq index plunged 50% by late November.

Declines of 70%, 80%, or 90% were common among stocks of small companies specializing in Internet businesses such as selling to consumers via sites on the World Wide Web. Shares of one heavily advertised Internet company, priceline.com, fell from $104 to just more than $2; Yahoo! dropped from above $250 to less than $40; and Amazon.com from $113 to below $20.

To some observers, this was simply the collapse of a speculative "bubble," a classic demonstration of pie-in-the-sky dreams colliding with reality. But many analysts said stock prices overall also were adjusting to the prospect of a significant economic slowdown induced by the Federal Reserve. The U.S. central bank, which had raised short-term interest rates three times in 1999, adopted another three increases in the first half of 2000. The Federal Reserve's target rate on federal funds, or overnight loans among financial institutions, rose a full percentage point to 6.5%.

Bonds. Not all U.S. interest rates rose, however. In the waning weeks of the year, yields on long-term Treasury bonds dropped below 5.7%, about a half-point below 12 months earlier. Other Treasury notes and bonds with maturities from two to 30 years also rose in price, pushing yields lower, as the U.S. government's budget surplus expanded dramatically. With the government taking in more in tax revenues than it was spending, the Treasury bought back some outstanding bonds early and cut back

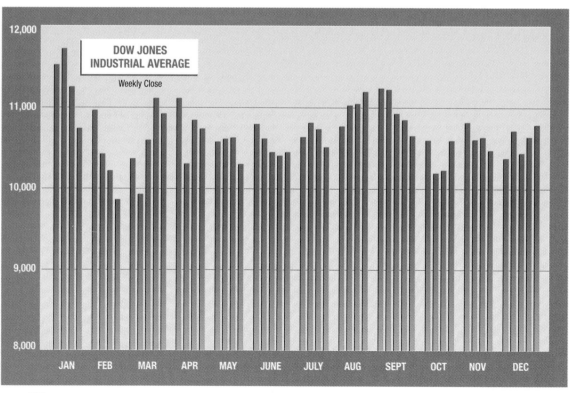

on new ones it issued. Some analysts even began looking for other securities to serve as a benchmark standard for the bond market as the event activity in long-term Treasuries dwindled to the point where T-bonds could no longer serve that function.

It was far different in the market for lower-quality corporate "junk" bonds, which had thrived in the 1990s, but now were suffering fallout from the "tech wreck" in the stock market and showing signs of slowing economic growth. Mutual funds specializing in high-yield corporate bonds showed a loss late in the year of more than 8%, as tracked by Morningstar.

Mutual Funds. Stock funds also had a rocky year, with a few Internet funds dropping 50% or more. For much of the year, diversified managed funds could at least boast that, on average, they were outperforming index funds. But that edge provided little comfort in the general decline that swept through the market in the autumn. Even so, investors kept putting money into funds, showing a willingness to take a long view and to pursue strategies of regular investing through vehicles such as tax-deferred 401(k) retirement plans sponsored by employers. In the first nine months of the year, according to the Investment Company Institute, stock funds attracted a net inflow of $272 billion from investors, more than they had ever received in any full year.

Money-market funds investing in interest-bearing securities with lives of a few days to a year also prospered, drawing inflows of just under $60 billion from January through September. Yields on money funds climbed above 6% in many cases. Some investors also looked to money funds as a haven from stock declines. Bond funds, by contrast, experienced outflows as their popularity waned. Investors in Treasury bonds, for example, often prefer to buy those securities direct.

On the whole, the fund industry seemed to hold its own as it coped with weaker markets and new competitive threats from the likes of exchange-traded funds, a type of index-based portfolio whose shares can be traded throughout the day. Most traditional mutual funds, by contrast, are priced just once a day, typically as of 4:00 P.M. New York time. Assets of exchange-traded funds climbed past $50 billion, still small compared with the $6.8 trillion in conventional mutual funds.

World Markets. International stock funds, for the most part, posted even bigger losses than domestic stock funds as markets in Asia, Europe, and elsewhere generally struggled through a dismal year. As of early December, the great majority of world markets showed losses exceeding 10%, as stated in U.S. dollars. Singapore was down 30%, Japan 24%, Brazil 23%, Mexico 19%, Hong Kong 18%, Britain 18%, Germany 14%, Australia 13%, and France 12%. One notable exception was Canada, up 2% in U.S. dollar terms and more than 8% higher in its local currency, benefiting from strength in energy stocks as the world price of oil rose.

The jump in energy costs jolted many world economies. Near-term crude oil futures on the New York Mercantile Exchange shot up from $23.70 a barrel in early April to $37.80 in late September. Analysts said higher costs for motor and heating fuel acted as a drag on economic activity in many parts of the world.

European markets also contended with weakness in the euro, the currency of the European Union (EU), which continued the disappointing performance that followed its introduction in January 1999. When it hit a new low of $0.825 U.S. in September, the euro showed a loss of 29% against the dollar, and 33% against the Japanese yen, since its inception.

For all the year's financial traumas, financial giants around the world were still eager to place large bets on future prosperity, as evidenced by their takeover bids for U.S. brokers, banks, and money-management firms. The big buyers on Wall Street included Credit Suisse Group of Zurich, which acquired Donaldson Lufkin & Jenrette, and another Swiss banker, UBS, which snapped up PaineWebber. The blue-chip bank J.P. Morgan & Co. said "yes" to a suitor closer to home, the U.S.-based Chase Manhattan Corporation.

In deals for U.S. fund managers, the Italian bank UniCredito Italiano agreed to buy Pioneer Group; France's CDC Asset Management went after Nvest; and Old Mutual, South Africa's biggest insurer, set its sights on United Asset Management Corporation.

Even the familiar look of the stock tables seemed to change as U.S. markets moved from price quotes in whole numbers and fractions to decimal dollar-and-cents figures. The gradual changeover began in 2000. The Securities and Exchange Commission (SEC) ordered that it be completed by April 9, 2001.

CHET CURRIER, *"Bloomberg News"*

Sudan

In 2000, Lt. Gen. Omar Hassan Ahmed al-Bashir remained the president of Sudan, but there were significant changes in the regime's structure. The seemingly endless civil war dominated Sudanese affairs.

Domestic Affairs. President Bashir used the state of emergency that he had declared in December 1999 to remove Hassan al-Turabi, the major ideologue of the regime since it came to power in 1989, from all public offices. Turabi was relieved of his position as secretary-general of the government's political party, the National Congress, and in June formed his own opposition party, the Popular Congress. The government stopped support for the Popular Arab and Islamic Conference, the Islamist regime's international organization under Turabi's leadership. By the end of the year, there were reports of a continuing process of removal of allies of Turabi from governmental posts. Nevertheless, Turabi and his supporters remained free to operate within the country.

Former opposition members of older northern Sudanese political parties continued the process of reconciliation with the Bashir regime. Sadiq al-Mahdi, head of the Umma Party and former prime minister, engaged in discussions with both Bashir and Turabi. Mahdi's party suspended participation in the National Democratic Alliance (NDA), the leading coalition of antiregime groups. Zayn al-Abidin al-Hindi, the secretary-general of the Democratic Unionist Party (DUP) inside Sudan, announced his support for Bashir in future presidential elections, while Muhammad Uthman al-Mirghani, the head of the DUP, remained the leader of the NDA in exile. Parliamentary and presidential elections occurred in December, with Bashir being reelected.

Civil War. During 2000 there were no significant changes in either the diplomatic or the military positions in the civil war. The most visible continuing fighting took place in the Unity Province, site of the major oil-producing areas in the southern region. Southern forces that were allied with the government fought major battles with the Sudan People's Liberation Army (SPLA) and other southern groups in a complex, ongoing struggle for control of the oil fields. Fighting continued in other areas as well, but neither side made any significant gains, strengthening the view that military victory was not possible for either the government or opposition forces.

```
┌─────────────────────────────────────────────┐
│         SUDAN • Information Highlights        │
│ Official Name: Republic of the Sudan.         │
│ Location: Northeast Africa.                    │
│ Area: 967,494 sq mi (2 505 810 km²).          │
│ Population (2000 est.): 35,079,814.           │
│ Chief Cities (1993 census): Khartoum, the     │
│   capital, 947,483; Omdurman, 1,271,403;      │
│   Khartoum North, 700,887; Port Sudan,        │
│   308,195.                                     │
│ Government: Head of state and government,      │
│   Omar Hassan Ahmed al-Bashir, president      │
│   (took power June 30, 1989). Legislature     │
│   (unicameral)— National Assembly.            │
│ Monetary Unit: Pound (1,670.0000 pounds       │
│   equal U.S.$1, Dec. 31, 2000).               │
│ Gross Domestic Product (1999 est. U.S.$):     │
│   $32,600,000,000 (purchasing power parity).  │
│ Foreign Trade (1999 est. U.S.$): Imports,     │
│   $1,400,000,000; exports, $580,000,000.      │
└─────────────────────────────────────────────┘
```

Negotiations among the various parties continued. The long-standing mediating role of the Inter-Governmental Authority on Development (IGAD), a trade group of African states, continued. Diplomatic initiatives by Egypt and Libya created opportunities for discussions, but these talks primarily involved northern Sudanese opposition groups and the government. The NDA held its second general conference in September in Massawa, Eritrea, and discussions involved condemnation of the Umma Party for withdrawal from the alliance and authorization of the NDA to engage in reconciliation talks with the Khartoum government.

International Affairs. The Bashir government continued to develop better relations with a number of countries, circumventing sanctions and restrictions set by the United States. Egyptian and Libyan initiatives in promoting national-reconciliation discussions among Sudanese reflected improved relations between Sudan and its northern neighbors. Despite some border tensions, relations with Eritrea and Ethiopia were better than in previous years.

In July, Canada reestablished diplomatic relations with Sudan. Despite pressure from the United States, Canada imposed no sanctions on Talisman Energy Inc., the Canadian oil company involved in developing Sudanese oil production. However, attempts to block stock offerings by Chinese oil companies involved in Sudanese projects met with some success.

The U.S. special envoy, Harry Johnston, discussed easing sanctions and reopening the U.S. Embassy in Khartoum. However, the United States maintained its strong condemnation of human-rights violations by the Sudanese government, and slavery remained a major concern among U.S. political leaders. The United States successfully defeated the Sudanese bid for a seat on the United Nations Security Council.

JOHN O. VOLL, *Georgetown University*

Sweden

The Swedish economy performed with strength in 2000. As a result, Sweden's Social Democratic government planned to cut income taxes moderately in 2001. Denmark's rejection of the euro, the European Union's (EU's) common currency, could postpone a Swedish referendum on the issue until 2005. Meanwhile, the new economy made strides in Sweden, posting key information technology (IT) figures comparable to those of the United States. Partial privatization of Telia, the state telecommunications corporation, was implemented, but disappointed investors.

Politics and European Affairs. Swedish opposition to joining the euro rose in reaction to the Danish "no" vote in a September referendum on the question. A November poll revealed that only 31% of Swedes favored participation in the euro—the lowest support in four years. Officially, Swedish policy remained unmoved by the Danish vote, and the government planned for a referendum on Swedish government policy remained unmoved by the Danish vote, and the government planned for a referendum on Swedish participation when feasible. In the spring, at a special congress of the Social Democratic Party, delegates voted 234 to 113 in favor of Prime Minister Göran Persson's proposal to adopt the euro. Polls, however, showed a 2% lead among "no" voters. A referendum is unlikely before mandatory

general elections in 2002, and members of the financial markets view 2005 as the earliest possible target date.

Sweden wants the EU to be ready for new members by 2003, and although Sweden is not a member of the North Atlantic Treaty Organization (NATO), its government was supporting the aspirations of Estonia, Latvia, and Lithuania to join.

Sweden maintains the highest tax ratio among industrialized countries, 57.8% of gross domestic product (GDP). The International Monetary Fund (IMF) warned that unless tax rates came down, long-term growth would be stymied. Finance Minister Bosse Ringholm defended the moderate tax cut (U.S. $1.3 billion), or the equivalent of $300 to $500 per worker, by trumpeting the need to cap consumption to prevent overheating of the economy and to continue to reduce public debt. Further tax cuts were promised, provided budget surpluses could be maintained above 2% of GDP. Spending was increased, especially on child care and education. This was done partly to gain the support of the Left Party, the successor of the Swedish Communist Party.

The Social Democratic government commanded only a minority in parliament, and a majority of Social Democratic voters indicated they wanted the Left Party to join the government. That party's leader, Gudrun Schyman, was not asked to join, but it remained a possibility following the 2002 elections. Though Schyman is a moderate, the anticapitalist platform of the Left Party would be difficult.

Economy. The Swedish economy showed unexpected strength in 2000, with the GDP growth estimated above 4%. Unemployment fell to 5.1%, a full percentage point less than in 1999. Volvo was not allowed by the European Commission to merge with its Swedish rival, Scania, but instead bought the truck division of French Renault.

The new economy made strong inroads in the Swedish economy, with software investments accounting for 10% of all investments in the 1996–99 period, compared with 11% in the United States. IT investments in the same period were estimated at about 25% of the total, similar to that of the United States, the global leader in the new economy. Telia, the state monopoly, was partially privatized, but investors were disappointed as telecoms and IT share prices fell sharply in the fall.

LEIF BECK FALLESEN
Editor in Chief, "Boersen," Copenhagen

SWEDEN • Information Highlights

Official Name: Kingdom of Sweden.

Location: Northern Europe.

Area: 173,732 sq mi (449 964 km²).

Population (2000 est.): 8,873,052.

Chief Cities (Dec. 31, 1998 est.): Stockholm, the capital, 736,113; Göteborg, 459,593; Malmö, 254,904.

Government: *Head of state,* Carl XVI Gustaf, king (acceded Sept. 1973). *Head of government,* Göran Persson, prime minister (took office March 1996). *Legislature* (unicameral)—Riksdag.

Monetary Unit: Krona (9.4158 kronor equal U.S.$1, Dec. 31, 2000).

Gross Domestic Product (1999 est. U.S.$): $184,000,000,000 (purchasing power parity).

Economic Indexes (1999, 1990 = 100): *Consumer Prices,* all items, 124.3; food, 98.8. *Industrial Production,* 129.7.

Foreign Trade (1999 U.S.$): *Imports,* $68,431,000,000; *exports,* $84,771,000,000.

Switzerland

National referenda, Holocaust victims' claims settlements, and the annnouncement of the resignation of Adolf Agi from the cabinet dominated Swiss concerns in 2000.

Referenda Issues. On March 12, Swiss voters approved plans for judicial reform, but rejected proposals to limit the processing period for initiative procedures to one year, ban sperm donation and in-vitro fertilization, establish quotas guaranteeing women a percentage of seats in parliament and public offices, and reduce traffic levels for environmental purposes. On May 21, 67.2% of those voting indicated support for seven bilateral agreements improving Switzerland's relations with the European Union (EU). On November 26, voters overwhelmingly rejected a proposal to cut the military budget by one-third ($1 billion).

On September 24, voters disapproved measures to foster development of renewable-energy resources. They (63.7%) also rejected a proposal to restrict foreigners living in Switzerland to 18% of the total population. The latter initiative, sponsored by the Swiss People's Party, reflected increased resentment toward immigrants from the Balkan states and Turkey. In March, voters in the city of Emmen had turned down 48 individual applications for citizenship from former residents of Turkey or Yugoslavia.

Political Dichotomy. Rising anti-immigrant sentiment and a shift by the increasingly popular People's Party to an ultraconservative, isolationist platform were counterbalanced by widespread support for the EU treaties, and the filing on March 6 of a 125,000–signature petition supporting Swiss membership in the United Nations (UN), ensuring a national referendum on this issue. An internationalist outlook also was evidenced by demands that English, rather than one of the four official languages of Switzerland, be taught as the primary "foreign" language in schools.

On October 18, Swiss President and Defense Minister Adolf Ogi announced that he would resign from the ruling seven-member cabinet on December 31. An advocate of Swiss membership in the EU and the UN, Ogi's views no longer coincided with those of the increasingly right-wing conservative Swiss People's Party, which he represented in the cabinet. His action threatened the continued existence of the four-party coalition that has cooperatively governed Switzerland since December 1959.

Holocaust Victims' Settlements. Negotiations regarding the 1998 $1.25 billion compensation agreement for victims of the Holocaust during World War II continued. On May 4 the two major Swiss banks, Credit Suisse and UBS, agreed to open records of 2.1 million accounts to facilitate the search for legitimate claimants. The final settlement was approved by U.S. Federal Court Judge Edward Korman on July 26, but protection and release from future claims was denied to Swiss banks who had not yet made their records available. On September 11, Judge Korman issued a plan for distributing the funds—$800 million for those providing evidence of family-held World War II Swiss bank accounts, and $450 million to other groups of Holocaust victims.

On May 20 the Swiss government agreed to pay $115,000 to the children of a couple who had been denied refuge in Switzerland in 1942, and had subsequently died in a Nazi concentration camp. The government also formally apologized to the family, the first admission of the wrongfulness of its World War II policy.

Banking Scandals. During 2000, Swiss bank investigators continued to uncover alleged cases of international bank fraud. The largest suspect account in Swiss banking history, $670 million, was held by the family of deceased Nigerian military ruler, Gen. Sani Abacha. On June 6 the general's son, Mohammed, was indicted by a Swiss court on charges of money laundering and corruption, and in July the first of several payments returning the funds was made to the Nigerian government.

PAUL C. HELMREICH
Wheaton College, MA

Syria

The year 2000 was one of change in Syria; questions remained, however, as to the extent of the change. The year was split neatly into two by the death on June 10 of Hafiz al-Assad (*see* OBITUARIES), for 30 years the president of Syria. He was succeeded by his son, Bashar al-Assad (*see* BIOGRAPHY), in a fashion so organized that it resembled dynastic succession rather than a political process. Bashar had been the heir presumptive since the accidental death of his elder brother, Basil, in 1994.

An Era Ends. Hafiz al-Assad had ruled Syria for so long, and had so undeniably given it stability—in marked contrast to the preceding series of political upheavals—that a future without him was dreaded. He had been in ill health for nearly 20 years, and this had increased apprehension, not only among his own countrymen. This generalized fear was perhaps the real source of an extraordinary rumor that circulated throughout the Middle East in 1999-2000. It was suggested that there was a plot by the Muslim Brotherhood, the ultraconservative Islamic order, to assassinate Assad; and that all sorts of chaotic disorders would follow throughout the Middle East. The rumor attracted the attention of the Central Intelligence Agency (CIA), and, like all the best of rumors, had a certain plausibility: The Muslim Brotherhood detested Assad, especially after he orchestrated the massacre of thousands of its followers at Homs in 1982.

The reality of what did happen was utterly different from such prognostications. Hafiz al-Assad died a natural death on June 10, and a series of steps, deftly executed, made Bashar the president of Syria. There was a substantial change in the Syrian constitution to permit Bashar to become president at the young age of 34; he was made chief of the Baath Party; and appointed president by the Syrian parliament, an action confirmed overwhelmingly by a popular vote on June 25. Bashar's uncle, Rifaat, who had been expected to oppose Bashar's succession or even prevent it, issued some pronouncements of protest, but these were totally ineffective.

If the succession proved flawlessly smooth, this was undoubtedly due to a series of wise steps taken earlier, presumably by the elder and the younger Assad acting in concert. Begun in earlier years, these were accentuated and became more numerous in the first half of 2000. Bashar strove to cut

the red tape—frequently linked to corruption—that hampered economic development. Computer access and use were facilitated. It became legal to own satellite dishes. Some cautious moves suggested that greater political freedom was coming, and one aspect of policy that was deliberately identified with Bashar's influence was the attack on corruption—a popular cause. In addition, Gen. Ali Duba, in charge of Syria's internal security since 1974, had retired in January and was replaced by Gen. Hassan Khalil who had been involved in negotiations with Israel for a period of time.

The most spectacular sign of reforms coming along under Bashar's influence was the appointment on March 14 by Hafiz al-Assad of a new prime minister and cabinet. The president named Muhammad Miru, formerly the governor of Aleppo and reckoned an able administrator, as prime minister. There were 22 new figures in the new administration, but the foreign minister and other leading figures were carried over from the previous cabinet.

An Era Begins. Mourning among the Syrian people for the deceased "lion of Syria" was intense and apparently sincere. In the first six months during which Bashar governed Syria, the new president's policies continued cautiously along the same lines already sketched. It was clear that, though the portents of reform were encouraging, there would be no rapid changes. Calm prevailed. The Syrian Social National Party, technically illegal since the 1970s, was permitted to raise its head, and some discussions between its leader and the governmental Baath Party occurred. Freedom of public debate increased. Bashar also released more than 600 political prisoners—out of a supposed total of some 1,500. The

---

SYRIA • Information Highlights

Official Name: Syrian Arab Republic.
Location: Southwest Asia.
Area: 71,498 sq mi (185 180 km²).
Population (2000 est.): 16,305,659.
Chief Cities (September 1994 census): Damascus, the capital, 1,394,322; Aleppo, 1,582,930; Homs, 540,133.
Government: *Head of state,* Bashar al-Assad, president (took office July 2000). *Head of government,* Muhammad Miru, prime minister (took office March 2000). *Legislature* (unicameral)—People's Council.
Monetary Unit: Pound (45.0000 pounds equal U.S. $1, Dec. 4, 2000).
Gross Domestic Product (1999 est. U.S.$): $42,200,000,000 (purchasing power parity).
Economic Index (Damascus, 1999; 1990 = 100): *Consumer Prices,* all items, 177.0; food, 156.0.
Foreign Trade (1999 U.S.$): *Imports,* $3,832,000,000; *exports,* $3,464,000,000.

amnesty celebrated the 30th anniversary of the coup that brought Bashar's father to power in 1970.

Foreign Relations. If a wind of change appeared to be blowing through Syrian domestic policies, no such modification was observable in the country's foreign relations—especially regarding Israel. In Bashar's few public pronouncements on relations with Israel, he insisted on the return of the entire Golan Heights as the precondition of any negotiations. This was the line his father had invariably taken, and the one that made Hafiz's one-day meeting with U.S. President Bill Clinton in Geneva on March 26 entirely futile.

Syrian relations with other Arab states, not always friendly under Hafiz, were clearly a high priority with Bashar. One symbol of this was a new trade agreement concluded with Jordan.

ARTHUR CAMPBELL TURNER
University of California, Riverside

Taiwan

In Taiwan, the year 2000 began with remarkable and unanticipated political change; it ended in political turmoil reminiscent of a badly scripted soap opera. Winning the island republic's second presidential election in March, Chen Shui-bian (*see* BIOGRAPHY) and the opposition Democratic Progressive Party (DPP) overturned 55 years of Nationalist Party rule. Their victory marked the first time a political opposition had taken power in a Chinese democracy. Nine months later, however, Chen and his government were under assault, with the threat of a recall vote being considered by the national legislature, where the Nationalist Party holds a majority of seats.

Inexperience and Indecision. Chen's slim victory brought into power the DPP, a party with 15 years of experience as a vociferous and often disruptive opposition, but no experience at all in governing at the national level. Chen chose Tang Fei, a widely respected military figure and a member of the Nationalist Party, as his prime minister. Not so wisely, the actions of the president during his first months in office created the impression of inexperience and indecisiveness.

A midsummer disaster in which construction workers were marooned and ultimately drowned in the flooding Pachang Creek resulted in Chen's government being blamed for the deaths; Tang Fei offered his resignation. Chen rejected Tang's offer, but accepted the resignation of Vice-Prime Minister Yu Hsi-kun.

A decision announced in late October seriously undermined Chen's credibility and, indeed, jeopardized his tenure in office. Having campaigned on a platform that included opposition to the further development of nuclear power on the island, Chen was confronted with the problem of what to do with a $3 billion nuclear plant under construction near Taipei. He had pledged to halt its construction, but waffled after taking office. The adverse effects of this indecision precipitated a second resignation by Tang Fei. This time his resignation was accepted, and a new cabinet was appointed. Tang's deputy, Chang Chun-hsiung, was named prime minister.

Chen finally made up his mind on the nuclear plant in October, and blundered seriously. In a televised fence-mending meeting with his Nationalist Party election rival, Lien Chan, he pledged to consult with Lien and the Nationalists before making a final decision on the plant construction. Then, less than an hour after the meeting ended, his newly appointed prime minister decided to terminate the project.

The Opposition Overreacts. This unfortunate sequence of events caused Chen's political opponents to overreact. Nationalist legislators decided to initiate a recall of the president and passed a series of procedural rules to make it as difficult as possible for their supporters to defect. The grounds for the recall were the constitutionally ambiguous question of whether the president had the authority to reverse the legislature's decision to build the nuclear plant.

Problems arose with the recall movement almost as soon as it was proposed by

---

TAIWAN • Information Highlights

Official Name: Taiwan.
Location: Island off the southeastern coast of mainland China.
Area: 13,892 sq mi (35 980 km²).
Population (2000 est.): 22,191,087.
Chief Cities (Dec. 31, 1998 est.): Taipei, the capital, 2,639,939; Kaohsiung, 1,462,302; Taichung, 917,788; Tainan, 721,832; Panchiaio, 520,286.
Government: *Head of state,* Chen Shui-bian, president (took office May 20, 2000). *Head of government,* Chang Chun-hsiung, prime minister (appointed October 4, 2000). *Legislature* (unicameral)—Legislative Yuan; (unicameral)—National Assembly.
Monetary Unit: New Taiwan dollar (33.0800 NT dollars equal U.S. $1, Dec. 4, 2000).
Gross Domestic Product (1999 est. U.S.$): $357,000,000,000 (purchasing power parity).

A Taiwanese stock investor watched—with some horror—the graph on his monitor as the volatile stock exchange closed 161.07 points down in early October. The market lost 50% of its value in 2000, but Taiwan's economy was strong.

120 opposition politicians. First, although Chen's decision on the nuclear plant brought opposition parties together, ill feelings still ran high in the Nationalist Party over James Soong's decision to run against Lien Chan, the party's designated candidate in the presidential election. Recalling that defeat, in turn, caused soberer minds among the Nationalists to reflect that a successful recall of Chen could result in a Soong presidency. Moreover, public opinion was not supportive of the recall.

As the recall movement began to unravel, the opposition changed its tactics, alleging that Chen was involved in a sexual relationship with a young female aide; Chen denied the allegations. As the year drew to a close, the situation turned bizarre: People First Party legislator Chin Huei-chu released a series of documents she alleged were copies of a series of letters exchanged between Chen and China's President Jiang Zemin, during the run-up to the March election. The letters purported to show that Chen had agreed to abandon his party's support of Taiwan independence in exchange for a payment of $5 million from Jiang. Government officials on both sides of the Taiwan Strait denounced the documents as highly implausible forgeries.

Cross-Strait Relations. From the perspective of the Taiwan side of the Strait, there was scant progress in sorting out the fraught relationship with the government in Beijing—a dilemma that has been raging for years. There was little reaction to mainland blustering in advance of the March elections, and differences among opposing candidates' stances on the question appeared to have very little effect on the outcome of the election. Chen distanced himself from his party's pro-independence position early in the campaign, and proposed an early resumption of cross-Straits talks as soon as he was inaugurated. But he refused to accept Beijing's precondition for resuming the talks, which was that he accept its "one China" position—in other words, that he capitulate before he began to negotiate. Instead, he proposed a return to the ambiguous situation of the early 1999s, in which both sides adopted a "one China" stance. His proposal pleased no one: Beijing rejected it, members of his own party reasserted their pro-independence position, and the opposition proposed that he relinquish control over cross-Straits negotiations to a new government of its choosing.

Economic Consequences. Although the Taiwan stock market reacted adversely to the year's political events, losing 50% of its value, the economy itself turned in a strong performance. Growth in gross domestic product (GDP) was projected to exceed 6.5% for the year. The consumer price index rose just under 1%, foreign trade was forecast to exceed that in 1999 by more than 25%, and foreign-exchange reserves stood at $113 billion at the end of the third quarter. Taiwan's investments in the mainland economy totaled in excess of $40 billion.

JOHN BRYAN STARR, *Brown University*

Tajikistan

During 2000, Tajikistan elected both houses of its new legislature, the Supreme Assembly (Majlisi Oli), which was established by the 1999 constitution. Elections for the lower house, the Assembly of Representatives (Majlisi Namoyandagon), were held on February 27 and March 12, 2000. Of the 63 seats at stake, 41 were allocated to candidates running as individuals, and the remaining 22 to political parties. Six parties participated in the elections.

The People's Democratic Party of Tajikistan (PDPT), headed by President Imomali Rahmonov, won more than 60% of the February vote. The Communist Party of Tajikistan finished second, with more than 20%, and the Islamic Rebirth Party received under 8%. The remaining parties each received less than 5% of the vote, and therefore did not win any seats allocated to parties. The United Nations (UN), among others, criticized the elections as unfair. Elections for the 33-member upper house, the National Assembly (Majlisi Milli), were held in March. Twenty-five of the seats were chosen by local assemblies; the other eight were appointed by the president.

Moving Forward. The elections marked a major turning point for Tajikistan. The National Reconciliation Commission (NRC)—established in accordance with the 1997 peace agreement, which ended Tajikistan's civil war—declared its mission complete once the Supreme Assembly had been elected, and finished its work in March. The UN mission to monitor the implementation of the peace agreement concluded its activities in May. The peacekeeping force established for Tajikistan in 1993 by Russia and several Central Asian states also ended operations. Russia continued its military presence in the country.

President Rahmonov removed Prime Minister Yahyo Azimov and appointed Oqil Oqilov to the post in December 1999. Azimov was named minister of economy and foreign economic relations in March 2000.

Census and Currency. Tajikistan's first census since 1989 was held in January. It showed the country's population had risen to about 6.1 million, and that 437,000 people had emigrated since the previous census.

The government introduced a new currency, the somoni (2.05 somoni = U.S.$1), in October, to replace the Tajik ruble, introduced in 1995. The exchange of the old currency for the new was scheduled to continue

through April 1, 2001. The change, endorsed by the International Monetary Fund (IMF), was intended to aid economic stabilization.

Border Relations. Relations with neighboring Uzbekistan became strained as Uzbekistan's government, citing fears of infiltration via Tajikistan by guerrillas and drug traffickers, criticized Tajikistan's government for not curbing the guerrillas, and tightened border controls. These measures included mining points along the border, which led to the death or injury of several Tajik citizens, and restricting travel along the roads linking Tajikistan via Uzbekistan to the wider world, which interfered with Tajikistan's ability to export and cost it millions of dollars.

MURIEL ATKIN
George Washington University

Tanzania

Presidential and parliamentary elections were held in Tanzania during 2000, but, as in 1995, voting in semiautonomous Zanzibar was marked by controversy. On the other hand, 2000 was also marked by positive economic outcomes.

Domestic Affairs. The presidential elections, held on October 29, pitted the incumbent Benjamin Mkapa of the ruling Chama Cha Mapinduzi (CCM) party against three challengers—Professor Ibrahim Lipumba of the Civic United Front (CUF), Augustine Mrema of the Tanzania Labour Party (TLP), and John Cheyo of the United Democratic Party (UDP). Mkapa won an overwhelming victory, gaining 71.7% of total votes cast and defeating his nearest rival, Professor Lipumba, by more than 4.5 million votes. President Mkapa was sworn in

© Sayyid Azim/AP/Wide World Photos

Supporters of Tanzania's President Benjamin Mkapa and the ruling Chama Cha Mapinduzi (CCM) dressed in CCM colors to celebrate an overwhelming victory in the Oct. 29, 2000, elections.

for his second, and final, five-year term on November 9. CCM won an even larger victory in the parliamentary and civic elections as it obtained more than 90% of all seats.

Nevertheless, the CCM victory in the Zanzibar elections was marked by huge controversy. An agreement brokered by the Commonwealth secretariat in 1999 was not implemented, and the October 29 elections on the island were so badly organized—and there were charges of vote rigging and intimidation—that the electoral commission ordered a rerun in 16 constituencies on November 5. The opposition CUF called for a completely new election and boycotted the November vote. The result of the elections thus did little to cool the political temperature as CCM won 35 seats in the Zanzi-

bar House of Representatives to 15 for CUF. The CCM candidate, Amani Karume, was declared victor in the race for Zanzibar's presidency over CUF's Seif Sharif Hamad. The CUF refused to recognize these elections, claiming that the CCM had rigged the outcome.

Economy. The year saw many positive indicators for the Tanzanian economy. An October United Nations (UN) report placed annual gross domestic product (GDP) growth at 5.3%, higher than anticipated. Growth in the agriculture and mining sectors led the way, and tourism experienced expansion as well. Inflation declined to 6% in May, the lowest in more than 20 years. The external sector also improved considerably over the previous year. This enhanced performance and the success of the government's fiscal and monetary policies in meeting goals led the International Monetary Fund (IMF) and the World Bank (WB) to approve a comprehensive debt-reduction package for Tanzania during the year. This provided $2 billion in debt relief along with loans to be used for poverty reduction. With the agreement of the donors, President Mkapa pledged implementation of a ten-year poverty-reduction plan. With widespread unemployment, HIV/AIDS emerging as a potential catastrophe, and slightly more than half of the population living below the WB poverty line, significant poverty reduction was providing a difficult challenge for Tanzania.

Foreign Affairs. Tanzania followed through in early September on its 1999 decision to formally withdraw from the Common Market for Eastern and Southern Africa (COMESA). In June, Tanzania became the last of the signatories to ratify the treaty that opened the way for the creation of a new East African Community (EAC). Formally established in November, EAC linked the nation with Kenya and Uganda.

ROBERT M. MAXON, *West Virginia University*

TANZANIA • Information Highlights

Official Name: United Republic of Tanzania.
Location: East coast of Africa.
Area: 364,900 sq mi (945 090 km²).
Population (2000 est.): 35,306,126.
Chief Cities (1985 est.): Dar es Salaam, the capital, 1,096,000; Mwanza, 252,000; Tabora, 214,000.
Government: *Head of state,* Benjamin Mkapa, president (took office Nov. 23, 1995). *Head of government,* Frederick Sumaye, prime minister (appointed November 1995). *Legislature* (unicameral)—National Assembly.
Monetary Unit: Tanzanian shilling (807.0000 shillings equal U.S. $1, Jan. 4, 2001).
Gross Domestic Product (1999 est. U.S.$): $23,300,000,000 (purchasing power parity).
Economic Index (Tanganyika, 1998; 1990 = 100): *Consumer Prices,* all items, 36,111.2; food, 42,146.4.
Foreign Trade (1999 U.S.$): *Imports,* $1,634,000,000; *exports,* $540,000,000.

Taxation

To supporters of tax reform, the year 2000 was one of much talk and little action. After pushing unsuccessfully in 1999 for a sweeping tax-cut plan—totaling $800 billion over ten years—the Republican-controlled 106th Congress decided to adopt a new strategy by offering several targeted tax-reduction proposals in 2000. Most of these went nowhere, however. President Bill Clinton, in his last year in office, vetoed several major tax bills, and their Republican sponsors were unable to muster enough votes to override the vetoes. That shifted the focus of tax policy to the presidential campaign. Both George W. Bush and Al Gore proposed very detailed and largely contradictory plans for changing the tax code.

Congressional Action. Lawmakers considered a number of targeted tax cuts in 2000. But two proposals—to eliminate the so-called marriage penalty and the estate tax—generated heated debates.

The marriage-penalty bill, by far the most expensive of the list of Republican-backed proposals, would have cost $292 billion over ten years. It was aimed at helping the 25 million married couples who were "penalized" because they paid more in income taxes than they would if they were single and filing separately. President Bill Clinton promised in his January State of the Union address to support legislation to eliminate the penalty. On July 20, Congress approved a bill, which had been the centerpiece of the ill-fated 1999 tax cut, that also would have cut taxes for the 21 million married couples not subject to the penalty. President Clinton cited the proposal's high cost when he vetoed it on August 5, calling it "the first installment of a fiscally reckless tax strategy." A House effort to override the veto failed by 16 votes; in the Senate, support for the measure fell short of the two-thirds majority needed to override the veto, and it never came to a vote.

Congress also passed a Republican-backed measure to phase out the estate tax, also known as the "death tax," which is levied on an estate after a person has died. Supporters of the repeal argued the tax hurt small-business owners and farmers by forcing heirs to sell family farms and close businesses in order to pay their tax bills. Critics claimed that the repeal would help only the wealthy because current law already exempted the first $675,000 of an estate from taxation. Because of that exemption,

scheduled to rise to $1 million by 2006, only 2% of heirs were liable for the estate tax in 2000. The estate-tax repeal would have cost $104 billion by 2010. Clinton vetoed the measure, saying it would favor the wealthy and erode the budget surplus. On September 8, the House failed to override the veto.

Clinton also vetoed a measure that would have eliminated the 3% federal excise tax on telecommunications. Also known as the "tax on talking," the tax was originally imposed in 1898 to help fund U.S. involvement in the Spanish-American War, and today is levied on local, long-distance, and wireless-phone bills, including dial-up access to the Internet. The measure, supported by the telecommunications industry, would have abolished the tax, costing about $5 billion a year in federal-tax revenues.

Republican lawmakers attached four popular tax proposals to a broader bill that would have boosted reimbursements to Medicare providers. One measure would have increased the amount taxpayers may contribute to 401(k) plans and other tax-deferred retirement savings accounts. Another would have raised the minimum wage by $1—to $6.15—over two years, while also cutting taxes on firms such as restaurants and retailers that employ low-income workers. A third measure would have lowered taxes and regulations on businesses that invest in low-income urban and rural communities. However, the uncertainty of the presidential-election results ultimately prompted lawmakers to shelve the broad measure and consider separately the fourth tax proposal—the repeal of a 16-year-old tax break for U.S. exporters who set up their offshore offices in tax havens such as the Bahamas and the U.S. Virgin Islands.

The law had enjoyed strong support from U.S. businesses, including such behemoths as Boeing and Cisco Systems, which had saved tens of millions of dollars a year in corporate-income taxes under its provisions. During its end-of-the-year, lame-duck session, however, Congress changed the tax provision in response to a charge by the European Union (EU), upheld in February by the World Trade Organization (WTO), that it amounted to an illegal subsidy of U.S. exports. The new law exempted from taxation a large portion of income earned abroad. On November 15, Clinton signed the measure—the only significant tax change that made it into law in 2000. However, because the new measure requires that at least half the value of exported goods

U.S. House Speaker Dennis Hastert of Illinois (left) and Capitol Hill staffers wave to a newlywed couple on Capitol Hill during a July rally encouraging Bill Clinton to sign the marriage-penalty bill. The president vetoed it, and efforts to override the veto failed.

contain U.S. components, it appeared likely that it, too, would be challenged as an unacceptable export subsidy.

State Initiatives. While the U.S. Congress failed to make significant headway on tax proposals, a number of initiatives took root at the state level. Some states enjoyed such hefty tax revenues that they were able to offer tax breaks to residents. Twenty-nine states cut taxes in 2000, for a total savings of almost $10 million. It was the sixth year in a row that states reduced taxes.

Most of the state-tax relief—accounting for more than $3 billion of total state-tax reductions—came in the form of personal-income-tax reductions, enacted in 24 states in 2000. Many states targeted their income-tax cuts to poor families by raising the income threshold for requiring them to pay the tax or by eliminating it altogether for families below the federally designated poverty level. Twenty-one states reduced sales taxes, while 17 cut corporate and business taxes.

In addition to permanent tax cuts, some states offered residents temporary relief by declaring a so-called sales-tax holiday, a period in which consumers could buy clothing, shoes, and certain other goods free of retail-sales tax. Seven states—Connecticut, Florida, Iowa, New York, Pennsylvania, South Carolina, and Texas—held tax holidays in 2000. In most cases, holidays lasted a

few days and coincided with the back-to-school shopping period.

Not all states were in a position to give back tax revenues to taxpayers. In Virginia, a flagging economy forced Republican Gov. James S. Gilmore III to take extraordinary steps to keep his promise to eliminate the hated "car tax." Gilmore had won a sweeping victory in the 1997 gubernatorial election on his campaign promise to eliminate the state's personal-property tax, used to help fund local governments. The Virginia Assembly approved Gilmore's plan, but conditioned its completion on the state's continued healthy economic growth. When the economy slowed in 2000, reducing state-revenue growth to a meager 3%, Gilmore announced he would use national tobacco-settlement funds to boost state revenues and thus keep the tax cut on track.

IRS Reform. Two years after lawmakers heard poignant reports of taxpayer abuse at the hands of agents of the Internal Revenue Service (IRS), efforts to reform the agency stalled amid funding shortfalls. The agency had requested funding to hire more than 2,000 new agents and modernize its aging computer systems. But Republicans balked at the request, arguing that the IRS had made insufficient progress toward improving its record to justify the expenditure. But in a letter to lawmakers, IRS Commissioner Charles O. Rossotti warned that unless the agency received more funding, it would have to reduce the number of tax returns it audits and would have to cut service on its toll-free taxpayer telephone lines.

In September the Senate confirmed seven individuals from the private sector as members of a nine-member panel authorized by the 1998 IRS reform law to monitor reports of taxpayer abuse and suggest ways to improve the agency's customer-service operations. The panel also included the secretary of the treasury and IRS commissioner as permanent members. Meanwhile, many of the allegations of abuse that had helped ensure the IRS reform law's passage failed to stand up to investigators' scrutiny. In August the Treasury Department inspector general for tax administration, a position created by the law, reported that investigations had turned up only four valid cases out of some 1,300 complaints of taxpayer abuse.

Campaign News. During the presidential campaign, Vice-President Al Gore (D) and Texas Gov. George W. Bush (R) offered starkly different proposals for revamping the tax code. Both candidates promised to use part of the record $237 billion federal-budget surplus to pay down the $3.1 trillion national debt, but Gore was more emphatic on this issue. His tax plan would have cost $500 billion over ten years; Bush's more sweeping plan proposed reducing federal tax revenues by $1.3 trillion over approximately the same time period.

Reflecting traditional Democratic goals, Gore's tax proposal included a number of new and expanded credits and deductions targeted mostly at couples who earned less than $70,000 and shouldered specific expenses. These included credits to help pay for day care, after-school care, and college tuition, as well as long-term care for the elderly. Gore's plan also proposed the creation of a tax credit for small businesses that joined purchasing pools to buy health insurance for their employees. The plan called for tax breaks to promote school construction, low-income housing, worker training, and land conservation. Gore also proposed expanding the earned-income tax credit to cover an additional 7 million low-income families, doubling the standard deduction for married couples, and exempting certain small-business heirs from estate taxes.

In contrast to Gore's targeted approach, the centerpiece of Bush's tax proposal was an across-the-board cut in the personal-income tax. It also called for a reduction in the number of income-tax rates from five to four, with the top rate set at 33%, in contrast with 39.6% under current law. Those changes would benefit higher-income taxpayers as well as the middle- and lower-income taxpayers targeted under Gore's proposal. Bush's tax plan would double the $500–per-child tax credit, make permanent a business tax credit for research and development, and raise from $500 to $5,000 the amount that can be deposited in a tax-free education-savings account. Bush also expressed strong support for repeal of the estate tax. After being declared president-elect in December, Bush made it plain that his new administration would push for his $1.3 trillion tax plan.

With virtually no movement on federal-tax proposals, some experts pinned their hopes for future action on an emerging compromise proposal. In late November, as the presidential-election results remained in limbo, tax experts met to hammer out a new tax proposal that promised to merge some of the goals set forth by both Gore and Bush. Meeting at the Brookings Institution in Washington, DC, the group of academic and government economists came up with a strategy that addressed Democrats' concerns over the tax code's treatment of middle-class taxpayers and the Republicans' quest to simplify the current law. The problem they addressed was a quirk in the system that left one group of taxpayers—married couples with children and a yearly income between $30,000 and $60,000—with fewer tax benefits than both poorer and wealthier taxpayers. At one end of the income spectrum, the earned-income tax credit enabled poor families with children to reduce their tax bills, but that benefit was phased out between incomes of $20,000 and $30,000. At the other end, wealthy families could cut their tax burdens by itemizing their deductions, an option that generally favored higher-income taxpayers.

Expanding on a proposal first advanced by economists Max Sawicky of the Economic Policy Institute and Robert Cherry of the City University of New York, former Clinton administration officials David Ellwood and Jeffrey Liebman proposed several options to eliminate tax discrimination against middle-income families. The options, which included raising the child tax credit and extending the earned-income tax credit, were seen as promising areas of consideration for the 107th Congress.

MARY H. COOPER
"The CQ Researcher"

Television and Radio

In a year marked more by its bad shows than its good ones, several issues and events involving television stood out in 2000. Game shows with potential big-money winnings continued to reign supreme, at least initially. The Olympics, which in previous years had drawn large numbers of viewers, failed to capture the same television audience in 2000. The U.S. Congress lambasted Hollywood for its promotion of violence. Movie stars turned to the small screen, while presidential voters turned as much to late-night talk shows for news as they did prime-time shows. And the art of voyeurism took on new meaning as "reality-based" television shows became the rage, especially the hit of the summer, *Survivor*.

Shows of 2000. Many of the favorite shows of 2000 were carryovers from 1999, including Emmy-winners *West Wing* and *The Sopranos* dominating many lists. Not to be ignored, however, were such new shows as NBC's *Ed*, the story of a big-city lawyer who returned to his hometown, stayed because of his high-school crush, and bought a bowling alley where he dispensed legal advice. David Kelley's new show on FOX, *Boston Public*, a serious-but-funny drama about life in a racially diverse and troubled Boston high school, fared much better than recent Kelley shows, such as the short-lived *Snoops* and *Chicago Hope*.

Mid-season replacements, which began airing in January, included a new hospital drama, *City of Angels*, produced by Steven Bochco, whose *NYPD Blue* was in its seventh year. The game-show craze was fueled by such *Who Wants to Be a Millionaire* wanna-be's as FOX's *Greed* and NBC's *21* (*see* THE QUIZ-SHOW CRAZE, page 90). Teen shows were popular, as FOX counted *Malcolm in the Middle* as a successful mid-season entrant. A syndicated talk/cooking show that featured British comic and TV chef Ainsley Harriott also debuted.

The fall season, with 30 new programs, was notable for the number of big-name film actors who tried their hand at television. Geena Davis and Bette Midler started eponymous shows, *The Geena Davis Show* and *Bette*, respectively. Robert Downey Jr., joined the cast of David Kelley's hit *Ally McBeal*. Charlie Sheen replaced Michael J. Fox on *Spin City* and Sally Field appeared for several weeks on *ER*. Other film stars joining the small-screen brigade included Gabriel Byrne in *Madigan Men*; Ellen Burstyn in *That's Life*; Oliver Platt, Tom Conti, Hope Davis, and Lili Taylor in *Deadline*; and Tom Everett Scott in *The Street*. And with TNT's made-for-TV movie *Baby*, Glenn Close showed that she was as skillful at producing as she was at acting.

Michael Richards of *Seinfeld* fame returned to television as an unconventional Los Angeles private detective in the *Michael Richards Show*; Delta Burke, formerly of *Designing Women*, returned as the first lady in the comedy *DAG*, also starring David Alan Grier, formerly of *In Living Color*. By year's end, Byrne, Platt, and Richards had their shows canceled, while the Midler and Davis projects struggled.

A number of shows were simply copies of earlier successes. *The Fugitive* returned on CBS with Tim Daly as Dr. Richard Kimble; Aaron Spelling tried to work his magic on another evening soap with NBC's *Titans*; and the WB Network sketch comedy *Hype* recalled *In Living Color* and *Laugh-In*.

Public and Cable Television. Cable TV broke new ground with the launch of *Queer as Folk*, the U.S. remake of a taboo-busting

© Monty Brinton/CBS Photo Archive

CBS's "reality adventure" series "Survivor" was the surprise hit of the summer. Richard Hatch (above) outlasted 15 other contestants stranded on an island to win $1 million.

© Ken Staniforth/NBC/Everett Collection, Inc.

NBC's comedy series "Ed," about a big-city lawyer who returns to his hometown, was a standout among the shows debuting in the fall of 2000. It featured (l-r): Josh Randall, Jana Marie Hupp, Lesley Boone, Tom Cavanagh, and Julie Bowen.

British series about gay life. The series began airing on Showtime in December. *BattleBots*, which featured remote-controlled robots fighting in an enclosed arena for $5,000 in prize money, made its way onto Comedy Central, while the *Naked Chef*, who brought food down to its bare basics, highlighted the Food Network.

Made-for-cable shows were popular. For example, A&E broadcast *Catherine the Great*, TNT produced *David Copperfield*, and USA ran a Halloween drama, *Dark Prince: The True Story of Dracula*.

On public television, *Antiques Roadshow* achieved an almost cult-like status (*see* SIDEBAR, page 529). The Public Broadcasting Service (PBS) named Pat Mitchell, a longtime Turner Broadcasting executive, as its new president.

Trends. One trend many critics viewed as disturbing was the growing number of reality-based television shows. Hitting what many considered an all-time low was FOX's *Who Wants to Marry a Multimillionaire*. The premise of the show was that a prospective bridegroom, who was also a multimillionaire, would select a bride from among 50 contestants. Seen by more than 22 million people, the show blew up in the network's face when, just days after the on-air wedding, it was learned that the groom was not a multimillionaire and that a former fiancée had a restraining order on him. Within weeks, the bride filed, and received, an

annulment. She later posed for *Playboy*. FOX vowed in February that it would not broadcast any more exploitative shows. But by year's end it was planning a new series, *Temptation Island*, in which supposedly committed couples journey to a tropical island filled with attractive singles to test the strength of their relationships.

The rage of the summer was CBS's *Survivor*, which put 16 contestants on an island in the South Pacific for 39 days and then set them up to outwit and outlast the others in a quest for $1 million. Like ABC's *Who Wants to Be a Millionaire* in 1999, it was a surprising hit. The show's final episode drew 50 million viewers—second only to pro-football's Super Bowl in 2000. A second *Survivor*, set in the Australian outback, was due to air in January 2001. Less successful was CBS's *Big Brother*, where ten people were confined to a house and connived to be the last-remaining contestant as viewers watched their every move.

A positive trend for the 2000–2001 season was the airing of plays on television. Led by PBS, productions included *The Man Who Came To Dinner*, A.E. Gurney's *Far East*, and Anna Deavere Smith's *Twilight: Los Angeles*. A&E aired *Peter Pan*, starring Cathy Rigby, and HBO broadcast *Wit* and *Dinner with Friends*.

The Olympics. From a U.S. television standpoint, the 2000 Olympics, played in Sydney, Australia, were a bust. Broadcast by NBC, the Sydney Olympics had the lowest ratings for any Summer or Winter Olympics since 1968. Particularly bad, according to Neilsen Media Research, were the final three nights. On the last Friday, for example, only 15.5 million people watched. Speculation on why viewership was low included the time difference between the United States and Sydney which resulted in many taped broadcasts; lack of a 2000 Winter Olympics; the late-season start; and the fact that the last Summer Olympics were in Atlanta, GA, had helped foster U.S. interest.

Issues and the Election. The promotion of violent entertainment to children via television and other methods became a 2000 presidential-campaign issue. In September the Federal Trade Commission (FTC) released a report stating that the majority of best-selling restricted movies, videos, and music were deliberately marketed to children aged 12 to 17. One example was the promotion of R-rated movies during the teen show *Dawson's Creek*. Hollywood executives pledged to curb such marketing, but said parents should prevent children from seeing the films. Democratic vice-presidential candidate Joseph Lieberman had been particularly vocal in his quest to keep R-rated material from children.

Politicians, however, embraced the television media when it came to getting their message out. Ever since 1992, when then-presidential-candidate Bill Clinton played his saxophone on *The Arsenio Hall Show*, candidates have sought spots on morning and late-night talk shows. The year 2000 was no exception, as candidates were both sought-after guests and comic fodder.

Controversy raged over television's early reporting of results on Election Night 2000; on two different occasions that night, network and cable-news programs miscalled Florida results,

possibly influencing, after the first miscall, voting in later time zones. The networks pledged to reexamine their poll-projection standards. (*See also* SPOTLIGHT FALLS ON THE ELECTORAL MACHINERY, page 29.)

Networks.   CNN, which pioneered the concept of all-day and all-night television news, celebrated its 20th anniversary in June. The network was relatively unknown until the Gulf War in 1991. Although it remained the most-watched all-news network in 2000, competition cut into its ratings. Executives hoped that a planned merger between America Online (AOL) and CNN's parent, Time Warner, would revitalize it.

© Len Irish/ABC/Photofest

© Photofest

The NBC comedy "Will & Grace" (cast above) won three Emmy Awards, including best comedy series, best supporting actress—Megan Mullally (far left), and best supporting actor—Sean Hayes (far right). Sela Ward (left) took home an Emmy as best actress in a drama for ABC's "Once and Again."

Competitors included MSNBC and FOX News, the all-news limbs of NBC and FOX, respectively. By third quarter 2000, CNN and CNN Headline News held 44% of the market, CNBC and MSNBC shared a combined 43%, and FOX News accounted for the balance, some 14%.

Coming and Goings.   David Letterman took a five-week break from his *Late Show* for quintuple bypass surgery. Kathie Lee Gifford left *Live! With Regis & Kathie Lee* in July. Michael J. Fox left *Spin City* in May to spend more time with his family and raise money for Parkinson's disease, with which he is afflicted. At NBC, the stars of *Friends* each agreed to take just $750,000 per

TELEVISION • 2000

Some sample programs

About Sarah—Drama about a student who, after the death of her grandmother, becomes the legal guardian of her developmentally disabled mother. With Kellie Martin, Marion Ross, Diane Baker, and Mary Steenburgen. CBS, Aug. 6.

A Father's Choice—Drama based on fact about a rodeo veteran who assumes parental responsibilities when his former wife is murdered. With Peter Strauss, Michelle Trachtenberg, Yvonne Zima, Susan Hogan, and Mary McDonnell. CBS, Jan. 12.

The American Experience: America 1900—A recollection of the past century narrated by David McCullough. PBS, Jan. 3.

The American Experience: George Wallace: Settin' the Woods on Fire—A documentary about a man who was a giant in Southern politics for 30 years. Narrated by Randy Quaid. PBS April 23–24.

The American Experience: Reagan—A two-part series about Ronald Reagan's background and his years as president. PBS, May 29–30.

The American Experience: The Rockefellers—A two-part profile that follows four generations of the Rockefeller family and covers their participation in politics and interest in art. Narrated by David Ogden Stiers. PBS Oct. 16 and Oct. 23.

American Masters: Mailer on Mailer—A television study of Norman Mailer, the Pulitzer Prize-winning author. PBS, Oct. 4.

Best Friends for Life— A drama about two longtime friends whose friendship is tested after the deaths of their husbands. With Gena Rowlands, Linda Lavin, and Richard Farnsworth. CBS, July 2.

Beyond the Prairie: The True Story of Laura Ingalls Wilder—A love story about the *Little House on the Prairie* book series writer who leaves the safety of her family and begins life in the Dakota territory as a wife and mother. With Richard Thomas, Meredith Monroe, and Lindsay Crouse. CBS, Jan. 2.

Bonhoeffer: Agent of Grace—A docudrama about a German minister who at great risk opposes Hitler. With Ulrich Tukur and Robert Joy. PBS, June 14.

Boston Public—An hour-long drama series about the personal and professional sides of the people who run our public high schools. With Chi McBride, Fyvush Finkel, Anthony Heald and Jesslyn Gilsig. Fox, Oct. 23 premiere.

Catherine the Great—Drama about the German princess who became the Empress of Russia. With Catherine Zeta-Jones and Paul McGann. A&E, Dec. 3.

Child Stars: Their Story—A documentary that focuses on child stars and the problems and successes they have had as they became adults. Narrated by Hayley Mills, and featuring Tony Dow and Melissa Gilbert. A&E, Sept. 4.

Clint Eastwood: Out of the Shadows—An "American Masters" Special that profiles the life and achievements of the famous actor and director. With Gene Hackman, Meryl Streep, and Clint Eastwood. PBS, Sept. 27

Common Ground—Drama about reactions to homosexuality in America during the past 50 years. Film written by Harvey Fierstein, Terrence McNally and Paula Vogel. With Edward Asner and Beau Bridges. SHOW, Jan. 29.

The Corner—A six-part miniseries that focuses on a Baltimore drug-addicted family. With Khandi Alexander, T.K. Carter, and Sean Nelson. HBO, April 16.

Critical Condition with Hedrick Smith—A documentary about America's health-care system. The topics covered deal with medical errors, patients with chronic ailments, and HMOs and people who do not have medical insurance. PBS, Oct. 18.

The Crossing—A historical drama about George Washington leading his army across the Delaware River to defeat the Hessian army. With Jeff Daniels and Roger Rees. A&E, Jan. 10.

Cupid & Cate—A "Hallmark Hall of Fame" drama about the dilemma an engaged woman feels after she is introduced by her sister to someone else to whom she is instantly attracted. With Mary-Louise Parker, Joanna Going, Peter Gallagher, and David Lansbury. CBS, May 7.

Custody of the Heart—A drama about a businesswoman, going through a divorce, who has to fight for the custody of her children when her husband accuses her of being an unfit mother. With Lorraine Bracco, Martin Donovan, and Dennis Boutsikaris. LIFE, Aug. 28.

Dark Prince: The True Story of Dracula—A suspense about the Romanian Prince Vlad Dracula. With Rudolf Martin and Michael Sutton, USA, Oct. 31.

Deadlocked—Drama about a father trying to overturn his son's conviction for the rape/murder of the wife of the younger man's boss. With Charles S. Dutton, David Caruso, and Jo D. Jonz. TNT, June 18.

Debating Our Destiny: 40 Years of Presidential Debates—A historical look at debates between presidential hopefuls. Hosted by Jim Lehrer. PBS, Sept. 24.

Don Quixote—Adaptation of the Cervantes novel about an eccentric Spanish gentleman who sets off on chivalric adventures. With John Lithgow, Vanessa Williams, Isabella Rossellini, Bob Hoskins. TNT, April. 9.

Dying to Be Perfect: The Ellen Hart Pena Story—Biography of a world-class runner who is forced to reveal her bulimia to her husband when she becomes pregnant. With Crystal Bernard and Esai Morales. ABC, July 17.

Enslavement: The True Story of Fanny Kemble—Drama about a woman who helps slaves escape from her in-laws' plantations. With Jane Seymour and Keith Carradine. SHOW, April 23.

The First Measured Century—A historical presentation about the 20th century that takes a clinical approach by using data and measurement. With pollster George Gallup and Sen. Daniel Patrick Moynihan commenting. PBS, Dec. 20.

Freedom Song—A civil-rights drama about a family man living in Mississippi in the early 1960s. His teenage son wants to get involved in trying to register black voters. With Danny Glover and Vicellous Reon Shannon. TNT, Feb. 27.

Geppetto—A "Wonderful World of Disney" musical about the wood-carver who created a son—Pinocchio—for himself. With Drew Carey, Julia Louis-Dreyfus, Seth Adkins, and Brent Spiner. ABC, May 7.

Hard Time: The David Milgaard Story—Docudrama about a Canadian man who is wrongfully convicted of a rape/murder and serves 23 years of his sentence before being proved innocent. With Ian Tracey and Gabrielle Rose. LIFE, August 3.

High Noon—This remake of the 1952 movie focuses on the role of the older Mexican woman, Helen Ramirez, and what she means to the town. With Tom Skerritt, Maria Conchita Alonso, and Susanna Thompson, TBS, Aug. 20.

A House Divided—Based on the life of Amanda America Dickson, this is a drama about a slave who is raped by the owner of the plantation. Amanda is born from this union and when her father dies, he leaves most of his estate to her. With Jennifer Beals, Sam Waterston, Ron White, and Tim Daly. SHOW, July 30.

The Hunley—Historical drama set during the Civil War about the first submarine to sink an enemy ship. With Armand Assante and Donald Sutherland. TNT, July 11.

The Huntress—A suspenseful drama about a bounty hunter's widow and daughter who are trying to catch his killer. With Annette O'Toole and Aleksa Palladino. USA, March 7.

If These Walls Could Talk 2—Drama in which three tales about lesbianism unfold in different decades. With Vanessa Redgrave, Marian Seldes, Michelle Williams, Chloe Sevigny, Ellen DeGeneres and Sharon Stone. HBO, March 5.

In His Life: The John Lennon Story—A biography which covers the early years of the Beatle's founder. With Phillip McQuillan, Blair Brown, Daniel McGowan, Mark Rice-Oxley and Kristian Ealey. NBC, Dec. 3.

KPFA on the Air—P.O.V. (Point of View) documentary about a radio station in Berkeley, CA, that has kept broadcasting since it was founded by a pacifist. PBS, Sept. 19.

King Gimp—Documentary profiling Dan Keplinger who has coped with cerebral palsy while displaying his talent as an artist. HBO, June 5.

La Boda—P.O.V. documentary about the marriage of two people from the border between the United States and Mexico. PBS, June 22.

The Last of the Blonde Bombshells—A story about a fictional World War II all-girl band, the Blonde Bombshells, who later reunite. With Joan Sims, Judi Dench, Billie Whitelaw, and Ian Holm. HBO, August 26.

Lost & Found—Comedy about a restaurateur who tries to start a romance with his neighbor by kidnapping her dog and helping her "find" it. With David Spade and Sophie Marceau. HBO, March 25.

Love Lessons—A drama about a 50-year-old woman who, when she discovers that she is pregnant, must face the difficult challenges and changes that this will bring to her marriage at a time when she and her husband had already made plans for their retirement. With Patty Duke, Ronny Cox, and Max Martini. CBS, Nov. 22.

The Man Who Came to Dinner— A "PBS showcase" about a critic who is not pleased about his long stay with a woman and her family. At the same time, the family is not happy with the critic's ludicrous acquaintances who visit him. With Nathan Lane and Jean Smart. PBS, Oct. 7.

The Mill on the Floss—Drama about a woman whose family loses its mill to a scheming lawyer whose son she loves. With Emily Watson, Nicholas Gecks, and James Frain. PBS, Jan. 2.

Missing Pieces—A "Hallmark Hall of Fame" drama about a man estranged from his son, who supposedly has committed suicide. The father becomes suspicious that his son is still alive when he goes to retrieve his body. With James Coburn, Lisa Zane, and Paul Kersey. CBS, Feb. 6.

The Moving of Sophia Myles—A story about a woman whose minister husband unexpectedly dies, causing her to question her faith and also deal with the possible loss of her home. With Della Reese and Rue McClanahan. CBS, Nov. 26.

Mystery! "The Wyvern Mystery"—The two-part season premiere of the 21-year-old anthology series opens with a story about a young woman who marries the heir of an estate and finds her life of privilege turning into one of terror. With Naomi Watts, Derek Jacobi, and Iain Glen. PBS, Oct. 12

The 1900 House—Four-part documentary that "transports" an actual modern family from 1999 back in time to life in 1900. PBS, June 12.

Nova: The Vikings—Historians place perspective on the history of the Vikings. PBS, May 9.

On Our Own Terms: Moyers On Dying—A four-part series about the end-of-life issues Americans face. With Mary Alice Williams, Rafael Pi Roman, Bill Moyers, and Judith Davidson Moyers, PBS, Sept. 10–13.

One Day in September—A recollection of the 1972 Olympics in Munich when Palestinian terrorists held Israeli athletes hostage. Narrated by Michael Douglas. HBO, Sept. 11.

Opening the Tombs of the Golden Mummies: Live!—A documentary, hosted by Hugh Downs, about an Egyptian excavation site where a fortune in gold is expected to be found in the underground tombs. Fox, May 23.

"Antiques Roadshow"

Part adventure, part history lesson, part treasure hunt, *Antiques Roadshow* claimed its spot in 2000 as the Public Broadcasting Service's (PBS') most-watched series, with a weekly viewing audience of an unprecedented 15 million.

The concept for the show is very simple. Each summer since 1995, a staff of appraisers,

Visitors to PBS' "Antiques Roadshow" await the verdict as their Chippendale chair, above, and violin, right, are appraised.

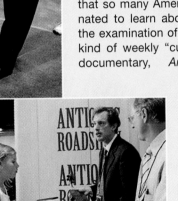

dealers, and auction-house representatives has been dispatched to cities across the United States, where countless thousands have gathered to await their arrival and to have their possessions valued. Standing in line for hours—with necklaces, porcelains, and even bookcases—the hopeful and anxious have offered up their belongings for very public—and not always flattering—appraisal.

Some of these objects truly have been judged to be treasures. One American table by Bostonian John Seymour in pristine condition,

complete with rare label, was discovered on the program and eventually sold for more than $500,000. Yet other objects—such as the shrunken head in a music box that, when opened, played "Raindrops Keep Falling on My Head"—simply were unique. Home viewers did their own "appraising," cheering every victory and wincing at defeats. For some attendees, their "gold" was gold filled, but television audiences—and disappointed owners—received useful lessons in the ways that Tiffany-glass vases, Native American artifacts, and antique jewelry can be convincingly faked. *Roadshow* became a stadium event on the road, and rivaled the most-popular television fare. With a new item on camera every three minutes, even hardened veterans of network television found themselves glued to their seats.

WGBH Boston, the public-television station that brought this successful format to the United States from England, was delighted and surprised by its unexpected success. Others were as well. Public-television stalwarts were pleased that so many Americans seemed fascinated to learn about the past through the examination of attic treasures. As a kind of weekly "cultural anthropology" documentary, *Antiques Roadshow* teaches U.S. history by bringing to light and informing the viewers about America's material culture. The participants are pleased to learn anything at all about their possessions, even when they turn out to be of no significant value, and viewers are encouraged to visit historical societies, libraries, and museums—frequently toured on the show—to learn more.

The program's prototype has been running in Great Britain since 1973. If one considers how many more attics there are in the United States than there are in Britain, the first episodes of *Antiques Roadshow* should be antiques by the time this show goes off the air.

CAROL PRISANT
Author, "Antiques Roadshow Primer"

Our House in Havana—P.O.V. documentary about a Cuban woman who returns to the home where she lived as a child and the difficulty she has in trying to adjust her recollections with the world Fidel Castro has created. PBS, July 25.

Peter Jennings Reports: The Search for Jesus—A documentary that traces the footsteps of Jesus while trying to present a balanced picture of Jesus as viewed through a reporter's eyes. ABC, June 26.

Rebecca—Two-part adaptation of 1997 "Masterpiece Theatre" story of a bride who feels eclipsed by her husband's dead first wife. With Diana Rigg, Emilia Fox, and Charles Dance. PBS, March 26 and April 2.

The Right Temptation—A suspense drama about a private detective who has to keep herself alive while seeking the person who murdered her client's husband. With Rebecca De Mornay and Kiefer Sutherland. HBO, Aug. 19.

The Runaway—A "Hallmark Hall of Fame" drama about racism in a small town in the 1950s. With Dean Cain, Maya Angelou, Cody Newton, and Duane McLaughlin. CBS, Dec. 10.

Running Mates—A drama about the happenings during a political convention in which the presidential nominee has to choose his vice-president. With Tom Selleck, Nancy Travis, Laura Linney, Teri Hatcher, Faye Dunaway, and Robert Culp. TNT, Aug. 13.

Sally Hemings: An American Scandal—Two-part saga about a slave who had an affair with Thomas Jefferson. With Sam Neill, Carmen Ejogo, Diahann Carroll, Mario Van Peebles, and Mare Winningham. CBS, Feb. 13 and Feb. 16.

Secrets of the Dead—Scientists investigate mysteries that have puzzled people throughout history. PBS, May 15–17.

The '70s—Two-part drama about a decade of politics and violence. With Brad Rowe, Vinessa Shaw, Guy Torry, and Amy Smart. NBC, April 30 and May 1.

Sidney Poitier: One Bright Light, an American Masters Special—Profile of the Oscar-winning actor. Narrated by Lee Grant. PBS, Feb. 2.

Songs in Ordinary Time—A story about a single mother who falls in love with a seemingly well-meaning con artist, who manages to disrupt her life by the time she becomes suspicious of him. With Sissy Spacek and Beau Bridges. CBS, Oct. 22.

Soul Food—Drama about three sisters who try to keep their family together after their mother dies. With Vanessa Williams, Nicole Ari Parker, Malinda Williams, and Irma P. Hall. SHOW, June 28.

Survivor—A "reality adventure" series where 16 Americans (8 men and 8 women) are stranded on an island in the South China Sea and are in competition with each other to be the final survivor who wins $1 million. To air in 13 episodes, premiering on CBS, May 31.

Take Me Home: The John Denver Story—Drama about the late singer-songwriter's life. With Chad Lowe, Kristin Davis, and Gerald McRaney. CBS, April 30.

Three to Tango—A comedy about an architect who is trying to gain a particular client, who thinks he is gay. The client asks him to watch over his mistress, with whom the architect falls in love. With Matthew Perry, Dylan McDermott, and Neve Campbell. HBO, Nov. 4.

Too Close to Home—Melodrama about an obsessive mother who becomes a major suspect when a major tragedy happens to her daughter-in-law. With Judith Light, Rick Schroder, and Sarah Trigger. CBS, July 9.

Twenty Years of Stories: This Is CNN—Two-part special, anchored by Larry King, recalling two decades of CNN coverage of the news. CNN, June 1–2.

Waking Ned Devine—Comedy in which two Irish senior citizens plot to cash in on a winning lottery ticket whose owner has died from the shock of winning. With Ian Bannen and David Kelly. MAX, Jan. 21.

What's Up With the Weather?—Traveling from opposite sides of the world, from Greenland to India, scientists study Earth's changing climate. PBS, April 18.

Who Killed Atlanta's Children?—A magazine reporter and his editor investigate a serial-murder case involving African-American youngsters in Georgia. With James Belushi and Gregory Hines. SHOW, July 16 and July 19.

---

episode rather than the $1 million plus they originally wanted.

NBC's *Today* dominated morning news shows, and added an extra hour with hosts Katie Couric and Matt Lauer. This followed an earlier, ill-fated attempt to have an hour-long *Later Today*.

Radio. A 75-year era in radio ended in September when John R. Gambling, a WOR-AM radio talk-show host, went off the air. The *Rambling With Gambling* morning program had been hosted by a member of the Gambling family since 1925, when John B. Gambling started the show. His son, John A. Gambling, and grandson, John R. Gambling, followed him. The youngest Gambling's contract was not renewed because the show had a disproportionate share of listeners who were 54 years or older, and this was not the age group sought by the majority of advertisers.

National Public Radio (NPR) decided to move into the digital age in February with the launch of *All Songs Considered*, an Internet-only radio program. The program featured full-length versions of the musical excerpts that are heard between segments of the news magazine *All Things Considered*.

Also trying the Internet was the former Channel 103.1 alternative, adult-format radio station. In September the station ceased on-air transmission and began broadcasting exclusively over the Web at www.channel1031.com.

KRISTI VAUGHAN

Patricia Heaton won an Emmy Award as best actress in a comedy for her portrayal of a suburban mother and wife in the hit series "Everybody Loves Raymond" on CBS. Comic Ray Romano is her costar.

© Everett Collection, Inc.

Terrorism

A series of disturbing acts of terrorism in 2000 illustrated how terrorists continually look for innovative ways to perpetrate their violence. Suicide terrorism at sea now must be considered a threat along with suicide car and truck bombings on land.

Disaster At Sea. A daring suicide attack at sea was the major anti-U.S. terrorist incident during the year 2000. The bombing of the USS *Cole* in Yemen on October 12 killed 17 sailors and injured 39 others. The *Cole*, a guided-missile destroyer, was attacked while refueling in the Yemeni port of Aden. Two men aboard a fiberglass skiff detonated several hundred pounds of explosives when they brought their small boat alongside the *Cole*. The terrorists, who were killed in the blast that blew a 60-ft- (18-m-) wide and 40-ft- (12-m-) high hole in the destroyer's side, were later identified as Saudi Arabian-born Yemenis who had surveyed the harbor for months prior to the attack. It was unknown whether they were affiliated with Saudi exile Osama bin Laden's international network of Islamic terrorists. Several people were arrested in Yemen in connection with the devastating bombing. (*See also* MILITARY AFFAIRS.)

Headline Incidents. In November, authorities in Kuwait uncovered 293 lb (133.2 kg) of high explosives that three Kuwaitis and a North African planned to use in attacks against U.S. installations in Kuwait and neighboring countries. The cache included 1,450 detonators and five grenades. Meanwhile, in Jordan, a military court sentenced six men to death on September 19 for a plot to kill U.S. and Israeli tourists during millennium celebrations. However, judges acquitted the men of charges that they were members of bin Laden's group, al-Qaida.

In October a former U.S. Army sergeant pleaded guilty in New York federal court to participating in a terrorist conspiracy against U.S. citizens. Ali A. Mohamed admitted that he conducted surveillance of U.S., British, French, and Israeli targets in Nairobi, Kenya, at the request of bin Laden. Among the targets was the U.S. Embassy, which was bombed in 1998 along with the U.S. Embassy in Tanzania. More than 200 people died in the two blasts.

The trial of two Libyans, Abdelbaset Ali Mohmed al-Megrahi and al-Amin Khalifa Fhimah, accused of planting a bomb that blew up Pan Am flight 103 in 1988, finally began in the Netherlands on May 3. The jet had exploded over Lockerbie, Scotland, killing 270 people in the air and on the ground. The trial was ongoing at the end of the year.

Federal officials in Charlotte, NC, arrested 18 people on July 21 for conspiracy to aid Hezbollah, the Islamic terrorist group based in Lebanon. It is a federal crime to give assistance to an organization, such as Hezbollah, that is designated by the U.S. government as a terrorist group. The suspects used the profits they made from illegal cigarette trafficking to send money overseas to Hezbollah leaders.

The investigation into the 1996 crash of TWA flight 800 over Long Island, NY, formally ended on August 23, when the National Transportation Safety Board (NTSB) issued its final report. The NTSB stated there was no evidence of a criminal act. The board ruled that the crash was the result of a short circuit in the plane's wiring that probably led to a fuel-tank explosion that tore the aircraft apart. All 230 people aboard the flight were killed.

In other developments, Muslim rebels from the Abu Sayyaf Group (ASG) kidnapped a U.S. citizen, Jeffrey Schilling, on the remote Philippine island of Jolo on August 30. Schilling stated in a telephone conversation with the U.S. Embassy that the Muslim rebels were demanding that $10 million be paid for his release. The Philippine military launched an operation against the ASG in September, but failed to rescue Schilling and a Filipino hostage.

In March a federal judge ordered the government of Iran to pay former hostage Terry Anderson and his family $341 million in damages. The judge ruled that Iran was behind the kidnapping of Anderson and several other U.S. citizens in Lebanon during the 1980s. Anderson was kidnapped in Beirut in March 1985 and held captive for nearly seven years.

Finally, a federal grand jury in Seattle indicted Ahmed Ressam in January on nine counts, including conspiracy to commit a terrorist act. Authorities stated that Ressam's apprehension and arrest broke up an intricate plot by Islamic Algerian terrorists to set off a bomb during millennium celebrations in the United States. If convicted of all counts, Ressam could face more than 90 years in prison. The trial was scheduled to begin in Los Angeles in March 2001.

JEFFREY SIMON, *Author*
"The Terrorist Trap"

Thailand

A new Thai Senate was elected at mid-year 2000. In November the House of Representatives reached the end of its term and was dissolved. The election of a new House was scheduled for January 2001.

Politics. Democratic Thailand's longest-serving legislature was dissolved by royal decree on November 9, just a week short of its full four-year term. New elections were scheduled for Jan. 6, 2001. Originally elected on Nov. 17, 1996, the outgoing House of Representatives had two prime ministers. The first, Chavalit Yongchaiyudh, leader of the New Aspiration Party (NAP), was forced to step down in the wake of the economic crash of 1997, after only a year in office. Chuan Leekpai,, leader of the opposition Democrat Party (DP), became prime minister. In July, 96 NAP parliamentarians, the majority of the opposition, attempted to force an early election by resigning their seats. This only had the effect of enhancing Chuan's coalition's majority for the last five months of the session.

The 500 members of the new House of Representatives will be the first elected under a new constitution and under the independent Election Commission. The task of the commission is to implement electoral laws designed to eliminate the fraud and money politics characteristic of Thailand's electoral history. If the 2000 election for the upper house—the theoretically nonpartisan Senate—was any guide, the Election Commission will be hard pressed. Because the Election Commission kept disqualifying winning candidates for voter fraud and illegal spending, it took five rounds of voting between March and June to fill the 200 Senate seats. Attempts to strip the commission of its power were turned back in October when the Constitutional Court ruled that the Election Commission could bar candidates found to have violated electoral law.

Chuan's Democrats faced strong opposition from the Thai Rak Thai (Thai Love Thai) Party led by telecommunications magnate Thaksin Shinawatra. The Thai Rak Thai replaced the NAP as the Democrats' principal opponent. Public-opinion polls through the second half of the year showed Thai Rak Thai and Thaksin consistently ahead of Chuan and the Democrats on issues of the economy, corruption, and environment. Chuan was further hurt when the Democrats' political manager, Interior Minister Sanan Kachornprasart, was indicted for cor-

ruption and then banned from politics for five years. Heading toward the polls, however, Thaksin himself was under multiple investigations about taxes, illegal share transfers, and incomplete asset disclosures—any of which, if proved, could disqualify him from office.

Economy. Thai economic recovery sputtered in 2000. The manufacturing-production index dropped sharply. Plants operated well below capacity. Exports faltered. The currency was under pressure. The stock market dropped. Public debt was 54% of gross domestic product (GDP) and rising. All of the macroeconomic indicators suggested that future growth would be slow. New investment was stalled as business awaited the outcome of the election.

In October, in a preelection effort to turn the economy around, the government initiated a stimulus package. The Thai Rak Thai Party seized upon mismanagement of the economy as a major campaign issue. Thaksin's message was that the Chuan government slavishly adhered to the economic-policy discipline of the International Monetary Fund (IMF), which favored the rich.

Foreign Affairs. In February, Thailand served as host for the Tenth United Nations Conference on Trade and Development (UNCTAD X). Ten thousand Thai police and military formed a tight security ring around the 3,000 delegates from 143 nations. It was the first major meeting on the global economy since the collapse of the 1999 Seattle World Trade Organization (WTO) meeting following street violence. The demonstrations in Bangkok were smaller than in Seattle, and order was maintained.

DONALD E. WEATHERBEE
University of South Carolina

Theater

Despite Broadway's movement toward mass entertainment with a concentration on musicals, the year 2000 also was marked by breakthroughs in the realm of more cerebral theater. The likelihood of either science or mathematics as the basis for a Broadway hit seemed slim. Yet, the imported British drama *Copenhagen*, winner of the 1999–2000 season Tony Award for best play, captivated audiences who had to pay close attention to a plot involving nuclear weapons, World War II, and discussions about loyalty and betrayal, truth and motivation, and personal relationships. Michael Blakemore was awarded the Tony for best director for *Copenhagen*, and Blair Brown won for best featured actress. The play *Proof*, which started off-Broadway and moved to Broadway after its initial success, dealt with the discovery of a math solution and the refusal to believe that a young woman could have solved a problem that had stumped the male establishment.

Even more unlikely was the making of a musical out of a math theorem, yet that was what the off-Broadway York Theatre Company presented under the title of *Fermat's Last Tango*, which featured Euclid, Pythagoras, and Sir Isaac Newton breaking into song in a fictional story related to the 1993 achievement of Andrew Wiles, the Princeton University professor who, after a false start, proved the renowned theorem of 17th-century mathematician Pierre de Fermat.

Other productions that appealed to audiences who sought more substantial fare included the return of Tom Stoppard's *The Real Thing*, which explored complicated marital and extramarital relationships. It was honored with a Tony for best play revival, a best actress Tony for Jennifer Ehle, and a best actor Tony for Stephen Dillane. A new production of Eugene O'Neill's emotionally powerful *A Moon For the Misbegotten* netted Roy Dotrice a Tony as best featured actor in a play. A revival of Sam Shepard's disturbing *True West* featured Philip Seymour Hoffman and John C. Reilly alternating the leading roles. Arthur Miller was back on Broadway with his drama *The Ride Down Mount Morgan*, previously presented off-Broadway by the Public Theater.

Popular revivals included Anton Chekhov's *Uncle Vanya*, which starred the renowned British actor Derek Jacobi, and Harold Pinter's *Betrayal*. Gore Vidal's acerbic *The Best Man* was revived in time to make its political shenanigans amusingly relevant in an election year. One of the most powerful dramas was August Wilson's *Jitney*, an off-Broadway entry dealing with struggling African-American characters connected to a Pittsburgh taxi service. Gregory Murphy's *The Countess*, an unusual, compelling play set in the 19th century and dealing with the scandal-scarred lives of art critic John Ruskin, his wife Effie, and artist John Everett Millais, had a substantial off-Broadway run.

In the comedy department, Neil Simon's *The Dinner Party* farcically examined what happens when former couples are brought together for a mysterious dinner in Paris. Linda Lavin, Michelle Lee, and Tony Roberts were quite amusing in Charles Busch's witty comedy *The Tale of the Allergist's Wife*, which got its start off-Broadway but moved to a Broadway theater as a result of its popularity. Lily Tomlin returned to Broadway with a freshly mounted production of her previous *The Search for*

© Joan Marcus

Broadway audiences were captivated by "Copenhagen," the British import which won the Tony Award for best play. Blair Brown (center) also won a Tony Award for best featured actress in the World War II-era drama.

Tom Stoppard's "The Real Thing," a complex look at marital and extramarital relationships, was honored with Tony Awards for best revival of a play and best actor in a drama. The play had a four-month run.

© Joan Marcus

Signs of Intelligent Life in the Universe. A revival of *The Man Who Came to Dinner*, starring Nathan Lane in the role of Sheridan Whiteside, was presented at the American Airlines Theatre, a renovated version of the old Selwyn Theatre and the new home of the Roundabout Theatre. Claudia Shear's *Dirty Blonde*, in which she starred both as Mae West and one of her fans, was yet another play that made the leap from off-Broadway to Broadway.

Musicals. A musical of exceptional quality was Meredith Willson's *The Music Man*, restaged with great flair by director-choreographer Susan Stroman and well acted by Craig Bierko and Rebecca Luker in the leads. *Contact*, the Tony best musical choice for the 1999–2000 season, with choreography by Stroman, made a striking impression on audiences as a three-part work described as a dance play. Other *Contact* awards included Tonys for Boyd Gaines as featured actor in a musical, Karen Ziemba as featured actress in a musical, and Stroman for her choreography.

The Tony for best actor in a musical went to Brian Stokes Mitchell for *Kiss Me Kate*, which opened in 1999. (The theater season has long had its own calendar, running from the fall of one year through the spring of the next.) The show also won a Tony for best revival of a musical, another for best direction of a musical by Michael Blakemore, and others for costumes and orchestration. The Tony for best book for a musical went to *James Joyce's The Dead*. An adaptation of the opera *Aida* received mixed reviews, but appealed to those who enjoyed the glitzy production—and there was general agreement that Heather Headley deserved her

Tony for best actress in a musical. Elton John and Tim Rice also won one for original score, and another coveted Tony was bestowed for the scenery. A musical revival that did not strike sparks was *Jesus Christ Superstar*.

The popular British film *The Full Monty* became the basis for a lively Broadway song-and-dance show by the same title. The scene switched from England to Buffalo, NY, as men hit by recession concocted a scheme to make money as strippers. Publicity about their appearing in the nude doubtlessly helped sell tickets. *Jane Eyre* was an ambitious musical adaptation of Charlotte Brontë's classic novel, and while the music left much to be desired, the strong story went far to make the show involving, and there was an impressive title performance by Marla Schaffel. *Seussical*, which underwent many changes before opening, was based on writings by Dr. Seuss (pseudonym of Theodore Geisel), but it stirred limited admiration, although it came across as a candidate for family entertainment. There were two versions of *The Wild Party*, both based on the 1920's poem by Moncure March: one on Broadway and another at off-Broadway's Manhattan Theater Club.

Holdover musicals that continued to draw audiences included the hot ticket *The Lion King*, the long-running *Phantom of the Opera, Chicago, Cabaret, Annie Get your Gun, Beauty and the Beast, Fosse, Les Miserables, Swing!*, and *Miss Saigon*. Alas, the phenomenal run of *Cats* finally ended after 7,485 performances seen by more than 10 million people.

Off-Broadway and Broadway. Over the years, the artistic line has been increasingly blurred between Broadway and off-Broadway. Tony Awards are confined to eligible Broadway shows, with the result that these prizes are largely promotions for main-stem productions, and enticing musicals are given prominence in Tony Award broadcasts. But the Drama Desk, a prestigious organization

© Joan Marcus

much British actors contribute to the U.S. theater, as Eileen Atkins and Alan Bates delivered superb performances as strangers who meet on a train. Another was the appearance of Ralph Fiennes in *Richard II* and *Coriolanus*, imported productions from England, staged at the Brooklyn Academy of Music.

A revival of Edward Albee's enigmatic *Tiny Alice* was lauded in its off-Broadway reincarnation. Lee Blessing's *Cobb* presented three actors confronting each other as baseball great Ty Cobb at various stages of his life, and the play made a strong dramatic impact. *Dinner With Friends*, Donald Margulies' clever play about the effect of a marital breakup on friends as well as on the troubled couple, won the 2000 Pulitzer Prize for

Although the play itself won mixed reviews, Heather Headley (above) earned wide acclaim—and a coveted Tony for best actress in a musical—for her performance in "Aida." More well-received was a restaging of Meredith Willson's rousing "The Music Man."

© Joan Marcus

of critics and journalists, combined Broadway and off-Broadway productions in giving awards. Many shows that open off-Broadway ultimately move to Broadway to accommodate more people and to potentially earn more money.

Some of the most striking shows of the year, including the ones noted above, enlivened the theater scene in general and off-Broadway in particular. One was Alan Ayckbourn's *Comic Potential*, a futuristic look at the world of television soap opera in which the cast members are played by programmed robots. British actress Janie Dee, who won awards in London when the play was staged there, repeated her dazzling performance as a robot who begins to have human feelings after meeting a young man who falls in love with her. In another import from London, Yasmina Reza's *The Unexpected Man* was a further example of how

Drama and was snapped up for a Home Box Office (HBO) movie, directed by Norman Jewison. Wendy Wasserstein's class-conscious play *Old Money* opened off-Broadway but was poorly received. Anne Meara, an actress-turned-playwright, wrote *Down the Garden Paths*. Anne Jackson, Eli Wallach, and John Shea starred in the comedy-drama that wittily examined what might have happened in a family if there had been different twists of fate.

One of the funniest plays was Becky Mode's *Fully Committed*, a one-man show that starred Mark Setlock as a would-be actor taking reservations in the basement of a four-star restaurant. There was yet another edition of the long-running *Forbidden Broadway*, which satirized Broadway shows

"Jane Eyre," an ambitious musical adaptation of Charlotte Brontë's classic novel, opened on Broadway in December 2000. Critics cited the impressive performances of Marla Schaffel in the title role and James Barbour as Mr. Rochester.

© Joan Marcus

and their stars. The latest production was called *Forbidden Broadway 2001*.

Off-Broadway is a lively place for ethnic-based theater. For example, the Irish Repertory Theatre, which presents an assortment of productions each season, revived Brendan Behan's *The Hostage*. The Folksbiene Yiddish Theatre brought back Sylvia Regan's play *An American Family*, a saga about Jewish immigrants building their lives in New York City, presented in Yiddish with the audience using earphones for simultaneous English translation.

Whether offered on or off-Broadway, there were some shows that defied easy classification. *Riverdance on Broadway* featured a company of talented Irish dancers doing showstopping steps. A special "live theatrical event" Tony award was presented for *Dame Edna, the Royal Tour*, starring Barry Humphries in his often-hilarious creation of the outrageous lady who becomes a full-fledged character, and not merely a man in woman's clothing. Another special Tony went to *Encores! Great American Musicals in Concert*, a series that has been in existence for seven years and offers scaled-down, concert-style versions of famous American musicals of the past. The sold-out presentations in 2000 included an especially fine treatment of *Wonderful Town*.

Regional Theater. Many regional theaters throughout the United States provide venues for developing fresh talent while enabling audiences to enjoy stage productions in their home cities. At the same time, regional theaters serve as launching pads for Broadway shows and major careers. The Utah Shakespearean Festival in Cedar City,

UT, received national recognition when it was honored with a Tony Award in the 2000 ceremonies for displaying "a continuous level of artistic achievement contributing to the growth of theater nationally." (Past honorees included the La Jolla Playhouse in California, the Seattle Repertory Theatre, the Guthrie Theatre in Minneapolis, the Steppenwolf Theatre in Chicago, and the Old Globe Theatre in San Diego.) The Utah Shakespearean Festival's 2000 season included *The Merchant of Venice, The Merry Wives of Windsor*, and an adaptation of *The War of the Roses*.

The esteemed Arena Stage in Washington, DC, recognized as one of the country's finest regional groups, celebrated its 50th anniversary in 2000. Its opening anniversary production was a revival of *The Great White Hope*. Another prime regional center is the Actor's Theatre of Louisville, KY, the location for the Humana Festival, which showcases new works and draws visitors from throughout the country. Productions of its own included *Wuthering! Heights! The! Musical!, Dracula, Wit, A Tuna Christmas*, and *A Christmas Carol*.

A sampling of other regional theater productions indicated a high level of activity in various parts of the country. The noted Alley Theatre of Houston, founded in 1947, delivered a varied program that included *Arsenic and Old Lace*, Agatha Christie's *Towards Zero*, Shakespeare's *A Midsummer Night's Dream*, and Patrick Marber's contemporary *Closer*. Among other institutions, New Jersey's busy theater activity included that of The Two River Theatre Company of Red Bank, which staged George Bernard Shaw's *Arms and the Man*. The New Jersey Shakespeare Festival's program included a production of *The Merchant of Venice*. In Florida, the Royal Palm Beach Dinner Theatre presented *Bells Are Ringing, High Society, Little Me*, and *Of Thee I Sing*, and The Actors' Playhouse of Coral Gables offered *The Amazing Technicolor Dreamcoat*.

BROADWAY OPENINGS • 2000

MUSICALS

Aida, book by Linda Woolverton; music by Elton John; lyrics by Tim Rice; directed by Robert Falls; choreographed by Wayne Cilento; with Heather Headley, Sherie René Scott, Adam Pascal; March 23–.

Contact, book by Susan Stroman and John Weidman; directed and choreographed by Susan Stroman; March 30–.

The Full Monty, book by Terrence McNally; music and lyrics by David Yazbek; directed by Jack O'Brien; choreography by Jerry Mitchell; with André De Shields, John Ellison Conlee, and Patrick Wilson; October 26—.

Jane Eyre, music by Paul Gordon; directed by John Caird and Scott Schwartz; with Marla Schaffel, James Barbour; December 10–.

Jesus Christ Superstar, book by Tim Rice; music by Andrew Lloyd Webber; lyrics by Tim Rice; directed by Gale Edwards; with Glenn Carter; April 16–September 3.

The Music Man, book, music, and lyrics by Meredith Willson; story by Meredith Willson and Franklin Lacey; directed and choreographed by Susan Stroman; with Craig Bierko, Rebecca Luker; April 27–.

The Rocky Horror Show, music by Henry Aronson; directed by Christopher Ashley; choreography by Jerry Mitchell; with Tom Hewitt, Joan Jett, Daphne Rubin-Vega, Jarrod Emmick, and Dick Cavett; November 16–.

Seussical, book by Stephen Flaherty and Lynn Ahrens; music by Stephen Flaherty; directed by Frank Galati; choreography by Kathleen Marshall; with Anthony Blair Hall, David Shiner, Michele Pawk; November 30–.

The Wild Party, book by George C. Wolfe and Michael John LaChiusa; music and lyrics by Michael John LaChiusa; directed by George C. Wolfe; with Toni Collette, Eartha Kitt, Mandy Patinkin, Yancey Arias, Tonya Pinkins; April 13–June 11.

PLAYS

The Best Man, by Gore Vidal; directed by Ethan McSweeny; with Charles Durning, Spalding Gray, Chris Noth, Elizabeth Ashley, Michael Learned; October 11–December 31.

Betrayal, by Harold Pinter; directed by David Leveaux; with Juliette Binoche, Liev Schreiber, John Slattery, Mark Lotito; November 14–.

Copenhagen, by Michael Frayn; directed by Michael Blakemore; with Philip Bosco, Blair Brown, Michael Cumpsty; April 11–.

The Dinner Party, by Neil Simon; directed by John Rando; with Henry Winkler, John Ritter, Len Cariou; October 19–.

Dirty Blonde, by Claudia Shear; directed by James Lapine; with Claudia Shear, Bob Stillman, Kevin Chamberlin; May 1–.

The Green Bird, by Carlo Gozzi; translated by Albert Bermel and Ted Emery; directed by Julie Taymor; music composed and orchestrated by Elliott Goldenthal; with Derek Smith, Didi Conn, Ned Eisenberg, Kristine Nielsen, Edward Hibbert; April 18–June 4.

The Man Who Came to Dinner, by Moss Hart and George S. Kaufman; directed by Jerry Zaks; with Nathan Lane; July 27–October 1.

A Moon for the Misbegotten, by Eugene O'Neill; directed by Daniel Sullivan; with Cherry Jones, Gabriel Byrne, Roy Dotrice; March 19–July 2.

Proof, by David Auburn; directed by Daniel Sullivan; with Mary-Louise Parker, Larry Bryggman, Ben Shenkman, Johanna Day; October 24–.

The Real Thing, by Tom Stoppard; directed by David Leveaux; with Stephen Dillance, Jennifer Ehle; April 17–August 13.

The Ride Down Mount Morgan, by Arthur Miller; directed by David Esbjornson; with Patrick Stewart, Frances Conroy, Shannon Burkett; April 9–July 23.

Rose, by Martin Sherman; directed by Nancy Meckler; with Olympia Dukakis; April 12–May 20.

The Tale of the Allergist's Wife, by Charles Busch; directed by Lynne Meadow; with Linda Lavin, Tony Roberts, Michele Lee; November 2–.

Taller than a Dwarf, by Elaine May; directed by Alan Arkin; with Matthew Broderick, Parker Posey; April 24–June 11.

True West, by Sam Shepard; directed by Michael Warchus; with Philip Seymour Hoffman, John C. Reilly; March 9–July 29.

Uncle Vanya, by Anton Chekhov; directed by Michael Mayer; with Derek Jacobi, Anne Pitoniak, Laura Linney, Brian Murray, Roger Rees, David Patrick Kelly; April 30–June 11.

Wrong Mountain, by David Hirson; directed by Richard Jones; with Ron Rifkin, Daniel Davis, Michael Winters; January 13–February 5.

OTHER ENTERTAINMENT

Riverdance, a revue; composed by Bill Whelan; produced by Moya Doherty; directed by John McColgan; March 16– .

The Search For Signs of Intelligent Life in the Universe, written by Jane Wagner; with Lily Tomlin; November 16–.

Squonk, a music-theater piece created and performed by Steve O'Hearn, Jackie Dempsey, T. Weldon Anderson, Kevin Kornicki, Jana Losey, Casi Pacilio; February 2–March 26.

Notes. For the most part, the box office boomed for the Broadway theaters. The League of American Theatres and Producers, the trade organization that negotiates union contracts and promotes Broadway theater, announced that the week of December 25–31 was "the highest grossing week in Broadway history." Indeed, some $19 million was taken in during that final week of 2000, representing an 18% increase over the same period in 1999. Theater attendance increased nearly 10%, with 286,357 persons attending a total of 30 shows.

Box-office figures for the 1999–2000 season totaled $603 million, a hike from the previous season's $588 million. Higher ticket prices accounted for some of the increase, as attendance was actually down slightly. There were 37 new productions staged.

There was also big business in road company tours of Broadway shows. In fact, money at the box office on the road almost equaled that on Broadway for the 1999–2000 season. The total box office take was $572 million with 11.7 million in attendance. By contrast, the Broadway shows drew 11.38 million in attendance.

A partial changing of the guard took place in New York at the influential Actors Studio, the workshop that played an important part in the development of talent during the second half of the 20th century. Three copresidents were named—Al Pacino, Ellen Burstyn, and Harvey Keitel; they replaced Arthur Penn. Estelle Parsons remained as artistic director.

WILLIAM WOLF
New York University

Transportation

The transportation industry experienced many milestones during 2000, but the year ended with the future of some of those changes mired in doubt. The world's largest airline announced plans for the industry's largest merger, while the biggest railroad merger in history was derailed. The fastest commercial jet was grounded after a fatal crash, while the most enormous cruise ship ever built set sail. Plans were made to build the largest passenger jet and an even more gigantic cruise ship. Rising fuel costs hit carriers in just about every mode, and labor unrest affected passengers on everything from planes to trains to city buses. It was also a year of tragedy, as transportation crashes cost hundreds of lives.

Aviation. On January 31 an Alaska Airlines flight from Puerto Vallarta, Mexico, to San Francisco crashed into the Pacific Ocean near Los Angeles. All 83 passengers and the five-member crew were killed. The crash shook the western carrier as it struggled to answer questions from the Federal Aviation Administration (FAA) about its ability to oversee its own maintenance program. The FAA announced nearly $1 million in fines against the airline late in the year. The crash investigation focused on a jackscrew controlling the tail's horizontal stabilizer, which controls the pilot's ability to adjust the altitude of the MD-80 aircraft.

Just more than six weeks after the crash, an Alaska Airlines flight on the same route had another scary incident and was forced to land when a passenger went out of control during the flight. The passenger, Peter L. Bradley, Jr., broke down the cockpit door before several passengers were able to subdue him. The incident brought new attention to the problem of "air rage," or incidents of violent or inappropriate actions by airline passengers. The U.S. Congress already had passed a law earlier in the year raising civil penalties for interfering with a flight crew to $25,000 from $1,100.

On May 24, United Airlines, the world's largest airline, announced it was making a $4.3 billion cash bid for US Airways Group, the sixth-largest airline in the United States, in what would be the largest merger in the airline industry's history. The move prompted speculation of further consolidation within the industry, with expectations that Number 2 U.S. carrier American Airlines and Number 3 Delta would be forced to make deals to purchase major carriers. Overseas,

British Airways and KLM Royal Dutch Airlines discussed what would have been the world's largest cross-border merger.

The proposed deals raised concerns that passenger service would suffer and fares would rise. United's unionized employees, especially its pilots, objected to the potential loss of seniority. This was a significant factor since United's parent, UAL, was the world's largest employee-owned company in 2000: Pilots held about a 25% stake, and members of the International Association of Machinists owned about 20%. The drumbeat of airline consolidation eventually quieted to a whisper. The British Airways–KLM discussions ended without a deal, and the year ended with the United–US Airways deal still pending. Early in 2001, that deal became more likely, though, as American Airlines announced plans to purchase the bankrupt Trans World Airlines, as well as some of US Airways' assets. The move could lessen regulators' concerns about the United–US Airways deal.

On July 25, Air France's supersonic jet, the Concorde, crashed into a hotel shortly after takeoff from Charles de Gaulle Airport near Paris, en route to New York's John F. Kennedy International Airport (JFK). All 100 passengers and nine crew members were killed, as were five people on the ground. Photographs showed fire shooting from the jet even before the plane lifted off. Investigators believe a metal strip on the runway, possibly dropped from another jet, caused a blowout in one of the supersonic jet's tires, which is believed to have sent heavy chunks of rubber into the fuel tanks located in the Concorde's wings. The investigation, and concerns about the aircraft's landing gear, resulted in both Air France and British Airways grounding the aircraft, the only supersonic commercial jet in the world. Both airlines hope to regain clearance to fly it again in 2001.

Another major crash that was apparently caused by runway debris was the October 31 crash of a Singapore Airlines 747 in Taipei, Taiwan. The plane, flying to Los Angeles, tried to take off into an approaching typhoon and apparently struck construction equipment on the runway, which was under repair. A total of 83 people on board died.

Once again a private-plane crash gathered nationwide headlines in 2000. On October 16, three men, including Missouri Gov. Mel Carnahan, were killed in the crash of a Cessna 335, about 25 mi (40.3 km) south of St. Louis. The other victims were his son

The sight of US Airways (background) and United Airlines (foreground) planes parked in the same gate could be a familiar one in 2001, as United again appeared poised to buy out its rival. Rumblings of such a deal in 2000 had US Airways employees in an uproar about their future, and airline customers concerned with a potential decline in service.

Roger, who was piloting the plane, and Chris Sifford, a top campaign aide. They were en route to a campaign event when Roger radioed that he was having trouble with the plane's instruments. Mel Carnahan, a Democrat, was campaigning for a U.S. Senate seat held by Sen. John Ashcroft. Because Carnahan's death came so close to the November 7 election, his name remained on the Missouri ballot. Despite his death, he managed to win the election, and his successor, Gov. Roger Wilson, named Jean Carnahan, Mel's widow, to take his Senate seat.

A number of major airlines found planes grounded by labor pains despite no formal strikes. United Airlines was involved in labor negotiations with its pilots and machinists. United settled a lucrative pact with its pilots, but went to court to try to force its mechanics to stop grounding planes. Delta sued its pilots for not agreeing to fly overtime during negotiations, and Northwest Airlines, the fourth-largest U.S. carrier, sued its mechanics' union to try to force it from grounding planes.

The various labor problems contributed to a growing delay problem at the nation's airports. FAA statistics showed that there were three delays per 1,000 flights from June through October. Delays per 1,000 flights were up 17% from the same period in

1999. Weather was the biggest problem, but aircraft volume and air-traffic-control problems played a role.

One choke point of the system was New York's LaGuardia Airport, which accounted for 23% of the nation's flight delays—more than half due to volume. The FAA long had restricted flights to LaGuardia, JFK, and Chicago's O'Hare International Airport, but those restrictions were loosened during the summer, under legislation that authorized new flights by carriers with fewer than 20 slots at LaGuardia, along with carriers serving small hubs and nonhubs. The rule was meant to promote competition and service, but caused gridlock instead, as airlines, especially the commuter arms of major carriers, rushed to begin new service into LaGuardia. Due to that airport's congestion, the FAA held a lottery in December to allocate landing and takeoff slots at LaGuardia, and limit the number of flights through September 2001, while the agency devised a new plan.

One solution that could move more passengers through major air hubs is the plan of European aircraft manufacturer Airbus Industrie to build the A380 jet, a two-level "superjumbo" jet that could carry 550 passengers. The first deliveries were expected in 2006. Competitor Boeing announced plans for a new version of its 747 jumbo jet, a smaller, wide-body jet with longer range.

Amtrak's Acela Express (above), *the nation's new high-speed train, began serving the heavily traveled Washington to New York City and New York City to Boston runs. New public light-rail service* (left) *should help reduce traffic in congested northern New Jersey.*

Railroads. In the world of railroads, U.S. regulators blocked the proposed merger between Burlington Northern Santa Fe (BNSF) and Canadian National (CN). The Surface Transportation Board, the U.S. body regulating railroads, issued a 15-month moratorium on rail mergers in March, saying it needed to study the rules.

When the $19 billion deal between BNSF and CN had been proposed in December 1999, it was seen as the first step in a final round of consolidation expected to eventually leave North America with only two major railroads, each serving most of the continent. Many rail customers objected to that prospect, saying the other major railroads had failed to solve service problems associated with previous mergers. Those railroads joined to object to the BNSF-CN deal, saying they were not ready for further mergers, but would be forced into deals by market realities if such a combination were approved.

In passenger rail, Amtrak started its long-delayed high-speed train service, Acela Express, between Boston and Washington in December. The train reached 135 mph (217.7 km/hr) between Washington and New York, and 150 mph (241.9 km/hr) between New York and Boston. The difference in speed was due to the condition of the tracks, but the speeds were well below the 190 mph (306.5 km/hr) achieved by bullet trains in Japan and Europe. At current speeds, Acela was only about 15 minutes quicker than the traditional Metroliner service from Washington to New York, although it saved closer to 45 minutes from New York to Boston. The service was seen as a key to Amtrak becoming self-sufficient. But service was not expected to be on full schedule until 2001, years later than originally planned.

Ocean Shipping. It was a generally profitable year for shipping lines, although U.S.

companies were no longer one of the major players. Lines benefited from strong rates, particularly on shipments to the United States, which gave the industry one of its most profitable years in quite a while. But there was industry concern that the boom could be short-lived, with a number of new, huge container ships—too large to fit through the Panama Canal—due to start calling on U.S. ports in 2001. Those mother ships could tip the balance on rates.

Larger passenger ships were on the horizon. On October 28, Royal Caribbean's *Explorer of the Seas* inaugurated service as the world's largest cruise ship. The 15-deck, 142,000-ton ship can carry 3,114 guests. Weeks later, Carnival Cruise Lines announced its Cunard Line would build the *Queen Mary 2*, a $780 million ship that at 1,132 ft (345.1 m) long would be 112 ft (34.1 m) longer than *Explorer of the Seas*, although it would carry only 2,620 passengers. The *Queen Mary* was due to be launched in 2003. That was one of about 50 cruise ships planned by the industry. Carnival had 15 other ships on order. Some suggested that the industry was already over capacity, and that finances could be difficult during 2001.

The year saw two high-profile bankruptcies when Florida-based Premier Cruise Lines went out of business in September, and Commodore Holdings, Ltd., the parent of Commodore Cruise Lines and Crown Cruise Line filed for bankruptcy in December. In the case of Premier, which operated the Big Red Boat ships, creditors seized its six ships, sending some passengers home mid-trip from ports ranging from Halifax, Nova Scotia; to Nassau, the Bahamas; to Cozumel, Mexico. In December, one of Premier's ships, *SeaBreeze*, was heading from Halifax to Charleston, SC, for engine repairs when its engines failed in heavy seas about 200 mi (322.6 km) off the Virginia coast. Fortunately, there were no passengers on board, and the crew of 32 was rescued by Coast Guard helicopter. The ship itself sank.

Public Transit and Trucking. Public transit installed new service during 2000, as a light-rail service started in Hudson County, NJ, when a 7.5-mi (12.1-km) stretch between Bayonne, NJ, and Jersey City, NJ, opened in March. It was expected to eventually run about 20 mi (32.3 km), reaching north to Ridgefield, NJ, at a cost of $1.1 billion. The new service was hailed as a way of relieving the chronic congestion and subsequent air pollution in the region.

Light-rail advocates hoped the New Jersey project might be a trendsetter. As the year ended, about 200 proposed systems nationwide vied for $6.3 billion in federal dollars. But some doubted that transit systems would be the answer. In late December, business and community groups withdrew support of a proposed light-rail system in Seattle when new estimates came out suggesting that the proposed 21-mi (33.9-m) project would take three years longer and cost $1 billion more to construct than originally planned.

Public transit suffered a setback when transit workers in Los Angeles went on strike in September. Officials with the Metropolitan Transportation Authority (MTA) sought concessions to save $23 million annually. As a result, the 4,400 members of the United Transportation Union stayed out 32 days, cutting off bus and light-rail service to about 450,000 riders. The deal to end the strike was eventually brokered by the Rev. Jesse Jackson.

Federal Express (FedEx) made a move to become a larger player in the world of trucking in 2000 as it announced plans to buy American Freightways, a carrier that moved pallet-sized shipments from different customers in the same truck—a sector of the industry known as less-than-truckload (LTL). FedEx had bought a smaller LTL as part of a 1997 deal for a national parcel-delivery service. With the American Freightways purchase, FedEx will have virtually national LTL coverage. The company also expanded its national parcel-delivery service and renamed it FedEx Ground.

The year ended with a major merger in the truckload-carrier sector, which moves trailer-sized shipments of freight directly from origin to final destination without the intermediate use of warehouses needed by the LTL sector. Swift Transportation Co., which had been an active buyer of smaller, privately held trucking companies, bought M.S. Carriers, a large, publicly traded carrier. The deal would establish the nation's third-largest truckload carrier.

FedEx, United Parcel Service (UPS), and other trucking companies responded to rising fuel prices by imposing fuel surcharges on their customers. Nevertheless, demand remained strong, and some trucking companies, particularly in the LTL sector, were able to report increased profits in the face of rapidly escalating fuel prices.

CHRIS ISIDORE
Freelance Transportation Writer

Travel

Although the U.S. share of the global travel market showed a slight decline in 2000, the nation remained the third-most-popular tourist destination—after France and Spain—with 46.4 million foreign visitors. The United States ranked first in terms of spending by inbound travelers, and U.S. travelers spent a record $81.4 billion on visits abroad. Thanks to a healthy economy and higher personal earnings, leisure travel led the industry, with more than 1 billion person-trips of 50 mi (80 km) or more away from home. Business travel edged up, accounting for 212.3 million person-trips.

Domestic Travel. Rising gas prices (*see* ENERGY—Gas Prices) did not put the brakes on U.S. travel plans in 2000. More than 80% of pleasure travelers drove their cars on family vacations, and recreational-vehicle (RV) travel increased sharply. Weekend trips accounted for more than one-half of all domestic travel, while vacationers on longer trips spent an average of ten nights on the road, up from 8.5 in 1999. The American Automobile Association (AAA) reported leisure-travel expenses held steady, with an average food and lodging cost of $213 per day for a family of four. Baby boomers (ages 35 to 54) generated the highest volume (more than 25 million trips), were more apt to fly, stay in a hotel or motel, and spend more than other group—averaging $460 per trip, excluding transportation.

Beaches remained the favorite destination, with 50 million travelers heading to the shore in summer 2000. Museums, historical sites, and cultural events drew another 66.6 million visitors. One in eight travelers played golf when they were on trips of 100 mi (160 km) or more away from home. Outlet shopping was a secondary interest for 78% of travelers. Nationwide, the number of hotel rooms grew 3% in 2000, while demand was up 3.5%. Average room rates were $85, a 4.4% increase over 1999. Florida, New York, Nevada, and California remained top vacation destinations for domestic and international travelers.

All forms of transportation showed growth for the year. Despite fuel surcharges, crowded planes, and unparalleled cancellations and delays, demand for air travel was at an all-time high. The nation's airlines transported about 670 million people, an increase of 6%, and anticipated net revenues of $2.5 billion. The average fare for a 1,000-mi (1 600-km) domestic trip rose 3.7%, with first-class fares up 5.9%. Amtrak touted ten-year highs in riders and revenues, with record-breaking summer sales. Acela Express high-speed trains were launched late in the year on the corridor between Boston, New York, and Washington.

International Travel. Bolstered by the U.S. dollar's continued strength against the fledgling euro, outbound U.S. travel was brisk. Although growth was somewhat limited by tight air capacity, arrivals were projected to reach 12.2 million to Britain and Western Europe, up 3.5%. It was the seventh straight year for record numbers. In addition, visitor counts were up 30% in Central Europe. Tourism was flat in most parts of the Middle East, but travelers began returning to Asia. Hong Kong was the top destination, with some 11 million visitors, followed by China, Thailand, Malaysia, Singapore, and Vietnam. Australia and New Zealand visitor counts were up in light of the Summer Olympics in Sydney. U.S. Treasury Department statistics showed U.S. visitors to Cuba up 47%. Americans also flocked across the borders to Canada and Mexico, helping raise tourism 3.7% in Canada and 4% in Mexico.

Travel in the United States was on track to end 2000 nearly 3% higher than in 1999, according to the Travel Industry Association of America. Domestic and international travel expenditures were expected to reach $557 billion. Canada and Mexico sent more travelers to the United States than other inbound destinations, with forecasted visitor counts of 14 million and 10 million from each country, respectively.

Cruising and General Trends. The cruise industry was in the middle of the biggest shipbuilding cycle in its relatively brief history, adding 9.9% more berths in 2000. According to the Cruise Line International Association, increased capacity would be absorbed by a 10.2% growth in passengers for the year, to 6.5 million. The year 2000 saw the demise of Premier Cruises and the birth of Hawaii's United States Lines.

Some 25 million Americans booked travel on the Internet, up 60% from 1999, with 82% using the Net to make air arrangements. E-tickets also accounted for roughly 60% of all airline tickets sold in the United States. Growth markets included spa visits, time-share vacations (*see* SIDEBAR), adventure travel, educational travel, multisport travel, and ecotourism.

BARBARA J. BRAASCH
Freelance Travel Writer

Time-Shares

Time-sharing—or vacation ownership, as it is called by the industry—has become the fastest-growing segment of the U.S. travel market, according to the American Resort Development Association (ARDA), an industry trade group. Nearly 2 million Americans have bought time-shares since the concept was imported from Europe in the early 1970s. The market has catapulted from a modest $300 million business in 1978 to an estimated $7 billion industry in 2000. The number of units sold in 1999 reached a record 318,000, up 8% from the previous year.

The Concept. The original time-share idea carved ownership of individual resort condominiums or hotel units into a series of time intervals, usually one or two weeks. Buyers paid an up-front purchase price for a specific time slot and annual maintenance fees. There were several drawbacks to early ownership. Buyers were locked into spending vacations in the same place year after year. And, unlike typical real estate, if buyers decided to sell their time interval, there was virtually no chance of recovering anything even close to the purchase price.

Options and Trends. In the 1990s, new options, particularly the increased flexibility of trading vacation periods and locations, spurred time-share sales. For a modest exchange fee, an owner could exchange a time slot in one place for a corresponding interval in another resort area anywhere in the world. In 1999, Resort Condominiums International (RCI), the first time-share exchange service, reported almost 2 million exchanges at more than 3,500 resorts in some 100 countries.

With the traditional two-week vacation being largely replaced by a series of shorter getaways, time-shares today are regarded as a good alternative to buying or renting a vacation home. Many owners split time intervals into two-, three-, or four-day pieces, carrying unused days into another year. Some canny traders even swap land-based time-shares for cruising vacations.

When deluxe hotel and resort properties—such as Marriott, Ritz-Carlton, Hyatt, Four Seasons, Ramada, and Disney—began offering time-shares, the industry acquired a new image and a new way of doing business. Often referred to as "vacation clubs" or "second-home experiences," the luxury resorts guaran-

Photos, Courtesy, Marriott Vacation Club International

The advantages of a vacation ownership—time share—at Marriott's newest vacation clubs, (such as the one above), are explained to an interested couple.

tee lifetime ownership of maintenance-free time-shares at well-sited, generously sized, and meticulously run properties that often include pools, spas, tennis courts, or golf greens. For a change of scenery, buyers can trade an allotted time for a stay at another of the companies' club properties.

The entry of major hotel companies into time-share development has brought the business credibility and visibility, but experts still warn buyers to be wary of scams. In the past, developers often used high-pressure sales pitches and lured people to presentations with offers of free hotel rooms, free airfares, or cash.

Although it typically takes a year for new time-shares to hit the resale market, savvy buyers can pick up previously owned time-shares for 50% to 70% of the developer's original price. On-line resale exchanges that bring together owners of unwanted units and prospective buyers are strengthening the market. In 1999, about 15% of time-share buyers in the United States purchased on resale.

BARBARA J. BRAASCH

Tunisia

While Tunisia continued to consolidate economic gains in 2000, it made no progress in the area of human rights and press freedom. Living conditions continued to improve, but the government's fear of Islamist opposition led to a crackdown on journalists and writers who have a different opinion on political manners.

Politics. In May 2000, Tunisians elected local officials. As expected, the ruling Constitutional Democratic Rally Party (RCD) won 94% of the 4,144 seats across the 257 districts. The RCD faced no competition in 193 districts. The opposition was represented by five symbolic parties that had struggled to survive following their defeat in the 1999 elections. The opposition won 6% of the seats at stake, a result viewed by some as important since it won only 0.14% in the previous election.

Economy and Labor. In 2000 the Tunisian economy was characterized by a rising trade deficit and increased foreign direct investment (FDI). In midyear, Tunisia's trade deficit rose by 12.4%, and FDI had increased by three times over the same period in 1999. The latter increase was attributed to the privatization sale of two cement companies.

To improve corporate competitiveness, Tunisia set up an industrial-modernization program known as the *mise à niveau*. The program, which was supported primarily by funding from the European Union (EU), focused on improving management skills and technology in industrial and manufacturing companies. A severe drought greatly affected Tunisia's agricultural output and caused domestic consumption to slow. Farm output declined by about 15%, resulting in an economic growth rate of just 4%.

The 1999 census figures, which were released in 2000, showed that Tunisia continued to improve its standard of living. Data revealed generalized access to drinking water and electricity in homes as well as increased ownership of automobiles and such durable goods as televisions, radios, refrigerators, and ovens. Tunisia's social and economic improvements led to declining demographic pressure. The population's growth rate declined to 1.15% from 1.7% in 1994.

Tunisia's only trade union, UGTT, witnessed a power struggle that ended with the ousting of its longtime leader, Ismail Sahbani. Sahbani had been a key figure in negotiating social and economic improvement for the nation's working class. His deputy and political opponent, Abdesslam Jerad, became the union's new leader. Sahbani was considered authoritarian and too collaborative with the government and employees. He was accused of putting in place measures to avoid disclosure of decisions and transparency in business affairs.

Human Rights and Press Freedom. In the area of human rights and free speech, the hunger strike of journalist Taoufik Ben Brick dominated the world media, putting immense pressure on the Tunisian government. Ben Brick was protesting government censorship of his writings and also was trying to free his brother, Jelal, from jail. Ben Brick ended his hunger strike when his brother was released.

Habib Bourguiba. Tunisia lost one of its first modern political leaders when former President Habib Bourguiba died on April 6. Bourguiba became the first president of the republic of Tunisia in July 1957 after decades of struggle against French occupation. He sought to modernize Tunisia by generalizing education and launching various social and economic programs that would benefit all social classes. Bourguiba served as president until his ouster in a November 1987 bloodless coup, which was led by the current president—Zine El Abidine Ben Ali.

Bourguiba's funeral ceremony was an opportunity for Ben Ali to salute his predecessor for "his role and sacrifices" for the liberation of Tunisia and its development. In reality, however, the current regime had worked to distance Tunisia from the legacy of President Bourguiba.

ROSE RYAN, *Executive Editor*
"The North Africa Journal"

TUNISIA • Information Highlights

Official Name: Republic of Tunisia.
Location: North Africa.
Area: 63,170 sq mi (163 610 km²).
Population (2000 est.): 9,593,402.
Chief Cities (1994 census): Tunis, the capital, 674,100; Sfax, 230,900.
Government: *Head of state,* Zine El Abidine Ben Ali, president (took office Nov. 7, 1987). *Head of government,* Mohamed Ghannouchi, prime minister (appointed November 1999). *Legislature* (unicameral)—Chamber of Deputies.
Monetary Unit: Dinar (1.4134 dinars equal U.S.$1, Dec. 21, 2000).
Gross Domestic Product (1999 est. U.S.$): $52,600,000,000 (purchasing power parity).
Economic Indexes (1999, 1990 = 100): *Consumer Prices,* all items, 150.8; food, 149.9. *Industrial Production,* 145.9.
Foreign Trade (1999 U.S.$): *Imports,* $8,340,000,000; *exports,* $5,788,000,000.

Turkey

The chief issues for Turkey in 2000 were the election of a new president, continuing tensions involving the Kurdish minority, and measures needed to join the European Union (EU).

Politics. As the seven-year term of office of President Suleyman Demirel neared an end, Turkish Prime Minister Bulent Ecevit supported a constitutional amendment that would have permitted his former rival to be elected a second time. In March, however, the parliament failed to approve the amendment by the necessary margin of two-thirds, voting in favor by only 253 to 236 votes in a secret ballot. Subsequent debates confirmed a lack of support for the amendment that would have had future presidents elected for a maximum of two terms of five years each.

Once it was clear that President Demirel was not eligible to run again, the Turkish parliament turned to electing a new president, finishing this process on May 5 with a third-ballot election of Ahmed Necdet Sezer. On May 16, Sezer took the oath of office as the tenth president of the Republic of Turkey. He had served as a judge on the Constitutional Court since 1983, and as chief justice since 1998, Sezer stated goals to regularize and reduce the powers of the presidency, claiming that "At the basis of all of Turkey's problems is the practice of not abiding by the rules."

Almost immediately, Sezer entered into a dispute with Prime Minister Ecevit and the armed-forces leaders about the constitutionality of emergency powers granted by parliament to the government, which had issued decrees allowing Islamic fundamentalists to be purged from the civil service. On August 30, Huseyin Kivrikoglu, chief of the general staff, called for eliminating Islamists from government employment, in accordance with a decree by the prime minister. President Sezer opposed this, arguing instead that such a measure would be legal only if approved by parliament. On September 27, Sezer broadened the dispute by refusing to sign a decree by Ecevit on privatizing state-owned banks, again citing a constitutional provision that he felt required parliamentary approval of such an action.

Curbing Islamic fundamentalists became a prominent public issue after the discovery of 52 bodies in several locations between January 19 and February 2. The killings were linked by the government to the Turkish Hezbollah organization, many of whose members were arrested later in the year. In September, police closed the offices of the

© Burhan Ozbilici/AP/Wide World Photos

On May 16, 2000, Ahmed Necdet Sezer reviewed the military honor guard before taking the oath of office as the tenth president of the Republic of Turkey. A political independent, the new head of state had been chief justice of the Constitutional Court.

National Youth Federation, a pro-Islamic fundamentalist group.

Kurdish Developments. On June 29, 1999, a Turkish court convicted the captured leader of the Kurdish separatist Kurdistan Workers Party (PKK), Abdullah Öcalan, of treason, sentencing him to be put to death. The two appeals of the sentence were turned down in November and December 1999. However, in January 2000 the government coalition agreed to allow Öcalan to appeal his sentence to the European Court of Human Rights, thereby delaying his possible execution.

In February, PKK spokesmen stated that they were unilaterally abandoning the use of violence, but added that this was contingent on the fate of Öcalan and the future of democracy in Turkey. Later in the month, authorities arrested the Kurdish mayors of three cities, who were associated with the People's Democracy Party (HADEP), a primarily Kurdish organization, charging them with assisting Öcalan. In June an Ankara court sentenced Ahmet Demir, the head of the HADEP, to one year in jail on the grounds that he had advocated an independent Kurdish state.

In August, Turkey signed two international covenants on human rights that had originally been drafted in 1966 and had already been approved by 130 other nations. Turkish reluctance to approve these covenants was based on concerns relating to rights that Kurdish groups might claim under them, especially in regard to the use of the Kurdish language. Signing the covenants became easier after the government on Dec. 14, 1999, decided to permit the use of Kurdish on television broadcasts.

Foreign Affairs. On Dec. 10, 1999, the EU officially invited Turkey and six other countries to join. Turkey accepted the invitation on December 16. However, full membership was unlikely to happen in the near future, since the EU insisted that Turkey first make major changes in human rights, judicial policies, relations with Greece, and economic issues. (*See also* EUROPE.)

In the new year, the Greek and Turkish foreign ministers met in both countries—the first such visits in about 40 years. Turkey and Greece signed agreements in January on investments, commerce, crime, immigration, tourism, and environmental issues. In June, Turkish troops taking part in North Atlantic Treaty Organization (NATO) maneuvers landed in Greece.

A crisis in U.S.-Turkish relations erupted when the International Relations Committee of the U.S. House of Representatives passed a resolution accusing the Ottoman Empire—which had earlier ruled the territory that is now Turkey—of genocide against Armenians during World War I. Turkish authorities saw this resolution as an attack against modern-day Turkey, and as a result threatened to cease armaments purchases from the United States and to stop military cooperation with the United States in regard to Iraq. After intense lobbying by the White House, House Speaker J. Dennis Hastert agreed in October to cancel a planned vote on the resolution by the full House of Representatives.

In June, Italy extradited Mehmet Ali Agca, who had shot and wounded Pope John Paul II in 1981, to Turkey. Italy's President Carlo Ciampi had pardoned Agca, but since Agca had been convicted of a 1979 murder in Turkey, he was immediately sent to prison upon his return to his homeland.

Economy. In 1999 the Turkish economy was adversely affected by a severe earthquake in August and another in November. Gross domestic product (GDP) for the year fell by about 5%, the government's fiscal deficit was about 11% of GDP, and inflation remained high at nearly 70%. On Dec. 6, 1999, the International Monetary Fund (IMF) approved an aid program aimed at reducing inflation.

From January to June 2000, the number of tourists grew by more than one-third, thereby somewhat countering the increased price of petroleum imports. Inflation declined to a degree, so that consumer prices as of September were up by only about 50% for the preceding 12 months, the lowest increase in 14 years.

Archaeology. On September 14 the U.S. archaeological explorer Robert Ballard said that he would seek permission to take samples from the floor of the Black Sea, near Turkey's northern coast. Ballard claimed to have found evidence of settlements from about 7,000 years ago, possibly associated with Noah's flood.

Turkish dam construction in the upper reaches of the Euphrates River basin at Birecik gradually started to flood the site of the ancient city of Zeugma between the months of May and October. Archaeologists from Turkey and from several other countries rapidly excavated a great deal of the site, thereby preserving many of its mosaics. (*See also* ARCHAEOLOGY.)

WILLIAM OCHSENWALD, *Virginia Polytechnic Institute and State University*

TURKEY • Information Highlights

Official Name: Republic of Turkey.
Location: Southeastern Europe and southwestern Asia.
Area: 301,382 sq mi (780 580 km²).
Population (2000 est.): 65,666,677.
Chief Cities (mid-1997 est.): Ankara, the capital, 2,937,524; Istanbul, 8,274,921; Izmir, 2,130,359; Adana, 1,131,198.
Government: *Head of state,* Ahmet Necdet Sezer, president (took office May 16, 2000). *Head of government,* Bulent Ecevit, prime minister (took office December 1998). *Legislature*—Grand National Assembly.
Monetary Unit: Lira (677,355.0 liras equal U.S. $1, Dec. 17, 2000).
Gross Domestic Product (1999 est. U.S.$): $409,400,000,000 (purchasing power parity).
Economic Indexes: *Consumer Prices* (1999, 1994 = 100): all items, 1,917.5; food, 1,162.0 (1998). *Industrial Production* (1999, 1990 = 100): 131.1.
Foreign Trade (1999 U.S.$): *Imports,* $40,692,000,000; *exports,* $26,588,000,000.

Uganda

Exhibiting some resiliency, Uganda generated continued economic growth in 2000, despite problems of drought and lingering threats posed by rebel activity in portions of the country. Unrest plagued the nation, as Uganda's military support for rebels in the Democratic Republic of the Congo led to outbreaks of fighting with Rwandan troops.

Politics and Security Issues. The major political event of the year was the June 29 referendum to determine the nation's future political system. Voters overwhelmingly endorsed President Yoweri Museveni's "movement system," which stresses zero tolerance for political parties. Advocates of political parties and multiparty politics argued that the voter turnout of just more than 50% suggested many Ugandans rejected Museveni's system. The outcome of the vote—a crucial one for the future of Uganda—indicated the presidential and parliamentary elections, set for 2001, would be contested outside the political-party system.

Ugandans and others were shocked at the March deaths of almost 1,000 people associated with the Movement for Restoration of the Ten Commandments. Some 530 members of the "doomsday cult" perished in a church fire at Kanungu, in southwestern Uganda. In following weeks, police discovered mass graves in other parts of the country, with the bodies of more than 400 individuals. A mid-October outbreak of the deadly Ebola virus in northern Uganda brought more death, and heightened concern that the disease be contained.

Rebel activity organized by the Allied Democratic Front (ADF), particularly in the southwest, continued during 2000.

Economy. The Ugandan economy grew at nearly 8%, despite the drought conditions in several parts of the country. Uganda also experienced more-substantial growth of capital investment than its neighbors, while donors continued to provide significant economic assistance, in reaction to Uganda's successful economic reforms.

In April the World Bank (WB) and the International Monetary Fund (IMF) agreed to provide funds to Uganda under the Highly Indebted Poor Countries initiative, aimed at reducing debt-service payments.

Foreign Affairs. Uganda continued to be involved in the civil war in the Democratic Republic of the Congo. During the year, Ugandan soldiers were involved in fighting—on at least three occasions—with

---

UGANDA • Information Highlights

Official Name: Republic of Uganda.
Location: Interior of East Africa.
Area: 91,135 sq mi (236 040 km²).
Population (2000 est.): 23,317,560.
Chief Cities (1991 census): Kampala, the capital, 773,463; Jinja, 60,979; Mbale, 53,634.
Government: *Head of state,* Yoweri Museveni, president (took office Jan. 29, 1986). *Head of government,* Apollo Nsibambi, prime minister (took office April 1999). *Legislature* (unicameral)—National Assembly.
Monetary Unit: Uganda shilling (1,840.00 shillings equal U.S.$1, Oct. 26, 2000).
Gross Domestic Product (1999 est. U.S.$): $24,200,000,000 (purchasing power parity).
Economic Index (1996, 1990 = 100): *Consumer Prices,* all items, 260.5; food, 226.6.
Foreign Trade (1999 U.S.$): *Imports,* $1,340,000,000; *exports,* $516,000,000.

---

troops from Rwanda, in and near Kisangani. The hostilities were the result of the former allies backing different rebel factions in the Congo. A July 2 summit between Presidents Museveni and Paul Kagame of Rwanda—the second meeting within three months—produced the promise of a truce and recognition of the need for mutual understanding between the neighbors, so as to avoid future confrontations in the Congo.

In April, Uganda signed a treaty with Kenya and Tanzania, forming the East African Community (EAC), which aims to unite the three nations through trade, customs, and East African law. It was agreed in October that each member state would have nine representatives in the community's Legislative Assembly. The EAC inauguration was set for November 2000.

ROBERT M. MAXON, *West Virginia University*

Ukraine

An intense political power struggle between the newly reelected president and parliament was waged in Ukraine for much of 2000. Simultaneously, the country experienced one of its best years economically, although the economy was still beset by serious problems. In foreign affairs, Ukraine was in conflict with the Council of Europe (CE) over its domestic politics, and with the International Monetary Fund (IMF) over its economic policies.

Domestic Politics. President Leonid Kuchma regarded his reelection in late 1999 as a mandate to restructure legislative-executive relations in Ukraine. The left opposition—in the Supreme Council, or Verkhovna Rada— which held a parliamentary majority previously had blocked a number of his reform initiatives designed to move the country toward a market economy. In response, the president declared his intent to call a spring 2000 referendum in which voters would be asked to approve restructuring the Verkhovna Rada into a bicameral legislature, downsizing the body as a whole, stripping the deputies of legal immunity, and giving the president a qualified power of dissolution. After the left opposition tried unsuccessfully to block the planned referendum legislatively, it sought relief from the Constitutional Court.

Meanwhile, the threat of Kuchma's assault split parliament into two wings—a propresidential majority of nearly 250 of 450 deputies, and a large minority dominated by the Communist Party. In the ensuing struggle, the two groups met in separate buildings as the minority left-wing speaker refused to turn over his office to the majority's choice, Ivan Plyushch. Police and troops were called in, albeit without violence, before Speaker Plyushch and the majority regained control of the parliament building. In March the Constitutional Court ruled against two of the six proposed questions, but declared the referendum constitutional. On April 16, in an enormous turnout of 29 million voters, the electorate overwhelmingly supported President Kuchma's proposals by an average margin of 86%. During the summer the proposals were converted into proposed constitutional amendments to be considered by parliament in the late fall.

The Economy. In spite of continuing serious problems, 2000 proved to be Ukraine's best year economically since independence in 1991. For the first time, the gross domestic product (GDP) turned positive and the GNP's growth rate was projected at more than 4% for the year. In the first nine months, industrial output was up 12%, helped by a revival of exports, which increased by 25%; disposable income rose by 12%, with retail sales up 9%; and fixed investment soared by an increase of 21%. All signs indicated a continuing recovery.

Still, the agricultural sector presented problems; an energy shortage loomed; unemployment remained high; and inflation continued to plague the economy. As the result of a drought, agriculture, after three quarters, was down 6% on a year-to-year basis. A low grain harvest—even less than 1999, which was the worst year since 1945—was forecast. Wheat imports were considered as well as economic controls to prevent a bread shortage.

There also were concerns of an impending energy shortage. Under domestic pressure, Prime Minister Viktor Yushchenko suggested that Ukraine might delay the planned December 15 closing of the damaged Chernobyl nuclear reactor as had been promised but a power failure in late November left the issue in doubt. Compounding these problems, high inflation continued to dog the economy. Driven by a loose monetary policy and the rising cost of food and energy, caused respectively by the drought and high world energy prices, inflation reached 32% by September.

Foreign Affairs. Ukraine's most significant foreign-policy problem was the IMF's suspension of its three-year loan in late 1999, still in effect a year later. President Kuchma had met some of the IMF's demands for more-extensive administrative and agricultural reforms, but the fund felt more needed to be done. At midyear the World Bank followed suit, tying its smaller loan programs to improved governmental performance. By late fall the bank, recognizing some progress, released $70 million.

Ukraine also had problems with the Council of Europe (CE). The CE kept up a drumbeat of criticism over the executive-driven referendum process, even threatening suspension of Ukraine's membership.

On the positive side, U.S. President Bill Clinton paid a brief visit to Ukraine in June, and during the summer the country hosted the largest joint North Atlantic Treaty Organization (NATO) military exercise to date in a post-Soviet country. Late in the year the president dismissed pro-Western Foreign Minister Borys Tarasyuk in a move thought to be intended to pacify Russia, with which relations were strained.

ROBERT SHARLET, *Union College*

UKRAINE • Information Highlights

Official Name: Ukraine.
Location: Eastern Europe.
Area: 233,090 sq mi (603 700 km²).
Population (2000 est.): 49,153,027.
Chief Cities (Jan. 1, 1995 est.): Kiev, the capital, 2,635,000; Kharkov, 1,576,000; Dnepropetrovsk, 1,162,000; Donetsk, 1,102,000; Odessa, 1,060,000.
Government: *Head of state,* Leonid Kuchma, president (took office July 1994). *Head of government,* Viktor Yushchenko, prime minister (took office December 1999). *Legislature* (unicameral)—Supreme Council (Verkhovna Rada).
Monetary Unit: Hryvnia (5.4373 hryvnias equal U.S.$1, Nov. 9, 2000).
Gross Domestic Product (1999 est. U.S.$): $109,500,000,000 (purchasing power parity).
Foreign Trade (1999 est. U.S.$): *Imports,* $11,846,000,000; *exports,* $11,582,000,000.

United Nations

During 2000 a new phenomenon—globalization—seemed to challenge the very existence of the United Nations (UN). At a time when the nation-state was appearing less and less important, when giant corporations had greater revenues than most nations' budgets combined, the UN itself was risking being bypassed. In 2000, the 55-year-old world body had to define its role in the face of this new global challenge.

Kofi Annan, the UN Secretary-General, began the effort when he invited world leaders to New York to attend the September 6-8 Millennium Summit to offer their vision of the UN's future. All leaders signed the Millennium Declaration pledging to strengthen the world organization. With a view toward the impact of globalization on the UN itself, the document called upon the United Nations to "develop strong partnerships with the private sector and with civil-society organizations, in pursuit of development and poverty eradication."

Annan wants the UN to play a major role in globalization. He believes that leaders of business, labor, and civil societies should work with the UN in supporting values of human rights, just labor standards, and protection of the environment. At the beginning of a new century, the UN faces a new agenda and must meet a challenge to its own survival.

Security Council. It was mainly an African year for the UN Security Council, the organization's most powerful body. Much of the African continent faced conflicts so complex that they appeared beyond the council's ability to resolve. (*See also* AFRICA: A CONTINENT OF PROBLEMS, page 44.)

Angola has been ravaged by civil war since its 1975 independence, and the Democratic Republic of the Congo (DRC), after civil war erupted, suffered invasion by neighboring countries Uganda and Rwanda. Fighting back, the DRC invited allies Namibia, Zimbabwe, and Angola to come to its aid; the Security Council subsequently asked all foreign forces to leave. Sierra Leone was another threat to African peace. Rebel forces terrorized the civilian population. When the UN sent a peacekeeping force, a large number of UN troops were held as hostages—a humiliation for the UN. Nelson Mandela, South Africa's former president, was the facilitator of a peace effort in Burundi, where armed groups refused to agree to a cessation of hostilities.

The council hoped to rehabilitate Somalia, which had been without a government for a decade while warlords competed for power. A temporary government was formed, and although it was not accepted by all parties, it offered some hope that Somalia might achieve normalcy. To dampen fighting in Angola and Sierra Leone, the council adopted international sanctions that prohibited the purchase of diamonds sold by rebels to pay for arms.

The use of sanctions by the Security Council has expanded since the early 1990s. Late in 2000 the council strengthened sanctions against Afghanistan's Taliban government, demanding that it turn over Osama bin Laden to a country where he had been indicted for terrorism. The sanctions were scheduled to commence in January 2001. Sanctions against Iraq, in their tenth year, somewhat eroded. These were the most comprehensive in UN history, but governments friendly to Iraq contributed to helping the country out of its isolation by flying planeloads of officials to visit Baghdad. The Security Council was divided over whether these flights violated the sanctions. An Iraqi delegation was expected in New York in February 2001 for talks with Annan, to try to break the impasse.

The council was divided again in December when its nonaligned members presented a draft resolution calling for the council to send a military and police observer mission to protect civilians from clashes between Palestinians and Israelis. The resolution fell short of the nine votes required to pass.

The council carefully watched over its two unprecedented operations—UN administrations in Kosovo and in East Timor. In both cases the UN created a government and was exercising authority, setting up judicial and tax systems, infrastructure, and everything else needed to run a country. In Kosovo the UN had little success in bringing the two rival ethnic groups together; in East Timor the situation was less tense.

General Assembly. The world faced a new century of unknown challenges in 2000, and the UN itself went through critical reappraisals of its place in the world. Annan decided that it was time to seek advice at the highest level. He sent invitations to all world leaders for a Millennium Summit. To make the next 100 years better, in Annan's words, he wanted leaders to "articulate a vision for the United Nations in the new century and propose system-wide institutional adaptations that will enable us to act

UN Secretary-General Kofi Annan (right) was greeted by Cuba's President Fidel Castro as he arrived in Havana for a summit of the leaders of the Group of 77 (G-77), an alliance of developing nations that was established in the 1960s and now includes 133 members.

on that vision." Answering Annan's call, approximately 150 kings, presidents, prime ministers, and princes arrived for the September 6–8 summit, the largest gathering of world leaders in history. Each stood before the General Assembly podium and proclaimed his or her vision of the future for humanity and the UN. All agreed that a world without the UN as the protector of peace, security, justice, equality, and freedom was impossible to imagine. If Annan had felt the need for world leaders to publicly affirm support for the organization, he was more than satisfied. As proof of that support, the world leaders signed what became the Millennium Declaration, spelling out what was expected of the organization and its members in the future.

Then the regular General Assembly opened, and foreign ministers gathered to present their government policies in the General Debate. The General Assembly elected Finland's former Prime Minister Harri Holkeri as its president and, in order to turn the Millennium Declaration's goals into reality, established a follow-up mechanism to oversee their implementation.

One of the first issues the General Assembly faced was the request that the Republic of China on Taiwan be granted UN membership. As in the past, it was rejected, with mainland China adamantly opposed to any recognition of independent status for Taiwan. But Tuvalu, a Pacific islet with a 10,000 population, was admitted as the UN's 189th and smallest member.

While the Millennium Summit was historic, history was also made when the two Koreas, South and North, together sponsored a draft resolution seeking the General Assembly's support for inter-Korean dialogue, reconciliation, and reunification on the Korean peninsula. One-hundred and fifty countries joined in sponsoring the resolution and passed it swiftly.

Peacekeeping. In a declaration signed at the September 6 Millennium Summit, 150 world leaders committed the international community "to make the United Nations more effective in maintaining peace and security by giving it the resources and tools it needed." That pledge was crucial. If it had not been implemented, the UN would have been unable to carry out its most important task: keeping the peace. Annan had difficulty obtaining the number of troops for peacekeeping in Sierra Leone that the Security Council recommended. In that beleaguered country, Revolutionary United Front (RUF) rebels failed to live up to a November 10 agreement to end a nine-year-old civil war and allow UN and government troops to take over diamond-producing and other areas the RUF controls. At year's end,

Annan waited to see whether the RUF would carry out the cease-fire agreement.

As the year drew to a close, the UN was overseeing 15 peacekeeping operations with a total strength of nearly 31,000 military personnel at a projected cost of about $2.5 billion. In the DRC, 245 UN military observers were monitoring ongoing hostilities. In Kosovo the UN had 4,145 civilian police, while the North Atlantic Treaty Organization (NATO) was responsible for military operations. But in East Timor the UN had 7,877 military personnel as well as 1,420 civilian police. Strengthening another peacekeeping operation, the UN might expand the UN Interim Force in Lebanon (UNIFIL) in 2001. UNIFIL has been in Lebanon since 1978.

Because of many problems in the past with UN peacekeeping—a difficult task in often-unpredictable conditions—Annan asked a panel of experts to draw up recommendations for improving the way peacekeeping is carried out. The 58-page Brahimi Report—named after the panel's chairman, former Algerian Foreign Minister Lakhdar Brahimi—said that peacekeeping "is the yardstick with which the organization is judged by the peoples it exists to serve." Without significant financial support, the report warned, the UN would be incapable of carrying out the peacekeeping that its members assigned to it.

The newest peacekeeping force was the UN Mission in Ethiopia and Eritrea (UNMEE), made up of 426 military personnel and 105 international civilian staff. In September the Security Council authorized the deployment of up to 4,300 troops to the area. Annan, who attended the December signing of the final peace accord ending a devastating war between Ethiopia and Eritrea, said it was "a victory for the voice of reason, for the power of diplomacy."

Finance. For years the UN had faced bankruptcy. Its financial situation was so desperate that in late December 2000, as the General Assembly was discussing a resolution on the Middle East, three protesters were able to get into the Assembly Hall, normally off-limits to anyone without a proper pass, because of the UN's zero-growth budget according to Holkeri. "There are not enough resources," he said, "to ensure security to prevent these kinds of actions or to be speedy enough to react."

The United States was the main culprit in the UN's financial disaster. It had refused to fully pay its assessment to the UN budget or its assessment for peacekeeping. UN members owed the organization $2.5 billion, including current and past assessments; of that amount, the United States owed $1.36 billion. The U.S. reneging of its dues to the UN violated the UN Charter, a treaty the United States had signed when it was one of the organization's founders. But the U.S. Congress attached stiff conditions to U.S. payments—the main one being that the amount it has been assessed must be reduced.

For years the United States had been expected to pay 25% of the UN's regular budget and 30% of its peacekeeping budget. What Washington demanded was a cut for regular-budget payments to 22%, and for the peacekeeping budget to 25%. The amount a country paid was based on a government's capacity to pay, which in turn was based on its gross national product (GNP), with some adjustments. For years, other members of the UN rejected Washington's demands, arguing that the assessment was obligatory under the Charter, an international treaty, and that the world's richest nation should be able to pay its dues. But the United States demanded that its assessment be reduced, and its refusal to pay undermined the organization.

At the end of December, the General Assembly approved lowering the U.S. share to 22% of the regular budget, and to approximately 26%–27% of peacekeeping expenses. Canadian Ambassador Paul Heinbecker said that the reduction "is a distortion in the capacity to pay but a politically necessary one." He said he looked forward to the UN's largest contributor "paying its arrears in full without delay and conditions."

But with the decision came the realization that with a lower U.S. payment, there would be a $34 million shortfall in next year's budget. This was solved by television magnate Ted Turner, who contributed this amount. Under UN rules, only governments can pay their assessments. To solve this problem, Turner agreed to donate the money to the U.S. State Department, which would pass it on to the UN.

The UN's long years of barely making ends meet could be over. For the new Republican administration scheduled to take office in Washington in January, this settlement offered hope for improved U.S.-UN relations.

See also HUMAN RIGHTS; LAW—International.

RUTH PEARSON
United Nations Correspondent

ORGANIZATION OF THE UNITED NATIONS

THE SECRETARIAT *Secretary-General:* Kofi Annan (until Dec. 31, 2001)
THE GENERAL ASSEMBLY (2000) *President:* Harri Holkeri, Finland

The 189 member nations were as follows:

Afghanistan	Central African	Germany	Latvia	Nicaragua	Somalia
Albania	Republic	Ghana	Lebanon	Niger	South Africa
Algeria	Chad	Greece	Lesotho	Nigeria	Spain
Andorra	Chile	Grenada	Liberia	Norway	Sri Lanka
Angola	China, People's	Guatemala	Libya	Oman	Sudan
Antigua and Barbuda	Republic of	Guinea	Liechtenstein	Pakistan	Suriname
Argentina	Colombia	Guinea-Bissau	Lithuania	Palau	Swaziland
Armenia	Comoros	Guyana	Luxembourg	Panama	Sweden
Australia	Congo	Haiti	Macedonia, The	Papua New Guinea	Syria
Austria	Congo, Democratic	Honduras	Former Yugoslav	Paraguay	Tajikistan
Azerbaijan	Republic of the	Hungary	Republic of	Peru	Tanzania
Bahamas	Costa Rica	Iceland	Madagascar	Philippines	Thailand
Bahrain	Croatia	India	Malawi	Poland	Togo
Bangladesh	Cuba	Indonesia	Malaysia	Portugal	Tonga
Barbados	Cyprus	Iran	Maldives	Qatar	Trinidad and Tobago
Belarus	Czech Republic	Iraq	Mali	Romania	Tunisia
Belgium	Denmark	Ireland	Malta	Russia	Turkey
Belize	Djibouti	Israel	Marshall Islands	Rwanda	Turkmenistan
Benin	Dominica	Italy	Mauritania	Saint Kitts and Nevis	Tuvalu
Bhutan	Dominican Republic	Ivory Coast	Mauritius	Saint Lucia	Uganda
Bolivia	Ecuador	Jamaica	Mexico	Saint Vincent and	Ukraine
Bosnia and	Egypt	Japan	Micronesia	The Grenadines	United Arab Emirates
Herzegovina	El Salvador	Jordan	Moldova	Samoa	United Kingdom
Botswana	Equatorial Guinea	Kazakhstan	Monaco	San Marino	United States
Brazil	Eritrea	Kenya	Mongolia	São Tomé and Príncipe	Uruguay
Brunei Darussalam	Estonia	Kiribati	Morocco	Saudi Arabia	Uzbekistan
Bulgaria	Ethiopia	Korea, Democratic	Mozambique	Senegal	Vanuatu
Burkina Faso	Fiji	People's	Myanmar	Seychelles	Venezuela
Burundi	Finland	Republic of	Namibia	Sierra Leone	Vietnam
Cambodia	France	Korea, Republic of	Nauru	Singapore	Yemen
Cameroon	Gabon	Kuwait	Nepal	Slovak Republic	Yugoslavia
Canada	Gambia	Kyrgyzstan	Netherlands	Slovenia	Zambia
Cape Verde	Georgia	Laos	New Zealand	Solomon Islands	Zimbabwe

COMMITTEES

General. Composed of 28 members as follows: The General Assembly president; the 21 General Assembly vice-presidents (heads of delegations or their deputies of Belarus, Bhutan, Burkina Faso, China, Comoros, El Salvador, France, Gabon, Guinea, Haiti, Kuwait, Maldives, Mozambique, Russia, Suriname, Tunisia, Turkey, United Kingdom, United States, Uzbekistan, Yemen) and the chairmen of the main committees below, which are composed of all 189 member countries.

First (Disarmament and International Security): U Mya Than (Myanmar)

Second (Economic and Financial): Alexandru Niculescu (Romania)

Third (Social, Humanitarian and Cultural): Yvonne Gittens-Joseph (Trinidad and Tobago)

Fourth (Special Political and Decolonization): Matia Mulumba Semakula Kiwanuka (Uganda)

Fifth (Administrative and Budgetary): Gert Rosenthal (Guatemala)

Sixth (Legal): Mauro Politi (Italy)

THE ECONOMIC AND SOCIAL COUNCIL
President: Makarim Wibisono (Indonesia)
Membership ends on December 31 of the year noted.

Andorra (2003)	Egypt (2003)	Peru (2003)
Angola (2002)	Ethiopia (2003)	Portugal (2002)
Argentina (2003)	Fiji (2002)	Republic of Korea
Austria (2002)	France (2002)	(2003)
Bahrain (2002)	Georgia (2003)	Romania (2003)
Benin (2002)	Germany (2002)	Russia (2001)
Bolivia (2001)	Greece (2002)	Rwanda (2001)
Brazil (2003)	Guinea-Bissau	Saudi Arabia (2001)
Bulgaria (2001)	(2001)	South Africa (2003)
Burkina Faso	Honduras (2001)	Sudan (2002)
(2002)	Indonesia (2001)	Suriname (2002)
Cameroon (2002)	Iran (2003)	Syria (2001)
Canada (2001)	Italy (2003)	Uganda (2003)
China (2001)	Japan (2002)	United Kingdom
Congo, Democratic	Mexico (2002)	(2001)
Republic of the	Morocco (2001)	United States
(2001)	Nepal (2003)	(2003)
Costa Rica (2002)	Netherlands (2003)	Venezuela (2001)
Croatia (2002)	New Zealand	
Cuba (2002)	(2000)	
Czech Republic	Nigeria (2003)	
(2001)	Norway (2001)	
Denmark (2001)	Pakistan (2003)	

THE SECURITY COUNCIL
Membership ends on December 31 of the year noted; asterisks indicate permanent membership.

Bangladesh (2001)	Jamaica (2001)	Singapore (2002)
China*	Mali (2001)	Tunisia (2001)
Colombia (2002)	Mauritius (2002)	Ukraine (2001)
France*	Norway (2002)	United Kingdom*
Ireland (2002)	Russia*	United States*

THE TRUSTEESHIP COUNCIL
Composed of the five permanent members of the Security Council: China, France, Russia, United Kingdom, United States. The Council meets as occasion requires.

THE INTERNATIONAL COURT OF JUSTICE
President: Gilbert Guillaume (France, 2009)
Vice-President: Shi Jiuyong (China, 2003)

Membership ends on the year noted.

Shigeru Oda (Japan, 2003)	Rosalyn Higgins (United Kingdom, 2009)
Mohammed Bedjaoui (Algeria, 2006)	Gonzalo Parra-Aranguren (Venezuela, 2009)
Raymond Ranjeva (Madagascar, 2009)	Pieter H. Kooijmans (Netherlands, 2006)
Géza Herczegh (Hungary, 2003)	José Francisco Rezek (Brazil, 2006)
Carl-August Fleischhauer (Germany, 2003)	Awn Shawkat Al-Khasawneh (Jordan, 2009)
Abdul G. Koroma (Sierra Leone, 2003)	Thomas Buergenthal (United States, 2006)
Vladlen S. Vereshchetin (Russia, 2006)	

INTERGOVERNMENTAL AGENCIES
Food and Agricultural Organization (FAO); International Atomic Energy Agency (IAEA); International Bank for Reconstruction and Development (World Bank); International Civil Aviation Organization (ICAO); International Fund for Agricultural Development (IFAD); International Labor Organization (ILO); International Maritime Organization (IMO); International Monetary Fund (IMF); International Telecommunication Union (ITU); United Nations Educational, Scientific and Cultural Organization (UNESCO); United Nations Industrial Development Organization (UNIDO); Universal Postal Union (UPU); World Health Organization (WHO); World Intellectual Property Organization (WIPO); World Meteorological Organization (WMO); World Trade Organization (WTO).

On Dec. 19, 2000, Bill Clinton, who admitted that he thoroughly enjoyed his eight years as the 42d president of the United States, maintained the tradition of receiving his successor, Texas Gov. George W. Bush (left), at the White House.

The year 2000 was a time of fresh starts and new horizons for Americans. The country prepared to close the door on the eight-year-long Clinton presidency and welcome its 43rd chief executive, though it took five tension-filled weeks after the election to establish who the new president would be. Even as Americans continued to adjust to what the turbulent 20th century had wrought, they braced for a new wave of change. *The New York Times* reported that by the middle of 2001, non-Hispanic whites would no longer make up a majority of the population in California, and that the nation's largest state would thus become a testing ground for what many foresee as the multiracial society of the future. Meanwhile, some members of minority groups were already forging ahead. The Texas Rangers of Major League Baseball's American League signed the Latino shortstop Alex Rodriguez to a ten-year $252 million contract, a new record for professional sports. And President-elect George W. Bush turned the man-

agement of the nation's foreign policy over to two African-Americans—retired Gen. Colin Powell as secretary of state and Condoleezza Rice as national security adviser. In addition, Bush picked a Latino—Texas Supreme Court Justice Alberto Gonzalez—as White House counsel.

Domestic Affairs

The Presidency. President Bill Clinton devoted 2000 to living down the scandals that had plagued his tenure and striving for accomplishments that would establish a positive legacy. Much of the time, though, the Democratic president was frustrated by the opposition of the Republican-controlled Congress and by the limitations of his own lame-duck status. His State of the Union address, delivered almost a year after the Senate acquitted him on impeachment charges, was the longest of his presidency. It was replete with proposals for action in areas traditionally favored by Democrats, such as education, health care, and gun control. "America again has the confidence to dream big dreams," the president declared. "Of course you can't gain ground if you're standing still," he chided the GOP lawmakers. "And for too long this Congress has been standing still on some of our most pressing national priorities."

The president's $1.8 trillion budget proposal submitted on February 7 backed up his ambitious rhetoric. The proposal's central premise was that the projected surplus of $184 billion would permit carrying out the domestic programs on which his heart was set, along with tax cuts and reductions in the national debt. "It is a balanced budget with a balanced approach to our national priorities," Clinton claimed. But to Republicans on Capitol Hill, the talk of fiscal discipline seemed intended to cloak plans for increased federal spending, and the opposition party dug in its heels.

Clinton's biggest legislative triumph had more to do with foreign policy than the domestic arena close to his heart—enactment of legislation normalizing U.S. trade ties with China. The measure, ending a prolonged debate, marked the most significant step in U.S. policy toward China since the two countries opened diplomatic relations in 1979. It set the stage for China's entry into the World Trade Organization (WTO), and granted China the open-door trade status that the United States extended to most other countries. (*See also* CHINA—U.S.-China Trade.)

The president broke new ground on another front, too. His appointment of Norman Mineta as secretary of commerce made the former Democratic congressman from California the first Asian-American to hold a cabinet post. As a child, the 68-year-old Mineta had been interned along with his family as part of the massive roundup of Japanese-Americans during World War II. He succeeded William M. Daley, who resigned to oversee Vice-President Gore's presidential campaign. President-elect Bush later chose Mineta as the sole Democrat in his cabinet, naming him to the position of secretary of transportation.

In late December, President Clinton appointed the first African-American to the U.S. Court of Appeals for the Fourth Circuit in Richmond, VA. In naming Roger Gregory, a corporate lawyer from Richmond, to the post, the president bypassed the Senate confirmation process temporarily. The recess appointment meant that Gregory would probably serve until at least the end of the first session of the incoming 107th Congress. Clinton previously had been stymied in his efforts to appoint an African-American to the Fourth Circuit.

Investigations. The final year of Clinton's presidency saw the culmination of investigations into the various charges of personal and official misconduct that had plagued his administration. The probes of the president and members of his cabinet by independent counsels cost more than $95 million—mostly on the Whitewater and Monica Lewinsky investigations conducted by Kenneth Starr and his successor, Robert W. Ray.

In April, Independent Counsel Ralph I. Lancaster cleared Labor Secretary Alexis Herman of charges of influence peddling. She was one of five cabinet members investigated by independent counsels during the Clinton presidency, none of whom was convicted of a major felony.

Independent Counsel Ray, the new leader of the Whitewater probe, dealt separately with each of the investigations involving the president and First Lady Hillary Rodham Clinton. In March, Ray announced that his prosecutors found no criminal wrongdoing when White House officials obtained hundreds of Federal Bureau of Investigation (FBI) personnel files early in the Clinton administration—a controversy that had come to be dubbed "Filegate" after it erupted in 1996.

In June, Ray wrapped up another case that also had begun in the early days of the Clinton presidency—the so called "Travelgate" affair, stemming from the summary dismissal of White House travel-office employees. Though he said he would not

---

UNITED STATES • Information Highlights

Official Name: United States of America.
Location: Central North America.
Area: 3,717,813 sq mi (9 629 091 km²).
Population (2000 est.): 275,562,673.
Chief Cities (July 1, 1998, est.): Washington, DC, the capital, 523,124; New York, 7,420,166; Los Angeles, 3,597,556; Chicago, 2,802,079; Houston, 1,786,691; Philadelphia, 1,436,287; San Diego, 1,220,666.
Government: *Head of state and government,* Bill Clinton, president (took office Jan. 20, 1993). *Legislature*—Congress: Senate and House of Representatives.
Monetary Unit: Dollar.
Gross Domestic Product (1999 est.): $9,255,000,000,000 (purchasing power parity).
Economic Indexes (1999, 1990 = 100): *Consumer Prices,* all items, 122.5; food, 124.6. *Industrial Production,* 138.6.
Foreign Trade (1999): *Imports,* $1,059,430,000,000; *exports,* $702,098,000,000.

seek criminal charges against the first lady, Ray was critical of her behavior. He found "substantial evidence" that the president's wife lied under oath in denying that she played a role in the 1993 White House travel-office firings, but he acknowledged that he could not prove beyond a reasonable doubt that any of her testimony was false.

In his final report of the year in September, Ray ended the six-year investigation into the complex financial dealings surrounding the Clintons' 1980s' investment in an Arkansas real-estate venture called Whitewater, with the announcement that he had found "insufficient" evidence to charge the president or his wife with criminal wrongdoing.

While that cleared the docket of probes involving the first lady, Ray was not finished probing the president. In April the independent counsel announced that he was continuing to investigate the president's relationship to White House intern Monica Lewinsky—the case that led to his impeachment. Ray also was considering seeking an indictment against Clinton for perjury or obstruction of justice after his presidency ended. In August it was disclosed that Ray had impaneled a grand jury to consider criminal charges against Clinton. "There is," he declared, "an important principle at stake: that none of us is above the law."

Clinton also faced the possibility of disbarment for his behavior in the Lewinsky affair. In June, in an unprecedented rebuke for a sitting president, an ethics panel of the Arkansas Supreme Court filed suit to strip the president of his law license, declaring that he lacked "overall fitness" to be a lawyer and that his conduct "damages the legal profession." The action by the committee stemmed from a suit brought by the Southeastern Legal Foundation, a conservative organization. On Jan. 19, 2001, the day before Clinton's term ended, the president reached what amounted to a plea-bargain agreement with Ray. In return for escaping possible indictment and disbarment Clinton admitted making false statements in the Lewinsky case, and agreed to pay a $25,000 fine and to have his Arkansas law license suspended for five years.

In addition to the investigations of the personal conduct of President Clinton and his associates, the year saw probes of the actions of the administration. In September, former Sen. John C. Danforth, the outside counsel who investigated the 1993 Branch Davidian siege near Waco, TX, said that he had found that top government officials did nothing wrong in the tragic affair, which claimed the lives of some 80 cult members. But Danforth asserted that lower-level FBI employees, by misleading the public and Congress about relatively minor details, had "undermined public confidence in government and caused real damage to our country."

The government also suffered a black eye as a result of yet another controversial case. This resulted from the unexpected release in September of former Los Alamos scientist Wen Ho Lee, who had been jailed late in 1999 and branded a major threat to national security. Lee, who had been under a 59-count federal indictment, denied bail, and held much of the time in solitary confinement, was released after pleading guilty to a single charge of mishandling nuclear secrets. He had been fired from the Los Alamos lab and accused of downloading nuclear information to unsecured computer tapes and was suspected of leaking nuclear secrets to China. The charges against Lee outraged many Chinese-Americans, who accused the government of acting out of racial prejudice. Federal Judge James A. Parker, who ordered his release, did not mention the racial aspects of the case, but charged that the government's handling of Lee's prosecution had "embarrassed the entire nation and everyone who is a citizen of it." In the face of this criticism, Attorney General Janet Reno and FBI Director Louis J. Freeh vigorously defended their conduct.

Congress. From start to finish, the 106th Congress was plagued by intense partisanship that limited its achievements. In 1999 it was the impeachment of President Clinton that intensified friction between the two parties. In 2000 it was the election campaign, and the prolonged ending to the battle for the presidency that made Republicans and Democrats more willing to fight than conciliate. Democrats labeled Republicans obstructionists for blocking the enactment of measures backed by President Clinton, such as gun control, Medicare prescription-drug benefits, health-maintenance-organization (HMO) reform, and a minimum-wage increase. Republicans countered that it was Clinton himself who was the chief stumbling block to accomplishment, pointing to his opposition to major tax-cut legislation, particularly his veto of tax cuts for married couples and for heirs.

Whoever was to blame, the extent of the gridlock on Capitol Hill was dramatized by Congress' failure to reach a budget agree-

The White House at 200

The White House

On Nov. 9, 2000, three former presidents and four former first ladies joined President Bill Clinton and First Lady Hillary Rodham Clinton in celebrating the 200th anniversary of the White House—the president's home at 1600 Pennsylvania Avenue NW in Washington, DC. A lavish dinner party for 190 guests featured striped bass and other foods that would have been readily available during the time of John Adams, the first president to live in the Georgian neoclassical house. At the celebration, Mrs. Clinton unveiled the first set of china to feature the White House itself in the center of a gold-edged plate.

During its 200-year history, the mansion, designed by James Hoban and not officially named "The White House" until 1901 during Teddy Roosevelt's residence, has become a symbol of leadership and continuity. War and peace have been debated inside its walls,

heads of state and government have been its guests, and children have grown up there.

The White House was originally conceived as "the president's palace" by Washington, DC, city planner Pierre L'Enfant, and its planned size was reduced substantially by President George Washington. Still when it opened, it was the largest home in the United States. The White House was burned down by the British in 1814 and has undergone several additions and renovations—including being completely gutted and renovated during the Truman years and redecorated by Jacqueline Kennedy in the early 1960s.

Of its rooms, 32 are bathrooms. There are six levels, 412 doors, 147 windows, 28 fireplaces, seven staircases, and three elevators. A recent addition was a jogging track installed during the Clinton presidency. More than 6,000 people tour the White House daily.

---

ment before the election, resulting in a lame-duck session. The budget, finally approved on December 15, boosted spending for education and medical research, allotted $35 billion to Medicare and Medicaid providers to help make up for cutbacks in recent years, and created new tax breaks to encourage investment in depressed urban and rural areas.

The agreement gave both parties something to crow about. Clinton was particular-

ly pleased with a boost in spending on education to expand federal initiatives in class-size reduction, school renovation, education for special-needs students, and grants for poor college students. Republican House Speaker J. Dennis Hastert of Illinois took satisfaction from the "New Markets" tax-incentive program, creating 40 enterprise zones in cities and rural areas—which he and Clinton jointly promoted in a rare instance of bipartisanship. Costing $25.9 million over ten years, the package included delicately balanced tax credits, regulatory relief, and economic development measures planned to breathe new life into urban and rural areas of the nation forgotten by the economic boom.

Congressional analysts generally agreed that Congress' most enduring accomplishment in 2000 was the approval of legislation normalizing trade relations with China. Other fields where the lawmakers took significant action:

• Social Security. By eliminating the previous earnings limits on Social Security for beneficiaries between 65 and 70, lawmakers enabled hundreds of thousands of Americans in that age group to earn as much money as they want without losing Social Security benefits. The measure repealed a law in which persons between 65 to 69 lost $1 in Social Security benefits for every $3 in wages above an annual limit of $17,000 in 2000. The cost of the repeal was estimated at $22.7 billion over ten years.

• Campaign Finance. Enacting the first major change in campaign-finance law in 21 years, Congress adopted legislation that would force disclosure of secret donors and the expenditures of a newly popular brand of tax-exempt political committee. The law closed a legal loophole that had permitted certain ideological and issue-oriented groups to raise and spend money on political campaigns without being subject to the contribution limits and disclosure requirements that applied to most political groups. The reform measure would force these groups to disclose the identity of donors of $200 or more and expenditures of $500.

• Third World Trade. To encourage trade with sub-Saharan Africa, Central America, and the Caribbean Basin, Congress enacted a law that allowed nations in those areas that comply with human-rights and labor standards to enjoy duty-free and quota-free status for shipments to the United States of apparel made with U.S. yarn and fabric. The bill covers 48 countries in sub-Saharan Africa and 25 in Central America and the Caribbean region.

Elections. The headline, "Divided States of America," on the cover of the postelection issue of *Congressional Quarterly*, the longtime chronicler of political events on Capitol Hill and elsewhere, summed up the message of the first national election of the new century. Just as the battle for the White House turned into an extended photo-finish (*see* THE 2000 U.S. PRESIDENTIAL ELECTION,

page 22), the struggle for control of Congress came down to the wire—and beyond, with recounts needed to resolve several tight races. The outcome of the battle for control of the House of Representatives amounted to a major disappointment for the Democrats. They entered the election with 210 seats to 223 for the Republicans with two independents and two vacancies; a net gain of eight seats would have given them a majority. Their prospects seemed bright because 26 Republican incumbents were leaving the House, creating open seats, against only nine Democratic open seats.

Democrats hoped to make the six-year Republican control of the House an issue, as they had in 1996 and 1998. But the late 1998 departure of former House Speaker Newt Gingrich, erstwhile leader of the conservative revolution, drained the issue of much of its heat. The Democrats were unable to develop any broad argument against the Republicans, and the election turned into a series of district-by-district skirmishes, in which the Republicans came close to holding their own. They kept control of 20 of the 26 open seats, while capturing six of nine open seats from the Democrats. The final tallies gave the Republicans 221 seats, a net loss of two, to 212 to the Democrats, along with two independents, each of whom was expected to enlist with one of the two majority parties. Soon after the election, the Democratic numbers were reduced to 211 by the death of Rep. Julian C. Dixon of California. It was the smallest House majority since Dwight Eisenhower won the presidency for the Republicans in 1952.

In the Senate, Republicans had an even closer call. They entered the election with a 54 to 46 majority, with 19 of their seats being contested against only 15 for Democrats. When the dust had cleared, the GOP had lost a net of four seats, creating a 50–50 standoff—a deadlock that could be broken in the GOP's favor by the vote of the newly elected Republican Vice-President Richard Cheney. Five Republican incumbents were defeated—three of whom had won their seats in the GOP's historic victory of 1994. In Michigan, Spencer Abraham was ousted by Democratic Rep. Debbie Stabenow; in Minnesota, Rod Grams was beaten by Democratic department-store heir Mark Dayton; in Missouri, John Ashcroft was defeated by a dead man, the state's popular governor Mel Carnahan, whose name remained on the ballot after he was killed in a plane crash during the campaign. Subsequently, in

© Kevin Siers/"The Charlotte Observer"/Reprinted with special permission of King Features Syndicate

Recalls of certain cold medicines and some Firestone tires were among the problems Americans faced in 2000. Meanwhile, they were inundated with politics and elections. By the time a presidential winner was declared—five weeks after Election Day—some Americans wanted to recall the political process, too.

December, Missouri Gov. Roger Wilson appointed Carnahan's widow, Jean, to serve a two-year term in the seat won by her husband. In Washington, Republican Slade Gorton, seeking a fourth Senate term, was defeated by Rep. Marie Cantwell in an election in which a lengthy recount was required to establish the winner. The fifth Republican incumbent to lose, William V. Roth, was 79, and his advanced years made him vulnerable to the successful challenge of Delaware's Democratic Gov. Thomas Carper. Democrats also captured the only open Republican seat—in Florida, where State Insurance Commissioner Bill Nelson defeated Republican Rep. Bill McCollum, to succeed retiring Connie Mack.

Republicans partly offset the loss of these six seats in Virginia, where former Gov. George Allen defeated Democratic incumbent Charles Robb, and in Nevada, where former Republican Rep. John Ensign defeated Democrat Ed Bernstein for the seat held by retiring Democrat Richard H. Bryan.

In the 107th Congress, the Senate would include some other intriguing new faces, most notably Hillary Rodham Clinton. She overcame carpetbagger charges and the scandals of the Clinton White House to succeed Democrat Daniel P. Moynihan in New York and become the first first lady to hold elective office (*see* THE FIRST LADY BECOMES SENATOR-ELECT, page 37). Also likely to attract attention on Capitol Hill was former Wall Street chief executive officer (CEO) Jon Corzine, a Democrat who replaced retiring Democrat Frank Lautenberg in New Jersey. Another Democratic new Senate face belonged to former Nebraska

Gov. Ben Nelson, winning the seat formerly held by Bob Kerrey. The 2000 campaign began with the Republicans holding 30 governorships, compared with 18 for the Democrats and two for the independents. Gubernatorial contests in 11 states left the balance of power altered only slightly—29 Republicans to 19 Democrats and two independents—as a result of Democrat Rep. Bob Wise defeating Republican Gov. Cecil Underwood of West Virginia. Control of state legislatures, a crucial factor in the forthcoming decennial reapportionment of congressional districts was as evenly divided as the rest of the political world. Each party controlled the legislatures in 17 states, with control divided in 15 other states. In Nebraska, the legislature is unicameral and nonpartisan.

Among the most notable of about 200 initiatives and propositions on state ballots around the country was an initiative adopted by California voters favoring a radical shift in the war on drugs by sending drug abusers to treatment centers rather than prison. Abortion-rights supporters prevailed in Colorado, defeating a proposal that would have imposed a 24-hour waiting period before an abortion. School-voucher proposals were soundly defeated in California and Michigan. Nevada and Nebraska voters backed bans on gay marriage and a Maine ballot measure to protect gays against discrimination failed. But gay-rights supporters in Oregon narrowly defeated a measure that would have banned "public-school instruction encouraging, promoting, or sanctioning homosexual or bisexual behavior." Alabama voters agreed to overturn a century-old constitutional ban against racial intermarriage. Despite strong opposition by the National Rifle Association (NRA), measures to require background checks on purchasers of weapons at gun shows easily passed in Oregon and Colorado, where parents of victims in the 1998 Columbine High School shootings campaigned in support of the proposal.

ROBERT SHOGAN
"Los Angeles Times"

The George W. Bush Cabinet

Shortly after being declared 43rd president of the United States, George W. Bush began announcing selections for his cabinet and key administration positions. As members of the White House staff, the president-elect chose Condoleezza Rice as national security adviser; Andrew H. Card, Jr., as chief of staff; Karen P. Hughes as counsellor to the president; Alberto R. Gonzalez as general counsel; Karl Rove as senior adviser; and Ari Fleischer as press secretary. For the two important posts of administrator of the Environmental Protection Agency (EPA) and U.S. trade representative, Bush turned to New Jersey Gov. Christine Todd Whitman and Robert B. Zoellick, a veteran of the Reagan and Bush administrations, respectively.

By early 2001, the president-elect had completed his cabinet selections. All faced approval by the U.S. Senate. Linda Chavez, the original pick as secretary of labor, withdrew her nomination after questions arose concerning her sheltering an illegal immigrant in her home. Elaine L. Chao was quickly chosen for the post. Biographical sketches of the 14 nominees follow:

Department of Agriculture: Ann M. Veneman was deputy secretary of agriculture under President George H. Bush. Born June 29, 1949, she earned a law degree from Hastings College of Law in San Francisco, worked as a public defender, and then as a lawyer for the Bay Area Rapid Transit system before joining the U.S. Department of Agriculture in 1986. She served as secretary of California's Department of Food and Agriculture (1995–99) and had been in private law practice in San Francisco since 1999.

Department of Commerce: Donald L. Evans, the chief executive and chairman of Tom Brown, Inc., an oil company based in Midland, TX, is a longtime Bush friend. He most recently served as chairman of the Bush-Cheney 2000 campaign. The Commerce post would be his first government position. The Houston native was born July 27, 1946. He earned undergraduate and graduate degrees from the University of Texas.

Department of Defense: Donald H. Rumsfeld served as secretary of defense (1975–77) under President Gerald R. Ford after being Ford's White House chief of staff (1974–75). During that time, he was a mentor to now Vice-President-elect Dick Cheney. After Ford lost his reelection bid, Rumsfeld became chief executive officer and then chairman of G.D. Searle & Company. He went into private business in 1993. Born on July 9, 1932, in Chicago, Rumsfeld was a U.S. Navy pilot following his 1954 graduation from Princeton University. He was a member of the U.S. House of Representatives (1963–69) and U.S. ambassador to NATO (1973–74).

Department of Education: Roderick R. Page was one of two African-Americans to be nominated to Bush's cabinet. As superintendent of Houston's public-school system, beginning in 1994, he tied principals' salaries and job security to student performance. Page was born on June 17, 1933, in Monticello, MS, the son of a librarian and a school principal. He was graduated from Jackson State University and earned a master's degree from Indiana University. Beginning in 1971, he served as head football coach and assistant professor at Texas Southern University and was dean of its School of Education (1984–90).

Department of Energy: Until he was defeated in November 2000 in a bid for a second term, Michigan's Spencer Abraham was the only Arab-American in the U.S. Senate. Born June 12, 1952, he was graduated from Michigan State University and earned a law degree from Harvard University. He first went to Washington as deputy chief of staff to Vice-President Dan Quayle.

Department of Health and Human Services: Governor of Wisconsin since January 1987, Tommy Thompson gained a reputation as an innovator in welfare reform by enacting the nation's toughest welfare-to-work program. A Wisconsin native, Thompson was born on Nov. 19, 1941. He was graduated and earned a law degree from the University of Wisconsin and was in private law practice (1966–87). He served in the Wisconsin Assembly (1966–86) before being elected Wisconsin's governor.

Department of Housing and Urban Development: Melquiades Rafael Martinez would be the first Cuban-American to hold a cabinet post. Born on Oct. 23, 1946, in Sagua la Grande, Cuba, Martinez served as chairman of Orange County, FL, before being tapped for the cabinet position. Previously, he was president of the Orlando Utilities Commission. He received a law degree from Florida State University and was in private law practice until 1998.

Department of the Interior: A lawyer since 1978, Gale Ann Norton worked in Washington as assistant to the deputy secretary in the U.S. Department of Agriculture (1984–85) and as an associate solicitor in the U.S. Department of Interior (1985–87). She was Colorado attorney general (1991–99). Born on March 11, 1954, in Wichita, KS, she earned her bachelor's and law degrees from the University of Denver.

Department of Justice/Attorney General: John Ashcroft was nominated for the post of attorney general after being defeated in his bid for a second term representing Missouri in the U.S. Senate. Born May 9, 1942, in Chicago, Ashcroft was Missouri's attorney general (1977–85) and governor (1985–92) before being elected to the Senate in 1994. Ashcroft was graduated from Yale and earned a law degree from the University of Chicago.

Department of Labor: Elaine Lan Chao, a Chinese immigrant is a former head of the Peace Corps and United Way. Born on March 26, 1953, in Taipei, Taiwan, she was graduated from Mount Holyoke College and received a master's degree in business administration from Harvard. She has worked for both Citicorp and BankAmerica, was a White House Fellow, and later joined the U.S. Department of Transportation. Since 1996, she had been a distinguished fellow at The Heritage Foundation. The secretary-designate is married to Sen. Mitch McConnell (R-KY).

Secretary of State: Colin L. Powell, who would be the first African-American to serve as secretary of state, is well known for his 35 years of military service. As chairman of the Joint Chiefs of Staff (1989–93), he directed U.S. military operations during the 1991 Persian Gulf War. Earlier, he had been national security adviser to President Reagan (1987–88). In 1997 the retired general was chairman of the Presidents' Summit for America's Future, a presidential conference on volunteerism. Born on April 5, 1937, he was graduated from City College of New York and received a master's degree in business administration from George Washington University in 1971.

Department of Transportation: Norman Y. Mineta, who served as commerce secretary under President Clinton, was President-elect Bush's sole Democratic nominee to the cabinet. Mineta, a Japanese-American who was held with his family in an internment camp during World War II, served in the U.S. House of Representatives (1975–95). Born Nov. 12, 1931, he was the first Asian-American to serve in a presidential cabinet. Mineta was with Lockheed Martin Corporation before joining Clinton's cabinet.

Department of the Treasury: For the treasury post, President-elect Bush named Paul H. O'Neill, a business executive with Washington experience. Born on Dec. 4, 1935, in St. Louis, O'Neill earned a bachelor's degree from Fresno State College and a master's from Indiana University. He was with the U.S. Bureau of the Budget and the White House Office of Management and Budget (1967–77). He then held various managerial positions with International Paper (1977–87), including president, and joined Alcoa aluminum in 1987, serving as chief executive (1987–98) and as chairman since 1987.

Department of Veterans Affairs: Anthony J. Principi would be returning to the Department of Veterans Affairs, having been deputy secretary (1989–92) and acting secretary under President George H. Bush (1992–93). Born on April 16, 1944, in New York City, Principi was graduated from the U.S. Naval Academy and was awarded a law degree from Seton Hall. He served as a U.S. Navy line officer (1967–72). In 1980 he was recruited as counsel for the Senate Armed Services Committee. Most recently he was president of QTC Medical Services Inc.

The 22d U.S. Census

The United States took its 22d decennial census in 2000 and counted a population of 281,421,906. The decennial population census was mandated in Article 1, Section 2 of the U.S. Constitution for the purpose of allocating seats among the states in the U.S. House of Representatives and the Electoral College. The federal government has conducted a population count every ten years in a year ending in "0" since 1790, when the population was only 3.9 million.

During the past 210 years, the census has marked the shift in political power that has resulted from changes and growth in population. As a result of the counting in 2000, 12 seats in the House shifted from ten states to eight other states. These results continued patterns evident over the previous 40 years of relative shifts in the population from the Northeast and Midwest to the South and West. The detailed results of Census 2000 are scheduled to appear in 2001. Congress uses the census data in funding formulas to distribute tax dollars to programs targeted to particular demographic constituencies. The private sector uses the census results for target marketing and for demographic analysis of business patterns.

© Chris Hondros/Newsmakers/Online/Liaison Agency

Method. The U.S. Census Bureau, an agency in the U.S. Department of Commerce, conducted Census 2000. The census was taken primarily by mailing a questionnaire to the roughly 120 million residential addresses in the United States. The Census Bureau asked each householder to complete the form with information about who lived at the address as of April 1, 2000, and to mail it in. The Census Bureau also conducted a second follow-up process and sent enumerators to the 33% of all addresses that did not return the form by late April 2000. In remote areas, the Census Bureau sent enumerators directly to the address in order to collect the information more quickly.

Eighty-three percent of households received a "short form" with six questions about the name, age, sex, race, ethnic status, and household relationship of all residents, and whether the house was rented or owned; 17% of households received a "long" form with a total of 53 more in-depth questions regarding the household and demographic characteristics, including labor force status, income, citizenship, level of education, disabilities, and language spoken. The Census Bureau used an optical-scanning system to read the results of the paper forms into a computer and then tabulated and published the results both in electronic and paper form.

Issues. Census 2000 was the subject of partisan controversy because the Republican majority in Congress distrusted many of the methods proposed by the Clinton administration. Previous censuses had a net "differential" undercount of some groups in the population, particularly minorities and residents of inner cities. Such an undercount can shortchange certain local areas. For 2000, the Census Bureau proposed increased use of statistical sampling to save money and to produce more accurate results. Congressional leaders disagreed with the plans and sued the Clinton administration. In 1999 the U.S. Supreme Court resolved the conflict by ruling that the current census law prevented the use of sample data for apportioning seats in the House but that sampling was legal for other census uses.

Although the Census Bureau tried to maintain the continuity of the format of the questions, it did make changes in 2000, including new instructions on the race question, which permitted people to select "one or more" races, and a question on the long form about grandparents caring for their grandchildren.

MARGO J. ANDERSON
University of Wisconsin—Milwaukee

The Economy

The slowdown of the long economic expansion in the United States—feared by many Americans, forecast by economists, and earnestly sought by the Federal Reserve—finally arrived in the waning months of 2000. Electronic-chip manufacturers announced production slowdowns, personal-computer sales fell, carmakers slowed their assembly lines, the growth of profits deteriorated, many stocks reached lows for the year, jobless claims rose, and consumer confidence sank.

Though long anticipated, the reality of an economy performing at less than its full powers jolted some Americans, and the media made the most of it. Negative news items, regarded just months before as oddities to be treated as such, were displayed prominently, amid sometimes-dire forecasts of the slowdown deteriorating into a recession rather than a so-called soft landing.

The reality perhaps was not as bad as the popular depiction of it. While a Federal Reserve survey released in early December showed some evidence of erosion, growth remained steady in four regions, with only isolated evidence of sharp declines elsewhere, mainly in manufacturing. The report also showed that inflation was remaining subdued, and Federal Reserve Chairman Alan Greenspan assured the public that his agency, which had raised interest rates six times since June 1999, was prepared to lift restraints. And, somewhat unexpectedly, the price of oil fell from a high of $37 a barrel earlier in the year to $28 in December. Such evidence reinforced the reminder made earlier by David Wyss, Standard & Poor's economist, that by the standards of the 1980s a cooling of the economy to a 3.5% growth rate would be characterized as a boom, suggesting that rates below that would still represent fair growth. While third-quarter gross domestic product (GDP) growth was lower than that—at an annual rate of 2.2%, less than half the rate of the spring quarter—some of it was the result of an apparent temporary drop in government spending. Excluding that category, the economy in the third quarter grew at a 3.3% rate, with GDP reaching nearly $9.4 trillion.

Big Spenders, Small Savers Most Americans reveled in the strong pace at which the economy grew, but the Federal Reserve grew increasingly worried. Following a jump of 8.3% in the final three months of 1999, a rise of 4.8% in the first quarter of 2000 disturbed the Fed even more, since it was accompanied by an intensification of inflation to an annual rate of 3.3%, the highest quarterly pace since the long expansion had begun in 1991. The economy's growth quickened further in the second quarter to 5.6%, seemingly in defiance of the Fed's slowdown efforts, before finally slowing in late summer and early fall. Over the 12-month period through September, growth had averaged better than 5%, an extraordinarily sprightly pace usually associated with a young expansion rather than one that, by earlier standards, was in its old age.

The "wealth effect" had much to do with the strong performance. The post–World War II baby boomers were now in their middle years and showing signs of concern about their looming retirement, but they were secure with steady jobs and incomes, and flush with big stock-market profits. Moreover, borrowing was easy, especially on the equity of homes whose value rose steadily. Some even justified borrowing on assets such as stocks and bonds, observing that the value of both was rising apace. Members of the following generation, sometimes called Generation X, emulated their parents' habits, documented by the second year in a row of car and small-truck sales near or above 17 million units, and near record-high home building and sales. The savings rate fell below zero, meaning consumers borrowed more than they earned, a pattern that deeply concerned economists. They repeatedly warned Americans that savings were the source of capital for continued expansion, and that the nation had become overly dependent on foreign investments. But others pointed to a quirk in the savings statistics: The biggest drop in the savings rate was among the growing number of elderly living off the accumulated savings and stock-market gains of a lifetime. In fact, the law required retirees to withdraw a percentage of savings amassed in 401(k) retirement plans.

The interaction of relatively easy credit terms, technological innovation, youthful enthusiasm, business and consumer confidence, and a low level of inflation—albeit rising—stirred the pot.

Total bank credit rose to an annual rate of more than $5 trillion during the summer months, more than a quarter of it backed by securities, a portion of which was volatile. Infrequent critics contended that, despite interest-rate increases, the Fed was maintaining an overly easy money policy, but the agency repeatedly cautioned that it sought a slowdown, not a recession. Consumer credit, much of it by means of credit cards, rose to nearly $1.5 trillion during the summer, more than $100 billion higher than in the comparable period of 1999. After rising briefly, the rate for 30-year home mortgages dropped in December to 7.17%—the lowest rate in 19 months—and the 30-year Treasury security, as high as 6.6% in January, remained below 6% for most of the year.

High productivity, meanwhile, was given much credit for maintaining price stability, although wages and prices showed some upward trend in the fall. Productivity gains averaged 5% for the 12 months through October, but consumer prices rose at annual rates of between 3% and 4% for much of the year, in spite of producers absorbing some higher costs.

Manufacturing activity rose nearly 6% through the summer before suddenly tapering off, still a surprising performance in view of the expansion's age, and especially so when matched against 1999's total gain of 3.6%. Nevertheless, the industry operated at little more than 80% of capacity, similar to the 1990 rate and a testament to the benefits of rising productivity. At least some of the higher productivity seemed to result from growing electronic commerce, especially of the business-to-business (B2B, as it was sometimes abbreviated) category, and, most markedly, in achieving lower prices and greater efficiency in the purchase of parts and services. Construction did not fare as well, although it, too, gained, with expenditures averaging an annual rate of more than $800 billion before slowing late in the year, compared with $764 billion in 1999. Indicative of continued high consumer confidence, the Commerce Department reported new-home sales running at a torrid annual rate of 928,000 in October, and averaging for the year only 1% lower than the previous year's record level.

Employment, wages, and profits remained healthy through much of the year. The civilian labor force rose to more than 140 million, and unemployment averaged 4%. Hourly earnings rose only slightly over those of 1999. Late in the year the average hourly wage, measured in constant (1982) dollars was close to $7.90, and more than $13.80 in current dollars. The wage and price stability, coupled with productivity increases, allowed corporate profits to remain strong through the third quarter, growing to a pretax annual rate of close to $950 billion,

adjusted for inflation, compared to slightly more than $800 billion in the previous 12-month period. The growth of individual-and corporate-tax accounts pushed the federal budget into an extraordinary surplus of $237 billion for fiscal year 2000, almost double the level of 1999 and the third straight year of excessive revenues. It fueled a congressional controversy over how the money was to be used: to lower taxes or to finance social and other government programs.

There were great exceptions to the mostly good news. The trade deficit with foreign countries continued to worsen as Americans imported far more than they exported. The shortfall for the year was estimated by the University of Michigan to hit an all-time high of $373 billion. While some economists rationalized that such deficits were the logical consequence of an economy growing faster than that of other nations, critics warned that it was leaving too many dollars abroad, meaning future claims on U.S. assets. While farmers participated strongly in exporting grains and other crops, they failed to reap strong financial benefits. Gross farm income rose to $243 billion during the summer, but net income continued to fall, and small farmers became increasingly distressed. Despite huge production gains, net farm income during the summer averaged no higher than that of a decade earlier.

While the economy continued to grow, more Americans were experiencing the bitter taste of the downturn. By year's end, the Standard & Poor's 500-stock index, widely used as a benchmark, was 10.1% lower than when the year began, and the Nasdaq composite index, heavily weighted in technology stocks, was off by 39.3%. Many stocks were down as much as 50%, and some high-technology issues, touted to individuals less than a year before as their personal rockets to higher living standards, were down by much more. For example, priceline.com fell from a 52-week high of more than $104 to less than $3. And Amazon.com, the largest of the new E-commerce merchandisers, still had not made a profit.

Increasing number of companies reported profits lower than anticipated. The Bank of America reported that it had $1 billion in uncollectible loans. Consumer confidence fell. And in its peculiarly vague way, the Federal Reserve held out the possibility of lower interest rates.

See also THE U.S. ECONOMY—THE GREAT EXPANSION, page 38.

JOHN CUNNIFF, *Associated Press*

Foreign Affairs

In the last year of his presidency, Bill Clinton immersed himself in foreign-policy issues and travels, rising above the fray of a relatively deadlocked domestic agenda and election campaign. Perhaps the president's greatest triumph was the long-awaited congressional passage of "permanent normal trade status" for China. Throughout the summer the president worked to win reluctant Democratic votes from those worried about the reaction of their constituents and organized labor.

Perhaps the greatest disappointment of the year was the near miss in mediating an Israeli-Palestinian peace settlement through two weeks of intense summer negotiations at Camp David. The administration also failed earlier to inspire an Israeli-Syrian agreement at talks in West Virginia. The Middle East situation blew up in October, with bloody confrontations and demonstrations spreading from Jerusalem throughout the Palestinian territories and surrounding Arab states. Seventeen U.S. sailors were killed in a terrorist attack on the naval destroyer *Cole* in the Yemeni port of Aden. The president continued to press for resumed peace negotiations.

For the first half of 2000, relations with Cuba swirled in the media whirlwind of the custody case of Elián González, a 6-year-old Cuban boy who had been picked up at sea after his mother had drowned escaping Cuba. The case continued until Attorney General Janet Reno and the Immigration and Naturalization Service forcibly reunited the child with his father and they were allowed to return to Cuba. In June, Congress approved limited direct food sales to Cuba for the first time in four decades.

Politics. Remarkably, these and other foreign-policy issues, such as the future of relations with such key states as Russia and China, were nearly invisible in the U.S. presidential campaign. The main topics to emerge were Republican charges, hotly contested by the White House and Joint Chiefs of Staff, that the armed forces were ill prepared for future demands. There was also brief concern over the declining value of the common currency of the European Union (EU), questions about peacekeeping in places such as the former Yugoslavia and Africa, and indirect references to "foreign oil" as responsible for mounting fuel prices.

In January the Democratic candidate, Vice-President Al Gore, presiding at a United Nations (UN) Security Council debate, promised increased funding to fight infectious diseases among the poorest countries. The administration later added plans for $1 billion in loans to fight AIDS in Africa, and U.S. drug companies pledged to cut prices on lifesaving medications. Questions about the vice-president's 1995 agreement with Moscow to limit arms sales to Iran emerged as the United States pressed Moscow over continued sales. In the context of Florida campaigning, Gore also broke with the administration by supporting U.S. residency status for Elián González. For his part, Texas Gov. George W. Bush, the GOP candidate, proposed unilateral nuclear reductions, while favoring development of a controversial antinuclear defensive shield. Basically, though, the two candidates adopted a bipartisan stand on most foreign-policy issues.

Presidential Travel. On his trips, President Clinton styled himself as a peacemaker, an advocate of democratic reforms, and a booster for the emerging global economy—the latter coming under growing worldwide criticism and protest. During his farewell European tours in June and December, the

© David Guttenfelder/AP/Wide World Photos

In October 2000, U.S. Secretary of State Madeleine Albright met with North Korean leader Kim Jong Il in Pyongyang. The precedent-breaking trip increased diplomatic contact between the two nations.

president received the Charlemagne Prize for European unity and continued to press for Irish peace. He also went to India, Bangladesh, and Pakistan in March and Africa and Colombia in the summer. In South Asia, he expressed hopes for technology and trade, and his concerns about the regional nuclear-arms race; about Kashmir and delays in Pakistan's return to democracy; and about controls on terrorists.

Late in the year the president attended the Asia-Pacific Economic Cooperation (APEC) summit in Brunei, where the agenda focused on renewed trade liberalization in 2001. The Clintons then toured Vietnam, capping the U.S.-Vietnamese trade agreement negotiated earlier in the year.

Asia. Officials such as Secretary of State Madeleine Albright and Defense Secretary William Cohen spent much of the year engaged in overseas talks to solidify relations and promote democracy and trade in East Europe and East Asia. Following the historic North-South Korean summit (*see* THE KOREAS—A RAPPROCHEMENT, page 54) in the spring and the visit of a leading North Korean general to Washington, Secretary Albright made a precedent-breaking trip to Pyongyang in October. She paved the way for renewed diplomatic relations and talks on eliminating North Korea's missile program in return for U.S. technical assistance and dropping of economic sanctions.

As the president attended the G-8 summit in Okinawa in July, Washington tried to talk Japan out of reducing payments for controversial U.S. military bases. Later the administration threatened Tokyo with sanctions over expanded whale hunting. Washington also pressured Indonesia to disarm the militias still marauding in Timor. Disputes over corruption and the pace of reform led to heated Indonesian charges of U.S. meddling. The U.S. Senate delayed approval of a new U.S. ambassador to the Philippines even as southern Philippine Muslim rebels held Americans and other foreign nationals hostage.

Europe. American diplomatic pressure extended with some success to other trouble spots. The State Department, which had issued a criminal "wanted" poster for Yugoslav President Slobodan Milosevic in March, moved toward renewal of diplomatic relations and lifting of sanctions when he was voted out of office in the fall. One hundred million dollars in aid was made contingent on the new Yugoslav government's cooperation in apprehending war criminals.

U.S. forces still patrolled in Bosnia and Kosovo, with no real progress toward ending ethnic tensions in that region. In January, U.S. troops were themselves accused of mistreatment of civilians. At home, Governor Bush indicated a desire for early withdrawal from these missions, but did not back Republican efforts to set time limits and restrict presidential discretion.

Early in the year, Washington supported the EU's opposition to government participation by Austria's far-right Freedom Party. However, the United States and the EU could not agree on any of their four outstanding trade disputes, and several U.S. partners within the North Atlantic Treaty Organization (NATO) expressed concern about U.S. missile-defense plans. In March, Clinton acquiesced to Germany's candidate to head the International Monetary Fund (IMF), while lecturing Ukrainian leaders about abuses of IMF loans. A long-sought agreement with Greece was signed in September, pledging cooperation in fighting crime and terrorism. In October, Congress withdrew a resolution blaming Turkey for the Armenian genocide in 1915 when the administration warned of severe consequences in U.S.-Turkish relations.

Middle East. While Iraq rejected renewed weapons inspections, and while sporadic U.S. and British air attacks continued on Iraqi installations, some progress was made with Iraqi President Saddam Hussein's agreement to allow limited International Atomic Energy Agency (IAEA) inspection and increased oil sales. In February the navy seized a Russian tanker suspected of illegal Iraqi oil shipments. Relations with Iran took further steps toward normalization, although the United States pressured Colombia in January to refuse Iranian investments, and later criticized Iran's trial of 13 Jews on espionage charges. In May, Washington was outvoted as the World Bank issued its first loans to Iran in seven years. In the autumn, Washington and Jordan negotiated a bilateral trade pact, the first to include integral pledges to protect workers and the environment.

Reflecting concern about terrorism and particularly Osama bin Laden's network, the administration added an Uzbek Islamic movement to the international terrorist list in September, and Washington and Moscow joined in pressuring Afghani Taliban Party leaders to suppress Islamic militant groups.

Russia and China. Relations with major powers such as Russia and China remained

Bill Clinton went on numerous diplomatic missions during his final year in the White House. On Aug. 30, 2000, the president was in Colombia to assure President Andrés Pastrana (right) of the U.S. commitment to help Colombia fight the drug trade.

open but troubled by fundamental disagreements over such issues as arms sales to and the status of Taiwan, Beijing's human-rights record, strong and pointed Chinese and Russian objections to U.S. missile-defense developments, and Russia's role in the breakaway republic of Chechnya. In an address to the Russian parliament in June, President Clinton promised to support Moscow's bid to enter the World Trade Organization (WTO) and receive IMF assistance. However, no major new initiatives were reached in a somewhat chilly meeting with Russia's new president, Vladimir Putin. Cooperation was to continue on aspects of arms control, but Washington pressed for Moscow's commitment to curtail the sale of laser technology to Iran. Moscow and Washington evidently did consult closely in orchestrating Milosevic's exit from office in Yugoslavia. Terms for China's entry into the WTO continued to be debated, and Washington sought Beijing's cooperation in stemming the tide of illegal immigrants entering the United States.

Latin America. Latin policy revolved around crime, drugs, security, and trade. In the summer the administration and the Senate agreed on a massive $1.3 billion, mainly military, aid program for Colombia, seeking to limit the drug trade and ease the threat of the ongoing antigovernment insurgency. Critics continued to note the potential for a Vietnam-like involvement and for a spreading war. Proposed U.S. military use of El Salvador's main airport also drew political protests in that country, and similar protests plagued U.S. naval operations in Puerto Rico. In September, Peru's President Alberto Fujimori sought Washington's backing as he announced plans to step down and hold new elections amid bribery scandals. The United States helped arrange a controversial brief asylum in Panama for the former Peruvian intelligence chief, reportedly tied to the U.S. Central Intelligence Agency (CIA). Secretary Albright pledged to declassify documents on Argentina's military kidnappings during the junta period from 1976–83. Meanwhile, Mexico's new president-elect, Vicente Fox, having called for more-open borders and reduced emphasis on drug certification, met with various U.S. officials in Washington.

Africa. Africans were angered at delays in America's airlift of humanitarian assistance to Mozambican flood victims in February-March, a problem that has dogged U.S. relief efforts, according to a State Department report issued in May. Making up for lost time, the administration finally spearheaded a UN Security Council arms embargo of Ethiopia and Eritrea as the two renewed fighting in the spring before finally reaching a settlement. Washington applied diplomacy, training, and logistical support, but no force, as the UN intervened in the volatile Sierra Leonean civil war. Washington also took part in UN Security Council efforts to end ethnic resettlement in Burundi, and pledged logistical assistance to a planned new 5,500–man African peacekeeping force for the Congo. (*See also* AFRICA: A CONTINENT OF PROBLEMS, page 44.)

United Nations. Ironically, even as Washington remained in arrears on UN dues and pressed to have assessments reduced for global peacekeeping operations, U.S. Ambassador Richard Holbrooke backed a larger and more effective military emphasis in the organization's peacekeeping department. In April, Holbrooke also indicated for the first time U.S. willingness to accept a significantly enlarged Security Council. A new UN financial plan, reducing U.S. dues to the world body, was reached in December.

In January, concerned about potential restrictions on U.S. sovereignty, Senate Foreign Relations Committee chair Jesse Helms warned the UN Security Council of a potential U.S. pullout if too many demands were made. Secretary of State Albright tried to smooth over relations, and Senator Helms continued the dialogue by hosting a Security Council delegation at the Capitol in March. Helms also put the administration on notice in April that no major new arms-control agreements, including any related to missile defense, would be passed by his committee during Clinton's final days in office.

At the UN General Assembly's Millennium Summit in September, the United States and the other major nuclear powers hedged on their earlier commitment to eliminate nuclear arms. In general, Washington was criticized abroad for preaching democracy and reform but arming human-rights abusers and failing to support undertakings such as the global land-mine treaty. At year's end, Clinton responded by signing the treaty for an international criminal court.

Arms Sales, New Issues. While the United States remained the world's preeminent arms exporter, Secretary Albright pledged not to trade arms to "areas of conflict," and to work to stem the tide of small-arms trafficking. The administration's arms priorities included trying to negotiate a protocol on illegal sale of firearms in the Organized Crime Convention, supplier agreement on shoulder-fired antiaircraft missiles, increased reporting of global arms transactions, and the control and destruction of surplus small-arms stockpiles. For its part, Congress opposed liberalization of commercial arms-related export-license approvals. In February, gun exports to Canada were suspended, and in April, Secretary Cohen strongly criticized Israel's proposed sale of advanced airborne radars to China. In the fall, Congress and the Clinton administration agreed to keep certain military export information secret despite charges that sensitive equipment had been sold to countries with nuclear potential since 1994. In November, economic sanctions on China were lifted and nominally applied to Iran and Pakistan as Beijing agreed to curtail future missile exports.

At the G-8 summit, President Clinton addressed new agenda issues such as the "digital divide" between rich and poor nations in information technology. The conference ended with commitments to fight infectious diseases and ease global debts. The meeting pledged to halve the number of those living in extreme poverty in the world by 2015. Year-end meetings on global warming broke down in a U.S.-European disagreement as the administration sought ways to meet greenhouse-gas targets for 2012 through a combination of domestic conservation, credits for forestation, new technologies, and investments abroad in return for pollution credits from less-developed states.

As globalization became more of an issue, the United States met opposition in certain international meetings, including the January gathering of 130 nations in Montreal, Canada, seeking a regulatory treaty on trade in genetically modified food products, a technology that U.S. companies have for the most part pioneered. Washington also strived strongly to please varied interest groups and foreign allies in Vienna negotiations on a treaty to ban international trafficking in women and children, and the Senate clamped down on the practice in October. U.S. prison conditions came under international criticism in May from the UN Committee Against Torture.

FREDERIC S. PEARSON
Wayne State University

Uruguay

In 2000, Uruguay's new President Jorge Batlle pledged a smaller role for the state in the economy, lower labor costs, and more access to international markets.

Politics and Government. A center-right coalition, formed by the traditional Colorado and National (Blanco) parties, was installed on March 1. On Nov. 29, 1999, Colorado Jorge Batlle had been victorious in his fifth run for the presidency, with nearly 52% of the popular vote. He was the fourth member of his family to gain the presidential office. The Broad Front, a center-left coalition that included former Tupamaro guerrilla militants, polled 44% of the presidential vote, after having won 40% of the seats in the General Assembly.

Accompanying Batlle was a cabinet of 12 members that allotted four ministries to the Blancos. Gen. Juan Carlos Geymonat became the new army commander, replacing Gen. Manuel Fernandez, a nationalist, after he had criticized the president's "revisionism." Batlle won high public-approval ratings for his inaugural promise of an 8% public-spending cut, and for pledging to address the mysterious disappearance of Uruguayan civilians more than two decades earlier.

In May, approximately 70,000 citizens marched in Montevideo, insisting that the truth about the missing be told. Once in office, Batlle acknowledged the disappearances under the infamous "Operation Condor," which had its origins in Chile, under the dictatorship of Augusto Pinochet (1973–1990). In agreement with his leftist opponents and the Catholic Church, Batlle met families of victims of military rule (1973–85), to clarify the victims' fate. A parliamentary commission indicated that l64 Uruguayans vanished during the dictatorship—127 in Argentina, 32 in Uruguay, three in Chile, and two in Paraguay.

Economy. Losses in agriculture and livestock exports spiraled to $500 million for the 1999–2000 harvest season. Tax relief was necessary in order to stimulate production, but recovery was slowed by an outbreak of foot-and-mouth disease that temporarily halted sales of beef to North America and Europe. International efforts to contain the disease were based in Montevideo. The crisis caused a rise in rural poverty and a marked exodus of farm labor into Montevideo. An economic-emergency bill moved swiftly through the General Assembly, giving Batlle his first legislative victory, in June.

URUGUAY • Information Highlights

Official Name: Oriental Republic of Uruguay.
Location: Southeastern coast of South America.
Area: 68,039 sq mi (176 220 km²).
Population (2000 est.): 3,334,074.
Chief City (May 1996 est.): Montevideo, the capital, 1,303,182.
Government: *Head of state and government,* Jorge Batlle, president (took office March 2000). *Legislature*—General Assembly: Chamber of Senators and Chamber of Representatives.
Monetary Unit: Peso (12.5850 pesos equal U.S.$1, Jan. 12, 2001).
Gross Domestic Product (1999 est. U.S.$): $28,000,000,000 (purchasing power parity).
Economic Index (Montevideo, 1999; 1990 = 100): *Consumer Prices,* all items, 1,943.5; food, 1,497.5.
Foreign Trade (1999 U.S.$): *Imports,* $3,357,000,000; *exports,* $2,232,000,000.

The administration's failure to achieve greater export growth (6.8% between January and July) produced calls for a peso devaluation, which were rejected. Urban unemployment had risen above 14% by August; and the 2000 projection for economic growth was lowered to 1.5%, with inflation in the 4–6% range.

Uruguay and Paraguay, partners in the Southern Cone Common Market (Mercosur), ultimately won a 23% tariff concession from Brazil and Argentina on autos imported from outside Mercosur, until 2006.

Foreign Affairs. In September, President Batlle visited Paraguay, Uruguay's partner in Mercosur. Batlle called for greater involvement of its associate members, Chile and Bolivia, in the regional trade bloc, currently the third-largest common market in the world. Both he and Paraguay President Luis Gonzalez Macchi supported new rules and mechanisms to resolve regional trade disputes and to protect Mercosur.

While visiting Argentina in February, Batlle and his host, President Fernando de la Rúa, addressed construction of a bridge across the Río de la Plata estuary, which divides the two countries. Subsequently, Batlle revealed that completion of the long-sought 28-mi (45-km) bridge was a goal of his term, which ends in 2006.

LARRY PIPPIN
University of the Pacific

Venezuela

Venezuela moved from legal limbo in the first half of 2000, to implementing the new constitution and choosing new leaders by year's end. Following seven votes in 18 months, President Hugo Chávez and the country turned attentions to the economic, social, and foreign-policy arenas.

Politics. After being elected twice—first in December 1998 and then "relegitimated" under his new constitution in a July 2000 vote—Hugo Chávez continued to define his revolution in 2000. Employing a hazy Bolivarian ideology of nationalism, integrity, and strong leadership, Chávez' Venezuela was increasingly characterized by a concentration of power in the presidency; an elimination of the institutions that had represented the political and socioeconomic elite; the empowering of the masses through popular consultation and referenda; and a new foreign policy that challenged the dominant West, particularly the United States.

The Bolivarian constitution approved in December 1999 led to new elections for all posts in the country. Presidential, legislative, gubernatorial, and mayoral elections were held on July 30, 2000, and local council elections were held December 3. Chávez was elected to a new six-year term with 58% of the vote; his coalition won 60% of the seats in the new unicameral legislature. Conflicts with the church, media, and civil-society organizations culminated with a referendum on December 3 to abolish the existing labor union leadership and require new, direct elections within six months.

Despite expressions of discontent from lower ranks of the military and retired officers, Chávez strengthened the participation of the armed forces in his government by placing active military leaders in such key-government positions as the head of the state-owned oil company (PDVSA) and vice-chancellor of foreign affairs. He also continued the Plan Bolívar 2000 involving troops in providing social services from road repair to school construction.

VENEZUELA • Information Highlights

Official Name: Republic of Venezuela.
Location: Northern coast of South America.
Area: 352,143 sq mi (912 050 km²).
Population (2000 est.): 23,542,649.
Chief Cities (1992 est.): Caracas, the capital, 1,964,846; Valencia, 1,034,033; Barquisimeto, 692,599.
Government: *Head of state and government,* Hugo Chávez Frias, president (inaugurated Feb. 2, 1999). *Legislature*—unicameral National Assembly.
Monetary Unit: Bolívar (699.0000 bolívares equal U.S.$1, Jan. 12, 2001).
Gross Domestic Product (1999 est. U.S.$): $182,800,000,000 (purchasing power parity).
Economic Index (1997, 1990 = 100): *Consumer Prices,* all items, 1,818.8; food, 1,559.7.
Foreign Trade (1999 U.S.$): *Imports,* $14,522,000,000; *exports,* $20,288,000,000.

Economics. In 2000, Venezuela benefited from an oil boom: The average price of oil reached nearly $27, compared with $16 in 1999, and $10 in 1998. Venezuela hosted an Organization of Petroleum Exporting Countries (OPEC) summit, assumed the leadership of OPEC, and continued to push for restricted production to maintain high prices. With the oil cushion, the government announced a job-creation program to lower the unemployment rate, which hovered between 14% and 18%. Meanwhile, economic growth improved from a negative 7% in 1999 to a positive 3% in 2000.

A reform of the tax code was planned, and enforcement of tax collection was a rallying cry of Chávez. If successful, these policies could reduce the government's dependence on oil revenues. The administration continued to pursue the privatization of the aluminum and telecommunications sectors.

Foreign Policy. President Chávez was controversial and provocative in his foreign policy. Early in the year, he clashed with the United States when he turned away a ship with military engineers that had been requested by his own defense minister to help rebuild roads washed away by the devastating floods of December 1999. His government continued to deny U.S. requests for drug-surveillance flights in Venezuelan airspace, citing national-sovereignty reasons. Chávez became the first elected world leader to cross the international sanctions line to meet with Iraq's President Saddam Hussein, and he gave a lavish reception for Fidel Castro during the Cuban president's five-day visit to Venezuela.

Venezuela worried its neighbors as it reopened an old claim to half of Guyana's territory, and appeared to support the Revolutionary Armed Forces of Colombia (FARC) guerrillas against the Colombian government. Venezuela opposed the U.S.-backed Plan Colombia and imposed unilateral trade barriers on Colombia. Relations with Colombia grew more tense in November when Venezuela issued visas to FARC representatives to speak in Venezuela's Congress building in Caracas. That action led to the withdrawal of ambassadors from each country. Other governments began to distance themselves somewhat from Venezuela as Chávez gave verbal—and allegedly more substantive—support to groups resisting government policy in Ecuador and Bolivia, a charge he denied.

JENNIFER L. MCCOY
Georgia State University

Vietnam

Vietnam celebrated the 25th anniversary of its reunification in April and May 2000. A U.S-Vietnamese trade agreement in July was followed by a visit by U.S. President Bill Clinton in November.

Politics and U.S. Relations. Vietnamese leaders rejected the basic message that President Clinton brought to their country—that political democracy and rapid economic growth go hand in hand. Clinton's nationally televised speech and the enthusiastic crowds that greeted him in Hanoi and Ho Chi Minh City may have confirmed the party leaders' fears about the threat of freewheeling, Western-style democracy to their carefully controlled political system.

According to a May report by Human Rights Watch, Vietnam continued to punish political dissent by religious leaders, academics, journalists, and even Communist Party members. The government continued to reject all foreign criticism of its human-rights record as interference in its domestic affairs. When Clinton raised the issue of human rights with Prime Minister Phan Van Khai, the latter replied that their countries held different concepts of human rights.

President Tran Duc Luong urged President Clinton to provide greater assistance in helping Vietnam locate and defuse 3.5 million mines still buried in its jungles, and in caring for people whom the Vietnamese claim suffered birth defects because of U.S. spraying of the defoliant Agent Orange. Although Clinton paid tribute to the suffering of both nations during the war, he did not apologize for U.S. involvement in the war.

In return for Vietnam's support in searching for the remains of U.S. military personnel, the United States provided Vietnam with equipment and documents to aid the nation in the search for its own soldiers' remains. The United States also launched a study to determine the effects of exposure to Agent Orange.

The only changes in Vietnam's leadership group during the year were the appointment of Nguyen Dy Nien as foreign minister and Vu Khoan as trade minister. Both men were career diplomats and Central Committee members.

Economy. Prime Minister Khai said in November that his country's inflation rate was below 6% and that the economy would register 6.7%, growth in 2000, despite the worst floods in 70 years. The floods killed hundreds of people in the Mekong Delta and left thousands without shelter. Australia provided a hospital ship to aid flood victims. Nongovernmental organizations provided a total of $80 million during the year for a wide range of socioeconomic causes.

While rice purchases by major domestic buyers were down by 25% in October, exports of 3.2 million tons maintained Vietnam's status as one of the world's top rice exporters. Overall food production was expected to set a record at 35.7 million tons, including large increases in the production of both fish and coffee.

Vietnam and the United States concluded a major trade agreement in July, which

Twenty-five years after the reunification of Vietnam, U.S. President Bill Clinton conferred with Vietnam's President Tran Duc Luong (right) in Hanoi in November 2000. A U.S.-Vietnamese trade agreement had been reached in July.

still had to be ratified by both governments. In return for Vietnam's agreement to further liberalize its economy, the United States promised to reduce tariffs to the same level it charged most other countries. The agreement was an important step toward Vietnam's goal of joining the World Trade Organization (WTO). Foreign investment during the year 2000 was more than $2 billion, including a $1.5 billion project to exploit Vietnam's offshore gas. The latter project, which was signed in December, would help Vietnam meet a large portion of its energy needs. Investors urged Vietnam to expand reforms of the banking and legal systems, speed privatization of state companies, and reduce bureaucratic red tape.

Despite concerns about free speech and globalization, Vietnamese leaders proclaimed the goal of linking their country to the information-technology (IT) revolution. It was estimated that 50,000 overseas Vietnamese work in IT jobs. But with only 2,000 software specialists and 700,000 computers, the country had a long way to go. Because of high service charges, there were only 90,000 Internet subscribers in Vietnam, but Internet cafés were being allowed to function in major cities, Telephone subscribers increased by 20% during the year, with more than half of the new subscribers owning mobile phones.

A Cuban company was hired by Hanoi to supervise building a 615-mi (985-km) section of a new north-south highway that will roughly follow the "Ho Chi Minh Trail" from Hanoi to Ho Chi Minh City. Critics claimed it would disrupt the environment of the western provinces; they argued that it would make more environmental and economic sense to strengthen the existing north-south highway.

VIETNAM • Information Highlights

Official Name: Socialist Republic of Vietnam.
Location: Southeast Asia.
Area: 127,243 sq mi (329 560 km²).
Population (2000 est.): 78,773,873.
Chief Cities (mid-1993, provisional): Hanoi, the capital, 2,154,900; Ho Chi Minh City, 4,322,300; Haiphong, 1,583,900.
Government: *Head of state,* Tran Duc Luong, president (took office September 1997). *Head of government,* Phan Van Khai, prime minister (appointed June 1997). *Legislature*—National Assembly.
Monetary Unit: Dong (14,498.0000 dongs equal U.S.$1, Nov. 30, 2000).
Gross Domestic Product (1999 est. U.S.$): $143,700,000,000 (purchasing power parity).
Foreign Trade (1999 est. U.S.$): *Imports,* $11,600,000,000; *exports,* $11,500,000,000.

Foreign Relations. The presidents of Vietnam and China signed an agreement in December that settled a long-standing border dispute in the Tonkin Gulf. Vietnamese and Cambodian officials also indicated that they hoped to finish defining their common border by the end of the year.

Vietnam continued in 2000 to play an active role in the Association of Southeast Asian Nations (ASEAN), the Asia-Pacific Economic Cooperation (APEC), the Francophone group of countries, and the United Nations.

PETER A. POOLE
Author, "Eight Presidents and Indochina"

Washington, DC

In 2000, Anthony Williams, the mayor of Washington, DC, extended efforts to return more power to city officials. In Williams' second year as mayor, he won voter approval to reconfigure the 11-member school board and return its policy-making authority in 2001—after more than four years of oversight from the financial-control board of the District of Columbia. Separately, the District witnessed a number of moves to restore historic landmarks and create new memorials in the U.S. capital.

Elections and Politics. In June, Williams won voter approval of a referendum to replace the 11-member school board with five elected members and four appointed by the mayor. In November, Peggy Cooper-Cafritz, the school-board candidate supported by Williams, won with 53% of the vote. The new board would likely address some serious issues, including finding a replacement for interim Superintendent Paul L. Vance, who said in July when he replaced departing School Superintendent Arlene Ackerman that he would serve only one or two years. In November, Democrat Eleanor Holmes Norton won a sixth term as the District's nonvoting delegate to Congress.

With the financial-control board scheduled to disband in September 2001, the board certified in September that the District had met federal requirements of improving its short- and long-term ability to borrow money. Williams' strong hand in guiding the District back to increased self-governance won the admiration of many on Capitol Hill.

In November, President Clinton signed a DC budget providing $445 million in federal funds and approved the spending of local

In July 2000, President Clinton proclaimed Anderson Cottage (above), the Washington, DC, home where President Abraham Lincoln spent summers during the Civil War, a national monument, the President Lincoln and Soldiers' Home National Monument.

funds. The bill's final version banned the use of federal or local funds for the privately run needle-exchange program and barred the program from operating within 1,000 ft (300 m) of schools.

Historic Landmarks and Memorials. The 115-year-old Washington Monument reopened in the summer after a three-year, $10 million restoration that repaired thousands of chipped stones, added protective glass in some areas, and created new exhibits. President Clinton announced in July that the Washington cottage where President Abraham Lincoln spent his summers during the Civil War would be named a national monument. It will be known as the President Lincoln and Soldiers' Home National Monument. Lincoln penned the final version of the Emancipation Proclamation there, and used the 2.3-acre (0.9–ha) hilltop retreat as a place to escape the sweltering city heat. Clinton announced the designation and restoration grants a month after the National Trust for Historic Preservation named the cottage one of the 11-most-endangered historic sites in the nation. A three-year renovation was initiated to preserve the 14-room Anderson Cottage, where Lincoln and his family stayed, and the surrounding area, which had been used as a veterans' housing compound for years.

Additionally, ground was broken for a World War II veterans' memorial at the National Mall and for a visitors' center at the nation's Capitol. In early November, the 200th birthday of the White House was officially celebrated (*see* UNITED STATES—The White House at 200).

New Archbishop. Also in November, Pope John Paul II appointed Theodore McCarrick, the archbishop of Newark, as the new head of the Roman Catholic archdiocese of Washington. Archbishop McCarrick, who was named a cardinal in January 2001, succeeded Cardinal James A. Hickey, 80, who had held the post since 1980.

National Zoo. Visitors to the National Zoo will have another pleasant reason to stop there beginning in January 2001: an exhibit featuring two Chinese giant panda bears. The new pandas—female Mei Xiang and male Tian Tian—arrived in December, after a ten-year loan was arranged in the spring between the zoo and the Chinese government. The zoo was to pay China $10 million for conservation projects in exchange for the pandas, and any cubs would be Chinese property. The pandas replaced two giant pandas that came to the zoo as a gift from China in 1972. Hsing-Hsing, the male panda, died in 1999; Ling-Ling, his female partner, had died in 1992 of heart failure. The pair had five cubs, none of whom lived more than a short period.

REBECCA ADAMS, *Reporter*
"CQ [Congressional Quarterly] Weekly"

Women

When the United Nations' (UN's) Fourth World Conference on Women, the largest ever, met in Beijing, China, in 1995, participants pledged to take action on poverty, education and health, wartime violence against women and children, and workplace equality. But five years later, when the conference reconvened in New York in June 2000, it was obvious that, while there had been some progress, much remained to be done. A visible showing of the lack of progress was a photograph of the 146 world leaders gathered at the UN Millennium Summit in September. Of the crown princes, prime ministers, and presidents pictured, only four were women—from Bangladesh, Finland, Latvia, and Sri Lanka. Of the 43 world leaders who did not attend the summit, only five were women. They were from Ireland, Panama, St. Lucia, San Marino, and Sri Lanka.

Goals for Progress. The scoreboard put on view at the June 5–9 General Assembly special session "Women 2000: Gender Equality, Development and Peace for the 21st Century" showed progress in several areas during the five-year period: Women are living longer and are healthier; they are better educated; they have more rights and better jobs; and, in most countries, they have the right to vote. The scoreboard also showed women lagging behind men in leadership roles, pay, and literacy. With Women 2000 participants realizing it would have been unrealistic to expect the world to drastically change its attitude toward women in just five years, new goals were set, and the international community was given another five years before another appraisal would occur. The goals included: closing the gender gap by the year 2005; improving adult literacy by 50% by 2015; having legislators remove discriminating provisions by the year 2005; and providing universal access to high-quality health care by 2015.

The session did not leave out the UN. The 1995 Platform for Action had called on the UN to set the standard by giving women 50-50 status throughout the organization by the year 2000. It repeated the demand in New York but set no deadline.

The Beijing Platform had asked that by 2000, the UN be the role model for gender equality throughout the world. According to UN Assistant Secretary-General Angela King, Annan's adviser on gender issues, the UN's rate of progress, "while not remark-able, has been better than in most countries with the possible exception of the Nordic countries." King said many of the UN's top agency heads are women, and the UN Population Fund achieved the goal of 50-50 gender distribution in staffing professional and higher-level posts. In the UN Secretariat, women in 2000 accounted for 39.2% of the professional staff on geographic appointments, and among the larger population of professional staff with appointments of one year or more, the percentage of women was 36.5%. Compounding the problem of gender equality, however, was a lack of female job applicants.

The UN had moved ahead in appointing women to high-level positions when, in 1998, it created the new post of deputy secretary-general. The post went to Louise Fréchette of Canada. She is second in rank to Secretary-General Annan, and in charge when he is away. One of her duties is to make certain that gender equality is a priority. "The increased number of women in the UN ranks is making a difference," said Fréchette. "Indeed, I don't see how it is possible to 'mainstream' gender considerations without an adequate number of women participating in policy-making." Mainstreaming means ensuring that women's needs are met in humanitarian programs and "making room for the participation of women in the new political institutions being rebuilt after a conflict, or promoting the education of girls in our development work," she said.

The Platform for Action also asked governments to give women an equal role in decision making. UN Secretary-General Kofi Annan recognized much of the problem when he said that "the actual participation of women in national and international decision-making had not significantly changed since the Fourth World Conference in Beijing in 1995."

Government and the UN. While women make up about one-half of voters in most countries, in mid-2000, they accounted for only 13.8% of legislators in national parliaments. Of the 189 ambassadors to the UN in July, only 11 (5.8%) were women. There, however, were 14 female foreign ministers worldwide. In the United States, prior to the November 2000 elections, there were nine women in the Senate and 56 women in the House of Representatives. After the balloting, however, a record number of women—13—would take senatorial seats, and 59 women would serve in the House beginning in January.

Challenges. Addressing the UN General Assembly in September, South Africa's Foreign Minister Nkosazana Dlamini Zuma noted that the equality of women and men still is a subject of great concern. "All we need to do is look around this hall to realize how far we are from realizing the vision of the founders of the UN. The feminization of poverty is of great concern. The marginalization of women in the

U.S. First Lady Hillary Rodham Clinton, above, was welcomed to a follow-up session of the United Nations' Fourth World Conference on Women by UN Secretary General Kofi Annan in June 2000. Clinton spoke on the progress of the world's women. Also speaking at the session was Salvadoran Secretary of the Family Lourdes María Rodríguez de Flores, left.

sovereign states and in multilateral forums means that our countries and organizations, including the UN, are functioning at half capacity and are deprived of the unique qualities, energies, and creativity that women would bring."

During 2000, women had the vote in most parts of the world, but they still faced poverty, violence, poor nutrition, and ill-health. UN statistics showed that while women's employment increased, their wages were still just 50% to 80% of those of men; two-thirds of 8.75 million illiterates were women; up to 80% of refugees fleeing conflicts were women and children; and domestic violence was claiming too many women's lives. In addition, every minute of every day, a woman died from direct complications of pregnancy and childbirth, and 45% of women in the developing world did not meet the World Health Organization's (WHO's) minimum daily caloric intake. Also, maternal mortality was still at an unacceptably high level; each minute, four women and girls underwent female genital mutilation; and the worldwide spread of HIV/AIDS had strongly impacted women.

There also were new challenges that did not exist in 1995. These included globalization and revolutions in communication and technology. The latter brought advantages to the fortunate women who were part of the technological revolution. Globalization also benefited that fortunate few by bringing "greater economic opportunities and autonomy to some women," said Assistant Secretary-General King. Science and technology had transformed production patterns, created new jobs and ways of working, and established a knowledge-based society. But the world's poorest women still did not have access to these facilities, and were at risk of becoming part of what King called the "digital divide" because they were excluded from the opportunities technology presented.

A victory of sorts arrived in October 2000, however, when the UN Security Council heard 42 diplomats, pledging their support for women serving in peacekeeping operations—in tasks ranging from negotiating accords to postconflict peace building. In an era that has seen large interstate wars replaced by ethnic and intrastate hostilities, Secretary-General Annan sees women as bearing more than their share of the burden. The Security Council passed a resolution urging Annan to expand the role of women in field-based operations, and called on all parties in armed conflicts to protect women and girls from gender-based violence.

RUTH PEARSON
United Nations Correspondent

Yugoslavia

For Yugoslavia, the year 2000 culminated in the ouster of President Slobodan Milosevic from power, following September's presidential and parliamentary elections. The new government, led by the democratic opposition leader Vojislav Kostunica (*see* BIOGRAPHY), faced a daunting task in conducting political and economic reforms, keeping the remnants of Yugoslavia together, and putting Serbia on track for international integration.

Countdown to Elections. Following the North Atlantic Treaty Organization's (NATO's) 1999 defeat of Serbia over the territory of Kosovo, protest actions against the repressive Milosevic regime were organized by the opposition in a number of Serbian cities. Their impact proved limited, however, as most citizens were either preoccupied with questions of economic survival or were fearful of police repression. Moreover, a majority of opposition leaders had lost credibility among wide sectors of the public. Apathy and despair were widespread, a sentiment promoted and exploited by the Milosevic administration.

The government staged periodic crackdowns on the alternative media and the young people's movement, *Otpor* (Resistance), and threatened to pass a new "antiterrorism" law that had the potential to transform Serbia into a police state. The regime's campaign against the independent media included takeovers, heavy fines, administrative measures, and direct police repression. By the summer, most of the opposition media were either under government control or had closed.

Organized crime was pervasive in the country, and a series of assassinations rocked Belgrade during the year. In January the most notorious indicted war criminal and gang leader, "Arkan," was gunned down by rivals. Yugoslav Defense Minister Pavle Bulatovic was assassinated in February. Then, during the summer, the former Serbian Communist Party leader, Ivan Stambolic, disappeared from his home and was believed to have been abducted and murdered by Milosevic's security forces.

Downfall of Milosevic. In July the federal parliament amended the Yugoslav constitution primarily to prolong Milosevic's term in office. According to the 1992 constitution, the president of the Federal Republic of Yugoslavia (FRY)—the republics of Serbia and Montenegro and the formerly autonomous regions of Kosovo and Vojvodina—was to be elected by secret ballot by the Federal Assembly. The same individual could not be reelected for a second term. However, according to amendments to the 1992 constitution adopted in July, the president was henceforth to be elected through direct elections, by a secret ballot, for a four-year term. As a result, Milosevic could stand for another term in office.

A second amendment to the federal constitution specified that members of the upper house would be elected proportionally by popular vote, instead of in equal numbers by the Serbian and Montenegrin parliaments. Montenegrin authorities considered these measures to be a "constitutional coup," and refused to participate in what they viewed as an illegitimate federal ballot.

Milosevic called for several elections in September, including federal parliamentary, federal presidential, municipal, and local ballots. After prolonged dispute, the coalition Democratic Opposition of Serbia (DOS) picked Kostunica as their joint candidate. Meanwhile, other opposition groups—including the Serbian Renewal Movement (SPO) led by Vuk Draskovic—decided to run their own candidate in the presidential vote. To assure Milosevic's regime of victory, the election commissions were tightly controlled by the ruling Socialist Party of Serbia (SPS) and the opposition was denied any significant resources or access to the mass media.

Despite these maneuvers, Milosevic seriously miscalculated the public's growing frustration and the popularity of the main opposition candidate. Kostunica, the leader of DOS, had not been discredited, corrupt-

---

YUGOSLAVIA • Information Highlights

Official Name: Federal Republic of Yugoslavia.
Location: Southeastern Europe.
Area: 39,518 sq mi (102 350 km²).
Population (2000 est.): 10,662,087.
Chief Cities (1991 census): Belgrade, the capital, 1,168,454; Novi Sad, 179,626; Nis, 175,391.
Government: *Head of state,* Vojislav Kostunica, federal president (sworn in Oct. 7, 2000). *Head of government,* Zoran Zizic, federal prime minister (took office Nov. 4, 2000). *Legislature*—Federal Assembly: Chamber of Republics and Chamber of Citizens.
Monetary Unit: Dinar (41.95 dinars equal U.S.$1, non-commercial rate, July 2000).
Gross Domestic Product (1999 est. U.S.$): $20,600,000,000.
Economic Indexes (1999, 1997 = 100): *Consumer Prices* all items, 187.7; food, 192.1. *Industrial Production* (1999, 1990 = 100): 38.9.
Foreign Trade (1999 U.S.$): *Imports,* $3,300,000,000; *exports,* $1,500,000,000.

KOSOVO

During 2000, Kosovo's security situation stabilized, and interethnic violence decreased. October's municipal elections reinforced the position of the largest Albanian party, which demanded independence for the region.

Security Issues. The North Atlantic Treaty Organization's (NATO's) presence proved increasingly effective in providing overall security in Kosovo. Nevertheless, few of the Serbs who fled or were forced out of the region by Albanian refugees following NATO intervention in 1999 `returned. It was estimated that out of a prewar population of some 200,000 Serbs, only 70,000 remained by the end of the 2000. Most of the Serbs lived in northern Kosovo, in or near Mitrovica. The rest remained scattered in isolated enclaves protected by Kosovo forces (KFOR). NATO had 38,550 troops in Kosovo; the U.S. contingent consisted of 5,600; and the number of foreign police officers stood at more than 4,000.

Local Elections. October's municipal elections resulted in a sweeping victory for the largest party, the Democratic League of Kosovo (DLK), led by Kosovo's shadow president, Ibrahim Rugova. Figures released by the Organization for Security and Co-operation in Europe (OSCE) showed that the DLK won 58% of the votes and 504 seats in 27 municipalities, gaining control over 21 local governments. The Democratic Party of Kosovo (PDK), led by the former leader of the Kosovo Liberation Army (KLA), Hashim Thaci, won 27.3% of the vote, 267 municipal seats, and control in six local councils. Rugova underscored that his goal remained the full independence of Kosovo; he stated that no political link with Serbia would be acceptable.

Final Status. The local elections were considered a valuable starting point for building statewide institutions. The United Nations (UN) administrator, Bernard Kouchner, urged the international community to prepare for general elections for a central authority in the spring of 2001. Albanian spokesmen asserted that a commitment to eventual independence would restore Kosovar confidence in the international community and prevent political radicalization. They emphasized that regardless of Serbia's progress toward democracy, NATO needed to remain in the territory with a substantial U.S. component.

JANUSZ BUGAJSKI

© Anja Niedringhaus/AFP/Corbis

The Democratic League of Kosovo (DLK) of Ibrahim Rugova swept to victory in municipal elections held in October. Rugova (center) had stressed that no political link with Serbia would be accepted.

ed, or co-opted by the Milosevic regime over the previous decade. According to observers, he won the federal presidency outright in the first round of voting, despite massive fraud by the Socialist administration. Opposition monitors claimed that Kostunica had gained more than 55% of the vote and Milosevic had managed only 35%.

The federal election commission controlled by the Socialists claimed that Kostunica had not passed the 50% threshold, and called for a second round of presidential elections. In response, the opposition declared it would boycott the ballot, and Zoran Djindjic, the DOS campaign manager, called for a general strike in Serbia. Public support for the protests grew; workers in several factories and offices staged strikes calling for the recognition of Kostunica as the country's new president.

Following large-scale demonstrations and the storming of the federal parliament and the state-run television in Belgrade in early October, Milosevic lost the loyalty of military and police forces and was unable to stage a massive crackdown. Under pressure both domestically and internationally, Milosevic finally resigned from office on October 6. The Constitutional Court ruled that Kostunica had been elected Yugoslav president

SARAJEVO INTERNATIONAL AIRPORT

Some two weeks after becoming president of Yugoslavia, Vojislav Kostunica (center) met briefly with members of the tripartite presidency of Bosnia and Herzegovina at the Sarajevo airport.

© Hidajet Delic/AP/Wide World Photos

Socially, the Serb authorities had to maintain a sufficient measure of popular backing while launching a painful but necessary reform program. The leaders needed to prevent a potential populist and nationalist reaction as a result of deflated public expectations over rapid economic progress and prosperity. A related danger was that under tough economic conditions, the coalition could disintegrate and paralyze decision making.

in the first round of voting, and he was formally inaugurated as president.

In return for recognition as the FRY president, Kostunica made an agreement with the security services that he would forgo personnel purges. Late in October, DOS representatives also reached agreement with officials of the Socialist Party on the composition of the federal administration and the transitional republican government for Serbia, pending general elections scheduled for late December. In early November a new federal government was installed, despite the protests of the Montenegrin authorities. Its prime minister was Zoran Zizic, a Montenegrin politician and former Milosevic supporter. The DOS went on to win the December elections.

Serbia's Challenges. The new government faced a legion of political, economic, and ethnic problems inherited from the Milosevic years. Politically, it confronted the daunting task of keeping together a disparate coalition of 18 parties with divergent interests and competing personal ambitions. The potential fragmentation of this coalition could leave the political space open to nationalist radicals, populists, criminal syndicates, and the postcommunist apparatus.

Economically, Belgrade needed a tough reform program involving wholesale macroeconomic restructuring, state budgetary discipline, and competitive reprivatization. To be successful in this endeavor, it also needed to eliminate the illicit interest groups that still controlled the Serbian economy. The absence of systemic reform would discourage Western investment.

Constitutionally, Serbia and Montenegro either had to reformulate their federal arrangement on a genuinely equal basis, or the government in Podgorica looked determined to move forward toward national independence. Such a step would effectively terminate the Yugoslav federation and extinguish the rationale for Kostunica's government and presidential office. (*See* SIDEBAR, page 577.)

Territorially, the conflict between Serbia and Kosovo looked set to continue because of the irreconcilable positions of Belgrade and Pristina on the question of Kosovo's independence. While Kostunica's administration sought to preserve Kosovo within Yugoslavia, the Albanian leadership remained adamant about achieving statehood. (*See* SIDEBAR, page 575.)

Economic Outlook. The Serbian and Yugoslav economies continued to deteriorate during the year. Although reliable statistics were hard to obtain, the country's inflation rate accelerated and stood at about 42% for the year. The gross domestic product (GDP) was estimated to have contracted by some 20%, with production growth in industry falling by approximately 22%, and the unemployment rate exceeding 35%.

International sanctions, economic mismanagement, and rampant criminality continued to isolate Belgrade from international financial institutions and foreign investments. However, even before the removal of Milosevic, the European Union

Montenegro

The October collapse of the Slobodan Milosevic regime encouraged Montenegro's government to push for a new political arrangement with Serbia. Montenegro also declared it would withdraw entirely from the Yugoslav federation if its various demands were not met by the new administration of Vojislav Kostunica in Belgrade.

Constitutional Conflicts. In July, Montenegro's position in the Federal Republic of Yugoslavia (FRY) was undercut by the Socialist-controlled Federal Assembly. The legislature dominated by Serbs altered the federal constitution by mandating direct elections for the upper chamber of parliament. Under the original constitution, 20 deputies each represented the Montenegrin and Serbian republican parliaments in the upper chamber. The introduction of direct elections further limited the influence of the Montenegrin legislature.

Milo Djukanovic's administration declared that President Milosevic had, in effect, staged a "constitutional coup." It announced that it would not participate in the Federal Assembly or presidential elections scheduled for September because it would serve to legitimize Milosevic and eliminate Montenegro's sovereignty. Only 24% of the Montenegrin electorate took part in the ballot; most cast their votes for the pro-Milosevic party of former Montenegrin President Momir Bulatovic.

Yugoslav Negotiations. Following the victory of Vojislav Kostunica and the Democratic Opposition of Serbia (DOS) coalition in the FRY elections, Montenegrin authorities refused to recognize Kostunica as the president of Yugoslavia. They argued that the June constitutional changes had effectively terminated the federation. To avoid a full-scale confrontation, Djukanovic offered to engage in negotiations with the next Serbian government following December's parliamentary elections in Serbia.

Montenegro proposed the creation of an alliance or confederation of two independent states that could share functions such as national defense and foreign policy. But in case the proposed talks failed, the republican government pledged to hold a referendum on independence during the first six months of 2001. According to opinion polls conducted in the fall, support for outright Montenegrin independence stood at some 55%, while more than 70% favored a loose association with Serbia,

Podgorica was pressed by Western governments into an accommodation with the new administration in Belgrade. The United States threatened to cut off economic assistance to Montenegro if Djukanovic moved toward statehood. Washington feared that the disintegration of Yugoslavia would imperil democratization in Serbia.

JANUSZ BUGAJSKI

(EU) pursued a program to bypass the government in Belgrade and provide energy and other resources to cities in Serbia that had democratic administrations.

Regional Relations. In the wake of Kostunica's election as president, hopes were raised that Serbia could rebuild its relations with neighboring states and settle several outstanding disputes. These issues included the unconditional acceptance of Croatia's full control over the Prevlaka peninsula on the Adriatic coast, the recognition of the Macedonian-Serbian border as inviolable, and the severing of Belgrade's assistance to nationalist and separatist forces in Bosnia and Herzegovina.

Belgrade was urged to move quickly on settling the succession question with all the former Yugoslav republics, in order to legitimately divide the assets and debts of the defunct Yugoslavia and to establish productive bilateral relations.

International Reactions. Following the ouster of Milosevic, the EU moved to remove a list of sanctions against Yugoslavia and to provide humanitarian aid for Serbia. EU leaders were concerned that a hard winter could undermine Kostunica's authority and even allow for the return of the deposed Socialists. In early November, and despite the protests of Montenegro that the federation was illegitimate, Yugoslavia was admitted to the United Nations and to the Organization for Security and Co-operation in Europe (OSCE). Nevertheless, Belgrade refused to cooperate with the war-crimes tribunal in The Hague on extraditing Milosevic and other indicted war criminals. The Kostunica government also focused on developing close relations with Moscow, while moving more cautiously in restoring Serbia's ties with the United States.

JANUSZ BUGAJSKI
Center for Strategic and International Studies

Zimbabwe

The year 2000 was perhaps the most turbulent in the political and economic history of Zimbabwe since it became independent in 1980. There were major challenges to the authority of President Robert Mugabe; the economy floundered, in part because of an ill-advised commitment of Zimbabwean troops to the Democratic Republic of the Congo; and the occupation of white-owned commercial farms threatened the country's commitment to law and order. An opinion survey in October indicated that 70% of Zimbabweans wanted Mugabe to resign. On a positive level, the emergence of a new and strong opposition party pointed the way to political reform.

A Constitutional Referendum and National Election. For the first time since he came to power in 1980, President Mugabe was rebuffed by the electorate. A referendum for a proposed new constitution, held on February 12 and 13, was rejected by nearly 700,000 voters—55% of those who voted. While opponents of the government were denied access to radio and television until a week before the polling, their campaign against the referendum was victorious. For many, the "no" vote represented deep dissatisfaction with the deteriorating economic and political situation. Voters also were concerned that the proposed constitution would have been a dangerous expansion of Mugabe's power, and other felt that it would have enabled him to seize white-owned farms without compensation.

On June 24 and 25, after a campaign of violence, nearly 40 deaths, and questionable voters' roles, Zimbabweans went to the polls and chose new members of parliament. The

Legislation that passed in November 2000 gave the Zimbabwe government authority to seize and redistribute white-owned farms. Earlier armed war veterans, below, had caused unrest by invading such farms.

© Alexander Joe/AP/Wide World Photos

months before the election were characterized by threats, intimidation, kidnapping, and deaths, allegedly instigated by supporters of the ruling Zimbabwe African National Union–Patriotic Front (ZANU-PF). A powerful new opposition, the Movement for Democratic Change (MDC), led by 48-year-old Morgan Tsvangirai, a former secretary-general of the Zimbabwe Congress of Trade Unions (ZCTU), challenged the government, which it maintained had bankrupted the country. Throughout the campaign, Tsvangirai received numerous death threats. The MDC emphasized that there was rampant unemployment, estimated at close to 50% of the workforce; inflation nearing 60%; and that the prices of basic staples were increasing by an estimated 200%. The deployment of 11,000 Zimbabwean soldiers (one-third of the army) to fight in the Democratic Republic of the Congo, on the side of President Laurent Kabila, cost the government millions of dollars each month. Mugabe's electoral promises included a commitment to voters that he would appropriate white-owned land and back the illegal seizure of farms by so-called war veterans.

On election day, June 25, there was a large turnout and long lines at the polling stations. More than 60% of the 5.1-million-person electorate voted. It is noteworthy that international monitors, such as the European Union (EU) observer team, decided the election was neither free nor fair because of the "high levels of violence, intimidation, and coercion" that led up to it. While ZANU-PF narrowly won the election, the MDC became the first real parliamentary opposition since

1980. The final result of the election was 62 seats for ZANU-PF and 57 seats for the MDC. One seat was won by the small Zanu-Ndonga. In the previous parliament, ZANU-PF controlled all but three seats. In addition to the 120 elected members, under the terms of the constitution, Mugabe appointed 30 additional members to the 150-member parliament.

When Mugabe opened the first session of the new Zimbabwean parliament on July 21, he was met by thousands of opposition supporters chanting "change" as he arrived in an open car. Seven cabinet members were not reelected and had to be replaced, including the powerful minister of justice, Emerson Munangagwa. Ten of the 19 ministers were new.

The "change" Mugabe's opponents so desired was given a chance in October, when the MDC began impeachment proceedings against Mugabe. While the MDC had the necessary one-third quota to call for impeachment, it lacked the two-thirds vote in parliament needed to actually impeach the president. The MDC maintained it had called for impeachment to publicly debate the shortcomings of the president. As the MDC launched impeachment proceedings, President Mugabe threatened to arrest Ian Smith, the former Rhodesian prime minister, and other whites for genocide during the guerrilla war of the 1970s. Such a move would have violated the amnesty guaranteed by the 1980 settlement.

Land Resettlement and the Economy. Land continued to be a source of conflict and unrest throughout the year as veterans of the guerrilla war intensified their illegal—and sometimes violent—occupation of the white-owned commercial farms. The government of Zimbabwe essentially ignored this breakdown of law and order and reportedly encouraged the takeovers, despite being ruled illegal by the Zimbabwe Supreme Court in March. In June the government submitted a list of 2,295 farms—out of a total of 4,500—as targets for court approval. However, war veterans had already illegally occupied 1,700 farms. An increasingly embattled Mugabe, facing a tough election, was using the land issue to garner support from landless blacks by promising them farms. The country's economy, already under severe economic pressure, suffered from the shutdown of farms, and from losses from the sale of tobacco, the largest single foreign-currency earner. In November, Zimbabwe's parliament passed the Land Acquisition

The authority of Zimbabwe's President Robert Mugabe was challenged by Morgan Tsvangirai, above, leader of a new opposition group, the Movement for Democratic Change (MDC), as it won 57 of 120 parliamentary seats in June 2000 elections.

Amendment bill, which gave President Mugabe power to seize white-owned farms for redistribution to landless blacks without paying compensation.

At the end of July, the MDC and white farmers backed a three-day national strike organized by the country's labor unions, in an effort to force the government to end the prevailing lawlessness. The ZCTU called for its more than 1 million members to go on strike; the Commercial Farmers' Union (CFU) also called for nonessential tasks to cease for the three-day period. In particular, the strikers called for the removal of troops from urban townships, and for the restoration of law and order on commercial farms.

Zimbabwe continued to be plagued by problems of unemployment, high interest rates, and an absence of foreign investment and exchange. While the Zimbabwe dollar traded at Z$38 to the U.S. dollar, many believed this was unrealistic, and called for a more drastic devaluation. In August a further devaluation took place, pegging the Zimbabwe dollar at Z$50 to the U.S. dollar. Inflation was estimated at 60%, and interest rates were close to 60%.

PATRICK O'MEARA
Indiana University

Zoos and Zoology

Aquariums continued to make headlines in the United States during 2000. Two brand-new aquatic complexes and another that underwent a major renovation opened in May on the East Coast. A number of U.S. zoos and aquariums participated in two major emergency rescue efforts for wildlife.

Aquariums. The South Carolina Aquarium made its public debut in Charleston. The $69 million, 93,000-sq-ft (8 649-m²) facility sits on a former Superfund site along the waterfront, which was reclaimed. More than 60 exhibits with 10,000 living animals and plants help visitors imagine they are a drop of water making its way from the mountains to the sea. Along the way, they encounter Blue Ridge Mountain waterfalls at the source of a freshwater river inhabited by river otters and alpine birds. Next come channel catfish and white bass as the water proceeds through the rolling hills of the Piedmont Plateau, then freshwater swamp and marsh ecosystems along the coast, and finally sea turtles, eels, and jellyfish that live in the Atlantic Ocean.

The Pittsburgh Zoo changed its name to the Pittsburgh Zoo and Aquarium to highlight the importance of its new aquarium. The $15.9 million facility explores the diversity of water. Species range from tiny African cichlids to leafy sea dragons, stingrays to sharks, and Amazon River dolphins to penguins. Habitats run the spectrum from the local Allegheny River to coral reefs of the tropics. The displays have been designed so that they can evolve over time, exhibiting different animals in different ecosystems.

The North Carolina Aquarium located on Roanoke Island reopened its doors after the first phase of a major renovation and expansion was completed. The focus of the new 68,000-sq-ft (6 324-m²) building is the Waters of the Outer Banks. Beginning at Alligator River, the exhibits highlight fresh- and saltwater marshes of northeastern North Carolina, with alligators, otters, and frogs; and offshore waters in the Gulf Stream, with bluefish, eels, and other nearshore animals. A special 180,000-gal (681 300-l) ocean tank houses a re-creation of the USS *Monitor*. Visitors can see large sharks, cobia, groupers, and sea turtles among the wreckage of the Civil War ironclad ship.

Other New Attractions. It is the little things that counted at the St. Louis Zoo, with the opening of its Monsanto Insectarium. Visitors learn about the importance of invertebrates—how they recycle waste materials, pollinate plants, and form the base support in the cycle of life—in interactive exhibits that include more than 100 species of live insects. A re-created kitchen in "Not Home Alone" is inhabited by houseflies and cockroaches. A tree that literally goes through the roof allows bees to come and go as they please. In a dark corner, visitors can "make a date" with a firefly by selecting

© Tom Uhlman/AP/Wide World Photos

Children go nose-to-nose with a polar bear frolicking underwater in the new "Kroger Lords of the Arctic" exhibit at the Cincinnati Zoo. The zoo celebrated its 125th anniversary in 2000 with the opening of several new exhibits.

lights that match the flash patterns of these beetles. The Butterfly Wing surrounds visitors with hundreds of flitting creatures, lush plants, and a waterfall.

Invertebrates also got top billing at the Florida Aquarium in Tampa, with the unveiling of No BoneZone. The main feature is the S.C.U.M. touch tank, where visitors can get up close to sea stars, crustaceans, urchins, mollusks, and other marine invertebrates. The Terrific Pacific highlights tropical corals, giant clams, and cleaner shrimp. The corals in this display have been either farm-raised or confiscated by the government from illegal shipments. Ocean Architects displays shells from around the world and explores how mollusks create their own homes. No Bonz X-ray compares vertebrates (animals with backbones, such as bony fish) with the invertebrate (animals lacking backbones, such as mollusks) stars of the exhibit.

Amphibians are not usually the focus of an entire zoo display, but the Detroit Zoological Institute decided that these creatures deserve special attention, particularly in light of recent reports of amphibian-population declines around the world. In June the zoo opened Amphibiville, the National Amphibian Conservation Center—dedicated to the conservation, preservation, exhibition, and interpretation of amphibian life—on the edge of an actual Michigan wetland habitat. The featured amphibians range from tiny dart-poison frogs of tropical America to the Japanese giant salamander.

The Cincinnati Zoo and Botanical Garden celebrated its 125th anniversary, and opened the new Schott-Unnewehr Vanishing Giants exhibit, which was named after Marge Schott, the longtime zoo supporter and former owner of the Cincinnati Reds baseball team. The new exhibit involved renovation of the historic 1906 Elephant House and features a 60,000-gal (227 100-l) pool and an outdoor forest habitat for the pachyderms. It also encompasses a 4.3-acre (1.74-ha) walking safari to see okapis and Masai giraffes.

Zoology. In June an oil spill off the coast of Cape Town, South Africa, affected more than 20,000 African penguins. Within days of the spill, an appeal went out to the Penguin Taxon Advisory Group (TAG) of the American Zoo and Aquarium Association (AZA)

At the Oregon Zoo in Portland, Steller Cove, a new $11 million exhibit that simulates the coastal habitat of the U.S. Northwest, opened in July 2000. Youngsters can take advantage of the cove's research center, above.

for assistance with handling the thousands of birds brought to a rehabilitation facility. About 1,000 volunteers from around the world—including staff from the Baltimore Zoo, Brookfield Zoo (Illinois), Disney's Animal Kingdom (Florida), Aquarium of the Pacific (Long Beach, CA), Mystic Aquarium (Connecticut), New England Aquarium (Boston), Riverbanks Zoo & Botanical Garden (Columbia, SC), SeaWorld, and Seneca Park Zoo (New York)—assembled in South Africa to supervise and help remove the oil from the birds. About 19,000 of the birds were cleaned and released. Only time would tell how many would survive. There are an estimated 150,000 African penguins left in the wild.

At a major breeding site for Caribbean flamingos in a reserve in Mexico, a jaguar began raiding the nesting colony. After a few nights of jaguar visits, about 1,000 of the adult flamingos began incubating their eggs only during the day, abandoning the nests and leaving the eggs unguarded during the night in fear of the predator. Biologists studying the flamingos decided to collect the eggs, artificially incubate them, and hand-raise the young. Before long, the biologists were overwhelmed by the number of hatchings, so the scientists contacted the AZA Ciconiiformes TAG, which in turn contacted zoos and aquariums for help. A number of U.S. institutions—including SeaWorld, Disney's Animal Kingdom, Fort Worth Zoo, and Miami Metrozoo—provided staff, technical advice, and equipment. The goal was to release the juvenile flamingos in Mexico.

See also PRIMATES IN PERIL, page 82.

DEBORAH A. BEHLER, *Executive Editor*
"Wildlife Conservation Magazine"

Statistical and Tabular Data

The United States: 100 Years of Growth and Change

The beginning of an new century seems an appropriate time to consider how the United States has changed statistically during the last 100 years.

DEMOGRAPHICS

U.S. POPULATION 1900 - 76,212,168

U.S. POPULATION 2000 (50 states and Washington DC) - 281,421,906

Most Populous States

1900	2000
New York – 7,283,000	California - 33,871,648
Pennsylvania – 6,313,000	Texas - 20,851,820
Illinois - 4,828,000	New York - 18,976, 457
Ohio - 4,161,000	Florida - 15,982,378
Missouri - 3,108,000	Illinois - 12,419,293
Texas - 3,055,000	Pennsylvania - 12,281,054
Massachusetts - 2,788,000	Ohio - 11, 353,140
Indiana - 2,518,000	Michigan -9,938,444
Michigan - 2,423,000	New Jersey - 8,414,350
Iowa - 2,231,000	Georgia - 8,186,453

Least Populous States

1900	2000
Nevada - 43,000	Wyoming- 493,782
Wyoming - 93,000	Vermont - 608,827
Arizona - 124,000	Alaska - 626,932
Idaho - 163,000	N. Dakota - 642,200
Delaware - 185,000	S. Dakota - 754,844
New Mexico - 196,000	Delaware - 783,600
Montana- 245,000	Montana- 902,195
Utah - 277,000	Rhode Island - 1,048,319
North Dakota - 321,000	Hawaii - 1,211,537
Vermont - 344,000	New Hampshire - 1,235,786

Most Populous Cities

1900	2000
New York - 3,437,202	New York - 7,380,906
Chicago - 1,698,575	Los Angeles - 3,633,591
Philadelphia - 1,293,697	Chicago - 2,799,050
St. Louis - 575,238	Houston - 1,845,967
Boston - 560,892	Philadelphia- 1,417,601
Baltimore - 508,957	San Diego - 1,238,974
Cleveland - 381,768	Phoenix - 1,211,466
Buffalo - 352,387	San Antonio - 1,147,213
San Francisco - 342,782	Dallas - 1,076,214
Cincinnati - 325,902	Detroit - 965,084

Population by Age

	1900	2000
0-14	26,100,000	58,500,000
15-34	27,100,000	76,000,000
35-64	19,700,000	106,000,000
65+	3,100,000	34,800,000

Population Characteristics

	1900	1999
male	38,816,000	133,276,559
female	37,178,000	139,414,254
white	66,809,000	224,697,230
black	8,834,000	34,904,424
other	351,000	13,089,159

	1900	1990
rural	45,997	61,656,386
urban	30,215	187,053,487

Household Size

1900	1999
4.76 people	2.62 people

Bathrooms

1940	1999
55% households with at least one private bath	7% 1.5 baths or less; 40% 2 baths; 53% 2.5 baths or more

ECONOMY

Gross Domestic Product

	1929	2000
current	$103.8 billion	$9,255 billion

Personal Consumption Expenditures

	1929	1998
Current	$77.5 billion	$5,807.9 billion
Chained	$593.9 billion	$5,153.3 billion

Change in Personal Consumption Expenditures as Percentage

	1929	1997
food and tobacco	27.4%	15.2%
clothing	14.5%	6.4%
personal care	1.4%	1.4%
housing	15.1%	15.1%
household operation	13.8%	11.3%
medical care	4%	17.4%
personal business	5%	8.4%
transportation	9.9%	11.6%
recreation	5.7%	8.4%

Per Capita Personal Income/Disposable Income Personal Consumption Expenditures

	1960	1990
personal income	$2,277	$26,386
disposable personal income	$2,008	$22,304
personal consumption expenditures	$1,838	$21,490

Personal Income Per Capita—Ten Highest States

1990	1998
Connecticut - $26,545	Connecticut - $37,598
New Jersey - $24,883	New Jersey - $33,937
Massachusetts - $23,210	Massachusetts - $32,797
New York - $23,210	New York - $31,734
Maryland - $22,482	Maryland - $29,814
Alaska - $21,073	Delaware - $29,814
California - $21,363	New Hampshire - $29,022
Delaware - $21,599	Illinois - $28,873
Hawaii - $21,529	Colorado - $28,657
New Hampshire - $20,728	Washington - $27,961

Personal Income Per Capita—Ten Lowest States

1990	1998
Arkansas - $14,025	Mississippi - $18,958
West Virginia - $14,176	West Virginia - $19,362
Utah - $14,214	New Mexico - $19,936
New Mexico - $14,480	Montana - $20,172
Louisiana - $14,773	Utah - $21,019
Montana - $15,038	Oklahoma - $21,072
Kentucky - $15,085	Idaho - $21,081
Alabama - $15,213	South Carolina - $21,309
North Dakota - $15,264	Louisiana - $21,346
Idaho - $15,346	Arkansas - $20,346

Labor

Number of Workers and Median Weekly Earnings

	1990	2000
Workers	118,793,000	135,836,000
male	65,104,000	72,534,000
female	53,689,000	65,907,000
Median wages	$415	$576
male	$485	$646
female	$348	$491

Labor

Occupations

	1929	2000
total working population	49,180,000	141,489,000
employed	47,630,000	135,836,000
agricultural	10,450,000	3,883,000
non-agricultural	37,180,000	131,953,000

Employment by Industry

	1919	1998
mining	1,133,000	575,000
construction	1,036,000	5,965,000
manufacturing	10,659,000	18,716,000
transportation and public utilities	3,711,000	6,549,000
wholesale trade	N/A	6,825,000
retail trade		22,475,000
finance, insurance, and real estate		7,341,000
services		37,525,000
government	2,676,000	19,862,000

Standard and Poor's 500 Composite

1900 - 6.2	1998 - 1,085.5	2000 - 1,320.3

Dow Jones Industrials (30stocks)

1920 - 72	1998 - 9,181.4	2000 - 10,786.9

Median Family Income

	1947	1997
current	$3,031	$44,568
constant	$20,102	$44,568

Number of Acreage of Farms and Ownership

	1900	1992	1997
total	5,740,000	1,925,000	1,912,000
acres	841,202,000		931.8 mil-lion
family or individually owned		1,653,000	1,643,000
partnership		187,000	169,000
corporate		73,000	84,000

Farms

	1900	1970
farm population	29,875,000	9,712,000
number of farms	5,740,000	2,954,000
percentage of U.S. population	41.9%	4.8%

Transportation

Miles of Federal Highways

1917-12,919	1970 - 895,208

Miles of Surfaced, Rural Roads, and Municipal Streets

	1904	1921	1970
rural		3,160,000	3,730,000
surfaced	154,000	387,000	2,946,000

Motor Vehicle Factory Sales

	1900	1904	1970
Passenger cars	4,100	2,210	6,546,800
Trucks and buses		400	1,692,400

Operating Railroads

	1900	1970
total	1,224	351
miles of track operated	258,784	360,330
passenger car trains in service	34,731	11,378
passengers	576,831,000	289,469,000
passenger miles total	16,038 million	10,786 million
commutation		4,592 million
coach		5,414 million
parlor and sleeping car		765 million

Foreign Versus Native Born

	1900	2000 (est)
all races		
male	46.3	74.2
female	48.3	79.9

Life Expectancy at Birth

	1900	2000 (est)
all races		
male	46.3	74.2
female	48.3	79.9

Marital Status

	1900		1998	
	male	female	male	female
total	25,493,000	24,176,000	101,123,000	108,168,000
never married	10,262,000	7,549,000	31,591,000	26,713,000
married	13,919,000	13,781,000	58,633,000	59,333,000
widowed	1,173,000	2,706,000	2,569,000	11,029,000
divorced	84,000	114,000	8,331,000	11,093,000

Education

Enrollment, Graduates, and Degrees

	1900	2000 (est)
total K-8	16,422,000	38,543,000
total 9-12	650,000	14,903,000
high-school graduate	95,000	2,708,000 (1997)
college enrollment	238,000	14,889,000
B.A. degree	28,700	1,173,000

Education Summary as Percentage of Population

	1900	1997
high-school graduate (as percent of 17-year-old pop)	6.4%	69%
B.A. degree (as percent of high-school graduates four years earlier)	36%	47%

Number of Two- and Four-year Colleges

1970	1995
2,556	3,706

Healthcare

	1909	1970	1997
hospitals	4,359	7,123	6,097
beds	421,065	1,615,771	1,035,000

Physicians, Surgeons, and Osteopaths

1900	1970	1998
131,000	282,000	740,000

Registered Nurses

1900	1998
12,000	2,032,000

Reportable Diseases

	1925	1997
measles	310 per 100,000 population	1 per 100,000
whooping cough	131.2 per 100,000	2.5 per 100,000
AIDS	N/A	21.9 per 100,000
tuberculosis	N/A	7.4 per 100,000
gonorrhea	149.3 per 100,000	141.4 per 100,000

Prisons and Prisoners

State and federal correctional facilities

1990	1995
1,287	1500

Prison inmates

1926	2000
96,125	1,284,894

NATIONS OF THE WORLD[1]
A Profile and Synopsis of Major 2000 Developments

Andorra, S.W. Europe

Population: 66,824 **Capital:** Andorra la Vella
Area: 174 sq mi (450 km²)
Government: Marc Forne Molne, head of government

In June, the Organization for Economic Co-operation and Development (OECD) named Andorra and 34 other countries as "unfair tax havens" and called on them to reform their tax systems or face "defensive measures."

Angola, W. Africa

Population: 10,145,267 **Capital:** Luanda
Area: 481,351 sq mi (1 246 700 km²)
Government: José Eduardo dos Santos, president; Fernando Jose da Franca Dias van Dunem, prime minister (See also AFRICA.)

Antigua and Barbuda, Caribbean

Population: 66,422 **Capital:** St. John's
Area: 170 sq mi (440 km²)
Government: James B. Carlisle, governor-general; Lester Bird, prime minister. (See also CARIBBEAN.)

Bahamas, Caribbean

Population: 294,982 **Capital:** Nassau
Area: 5,382 sq mi (13 940 km²)
Government: Sir Orville Turnquest, governor-general; Hubert A. Ingraham, prime minister. (See also CARIBBEAN.)

Bahrain, W. Asia

Population: 634,137 **Capital:** Manama
Area: 239 sq mi (620 km²)
Government: Hamad bin Isa Al Khalifa, emir; Khalifa bin Salman Al Khalifa, prime minister

The Organization of Economic Co-operation and Development (OECD) listed Bahrain as one of 35 countries that were "unfair tax havens," calling on the country to reform its tax system or face "defensive measures." A Gulf Air passenger jet crashed just before landing at Bahrain on August 23, killing all 143 people aboard. In December, the government announced plans to restore an elected parliament and establish a constitutional monarchy.

Barbados, Caribbean

Population: 274,540 **Capital:** Bridgetown
Area: 166 sq mi (430 km²)
Government: Sir Clifford Husbands, governor-general; Owen Arthur, prime minister. (See also CARIBBEAN.)

Benin, W. Africa

Population: 6,395,919 **Capital:** Porto Novo
Area: 43,483 sq mi (112 620 km²)
Government: Mathieu Kerekou, president

Hubert Coutoucou Maga, the first president of Benin (then called Dahomey) after it won independence from France in 1960, died at age 83.

Bhutan, S. Asia

Population: 2,005,222 **Capital:** Thimphu
Area: 18,147 sq mi (47 000 km²)
Government: Jigme Singye Wangchuck, king

Botswana, S. Africa

Population: 1,576,470 **Capital:** Gaborone
Area: 231,803 sq mi (600 370 km²)
Government: Festus Mogae, president

Cyclone Eline caused extensive damage and flooding in Botswana in February, leaving thousands of people homeless. It was reported that Botswana has an HIV infection rate exceeding 25%, one the highest in the world. The Merck pharmaceutical company and the Bill and Melinda Gates Foundation promised Botswana $100 million in money and medicine during the next five years.

Brunei Darussalam, S.E. Asia

Population: 336,376 **Capital:** Bandar Seri Begawan
Area: 2,288 sq mi (5 770 km²)
Government: Hassanal Bolkiah, sultan and prime minister

The government announced that a lawsuit against Sultan Hassanal Bolkiah's brother, Prince Jefri Bolkiah, had been settled out of court. It was alleged that the prince had misused more than $40 billion in government funds while he was head of the Brunei Investment Agency. In mid-November, Brunei was host to the annual Asia-Pacific Economic Cooperation (APEC) forum.

Burkina Faso, W. Africa

Population: 11,946,065 **Capital:** Ouagadougou
Area: 105,869 sq mi (274 200 km²)
Government: Blaise Compaoré, president; Paramango Ernest Yonli, prime minister

The United States and Britain accused Burkina Faso of routing diamonds from Sierra Leone into the international market. The proceeds from the sale of the diamonds financed arms sales by the Revolutionary United Front, a Sierra Leonean rebel group.

Burundi, E. Africa

Population: 6,054,714 **Capital:** Bujumbura
Area: 10,745 sq mi (27 830 km²)
Government: Pierre Buyoya, president. (See also AFRICA.)

Cameroon, Cen. Africa

Population: 15,421,937 **Capital:** Yaoundé
Area: 183,568 sq mi (475 440 km²)
Government: Paul Biya, president; Peter Mafany Musonge, prime minister

In June the World Bank approved a $193 million loan for the construction of an oil pipeline to run from Chad through Cameroon to the Atlantic Ocean. (See also AFRICA.)

Cape Verde, W. Africa

Population: 401,343 **Capital:** Praia
Area: 1,557 sq mi (4 033 km²)
Government: Antonio Mascarenhas Monteiro, president; Carlos Wahnon Veiga, prime minister

Central African Republic, Cen. Africa

Population: 3,512,751 **Capital:** Bangui
Area: 240,534 sq mi (622 984 km²)
Government: Ange-Félix Patasse, president; Anicet-Georges Dologuele, prime minister

The health-care system of the Central African Republic was ranked among the worst in the world by the World Health Organization (WHO).

Chad, Cen. Africa

Population: 8,424,504 **Capital:** N'Djamena
Area: 495,753 sq mi (1 284 000 km²)
Government: Idriss Déby, president; Nagoum Yamassoum, prime minister

Hissene Habré, the ruler of Chad from 1982 to 1990, was indicted for human-rights violations by a court in Dakar, Senegal, where he had been living in exile. According to a Chadian commission, 40,000 opponents of Habré had been killed, and 200,000 tortured during his nine-year reign. In June the World Bank approved a $193 million loan for the construction of an oil pipeline from Chad through Cameroon to the Atlantic Ocean. (See also AFRICA.)

Comoros, E. Africa

Population: 578,400 **Capital:** Moroni
Area: 838 sq mi (2 170 km²)
Government: Assoumani Azali, president; Hamada Madi, prime minister

The three-island Indian Ocean nation of Comoros continued to deal with separatist demands by inhabitants of the island of

---

[1]*Independent nations not covered in pages 96–583.*

Anjouan. In January, according to Anjouan leader Col. Said Abeid, the Anjouanese voted to go ahead with plans for independence, but some observers called the vote fraudulent.

Congo, Republic of, Cen. Africa

Population: 2,830,961   **Capital:** Brazzaville
Area: 132,046 sq mi (342 000 km²)
Government: Denis Sassou-Nguesso, president

In December, a year after the government and rebel factions agreed to a cease-fire, President Omar Bongo of neighboring Gabon continued to mediate a peace agreement.

Djibouti, E. Africa

Population: 451,442   **Capital:** Djibouti
Area: 8,494 sq mi (22 000 km²)
Government: Ismail Omar Guelleh, president; Barkat Gourad Hamadou, prime minister

In February the Issa-dominated government and the rebel Afar Front for the Restoration of Unity and Democracy signed a peace agreement, ending a ten-year conflict between Djibouti's two ethnic groups. President Ismail Omar Guelleh hosted a meeting of Somalian clan representatives that resulted in the establishment of Somalia's first central government since 1991.

Dominica, Caribbean

Population: 71,540   **Capital:** Roseau
Area: 290 sq mi (750 km²)
Government: Crispin Anselm Sorhaindo, president; Pierre Charles, prime minister. (See also CARIBBEAN.)

Dominican Republic, Caribbean

Population: 8,442,533   **Capital:** Santo Domingo
Area: 18,815 sq mi (48 730 km²)
Government: Rafael Hipólito Dominguez Mejía, president. (See also CARIBBEAN.)

Equatorial Guinea, Cen. Africa

Population: 474,214   **Capital:** Malabo
Area: 10,830 sq mi (28 050 km²)
Government: Teodoro Obiang Nguema Mbasogo, president; Angel Serafin Seriche Dougan, prime minister

Eritrea, E. Africa

Population: 4,135,933   **Capital:** Asmara
Area: 46,841 sq mi (121 320 km²)
Government: Isaias Afworki, president

The two-year-old border war between Eritrea and Ethiopia, which claimed thousands of lives and displaced millions of people, ended in June with the signing of a preliminary cease-fire agreement. A comprehensive peace agreement was reached in December. (See also ETHIOPIA—Ethiopia-Eritrea War.)

Gabon, Cen. Africa

Population: 1,208,436   **Capital:** Libreville
Area: 103,346 sq mi (267 667 km²)
Government: El Hadj Omar Bongo, president; Jean-François Ntoutoume-Emane, prime minister

Gambia, W. Africa

Population: 1,367,124   **Capital:** Banjul
Area: 4,363 sq mi (11 300 km²)
Government: Yahya Jammeh, head of state

Ghana, W. Africa

Population: 19,533,560   **Capital:** Accra
Area: 4,363 sq mi (238 540 km²)
Government: John Agyekum Kufuor, president

In the December presidential election, John Agyekum Kufuor of the opposition New Patriotic Party (NPP) defeated John Atta Mills of the ruling National Democratic Congress (NDC). Mills had been vice-president under longtime President Jerry Rawlings, who was constitutionally barred from seeking a third term.

Grenada, Caribbean

Population: 89,018   **Capital:** St. George's
Area: 131 sq mi (340 km²)

Government: Daniel Williams, governor-general; Keith Mitchell, prime minister. (See also CARIBBEAN.)

Guinea, W. Africa

Population: 7,466,200   **Capital:** Conakry
Area: 94,925 sq mi (245 857 km²)
Government: Lansana Conté, president; Lamine Sidime, prime minister

In September, President Lansana Conté accused refugees from neighboring Sierra Leone and Liberia of aiding Guinean rebel groups. Guinean civilians and the Guinean government were accused of abusing the refugees. Prime Minister Lamine Sidime visited China in September. (See also AFRICA.)

Guinea-Bissau, W. Africa

Population: 1,285,715   **Capital:** Bissau
Area: 13,946 sq mi (36 120 km²)
Government: Koumba Yalla, president; Caetana N'Tchama, prime minister

Koumba Yalla, head of the Social Renewal Party, was sworn in as Guinea-Bissau's new president on February 17 after defeating acting President Malam Bacai Sanha in the January 16 presidential election. (See also AFRICA.)

Guyana, N.E. South America

Population: 697,286   **Capital:** Georgetown
Area: 83,000 sq mi (214 970 km²)
Government: Bharrat Jagdeo, president; Samuel Hinds, prime minister. (See also CARIBBEAN.)

Haiti, Caribbean

Population: 6,867,995   **Capital:** Port-au-Prince
Area: 10,714 sq mi (27 750 km²)
Government: Jean-Bertrand Aristide, president. (See also CARIBBEAN.)

Ivory Coast (Côte d'Ivoire), W. Africa

Population: 15,980,950   **Capital:** Yamoussoukro
Area: 124,502 sq mi (322 460 km²)
Government: Laurent Gbagbo, president

On December 10, in elections marred by ethnic conflicts, President Laurent Gbagbo's ruling Ivorian Popular Front won 91 of the 225 contested seats in parliament. The former ruling party, the Democratic Party of Ivory Coast, won 70 seats, and independent candidates won 15 seats. Many parliamentary seats in northern, mostly Muslim, Ivory Coast went unfilled because backers of Muslim candidate Alassane Ouattara, who was prevented from running, boycotted the elections. (See also AFRICA.)

Jamaica, Caribbean

Population: 2,652,689   **Capital:** Kingston
Area: 4,243 sq mi (10 990 km²)
Government: Sir Howard Cooke, governor-general; P.J. Patterson, prime minister. (See also CARIBBEAN.)

Kazakhstan, Cen. Asia

Population: 16,733,227   **Capital:** Astana (Akmola)
Area: 1,049,155 sq mi (2 717 300 km²)
Government: Nursultan A. Nazarbayev, president; Kasymzhomart Tokayev, prime minister

A consortium of oil companies, including U.S.-based Exxon Mobil and Britain's BP Amoco, announced in July that major oil and gas deposits had been discovered in the Caspian Sea. The consortium—Offshore Kazakhstan International Operating Company—estimated the field at 50 billion barrels of oil, one of the largest in the world.

Kiribati, Oceania

Population: 91,985   **Capital:** Tarawa
Area: 277 sq mi (717 km²)
Government: Teburoro Tito, president

Kuwait, W. Asia

Population: 1,973,572   **Capital:** Kuwait
Area: 6,800 sq mi (17 820 km²)
Government: Jabir al-Ahmad al-Sabah, emir; Saad al-Abdallah al-Sabah, prime minister

The UN Security Council approved a $15.9 billion compensation claim by the Kuwaiti Petroleum Corporation against Iraq for destruction of Kuwaiti oil fields during the Gulf war.

Kyrgyzstan, Cen. Asia

Population: 4,685,230   **Capital:** Bishkek (Frunze)
Area: 76,641 sq mi (198 500 km²)
Government: Askar Akayev, president; Kurmanbek Bakiyev, prime minister

Kyrgyzstan held parliamentary elections in February and a presidential election in October; both were criticized as flawed and undemocratic by the Organization for Security and Cooperation in Europe and other election monitors. In the presidential election, Askar Akayev won a third term with 75% of the vote.

Lesotho, S. Africa

Population: 2,143,141   **Capital:** Maseru
Area: 11,720 sq mi (30 355 km²)
Government: Letsie III, king; Pakalitha Mosisili, prime minister

Liberia, W. Africa

Population: 3,164,156   **Capital:** Monrovia
Area: 43,000 sq mi (111 370 km²)
Government: Charles Taylor, president

President Charles Taylor continued to support the rebels of the Revolutionary United Front (RUF) in neighboring Sierra Leone. Taylor was able to obtain the release of many United Nations peacekeepers who had been taken hostage by the rebels, but he also supplied the rebels with arms and other war matériel. In return, Taylor made a fortune from the diamonds smuggled out of Sierra Leone by the rebels in order to pay for military equipment. Taylor's actions led the European Union (EU) to put off a $43 million aid package to Liberia.

Liechtenstein, Cen. Europe

Population: 32,207   **Capital:** Vaduz
Area: 62 sq mi (160 km²)
Government: Hans Adam II, prince; Mario Frick, prime minister

In June, the Organization for Economic Co-operation and Development (OECD) named Liechtenstein and 34 other countries as "unfair tax havens" and called on them to reform their tax systems or face "defensive measures." In addition, a task force established by the Group of 7 industrialized nations named Liechtenstein as a "potential base" for money laundering by drug dealers and other criminals. Liechtenstein then took several steps to fight money laundering.

Luxembourg, W. Europe

Population: 437,389   **Capital:** Luxembourg
Area: 998 sq mi (2 586 km²)
Government: Henri, grand duke; Jean-Claude Juncker, prime minister

Crown Prince Henri, 45, became Luxembourg's new grand duke on October 7, following the abdication of his father, Grand Duke Jean. Jean, 79, had been grand duke for 35 years.

Madagascar, E. Africa

Population: 15,506,472   **Capital:** Antananarivo
Area: 226,656 sq mi (587 040 km²)
Government: Didier Ratsiraka, president; Tantely Andrianarivo, premier

In February and March, Cyclones Eline and Gloria caused extensive flooding and damage in Madagascar.

Malawi, E. Africa

Population: 10,385,849   **Capital:** Lilongwe
Area: 45,745 sq mi (118 480 km²)
Government: Bakili Muluzi, president

In November, amid allegations of corruption and fraud, President Bakili Muluzi fired his entire cabinet. He named a new 25-member cabinet on November 5. (See also AFRICA.)

Maldives, S. Asia

Population: 301,475   **Capital:** Malé
Area: 116 sq mi (300 km²)
Government: Maumoon Abdul Gayoom, president

Mali, W. Africa

Population: 10,685,948   **Capital:** Bamako
Area: 478,764 sq mi (1 240 000 km²)
Government: Alpha Oumar Konare, president; Mande Sidibe, prime minister

Prime Minister Ibrahim Boubacar Keita resigned in February and was replaced by Mande Sidibe, an economist.

Malta, S. Europe

Population: 391,670   **Capital:** Valletta
Area: 122 sq mi (316 km²)
Government: Guido De Marco, president; Edward Fenech Adami, prime minister

Marshall Islands, Pacific Ocean

Population: 68,126   **Capital:** Majuro
Area: 70 sq mi (181 km²)
Government: Kessai Note, president

In June a task force established by the Group of 7 industrialized nations named the Marshall Islands as a "potential base" for money laundering by drug dealers and other criminals.

Mauritania, W. Africa

Population: 2,667,859   **Capital:** Nouakchott
Area: 397,954 sq mi (1 030 700 km²)
Government: Maaouya Ould Sid Ahmed Taya, president; El Avia Ould Mohamed, prime minister

As the year ended, Prime Minister El Avia Ould Mohamed announced that Mauritania had experienced an economic growth rate of 5% in 2000.

Mauritius, E. Africa

Population: 1,179,368   **Capital:** Port Louis
Area: 718 sq mi (1 860 km²)
Government: Sir Cassam Uteem, president; Anerood Jugnauth, prime minister

In October the United Nations General Assembly elected Mauritius to a nonpermanent seat on the 15-member Security Council. During the year, Mauritius restated its claim to the British-ruled Chagos Islands, where the United States maintains a military base on Diego Garcia, the largest island in the Indian Ocean archipelago. (See also AFRICA.)

Micronesia, Federated States of, Pacific Ocean

Population: 133,144   **Capital:** Palikir
Area: 271 sq mi (702 km²)
Government: Leo A. Falcam, president

Moldova, Europe

Population: 4,430,654   **Capital:** Chisinau (Kishinev)
Area: 13,067 sq mi (33 843 km²)
Government: Petru Lucinschi, president; Dumitru Braghis, prime minister

It was announced in December that President Petru Lucinschi would probably dissolve parliament in January 2001 and call for a presidential election to determine his successor.

Monaco, S. Europe

Population: 31,693   **Capital:** Monaco
Area: 0.7 sq mi (1.9 km²)
Government: Prince Rainier III, Chief of State; Patrick Leclercq, minister of state

Monaco's new minister of state, Patrick Leclercq, addressed the United Nations on September 12.

Mongolia, N. Asia

Population: 2,650,952   **Capital:** Ulan Bator
Area: 604,247 sq mi (1 565 000 km²)
Government: Natsagiyn Bagabandi, president; Nambariin Enkhbayar, prime minister

In July elections, the Mongolian People's Revolutionary Party (MPRP), formerly the Communist Party, regained power by winning 72 of the 76 seats in parliament. MPRP leader Nambariin Enkhbayar was named prime minister.

Mozambique, E. Africa

Population: 19,104,696 **Capital:** Maputo
Area: 309,496 sq mi (801 590 km²)
Government: Joaquim Chissano, president; Pascoal Mocumbi, prime minister

At the Summer Olympic Games in Australia, Maria Mutola became the first Mozambican to win an Olympic gold medal when she placed first in the women's 800-m race. (See also AFRICA.)

Namibia, W. Africa

Population: 1,771,327 **Capital:** Windhoek
Area: 318,696 sq mi (825 418 km²)
Government: Sam Nujoma, president; Hage Geingob, prime minister.

Namibian troops continued to be involved in the civil war in neighboring Democratic Republic of the Congo. The Namibians supported Congo President Laurent Kabila in his battle against Ugandan- and Rwandan-backed rebel groups. (See also AFRICA.)

Nauru, Oceania

Population: 11,845 **Capital:** no official capital
Area: 8 sq mi (21 km²)
Government: Bernard Dowiyogo, president

In June, a task force established by the Group of 7 industrialized nations named Nauru as a "potential base" for money laundering by drug dealers and other criminals.

Nepal, S. Asia

Population: 24,702,119 **Capital:** Katmandu
Area: 54,363 sq mi (140 800 km²)
Government: Birendra Bir Bikram Shah Deva, king; Girija Prasad Koirala, prime minister

Prime Minister Krishna Prasad Bhattarai, who had been criticized for failing to end a Maoist guerrilla rebellion, resigned under pressure in March and was replaced by Girija Prasad Koirala, president of the Nepali Congress Party. In December, however, Koirala himself faced the same criticism, and his ability to remain in office was in doubt at year's end. He survived a no-confidence motion on December 28. Nepal completed negotiations to join the Poverty Reduction Growth Framework (PRGF), sponsored by the International Monetary Fund (IMF).

Niger, W. Africa

Population: 10,075,511 **Capital:** Niamey
Area: 489,189 sq mi (1 267 000 km²)
Government: Mamadou Tandja, president; Hama Amadou, prime minister

Mamadou Tandja, who was elected president in late 1999, traveled to France in January. France subsequently gave Niger some $10 billion in budgetary assistance. The government announced in November that 4 million people faced famine because of a poor harvest. (See also AFRICA.)

Oman, W. Asia

Population: 2,533,389 **Capital:** Muscat
Area: 82,031 sq mi (212 460 km²)
Government: Qaboos bin Said Al Said, sultan and prime minister

Palau, N. Pacific Ocean

Population: 18,766 **Capital:** Koror
Area: 177 sq mi (458 km²)
Government: Kuniwo Nakamura, president

Papua New Guinea, Oceania

Population: 4,926,984 **Capital:** Port Moresby
Area: 178,259 sq mi (462 840 km²)
Government: Sir Silas Atopare, governor-general; Sir Mekere Morauta, prime minister

The government announced in February that it would privatize the nation's airlines and other state-owned enterprises. In April, the government announced that it had agreed to let the people of Bougainville—an island where there is strong sentiment for secession—hold a referendum on independence. Australia agreed to lend Papua New Guinea $55.9 million as a sign of support for the reforms initiated by Sir Mekere Morauta, who had become prime minister in July 1999.

Qatar, W. Asia

Population: 744,483 **Capital:** Doha
Area: 4,416 sq mi (11 437 km²)
Government: Hamad bin Khalifa Al Thani, emir; Abdallah bin Khalifa Al Thani, prime minister

Rwanda, E. Africa

Population: 7,229,129 **Capital:** Kigali
Area: 10,169 sq mi (26 338 km²)
Government: Paul Kagame, president; Bernard Makuza, prime minister

Following the March resignation of President Pasteur Bizimungu, Maj. Gen. Paul Kagame was elected president by government ministers and legislators and sworn in on April 22. President Kagame continued Rwanda's support of rebels in the neighboring Democratic Republic of the Congo in their effort to oust President Laurent Kabila. In December, after Rwandan troops staged large-scale offensives against Kabila's forces, the United Nations Security Council called on Rwanda to withdraw its forces from the country. Bernard Makuza, a 39-year-old diplomat, was named prime minister in March. (See also AFRICA.)

Saint Kitts and Nevis, Caribbean

Population: 38,819 **Capital:** Basseterre
Area: 101 sq mi (261 km²)
Government: Cuthbert M. Sebastian, governor-general; Denzil Douglas, prime minister. (See also CARIBBEAN.)

Saint Lucia, Caribbean

Population: 156,260 **Capital:** Castries
Area: 239 sq mi (620 km²)
Government: Perlette Louisy, governor-general; Kenny Anthony, prime minister. (See also CARIBBEAN.)

Saint Vincent and the Grenadines, Caribbean

Population: 115,461 **Capital:** Kingstown
Area: 150 sq mi (389 km²)
Government: David Jack, governor-general; Arnhim Eustace, prime minister. (See also CARIBBEAN.)

Samoa, Oceania

Population: 179,466 **Capital:** Apia
Area: 1,104 sq mi (2 860 km²)
Government: Malietoa Tanumafili II, head of state; Sailele Malielegaoi Tuilaepa, prime minister

San Marino, S. Europe

Population: 26,937 **Capital:** San Marino
Area: 23 sq mi (60 km²)
Government: Loris Francini and Alberto Cecchetti, captains-regent

São Tomé and Príncipe, W. Africa

Population: 159,883 **Capital:** São Tomé
Area: 386 sq mi (1 001 km²)
Government: Miguel Trovoada, president; Guilherme Posser da Costa, prime minister

Senegal, W. Africa

Population: 9,987,494 **Capital:** Dakar
Area: 75,749 sq mi (196 190 km²)
Government: Abdoulaye Wade, president; Niasse Moustapha, prime minister

In March, Abdoulaye Wade was elected president with 60% of the vote. The leader of the opposition Senegalese Democratic Party, Wade defeated incumbent President Abdou Diouf, who had been president since 1980 and whose Socialist Party had been in power since Senegal gained its independence from France in 1960. The new president named Niasse Moustapha as prime minister. Late in the year, the government and the southern separatist Movement of the Democratic Forces of Casamance held talks to end the conflict.

Seychelles, E. Africa

Population: 79,326 **Capital:** Victoria
Area: 176 sq mi (455 km²)
Government: France Albert René, president

Sierra Leone, W. Africa

Population: 5,232,624 **Capital:** Freetown
Area: 27,699 sq mi (71 740 km²)
Government: Ahmad Tejan Kabbah, president. (See also AFRICA.)

Solomon Islands, Oceania

Population: 466,194 **Capital:** Honiara
Area: 10,985 sq mi (28 450 km²)
Government: Sir John Ini Lapli, governor-general; Mannasseh Sogavare, prime minister

Tensions on Guadalcanal between Guadalcanalese and settlers from the nearby island of Malaita continued. In mid-June, a paramilitary group from Malaita invaded Guadalcanal, kidnapped Prime Minister Bartholomew Ulufa'alu, and forced him to resign. On June 30, an emergency session of parliament elected Mannasseh Sogavare as the new prime minister. Solomon Mamaloni, prime minister of the Solomon Islands from 1983 to 1997, died January 13 at the age of 56.

Somalia, E. Africa

Population: 7,253,137 **Capital:** Mogadishu
Area: 246,199 sq mi (637 657 km²)
Government: Salad Hassan Abdikassim, acting president; Khalifa Galaydh Ali, premier. (See also AFRICA.)

Suriname, S. America

Population: 431,303 **Capital:** Paramaribo
Area: 63,039 sq mi (163 270 km²)
Government: Runaldo Ronald Venetiaan, president

Suriname's border dispute with Guyana continued. (See also CARIBBEAN (GUYANA).)

Swaziland, S. Africa

Population: 1,083,289 **Capital:** Mbabane
Area: 6,703 sq mi (17 363 km²)
Government: Mswati III, king; Sibusiso Barnabas Dlamini, prime minister

The Joint United Nations Program on HIV/AIDS (UNAIDS) reported in June that Swaziland had an HIV infection rate of 25%, one of the highest in the world. Prodemocracy groups continue to stage regular protests.

Togo, W. Africa

Population: 5,018,502 **Capital:** Lomé
Area: 21,925 sq mi (56 785 km²)
Government: Gnassingbé Eyadéma, president; Agbeyome Kodjo, prime minister

President Gnassingbé Eyadéma appointed Agbeyome Kodjo prime minister in late August.

Tonga, Oceania

Population: 102,321 **Capital:** Nuku'alofa
Area: 289 sq mi (748 km²)
Government: Taufa'ahau Tupou IV, king; Prince Lavaka ata Ulukalala, prime minister

Trinidad and Tobago, Caribbean

Population: 1,175,523 **Capital:** Port-of-Spain
Area: 1,980 sq mi (5 128 km²)
Government: Arthur Robinson, president; Basdeo Panday, prime minister

In December elections, Prime Minister Basdeo Panday's ruling United National Congress (UNC) won 19 of the 36 seats in the House of Representatives. The opposition People's National Movement (PNM) won 16 seats, and the National Alliance for Reconstruction (NAR) won one seat. (See also CARIBBEAN.)

Turkmenistan, Cen. Asia

Population: 4,518,268 **Capital:** Ashgabat
Area: 188,457 sq mi (488 100 km²)
Government: Saparmurat Niyazov, president

Turkmenistan became the 59th country to become a member of the Asian Development Bank (ADA). Russia's President Vladimir Putin and China's President Jiang Zemin both visited Turkmenistan in 2000.

Tuvalu, Oceania

Population: 10,838 **Capital:** Funafuti
Area: 10 sq mi (26 km²)
Government: Sir Tomasi Puapua, governor-general; Ionatana Ionatana, prime minister

Tuvalu became the 189th member of the United Nations on September 5, 2000, and held the further distinction of being the organization's smallest member state.

United Arab Emirates, W. Asia

Population: 2,369,153 **Capital:** Abu Dhabi
Area: 32,000 sq mi (82 880 km²)
Government: Zayid bin Sultan Al Nuhayyan, president; Maktum bin Rashid Al Maktum, prime minister

Uzbekistan, Cen. Asia

Population: 24,755,519 **Capital:** Tashkent
Area: 172,742 sq mi (447 400 km²)
Government: Islam Karimov, president; Otkir Sultonov, prime minister

Islam Karimov was inaugurated for a second term as president on January 22 after winning reelection overwhelmingly. U.S. Secretary of State Madeleine Albright visited Uzbekistan in April. The secretary declared that she and President Karimov had "had a frank discussion of the importance of [Uzbekistan] meeting international norms on a variety of human-rights issues." In December, Kenneth Roth, executive director of Human Rights Watch, characterized the situation regarding torture in Uzbekistan as "very serious."

Vanuatu, Oceania

Population: 189,618 **Capital:** Port-Vila
Area: 5,699 sq mi (14 760 km²)
Government: John Bani, president; Barak Sope, prime minister

Residents of Vanuatu were shocked by the murder of an Australian businessman in the capital of Port-Vila in June. Violent crime is relatively rare in this Pacific nation.

Vatican City, S. Europe

Population: 880 **Capital:** Vatican City
Area: 0.17 sq mi (0.438 km²)
Government: John Paul II, pope

In June, Italy's President Carlo Ciamp pardoned Mehmet Ali Agca, who had been serving prison time after being convicted of shooting Pope John Paul II in an assassination attempt in 1981. Agca then was extradited to his native Turkey, where he began serving a ten-year sentence for the murder of a journalist in 1979.

Yemen, W. Asia

Population: 17,479,206 **Capital:** Sanaa
Area: 203,850 sq mi (527 970 km²)
Government: Ali Abdullah Saleh, president; Abdul Ali al-Karim al-Iryani, prime minister

Yemen was the scene of kidnappings and terrorist actions in 2000. In March the Polish ambassador was kidnapped but later released. In June a Norwegian diplomat was kidnapped and killed. And in October a terrorist attack against the U.S. Navy destroyer Cole in the port of Aden killed 17 sailors and wounded 37 others.

Zambia, E. Africa

Population: 9,582,418 **Capital:** Lusaka
Area: 290,584 sq mi (752 614 km²)
Government: Frederick Chiluba, president

Zambia was involved in the civil wars of three other African nations. More than 200,000 Angolan refugees found refuge in Zambia, and Angola accused Zambia of harboring rebels of the União Nacional para a Independencia Total de Angola (UNITA). Peace talks aimed at ending the civil war in the Democratic Republic of the Congo were held in Zambia's capital, Lusaka, in August. And Zambian troops took part in the UN peacekeeping force in Sierra Leone. In May, 400 of them were captured by the rebels of the Revolutionary Front (RUF); four were killed and the rest released. Former President Kenneth Kaunda ended his political career, and his citizenship, which had been taken away from him in 1999, was restored. (See also AFRICA.)

The 107th CONGRESS
First Session

SENATE MEMBERSHIP

(As of January 2001: 50 Republicans, 50 Democrats.) Letters after names refer to party affiliation—D for Democrat, R for Republican, I for Independent. Single asterisk (*) denotes term expiring in January 2003; double asterisk (**), term expiring in January 2005; triple asterisk (***), term expiring in January 2007; quadruple asterisk (****), appointed for two years.

Alabama
R. Shelby, R**
J. Sessions, R*

Alaska
T. Stevens, R*
F. Murkowski, R**

Arizona
J. McCain, R**
J. Kyl, R***

Arkansas
T. Hutchinson, R*
B. Lincoln, D**

California
D. Feinstein, D***
B. Boxer, D**

Colorado
B. N. Campbell, R**
W. Allard, R*

Connecticut
C. Dodd, D**
J. Lieberman, D***

Delaware
T. Carper, D***
J. Biden, Jr., D*

Florida
B. Graham, D**
B. Nelson, D***

Georgia
M. Cleland, D*
Z. Miller D**

Hawaii
D. Inouye, D**
D. Akaka, D***

Idaho
L. Craig, R*
M. Crapo, R**

Illinois
R. Durbin, D*
P. Fitzgerald, R**

Indiana
R. Lugar, R***
E. Bayh, D**

Iowa
C. Grassley, R**
T. Harkin, D*

Kansas
P. Roberts, R*
S. Brownback, R**

Kentucky
M. McConnell, R*
J. Bunning, R**

Louisiana
J. Breaux, D**
M. Landrieu, D*

Maine
O. J. Snowe, R***
S. Collins, R*

Maryland
P. Sarbanes, D***
B. Mikulski, D**

Massachusetts
E. Kennedy, D***
J. Kerry, D*

Michigan
C. Levin, D*
D. Stabenow, D***

Minnesota
P. Wellstone, D*
M. Dayton, D***

Mississippi
T. Cochran, R*
T. Lott, R***

Missouri
C. Bond, R**
J. Carnahan, D****

Montana
M. Baucus, D*
C. Burns, R***

Nebraska
B. Nelson, D***
C. Hagel, R*

Nevada
H. Reid, D**
J. Ensign, R***

New Hampshire
B. Smith, R*
J. Gregg, R**

New Jersey
J. Corzine, D***
R. Torricelli, D*

New Mexico
P. Domenici, R*
J. Bingaman, D***

New York
H. Clinton, D***
C. Schumer, D**

North Carolina
J. Helms, R*
J. Edwards, D**

North Dakota
K. Conrad, D**
B. Dorgan, D**

Ohio
M. DeWine, R***
G. Voinovich, R**

Oklahoma
D. Nickles, R**
J. M. Inhofe, R*

Oregon
R. Wyden, D**
G. Smith, R*

Pennsylvania
A. Specter, R**
R. Santorum, R***

Rhode Island
L. Chafee, R***
J. Reed, D*

South Carolina
S. Thurmond, R*
E. Hollings, D**

South Dakota
T. Daschle, D**
T. Johnson, D*

Tennessee
W. Frist, R***
F. Thompson, R*

Texas
P. Gramm, R*
K. B. Hutchison, R***

Utah
O. Hatch, R***
R. Bennett, R**

Vermont
P. J. Leahy, D**
J. M. Jeffords, R***

Virginia
J. Warner, R*
G. Allen, R***

Washington
M. Cantwell, D***
P. Murray, D**

West Virginia
R. Byrd, D***
J. Rockefeller IV, D*

Wisconsin
H. Kohl, D***
R. Feingold, D**

Wyoming
C. Thomas, R***
M. Enzi, R*

HOUSE MEMBERSHIP

(As of January 2001: 221 Republicans, 211 Democrats, 2 Independents, 1 vacancy.) "At-L" in place of congressional district number means "representative at large." *Indicates elected in 2000; all others were reelected.

Alabama
1. S. Callahan, R
2. T. Everett, R
3. B. Riley, R
4. R. B. Aderholt, R
5. R. E. Cramer, Jr., D
6. S. Bachus, R
7. E. F. Hilliard, D

Alaska
At-L. D. Young, R

Arizona
1. J. Flake, R*
2. E. Pastor, D
3. B. Stump, R
4. J. B. Shadegg, R
5. J. Kolbe, R
6. J. D. Hayworth, R

Arkansas
1. M. Berry, D
2. V. Snyder, D
3. A. Hutchinson, R
4. M. Ross, D*

California
1. M. Thompson, D
2. W. Herger, R
3. D. Ose, R
4. J. T. Doolittle, R
5. R. T. Matsui, D
6. L. C. Woolsey, D
7. G. Miller, D
8. N. Pelosi, D
9. B. Lee, D
10. E. O. Tauscher, D
11. R. W. Pombo, R
12. T. Lantos, D
13. F. P. Stark, D
14. A. G. Eshoo, D
15. M. M. Honda, D*
16. Z. Lofgren, D
17. S. Farr, D
18. G. A. Condit, D
19. G. Radanovich, R
20. C. M. Dooley, D
21. W. M. Thomas, R
22. L. Capps, D
23. E. Gallegly, R
24. B. Sherman, D
25. H. P. McKeon, R
26. H. L. Berman, D
27. A. B. Schiff, D*
28. D. Dreier, R
29. H. A. Waxman, D
30. X. Becerra, D
31. H. L. Solis, D*
32. Vacant
33. L. Roybal-Allard, D
34. G. F. Napolitano, D
35. M. Waters, D
36. J. Harman, D
37. J. Millender-McDonald, D
38. S. Horn, R
39. E. R. Royce, R
40. J. Lewis, R
41. G. G. Miller, R
42. J. Baca, D
43. K. Calvert, R
44. M. Bono, R
45. D. Rohrabacher, R
46. L. Sanchez, D
47. C. Cox, R
48. D. E. Issa, R*
49. S. A. Davis, D*
50. B. Filner, D
51. R. Cunningham, R
52. D. Hunter, R

Colorado
1. D. DeGette, D
2. M. Udall, D
3. S. McInnis, R
4. B. Schaffer, R
5. J. Hefley, R
6. T. G. Tancredo, R

Connecticut
1. J. B. Larson, D
2. R. Simmons, R*
3. R. L. DeLauro, D
4. C. Shays, R
5. J. H. Maloney, D
6. N. L. Johnson, R

Delaware
At-L. M. N. Castle, R

Florida
1. J. Scarborough, R
2. A. Boyd, D
3. C. Brown, D
4. A. Crenshaw, R*
5. K. L. Thurman, D
6. C. Stearns, R
7. J. L. Mica, R
8. R. Keller, R*
9. M. Bilirakis, R
10. C. W. B. Young, R
11. J. Davis, D
12. A. H. Putnam, R*
13. D. Miller, R
14. P. J. Goss, R

15. D. Weldon, R
16. M. Foley, R
17. C. P. Meek, D
18. I. Ros-Lehtinen, R
19. R. Wexler, D
20. P. Deutsch, D
21. L. Diaz-Balart, R
22. E. C. Shaw, Jr., R*
23. A. L. Hastings, D

Georgia
1. J. Kingston, R
2. S. D. Bishop, Jr., D
3. M. Collins, R
4. C. A. McKinney, D
5. J. Lewis, D
6. J. Isakson, R
7. B. Barr, R
8. S. Chambliss, R
9. N. Deal, R
10. C. Norwood, R
11. J. Linder, R

Hawaii
1. N. Abercrombie, D
2. P. Mink, D

Idaho
1. C.L. Otter, R*
2. M. K. Simpson, R

Illinois
1. B. L. Rush, D
2. J. L. Jackson, Jr., D
3. W. O. Lipinski, D
4. L. V. Gutierrez, D
5. R. R. Blagojevich, D
6. H. J. Hyde, R

7. D. K. Davis, D
8. P. M. Crane, R
9. J. D. Schakowsky, D
10. M. S. Kirk, R*
11. J. Weller, R
12. J. F. Costello, D
13. J. Biggert, R
14. J. D. Hastert, R
15. T. V. Johnson, R*
16. D. A. Manzullo, R
17. L. Evans, D
18. R. LaHood, R
19. D. D. Phelps, D
20. J. Shimkus, R

Indiana
1. P. J. Visclosky, D
2. M. Pence, R*
3. T. Roemer, D
4. M. E. Souder, R
5. S. Buyer, R
6. D. Burton, R
7. B. D. Kerns, R*
8. J. N. Hostettler, R
9. B. P. Hill, D
10. J. Carson, D

Iowa
1. J. A. Leach, R
2. J. Nussle, R
3. L. L. Boswell, D
4. G. Ganske, R
5. T. Latham, R

Kansas
1. J. Moran, R
2. J. Ryun, R
3. D. Moore, D
4. T. Tiahrt, R

Kentucky
1. E. Whitfield, R
2. R. Lewis, R
3. A. M. Northup, R
4. K. Lucas, D
5. H. Rogers, R
6. E. Fletcher, R

Louisiana
1. D. Vitter, R
2. W. J. Jefferson, D
3. W. J. Tauzin, R
4. J. McCrery, R
5. J. Cooksey, R
6. R. H. Baker, R
7. C. John, D

Maine
1. T. H. Allen, D
2. J. E. Baldacci, D

Maryland
1. W. T. Gilchrest, R
2. R. L. Ehrlich, Jr., R
3. B. L. Cardin, D
4. A. R. Wynn, D
5. S. H. Hoyer, D
6. R. G. Bartlett, R
7. E. E. Cummings, D
8. C. A. Morella, R

Massachusetts
1. J. W. Olver, D
2. R. E. Neal, D
3. J. P. McGovern, D
4. B. Frank, D
5. M. T. Meehan, D
6. J. F. Tierney, D
7. E. J. Markey, D
8. M. E. Capuano, D
9. J. J. Moakley, D
10. W. D. Delahunt, D

Michigan
1. B. Stupak, D
2. P. Hoekstra, R
3. V. J. Ehlers, R
4. D. Camp, R
5. J. A. Barcia, D
6. F. Upton, R
7. N. Smith, R
8. M. Rogers, R*
9. D. E. Kildee, D
10. D. E. Bonior, D
11. J. Knollenberg, R
12. S. M. Levin, D
13. L. N. Rivers, D
14. J. Conyers, D
15. C. C. Kilpatrick, D
16. J. D. Dingell, D

Minnesota
1. G. Gutknecht, R
2. M. R. Kennedy, R*
3. J. Ramstad, R
4. B. McCollum, D*
5. M. O. Sabo, D
6. W. P. Luther, R
7. C. C. Peterson, D
8. J. L. Oberstar, D

Mississippi
1. R. F. Wicker, R
2. B. G. Thompson, D
3. C. W. Pickering, R
4. R. Shows, D
5. G. Taylor, D

Missouri
1. Wm. L. Clay, D*
2. W.T. Akin, R*
3. R. A. Gephardt, D
4. I. Skelton, D
5. K. McCarthy, D
6. S. Graves, R*
7. R. Blunt, R
8. J. A. Emerson, R
9. K. C. Hulshof, R

Montana
At-L. D. R. Rehberg, R*

Nebraska
1. D. Bereuter, R
2. L. Terry, R
3. T. Osborne, R*

Nevada
1. S. Berkley, D
2. J. Gibbons, R

New Hampshire
1. J. E. Sununu, R
2. C. F. Bass, R

New Jersey
1. R. E. Andrews, D
2. F. A. LoBiondo, R
3. J. Saxton, R
4. C. H. Smith, R
5. M. Roukema, R
6. F. Pallone, Jr., D
7. M. Ferguson, R*
8. W. Pascrell, Jr., D
9. S. Rothman, D
10. D. M. Payne, D
11. R. P. Frelinghuysen, R
12. R. D. Holt, D*
13. R. Menendez, D

New Mexico
1. H. Wilson, R
2. J. Skeen, R
3. T. Udall, D

New York
1. F. J. Grucci, Jr., R*
2. S. Israel, D*
3. P. T. King, R
4. C. McCarthy, D
5. G. L. Ackerman, D
6. G. W. Meeks, D
7. J. Crowley, D
8. J. Nadler, D
9. A. D. Weiner, D
10. E. Towns, D
11. M. R. Owens, D
12. N. M. Velázquez, D
13. V. Fossella, R
14. C. B. Maloney, D
15. C. B. Rangel, D
16. J. E. Serrano, D
17. E. L. Engel, D
18. N. M. Lowey, D
19. S. W. Kelly, R
20. B. A. Gilman, R
21. M. R. McNulty, D
22. J. E. Sweeney, R
23. S. L. Boehlert, R
24. J. M. McHugh, R
25. J. T. Walsh, R
26. M. D. Hinchey, D
27. T. M. Reynolds, R
28. L. M. Slaughter, D
29. J. J. LaFalce, D
30. J. Quinn, R
31. A. Houghton, R

North Carolina
1. E. M. Clayton, D
2. B. Etheridge, D

3. W. B. Jones, R
4. D. E. Price, D
5. R. Burr, R
6. H. Coble, R
7. M. McIntyre, D
8. R. Hayes, R
9. S. W. Myrick, R
10. C. Ballenger, R
11. C. H. Taylor, R
12. M. L. Watt, D

North Dakota
At-L. E. R. Pomeroy, D

Ohio
1. S. Chabot, R
2. R. Portman, R
3. T. P. Hall, D
4. M. G. Oxley, R
5. P. E. Gillmor, R
6. T. Strickland, D
7. D. L. Hobson, R
8. J. A. Boehner, R
9. M. Kaptur, D
10. D. J. Kucinich, D
11. S. T. Jones, D
12. P. J. Tiberi, R*
13. S. Brown, D
14. T. Sawyer, D
15. D. Pryce, R
16. R. Regula, R
17. J. A. Traficant, Jr., D
18. R. W. Ney, R
19. S. C. LaTourette, R

Oklahoma
1. S. Largent, R
2. B. Carson, D*
3. W. Watkins, R
4. J. C. Watts, Jr., R
5. E. J. Istook, Jr., R
6. F. D. Lucas, R

Oregon
1. D. Wu, D
2. G. Walden, R
3. E. Blumenauer, D
4. P. A. DeFazio, D
5. D. Hooley, D

Pennsylvania
1. R. Brady, D
2. C. Fattah, D
3. R. A. Borski, D
4. M. A. Hart, R*
5. J. E. Peterson, R
6. T. Holden, D
7. C. Weldon, R
8. J. C. Greenwood, R
9. B. Shuster, R
10. D. Sherwood, R
11. P. E. Kanjorski, D
12. J. P. Murtha, D
13. J. M. Hoeffel, D
14. W. J. Coyne, D
15. P. Toomey, R
16. J. R. Pitts, R
17. G. W. Gekas, R
18. M. F. Doyle, D
19. T. R. Platts, R*
20. F. Mascara, D
21. P. English, R

Rhode Island
1. P. J. Kennedy, D
2. J. R. Langevin, D*

South Carolina
1. H. E. Brown, Jr., R*
2. F. Spence, R
3. L. O. Graham, R
4. J. DeMint, R
5. J. M. Spratt, Jr., D
6. J. E. Clyburn, D

South Dakota
At-L. J. R. Thune, R

Tennessee
1. W. L. Jenkins, R
2. J. J. Duncan, Jr., R
3. Z. Wamp, R
4. V. Hilleary, R
5. B. Clement, D
6. B. Gordon, D
7. E. Bryant, R
8. J. S. Tanner, D
9. H. E. Ford, Jr., D

Texas
1. M. Sandlin, D
2. J. Turner, D
3. S. Johnson, R
4. R. M. Hall, D
5. P. Sessions, R
6. J. Barton, R
7. J. A. Culberson, R*
8. K. Brady, R
9. N. Lampson, D
10. L. Doggett, D
11. C. Edwards, D
12. K. Granger, R
13. M. Thornberry, R
14. R. Paul, R
15. R. Hinojosa, D
16. S. Reyes, D
17. C. W. Stenholm, D
18. S. Jackson-Lee, D
19. L. Combest, R
20. C. A. Gonzalez, D
21. L. S. Smith, R
22. T. DeLay, R
23. H. Bonilla, R
24. M. Frost, D
25. K. Bentsen, D
26. R.K. Armey, R
27. S. P. Ortiz, D
28. C. D. Rodriguez, D
29. G. Green, D
30. E. B. Johnson, D

Utah
1. J. V. Hansen, R
2. J. Matheson, D*
3. C. Cannon, R

Vermont
At-L. B. Sanders, I

Virginia
1. J. A. Davis, R*
2. E. L. Schrock, R*
3. R. C. Scott, D
4. N. Sisisky, D
5. V. H. Goode, Jr., I
6. B. Goodlatte, R
7. E. Cantor, R*
8. J. P. Moran, D
9. R. Boucher, D
10. F. R. Wolf, R
11. T. M. Davis, R

Washington
1. J. Inslee, D
2. R. Larsen, D*
3. B. Baird, D
4. D. Hastings, R
5. G. R. Nethercutt, Jr., R
6. N. D. Dicks, D
7. J. McDermott, D
8. J. Dunn, R
9. A. Smith, D

West Virginia
1. A. B. Mollohan, D
2. S. M. Capito, R*
3. N. J. Rahall II, D

Wisconsin
1. P. Ryan, R
2. T. Baldwin, D
3. R. Kind, D
4. G. D. Kleczka, D
5. T. M. Barrett, D
6. T. E. Petri, R
7. D. R. Obey, D
8. M. Green, R
9. F. J. Sensenbrenner, Jr., R

Wyoming
At-L. B. Cubin, R

AMERICAN SAMOA
Delegate, E. F. H.
Faleomavaega, D

DISTRICT OF COLUMBIA
Delegate, E.H. Norton, D

GUAM
Delegate, R. A. Underwood, D

PUERTO RICO
Resident Commissioner, A.
Acevedo-Vilá, PPD*

VIRGIN ISLANDS
Delegate, D.M. Christensen, D

Contributors

ADAMS, REBECCA, Reporter, "Congressional Quarterly" : *Washington, DC*

ALLEN, THOMAS B., Freelance Writer, Bethesda, MD; Coauthor, *America at War 1941–45, CNN: War in the Gulf*: **The Koreas—A Rapprochement**—*The Korean War—50 Years Later*

AMICK, GEORGE, Author, *Linn's U.S. Stamp Yearbook*: **Stamps and Stamp Collecting**

ANDERSON, JIM, Freelance Writer and Editor: **Biography**—*Wen Ho Lee*; **States**—*(in part)*

ANDERSON, MARGO, Professor, Department of History, University of Wisconsin—Milwaukee; Author, *The United States Census and Labor Force Change, The American Census: A Social History*: **The United States**—*The 22d U.S. Census*

ARNOLD, ANTHONY, Author, *Afghanistan's Two-Party Communism: Parcham and Khalq, The Fateful Pebble: Afghanistan's Role in the Fall of the Soviet Empire*: **Afghanistan**

ASSEO, LAURIE, Legal Affairs Journalist, Washington DC: **Crime; Crime**—*Capital Punishment*; **Law**—*U.S. Law*

ATKIN, MURIEL, Professor, Department of History, George Washington University: **Tajikistan**

ATTNER, PAUL, Senior Writer, *The Sporting News*: **Biography**—*Phil D. Jackson*; **Sports**—*Basketball, Football, The XXVII Summer Games*

BALDWIN, LOU, Staff Writer, *The Catholic Standard & Times*: **Religion**—*Roman Catholicism*

BEHLER, DEBORAH A., Executive Editor, *Wildlife Conservation* magazine: **Zoos and Zoology**

BEST, JOHN, Canadian Freelance Writer: **Obituaries**—*Pierre Elliott Trudeau*

BETTELHEIM, ADRIEL, Medical and Science Writer, *CQ Researcher*: **Environment**

BRAASCH, BARBARA, Freelance Travel Writer, Palo Alto, CA: **Travel; Travel**—*Time-Shares*

BRUSSO, CHARLENE, Member, New England Science Writers: **Physics**

BUCKLEY, ANNE M., Editor, *Catholic New York*: **Obituaries**—*John Joseph O'Connor*

BUGAJSKI, JANUSZ, Director of East European Studies, Center for Strategic and International Studies, Washington, DC; Author, *Ethnic Politics in Eastern Europe: A Guide to Nationality Policies, Organizations and Parties*: **Albania; Biography**—*Vojislav Kostunica*; **Bosnia and Herzegovina; Bulgaria; Croatia; Hungary; Macedonia; Romania; Slovenia; Yugoslavia; Yugoslavia**—*Kosovo*; **Yugoslavia**—*Montenegro*

BURKS, ARDATH W., Professor Emeritus, Asian Studies, Rutgers University; Author, *Third Order of the Rising Sun*: **Biography**—*Yoshiro Mori*; **Japan**

BUSH, GRAHAM W. A., Associate Professor of Political Studies, University of Auckland; Author, *Advance in Order: The Auckland City Council 1971–89*: **New Zealand**

CHAMETZKY, PETER, School of Art and Design, Southern Illinois University: **Art**

CHARLA, STEPHEN, Curator, International Museum of Cartoon Art: **Cartooning: The Comics Are Here To Stay**

COLLINS, BUD, Sports Columnist, *The Boston Globe*; Author, *My Life with the Pros*: **Sports**—*Tennis*

CONRADT, DAVID P., Professor of Political Science, East Carolina University; Author, *The German Polity, West European Politics*: **Germany**

COOPER, ILENE, Children's Book Editor, *Booklist Magazine*: **Biography**—*J[oanne] K[athleen] Rowling*; **Literature**—*Children's*

COOPER, MARY H., Staff Writer, *CQ Researcher*; Author, *The Business of Drugs*: **Energy; Energy**—*Gas Prices*; **International Trade and Finance; Taxation**

CUE, EDUARDO, Freelance Writer, Paris, France; Correspondent in France for *U.S. News & World Report*: **France**

CUNNIFF, JOHN, Business News Analyst, Associated Press; Author, *How to Stretch Your Dollar*: **The U.S. Economy**—*The Great Expansion*; **Business and Corporate Affairs; Industrial Production; United States**—*The Economy*

CURRIER, CHET, Financial Writer, *Bloomberg News*; Author, *The Investor's Encyclopedia, The 15-Minute Investor*; Coauthor, *No-Cost/Low-Cost Investing*: **Stocks and Bonds**

CURTIS, L. PERRY, Professor of History, Brown University: **Ireland**

DAVID, LEONARD, Director, Space Data Resources and Information: **Space Exploration**

DENNIS, LARRY, Freelance Golf Writer: **Sports**—*Golf*

DETMER, DON E., Gillings Professor of Health Management, Judge Institute of Management, University of Cambridge, England: **Medicine and Health**—*Medical Mistakes*

Di SCALA, SPENCER M., Research Professor, University of Massachusetts—Boston; Author, *Italy: From Revolution to Republic, 1700 to the Present*: **Italy**

DOMINGO, PILAR, University of London: **Bolivia**

DUFF, ERNEST A., Professor of Politics, Randolph-Macon Woman's College; Author, *Agrarian Reform in Colombia, Violence and Repression in Latin America, Leader and Party in Latin America*: **Colombia**

DYER, RICHARD, Chief Classical Music Critic, *The Boston Globe*: **Music**—*Classical*

EBERHART, GEORGE, *American Libraries* magazine, American Library Association: **Libraries; Libraries**—*The Library of Congress Is 200*

ENSTAD, ROBERT, Writer, Formerly, *Chicago Tribune*: **Chicago**

FALLESEN, LEIF BECK, Editor in Chief, *Boersen*, Copenhagen: **Denmark; Finland; Iceland; Norway; Sweden**

FISCHER, MARTIN, Assistant Professor, Terman Engineering Center, Stanford, CA: **Civil Engineering**

GOODMAN, DONALD, Associate Professor of Sociology, John Jay College of Criminal Justice, City University of New York: **Prisons**

GORDON, MAYNARD M., Senior Editor, *Ward's Dealer Business* magazine; Author, *The Iacocca Management Technique*: **Automobiles; Automobiles**—*The Ford-Firestone Tire Story*

GRAYSON, GEORGE W., Class of 1938 Professor of Government, College of William and Mary; Author, *The Politics of Mexican Oil, The United States and Mexico: Patterns of Influence, Oil and Mexican Foreign Policy*: **Biography**—*Vicente Fox Quesada*; **Brazil; Mexico; Portugal; Spain**

GROHOL, JOHN M., Psychologist, HelpHorizons.com; Author, *The Insider's Guide to Mental Health Resources Online*: **Medicine and Health**—*Mental Health*

GROSSMAN, LAWRENCE, Associate Director of Research, The American Jewish Committee; Editor, *American Jewish Year Book*: **Religion**—*Judaism*

GROTH, ALEXANDER J., Professor Emeritus of Political Science, University of California, Davis; Author, *Contemporary Politics: Europe, Comparative Resource Allocation, Public Policy across Nations*: **Poland**

591

HELMREICH, JONATHAN E., Professor Emeritus of History, Allegheny College; Author, *Belgium and Europe: A Study in Small Power Diplomacy, United States Relations with Belgium and the Congo 1940–1960*; Coauthor, *Rebirth: A History of Europe Since World War II*: **Belgium; Netherlands**

HELMREICH, PAUL C., Professor Emeritus of History, Wheaton College; Author, *From Paris to Sèvres: The Partition of the Ottoman Empire at the Peace Conference of 1919–1920*; Coauthor, *Rebirth: A History of Europe Since World War II*: **Switzerland**

HERZOG, BRAD, Author and Freelance Writer, *States of Mind, The Sports 100*: **The Quiz-Show Craze**

HOLLOBAUGH, JEFF, Track Columnist, ESPN.com; Author, *100 Stars of American Track & Field*: **Biography—Marion Jones; Sports—Track and Field**

HOPKO, THE REV. THOMAS, Dean, St. Vladimir's Orthodox Theological Seminary, Crestwood, NY: **Religion—Orthodox Eastern**

HORN, WADE F., President, National Fatherhood Initiative: **Family—The Fatherhood Movement**

HOWARD, DAVE, Freelance Writer and Photographer: **Photography**

HOWE, HERBERT M., Research Professor on African Politics, School of Foreign Service, Georgetown University, Washington DC: **Nigeria**

HOYT, CHARLES K., Fellow, *American Institute of Architects*; Author, *More Places for People, Building for Commerce and Industry*: **Architecture**

HUFFMAN, GEORGE J., NASA/Science Systems and Applications: **Meteorology**

ISIDORE, CHRIS, Freelance Transportation Writer: **Transportation**

JENNERMANN, DONALD L., Director, University Honors Program, Indiana State University; Author, *Born of a Cretan Spring, Literature for Living*: **Literature—English**

JOHNSON, LONNIE, Author, *Central Europe: Enemies, Neighbors, Friends*: **Austria**

JOHNSON, RHETA GRIMSLEY, Columnist, *The Atlanta Journal/Constitution*; Author, *Good Grief: The Story of Charles M. Schulz*: **Cartooning: The Comics Are Here To Stay—The Life and Legacy of Charles M. Schulz**

JONES, GRAHAME L., Soccer Columnist, *Los Angeles Times* and ESPN's *SportsZone*: **Sports—Soccer**

JONES, STEPHEN F., Associate Professor of Russian and Eurasian Studies, Mount Holyoke College: **Armenia; Azerbaijan; Georgia**

KANNAPELL, ANDREA, *The New York Times*: **The 2000 U.S. Presidential Election—One Unlike Any Other—The First Lady Becomes Senator-elect; New York City**

KARNES, THOMAS L., Professor of History Emeritus, Southwestern University; Author, *Latin American Policy of the United States, Failure of Union: Central America 1824–1960*: **Central America**

KERMOND, JOHN, Office of Global Programs, National Oceanic and Atmospheric Administration: **Oceanography**

KESSLER, ANN, American Bankers Association: **Banking and Finance**

KIM, HAN-KYO, Professor Emeritus, Political Science, University of Cincinnati; Author, *Korea and the Politics of Imperialism 1876–1910, Studies on Korea: A Scholar's Guide*: **The Koreas—A Rapprochement; Korea**

KISSELGOFF, ANNA, Chief Dance Critic, *The New York Times*: **Dance**

KLINGER, DAVID A., Associate Professor, Department of Criminology and Criminal Justice, University of Missouri–St. Louis: **Policing—A Problematic Enterprise**

LAWRENCE, ROBERT M., Professor of Political Science, Colorado State University; Author, *The Strategic Defense Initiative*: **Military Affairs; Military Affairs—The Sinking of the Kursk**

LEEPSON, MARC, Freelance Writer: **Drugs and Alcohol; Social Welfare**

LEVINE, LOUIS, Professor, Department of Biology, City College of New York; Author, *Biology of the Gene, Biology for a Modern Society*: **Biotechnology; Genetics; Genetics—Human Genome Project; Microbiology**

LIEBERMAN, ABRAHAM, Executive Director, Muhammad Ali Center, National Parkinson Foundation, Inc.: **Medicine and Health—Parkinson's Disease**

LOESCHER, GIL, Professor of International Relations, University of Notre Dame; Author, *Refugees and International Relations, The Global Refugee Crisis: A Reference Handbook*: **Refugees and Immigration**

LOVEMAN, BRIAN E., Professor, Department of Political Science, San Diego State University: **Chile; Chile—Ricardo Lagos Escobar**

MacLEOD, ALEXANDER, British Isles Correspondent, *The Christian Science Monitor*, London: **Biography—Cherie Booth Blair; Great Britain**

MAMMANA, DENNIS L., Astronomer, Reuben H. Fleet Science Center, San Diego, CA; Author, *The Backyard Astronomer: A Guide to Stargazing*: **Astronomy**

MARCOPOULOS, GEORGE J., Professor of History, Tufts University: **Cyprus; Greece**

MARKS, JONATHAN, Professor, Department of Sociology/Anthropology, University of North Carolina at Charlotte: **Anthropology**

MARPLES, DAVID R., Professor of History, University of Alberta, Canada; Author, *Belarus: A Denationalized Nation*: **Belarus**

MATHESON, JIM, Sportswriter, *Edmonton Journal*: **Sports—Ice Hockey**

MATHEWS, JAY, Education Reporter and Columnist, *The Washington Post*; Coauthor, *One Billion, Escalante, A Mother's Touch, Class Struggle*: **Education**

MAXON, ROBERT M., Professor of History, West Virginia University; Author, *Conflict and Accommodation in Western Kenya, East Africa: An Introductory History, Struggle of Kenya: the Loss and Reassertion of Imperial Initiative, 1912–23*: **Kenya; Tanzania; Uganda**

MAYERCHAK, PATRICK M., Professor of Political Science, Virginia Military Institute; Author, *Scholar's Guide to Southeast Asia*; Coauthor, *Linkage or Bondage: US-ASEAN Economic Relations*: **Malaysia; Singapore**

McCLINTOCK, CYNTHIA, Professor of Political Science and International Affairs, George Washington University; Author, *Revolutionary Movements in Latin America: El Salvador's FMLN and Peru's Shining Path*: **Peru**

McCONNELL, SHELLEY A., Associate Director, Latin American and Caribbean Program, The Carter Center; Adjunct Assistant Professor of Political Science, Emory College: **Ecuador; Latin America**

McCORMICK, HERB, Editor, *Cruising World* magazine; Boating Writer, *The New York Times*; Coauthor, *Out There*: **Sports—Yachting**

McCOY, JENNIFER L., Associate Professor of Political Science and Senior Associate at the Policy Research Center, Georgia State University; Senior Associate, The Carter Center; Author, *Venezuelan Democracy under Stress*: **Venezuela**

McGEE, GLENN, Center for Bioethics, University of Pennsylvania School of Medicine; Author, *The Perfect Baby*: **Medicine and Health—Bioethics**

MICHIE, ARUNA NAYYAR, Department of Political Science, Kansas State University: *India; Sri Lanka*

MILLER, RANDALL M., Department of History, St. Joseph's University; Author, *Shades of the Sunbelt: Essays on Ethnicity, Race and the Urban South*: *Ethnic Groups*

MILWARD, JOHN, Freelance Writer and Critic: *Biography—Carlos Santana; Music—Popular and Jazz*

MINAGAR, ALIREZA, Neurology Fellow, University of Miami School of Medicine: *Medicine and Health—Parkinson's Disease*

MORRIS, BERNADINE, Fashion Journalist, Author, *The Fashion Makers, American Fashion*: *Fashion*

MORTIMER, ROBERT A., Professor, Department of Political Science, Haverford College; Author, *The Third World Coalition in International Politics;* Coauthor, *Politics and Society in Contemporary Africa*: *Algeria*

MORTON, DESMOND, Director, McGill Institute for the Study of Canada; Author, *Working People: An Illustrated History of the Canadian Labour Movement, A Military History of Canada, Bloody Victory: Canadians and the D-Day Campaign, 1944*: *Canada*

NASATIR, JUDITH, Freelance Design Journalist and Editor, Former Senior Editor, *Interior Design* magazine: *Interior Design*

OCHSENWALD, WILLIAM, Professor of History, Virginia Polytechnic Institute and State University; Author, *The Middle East: A History, The Hijaz Railroad, Religion, Society and the State in Arabia*: *Saudi Arabia; Turkey*

O'MEARA, PATRICK, Dean of International Programs, Indiana University; Coeditor, *Africa, International Politics in Southern Africa, Southern Africa, The Continuing Crisis*: *Africa—Mozambique; South Africa; Zimbabwe*

PAUL, BIMAL KANTI, Kansas State University: *Bangladesh*

PEARSON, FREDERIC S., Director, Center for Peace and Conflict Studies, Wayne State University, Detroit; Coauthor, *International Relations: The Global Condition, Fuel on the Fire? Effects of Armament During Warfare*: *United States:—Foreign Affairs*

PEARSON, RUTH, United Nations Correspondent: *United Nations; Women*

PERETZ, DON, Professor Emeritus of Political Science, State University of New York at Binghamton; Author, *The West Bank—History, Politics, Society and Economy, Government and Politics of Israel, The Middle East Today*: *Egypt; Israel*

PERKINS, KENNETH J., Professor of History, University of South Carolina: *Libya; Religion—Islam*

PERRY, DAVID K., Associate Professor, Department of Journalism, The University of Alabama: *Publishing*

PIPPIN, LARRY L., Professor of Political Science, University of the Pacific; Author *The Remón Era*: *Argentina; Paraguay; Uruguay*

POOLE, PETER A., Author, *The Vietnamese in Thailand, Eight Presidents and Indochina;* Coauthor, *American Diplomacy*: *Vietnam*

POUST, MARY ANN, News Editor, *Catholic New York*: *Biography —Edward Michael Egan*

PRISANT, CAROL, Author, *Antiques Roadshow Primer*: *Television and Radio—"Antiques Roadshow"*

REBACK, MARILYN, American Numismatic Association: *Coins and Coin Collecting*

RICHTER, LINDA K., Professor of Political Science, Kansas State University; Author, *Land Reform and Tourism Development, Policy Making in the Philippines*: *Myanmar; Philippines*

RICHTER, WILLIAM L., Associate Provost for International Programs, Kansas State University: *Pakistan*

RIGGAN, WILLIAM, Associate Editor, *World Literature Today*, University of Oklahoma; Author, *Pícaros, Madmen, Naïfs, and Clowns, Comparative Literature and Literary Theory*: *Literature—World*

ROSE, MARK, Managing Editor, *Archaeology*: *Archaeology*

ROVNER, JULIE, Health-Policy Writer: *Medicine and Health—Health Care, Prescription Drugs*

RYAN, ROSE, Executive Editor, *The North Africa Journal*: *Morocco; Tunisia*

SCHLOSSBERG, DAN, Baseball Writer; Author, *The Baseball IQ Challenge, The Baseball Catalog, The Baseball Book of Why, Cooperstown: Baseball's Hall of Fame Players*: *Sports—Baseball*

SCHUYLER, ED, JR., Freelance Boxing Writer: *Sports—Boxing*

SCHWAB, PETER, Professor of Political Science, Purchase College, State University of New York; Author, *Ethiopia: Politics, Economics, and Society, Human Rights: Cultural and Ideological Perspectives*: *Africa: A Continent of Problems; Africa; Democratic Republic of the Congo; Ethiopia; Ethiopia—Ethiopia-Eritrea War*

SEIDERS, DAVID F., Chief Economist and Senior Staff Vice-President, National Association of Home Builders, Washington, DC: *Housing*

SENSER, ROBERT A., Editor, *Human Rights for Workers*: *Human Rights*

SEYBOLD, PAUL G., Professor, Department of Chemistry, Wright State University: *Chemistry*

SHAPIRO, WILLIAM E., Freelance Writer and Editor, New York City: *Fiji; Nations of the World*

SHARLET, ROBERT, Chauncey Winters Professor of Political Science, Union College; Author, *Soviet Constitutional Crisis*: *Baltic Republics; Biography—Vladimir Putin; Russia; Ukraine*

SHOGAN, ROBERT, Former National Political Correspondent, Washington Bureau, *The Los Angeles Times*; Author, *A Question of Judgment, Promises to Keep, The Forthcoming Bad News: Where the Press Goes Wrong in the Making of the President*; Adjunct Professor, Johns Hopkins University Washington Center: *The 2000 U.S. Presidential Election—One Unlike Any Other; Biography—George W. Bush, Al Gore, Dick Cheney, Joe Lieberman, John McCain; United States—Domestic Affairs*

SIMON, JEFFREY D., Freelance Writer; Author, *The Terrorist Trap*: *Terrorism*

SIMON, SHELDON W., Professor of Political Science, Arizona State University–Tempe; Author, *The Future of Asian-Pacific Security Collaboration*: *Asia*

SIMPSON, SARAH, Editor and Writer, *Scientific American* magazine: *Geology; Geology—"Sue"—The World's Largest T. rex*

SNODSMITH, RALPH L., Ornamental Horticulturist; Author, *Ralph Snodsmith's Tips from the Garden Hotline*: *Gardening and Horticulture*

STARR, JOHN BRYAN, Managing Director, Annenberg Institute for School Reform, Brown University; Author, *Continuing the Revolution: The Political Thought of Mao*; Editor, *The Future of U.S.-China Relations*: *Biography—Chen Shui-bian; China; China—U.S.-China Trade; Taiwan*

STEIN, LANA, Associate Professor of Political Science, University of Missouri–St. Louis; Author, *Holding Bureaucrats Accountable: Politicians and Professionals in St. Louis*: *Cities and Urban Affairs*

STIEBER, JACK, Professor Emeritus, School of Labor and Industrial Relations, Michigan State University; Author, *U.S. Industrial Relations: The Next Twenty Years, Governing the UAW, Public Employee Unionism*: *Labor*

STUART, ELAINE, Managing Editor, *State Government News*: *States, U.S.*—(in part)

SUTTON, STAN, Freelance Sportswriter based in Bloomington, IN: *Sports*—Auto Racing, Horse Racing

TAYLOR, PAUL, Executive Director, Alliance for Better Campaigns: *The 2000 U.S. Presidential Election—One Unlike Any Other*—Spotlight Falls on the Electoral Machinery

TESAR, JENNY, Freelance Science Writer; Author, *The New Webster's Computer Handbook, Introduction to Animals, Mammals, What on Earth is a Tuatara?*: *Primates in Peril; Computers and Communication; Medicine and Health*—Overview

TULLY, JUDD, Editor-at-Large, *Art & Auction*: *Art*—Art Market

TURNER, ARTHUR CAMPBELL, Professor Emeritus of Political Science, University of California, Riverside; Coauthor, *Ideology and Power in the Middle East*: *Biography*—Bashar al-Assad; *Iran; Iraq; Jordan; Lebanon; Middle East; Middle East*—Jerusalem; *Obituaries*—Hafiz al-Assad; *Syria*

VAN ZANDT, CHRISTINE, U.S. Government Analyst on East Asian Affairs, Washington, DC: *Cambodia; Laos*

VAUGHAN, KRISTI, Freelance Writer: *Biography*—Laura Welch Bush, Laura Schlessinger; *Family; Religion*—Far Eastern; *States, U.S.*—(in part); *Television and Radio*

VOLL, JOHN O., Professor of History, Georgetown University; Author, *Islam: Continuity and Change in the Modern World*; Coauthor, *Sudan: Unity and Diversity in a Multicultural Society*; Editor, *Sudan: State and Society in Crisis*: *Sudan*

VOLSKY, GEORGE, North-South Center, University of Miami: *Cuba; Cuba*—The Saga of Elián González

WALTON, DAVID, British Antarctic Survey; Author, *Antarctic Science*: *Polar Research*

WEATHERBEE, DONALD E., Department of Government, University of South Carolina: *Indonesia; Thailand*

WHITE, GAYLE, Religion Writer, *The Atlanta Journal Constitution*; President, Religion Newswriters Association: *Religion*—Protestantism

WHITTEN, PHILLIP, Editor in Chief, *Swimming World*: *Sports*—Swimming

WILLIAMS, PAUL R., Assistant Professor of Law, Washington College of Law, American University: *Law*—International Law

WILLIS, F. ROY, Professor Emeritus of History, University of California, Davis; Author, *France, Germany and the New Europe, 1945–1968, Italy Chooses Europe*: *Europe*

WILMETH, DON B., Asa Messer Professor; Chair, Department of Theatre, Speech and Drama, Brown University; Author and Editor, *The Cambridge Guide to American Theatre, Cambridge History of American Theatre, Staging the Nation: Plays from the American Theater, 1787–1909*: *Obituaries*—Sir John Gielgud

WISNER, ROBERT N., Professor, Iowa State University; Coeditor, *Marketing for Farmers*; Author, *World Food Trade and U.S. Agriculture*: *Agriculture; Food; Food*—Genetically Modified Foods

WOLCHIK, SHARON LEE, Director of the Russian and East European Studies Program and Professor of Political Science, George Washington University; Author, *The Social Legacy of Communism, Czechoslovakia in Transition: Politics, Economics and Society*: *Czech Republic; Slovakia*

WOLF, WILLIAM, New York University; Author, *The Marx Brothers, Landmark Films, The Cinema and Our Century*: *Biography*—Annette Bening; *Motion Pictures; Theater*

WOLFE, JOHN, Senior Vice-President, American Association of Advertising Agencies: *Advertising*

WOOD, DANIEL B., Los Angeles Bureau Chief, *The Christian Science Monitor*: *Los Angeles*

WOODS, MICHAEL J., Science Editor, *The Toledo Blade* and *The Pittsburgh Post-Gazette*; Author, *What's Happening in Chemistry*: *Biochemistry*

YARBROUGH, SCOTT, Assistant Professor of English, Charleston Southern University: *Literature*—American

YEARWOOD, TREVOR, Chief Editor, *CANA*; Creative Writers Group, Barbados Association of Journalists: *Caribbean*

YOUNGER, R. M., Journalist and Author; Author, *Australia and the Australians, Australia! Australia! A Bicentennial Record*: *Australia; Australia*—Sydney—An Olympic City

ZELENAK, MEL J., Department of Family/Consumer Economics, University of Missouri–Columbia: *Consumer Affairs; Consumer Affairs*—Credit-Card Skimming; *Retailing*

ZIMBALIST, ANDREW, Department of Economics, Smith College: *Sports*—Escalating Ticket Prices

Acknowledgements

We also wish to thank the following for their services: color separations and electronic file output, Que-net Media; text stock printed on 60# Somerset Matte; dust jacket and covers printed by Fortran Printing Inc.; cover materials provided by Ecological Fibers, Inc.; and printing and binding by Quebecor World Book Services, KY.

INDEX

Main article headings appear in this index as bold-faced capitals; subjects within articles appear as lower-case entries. Bold-faced page numbers indicate the location of the article about the subject. Both the general references and the subentries should be consulted for maximum usefulness of this index. Illustrations are indexed herein. Cross references are to the entries in this index.